THE LETTERS OF
T. S. ELIOT

EDITED BY

VALERIE ELIOT

AND

HUGH HAUGHTON

VOLUME 2

1923–1925

GENERAL EDITOR

JOHN HAFFENDEN

Yale
UNIVERSITY PRESS
New Haven & London

First published in the
United States in 2011 by Yale University Press.
First published in
Great Britain in 2009 by Faber and Faber Limited.

Yale University Press books may be
purchased in quantity for educational, business, or
promotional use. For information, please e-mail sales.press@yale.edu
(U.S. office) or sales@yaleup.co.uk (U.K. office).

Printed in the United States of America.

Library of Congress Control Number: 2011928725
ISBN 978-0-300-17686-5 (hardcover: alk. paper)

A catalogue record for this book is available from the British Library.

This paper meets the requirements of
ANSI/NISO Z39.48-1992 (Permanence of Paper).

10 9 8 7 6 5 4 3 2 1

i.m. John Bodley (1930–2004)

CONTENTS

ILLUSTRATIONS

ACKNOWLEDGEMENTS

I owe a special debt of gratitude to both Dr William H. Bond, formerly Librarian, and Rodney G. Dennis, Curator of Manuscripts, at the Houghton Library, Harvard University; to Dr Donald Gallup, bibliographer of Eliot and Pound, who has answered innumerable questions with grace; and to Matthew Evans with my editor, John Bodley, for their generous support and encouragement.

For permission to print letters and quote from copyright material, I wish to thank Alain Rivière (Alain-Fournier), Alastair Kershaw (Richard Aldington), Professor Charles W. Eliot (President Eliot), Mme Catherine Gide (André Gide), The Ezra Pound Literary Property Trust, and James Laughlin (Ezra Pound), The Bertrand Russell Estate and McMaster University (Bertrand Russell), Francis Wyndham (Sydney Schiff), Françoise Valéry (Paul Valéry), Harvard University Libraries (J. H. Woods).

I am grateful to Professor John Weightman for translating all letters in French, and to the following for help in various ways: Joan Bailey; Anne Olivier Bell; Kenneth Blackwell, McMaster University; Michael Harry Blechner, McFarlin Library, University of Tulsa; Mary Boccaccio, McKeldin Library, University of Maryland; Dr J. M. L. Booker, Lloyds Bank Archivist; Penelope Bulloch, Balliol College Library; William R. Cagle, Saundra Taylor, Lilly Library; Douglass Campbell; Dr Joseph Chiari; the late Marguerite Cohn; Joyce Crick; Arthur Crook; Roy Davids; Dr A. Deiss, General Secretariat, Swiss Medical Institutions; Giles de la Mare; Peter du Sautoy; Donald D. Eddy, Cornell University Library; Barclay Feather, Director of Libraries, Milton Academy; K. C. Gay, Lockwood Memorial Library, Buffalo; Herbert Gerwing, Special Collections, University of Victoria; Mrs Ghika; R. C. Giles, T. G. Mallinson, Highgate School; Robert Giroux; Sir Rupert Hart-Davis; Professor E. N. Hartley, Institute Archives, MIT; Cathy Henderson, Humanities Research Center, University of Texas; the late Robert Henderson; Dr Roger Highfield, Merton College Library; Robert W. Hill, New York Public Library (Manuscript Division); Penelope Hughes-Hallett; J. W. Hunt, Royal Military Academy, Sandhurst; Lord Hutchinson; Carolyn Jakeman; Professor Dorothy O. Johansen, Reed College, Portland, Oregon; William Jovanovich; Monique Kuntz, Bibliothèque Municipale,

Vichy; the staff of the London Library; Richard M. Ludwig, Princeton University Library; R. Russell Maylone, Northwestern University Library; Professor B. K. Matilal; Joe Mitchenson; Mary C. McGreenery, Harvard Alumni Records; Lord Quinton; Angela Raspin, London School of Economics; Benedict Read; Dr R. T. H. Redpath; Helene Ritzerfeld; Rosenbach Museum & Library; Anthony Rota; Samuel A. Sizer, Special Collections, University Libraries, University of Arkansas; Lola L. Szladits, Berg Collection; Theodora Eliot Smith; Kendon L. Stubbs, University of Virginia Library; Barbara Sturtevant; Elizabeth Stege Teleky, Joseph Regenstein Library, University of Chicago; Professor Kathleen Tillotson; Dr George Watson; the late Helen Willard; Professor David G. Williams; Patricia C. Willis, Beinecke Library, Yale University; Dr Daniel H. Woodward, Huntington Library.

It is a pleasure to record my heartfelt appreciation of the Faber team: Ron Costley, designer, Mark Massingham, typesetter, Jane Robertson, managing editor, Hazel Orme, copy-editor, and Gillian Bate, proof reader, who have combined their skills to produce such an elegant tribute to TSE in his centenary year.

1988

The acknowledgements above are those made by Valerie Eliot in the first edition of Volume 1. Sadly, a number of those mentioned are now deceased (as are some of those we will add below). The editors would like also to thank: Owen Barfield; H. Baugh; Jewel Spears Brooker; Robert Brown; Andrew Boxer; Ronald Bush; François Chapon; Mrs Charlton; Alan Clodd; the Literary Trustees of Walter de la Mare; J. P. G. Delaney; the estate of Geoffrey Faber; Toby Faber; Jennifer Formichelli; Mrs Burnham Finney; Estate of Enid Goldsmith; Herbert T. Greene; Warwick Gould; Michael Halls; Saskia Hamilton; Hal Hlavinka; Michael Hofmann; Michael Holroyd; Steven Isenberg; P. D. James; Iman Javadi; Emeline Jouvé; Paul Keegan; Kenneth A. Lohf; Jim McCue; Tessa Milne; Tim Munby; Mary Middleton Murry; Anne Owen; Craig Raine; Carol Rothkopt; Gerd Schmidt; Rev. Karl Schroeder, SJ; Ronald Schuchard; Jesse Cordes Selbin; Timothy and Marian Seldes; Prue Shaw; James Strachey; M. J. Tilby; François Valéry, Judith Robinson-Valéry; David Van Ness; Michael J. Walsh; Jemma Walton, J. Waterlow; Dave Watkins; Kieron Winn; Susan Wolfson; John Worthen and Michael Yeats. Special thanks go to Ron Costley, Donald Sommerville for his copy-editing, Jenny Overton for proofreading, Alison Worthington for indexing, and to Debbie Whitfield (PA to Mrs Eliot) for her commitment to this project.

We are grateful in addition to: Leslie Morris and Elizabeth A. Falsey (Houghton Library); Dr P. Kelly (National Library of Scotland); Robin Carlaw (Harvard University Archives); Eamon Dyas (News International); Moira A. Fitzgerald and Eva Guggemos (Beinecke Library, Yale); Thomas Lannon (New York Public Library); Molly Schwartzburg (Harry Ransom Research Center, University of Texas); Claire Nicholas-Walker (British Library); Thomas Whitehead (Temple University Libraries); Stephen Young (Regenstein Library, University of Chicago); Bibliothèque Littéraire Jacques Doucet; Bibliothèque Nationale, Paris; Bodleian Library, Oxford; University of Bonn Library; British Library; Bundesarchiv (German Federal Archives), Koblenz; Rare Books and Manuscripts Division, Butler Library, Columbia University, New York; University of California, Los Angeles; Fondazione Camillo Caetani, Rome; Clare College, Cambridge; Fondren Library, Woodson Research Center, Rice University; Galleria Nazionale d'Arte Moderna, Rome; Harvard University Archives; Special Collections, Isabella Stewart Gardner Museum, Boston, Mass.; Hornbake Library, University of Maryland; Special Collections, Keele University; Modern Archives Centre, King's College, Cambridge; Magdalene College, Cambridge; Marshall Library, Cambridge; Massachusetts Institute of Technology; Lockwood Memorial Library; University Library, Missouri History Museum; Morris Library, Southern Illinois University at Carbondale; Mugar Memorial Library, Boston University; National Library, Scotland; New College, Oxford; Pennsylvania University Library; Reading University Library; Real Academia de la Historia; Schiller-Nationalmuseum, Marbach am Neckar; Schweizerisches Literaturachiv (Swiss National Archives), Berne; University of Sussex Library; Trinity College, Cambridge; Trinity College, Dublin; University of Virginia Library; Washington University Library, St Louis, Missouri; Widener Library, Harvard University; Chapin Library, Williams College, Williamstown, Massachusetts; Yale University Archives.

2009

The editors and publishers apologise if any person or estate has been overlooked. They would be grateful to be informed if any copyright notice has been omitted, or if there have been any changes of ownership or location.

PREFACE

Volume 1 of the *Letters of T. S. Eliot* effectively covers the years from 1914 to the end of 1922. Volume 2 covers a shorter period, from 1923 to 1925. They are years of crisis and consolidation, of severe domestic collapse and hard-won professional recovery. The collection tells us a great deal about the intellectual culture in which Eliot established himself in postwar England; it also reveals his constant struggles with ill health and a distressed marriage – personal anguish is a keynote, most evidently in the candid and terrifying letters that he despatched to John Middleton Murry in 1925 – as well as the strains of balancing full-time employment at Lloyds Bank with his consummate vocation as poet, critic and editor. These are the years of 'The Hollow Men', that elusive, repetition-haunted ghost sequence, and the satirical and worldly knockabout of his melodrama, *Sweeney Agonistes*, which would inaugurate Eliot's lifelong engagement with poetic theatre. The major critical volume he produced in these years was *Homage to John Dryden* (published by Leonard and Virginia Woolf at the Hogarth Press), which is centred upon three essays first printed in the *Times Literary Supplement.*

Most importantly, this second volume documents the founding and early years of *The Criterion*, the periodical that Eliot launched with the financial backing of Viscountess Rothermere in late 1922, and which became a sometimes overwhelming undertaking throughout the eighteen years of its duration. If Volume 1 of the *Letters* shows the emergence of Eliot as poet and critic, in the period covered by Volume 2 he assumes a broadening responsibility as editor, publisher and arbiter. Though he had played a notable part as literary editor of *The Egoist* in the late 1910s, Eliot came into his own as cultural commentator only from the mid-1920s, in a role he would continue to play for the rest of his life.

Eliot's biography cannot be understood apart from his work as editor, and the letters in this volume reveal the dedicated and exacting day-to-day and quarter-to-quarter work of producing *The Criterion.* For most of the period spanned by these letters, he earned his living at the bank; the work of *The Criterion* – conjuring up ideas, cultivating contributors, revising submissions, fashioning each and every issue, working out due payments, lobbying for subscriptions – drew relentlessly on nearly all the available hours of his evenings and weekends, and on his statutory holidays: such were the demands of the periodical. He wrote in 1924: 'Conducting a Review after 8 p.m. in the back room of a flat, I live *qua* editor very much from hand to mouth, get myself into all sorts of hot water and predicaments, and offend everybody. At the end, the review is squeezed together somehow, and is never the number that I planned three months before.' As these letters demonstrate, it was a blend of high intellectual commitment, pragmatism, diplomacy, happenstance and perversity that brought about the appearance of each issue. And as an 'organ of documentation' seeking to illuminate 'the time and the tendencies of the time', *The Criterion* would become an influential cultural institution in the changing landscape of the 1920s and 1930s, and would go far to shape what W. H. Auden called 'the whole climate of opinion' of the period.

In a letter to Geoffrey Faber dating from 1938, Eliot would recall the large emotional and moral price he had paid for *The Criterion*: 'when one is young, one can say things in one's own periodical which one would not be at liberty to say elsewhere . . . And there are some bitter memories of the early years – before your time! – it was in no mood of enthusiasm, but more nearly of desperation, that I consented to launch the review . . . Incidentally, I do not forget that it was on the pretext of the *Criterion* that I was insinuated – with some difficulty – into Faber & Gwyer's.' The year 1925 marked a major turning-point in Eliot's life, with his resignation from Lloyds Bank and his decision to be recruited into the newly launched publishing firm of Faber & Gwyer (later Faber & Faber). In a letter to Faber of 22 March 1925, he indicated: 'With what you say about the situation of the Publisher I am in agreement. And the Editor has to combine and reconcile principle, sensibility, and business sense.'

The correspondence in Volume 2 testifies to these reconcilings in Eliot's work, letter by letter, and to the continuities between the poet, the critic and the editor. It ends with Eliot starting out at Faber & Gwyer, completing a draft of four of the Clark Lectures on *The Varieties of Metaphysical Poetry* that he was to deliver at Cambridge early in 1926, and publishing *Poems 1909–1925*, a volume which brought together all of his verse from *Prufrock and Other Observations* to *The Waste Land* and beyond. It was one of the first books to be published by the fledgling Faber & Gwyer: a symbol of Eliot's identification with the firm for which he would work for the rest of his life, and which would publish the rest of his work.

HUGH HAUGHTON

BIOGRAPHICAL COMMENTARY 1923–1925

1923 JANUARY – TSE works full-time at Lloyds Bank, where he runs an intelligence department specializing in 'Enemy Debts under the Peace Treaties', with 'Four girls and three men under me'. He is exhausted by all the 'planning and tact and supervision'; but he later explains: 'I simply could not resign in January because just then the bank started this department which they would not have started at all except for me, because there is no one else available in the bank who has the education and width of experience to run such a thing.' He deposits in his bank the *Dial* (New York) prize of $2,000; and receives a cheque for £50, signed by Ottoline Morrell and Virginia Woolf on behalf of 'Bel Esprit' (the 'Eliot Fellowship Fund'), which is intended to provide an income to enable him to leave the bank: as Ezra Pound puts it to him, it represents 'an emergency measure to save or utilize your particular talent'. TSE considers it as a 'trust fund' and invests the money in 'gilt-edged securities'. He takes out a lease on 'a tiny suite of two rooms', primarily for use as an office for the *Criterion*, at 38 St Martin's Lane, London. He writes of his other work, editing the *Criterion*, 'if one is going to edit a review at all I think the best one can do is to follow one's own faith and let things rip'. Subscriptions run to between 800 and 1000 copies. Lady Rothermere – who funds the periodical to the tune of £600 a year, and whom TSE respects as 'a woman of the world' – finds the *Criterion* 'a little high-brow & grave'. But she never interferes. TSE tells his brother: 'She has given me an absolutely free hand, has made no criticisms, has agreed to every suggestion and has lately slightly increased the sum which she at first stipulated would be the utmost to which she could go for its expenses.' Yet he grumbles too, 'The present position with the *Criterion* is a farce to make one laugh, if any Eliot could ever laugh. I am running a quarterly review which has to make the same appearances, get as good contributors, and give as good value as any other quarterly . . . The *Criterion* is run without an office, without any staff or business manager, by a sickly bank clerk and his wife. The latter has had to be on her back half of the time and the former has conducted all his work in the evening in his own sitting room, without even a *desk*, till Christmas! after a busy and tiring day, and subject to a thousand interruptions. Until the last few months I have paid my own secretary, a woman who came in three evenings a week. When I finally add that I have not only taken no salary but have actually been considerably out of pocket for payment of a secretary, and for the time that I might have spent on writing for other papers, it is enough to make any outsider believe that I ought to be certified a lunatic.' In 1924 he will write further of the fortunes of the *Criterion*: 'The ideal which was present to the mind of Lady Rothermere at the beginning was that of a more chic and brilliant *Art & Letters*, which might have a fashionable vogue among a wealthy few. I had and have no resentment against her for this. . . I have I think given her as much as possible of what she wants, and she has given me the possibility of an organ. It is true that I have laid myself open to the censure both of persons who assumed that I was making money out of the work, and of those who knew that I was taking nothing for it – and who consequently believe that I am running the paper for other discreditable reasons – which latter group of persons, by the way, includes my relatives in America. One does not like to explain oneself only to arouse the accusation of hypocrisy, to be associated with the other causes of impeachment, and one learns to keep silence. I have another reason for keeping silence, and that is that I find that I sometimes give people an impression of arrogance and intolerant self-conceit. If I say generally that I wish to form a "phalanx", a hundred voices will forthwith declare that I wish to be a leader, and that my vanity will not allow me to serve, or even to exist on terms of equality with others. If one maintains a cause, one is either a fanatic or a hypocrite: and if one has any definite dogmas, then one is imposing those dogmas upon those who cooperate with one . . . When I *write*, I must write to the limit of my own convictions and aspirations: but I don't want to impose these on others, any more than I should be willing to reduce myself to the common denominator of my colleagues. What is essential is to find those persons who have an impersonal loyalty to some faith not antagonistic to my own . . . My conception of "leader" or "organiser" is simply of a necessary organ in a body, which has no superiority at all, but simply exercises a particular function, and makes it possible for the others to do their best work.' He contributes '*Ulysses*, Order, and Myth' to the *Dial*. FEBRUARY – Following a visit from TSE ('costive, agonised'), Virginia Woolf suggests to John Maynard Keynes that TSE might become literary editor of *The Nation*. Woolf writes in her diary, of TSE: 'I could wish that poor dear Tom had more spunk in him, less need to let drop by drop of his agonized perplexities fall ever so finely through pure cambric. One waits; sympathises, but it is dreary work. He is like a person about to break down – infinitely scrupulous, tautologous, & cautious.' 23 MARCH – TSE turns down the *Nation*. Woolf notes: 'Here I have been toiling these 3 weeks to make Eliot take it; finally he shied . . .' (Leonard Woolf takes up the position at the *Nation*.) TSE and Vivien rent a small semi-detached retreat at 2 Milestone Cottages, Old Fishbourne, Sussex, on the road between Chichester and the coast at Bosham, and move in on 24 March. In time, TSE will come to think of the cottage as 'miserable . . . a hole'. Vivien has 'electric treatment' and 'Plombières treatment' (colonic irrigation). She relates, 'it is my opinion that Tom is right in refraining at this point from taking steps which would make our common dwelling place a four-roomed country cottage or an attic in London, and which would deprive me of medical assistance. (Of course there are the *nice* hospitals, I know.) Indeed, if he did take such steps I should bear him a considerable grudge.' It is reported that Boni & Liveright (New York) has to date sold 1,250 copies of *The Waste Land*. TSE reports in mid-March: 'I have sunk the whole of my strength for the past eighteen months into this confounded paper [*The Criterion*], when I ought to have been minding my business and doing my own writing. The paper has therefore done me more harm than good.' APRIL – Vivien suffers a violent crisis of health – at first she is 'completely numb, [with] terrible palpitations, and gasping for every breath'; then she endures 'a terrific colitis explosion', followed by others over succeeding days – and is laid up in Fishbourne for many weeks. The local doctor and the Eliots' London doctor, Hubert Higgins, are called in. There is talk of 'entero-colitis', 'enteric influenza', 'septic influenza'. 'My wife nearly died of influenza,' TSE will say at the end of May. He reports that 'malnutrition' is at the heart of her problems. Vivien is treated with 'serum and Bulgarian bacillus'. Her brother Maurice visits them. TSE uses up a month of his annual holiday entitlement in caring for Vivien; he feels 'dilapidated'. MAY – TSE writes to Ezra Pound that Vivien was 'contemplating suicide a short time ago . . . Hell.' 5 MAY – TSE lectures on criticism to an undergraduate society at Oxford. Vivien is 'extremely feeble and still in a precarious condition'. He blames himself: 'her mind was utterly worn out and *ruined* by my indecision over the *Nation* – which went on so *long* too - I know that the strain of that was deadly to her.' (In the opinion of his mother, Vivien 'eats his life out'.) TSE travels back and forth from Fishbourne to London, to meet his professional commitments at the bank and for the *Criterion*. Richard Aldington ('very useful and hard-working') is retained as TSE's paid assistant on the *Criterion*. JUNE – Vivien reports that since getting back to London she has been 'in . . . real despair, which isolates and freezes one . . . paralysing.' 17 JULY – TSE and Vivien visit Virginia Woolf, who notes that Vivien is 'very nervous, very spotty, much powdered'. Acting on a recommendation from Morrell, TSE and Vivien have consultations with a 'great German doctor', Karl Bernhard Martin, who is visiting London. TSE salutes him as 'the wisest, as well as the most scientific Doctor that I have ever met'. Dr Martin claims to discover in Vivien 'an extraordinary excess of streptococcus fecalis, and other mischievous cocci'. Vivien has a relapse. TSE enjoys socialising with James Joyce, who is holidaying in Sussex. SUMMER – Vivien is waited on by a Swedish woman doctor named Cyriax, who treats her with 'manipulation and hand vibration'. 'It is a wonderful system', says TSE. He himself consults the male Dr Cyriax, who seeks 'three times a week' to treat the nerves of TSE's head, neck, spine and stomach. The Cyriax treatment eventuates in two years of starvation dieting for Vivien. Dr Martin encourages her to stick at it. Virginia Woolf tries to find a teaching appointment for TSE at Oxford. Irene Pearl Fassett becomes TSE's secretary. 12 SEPTEMBER – *The Waste Land* is published by Leonard and Virginia Woolf at the Hogarth Press: 330 copies (of a print run of 460) are sold by the end of March 1924, and TSE receives a royalty cheque for £7. 5s. 7d. Vivien visits Eastbourne. NOVEMBER – Aldington resigns as TSE's assistant on the *Criterion*. CHRISTMAS – TSE and Vivien hold a party at 38 Burleigh Mansions; St John and Mary Hutchinson, Roger Fry, and the Woolfs are in attendance. Virginia Woolf: 'We went to a flat in an arcade, & asked for Captain Eliot. I noticed that his eyes were blurred. He cut the cake meticulously. He helped us to coffee – or was it tea? Then to liqueurs . . . We discussed the personal element in literature. Tom then quietly left the room. L. heard sounds of sickness. After a long time, he came back, sank into the corner, & I saw him, ghastly pale, with his eyes shut, apparently in a stupor. When we left he was only just able to stand on his legs.' TSE apologises the next day. TSE and Vivien spend 'a queer sort of Christmas' driving around Sussex in search of a new retreat.

1924 FEBRUARY – Vivien suffers from 'anaemia and complete exhaustion'. TSE writes to his brother, 'I am really in such a state that my mind and judgment and will are paralysed.' He is bed-ridden with flu; Vivien suffers likewise. TSE publishes in the *Criterion* passages from Wyndham Lewis's novel *The Apes of God*, and so antagonises friends including Sydney Schiff and the Sitwells who are satirised in barely disguised form. MARCH – TSE and Vivien collaborate in preparing the *Criterion*. Vivien publishes the first of her sketches, 'Letters of the Moment – I', in February; then 'Letters of the Moment – II' (which includes some verses rescued from the draft of *The Waste Land*) in April – using a series of pseudonyms. 'I have a very strong feeling,' she tells Schiff, 'that this is a sort of flash in the pan – that it won't *go on* – that, in fact, it is being done *faute de mieux* . . . No-one will persuade me that writing is a substitute for living.' The device at least helps her, as she says, to make money from the *Criterion*, which TSE is unable to do (in September 1924, the publisher Richard Cobden-Sanderson sends 'Miss Fanny Marlow' a cheque for £1. 10. 0d.) Vivien writes of her pseudonymous selves: 'There is no *end* to Fanny! But Feiron will never make money . . . He is a nasty fellow.' TSE informs his mother: 'There is no doubt whatever that [Vivien] has talent . . . She has already a very exceptional and individual style.' A year later, TSE advises Aldington: 'She is very diffident, and is very aware that her mind is quite untrained, and therefore writes only under assumed names: but she has an original mind, and I consider not at all a feminine one; and in my opinion a great deal of what she writes is quite good enough for the *Criterion* . . . I intend to see that she gets training and systematic education, because there are so few women who have an un-feminine mind that I think they ought to be made the most of.' TSE goes with Virginia Woolf to a performance of *King Lear*: he admires it, she despises it (though according to her testimony both of them had giggled throughout the performance). TSE looks back at his recent life: 'My history since this time last year is simply a record of one perpetual struggle with serious illness, expense far beyond my means and overwhelming work, done against every kind of obstacle and vicissitude. The *Criterion* itself has been torturingly uphill work, as one must expect with a purely literary quarterly which offers no political or other excitement and panders to no common taste and makes no bid for popularity.' Vivien has a further attack of colitis. SPRING – TSE's brother Henry sends $2,000. MAY – TSE and Vivien again consult Dr K. B. Martin: 'I have never met a Doctor of such wide special knowledge . . . a very charming man.' JUNE – Woolf writes of Vivien: 'Mrs. Eliot . . . making me almost vomit, so scented, so powdered, so egotistic, so morbid, so weakly.' TSE takes pains to cultivate personages such as Morrell and Woolf. He jokes about the danger of overstaying his welcome during country-house weekends: 'I know my failings. Insensitive persons can endure me for 24 hours; there is one old gentleman who, kept up by Port Wine, can even survive until the first Monday morning train: but 19½ hours is precisely the limit for less coarse and hardy natures.' MID-JUNE: 'I am giving up my cottage at Fishbourne as soon as I can get rid of it. The house next door has been turned into a garage which also sells lemonade and sweets; what with being on the Portsmouth Road, the place has become quite uninhabitable.' JULY – TSE takes over the offices of the Egoist Press (which Harriet Shaw Weaver is closing down) at 2 Robert Street, London. Suffers abscess under a finger nail and undergoes an operation involving the removal of a piece of bone from the finger. The summer also sees a stressful visit from TSE's mother, who occupies (with his sister Charlotte) the flat at 9 Clarence Gate Gardens while TSE and Vivien move into separate quarters. They visit Eastbourne, but TSE succumbs while there to what he terms a 'recrudescence' of the flu. 'It has been very trying', says TSE of his mother's visit. To Woolf he laments, 'I have been boiled in a hellbroth.' To Mary Hutchinson: 'I have been living beyond my income for five months, and eating up my savings. Vivien's illness and the cost of running *two establishments at once*, doctors, food, medicines, constant railway fares etc. have run me into colossal expense.' 23 AUGUST – Mrs Eliot and Charlotte sail back to the USA. OCTOBER – Vivien publishes 'Thé Dansant' (as Feiron Morris). TSE's *Homage to John Dryden: Three Essays on Poetry of the Seventeenth Century* appears from the Hogarth Press on 30 October. He also publishes

'Poème' (a version of Part I of 'The Hollow Men' I) in *Commerce*, and 'Doris's Dream Songs' in *Chapbook*. NOVEMBER – TSE and Vivien spend a weekend in Paris, staying at Lady Rothermere's apartment on the Quai Voltaire; they are disappointed by the Russian ballet. DECEMBER – TSE contributes an introduction to Paul Valéry's *Le Serpent* (trans. by Mark Wardle; printed by Cobden-Sanderson). TSE gets on very well with Geoffrey Faber, who will note in 1925 that he finds TSE 'a most attractive fellow, and . . . I am convinced that he will make a considerable name for himself.'

1925 JANUARY – TSE publishes in the *Criterion*, over his own name, a story entitled 'On the Eve: A Dialogue' (though it is principally written by Vivien). Vivien reviews Virginia Woolf's *Mr. Bennett and Mrs. Brown*. TSE contracts influenza, and is 'released from the basement [at the bank] for a month'. He and Vivien go to the country: 'my wife has broken down as the result of the long strain'. FEBRUARY – To Morrell: 'Vivien collapsed just a fortnight ago – my illness coming on top of a very hard and worrying winter of great strain and anxiety. She simply got out of bed and fell down – both exhaustion of body and spirit like two years ago.' MARCH – To Woolf: 'For the last three days Vivien has been in such agony as I have never seen, with the most terrific rheumatism all over her body. It came on quite suddenly, with no apparent cause, just as she was beginning to show signs of real progress. The doctor calls it rheumatism, but says that it is a most uncommon and peculiar variety, and she admits that she has never seen a case like it.' The doctors are puzzled: bronchitis, general neuritis – 'torture'. Vivien spends eleven weeks in bed. TSE publishes parts of 'The Hollow Men' in the *Dial*. On John Middleton Murry's recommendation, TSE is to be appointed (for a fee of £200) Clark Lecturer at Cambridge for 1926 – it came, wrote TSE, 'just at the blackest moment in my life'. 6 APRIL – TSE is invited by Geoffrey Faber – at the new general publishing firm (successor to the Scientific Press) that will be called Faber & Gwyer – to become the editor of a 'new quarterly review', for an initial five-year term, at a salary of £400; there is also the prospect that he could be made a director. Two weeks later, on 23 April, TSE is invited to join the board of directors: his salary is to be £325 as editor of a periodical to take over from the *Criterion*, with an additional sum of £150 as director of the publishing house. (In the event, there is a six-month interim between the last issue of the *Criterion* (July 1925) and the first issue of the *New Criterion* (January 1926.) TSE's job is to begin on 1 July 1925, and his first proposal is for a series of monographs on foreign writers. MID-APRIL – Vivien is gravely ill, with 'violent neuralgia and neuritis . . . Only her brain [is] alive.' TSE sends an alarming letter to Middleton Murry: 'In the last ten years – gradually, but deliberately – I have made myself into a *machine*. I have done it deliberately – in order to endure, in order not to feel – *but it has killed V* . . . I have deliberately killed my senses – I have deliberately died – in order to go on with the outward form of living – This I did in 1915 . . . But the dilemma – to kill another person by being dead, or to kill them by being alive? . . . Does it happen that two persons' lives are absolutely hostile? . . . Must I kill her or kill myself? I have *tried* to kill myself – but only to make the machine which kills her . . . I feel now that one cannot help another by *ruining* one's own soul – I have done that – can one help another and save it? Does she want to die?' Vivien writes what TSE calls a 'wonderful and terrible' story: 'The Paralysed Woman'. In May TSE sends the story – 'It seems to me amazingly brilliant and humorous and horrible' – to the *Dial*, but it is rejected by the editor, Marianne Moore. TSE becomes enraged with both Dr Martin (whom he later describes as a 'German brute') and Dr Cyriax: 'These people have done [Vivien] damage that will take a *very long* time to repair. Irritating and weakening the stomach, over-stimulating and exhausting the nerves. . . . in *agony* . . . almost blind.' APRIL – TSE publishes Vivien's 'Necesse est Perstare?', and writes to Morrell on 1 May: 'Yes, it is true that Vivien wrote that poem. In fact she has been writing for a long time – and I have always suspected that you knew it! And *I* think that she is a *very* clever and original writer, with a mathematical and abstract mind which ought to be trained – and I intend that it shall.' 1 MAY – TSE tells Morrell: 'The fact is that I have been very much more ill than I knew – it was a real breakdown. I *had* to make a change. And I shan't be fit for any brain work for a long time.' 7 MAY – He appeals for help from Bertrand Russell: 'I need the help of someone who understands her – I find her still perpetually baffling and deceptive. She seems to me like a child of six with an immensely clever and precocious mind. She writes *extremely* well (stories etc.) and [with] great originality. And I can never escape from the spell of her persuasive (even coercive) gift of argument.' He is 'desperate'. JUNE – a new doctor says of Vivien that 'he had never seen so bad a liver on a woman, or an intestine so nearly dead'. JULY – TSE publishes Vivien's sketch 'Fête Galante', which satirises the Hutchinsons and the Sitwells – according to Osbert Sitwell, St John Hutchinson protests to TSE. AUGUST – Vivien has shingles. SEPTEMBER – TSE undergoes an operation on his jaw: several teeth are extracted. The Woolfs are angry that Faber & Gwyer is to publish TSE's poems, including *The Waste Land* which they have issued from Hogarth. TSE is criticised too for seeming to poach other authors they have published. Woolf writes, 'To-day we are on Tom's track, riddling him and reviling him . . . L. thinks the queer shifty creature will slip away now.' 2 NOVEMBER – TSE resigns from Lloyds Bank, writing to Aldington later in the month: 'I am a director of Faber & Gwyer and a humble publisher at your service.' 23 NOVEMBER – *Poems 1909–1925* is published. 'The book gives me no pleasure – and I think *The Waste Land* appears at a disadvantage in the midst of all this other stuff, some of which was not even good enough to reprint. But I regard the book merely as an ejection, a means of getting all that out of the way.' Vivien is sent away to recover her health: first to an institution near Southampton, then to a sanatorium called The Stanboroughs – 'A Modern Hydrotherapeutic Health Institution'. 'I am sorry I tortured you and drove you mad,' she writes to TSE. 'I had no notion until yesterday afternoon that I had done it. I have been simply raving mad.' DECEMBER – TSE goes to rest at the Hôtel Savoie, La Turbie, in the Alpes Maritimes. He then visits Ezra Pound in Rapallo, and drafts three of the lectures he is to give at Cambridge. Vivien writes to her servant, of TSE: 'tell him his wife does love him and still loves him and always always has loved him, (*he does not believe I do*). Ask him to be kind to me, and to forgive me for any wrongs I've done him.' And to her doctor: 'When I think of all that my husband has done for me, and of all the life I smashed up (as I do think of it, all night and much of the day) I do not know why I don't go out and hang myself.'

ABBREVIATIONS AND SOURCES

PUBLISHED WORKS BY T. S. ELIOT

ASG	*After Strange Gods* (London: Faber & Faber, 1934)
AVP	*Ara Vos Prec* (London: The Ovid Press, 1920)
CP	*The Cocktail Party* (London: Faber & Faber, 1950)
CPP	*The Complete Poems and Plays of T. S. Eliot* (London: Faber & Faber, 1969)
EE	*Elizabethan Essays* (London: Faber & Faber, 1934)
FLA	*For Lancelot Andrewes: Essays on Style and Order* (London: Faber & Gwyer, 1928)
FR	*The Family Reunion* (London: Faber & Faber, 1939)
HJD	*Homage to John Dryden: Three Essays on Poetry of the Seventeenth Century* (London: The Hogarth Press, 1924)
KEPB	*Knowledge and Experience in the Philosophy of F. H. Bradley* (London: Faber & Faber, 1964; New York: Farrar, Straus & Company, 1964)
IMH	*Inventions of the March Hare: Poems 1909–1917*, ed. Christopher Ricks (London: Faber & Faber, 1996)
OPP	*On Poetry and Poets* (London: Faber & Faber, 1957; New York: Farrar, Straus & Cudahy, 1957)
P	*Poems* (London: The Hogarth Press, 1919)
P 1909–1925	*Poems 1909–1925* (London: Faber & Gwyer, 1925)
POO	*Prufrock and Other Observations* (London: The Egoist Press, 1917)
SA	*Sweeney Agonistes: Fragments of an Aristophanic Melodrama* (London: Faber & Faber, 1932)
SE	*Selected Essays: 1917–1932* (London: Faber & Faber, 1932; 3rd English edn., London and Boston: Faber & Faber, 1951)
SW	*The Sacred Wood: Essays on Poetry and Criticism* (London: Methuen & Co., 1920)
TCC	*To Criticize the Critic* (London: Faber & Faber, 1965; New York: Farrar, Straus & Giroux, 1965)

TUPUC	*The Use of Poetry and the Use of Criticism: Studies in the Relation of Criticism to Poetry in England* (London: Faber & Faber, 1933)
TWL	*The Waste Land* (1922, 1923)
TWL: Facs	*The Waste Land: A Facsimile and Transcript of the Original Drafts*, ed. Valerie Eliot (London: Faber & Faber, 1971; New York: Harcourt, Brace, Jovanovich, 1971)
VMP	*The Varieties of Metaphysical Poetry*, ed. Ronald Schuchard (London: Faber & Faber, 1993; New York: Harcourt Brace, 1994)

PERIODICALS AND PUBLISHERS

A.	*The Athenaeum* (see also *N&A*)
C.	*The Criterion*
F&G	Faber & Gwyer (publishers)
F&F	Faber & Faber (publishers)
IJE	*International Journal of Ethics*
N.	*The Nation*
N&A	*The Nation & The Athenaeum*
NC	*New Criterion*
NRF	*La Nouvelle Revue Française*
NS	*New Statesman*
TLS	*Times Literary Supplement*

PERSONS

AH	Aldous Huxley
BD	Bonamy Dobrée
BR	Bertrand Russell
CW	Charles Whibley
CWE	Charlotte Ware Eliot, TSE's mother
DHL	D. H. Lawrence
EP	Ezra Pound
EVE	(Esmé) Valerie Eliot
GCF	Geoffrey (Cust) Faber
HR	Herbert Read
HWE	Henry Ware Eliot (TSE's brother)
IPF	Irene Pearl Fassett (TSE's secretary)
JDH	John Davy Hayward
JJ	James Joyce

JMM	John Middleton Murry
LW	Leonard Woolf
MH	Mary Hutchinson
OM	Ottoline Morrell
RA	Richard Aldington
RC-S	Richard Cobden-Sanderson
SS	Sydney Schiff
TSE	T. S. Eliot
VHE	Vivien Haigh Eliot
VW	Virginia Woolf
WBY	W. B. Yeats
WL	Wyndham Lewis

ARCHIVE COLLECTIONS

Arkansas	Special Collections, University Libraries, University of Arkansas
BL	British Library, London
Beinecke	The Beinecke Rare Book and Manuscript Library, Yale University
Berg	Henry W. and Albert A. Berg Collection of English and American Literature, New York Public Library
Doucet	Fonds Bibliothèque Littéraire Jacques Doucet
Bodleian	The Bodleian Library, Oxford University
Bonn	Universitäts und Landesbibliothek, Bonn University
Brotherton	The Brotherton Collection, Leeds University Library
Buffalo	Lockwood Memorial Library, State University of New York at Buffalo
Butler	Rare Books and Manuscripts Division, Butler Library, Columbia University, New York
Caetani	Fondazione Camillo Caetani
Clare	Clare College, Cambridge
Cornell	Department of Rare Books, Olin Library, Cornell University
Faber	Faber & Faber Archive, London
Harvard	University Archives, Harvard University
Houghton	The Houghton Library, Harvard University
Huntington	Huntington Library, California
Keele	Special Collections, Keele University
King's	Modern Archive Centre, King's College, Cambridge
Lilly	Lilly Library, Indiana University, Bloomington

Marshall	Marshall Library, Cambridge
McMaster	Mills Memorial Library, McMaster University. Hamilton, Ontario
Morris	Morris Library, Southern Illinois University at Carbondale
Mugar	Mugar Memorial Library, Boston University
NYPL (MS)	New York Public Library (Manuscripts Division)
Northwestern	Special Collections, Northwestern University Library, Evanston, Illinois
Pennsylvania	Pennsylvania University Library
Princeton	Department of Rare Books and Special Collections, Princeton University Library
Reading	Reading University Library
Rosenbach	Rosenbach Museum and Library, Philadelphia, Pennsylvania
TCD	Trinity College, Dublin
Texas	The Harry Ransom Humanities Research Center, University of Texas at Austin
Tulsa	Department of Special Collections, McFarlin Library, University of Tulsa, Oklahoma
UCLA	University of California at Los Angeles
VE Papers	Vivien Eliot Papers, Bodleian Library, Oxford
Vichy	Bibliothèque Municipale, Vichy
Victoria	Special Collections, McPherson Library, University of Victoria, British Columbia
Virginia	Alderman Library, University of Virginia Library
Washington	Washington University Library, St Louis, Missouri

EDITORIAL NOTES

The source of each letter is indicated at the top right. CC indicates a carbon copy. Where no other source is shown it may be assumed that the original or a carbon copy is in the Valerie Eliot collection or at the Faber and Faber Archive.

del.	deleted
MS	manuscript
n. d.	no date
PC	postcard
sc.	*scilicet*: namely
TS	typescript
< >	indicates a word or words brought in from another part of the letter.

Place of publication is London, unless otherwise stated.

Ampersands and squiggles have been replaced by 'and', except where they occur in correspondence with Ezra Pound.

Some obvious typing or manuscript errors have been silently corrected.

Dates have been standardised.

Some words and figures which were abbreviated have been expanded.

Punctuation has occasionally been adjusted.

Editorial insertions are indicated by square brackets.

Words both italicised and underlined signify double underlining in the original copy.

Where possible a biographical note accompanies the first letter to or from a correspondent. Where appropriate, this brief initial note will also refer the reader to the Glossary of Names at the end of the text.

Vivienne Eliot liked her husband and friends to spell her name Vivien; but as there is no consistency, it is printed as written.

THE LETTERS
1923–1925

1923

TO *Henry Eliot*[1] TS Houghton

2 January 1923 9 Clarence Gate Gdns, London N.W.1

My dear Henry,

I have so much to write to you about that I must divide it into two or three letters. The three chief subjects are

Hydraulic[2]
the Bank
Mother's visit

I will only deal in this letter with the latter two.

Of course I must thank you for your goodness in writing so often, and keeping me posted about finance in America, and for your last admirable letter. And most of all for your latest extraordinary generosity. About your cheque: I imagine that you sent it under the impression that I had either just left the bank, or that I was just about to leave.[3] There are three reasons why I have not yet done so and cannot at the present time. But I feel that I ought to return it to you: I will either do that, or else invest it until needed, as you prefer. Please say. I do not want to take it under any misapprehension on your part. But if I invest it, I think I shall return it to you to invest for me in America, as I do not like sinking any more money in England at the present juncture.

I cannot possibly leave the bank at present, because of the way in which they have treated me. In spite of the fact that I have been absent about ten or eleven weeks during the past year, owing to Vivien's illness, and constantly late, they have raised my salary to five hundred pounds, at a time when they are raising very few salaries indeed. But this is not the main point. That is that they have shown me in word and deed that they value my services very highly indeed, and have placed me in a position of responsibility such that I cannot resign now without letting them down very badly and behaving with ingratitude. I am now head of an Intelligence

1 – Henry Eliot: see Glossary of Names.
2 – The Hydraulic-Press Brick Company, established in St Louis in 1864. TSE's father Henry Ware Eliot had been chairman of the company from 1909 until his death in 1919.
3 – TSE was considering leaving Lloyds Bank (where he had started work in the Colonial and Foreign Department in Mar. 1917), but did not ultimately do so until late 1925.

Department with a number of clerks under me, and in sole charge. I have had to organise the department, and the organisation is still far from complete. On the contrary, they are just on the point of enlarging the scope of the department much more. The heads of the bank are anxious to make a big thing of it; and I know quite well that there is at present no one else in the bank but myself who can do it for them – that is, the one or two men who might do it are not available for this post. This is not a boast: it is simply the fact that there happens to be no one available with the proper qualifications, and as a matter of fact they had me in view from the inception of the idea. The bank is getting bigger and bigger, with interests practically all over the world, and affiliated banks everywhere, and there is the opportunity to create a service of Intelligence which would be quite unique. It has involved very heavy work so far: I have had to draft schemes, and at the same time attend to a mass of detail, such as the running of a printing press (which is always breaking down) and the holidays and attendances and personal grievances of the clerks; and although I have much more liberty of movement than before, I have had to be at the bank early and late to get the work done. And with it all I have to read ten or fifteen papers a day to try to keep myself posted on all sorts of subjects, such as foreign budgets, movements of crops, agricultural banks, oil developments, and what not. In addition, I am still unfortunately the only person in the bank who knows anything about the Peace Treaties, and there are two or three big lawsuits with Germans coming on this winter which involve an intimate knowledge of their history for the past four years, which no one else possesses. You will think that I have got excited about all this, but the fact remains that if I left the bank now I should simply be hanging another millstone round my conscience. The bank took me in without knowing anything about me whatever, when I was absolutely on the rocks in 1917, and has treated me with extraordinary kindness ever since. Of course this big expansion of the Intelligence work has only happened since my decision to leave: this summer I was merely running a daily newspaper of extracts from the foreign press, with another man, and it would not have been nearly so disconcerting for the bank if I had left then.

This is my main reason. Another reason is the social uncertainty, owing to the alarming rise of the Labour Party to power.[1] It has thrown England into great anxiety and confusion: no one knows what sort of living

1 – At the General Election on 6 Dec. 1923 the Conservatives were defeated, and on 23 Jan. 1924 Ramsay MacDonald formed the first Labour government in Britain.

conditions we shall have in six months from now. I have been working toward getting a position in journalism under Lord Rothermere.[1] I am in sympathy with his views, in general, and he is one of the very richest and most powerful men in England. This, of course, is the reason why I have stuck so hard to the *Criterion*; the support and backing of the Rothermeres is something which is worth working for. I have not worked for immediate profit – for in fact I have not had a penny from it, except ordinary payments for contributions – but with a view to solidifying myself with the Rothermeres. I saw Lord Rothermere today, and he said that the political situation was so dangerous that he would not consider inviting me to leave the bank, or indeed consider any expansion of his interests or development of his papers, until the situation had cleared up, and he told me to see him again at the middle of March.[2]

Perhaps it is as well that I should not leave just now, from some points of view. I am so jaded, with the anxiety of the past year, that I simply cannot write decent prose: my last articles in the *Dial* are deplorable;[3] and until I can get my mind into better shape I should simply ruin my reputation by writing at all.

Now about mother. This time, I feel that it [is] impossible for me to take the responsibility either of urging her to come or urging her to remain. We have been keeping on our flat, and Ellen,[4] simply because we felt that mother would not want to come to any other place; we should otherwise have disposed of it a year ago and found a place which [would] both have been cheaper and more pleasant to us, but we could have found nothing so suitable in comfort and convenience for mother. Or we should have let this flat profitably on a long lease. If the Labour Party come in, and there is a big panic and depression, we may find it very difficult to dispose of. But if mother comes, what I should do is this. I have a very nice, intelligent, serious Scotch woman [Miss Duff], who has been coming to me about twice a week for the past year to do secretarial work. She is engaged in the

1–Harold Sidney Harmsworth, first Viscount Rothermere (1868–1940): proprietor of the *Daily Mirror*, *Sunday Pictorial*, *Glasgow Daily Record*, *Evening News* and *Sunday Mail*. Harold Harmsworth also shared ownership of Associated Newspapers with his elder brother, Alfred, first Viscount Northcliffe. On the death of his brother in 1922, Harold acquired his controlling interest in Associated Newspapers, including the *Daily Mail*, for £1.6 million.

2–Since Viscount Rothermere was estranged from his wife, Lilian (she had had an affair with his younger brother), who was the sole financial backer of the *Criterion*, it is possible that he might have been disingenuous in his dealings with TSE.

3–TSE, 'Letters from London', *Dial* 73: 3 & 6 (Sept. & Dec. 1922).

4–Ellen Kellond, who had been the Eliots' maid since 1918.

daytime as a typist in a city office, but she is tired of city work. She is about forty, and has for me the great advantage of knowing French well. I should engage her as a resident secretary–housekeeper. I should put her in to Clarence Gate to look after mother, with Ellen to cook, and Miss Duff could go about with mother and would be a much better person than Marion[1] – tactful and placid. Marion could thus get some holiday out of it, and perhaps could go into the country for a bit with Vivien. Then I should engage a car so that mother need do nothing on foot or in buses, and I would go away with her sometimes for weekends.

And I think that I could come and fetch mother. I could only come to New York and meet her at the boat, and leave *immediately* (I don't know whether there is any passport or other red tape to interfere). I don't conceal that this would be a considerable sacrifice. I would take most of my holiday (which is three weeks and three days and not a day more in a year) to do that, and it would mean giving up certain other plans of which I shall speak later. But the immediate point is this: I do not see any point in arranging a convoy for mother one way, if she has to be alone the other. I could not possibly make two voyages. If I brought mother over, *could you come and take her back*? It would of course be a big sacrifice for you too, and tantalising to come all the way to Europe and not be able to stay, but unless you can do this I do not see how mother can come.

What I want you to do is to think over the plan for mother's stay[2] which I have outlined, and consider whether you think it feasible, and also whether you could escort mother *either* to England or back from England, and *wire me yes or no* at once. I cannot afford to remain in a state of suspense, as important plans of my own depend on this; and I cannot make the arrangements for Miss Duff etc. without knowing your opinion. In fact, our whole life is in suspense on account of the uncertainty of mother's visit.

If mother could not come – and if you think she should not come – I would come to America; but I have always felt that a visit of four or five days, such as mine must be limited to, would be more pain than pleasure to mother.

Please wire me as quickly as you can.

1–Marion Cushing Eliot (1877–1964) was the fourth child of Henry Ware and Charlotte Champe Eliot; TSE's favourite sister, she had travelled with her mother to visit him in London in 1921.

2–After the success of her visit to England in 1921, TSE was counting on his mother returning in the summer of 1923. This proved impossible, and she made her second visit only in 1924.

I shall try to write about other subjects within a few days. I am very tired. My fatigue, which has been growing for years, is not solely due to overwork and anxieties: it is largely due to the kink in my brain[1] which makes life at all an unremitting strain for me, and which is at the bottom of a good many of the things about me that you object to.

Affectionately your brother

Tom[2]

TO *Richard Aldington*[3]

MS Texas

4 January 1923 — 9 Clarence Gate Gdns

My dear Richard

The best wishes for the New Year to you!

I was going to write – but I am delighted to see you on Wednesday, as I have a great deal to speak about, and it is more satisfactory than writing. Could you manage to fetch me at twelve at my office? We could lunch nearby – I only have *one hour!* – and would save time. It is Bank Station – Central London – 75, Lombard Street, 1st floor – Information Dept opposite clock of St Mary Woolnoth. I am sorry you are only here for the day. But it will be delightful.

Yours

Tom

1–Cf. TSE's letter to RA, 6 Nov. 1921, which spoke of suffering from 'an *aboulie* and emotional derangement which has been a lifelong affliction'. Cf. also Celia in *CP*, II, 559–69: 'Well, my upbringing was pretty conventional – / I had always been taught to disbelieve in sin. / Oh, I don't mean that it was ever mentioned! / But anything wrong, from our point of view, / Was either bad form, or was psychological. / And bad form always led to disaster / Because the people one knew disapproved of it. / I don't worry much about form, myself – / But when everything's bad form, or mental kinks, / You either become bad form, and cease to care, / Or else, if you care, you must be kinky.'

2–At the foot , HWE wrote: 'Mother's going inevitably uncertain. Could bring her back. Would keep flat a while if possible [*del.*]. Write Mother direct. Writing. Wired TSE.'

3–Richard Aldington: see Glossary of Names.

TO *Ottoline Morrell*[1] MS Texas

5 January 1923 9 Clarence Gate Gdns

My dear Ottoline,

I am writing to tell you – in confidence, as you will see – that I have just by an extraordinary piece of good luck come across a tiny suite of two rooms which are amazingly cheap, and which I intend to take if nothing goes wrong. My idea is to use them as an office for the *Criterion* work at once, and when the lease of this flat is up, which will be before very long, I expect to give it up.[2] We want to decrease expenses of living, and settle ourselves in a way that would be adaptable to any kind of life. I took the liberty of giving you as a reference for my respectability, because I knew that I could depend upon your not mentioning it to anyone *at all*, – and there are so few of one's friends of whom one can be sure in that way! You see, this arrangement is so intimately bound up with all of my plans, and so personal, that I do not want anyone to know about it. I hope you will not mind the bother of replying at once to the agent, because my only chance of getting this is to be *very quick* about it. I shall be very grateful to you, because there are so few people whom I should care to ask.

I have received from Virginia Woolf a cheque for £50 signed by you and her. I have written to thank her, and to ask her to express my gratitude and appreciation to the others whose names I do not know.[3] I am really overwhelmed at what you and a few others do, and by the difficulty of expressing what I feel. I think the best way of showing in what way I take this gift is this: I have placed this cheque, together with the *Dial* prize in a special account, to which I shall add all the money that I can save.[4] I shall keep this fund intact, by investing it and having the interest accumulate in the same fund, and I shall not touch it, until the interest upon the savings is enough to use to alter my way of life in such a direction as I know the givers would most desire. I shall consider it, in other words, as a Trust.

1 – Lady Ottoline Morrell: see Glossary of Names.

2 – This is the first reference to TSE's renting a small flat, 38 Burleigh Mansions, St Martin's Lane, nr. Trafalgar Square. Arthur Grover & Co., letting agents, referred to the premises as an 'office' (letter to TSE, 16 Jan. 1923). Its existence was known only to close friends. VW describes (19 Dec. 1923) going to a 'flat in an arcade' and asking for 'Captain Eliot' (*Diary of Virginia Woolf*, II, *1920–1924*, ed. Anne Olivier Bell [1978], 278). VHE was to ask MH to meet her there in Oct. 1924.

3 – The cheque from OM and VW was from the Eliot Fellowship Fund, set up in July 1922 by OM, RA, Harry Norton, LW and VW. It was designed to enable TSE to leave Lloyds Bank.

4 – TSE had been given the 1922 *Dial* award (founded by Scofield Thayer in 1921) worth $2,000, for *TWL*. The poem had been first published in the USA in *Dial* 73: 5 (Nov. 1922).

With very many wishes for the new year for you in every way.

Affectionately yours,
Tom

TO *The Editor of the Daily Mail*[1]

Published 8 January 1923 9 Clarence Gate Gdns

Sir,

It is so remarkable to find oneself in agreement with the policy of any newspaper on more than one point that I am writing to express my cordial approval of your attitude on nearly every public question of present importance.

Nothing could be more salutary at the present time than the remarkable series of articles which you have been publishing on Fascismo;[2] these alone constitute a public service of the greatest value and would by themselves have impelled me to write to thank you.

On the Ilford murder[3] your attitude has been in striking contrast with the flaccid sentimentality of other papers I have seen, which have been so impudent as to affirm that they represented the great majority of the British people.[4]

1–The text is from the *Daily Mail* (8 Jan. 1923, 8), under the heading 'Right on all Points'.

2–On 19 Dec. 1922, the *Daily Mail* launched a series of articles on Italian politics by Sir Perceval Phillips: 'The "Red" Dragon and the Black Shirts' recorded the 'wonderful epic' of the Fascist Revolution in Italy, and described 'the war against Bolshevism' of 'the Crusaders of the Black Shirt'. The series concluded on 5 Jan. 1923 with an account of the Italian Fascist government as 'the greatest experiment we have witnessed since Lenin overthrew the Romanoffs', and a portrait of Mussolini as 'A solitary and terrible figure, with the weight of Italy on his shoulders'. In an editorial 'The Saviours of Italy' at the start of the series, the *Mail* observed: 'The rescue of Italy from the Bolsheviks by the unselfish devotion of the Fascisti is not only a romance in itself; it is also one of the most important events of our time.' Roger Kojecky suggests that TSE's 'Triumphal March' draws on 'the poet's recollections' of these accounts of Mussolini's March on Rome (*Social Thought of T. S. Eliot* [1971], 101).

3–The *Daily Mail* gave detailed coverage of the 'Ilford Murder Trial', in which Frederick Bywaters and Edith Jessie Thompson were accused of 'the murder of the woman's husband . . . stabbed in the streets near his home at Ilford, Essex, when returning with his wife from the theatre in the early hours of October 4 [1922]'. Found guilty on 11 Dec., the two lovers were sentenced to death. The case aroused huge public interest, with Edith Thompson being described in the papers as 'the Madame Bovary of North-East London and the Messalina of Ilford'. Both were hanged on 9 Jan. 1923. Thompson was the first woman to be hanged in Britain since 1907. Dorothy L. Sayers and Robert Eustace's *The Documents in the Case* (1930) was based on accounts of the crime in the *Daily Mail* and other papers.

4–The *Daily Sketch* organised a petition for the quashing of the death sentence on the 'blameless' Bywaters that was allegedly signed by a million people but disregarded by the Home Office. In contrast, the *Daily Mail* opposed 'the crusade of the sentimentalists'.

On the Turkish question,[1] and on other matters of foreign policy, you have manifested a temperance, sanity, and consistency which can but rarely be attributed to the Press – virtues, however, in which the Press ought to lead the public. In an age when the intellect is eclipsed alternately by passion and apathy such virtues can hardly be over-estimated.

T. S. Eliot

TO *Ottoline Morrell* MS Texas

9 January 1923 9 Clarence Gate Gdns

My dear Ottoline,

It was *most kind* of you to reply *immediately* to my request, and if I get this I shall feel that it is very largely by your aid and under your benediction.[2] Thank you a thousand times. Vivien is at Eastbourne – it is an experiment of course – it means partly giving up the diet which has proved so admirable, in exchange for sea air and change. So I shd be very glad if I mt. come to tea with you on Tuesday?

Affectionately yours
Tom

FROM *Vivien Eliot*[3] MS Valerie Eliot

Thurs. [Postmark 11 January 1923] [Eastbourne]

Dearest darling Wing

I wired this morning. Yesterday I was so dead tired I dozed most of the afternoon, and it was early closing day so that to send a wire one of us wd. have had to stump all the way to the G.P.O. and I was somehow even too tired to ask Pearl [Fassett] to do it. My fatigue is *immense*, but quite

1–The British government, represented by Lord Curzon, was a key participant in the Lausanne conference, set up to resolve a number of vexed issues in the aftermath of the Greco-Turkish war of 1919–22. These included the fate of Greeks in the new Turkish Republic, the Turkish claim to Mosul, and Turkish proposals that 'foreign warships in the Black Sea . . . shall not exceed the strength of the strongest Black Sea fleet'. The *Mail* supported Curzon's view that the proposals were designed to be 'favourable to Russia', noting that 'the Russians are posing at being more eager to protect Turkish interests than are the Turks themselves' (19 Dec.). On 30 Dec., it advised: 'Talk plainly to the Turks but do not talk War! The country will not tolerate a war with the Turks on any pretext whatsoever.'

2–OM had written a reference for his second flat (see TSE's letter of 5 Jan.).

3–Vivien Eliot: see Glossary of Names.

healthy. At night I just [get] into bed and am half asleep before that. Last night I slept like a dog without moving. Thank you for yr. very sweet satisfying letters. Funnily – I have had Katherine M. perpetually in my mind the last two days. – *and*, last night I dreamed of her *all night*! This a.m. when I read yr. letter that she was v. ill I felt that there is indeed something psychic going on. I think Rother. shd. be blamed if anything happens to K. M. for if she was not mad and irresponsible she wd. not have allowed K. M. to stay in that bug-house. And *Murry* – !!

Well dear *please* come down for the weekend and bring me back on Sunday. *Could you* get Sat. morning off – and come on *Friday night*? Bring the suitcase.

Wang I'm just pining to see that flat – just *mad* to see it. There is no denying I'm better already altho' hideous green and blotched. Wire me tomorrow morning, dearest.

<Please address this letter have forgotten the address.>

I think Waste Land book *very nice*.

Have you sent Lewis's drawing yet to *Vanity Fair* if NOT DO *AT ONCE*. You *must*. *Register it*. *Criterion not bad*.

Jack has written and wired each day in wild attempts to make up.

Of course P. has caused me extra fatigue, but yet has stood between me and unpleasant contacts.

Please send this letter[1] at once and register, and put please forward in Eyetalian on it. *Forgotten number*.

Do come Friday night if poss.

[Vivien]

TO *S. S. Koteliansky*[2] MS BL

11 January 1923 *The Criterion*, 9 Clarence Gate Gdns

Dear Mr Koteliansky

I hope I have not taken too much time over the essay on Dostoevski? I have been very much interested in it, but I think it would not be suitable

1 – Enclosure no longer present.

2 – Born in a Jewish *shtetl* in the Ukraine, S. S. Koteliansky (1882–1955) – 'Kot', as he was known to friends – moved in 1911 to London where he befriended DHL, LW, VW, JMM, and Katherine Mansfield (whom he adored), and the artist Mark Gertler. From 1923 to 1924, he was business manager of *The Adelphi*. He translated into English several Russian writers including Dostoevsky and Chekhov. See John Carswell, *Lives and Letters: A. R. Orage, Beatrice Hastings, Katherine Mansfield, John Middleton Murry, S. S. Koteliansky: 1906–1957* (1978).

for the *Criterion* for some time to come. In such a small review one has to proportion and balance very carefully, and as we have just had one very conspicuous and important Dostoevski contribution[1] – certainly the most important thing in no. 1 – I think it would be better if the next thing representing Russia were on quite another subject.

You will think that I should have thought of this before giving you the trouble. I did. But I was so anxious to satisfy my curiosity about anything you thought it worth your while to translate, that I asked for it. I am, for my own sake, very glad I did. But I shouldn't want to publish it for some time to come, and I am very keen to see the other thing you have promised to show me.

With cordial wishes

Yours sincerely
T. S. Eliot

TO *Edmund Wilson*[2]

MS Beinecke

11 January 1923 — *The Criterion*, 9 Clarence Gate Gdns

Dear Mr Wilson,

Thank you for your letter of the 18th December, which has lain on my table for less time than most of my correspondence! I shall send you a copy of the Wyndham Lewis drawing[3] in a few days, as soon as I have time to do it up.

There is one favour I wish to ask you, and that is, that in using my picture, or in any other mention of me, you see that I am not referred to as 'editor' of the *Criterion*. It is true that the fact has been stated in several places, but that is because I have been too occupied to warn my friends, and others will do so anyway (but it can be denied if necessary). The reason is that I already occupy one 'official' position – in a bank; and it is inconsistent with the obligations of that position to occupy any other, and the continued or conspicuous publication of my name in that capacity might be troublesome for me. My conscience is quite clear, because the

1–F. M. Dostoevsky, 'Plan of the Novel *The Life of a Great Sinner*', trans. S. S. Koteliansky and VW, C. 1: 1 (Oct. 1922).

2–Edmund Wilson (1885–1972), US journalist and critic; author of *Axel's Castle: A study of Imaginative Literature 1890–1930* (1931) and *To the Finland Station* (1940). Managing editor of *Vanity Fair* from 10 July 1922 to 5 May 1923, he later worked for the *New Republic*.

3–WL's 1921 pencil portrait of TSE.

one work does not in fact interfere with the other, and furthermore I am not taking any money for the *Criterion* work; but I am sure that I can rely upon your discretion. I had neglected to mention this to Mr Seldes,[1] but I shall do so when next writing.

Please accept my cordial thanks for your more than generous appreciation of *The Waste Land*.[2] I think you have understood it remarkably well, perhaps a little over-understood it! I mean read more into it than it contains here and there. I am very sensible of its fundamental weaknesses, and whatever I do next will be, at least, very different; I feel that it [is] merely a kind of consummation of my past work, not the initiation of something new, and it will take me all my courage and persistence, and perhaps a long time, to do something better. But 'something' must be better. *The Waste Land* does not leave me well satisfied.

May I raise one objection, since I feel it strongly? It gives me great pain to have my work used to belittle that of Ezra Pound.[3] It is not merely a question of friendship – or of my vast indebtedness to him – but of justice; I admire the *Cantos* very much myself, and I think that he never receives the recognition he deserves. And at the least there are unquestionably respects in which he is far more a master than I am.

With cordial thanks,

Sincerely yours
T. S. Eliot

PS Lady Rothermere has asked for my photograph to be sent to *Vogue*. As I am under the impression that *Vogue* and *Vanity Fair* are part of one and the same firm, could not the one you have be handed on to *Vogue* if necessary?[4] Subject, of course, to the silence about the *Criterion* explained in my letter.

T. S. E.

1 – Gilbert Seldes: see Glossary of Names.
2 – 'The Poetry of Drouth', *Dial* 73: 6 (Dec. 1922), 611–16.
3 – Wilson had contrasted TSE's use of allusion to 'the extremely ill-focused *Eight Cantos* of his imitator Ezra Pound, who presents only a bewildering mosaic with no central emotion to provide a key'.
4 – *Vanity Fair* and *Vogue* were both owned by Condé Nast (1873–1942).

TO *Scofield Thayer*[1] TS Beinecke

12 January 1923 *The Criterion*, 9 Clarence Gate Gdns

Dear Scofield,

Thank you very much for your letter of 29th December and the enclosed essay by Hofmannsthal.[2] I think it is considerably shorter than 5000 words and we shall have no difficulty in getting it in to the July number to which it will add distinction. I shall probably take the liberty of cutting out the long quotation from Barrès[3] as it is out of proportion to the length of the charming essay and I think we have had nearly enough of Barrès in our generation. Will you communicate our pleased acceptance of the article to H. I will write to him direct later.

Since I wrote you I received my copies of the *Dial*[4] and I have now received two additional copies for which I thank you.

If any more [simple *del.*] central! European writers are recommended to me I will consult you about them. Bertram[5] is a professor at Bonn who was recommended to me by Curtius[6] and who has written what is said to be a very good book on Nietzsche[7] which I possess but have not read. I am glad to hear that you are remaining in Vienna for some time to come.

With best wishes for the New Year,

Yours ever,
Tom

1–Scofield Thayer: see Glossary of Names.

2–Hugo von Hofmannsthal: see Glossary of Names. His essay appeared as 'Greece' in *C.* 2: 5 (Oct. 1923), 95–102.

3–Maurice Barrès (1862–1923): French novelist, journalist and politician; he served in the Chamber of Deputies, 1889–93, and became a nationalist. He was an anti-Dreyfusard during the period of the Dreyfus Affair (1897–9), and an ally of Charles Maurras in the French Nationalist Party. See Michael Curtis, *Three against the Third Republic: Sorel, Barrès, and Maurras* (1959).

4–TSE's 'London Letter' on Marie Lloyd appeared in *Dial* 73: 6 (Dec. 1922).

5–Ernst Bertram (1884–1957), poet and scholar, was a lecturer at the University of Bonn until 1922, when he was appointed Professor of German Literature at Cologne University; author of *Nietzsche: An Attempt at Mythology* (1918), and essays on literary figures including Hugo von Hofmannsthal, Stefan George, and Thomas Mann (who became his friend and correspondent).

6–E. R. Curtius: see Glossary of Names. Curtius became a contributor to *C.* and translator of *TWL*.

7–Ernst Bertram, *Nietzsche: Versuch einer Mythologie* [*Nietzsche: An Attempt at Mythology*] (Berlin, 1918).

TO *Edmund Wilson* TS Beinecke

12 January 1923 *The Criterion,* 9 Clarence Gate Gdns

Dear Mr Wilson,

I have sent you a copy of the drawing by Wyndham Lewis,[1] but it occurs to me that of course I have no right to authorise its publication and that the copyright resides with him. He is entitled, I suppose, to a fee for its use. May I leave it to you to settle that matter with him? and will you return the copy to me if you do not use it?

In haste,

Yours sincerely,
T. S. Eliot

TO *Mrs Walter Edward McCourt*

TS Missouri History Museum

12 January 1923 9 Clarence Gate Gardens

Dear Mrs McCourt,

Thank you very much indeed for your kind letter of December 17th. It is rare for me to receive letters of this sort, and this is the first letter I have received from my native city. Indeed, it is the first intimation that I have had that my work is known there, and you must know that in spite of the admonition of the old proverb, or perhaps because of it, a prophet always particularly hankers after honour in his own country. At least, this is true of the minor prophets.

It is many years since I have been in St Louis. Men's memories are short, especially in a growing and changing town, and I doubt if many of those who owe most to the university there even now know that it was named after my grandfather (and later changed at his insistence) or have ever noticed his portrait hanging there. But I am very proud of all that he did for the city and for all that he did for the nation at the most critical moment in its existence. And these feelings give me still more pleasure in having this letter from you to which to reply.

Yours very truly,
T. S. Eliot

1–On 14 Aug. 1922 TSE had suggested that Wilson use the WL portrait of him alongside his article on 'Contemporary English Prose' (*Vanity Fair* 20: 5, July 1923). The prose of WL was one of the subjects of the essay, which describes Lewis's imagination as 'primarily visual'. Wilson responded on 26 Feb. to say that the portrait was 'too faint' to reproduce.

TO *Jacques Rivière*[1] CC

18 January 1923 [London]

Cher Monsieur,

Je m'empresse de vous écrire pour vous féliciter sur le numéro de la *Nouvelle Revue Française* en hommage à Proust.[2] C'est une chose remarquable que vous avez fait, chose (je pense) unique dans l'histoire des revues littéraires. Puisque je suis moi-même chargé de la rédaction d'une petite revue, je suis capable d'apprécier le travail dévoué qui a préparé une telle oeuvre.

Vous m'enverrez plus tard un petit mot pour me dire à quel moment vous désirerez une autre chronique.

Plus instamment, je vous rappelle que nous convoitons l'article que vous avez généreusement promis,[3] et je ne lasserai pas de vous en demander des nouvelles!

Croyez, cher monsieur, à ma sympathie cordiale.

[T. S. E.][4]

TO *Richard Cobden-Sanderson*[5] CC

18 January 1923 [London]

Dear Cobden-Sanderson

I enclose two more articles for No. 3 and I hope that the printers won't balk at Charles Whibley's writing.[6] This is nearly everything; there will

1 – Jacques Rivière: see Glossary of Names.

2 – The most recent *NRF* (1 Jan. 1923) was a Proust memorial issue, with articles by André Gide, Albert Thibaudet, Arthur Symons, E. R. Curtius, Joseph Conrad and others. Rivière, one of the first critics to recognise Proust, published extracts from *À la recherche du temps perdu* in *NRF*.

3 – On 7 Nov. 1922, Rivière wrote that he was due to lecture on Freud and Proust in Jan. 1923; his 'Notes on a Possible Generalization of the Theories of Freud' appeared in *C.* 1: 4 (July 1923).

4 – *Translation*: Dear Sir, I am writing at once to congratulate you on the issue of *La Nouvelle Revue Française* in homage to Proust. You have done something remarkable, something unique (I think) in the history of literary reviews. Since I myself am responsible for the editing of a little review, I am able to appreciate the devoted work involved in the preparation of such an issue.

Please send me a note later to tell me at what date you would like another letter.

More urgently, I remind you that we are eagerly awaiting the article you generously promised us, and I shall not weary of asking you how it is coming along!

With my warmest and most cordial regards. [T. S. E.]

5 – Richard Cobden-Sanderson: see Glossary of Names.

6 – See CW, 'Bolingbroke, Part 1', in *C.* 1: 3 (Apr. 1923), 203.

certainly be one more if not two but not more than two; one possibly from myself. I should like to know the number of words in each contribution as soon as possible. Also I have not yet heard from Hazell[1] the number of words in the various other articles in No. 2. I don't want to know how many in Marie Lloyd;[2] as I told you some days ago on the telephone, I am not taking any money for that.

Can you send me a few, ten or fifteen, of the slips of contents which went in to No. 2.

I saw the advertisement in the *TLS*[3] and now await reviews with anxiety.

Yours ever

[T. S. E.]

I think the contributors ought to be paid as soon as possible. Please note that Curtius has written to ask that his money be sent to him: *c/o Freiherr E. von Weizsäcker, Deutsche Consulat, Basle, Switzerland.*

Curtius	5430	words	10:16/-
Gómez	1600	"	3:4/-
Robertson	4847	"	9:12/-
*Pound	3545	"	7:12/-
Moore	5714	"	11:8/-
Hudson (SCHIFF)	1346	"	2:12/-
Flint (trans)	7030	"	5:5/-

I still want the no. of words for FRY and PIRANDELLO.
Please check my figures before paying!

* Plus 2 preface????

TO *Mrs S. A. Middleton*[4] CC

18 January 1923 [*The Criterion*, London]

Dear Madam,

Thank you for your letter, which gave me great pleasure. I have enjoyed seeing your son, and it would be a delight to me to be the means of his

1–Hazell, Watson & Viney Ltd, printers of C.

2–TSE, 'In Memoriam: Marie Lloyd', C. 1: 2 (Feb. 1923); reprinted from *Dial* 73: 6 (Dec. 1922).

3–The *TLS* advertisement (18 Jan. 1923, 45) listed the contents for Jan. 1923: J. M. Robertson, 'Flaubert'; Roger Fry, 'Mallarmé's "Herodiade"'; E. R. Curtius, 'Balzac'; EP, 'On Criticism in General'; Luigi Pirandello, 'The Legend of Tristram and Isolt, II'; Stephen Hudson, 'The Thief'; TSE, 'In Memoriam: Marie Lloyd'; Ramón Gómez de la Serna, 'From "The New Museum"'.

4–S. A. Middleton, a translator, did a number of translations from Spanish for C.

finding the place he is looking for.[1] We must go on looking and trying; I am a great believer in things 'turning up'. And I have been in a similar position myself, and when I was some years older than he is!

I enclose the MSS. of [Antonio] Marichalar,[2] and shall be very grateful if you will translate for us.

Yours very truly,
[T. S. E.]

TO *J. B. Trend*[3] CC

18 January 1923 [*The Criterion*, London]

Dear Mr Trend,

Thank you very much indeed for your letter of the 13th. I am communicating your praise of the Gómez translation to Mr Flint, who had a very tough tussle to make it presentable. It seemed almost untranslatable, and I was in despair, as I had asked Gómez to contribute, on the strength of very enthusiastic recommendations.[4] I am glad, too, that you like the Pirandello, for I was delighted with it myself.[5]

But I had been wondering whether I should hear from you, and whether you had returned from Spain (though I had seen one or two things I thought must be by you, in the *TLS*) and had been for some time on the point of writing to you. Remember that I have been counting on you, if on

1–TSE took a kindly interest in advising Mrs Middleton's son about his job prospects; he even interviewed him in Jan. 1923. Then, in a letter of 14 Feb., Ian C. Middleton offered his services to TSE – 'with someone to lick your stamps and envelopes and play office boy generally, you might gain a little more time for more important work' – but TSE counselled him first to study French, as well as shorthand and typing. VHE too talked to him encouragingly over the phone.

2–See Antonio Marichalar, 'Contemporary Spanish Literature', trans. by 'Mde S. A. Middleton', *C.* 1: 3 (Apr. 1923), 277–92.

3–J. B. Trend (1887–1958): British Hispanist, with interest in history of music; first Professor of Spanish at Cambridge University; author of *Manuel de Falla and Spanish Music* (1929). He first met TSE in the summer of 1922, and had a regular music column in *C.*, 1924–33.

4–Trend praised F. S. Flint's translation of 'From "The New Museum"', in *C.* 1: 2 (Jan. 1923): 'The translation of Gómez de la Serna has the surprizing result of making him read better in English than he does in Spanish . . . But I rather wish that it had been some other writer. Gómez de la Serna is amusing enough; but his humour is not in the least Spanish. To a Spanish mind it would seem very Gallic – imitation Gallic, I mean . . . The Pirandello story, on the other hand, is a glorious contrast. It is a brilliant piece of work; and yet no one but an Italian would have thought it.'

5–Luigi Pirandello, 'The Shrine', *C.* 1: 2 (Jan. 1923), 157–70.

anyone, to report to me some treasure from Spain which might be exploited by the *Criterion*. Unless Spain is absolutely barren – can we not meet before very long and talk about it again?

Sincerely yours,
[T. S. E.]

TO *F. S. Flint*[1]

TS Texas

18 January 1923 — *The Criterion*, 9 Clarence Gate Gdns

Dear Flint,

I have a letter from Trend, the Spanish literature specialist on the *TLS*, who says:

'The translation of Gómez de la Serna has the surprizing result of making him read better in English than he does in Spanish'.

I hope this will go to comfort you for what must have seemed thankless work! Cheque in a few days. With many thanks for helping us out of that difficulty so triumphantly.

Yours
T. S. Eliot

TO *John Middleton Murry*[2]

MS Valerie Eliot

18 January 1923 — 9 Clarence Gate Gdns

Dear John,

Forgive me for writing to you at all, but one must express oneself if only by a sheet of paper. There is, of course, nothing that I can say, except to remind you that I feel very very deeply, and that this has hardly left my thoughts for ten days, and that my sympathy with your suffering is something that cannot be written.[3]

Yours always
Tom

1–F. S. Flint: see Glossary of Names.
2–John Middleton Murry: see Glossary of Names.
3–JMM's wife, the author Katherine Mansfield (1888–1923), had died at Fontainebleau on 9 Jan.

Sometime – *later* – just write and say that you did not mind my writing you this. Later still, when you are working again, I want your article.[1] I shall have done a critical article on K's work.[2]

TO *Daniel Halévy*[3] CC

18 January 1923 [London]

Monsieur,

Je vous remercie de votre lettre du 15 janvier, et du manuscrit de l'article qui fera grand honneur au *Criterion*. Je vous prie de rendre à Monsieur Benda[4] l'expression de ma vive reconnaissance. Est-ce que le *Criterion* a le merite d'être la première revue en Angleterre de publier quelque chose de lui?

Veuillez bien me dire si je devrais envoyer les épreuves à vous ou directe à M. Benda. La traduction paraît bien faite, mais j'aurai la temerité de proposer deux ou trois mots alternatifs . . . il y a seulement deux ou trois phrases d'un presqu'argot qui, en anglais, sentent un peu la banlieue (the suburbs) – toujours sujet à l'autorité de M. Benda.

Recevez, Monsieur, avec mes remerciements, mes salutations les plus distinguées.

[T. S. E.]

1 – TSE had written to JMM the previous year, asking for a contribution, possibly on Shakespeare. JMM's 'Romanticism and Tradition' appeared in C. 2: 7 (Apr. 1924), 272–95.
2 – Writing to EP in Dec. 1922, TSE had called Mansfield a 'sentimental crank' he had 'no time for'. An obituary notice appeared in C. 1: 3 (Apr. 1923).
3 – Daniel Halévy (1872–1962): French social historian and man of letters; friend and colleague of Péguy, Sorel and Rolland; acute and dispassionate chronicler of the Third Republic; biographer of figures inc. Nietzsche, Péguy and Sorel, plus a two-vol. life of Proudhon; author of *Les Visites aux paysans du Centre* (1921) and *Charles Péguy et les 'Cahiers de la quinzaine'* (1919); editor of *Les Cahiers Verts*, 1921–3. See Alain Silvera, *Daniel Halévy and His Times* (1966).
4 – Julien Benda: see Glossary of Names.

Je viens de lire un article de vous, dans la *Revue de Genève*, qui m'a interessé au plus haut point.[1] C'est une critique merveilleusement bien equilibrée.[2]

TO *Richard Cobden-Sanderson* MS Beinecke

19 January 1923 [London]

Dear Cobden-Sanderson

Yes, send a copy to the *Freethinker*. I trust you got my registered letter with two more articles. H.W. and V. will I hope let you know quite soon how many words.

I am only waiting for no. of words of Pirandello.

Fry will be £3.12/- as I make it – (1805 words).[3]

Yours ever
T. S. E.

Pirandello (The Shrine) 4517 words £9.00.

1 – Daniel Halévy, 'France', *La Revue de Genève*, 5: 30 (Dec. 1922), 747–70. This was one of the review's regular 'Chroniques Nationales': its sub-headings were: 'On the Religious Question – Contrasts of Thought – Recent Works by MM. Georges Goyau and Henri Brémond – Another Contrast – The Career of M. Maurice Barrès and Catholic Criticism – A Mystical Expression of Contrast'. The paper was a concise discussion of French religious history, commenting on contemporary thinkers including Jacques Maritain, Charles Maurras and Charles Guignebert.

2 – *Translation*: Sir, Thanks for your letter of 15 January, and for the manuscript of the article which will bring great honour to the *Criterion*. I ask you to send Monsieur Benda my hearty thanks. Does the *Criterion* have the merit of being the first review in England to publish something of his?

Would you please tell me whether I should send the proofs to you or directly to M. Benda. The translation appears well done, but I will have the temerity to suggest two or three alternative words . . . there are only two or three half-slang phrases which in English smell of the suburbs – always subject to the authority of M. Benda.

Please accept, with my thanks, my greetings. Yours very sincerely [T. S. E.]

P.S. I have just read an article of yours in the *Revue de Genève* which interested me intensely. It is a beautifully balanced piece of criticism.

3 – Roger Fry, 'Mallarmé's "Herodiade"', *C.* 1: 2 (Jan. 1923).

TO *Richard Cobden-Sanderson* MS Beinecke

21 January 1923 [London]

Thanks for your letter and circulars. Will you tell this man that we will reconsider the matter next time?* I don't follow his reference to the *Pioneer.*

T. S. E.

* I gave that to you!

TO *W. B. Yeats*[1] TS Michael Yeats

23 January 1923 [9 Clarence Gate Gdns]

Dear Mr Yeats,

It has been a great disappointment to me not to have received for the third number of the *Criterion* the paper, or one of the papers, which we discussed in London.[2] But of course you did not promise it definitely and it was only a hope on my part that I might hear from you. I trust, however, that your silence is not due to political or other worries. I congratulated the Free State on hearing that you had accepted the Senatorship,[3] but I cannot deny that it caused me some alarm both for literature and for yourself.

May I still hope that we can pride ourselves on having a contribution from you in No. 4? I do not wish to boast of the *Criterion*, but you know that I consider it the only periodical in England which ought to have the privilege of publishing your work.

Sincerely yours,
T. S. Eliot

1 – W. B. Yeats: see Glossary of Names.

2 – Writing to OM on 12 Dec. 1922, TSE recorded meeting WBY at the Savile Club – adding that he was 'one of a very small number of people with whom one can talk profitably of poetry'. The same day, he told EP that WBY 'has promised a contribution in prose' for the next C.

3 – WBY was elected to the Senate in the Irish Free State on 11 Dec. 1922, serving until 1928.

TO *Mark Wardle* CC

23 January 1923 9 Clarence Gate Gdns

Dear Mr Wardle,

Thank you for your letter of the 14th inst. I have spoken to some friends who run the Hogarth Press[1] about the *Serpent*[2] and they appeared to be interested in it. I have promised to show them a copy of the proof of your version as soon as I get it from the printers in a few days, and I will also show them the edition which you have sent me and which I will take care of and return to you.[3] I should like to know whether Valéry has any personal choice in mind of an English writer to provide the preface. Of course, as an admirer of his work, I should be very happy to do it myself, but there are others more competent and I think that Valéry himself ought to indicate someone to be approached among those who have already written the most intelligent criticism of his work. The choice might depend partly upon the choice of publisher, as of course different writers have different standing among the patrons of different publishing firms.

If the Hogarth Press decides against publishing the *Serpent* I have one or two other presses in mind whom I should like to approach.[4] I should think myself that an edition of about 250 copies, well got up, would be right, but that is merely a suggestion.

Please give my respects to Valéry when you see him.

With best wishes to yourself.

Yours very truly,
[T. S. E.]

1 – LW and VW had founded the Hogarth Press in 1917.

2 – 'Le Serpent', a poem by Paul Valéry (1871–1945), first published in *Charmes* (1922). TSE wrote to Valéry on 17 Aug. 1922 to say the *Criterion* was proud to be publishing Wardle's 'excellent' translation.

3 – Wardle had sent his own copy of *Charmes*: 'for Heaven's sake don't lose it'.

4 – When the Hogarth Press turned it down, TSE arranged for it to be published as *Le Serpent par Paul Valery*, trans. Mark Wardle and with intro. by TSE (Cobden-Sanderson, 1924).

TO *W. B. Yeats* TS Michael Yeats

23 January 1923 [9 Clarence Gate Gdns]

Dear Mr Yeats,

I was delighted to get your letter.[1] I wired you because my letter to you was posted just before I received yours, and I was afraid that you might be puzzled on receiving it. I shall be very happy to have your manuscript as soon as you can send it. I am not absolutely certain of being able to get it into this number, as I had given up hope, and made other arrangements; and nearly the whole of the number has already been set up but if I can get your essay within a few days I shall do my best to include it in this next number, which in that case will be the best number of the year.[2] If it is impossible, I shall have to content myself with announcing it for the third number.

It is very thoughtful and kind of you to have taken so much trouble in the midst of such disturbing circumstances which I hope are now giving you less anxiety. It is a very great satisfaction to me to know that you like *The Waste Land*.[3] When it is brought out in this country in a month or two as a book, with notes, I shall send you a copy and hope to have at some time either in conversation or by letter, a detailed statement of your criticism.[4] It is quite possible that the passages ought to be repaired.[5]

Sincerely yours,
T. S. Eliot

1–Writing from the Savile Club, London (23 Jan.), WBY explained that he had been unable to 'do the Dante around our destructive Dublin life': a 'child's illness and nurses in the house' had prevented Mrs Yeats from reading Dante to him in the evening. In place of the promised article, he offered an extract from his autobiography, *The Trembling of the Veil*, dealing with a 'strange psychic experience'. He considered it 'better from your point of view than the Dante'.

2–It appeared as WBY, 'A Biographical Fragment', *C.* 1: 4 (July 1923), 315–21.

3–In a postscript, WBY wrote: 'I find *The Waste Land* very beautiful, but here and there are passages I do not understand – four or five lines.' Yeats had read the unannotated text published in *C.* 1: 1 (Oct. 1922).

4–The first UK book publication of *TWL* (Hogarth Press, 1923). Published in Sept., it included the 'Notes' added to the New York Boni & Liveright edition the previous Dec.

5–Whatever 'passages' Yeats did not understand, TSE never 'repaired' them.

TO *E. M. Forster*[1] CC

23 January 1923 [London]

Dear Forster,

I hope that you remember that when we met at Rodmell[2] I succeeded in extracting from you a promise – which I hope was not a reluctant one – for a contribution this year to the *Criterion.* The time has now come when I must endeavour to make you realise that promise. I hope that my request did not make such a faint impression upon you as to be quite obliterated by time, and I hope that you have on hand something which you will be willing to give me. It is for the number which will appear in July; I am particularly anxious to have it for that number, as I wanted the pleasure of including you in the first volume of the review.[3]

Anything from you, within the general and elastic scope of the *Criterion* will be welcome; but I may hint that I have not asked anyone else for a story or sketch for that number, and we like to have one (or at most two) stories or sketches in each number. But also, I should like very much to have some of your Indian material.[4]

I do not know whether you have seen the *Criterion.* If not, I will send you a copy of number 2. I am using a very charming thing of Virginia's in No. 3 which will appear in April.[5]

May I say that whenever you should happen to be in town, especially if you are in town at the end of the week, I should enjoy very much the opportunity of seeing you again.

Sincerely yours,
[T. S. E.]

1–E. M. Forster: see Glossary of Names.
2–Forster and TSE had visited the Woolfs on the weekend of 23 Sept. 1922.
3–Forster contributed 'Pan', an essay celebrating the consumption of '*pan*' in the face of the disapproval of Anglo-Indians, to *C.* 1: 4 (July 1923), 402–8; reprinted as 'Adrift in India' in *Abinger Harvest* (1936). Forster's only other contribution was a review essay on 'The Novels of Virginia Woolf' in *NC* 4: 2 (Apr. 1926).
4–Forster had made a second visit to India in 1921–2, working as secretary for the Maharajah of Dewas, and was just completing *A Passage to India*, which came out in 1924.
5–Virginia Woolf, 'In the Orchard', *C.* 1: 3 (Apr. 1923).

TO *John Middleton Murry* — TS Valerie Eliot

26 January 1923 — 9 Clarence Gate Gdns

Dear John,

I am very glad to have a word from you.[1] I hope you will not forget that it is a long time since we have met and that I am looking forward to our next meeting when you are in town and find it convenient and when you care to see me. I wish that there was something that I could do to help you, but be assured at least that I constantly think of you.

Yours
Tom

TO *Alec Randall*[2] — TS Tulsa

26 January 1923 — *The Criterion*, 9 Clarence Gate Gdns

Dear Randall,

Thank you for your letter of 19th January. You are quite right in thinking that what I was interested in was a *translation* of selected letters, although I hoped that you would provide some explanatory matter, as much or as little, as you thought fit, for the benefit of the majority of English readers who are probably unacquainted not only with Madame Gontard but with Hölderlin.[3] So I shall look forward to seeing your article in the *Fortnightly*[4] and also hope that you will let me see either the German text or a translation of some of the letters. But by all means go ahead with your *Fortnightly* article and publish it first.

1–On 25 Jan., JMM replied to TSE's letter of 18 Jan. about Katherine Mansfield's death. 'I should have missed it, very badly, had I had no sign from you. It seems to me that terrible things are happening to me of which Katherine's death is only the beginning.'

2–Alec (later Sir Alec) Randall (1892–1977), diplomat, entered the Foreign Office in 1920. In the early 1920s he was Second Secretary to the Holy See. He ended his career as Ambassador to Denmark, 1947–52. He was a regular reviewer of German literature for both C. and the *TLS*.

3–Friedrich Hölderlin (1770–1843) wrote a number of poems to Susette Gontard, the love of his life, under the name of Diotima. Her letters to him had recently been published as *Die Briefe der Diotima an Hölderlin*, ed. Carl Viëtor (Leipzig, 1922). Randall had been given the English rights for these love letters

4–Randall thought TSE was potentially interested in his translations rather than 'an article about them'. As a result, he had promised an article about them among other recent literary discoveries to *The Fortnightly Review*.

I have heard of George's[1] war poems and should certainly be interested to see a specimen of them. I have one of his books, (but not that one) which I confess I have not yet looked at.

I am sorry to hear that you have been ill and I hope that your letter means that you are now recovered. The weather has been very unfavourable to invalids.

With many thanks

Yours sincerely,
T. S. Eliot

TO *John Gould Fletcher*[2] CC

29 January 1923 [London]

Dear Fletcher,

I must beg your pardon for not having replied about your manuscript for such an unconscionably long time. I was very much interested in your poems both in themselves and of course they seem to indicate a new direction in your work. But I think I had better return them to you because we are so choked up with things that I have asked for and have got to publish that it will be a long time – I mean six or nine months – before anything else can be considered. But if you do not publish them elsewhere in the meantime, I shall remember them and I hope that you will continue to send both verse and prose.[3] If the review can get really on its feet we may be able to make the public treat with respect the sort of things that it has hitherto laughed at when it has been allowed to see them at all.

1–Stefan George (1868–1933), poet. Randall suggested 'an English translation of the remarkable "War-poems" of Stefan George which appeared last year'; this must refer to *Drei Gesänge: An die Toten, Der Dichter in Zeiten der Wirren, Einem jungen Führer im ersten Weltkrieg* [*Three Songs: To the Dead, The Poet in Time of Turmoil, To a Young Leader in the First World War*] (Berlin, 1921). Neither the Gontard letters nor the Stefan George poems came out in *C.*

2–John Gould Fletcher (1886–1950), American poet and critic, scion of a wealthy Southern family, dropped out of Harvard in 1907 (his father's death having secured him independent means) and lived for many years in Europe, principally in London; a friend of EP, he became one of the mainstays of Imagism. In later years he returned to his native Arkansas and espoused agrarian values; his *Selected Poems* won the Pulitzer Prize, 1938. See Fletcher's autobiography, *Life Is My Song* (1937); *Selected Letters of John Gould Fletcher*, ed. Leighton Rudolph and Ethel C. Simpson (1996); Glenn Hughes, *Imagism and the Imagists* (1931); and Lucas Carpenter, *John Gould Fletcher and Southern Modernism* (1990).

3–Fletcher became a frequent contributor to C., writing essays and reviews, as well as three poems. His first contribution was a poem, 'The River Flows', in *NC* 4: 1 (Jan. 1926).

I have often felt a desire to see you but in the prison-like limitation of my time it has been almost impossible for me to see anyone except for such interviews as necessity forces upon one. I hope, as I have been hoping for some time, that a month or so will see a little more leisure.

Sincerely yours,
[T. S. E.]

TO *Mark Wardle* CC

29 January 1923 [London]

Dear Captain Wardle,

I am sending you herewith a copy of your proof.[1] Will you correct it and return it as soon as possible to R. Cobden-Sanderson, 17 Thavies Inn, Holborn, E.C.1? I have sent another copy to the Hogarth Press and I am letting them see your copy of the *Serpent* which you have lent me.

I am very glad to get another manuscript from you. I have not yet had time to look at it, it lies with a pile of others waiting my attention, but I have placed yours on the top of the pile.

Yours very truly,
[T. S. E.]

TO *F. S. Flint* TS Texas

29 January [1923][2] *The Criterion*, 9 Clarence Gate Gdns

Dear Flint,

I am proposing to have a regular series of short notes dealing with any foreign reviews with which we may exchange. They will be very brief and my idea is not to give a cut and dry synopsis or table of contents of each review, but merely to acknowledge the receipt and to publish a brief critical notice of anything in any review which strikes the reviewer as good and germane to the interests of the *Criterion*. The notes should therefore be rather elastic and the length would depend on what the reviewers found there was of interest.[3]

I should be highly pleased if you would consent to let me have sent to you any Spanish, German or Norwegian periodicals which we may receive.

1 – Wardle's transl. of Paul Valéry, 'The Serpent', for C. I: 3 (Apr. 1923).
2 – Misdated 1922.
3 – Regular 'Notes' on foreign periodicals began with C. I: 3 (Apr. 1923).

It is obvious that what remuneration we can give *pro rata* for such notes is hardly an inducement, and it will not interest you unless you care to get the reviews and have the curiosity to see what is in them. On the other hand, if the idea interests you, it ought not to take very much of your time. It would merely mean looking over the reviews as they came in and sending me a few notes once a quarter. I propose that the reviews should be initialled by the writers.

So far I am trying to get the *Neuer Merkur*[1] and the *Neue Rundschau*.[2] I shall try to find out what Spanish and Scandinavian literary reviews there are and if there are any reviews in any of these languages which you would specially like to have, I would try to get them for you.

I hope that you have received a cheque from Cobden-Sanderson; if not, I know that you will get it this week.

Yours ever,
T. S. Eliot

TO *Virginia Woolf*[3] CC

29 January 1923 [London]

Dear Virginia,

I am sending you herewith a proof of 'In the Orchard'.[4] Will you return the corrected copy direct to Cobden-Sanderson, 17 Thavies Inn, Holborn, E.C.1?

I am also sending, as I promised, a galley proof of the translation of Valéry's poem [*Le Serpent*] which I discussed with you and Leonard. The thing looks perhaps a little preposterous unless one has a French version with which to compare it. I don't think that the translation has enough strength to stand entirely on its own legs and I should have liked to print the French text in the *Criterion* as well; but as the translation of a difficult poem to translate it seems to me to have a great deal. I shall send you in a day or two a copy of the original edition, now out of print. This copy belongs to Captain Wardle, and he sent it to me to look at, with strict command to use it well and not to lose it and to return it to him as soon

1–*Neue Merkur* [*New Mercury*], an influential German literary periodical edited by Efraim Frisch, ran from 1915 to 1925.
2–*Die Neue Rundschau* [*New Panorama*] founded in 1890, a literary periodical.
3–Virginia Woolf: see Glossary of Names.
4–VW's sketch was published in C. 1: 3 (Apr. 1923).

as possible. He sent it because as a book production it is the sort of thing that Valéry has in mind. What Valéry wants is to have an introduction by some English writer, which presumably would give it a somewhat larger English public. He has not yet suggested, however, any name which he would prefer.

I am very anxious to know how you are, and have had you on my mind ever since I last saw you. I feel so sure that there is some treatment or probably simply some regime to which these temperatures would yield. Apart from anything else, it must be such a drain upon your strength and such an interruption to your work.

Yours always,
[T. S. E.]

PS I wrote to Morgan Forster last week and sent it care of the Hogarth Press. Please forgive the trouble of forwarding it that I imposed upon you.

TO *Richard Aldington* TS Texas

29 January 1923 *The Criterion*, 9 Clarence Gate Gdns

Dear Richard

Thank you very much for your letter of the 21st inst. with the statement which you have prepared.[1] Thank you, again, for the trouble you have taken. I shall write to you again about this as soon as I can.

I am simply writing to say that I contemplate a very brief review of foreign reviews as a permanent feature of the *Criterion*. That is to say, brief but more or less critical notices of anything in the foreign reviews that might be of interest to the readers of the *Criterion*, assuming that they can read the language. Every review received shall be mentioned, but if there is nothing of any interest in it there is no need to say any more than that it has been received. Would you care to take over such French and Italian reviews as come in? There would not be much in it, as income, because the reviews would be so very short. It would only be worth your while, I say frankly, if you were interested to receive the reviews and to glance over them out of curiosity. It need not take you very much time.

1 – With his letter of 21 Jan., RA enclosed a statement (1 Jan.) of subscriptions to the 'Bel Esprit' (English section) scheme, or 'Eliot Fellowship Fund'. The statement records seven subscriptions from 'Capitalists', one from 'Status Unknown', and three from 'non-Capitalists', for figures from £2 to £25 (the bulk are for £10). It is signed by RA as 'Treasurer of the Fund'.

I daresay you receive most of the French periodicals already. If you cared to do it I should be grateful and the paper will pay what it can. But if you do not care to do it please do not think of doing it as a favour to me. I propose to offer Flint the Spanish, Norwegian (if any) and perhaps the German reviews, and Herbert Read any American ones.

I did not realise when I saw you that the £50 idea was really yours and that you were the only person who knew anything about it. If so, I should have discussed it with you at more length, although the time was so short and must be until you can spend a night in town.

Yours ever
Tom

PS The reviews to which I propose writing are:-

La Nouvelle Revue Française,[1]	*L'Action*
Le Mercure de France	*Il Convegno*
Les Ecrits Nouveaux	*La Ronda*
L'Esprit Nouveau	*Esame*

Should you want any others, or should you prefer not to have any of these, would you let me know, as if there are any you receive already it would probably be only a nuisance to you to get another copy.

TO *Herbert Read*[2] CC

2 February 1923 [*The Criterion*]

Dear Read,

Thank you for your letter of the 30th January. I am very much pleased that you consent to do the American periodicals. I will send you what I have on hand and I will ask the *Dial* to send you a copy regularly.[3] If there is anything that you would like particularly I will see if I can get it for you in exchange.

1–The French periodicals are *Nouvelle Revue Française*, founded in 1908 and ed. by Jacques Rivière; *Le Mercure de France*, a prestigious literary review founded in 1890; *Les Ecrits Nouveaux*, a monthly review founded in 1917; *L'Esprit Nouveau*, an avant-garde journal which ran from 1920 to 1925; *L'Action Française*, founded in 1898, the journal of l'Action Française. Of the Italian journals, *Il Convegno* was founded in Milan after WW1, heavily featuring the Futurist Marinetti; *La Ronda* was a literary review, founded in 1919 and published in Rome, which closed in the course of 1923 in response to the new Fascist regime. RA agreed to do the notes on French periodicals.
2–Herbert Read: see Glossary of Names.
3–HR's regular notes on American periodicals began in *C.* 1: 3 (Apr. 1923), where he dealt with *The Dial*, *Secession* and *Rhythmus*.

I am very much obliged to you for seeing Mr Middleton[1] and I am sure that he will be grateful to you whether anything comes of it or not.

I am sending you your manuscript and proof herewith.[2] Will you return the corrected copy direct to R. Cobden-Sanderson, 17 Thavies Inn, Holborn, E.C.1 as soon as you can.

Yours ever,
[T. S. E.]

TO *Richard Aldington* TS Texas

2 February 1923 *The Criterion*, 9 Clarence Gate Gdns

Dear Richard

I am very much gratified to receive your acceptance of my proposal. You mention however only the French reviews. Am I to understand that you would prefer not to touch the Italian? I hope you do not mean that. There will be very few and I hardly hope that they will contain very much of interest.[3]

I will try to get for you all the papers you ask for, although I cannot promise that they will all agree to exchange with a rather small quarterly review. I certainly agree that one ought to be perfectly fair and search as diligently in the older periodicals as in the newer ones.

I am very much obliged for your criticisms of the article on Rétif.[4] It did not look to me very original or very intelligent, but I wanted to assure myself from an authority before returning it. Besides, I have no particular desire to boom the stock of any disciple of Rousseau.

Yours always,
Tom

1–HR said he 'gave him [Ian Middleton] what few crumbs of comfort there were in the situation'; he wished he could have 'done something more definite.'

2–HR, 'The Nature of Metaphysical Poetry', C. 1: 3 (Apr. 1923), 246–66. TSE made numerous queries and suggestions on HR's outline for this essay in 1922 (Victoria).

3–RA provided notes only on the French reviews, not the Italian ones. In July, TSE noted, 'Italian periodicals are held over until the next number' (C. 1: 4, 427).

4–Rétif (or Restif) de la Bretonne (1734–1806): French author of rambling novels and memoirs, including *Les nuits de Paris* (1788–90); usually viewed as a follower of Jean-Jacques Rousseau.

TO *Harold Monro*[1] TS Beinecke

2 February 1923 9 Clarence Gate Gdns

Dear Munro [*sic*],

Thank you for your letter of the 28th January. I was not only pleased to receive the *Chapbooks* but I actually have read your morality, and for me to read anything is a very exceptional event.[2] As a matter of fact, like other people, I hardly read anything that is sent me for fear of the difficulty of saying anything nice about it afterward, but I felt fairly safe on account of my opinion of your poetry, and I can say with a clear conscience that I enjoyed your play very much and compliment you on it. I think it might also be very entertaining if performed on a small stage.

I thank you for your compliments on the *Sacred Wood*.[3] I have not looked at it myself for many months but I know very well that there are many statements in it which I no longer believe, and sooner or later I suppose I shall have to publish a more careful revision of many of the points I discussed. But when one reads one's own dicta later one is always impressed by one's own temerity at the time.

I am glad to hear that the *Chapbook* is going so well and to hear such good news of Sacheverill [*sic*] Sitwell.[4] I always believed that he had a genuine poetic source in him and I think I was one of the first to say so;[5] I was not certain whether it would develop into a river or disappear in sand. I shall look forward to the March *Chapbook* and of course to the second.[6]

1–Harold Monro: see Glossary of Names.
2–Monro was editor of *The Chapbook*. TSE contributed 'A Brief Treatise on the Criticism of Poetry' to *Chapbook* 2: 9 (Mar. 1920), and 'Prose and Verse' to 22 (Apr. 1921). With his letter to TSE of 28 Jan., Monro sent a 'poor little play' entitled *One Day Awake*, published in *Chapbook* 32 (22 Dec. 1922). Having just read *SW*, Monro wondered how he dared send it, but remarked that it was at least 'a human document'. He also sent the Jan. issue.
3–Monro wrote that *SW* 'has been a startling revelation to me. I did not know there was a living writer capable of such a book. I wish I'd read it earlier. It has made a whole lot of problems clear to me (even if it is only the problem, and not the solution). I offer you my homage.'
4–Monro said that the Mar. *Chapbook* would contain 'a charming long poem by S. Sitwell, who is developing': the poem was 'Bolsover Castle'.
5–TSE reviewed Sacheverell Sitwell's *The People's Palace* in *Egoist* 5: 6 (June/July 1918): 'We have attributed more to Mr Sitwell than to any poet of quite his generation; we require of him only ten years of toil.'
6–Monro said he had written some notes on *TWL* in the Feb. issue. He thought, 'after the many times I have read it, I do really know something about it, but confidence fails me when I try to express myself on paper'.

I will ask Lady Rothermere to approve of sending you the *Criterion* regularly in exchange,[1] but I am no longer able to give assurances myself, as Cobden-Sanderson is on the side of economy in distributing exchange copies. If we print a larger edition of the third number it may be more possible to do as a well-conducted review ought in these matters.

As for verse – I swear to you that I have not produced the slightest scrap for a year; I have nothing which I could offer you, or anyone else, or which I could even light my pipe with. I only hope for conditions under which it may be possible for me to begin to want to do something![2]

Sincerely yours
T. S. Eliot

TO *F. S. Flint*

TS Texas

2 February 1923 — *The Criterion*, 9 Clarence Gate Gdns

Dear Flint,

I am very pleased at your acceptance of my proposal.[3] I will send you directly what I have on hand and will ask you to let me have your notes as soon as possible for No. 3. As I have said, you must use your discretion: if a review contains nothing worth mentioning we will simply acknowledge it. If on the other hand it contains something of merit notice it at a length proportionate to its value, and should you ever come across anything which strikes you as so good that the author ought to be asked to contribute to the *Criterion*, I will trust you to advise me.

The arrangement you suggest is perfectly convenient but will you let us make the financial arrangements solely with you and will you arrange the distribution with your colleague? You see we shall not know how much of the labour is contributed by each, and I think it would be more satisfactory to us to recognise officially only yourself.

Thank you for your favourable comments on the present number. I hope that the third one will be better.

Yours ever,
T. S. Eliot

1 – Monro asked whether he might have C. in exchange for *The Chapbook*.
2 – Monro asked whether TSE could 'spare even a short poem'. After *TWL* in C. 1: 1 (Oct. 1922), TSE's next published poems were 'Poème' (later 'The Hollow Men' I) in *Commerce* 3 (Winter 1924/25) and 'Doris's Dream Songs' in *Chapbook* 39 (Nov. 1924).
3 – Flint had agreed to provide 'Notes' on German periodicals for C. 1: 3.

TO *Julien Benda*[1] CC

2 February 1923 [*The Criterion*, 17 Thavies Inn, London E.C.1]

Monsieur,

J'ai l'honneur de vous envoyer ci-inclus épreuves de votre Préface.[2] J'ai expedié un autre exemplaire à Mademoiselle Robinson. Veuillez bien s'il vous plaît faire renvoyer à moi l'un ou l'autre exemplaire après la révision?

Au marge j'ai indiqué quelques suggestions en fait de la traduction de plusieurs mots, mais vous aurez naturellement tous droits de conserver la traduction intégralement.

Nous nous félicitons sur l'occasion de présenter un morceau de votre oeuvre aux lecteurs anglais, et nous allons parler de vous plus tard.

Le numéro du *Criterion* qui contient votre Préface paraîtra le 15 Avril et vous recevrez un exemplaire et la rémunération aussitôt après cette date que possible.

Recevez, Monsieur, l'assurance de mes hommages devoués.

[T. S. E.][3]

1 – Julien Benda: see Glossary of Names

2 – Julien Benda, 'A Preface', *C.* 1: 3 (Apr. 1923), 227–42.

3 – *Translation*: Dear Sir, Please find enclosed the proof of your Preface. I have sent another copy to Miss Robinson. Be so kind as to return one or other of the copies to me, after checking.

In the margin I have made some suggestions relating to the translation of certain words, but naturally you have every right to leave the translation just as it stands.

We are very pleased to have this opportunity of presenting an extract from your work to English readers, and we intend to speak about you later.

The issue of the *Criterion* containing your Preface will appear on 15 April, and you will receive a copy and payment as soon as possible after that.

Yours faithfully, [T. S. E.]

TO *Ford Madox Ford*[1] TS Cornell

2 February 1923 9 Clarence Gate Gdns

Dear Mr Ford,

Many thanks for your charming letter of the 25th January. I gather from the opening phrases that you feel a slight suspicion of me as an editor and a prose writer, but your compliments on *The Waste Land*, which I prize very highly coming from you, more than restore my composure.[2] In any case, my suspicion of your suspicion does not disturb my desire which Ezra has reported correctly. I do not expect to see eye to eye with anybody, but I am anxious to discover a few people with whom it is worth while to disagree and to expose the agreements and disagreements of these people in the *Criterion*. I saw not long ago in a periodical which I did not otherwise admire, an essay of yours on Shelley[3] which was at least much nearer to my own opinion of that poet than any other I have read. I have myself outraged public opinion in England by my remarks on a greater than Shelley,[4] so that I should very much like to see your immense history of British literature.[5] The only question is, how immense is it? I have ordered the *Criterion* to be sent to you and it will give you an idea of the suitable length of articles, even if it gives you no other idea. For me, English literature ends well before 1800, (at least that part of it which is written in verse)[6] but I can see that for the purpose of improving the public mind,

1–Ford Madox Ford: see Glossary of Names. In Oct. 1922, TSE had told EP he did not want Ford 'for several numbers yet because there are a great many other people beside myself who do not like him'.

2–Ford had been surprised to learn from EP that TSE would like something for *C.* 'for we can't see eye to eye, I fancy, on many things'. Since he wanted to help with 'the good work', and thought TSE probably didn't want 'poems' or 'novels', he wondered what he should write about. He was 'a quite real admirer of *Prufrock* and *Waste Land* – which is, curse you! – the real thing. I say curse you! – because for months before *The Waste Land* appeared I was labouring with an immense Poem on the same lines and have had to cut, hack, dismantle and alter it.' Ford's poem was *Mr Bosphorus and the Muses* (1923).

3–Ford, 'Third Rate Poet', *Golden Hind* I (Oct. 1922), 15–20. TSE wrote later that 'an enthusiasm for Shelley seems to me also to be an affair of adolescence: for most of us, Shelley has marked an intense period before maturity, but for how many does Shelley remain the companion of age?' (*TUPUC*, 89).

4–Presumably a reference to his remarks on *Hamlet* as 'artistic failure', in 'Hamlet and His Problems' in *SW* (1920).

5–Ford spoke of 'an immense history of British Literature which Ezra wanted' him to send TSE; this was to be *The Long March of Literature* (1938).

6–In 'The Metaphysical Poets', *TLS* (20 Oct. 1921), TSE speaks of 'something which had happened to the mind of England between the time of Donne or Lord Herbert of Cherbury and the time of Tennyson and Browning; it is the difference between the intellectual poet and the reflective poet'. These views were developed further in 'Andrew Marvell', *N&A* 33: 26 (29 Sept. 1923). Both essays were reprinted in *Homage to John Dryden* (1924).

if it is to be improved, there is something to be said about the rest. I think that your history of British literature is what we want, or, if it is too immense, the more important parts of it. Can I see it, part of it, or an outline of it?

As for your pro-French policy,[1] that is one with which I am in sympathy, united (politically) within hereditary and ineradicable toryism.

Will you not let me receive some manuscript, or at least continue these conversations, as soon as anyone under the influence of the Mediterranean climate can manage to do so?[2]

With many thanks,

Yours very sincerely,
T. S. Eliot

TO *Jacques Rivière* CC

2 February 1923 [London]

Cher Monsieur,

Merci bien de votre aimable lettre du 27 passé. J'attendrai avec impatience l'article dont vous me parlez.[3] Est ce que je peux le recevoir vers le 1° Avril, ou le cas échéant plus tôt puisqu'il y a encore le travail de traduction.

J'espère pouvoir vous donner une chronique vers le 15 février.[4]

Agréez, cher Monsieur, l'assurance de ma sympathie cordiale.

[T. S. E.][5]

1–Ford was contemplating 'a reviewerish sort of article on the differences between the French & British temperaments'; 'his pro-Frenchness' was 'so absolute' he didn't try to 'keep any balance'.
2–See Ford's impressionistic essay 'From the Grey Stone', in C. 2: 5 (Oct. 1923).
3–Jacques Rivière, 'Notes on a Possible Generalisation of the Theories of Freud', C. 1: 4 (July 1923), 329–48.
4–TSE's next 'Lettre d'Angleterre' did not appear until *NRF* 21: 122 (1 Nov. 1923).
5–*Translation*: Dear Sir, Thank you for your kind letter of the 27th of last month. I shall wait impatiently for the article you speak of. I wonder if I could have it by 1 April or, if possible, even earlier, since some time must be allowed for the translation.
I hope to be able to send you my chronicle round about 15 February.
Please accept, dear Sir, my cordial regards. [T. S. E.]

TO *Charles Whibley*[1] CC

2 February 1923 [*The Criterion*, London]

My dear Whibley,

This letter is to send you the proof of Bolingbroke.[2] When you have corrected it will you return one copy direct to R. Cobden-Sanderson, 17 Thavies Inn, Holborn, E.C.1. Of course he would like to have it as soon as possible but I hope you are now well enough for proof-correcting to be not too intolerable a nuisance.

I hope to have better news and to see you before very long.

Yours always,
[T. S. E.]

PS I am returning you the envelope of your letter as you asked me to do. It appears to have left Bletchley[3] in the morning!

TO *Mrs S. A. Middleton* CC

2 February 1923 [*The Criterion*, London]

Thank you for your letter of the 29th ulto. enclosing translation of the note by Marichalar[4] and thank you also for your promptness.

I will certainly keep you in mind in case of hearing of any Spanish translations to be done.

Yours sincerely
[T. S. E.]

1–Charles Whibley: see Glossary of Names.
2–'Bolingbroke, Pt. I', *C.* 1: 3 (Apr. 1923), 203–16.
3–Whibley lived in Broomhill House, Brickhill, Bletchley.
4–Antonio Marichalar, 'Contemporary Spanish Literature', *C.* 1: 3 (Apr. 1923) concluded with a Note on 'The Nobel Prize and Benavente' by 'A. M.'; trans. by Mrs Middleton. See TSE's letter to Marichalar, 14 May 1923.

TO *Charles Caffrey*[1] CC

2 February 1923 [*The Criterion*, London]

Dear Mr Caffrey,

I am enclosing herewith the first German manuscript which I have had since corresponding with you, a fragment of a Greek voyage by Hugo von Hofmannsthal.[2]

You will observe at the end I have marked a line after which the essay consists almost wholly of a long quotation in German from Maurice Barrès. The length of the quotation is out of proportion to the length of the article and you therefore need not translate after the line which I have drawn.

Will you return the original as well when you send me the translation.

You need not hurry over this, but I should be obliged if you would let me have it within six weeks, and also if you will acknowledge receipt immediately.

As I said before, I only regret that we have so little material to offer you.

[T. S. E.]

TO *Ford Madox Ford* MS Cornell

4 February 1923 *The Criterion*, 9 Clarence Gate Gdns

Dear Mr Ford,

I see on looking over our correspondence that I did not make clear that any form of literature (except a novel, which could hardly appear in a *quarterly*) would be welcome from you, and *of course verse*. But I was excited by the history of British literature, which seemed to fit in to my critical programme so well. It must depend on your wishes at the moment. Have you any *contes*? *Is April 15 a possible date?*

Cordially and again with thanks

T. S. Eliot

1–Charles Caffrey did a small number of translations from the German for *C.*

2–Hugo von Hofmannsthal, 'Greece', *C.* 2: 1 (Oct. 1923), 103.

TO *George Saintsbury*[1] CC

6 February 1923 [London]

My dear Sir,

The publication of your 'Dullness'[2] gave the *Criterion* such a triumphant start that I am now bold enough to write to you again. The suggestion which I wish to put to you has been made to me by the editor of *The Dial* of New York (a paper which I think you know) and it is one which I cordially accept and endorse, if it receives your approval.

Would you be willing, at your leisure and convenience, to discuss the style and the prose rhythms of Mr James Joyce's *Ulysses*? *The Dial* and the *Criterion* would then arrange to publish your essay simultaneously, and each would pay its full rates.

(*The Dial* would pay much more handsomely than we can, at the rate of 2 cents a word.)

The Dial cannot publish quite such long articles as the *Criterion*, so that I should think that the limit should be about 4000 words; but if you wished to take more space I think that to you it would be conceded, as they are very anxious to publish some of your work.

For my part, I should be delighted if you would accept, and I should then hope that you could let us have it in time for the October number of the *Criterion* and the November number of *The Dial*, which appear within a few days of each other.

If you yield to our persuasion, please let me know whether you have a copy of Mr Joyce's book, as I should wish to arrange to have one sent to you if you are not already the possessor of the book.[3]

I have myself promised to write something about the book for *The Dial*, but I shall limit myself to a discussion of the significance of the association of the myth with the contemporary action.

1 – George Saintsbury (1845–1933): literary critic and historian; Regius Professor of Rhetoric and English Literature, Edinburgh University, 1895–1915. TSE, in his preface to the Collected Edition of *C.* (1967), was to call Saintsbury 'that genial doyen of English letters'.

2 – George Saintsbury, 'Dullness', *C.* 1: 1 (Oct. 1922), 1–15.

3 – Saintsbury had been surprised to receive a press copy of the novel from JJ, who wrote to Harriet Shaw Weaver (17 Nov. 1922): 'I am old-fashioned enough to admire him though he may not return the compliment. He is however quite capable of flinging the tome back through your window, especially if the 1922 vintage has not matured to his liking.' (James Joyce, *Letters,* ed. Stuart Gilbert, 1957, vol. I, 195.)

With my renewed thanks for your kindness to our first number, and the fervent hope that you will accede to the present request.

I am,
Yours sincerely,
[T. S. E.]

TO *Gilbert Seldes*[1] CC

6 February 1923 [London]

My dear Mr Seldes,

I have your letter of the 30th ulto. and like your proposal very much. I have just written to Mr Saintsbury and will let you know as soon as he has replied.[2] He is a very charming and amiable person and I hope that he will consent, although I have no idea what may be his opinion of Joyce.

You are quite right in assuming that I shall not go into the question of style and rhythm in *Ulysses*: I intend chiefly to occupy myself with the question of the value and the significance of the method of moulding a contemporary narrative upon an ancient myth, a question which I think is of interest to Yeats, Pound and myself, though I have not yet found that it interests anyone else![3] I should suggest, if we get the paper in time, that it be published in the *Criterion* of the 15th October and in the *Dial* of the 1st November which I assume will be on the bookstalls by the 25th October. We should endeavour to post the American copies of the *Criterion* on a date such that they would be received in New York about the 25th.

I see that you have not yet received at least one letter which I posted to you in New York, but that it has been forwarded to you. In one letter I expressed my warm appreciation of your notice of *The Waste Land*.[4]

1–Seldes later wrote a number of 'New York Chronicles' for *C*.
2–Seldes had proposed that Saintsbury should write an essay on 'the prose rhythms' of *Ulysses*.
3–Seldes assumed TSE 'would not have space to go into this special subject' when writing his essay on JJ for *The Dial*. This appeared as '*Ulysses*, Order and Myth', *Dial* 75: 5 (Nov. 1923).
4–Seldes hoped TSE was 'not entirely disappointed' with his notice, 'T. S. Eliot' (*Nation* [NY] 115, 6 Dec. 1922, 614–16), which emphasised the poem's 'historical sense', its 'alternation between the visionary . . . and the actual', and its 'hidden form'. He saw it as 'the inversion and complement of *Ulysses*'.

I am glad that you are having a holiday, I trust not in a sanatorium[1] but on skates or skis.

Sincerely yours
[T. S. E.]

TO *E. M. Forster* CC

6 February 1923 [London]

Dear Forster,

I am sure neither my letter nor my wire reached you in time.[2] But I hope you will let me know. I feel extremely apologetic about my delay. In any case, I trust that my letter was forwarded to you from the Reform Club if you did not call and find it there. I hope that you will be coming up to London soon on a Saturday or at some time when we can meet.

Meanwhile, I repeat my pleasure at hearing that I may count upon something from you before the end of March.[3]

[T. S. E.]

TO *J. M. Robertson*[4] CC

6 February 1923 [London]

Dear Mr Robertson,

I am very much delighted at receiving your kind letter and the manuscript which you enclosed.[5] Your writing is very legible, but in any case I have passed the severest test known, by reading through a manuscript of Saintsbury's which the printers refused to examine, and taking [typing] the whole thing out for them.

I shall read through your manuscript at the earliest possible moment, but meanwhile you need not wait to be told that we shall be happy to have it. I should like to publish it in the October number, or if I have not already committed myself to too much material, in the July number.

1 – Seldes had written from Südbahn Hotel, Semmering, Austria.
2 – On 29 Jan. Forster invited TSE to lunch with him at the Reform Club on Friday, 2 Feb.
3 – Forster, 'Pan', *C.* 1: 4 (July 1923), 402–8.
4 – J. M. Robertson: see Glossary of Names.
5 – Robertson had submitted (5 Feb.) a handwritten copy of his article on 'English Blank Verse'; it appeared as 'The Evolution of Blank Verse', *C.* 2: 6 (Feb. 1924), 171–87.

I will try to see Mr Cobden-Sanderson as soon as I can and shall certainly urge him to publish your book.[1] He ought to realise that it is an opportunity which he should not miss. It is scandalous that you should have had to publish *The Shakespeare Canon*[2] at your own expense: it is the sort of thing that the Oxford press ought to do, instead of publishing so many anthologies, of little or no scholarly interest.

With very many thanks,

Yours sincerely,
[T. S. E.]

TO *Alfred Kreymborg*[3] CC

6 February 1923 [London]

Dear Kreynborg [*sic*],

Thank you for your letter. I also was disappointed not to see you again;[4] It is my responsibility but not my fault, as I was constantly waiting for a free evening when I could suggest something to you and as constantly was baulked. Then just as I was going to write to you I learned that you had left London the week before.

1. I have just received a copy of your magazine[5] and indeed wish that I had even half a line which I could send, but I have written absolutely not a word since the *Waste Land* was finished and everything that I wrote before that is either published in my book[6] or will never, I hope, be published at all. And I think it will take me a year or two to throw off the *Waste Land* and settle down and get at something better which is tormenting me by its elusiveness in my brain.

1–Robertson said his 'book on Hamlet is just about finished – after many revisions', and wondered if RC-S would consider publishing it. It appeared as *Hamlet Once More* (1923).
2–Robertson had published his *The Shakespeare Canon* (5 vols, 1922–5) at his 'own expense', which he said was 'repugnant to [his] financial status'.
3–Alfred Kreymborg (1883–1966): American poet, playwright, and puppeteer.
4–In his autobiography, Kreymborg describes meeting TSE at home at 9 Clarence Gate Gardens: 'The man was as clearly the expression of the artist as the artist was of the man. The suave intelligence was given over to the pursuit of a refinement of experience from which unnecessary details dropped away with an ironical though almost imperceptible smile' (*Troubadour* [1925], 396–7). Remarking that 'The man was beautiful to look at as well as to listen to', he noted too: 'Eliot was the high priest of the best of the younger English poets and essayists.'
5–*Broom: An International Magazine of the Arts*, ed. Kreymborg and Harold Loeb; the first issue was published in Nov. 1921, the last in Jan. 1924.
6–*Ara Vos Prec* (London: Ovid Press, 1920).

2. I have no objection, from what you tell me, to your including 'The Portrait of a Lady' in your anthology[1] to be published in English in Munich. I hope, however, that the anthology is really and truly for German and central European consumption, as I do not want to appear in any more Anglo-Saxon anthologies – for one has seen the same poems of mine turn up again and again in one anthology after another[2] – and people must be pretty well sick of them.

3. I am looking forward to the book of yours which I see Secker is about to produce,[3] but will you not let me hear from you about the other article on the marionette theatre which you promised me and appear to have forgotten?[4]

Sincerely yours,
[T. S. E.]

TO *Charles Whibley* CC

6 February 1923 [*The Criterion*, London]

My dear Whibley,

Many thanks for your letter. I should of course be delighted to have Mr Ker's article on Byron,[5] and am more than grateful to you for the trouble you have taken and for the use of your influence.[6] May I trouble you still further to tell him that I should be glad to have it as soon as he can send it to me?

I venture to suggest to you an idea I have had in my mind: would you care at some time or other to write something for us about Charles Maurras?[7] The political implications would of course have to be handled

1–Having edited a series of annual *Others* anthologies (1915–19), Kreymborg's next volumes were *Others: An Anthology of New Verse* (1927) and *Lyric America: An Anthology of American Poetry* (1930).

2–'Portrait of a Lady' had appeared, with 'Prufrock' and three other poems, in EP's *Catholic Anthology*, in *Others* (1916), and in Harriet Monroe and Alice Corbin Henderson's *The New Poetry: An Anthology* (1917). Methuen published 'La Figlia Che Piange'; and Louis Untermeyer's *Modern American Poetry* (1921) included extracts from 'Prufrock' and 'Portrait of a Lady'.

3–*Puppet Plays*, with a preface by Gordon Craig (1923).

4–On 6 Aug., Kreymborg sent to TSE the typescript of 'Writing for Puppets', but it was never published (see TSE's letter of 23 Aug.).

5–For W. P. Ker, see note to TSE's letter of 20 Mar.

6–Ker, 'Byron: An Oxford Lecture', C. 2: 5 (Oct. 1923), 1–15.

7–Charles Maurras (1868–1952): French poet, critic, political philosopher and polemical journalist; founding editor and moving spirit of the reactionary and extreme monarchist

delicately in a literary review – partly for obvious reasons of discretion but partly also because I believe the review can only maintain its literary usefulness by keeping outside of political [discussion][1] – and these implications will have to be left implicit in discussing the general philosophic position; but of course there is a good deal to be said about his literary criticism and his conception of the qualities and the place of literature. Of course I do not want you in any case to bother about this at all until I have extracted the second part of Bolingbroke from you which I hope will be soon:[2] I merely put this forward tentatively to see how it strikes you.

You say nothing about your health so I hope the peace and seclusion of the country are performing good work.

Yours ever,
[T. S. E.]

TO *W. W. Worster*[3] CC

6 February 1923 [*The Criterion*, London]

Dear Mr Worster,

Very many thanks for your letter of the 29th January and for the article and story which you have sent.[4] I appreciate very keenly the interest you are taking and the trouble you have given yourself to provide me with such

—

paper, *L'Action Française* (1908–44), which was to support Pétain and Vichy during WW2. Building on 'three traditions' – classicism, Catholicism, monarchism – the thrust of Maurras' ideology became increasingly, and intransigently, right-wing, authoritarian and anti-democratic. While CW did not complete his piece on Maurras, in 1925 TSE planned to write a book on him. He later wrote 'The *Action Française*, M. Maurras and Mr Ward', in *NC* 7: 3 (Mar. 1928), an issue that included his translation of Maurras's essay 'Prologue to an Essay on Criticism'. TSE said he had been 'a reader of the work of M. Maurras for eighteen years', and, far from 'drawing him away from' Christianity – in 1926 Maurras was even condemned by the Pope, with five of his books being placed on the Index – it had had the opposite effect. In a later essay TSE named CW, Léon Daudet, and Maurras as the 'three best writers of invective of their time' (*SE*, 499).

1 – Word missing. See Kenneth Asher, 'T. S. Eliot and Maurras', *ANQ* 11: 3 (Summer 1998).

2 – Whibley, 'Bolingbroke, Pt. II', *C.* 1: 4 (July 1923).

3 – W. W. Worster, a translator from Norwegian and Danish, was to become well known for his translations of the Norwegian Nobel laureate Knut Hamsun, inc. *Growth of the Soul*.

4 – Worster submitted for consideration an article 'Four Icelandic Poets' (albeit the writers in question were not poets) and 'a short story which my agent has been vainly trying to dispose of' – 'Bohème' (the latter in the name of 'W. Williamsson', his nom-de-plume for fiction).

full and useful information. I am hoping to be able to read your contributions this week; the influx of material is now pretty heavy for me to deal with singlehanded, but I am looking forward to reading your manuscript with pleasure.

I have not yet approached any of the writers whose names you have given me simply for the reason that there have been such a number of English and French writers and a few German, Italian and Spanish, whose absence from the first year of the review would be remarked as a defect.[1] It is difficult to know when to invite contributions and when to accept them, with a quarterly, for one does not like to ask people to wait six months or a year before their contribution is published.

With very grateful thanks and best wishes for improved health,

Yours very truly,
[T. S. E.]

TO *Egdar Jepson*[2] — TS Beinecke

6 February 1923 — 9 Clarence Gate Gdns

My dear Jepson,

It is indeed a very long while since we met, and it is a pleasure to me [to] think you occasionally remember me and wish to see me, and I have very often thought of you and then waited before writing until I could definitely fix an agreement. The combination of having had my wife very ill during nearly the whole of 1922, and the *Criterion* review, left me very little time to see people merely because I wanted to see them. Even now I cannot accept for this Sunday; I have finally made an engagement for Sunday with friends whom I have not seen for months, and who think that I have neglected them. May I, however, be allowed to write and suggest my presence – at supper or after supper or before supper – the first Sunday I can, on the understanding that you will put me off till the following Sunday if you find it inconvenient?

I have had it on my mind also to send you the *Criterion* in order to submit my poem to your judgement, but even a little paper and paste, is

1 – Worster included with his letter of 29 Jan. a list of Danish publishers and writers.
2 – Edgar Jepson (1863–1938): British novelist; vocal advocate and friend of EP and TSE.

more than I often have time for. But you shall receive it, as I am waiting your opinion.[1]

With many thanks. Yours sincerely,

T. S. Eliot

TO *John Middleton Murry* MS Northwestern

7 February 1923 9 Clarence Gate Gdns

Dear John

I am very grateful to you for putting me in the way of the Dostoevski letters.[2] From what you say I should not hesitate to use them as soon as possible, and I am writing at once to Koteliansky. Thank you very much.

I am asking Cobden-Sanderson to send you a *Criterion*. I was under the impression that one had been sent to you.

I want very much to see you; and I have several matters of importance I am anxious to discuss with you as soon as possible. And it would be delightful to visit you in the country. Could I come weekend after next (Feb. 17)?

Yours ever
T. S. E.

TO *S. S. Koteliansky* MS BL

7 February 1923 *The Criterion*, 9 Clarence Gate Gdns

Dear Mr Koteliansky

I have just heard from Murry, telling me about some Dostoevski letters you have just translated, and recommending me to try to get them, if you are willing, for the *Criterion*. I should very much like to publish them, and hope you will consent. The letters he mentions are

1. Full text of letter of D. to his brother after his reprieve.
2. D's letter to Maikov outlining a scheme for a great poem on Russian history.

1–Jepson wrote to thank TSE for *TWL*, saying he had 'already read it a good many times' and would be using it in 'a lecture – unsympathetic – on modern poetry', though he had said 'several pleasing things' about TSE. In the event, rather than commenting on the poem itself, Jepson preferred to discuss *From Ritual to Romance*, *The Golden Bough* and Cabell's *Jurgen*.
2–See following letter to Koteliansky.

3. D's letter to Poliedmoszer (no. 3) from Bad-Ems, 24 Aug. 1922 (??)[1] explaining part of *Brothers Karamazov*.

I should use these in the no. of *July 1st.* (In a case like this, of translation of a dead author, we can pay at the rate of £10 per 5000 words.)[2]

I hope you have no objection, as it would be a great honour for the paper. I understand from Murry that the letters have never been translated before.

Sincerely yours
T. S. Eliot

TO *Richard Aldington* TS Texas

9 February 1923 *The Criterion*, 9 Clarence Gate Gdns

Dear Richard

Referring to your letter of the 30th January would you let me know the addresses to which to write for the following periodicals which you have recommended:-

Revue de l'Amérique Latine[3]
Intentions
La Revue des deux Mondes
Supplément Littéraire du Figaro
La Revue de Paris
La Revue Hebdomadaire

Would you care at your leisure, to use as the pretext for an essay on Greek verse translation, or on Aeschylus, or on any cognate subject that you choose, a book of translations of the Oresteia by Robert Trevelyan

1–This should read 'to Pobiedonoszev', and the date should read '24 Aug. 1879'.

2–Koteliansky replied that he would be willing to have the first and third of these published, but that his publisher would not allow him to publish the other in a periodical. He asked for them to be published 'immediately' in the Apr. number: his translations duly appeared as 'Two Unpublished Letters of F. Dostoevsky', C. I: 3 (Apr. 1923), 217–26.

3–*Revue de l'Amérique Latine*, was a Paris-based review on Latin America ed. by E. Martinenche; *Intentions* a monthly literary review ed. by Pierre-André May, 1922–4; *La Revue des deux Mondes* a monthly cultural and literary magazine founded in 1829; *Supplément Littéraire* the weekly literary supplement of *Le Figaro*, a newspaper founded in 1826; *La Revue de Paris* a literary magazine founded in 1829, bought by the parfumier Coty in 1922; *La Revue Hebdomadaire* a newspaper of the right-wing group Redressement Français. In his notes on 'French Periodicals' in C. I: 3 (Apr. 1923), RA commented on *NRF*, *Mercure de France*, *La Revue Musicale*, *Les Marges*, *Revue de l'Amérique*, *Les Cahiers Idéalistes* and *La Vie des Lettres*.

which I have received?[1] If the idea at all appeals to you I will send the book on to you. It may be good or *bad*, haven't looked.

Yours in haste
[T. S. Eliot *del.*] T

PS Can you tell me anything about the work of Daniel Halévy? There is a chronique by him in the *Revue de Genève* which I am sending you with other periodicals.[2] He appears to act as Benda's secretary and go-between in the negotiations I have had over Benda's article. I mentioned in writing to him that I was interested in what he said about the Abbé Brémond and he promptly wrote and offered to write an article about him! All I know of Halévy is an impression that he was a friend of Péguy and contributed to the *Cahiers de la Quinzaine* and that he now edits some *Cahiers* of his own. Read his chronique and tell me what you think of him. Du Bos[3] sometimes writes intelligently, but somewhat desiccated, I think. Was it you who reviewed his book in *The Times*?[4]

Please let me know whether you receive *La Nouvelle Revue Française* regularly. If not I will lend you my own copies for the last two months, including the Proust Memorial,[5] and will ask Rivière to send a copy regularly direct. It is a review that I like to see myself.

TO *Richard Cobden-Sanderson* TS Texas

9 February 1923 *The Criterion*, 9 Clarence Gate Gdns

Dear Sanderson

I enclose herewith a corrected proof from Julien Benda[6] and also the note which I warned you would arrive to be added at the end of the article by Marichalar.[7] Can you have this note set up to go at the end of the article, in small type, but preferably not quite so small as the italicised

1–Aeschylus, *The Oresteia*, trans. R. C. Trevelyan (1922).
2–Daniel Halévy, 'France', *La Revue de Genève* 5: 30 (Dec. 1922), 747–70: a review of the contemporary religious situation in France. Halévy also edited *Les Cahiers Verts*.
3–For Charles du Bos, see TSE's first letter to him, 1 May 1923.
4–'A French Critic', *TLS*, 11 Jan. 1923, 23 (rev. of Charles du Bos, *Approximations: Essays on French writers* (Paris, 1922). TSE praised du Bos's essay on Baudelaire (in *Approximations*) as 'the finest study of Baudelaire that has been made' ('Baudelaire In Our Time', *FLA*, 75).
5–The Jan. issue of *NRF* was dedicated to the memory of Marcel Proust.
6–Julien Benda, 'A Preface', *C.* 1: 3 (Apr. 1923).
7–Marichalar's article 'Contemporary Spanish Literature' appeared in *C.* 1: 3 (Apr. 1923), as did his note on 'The Nobel Prize and Benavente'.

introduction to Pound's article in the last number? I shall send you a corrected proof of the article itself and The Obsequies[1] in the course of a few days. You tell me you have received a proof of the 'Serpent' and 'In the Orchard'.[2] You should also have received by this time direct the corrected proof of the articles by Herbert Read and Charles Whibley.[3]

With regard to Pound's complaint,[4] I was under the impression that I had informed him that the sum of £10 was for 5,000 words and the payment was pro rata. I have not yet had a moment to look through my previous correspondence with him on this point, but as he was under the impression that he would get £10 for the article I propose that he should on this occasion have it. I am writing to him to explain the situation and to make it clear that in future we must stick to the rates at which everybody is paid, but I should be obliged if you would on my responsibility send him a cheque for the balance of £2.8.0. [2.12.0 *del.*] You need not raise the point in your own letter to him as I shall explain that fully.

There is also a sum owing on account of the translation of the Marichalar article, which as it happens is owing to me. I had the translation made long before we could use it and as the translator is a needy person I paid her out of my own pocket in order that she might not have to wait. I am simply warning you that I shall send you her receipt and claim £4.11.4. from you when No. 3 comes out.

I hope at least to ring you up shortly and to find how things are going.

How long does it take to get *Criterion* letter paper printed? I have enough to go on with, I think, for about a month, but I should like to know how long ahead I should apply for a new supply in order that I may not be caught without any.

Yours ever
T. S. Eliot

<*Whibley's* article is to start the No. 3>[5]
There will be a *short* note in a few days for End of Benda.[6]

1–A short story by B. M. Goold Adams in C. 1: 3 (Apr. 1923), 293–302.
2–Paul Valéry, 'The Serpent'; Virginia Woolf, 'In the Orchard', in the same issue.
3–Herbert Read, 'The Nature of Metaphysical Poetry' and Charles Whibley, 'Bolingbroke, Pt. I'.
4–EP had complained about the rate of payment for his essay 'On Criticism in General' in C. 1: 2 (Jan. 1923). See following letter.
5–Scribbled by TSE by hand at head of letter. Whibley, 'Bolingbroke, Pt. I' was the first article in C. 1: 3 (Apr. 1923).
6–The note explaining the context of Benda's 'A Preface' ends the article in 1: 3 (Apr. 1923).

TO *Ezra Pound*[1] CC

9 February 1923 9 Clarence Gate Gdns

Cher Ezra

Point 1

I thought that I had made it quite clear that the payment was at the rate of £10 per 5000 words. Your essay came to 3545 words.[2] That accounts for the difference. I have not had time to look through our correspondence, but it is quite possible that I neglected to mention this important detail to you, and therefore I have instructed Cobden-Sanderson to send you a further cheque for £2.8.0, which please accept for value received.

Point 2

Thank you for your letter A containing statement about Bel Esprit.[3] I gathered that you agreed that the minimum possible is £300 guaranteed. If there was more than that, as I have said all along, the guarantee for everything over the initial £300 need not be so solid.

Do you propose to collect a capital sum of round about £3000?

If you collect only part of this sum is there any other method of guaranteeing the rest of the income up to £300?

How long do you suppose it will take before matters are settled? I mean before you know how many of the present subscribers will realise their promises in a durable form.

If you can't answer this last question you can't, but if you can answer it I am naturally interested to know how long it will be before the scheme arrives or collapses.

Point 3

Re letter B. The book by Vivante has arrived.[4] I am endeavouring to acquire the first two chapters as fast as extremely limited time and limited

1 – Ezra Pound: see Glossary of Names.

2 – EP, 'On Criticism in General', C. 1: 2 (Jan. 1923), 143–56.

3 – EP sent two letters, marked A and B in late Jan. In letter A (29 Jan.), EP told TSE that Bel Esprit was 'an emergency measure to save or utilize *your* particular talent' but also an *idea*: 'the germ of a reorganisation of civilization', representing 'the proper way to get work out of artists'. Bel Esprit was a scheme launched in 1922 by RA, EP and others to buy TSE independence from Lloyds Bank.

4 – In letter B, EP said he was sending a book by Leone Vivante, which TSE 'might use' in C. This was Vivante's *Della Intelligenza nell'Espressione* (Rome, 1922): the English translation, *Intelligence in Expression*, was to be reviewed by W. A. Thorpe in C. 3: 11 (Apr. 1925), 463–4. According to EP, the 'Value of Vivante is that one can argue against Hueffer without arguing for Gosse, Pisswallow Murry or the academic imbeciles'. It was 'not that he tells one anything one didn't know before, but that he makes a full verbal statement of something one cdn't be bothered to write out'.

knowledge of Italian will let me. It might be better to do some sort of general article first dragging in Vivante and perhaps publish chapters one and two afterward, but I am pretty well in the dark until I have read these two chapters which I attempt to do during my lunch. I recognise the need for a small, concentrated and distinct corpus of criticism. Will you tell me what critical writings of Hueffer[1] are available and in what form.

Discussions could be pursued in the *Criterion* and the results should be published in book form concentrated to the greatest brevity compatible with clarity.

Yrs
[T. S. E.]

Gómez[2] is in my opinion quite futile. I will have the Criterion sent to Vivante. Who is Adolfo de Bosis?[3] Will you give me the correct title and address of Mrs, Miss or Mr Goold Adams[4] in order that the necessary cheque may pass on the publication of No. 3.

TO *Jacques Rivière* CC

9 February 1923 [London]

Cher Monsieur,

J'espère que les deux propositions suivantes recevront votre accueil favorable; en tout cas, pardonnez moi si vous les trouvez ennuyeuses.

Nous proposons de présenter dans chaque numéro du *Criterion* une revue des revues étrangères qui indiquerait aux lecteurs anglais ce que chaque revue contient de plus remarquable. Naturellement, nous voulons que la *Nouvelle Revue Française* y fasse figure d'importance. Monsieur Richard Aldington qui soigne la littérature française dans le *Times Literary Supplement*, et qui est de tous les critiques anglaises le mieux doué pour

1–In his letter, EP sought to establish 'authority. I.e. a circle of critics – serious characters, with honest, divergent views, who will refer to each other's ideas.' Referring to Ford Madox Ford under his original name of Hueffer, he told TSE: 'I don't see anyone save Hueffer you & myself capable of understanding the job.' He thought Vivante would help argue against 'Hueffer's attempt to lump verse & prose into a single concept'.

2–EP had not yet seen Gómez de la Serna's 'From "The New Museum"' but found him 'very insignificant in Larbaud's translation'.

3–EP had suggested sending a copy of C. to Vivante and Adolfo de Bosis in Rome. Adolfo de Bosis (1863–1924) was a minor Italian poet, translator of Shelley, and editor of the literary review *Convito*.

4–B. M. Goold-Adams: author of the story 'Obsequies' in C. I: 3 (Apr. 1923).

cette besogne, s'occupera des revues françaises. Pouvez-vous lui faire expédier régulièrement la *Nouvelle Revue Française*? Il commentera le contenu des trois numéros de la *Nouvelle Revue Française* dans chaque numéro (trimestriel) du *Criterion.* Puisque je vous envoie déjà régulièrement le *Criterion,* je ferai envoyer régulièrement un autre exemplaire à la *Nouvelle Revue Française* en continuant l'envoi du *Criterion* à vous personnellement.

Voici la seconde affaire. Plusieurs mois avant sa mort, qui nous a désolé tous, Monsieur Proust a promis de nous envoyer quelque chose.[1] Dernièrement j'ai causé avec Monsieur Scott Moncrieff[2] qui s'est fait un succès éclatant par sa traduction de *Swann*, et qui traduira probablement *A l'ombre des jeunes filles en fleurs*. Je vous écris avec son accord et son approbation: Est ce que nous pourrions espérer la permission de publier un morceau ou de l'oeuvre que Monsieur Scott Moncrieff va entamer, ou même de quelque chose d'inédit?[3] Ça serait naturellement traduit par Monsieur Scott Moncrieff, et je crois que la traduction des morceaux dans le *Criterion* serait avantageuse aux traductions que font publier Messrs. Chatto et Windus. Si vous en approuvez vous-même voulez-vous me mettre sous une obligation profonde en proposant l'idée à Monsieur Gallimard?[4] Je vous prie de me pardonner en vous faisant une telle demande. Croyez moi toujours prêt à réciproquer en toute manière possible.

1–As early as 9 July 1922, TSE told EP he was 'fishing' for something from Proust ('the only name worth getting' in France). Proust died on 18 Nov. 1922.
2–C. K. Scott Moncrieff (1889–1930): Scottish translator. Educated at Edinburgh University, he served with distinction in WW1 (King's Own Scottish Borderers), being awarded the Military Cross for gallantry. (During 1918 he was to become an intimate friend of Wilfred Owen.) From 1919 he set himself to translate the entirety of Marcel Proust's sequence *À la recherche du temps perdu* [*Remembrance of Things Past*] (though the final volume was undertaken by Sydney Schiff following Scott Moncrieff's premature death from cancer). His other translations included *Chanson de Roland* (1919); *Beowulf* (1921); the Latin letters of Abelard and Héloise; novels by Stendhal, and three vols of Pirandello. At the time of his meeting with TSE, Scott Moncrieff had translated the first vol. of *À la recherche du temps perdu*: it came out as *Swann's Way* (2 vols, 1922). This was to be followed by his translation of Proust's second vol., *A l'ombre des jeunes filles en fleurs* [*Within a Budding Grove*] (1924). See Scott Moncrieff, *Memories and Letters*, ed. J. M. Scott Moncrieff and L. W. Lunn (1931).
3–Marcel Proust, 'The Death of Albertine', trans. by C. K. Scott Moncrieff, came out in C. 2: 8 (July 1924), 376–94. This was an extract from the penultimate book, *La Fugitive* or Second Part of *Sodome et Gomorrhe*.
4–Gaston Gallimard (1881–1975): French publisher who founded *Les Éditions de la Nouvelle Revue Française* in 1911. This later became Éditions Gallimard, the most important French literary publishing house.

J'espère bientôt recevoir des nouvelles sur votre article.
Recevez, cher Monsieur, l'assurance de mes sentiments dévoués.

[T. S. E.][1]

TO *Gilbert Seldes* CC

9 February 1923 [*The Criterion*, London]

Dear Mr Seldes,

I have written to Mr Saintsbury and have received the following reply, as nearly as I can decipher his handwriting.

'Dear Mr Eliot,

Oddly enough I received an "Author's Copy" of *Ulysses* but wrote back saying that I only kept it on the understanding that I was not to be expected to write about it. That wouldn't interfere of course. But to tell you the truth I have read very little of it – coming on things not at all "obscene" but what I risk meaning by nasty. What they call obscenity can be quite nice, but nastiness obviously cannot. A and not-A may sometimes coincide – but not *those*! However, if

1 – *Translation*: Dear Sir, I hope that the two following proposals will meet with a favourable response from you; anyway, please forgive me, if you find them troublesome.

We plan to publish in each issue of the *Criterion* a review of foreign reviews, aimed at bringing to the notice of English readers the most important articles of each of these reviews. We naturally wish the *Nouvelle Revue Française* to occupy an important place in this chronicle. Mr Richard Aldington, who is in charge of French books in the *Times Literary Supplement*, and who is better equipped than any other English reviewer for this task, will be in charge of the French reviews. Could you make arrangements for a copy of the *Nouvelle Revue Française* to be regularly sent to him? Each issue of the *Criterion*, which is a quarterly, will carry his comment on three issues of the *Nouvelle Review Française*. I already send you regularly a copy of the *Criterion*; I shall from now on do the same for the *Nouvelle Revue Française*, while of course continuing to send you your personal copy.

Now for the second proposal. A few months before his death, which has grieved us all, M. Proust had promised to send us something. I recently had occasion to talk to Mr Scott Moncrieff who has scored a brilliant success with his translation of *Swann* and who will probably translate *A l'ombre des jeunes filles en fleurs*. I write to you with his support and approval, in order to ask you whether it might not be possible to obtain permission to print an extract from the work which Mr Scott Moncrieff is about to translate, or even something from Proust which has not yet been published. This would naturally be translated by Mr Scott Moncrieff, and I am sure that the publication of such extracts in the *Criterion* would benefit the sales of the translation to be published by Chatto & Windus. If you approve my proposal, you would greatly oblige me by submitting this project to the attention of M. Gallimard. I beg you to forgive me burdening you with such a task, and I beg you to believe that I shall always be ready to do the same for you in whatever way I can.

I hope to hear soon about your article.

Please believe me, dear Sir, yours faithfully, [T. S. E.]

you will give me a day or two I'll continue explorations and let you know . . . .[1] Joyce has *power* of course . . . .

Yours sincerely,

G. S.'

So there it is at present, and I will let you know if he succeeds in making up his mind one way or the other.

Sincerely yours,

[T. S. E.]

FROM *George Saintsbury* — MS Valerie Eliot

11 February 1923 — 1 Royal Crescent, Bath

Dear Mr Eliot

I'm afraid it's no go. There is no prudery in me but I have what the doctors I believe call an 'irritable vomiting centre' and Mr Joyce unfortunately acts on it like ipecacuanha or a feather. It is a pity: for not only are his more serious or serious-parodist pieces sometimes very good, but he has an odd faculty of more pictorial or musical than purely literary *composition.* The long bar room piece in the middle is a sort of sonata with the two girls being in and out of it like mottoes.[2] But when you're always expecting to have to run to the side of the ship as you turn the page it ceases to be delightful. So I must decline to be happy with either of the two ladies who offer themselves so generously and together on this occasion.

Yours none the less sincerely

George Saintsbury

TO *James S. Watson*[3] — TS Berg

12 February 1923 — 9 Clarence Gate Gdns

Dear Mr Watson,

Mr Seldes told me that he was to be away and that I should address anything of a personal nature to you. As I conceive the acknowledgement

1–TSE omits Saintsbury's remark, 'Many thanks for what you say about the "*Dullness*"', referring to TSE's comments on his essay in C. 1: 1 (Oct. 1922).

2–'The Sirens': episode 11 of *Ulysses*.

3–Dr James Sibley Watson (1894–1982): New York philanthropist, who, at the suggestion of his friend Scofield Thayer, purchased *The Dial* in 1919 and supported it until its demise in 1929.

of your cheque for the *Dial* prize[1] to be in the nature of a personal communication, and to require my expression of appreciation not only to the *Dial* as an institution but to all of its proprietors and editors severally, I am therefore writing to you. I cannot however express adequately my appreciation of the kindness and generosity which I have received from you from beginning to end. I can only say that the *Dial* is exceptional in having such persons to manage it and that its managers are exceptional in themselves and for having a paper like the *Dial* which is certainly unique in the world. Please accept this letter as a weak and partial attempt to express what I feel.

I shall always give the *Dial* the refusal of whatever I consider my best work, and needless to say especially of my verse.[2]

Believe me,

My dear Mr Watson,
Yours very gratefully
T. S. Eliot

TO *George Saintsbury* CC

15 February 1923 [*The Criterion*, 17 Thavies Inn]

Dear Mr Saintsbury,

Thank you for your letter of the 11th. I am of course very sorry that you cannot write this paper, for I am sure that such an essay from you would be an event of great importance. While I do not see eye to eye with you on this subject, I fully realise the difficulties and sympathise with your attitude. I can only say that the *Criterion* will always be glad to publish anything you care to offer; and I should be very happy if you would propose some subject of your own choice, for either the October or December number next. Please believe, for what my opinion is worth, that I recognise and appreciate the most eminent English critic of our time.[3]

Yours very sincerely
[T. S. E.]

1–TSE had been awarded the second annual *Dial* award of $2,000 for *TWL*.
2–TSE contributed '*Ulysses*, Order and Myth' to *Dial* 75: 5 (Nov. 1923), and 'Marianne Moore' to 75: 6 (Dec. 1923). The next poem to appear there was 'The Hollow Men', Parts I–II and IV, in Mar. 1925.
3–In 1924 TSE was to dedicate *HJD* to Saintsbury, whose monograph on the same subject had appeared in the 'English Men of Letters' series (1881).

TO *Charles Whibley* CC

15 February 1923 [London]

My dear Whibley

Thank you for your kind letter. It is a very great pleasure to me to say that I shall be delighted to come on the 10th of March and I shall look forward very keenly to seeing you and hope to find you quite restored in health.

Thank you also for returning the Bolingbroke proof so promptly. I am anticipating very eagerly the effect which I am sure it will have, and I think that the next number will be one of the best.

Yours always
[T. S. E.]

TO *Lady Rothermere*[1] CC

15 February 1923 [9 Clarence Gate Gdns]

Dear Lady Rothermere,

I have at last come to the conclusion that I must ask you about something which I have been hesitating to ask you for many months.

Since seeing you, I have become more and more convinced that I must leave the Bank ultimately: and therefore the sooner I can do so, obviously the better. I find that I have always more and more work to do in the hours outside the Bank, and my health gives me less and less time and strength to do it. I cannot help seeing all the time what an infinitely greater success I could make of the *Criterion* if only I had sufficient time to give it. It seems to me already such an astonishing success (I hope this is your opinion) that I find it so much the more tantalising to have to spend the best eight hours of the day in the Bank, doing work which can lead to nothing, and give the *Criterion* only the evening when my mind is worn out.

Of course, I never imagined that Bel Esprit would enable me to leave the Bank with security and lack of anxiety, immensely as I have appreciated the unselfish work done in the matter by my friends. Besides which I think that even if the scheme did come off I should never really be happy to live on unearned money. I know that people think me absurd in this direction, but I cannot help having strong feelings about it.

1–Viscountess Rothermere: see Glossary of Names.

This rather long winded preface leads me to what I have come to the conclusion I will ask, trusting you will take it in the spirit in which it is meant, and fully realising how unlikely it is that such a thing should be in anybody's power to help me to.

Is it, do you think, possible that Lord Rothermere could give me a literary post (even a small one) on one of his journals? You know that I am accustomed to work, so that the usual work of a literary editor would, after the pressure under which I have lived for years, seem to me in comparison to give all the leisure I could ask. At the Bank alone I work forty-four hours a week, and including the time spent in coming and going, it takes fifty hours altogether, so that I am not asking for a sinecure!

One naturally wishes to work for a paper with which one has a general sympathy; I have a great deal of admiration for the way in which Lord Rothermere conducts his papers and have remarked an obvious improvement since he took them over.

A crisis which has appeared in my affairs[1] has forced me to write now and if you think it any good at all to make an attempt, it would make all the difference in the world if you could do it at once. I should be very glad and grateful if I might hear from you, as I am rather anxious at this moment.

Of course I know I need not tell you that what I have said is quite confidential, as I am sure that you will treat it as such.

Always sincerely yours
[T. S. E.]

TO *J. B. Trend* CC

15 February 1923 [*The Criterion*, London]

Dear Trend,

Thank you for your letter of the 8th. I have only been waiting for a free evening in order to propose that evening to you, but business and literary affairs have been increasingly complicated this last month. So, at the moment I can only say that I hope that you are settled in London for some time to come, as I shall propose a meeting at the first opportunity.

1–TSE had been confidentially offered the literary editorship of *The Nation* by the economist John Maynard Keynes, who was in the process of acquiring it (see letters below to SS and John Quinn of 12 Mar.).

Yes I think that Azorín sounds very interesting,[1] and I shall look forward to reading your articles on the other two men you mention.[2] I have not even had time to look at the *Supplement* lately and have let it accumulate until I have had time to do so. I should be delighted if you would let me have specimens, whenever you can, of some of the work of the men you name.

With many thanks,

Sincerely yours
[T. S. E.]

TO *Herbert Read* CC

20 February 1923 [*The Criterion*, London]

Dear Read,

Forgive me for not answering your postcard at once, and indeed for not having written to you before that, but I have been of late exceptionally busy and exceptionally worried, even for me. I should very much like to have a few notes from you for the next number, if possible by the end of the month.[3] Can you manage it? As I have not yet had time to arrange for the *Dial* to be sent to you regularly I will send you also the last number, and hope you will not mind letting me have it back when you are done with it.

Yours always,
[T. S. E.]

TO *W. W. Worster* CC

20 February 1923 [*The Criterion*, London]

Dear Sir,

I have certainly been dilatory in examining and reporting on your manuscript, but no more so than I have been of late in all my obligations.[4]

1 – Azorín was the pseud. of José Martínez Ruíz (1894–1967), Spanish essayist, novelist and critic, and a central figure, with Miguel de Unamuno, of the Generation of 1898; author of *Al margen de los clásicos* (1914).

2 – Trend noted in his letter: 'The *Lit. Sup.* have had articles of mine on E. D'Ors and J. R. Jimenez lately: & I suppose they will appear in a week or so.'

3 – In addition to his essay on 'The Nature of Metaphysical Poetry', HR contributed notes on 'American Periodicals' for *C.* 1: 3 (Apr. 1923).

4 – Worster was pressing (19 Feb.) for a decision on the article on Icelandic literature he had submitted on 2 Feb.

My only excuse is that I am singlehanded and that my free time has been almost entirely claimed by private business for several weeks past. I hope to let you know definitively in a week, but if there is any special reason for haste will you let me know and I will make time somehow to read and consider your manuscripts.

Yours very truly,
[T. S. E.]

TO *Richard Aldington* TS Texas

20 February 1923 *The Criterion*, 9 Clarence Gate Gdns

Dear Richard

Would it be possible for you to let me have some brief notes about the end of this month? I am sorry to ask you if it is going to be a nuisance to do them at such short notice, but really brief notes will do unless you find anything of special importance.[1] I have arranged for the *Nouvelle Revue Française* to come to you direct in future, but I am sending you my copy of the Proust number as they are out of it. Will you return it some time to me when you have done with it.

If you cannot manage to do a few notes on the stuff I sent you, please let me know at once.

I have been fearfully rushed and overwhelmed with several pieces of important business, besides the *Criterion*, and have literally not had a moment in which to write to you. Please be sure that I want very much to write to you at the first opportunity I can get.

I am feeling pretty well worn out at present and I am convinced that I cannot keep at this kind of life for very long.

Affectionately,
Tom

1 – 'French Periodicals', *C.* 1: 3 (Apr. 1923).

TO *Raymond Mortimer*[1] TS Beinecke

20 February 1923 9 Clarence Gate Gdns

Dear Mortimer,

I should have been delighted to dine with you on Saturday, but alas I have to go out of town to look at a country cottage[2] which I have heard about and I shall not be back until late in the evening. This is only one of several important and difficult pieces of business which I have had on my hands lately, else I should have dropped you a line to remind you to let me know when you were in town again. It is distressing to have to decline another opportunity of seeing you. Would you care to look in on me in the city one day next week and have lunch? I make the suggestion timidly, first because I am obliged to lunch at 12.00 o'clock, and second because I cannot offer a very good lunch in my neighbourhood, and third because I am ashamed to ask anyone to make that journey for a meeting which is strictly limited to an hour. But this is the only thing I can do for the next fortnight or so, and I therefore make the suggestion and should be *very glad* if you would care to come.

In haste
Yours sincerely
T. S. Eliot

TO *F. S. Flint* TS Texas

20 February 1923 *The Criterion*, 9 Clarence Gate Gdns

Dear Flint,

If humanly possible, I should be glad if you could let me have a couple of brief notes from the two German papers I sent you, by the end of the month.[3] They will be too far out of date by the following number to review at all. I cannot make out whether the *Merkur* intends to send to us regularly or not, but if so, I will ask them to send it direct to you.

I hope this will not be a nuisance to you. I have been so rushed these last weeks that I have not been as businesslike as I should have been. I ought certainly to have let you know before and if you cannot do the notes it

1 – Raymond Mortimer (1895–1980): literary critic and journalist; prolific literary reviewer.
2 – TSE and VHE were urgently looking for a country retreat from London.
3 – See Flint's notes on 'German Periodicals', signed 'T.-F.', C. 1: 3 (Apr. 1923), 310–11.

will be my own fault. I expect that a short paragraph will be enough for each.

Yours in haste,
T. S. Eliot

TO *Lady Rothermere* CC

20 February 1923 [London]

Dear Lady Rothermere,

Thank you very much for your kind and understanding letter and for your expressions of sympathy.[1] I wish that I had [been able] to discuss the matter with you in London because I am aware now that it would have been better from every point of view if I had come to this decision sooner. I am now within measurable distance of the end of my tether and I may find before very long that I no longer have time to pick and choose. I should be very sorry to have to decide on something which I should find less congenial than work in connection with one of Lord Rothermere's papers, and that was why I wanted to find out what possibilities there are in that direction, before I had to make such a choice. You see that I have something in mind which may or may not become a definitive offer to me and I am at present very much perplexed.[2] I am glad however that you do not appear to regard my wishes as wholly impossible.

I am doing everything I can in other directions, but I do not see any prospect of anything which would be as satisfactory to me as what I asked you. I will keep you in touch with any progress I may make.

I certainly feel the need of a long rest and a complete change, you are quite right, and if I could get it I should certainly make use of your kind offer. My mind is completely stale from having to think of many things at once, and from having to wait eight hours a day in the knowledge that I must redouble my activity at the end of it, and I am beginning to feel very definitely the effect of many months of insufficient sleep. It would certainly be unfortunate if I had to tackle new work in my present condition. I hope that no choice will be forced upon me until you have been able to find out from Lord Rothermere whether there is any chance.

I hope, in spite of everything, that the third number of the *Criterion* will be a good one and am very much gratified and encouraged by what you

1 – A reference to her reply to his letter of 15 Feb., asking about a possible opening for him on one of Lord Rothermere's papers.
2 – The literary editorship of *The Nation*.

say about my connection with the paper. But as I said before the *Criterion* has not yet given me real satisfaction, because I feel how much better it ought to be and could be if I could devote enough energy to it.

Always sincerely yours,
[T. S. E.]

TO *Mark Wardle* CC

26 February 1923 9 Clarence Gate Gdns

Dear Captain Wardle,

I am awfully sorry to return your story,[1] because I think it is a very good one. Half a dozen papers would snap at it, but – partly for that reason – it does not fit in with the programme of the *Criterion*. The *Criterion* aims to publish only fiction mirroring some phase of the modern world or the modern spirit, or illustrating some new development of the modern mind and sensibility. The sort of fiction, in fact, which would repel most editors.

With regard to the two versions of the 'Serpent', I cannot find space in the *Criterion*, but think they should *both* go into the book.[2] I shall try to get an early decision from the press to which I have submitted the poem,[3] and if it is unfavourable, will try another. I am most anxious to get the book done.

Sincerely yours,
[T. S. E.]

TO *Jacques Rivière* CC

26 February 1923 9 Clarence Gate Gdns

Cher Monsieur,

J'étais désolé à la fin d'être forcé de vous télégraphier mes mauvaises nouvelles. J'espérait jusqu'au dernier moment trouver le temps pour rédiger mes notes.[4] Mais pendant les dernières quatre semaines j'ai été

1 – On 14 Jan. Wardle said he was sending 'a rather macabre story'.
2 – Wardle's transl. of Valéry's 'The Serpent' appeared in English in *C.* 1: 3 (Apr. 1923), 267–76, and in tandem with the original when published as a book. 'Le Serpent' had been published with two different endings: TSE published only the revised version in *C.* 1: 3, but the original was included as an appendix in *Le Serpent par Paul Valéry* (1924), trans. by Wardle and with intro. by TSE.
3 – The Hogarth Press.
4 – Following on the 'Lettre d'Angleterre' in *NRF* 19: 111 (Dec. 1922), TSE had promised a second one for the spring. In the event, it did not appear until *NRF* 21 (1 Nov. 1923).

complètement écrasé par deux affaires personelles qui ne m'ont pas laissé même le temps de mettre deux notes debout. Je suis navré si je vous ai embarrassé ou gêné dans la préparation du numéro d'avril. J'espère vous envoyer quelque chose vers le milieu du mois de mars et j'espère que cette fois vous me pardonnerez.

Je vous remercie de votre letter du 17 fevrier et de votre réponse si favorable.[1] Dorénavant voulez vous envoyer regulièrement l'exemplaire de la *Nouvelle Revue Française* à l'adresse suivante:-

Monsieur Richard Aldington,
Malthouse Cottage,
Padworth,
near Reading, Berks.

J'espère que vous continuerez de me l'envoyer aussi et je ferai envoyer deux exemplaires du *Criterion* regulièrement en échange à *La Nouvelle Revue Française* et à vous personnellement.

J'attends avec une impatience agréable la réception de votre article vers le 15 Mars, un article qui fera grand honneur à notre numéro de Juillet.[2]

Recevez cher Monsieur avec toutes mes excuses et ma reconnaissance impressée, l'assurance de ma sympathie loyale.

[T. S. E.][3]

1 – Rivière said he would be willing to give TSE a fragment of Marcel Proust for a future number of *C.*, but would need to get permission from Dr Proust, his executor.

2 – Rivière, 'Notes on a Possible Generalisation of the Theories of Freud', *C.* 1: 4 (July 1923).

3 – *Translation*: Dear Sir, I was extremely sorry to be eventually obliged to telegraph the bad news to you. I had hoped until the last moment to find time to write up my notes. But during the last four weeks, I have been completely overwhelmed by two personal matters which did not leave me time to put together even a couple of notes. I would be upset to think I had caused you any embarrassment or inconvenience in connection with the preparation of the April number. I hope to send you something towards the middle of March, and I hope you will forgive me on this occasion.

I thank you for your letter of 17 February and for your favourable reply. Henceforth, could you send a copy of *La Nouvelle Revue Française* regularly to the following address: Mr Richard Aldington, Malthouse Cottage, Padworth, near Reading, Berks.

I hope you will continue to send me the review as well and, in exchange, I will arrange for two copies of the *Criterion* to be sent regularly, one to *La Nouvelle Revue Française* and the other to you personally.

I look forward, with pleasurable impatience, to receiving your article around 15 March; it will be a great honour to have it in our July number.

With all my apologies, my warmest gratitude and faithful regards. [T. S. E.]

TO *Owen Barfield*[1] CC

26 February 1923 [*The Criterion*, London]

Dear Sir,

I have received your story which I am prepared to accept, if you would be so good as to change the title as the present title ['Dope'] is not suitable for the *Criterion* and is not, in our opinion, a good enough one.[2]

With regard to the final paragraph commencing 'On on on on', we should be glad to know whether you would object to only one 'on' instead of the four as we consider this would be an improvement.[3]

The story will probably appear in the July issue of the *Criterion*.

I am returning the manuscript and would like to know by return if you will make these alterations.

Yours truly,
[T. S. E.]

TO *W. B. Yeats* CC

26 February 1923 [9 Clarence Gate Gdns]

Dear Mr Yeats,

Not having heard from you since you were last in London I am beginning to be somewhat apprehensive about the autobiographic fragment which you promised me and hope that I shall soon receive a re-assurance from you.[4] I have been counting upon it as the most important contribution for the July number, and also counting upon the satisfaction of announcing it in the April number.

May I hope to receive it by the end of March? and I should like to suggest that the earlier we receive it the better, as it will need to be set up, and the proof will be forwarded to you without delay.

I hope that neither political duties nor domestic anxieties will be too oppressive to permit of your conferring this great benefit upon the

1–Owen Barfield (1898–1997), author and anthroposophist, was at this time a freelance writer; later publications include *History in English Words* (1926) and *Poetic Diction* (1928).
2–Barfield replied (27 Feb.) that he would accept a changed title, but that it 'was originally conceived to fit that title' which he thought 'exactly expresses its angle of vision'. TSE's secretary wrote back on 4 Apr. to say that 'on careful re-reading' TSE agreed 'the original title' of the story was 'the best possible'. It appeared as 'Dope' in *C.* 1: 4 (July 1923), 322–8.
3–In his letter of 27 Feb., Barfield thought this 'a definite improvement'.
4–See WBY, 'A Biographical Fragment', *C.* 1: 4 (July 1923), 315–21.

Criterion. I cannot say too often how warmly I appreciate the magnitude of the favour you will be doing us.

Yours always sincerely,
[T. S. E.]

TO *Herbert Read* CC

2 March 1923 [*The Criterion*, London]

Dear Read,

Thank you for your notes[1] which are excellent. If possible they shall be published entire, and I hope to collect a more interesting lot for you in future.

Yours ever
[T. S. E.]

TO *Ottoline Morrell* TS Texas

2 March 1923 9 Clarence Gate Gdns

My dear Ottoline

I am very sorry that I could not keep my promise to write to you sooner, but I have had more to think of and to decide during the last ten days than at almost any moment in my life.[2] I do hope that your cold is better and that there is a touch of spring in the Garsington air; here there have been occasional moments of warm sunshine among days of constant rain.

Vivien is sleeping a little better, although it is a hard struggle at best. It remains to be seen whether the treatment she has been having is not too drastic for her; it is not at all pleasant and she finds it *extremely* exhausting. One never knows whether the benefits of this sort of thing compensate for the strain which she must put upon herself in order to undergo them. They have been giving her, as well as the electric treatment, the Plombières treatment,[3] which is the most disagreeable of all; she feels in a state of complete exhaustion. I will let you know how she progresses.

1 – HR's notes on 'American Periodicals' (*C.* 1: 3, Apr. 1923, 311–13) were devoted to issues of *The Dial*, *Secession* and *Rhythmus*.

2 – TSE is referring to his indecision over whether to leave Lloyds Bank to take the literary editorship of *The Nation* or else money from the Bel Esprit scheme.

3 – A form of colonic irrigation used to treat chronic constipation, colonic catarrh and colitis; it was first introduced by Dr Langenhagen at Plombières.

I have finally secured a tiny cottage in Sussex[1] which we shall use as much as possible this summer and which we intend to get into the moment she is out.

I wish I could promise myself a weekend with you soon, but I have so much to do that I have no right to look forward to such a luxury before the middle of April. As I told you I have promised to lecture [to the undergraduate Ordinary Society] at Oxford on the 5th of May, and it will take me all my spare time for a fortnight beforehand to prepare the lecture. I regret now that I promised it so soon because I have three articles that I ought to write first. I look forward to staying with you then, in fact it is one of the chief inducements. I have promised to speak on Saturday evening: I suppose that I shall have to dine in Oxford.

I should like *very much* to meet Dr Bridges[2] some time as I have never seen him and believe that I should like him.

I enjoyed our dinner very much indeed. It was the *last* occasion on which I have seen anybody except for business reasons,

Affectionately
Tom

Vivien Eliot TO *Mary Hutchinson* — TS Texas

Sunday, 4 March [1923] — London N.W.1

My dear Mary

It is very sweet of you to show so much interest and pleasure in my having secured my cottage. It is really settled, and I can move my furniture in a fortnight. Won't that be fun?

Meanwhile, since last week and for at least the next fortnight I am having Plombières treatment. I do not suppose you know what that is, but perhaps Jack does. It is extremely exhausting for me as I am already very weak. So I am going to give myself up to it, in order to be ready to go to the country directly my cottage is ready to receive me.

I am having a Plombières tomorrow so I should not be able to see you in any case, and therefore I will not telephone.

1–TSE had found a cottage at Fishbourne, only a few miles from Bosham where they had stayed the year before.

2–Robert Bridges (1844–1930): doctor and poet; friend and editor of Gerard Manley Hopkins, and from 1913 Poet Laureate. In an unpublished lecture, TSE called him 'a traditional Victorian poet': 'his greatest distinction is that, in the position of Poet Laureate, he maintained with dignity the status of the poet as craftsman' ('The Last Twenty-Five Years of English Poetry', 1940).

In passing, if anyone asks you what is the matter with me I should be so much obliged if you will reply – in crude words – 'Catarrh of the intestines, with occasional enteritis'. That is, if your delicacy will allow you to frame such an intolerable statement of fact. If you cannot bring yourself to utter it, will you have the kindness of heart to refer enquiries to me. To my cynical and unromantic mind a statement of fact presents no difficulties.

Again, in passing, it is my opinion that Tom is right in refraining at this point from taking steps which would make our common dwelling place a four-roomed country cottage or an attic in London, and which would deprive me of medical assistance. (Of course there *are* the nice hospitals, I know.) Indeed, if he did take such steps I should bear him a considerable grudge.

I know, too well, that in your view the poet's wife dying in a humble cot would be a pretty sight – almost a nosegay. Alas! that you should never have the opportunity to experience such a pathetical situation.

But Mary, take my advice and find an artist for a lover.[1] Meanwhile be bold – and not too ardent. Conquer Cambridge, then the world (there *is* a world).

Your unromantic friend
Vivien

TO *Ottoline Morrell* — MS Texas

4 March [1923] — 9 Clarence Gate Gdns

My dear Ottoline

Since I saw you I have reached a critical point about the bank and the *Criterion*. I must either give it up or get a minimum salary from Lady R[othermere] (£300 a year is little enough, God knows) so that we can go away and save what remains of our health.

It is a question of my seeing her as soon as possible and getting a contract. I think it more than likely that she will prefer to drop it, and me. But she would be much more likely to give me what I ask if I could tell her that other people (a group) would run a quarterly if she won't. It is simply a matter of getting the consent to use names (not definite sums). For my present purpose it would be enough if I could mention people who agree to back me *if she backs out*. The promise might be purely nominal as no sums each need be specified.

1 – Mary Hutchinson's lover was Clive Bell, nephew of VW.

Could I say, if necessary, that *you* (with other names) were one of the group?

And could you get your brother Henry[1] to allow the use of his name also. It is *names* (preferably titles) which will impress Lady R., not figures.

This would not actually commit either you or your brother to *anything*. *If* she refused to give me my contract and salary, I *should* get twenty or twenty-five people to contribute in this way to subsidize the paper as a *literary* and critical, non-political review. But they needn't include all the people mentioned first. I only want to say to Lady R. 'So and so and so and so and so and so are among the people who have agreed to subsidize a quarterly review; if you don't choose to do it yourself, and at once, the review will be done by others.'

If this is clear to you, and you agree, and can get your brother to agree, and anyone else! I should be very very grateful. I want to act quickly.

There is 1) the people who allow their names to be used now.

2) the people I should get together *if* she refused. This would be far more sympathetic than Bel Esprit scheme, because I should be giving my services to a literary review instead of receiving charity.

How I wish you were in town, and I could talk to you! It was very disappointing to see you only once.

In haste,

Affectionately
Tom

Bruce Richmond[2] is confident of getting a number of people. £1000 a year would do it altogether, and some could give a good deal and some very little.

TO *W. W. Worster* cc

12 March 1923 [*The Criterion*, London]

Dear Sir,

I must apologise for the long delay which is entirely owing to the fact that I have been working under extreme pressure for some weeks past and have had no time to write any letters. I was very much interested by your

1–Lord Henry Bentinck (1863–1931): OM's favourite brother; Conservative MP for North-West Norfolk 1886–92 and for South Nottinghamshire (with one interruption) from 1895 to 1929.

2–Bruce Richmond was editor of the *TLS*: see Glossary of Names.

article [on Icelandic literature] which I think succeeds in the difficult task of making entirely unknown and practically inaccessible authors interesting. What I have to suggest is this, and if it is not acceptable to you please say so frankly.

The aim of the *Criterion*, in dealing with foreign literature, is to attempt to introduce foreign authors themselves and to criticise only such authors as are either known to our public or can be made known through the *Criterion*. What I should like very much would be if you could divide your article and take for the moment whichever one of your four authors seems to you the most suitable and expand what you have said about him. We should then want to get some specimen of his work suitable in character and in length for the *Criterion* and present it at the same time. I do not know whether you would care to undertake the translation as well as the selection of such a specimen, and I suggest it rather diffidently; but at the same time I suggest that you are certainly the most suitable person to introduce such work in this country.[1]

If, however, you prefer to publish your essay as it stands I do not wish to stand in your way, as I am sure that several other reviews would be very glad to have it. I should very much appreciate the honour of having the first inspection of it and I hope very much that my proposal will appeal to you.

With many thanks,

I am,
Yours faithfully,
[T. S. E.]

TO *Sydney Schiff*[2] — TS Valerie Eliot

12 March 1923 — 9 Clarence Gate Gdns

My dear Sydney,

I am very much disappointed that I cannot dine with you on Wednesday, and this letter will explain why. Ever since I saw you last I have been in a state of worry to the point of complete paralysis over a crisis in my affairs which has of course been impending had I not refused to see it for a very long time. The work of the *Criterion* has been steadily increasing week by week to such a point that I have steadily come nearer and nearer to

1 – Despite TSE's suggestions, Worster never became a contributor to the *C*.

2 – Sydney Schiff, see Glossary of Names. SS's short story 'The Thief' was published under the nom-de-plume Stephen Hudson in *C.* 1: 2 (Jan. 1923), 188–91.

exhaustion; so that now when I am suddenly faced with a decision, I hardly feel capable of making one or carrying it out when made. I have refused always to recognise that there are any limitations to my capacity for work and now I am faced with the consequences. I have for a long time been living under such strain that I lost all power to realise how abnormal the strain was.

The situation has now come to this: That I must now either give up the *Criterion*, and that without any delay, or I must give up the bank and find some work that I can fit in with the *Criterion*. After having sunk the whole of my strength and all my time gratuitously into the *Criterion* for eighteen months, and put the whole of my life into this work, it will be a terrific blow to me to have to admit that it has all been a complete waste of time and a fatal mistake; but it would be better to make this admission now than to go on and collapse or that I could no longer carry on the work which has been my sole source of livelihood.

I am at present faced with this choice. I am offered the literary editorship of a paper whose name I am not yet at liberty to mention, at a salary of 300 a year with only six months guarantee of security.[1] On the one hand it would allow me the time to run the *Criterion*; on the other hand it would be a serious drop of half my income, and I should have to use the rest of my time in making up my income by other journalism, so that my actual leisure for poetry and for ordinary living would be no greater than it is at present. And furthermore I should have to work with the uncertainty whether the post would last more than six months, and if it did last six months, I might still be dismissed at three months' notice, leaving me in a worse position than I have ever been in my life. This would be the price for the necessary time in which to carry on the *Criterion*; otherwise I must abandon the *Criterion* at a moment when there seems to be a definite prospect of its ultimate success. For that success, however, I cannot afford to wait; I cannot live as I have been living for many more weeks; the persons in whose hands this unmentioned paper is, are coming to town this week; I do not know which day, but I must hold any time open for the final interview at which all difficulties will be discussed and my final offer made. That is why I cannot come to dinner on Wednesday. It is quite likely

1–In her diary (19 Feb.), VW said she had been 'trying to pull wires, to seat Tom at the Nation as literary editor, & unseat my foe Miss Royde-Smith'. She wished 'poor dear Tom had more spunk in him, less need to let drop by drop of his agonised perplexities fall ever so finely through pure cambric. One waits; sympathises, but it is dreary work. He is like a person about to break down – infinitely scrupulous, tautologous, & cautious' (*Diary*, II, 236).

that I shall be free that evening, but I should not care to promise and then disappoint you at the last minute. But if I am free Wednesday evening I will *certainly* come in after dinner, and too I am very anxious to see Murry[1] and it may be the only opportunity to see him. So it is quite possible, and I hope, that I may see you on Wednesday.

Vivien is very disappointed that you are not taking a house in Sussex;[2] she had been very much looking forward to it and we settled on the cottage half in the hope that you would not be far away.

I cannot write more now: You will see from this letter what I have been going through in the interval since I saw you last,

Affectionately,
Tom

TO *John Quinn*[3] — TS Berg

12 March 1923 — 9 Clarence Gate Gdns

My dear Mr Quinn,

I was delighted to get your long and kind letter after having heard nothing of you for many months.[4] I had become concerned about you, because I had recently heard from Pound saying that he had had no news of you for a long time and I feared that it indicated some severe breakdown.[5] My wife has had so much and so severe illness, and has borne it and struggled for health with such heroic fortitude, that I think I can understand the tortures of ill-health better than most people.

I consider your payment for the manuscript very generous indeed,[6] and feel that you have thwarted me in my attempt to repay you in some way for all that you have done.

1 – JMM, as one-time literary editor of the *Athenaeum*, was in a good position to offer advice.
2 – Sydney and Violet Schiff had previously spent summers in Eastbourne.
3 – John Quinn: see Glossary of Names.
4 – In a letter of 26 Feb., Quinn had thanked TSE for the MSS of *TWL* and the 'leather bound notebook', which TSE sent him in Dec. 1922. He found the manuscript of 'great interest', and noted the 'evidence of Pound's criticisms on the poems': he personally would not have cut out 'some of the parts that Pound advised you to cut'. He would hold these MSS 'in trust' and provide 'copies of the original manuscript with any unpublished poems' if required.
5 – Quinn said that in early Jan. he had had an 'attack of some sort, probably due to the accumulation of toxins in the system'. He took two weeks of convalescence in Hot Springs, Virginia, and returned at the end of Jan. feeling better. He had not written to EP 'all autumn' and was going to write in a few days.
6 – Quinn had the MSS valued by James F. Drake, who 'thought a payment of about $2 a page, which would be about $120, would be "about right"'. Quinn considered these figures

I am interested to hear that Liveright has sold 1250 copies of my book already and am glad that it has exceeded his expectations.[1] At the same time I am all the more surprised that I have had so far had [*sic*] not a penny from him. I have just looked at the two contracts which you prepared, and it seems to me clear that the first contract assured me of $150 on publication, and that the supplementary contract did in no way affect this clause. I remember also that you pointed out this advantage in a letter, so I do not think I can be mistaken. I am very annoyed about this, although it is the sort of behaviour which I have been led to expect from Liveright. I am sick of doing business with Jew publishers who will not carry out their part of the contract unless they are forced to;[2] I have not the time nor can I at this distance keep my eye on him incessantly and I hate to bother you with these affairs. I wish I could find a decent Christian publisher in New York[3] who could be trusted not to slip and slide at every opportunity. I should be very grateful if you would just confirm my reading of the contract and drop a line to Liveright unless I am quite mistaken. As I say, I hate to impose another burden on you, but who else is there who would do what you have done?

—

'somewhat conservative', and sent TSE a draft for '£29.14.10, the equivalent at the present rate of exchange of $140', which he thought 'fair and reasonable'.

1 – Horace Liveright, see Glossary of Names. TSE had met Liveright with EP in Paris on 4 Jan. 1922, and Quinn set up the contract for him to publish *TWL* the following summer. In his Feb. letter, Quinn recorded that when ordering some additional copies of *TWL* from Boni & Liveright, he 'found the first edition of 1,000 copies had been exhausted and that a second edition of 1,000 copies was sold up to some 240 copies' (this was properly a 'second impression' rather than a 'second edition').

2 – Liveright's biographer Tom Dardis notes: 'The presence of Jews in American publishing was an anomaly in the pre-World War I years. When Horace [Liveright] and Albert Boni created their firm in the late spring of 1917, they were entering a Christian industry – owned by Christians and staffed by them' (*Firebrand: The Life of Horace Liveright*, 1995). Dardis points out that many of the major works of the modernists were published in the US by Jewish firms, citing JJ's *Dubliners* and *A Portrait of the Artist* (Huebsch), DHL's *The Rainbow* and *Women in Love* (Seltzer), TSE's *Prufrock* (Knopf), and EP, Eugene O'Neill, Ernest Hemingway, Djuna Barnes, as well as TSE's *TWL* (Boni & Liveright). TSE's comment is a response to the openly prejudiced Quinn, who wrote to EP in 1920 of 'the damned Jew spewing-up of the Untermeyers, the Oppenheims, the Waldo Franks' (*Selected Letters of Ezra Pound and John Quinn*, 175). In his previous letter to TSE, Quinn wrote that on Broadway 'the streets and sidewalks are infested . . . with swarms of horrible looking Jews, low, squat, animal-like' (26 Feb. 1923).

3 – TSE wrote again to Liveright on 23 Aug. about a companion book of prose, which was never realised. TSE did subsequently change US publishers, with *Ash-Wednesday* being brought out by G. P. Putnam's (1930); *Poems 1909–1925* (1930) and *Selected Essays* (1932) by Harcourt, Brace & Company. By that time, however, Liveright had been forced out of business.

In the circumstances, I do not feel particularly disposed to come to any arrangement with Liveright about the *Criterion*. It would apparently be necessary to keep a collector at his door the whole time and God knows what other tricks he might play with the paper.

Anyway, I am now in the midst of a terrific crisis. I wish to heaven that I had never taken up the *Criterion*. It seemed a good thing and it is a good thing, but although it is a pity to drop at such a promising beginning I may very soon have to drop it and I am quite sincere when I wish that I had never undertaken it. It has been an evergrowing responsibility; it has been a great *expense* to me and I have not got a penny out of it. There is not enough money to run it and pay me too. I hoped it would be a solid thing for me, but there is no longer *time* to wait for that. I think the work and worry have taken ten years off my life. I have sunk the whole of my strength for the past eighteen months into this confounded paper, when I ought to have been minding my business and doing my own writing. The paper has therefore done me more harm than good. The present situation is this: That I must either give up the bank at once and find some work which would take less of my time – thereby sacrificing part of an income every penny of which I need – or else I must give up the *Criterion* before my health crashes and I am no longer able to perform my bank work. I am now offered the post of literary editor of the *Nation*, at £200 a year less than my present salary and with no assurance that the job will last longer than six months, and if I take that I shall have to go straight into new work, which for the first six months will be very difficult and worrying, at a moment when I feel much more like going into a sanatorium. In order to carry on the *Criterion* I have had to neglect not only the writing I ought to be doing but my private affairs of every description which for some time past I have not had a moment to deal with. I have not even time to go to a dentist or to have my hair cut, and at the same time I see the *Criterion* full of most glaring defects which I could only avoid by having still more time for it to devour,[1] and at the same time I am simply unfit to take risks which in any case I should not be justified in taking. <I am worn out, I cannot go on>.[2]

1 – Ovid, *Met.* 15: 234: '*Tempus edax rerum*'; Shakespeare, sonnet 19: 'Devouring time'
2 – Added in ink.

I should like to write to you much more fully than this – but I have not the time.

Always sincerely yours,
T. S. Eliot[1]

TO *Ottoline Morrell* TS Texas

12 March 1923 9 Clarence Gate Gdns

My dear Ottoline,

Has mischief been made? If so, I ask you to write and tell me frankly, and I will clear it up.[2]

Affectionately,
Tom

1 – Quinn responded to TSE's letter on 27 Mar. Not only had he immediately and successfully chased Liveright for the $150 that he owed to TSE on publication, he agreed to guarantee to TSE $400 a year for five years, and he had persuaded Otto H. Kahn to subscribe a further $200 for five years. (Otto Kahn [1867–1934], German-born investment banker, philanthropist and patron of the arts, took British citizenship before moving to the USA in 1893, whereupon he became a partner in Kuhn, Loeb & Company and a hugely successful banker. He supported artists such as Hart Crane and George Gershwin, and was the author of many books including *Reflections of a Financier: A Study of Economic and Other Problems* [1921]. Quinn had sent Kahn copies of *Poems*, *TWL* and *SW*.) 'If you accept the offer of the *Nation*, at £200 less than your present salary, the $600 which I can guarantee at once and begin to send you at once for five years would nearly make up that £200, and I think you could count with reasonable safety upon my getting $200 or even $400 more, making it $800 or $1,000 for five years.' He added a consideration that was to prove crucial in TSE's calculations: 'It seems to me that if you accept the post of literary editor of the *Nation* you ought to have a provision for at least a year's notice or a year's pay in case the job is terminated.' He counselled too: 'Now, take off the time and go to your dentist. That is rather important, much more important than having your hair cut'; and closed with this advice: 'It seems to me that if the post of literary editor of the *Nation* is with decent white men, if you would not kill yourself doing the work, and if it would give you time for your own creative work, that is possibly the best thing that you could do.'

2 – The 'mischief' is not known, but may refer to the Bel Esprit scheme discussed in his letter to OM of 4 Mar. VW wrote to OM on 28 Feb. that TSE was 'very anxious that I should write . . . and ask you not to take any further steps about getting subscriptions to the Fund. He says he can't take any more money so long as he is in the Bank' (*Letters*, III, 17).

TO *Virginia Woolf* MS Berg

13 March [1923] [London]

My dear Virginia

This is just to thank you for your kind and encouraging letter.[1] In the midst of this destroying strain it has been a great joy to have such tireless and generous friendship and understanding as you have given.

Keynes rang up this evening, and I am to see him Thursday, if he cannot see me tomorrow. He asked me to lunch, but with a *strict* 12 to 1 in the City (I cannot be ten minutes over time) there will not be time to say anything, especially if I come to the West End to see him. So I *hope* he can arrange a meeting *after* bank hours. If our meeting is very brief, it will be a great advantage that he should have had your letter first.[2] Thank you again. I will let you know immediately I have seen him.

Yours always
Tom

FROM *Henry Eliot* TS Houghton

March 1923 [Chicago]

[Dear Tom]

Regarding the enclosed comment of Hecht's,[3] which was passed round the office, Buchen and Needham, neither of whom be could be convicted of snobbery or faddishness, are strong admirers of *The Waste Land*, and disagree with Hecht's conclusions. I do myself to a great extent, but I see in the poem considerable 'spoofing'. However, that may be considered legitimate. There is much 'spoofing' in Cabell's work,[4] and perhaps in all good satire. I have never seen it carried to quite the extent that it appears in *The Waste Land*; it wearies me a little, like the continual exploits of a

1–This letter does not appear to survive.

2–VW wrote to J. M. Keynes (see TSE's letter to him of 21 Mar.) on 13 Mar.: 'Eliot rang me up last night, (apparently on the verge of collapse, but that is neither here nor there) and explained the present, and very satisfactory, state of affairs. But there still remains the one great obstacle which makes us hesitate to advise him to accept – the question of guarantee' (VW, *Letters*, III, 20). In her diary (17 Mar.), she noted: 'Poor Tom the other day actually couldn't speak for tears (thanking us) on the telephone. He is broken down, & yet must buckle to & decide shall he take the *Nation*? can he defeat Maynard? I am tired of writing the word guarantee – which is what he claims' (*Diary*, II, 239).

3–See below for notes to TSE's letter of 20 Mar. to *Chicago Daily News*.

4–James Branch Cabell (1879–1958), whose fantastical novel *Jurgen: A Comedy of Justice* was published in 1919 and immediately suppressed for obscenity.

practical joker. The obscurantism, moreover, seems to me a little too wilfully striven for – '*trop voulu.*'[1]

The question of how much intent to attract notice there is in the poem is a good deal similar to the question of the same intent in women's dress. No nice woman, of course, will admit any reasons for the open bosom, the sheer waist fabric, the gauzy stockings, the high heels, the skirt drawn tight over the haunches, the cosmetics, the aphrodisiac perfumes, save that these things are the fashion, and that she likes to look sweet and dainty. Strong sub-conscious inhibitions to frankness, and world-old hypocritical complexes prevent her having any conscious knowledge of her motives. Of course, most people, like Ben Hecht, recognize no motives except conscious and deliberate motives.

I believe that you contend that the matter of motive is not relevant to literary criticism.[2] That seems to me to be a superficial psychology. The whole question of a thing being '*trop voulu*' – which often spoils a work of art – is one of too apparent motives. If a petty motive is discernible it lowers the dignity of a work of art. Petty motives inevitably produce bad art, and it is perhaps a matter of only metaphysical importance whether it is the motive or the result that offends. To say that it is of no importance whether the motive of the poet is to buy whiskey for himself or bread for his baby, is quibbling. Such motives, being on an entirely different plane of consciousness, are of course irrelevant. But if his motive is to win cheap popularity it will inevitably be apparent in his work. Neither is the personality of the artist irrelevant, as you claim.[3] *Le style, c'est l'homme.*[4]

The only other criticism I have to make of the poem is that it is too excessively allusive. I have always regarded the habit of quoting as a vice to be tolerated only to a limited extent. It is a substitute for original thought, and a fatally easy vice for a learned man to fall into. Huxley's hero, quoting from some poet, wonders disgustedly whether he has a brain or only an education.[5] I do not like a poem to be a scrap book.

1–'Too willed' (French).

2–See 'Tradition and the Individual Talent': 'It is not in his personal emotions, the emotions provoked by particular events in his life, that the poet is in any way remarkable or interesting' (*SE*, 57).

3–'The poet has, not a "personality" to express, but a particular medium, which is only a medium and not a personality, in which impressions and experiences combine in peculiar and unexpected ways' ('Tradition and the Individual Talent', *SE*, 56).

4–'Style is the man', a quotation from Buffon.

5–Denis, in *Crome Yellow* (1922), after quoting some verse, exclaims inwardly: 'Oh, these rags and tags of other people's making! Would he ever be able to call his brain his own? Was there, indeed, anything in it that was truly his own, or was it simply an education?' (Ch. xxv).

The trivial passages of the poem certainly do not stand on their own merits as poetry, and can only be justified as producing a certain psychological effect. They are the sort of things that one is rather ashamed of thinking, and that are extracted from people's minds only by psychiatrists employing hypnotism. Their introduction seems to me as dadaistic as sticking a piece of glass, a piece of wood or cloth, to a painting. They have practically no selective value; for instance, 'hey, diddle, diddle,' is as good as 'fe, fi, fo, fum,' for these purposes. However, I am no quibbler about means, if they attain a successful effect.

On the other hand, my sensibility has become dulled to these things by repeated reading, and my appreciation of the merits of the poem enhanced. I am skeptical about the value of the thought in the poem (did you not once say that ideas were a handicap? I agree with you). But I believe *The Waste Land* the best approach to a highly serious mood that I have seen in modern poetry. It approaches at times to Biblical seriousness, than which there is none finer. And the Bible is certainly not burdened with 'ideas'.

I expect your next poem to be either much finer or much more obscure and perverse. Heaven direct your steps.[1]

[Henry]

TO *Charles Whibley* CC

20 March 1923 [London]

My dear Whibley,

I have been hoping daily to write to you, but I have been postponing it until I had definite news of myself to report. At present, matters are still in suspense, but I must tell you that in any case I shall hold out for the two years which you so strongly advised.[2]

I will write to you again and only write now to tell you that I enjoyed my weekend with you more than any occasion on which I have seen you before which is an expression of very great pleasure indeed. You do not know what a comfort and satisfaction it has been to me to know you.

Yours ever,
[T. S. E.]

1 – 'He shall direct thy paths' (Proverbs 3: 50).

2 – To secure a guaranteed two-year contract at the *Nation*. Replying on 24 Mar., Whibley was glad TSE was 'sticking out for two years'.

TO *Gilbert Seldes* CC

20 March 1923 9 Clarence Gate Gdns

Dear Seldes,

I am feeling a little steadier, but was unable to write you last night. What I chiefly wanted to say was first, to make clear that the whole matter is extremely tentative. What I put to you is merely a possible scheme which depends upon a combination of circumstances. As I said, it is absolutely vital that the matter should be kept between ourselves, that is you, Thayer, Watson, and myself, until I myself have discussed it with Lady Rothermere, and if any hint of it should reach her through any other channel but myself at the proper moment it would be fatal to the scheme and to the existence of the *Criterion* as well. In the first place, I can only put it to her that I can show her good reason for its being the best course, and in the second place it is quite likely that the scheme will not appeal to her even then. For several weeks the situation must be left in complete suspense except of course for discussion between Thayer and yourself.

The other point is that I did not wish to give you the impression that Lady Rothermere's attitude toward the paper had been in the least indifferent or miserly. There was no reason why she should have started a paper at all except her desire to do so. She was told that it could be done for the sum which she was able and willing to guarantee and I took it up as an interesting venture on the basis of that amount. She was quite prepared, and indeed desired, that I should take a certain amount of the money in payment for the work, but I was anxious to make the best of the paper and I preferred to have the whole of the money employed in bringing out the *Criterion* properly and in paying contributors at the best rates we could. As a matter of fact, she gave me £25, which was outside of the sum guaranteed for the paper, for publishing my poem and I preferred not to take anything for minor obligations.

I am sure of course that the paper could progress faster and secure a larger circulation more quickly if it had more capital at its disposal. I think these are the only points which I wish to make at the moment, but I am feeling very exhausted and my nerve is not in very good order so I may want to write to you again very soon.

I was very glad to have had the pleasure of seeing something of you on Monday and do not forget to let me have your address as soon as you are settled. I hope that you will be able to get to work on your book under the best conditions.[1]

Sincerely yours,
T. S. E.

TO *W. B. Yeats* CC

20 March 1923 9 Clarence Gate Gdns

Dear Mr Yeats,

Forgive me for not having written immediately to thank you for your letter, and again on receipt of your script from your agent.[2] I have been so overwhelmed with personal affairs of the most vital nature that I am forced to appear unbusinesslike as well as rather ungrateful. It is of course an immense satisfaction and benefit to the *Criterion* to have the honour of being the review to publish anything of yours in this country. Of course the American publication is a complication[3] which has to be worked out in such a way as to bring no disadvantage to the contributors, as the *Criterion* is unfortunately not yet sufficiently remunerative to be able to purchase from its contributors the exclusive rights in the English language.

I am very happy indeed to have received this essay from you and assure you that the *Criterion* fully appreciates your kindness and generosity.

I hope that I may see you again in London before very long.

Sincerely yours,
[T. S. E.]

His Mother TO *Henry Eliot* CC Houghton

20 March 1923 24 Concord Ave, Cambridge, Mass.

Dear Henry:

I have just received from Tom the letter he told me he was writing. I will write in part what he says: 'I have been looking in every letter from you for some word about your plans for this summer. You must have known, as

1 – Seldes's pioneering study of American popular culture, *The Seven Lively Arts* (1924).
2 – On 5 Mar., Yeats wrote that his agent Watt would send 'that article of mine'. In a letter to the *Dial*, TSE refers to it as 'describing a kind of vision'. Yeats said that TSE might 'find it dry but at the worst it records a new kind of cross corroboration'.
3 – Yeats wanted to publish it in 'the American *Dial*': it appeared as 'A Biographical Fragment' (*Dial* 75: 1, July 1923, 13–19), and was the first item in C. 1: 4 (July 1923), 315–21.

I have mentioned it in nearly every letter, that I have been counting on seeing you this year. If you had made up your mind not to come, you would, I am sure have told me so and explained the reasons, as it would be unkind to keep me in unnecessary suspense and deluded hope. If on the other hand you were merely considering coming and were weighing reasons on both sides, I should have hoped that you [would] have expressed to me something of what you were thinking, in order that I might know the situation and discuss it with you. So I cannot understand your complete silence on the subject. I am sure you do not realise our state of suspense and anxiety, or that it would be a greater disappointment now to learn that you were not coming than it would have been four months ago. Unless there are strong reasons to the contrary – and if there were strong reasons you would certainly have told me of them – and if you really want to see me as much as I want to see you, you will surely come this year. Your stock is now, and will probably be for some time to come, paying better than anyone expected; at the present time all the family are comparatively affluent. From everything that Henry tells me this is a season of prosperity in America, and some of your land is he tells me appreciating in value. You are, unless facts have been concealed from me, in very good health, and there is nothing to prevent you from coming if you want to come. If you do not care to come without Henry, I feel perfectly sure that he could get a long enough holiday either to come with you and go back first or to come later and return with you, and perhaps his coming would be a greater inducement, if it did not seem worth while to take such a journey otherwise.

'I cabled you in order to prepare you for this letter and so that you might be thinking about the question until this letter arrived. If you knew how I long to see you you would not postpone this decision another day. I know, because I saw it, and because you and all of the family spoke of it afterward, how much you enjoyed the trip two years ago.[1] Of course you had then the pleasure of seeing England for the first time as well as seeing Vivien and myself, and I cannot offer you the same novelty twice. But I remind you of how much you enjoyed it because you may have forgotten how much urging it took on my part and how many letters I had to write in order to induce you to come then.

'We have carefully thought out plans. Vivien is much better than last time, and I can assure you that you would find our arrangements much

1–CCE wrote a detailed diary of her first trip to England to visit TSE and VHE in 1921, which she copied out later and presented to them as a souvenir of her stay (Valerie Eliot).

better than they were the last time. I should live here at Clarence [Gate Gardens] with you so I should be with you a great deal more than last time. You would of course have this flat; Vivien would be part of the time in London and part at a small cottage we have taken near Chichester. It is unnecessary to go into details, I only assure you that we have worked them out. And I may assure you that you have not the slightest idea what a happiness it would be to Vivien to have you here. You will never know how much your last visit meant to her, and you can have no idea how much she cares that you should come again.

'I can write no more and I do not want to mention anything else in so important a letter. But please try to realise how much this matters and how incessantly it has been in my mind.'

Tom's letter I find distressing to me. I should have written sooner that I did not feel as if I ought to come this summer. I cannot cross the ocean more than once more and if I go again it must be next summer. I am sorry I did not write Tom decidedly that I should not come this summer. I feel as if I had all too little to divide among my children. But I should like to feel I could go next summer. I shall never be able if I do go again abroad to do as much as I did two years ago. You could not possibly go this summer but next summer you might go with me for a few weeks. I do not think Marian cares much about it, if Margaret went with me she would be more of a care than a help.[1] She does not realize my infirmity of age. I should prefer to stay a short time with you rather than a long time with one of my daughters.

I do not know what to write to Tom. I can only tell him that if it is a possible thing I will come next spring. That will be for the last time.

I am continually afraid of your taking a cold in your fatigued condition. The papers say it has been fearfully cold in Chicago, and today the cold wave is here. Tomorrow, 'cloudy and warmer'.

Write me what you think. I have never given Tom reason to think I was going to London this year, but I ought to have told him decidedly that I was not coming. I do not know whether I ought to have planned to go. It is too late now. Marian is spending ten days with Charlotte[2] because she is so tired all the time. She hardly seems to me fit to go with me as a caretaker. I do not think she cares much for sight-seeing. And I could not do much.

1 – Margaret Dawes Eliot (1871–1956) was the second Eliot child: TSE's second-oldest sister.
2 – Charlotte Eliot: see Glossary of Names.

Tell me whether I ought to risk anything on the *Savonarola*.[1] I fear Houghton & Mifflin would not assume the expense. I will take this out and mail it. I hope you will get a pleasant lodger in Sheldon's place.

With love,
[Mother]

TO *Stanley Rice*[2] CC

20 March 1923 [London]

Dear Sir,

I am much in the wrong not to have written to you before about your article[3] for I can only excuse myself by pressure of business of the gravest nature. There has been much difficulty in fitting in various contributions, some of which had been requested but not expected, and therefore it has only been possible to assure printing your article in the number which will appear at the beginning of July. I send you the proof herewith and hope sincerely that appearance in that month will be satisfactory to you. I shall be very glad to hear from you on the matter as the issue for July is now being put together.

Yours faithfully,
[T. S. E.]

TO *The Editor of* The Dial CC

20 March 1923 [*The Criterion*, 17 Thavies Inn]

Dear Sir,

Mr William Butler Yeats has sent us what he calls 'A Biographical Fragment' describing a kind of vision. He tells me that he is sending it to the *Dial*, according to his arrangements with you. I have spoken to Mr Gilbert Seldes, who was in London until yesterday, and he has authorised me to write to you asking you if you would be so kind as to print it in the July number, as the *Criterion* will be unable to print it until its issue of that

1–Her poem was ultimately published with an intro. by TSE (Cobden-Sanderson, 1926).
2–Stanley Rice (1869–1944), Indian civil servant and orientalist, published *Tales from the Mahabharata* (1924) as well as studies of Indian religion.
3–'Alcestis and Savitri: A Suggestion' (*C.* 1: 4, July 1923) compared the Greek story of Alcestis (which TSE was later to draw on in *CP*) to a similar tale in the Indian epic *The Mahabharata*.

month. This would still give you the advantage of a few days before the *Criterion* is on sale in America and we should therefore much appreciate your generosity if you could arrange publication in that number. The *Criterion* on the other hand, would always be glad to arrange that no contribution which you also were using should appear in the *Criterion* before it appeared in the *Dial*.

Yours sincerely,
[T. S. E.]

TO *W. P. Ker*[1] CC

20 March 1923 [London]

Sir,

I have received from Mr Charles Whibley your Essay on Byron which the *Criterion* will be very happy to have the honour of publishing in its July number.[2] It is extremely gratifying, as we have been anxious for a long time to secure something from you, and I am afraid that I have bothered Mr Whibley more than I ought to have in begging him to intercede with you.[3]

You will receive proofs in due course.

I am sorry to say that the *Criterion* is able to pay so little that it can make no discrimination between contributors and must pay at the uniform rate of £10 per 5,000 words.

Mr Whibley has promised me, when he next comes to town, to arrange that I will have the pleasure of meeting you one evening. I cannot in good conscience urge him to come to town, because his health lately has suffered so much from his occasional visits, but I earnestly hope that when he does come he will carry out his promise.[4]

With most grateful thanks,
I am, Sir,

Your obedient servant,
[T. S. E.]

1–W. P. Ker (1855–1923): polymathic Scottish scholar and historian; Fellow of All Souls College, Oxford; Quain Professor of English Language and Literature, University College, London, 1889–1922; Professor of Poetry, Oxford University: see *The Art of Poetry: Seven Lectures, 1920–1922* (1923); author of *Epic and Romance* (1897), *The Dark Ages* (1904), *Essays on Medieval Literature* (1905), and *Collected Essays*, ed. Charles Whibley (1925).
2–In fact, Ker's 'Byron: An Oxford Lecture' appeared in C. 2: 5 (Oct. 1923), 1–15.
3–In Nov. 1922, Whibley said he had asked W. P. Ker to write for *C.*
4–Ker replied on 24 Mar. that he did 'not expect to be in London before October'. In the event, he died before they could meet.

TO *The Literary Editor of the* Chicago Daily News CC

20 March 1923 9 Clarence Gate Gdns

Sir,

According to your issue of the 21st of February,[1] Mr Ben Hecht[2] has stated that he met me in London, and added that he knows that I thoroughly hate Americans and everything they write and read. Mr Ben Hecht has never met me in London or anywhere else, and I hope that you will kindly publish this fact as I think that if it is brought to Mr Hecht's notice he is not likely in future ever to want to meet me. I do not know what credit is usually given in Chicago to Mr Hecht's statements but I trust that your readers will observe that as Mr Hecht has on a point of fact said a thing that is not,[3] it is superfluous for me even to contradict the further statements which Mr Hecht has made about me.

I am, Sir,

Your obedient Servant,
[T. S. E.]

TO *Jacques Rivière* CC

20 March 1923 [London]

Cher Monsieur,

Je suis désespéré quand je pense que j'ai demandé une faveur à vous et que je n'ai pas encore rempli mes devoirs envers la *Nouvelle Revue*

1–The literary editor gossiped ('The Literary Scene', *Chicago Daily News*, 21 Feb. 1923, 14): 'In speaking about *The Waste Land*, T. S. Eliot's much-discussed modernist poem, Ben Hecht said on Saturday at Schlogl's that he considered it a subtle joke by Eliot on the American critics. "The poem has certain merits in it," said Hecht, "as is natural in a poem written by a big man like Eliot, but it differs so radically from his work in *Prufrock* and other poems that I have no doubt that it was carefully planned by Eliot as a hoax on the American public. I met Eliot in London and know that he thoroughly hates Americans and everything they write and read and would consider him wholly capable of hoaxing the *Dial* and all its friends."'

2–Ben Hecht (1894–1964), novelist and dramatist, made his name as a maverick newspaperman on the *Chicago Daily News*, where he wrote a column *1001 Afternoons in Chicago*, before founding the *Chicago Times* in 1923. He was a friend of Maxwell Bodenheim and published a novel *The Florentine Dagger: A Novel for Amateur Detectives* (1923). In 1926 he moved on to Hollywood, where he wrote a series of successful film scripts, including *The Front Page* (1928). In Sept. 1922 Edmund Wilson had spoken of Seldes putting him 'in a class with Eliot, Joyce, and Ben Hecht'; and on 30 Aug. 1922 EP asked, in relation to contemporary prose writers, 'Is there anyone but Hecht and Sherw. Anderson?'

3–Jonathan Swift's Gulliver, recalling his stay in the land of the Houyhnhnms, reports: 'I said the thing which was not. (For they have no word in their language to express lying or falsehood)' (*Gulliver's Travels*, Bk IV, ch. 3).

Française.[1] Depuis deux mois j'ai eu à lutter avec une santé affaiblie contre des problèmes personnels qui ont tous synchronisé à un moment fatal. J'ai du même laisser le travail nécessaire pour le *Criterion* et je ne peux dans le prochain numéro démontrer que trop clairement le temps exigu, que j'y ai dépensé. Ces sont des difficultés qui auraient du se résoudre et qui devraient encore se résoudre en quelques jours. Mais, selon le conseil de mon médecin, il est probable que je pars en quelques semaines de vacance aussitôt que possible.

Dans ces circonstances que j'ai signalées, vous me trouverez peut-être dévergondé, parce que j'espère que nous allons recevoir votre article important dans peu de jours.[2] Croyez au moins que pour nous c'est un espoir qu'il serait cruel de decevoir.

Je n'ai pas encore répondu à la question que vous m'avez posée au sujet de la remunération pour un morceau de Proust. Je ne peux offrir que la même que nous offrons à tous nos collaborateurs – £10 par 5000 mots. Si la *Nouvelle Revue Française* ne peut pas accepter, je devrais remettre les négociations jusqu'à la retour de Lady Rothermere au mois d'avril.

Croyez, Monsieur, à mes sentiments les plus cordiaux, et à la haute valeur que nous mettons sur n'importe quels écrits de vous.

T. S. Eliot

PS Le Directeur de périodique de New York, *Vanity Fair*, m'a demandé la permission de ré-imprimer (en anglais naturellement) la dernière chronique à la *Nouvelle Revue Française*.[3] Puisque cet article a été commandé par la *Nouvelle Revue Française* je ne voudrais pas le faire paraître ailleurs sans avoir préalablement votre permission. Je vous prie donc de me laisser avoir un petit mot, mais j'espère que vous n'y voyez aucune objection.[4]

1 – TSE had not yet submitted the 'chronicle' for *NRF* he had promised on 2 Feb.; it would be submitted by 15 Mar.

2 – Jacques Rivière, 'Notes on a Possible Generalisation of the Theories of Freud', C. 1: 4 (July 1923), 329–47.

3 – Edmund Wilson wrote (26 Feb.): 'I have just seen your thing on English prose in the *Nouvelle Revue Française* and I wish you could let us reprint it in *Vanity Fair* . . . I think it is so admirable that it would be a great pity for it not to appear in English. We could pay you about $75.'

4 – *Translation:* Dear Sir, I am in despair when I think that I asked a favour of you, and that I have not yet carried out my obligations towards the *Nouvelle Revue Française*. During the last two months I had to struggle, in a weakened state of health, with personal problems which all coincided at a fateful moment. I have even had to neglect the work required for the *Criterion*, and the next number will betray only too clearly the inadequately short time I spent on it. The difficulties are of a kind that ought to have been resolved and should even now be resolved in a few days. But, following my doctor's advice, I shall probably go away for a few weeks' holiday as soon as possible.

TO *John Maynard Keynes*[1] TS Marshall

21 March 1923 9 Clarence Gate Gdns

Dear Mr Keynes,

I so completely realise what must have been the effect on you of my inconceivable delay in replying to your offer of the literary editorship of the *Nation*, that I feel that the only thing I can now do is to give you the satisfaction of turning me down. For this reason I am writing the following statement, although knowing that it is obviously impossible for you or any paper to accept:

1. that I receive a guarantee of at least two years.
2. that I give the bank three months notice, with a [further *del.*] fourth month of absence.
3. as I have already explained to you, I have been engaged for three years on special work (Enemy Debts) which is coming to an end, but some of the most important part of this work is still to be done, and there is no one else in the bank with the necessary experience and training to do it. I cannot myself approach, or allow anyone else to approach on my behalf, any official of the bank with a view to releasing me before the end of the three months.
4. I cannot engage to do any work for the *Nation* while still at the bank, as I must on the contrary cease all possible work for some

---

Given the circumstances I have just outlined, you will perhaps find it shameless on my part to hope that we shall receive your important article during the next few days. Please believe at least that the disappointment of this hope would affect us cruelly.

I have not yet answered the query you put to me about payment for a piece of Proust. I can only offer the same rate as for all our contributors – £10 per 5000 words. If this is not acceptable to *La Nouvelle Revue Française*, I must postpone negotiations until Lady Rothermere's return in April.

I send you my most cordial greetings and assure you of the great value we attach to all your writings. T. S. Eliot

PS The editor of the New York periodical *Vanity Fair* has asked for my permission to reprint (in English naturally) my last letter to the *Nouvelle Revue Française*. Since the article was commissioned by the *Nouvelle Revue Française*, I would not like to publish it elsewhere without your prior authorisation. Please send me a word to this effect; I trust that you have no objection.

1–John Maynard Keynes (1883–1946), economist – author of *Economic Consequences of the Peace* (1919), which was much admired by TSE, and *Treatise of Probability* (1921) – had recently become chairman of the Liberal periodical *The Nation*. Following the crash of 1929, he was to write *General Theory of Employment, Interest and Money* (1935).

> time to come. I have been obliged to consult a specialist in Harley Street, who urged most emphatically the necessity for an immediate and long rest. I could not possibly ask the bank for leave of absence after I had given them notice, so I had intended to take this holiday at the end of the three months. However, although the consultant declared this period of rest to be essential, I was prepared to forego it, in order to join the *Nation* at the end of the three months. But I have just had news from America, connected with my private affairs, which makes it of the utmost importance that I should go to America, at the first possible moment, even if only for a week. I should not be able to leave for three months, having given notice at the bank, and must then make the visit to America, instead of taking the rest which the doctor insists is essential for the recovery of my health.

On these conditions I would give notice to the bank on receiving your formal contract.

Realising perfectly that my behaviour in this matter will always be incomprehensible to those of my friends who have worked so hard on my behalf, and that it can have no other effect than to forfeit your good will and that of many others,[1]

I am,

Yours faithfully,
T. S. Eliot

His Mother TO *Henry Eliot* — TS Houghton

22 March 1923 [24 Concord Ave]

Dear Henry:

I am loathe to trouble you when you are so driven with work, but I do not know to whom else of the family to go. I have been much distressed by Tom's letter,[2] and have hardly known what I ought to do. I suppose he is justified in reproaching me because I have not written to him decidedly about going to London this summer, and I should hate to have him

1–RA was to write to HR, 19 June 1925: 'Eliot has funked his responsibilities to us since 1921. At that date he could have had the *Nation* . . .' ('Richard Aldington's Letters to Herbert Read', ed. David S. Thatcher, *The Malahat Review* 15, July 1970, 17).
2–The letter in question is missing.

disappointed. Several times he has referred to my coming this year, but I have not given the least intimation that I should do so. As, however, I had not planned to go, [I] should have so written him decidedly.

Do you not receive the impression from his letter that he expects me to come without Marian? He speaks of my staying with him at Clarence Gate Gardens, but there are only two bedrooms, and if Marian were with me he would be obliged to sleep on the lounge in the sitting-room, which, I fear would not be very restful. I have the impression that Tom thinks I am a great deal stronger than I am. He does not realize my age. I do not know whether he thinks I can cross the ocean alone. If I thought there was any possibility of your being able to take a month off next summer and could go with me, I should prefer to wait until then. We had a very smooth passage to London and back two years ago, but a rough passage or a storm would be a severe strain on me, and I should feel much better to have you with me than simply Marian, as she is timid and liable to break down in an emergency. Just now and for the entire winter she has been quite weak and not at all well. Tomorrow she will have spent ten days with Charlotte for a change. She has almost nothing to do for me, but takes me as a heavy responsibility, and it seems to wear on her nerves. This is hard for me as well as herself.

I thought to consult with Ada[1] last night, as she came in unexpectedly and did a very unfortunate thing. I had intended *to read* Tom's letter to her, but am so forgetful I put the letter in her hands, and she became very angry when she read what he wrote about the family's objecting to my going to London. She said she would not express an opinion either way. Margaret came into the room while she was talking and expressed the opinion which Ada agreed, that I was the only one of the family Tom cared for. All this distressed me greatly. I could not ask Ada to attend to any finance while I was away.

Charlotte has just been here and says she would go with me, but I should be sorry to have her leave her family. And I do not know whether they would want her. I think one thing is pretty certain and that is that I ought not to cross the ocean alone. And if I was alone with Tom and he gone all day, I should be pretty lonely. I had rather wait and go with you for a short visit than to be alone there.

Now I want you to write and tell me what you think I ought to do. I do not think I am as hale and hearty as Tom thinks. I am sorry for him, more sorry than I can tell. Do you not think you might get off for a month next

1–TSE's sister Ada Sheffield (1869–1943).

summer? I might pay your expenses if I do not have to pay Marian's. If you have not already written expressing your judgment and your understanding of the plan when this reaches you, will you send a night message for which I will repay you?

Your perplexed
Mother

FROM *John Maynard Keynes* MS Valerie Eliot

23 March 1923 46 Gordon Square, Bloomsbury

Dear Eliot,

I have shown your letter to my associates, and, as you rather anticipated, they feel with great regret that they cannot meet you. The vital point is of course the four months' delay *plus* the doubt as to what your health may be at the end of that time. So I am afraid the proposal must definitely lapse and we must set about making other arrangements.[1]

I am very sorry. I think we could have worked together and made a good thing of it. I appreciate deeply your difficulties. You mustn't think that the last paragraph of your letter to me is anything but the exact opposite of the truth. Please believe that my sympathy and goodwill is not diminished but increased. If I can ever be of any assistance to you on a future occasion, I hope you will call on me.

Yours sincerely,
J. M. Keynes

TO *Mary Hutchinson* MS Texas

Friday, 23 March 1923 [Postmark N.W.1]

My dear Mary

It is very sweet of you to ask us to the boat race – but when is it? is it tomorrow?[2] if so, my question need not be answered, because we shall be Away. You know, we have got a country cottage, a tiny one; today has been spent in packing furniture, and tomorrow we go down early to arrive

1 – Keynes offered the post to Leonard Woolf. VW noted: 'Here I have been toiling these 3 weeks to make Eliot take it; finally he shied; & this is the result. No doubt there are drawbacks, but it means safety for the moment, indeed luxury' (*Diary*, II, 240).

2 – The Oxford and Cambridge boat race was held on Sat., 24 Mar.

before the van and get the furniture in.[1] It will be such a day's work. Well, anyway, there will be the summer – if there is to be any summer – with a chance, I hope of *meeting*, in aquatic leisure?

Always aff'tly
T.

His Mother TO *Henry Eliot* — TS Houghton

25 March 1923 — 24 Concord Ave, Cambridge, Mass.

Dear Henry:

I shall expect a letter from you tomorrow. I wrote to Tom yesterday telling him I should probably cable him before he received my letter. It is evident to me that he expects me without Marian. And I have written him that I could not go to London without you or Marian not only to accompany me but to remain with me. I would not like to be alone there. I am aware there is not one chance in a hundred you could go with me this year.

He writes that I will be with him at 9 Clarence Gate Gardens while Vivien is at a cottage near Chichester. You know there are only two bedrooms at their apartments [so] there would be no room for Marian. I should be alone all day while Tom was at the Bank, and surely Vivien would expect him at week ends at Chichester. It makes me feel homesick to think of it. I should feel very helpless especially if I should for any cause break down.

I looked through all Tom's back letters last night and found only one in which he spoke of my coming on. Vivian [*sic*] however, in her last letter said they expected me and that Tom or she could get a room outside, so that I could come. That remark I should have taken more seriously, and I greatly reproach myself that I did not write Tom I did not expect to go this year. It at the time seemed to me impossible that I should allow either Vivien or Tom to sleep outside so as to give me a room. I have done wrong but I do not feel that Tom is justified in reproaching me as bitterly as he is doing. It simply seems to me as if I could not be alone in London without you or Marian. And if he cables for Marian to come with me, I shall hate to think of his leaving his own home to make a place for her, and it will be uncomfortable for her to feel that she is not wanted. I would like to please Tom, for I feel from the tone of his letter that he is sore tried. If I went I should want to go from Boston and that late in June. The *Winifredian* sails the last of May or first of June, and I should not want to go until the last

1 – TSE and VHE moved into their rented cottage at Fishbourne, nr. Chichester, on 24 Mar.

of June. Another 'sister' ship under a new name is likely to be put on, but they do not know when the sailing will be. The *Winifredian* is much cheaper than the New York steamers, the highest price for two being $180.00 for an outside state room.

Tom writes Mr and Mrs Haigh-Wood[1] will be in London and will be glad to take me around. Mrs Haigh-Wood is very pleasant, but she is not congenial to me, and I can not forget. She is not a person of high principle and I should not want to be much with her. I do not think Tom entirely trusts her. He makes the very best of his marriage which was a great misfortune, and becomes more and more so. I can not bear to look forward for him. The standards in the female branch of that family are not as high as they should be. I think it is different with the men.

Do you think there is any prospect you could be absent a month next summer and go with me? I had planned to make the attempt next year but not this. Do you think I ought to go this to atone for not having written Tom this year that I was not coming? And ought I to allow him to change his plan and live outside to make room for Marian? This matter lies heavy on my mind. Then I had wanted when you came on, to see about the printing or publishing of the *Savonarola*. I am hesitating about writing to Professor Lowes[2] to ask if he thinks it worthy of publication. I would give it to Houghton & Mifflin[3] in the summer (if they will accept it at my risk), and have it published in the late fall.

I hope to hear from you and obtain some expression of opinion tomorrow morning. I shall be more or less influenced by your judgement as to what it is my duty to do. If I go to England this summer it is not probable that I shall ever go again. Tom will have to come here if I feel the end approaching. I should like to live as long as I can keep my faculties.

I can not bear to think of long days alone in London, and I do not want to go to Chichester. Itchenor was a nightmare save that we were with dear Tom.[4]

1–Charles Haigh-Wood (see Glossary of Names) and Rose Haigh-Wood (neé Robinson), Vivien's parents, whom Charlotte Eliot had met in London in 1921.

2–John Livingston Lowes (1867–1945) taught at Washington University before becoming Professor of English at Harvard, 1918–30; best known for his remarkable study of Coleridge's sources, *The Road to Xanadu: A Study in the Ways of the Imagination* (1927), a work discussed in TSE's *TUPUC*, 78–9.

3–Houghton & Mifflin was Lowes's Boston publisher.

4–In her 1921 memoir, CCE wrote: 'For a short time in Tom's vacation we went together to a small town called Itchenor.' They visited the country home of St John and Mary Hutchinson.

I asked Mr Hight about the 4% and the 5% Tel & Tel, and he said the 4% appreciated in value so that they would be worth more at the end of the six years. But of course they would meantime give me less income. My own feeling is that I prefer the 5% income *now*. He said that Tel & Tel was allowable for trust funds – that it was regarded as a safe investment. So my own preference is for four 5% Tel & Tel. I will then purchase one US Rubber if I have enough left and you desire.

Nichols wrote to know if Halverson was sole Agent for Block 17, and what I would sell it for. I have just written that I informed Halverson I would sell at the same price as that obtained for Block 13. And that since receiving this last letter of theirs I had informed him that I would like to have them (the Nichols firm) also try to sell it, and if they could get a better offer than he, I would pay him the half commission. I wrote Halverson also that I would prefer he should secure a purchaser if he could, but I would like to double my opportunity. Was not that right? I think the Nichols Company is waking up. If you do not approve of this let me know.

I am hesitating now about addressing Professor Lowes. What do you think of it? I think I could say to the publisher Grandgent[1] and Lowes endorsed my book.

I wish you were here and I could talk with you. How are things going – business? I shall be anxious to know whom you take in Sheldon's place. I hope an agreeable person. It will be expensive while there are only you and Peckham. I suppose if the latter married you would break up.

Ever with love,
Mother

TO *Horace B. Liveright*[2] CC

27 March 1923 [London]

Dear Mr Liveright,

I like your production of my book but I do not like your business methods. I intentionally allowed two months to pass without mentioning the advance royalty of $150 to you, in order to know whether you would fail to remember it until I reminded you of it.[3] I should be glad to receive

1 – Charles Hall Grandgent (1862–1939), Professor of Romance Languages at Harvard, 1896–1932; editor of Dante, and author of *The Power of Dante* (1918).
2 – Horace Liveright: see Glossary of Names.
3 – Valerie Eliot has seen a photocopy (now lost) of the cheque, dated 15 Mar. 1923 (when *TWL* was in its second impression). TSE had to countersign it twice because it was made out to 'F. S. Eliot'.

some explanation of this absence of mind, as I shall have to discuss with Lady Rothermere, immediately on her return to this country, the question of contracting for the publication of the *Criterion* in America.

Yours very truly,
[T. S. E.]

TO *Sydney Schiff* — MS Valerie Eliot

Tuesday [27 March 1923] — 9 Clarence Gate Gardens

My dear Sydney,

This is just a line to tell you that the final decision is: I am staying at the Bank. I will ask you to keep this *to yourselves* for a week, as I do not want discussion going on about it.

We are both very tired – *tired* does not express it – we are too tired to go away at present and shall not go away over Easter.

I do hope the Surrey air is doing you good and giving peace. With love to both.

Yrs. aff.
Tom

FROM *His Mother* — TS Valerie Eliot

29 March 1923 — 24 Concord Ave, Cambridge, Mass.

My very dear Tom:

I received last evening your letter of the 19th inst., and conscious or subconscious it has not been out of my mind since. I had not altogether given up the idea of going late in June. Of one thing I was certain I could not safely cross the ocean alone. I knew that Henry could not go, and that Marian must, not only for the voyage but in London. Henry has not influenced me against going. I did not even know you had written to him or he to you, until I sent him a copy of your letter to me, and asked his advice. I was already sure he could not leave this year, and he wrote:

'The honest truth is that it would be a very bad thing for me to go abroad to take three or even two months this summer, for this is an important stage in the progress of my business affairs, and I do not see how the other two men could possibly get along without me. The thing means too much to me right now, when prospects are bright, and it looks like the solution of my whole future. It is exactly the opposite of the case in 1921, when I thought I had practically nothing to lose by going away.' He also wrote that he had vaguely in mind 'the possibility of making a trip next summer.'

I think I have already written you some of the details of Henry's business. He is working very hard. I was sure he could not go with me this year, and knew there was no place for Marian, unless I went to a hotel with her. Even if Vivian were in London I should not like to call upon her as I do upon Marian. I will promise you to come next summer if it is a possible thing and may go to some private hotel where I could see you every day – one of the not most expensive.

As soon as I had read your letter I started right down to the Square and sent you a cablegram. It seems to me if I do not go to England this summer, not until next, it would do you good to come here. If instead of two vacations you could have a month at one time, you would have ten days or so here. The ocean trip would quiet your nerves which seem to me unstrung, and I think would do you more good than travel by land. I would be only too glad to pay the expense of the trip. I hope Vivian will urge you to do this. I did wrong not to reply to her very kind invitation to me to visit you this summer, proposing that one of you should sleep at the office of the *Criterion*. It seemed to me that I could not allow that. But I should have told her so at the time, and I reproach myself that I did not.

Do not think for a moment that Henry does not care for you. He loves you next to me better than any one else. He has had cruel disappointments in his love affairs, and the last time cruel treatment. He sends me every item about you he finds in the papers, and has sent two magazines with pictures I have cut out. In these pictures and the large one you sent you look so smiling, I cannot realize how troubled you are. Will you not write and tell me what these troubles are, and what are 'the vital decisions affecting your whole future.' What is 'crumbling away?' You alarm me and I hope you will soon write again and tell me your troubles. You know I will do anything I can.

I do not of course understand the situation as you do, or one on the spot. I have felt regret right along that you undertook the editorship, of the *Criterion*. I judge from what Vivian said [the] summer before last, that the salary is small, and unless it will be increased so that you could give up the Bank, it does not seem worth while – Nay more, it seems to me a positive injury to you. For evidently you are in a very nervous condition and I fear will break down again unless relieved. You give to it time that might more profitably be given to original work waiting for you to do. I have read in several notices of your work that it has made a great impression considering the size of your 'output.' You would not accept, I remember, the Assistant Editorship of the *Athenaeum*, because you wrote it conflicted with original work.[1]

I will write you every Sunday except the coming one, Easter, if it would give you any pleasure. I stopped because I wrote two or three letters to your one. I shall not have much to tell you, but I can at least express affection.

Give my love to Vivien and tell her I should have thanked her for her very unselfish offer to have one of you sleep outside that I might be with you, in your dear home. It was so good in both of you to let us have it in 1921, while you moved to much less attractive rooms.[2] I do hope you will renew your lease, although seven years seems a long time to look ahead. Too bad Vivien has to go to country places in the summer, but I suppose London air is smoky. She must find it lonely.

If I have forgotten anything in this I will write Sunday. Do consider if you can get a month's vacation, coming on here, and I will come next summer to London. Remember that you are very dear to me. You are in my heart of hearts. Do not blame me if I do not dare to go alone to London, and want someone there with me as you are so occupied. If you are ill I will come and go with Marian to a hotel. If you should break down, get Vivian to cable me. You are working too hard I am sure.

The dividends ought to come in a few days, and I will send yours. I hope the cable address was right. I was sorry afterwards I did not send to 9 Clarence Gate Gardens. Remember if you are ill and need me you must cable and I will come right on and go to a hotel.

Ever and ever yours,

Mother

His Mother TO *Henry Eliot* — TS Houghton

29 March 1923 — 24 Concord Ave

Dear Henry:

I had no sooner taken your letter to the mail box yesterday than I received a very despondent and tragic letter from Tom. I am afraid he is near a nervous breakdown. He does not see any reason why I should not

1–See TSE's letter, 29 Mar. 1919 (*Letters*, 1).
2–TSE and VHE moved into a flat at 12 Wigmore Street during her visit in 1921.

come on. He says Vivien would have gone about with me a great deal, and so would her father and mother. Now I would not like to be dependent on them. I do not doubt they would be very kind. And Vivien! Tom had written they had taken a cottage near Chichester. I had supposed that her absence there made it possible for me to occupy a room at Clarence Gate. And if she were in London I should not want, invalid as she is, to call upon her.

As soon as I received Tom's letter I went down to the Square in a cold wind to cable Tom. I cabled: 'Hope keep apartments. Come summer or fall. Will pay expenses both ways. Long to see you.' I think if he could take all his vacation at one time, he might have a month, which would give him ten days here. I have written him this morning that I think the ocean voyage would be good for his nerves. I should think he could come in October. It would depend on Vivien. Would she let him come without her? He generally goes with her in October.

Tom seems to think that I am not coming in deference to your wishes, and I have written that I had not known there had been any correspondence between him and you, until I have sent you a copy of his letter and that you had nothing to do with my not going. I have told him again I could not go on alone, and that as there was no place for Marian if I went on with her we would go to a hotel. Marian felt last summer that Vivien did not want her. Whether she was right I do not know. Anyhow there would not be room for her at 9 Clarence Gate Gardens.

Tom writes: 'I have several other matters to write to you about – some about you and some about me – and as for my own, I am simply distracted and destroyed – everything seems to be crumbling away about me and under me, and I am faced with most vital decisions deciding my whole future. But those I must tell you about separately and face as best I can: they come at a time when I want you very much. You will never know how constantly I think of you, and how at every moment of anxiety or despair, as well as in success or happiness, I have longed for your presence.'

All this is very distressing to me, and if I thought Tom was breaking down, I would go with Marian and stay at a hotel a few weeks. I cabled: 'Hope keep apartments', because Tom had written 'The lease of this flat ends on June 25th. I have been hanging on keeping matters in suspense about signing a new lease, and in some difficulty with the landlord, – simply in order to have it for you to come to, which would have made it worth while to have taken it on for another long lease of five or seven years. The new lease is to be a long one, probably seven years.'

If you do not object I will purchase 5% Tel. & Tel. That would give me more income than the 4% and when I have sufficient income from bonds I will transfer rest of the Hydraulic. If I can sell Block 17, Kansas City, I shall be able to sell 812 North Broadway, for the rental of 2635 Locus will then pay taxes.

Unless Tom was ill I should not want to go to London until after your vacation. I hope it is in June. I have quoted from your letter and told Tom I knew it would have been impossible for you to go to London now.

Ever yours
Mother

[Indecipherable ink half sentence in margin]

FROM *His Mother* TS Valerie Eliot

30 March 1923 24 Concord Ave

Dearest Son:

I wrote you yesterday but have been so troubled about you I have cabled this morning to ask you to write more fully, and have written to Vivien hoping she would tell me more about your condition than you yourself do. Indeed the intimations in your letter cause me anxiety. What are the 'vital decisions' you will soon be called upon to make, that will 'decide [your] whole future.)' Such an expression alarms me. And I feel that you are overwrought as a result of overwork. I am hoping that at the end of the year you will turn over the *Criterion* to some other editor. If Lady Rothermere wants it she ought to pay a 'living wage.'

If you could get away for a month and come over here, I feel it would do you much good. I shrink from crossing the water alone, but if it would help you very materially I would cross with Marian and go to a hotel. I should not go until late and make a shorter stay. Your health both nervous and physical is of much more importance than sight-seeing. I have for some time feared your breaking down again from overwork. I think the *Criterion* involves more work than you had realized. And it keeps you from creative work.

When does Vivian go to Chichester? Not until July? I am glad she is to have her Father and Mother in London this summer. They have such a lovely house and environment. I do not know what you would do if you gave up your apartments. The papers, including *Punch*, speak of the dearth of houses. I fear you and Vivian would be adrift. And the rooms you have are exceptionally pleasant. Seven years is a long time. Will not your landlord compromise on five? Do write me about your affairs. I will go late and stay a few weeks if you need me badly.

Very affectionately
Mother

TO *Sydney Schiff* MS BL

30 March [1923][1] *The Criterion*, 9 Clarence Gate Gdns

My dear Sydney

This is just a line to thank you for your very kind and sympathetic letter[2] and to say that I do indeed appreciate all the thought that you have given to my affairs. I hope we shall have good news of your health. I am too tired to write more.

Always affectionately
Tom.

I had tea with [Wyndham] Lewis today and had a good talk with him, and found him much more sympathetic than when I spoke to him before.

His Mother TO *Henry Eliot* TS Houghton

30 March 1923 24 Concord Ave

Dear Henry:

I have been so stirred up by Tom's letter that I cabled again this morning: 'Write more fully. Anxious.' I do not know how much of his letter I quoted to you. I think I copied this: 'I have several other matters of the most vital importance to speak to you about – some about you and some about me – and as for my own, I am simply distracted and destroyed – everything seems to be crumbling away about me and under me, and I am faced with most vital decisions affecting my whole future. But these I must tell you about separately and face as best I can: they come at a time when I want you very much.'

I cannot think what Tom means nor why it is so vital to him to have me in London. I have written him and Vivian again today, telling Vivian that from the tone of Tom's letter I feared he was facing another nervous breakdown. I suggested his getting if he could, a month's vacation and

1 – Written over '27 mars 1923'.
2 – A reply to TSE's of 27 Mar. confirming he was 'staying at the bank'.

coming here. I had already cabled him as I told you, that I would pay expenses both ways. I wrote Vivian it would involve some self-denial on her part but it was better than a nervous collapse. I also said in case of necessity I would come on late with Marian and go to a hotel. I said I was nervous about crossing alone. What do you think of my going alone? I had written Tom it was absolutely impossible for you to go. What I am afraid of is, of Tom's injuring his brain and nerves by overwork. I think the *Criterion* is a great mistake, and I have told them so.

You have so much to think about in the condition of your own affairs, I do not know that I ought to trouble you. If I went it would be by preference late in June, as I hope your vacation is in June. I hope to hear in a day or two.

It seems to me as if Vivian was enough of a support to him, Tom would not need me. She is very fond of him, but at the same time an awful drag on him, she requires so much. She would wear me all out, and I fear she does Tom. But what can anyone do?

I do not know that I am writing this to any purpose, but just as a relief and to get your judgment.

Perhaps to relieve myself, for I am very much concerned.

Ever yours
Mother

TO *Violet Schiff* — MS BL

1 April [1923?] — 9 Clarence Gate Gdns

My dear Violet

Thank you so much for your letter. At the moment, Vivienne is not suffering from actual neuritis, but from very peculiar after effects, which are very worrying indeed – a sort of utter prostration and general numbness; and the effect of the treatment[1] now seems to be merely *irritant* and disturbing. If this goes on after a day or two I think the treatment will have to be dropped. You will understand how very worrying and depressing this is for her. I simply don't know what to do.

I'll write or telephone in a few days and let you know. It is quite impossible for Vivienne to go out to lunch – she only *hopes* to slip round one afternoon and see you and Sydney alone. Just now the treatment is all she can manage (and a bit more) in a day.

1 – Presumably 'the Plombières treatment' referred to in his letter to OM of 2 Mar.

I should have liked very much to meet Beerbohm,[1] although it would not take the place of seeing you by yourselves. But Sunday is now our one day of real rest – we shut ourselves up, and don't have our servant come, and I know I could not be up for lunch. You will understand that we are just *keeping alive* and no more. I doubt if I could even get in later in the afternoon – but I *do* want to see you both soon.

With love from both
Tom.

FROM *John Quinn*

TS copy Valerie Eliot

2 April 1923 [New York]

My dear Eliot:

I received this morning your cable reading as follows:

'London

Quinn
3 Nassau Street
New York

Nation off failing guarantee. Also unable wait necessary notice bank. Does extraordinarily generous offer hold if bad health forces leave bank without alternative position. Thank Kahn. Await letter.'

If the *Nation* is not willing to give you a guarantee I think you were right not to take up with it.

I am not certain about the meaning of the second phrase in your cable, 'Also unable wait necessary notice bank'. But I take it that that means that you had to accept or decline the *Nation* at once without giving the necessary notice to the bank.

As I wrote you, I am still hoping to get two or three or possibly four hundred dollars more in addition to the four hundred which I have guaranteed and the two hundred which Kahn guaranteed for five years.

I am cabling you today as follows:

1 – Max Beerbohm (1872–1956): caricaturist and writer; contributor to *The Yellow Book* in the 1890s; author of *Zuleika Dobson* (1911). On 24 Aug. 1952 TSE was to contribute to an 80th Birthday Album for him.

'April 2, 1923

Eliot
9 Clarence Gate Gardens
London
Offer holds for five years, unconditional. Writing.
(Sgd) Quinn'

I will send you the first check in response to your letter, if that is satisfactory to you.

Sincerely yours,
[John B. Quinn]

TO *Messrs. Hazell, Watson & Viney* CC

2 April 1923 [*The Criterion*, London]

Dear Sirs,

I send you herewith my delayed copy for the six pages.[1] In order to save time, you need not send proof unless it exceeds the limit, which I do not think likely. If it is necessary to save space, and if printing in smaller type will save space, please do so. And if there is not enough room the obituary note on Miss Mansfield can be put at the bottom of the last page of 'The Obsequies' but I prefer that it should have a page to itself.[2]

Yours faithfully
[T. S. E.]

1–Presumably the 'Foreign Reviews' in C. 1: 3 (Apr. 1923), 308–13. This was the first time this regular feature appeared.

2–Katherine Mansfield (1888–1923) had died at Fontainebleau on 9 Jan. The obituary did have a page to itself: 'The *Criterion* desires to express profound regret at the death of Katherine Mansfield. It had been hoped that Miss Mansfield would be a contributor to these pages. A study and appreciation of her work will be reserved until the appearance of her collected works; at the moment we can only register our conviction of the great loss to English letters.' 'The Obsequies' was a story by B. M. Goold-Adams, in the same issue, 293–302.

TO *Jacques Rivière* CC

4 April 1923 [London]

Cher Monsieur,

Merci bien de votre amiable et généreuse lettre du 24 mars.[1] J'apprécie fort bien votre indulgence et je ferai de mon mieux pour la justifier.

Je vous remercie aussi de votre aimabilité à l'egard de *Vanity Fair* et j'écris à la Direction de cette revue qu'il faut indiquer que mon article a déjà paru dans la *Nouvelle Revue Française*.[2] Je vous remercie aussi de vos soins à propos de *La Prisonnière* et je vous remercie de tout mon coeur des efforts que vous aurez fait auprès du Docteur Proust.[3] Vous m'avez comblé d'actions et d'expressions généreuses.

À ce moment je pars en villégiature pour quelques semaines dans l'espoir de rétablir ma santé, mais on fera suivre toute lettre qui est addressée ici.

Recevez cher Monsieur l'[4]

TO *Edmund Wilson* TS Beinecke

4 April 1923 *The Criterion*, 9 Clarence Gate Gdns

Dear Mr Wilson,

Thank you for your letter of 26th February. I should have replied to it before but I thought it best to write to *La Nouvelle Revue Française* before accepting your proposal. *La Nouvelle Revue Française* now tell me that

1 – Rivière said TSE should not be too anxious about his delayed chronicle for *NRF*, wished him a restful convalescence, and asked for a little notice before TSE submitted his piece.

2 – Rivière was happy for TSE's Dec. 'Lettre d'Angleterre' to be republished in *Vanity Fair* with a note explaining it had already appeared in *NRF*. It appeared as 'Contemporary English Prose', *Vanity Fair* 20: 5 (July 1923).

3 – Rivière was looking for an extract from Proust's *La Prisonnière* for publication in *C.*, as TSE wanted. 'The Death of Albertine' appeared, in Scott Moncrieff's translation, in *C.* 2: 8 (July 1924).

4 – The letter breaks off here.

Translation: Dear Sir, Thank you for your kind and generous letter of the 24th March. I sincerely appreciate your understanding, and I shall endeavour to justify it.

I thank you also for your kind acceptance of my suggestion about *Vanity Fair*. I am writing to the Editor to let him know that he must state clearly that the article has already been published in the *Nouvelle Revue Française*. I thank you also for all the trouble you have taken about *La Prisonnière*, and I thank you most sincerely for all the negotiations you have carried out with Dr Proust. You have showered me with good deeds and generous comments.

I am about to go on holiday for a few weeks, in order to improve my health, but my mail will be forwarded to me.

Please believe, dear Sir

they have no objection to your using the article which appeared in that paper, providing that you make acknowledgement at the beginning or end of the article that it has appeared with them first. I am pleased that you should like this article and accept your terms of $75.[1]

I have an informal arrangement with *La Nouvelle Revue Française* to write three or four of these articles a year and if you cared to publish them regularly I could doubtless arrange with *La Nouvelle Revue Française*. If this appeals to you, I should be very glad to hear from you on the subject.

I am afraid that it is impossible to get a heavier copy of the [Wyndham] Lewis drawing from this block. I have spoken to Lewis about it and he will perhaps take steps to obtain a heavier impression. If not, I will see about it myself as soon as I have time, but I have been fearfully rushed lately and am very worn out and am going to the country for several weeks' rest.

I shall have pleasure in taking with me your manuscript to read; I have been so busy that I have had to lay upon myself a rule to read no manuscript at all until I can get away with nothing on my mind. I shall write to you about it later. Thank you for sending it.

Sincerely yours
T. S. Eliot

TO *Charles Whibley* CC

4 April 1923 [London]

My dear Whibley,

I thank you very much for your two kind letters and particularly for your kindness and loyalty in sending me your manuscript.[2] I confess that I have had it somewhat on my mind and conscience, and had been feeling that I ought to write to you to ask you not to bother about it until you were well again.[3] I do very keenly appreciate your thoughtfulness and kindness because I am sure that it must have been a burden to you to have had this piece of work to do when you were feeling so ill. I can only say that this and everything that you will contribute will be of inestimable benefit to the *Criterion*.

1–TSE's article appeared as 'Contemporary English Prose', *Vanity Fair* 20 (5 July 1923), 51, 98) and was the revised English text of 'Lettre d'Angleterre: Le style dans la prose anglaise contemporaine', *NRF* 19: 111 (1 Dec. 1922), 751–6.
2–'Bolingbroke, Pt II', *C.* 1: 4 (July 1923).
3–On 24 Mar., CW said he had not 'been very well' and 'was going to Bath after Easter to see what a cure will do'.

I do hope that you will write to me after you have been at Bath a little while and tell me what it has done for you. Very likely it will quite set you up, but if not, I am indeed very much in earnest in my suggestions.

[Yours sincerely
T. S. E.]

FROM *Messrs. Methuen & Co* — TS Valerie Eliot

5 April 1923 — 36 Essex St, London W.C.2

Dear Sir,

We are sorry to say that the demand for your book *The Sacred Wood* [1920] is not very good, during the last three months we have only sold about twenty copies. There are about 850 copies in our warehouse and as at the present rate of selling it will be a very long time before we are able to make any considerable reduction in this stock we propose, as we must relieve our store, to try to sell some at reduced prices crediting your account with 5% of the amount realised as mentioned in clause 8 of the agreement. Of course this does not mean that the book will be removed from our catalogues and lists as we propose to keep a good supply to meet any demand there may be in the ordinary way. We shall be glad to hear whether you wish to purchase any at 2/3 each.

We are, dear Sir,

Yours faithfully,
Methuen & Co Ltd

TO *Sydney Schiff* — MS Valerie Eliot

6 April 1923 — 9 Clarence Gate Gdns

My dear Sydney

This is in answer to Violet's letter to Vivien. She is too ill and exhausted with battling in the face of obstacles to write. We have not yet left here and I do not know when we shall, and every hour adds to the difficulties. When we do get to the country we shall simply have to bury ourselves completely in order to save our lives, otherwise we could die with less effort in London. The time has really come when we must consider nothing but self-preservation: Vivien is an *extreme* example of a person who has never learned to put herself first. She has always put other people first – and that is *one* way in which I myself have done her great harm. She has always been burdened – even when so ill that she needed every ounce of energy she had just to keep alive – with me and my affairs.

This is what Dr [Hubert] Higgins has tried to teach her all the winter: *to consider herself* – he says (and he is a man who never exaggerates, and speaks quite coldly) that otherwise she will *certainly die*.

Every doctor she has ever had (Higgins more clearly and cogently) has urged upon her that she *ought to be alone*, as she is too sensitive to be battened on by impressions, and cannot refrain from giving herself altogether.

I know that you are one of the exceptional people who are intelligently interested in health and disease, medecine and hygiene; – nearly everybody is ignorant of everything but measles, appendicitis and 'nerves' as they call them. Nobody has ever heard of *malnutrition* – the root and core of Vivien's illness – of which *colitis* is only a symptom. I *must* write again, as I must stop now, and have so much to say to you.

Yrs affectionately
Tom

TO *The Literary Editor of the* New York Globe[1] CC Berg[2]

6 April 1923 9 Clarence Gate Gdns

Sir,

I have received a cutting from your issue of 6th March in which you quote from the *Chicago News* some statements about myself which are asserted to have been made by Mr Ben Hecht. According to this cutting, Mr Hecht says that he met me in London, and knows that I thoroughly hate Americans and everything they write and read, and that he considers

1–N. P. Dawson, who quoted this letter in 'Books in Particular' in the *Globe and Commercial Advertiser* (17 Apr. 1923, 16), commented: 'This sounds exciting. But if we were Mr Eliot we should rather have Mr Ben Hecht say about him what he was quoted as saying in the *Chicago News* than witness the swooning ecstasies into which his poem sent some of the critics. As for ourself, we never for a moment thought that Mr Eliot planned *The Waste Land* as a hoax. But the "psychological phenomena" which reading the poem produced on some of the critics seemed to us funny. And we were sufficiently flattering to Mr Eliot to think the exhibits of these critics would seem funny to him too. *The Waste Land*, of course, is just the kind of poem to which the *Dial* would give an award. Although we recall that one of Mr Eliot's swooning admirers said (or we thought he said) that the award was not given to Mr Eliot because of *The Waste Land* but because of – er – er – a number of things. *The Waste Land* will always remain for us a joyous episode.'

2–The carbon was sent to John Quinn, with a note: 'Writing in two days – going to the country for an essential rest. *Very* grateful to you. TSE.'

me wholly capable of hoaxing the *Dial* and all its friends. In case there may be anyone in America who believes this statement, I wish to inform you that if Mr Hecht made the remarks attributed to him in the *Chicago News*, he is a liar. I should be glad if you would make this public.

Mr Hecht has never met me in London or anywhere else. He has not the slightest ground for the opinions which he assigns to me, and he must be perfectly aware of this fact. I can only presume that Mr Hecht believes that my being 3000 miles away will protect him from any legal action, as it certainly protects him from any physical action on my part. I do not know whether Mr Hecht is the author or merely the supporter of the libel which charges me with having hoaxed the *Dial*, but at least he appears to have found it necessary to lie about me in order to give substance to this rumour. If Mr Hecht has succeeded in hoaxing anybody with such a clumsy falsehood as that reported in the *Chicago News*, it would hardly be worth my while to spend two years' labour upon a poem in order to hoax the *Dial*.

I am, Sir,

Yours faithfully,
[T. S. E.]

FROM *Henry Eliot* — TS Valerie Eliot

7 April 1923 — 1037 Rush St, Chicago

Dear Tom:

This has been a frantic week, with telegrams and radiograms flying back and forth. I cabled you yesterday to cable Mother that you were well, for she is in a way to work herself into a nervous collapse. Your letter, in which you refer to things 'crumbling away', has thrown her into a state of alarm and self-reproach and general consternation. Why, oh why, were you not more specific? Now it will be at least a month before she will be free of worry. I have eight letters of hers on my desk, concerned almost exclusively with her doubts and worries, her plans made and unmade for sailing, her imaginings of a nervous or physical breakdown on your part, and her hopes that you do not feel bitterly towards her (the last being a most extraordinary flight of imagination). She has made a reservation on the *Samaria*. The crossing is very rough; a letter from Thomas [a colleague] in New York says he has spent two days recovering from sea-sickness.

For me to come this summer is out of the question, unless I wanted to 'chuck up' this business entirely. I am temporarily at least the financial prop of the whole thing. I have no fears of losing money, for we made $1800 in March, and should make more than that in April. We may earn 50% on our stock for the year. Things are going well. But I may, in part, have to finance the purchase of the company. I have only mentioned the suggestion of yours to Buchen, but could see his concern over it.

It would be an act of consideration to Mother for you to come over here for two or three weeks, though I do not know whether you can arrange it. It would seem more appropriate, also, and would have a good effect on the rest of the family, who, I understand, are disposed to observe that Mother is the only one whom you want to see. I can understand and to a great extent sympathize with any objections that you might have to coming over here, your attitude to the country probably being something like mine toward Winnetka, Ill., or the University Club of Chicago. You will experience some of the inconveniences of being well known, and having to be decent to a great many silly people. You could, however, make some money lecturing; and you will learn what free publicity is, in the country which invented advertising.

Your letter, or the part of it which Mother quotes to me, is, one must admit, rather reproachful in tone. The passages about everything crumbling suggest a great many vague and disturbing things. I have myself lost some sleep over it, as I cannot imagine the letter being written except in the stress of desperate emotion, such as might be caused by some financial disaster or disgrace, or being in love with another man's wife, or being blackmailed, or seeing Vivien in mortal illness, or anything calamitous. Not knowing the circumstances, none of us knows how to help, which any of us would be ready at once to do. In any of the contingencies suggested, Mother would be a frail reed, physically, to lean on. The length of her life, I think, depends on her keeping happy and contented. Anxiety will surely affect her general health seriously.

I do not know how to write until I know what your difficulties are. Hydraulic[1] has sagged off to about 56, which is not an alarming phenomenon in a 'thin' market, but I see that yesterday 290 shares were sold at a slightly higher price, which may be 'accumulation', for a possible rise before the June directors' meeting. I will write about Hydraulic later. I doubt not that you are a better investor than I, but when you do invest the proceeds, I hope you will see me first. Of course you will invest in British securities, which I know nothing about. But in the last four years I have sown a most fancy variety of wild oats, and have made nearly every

1 – Hydraulic-Press Brick Company, their father's company.

mistake that can be made, including buying on margin, with borrowed money, and seeing my collateral go down, and the bucket shops blow up (after I was out); and the net of it all is, that the smarter you are and the more you know, the harder you fall; and it has cost me very little, owing to a natural timidity; and it is the cheapest and from a practical standpoint the most valuable education I possess. Had I studied literature with half the zeal I have the security markets, I should not now be naked to the shafts of the literate. I hope that in ten years, at least, none of the family will hold any stocks or any real estate. Short term bonds yielding 5½ to 6%, at present – and watch them!

I hope that meanwhile you are writing me or Mother fully.

Affectionately,
Henry

I have mailed you a copy of the *Literary Digest Book Review*, containing a long and sensibly balanced critique of *The Waste Land*.[1] It is undoubtedly the literary sensation over here, outstripping, I think, *Ulysses* – which derives part of its fame from the fact that nobody can get hold of it, just as *Jurgen*[2] did.

TO *Ottoline Morrell* — MS Texas

[?mid April 1923]

2 Milestone Cottages,
Old Fishbourne, nr Chichester

My dear Ottoline,

We have been through such a terrific crisis that I have hardly had a moment even to *read* a letter, much less write one. We were to have come here ten days ago; we only got off on Thursday. First Vivien got an attack of bronchitis, so that we waited over – in very uncomfortable conditions, as we were on the point of starting. Vivien got more and more fatigued and exhausted, and I wanted to get her away from London at the first possible moment. So I engaged a *car* for Wednesday, but on Tuesday she was so ill that I postponed it till Thursday. And on Wednesday she had the worst crisis, after tea, that I have *ever* seen, the worst she has ever had. I am sure that she was on the point of death. She went completely numb, terrible palpitations, and gasping for every breath. I telephoned to *four* doctors –

1–Herbert S. Gorman, 'The Waste Land of the Younger Generation', *Literary Digest International Book Review* 1 (Apr. 1923).

2–*Jurgen* (1919) by James Branch Cabell was, like Joyce's *Ulysses*, subject of an obscenity trial in 1922.

all out – finally one came. But before he came she suddenly had a terrific colitis explosion – poison that must have been accumulating for two or three weeks <owing to the terrible strain over the *Nation* and over getting ready to come here> – and the doctor, and also Dr [Hubert] Higgins, who had been out but came later, both said that this saved her life. Otherwise, she would have died of acute toxaemia, or of the strain on the heart from the effort to resist it. The doctor, and Dr Higgins, both said that the danger was over for the moment, and she had better get away at once. So we came down in a car on Thursday . . . I can't write more now because I am so very tired – but instead of the crisis being over, Vivien had two more, all Friday night, and on Saturday, so that I had to send for her mother. Tonight for the first time she begins to show a little sign of being alive. She has not had any meal at all since last Tuesday and for the last three days has been fed on little drops of milk and teaspoonfuls of brandy to keep her alive. I *think* we are through now, but she has wasted in this week to an absolute skeleton, and it will take weeks to build her up.

I will begin using your bectine tomorrow when I shall get into Chichester to buy a syringe. I will send you the cheque in a day or two.

We haven't dared, of course, to try Vivien with any new thing during this crisis, but she will begin taking it directly she is able – Higgins was interested in it.

[Unsigned]

TO *Richard Cobden-Sanderson* MS Beinecke

[?16 April 1923] *The Criterion*, 9 Clarence Gate Gdns

Dear Cobden-Sanderson,

Copies should go of No. 3 to:[1]

Whibley)	
Koteliansky)	whose addresses you have
Mrs Woolf)	
Read)	
Marichalar)	
Paul Valéry	40, rue de Villejust, Paris XVI
Capt. Mark Wardle	13 rue de Mademoiselle, Versailles, S. et O., France
Ezra Pound	70 bis rue de Notre Dames des Champs, Paris VI

1 – The first six names are of contributing authors and translators in C. I: 3 (Apr. 1923).

Jacques Rivière 3 rue de Grenelle, Paris VI
(as well as to the *N. R. Française*)
Dr Wilhelm Lehmann,[1] Holzminden (Braunschweig), Landschulheim 2, Germany

Also one to
Leonid Massine[2]
c/o Manager
Covent Garden Opera House
if possible marked

'See page 305'
yrs
T. S. E.

TO *John Middleton Murry* MS Valerie Eliot

20 April 1923 2 Milestone Cottages, Old Fishbourne

My dear John,

I should have written to you at once on hearing of your address, but things have been, up to this moment, in too desperate a state to write any letters. Vivien did send you a rare and precious postcard, which she hopes is awaiting you at the farmhouse.[3] If, since you wrote, you have gone there, I assume that this will be forwarded from Selsfield House, and I am asking Cobden-Sanderson to send you the *Criterion* to that address.

Vivien was very ill indeed, in fact for several hours was at the point of death, last week before we came. The doctors advised coming nonetheless, as they said the crisis was over, and she ought to get into the country. So I brought her down in a car. She had a series of intestinal crises throughout the week, and we have had her specialist down from London for two days, and have a nurse who comes in. It is the worst time she has ever had – she has just escaped, by indomitable pluck in the face of terrible difficulty, so far.

1–Wilhelm Lehmann (1882–1968): German poet, critic and novelist; author of *Weingott* (1921). TSE received a letter from him on 16 Apr. He was never a contributor to *C.*

2–Léonide Massine (1896–1979); Russian choreographer and ballet dancer; chief choreographer and subsequently (following the departure of Vaslav Nijinsky) principal dancer of Diaghilev's Ballets Russes. The note 'See page 305' refers to TSE's 'Dramatis Personae' in which he called Massine 'the greatest actor whom we have in London', adding: 'Massine, the most completely unhuman, impersonal, abstract, belongs to the future stage' (*C.* 1: 3, Apr. 1923, 305).

3–JMM had moved from Selsfield House to a cottage at Boxgrove, nr. Chichester.

Most unfortunately, this cottage, which I took only because I was in despair at finding anything else – having tried all the winter – is not at all the proper place for her. It is insanitary, and the noise is terrific – besides the traffic on the Portsmouth road[1] – the man next door is rebuilding his house and has been laying floors for the last three days. And three small children.

So I *must* find another (unfurnished) cottage or house as soon as possible. Do you think you could find anything in your neighbourhood, or near Chichester? Or turn out one of your tenants!

Let me hear from you. I want to know whether you can let me have something by July for the *Criterion*?[2] You know I have been waiting patiently for a long time.

It is hard to think, in the midst of such troubles. But it would be a comfort to have a letter from you.

Yours ever
Tom

TO *Richard Cobden-Sanderson* PC Texas

[Postmark 20 April 1923] [Bosham, Chichester]

Many thanks for *Criterion*[3] and card. Shall write you in a day or two – have had incredible difficulties and anxieties here.

Yours
T. S. E.

TO *John Middleton Murry* MS Valerie Eliot

25 April 1923 2 Milestone Cottages,
Old Fishbourne

Thanks, dear John, for your adorable letter. Will you wire me please, what you are going to do and where you are to be each day of this week, and give me a chance to reply by wire. Vivien is so dangerously ill that there is

1 – Fishbourne lies between Chichester and Bosham, where their previous cottage had been, by the route of the current A27 to Portsmouth. JMM at Boxgrove was not far away.
2 – JMM's first contribution was to be 'Romanticism and the Tradition', C. 2: 7 (Apr. 1924).
3 – C. 1: 3 (Apr. 1923), which had just been published.

a fresh consultation of doctors every day to decide whether she can be moved to London in a closed car.[1]

I feel a kind of dependence on you, and it will be a great comfort to know every day where you are. You are the only person I want to be in touch with.

Vivien is so ill that of course nobody could see her for a minute. *Of course* I should love her to have a cottage near you whatever it was like, but don't bother and worry yourself about it for the moment – just see how the land lies.

Ever yours
Tom

Vivien sends you her best love. If she is taken back to town on Sat. or Sun. she wd love to see you in London: if not, she wd like to see you here for a moment one day next week. Everything is utterly undecided.

TO *Ottoline Morrell* — MS Texas

[April 1923] — 2 Milestone Cottages

My dear Ottoline

I have wanted to write to you for some time, and now that I am back again in Fishbourne it is my first opportunity. I came up to London for a week, and tried to attend to all the matters that I had to neglect for six weeks – with an intensification of the familiar feeling of trying to do twice as much as one can. Now I am back for a fortnight by my doctor's orders (he *said* three weeks) and the kindness of the bank. I was not to do any work here, and tried to clear my path while I was in London; but I still have my Oxford paper to put into shape. It would have been done, but I spent so much time on writing an article for the *Nation*,[2] which Leonard Woolf asked me to do at once[3] – and the effort of concentration to write anything takes me twice as long as it used to – but now that it is done he says he cannot print it yet – so I might better have been getting my Oxford

1 – An enclosed car, with roof and side windows, rather than the more usual open car of the time: cf. 'a closed car at four' (*TWL*, 136).

2 – TSE, 'John Donne' (rev. of *Love Poems of John Donne*), *N&A* 33: 10 (9 June 1923).

3 – LW was offered the job of literary editor of the *Nation* on 23 Mar. The Woolfs sailed on 27 Mar. for a month's holiday in Spain and Paris, and LW returned on 24 Apr. While LW was away, Maynard Keynes wrote to TSE on 10 Apr.: 'we should like something from you for one of the early numbers'. He asked TSE to suggest 'any subject of criticism or book to review'. In a letter of 4 May, VW said that when they returned they were 'bombarded with proofs, reviewers, books and turmoil' (*Letters*, III, 34).

paper written, and only did the other first because he said he would like to have it at once. I am looking forward eagerly to coming down to Oxford. One always has hopes of undergraduates – almost the only kind of audience that is interesting to talk to. It would be a pity if we quite lost *that* hope, wouldn't it. The most hopeless of them are more intelligent and interesting than the same sort of man ten years later.

Vivien is still *very* weak, and the weather – *no* sun ever – is a great handicap. She has such faint spells, and so much pain, that it is a struggle to get through every day, and the slightest exertion of mind or body is a setback. I am wondering if you are away, and whether you got a letter she wrote you a week ago. She can write very little – about one letter a week altogether. But you will be at Garsington now, I suppose: for Vivien had a letter from Virginia Woolf – such a curious letter – saying that she was coming to spend the weekend with you.[1] I could not understand her letter, what was at the back of her mind, but people are very mysterious and changeable, ain't they, in their moods? And she seemed to misinterpret remarks so surprisingly – so I don't know what you will hear!

It will be a great pleasure to see Garsington again. I am only sorry that my visit will be shorter than ever. I suppose I shall have to go to Oxford direct, dine there Saturday, and not see you till after the meeting. I shall come out as early as I can, in a taxi.

Vivien hopes she may have a line for you soon, – although she is such a poor correspondent now, and feels that she cannot express anything without risk of its being misconstrued. But you have suffered so much yourself that you know what it means to have just gone through a life-or-death illness, and can allow for it – so few people seem to know what it means!.

Affectionately
Tom

FROM *Henry Eliot*

TS Valerie Eliot

26 April 1923 — 1037 Rush St, Chicago

Dear Tom:

I received your radio [telegram] today and answered suggesting having Vivien go to a hospital. I do not know about England, but the tendency

1 – This letter does not seem to survive, and its date is not known.

here is more and more to treat all serious illnesses in the hospital, where better care can be exercised and better facilities are at hand.

A letter from Mother today says that she has received an affectionate letter from you in which you speak of Vivien's having bronchitis. I hope it has not developed into any more serious form of illness.

If you need money I hope you will cable me. I am not entirely free yet of the temporary financial burdens of the company, but there are always ways to raise money.

I have been hoping to hear from you, and perhaps shall before long. I think it is nearly three weeks since you cabled you were writing, but I do not know whether you meant writing me or Mother.

I have not really heard from you since January, and not much news for longer than that. I am much in the dark and should like to know what your circumstances are; whether the burden of the *Criterion* is proving insupportable, together with worry over Vivien's illness.

Your letter to the [*New York*] *Globe* in regard to Hecht was very good, though I doubt the advisability of mentioning physical punishment. There is a possibility also that Hecht never said that he had met you. I was much surprised that you treated the matter so seriously, as the accusation of fraud (if hoax means that) is obviously absurd, and if it means concealed satire, is not derogatory. I do not know Hecht, but understand he is a man of no fine scruples.

I have passed through four months of work under high pressure, complicated recently by a bronchial cold and deafness, and a quarrel between my two partners over apparently nothing – a tone, a look, an inflection. I had thought them exceedingly rational persons hitherto. Now every remark one makes is suspect to the other, thought to be innuendo or irony, which is a terrible state which feeds on itself. I suppose the sanest of us is not exempt from that. I have wasted many hours arguing with them. I think it will wear off in time.

I enclose data on Hydraulic and on business in general, which I have sent to various members of the family.

I hope you have written or will shortly snatch time to write. If Vivien's illness becomes more serious I hope you will cable.

Affectionately
Henry

TO *Ottoline Morrell* MS Texas

Thursday [?26 April 1923] 9 Clarence Gate Gardens

My dear Ottoline,

I am writing for Vivien to thank you for your kind letter. We are going to the country tomorrow, somehow – Vivien is very ill and I don't know which is worse for us, to make this great effort or to delay in town. We want to get away and have just solitude and peace – and people won't let one alone and won't understand and take offence: and we feel as exposed to them in Sussex as in Regent Street. If we could only go *abroad* for a long time and hide and forget everything!!

Vivien is *very much interested* in what you say and would be very grateful if you would send a tin of the Amidal[1] – it is

2 Milestone Cottages, Old Fishbourne, near Chichester, Sussex

and I should very much like to know how I could get the Hectene [?Bectine] and how to take it.

I am looking forward to coming on May 5 and lecturing and staying with you. I do wish that I could get a connection with Oxford. Will you *advertise* me, when you can?

Affectionately
Tom

We did not know Maria Huxley had been ill, as we never see them and have not seen them or even heard of them for years.

Vivien has had terrible pain in the *back of her head* lately, with great stiffness and dizziness. Have you ever had these symptoms? It is caused by *glands* in the back of the neck.

TO *Mary Hutchinson* MS Texas

[Postmark 26 April 1923][2] 2 Milestone Cottages,
Old Fishbourne

Dear Mary

I am writing this for Vivien as she is not up to writing a letter today. She says she is so sorry that she invited you to come and see her while she has malignant influenza, but she was too ill to realise what she was doing. If

1 – Amidal is a combination medication used to treat symptoms (coughing, runny/stuffy nose, congestion) caused by the common cold, allergies, asthma, bronchitis, sinusitis, and other breathing illnesses.

2 – The same morning, TSE sent a telegram to Hutchinson: 'STILL ILL HAVE WRITTEN TOM'.

you had come, though, of course I should not have allowed you to go into her room. She wants to say that she looks forward to seeing you very much and has a lot to talk to you about, but that unfortunately next weekend is not possible in any way, as the doctor from London is coming again to stay from Saturday over Sunday. There is also some question of moving her away from here in a car the moment she can be moved. We have never been able even to arrange the furniture, and it is extraordinarily uncomfortable and inconvenient for a case of serious illness.

My successful holiday will shortly be at an end, so that perhaps I may look forward to the pleasure of seeing you in London in the near future. With love from us both, to you and Jack.

Yours ever
Tom

TO *John Quinn* MS Berg

26 April 1923 as from 9 Clarence Gate Gdns

Dear Mr Quinn,

I cabled you yesterday,[1] as you must have thought it very extraordinary that I had not written at all. I have had it on my mind to write to you, almost from hour to hour, for the last four weeks: during that time I have not written a single letter, and have had to allow my affairs to drift into complete chaos.

I am writing this from a small cottage near Chichester, which I took for a year because it was essential that my wife should be in the country. I took my three weeks annual holiday in order to get her started here. Unfortunately, she had a very bad colitis attack just before we came, and has been ill here – under most uncomfortable conditions – ever since; having the specialist from London twice a week, and the local man twice a day, and her mother most of the time. Another man is coming from London on Saturday. They have called it septic influenza and then thought it was turning to pneumonia, and have been taking analyses. Meanwhile she has wasted away to a skeleton, and my holiday is gone, and I feel a good deal more ill than when it started, and I shall not get a day more for a year. And I don't suppose this cottage will be of much use; my wife ought to be in the country, but she won't be fit to be left here for a long time.

1 – Telegram received by Quinn on 26 Apr.: 'WIFE ILL PNEUMONIA BEEN UNABLE TO WRITE ELIOT.'

As we have been two miles out in the country in a labourer's cottage, and my wife could not possibly be moved, the conditions have been the most inconvenient possible, and I have had to work like a nigger, and have had not a minute to attend to anything. I give you this very brief history of the last three weeks – only to make clear why I have not written. I feel pretty well knocked out: the shock of thinking ~~two~~ seven or ~~three~~ eight times over that my wife was ~~dying~~ at the point of death was enough in itself.

Her fundamental trouble is malnutrition, of which entero-colitis is a symptom; but there is always risk, in these attacks, of appendicitis or peritonitis. It is a condition which must have begun many years ago, and which will take years, with favourable conditions, to set right.

You were right in your interpretation of my cable. The *Nation* did not want to give more than six months guarantee and they wanted me *at once* if at all. I pointed out that this might be allright for a man who was already in journalism, but that it is quite different for a man who had to give up a secure post. I don't know whether I have ever explained this to you, but the Bank is a secure job for life, with a pension at sixty, and a year's salary and a pension for my wife in the event of my death. The main point, in any question of leaving the Bank, is (as I explained to Pound) the security for my wife. She will never be strong enough to shift for herself, or to endure great privation, she will inherit very little, and not in the ordinary course for many years, and I must make reasonable provision for her before undertaking any adventures. I must explain also that owing to the terms of my father's will any property coming to me is in trust, and reverts to the family on *my* death – instead of being left outright, as to my brother and sisters.[1] Thus my wife can get no benefit from my inheritance in the event of my death. My father disapproved of my residence in England.

I have gone into these details, for the first time, because it might appear, and I daresay has appeared to people who do not know my circumstances, that I am either very cowardly or very grasping.[2] If I appear in this light to you, please let me know.

I do regard it as a *disaster* that I could not come to an arrangement with the *Nation*, and if the same post, or any similar post, should be open to me in the future, I should take it. I *mean to* leave the bank, and I *must* leave the bank, but I cannot say *how soon* or in what way.

1 – TSE had written to HWE on 5 Nov. 1916 that their father had warned him that TSE's life insurance was 'probably all there will be for Vivien'. TSE was 'very anxious about her future in the event of my death', since their father's will left his inheritance to TSE on condition that it reverted to the Eliot family in the event of TSE's death.

2 – VW noted on 6 Mar.: 'Eliot slightly disillusions me too; he is peevish, plaintive, egotistical; what it amounts to is that poverty is unbecoming' (*Diary*, II, 238).

I am at present trying to lay a foundation by investing every penny I can save. This is a very slow process, with the expenses which I have – the cost of the last fortnight, with the specialist down twice a week from London, local doctor twice daily etc. etc. have been almost ruinous, and I shall not be able to put by any more for a long time to come. But I have put the *Dial* award, and a little other money, into a *separate* account, which I gradually invest in gilt-edged securities, and have the income from these securities paid into the same account, so that *none* of these savings goes on expenses, but it is *all* put by for *capital* against the day when I leave the bank. I regard this as a *trust fund*, and any money that comes to me beyond my current income, I shall deal with in this way.

In your letter you said that you would 'send me a cheque as soon as I acknowledged receipt of your letter'. If you did that, I should of course put it to my 'trust fund' and invest it. *But if you assumed that I was leaving the bank at once in any case*, and meant the money to be payable on my leaving the bank only, then I should like to know whether the guarantee of this $600 p.a. for five years holds good whether I leave the bank to go into another job such as an editorship or whether my health forces me to leave without any job at all.

None of the literary jobs, such as there are, is very well paid or very secure, but I should take anything it was possible to accept.

In any case, I want to be sure that you understand and approve my point of view and my line of action.

I have said nothing so far to show an atom of my appreciation of your extraordinary generosity and kindness. When I think of all you have done for me for years past in other ways, I do not know what more to say to convince you of the strength of my recognition. Perhaps I can only say that it is the greatest stimulus to me to commence the work I have in mind, which is more ambitious than anything I have ever done yet.[1] And a stimulus to do my part to bring about the conditions which will make this work possible.

I hope you will also express to Otto Kahn *my very deep gratitude*. To have one of the greatest international bankers interested in me is a reassurance in itself.

Yours always gratefully
T. S. Eliot

1 – Quinn averred, 'your own writing is the most important, much more than propaganda work' in C., and noted too that 'an artist was to be judged [by] what he painted and a sculptor by what he sculpted and a writer by what he wrote'.

Vivien Eliot TO *Virginia Woolf* MS Berg

27 April [1923] 2 Milestone Cottages,
Old Fishbourne

Dear Virginia

I hope this is in time to welcome you home.

Your letter came in a very bad [?time] and made me happy for a whole day. You have had a wonderful time, havent you? Of course I should love to live abroad.

I am very ill at present. I have been really frightfully ill for three weeks and have nearly died about seven times. It has been dreadful to have it here, and the *ruin* of Tom's holiday! and the incredible expense!

I cannot write much now. Tom will write to you. When he is able to go back to London be kind to him. Not getting the *Nation* was a disaster for us both – indeed, we cannot bear to think of that, at all.

It is so charming of you to say you want to see me. I need hardly say how much I look forward to seeing you again.

With love from Vivien

TO *John Middleton Murry* MS Valerie Eliot

Undated [? April 1923] [London]

Dear John

I was very disappointed not to see you this week, but I have had to set to at masses of correspondence – private and otherwise – and attend to innumerable domestic details, and I have not had one free evening. But believe that I want to see you, and have thought of you daily.

I am devoured by worry too – Vivien's progress is so slow, and with so many relapses, and I am anxious every minute. I am just going down there [to the cottage at Fishbourne].

I have *lost* yr telephone no (York Bldgs).

Aff. always
Tom

[On back of envelope]
What I do not say, but am always thinking, is the most important. But I don't know whether you have ever got to *such* a low point – this is an ebb-tide, in *every* respect. I have no longer any confidence in *my* . . .

You have got further, in your own way, than I in mine.

TO *Mary Hutchinson* PC Texas

[Postmark 30 April 1923] [Fishbourne]

Many thanks for your good offices. V is much too ill to see anybody, and is being kept going on serum and Bulgarian bacillus. When she can, I am sure she will write to you, but at present she cannot sit up even. We have the London doctor down twice a week and a local man daily. I will let you know when things are a little better.

Yrs
T

TO *Charles du Bos*[1] MS Texas

1 May 1923 2 Milestone Cottages,
Old Fishbourne

Dear M. du Bos

I am very happy to hear that you are coming to London. I should be there now, but have been delayed in the country, as my wife has been seriously ill here. I expect to be in London toward the end of next week, and will write to you to propose a meeting. I look forward keenly to seeing you.

Very sincerely yours
T. S. Eliot

TO *John Middleton Murry* MS Valerie Eliot

[?1 May 1923] 2 Milestone Cottages

Dear John,

If you are in this neighbourhood, will you come over and see me Friday Saturday or Sunday. I can't promise about V. but I am practically certain

1 – Charles du Bos (1832–1939), French man of letters of French and English literature – his mother was English, and he studied at Oxford – wrote one review for *C.* in 1935. He published *Réflexions sur Mérimée* (1920), and was later famous for his posthumously published journals (6 vols, 1946–55). He contributed some 'Remarques' on Henry James to *La Revue de Genève* 5: 30 (Dec. 1922), 818–21, introducing the French translation of *The Figure in the Carpet*.

to be here myself and want badly to see you.[1] You might give me a look at your cottage. With love from us both and thanks for wire.

In great haste
Yrs
Tom

TO *Ottoline Morrell* MS Texas

Tuesday [1 May 1923] 9 Clarence Gate Gdns

My dear Ottoline

I was very glad to get your sweet letter, but dreadfully disappointed about your health. It is like a horrible treadmill, isn't it? going on struggling and fighting for health only to be knocked over again and begin at the beginning. And how few people understand what delicate people have to put up with, and how much courage and *character* they have to exercise at every minute.

I was very troubled at the idea of imposing myself on you at this time – my 'lecture' is on Saturday, and by the idea of abusing your hospitality by keeping you up and coming out in a taxi so late, at or after bedtime. So I jumped with relief at the invitation to stay in Balliol [College] – so I can come out directly after breakfast – if indeed that is not too much. I feel that you ought not to have visitors at all, but I want so much to see you, and stay to lunch? I shall see just as much of you that way, and with an easier conscience. But I hope that my visit at all will not be too much for you.

It will be the first night that I shall have left Vivien without a proper attendant. I am bringing her to London – it couldn't be helped – she naturally *hates* to leave the country – but I hope she can get away again soon. I am not at all happy about bringing her back or leaving her.

I do *hope* you are getting better, and so look forward to seeing you.

Affectionately
Tom

1 – The letter is dated in relation to the next one to JMM, which is clearly dated 2 May 1923 and appears to follow on from this one. However, TSE was lecturing at Oxford on Sat., 5 May, and so must be referring here to the following weekend of 12 May.

TO *John Middleton Murry* MS Valerie Eliot

2 May 1923 2 Milestone Cottages,
Old Fishbourne

Dear John

Many thanks for your letter. Referring to mine (which you had not received) – *if* you are at your cottage and can and will come over, *Sunday* would be the best day – but come when you can on Friday – Sat. or Sunday and I hope you can. Do let me know in advance, by card or wire.

Yours
Tom

TO *Mary Hutchinson* PC Texas

[Postmark 3 May 1923] 2 Milestone Cottages

If you come to Wittering, I shd be delighted if you would look in and see me for half an hour on Sunday afternoon?[1] V won't be able to see anybody yet, but sends love.

T.

TO *Richard Aldington* MS Texas

Friday [4 May 1923] 9 Clarence Gate Gdns

My dear Richard

I was very sorry to miss you on Wednesday, but did not arrive in London till nearly 7. I am very much obliged to you for having settled matters with C-Sanderson, and with such discretion.[2] Of course, before another number, I shall be able to arrange with you the division of labour in an orderly way; but I have had so much on my mind and my time so taken up the last three months that I have had to be very disorderly. It is unnecessary to say that your prompt action has saved No. 4, as you must know that.

1 – As with the letter to JMM of 2 May, the postmark poses a problem, since TSE was at Oxford the following Saturday, 5 May, and due to lunch with Ottoline Morrell at Garsington on Sunday.

2 – As assistant editor, RA took responsibility during TSE's emergency absence in Sussex for some of the arrangements with RC-S for the next issue of C.

Ezra's poem is much too long for us, but he insists that it is a unit, and I believe in respecting the wishes of poets.[1] I have got the proof from you tonight and will let you have my observations in a couple of days.

I have to go to Oxford tomorrow to address some undergraduates on the subject of criticism – I told you about this. And if I am to do *any writing at all* this summer, I must deny myself *any* more weekends for many weeks to come. I shd have enjoyed the anticipation of a weekend with you – may I be allowed to propose myself, *when* it is possible, on the understanding that you tell me if it is inconvenient.

Are you taking a holiday this year, and if so when and where?

I think we ought to subscribe to a few reviews. I doubt if the Germans will exchange – and the cost is not much.

I am not keen on Scandinavians and Czechoslovaks, but we want to do something to extend the Empire – and although I am gallophile in essentials – to check the French hegemony of Europe.[2] And Norway and Holland have always been susceptible to British influence.

I wrote to Richmond [Bruce Richmond, editor of the *TLS*] (at 3 Sumner Place) but have no answer.

I have at last got definite promise of an *inédit* of Proust, and Scott Moncrieff will translate it.[3]

I shall initial *my* editorial;[4] I can't touch this or the circular[5] till after my talk tomorrow.

I shall be writing you early next week.

Again thanks
Yrs
T.

1 – Four of EP's Cantos were published, as '"Malatesta Cantos" (Cantos IX to XII of a Long Poem)', in *C.* 1: 4 (July 1923), 363–84. When EP sent the same texts to the *Dial* on 4 Jan., arranging simultaneous publication in the USA, he wrote: 'I DON'T see how the four /// cantos can be separated, riven in sunder, without very considerable damage and diminuation [*sic*] of interest' (*Pound, Thayer, Watson, and The Dial*, 255).

2 – Dutch and Danish periodicals were added to the review of periodicals in *C.* 2: 6 (Feb. 1924). TSE's notion of 'Empire' may be related to his later claim, 'We are all, so far as we inherit the civilization of Europe, still citizens of the Roman Empire' ('Virgil and the Christian World' [1951], *OPP*, 130).

3 – See Proust, 'The Death of Albertine', trans. Scott Moncrieff, *C.* 2: 8 (July 1924).

4 – There was no 'Editorial' as such in the next *C.*, only two pages of 'Notes' placed between the articles and 'Foreign reviews'. TSE's piece, flagged as 'The Function of a Literary Review', concludes: 'It is the function of a literary review to maintain the autonomy and disinterestedness of literature, and at the same time to exhibit the relations of literature – not to "life", as something contrasted to literature, but to all the other activities, which, together with literature, are the components of life' (*C.* 1: 4, July 1923, 421).

5 – A new advertising circular for *C.*

TO *Ottoline Morrell* MS Texas

[Monday 7 May 1923] [London]

My dear Ottoline

This is a hasty paragraph to tell you how very keenly I enjoyed meeting the young men – all of them – and how I appreciate the trouble and thought you took.[1] I enjoyed every moment: I wish I might see them all again! It means so much to find fresh and untried minds, and unspoiled lives: one doesn't meet many in London. I should like nothing better than to give a course of lectures in Oxford, if we can arrange it.

I don't know if I made clear that Vivien is not suffering primarily from *colitis,* now: she is suffering from the after effects of the devastating influenza pneumonia – very very low vitality, and consequent depression of mind. I am sure that what she needs is air, and the country, and peace, and *no mental* strain, and this Scotch doctor in Chichester is *very good* indeed. So I am doubtful of exposing her to the strain of a new doctor, esp. as he will not have time to go into it thoroughly here – but I hope you will see Martin[2] soon and let me know all about it and how he impresses you. I am *very grateful* for all your sympathy and thoughtfulness. I cannot tell you how much I enjoyed seeing you before lunch.

V. aff
Tom

She seems to have almost no colitis at present.
PS I posted your letters. Monday.

Charlotte C. Eliot TO *Thomas Lamb Eliot*[3] TS Houghton

7 May 1923 24 Concord Ave, Cambridge, Massachusetts

Dear Brother Tom

Because in your letter you say you do not understand Tom's poem, *The Waste Land*, I am sending you one of the critiques I have which I will ask

1 – A reference to his trip to Oxford and lunch at Garsington the previous weekend. Thanking OM after a visit to Garsington later the same month, on 7 May VW praised the hostess's 'genius': 'I think of the thirty seven young men, and you waving your wand among them.' In a letter to TSE of 4 June, VW said she had met at dinner 'a young Lord at Oxford who said that Mr Eliot was his favourite poet, and the favourite of all his friends' (*Letters*, III, 45; she was referring to Lord David Cecil).

2 – Dr Karl Bernhard Martin: see Glossary of Names.

3 – Thomas Lamb Eliot (1841–1936): brother of TSE's father; Unitarian Minister, educated at Washington University, St Louis, and Harvard; Pastor, First Unitarian Society, Portland,

you to return in the enclosed envelope.[1] The poem puzzled me at first, but now I think I understand it better. Tom wrote me before it was published that he had put so much of his own life into it.[2] Certainly up to the time of his marriage and residence in England, he dwelt in an ideal world. Since that time he has had pretty hard times. He had made a splendid record in Philosophy at Harvard, and they intended to advance him as fast as they could. After he married his wife she and her mother were very averse to her coming to America, although we urged it all we could. For a year he taught small boys. In addition he gave courses of extension lectures and reviewed books. Then he obtained the position at Lloyds he now holds, and all his literary work has been done in the evening. I was much opposed to his undertaking the editorship of the *Criterion*, and indeed he broke down that fall and had to take three months rest at Lausanne. This year, however, he finally consented, and is at present very much overworked and tired. One of his greatest misfortunes has been the invalidism of his wife. It was not an eugenic marriage.[3] He wrote me at Christmas she had not been to the table for six months. Then she was 'better', next she had Bronchitis, and a recent cablegram says: 'Vivien recovering Pneumonia.' Tom has been a perfectly devoted husband, but it is very hard on him.

Under these circumstances you can easily imagine some of his ideals are shattered. I would like him to supplement *The Waste Land* by its natural sequence 'The coming of the Grail'. He has had for some time the plan for another poem in his mind but has no time. I earnestly hope he will give up the *Criterion*. Love to Etta,

Most affectionately yours,
Lottie Eliot

—

Oregon, 1867–93; author of *The Radical Difference between Liberal Christianity and Orthodoxy*. TSE wrote to him on 4 Dec. 1922, thanking him for a letter about his father, and saying 'how very much touched and pleased I am at the memorial of which it forms a part'. See Earl M. Wilbur, *Thomas Lamb Eliot, 1841–1936* (Portland, Oregon, 1937).

1 – Not identified.

2 – The letter does not appear to survive. The editors have been unable to trace any letters of TSE to his mother between the end of Aug. 1921 and Oct. 1923.

3 – W. Grant Hague in *The Eugenic Marriage: A Personal Guide to the New Science of Better Living and Better Babies* (1913) argued: 'The eugenic ideal is a worthy race – a race of men and women physically and mentally capable of self-support. The eugenist, therefore, demands that every child born shall be a worthy child – a child born of healthy, selected parents.'

TO *Richard Aldington* TS Texas

11 May 1923 *The Criterion*, 9 Clarence Gate Gdns

Dear Richard,

I feel a special obligation to write to you because you are one of the very few people who have the constancy to persist in writing to me whether I answer or not. We have had a terrible month of it and in short my wife's progress has been set back for a year, I have been at great expense, and I have exhausted the whole of my holiday and ten days more which the bank allowed me, without extracting anything but exhaustion. However I am thankful to say that my wife appears to be recovering; she is beginning to gain a little strength. For the first two weeks she was frequently not expected to live; a mysterious form of what the doctors call influenza – the name is perhaps no more than a synonym for ignorance – and which almost became pneumonia, reduced her to a skeleton.

But I will not say more now because I am looking forward to seeing you on Wednesday. I will do my best to keep the evening free to devote to you: In case anything should turn up to interfere, will you let me know where to communicate with you some time on Wednesday? As a matter of fact I expect to have several things to talk about, besides my desire to see you.

Yours always,
Tom

TO *Charles du Bos* TS Texas

11 May 1923 *The Criterion*, 9 Clarence Gate Gdns

Dear Mr Du Bos,

I got back to London yesterday and after several attempts finally succeeded in getting Mr Beresford on the telephone this evening. He informed me of what I feared would be true, that you had only stayed four days and that you had left England a week ago. I must count this as another misfortune in a disastrous holiday. My wife has been so critically ill that it was impossible for me to leave her even for a day or even to attend to my correspondence, and I am not yet certain that she is safe. I am very much disappointed at having missed you. I cannot even feel any secure hope of seeing you in Paris as I have run through the whole of my annual holiday and can now only look forward to a short weekend in Paris later in the year, but I trust that your having mastered so completely the English language – if I may say so – is evidence that you are a not infrequent visitor to London; and as I am certain to be fixed to London for the next year without interval I pray that you will let me know of your next visit.

It has occurred to me that it would be interesting to have from you at some time for the *Criterion* a critical study of some English writer. We have already published a German critic on Balzac,[1] a Scotch critic on Flaubert,[2] and I find these critical studies by writers of different nationality very illuminating.[3] Larbaud, also, has promised us some papers on Walter Savage Landor.[4] I am sure that no one in France is more competent to write about English literature, either present or past, than yourself. Would you not suggest a subject?

Yours sincerely,
T. S. Eliot

TO *Edmund Wilson* CC

11 May 1923 [London]

Dear Mr Wilson,

Thank you for your letter of 23rd April with enclosed cheque of $100 for which I enclose your formal receipt.[5] I note that your receipt stipulates that you retain all rights including those of translation, but of course it is understood that the right of translation into French does not apply to these articles which are written for the *Nouvelle Revue Française*.

Of course you will understand that this article and articles of the same series are written primarily for a French public and therefore it is rather to my advantage that this limitation should be evident. I do not know whether the *Nouvelle Revue Française* would have any objection to your publishing them simultaneously. At the moment I am under too much obligation to Monsieur Jacques Rivière to care to ask such a concession from him; but I will ask him whether he objects to your using them regularly the following month. The fact is that at present, and so far as I can see indefinitely, I have not the time to write two separate sets of

1 – Ernst Robert Curtius, 'Balzac', *C.* 1: 2 (Jan. 1923), 105–18.
2 – J. M. Robertson, 'Gustave Flaubert', *C.* 1: 2 (Jan. 1923), 127–42.
3 – TSE later wrote, 'We cannot determine the true status and significance of the significant writers in our own language, without the aid of foreign critics with a European point of view.' ('Brief über Ernst Curtius', *Freundesgabe für Ernst Robert Curtius* [1956], 27.)
4 – See TSE's letter to Valery Larbaud, 8 Nov. 1922, in Vol. 1 of these *Letters*.
5 – Wilson (26 Feb.) had offered 'about $75' for the translation of TSE's 'Lettre d'Angleterre' from *NRF* 19: 111 (1 Dec. 1922).

articles.[1] I do not see why your acknowledgement should not be in some such form as the following: 'Published only in the *Nouvelle Revue Française* and *Vanity Fair*'.

What the *Nouvelle Revue Française* asked me to do, and what I am going to do, is a series of chronicles dealing with the contemporary condition of literature in England. I am allowed to include American affairs also, but as I am not on the spot I only propose to deal with a few people and a few books. I intended in the next paper to deal with the intellectual influences of the older generation upon our own.[2]

Yours very sincerely,
[T. S. E.]

TO *W. P. Ker* CC

11 May 1923 [London]

Dear Mr Ker,

I should have written to you several weeks ago but I have been detained in the country by a very critical illness of my wife and I did not have your address by me, or indeed the time for any correspondence whatever. I am writing to ask you if you would have any objection to our using your paper on Byron in the October number of the *Criterion* instead of in July.[3] The reason is simply that I do not want to spread the butter too thick by putting all the star performers in one number. Mr Whibley's Bolingbroke must be published in July because it is a continuation from April; and Mr William Butler Yeats' Reminiscences must be published in July for the reason that he has arranged simultaneous publication in America.[4] If we publish you

1–On 23 Apr., Wilson said they would be 'delighted to have the other articles too', possibly simultaneously with *NRF*. After Wilson's departure in May, the editor Frank Crowninshield asked TSE on 22 June whether he would write a 'few articles' for *Vanity Fair*. On his copy of the letter, TSE jotted 'first *Nouvelle Revue* article' and 'third', followed by 'Future of Poetry', 'The need for experimentation in the arts', and 'The French'. 'Lettre d'Angleterre: le style dans la prose anglaise contemporaine' (*NRF* 19), became 'Contemporary English Prose' (*Vanity Fair* 20: 5, July 1923), followed by 'A Preface to Modern Literature: Being a Conspectus Chiefly of English Poetry, Addressed to an Intelligent and Inquiring Foreigner' (*Vanity Fair* 21: 3, Nov. 1923), which was a translation of the earlier 'Lettre d'Angleterre' (*NRF* 18: 104, 1 May 1922).

2–The next 'Lettre d'Angleterre' (*NRF* 21: 122, 1 Nov. 1923) was later published as 'A Prediction in Regard to Three English Authors, Writers Who, though Masters of Thought, Are likewise Masters of Art', in *Vanity Fair* 21: 6 (Feb. 1924). The three writers considered were Henry James, Sir James Frazer and F. H. Bradley.

3–W. P. Ker, 'Byron', *C.* 2: 5 (Oct. 1923), 1–15.

4–WBY, 'A Biographical Fragment', *C.* 1: 4 (July 1923), and *Dial* 75: 1 (July 1923).

in the same number we shall find it very difficult to keep the October number to the same level; so I hope that you will have no objection. I am in any case disappointed at postponing anything so desirable as your essay.

I hope that when you return in October I may have the pleasure of seeing you.

Yours sincerely
[T. S. E.]

TO *Ford Madox Ford* TS Cornell

11 May 1923 *The Criterion*, 9 Clarence Gate Gdns

Dear Mr Ford,

I have your card and should have written to you long ago but that a very critical illness of my wife has interrupted all my activities for over a month. I like your essay 'From this Grey Rock'[1] very much. Had it been possible I should have printed it in the April number, indeed it ought to have appeared three months ago; I purpose to use it in July. It is an admirable statement of the Anglo-French policy which I myself strongly advocate and which needs re-assertion at the present time.[2] In fact, it was never needed more.

As I am so pleased with this article,[3] and as I have not had a moment for reading of any kind, even the newspapers, I have not yet progressed to your History of British Literature.[4] I want to keep it by me if you will let me for some time and read the whole thing; I am sure that there will be a great deal which we should be very anxious to publish.

Sincerely yours
T. S. Eliot

1–See Ford, 'From the Grey Stone', *C.* 2: 5 (Oct. 1923). TSE's slip recalls 'Come under the shadow of this grey rock' from 'The Death of St Narcissus'. Ford reprinted his article as the last chapter of *A Mirror to France* (1926).

2–Ford wrote: 'what stands out in the world of Thought and the Arts is this: It is only England and France that matter – England for all the finenesses that she has produced and ignored; France for all the glories that would have been for ever hers had she not owned Provence.'

3–For a different view, see TSE's letter to EP of 4 Oct.

4–Ford sent in his 'history' on 18 Feb. – 'as much of it as is written at all' – telling TSE to print what he wanted. After 'From the Grey Stone', however, TSE published nothing else by Ford.

TO *Natalie Clifford Barney*[1] TS Doucet

11 May 1923 [9 Clarence Gate Gdns]

Dear Miss Barney,

April is indeed the cruellest month, and the fact follows the word.[2] This is the first moment I have had to sit down and follow my telegram with a letter. Please accept my very sincere regrets and apologies.

I have been in the country for the last five weeks, having intended to be there only three. My wife was taken very ill, indeed was very ill when we went, although the doctors urged me to take her. She was in bed for a month, and during the first part of the time we did not expect her to live. The doctors called it enteric influenza, which was narrowly prevented from becoming pneumonia. We had to have a local doctor in constant attendance as well as a London specialist twice a week, and I am sure you will understand that under the conditions, in a half-furnished and not very comfortable country cottage several miles outside of Chichester, the situation was one of the very greatest anxiety. My wife is apparently recovering though very slowly, and it will at best be many months before she recovers from this illness. It has been very unfortunate in every way. I have used up the whole of my annual holiday and a little more; a month of the year which the doctors have been relying upon for my wife to make the most progress must be spent in slow recuperation, and a complete restoration is delayed by at least a year. Also, I have had to allow *affaires* of the great[est] importance to remain untouched, and I find myself again in London after great expense with a month's arrears of work.

I am so late in replying to your letter of the 4th April that it seems useless for me to attempt to reply to your questions.[3] I do not know what Lady

1–Natalie Clifford Barney (1876–1972), a wealthy expatriate American writer in Paris, hosted for several decades (from 1909) a brilliant, legendary salon at a sixteenth-century pavilion, 20 rue Jacob, on the Left Bank – her '*temple de l'amitié*' – attended by innumerable writers inc. EP, André Gide, Anatole France, Paul Valéry, Jean Cocteau, Colette, Gabriele D'Annunzio and Peggy Guggenheim. She also helped to raise funds for certain gifted but indigent writers including TSE and Valéry. A lesbian, she was the addressee of Rémy de Gourmont's *Lettres à l'Amazone* (1914); and in 1927 she founded an *Académie des Femmes* to honour women writers. See *A Perilous Advantage: The Best of Natalie Clifford Barney* (1992) and Diana Souhami, *Wild Girls: Paris, Sappho and Art: The Lives and Loves of Natalie Barney and Romaine Brooks* (2004).

2–Barney opened her letter of 4 Apr. with an allusion to the opening line of *TWL*: 'April is the cruelest month'. C. and the *Dial* had brought her TSE's 'waste lands', and she wished 'the energy of so stimulating a poet might be liberated'.

3–In addition to wanting to discuss 'Bel Esprit' in relation to Paul Valéry, Barney asked TSE if he could recommend an 'anglo-american' editor and publisher for her *Pensées d'une amazone* which had been translated by EP and others.

Rothermere had in mind in suggesting that the variety of my interests was a bar to my liberation – the only bar that I know of is the difficulty of combining liberation with a secure income for my wife in the event of my death or incapacity.[1]

As I said, I have used up the whole of my holiday, and therefore the most I can hope for is a hasty weekend in Paris later in the year. If I am able to come over for a day or two I hope that I may find you there and call on you, and I shall be very glad to know whether you expect to be away from Paris the whole of the summer.

Richard Aldington by the way is living in the country: his address is Malthouse Cottage, Padworth, near Reading, Berks.[2]

I have been trying to find a publisher for Valéry's *Le Serpent* together with Captain Wardle's translation.[3]

Will you write to me again?

Yours sincerely,
T. S. Eliot

TO *F. S. Flint* CC

[13?] May 1923 [London]

Dear Flint,

Would you be willing to undertake for the next number the translation of an article by Jacques Rivière on Freud?[4] I have not had time to read it myself but I think that it ought to be of some interest.

I must explain in passing that the payment to contributors for the number 3 and a great deal of other business has been delayed owing to the fact that I have had to throw up everything for the time and remain for the past month in the country with my wife who has been very dangerously ill.

Yours in haste,
[T. S. E.]

1 – Barney said Lady Rothermere had told her that it was not as easy as EP and she had hoped to free TSE from the Bank – 'because of the many occupations' he seemed interested in.
2 – Barney wanted RA to telephone her to discuss her conversations with Rémy de Gourmont.
3 – The English translation of Valéry's poem was ultimately published by RC-S (1924). Barney was considering ways of subsidising Valéry as well as EP.
4 – On 16 May, Flint said he thought Rivière 'a good critic' but inclined 'to the high-falutin' style'. Flint's translation appeared as Rivière, 'Notes on a Possible Generalisation of the Theories of Freud', C. 1: 4 (July 1923).

TO *Antonio Marichalar*[1] TS Real Academia de la Historia

14 May 1923 *The Criterion*, 17 Thavies Inn

Cher Monsieur,

Merci de vos deux lettres et de l'envoi du résumé de votre Conférence.[2] J'avais l'intention de vous écrire il y a longtemps – mais pendant les dernières 5 semaines j'ai dû laisser toutes mes affaires et rester à la campagne près du lit de ma femme qui a été dangéreusement malade. Pour cette raison aussi, puisque je n'avais laissé aucun remplaçant à Londres, la bonification des collaborateurs est en retard. Je vous fais toutes mes excuses. Je suis rentré hier à Londres où je me trouve comblé d'affaires importantes arriéreés.

Je suis bien content que vous êtes satisfait de la traduction de votre article.[3] C'est facheux qu'on a dû découper l'article mais on a dû restreindre l'étendue du numéro 3 et plusieurs de nos collaborateurs ont souffert. J'espère plus tard pouvoir disposer de plus nombreuses feuilles et vous rendre justice la prochaine fois.

J'étais bien intrigué par le compte-rendu de votre Conférence. *Est ce qu'il vous serait possible de m'en laisser voir le texte intégral?*

Avec toutes mes félicitations sur le succès de votre article, croyez moi, bien à vous,

T. S. Eliot[4]

1 – Antonio Marichalar, Marqués de Montera (1893–1973), Spanish author, wrote articles for *Revista de Occidente* (his subjects including Joyce, Valéry and Virginia Woolf).

2 – Marichalar's letters do not seem to survive; the subject of the lecture is not known.

3 – 'Contemporary Spanish Literature', trans. Mde S. A. Middleton, C. 1: 3 (Apr. 1923), 277–92. Marichalar (19 Apr. 1923) thought the translation '*excellente*', and the cuts '*sans importance*'.

4 – *Translation*: Dear Sir, Thank you for your two letters and for the abstract of your lecture. I intended to write to you some time ago but, during the last five weeks, I have had to interrupt all my activities in order to stay in the country at the bedside of my wife who has been dangerously ill. This is also the reason why payment to contributors has been delayed, since there was no one to replace me in London. I sincerely apologise for this. I returned to London yesterday and find myself overwhelmed by important matters waiting to be settled.

I am pleased that you are satisfied with the translation of your article. It is a pity we had to make some cuts, but we had to reduce the length of the third number and several of our contributors have had to suffer. I hope to have more pages available later and to do full justice to your contribution next time.

I was most interested by the abstract of your lecture. *Would it be possible for you to let me see the full text?*

With all my congratulations on the success of your article, Yours ever, T. S. Eliot

TO *Iris Barry*[1] TS Buffalo

14 May 1923 *The Criterion*, 17 Thavies Inn

Dear Miss Barry,

I have read your story with interest and amusement but I am returning it because I think that in its present form at least it is not quite suitable for the *Criterion*. It seems to me that you have a very good and amusing idea but that the point ought to be made more quickly and sharply. That is, the whole thing needs a good deal of condensation. For instance, it appears to me that the description of the lady's appetite is an unnecessary addition. Having stated the personality of the hero and the heroine the point should be more quickly concentrated on the episode on the staircase. This does not mean however that the story might not be extremely suitable in its present form for some paper with more space at its disposal.

Be sure that we shall always be glad to consider anything you submit and that it would have been a pleasure to me, had I not been exceptionally pressed for time, to have criticised this contribution in much greater detail. Will you send something soon?

Yours very truly,
T. S. Eliot

TO *Wilhelm Lehmann* TS Texas

14 May 1923 *The Criterion*, 17 Thavies Inn

Dear Sir,

Thank you for your letter of the 16th April which I have been unable to answer because of absence in the country. I have ordered a copy of No 3 of the *Criterion* to be sent to you and I shall send you as soon as possible a copy of *The Sacred Wood* with my compliments. I am glad to hear that you have received some numbers of the *Dial*. If your subscription does not include the November number in which *The Waste Land* was printed, please let me know.

I am very much interested in what you say about contemporary German literature, as I had suspected that the *Dial* had perhaps made a few

1–Iris Barry (1895–1969): British writer, now known principally for her film criticism: in 1935 she was to become a curator at the Museum of Modern Art, New York, where she inaugurated film study. She wrote criticism for the *Spectator*, 1923–30, and was film critic of the *Daily Mail*, 1926–30; author of *Let's Go to the Movies* (1926) and *Splashing into Society: A Humorous Tale* (1923).

mistakes.[1] It would be a great favour if you could arrange to have sent me a representative book by each of the two men you mention, Moritz Heimann and Oscar Loerke.[2] It is impossible in any country to find out through the official press who are the really important people; the German writer who has been the most spoken of here lately is Ernst Toller[3] whose work seems to me somewhat overrated. I should be very glad also if you would send me some book of your own. Of course I shall be glad to pay for anything you are kind enough to send me; for it is very difficult and very tedious getting anything through London booksellers.

I am pleased that you should have liked my article in the *Nouvelle Revue Française*.[4] Had time and anxieties permitted, I should already have followed it up with another one.

If you are in communication with Curtius will you please give him my cordial salutations.

Sincerely yours
T. S. Eliot

I shall be glad of your opinion on *The Waste Land* when you see it, because I think it might translate better into German than into any other tongue.[5]

TSE

TO *Ezra Pound* — TS Lilly

14 May 1923 — 9 Clarence Gate Gdns

Dear Ezra

Your letters of the 6th and 11th received *with many thanks*. Before dealing with the enclosed cheques I wish first to ask whether these funds in any way affect your own pocket. This is important and deserves a

1–On 28 Aug. 1922 TSE had told E. R. Curtius, 'I know almost nothing of German literature since 1914.' Under the influence of Scofield Thayer in Vienna, the *Dial* published work by Arthur Schnitzler, Hugo von Hofmannsthal, Hermann Hesse, Thomas Mann, Stefan Zweig and Gerhart Hauptmann.
2–Moritz Heimann (1868–1925): German-Jewish playwright, fiction-writer and journalist. Oscar Loerke (1884–1941): German poet, whose *Naturlyrik* was widely influential, particularly on Lehmann; his most recent collection was *Die Heimliche Stadt: Gedichte* (Berlin, 1921).
3–Ernst Toller (1893–1939): German dramatist, initially associated with Expressionism; later responsible for more realistic political theatre such as *Die Maschinenstürmer* [*The Machine-Wreckers*] (1922).
4–TSE, 'Lettre d'Angleterre', *NRF* 19: 111 (1 Dec. 1922).
5–*TWL* was translated into German by E. R. Curtius as *Das Wüste Land*, in *Neue Schweizer Rundschau* (1 Apr. 1927), reprinted in T. S. Eliot, *Ausgewählte Gedichte* (Frankfurt, 1951).

truthful and not misleading reply. I wish also to make quite clear that I am not *at the moment* forced to borrow money or to realise any of the trust fund which I believe I have explained to you. If this £20 is to cover immediate and inevitable expenses I must let you know that even without it I shall not be quite penniless within the next few weeks. <Not that [it] wd not be very useful – but I wish to be quite clear.> It is true that expenses have been [very *del.*] <ruinously!> heavy and likely that they will continue to be heavy. If you wish me to keep the money I will again explain – in case I have not done so before – the nature of the special fund.

The *Dial* prize, and any other voluntary contributions which I receive while still in the bank, and any money I can save out of my ordinary income, are placed to a special account which is invested in securities of the highest class as it accumulates. The income from such investments will be paid into the same account and capitalised for reinvestment. A fund is thus constituted upon which I do not propose to draw so long as I have my regular salary*. <*exc. to keep out of debt.> It will constitute a small foundation but at least reliable as long as the capitalist system continues.

Vivien does not seem to improve with any rapidity and the situation is rather a dilemma; she is hardly well enough to remain in the country but hardly seems likely to get better if brought back to town. Later on, I should like her to get abroad, especially as like all sensible persons she finds the civilisation of England extremely depressing; but for some time it is extremely unlikely that she will be fit to travel. At best, she has in a few weeks lost more than all the benefit she gained from a year's strict and detestable regime, and of course it takes anybody a very long time to recover from the shock of having been consciously so very near to death. <Still very anxious.>[1]

Thanks for miscellaneous information. Is the *Dial* going to pieces? It will sooner or later ruin itself by its mania for popular names and by its lack of any one genuine intelligence directing its policy. I am assured by a German correspondent that up-to-date Germans consider it all wrong in its Teutonic selections; I give this merely for what it may be worth, but it

1 – EP wrote to Ford Madox Ford at about this time: 'Eliot's wife was at the point of death for three weeks during the time when he would, otherwise, have been making his calculations for July contents. Consequently he has got to break his promise to someone IF he is to save me from extinction. <I mean he has promised more space than he has.>' *Pound/Ford: The Story of a Literary Friendship*, ed. Brita Lindberg-Seyersted (1982).

does strike me that there is too much Hauptmann.[1] Gide is exactly the sort of person whom one would expect Scofield to respect.

I shall see whether I can press for subsequent publication with any success. (Am anxious to publish & damn the *Dial*. Does not affect it so far as *I* am concerned.)[2] Thirty pages is rather a lot, but perhaps we could use slightly smaller type without affecting the rates of payment.[3] The payment *must* be increased to select contributors for select work. Anyway, I will write you about this again.

Yrs
T

<Have rcd. 3 Mntns autobiog.>[4] But have literally read nothing for six weeks. Saving this up.

TO *Herbert Read* — TS Victoria

14 May 1923 — *The Criterion*, 17 Thavies Inn

Dear Read,

This is just a note to congratulate you on the success of your essay in the April *Criterion*.[5] Newspaper notices, such as they are, do not give much evidence of the comparative success of the contributions of a quarterly review, so I wanted to let you know that your essay has been praised to me from several different quarters and I am sure it has contributed largely to the good opinion that seems to be held of this number. I hope to have something more from you soon and will before very long suggest a book as a possible [egg *del.*] peg for an article.[6]

1–Gerhart Hauptmann (1862–1946): dramatist, novelist and poet, whose 'The Heretic of Soana' (an extract from his novel *Der Ketzer von Soana* [1918] had appeared in *Dial* 74: 4 (Apr. 1923) and 74: 5 (May 1923).

2–Scofield Thayer was deeply sceptical about EP's *Cantos*, which were due for simultaneous publication in the *Dial* and C. but were never in fact published in the *Dial*. Making use of the famous phrase 'Publish and be damned' (attributed to the Duke of Wellington when threatened with blackmail), TSE plays the two magazines off against each other. EP published a 'Paris Letter' in *Dial* 74: 3 (Mar. 1923); but thereafter, owing to Thayer's dislike of his work, nothing further until 'Part of Canto XXVII' in 84: 1 (Jan. 1928).

3–Pound's 'Malatesta Cantos', in *C.* 1: 4 (July 1923), 363–84, were not printed in smaller type.

4–The Three Mountains Press, a small press set up in 1922 by Bill Bird (1888–1963), brought out EP's *Indiscretions: or, Une Revue de Deux Mondes* (1923), the first of the 'Inquest' series.

5–HR, 'The Nature of Metaphysical Poetry', *C.* 1: 3 (Apr. 1923), 246–66.

6–HR became a regular contributor to *C.*, his next major article being 'Psycho-Analysis and the Critic', *C.* 3: 10 (Jan. 1925).

I am looking forward to the appearance of your *Phoenix*.[1]

Sincerely
TSE

Payment soon – Delayed. I have been in the country – my wife has been dangerously ill there.

TO *E. R. Curtius*[2] CC

14 May 1923 [9 Clarence Gate Gdns]

Dear Mr Curtius,

I have been too occupied with business and personal anxieties for some time to be able to write to you, but I have wished to say this; I believe that you are a member of the Faculty of Marburg University, and if you think that it would be of interest to a sufficient number of the Faculty or of the undergraduates, I should be glad to arrange to have a copy of the *Criterion* sent regularly to the library of the University. This is in memory of my affection for the town and my respect to the University where but for the war I should have been a student.[3]

Please remember I shall always be glad to hear from you and to send you any book that you specially desire.

Sincerely yours
[T. S. E.]

TO *Aldous Huxley*[4] CC

14 May 1923 [London]

Dear Aldous,

In the course of several upheavals I have again lost your address but I am sure this will reach you. It is just to remind you that you have promised me your essay on Wit[5] by the beginning of July, and that I hope we may have it even sooner. Will you let me know what the title will be?

1 – HR, *Mutations of the Phoenix* (1923), published in May.
2 – Ernst Robert Curtius: see Glossary of Names.
3 – TSE went to Marburg in 1914 as a postgraduate student in philosophy, only to have his stay cut short almost immediately by the outbreak of WW1.
4 – Aldous Huxley: see Glossary of Names. TSE had known Huxley since 1917.
5 – AH's essay on 'Wit' never appeared in C. He had earlier published 'On Wit' – a review of Paul Elmer More, *With the Wits* – in *A.* (28 May 1920); reprinted in 'Aldous Huxley's Early Excursions into Literary Criticism: Some Lesser-Known Essays', ed. James Sexton, *Aldous Huxley Annual* 2 (2002), 24–7.

I have just returned to London after a most awful month of anxiety in the country and I am overwhelmed with arrears of work. Will you lunch with me some day in the city, as I see no immediate prospect of seeing anybody in any other way.

Yours ever,
[T. S. E.]

TO *Sydney Schiff* PC Valerie Eliot

[Postmark 15 May 1923] [9 Clarence Gate Gdns]

Vivien improves *very* slowly, and is weak to the last point, and has relapses, so we are by no means at ease. The Chichester doctor comes daily. I am going down as early in the week as I can get away. Crushed with pressure of affairs, and in great haste

Yrs. aff.
T

TO *Valery Larbaud*[1] TS Vichy

16 May 1923 *The Criterion*, 17 Thavies Inn

Dear Larbaud,

Had time and anxieties permitted I should have written to you already some weeks ago. You must remember that you promised the *Criterion* an essay or a series of essays, or part of what might become a book, on Walter Savage Landor.[2] *The Criterion* is counting upon this to start its autumn season. Have you been able to make progress with it, and do you think that you could let us have it – or a section of it, if what you will let us have is long – by July? I have hoped, as you know, that you might introduce in the *Criterion* what would develop into a book which I feel pretty sure I could get published in this country – possibly under the auspices of the *Criterion* itself.

1 – Valery Larbaud: see Glossary of Names.

2 – On 20 Mar. 1922 TSE had told Larbaud he 'would be particularly pleased at having the honour of publishing first something of yours on Landor'. (Larbaud had begun a doctorate on Landor.) He reiterated this on 8 Nov. 1922, but nothing else by Larbaud was published in *C.*

I have just received the 14th edition of the *Poésies de A. O. Barnabooth*.[1] I had never seen them before – I read *Barnabooth* as it came out in the *NRF*[2] – and I read every word of the book last night in the train coming up from Chichester. They interested me so much that I cannot understand why I have never read them before. If I may say so, there is one poem in particular which struck me as saying something which had never been said before but as expressing a feeling which I have felt myself very strongly: '*Le don de soi-même*'.[3] But furthermore I think I see in this book the parentage of what is now a very distinct frame of mind among our contemporaries.[4]

Is there any possibility of your coming to London this year?

Sincerely yours,
T. S. Eliot

TO *Herbert Read* MS Victoria

[? Late May 1923] [London]

Dear Read

Many thanks for the *Phoenix*.[5] It is beautifully done, and I am looking forward to reading it with the care it demands and deserves. The Donne[6] has struck me (at a mere glance) as containing undigested Browning (it is hard to get away from him) and less ripe than the rest.

Jargon – yes – it is very difficult to write good prose nowadays on a technical study.[7] Psychology is worse than anything because it is a young science (if it be a science)[8] and hardly born before jargonising was well

1–Larbaud published the *Poèmes* of A. O. Barnabooth in 1908 in a two-vol. '*Oeuvres françaises complètes*'. It was reprinted as *A. O. Barnabooth: ses oeuvres complètes, c'est-à-dire un conte, ses poésies et son journal intime* in 1913. The 13th and 14th editions came out in 1923.
2–*A. O. Barnabooth: Journal d'un milliardaire* was serialised in four parts in *NRF* 50–54 (1 Feb.–1 June 1913).
3–TSE wrote, in a later year: 'The poetry of flight . . . in contemporary France, owes a great debt to the poems of the A. O. Barnabooth of Valery Larbaud' ('Baudelaire', 1930; *SE*, 428.
4–Larbaud replied (14 June) that TSE's letter made him feel 'very proud': it gave him 'the incentive' he wanted to 'go on writing at all'.
5–HR, *Mutations of the Phoenix* (1923).
6–HR's poem, 'John Donne Declines a Benefice', 19–24.
7–TSE developed his ideas about modern prose in 'Contemporary English Prose', sub-titled 'A Discussion of the Development of English Prose from Hobbes and Sir Thomas Browne to Joyce and D. H. Lawrence', *Vanity Fair* 20: 5 (July 1923).
8–HR was interested in psycho-analysis and went on to publish 'Psycho-Analysis and the Critic' in *C.* 3: 10 (Jan. 1925). TSE's scepticism towards psychology was evident as early as

advanced. There are Berkeley and Hume,[1] of course. Economics is ruined by it, although Adam Smith could write well.[2]

Yours in haste
T. S. Eliot

TO *Ezra Pound* MS Lilly

20 May 1923 9 Clarence Gate Gdns

Cher E

Very many thanks for your explanation and for your letter. The money will either join the investment fund or be used to prevent my breaking into it. Apart from expenses already incurred, and only partly paid, this disaster is certain to necessitate more expense for a long time to come. It will take Vivien a year to get over this. She won't be able to rough it in a small cottage, and she must go abroad as soon as fit to do so.

If possible, I want to use your cantos in the July no.[3] I am finding out how much space is needed for contributions ordered six months ago & definitely accepted for July, & will then see what can be chucked out, & will put it up to Lady R. If successful, I will wire you for MSS.

I am delighted that you have a period of time which the *Criterion* can profit by. Do you want to do something about Vivante,[4] or about the general subject including Vivante and the establishment of a small critical canon (as discussed by us some time ago).[5] Hurry up and write something before you are too busy or go off on yr. Travels.

---

his PhD thesis *Knowledge and Experience in the Philosophy of F. H. Bradley*, where he wrote: 'popular psychology . . . is the only psychology there is' (81).

1–The idealist Irish philosopher George Berkeley (1685–1753), author of *A Treatise Concerning the Principles of Human Knowledge* (1710), and the sceptical Scottish philosopher David Hume (1711–76), author of *An Enquiry Concerning Human Understanding* (1748).

2–Adam Smith (1723–90): Scottish political economist; author of *An Inquiry into the Wealth of Nations* (1776).

3–On 18 May, EP suggested TSE provide 'a note saying they are IX to XII in a long poem' to explain 'the bewildering numerals above each canto'. 'Think it needs to be read aloud, rather rapidly, in plain matter of fact voice; to get full general swing.' The verses were published as 'Malatesta Cantos (Cantos IX to XII of a Long Poem)' in *C.* 1: 4 (July 1923), 363–84; reprinted, with revisions, as Cantos VIII–XI.

4–On 28 Jan., EP had sent TSE a book by Leone Vivante, *Della Intelligenza nell'Espressione* (1922). The English translation, *Intelligence in Expression*, was reviewed by W. A. Thorpe in C. 3: 11 (Apr. 1925), 463–4.

5–On 28 Jan., EP told TSE he wanted to establish 'a circle of critics – serious characters, with honest, divergent views, who will refer to each other's ideas'. He stipulated: 'There has to *be a recognisable body of discussable criticism* as an instrument to this revaluation.'

More about *Criterion* etc. later. Vivien still in country, as impossible to move her. I have had to leave her entirely in the care of her mother and the young man.[1] She sends her love to you and D[orothy, Pound's wife] and is counting on seeing you this summer *and* again in the winter. On contemplating suicide a short time ago she was going to leave you a letter. Hell.

Yrs
T

<I may be able to make a proposal for book pub. also, later.>

Vivien Eliot TO *Ottoline Morrell* — MS Texas

20 May [1923] — 2 Milestone Cottages, Old Fishbourne

Dearest Ottoline

How are you my dear? I have been longing to write to you – and to hear from you.

I still feel so ill, so intolerably unsteady, weak, dizzy – *reeling*, that life is a fearful burden.

I hardly know where I am, now. After so great a shock – so many shocks – it is coming back from death and I am still gasping for breath – just *hanging on*. It is not life, I don't know what it is. Time passes, it seems the summer is going – and I can't grasp it. I only wake up and realise every now and then how time is passing.

I don't feel I could ever pick up the old life again. I feel so many hundred miles now from everyone and everything. You understand this don't you?

I found that one of the very few *really happy, stable*, memories I had to hang on to was Garsington. You and Garsington, there is something definite there. *You* have *made* something real, comforting. A form. Excuse incoherence.

My love
Vivien

1 – Unidentified.

TO *Richard Cobden-Sanderson* MS Beinecke

24 May 1923 *The Criterion*, 9 Clarence Gate Gdns

Dear Cobden-Sanderson

I enclose my list of payments – will you check it? please.

I have a parcel of MSS. ready whenever your man can call.

It strikes me that if the *Criterion* is published in America (e.g. as by Liveright) we shall have to extract *American* rights from all contributors – in self protection. Is that not so? and in that case some of the contributors will want more money![1]

Yrs in haste
TSE

TO *Ezra Pound* MS Lilly

Sunday [27 May? 1923] (Returning to) 9 Clarence Gate Gdns

Dear E

I cabled to say we will print poem in July & it will come to about £20. That is the best we can do, esp. *as* it is appearing in the *Dial*.[2] I object strongly on tactical grounds to yr 1st line.[3] People are inclined to think that we write our verses in collaboration as it is, or else that you write mine & I write yours. With your permission we will begin with line 2. No time to write more, still having a hell of a time.

Yrs
T

Will you explain to Ford – I don't know where he is – why we postpone him till October.[4]

I have got Richard [Aldington] to assist, do proof, run exchanges, write letters, & help generally – he is the only person in England I could think of, & I believe will be extremely useful in many ways.

1–US publication did not come to pass.

2–EP replied on 12 June, 'Not the least sure that Cantos *are* appearing in *Dial*'.

3–The opening line of Canto IX (later Canto VIII) was 'These fragments you have shelved (shored)'. When TSE objected to EP's overt allusion to the end of *TWL*: 'These fragments I have shored against my ruins' (l. 430), EP replied on 12 June, 'All right, delete first line, if it worries you.' TSE did so, but EP restored the line in *A Draft of XVI Cantos* (Paris 1925) and in subsequent editions.

4–EP told TSE that Ford's 'present spouse' thought he would not mind his piece being 'postponed'. See also note to TSE's letter to EP of 14 May.

I like cantos immensely, exc. few details of personal fancy. Certainly a great pioneer invention in method.

TO *Jacques Rivière* CC

27 May 1923 [London]

Cher Monsieur,

A propos des inédits de Proust dont nous avons déjà parlé,[1] je viens de voir Lady Rothermere. Je suis maintenant dans une position de proposer une considération au taux de £15 les 5000 mots au lieu de notre taux ordinaire de 10 les 5000 mots. Nous ne pourrons guère dépasser 15, puisque nous devrions payer aussi Monsieur Scott Moncrieff pour la traduction. Je vous saurai bien gré si vous aurez la bonté de soumettre cette proposition au Docteur Proust, parce que si nous parvenons à nous entendre là-dessus je voudrais bien annoncer que le morceau inédit de Proust paraîtra dans notre numéro d'Octobre.

Monsieur F. S. Flint s'est chargé de l'oeuvre de la traduction de votre article et j'ai toute confiance que sa traduction vous plaira.

Ma femme commence à se rétablir très lentement, mais elle ne peut pas encore se déplacer. Je vais la rejoindre à la campagne mercredi pour quinze jours de repos qui me sont devenus essentiels.

Si vous m'écrivez pendant la quinzaine je vous prie d'adresser votre lettre à 2 Milestone Cottages, Old Fishbourne, Chichester, Sussex.

Recevez, cher Monsieur, l'assurance de mes sentiments devoués.

[T. S. E.][2]

1 – M. Proust, 'The Death of Albertine', *C.* 2: 8 (July 1924), 376–94.

2 – *Translation*: Dear Sir, I have just seen Lady Rothermere concerning the articles from Proust's unpublished work which we have already discussed, and I am now able to offer you £15 per 5000 words, instead of the usual rate of £10 per 5000 words. As we also have to pay Mr Scott Moncrieff for the translation, we would find it rather difficult to go beyond £15. I should be grateful to you if you would be kind enough to submit this new proposal to Dr Proust for, if we could reach agreement about it, I should very much like to announce the appearance of this unpublished Proust extract for the October issue.

Mr F. S. Flint has been given the task of translating your article and I am confident that the result will please you.

My wife is beginning very slowly to recover, but she is not yet fit to move about; I am therefore joining her in the country on Wednesday for a fortnight's rest, which has become absolutely necessary for me.

If you wish to write to me during this fortnight, would you please address your letter to 2 Milestone Cottages, Old Fishbourne, Chichester, Sussex.

Please accept, dear Sir, my very kind regards. [T. S. E.]

TO *Richard Aldington* CC

27 May 1923 [London]

Dear Richard,

I have now seen Lady Rothermere and have pleasure in confirming the proposals which I made to you the other night. She has agreed to them verbally without hesitation and I am only awaiting the return of an explicit statement which I am sending to her for her signature.

You will be offered a consideration at the rate of £50 a year to act as secretary, managing editor, or some similar designation [with] the following duties and any other work agreed upon between you and myself: To take charge of the translation of manuscript accepted in foreign languages, to read the proof and fit together the accepted material, to write a page or so of editorial matter for each number over your initials.

The work of managing the foreign reviews comprehends arranging for exchange with such periodicals as you select, correspondence on the subject with these periodicals and distributing for review to whomever you think fit such periodicals as you do not wish to review yourself. As in [*sc.* 'I'] informed you, I have been sending American periodicals to Read and German periodicals to Flint. Flint is also prepared to undertake Spanish, Dutch and Scandinavian periodicals in collaboration with a colleague of his in his ministry. It is understood that you will be paid separately for such reviews of periodicals as you write yourself and for all of your contributions to the paper excepting the editorial page which is included in the consideration named above.

I think that reviews of foreign periodicals should be paid at the same rate as other contributions, i.e. at the rate of £10 per 5,000 words. But they should be kept as short as possible and limited to about four pages of small print, (see *Criterion* No. 3)[1] in each number. Reviewers are not expected to consider any but the most important articles, and doubtless it will often be sufficient to give only a partial list of contents of many of the reviews received. Reviewers should keep their eyes open for anything they see of exceptional merit in order that we may come to know of new foreign writers who would be desirable contributors to the *Criterion*.

I will ask Cobden Sanderson to send you a supply of *Criterion* letter paper.

1 – 'Foreign Reviews', devoted to French, German and US publications, occupied pp. 308–13 of C. 1: 3.

I hope it will be possible to increase the emolument later. At present of course I am not taking anything out of the paper myself, but I think that in future I shall have to be paid for my own contributions at the regular rates.

I am sending you such correspondence as I have had with foreign reviews.

I do not think that we can afford at present to exchange with more than about twenty-five reviews. The list at present is:

Mouton Blanc,[1]
Indice,
Reine de Genève,
Ecrits du Nord,
Convegno,
Neue Rundschau,
Neue Merkur,
Nouvelle Revue Française,
Nation, N.Y.
New Republic,
Dial.

I am not sure that the *Mouton Blanc* is worth while, and *Indice* never appears, but it is desirable to be in touch with somebody in Madrid. If you can find out the names of any other reviews in Spain, Italy, Germany and other countries with which it would be desirable to exchange, it would be a good thing to do.

I have got a fortnight's more leave very generously from the bank and shall be at 2 Milestone Cottages, Old Fishbourne, Chichester, from Wednesday next. I shall tell Sanderson to send proof direct to you.

I enjoyed immensely seeing you the other night and I wish very much that we could meet more often.

Yours,
[T. S. E.]

1–*Mouton Blanc*, an 'organ of modern classicism', was a French review ed. by J. Hytier; *Indice* a Spanish review; '*Reine de Genève*' is a slip for '*Revue de Genève*', a French-language Swiss 'review of the European elite' which ran from 1920 to 1924; *Écrits du Nord*, a monthly review of literature published in Brussels and Paris; *Il Convegno* an Italian review with a strong Futurist presence; *Neue Rundschau* a well-established German literary review founded in 1890; and *Neue Merkur* a German literary periodical, ed. by Efraim Frisch, 1915–25. *The Nation* and *New Republic* were US newspapers with serious literary review sections.

TO *Richard Cobden-Sanderson* MS Beinecke

27 May 1923 *The Criterion*, 9 Clarence Gate Gdns

Dear Cobden-Sanderson,

I have arranged with Lady Rothermere to have Richard Aldington as secretary or assistant editor of the *Criterion* at the rate of £50 per annum, payable quarterly.[1] He is to take entire charge of foreign reviews, proof reading, translations, and any other routine business that I cannot manage myself. This will ensure the continuance of the *Criterion* should I have any more disasters like the one I have just been through, and I believe that it will be a help to you as well as to myself. The amount of routine work and correspondence has increased so much that at best I simply have no time to write myself or to do other things for the paper that I should like to do; and so we have adopted this plan.

Will you send Aldington some *Criterion* letter paper in order that [he] may correspond direct with foreign reviews? I shall continue to select contributions and to approach people who are desirable as contributors, so you may continue, alas, to send me the contributions that come in.

Will you also, when you get a slip proof, please send two copies direct to the author or translator as the case may be and one copy to Aldington instead of to me?

I send you herewith manuscript of a long poem by Ezra Pound and I should like to know as soon as possible how much space it would take, i.e. the number of words that a prose article occupying the same space would contain – in order that I may compare it for length with the contributions we have. If it is possible to get it in, I should like it to go in to the July number. As it will be published in America it must go in the July number or not at all.[2]

Hazells had better go straight ahead setting up all of the ms. If there is too much for this number, it will go into the October number, in any case, so that the galley will not be wasted.

I have got two weeks' more leave from the bank, as I am feeling completely knocked up, and am going back to Fishbourne on Wednesday. So you can write to me there and I will see you about the 15th of June. Meanwhile I shall ask Aldington to carry on with all the things that he

1 – RA had been literary editor of the *Egoist* and worked on the *TLS*.
2 – In the event it was not published in the *Dial*.

can deal with himself. There is a parcel of rejected manuscript waiting here for you.

Yours ever,
TSE

Did you get my statement of amts. due to contributors? (G. Adams[1] c/o Ezra Pound)

TO *Leonard Woolf*[2]

TS Berg

27 May 1923 9 Clarence Gate Gdns

Dear Leonard,

I tried twice to ring up Hogarth House today, but got no reply.[3] I wanted to explain that I have put a good deal of time on this paper[4] – all I had to give – but that I am quite aware that it is a failure, incoherent, badly written, and not long enough for your purpose. Never has my brain been so costive. I only send it in earnest of my good intentions. If you do not think it is good enough to print, send it back.[5] But I cannot attempt anything else for several weeks. I have had to go to the bank and ask for more time, and am going back to Fishbourne on Wednesday for a fortnight's rest, with a prescription and a certificate. During the last week I have been trying to get through business of every sort, and feel completely done up.[6]

How are things going with you, and how is Virginia? I should like to have seen you or at least spoken to you before I left, but it seems impossible.

Yours ever
Tom

1–B. M. Goold-Adams.
2–Leonard Woolf: see Glossary of Names.
3–The Woolfs lived at Hogarth House from Jan. 1920 to Mar. 1924.
4–'John Donne' (rev. of *Love Poems of John Donne*), *N&A* 33: 10 (9 June 1923): TSE's first review since the publication of *TWL* in Oct. 1922.
5–LW offered TSE more time to revise the article (see TSE's letter of 3 June).
6–TSE had dined with the Woolfs on 17 May. On 18 May, VW told Roger Fry that 'strange figure Eliot' had been with them the night before: 'I feel that he has taken the veil, or whatever monks do. He is quite calm again. Mrs Eliot has almost died at times in the past month. Tom, though infinitely considerate, is also perfectly detached. His cell is, I'm sure, a very lofty one, but a little chilly.' (*Letters*, III, 38.)

TO *F. S. Flint* TS Texas

27 May 1923 *The Criterion*, 9 Clarence Gate Gdns

Dear Flint,

I should be glad to know that you received the typed script of Rivière's article on Freud which I sent you some days ago.[1] When the translation is ready will you send it to Richard Aldington? He has accepted the position as secretary to the *Criterion* and will have charge of all the business in connection with translations and with foreign reviews. I am trying to get recent numbers of the two German reviews for you,[2] and will ask you to send your notes to him by the 15th of June. If you come to know of any desirable reviews in German or any of the other numerous languages which you manipulate, will you write to him and recommend them for exchange?

And do not forget that I should welcome from you any suggestions both for an article or for brief notes by you of a more editorial character.[3]

Yours ever,
T. S. Eliot

TO *Charles Whibley* CC

27 May 1923 [London]

My dear Whibley,

When I suggested to you some months ago that it would be a very useful thing and a great kindness if you would write at your leisure an article on Charles Maurras for the *Criterion*, I think that you did not receive the proposal unfavourably. I am now writing in the hope that you have not changed your mind and that you will let me mention among other contributions that we expect in six months or so to have this important contribution from you.

I should like however to suggest an alternative; at one time you proposed writing an essay on Chesterfield[4] and this would be equally acceptable.

1 – 'Notes on a Possible Generalisation of the Theories of Freud', trans. by Flint, in *C.* 1: 4 (July 1923).

2 – Flint reviewed *Neue Rundschau*, but not *Neue Merkur*, in *C.* 1: 4 (July 1923).

3 – Though a frequent contributor to *C.* as reviewer and translator, Flint published little in the way of articles or editorial comments.

4 – Stanhope, Philip Dormer, fourth earl of Chesterfield (1694–1773): politician and diplomat; author of *Letters to his Son*. CW's previous contribution was on Bolingbroke (Henry St John, 1st Viscount Bolingbroke, 1678–1751), whom he described as 'the wisest and most eloquent of the Tories'. CW wrote too: 'Chesterfield, by no means the worst critic of his time, thought

I will tell you frankly what I have in mind. The *Criterion* proposes next year to begin the publication of a very small number of books, exclusively by contributors to the *Criterion* and often composed of or including contributions to the *Criterion.* The first will be a very small book indeed, Valéry's *Serpent* with the translation and introductory essay by myself. What I should very much like would be to have a book of three or four essays by yourself, some of which should have appeared in the *Criterion.* You will see that a book by yourself containing essays on subjects having some[thing] in common with the subject of Bolingbroke, would be an important statement of a position, whether it was Bolingbroke, Chesterfield, Maurras and one or two others and nothing could be more desirable in indicating the standpoint of the *Criterion.*[1]

Of course I do not know what your engagements are, or whether you would in any case consider publishing with anyone but Macmillan.[2] In the state of my ignorance please excuse my having presented to you what may be a wholly unacceptable suggestion, and accept it, if you like, merely as the expression of an impossible wish.

In any case, I am very anxious to have another essay by you in the *Criterion* next winter.

My wife is still extremely feeble and still in a precarious condition, although she is gaining strength. I have obtain[ed] another extension of leave, very generously given by the bank – and am going back to 2 Milestone Cottages, Old Fishbourne, Chichester, on Wednesday for a fortnight. Indeed, I very much need rest; this has been the greatest strain I have ever undergone, and I do not feel any the better for having attempted to make up for the six weeks' arrears of work and correspondence during the fortnight I have been in town.

The work of the *Criterion* will be somewhat relieved, as I have secured Richard Aldington, (whose principles political and literary are nearer to mine than those of anyone whom we could get) to act as secretary to the *Criterion* and take charge of much of the routine.

—

Bolingbroke's style superior to anybody's.' This may have prompted TSE to suggest a companion study of Chesterfield, another eighteenth-century Tory. CW duly contributed 'Lord Chesterfield' to C. 2: 7 (Apr. 1924), 236–57.

1 – TSE's idea that CW's studies of English Tory writers and of Maurras would represent 'the standpoint of the *Criterion*' anticipates his publicity circular of Dec. 1924 which identified the *Criterion* with a philosophy of 'pure Toryism'.

2 – CW's books *Political Portraits* (1917), *Literary Studies* (1919), and *Literary Portraits* (1920) were all published by Macmillan.

I should like to have a word from you to let me know how you are and whether you have been able to make headway against this disastrous season of bad weather.

Yours ever
[T. S. E.]

PS Do you remember that more than six months ago you told me that Stanley Baldwin would be the next Prime Minister?[1]

TO *Lady Rothermere* CC

27 May 1923 [London]

Dear Lady Rothermere

I enclose a letter which embodies all the arrangements we made, as I understand them. If I am wrong, will you let me know; if not, will you sign one copy and return it to me?

I also enclose a sketch of my idea for a monogram for *Criterion* publications; it seemed to me that something bold and simple would be most effective, and I do not greatly admire Cobden-Sanderson's own monogram. What do you think? If this is on the lines you approve, will you tell him so?

I also enclose a list of *Egoist* publications, which is not up to date.[2] But there are only three or four things since: Marianne Moore, and Pound, and H. D., so far as I know.[3] Of course I can do nothing about this until my return.

I presume Cobden-Sanderson will write to you about the cost of printing Valéry [*Le Serpent*], and submit specimens of paper and binding. I have told Wardle to write to him, or to tell Valéry to write to him, about the terms of publication.

I understand from you that your offer to me of a salary of £300 (with a three years guarantee) for editing the *Criterion* in the event of my leaving the bank, will hold good notwithstanding the increase of your guarantee

1–Stanley Baldwin (1867–1947), Chancellor of the Exchequer in 1922, succeeded Bonar Law as Conservative Prime Minister on 22 May 1923.

2–In addition to being a literary review, the *Egoist* had published books by contributors, most notably JJ, *A Portrait of the Artist as a Young Man* (1917), WL, *Tarr* (1918) and TSE, *Prufrock and Other Observations* (1917).

3–Marianne Moore's *Poems* (1921), Ezra Pound's *Quia Pauper Amavi* (1919), and H. D.'s *Hymen* (1921) were all published by The Egoist Press.

for the *Criterion* itself from £600 to £750.[1] I should like to know whether I am quite right – as I may be making plans on this assumption.

From Wednesday, I shall be at 2 Milestone Cottages, Old Fishbourne, near Chichester, Sussex. Your address is 33 quai Voltaire, after this week? I hope I may hear from you in Paris. But I shall ring you up, to say good-bye, before I go!

Always sincerely yours
[T. S. E.]

TO *Herbert Read* CC

27 May 1923 [London]

Dear Read,

I have got Richard Aldington to take charge of the foreign reviews of the *Criterion* and generally to act as secretary of the paper, because there is now much more to do than I am able to cope with myself. Will you therefore send some notes on American periodicals to him at Malthouse Cottage, Padworth, near Reading, Berks, by the 15th of June?[2] I am afraid there is not much for you to write about. If you know of any interesting American reviews which you would like to have will you write to Alding[ton] and ask him to try to get them? I am hoping later to have more brief editorial notes, comments, favourable or damnatory, on current work etc. in the *Criterion* during its second year.[3] I hope that you are willing to associate yourself closely enough with the redaction of the paper to do a certain amount of this, as well as contribute full-dress articles.[4]

Yours ever,
[T. S. E.]

1–Lady Rothermere responded (29 May): 'Yes, *certainly* – my offer holds good – despite of increased expenses!'

2–HR wrote about the latest issues of the *Dial* from Mar. to May 1923, and gave a brief report on the Jan. issues of *Secession*, *Poetry*, *Rhythmus* and *The Double Dealer*.

3–A feature entitled 'Books of the Quarter' began a year later, in C. 2: 8 (July 1924).

4–On 4 June, HR said he was 'very willing to associate myself with the *Criterion* during its second year'.

TO *Harold Monro* TS Beinecke

27 May 1923 9 Clarence Gate Gdns

Dear Monro,

I have had it in mind to write to you for a long time but circumstances of my wife's illness have stopped all correspondence in the last two months. She has had a very dangerous illness under appallingly inconvenient conditions in the country and I have been with her as much as I possibly could. I am returning on Wednesday for a fortnight, having got an extended leave of absence on the ground of my own health which of course has suffered incidentally.

So I am extremely sorry that I shall be unable to come and make the acquaintance of Mr Robinson.[1] I should very much have liked to meet him. I can only hope that he as well as yourself will be in town after June 15th. Will you tell him how very sorry I am that circumstances prevent me coming.

I have wanted to express my appreciation of your comments on *The Waste Land* in *The Chapbook*.[2] They have given me a great deal of pleasure, especially as so much nonsense has been written about the poem in America.

I have received from America a book about Wordsworth[3] which I think might interest you. It is by a professor in the university of Wisconsin and is of course the usual American heavy professional production, but I saw one or two pages which struck me as not unintelligent. You are one of the few persons to recognise the merit of Wordsworth's prefaces and I wonder if it would amuse you to use this book as a peg for a note or a short essay on Wordsworth to appear in the *Criterion*.[4] I hope the idea interests you, and if you let me know at once I should like to send you the book before I go away.

1–Edwin Arlington Robinson (1869–1935), US poet. On 25 May, Monro said Robinson wished to meet TSE, and suggested supper at the Poetry Bookshop on 4 or 5 June.

2–Monro, 'Notes for Study of *The Waste Land*: an Imaginary Dialogue with T. S. Eliot', *Chapbook* 34 (Feb. 1923), 10–24. 'Most poems of any significance leave one definite impression on the mind. This poem makes a variety of impressions, many of them so contradictory that a large majority of minds will never be able to reconcile them, or conceive of it as an entity.'

3–Arthur Beatty, *William Wordsworth: His Doctrine and Art in their Historical Relations* (1922).

4–See Monro's 'Wordsworth Revisited', which touched on Beatty's book, as well as on Emile Legouis, *Wordsworth in a New Light*, and H. W. Garrod, *Wordsworth*, in *C.* 2: 8 (July 1924).

I wish that you would tell me about the preparation[1] you mention and its properties and what it is for. Many thanks indeed.

Sincerely yours
T. S. Eliot

TO *Harriet Monroe*[2] TS Houghton

28 May 1923 9 Clarence Gate Gdns

Dear Miss Monroe,

Thank you for your letter. I shall be very glad indeed to see you as soon as it is possible for us to meet. It has been impossible for me lately to see anyone: I had to be in the country for a month with my wife who has been very dangerously ill there; I have been in London for a few days but I am returning to the country on Tuesday to be with my wife and to get a rest which I very much need. But as you say in your letter that you will be in London throughout June I shall look forward to seeing you upon my return in the latter part of the month.[3] Meanwhile I hope that the English climate will be more friendly toward you than it has been these past weeks. We have had the dreariest month of May that I have ever known here.

Yours sincerely,
T. S. Eliot

TO *Captain Mark Wardle* CC

28 May 1923 [9 Clarence Gate Gdns]

My dear Wardle,

I think that at last I am in a position to give you something definite about the *Serpent*. The Woolfs went away to Spain for a month before making a decision and I myself – you will remember you rang me up on the telephone shortly before I left – have been through a most terrible experience, having had my wife very ill, at the point of death, in a small cottage in a remote part of the country. I was with her continuously for five

1 – In his letter of 25 May, Monro suggested VHE might benefit from 'an amazing and quite genuine thing called Yahdil' which cured people with apparently chronic troubles. On 25 June, he said he was sending *The Yadil Book*, a 'sumptuous volume' with more about this 'panacea'.

2 – Harriet Monroe: see Glossary of Names.

3 – Monroe was staying at 58 Bloomsbury St, London.

weeks. She improves very slowly and not without relapses. I am completely exhausted myself having been wholly unable to attend to business during that time and having endeavoured to attend to the arrears during the last fortnight. I am returning to the country on Wednesday for another fortnight, having secured leave of absence from the bank on account of my own very dilapidated condition.

The Woolfs would have liked to publish the *Serpent* but owing to prior commitments would be unable to do so until some time this winter. I can now tell you that Lady Rothermere is very anxious to publish it and will have it published for the *Criterion* by Cobden-Sanderson, as the first of a projected series of publications by contributors to the review. Cobden-Sanderson knows all there is to know about book-making, and Lady Rothermere is very anxious that the book should be very well done. As for the terms of publication, may I suggest that you put yourself in touch with Cobden-Sanderson and make the necessary arrangements, or that Valéry should do so himself. I should be glad to help further but it is impossible at the present time for me to undertake such negotiations.

The Hogarth Press, I believe, does not usually make contracts but simply pays royalties as it gets money in hand. I think that the *Criterion* would prefer a more business-like arrangement and would either pay a sum down for the rights in the English language or a royalty by contract.

It is proposed to publish the book in October. I wonder if you would be so good as to get me, if it is acceptable to Valéry that I should write the preface,[1] or ask Valéry to have sent me, copies of some of his works which I have not got. I have *Charmes*[2] but I should like to have the introduction to *Lionado*[3] and the *Soirée avec Monsieur Teste*[4] as well before writing about either of them. Is there anything else that I ought to know?

My address after Wednesday will be 2 Milestone Cottages, Old Fishbourne, Chichester, Sussex, for a fortnight only, and I should be delighted to hear from you.

Sincerely yours,
[T. S. E.]

1–On 19 Mar., Wardle said Valéry initially wanted Lytton Strachey to write a preface for *Le Serpent* but had accepted TSE's offer 'with gratitude'.

2–Paul Valéry, *Charmes ou Poèmes* (1922), his major collection of poems after *La jeune parque* (1917), included *Le cimetière marin* which TSE thought 'one of his finest poems'.

3–Valéry, *Introduction à la méthode de Léonard de Vinci* (1895), his first important publication: an investigation into the psychology of creation.

4–Valéry, *La soirée avec monsieur Teste* (1896). In his 'Brief Introduction to the Method of Paul Valéry' TSE observed that a 'poet who is also a metaphysician' would be 'a monster, just as (in my opinion) M. Valéry's Monsieur Teste is a monster'.

TO *Richard Cobden-Sanderson* TS Beinecke

28 May 1923 *The Criterion*, 9 Clarence Gate Gdns

Dear Cobden-Sanderson,

Thank you for your kind letter. I ought to have explained that I like to pay more for verse than for prose and that I am allowing more to Captain Wardle than is usual because his translation is more important, i.e. is responsible for a larger proportion of the interest than in the case of most translations. Also with regard to the Koteliansky and similar cases where the translator has the right to some valuable manuscript of a dead author,[1] and so that through the translator we get the advantage of a 'scoop', I think that the translator ought to be paid at the ordinary prose rates.

You are always very considerate about bothering me, but I hope that you will let me know as soon as you hear from Hazell the particulars about the Ezra Pound poem. I shall have to deal at least with this one matter while I am away in order to decide finally on the makeup of No. 4.

As soon as you have some more of the *Criterion* letter paper with the Cobden-Sanderson address on it I shall be glad if you will let me have a supply – I shall be sorry to think that my absence from town will be putting more labour or worry upon you.

Yours ever,
TSE

PS Would you grudge sending copies of No 3 to the following persons whom I have invited to contribute:

Professor G. Elliot Smith, 31 Belsize Gardens [Crescent], N.W.3.
Miss Rebecca West, 36 Queens Gate Terrace, S.W.
Professor A. B. Keith, 4 Crawford Place, Craigmillar Park, Edinburgh.
F. M. Cornford Esq, Trinity College, Cambridge.
W. Trotter Esq, c/o T. Fisher Unwin Ltd, 1 Adelphi Terrace.
Professor A. S. Eddington, The Observatory, Cambridge.

1 – See Koteliansky's translation of Dostoevsky's 'Plan of the Novel *The Life of a Great Sinner*', C. 1: 1 (Oct. 1922), and of 'Two Unpublished Letters' in C. 1: 3 (Apr. 1923).

TO *S. S. Koteliansky* TS BL

28 May 1923 *The Criterion*, 9 Clarence Gate Gdns

My dear Koteliansky,

I have had to be out of London almost continuously since the time when you sent me your translation of the *Reminiscences of Andreyev*.[1] I do not know whether you have heard any news of me so I will explain that my wife nearly died of influenza in the country and that I had to drop all business and be with her for five weeks. During the last week I have been in town endeavouring to rescue my affairs from the disorder into which they have fallen, and especially affairs of the *Criterion*. But I now find my own health so bad that I must return to the country on Wednesday for a fortnight's complete rest.

On returning to town I have discovered among other misfortunes that there is so much material from authors whom I have *asked* to contribute which will either have to go into the July number or not at all, that I should be unable after all to use but an insignificant fragment of Gorki at best. It is a very long thing but I do not think that it ought [to] be cut more than half. It would be a pity to cut it as much as that. If you approve, I will retain the manuscript and use half of it in the October number; if not I can only offer my apologies for a muddle which I hope will not occur again.

I am sorry not to have the opportunity of seeing you but I shall again look forward to a meeting on my return in June.

Sincerely yours,
T. S. Eliot

TO *G. Elliot Smith*[2] CC

28 May 1923 [*The Criterion*, London]

Sir,

I take the liberty of writing to you on behalf of the *Criterion*. As it is possible that you have not seen or heard of this review, which was started

1 – *Reminiscences of Leonid Andreyev* by Maxim Gorky (1868–1936) trans. S. S. Koteliansky and Katherine Mansfield, was published by Heinemann in 1922.

2 – Sir Grafton Elliot Smith (1871–1937), anatomist and anthropologist, was appointed in 1919 Professor of Anatomy at University College, London, where he set up the Institute of Anatomy which developed rapidly in renown and influence. He was awarded the Royal Medal of the Royal Society, 1912; the Honorary Gold Medal of the Royal College of Surgeons, 1930; and the Huxley Medal, 1936; and he was knighted in 1934. His books include *The Ancient Egyptians* (1911) and *Evolution of the Dragon* (1919). By his middle

in October last, I enclose a copy of a circular which was issued at the time, which will give you some notion of the character of the paper and its contributors. A further circular reviewing the first year's accomplishment will be issued in July. It is desired during the second year to extend the scope of the paper and include work not only by the most important men of letters, both English and foreign, but also by distinguished scholars and men of science. Professor W. P. Ker has contributed a paper for the October number,[1] and Sir James Frazer[2] has promised his collaboration also.

The *Criterion* does not aim at a very large circulation, but aims solely at publishing the highest class of work. While a contribution to this paper does not reach a very large audience, it probably receives more intelligent attention than a contribution to any other review and the audience is not limited to Great Britain. The *Criterion* would be very greatly honoured by a contribution from you on some ethnological or anthropological subject. While we cannot, of course, publish papers which are only intelligible to the readers of technical reviews, we believe that distinguished scientists ought occasionally to address themselves to the cultivated public in general. There is of course no question of including 'popular science' articles in the *Criterion*. Our rates of payment must at present be very modest, at the rate of £10 per 5000 words, and articles should not greatly exceed that length.

Should you consent to promise a contribution for next winter I should be extremely grateful; and if you accept in principle, I will ask the secretary, Mr Richard Aldington, to discuss any details with you later.[3]

—

years, as a result of his fascination with the anthropology and customs of ancient Egypt, he became a proselytising 'diffusionist' – all human culture evolved out of Egypt – and published a series of popularising books on the subject, inc. *The Evolution of Man: Essays* (1924) and *The Search for Man's Ancestors* (1931). TSE said his 'recent theories' were 'of interest and importance to every student or practitioner of the arts, as indeed they should be to everyone who would pay any attention to the history and the future of the human race' (*C.* 2: 8 [1924], 489), and invited WL to review *The Evolution of Man* and *Egyptian Mummies* (written by Elliot Smith and Warren R. Dawson) in *C.* 3: 10 (Jan. 1925).

1–W. P. Ker, 'Byron: An Oxford Lecture', *C.* 2: 5 (Oct. 1923).

2–Sir James Frazer (1854–1941): social anthropologist and classical scholar; author of *The Golden Bough* (first edn pub. 1890), which TSE hailed as 'a work of no less importance for our time than the complementary work of Freud – throwing its light on the obscurities of the soul from a different angle'. TSE thought Frazer's 'vision' and 'fine prose style' gave him 'an inevitable and growing influence over the contemporary mind' ('A Prediction in Regard to Three Authors', *Vanity Fair* 21: 6 [Feb. 1924]). TSE's first note in *TWL* acknowledged that he was 'indebted in general' to *The Golden Bough*, a work which he says 'has influenced our generation profoundly'. However, nothing by Frazer appeared in *C.*

3–See G. Elliot Smith, 'The Glamour of Gold', *C.* 3: 11 (Apr. 1925).

Hoping that I may hear from you.

I am,
Sir,
[T. S. E.]

TO *S. S. Koteliansky* MS BL

29 May 1923 *The Criterion*, 17 Thavies Inn

My dear Koteliansky

Your letter crossed mine. Of course I should not object – I shd have no right to object – to your using part in the *Cassell's Weekly*.[1] I think there is really far too much for our small size and infrequent appearance anyway, and we should simply not use that part. So I imagine that you would like to have MSS. back for the time and send it regd. tomorrow. Excuse haste – I leave in the morning and I hope to see you late in June.

Sincerely yours
T. S. Eliot

TO *May Sinclair*[2] CC

29 May 1923 [London]

Dear Miss Sinclair,

It is a long time since I have seen you or communicated with you but this winter and spring have been a very crowded and anxious time for me divided between domestic anxieties and *Criterion* business routine and I have seen myself forced to sacrifice each to the other. At the beginning of April my wife had a disastrous attack of influenza in the country from which she nearly died and I have had to be out of town most of the time since then.

I am hoping that things will proceed more smoothly, because I have secured the assistance of Richard Aldington to take over a great deal of the work and help me in various ways with the *Criterion* and I am sure you will agree that there is no one better I could have found.

1 – A reference to *Reminiscences of Leonid Andreyev* by Maxim Gorky, which Koteliansky had offered to C. *Cassell's Weekly* ran from 21 Mar. to 27 Oct. 1923, before metamorphosing into *T. P.'s and Cassell's Weekly*, 1923–9.

2 – May Sinclair: see Glossary of Names.

In July we expect to issue a circular in the attempt to secure a larger circulation. At present it fluctuates, so far as we can judge, between 800 and 1000. A thousand copies of the first number have been sold and the sales of all three numbers continue. I should like to see the circulation doubled in this country and see it reach a thousand in America as this does not seem to be beyond the bounds of possibility. The circular will sum up the performance of the first year and outline the work of the second year. May we hope to receive a story from you for one of the numbers of the second year?[1] I say a story, not an article, simply because it is a hundred times more difficult to secure a story up to the standard which we have set ourselves – and which you set for us in the first number[2] – four times a year, than it is to get half a dozen good articles. I am painfully aware that any contribution from you is a kindness at a financial sacrifice to yourself, because there are so many other periodicals which would be only too glad to pay you very much more. To a few contributors like yourself, we shall be able to give double rates – i.e. £20 for 5000 words, but only [on] the condition that we have first serial rights for both England and America.

I should always be interested to hear from you, and grateful for any criticisms or suggestions you have to make on the numbers of the *Criterion* that have appeared.[3] They would be most valuable.

Yours always sincerely,
[T. S. E.]

TO *A. S. Eddington*[4] CC

29 May 1923 [*The Criterion*, London]

Sir,

I take the liberty of writing to you on behalf of the *Criterion*. As it is possible that you have not seen or heard of this review, which was started in October last, I enclose a copy of a circular which was issued at the time, which will give you some notion of the character of the paper and its contributors. A further circular reviewing the first year's accomplishment

1 – Sinclair's 'Jones's Karma', *C.* 2: 5 (Oct. 1923) – 'a story TSE always admired' (EVE).
2 – 'The Victim', *C.* 1: 1 (Oct. 1922) was the first piece of new fiction published in *C.*
3 – On 3 Nov. 1923, Sinclair wrote to thank TSE for *TWL*, saying he had 'never done anything more purely *beautiful*, more haunting & more terrible'.
4 – Sir Arthur Eddington, OM (1882–1944): English theoretical physicist and astrophysicist, whose *Space, Time and Gravitation* (1920) helped to popularise Einstein's theory of relativity. His later works include *The Mathematical Theory of Relativity* (1923).

will be issued in July. It is desired during the second year to extend the scope of the paper and include work not only by the most important men of letters, both English and foreign, but also by distinguished scholars and men of science. Professor W. P. Ker has contributed a paper for the October number, and Sir James Frazer has promised his collaboration also.

The *Criterion* does not aim at a very large circulation, but aims solely at publishing the highest class of work. While a contribution to this paper does not reach a very large audience, it probably receives more intelligent attention than a contribution to any other review and the audience is not limited to Great Britain. The *Criterion* would be very greatly honoured by a contribution from you on some subject within your own field which educated and intelligent persons of only the ordinary mathematical training could understand. While we cannot, of course, publish papers which are only intelligible to the readers of technical reviews, we believe that distinguished scientists ought occasionally to address themselves to the cultivated public in general. There is of course no question of including 'popular science' articles in the *Criterion*. Our rates of payment must at present be very modest – at the rate of £10 per 5000 words – and articles should not greatly exceed that length.

Should you consent to promise a contribution for next winter I should be extremely grateful; and if you accept in principle, I will ask the secretary, Mr Richard Aldington, to discuss any details with you later. I have asked Mr Cobden Sanderson to send you a copy of the April number.

Hoping that I may hear from you.[1]

I am, sir, your obedient servant

[T. S. E.]

TO *Jane Harrison*[2] CC

29 May 1923 *The Criterion*, 17 Thavies Inn

Madam,

I take the liberty of writing to you on behalf of the *Criterion*. As it is possible that you have not seen or heard of this review, which was started

1–Replying on 3 June, Eddington said that while he shared TSE's 'wish that science may be adequately represented in reviews appealing to the cultivated public', he had 'little time and energy for all I should like to attempt'. He did not contribute to C.

1–Jane Harrison (1850–1928): pioneering scholar of Greek religion, with anthropological interests. She was a fellow of Newnham College, Cambridge, until 1922, when she went to live with Hope Mirrlees in Paris. Her *Epilegomena to Greek Religion* had appeared in 1921.

in October last, I enclose a copy of a circular which was issued at the time, which will give you some notion of the character of the paper and its contributors. A further circular reviewing the first year's accomplishment will be issued in July. It is desired during the second year to extend the scope of the paper and include work not only by the most important men of letters, both English and foreign, but also by distinguished scholars and men of science. Professor W. P. Ker has contributed a paper for the October [number], and Sir James Frazer has promised his collaboration also.

The *Criterion* does not aim at a very large circulation, but aims solely at publishing the highest class of work. While a contribution to this paper does not reach a very large audience, it probably receives more intelligent attention than a contribution to any other review and the audience is not limited to Great Britain. The *Criterion* would be very greatly honoured by a contribution from you on some subject which would be of interest to general readers of *Themis* and *The Prolegomena*.[1]

Our rates of payment must at present be very modest, at the rate of £10 per 5000 words, and articles should not greatly exceed that length.

Should you consent to promise a contribution for next winter,[2] I should be extremely grateful; and if you accept in principle, I will ask the secretary, Mr Richard Aldington, to discuss any details with you later.

I have asked Mr Cobden Sanderson to send you a copy of the April number.

Hoping that I may hear from you,

I am, Madam, your obedient servant,
[T. S. E.]

TO *Rebecca West*[3] CC

29 May 1923 [*The Criterion*, London]

Madam,

I do not know whether you have seen this periodical of which I send you the prospectus which was issued last October, but I hope at least that you have heard of it and if so that you have heard well of it. The *Criterion*

1–Harrison's most influential books were *Themis* (1912), an attempt to interpret Greek religion in terms of totemism and fertility rituals, and *Prolegomena to the Study of Greek Religion* (1903).

2–Harrison never published in C.

3–Rebecca West (pseudonym of Cicily Andrews, née Fairfield) (1892–1983): British novelist, feminist, journalist and political commentator; author of *The Return of the Soldier* (1918).

likes to publish one piece of fiction in each of its four numbers during the year. It is extremely difficult to obtain four short pieces of fiction at the quality required, although great numbers are submitted. At the end of the first year, which ends with the number to appear in July, we shall have published stories by Miss May Sinclair, Miss Virginia Woolf, Signor Luigi Pirandello, Stephen Hudson, and two writers hitherto unknown, Mr Owen Barfield and Mrs Goold Adams.[1]

I was very much struck by your novel *The Judge* and I am sure that if you write shorter fiction at all it must be what the *Criterion* wants. I should be very happy to receive a story from you, of anything from 1500 to 5000 words, or at least the assurance that we may hope to receive one from you during the summer or autumn.

Our rates of payment are unfortunately limited to £10 per 5000 words. We hope that the success of the *Criterion* will enable it to increase these rates but at present we must rely for attracting the best writers upon our maintenance of the severe standards which we have set ourselves.

Should you be able to gratify us immediately, or at least to appease our request with a promise, I will ask the secretary, Mr Richard Aldington, to communicate with you.[2]

I have asked Mr Cobden Sanderson to send you a copy of the April number.

I am, Madam, Your obedient servant,

[T. S. E.]

TO *F. M. Cornford*[3] CC

29 May 1923 [*The Criterion*, London]

Sir,

I take the liberty of writing to you on behalf of the *Criterion*. As it is possible that you have not seen or heard of this review, which was started in October last, I enclose a copy of a circular which was issued at the time,

1–May Sinclair, 'The Victim', *C.* 1: 1 (Oct. 1922); VW, 'In the Orchard', 1: 3 (Apr. 1923); Luigi Pirandello, 'The Shrine', and Stephen Hudson, 'The Thief', 1: 2 (Jan. 1923); Owen Barfield, 'Dope', 1: 4 (July 1923); B. M. Goold-Adams, 'The Obsequies', 1: 3 (Apr. 1923).

2–Nothing by West appeared in *C.*

3–Francis MacDonald Cornford (1874–1943), classical scholar associated with the Cambridge 'ritualists' Jane Harrison and Gilbert Murray, was author of studies of Greek art and thought including *From Religion to Philosophy: A Study in the Origins of Western Speculation* (1912).

which will give you some notion of the character of the paper and its contributors. A further circular reviewing the first year's accomplishment will be issued in July. It is desired during the second year to extend the scope of the paper and include work not only by the most important men of letters, both English and foreign, but also by distinguished scholars and men of science. Professor W. P. Ker has contributed a paper for the October number, and Sir James Frazer has promised his collaboration also.

The *Criterion* does not aim at a very large circulation, but aims solely at publishing the highest class of work. While a contribution to this paper does not reach a very large audience, it probably receives more intelligent attention than a contribution to any other review and the audience is not limited to Great Britain. The *Criterion* would be very greatly honoured by a contribution from you on some subject which would be of interest to readers of your *Origin of Attic Comedy*.[1]

Our rates of payment must at present be very modest – at the rate of £10 per 5000 words – and articles should not greatly exceed that length.

Should you consent to promise a contribution for next winter I should be extremely grateful; and if you accept in principle, I will ask the secretary, Mr Richard Aldington, to discuss any details with you later.[2]

I have asked Mr Cobden Sanderson to send you a copy of the April number.

Hoping that I may hear from you.

I am, sir, your obedient servant

[T. S. E.]

TO *A. Berridale Keith*[3] CC

29 May 1923 [*The Criterion*, London]

Sir,

I take the liberty of writing to you on behalf of the *Criterion*. As it is possible that you have not seen or heard of this review, which was started

1 – *The Origin of Attic Comedy* (1914) identified a ritual sequence lying behind Aristophanes' plays. On 18 Mar. 1933 TSE told Hallie Flanagan, who was directing at Vassar College a production of his fragmentary play *Sweeney Agonistes* (sub-titled *Fragments of an Aristophanic Melodrama*): 'See also F. M. Cornford, *Origins of Attic Comedy*, which is important to read before you do the play.'

2 – Cornford never contributed to *C*.

3 – Arthur Berriedale Keith (1879–1944): constitutional lawyer and Sanskrit scholar; from 1914, Regius Professor of Sanskrit at Edinburgh University.

in October last, I enclose a copy of a circular which was issued at the time, which will give you some notion of the character of the paper and its contributors. A further circular reviewing the first year's accomplishment will be issued in July. It is desired during the second year to extend the scope of the paper and include work not only by the most important men of letters, both English and foreign, but also by distinguished scholars and men of science. Professor W. P. Ker has contributed a paper for the October number, and Sir James Frazer has promised his collaboration also.

The *Criterion* does not aim at a very large circulation, but aims solely at publishing the highest class of work. While a contribution to this paper does not reach a very large audience, it probably receives more intelligent attention than a contribution to any other review and the audience is not limited to Great Britain. The *Criterion* would be very greatly honoured by a contribution from you on some subject in the field of Indian mythology, folklore, or classical literature.

Our rates of payment must at present be very modest – at the rate of £10 per 5000 words, and articles should not greatly exceed that length.

Should you consent to promise a contribution for next winter I should be extremely grateful; and if you accept in principle, I will ask the secretary, Mr Richard Aldington, to discuss any details with you later.

I cannot forbear mentioning that I first heard your name many years ago from my honoured teacher, Professor Charles Rockwell Lanman,[1] of Harvard, when I was beginning the study of Sanskrit with him. I remember that he referred to you as knowing more Sanskrit than any man in England, and mentioned you in the same sentence with Jacobi and Lévy.[2]

Hoping that I may hear from you.[3]

I am, Sir, Your obedient servant,

[T. S. E.]

1–C. R. Lanman (1850–1941), Professor of Sanskrit, was founding editor of Harvard Oriental Series; author of *The Sanskrit Reader* (1884); the foremost authority in the USA.

2–Hermann Jacobi (1850–1937): pioneering German Indologist and Sanskrit scholar; Sylvain Lévy (1863–1935), French Sanskrit scholar; Professor at the Collège de France; author of *Le théatre indien* (1890) and *Doctrine du sacrifice dans les Brahmanas* (1898).

3–On 3 May, Keith replied that he was pleased to hear 'from a pupil of my old friend, C. R. Lanman', and promised a contribution on 'Indian classical literature'. TSE was to tell RA in Sept. 1923 they had an article of his for publication, but nothing by Keith ever appeared in C.

TO *Harold Monro* MS Beinecke

[?2 June 1923][1] [9 Clarence Gate Gdns]

You will think me very dilatory but I have not even had time to wrap up the Wordsworth book yet. I will try to get you the new Legouis book on him too.[2] We shd. like *article*, if it suits you to write 3000 words or so.[3]

Yours ever
T. S.E.

TO *Leonard Woolf* TS Berg

Sunday, 3 June 1923 [9 Clarence Gate Gdns]

Dear Leonard,

Thank you for your letter of the 29th. I am very much relieved to hear that you do not have to use my article at once after all.[4] It was written in a hurry and under great pressure, and I quite realised how badly it was written; I only sent it in that form because I had promised it that week and thought that you wanted it at once. It shows evidence of pressure and haste, and I fear, mental fatigue. So, as you are not using it immediately, will you let me have it back to re-write for you? Please be sure that I should not have allowed such a piece of work to go out of my hands, and certainly not into yours, but that I had promised it, and thought that it would be inconvenient for you not to get it. I do not want to add to your editorial troubles! So please let me have it back to remodel.

1–The date in pencil was added later, probably by Donald Gallup.
2–On 10 Jan. 1924, Monro told TSE that RA had obtained for him both Emile Legouis, *Wordsworth in a New Light*, and H. W. Garrod, *Wordsworth: Lectures and Essays* (1923).
3–See Monro, 'Wordsworth Revisited', *C.* 2: 8 (July 1924).
4–TSE's (revised) review of *Love Poems of John Donne* – 'John Donne', *N&A* 33: 10 (9 June 1923) – contended that 'those who take Donne as a contemporary will be taking him as a fashion only'. Proposing that 'Our appreciation of Donne must be an appreciation of what we lack, as well as of what have in common with him', he went on: 'A style, a rhythm, to be significant, must embody a significant mind, must be produced by the necessity of a new form for a new content . . . And for this reason, I suspect, most contemporary verse is so uninteresting in rhythm and so poor or so extravagant in vocabulary . . . we cannot return to sleep and call it order, and we cannot have any order but our own, but from Donne and his contemporaries we can draw instruction and encouragement.'

After I have got off my mind all the arrears of work and business that ought to have been attended to weeks ago I am sure that I can do you a much better article than this.

Yours ever
Tom

TO *Richard Cobden-Sanderson* MS Beinecke

Sunday, 3 June 1923 2 Milestone Cottages

Dear Cobden-Sanderson

About Wardle – my idea was that the offer to Valéry should be based on cost and probably receipts. This of course is outside of the financial arrangements of the *Criterion* proper and Lady Rothermere will have to approve such estimates as you lay before her and authorise you to incur the necessary expenses. When the amount of payment to Valéry is settled I suggest that you draft a letter to him for her to sign. I suggest that you work out estimates including your commission on sales and send her your recommendations. As I have never been a publisher I don't think I should intervene.

Tell Wardle that you are submitting estimates to Lady R. and will make a proposal approved by her when she has seen them.

Will write about the *Criterion* in a day or two.

Yours in haste
TSE

TO *Mary Hutchinson* TS Texas

4 June [1923?] [London]

Dearest Mary

Je suis tres affairé[1]
And Bucktooth Maclaggan[2]
An undernourished bagman

1–'I am very busy' (French).

2–Eric Robert Dalrymple MacLagan (1879–1951): an authority on textiles and Italian sculpture; later Director of the Victoria & Albert Museum, 1944–5. TSE alludes to the description in JJ's *Ulysses* of Buck Mulligan as 'Bucktooth Mulligan'.

And Mrs H (though rich)[1]
A dreary kind of bitch
But the Hope of meeting Rodger[2]
The Aphrican artful Dodger
And the magnetic
Sympathetic pathetic aesthetic
Quality
Of your own personality
And because Im wishin
To see the Great Politician[3]
Who is Quite Above Suspicion
Attract me

T. S. E.

Vivien would have made the party brighter
Its a Pity you didnt Invite her
But she wouldnt have Come if you had

[envelope] Take, postman, take your little skiff
And ply upstream to HAMMERSMIFF,[4]
And rest your oar (nay, but you shall),
By RIVER HOUSE, at UPPER MALL;
This letter, when all's said and done,
Is meant for Mrs HUTCHINSON.
w.6

1–Violet Mary Hammersley (1878–1964): society hostess whose late husband had been a partner in Cox's Bank.
2–Roger Fry (1866–1934): art historian and critic; author of *Vision and Design* (1920); a close friend of the Hutchinsons. TSE's description of Fry as 'The Aphrican artful Dodger' associates him with the sweet-talking Cockney pick-pocket in Dickens's *Oliver Twist*, Aphra Behn and Africa (whose art had been taken up by the Post-Impressionists whom Fry championed).
3–Herbert Asquith (1852–1928): Liberal Prime Minister, 1908–16. On 29 Dec. 1918, after the General Election, TSE said it was 'most deplorable that men like Asquith . . . should have been defeated'.
4–The Hutchinsons lived at River House, Hammersmith, London, w.6. TSE's rhyming address takes after the neo-classical style of Pope (associated with nearby Burlington House), and after Rimbaud.

TO *Ottoline Morrell* MS Texas

Tuesday [5 June 1923] 2 Milestone Cottages

My dear Ottoline

I am afraid you are very ill – the more so as I had a feeling that something was wrong with you, for days before you wired. I am very anxious. I don't want you to write, but if you could get somebody to send me – a line – a card to say how you are, it would be a great relief.

With much sympathy and love –
Tom

TO *Richard Cobden-Sanderson* MS Beinecke

9 June 1923 2 Milestone Cottages

Dear Cobden-Sanderson

I am returning to town this week Wed. or Thurs. and will see you as soon as possible – I know there is a great deal to be discussed. I don't want to see proofs; but one copy of each and of page proof should go to Aldington. I expect to be in town for good after this, or for better or worse.

Yours
TSE

TO *Richard Aldington* MS Texas

Sunday [10 June 1923]

Dear Richard

I am returning to town on Wednesday or Thursday.

Do you mind writing to Constable for a copy of Katherine Mansfield's book for me when it comes out.[1] I think her inflated reputation ought to be dealt with.[2]

1–Katherine Mansfield, *The Dove's Nest and Other Stories* (1923).

2–On 7 Nov. 1922, TSE told EP that Mansfield was 'one of the most persistent and thickskinned toadies and one of the vulgarest women', and 'a sentimental crank'. There was no review of *The Dove's Nest* in *C.*, but Mansfield's letters and journals were sympathetically reviewed by Orlo Williams in *NC* 8: 32 (Apr. 1929). Much later, TSE wrote a foreword to JMM, *Katherine Mansfield and Other Literary Studies* (1959).

I have told C-S to send one copy of Ezra's proof [of 'Malatesta Cantos'] to you. Ford[1] will have to wait till October, as you say, we can't have him and EP together. And we must get that good article on Dizzy[2] – but there isn't much time.

I am writing to EP to say his first line (quotation from me) must come out[3] – you will see why. Possibly the phrase 's.o.b.'[4] may give offence and is an unnecessary insult in my opinion.

Yours ever
T

Vivien Eliot TO *Virginia Woolf* — MS Berg

18 June [1923] — 2 Milestone Cottages

Dear Virginia

It so stunned me to find that my mental condition was one in which anything I could write could be construed into a statement that Maynard Keynes was bankrupt that I immediately ceased to write letters and even telegrams. It is evidently quite hopeless, and I must accept my fate and remain cut off from any communication with the civilised world.

Some day I may return to London and try my luck, but at present I am too timid to return as the instigation of such a rumour.

It becomes more and more pleasant to be in the country, and I spend some of my time driving about and searching for a really nice cottage, for this is not one.

Murry has a most beautiful cottage four miles away, but it is too isolated for me just now. But of course nothing I see is ever quite so perfect as the Hutchinsons' 'Eleanor', nor could be I am sure.

1 – Ford Madox Ford's 'From the Grey Stone' was held over to C. 2: 5 (Oct. 1923).
2 – F. W. Bain, 'Disraeli', appeared only in C. 2: 6 (Feb. 1924).
3 – Canto IX opened with the line 'These fragments we have shelved (shored)', an allusion to *TWL*, l. 430: see TSE's objections on 27 May above.
4 – In Canto XI (later renumbered X), EP referred to 'that monstrous swollen, swelling s.o.b. / Papa Pio Secundo'. RA, in his autobiography, recalled that when he noted in the proofs that EP had 'called the Pope a s.o.b', he considered the severe 'law of libel', and the sensitivity of Roman Catholics, and thought it was not 'urbane to call the Pope a s.o.b': 'So I cut it out; whereupon Ezra transferred the epithet to me by mail' (*Life for Life's Sake* [1941], 266). In C., the line read 'that monstrous swollen, swelling / Papa Pio Secundo'. EP restored the epithet in *A Draft of XXX Cantos* (1930). In Canto XII (later XI), EP referred to Federigo da Montefeltro as 'that nick-nosed s.o.b. Feddy Urbino'. In that case, the line was printed without bowdlerization in C.

Tom has, alas, gone back to London and on Saturday is going to Oxford to lecture to the undergraduates.

I should love to go with him, and on to Garsington the next day, but perhaps it would be wiser to refrain.

I do hope I shall see you soon. A meeting in the country would be very delightful.

Yours ever
Vivien Eliot

TO *Dorothy Pound*[1]

MS Lilly

Friday 22 June [1923] 9 Clarence Gate Gdns

Dear Dorothy

I shall be delighted if you will lunch with me on Thursday the 28th, at Simpsons in *Cheapside* (where Cheapside joins Poultry [Street])[2] at 12 o'clock. I say 12 o'clock because I *have* to lunch from 12 to 1. If you take bus or tube to the Bank you walk back (*west*) along Poultry (i.e. Cheapside) about a block and Simpsons is on the left facing west. I will wait at the entrance to the court. Simpsons is up a little court.

I shall be able then to give you a small present which Vivien has for you. She was going to send it to Paris, but it is better to give it to you.

Yours always,
T. S. E.

TO *The Editor of* The Nation and The Athenaeum[3]

23 June 1923 9 Clarence Gate Gdns

Sir,

In some interesting remarks on Ben Jonson in the *Nation and Athenaeum* of June 23rd – with which I am otherwise in accord – I observe that you refer to me as seeming to have praised Jonson 'apologetically'.[4]

1 – Dorothy Pound: see Glossary of Names.

2 – Cheapside turns into Poultry St close to Bank tube station, nr. TSE's office at Lloyds Bank.

3 – Text taken from TSE, 'Ben Jonson', *N&A* 33: 13 (30 June 1923), 426.

4 – In 'The World of Books: Ben Jonson', LW had written: 'But even Mr T. S. Eliot, and after him Mr Aldous Huxley, seem to praise Jonson apologetically. The tone seems to be incongruous and unnecessary', *N&A* 33: 12 (23 June 1923).

My article[1] was intended as a 'defence' only in so far as I believed Jonson's reputation – as evidenced by manuals of literature, such as you yourself quote – was a mis-representation; and in this belief, I should imagine, you concur. And theoretically I agree that the only 'defence' necessary for Jonson is to 'tell people to read him'.[2] But this is equally the only defence necessary for a number of other writers; and a great deal depends on the persuasiveness of the way in which one tells people to read them. But if any defence, further than an oracular invitation to the public to read an author, implies that the author defended is weak or vulnerable, then my paper on Jonson was by no means intended as a defence or an apology. On the contrary, Jonson seems to me to have a particularly strong position.

Yours, &c.,
T. S. Eliot.

Vivien Eliot TO *John Middleton Murry* MS Valerie Eliot

24 June [1923] 9 Clarence Gate Gdns

Dear John

Ever since I saw your beautiful cottage I have wanted to write to tell you how much I like it. I was 'dumbstruck' – as Ellen [Kellond] calls it. The bedrooms particularly touched me. And your furniture is perfect.

To speak the truth to you – and you must take this please as my answer to what you tell me of your feelings about me and Tom – since coming back to London I have been in despair. I mean real despair, which isolates and freezes one. (I don't much believe in despair which seeks sympathy and comfort, do you?)

In addition, I am trying to come to a decision. It is an old indecision, really, but the conclusion becomes always more urgent. My despair is paralysing me. There, John, there is no-one else in this world today to whom I would make an explanation.

So I can't see you just now, my dear. But if you are what you *must* be, you will let me call on you the moment I smash a chair or two, and will come then quickly, before I have time to get re-bound.

Vivien

1 – TSE, 'Ben Jonson', originally published anonymously in the *TLS* (13 Nov. 1919), was reprinted in *SW* (1920). TSE said, 'Jonson behaved as the great creative mind that he was: he created his own world, a world from which his followers, as well as the dramatists who were trying to do something wholly different, are excluded' (*SW*, 117).
2 – LW wrote: 'The only defence of Jonson which is necessary is to tell people to read him.'

TO *Dorothy Pound* MS Lilly

Sunday [24 June 1923] 9 Clarence Gate Gdns

Dear Dorothy

I hope you can use this ticket to the Phoenix performance of the *Faithful Shepherdess* tomorrow (Monday) afternoon.[1] I have given the other ticket to James Joyce.[2] I think it should be interesting. I look forward to seeing you on Thursday.

Yours ever
T

TO *James Joyce*[3] MS Buffalo

Monday, 25 June 1923 9 Clarence Gate Gdns

My dear Joyce

Can you and Mrs Joyce have tea with me tomorrow (Tuesday) at 5.30 at Frascati's (Oxford St near the corner of Tottenham Court Road)? There will only be Lady Ottoline Morrell, who is very anxious to meet you and is only here for a day or two. I hope you can come. If you will leave word, I will ring up your hotel in the morning.

Very sincerely
T. S. Eliot

Excuse short notice – I was not sure till today that Lady O. M. was coming, and I knew you were out this evening.

PS Please do not mention to Lady O. M. (if you come, as I hope you will) that you saw my wife. She is not strong enough to see many people yet.

1–John Fletcher, *The Faithful Shepherdess*, was performed by the Phoenix Society at the Shaftesbury Theatre. The cast included Isabel Jones, Cathleen Nesbitt and Harcourt Williams, with music arranged by Sir Thomas Beecham. 'The Phoenix gave us yesterday afternoon three hours in Arcady. At the end of the performance of Fletcher's pastoral play . . . each member of the audience could truthfully say to himself, *Et ego in Arcadia vixi*, and there can have been few who regretted their sojourn at the Shaftesbury' (*The Times*, 26 June, 1923, 10).
2–JJ was on holiday in England with his family, 15 June – 9 Aug.
3–James Joyce: Irish novelist and poet, see Glossary of Names.

TO *James Joyce* PC Buffalo

[Wednesday, 27 June 1923] 9 Clarence Gate Gdns

I will call for you at your hotel tomorrow (Thursday) at 7. I am sorry I was out this afternoon. I rang you up this evening but you were out also.

Sincerely
T. S. Eliot

TO *James Joyce* MS Buffalo

Friday [?29 June 1923] *The Criterion*, 9 Clarence Gate Gdns

My dear Joyce

Don't forget to write to me here your address in Bognor.[1] I hope you will have no trouble in finding a good hotel. I want to get a car one day when I am at Fishbourne and fetch you over and show you some of the waste lands round about Chichester.

Yours ever
T. S. Eliot

TO *Richard Cobden-Sanderson* MS Beinecke

Sunday [1 July 1923][2] *The Criterion*, 17 Thavies Inn

Dear Cobden-Sanderson

I have the first set of page proof. Is it too late to alter the order so as to put *Rivière second* and 'Dope' third?[3] I think it is too much of a contrast with Yeats.

I am sorry to be a nuisance, having left it so late, but if it *can* be done without delay *please* do. And the last sentence of 'Dope' ought to read – 'Hide me from *this* bloody world'.[4]

Don't answer. I will see you on Tuesday.

Yours ever
T. S. E.

1 – JJ with his wife and daughter stayed at Alexandra House, a boarding house in Clarence Road, Bognor Regis, Sussex.
2 – Dated by Cobden-Sanderson.
3 – No change was made in C. 1: 4 (July 1923). The running order remained Yeats, 'A Biographical Fragment', Barfield, 'Dope', Rivière, 'Notes on a Possible Generalisation of the Theories of Freud'.
4 – These are the last words of the story as published.

TO *L. A. G. Strong*[1] MS Texas

3 July 1923 9 Clarence Gate Gdns

Dear Mr Strong

Thank you for your kind and flattering letter.[2] I am afraid, however, that I must decline your offer, however much honour it does me. For one thing, *The Waste Land* is intended to form a whole, and I should not care to have anyone read *parts* of it; and furthermore I am opposed to anthologies in principle.[3] I wrote one or two letters to the *Times Literary Supplement* on this subject two years ago.[4] I do not know why authors should make a present of their works to publishers and editors, in a form which does not lend itself to understanding, and for an undiscriminating public – for if it discriminated, it would not buy anthologies. Especially as the appearance of verse in anthologies is likely to reduce the sale of the collected works of the authors included. I must, therefore, decline the pleasure of inclusion in your book.

Yours very truly
T. S. Eliot

1–L. A. G. Strong (1896–1958): novelist, journalist, editor and poet; later a director of Methuen. He edited *Eighty Poems: An Anthology* (1924) and published *Doyle's Rock and Other Stories* (1925). With C. Day Lewis, he edited *New Anthology of Modern Verse* (1940).
2–Strong had asked to include an extract from *TWL* in an anthology of contemporary verse. This may refer to *The Best Poems of 1923*, ed. L. A. G. Strong (Boston, 1924), which included poems by RA, H. D., De La Mare, E. E. Cummings, Harriet Monroe, Osbert Sitwell and J. C. Squire; or to *Eighty Poems: An Anthology*, ed. L. A. G. Strong (1924).
3–TSE consistently refused to allow the publication of extracts from *TWL* and other poems.
4–In a letter to the *TLS* (24 Nov 1921), 'Poets and Anthologies', TSE objected to the inclusion of extracts from his work in *Modern American Poetry*, ed. Louis Untermeyer. 'Some months ago I discussed the general question of anthologies with a poet (of a very different school and tradition from mine) whose name is more widely known than mine is. We agreed that the work of any poet who has already published a book of verse is likely to be more damaged than aided by anthololgies.' Robert Graves, among others, wrote in support; and the case was developed later in Robert Graves and Laura Riding, *A Pamphlet Against Anthologies* (1928).

TO *Richard Cobden-Sanderson* MS Beinecke

5 July 1923 [London]

If this[1] won't go on three pages, let me know – and if there is room, I think it would be good to have a list of contents of the Nos 1–2–3–4 attached.

T. S. E.

I saw Aldington. Yes, print 1260 and give [W. H.] Smith 300.

TO *Richard Cobden-Sanderson* MS Beinecke

Friday, 6 July 1923 9 Clarence Gate Gdns

Dear Cobden-Sanderson

Many thanks for letter and addressed envelope. I shall be very pleased, for my part, with the Circular as proposed, and am very glad the Contents will go in. I hope the type will not have to be very small. I'm sorry if we can't come out punct. on the 15th, as it is July especially, but that is my fault – still, I hope we will not be many days out.

We ought to have enough of the circular to be able to send it out again, in October. Therefore I wish you would change 1st sentence of the circular to

'With the October 1923 number the *Criterion* begins its second volume'.

Don't you think that is better?

1 – 'This' refers to the following circular for C.:

'The July number of the *Criterion* just published, completes the first volume of this interesting literary review. It is likely that the first volume of this brilliant quarterly will be eagerly sought after by bibliophiles; we understand that the first numbers are out of print and are only to be obtained at a premium.

'A circular issued with this number summarises the achievement and outlines the next year, which will show some interesting developments. The contents of Vol. I show a list of distinguished names, of both older and younger writers, such as any literary review might envy. The July number is in no wise inferior to the three previous. It includes some fascinating reminiscences by William Butler Yeats; a charming sketch by E. Morgan Forster; the second part of an essay on Viscount Bolingbroke by Charles Whibley, one of the greatest authorities on the subject; an essay on Freud by Jacques Rivière, the editor of *La Nouvelle Revue Française*; an essay on Italian Renaissance poetry by Richard Aldington; an examination of Indian drama by Stanley Rice; and for those who are capable of appreciating the most modern literature, some amazing 'Cantos' by Ezra Pound, and a curious story called 'Dope'. The review is remarkable in the discrimination and skill with which it combines writers of widely different type, selecting only according to merit, and it deserves praises for introducing important foreign writers to this country. It is obtainable at booksellers for 3/6, or from the publisher, R. Cobden-Sanderson, 17 Thavies Inn, E.C.1.'

The extra cost of red type is a nuisance, but as it is so distinctive of the *Criterion* I think *it is worth* the money.[1]

Yours ever
T. S. E.

PS I have just discovered two paragraphs I want to alter. So will you please hold over and you shall have corrected copy by Monday morning. I *swear* I can't let it go out in this form. I'm awfully sorry.

TO *James Joyce* PC Buffalo

[Postmark 9 July 1923] 9 Clarence Gate Gdns

I'm awfully sorry – but we shall not be able to get to Fishbourne for another week or so. I will drop you a line when we arrive, so *please* keep me posted of your movements. With kind regards to your wife.

Yours ever
TSE

I hope Bognor suits all of you?[2]

TO *Ottoline Morrell* MS Texas

10 July 1923 9 Clarence Gate Gdns

My dear Ottoline

I was very glad to hear from you, but of course disappointed that you are not stopping over in London. We have had two long interviews with Dr Martin. He was very much interested indeed and kept Vivien a long time. He has discovered, by having bacteriological analyses made, an extraordinary excess of streptococcus fecalis, and other mischievous cocci. He has promised to send over cultures from Germany. But he says it cannot be *properly* done in this country, and it is much as I expected – he can't do much for her unless she can go to Freiburg in the autumn.[3] This is what it comes to. And I have been run into such ruinous expenses with this illness already that I don't see how I can undertake such a new adventure.

1–RC-S asked (6 July) whether it was really necessary to have *Criterion* on p. 1 printed in red ink? It would 'add another 30/- or so to the cost of printing'. On 7 July, however, he said he 'would see that the title is printed in red ink'.
2–JJ wrote to Harriet Shaw Weaver (5 July): 'I like it [Bognor] very much . . . The weather is very fine and the country here very restful.'
3–OM went for treatment at Freiburg in the autumn, but VHE was unable to go.

It has been terribly exhausting – two visits and three analyses – and Vivien is utterly worn out. We hope to get back to the country on Saturday, and I shall stay as long as I can, for I am utterly worn out. I do hope that Dr Martin has done you good. We liked him very much.

I'll write to you from Fishbourne.

Always aff.
Tom

TO *Richard Cobden-Sanderson* MS Beinecke

15 July 1923 *The Criterion*, 9 Clarence Gate Gdns

Dear C-S

Could you send tomorrow morning for two parcels? They are for Aldington (MSS) but I don't want to send them to him till he returns home, and I don't want to have them here. If you'd keep them and send them to him (registered) at the *Criterion*'s expense when he gets back I shd be *very grateful.*

Shall send you 'copy' [for advertisement] for Rothermere press in a few days.

Yours ever,
T. S. E.

Sunday

TO *Robert Graves*[1] MS Morris

[Postmark 16 July 1923] 9 Clarence Gate Gdns

Many thanks for J. C. R. MSS.[2] After I have gone over them I will certainly talk to the Woolfs[3] about them, and let you hear.

In haste
T. S. E.

1 – Robert Graves (1895–1985): poet, novelist, critic, mythologist; served during WW1 with the Royal Welch Fusiliers, and was wounded in June 1917; later author of the modern classic, *Goodbye to All That* (1929). After the early war poems of *Over the Brazier* (1916) and *Fairies and Fusiliers* (1917), he produced a series of collections, inc. *The Pier Glass* (1921). He had also written *On English Poetry: being an irregular psychological approach to this art* (1922).

2 – John Crowe Ransom (1888–1974), poet and critic associated with the Fugitives, had published two books of poems in the USA. Graves was one of the first to admire Ransom's poetry, and had sent TSE a selection of poems from Ransom's volumes for possible publication in C. and advice about publication elsewhere.

3 – LW and VW had published Graves's *The Feather Bed* (1923). Ransom's poems eventually appeared from the Hogarth Press as *Grace After Meat*, with intro. by Graves (1924).

TO *Sydney Schiff* TS BL

Thursday [19 July? 1923] *The Criterion*, 17 Thavies Inn

My dear Sydney,

I have long had it in mind to ask you to do something for Volume II of the *Criterion*. But knowing how hard you have been working for the past six months and more I have purposely delayed mentioning it until a more seasonable time appeared. But now that your book is finished,[1] and before your next book has completely claimed your time I venture to remind you that we should like very soon a short sketch or story from you. <(Have you any of your short things?)> I say a sketch or story to give you as much scope as possible and to allow myself to make a suggestion. I think that you could do a very amusing satirical sketch of present times and manners; you know the sort of thing I mean. Yours is a very satirical and observant mind and you might write some very caustic sketches of the sort of people who are typical of our time. This is a sort of thing that the *Criterion* needs. Can you do something for us *now*?[2]

I am sorry to tell you that Vivienne has been quite ill again for the past two weeks and in fact has had a bad relapse.[3] This is a very bitter disappointment as up till then she had seemed to be making real progress under the Swede. She has seen no one, but should you be in London and free on Saturday afternoon, she wants me to tell you that she would like to see you about 4.30 or 5 just for a short time.

Affectionately,
Tom.

This sounds very dreary when I read it over – and comes from dictating to a *new* secretary. I could have said simply that Vol. II *must* have something from you! There are *only* half a dozen writers of fiction, and I *depend* on you.

1 – SS's novel *Prince Hempseed* (1923), written under his nom-de-plume of Stephen Hudson.
2 – SS's 'Céleste' appeared, under his pseudonym Stephen Hudson, in C. 2: 7 (Apr. 1924), 332–48; it was later the title story of his collection *Céleste and Other Sketches* (1930).
3 – In a letter of 10 Aug., VW mentions that several recent letters by her had 'semi-fatal results': for instance, 'poor Mrs Eliot had a relapse'.

TO *Ezra Pound* MS Lilly

23 July 1923 as from 9 Clarence Gate Gdns

Mon cher

This from Chichester, but letters are forwarded. I most humbly apologise. There is no justification for such negligence.[1] I have not your original receipt by me, so please date this to suit yourself.[2] The fr. 1000 will of course be kept in trust fund & can be accounted for.

The *Criterion* cantos[3] I am afraid are not perfect in typography, owing to the muddle in which this no. was produced. I am asking C-S to send you ten copies.

Will write further as soon as possible.

Tout à toi
TSE

TO *Wyndham Lewis*[4] TS Cornell

26 July 1923 2 Milestone Cottages, Old Fishbourne

Dear Lewis

I got your letter forward[ed] this morning. I am awfully sorry I missed you, and that you are going away;[5] as I do not expect to return to town for ten days. I am delighted to hear about the manuscript.[6] Could you send it to me, here, *registered*, and if you wish I will post it back within twenty-four hours. Or if you can leave it with me longer I will keep it locked up and not let anybody know of its existence. We want to print it, of course.[7] If you can have it typed out in duplicate and send me one copy, so much

1–On 19 July, EP wrote: 'Have tried in VAIN to get you to send me receipt for B.E. twenty pounds stg/ remitted some weeks ago. Do try.' EP wanted to keep his own name 'unpolluted' in regard to the Bel Esprit fund but also to uphold the 'idea' of it.

2–The receipt read: 'Received from Bel Esprit per Ezra Pound Esq. £20 (twenty pounds). T. S. Eliot', June 1923.

3–EP, 'Malatesta Cantos', *C.* 1: 4 (July 1923).

4–Wyndham Lewis: see Glossary of Names.

5–On 24 July, WL wrote that he was leaving for France the following Monday.

6–Drafts of what became *The Apes of God*, WL's first major work of fiction since *Tarr* (1917). WL wanted to discuss a 'section of Book (of which I spoke to you) with view to publication in *CRITERION* ETC.'

7–TSE initially advised WL to avoid periodical publication of the novel, but later published extracts from *The Apes of God* in *C.* 2: 6 & 7 (Feb. & Apr. 1924).

the better. I hope France will do you good. You do not say how long you intend to be away. Please let me hear from you on receipt of this, and if possible send the MSS. at once.

Yours ever
TSE

TO *Sydney Schiff* MS BL

28 July 1923 2 Milestone Cottages

My dear Sidney,

It has been a great pleasure to us to have your and Violet's letters, you must know; and I am sure that you if anyone will realise that if we have not answered sooner it is a case of *höhere Gewalt.*[1] I am very glad to know that you like the *Criterion* and when you have read it I look forward to your detailed observations. I also hope you like the prospectus for next year. It must have been most stimulating to you to have Lewis read you part of his book.[2] I am convinced that it will be a great work. As he took you so much into his confidence I am surprised that he did not let you know that I discussed with him the possibility of publishing part of the book in the *Criterion*, [and] finally was forced to agree with him that the book might make a more impressive appearance if none of it had previously been printed. Thus I sacrificed the *Criterion* to his interest. I am very anxious that the book shd make a great success, but had he consented, I shd have jumped at it for the Quarterly.

It has been a great upheaval again, moving back to the country, and the first effects have been that Vivien is not *nearly* so well, has fallen back. Every time she has to move she loses several weeks, [and] you cannot – no one – can imagine, what a great undertaking this moving is. She needs every ounce of strength she has, merely to live from day to day, which is all we do, keeping out of doors as much as possible. She has been far too weak to write letters, but has appreciated very keenly, as have I also, Violet's letters. People pretend that they don't expect letters to be

1 – 'Act of God' (German).

2 – WL's biographer Jeffrey Myers notes, 'Sydney Schiff was Lewis' generous patron during the 1920s and a major victim of *The Apes of God*' (*The Enemy: A Biography of Wyndham Lewis* [1980], 126). SS called WL 'the only definitely creative artist this country possesses', purchased a number of his works at the 'Tyros and Portraits' exhibition (1921), and commissioned from him a portrait of his wife Violet for which he paid £712. In his novel, WL satirised SS mercilessly in the figure of Lionel Klein, the rich Jewish patron of the arts.

answered, but very few really carry out the pretensions, as you [and] Violet do, by continuing to write, [and] Vivien wants Violet to know how highly she appreciates it. She often feels that she must have lost all her friends, by having been unable to see or even to write to anyone for so many months.

It is good to hear that you are writing again, and I do hope you will be able to stay in the delightful solitude you are in, [and] get well under way something even better than *Prince Hempseed*. With love from both to both

Always yours aff.
Tom

I have enjoyed seeing Joyce of late, very much – a near neighbour.[1] It is very sad about poor W. P. Ker.[2]

TO *Richard Cobden-Sanderson* PC Texas

31 July 1923 Fishbourne

Stanley Rice[3] is clamouring for a copy of the *Criterion*. Have you sent one? His address is New Cottage, East Sheen S.W.14. When I get back, next week, I will ring you up. I shall want fifty copies of the *Criterion* then. Hope all well with you.

T. S. E.

FROM *Paul Valéry* TS Valéry Estate

4 August 1923 Paris, 40 Rue de Villejust XVI

Cher Monsieur,

J'ai trouvé votre lettre en revenant d'un petit voyage. Il est exact que j'ai convenu avec le Capitaine Wardle de partager les droits à provenir de la publication du *Serpent* avec traduction anglaise, dans la proportion de 5/11 pour lui et de 6/11 pour moi.[4]

1 – On 17 July, VW recorded VHE saying 'I'm living between [JMM] and Mr Joyce. Mr Joyce is very nice', and TSE adding: 'His wife is very nice too – & the children' (*Diary*, II, 256).
2 – W. P. Ker had died suddenly while climbing at Macagnaga, Italy, on 17 July.
3 – Rice's 'Alcestis and Savitri: A Suggestion' appeared in *C.* 1: 4 (July 1923).
4 – See TSE's letter of 28 May to Mark Wardle.

Mais je désirerais savoir si l'édition que vous comptez faire de ce poème[1] est à tirage limité, ou si l'arrangement concerne toute publication future du *Serpent* en anglais et français juxtaposés, et s'étend à un tirage *illimité*?

Je voudrais savoir aussi si la somme de 800 francs que vous proposez est entièrement pour moi, ou si elle doit se partager avec Wardle, dans la proportion indiquée ci-dessus?

Quant aux gravures sur bois, vous ferez ce qu'il vous plaira.[2] Et quant aux épreuves, je pense que Wardle pourra fort bien les corriger. Je l'aiderai, s'il le désire, bien volontiers.

Veuillez agréer, Monsieur, mes salutations très distinguées.

Paul Valéry[3]

TO *Richard Cobden-Sanderson* — PC Beinecke

[Postmark ?4 Aug. 1923] — 2 Milestone Cottages, Fishbourne

Excellently produced number![4] Will you send ten copies to Ezra Pound, please? Circular admirable[5] –

Hope things are going well and not giving you too much work.

Yrs

T. S. E.

Don't send your man with any parcels to C.G.G. till I return.

1 – Valéry published a limited edition of *Le Serpent*, illustrated by Jean Marchand (Paris: Éos, 1926).

2 – The English edition was not illustrated.

3 – *Translation*: Dear Sir, I have found your letter waiting for me on returning after a short absence. It is correct that I have agreed with Captain Wardle to share the royalties from the publication of the *Serpent* with the translation into English, in the ratio 5/11 for him and 6/11 for me.

But I would like to know if the edition of the poem you propose to bring out will be a limited one, or whether the arrangement relates to all future publications of the *Serpent* with the French and English texts juxtaposed, and extends to an *unlimited* number of copies?

I would also like to know if the sum of 800 francs you suggest is entirely for me, or whether it is to be shared with Wardle, according to the above-mentioned ratio.

As for the wood cuts, do exactly as you please. And as regards the proofs, Wardle can correct these perfectly well, I think. I am willing to help, if he wants me to.

Yours sincerely, Paul Valéry

4 – *C.* 1: 4 (July 1923).

5 – The *C.* circular (see TSE's letter of 5 July).

Vivien Eliot TO *Virginia Woolf* MS Berg

Sunday 5th [August 1923] Milestone Cottages,
Old Fishbourne, Sussex

Dear Virginia

I expect you are now at Rodmell. I have been waiting to be sure you were there before writing to you. I don't like my letters to be wandering the world (they are so precious, & *really important*).

I hope you are enjoying the country more than I am. I have been in bed nearly the whole time I have been here & Tom & I are completely out of love with the country & country cottages & the whole *country cottage idea*.

We are now convinced that we ought to & must have a house in London with a garden. This will be instead of the Citroen car which was never more than a dream, I think.

We have had young people staying with us – 'to *help!*' & we are now out of love with young people too, especially when they have literary aspirations.

In my experience all young people nowadays do have literary aspirations; & where they used to go harmlessly about with a box of water colours & a sketching block they now immerse themselves in ink & shout their ideas at meal times giving their hosts no chance to digest their food.

I do hope you will relent & answer this letter although I know well enough it merits no reply.

Tom is thankfully returning to London on Thursday (tomorrow) & my present hope is that I may soon follow him.

I have seen no one at all here, but I still will hope that we shall be able to have a meeting. It [seems] Tom will be here for weekends. Next weekend my doctor is coming down, which is a trial, but after that they will be, I hope, all free & with possibilities of seeing you.

Much love from us both
Yrs ever,
Vivien Eliot

TO *Mary Hutchinson* MS Texas

Wednesday [?8 August 1923] *The Criterion*, 17 Thavies Inn

My dear Mary

Many thanks for your sweet letter. I got it this morning just before I left. I am really certain that Vivien will not be fit for anything or anybody this week, or for some days. She has only been out for half an hour and comes back very dizzy and faint. I hate to leave her in that hole,[1] and hate to bring her back to this. We must get that small house with a garden *soon*! Can you help me?

She is frightfully depressed – cooped up and unable to see anyone. I may bring her back. But we both want to see you *soon* – that was an unsatisfying glimpse the other day. I'll write on Sunday or Monday and let you know how things are.

I assure you, Mary, of my faithful affection.

Tom

TO *Richard Cobden-Sanderson* — MS Beinecke

8 August 1923 — 9 Clarence Gate Gdns

Dear Cobden-Sanderson,

I have come back today for two days only. But I will telephone you early next week and arrange a meeting. Meanwhile, thanks for your letter and for circulars. Will you please send me (here) some more letter paper and five *Criterions*?

Aldington sent me a schedule of payments. I have two qualifications – Pound must be paid £18[2] (Eighteen) on the no. of words stated by Aldington *(not* £15) and Rivière must be paid in full,[3] *without* deduction of translator's fee, because I have promised him.

Barfield's address is

9 New Street
Dorset Sq.
N.W.1

Yes, send copy to the *Cherwell*[4] – I shall be very glad if you would take up this Valéry matter[5] with Lady R. Having just returned, I don't know whether she has left London or not.

Will try to telephone you on Monday.

Hope your affairs are going smoothly.

Yours ever
T. S. Eliot

1–2 Milestone Cottages, Old Fishbourne, their rented cottage.
2–For 'Malatesta Cantos'.
3–For 'Notes on a Possible Generalisation of the Theories of Freud', C. 1: 4 (July 1923).
4–An Oxford student magazine founded in 1920.
5–See TSE's letter of 4 Aug. to Valéry.

TO *Mary Hutchinson* Telegram Texas

10 August 1923

IF ALONE CAN YOU PICNIC SUNDAY MEET THREE THIRTY – BLACK BOY[1] FISHBOURNE REPLY FISHBOURNE

TOM

TO *Dr Wilhelm Lehmann* MS Texas

14 August 1923 9 Clarence Gate Gdns

Dear Dr Lehmann

Please forgive this long long delay. I have meant to write you many a time, but have been distracted for months by my wife's severe illness – in the country. I have not had a moment – even to read the books you so kindly sent, a pleasure I promise myself still. I send you the *Faktura*,[2] with Mk 50,000 because I do not think it is enough – I want to pay for the *books*[3] although they are marked *Rezension*.[4] Will you help me to do so.

You may count on hearing from me again when I have had time to read them. Meanwhile I shd be delighted to hear from you about German literature or anything!

Forgive this scrawl

Sincerely
T. S. Eliot

Perhaps our announcement will interest you.

Shall we ever meet? I want next year to bring my wife to Freiburg i/B. There is a great doctor there – *Martin* – have you ever heard of him?

1 – The Black Boy Inn, Main Road, Fishbourne.
2 – 'Invoice' (German).
3 – On 14 May, TSE asked Lehmann to send him books by Moritz Heimann and Oscar Loerke, the writers he had previously mentioned.
4 – 'For review' (German).

TO *Henry Eliot* — MS Houghton

14 August 1923 — 9 Clarence Gate Gdns

My dear Henry

This is just a note to begin with. I have written twice to mother – thank God – that deficit had been eating into me. You have been with her – I wish you would let me know how you are. She said you looked ill.

I am an ungrateful dog not to have written and thanked you for everything. I was examined by the doctor for the Life Insurance.[1] He said my hernia was worse (on the *other* side) and I should wear a truss and perhaps have an operation.[2] I am going to see my doctor about it. Since then he has written to say that the Company want him to see me again, so I suppose there is something wrong. I will let you know.

Things have been very bad – I cannot write more now – only to thank you and remind you that I am always

Your affectionate brother
Tom

TO *E. R. Curtius* — MS Bonn

14 August 1923 — 9 Clarence Gate Gdns

My dear Curtius

It is very rude of me not to have answered your letter before. I can only say that I have been mostly preoccupied, in the country, with my wife's illness, and have neglected everything and everyone. I have at least sent off *Imaginary Portraits*[3] and hope it will reach you quickly. I should have at once suggested that you should write us an essay on Pater, but Charles du Bos[4] (whom I think you know) had just suggested that subject for himself, and I had accepted! *But will you let us have an essay on a subject of your own choosing, in the next six months?*[5] Do, please. We hope that

1–On 30 July the Canada Life Assurance Company sent HWE a life insurance policy on TSE's life; the beneficiary was 'Vivien Haigh-Wood Eliot', and the sum insured $20,000. The first premium of $558 was paid on 28 July by HWE himself.

2–TSE had a congenital hernia, and had had to wear a truss since childhood (see CCE's letter to Mr Cobb of end Sept. 1905, in Vol. 1 of these *Letters*).

3–Walter Pater, *Imaginary Portraits* (1887). TSE discussed Pater's influence in 'Contemporary English Prose', *Vanity Fair* 20: 5 (July 1923). On 30 May, Curtius (who loved and admired Pater) said that, though he had most of Pater, he did not possess this volume.

4–Du Bos's projected study of Pater was never written.

5–Curtius next published 'On the Style of Marcel Proust' in C. 2: 7 (Apr. 1924).

eventually we may have the honour of bringing out a book of your essays here in English. I wish you wd do a series of *English Wegbereiter*[1] – very much and *my* choice wd be[2]

Henry James
Joseph Conrad
Rudyard Kipling
Lytton Strachey
James Joyce
Wyndham Lewis
Ezra Pound

I shd be tempted to add *Frazer* and *Bradley*

but *this* is merely to amuse you.

Have you ever heard of a poet named Kühlemann? I have seen his *Tristan da Cunha* which I liked.[3]

Do let me hear from you.

Sincerely always
T. S. Eliot

By some inconceivable stupidity I addressed the book Roten*proben* 15A![4] I can't think why, when I was thinking of Berne! Let me know if it does not arrive, and warn your Post Office.

I must wait to write about yr beautiful *Balzac*.[5] I am sending the *Criterion* to the university.[6]

1–Curtius had published *Die literarischen Wegbereiter des neuen Frankreich* [*The Literary Precursors of the New France*] in 1919. He never did a comparable study of English literature.
2–TSE's list of English-language precursors includes his modernist allies alongside Henry James, Sir James Frazer and F. H. Bradley, who were the subject of his next 'Lettre d'Angleterre' in *NRF* 21: 122 (1 Nov. 1923), later translated as 'A Prediction in Regard to Three English Authors', *Vanity Fair* 21: 6 (Feb. 1924). TSE had originally chosen an epigraph for *TWL* from Conrad's *Heart of Darkness* ('The Horror! The Horror!'), and Conrad and James are mentioned in 'Contemporary English Prose' as 'distinguished aliens' with 'very personal and incommunicable styles'. The mention of Kipling anticipates the admiration expressed by TSE in *A Choice of Kipling's Verse* (1942).
3–Johannes Theodor Kühlemann (1891–1939): poet and journalist associated with the Cologne Dadaist scene. TSE would later refer, in a letter to the *NS* ('Tristan da Cunha', 22 Oct. 1927), to 'a German poem which is almost unknown even in Germany, the Tristan da Cunha of Johannes Th. Kuhlemann (Der Strom, Cologne, 1919). I once attempted to translate this poem, which is very fine, but abandoned the attempt.' TSE's attempt at translation has not been discovered.
4–Curtius's address was Rotenburg 15A.
5–Following his essay 'Balzac', in C. 1: 2 (Jan. 1923), Curtius had published *Balzac* (Bonn, 1923).
6–On 30 May, Curtius said the Director of Marburg University Library would welcome C.

TO *Glen Walton Blodgett*[1] MS Texas

14 August 1923 *The Criterion*, 9 Clarence Gate Gdns

Dear Sir

I am very glad to send you my autograph, and hope in return for this trifling favour you will make me happy by ceasing to *split infinitives*. But as for a poem – I have disposed of my MSS.[2] and I don't think I ought to *forge* new ones!

I am, dear Sir,

Yours faithfully
T. S. Eliot

TO *Charles du Bos* MS Texas

14 August 1923 *The Criterion*, 9 Clarence Gate Gdns

My dear Du Bos,

Pray forgive my intolerable delay, due to grave domestic anxieties – Alas! I shd have liked nothing better than Pontigny, but I have had to be absent so much from London this year that a holiday of any sort is out of the question – Perhaps next year?[3]

I have the temerity to send you our circular, from which you will see I have taken you at your word. May we hope for it *sooner* than 'spring'?[4]

I want now to *entamer*[5] my next long delayed [article] for the *NRF*,[6] but my brain is hardly fit to cope with it.

With most cordial thanks – I shd have been very happy at Pontigny.

Yours very sincerely
T. S. Eliot

1 – Glen Walton Blodgett: an autograph hunter from Buffalo, New York.
2 – TSE had sold the MSS of *TWL* to John Quinn; he had given him *Inventions of the March Hare*.
3 – On 5 July, Du Bos invited TSE to participate in the annual literary conference at Pontigny (Yonne). He enclosed the booklet *Des Entretiens d'Été de Pontigny*, and pointed out that other participants included Gide, André Maurois, Roger Martin du Gard and Edith Wharton.
4 – Du Bos suggested an extract from a future book, *Walter Pater ou l'ascète de la beauté*, which would be 'ready by next spring'. In the event, he did nothing for TSE until 'On "Introduction à la Méthode de Léonard de Vinci" by Paul Valéry', *NC* 14: 55 (Jan. 1935).
5 – 'Begin' (French).
6 – 'Lettre d'Angleterre', *NRF* 21: 122 (1 Nov. 1923).

TO *Natalie Barney* MS Doucet

14 August 1923 9 Clarence Gate Gdns

Dear Miss Barney

I am trying shamefacedly to make up arrears of correspondence – the debt to you is one of the first and most disgraceful.[1] I see no prospect of getting to Paris for a long time – affairs public and domestic keep me even from a weekend. One of the first things I shall do will be to call on you – and as it will not be till autumn at least, I have some hope of finding you.

With grateful thanks
believe me

Sincerely yours
T. S. Eliot

TO *Ford Madox Ford* MS Cornell

14 August 1923 9 Clarence Gate Gdns

Dear Ford

Forgive my intolerable (but universal) delay. Your essay shall definitely appear in October – prominently – and more timely than ever.[2]

Had I been able to do anything about the Viscount[3] I shd have done already. I don't know him, have never seen him, and he is very shy – is never in London, or if so is well-protected by his vassals, cannot be got at. But I will keep my eyes open for the sake of the Cause, and perhaps something could be done in October. It *ought* just to suit his book, and I wish [it] with all my heart.

I'm waiting to see the immense poem.[4] There are I think about thirty *good* lines in *The Waste Land*, can you find them? The rest is ephemeral.

Yrs ever
T. S. Eliot

1 – Barney wrote on 20 June in reply to TSE's letter of 11 May, inviting him to visit when next in Paris, and hoping to 'find a capitalist' to free him from the bank.

2 – 'From the Grey Stone', C. 2: 5 (Oct. 1923), 57–76.

3 – Thinking that TSE knew Lord Rothermere, Ford had asked TSE to tell him that he (Ford) would 'be glad to write some horse-sense about France' for one of his periodicals.

4 – *Mister Bosphorus and the Muses, or a Short History of Poetry in Britain: Variety Entertainment in Four Acts; Words by Ford Madox Ford, Music by Several Popular Composers, with Harlequinade, Transformation Scene, Cinematographic Effects, and Many Other Novelties, as well as Old and Tried Favourites. Decorated with Designs on Wood by Paul Nash* (1923). Ford thought of asking TSE's permission to dedicate it to him, 'Pereant qui

TO *Richard Cobden-Sanderson* TS Beinecke

22 August 1923 *The Criterion*, 9 Clarence Gate Gdns

Dear Cobden-Sanderson,

Many thanks for the Cotton;[1] it is a beautiful book, and does you very great credit. I am very happy to possess it. I have promised to review it for the *Nation* if Saintsbury does not want to do it, but I advised them to try him first.[2]

I have just bought a new typewriter for which the *Criterion* must pay.[3] As I have worn out my Corona in the service of the paper I consider myself entitled to this relief. It is only £10, and guaranteed for two years.

I hope you are making the most of your holiday in spite of the unsettled weather. With best regards to your wife and yourself,

Yours ever
T. S. Eliot

TO *Antonio Marichalar* TS Real Academia de la Historia

23 August 1923 9 Clarence Gate Gdns

Cher collègue,

Merci mille fois pour la *Revista de Occidente*, qui est vraiment une belle production;[4] j'ai lu avec un grand intérêt vos paroles très justes sur Cocteau.[5] Succès à la Revista: mais puisse-t-elle vous laisser le temps et la force de réveiller *Indice* de son sommeil qui dure un peu trop longtemps.[6]

Tout ce que vous me dîtes du *Criterion* me donne beaucoup de plaisir; si la revue peut satisfaire une petite élite internationale, je serai recompensé du travail. En somme, nous avons completé le premier volume sans gaspiller trop d'argent.

—

ante nos . . .' (An abbreviation of the dictum by the Latin grammarian Donastus: 'Pereant qui ante nos nostra dixerunt': 'May they perish who expressed our bright ideas before us'). Ford's long dramatic poem uses music-hall style and historical pastiche to trace the life and death of a poet called Bosphorus all the way from a garret to Poets' Corner.

1–*Poems of Charles Cotton 1630–1687*, ed. John Beresford (Cobden-Sanderson, 1923).

2–George Saintsbury, 'Charles Cotton', *N&A* 33: 22 (1 Sept. 1923), 689.

3–HWE had left TSE his typewriter at the end of his visit to England in 1921.

4–The first number of a Spanish review ed. by José Ortega y Gasset. On 8 Oct., Marichalar thanked TSE for the keen notice of it by F. S. Flint in 'Spanish Periodicals', C. 2: 5 (Oct. 1923).

5–Marichalar, 'Jean Cocteau, *Le Grand Écart*', *Revista de Occidente* I: 1 (July 1923), 123–6.

6–The review *Indice* ran for only four numbers in 1921–2.

Des inquiétudes personnelles toujours chez moi; et des travaux commencés et délaissés. J'ai votre conférence toujours a côté; cela a été precisément une conférence de chevet – pas encore terminée – j'espére en revenir et vous écrire dans un avenir très proche.

Toujours cordialement vôtre

T. S. Eliot[1]

TO *Horace Liveright* CC

23 August 1923 9 Clarence Gate Gdns

Dear Mr Liveright,

Thank you for your letter of 7th instant.[2] I am afraid that rumour, as always, is a little too soon; I hope to have enough material for a miscellaneous book of essays – I suppose about the length of the *Sacred Wood*[3] – in the spring. If so, I should [like] it to be uniform with that volume. I shall be able to give you a provisional list of contents later.[4]

Yours truly,

[T. S. E.]

1 – *Translation*: Dear Colleague, Very many thanks for the *Revista de Occidente*, which is a truly fine production; I have read with great interest your very accurate comments on Cocteau. All success then to the *Revista* but let us hope that it will leave you the time and the energy to awaken *Indice* from a slumber that has lasted rather too long.

Everything you say about the *Criterion* pleases me greatly; if the review can satisfy a small international elite, I shall be compensated for the work involved. On the whole, we have completed the first volume without wasting too much money.

I am still involved in personal anxieties and in projects begun and then abandoned. I still have your lecture beside me; it has actually become my unfinished bedside reading – I hope to come back to it and to write to you in the near future.

As ever, yours cordially, T. S. Eliot

2 – Liveright's letter has not been traced.

3 – TSE's *SW*, published in London in 1920, appeared in the USA from Alfred Knopf in 1921.

4 – On 5 Sept., Liveright agreed the 'new book should be uniform with *The Sacred Wood*', and was 'eager to get a squint at the table of contents'. He also wanted TSE's advice on work to publish in the USA, and suggested meeting in London in Dec. TSE's next book of essays, *For Lancelot Andrewes: Essays on Style and Order* was published by Faber & Gwyer in 1928, and by Doubleday, New York, the following year.

TO *Richard Aldington* CC

23 August 1923 9 Clarence Gate Gdns

My dear Richard

I have been waiting to hear when you were coming to town, to save me the trouble of writing to you. However, I must write one line. I enclose two letters and pray you to answer. I have a card from Monro from Mürren to say that he has not got the Legouis book[1] – did you send for it?

Clyne of Pascal writes in a fury.[2]

Will you work out how much is due to Caffrey for translating Hofmannsthal and tell Cobden to send it to him?[3] It isn't right that the poor man should have to wait since February until next October. His address is now [Charles] Caffrey Esq., Manno, near Lugano, Switzerland.

Have you any ANY notion of anyone to ask for a STORY for January?[4] I have here a load of poems by one John Crowe Ransom, and can't make up my mind how good they are.[5] They are better than most.

What has Levi-Bruhl[6] written about? Whibley has offered me £50 for my introduction;[7] have you heard from him yet?

When I see you we will discuss ways and means of managing in your absence;[8] can you think of anybody whom I could get on with who cd

1–Harold Monro agreed to write an essay on Wordsworth, and asked for a copy of Emile Legouis, *Wordsworth in a New Light* (1923). RA told Monro on 23 June that TSE was 'counting on' his Wordsworth article and would 'jog his memory about the book'. RA also took the opportunity to calm Monro's jealousy: 'I don't see that the *Criterion* and *Chapbook* clash at all. The *Chapbook* is now almost entirely new poetry, isn't it? The *Criterion* is almost wholly critical. I am urging Eliot to use poetry as rarely as possible' (*Richard Aldington: A Life in Letters*, ed. Norman T. Gates [1992], 70). See 'Wordsworth Revisited', *C.* 2: 8 (July 1924).

2–Anthony Clyne had submitted an article on Pascal: it was never published.

3–On 21 Aug., Charles Caffrey complained that his translation of Hofmannsthal, sent the previous Feb., had not been acknowledged: see 'Greece', *C.* 2: 5 (Oct 1923).

4–Apart from WL's 'Mr Zagreus and the Split-Man', the only fiction in the New Year issue was by VHE, under the pseudonym 'F. M.': 'Letters of the Moment – I', *C.* 2: 6 (Feb. 1924).

5–Robert Graves had sent a selection of poems by John Crowe Ransom. The volume ultimately came out as *Grace After Meat*, with Intro. by Graves (Hogarth Press, 1924).

6–Lucien Lévy-Bruhl (1857–1939): French sociologist and anthropologist; Professor at the Sorbonne. TSE was familiar with his work, and in his 'A Prediction in Regard to Three English Authors' saluted the 'brilliant theories of human behavior' of 'MM Durkheim and Levy-Bruhl' (*Vanity Fair* 21: 6, Feb. 1924). Lévy-Bruhl's 'Primitive Mentality and Gambling' appeared in C. 2: 6 (Feb. 1924), 188–200.

7–TSE's intro. to *Seneca: His Tenne Tragedies, translated into English, edited by Thomas Newton* (1927). This was part of the Tudor Translations Series, which CW edited.

8–On 16 Aug., RA said he had 'a great longing to winter in Italy', and could do his work for *C.* and the *TLS* 'just as well in Florence as in Padworth'.

surrogate for you for the more mechanical work? You continuing to deal with mss. correspondence, etc.

yours ever
[T. S. E.]

TO *Alfred Kreymborg* CC

23 August 1923 9 Clarence Gate Gdns

Dear Kreymborg,

Many thanks for your letter of the 6th and your previous letter, and your manuscript.[1] I hope we shall be able to publish it in January – if not it would be April – Aldington has got January as well as October next nearly made up, but I want to squeeze it in.

I have not told you yet how much I enjoyed the Secker puppet plays.[2] I think you have really got hold of something new and fruitful in rythym – at any rate they have been a great stimulation to me and I have read them several times.[3] They are very different indeed from what I have in my mind to attempt, yet they are more like it than anything else I know. I am trying to get at a dominant rythym and subordinated rythyms for the thing – I expect it will be called jazz drama.[4] Anyway, you encourage me to continue.

By the way, how do you make a puppet? As I think I told you,[5] I want to build a small theatre – a box small enough to stand on a table 3 x 3 ft.

1–On 6 Aug 1923, Kreymborg submitted to TSE the article, 'Writing for Puppets', that he had been promising for many months.

2–Kreymborg, *Puppet Plays*, with preface by Gordon Craig (1923). In *Troubadour*, Kreymborg describes his post-war years touring the USA with his wife Dorothy, as 'Puppet People', performing experimental puppet-shows and playing the 'mandolute'. During his visit to London he had conceived the idea of issuing a new edition of the privately printed 'Poem-Mimes', and Martin Secker agreed to publish the volume.

3–TSE's tribute to Kreymborg's texts for puppets has a bearing on the theatrical experiments he had in mind at this time. On 14 Jan. 1924, Kreymborg told TSE the paragraph in his letter 'about Puppet plays was most encouraging. The book has had a very small audience – the usual happening in my case – but your interest, alone, would be enough . . . That you are planning plays of your own – also with puppets – was and is an exciting bit of news.'

4–A ref. to what became *SA* (1932), the first section of which was published as 'Fragment of a Prologue' in *NC* 4: 4 (Oct. 1926), 713–18. As early as 20 Sept. 1920, VW recorded TSE saying he wanted 'to write a verse play in which the 4 characters of Sweeny act the parts' (*Diary*, II, 68).

5–In *Troubadour*, Kreymborg records meeting TSE in his Clarence Gate flat. TSE fixed him with 'a probing eye' while drinking Scotch and soda, and 'asked him a casual question about writing for puppets'. As a result, 'the man from Manhattan lost himself in a subjective

– and preordain every move and gesture and grouping. How do you make faces for the little devils?[1]

I am very curious to know what a symphonic comedy is.[2]

Yours ever,
[T. S. E.]

TO *J. B. Trend* CC

23 August 1923 [*The Criterion*, London]

My dear Trend,

I have not heard from you for so long that I imagine you must have lost all interest in the *Criterion*. I am however impelled to write to you by a remark that Bruce Richmond let drop when I saw him last, some weeks ago. He said that he had heard from you from Spain and that you had discovered manuscripts of very early English music in the library – in Madrid I think.[3] It occurred to me that if you would write a paper about your discovery it would be immensely interesting for the *Criterion* – which wishes somewhat to widen its scope.[4] Even a short paper, or as much as you care to make of it, would be very acceptable.

I do hope you will consider this and let me hear from you. I was deeply interested by an account you gave of a ceremony of Astarte worship in Spain – I wish you would do more of that sort of thing too.

Always sincerely
[T. S. E.]

—

dithyramb no conscious regard for objectivity could control' while 'Eliot smiled his sphinx-like smile and nodded in a friendly fashion' (397).

1–Replying on 14 Jan., Kreymborg recommended using papier mâché and chess pieces, and reading Mrs Joseph's *The Book of Marionettes*. He enquired when his article on puppets was due to appear in *C*. In the event nothing by Kreymborg appeared in *C*.

2–On 6 Aug., Kreymborg said his article had been delayed 'due to an interruption on the part of a clamorous idea for a symphonic comedy (in four acts)'.

3–Trend reported (7 Sept.) that he had discovered 'in the Escurial, an English composition of about 1500 . . . but I haven't seriously tried to identify the words . . . I will try to track it down.'

4–See Trend, 'The Moors in Spanish Music', *C*. 2: 6 (Feb. 1924), 204–19. Trend's essay, the first serious treatment of music in *C*., does not draw on the newly discovered manuscripts.

TO *R. O. Morris*[1] CC

23 August 1923 9 Clarence Gate Gdns

Sir,

I have the permission of my friend Mr Bruce Richmond to use his name in writing to you. Some little time ago I asked him, as somewhat of an authority on the subject, who there was who could write on early English music; he immediately mentioned you, and subsequently sent me an article of yours in *Music & Letters* which interested me very much indeed.[2]

I enclose a circular of the *Criterion* which will give you some notion of the nature of the reviews. You will see that we propose to publish from time to time essays on English painting and on English music. Would you be willing to write for us a paper on some subject in early English music – I suggest Weelkes, for instance.[3] The *Criterion* would consider itself very fortunate in securing such a contribution from you.[4]

I may say that the proper length for an article in the *Criterion* is not more than 5000 words; and that our rates are £10 per 5000 words and pro rata.

Hoping that I may hear from you in a favourable sense,
I remain, Sir,
Your obliged obedient servant,

[T. S. E.]

TO *Anthony Clyne*[5] CC

23 August 1923 [*The Criterion*, London]

Sir,

I am sincerely grieved by your letter of the 15th instant. Your essay was not read by me, but by Mr Aldington, who is now editing the *Criterion*,

1–R. O. Morris (1886–1948): British composer and musicologist; Professor of Counterpoint and Composition at the Royal College of Music, London; author of *Introduction to Counterpoint*, *Contrapuntal Technique in the Sixteenth Century* (1922). Renowned as a teacher of counterpoint, he had among his pupils Gerald Finzi, Sir Michael Tippett and Constant Lambert.

2–Morris published two articles in *Music & Letters* in the early 1920s: 'Hubert Parry' in 1: 2 (Apr. 1920), 94–103; 'Maurice Ravel' in 2: 3 (July 1921), 274–83.

3–Thomas Weelkes (1576?–1623); English composer.

4–Morris did not contribute to C.

5–Anthony Clyne was a freelance critic who wrote for *Music & Letters* and other journals.

and who I presume returned your essay to you. As for the delay, I am heartily sorry, especially if you have thereby been the loser; the fact is that I have had to neglect all my affairs in order to be in the country with a member of my family who was for a long time at the point of death. Thus the MSS. in hand did not reach Mr Aldington for many weeks. I cannot understand, however, why you should not have written the other article on Pascal of which you speak: journalists frequently write two articles on the same subject.[1] And I certainly cannot admit that the *Criterion* did more than express its willingness to read your essay; or that delay in return implies any obligation to print. If such has been your experience, it has been happier than mine: but you have written for more papers than I have.[2] And I must, without prejudice, deny the existence of a parallel between yourself and my grocer.[3]

I am, Sir, your obedient servant,

[T. S. E.]

TO *Charles Caffrey* CC

23 August 1923 [*The Criterion*, London]

Dear Sir,

I have your note of the 21st instant and am humiliated to think that I failed to acknowledge the receipt of your admirable translation of Hofmannsthal.[4] Please accept my apologies. I am asking Mr Aldington to see that the small emolument is paid to you at once. The essay will be published in October, and a copy will be sent you.[5] I did not anticipate that there would be so long a delay in publication.

During this winter I hope to receive articles from Ernst Curtius[6] and from Ernst Bertram;[7] possibly from Hermann Hesse,[8] who is, by the way,

1–Clyne had submitted an article on Pascal, and in his letter of 15 Aug. said he 'could have written a similar article for another magazine in connection with the centenary', had he not been led to understand it had been accepted by C.

2–Clyne's headed paper included a list of eighty-nine titles of papers, from *The Bookman* and *The Contemporary Review* to *The Gas World* and *The Sunday School Times*.

3–In his letter Clyne asked, 'Why should journalists be treated worse than grocers?'

4–Caffrey complained (21 Aug.) that his translation of Hofmannsthal, submitted in Feb., had never been acknowledged.

5–See Caffrey's transl. of Hugo von Hofmannsthal, 'Greece', C. 2: 5 (Oct. 1923), 95–102.

6–E. R. Curtius, 'On the Style of Marcel Proust' (trans. F. S. Flint), C. 2: 7 (Apr. 1924).

7–Ernst Bertram never contributed to C.

8–Hermann Hesse contributed on 'Recent German Poetry', C. 1: 1 (Oct. 1922).

a neighbour of yours, living at Montagnuola; and any of these that come in I will send to you for translation if you will kindly accept them.

I am, Dear Sir,

Yours faithfully
[T. S. E.]

TO *Leone Vivante*[1] CC

23 August 1923 [*The Criterion*, London]

Dear Sir,

I owe you my humble apologies for not having replied to your earlier letters, but I have had to be in the country, on account of my wife's serious illness, and have neglected all correspondence.[2]

We expect to publish Part I of your essay in the January number of the *Criterion*.[3] It is only because the review is a small one, and appears only quarterly, that we are obliged to defer it so long. A copy will be sent you immediately on publication.

We are very much obliged to you for allowing us the honour of introducing such a work to this country.

I am, Dear Sir,

Yours faithfully
[T. S. E.]

1–Leone Vivante (1887–1970): Italian philosopher; author of a series of works on ethics and the theory of knowledge, inc. *Della intelligenza nell'espressione* (1922; trans. as *Intelligence in Expression* [1925]); *Note sopra l'originalita del pensiero* (1925; *Notes on the Originality of Thought* [1927]); *A Philosophy of Potentiality* (1955), and the posthumous *Essays on Art and Ontology* (1980). 'The Misleading Comparison Between Art and Dreams' appeared in *NC* 4: 3 (June 1926); and TSE was to write a preface to *English Poetry* (1950), Vivante's own translation of *La Poesia Inglese ed il suo contributo alla conoscenza dello spirito* (1947).

2–Vivante wrote twice (6 July, 6 Aug.) to ask whether his essay 'The Relation between concept and expression in poetry and prose' (which EP had forwarded) was soon going to be published in C. (Prof. Bullock, at Rome University, had been suggesting improvements to the translation.)

3–In the event, this essay did not appear, and correspondence lapsed until 19 Aug. 1924. *Della intelligenza nell'espressione* was reviewed by W. A. Thorpe in C. 3: 11 (Apr. 1925), 463–4.

TO *Charles Whibley* CC

23 August 1923 [9 Clarence Gate Gdns]

My dear Whibley, I return herewith Kipling's letter.[1] I am extremely grateful to you for your efforts, in addition to all the other kindnesses you have shown the paper, and shall remember each instance. Of course I am disappointed at Kipling's refusal; because he would fit in very well to our cadre;[2] but perhaps there may be justification for trying him again later.

I have been in communication with Bain:[3] he is evasive, and I have been waiting for an opportunity to go to see him. If at any time the name occurs to you of anyone who could write well about Burleigh,[4] I hope you will let me know. I wish you had not already written about Clarendon.[5] I should like to get Oliver on Carteret,[6] as you suggest; I only doubted whether this was a suitable time for Carteret, whom I always imagined as, in his day, a pro-German. But is this a libel?

I am glad you think the *Criterion* is beginning to have character:[7] it was hardly visible in the first numbers; but this was partly due to lack of time and partly to cautiousness.

£50 seems quite ample for the introduction to Seneca.[8] Will you let me know about how long you think it ought to be, and how much ground it

1–On 26 July, CW said he had written to Kipling on TSE's behalf, apparently requesting a contribution to C. On 2 Aug., he enclosed Kipling's letter, saying 'I am sorry the answer is not favourable'. CW hoped that 'at a later date' he might persuade Kipling to change his mind.

2–TSE wrote a sympathetic review of Kipling's *The Years Between* in 'Kipling Redevivus', *A.* (9 May 1919), praising him as 'a very nearly great writer': 'The admired creator [G. Flaubert] of Bouvard and Pécuchet would not have overlooked the Kipling *dossier*.'

3–For F. W. Bain, see note to letter of 3 Sept. On 26 July, CW reported that the 'diffident' Bain 'would like to write about Disraeli'. See his 'Disraeli', C. 2: 6 (Feb. 1924).

4–Alexander Hugh Bruce, sixth Lord Balfour of Burleigh (1849–1921): Conservative politician.

5–CW, 'Edward Hyde, Lord Clarendon', in *Political Portraits* (1917).

6–F. S. Oliver (1864–1934); political polemicist (see note to letter of 3 Sept.); John Carteret, Earl of Glanville (1690–1763), statesman; Lord Lieutenant of Ireland 1724–30; Secretary of State 1742–4; Lord President of the Council, 1751–63. In Dec. 1762, Chesterfield wrote that 'when he [Carteret] dies, the ablest head in England dies too, take it for all in all'.

7–On 2 Aug., CW found 'much that was interesting' in the July C.: 'it has character, above all, & I liked your pronouncement at the end'. TSE's 'pronouncement' was his 'Notes' on 'The Function of a Literary Review', *C.* 1: 4 (July 1923), his first editorial comment.

8–CW had asked TSE to write an introduction to Seneca's tragedies for his Tudor Translations Series. He had 'found a copy', and asked whether '£50 for the introduction' would be 'agreeable'. It appeared as *Seneca: His Tenne Tragedies translated into English, edited by Thomas Newton* (1927): TSE's introduction was reprinted, as 'Seneca in Elizabethan Translation', in *SE* (1934).

ought to cover. I do not suppose you want much textbook information put into it; but I should like to utter a defense of the merit of Seneca as a dramatist and as a poet, in comparison with Euripides. And something ought to be said about the general influence of Seneca on English drama and the influence of this translation.[1] I am looking forward to this piece of work. As there is only one edition, I don't suppose there is any textual emendation to be done?

I have been to and fro incessantly: my wife is fighting pluckily to stick it out in the country, but against every discouragement. – You say nothing of your health; may I infer that you are stronger?

Always yours,
[T. S. E.]

TO *Mary Hutchinson* MS Texas

Sunday [26 August 1923] [London]

My dear Mary

Very many thanks for your sweet letter, you are an angel and give me confidence that we *shall* get a house. The fact is, that it involves so much that I can do nothing about it *at present*: because I cannot possibly afford to take a house *unless* I can sell the lease of the flat, and get a good price for it, *at the same time*. I cannot pay the rent on two dwellings at once.[2] My point however is that just now *I haven't time* to attend to all the business this involves. You see, Mary, I *must* settle down and write a *lot* of articles at once,[3] because I *must* find the money, and I can't do anything else. I tell you this in confidence: I have been living beyond my income for five months, and eating up the savings: Vivien's illness, and the cost of running *two establishments at once*, doctors, food, medicines, constant railway fares etc. have run me into colossal expense, and I must try to find

1 – TSE's introduction opened: 'No author exercised a wider or deeper influence upon the Elizabethan mind or upon the Elizabethan form of tragedy than did Seneca.'

2 – Their London flat at Clarence Gate Gardens and their rented cottage in Fishbourne. (Since Jan. 1923 he had also been paying for the flat at 38 Burleigh Mansions.)

3 – With the exception of his 'London Letters' in *The Dial*, his 'Lettres d'Angleterre' in *NRF*, and a couple of contributions to *C.*, TSE had been unproductive as a journalist since late 1922: he had published only one review, 'John Donne' in *N&A* 33: 10 (9 June 1923). In the autumn he went on to publish 'Andrew Marvell' and 'The Beating of a Drum' in *N&A*, substantial essays on '*Ulysses*, Order and Myth' and 'Marianne Moore' in the *Dial*, a couple of essays in *NRF* and *Vanity Fair*, and two pieces (inc. 'The Function of Criticism') in *C.* 2: 5 (Oct. 1923).

£50 by writing in a month, and more later. (All this time it has been of course quite impossible to write, and I must do it *now*.)

Of course it wd have been much less trouble, taking a house a year ago than it wd be now. But one *important* thing that deterred us is that we should lose Ellen. She has varicose veins and won't stand for stairs etc. But in any case, with the necessity for two sets of negotiations, buying and selling, and perhaps immediate moving to do, I don't see how *I can do anything about a house until Vivien comes back to London*. But I should be very grateful if you would see this house on Chiswick Mall[1] and tell me about it. I think we shall depend on you to get us into the house when it is found!

I am delighted to hear that you are going to give Vivien a course of reading – only don't feed her too *fast*. Her illness has reduced her vitality so low that she can only read a very little at a time – it is too tiring and too exciting. I like her to do as much *manual* work as she can, when she cannot be out of doors. She has been painting furniture very beautifully: and while this is physically tiring, it is mentally restful. And also her *eyes* are so bad that she ought not to read *much*.

I am sure also that her mind was utterly worn out and *ruined* by my indecision over the *Nation* – which went on so *long* too – I know that the strain of that was deadly to her. No one will ever know what she went through.

I should love to see you and discuss everything in London when you are there – it can't be done satisfactorily in Sussex – we don't want to think about practical affairs on our picnics, and meanwhile I hope to see you and Jack there. I will write before the weekend –

What a lovely bonnet.

With much affection
Tom

His Mother TO *Henry Eliot* — TS Houghton

28 August 1923 — [24 Concord Ave]

Dear Henry:

It seems almost cruel to bring to you all my problems, when you are so busy in your daily business affairs. Yet you are the only person to whom I can go.

1 – A house on Chiswick Mall would have been close to the Hutchinsons at Riverside House.

To begin with a small matter of business, I received a note from Miss Gerlach this morning asking if Brinker could be allowed to stay if he would confine himself to that portion of Spring Avenue not leased.[1] I wrote her I thought it safest to let him go if Zeibig had so requested as probably the Southern Wheel Company had complained. Brinker is three months behind with rent, and I think I will add a postscript to my letter to Miss Gerlach asking her to try and collect back rent before giving notice to vacate.

The next matter is personal and business both, and relates to a letter received from Tom yesterday. I had written him that his share of the estate had been left in trust.[2] This causes him concern. I will copy most of the letter before discussing it. He says referring to his not writing: 'It hasn't been simply lack of time but a paralysis from misery'. This is about what I supposed. And it is difficult to say anything to encourage him, for Vivian's seems about the most hopeless case I know of. Then he goes on: 'Vivien is still at the cottage – sticking it out by pure pluck. It is a dilemma. She ought to be out of London, but she cannot go to a hotel so long as the doctors insist on her having her meat minced in a mincing machine. And *somebody* must inspect the machine every day to see that it is kept clean.'

'I must explain about brickstock.[3] Until I can convert it into Bonds, I cannot feel that I can depend on it, useful as it has been. *I do not know how I should have got through without it*, yet it might for a year *or more* at a time pay no dividends. The point is that I cannot – no honourable man could – take risks until I know that in case of my death I could leave Vivien provided for, with just enough to live upon. She will get *very little* from her parents. The estate has dwindled very much since [the] war – it was chiefly in Irish property and you can realize what that means now,[4] and as it is her father and mother cannot afford to live in England all the year round. And death duties are immensely heavy here, that is two death duties before the money is divided between Vivien and Maurice. So that I am only taking the precaution that any man would take, especially as it will be a long time before Vivien is quite cured. Malnutrition which only

1–A rental property that Mrs Eliot owned in St Louis.

2–In her letter to TSE of 5 Aug., Mrs Eliot explained that Margaret's and his share of their father's estate was 'left in trust'.

3–His stocks in the Hydraulic-Press Brick Company. In her letter of 5 Aug., she reminded TSE that, in addition to his income from the bank, he had (like Henry) 275 shares in Hydraulic, and she intended to give him fifty more. She had turned these over to Henry in case of her sudden death.

4–The Haigh-Wood income derived largely from their Irish property at Ballsbridge, nr. Dublin. Since the founding of the Irish Free State in 1922, however, Ireland had been convulsed by civil war between government forces and irregulars opposed to the treaty.

French and German doctors really understand, is years coming on and hence a long time to cure.'

'You tell me that my share of the estate is *left in trust*. Does this mean that when I die it reverts? This is important to me because what I need, in order to feel free to accept a literary post, is assurance of an income, to cover not *my* duration of life, but Vivien's. In other words I want her to have a life interest for the duration of her life, not mine, just in case she outlives me (which is highly improbable). I think it ought to revert to the family after her death. This is only fair and indeed I should not want any inheritance that discriminated for me against her.[1]

'What I want is for you to have enough money to make your visit to me to us next year without pinching. Let me look forward to that – we both talk of it so often. I am going to write to Henry.'

[incomplete]

TO *Virginia Woolf* TS Berg

Wednesday, 29 August [1923] 9 Clarence Gate Gdns

My dear Virginia,

I am immensely pleased – more than you realise – by your invitation. I do want to see you, more than anyone, but I don't feel that I can accept either for the 15th or the 22nd,[2] because matters are so unsettled at present – as long as Vivien is at Fishbourne I shall go there every weekend; and she may be back any day or she may stay into October – that is the only safe way to leave it. So I shall simply wait and let you know – and of course in return I shall want you to say simply that you cannot have me: I put it this way simply because I want very much indeed to see you, and because I should like to feel that if at any moment I proposed myself you would not have the slightest *gêne* [difficulty] in saying that it was not convenient. If you don't agree to this I can only say: may I spend a night with you (instead of calculating trains) at Richmond?[3]

Yours always
Tom

1 – Since his marriage, and particularly since knowing of his father's will, TSE had been preoccupied by the need to support VHE during her illness and in the event of his death.
2 – On 10 Aug., VW told Gerald Brenan she had 'seen Lytton and Eliot' at Rodmell. 'Eliot will come and stay with us. At first I shall find him very pompous and American. Later, rather young and simple' (*Letters* III, 65). *TWL* was due from the Hogarth Press 'in a week or two'.
3 – At Hogarth House, the Woolfs' town address.

TO *Valery Larbaud* TS Vichy

[Early September 1923] 9 Clarence Gate Gdns

My dear Larbaud,

Many thanks for your wire. I am very sorry to have worried you about this while you were ill;[1] please accept my sympathy and hopes (not altogether disinterested) for your rapid recovery. It is of course a great disappointment not to be able to start volume II with Landor; but the January number will be all the brighter, if you can get your first section finished by the 1st of December.

I hope we may see you in London this winter. The English edition of my *Waste Land* appears next week,[2] and I shall see that a copy is sent to you and to the *Revue Européenne*.

Yours very sincerely,
T. S. Eliot

TO *Virginia Woolf* TS Berg

[3? September 1923] *The Criterion*, 9 Clarence Gate Gdns

Dear Virginia

Of course you cannot keep space for me on the possibility of my being able to come – I was afraid afterwards that I might have put it that way. But I want to say that I shall miss my annual visit to Rodmell very much; but if Vivien can stick it out in the country, I should not like to go so long as a fortnight without seeing her. I may look forward, however, to spending the night some time in Richmond?

I am delighted with the *Waste Land* which has just arrived.[3] Spacing and paging are beautifully planned to make it the right length, far better than the American edition.[4] I am afraid it gave you a great deal of trouble.

1–On 14 June, Larbaud told TSE he hoped to send the 'first article' on Landor at 'the end of August'. This elusive article, first solicited in autumn 1922, never appeared.
2–The English edn of *TWL* was to appear from the Hogarth Press on 12 Sept. 1923.
3–The first publication of *TWL* in book form (and with notes) in the UK; hand-set by LW and VW, with a print run of 460 copies, it was priced 4s. 6d.
4–The US edn, published by Boni & Liveright in Dec. 1922, had only 12 or so lines per page, and the poem occupied 49 pages, followed by 11 pages of notes. In contrast, the Hogarth edn had up to 27 lines per page, so that the poem occupied 20 pages and the notes just six. This gave a different sense of the poem's distinctive form and typographical layout, closer to that in its first appearance in C. 1: 1 (Oct. 1922), where the poem occupied 15 pages without notes.

You also had to contend against my abominable proofreading: I see one dreadful oversight for which I owe apologies: p. 7, I left *under* London Bridge instead of *over*![1] Will you tell Leonard how much I like the book? Also that if you can, I should like review copies to go to the *Nouvelle Revue Française* and *La Revue Européenne*, which *ought* to review it.[2] But if that exceeds your limit I will send them; I shall probably have to take most of my royalties in complimentary copies, I have so many I must send. I think it is simpler if I order a certain number from you and settle it with you quite apart from royalties, however.

When I see you next I shall attack you again on the subject of a story or sketch from you for the 1923 *Criterion* – so be prepared with an *ébauche* [outline].[3]

Always yours
Tom

TO *Charles Whibley* CC

3 September 1923 9 Clarence Gate Gdns

My dear Whibley,

I am writing, as usual, to ask you for a favour. You promised an obituary note on Ker,[4] and although you have already given your testimony in *Blackwoods*[5] – I read that with great interest, and the Musings, as usual, with great pleasure – I am wholly in agreement about the nature of the German – I hope you will not shrink from the opportunity of doing so again. As for the collaborate testimony, which I contemplated, I fear it is now too late to consider such an attempt; but the *Criterion*, especially as it is so fortunate as to publish Ker's essay,[6] as leader, must have some

1–In the Hogarth text, l. 62 read 'A crowd flowed under London Bridge, so many' rather than 'A crowd flowed over London Bridge, so many'; l. 96 read 'In which sad light a coloured dolphin swam' rather than 'In which sad light a carvèd dolphin swam', as in C. and later editions. In most of TSE's presentation copies, he corrected these mistakes in the text, as well as, in the notes, substituting 'Cambridge' for 'Macmillan' as the publisher of Jessie Weston's *From Ritual to Romance* (a mistake that was taken over from the Boni & Liveright edn). These corrections were incorporated on the poem's republication in *P 1909–1925*.
2–There was no review in *NRF*.
3–VW's next contribution was 'Character in Fiction' (later 'Mr Bennett and Mrs Brown') – a paper read to the 'Heretics', Cambridge, in May 1924 – in C. 2: 8 (July 1924).
4–On 26 Sept., CW told TSE that W. P. Ker, who had died in July, was 'a great scholar & a great man', and his 'closest friend' for many years.
5–CW, 'W. P. Ker', *Blackwood's Magazine* 214 (Sept. 1923), 386–93.
6–W. P. Ker, 'Byron: An Oxford Lecture', C. 2: 5 (Oct. 1923), 1–15.

tribute to him. And of course – apart from the fact that you were responsible for his appearing here – you are the only person to do it. Could you then let us have – within the fortnight – about 300 words, to be printed with the editorial paragraphs at the end.[1] Thus printed, it would have the effect of suggesting a close connexion between yourself and the review: I hope you will not mind that.

I have seen and enjoyed F. W. Bain;[2] I am trying to persuade him to write on Disraeli, and controvert Strachey;[3] he is under the mistaken impression that the subject, and what he wants to say about it, are not sufficiently literary.

If I write to Oliver[4] or to Kerry,[5] both of whom you suggested for their subjects, may I mention your name? I suppose I shall have to attack J. A. Smith[6] for Aristotle, but I doubt if it is possible to get anything out of him. Do you happen to know what John Burnet's political views are?[7] I want to get something from him on Greek philosophy, but I will not ask him for Aristotle or Plato if his politics are at all romantic.

If Bain is obdurate, would you be able to have your Maurras in time for the January number?[8] Otherwise I should like to publish it in April.

I hope you are in good health. I am tired and dejected. I feel that I ought for the obvious reasons to have accepted the *Nation*, last spring; if there is ever any chance – I do not hope for such good fortune – on a more sympathetic paper I shall take it.[9]

1–This appeared as 'W. P. Ker (1855–1923)', *C.* 2: 5 (Oct. 1923), 103.
2–See following letter.
3–As Michael Holroyd notes, Lytton Strachey's portrait of Disraeli, in *Queen Victoria* (1921), was 'almost as sympathetic as his Melbourne' (*Lytton Strachey: The New Biography*, 493). Strachey said the 1874 Tory victory was 'pre-eminently due to the skill and vigour of Disraeli. He returned to office, no longer the dubious commander of an insufficient host, but with drums beating and flags flying, a conquering hero' (*Queen Victoria*, VIII). TSE noted, 'Disraeli appears to be too consciously playing a *rôle* for Mr Strachey to extract much fantasy from him' ('London Letter', *Dial* 71: 2, Aug. 1921). See Bain, 'Disraeli', *C.* 2: 6 (Feb. 1924).
4–F. S. Oliver (1864–1934): a partner in the Debenhams drapery firm; a formidable political polemicist. He was author of *Alexander Hamilton* (1906), *The Ordeal of Battle* (1915), and *The Endless Adventure*, a study of parliament in the age of Walpole (3 vols, 1930–5).
5–Lord Kerry. See TSE to RA, 20 Sept.
6–J. A. Smith (1863–1939): philosopher and classical scholar; Waynflete Professor of Moral and Metaphysical Philosophy at Oxford, known for his contribution to Aristotelian scholarship; author of *The Nature of Art* (1924). TSE had attended his lectures on *De Anima*.
7– For Burnet see note to TSE's letter of 1 Oct.
8–Whibley said he could not possibly write on Maurras by Jan. (in fact he never did). His 'Lord Chesterfield' appeared in *C.* 2: 7 (Apr. 1924).
9–This is the first indication that the Liberal-leaning political stance of *N.* had any bearing on TSE's rejection of Keynes's offer of its literary editorship. In reply, CW said TSE was 'right

Ker's 'Byron' is extraordinarily good.

[T. S. E.]

TO *F. W. Bain*[1] CC

3 September 1923 9 Clarence Gate Gdns

Dear Mr Bain

After our conversation – which I otherwise much enjoyed – I rather anticipated your refusal, but I was going to write to you tonight in any case to put you right. I was aware that I had given you a mistaken impression of our purposes. It is not contemplated merely to treat subjects of literary interest only. We have in view treatment not only of statesmen like Bolingbroke, who belong to literature, and statesmen like Disraeli who touch literature, but others who have no literary interest whatever. I have wished to get something on Burleigh, if I can find the man to write it; and Whibley has also suggested Carteret – which I should be very glad to have.

The point which I put in a misleading way is this: we want it to be clear that the *Criterion* is apart from current political controversy, that it is independent of party politics, and leagued with an ideal rather than with the actual Tory party. There is no other periodical extant which pursues the discovery and maintenance of the philosophy and history of politics; and a Conservative review which is founded rather on Aristotle than on the views of Viscount Younger[2] is somewhat of a novelty. I do not want people to think that the *Criterion* has become a party organ, or that it is pursuing politics miscellaneously alongside of literature. We have no views on the occupation of the Ruhr[3] or Corfu,[4] or tariffs, but we have views on the nature of *to douleion*.[5] If it were supposed that the *Criterion* was interested directly in politics, it would lose its usefulness. My belief is that if one has

---

not to have anything to do with the *Nation*': he would have been disgusted by Keynes's 'stock-jobbing point of view'.

1–Francis Bain: see Glossary of Names.

2–George Younger (1851–1929), chairman of the Unionist party, 1917–23, was made Viscount Younger of Leckie in 1923, and was party treasurer of the Conservative and Unionist Party in the House of Lords until his death.

3–In Jan. 1923, French and Belgian troops occupied the Ruhr in response to the Weimar Republic's failure to pay reparations in the aftermath of WW1. The British government deplored the occupation, which lasted until 1925.

4–The Greek island of Corfu was occupied by Italian forces on 31 Aug. 1923 in protest against the assassination of General Tellini.

5–'the slavish' (Greek).

principles at all, they will have their consequences in both literature and politics, they will apply to both. I should like too to give to Toryism the intellectual basis with the illusion of which Socialism has so long deceived the young and eager. And I believe that the intellectual hold of socialism on the young is weakening, and that there is the chance of establishing an austere classicism.[1] Toryism is a view of life; and Tory and Whig (I am not interested in the superficial distinction of Conservative and Liberal) will [TSE's typing has here run off the page] literature I include things as discrepant as Gilbert Murray and Lytton Strachey, and Middleton Murry.[2] I mean romantic, opposed to classical, to Greek culture.

I want to make it clear therefore that the limitations I sketched the other day are not limitations to literary subject matter, but limitations to a somewhat uncommon approach to politics. We shall have many contributions no more literary, in the narrow sense, than yours: Guignebert on the Devil,[3] and Lévy-Bruhl on Gambling in Primitive Society,[4] and Elliot-Smith on the movements of races.[5]

So I hope that this letter will persuade you to reverse your decision – you cannot maintain it on the ground you have taken.[6]

Yours sincerely
[T. S. E.]

TO *Richard Cobden-Sanderson* TS Texas

3 September 1923 *The Criterion*, 9 Clarence Gate Gdns

Dear Cobden-Sanderson,

Many thanks for your letter. Yes, I should be grateful for the £10 as soon as you can let me have it, as it is a little difficult to keep my bank account in funds at present, and I have already paid for this machine.

1–TSE's espousal of 'Classicism' is given further definition in 'The Function of Criticism' in *C.* 2: 5 (Oct. 1923), where he opposes it to both 'Romanticism' and 'Whiggery'.
2–TSE mounted a critique of the Cambridge classical scholar Gilbert Murray in 'Euripides and Professor Murray' in *SW* (1920), portraying his style as 'a vulgar debasement of the eminently personal idiom of Swinburne'. In one of his London Letters, TSE characterised Strachey as a 'romantic mind', dealing 'with his personages, not in a spirit of "detachment", but by attaching himself to them, *tout entier à sa proie attaché*', *Dial* 71: 2 (Aug. 1921), 215. He dealt with JMM in 'The Function of Criticism', in *C.* 2: 5 (Oct. 1923), opposing himself as a Classicist to JMM as a representative of Romanticism, Whiggery and the 'Inner Voice'.
3–Professor Charles Guignebert, 'Concerning the Devil', *C.* 2: 5 (Oct. 1923), 16–30.
4– L. Lévy-Bruhl, 'Primitive Mentality and Gambling', *C.* 2: 6 (Feb. 1924), 188–200.
5–Elliot Smith's essay did not appear; but see 'The Glamour of Gold', *C.* 3: 11 (Apr. 1925), 345–55.
6–Bain did reverse his decision: his 'Disraeli' appeared in *C.* 2: 6 (Feb. 1924), 143–66.

I hope you are enjoying your holiday without thought of the *Criterion* or other troubles; and I *think* that No. 1[1] will be in a state not to disturb your serenity when you return.

Yours ever,
T. S. E.

TO *Ezra Pound* — TS Lilly

3 September 1923 — *The Criterion*, 9 Clarence Gate Gdns

My dear Ezra

Enclosed is returned to you for full particulars. I am not sensitive enough to grasp the meaning.[2] Wasnt cheque enclosed or isnt it enough. If latter will do what I can, but must have more than a hint.

Now what the devil do you want me to print.[3]

Have done my best to get Joyce and Lewis.[4] Cocteau[5] has promised (in conversation with Lady R.) should be glad of a reminder. Hemingway[6] you know I have never seen, cant order things without knowing what to expect, if he sends shall receive careful a tention; Mac Almon[7] may be coming on, but I havnt been privileged to see him come, he was pretty callow when I knew anything about it, but same applies to him as to Hemingway; Barfield is I think better than Goold Adams, but they are

1–The first issue of *C.* 2 was dated 'October 1923' but numbered 'Vol. II. No. 5'.
2–Presumably a ref. to a complaint about payment for 'Malatesta Cantos'.
3–On 30 July, Pound sent TSE a five-page diatribe against *C.* 2: 4. With the exception of his own work, the rest of the number was 'unreadable, save the Yeats (unimportant and already read in *Dial*)'. He told TSE: 'But for yr. connection with the review I couldn't go on appearing with this bunch of dead mushrooms . . . *Franchement* (tautology perhaps for me to use the term) *c'est pire que le Dial*. I mean the *Criterion* is worse than the *Dial*.'
4–See JJ, 'Fragment of an Unpublished Work', *C.* 3: 12 (July 1925). Extracts from WL's *The Apes of God* appeared in *C.* 2: 6 & 7 (Feb. & Apr. 1924). EP anathematised all the writers who appeared in *C.* 1: 4 (July 1923), and suggested: 'Lewis (i.e. Wyndham not Sinclair Lewis) Hemingway, Mac Almon, also Joyce (I take it the answer to the last is in the affirmative). Cocteau? (at any rate lucid) Cros?'
5–Jean Cocteau: see Glossary of Names. His 'Scandales' appeared in French in *NC* 4: 1 (Jan. 1926). He had promised Lady Rothermere he would contribute something.
6–Ernest Hemingway (1899–1961) formed part of EP's expatriate circle in Paris, but had not yet published much. He published *Three Stories and Ten Poems* in 1923, and made his name with *In Our Time* (1925) and *The Sun Also Rises* (1926). He never published in *C.*
7–Robert McAlmon (1896–1956): poet and publisher, an expatriate American in Paris. He published a book of stories called *A Hasty Bunch* (1922), and the autobiographical *Post-Adolescence* (1923); and he founded Contact editions which published Hemingway, Stein and others. He did not appear in *C.*

much in the same class;[1] have no objection to her translation of Picabia,[2] but cannot accept without seeing. You are very wide of the mark about bloomsbury. If you want to cite facts about Whibley's character[3] (which you have not yet done) they may or may not be relevant; he writes fairly decent English, and is an enemy of the *Mercury*, Gosse, G. Murray, bloomsbury[4] and a number of other things. He compares favourably with your friend Clutton Brock,[5] who is the dirtiest shit with the worst mind in London, which is saying a good deal. May I mention that Robertson, who has annihilated Brock and Murry as no one else has done, has suffered through association with me and that he is NOT reviewed any longer by *The Times* or the bloomsbury press in consequence, and that although he is a whig the whig vermin will not associate with him. These points may not interest you. I ask you to cite one writer of first merit whom I have not tried to get? It would be useful to know. Of course I don't think ¾ of the stuff worth printing, but ¼ is a larger proportion than any other paper can show.[6] *Waste Land* and *Cantos* do more good in this society than in the company of cummings cowley hauptmann etc.[7] Please remember that the *Dial,* not the *Criterion,* is the bloomsbury organ, owing to Mortimer, birrell garnett etc.[8] Programme not all there is to say by any means but authentic so far as it goes.[9] More presently.

1–Owen Barfield's 'Dope' appeared in the July *C.*, prompting EP to say: 'Barfield is *merde*'. At EP's prompting, TSE published Goold-Adams's story 'The Obsequies' in *C.* 1: 3 (Apr. 1923).
2–EP said, 'I take it there is no use submitting Adams's trans, of Picabia's *J. C. Rastaquouere*, even after I have gone over it?' Francis Picabia published *Jésus-Christ Rastaquoère* in 1920.
3–EP referred to CW as 'The petrified shit Whibley', and praised Wickham Steed as 'less stupid than H. Read and less corrupt than Whibley'.
4–In his July letter EP said: 'I can stand your conservatism, and scholarship, but not the Bloomsbury mush that seems to get between yr. chinks.'
5–Arthur Clutton-Brock (1868–1924): journalist, critic, essayist; author of *Shelley: The Man and the Poet* (1911). His *Shakespeare's Hamlet* (1922) took TSE to task for his account of *Hamlet* (in 'Hamlet and His Problems') as 'an artistic failure', saying his 'arguments are partly taken from Mr [J. M.] Robertson, though not stated with his accuracy'.
6–EP reprimanded TSE: 'You CANT possibly think ¾th of the stuff in this years *Crit.* has been *in se* worth printing.' Writing to WL on 6 Sept., EP related that TSE 'has replied in a rather satisfactory manner, admitting that ¾ths of the stuff isn't worth printing' (*Pound/Lewis: The Letters of Ezra Pound and Wyndham Lewis*, ed. Timothy Materer (1985), 137).
7–In his diatribe against *C.*, EP conceded: 'On the other hand, the achievement of having printed *Waste Land* and *Cantos,* in London in one year . . . but do we need to bury or embed it in such diarrhoetic and flowing merde'. Malcolm Cowley, E. E. Cummings and Gerard Hauptmann, who are mentioned by TSE, all appeared in the *Dial* in the first half of 1923.
8–Raymond Mortimer had published 'London Letters' in the 1923 *Dial*, and Francis Birrell an essay on 'Proust: Prophet of Despair', while David Garnett's *Lady into Fox* (1922) was mentioned in a review. All three writers were associated with Bloomsbury. Garnett and Birrell ran a bookshop in Bloomsbury.
9–In his letter, EP asked: 'This published programme of yours??? is that all there is to say?? Is it what you mean?? or is there a private programme?'

Je tembrasse sur les 2 joues.[1]

have mapt out Aristophanic comedy,[2] but must devote study to phallic songs, also agons.[3]

King Bolo's big black basstart queen[4]
  Was awfly bright and cheerful
Well fitted for a monarch's bride
  But she wasn't always keerful.
Ah yes King Bolo's big black queen
  Was not above suspicion;
We wish that such was not the case –
But whats the use of wishin?

The dancers on the village green
They breathed light tales of Bolo's queen

The ladies of King Bolo's court
  They gossiped with each other
They said 'King Bolo's big black queen
  Will soon become a mother[']
They said 'an embryonic prince
  Is hidden in her tumbo;
His prick is long his balls are strong
And his name is Boloumbo'.

Basstart is the feminine form of bassturd. Brock is a bassturd.[5]

1 – 'I kiss you on both cheeks' (French).

2 – *SA* was sub-titled 'Fragments of an Aristophanic Melodrama' (1932).

3 – In the *The Origin of Attic Comedy* (1914), F. M. Cornford discusses Aristotle's account of the origins of comedy as deriving from 'phallic songs'. 'What is now generally called the *Agon*' is 'a fierce "contest" between the representatives of two parties or principles, which are in effect the hero and villain of the whole piece'. TSE drew on Cornford when devising his own 'Aristophanic' *SA*; and on 18 Mar. 1933 he would tell the producer Hallie Flanagan, 'See also F. M. Cornford. *Origins of Attic Comedy*, which is important to read before you do the play.'

4 – TSE's Bolo poems go back to his student years at Harvard, as recalled in Conrad Aiken's memoir, 'King Bolo and Others', where they are described as 'hilariously naughty *parerga* . . . devoted to that singular and sterling character known as King Bolo, not to mention King Bolo's Queen, "that airy fairy hairy – 'un"' (in *T. S. Eliot: A Symposium*, ed. R. March and Tambimuttu [1948], 22). Some early versions are reprinted in *IMH* (315–20). These latest variants respond to the scatological abuse in EP's letter, and are themselves an instance of modern 'phallic songs'.

5 – A reference to Arthur Clutton-Brock, described earlier as 'the dirtiest shit' in London.

TO *Bruce Richmond* CC

3 September 1923 9 Clarence Gate Gdns

My dear Richmond,

I arise from the grave only to make appeals. You will remember that you recommended R. O. Morris and that I wrote to him.[1] Now he writes to say that he is not at present, for private reasons, undertaking musical criticism; he advises me to try Miss Townsend Warner.[2] I have the impression that you mentioned her name, but I made no note of it, and I am not sure that she was not one of the persons who you said were keeping the pot of controversy bubbling. Would you mind reminding me, and if you do not think her suitable would you suggest another? I should be very grateful.

I wrote also Trend,[3] at New Quebec Street, but have no reply. Is he possibly still in Spain?

Also, I think you offered to write to Burnet. I do want Burnet (I have just lent his books to Richard, who is delighted with them).[4] Might I ask you to write, and if so should I write simultaneously or wait?

I am placed now (I am moved to the Colonial and Foreign Department, 30 King William Street) so that it is somewhat easier for me to slip away for lunch, for a shade longer than the statutory hour, and if ever convenient to you, I should be delighted if you would lunch with me one day at some place most accessible to yourself.

If you are frightfully busy, forgive me and don't bother to write.

Yours always,
[T. S. E.]

1 – See TSE's letter to Morris, 23 Aug.

2 – Sylvia Townsend Warner (1893–1978): English novelist and poet, whose poems *The Espalier* (1925) and first novel, *Lolly Willowes* (1926), were still to come. At this time, she was an editor of *Tudor Church Music* (1922–9). She did not contribute to *C*.

3 – See TSE's letter to J. B. Trend, 23 Aug.

4 – John Burnet's books included *Early Greek Philosophy* (1892) and *Aristotle on Education* (1903).

TO *W. R. Lethaby*[1] CC

5 September 1923 [*The Criterion*, London]

Dear Professor Lethaby,

I think that it is over a year ago that I wrote to you about the *Criterion*, so that you cannot complain that I have plagued you. You will see from this circular that your name represents a defect in what seems to me an otherwise brilliant list. I am sending you the essay[2] on architecture which I enclose, in the hope that it may stimulate you to write at least a little paper for us. But remember that any subject in connexion with art or architecture that you choose would be welcome to us; and if this essay does not interest you, or if you are too busy, or for any other reason, do not bother to return it. There is no one else whom we should ask to write about these subjects.

Sincerely yours,
[T. S. E.]

TO *Richard Cobden-Sanderson* TS Texas

7 September 1923 *The Criterion*, 17 Thavies Inn

Dear Cobden-Sanderson

Thank you for the cheque, for which I enclose your receipt herewith. For God's sake do something at once about Lady Rothermere, and get enough money to cover the October number too: Wire her at the quai Voltaire address – 33 isn't it?

I am writing to Wardle in Paris, as he does not seem to have come to London.

I am very glad you are having a lotophagic holiday.

Yours ever
TSE

We shall get a nasty reputation if we can't pay contributors promptly.

1 – William Richard Lethaby (1857–1931): educationist and architect; disciple of John Ruskin and William Morris; first director of the Central School of Arts and Crafts, London, 1896–1911; and from 1900 professor of the School of Ornament and Design at the Royal College of Art; surveyor of the fabric of Westminster Abbey from 1906; author of *Architecture, Mysticism and Myth* (1891), and *Westminster Abbey and the King's Craftsmen: A Study of Medieval Building* (1906).

2 – Not identified.

TO *Mary Hutchinson* — Telegram Texas

11.00 8 September 1923 — Fishbourne

WOULD YOU LIKE PICNIC ITCHENOR FERRY SEVEN O'CLOCK BRINGING OWN FOOD

TO *Richard Cobden-Sanderson* — TS Beinecke

14 September 1923 — *The Criterion*, 9 Clarence Gate Gdns

Dear Cobden-Sanderson.

I am glad to hear that you are back in London. If you have not yet heard from Lady Rothermere, please write to her at once at Hotel de l'Europe, VENICE, whence I have just heard from her. Will you, at your convenience, send copies of No. 4 to

Herrn Dr Ernst Robert Curtius,
M a/L,
Rotenberg 15 a,
Hessen, Germany,

and to

Dr Wilhelm Lehmann,
HOLZMINDEN (Braunschweig)
Landschulheim 2,
Germany,

and send the *Criterion* (for one year) with Vol. II no. 1 to

Miss Hale,[1]
Johnston Hall,
Milwaukee-Downer College,
Milwaukee, Wis. U.S.A.

No. 1 is all in, except 300 words small type from Chas. Whibley.[2] I hope no. 4 has been going well, but we shall meet next week – I will ring you up on Monday.

Yours always
T. S. E.

1 – Emily Hale (1891–1969), with whom TSE had fallen in love while at Harvard.
2 – Whibley, 'W. P. Ker', C. 2: 5 (Oct. 1923).

TO *Ottoline Morrell* TS Texas

14 September 1923 *The Criterion*, 17 Thavies Inn

My dear Ottoline,

Thank you very much for your letter and for the enclosure from Lady Margaret Levett.[1] I have no time to write, this is just a line to thank you for your thought and efforts, and to say that I wait eagerly to hear. Of course, if I could get such a post, to start with the winter term, I should be able to leave London and take Vivien to Freiburg, if she would go with me; but I feel so little hope of eligibility that I do not think about it. Everything you can say and express is a genuine help, be sure.

With much affection
Tom

TO *Virginia Woolf* TS Berg

Friday, [14 September 1923] 9 Clarence Gate Gdns

My dear Virginia,

This is very kind of you and distressing: I shall be very sorry not to see Rodmell this year. But I can only say that I hope that you are coming back to Richmond soon; I want very much to see you as soon as you do. Vivien is only staying on as long as the weather makes it possible, so that we have no idea how long it will be.

I have received the six copies of the *Waste Land*. Now may I order from you twelve more copies? I want to pay for them when I get them; it is much simpler. There are a number of people to whom I must send it.

I have been in to Jones & Evans and corrected the copies they have (they say they have sold three). There are three mistakes I left: 'under' for 'over' London Bridge; 'Coloured' for 'carven' dolphin; and Macmillan for Cambridge University Press for Miss Weston's book.[2] I hope you will forgive me.

Will you tell Leonard that I got a note from Miss Jones asking me for Marvell,[3] and sent it off the next day. I have just corrected the proof. I will try to do you a thing on Elizabethan prose[4] next week if I can, to use at your convenience; because after that I want to clear two or three months

1–Lady Margaret Levett was TSE's English contact with Dr K. B. Martin of Freiburg.
2–See letter to VW of 3? Sept.
3–'Andrew Marvell', *N&A* 33: 26 (29 Sept. 1923), 809.
4–'The Beating of a Drum', *N&A* 34: 1 (6 Oct 1923), 11–12.

to work more or less connectedly on two rather difficult things, prose and verse.[1]

I am very pleased that you cared to write to me again about Sunday, and I wish I could be at Rodmell and at Chichester at once. But do let me know when to expect you in London.[2]

Affectionately
TSE

TO *Ezra Pound*

TS Lilly

14 September 1923 — *The Criterion*, 17 Thavies Inn

Dear E. P.

Very well. Please tell me what – within possibilities – you consider a reasonable payment.[3] I remember wiring to you that it would be 'about £20'. It was £18. I can go the extra £2 but I dont think we can go beyond. As you did not demur at the time I presumed that you were satisfied. Remember that it is not a question of absolute values at all but of what we can afford. Otherwise it would be £50.

Re our recent conversation, I have some hope of something from Wyndham [Lewis].[4] Wickham Steed NO![5] He created Czechoslovakia, I am told; and I, on the other hand, am anxious to see the Hapsburgs restored.[6]

1–The verse is probably a reference to what became *SA*; the prose probably '*Ulysses*, Order and Myth' for *Dial* 75: 5 (Nov. 1923), or 'Lettre d'Angleterre' for *NRF* 21: 122 (1 Nov. 1923). After 'The Beating of a Drum' he published nothing else in *N&A* for three years.
2–The Woolfs returned from Rodmell to London on 30 Sept.
3–In response to TSE's question (3 Sept.), 'Wasnt cheque enclosed or isnt it enough', EP wrote 'Answer to first question is emphatically in the negative. £18–0–0 is insufficient payment for 11 months work.'
4–On 3 Sept., TSE told EP he had done his 'best' to 'get Joyce and Lewis'. WL had evidently written since then, thanking TSE for *TWL*, and saying he had been 'hanging on – and [had] not written – because undecided about a title for fragment'. He settled on 'Mr Zagreus and the Split-Man', which appeared in *C.* 2: 6 (Feb. 1924).
5–Henry Wickham Steed (1871–1956): foreign editor of *The Times* 1914–19; editor 1919–22. On 30 July, EP told TSE: 'Wickham Steed, might be better than some of yr. contributors' and 'was out of a job'.
6–TSE's jocular declaration of allegiance to the defunct Hapsburg Empire may have a bearing on *TWL*, in which he drew on the recollections of Countess Marie Larisch ('Marie, Marie, hold on tight', ll. 15–16). Cf. TSE's declaration that he was 'royalist in politics', in the Preface to *FLA* (1928).

Did I point out that a Tory policy is in no wise acceptable to Bloomsbury.

Do you think 'Eeldrop and Appleplex' worth continuing?[1] As a kind of deversoir for a variety of thoughts and feels: neither Poetry nor Criticism. When I suggested this to Richard [Aldington] he said why not write some historical dialogues. Some people are like that. Please say something different, at least.

Is it true that the Wild Man dal Bornio[2] (*che diedi i mai conforti*)[3] is coming to London in Oct–Nov? I hope so – I may have some things to say (*tu di me novelli porti*)[4] which I do not care to confide to type.

Yours klansmanikally
T

TO *Frederic Manning*[5] CC

16 September 1923 9 Clarence Gate Gdns

My dear Manning,

Thank you for your letter. I am sending the Fernandez to Richard, who has kindly agreed to do it.[6] I am sorry to hear that you are still weak and are very busy, and also that you are likely to sell your place and go abroad. That disposes of the hope that I still entertained of coming to spend a weekend with you during this winter. But you are right to leave England for the winter.

I should like to have a Newman article from you very much – not of course, immediately after this one, but within a year of it.[7] So will you keep it in mind in the knowledge that I want it?

1–TSE's 'Eeldrop and Appleplex ' appeared in two parts in *Little Review* 4: 1 (May 1917) and 4: 5 (Sept. 1917). They were satirical dialogues between fictional versions of himself and EP.
2–Ezra Pound. The reference is to both Dante's *Inferno* XXVIII, 133 – 'i' son Bertram dal Bornio' ('I am Bertran de Born') – and the 'Wild Man of Borneo'. According to an article in *Illustrated World* (Jan. 1922), 'Wild men of Borneo' appeared in Barnum's and other circuses, and were 'mostly negro canvasmen painted with brick dust or vermilion red, chained, and their mouths fitted with a false bridge, from which two tusks protruded'.
3–'He who gave evil counsels', Dante, *Inf.*, XXVIII, 135. Dante's Bertran de Born 'gave evil counsels to the young king'.
4–'Thou mayest carry tidings of me' (ibid. 133). Bertran says 'E perché tu di me novella porti, / sappi ch'i'son Bertram dal Bornio' ['So that you may carry tidings of me, / Know that I am Bertran de Born'].
5–Frederic Manning: see Glossary of Names.
6–Ramón Fernandez, 'The Experience of Newman' (trans. RA), *C.* 3: 9 (Oct. 1924).
7–See Manning, 'A French Criticism of Newman', *NC* 4: 1 (Jan. 1926).

Inadvertently, I have not replied to you about [Lionel] Johnson. I should very much like to see the letters and to publish some of them. May I have them, or some letters, to read? It is very kind of you to suggest them.[1] He is a writer for whom I have a deep respect: with all the faults of writing which he has, as a writer of that epoch, he is one of its most dignified figures, and he ought to be more studied than he is.

Yours ever sincerely,
[T. S. E.]

TO *Mrs Bartholomew* CC

20 September 1923 [*The Criterion*, London]

Dear Mrs Bartholomew,

Please excuse my not having written to you before, but I have unfortunately very little time for correspondence and also I wanted to read your essay with the attention it deserves before writing to you.[2] It certainly has much more than a personal interest for me and I shall consider it a favour if you will let me keep it longer to read carefully again. I certainly feel very timid about offering any advice to a writer in fields with which I am not myself very familiar, but if I can really be of any use to you as a critic I shall be most happy, only, it will take me some time. I hardly know whether the subject is suitable for us. It is likely to be more suitable later on, for the reason that we are anxious to widen the scope of the paper to include well-written articles on any subjects, except the dreariest one of economics. But so far we have not had space to include essays on music and painting and architecture, with which we really ought to deal, and with which we have promised to deal. The question of expense makes it imperative to keep the paper down to as small a size as possible until it is better established, so that our programme at present is an amputated one.

I am very grateful to you for letting me see your essay and shall be very disappointed if you do not allow me the opportunity for reading it again at greater leisure.

I am,

Yours very sincerely,
[T. S. E.]

1–Lionel Johnson (1867–1902): poet of the 1890s associated with the Rhymers' Club; author of *Poems* (1895) and *Ireland and Other Poems* (1897). His essays appeared posthumously as *Post liminium* (1911). See 'Some Letters of Lionel Johnson', C. 3: 11 (Apr. 1925), 356–63.

2–On 5 Sept., Mrs Bartholomew wrote that her sister Lady Rothermere had suggested she send an extract from a book she was writing.

TO *Owen Barfield* CC

20 September 1923 [*The Criterion*, London]

Dear Sir,

I have your letter of the 17th inst. I have indeed received your second sketch and have kept it in the hope of being able to see you or write to you at some length about it.[1] I must tell you frankly that I do not like it nearly as much as the one which we published.[2] The latter impressed me as having a distinct individual rythym which made it remarkable; the former seems to me to have the defects of the method without this rythym. The story which we published, however, interests me so much that I shall follow with the greatest interest anything you write and hope that you be as good as to let me see other things which you have written.

Yours faithfully
[T. S. E.]

TO *Leone Vivante* CC

20 September 1923 [*The Criterion*, London]

Dear Sir,

Thank you very much for your letter of the 17th inst. and for your manuscript which has arrived at the same time.[3] I am very grateful to you for giving us the opportunity of printing it and hope that it may be possible for us to do so, as it would be only fair to you and to our readers after printing the first part.[4] The difficulty is that we have accepted so much material for the next three numbers that I cannot at present say when or whether it will be possible, but I will let you know at the earliest possible moment.

Faithfully yours,
[T. S. E.]

1–On 17 Sept., Barfield asked TSE to return his story 'The Devastated Area' if he was not going to use it.
2–'Dope', C. 1: 4 (July 1923), 322–8.
3–Vivante wrote that he was sending 'for any emergency' the corrected copy of "The Original Reality of Poetic Thought"' – i.e., the second chapter of his book *Intelligence in Expression*, which EP had recommended for publication in C.
4–On 23 Aug. TSE told Vivante he intended to publish Part I in C. 2: 2 (Jan. 1924), but it never appeared. Vivante's 'The Misleading Comparison Between Art and Dreams' appeared in *NC* 4: 3 (June 1926).

TO *Richard Aldington* CC

20 September 1923 [London]

My dear Richard

I was very much pleased and flattered by receiving your translation of *Cyrano* with the inscription.[1] It is a book which I should have wanted to possess even without the pleasure of receiving it as a gift, and I congratulate you on such a scholarly piece of work and such an interesting introduction. I like the translation although of course I cannot compare it with an original which I have never seen or read. What article of Croce have you accepted?[2] I hope you did not promise Ainslie[3] that it would appear in any particular number, because I am beginning to be worried by the amount of stuff that may come in for the January number. We have already got Robertson and Keith and Levy-Bruhl; Larbaud [on Walter Savage Landor] may turn up; Bain's I expect to get in December.[4] I do not know whether the Marcel Proust fragment will come in (I wrote to Rivière a week ago about another matter and have had no answer.[5] I presume you have written to him about this.) Finally I have accepted as much as we can possibly print, and I want to print a good deal, of a very brilliant novel Wyndham Lewis is now writing[6] and of which he read me parts the other night, and there is also this Italian of Ezra's[7] whom I cannot read and whom you cannot read. I think we must be prepared to postpone both

1–Cyrano de Bergerac, *Voyages to the Moon and Sun*, trans. RA (1923): the first modern English translation of the work of the seventeenth-century French writer, Savinien Cyrano, the inspiration for Rostand's verse drama.

2–Benedetto Croce (1866–1952): critic, idealist philosopher, politician; author of *Breviario di estetica* (1912). RA wrote on 17 Sept. that he had 'accepted Ainslie's Croce article'. On 18 Aug., Douglas Ainslie had written to RC-S (believing him to be the editor of C.) to ask 'whether or no you would care to see my versions hitherto unpublished in English of Benedetto Croce's *Heine, Balzac & Zola*? They form part of his *Poesia e non poesia* which I shall eventually publish complete.' RC-S must have forwarded Ainslie's letter to RA, TSE's assistant on C.

3–Douglas Ainslie (1865–1948): Scottish poet, translator, critic and diplomat; associated in the 1890s with such personages as Aubrey Beardsley and Walter Pater; contributed to the *Yellow Book*. He was the first to translate into English the work of the Italian philosopher Benedetto Croce, inc. *European Literature in the Nineteenth Century* (1924). See Croce, 'On the Nature of Allegory', trans. Douglas Ainslie, in C. 3: 11 (Apr. 1925).

4–See J. M. Robertson, 'The Evolution of English Blank Verse', Lévy-Bruhl, 'Primitive Mentality and Gambling', and Bain, 'Disraeli': all in C. 2: 6 (Feb. 1924). Neither Keith's nor Larbaud's essays materialised.

5–Proust, 'The Death of Albertine', C. 2: 8 (July 1924).

6–*The Apes of God*, WL's satirical account of the post-war London art world.

7–Vivante (see previous letter). On 30 Aug., RA said: 'Vivante I can't read; it bores me.'

Keith and Joachim[1] to April, and perhaps other things as well. Ezra has now offered me an article for the January number; as you are familiar with Ezra's style of letterwriting you will quite understand that I am not certain what this article is about; but it appears to concern itself with some new German musician with whom he is very friendly and who he naturally assumes to be so illustrious that there is no need to tell me anything about him.[2] Ezra seems to be showing a certain tenderness toward the Huns at present. As I want to put in as much as I can of Lewis it will be an excellent excuse for excluding Ezra, one of the very few excuses which Ezra may accept.

Lewis rather astonished me by telling me that Ezra had written to him to say that he was assembling a number of the *Criterion* and asked Lewis to contribute to his number.[3] This Lewis did not appear particularly anxious to do, so that he asked me what arrangement I had made with Ezra for compiling a *Criterion*. I told him that this was the first I had heard about it and that I supposed that this was the effect on Ezra's imagination of my having invited him to send for inspection any of the brilliant works which to judge from his recent strictures on the paper we were apparently excluding.[4]

I should like very much to get something from Maurras for the April number for which I expect Whibley's article on him. But is it any use writing to Maurras if he is still in Jail?[5] I think your suggestions are excellent and I shall write to the *cher maître* in that tone.[6]

1–Harold Joachim: see Glossary of Names. Nothing by him was published in C.

2–On 16 Sept., EP said he was 'doing an article on Antheil, who is really of some interest. Trust you will hold space for it in Jan. number'. George Antheil (1900–59) was an American avant-garde pianist and composer, of German extraction. See 'George Antheil', *C.* 2: 7 (Apr. 1924).

3–On 6 Sept, EP told WL: 'At any rate, I am putting together a more lefterly outburst for some future number of his organ' (*Pound/Lewis*, 137).

4–See TSE's letter of 3 Sept.

5–CW's article never appeared. In June, Maurras and three members of the Camelots du Roi were tried for assault upon three men, two of whom were deputies in the Chamber of Deputies. On 27 June, Maurras was sentenced to a fine and four months in prison. *The Times* reported that Maurras, as 'one of the directors of the Royalist newspaper *L'Action Française* . . . voluntarily presented himself before the examining magistrate, and declared that he had ordered the attacks of 31 May to be made and took full responsibility for them . . . he refused to make any apology' (*Times*, 28 June 1923, 13). RA said he was 'still climbing up the ever climbing way of the treadmill'.

6–On 17 Sept., RA advised TSE to '"Cher Maître" him vigorously, discourse of the iniquity of "La democrasserie", express the homage of England to le grand Maurras.' See TSE's letter to Maurras of 4 Oct.

Of course the articles on music and painting that we promised must go by the board for a number or two. I consider them incidental, valuable but incidental, to the main programme of literary, social and political reform. I have just been looking at Frederick Scott Oliver's book on Alexander Hamilton and I think it is very good.[1] I think he might be a very good man to have, whether he wrote on part of it or on any other subject. The only other political article that I have in mind is one which I may have mentioned to you to be got from Lord Kerry on Shelburne.[2] But it would be more important to get someone to write about Burke.[3]

If you can come up to town next week will you drop a line to Whibley as well as myself saying what night it will be – any night except Monday or Saturday. I should be delighted to offer you my roof, my only difficulty is this: that I keep everything ready here in case it should at short notice be necessary or desirable for my wife to return from the country. Therefore I cannot offer a bed very far ahead; but I can always be pretty certain within a day or two; so that if you have an alternative lodging I should be able to let you know the day before whether I am certain to have room. It would be much more satisfactory if you could stay the night here.

Yours ever affectionately
[T. S. E.]

TO *Lady Rothermere* CC

20 September 1923 [London]

My dear Lady Rothermere,

Thank you very much for your letter. I was beginning to wonder where you were as I knew that by this time you must have left Evian where I am happy to hear that you have thriven. I have been very busy this summer and had to be a great deal up and down between here and the country. Only within the last two or three weeks my wife has been a little better but

1–F. S. Oliver, *Alexander Hamilton* (1906). The book presented the early United States as a model for British imperial federation.

2–Lord Edmond Fitzmaurice, Baron Fitzmaurice (1846–1935): Liberal politician, under-secretary in Foreign Office, historian. His three-vol. *Life* (1875–6) of his ancestor William, Earl of Shelburne established his reputation as a historian. William Petty (1737–1805) was second Earl of Shelburne and first Marquess of Lansdowne; politician and prime minister.

3–Edmund Burke (1729/30–97): Irish politician and author, whose *Reflections on the Revolution in France* (1790) had become a classic of counter-revolutionary thought. The only discussion of Burke to appear was a review by K. Pickthorn of B. Newman's *Edmund Burke*, in *NC* 6: 6 (Dec. 1927).

she has had to make a terrible fight of it all this summer. But had I at any particular moment been certain that a letter from me would reach you I should have written to you some time before.

The October number is now quite ready. I think it is good on the whole and I have written a long essay for it in the attempt to give the liveliness of controversy and the noise of battle.[1] We have had one very fortunate stroke. W. P. Ker sent an article in and a few weeks later died of heart failure in the Alps, and as his death has attracted a great deal of attention and notice, and as I think we shall be the first if not the only review to publish anything by him since his death, it ought to be a very good advertisement.[2] There is one dreadful failure of which [to] warn you, otherwise you will wonder at my lack of judgement. On this occasion at least you shall have no reason to complain that I have not explained fully in advance. Over a year ago, when I was still wondering where the contributions were to come from and how the paper was to be filled, I accepted an article by a learned and well-known Shakespearian scholar named Lawrence.[3] Had filling the paper proved as difficult as I then feared, this article would have been very good stuff, but as things turned out, it simply means postponing much better stuff. The article is terribly dull. I have managed to put him off from one number to the other for nearly a year, but unfortunately the poor man has made some discovery which he is afraid somebody else will make and get the credit for, so he is beginning to get a bit impatient, and I find myself simply forced to print it. Do not think that this mistake will occur again; for now the difficulty is to keep the paper down to the right size, not to keep it up. But the January number will have to be a very big one, because I have accepted a large piece of a new work by Wyndham Lewis which I think will be somewhat of a sensation although not (at any rate the part I am going to print) a scandalous sensation.[4] And it is also likely that the thing from Proust will turn up for the same number.[5]

I am very annoyed with Sanderson for his unbusinesslike methods. I find that he delayed writing to you about the finances of the paper until very late, and then apparently kept writing to the wrong addresses: with the result that the July printers' bill is still unpaid. I have urged upon him the

1–TSE, 'The Function of Criticism': an attack on JMM and 'Whiggery'.

2–'Byron: An Oxford Lecture', C. 2: 5 (Oct. 1923).

3–W. J. Lawrence, author of *The Elizabethan Playhouse and Other Studies* (1912). See his 'A New Shakespeare Test', C. 2: 5 (Oct. 1923), 77–95.

4–'Mr Zagreus and the Split-Man', in C. 2: 6 (Feb. 1924), did create a scandal.

5–Proust, 'The Death of Albertine', C. 2: 8 (July 1924).

necessity for looking a little farther ahead, especially as it is important for the credit of the paper that contributors be always paid on the nail.

Of course there are no returns yet from the July number, but we shall know in a couple of weeks whether Smiths have disposed of the 300 copies which they took. Unless I am entirely mistaken, the next three numbers ought to sell better than any of the previous. Now that Aldington has taken so much of the routine off my hands, I have been able to devote much more time to plotting out the contents, and I think that these numbers will provide more excitement and stimulate more curiosity and discussion than any of the previous.

You say you are going to Paris in October but I hope you will also pay your usual quarterly visit to London about the time that the *Criterion* comes out. May I look forward to seeing you then?

Yours always sincerely,
[T. S. E.]

TO *H. Dugdale Sykes*[1] CC

20 September 1923 [*The Criterion*, 17 Thavies Inn]

Dear Mr Sykes

I am an ungrateful dog not to have written to you for such a long time to express my appreciation of your essay on Middleton[2] and my entire agreement with its conclusions. I must tell you frankly that the reason why I clung so long to your paper was that I had the desire to get it published in a quarterly review, the title of which you see above, in which I take a keen interest. But we have been forced to forego, on account of lack of space, the publication of a great many things which interest me extremely, and in this way I am afraid that your paper is too technical to give me the right to include it to the exclusion of certain other things. It is with great regret that I release it to you. I must explain that in consequence of many requests I have consented to contribute to this paper four essays on Elizabethan dramatists so that for the next year we shall not be able to

1–Henry Dugdale Sykes (1874?–1932): author of *Sidelights on Shakespeare* (1919) and *Sidelights on Elizabethan Drama* (1924). In his essay 'Cyril Tourneur' TSE called Sykes 'perhaps our greatest authority on the texts of Tourneur and Middleton' (*SE*, 186).

2–In 'John Ford the Author of *The Spanish Gypsy*' (*Sidelights on Elizabethan Drama*), Sykes argued that a number of plays ascribed to Middleton were 'patently by other people'. In 'Thomas Middleton' (1927), TSE cites Sykes as having 'written authoritatively on this subject' (*SE*, 161).

include much else in the same field. The four whom I have chosen are Webster, Middleton, Chapman and Tourneur,[1] and I shall take the opportunity of having sent to you each of these numbers as they appear in the hope that they may provoke some correspondence from you which we will publish in the *Criterion*[2] or by which I may correct my conclusions when I come to make the articles into a book.

I hope that you will give me the opportunity of seeing anything you write on the subjects which interest us both and I should be very glad to resume contact with you again.

Sincerely yours
[T. S. E.]

TO *Wyndham Lewis* — MS Cornell

26 September 1923 — 9 Clarence Gate Gdns

Dear Lewis

Many thanks. May I take it that we shall have definitely

1. Mr Zagreus[3] for Jan. number
2. An essay for March[4]

?

If so, how soon Zagreus? I must tell you again I think this will be a great book[5] – don't let *anything* interfere with it.

I understand that you encourage me to go on with the Sweeney play[6] – I hope that is what you mean. 'Eeldrop'[7] was only intended as a fill up or an occasional release of otherwise useless cerebration.

1–'Four Elizabethan Dramatists I: A Preface' appeared in C. 2: 6 (Feb. 1924), but the promised essays on Webster, Middleton, Chapman and Tourneur did not follow. TSE wrote later 'Mr Lucas's Webster', *NC* 7: 4 (June 1928), 'Thomas Middleton', in *TLS* (30 June 1927), 'The Sources of Chapman', *TLS* (12 Feb. 1927), and 'Cyril Tourneur', *TLS* (13 Nov. 1930). The second and fourth of these were republished in *SE* (1932) and *EE* (1934).
2–Sykes did not appear in C.
3–'Mr Zagreus and the Split-Man', *C.* 2: 6 (Feb. 1924).
4–A second instalment of the novel appeared as 'The Apes of God', *C.* 2: 7 (Apr. 1924). WL's first essay was an 'Art Chronicle', *C.* 3: 9 (Oct. 1924).
5–*The Apes of God* did not appear in book form until 1930.
6–A ref. to what became *SA*. In his letter, WL said: 'perhaps the play should come next'.
7–'Eeldrop and Appleplex', *The Little Review* 4: 1 & 5 (May & Sept. 1917). WL told TSE to 'develop what he started' in *TWL*, but this did not mean 'I squint at EELDROP' (*Selected Letters of Wyndham Lewis*, 135).

Disgusting and filthy article on me by Clive Bell in *Nation*[1] – sort of thing one can only receive in silence.

Let me know when to expect Zagreus. I should like to get it set up quite soon.

Have you arranged publication of your book of essays?[2] If not, I shd like to get the *Criterion* to do it as a book. That is where it ought to appear. We bring out Valéry in December,[3] & yours could appear in the spring. Let me know what sort of terms you expect for it. I'm sure Lady R wd be keen about it. *Give us the first chance.* & Let me know about Zagreus.

Please answer.

Yours ever
T. S. E.

I wrote to the *Dial* & gave them your address and told them they had the chance of getting something from you if quick.[4]

TO *W. B. L. Trotter*[5] CC

29 September 1923 [*The Criterion*, London]

Sir,

I take the liberty of writing to you on behalf of the *Criterion*. As it is possible that you have not seen or heard of this review, which was started in October last, I enclose a copy of a circular which was issued at the time, which will give you some notion of the character of the paper and its contributors. A further circular reviewing the first year's accomplishment will be issued in July. It is desired during the second year to extend the scope of the paper and include work not only by the most important men of letters, both English and foreign, but also by distinguished scholars and

1 – Clive Bell, 'T. S. Eliot', *N&A* 33 (22 Sept. 1923), 772–3. Bell attacked *TWL* as a case of the poet 'more or less repeating himself'; 'lack of imagination' being the 'essential defect'. TSE was one of 'that anything but contemptible class of artists whose mills are perfect engines in perpetual want of grist'; 'an exceptional critic'; 'Unluckily he is a Cubist'. Bell deplored above all TSE's 'indiscreet boosting of the insignificant Miss Sinclair and the lamentable Ezra Pound'.

2 – WL published no polemical books between *The Caliph's Design* (1919) and *The Art of Being Ruled* (1926).

3 – In fact, *Le Serpent par Paul Valéry* came out in Dec. 1924.

4 – Although he had published 'Paris versus the World' in *Dial* 71: 1 (July 1921), WL did not publish there again.

5 – W. B. L. Trotter (1872–1939): surgeon and social psychologist; Professor of Surgery at University College Hospital, London, and pioneering neurosurgeon; serjeant-surgeon to King George V; author of *The Instincts of the Herd in Peace and War* (1916).

men of science. Professor W. P. Ker has contributed a paper for the October number, and Sir James Frazer[1] has promised his collaboration also.

The *Criterion* does not aim at a very large circulation, but aims solely at publishing the highest class of work. While a contribution to this paper does not reach a very large audience, it probably receives more intelligent attention than a contribution to any other review and the audience is not limited to Great Britain. The *Criterion* would be very greatly honoured by a contribution from you on some subject which would interest the readers who like myself have gained so much from the study of 'Instincts of the Herd in Peace and War'. While we cannot, of course, publish papers which are only intelligible to the readers of technical reviews, we believe that distinguished scientists ought occasionally to address themselves to the cultivated public in general. There is of course no question of including 'popular science' articles in The *Criterion*.

Our rates of payment must at present be very modest, at the rate of £10 per 5000 words, and articles should not greatly exceed that length.

Should you consent to promise a contribution for next winter I should be extremely grateful; and if you accept in principle, I will ask the secretary, Mr Richard Aldington, to discuss any details with you later.

I have asked Mr Cobden Sanderson to send you a copy of the April number.

Hoping that I may hear from you.[2]

I am, sir, your obedient servant
[T. S. E.]

TO *Wyndham Lewis* — TS Cornell

[Early October? 1923] — *The Criterion*, 17 Thavies Inn

Dear Lewis

Send the essays along as soon as you can, and give me a few days to read them carefully, then we will discuss them.[3] It seems a pity if (as I understand from you) the book of essays must come out in March, because thus you [pass up] the profit of selling some to *Vanity Fair*, the *Dial* and the *Criterion*.[4] But perhaps I am mistaken, or at any rate you will have

1 – Despite CW's assurance that Sir James Frazer was willing to contribute, he never did so.
2 – Trotter never contributed to C.
3 – See TSE's letter of 26 Sept.
4 – No book of essays appeared, and Lewis published no other periodical pieces in 1923 or 1924.

some more afterwards? At any rate, the *Criterion* wants the first chance at publishing the book. We can certainly do better for you than Miss Weaver[1] could and perhaps as well as others.

Remember that I want Zagreus[2] by November 1st. see enclosed.

I will not mention your movements to Schiff or to any one.[3] I presume that your movements include your new address,[4] which I will not mention either.

Yours
TSE

Yes, Huffer[5] is starting a paper.

TO *Wyndham Lewis* CC

1 October 1923 [London]

Dear Lewis

Many thanks indeed. I will give you as long as I can, but I should like to have 'Zagreus' in a month. Meanwhile, will you send me the essays you speak of and we will then arrange a meeting and discussion. I have not yet written to Crowninshield[6] but I will do so very soon. We are advertising 'Zagreus' for the January number.

I don't propose to pick a quarrel with the *Nation* on this point.[7] I shall leave it alone – they have one article of mine[8] – but I expect that after the

1–Harriet Shaw Weaver had published Lewis's *Tarr* at the Egoist Press.
2–'Mr Zagreus and the Split-Man', *C.* 2: 6 (Feb. 1924).
3–SS was one of WL's most generous patrons. In an undated letter to TSE, WL said: 'Don't inform Schiff about my movements, there's a good fellow' (*Letters of Wyndham Lewis*, 126).
4–Lee Studio, Adam & Eve Mews.
5–Ford Madox Ford (formerly 'Hueffer') launched the short-lived *Transatlantic Review* in Paris in Jan. 1924. In his undated letter, WL wrote: 'Letter from Pound saying Hueffer and he starting paper. No answer of course to that' (*Letters*, 126).
6–Frank Crowninshield (1872–1947), scion of a Boston Brahmin family and editor of *Vanity Fair*, to whom WL proposed to send one of his essays. The sophisticated 'Crownie', who was hired by his friend Condé Nast, published many of the leading writers of the era including AH, TSE, Gertrude Stein, F. Scott Fitzgerald, and Dorothy Parker; he also cultivated modern artists.
7–Having read Clive Bell's 'clearly personal' review, WL thought it betrayed the *Nation*'s attitude towards TSE. He advised withdrawing any articles already sent or cancelling any writing arrangement with *N.* (*Letters of Wyndham Lewis*, 135).
8–'The Beating of a Drum', *N&A* 34: 1 (6 Oct. 1923). TSE made no further contribution until Dec. 1926.

next two or three numbers of the *Criterion* there will be attacks enough from that quarter. The *Criterion* policy will probably be put down to a splenetic rage on my part and I therefore state to you beforehand that it has nothing to do with my personal relations past or future. I like to keep literary controversy completely impersonal.[1]

The articles that I have been writing lately are simply wiping out old commissions that I have undertaken in some cases as much as a year ago.[2] In addition, I happen to want just now any money that I can get by journalism. But I hope to get myself clear this week and thereafter to write no articles at all for the next year except a quarterly article for the *Criterion*. I shall thus have time, I hope, for the play[3] and for other activities besides writing. Let me hear from you soon.

Yours ever
[T. S. E.]

TO *J. M. Robertson* CC

1 October 1923 9 Clarence Gate Gdns

My dear Mr Robertson,

I am very sorry that my occasion for writing to you is what it is; but I have come to depend on you as one of the chief supporters and distinctions of the *Criterion*: therefore I hope you will consent to our postponing your blank verse article to the January number,[4] when I will explain to you the reasons.

Over a year ago, when I was in terror lest it should be impossible to secure enough contributions to keep the *Criterion* going, I accepted a very long, very dull, and very badly-written article on the Elizabethan theatre.[5] I had it set up in type, but have managed to postpone it from number to number on the theory that the longer the delay the better the position of the *Criterion* to bear such a weight. Unfortunately, Mr Lawrence has made a kind of discovery which may be useful to scholars in fixing the dates of

1–Cf. TSE's insistence in 'Tradition and the Individual Talent': 'The emotion of art is impersonal' (*SW*, 53; *SE*, 22).
2–Lewis wrote: 'I hope to hear soon you are getting your play done. Why don't you stop writing articles for a bit and do nothing but work of your own?'
3–*SA*.
4–'The Evolution of English Blank Verse', *C*. 2: 6 (Feb. 1924), 171–87.
5–W. J. Lawrence, 'A New Shakespearean Test', *C*. 2: 5 (Oct. 1923), 77–94.

Elizabethan plays;[1] and he is justly anxious that his article should be published before anyone else makes the same discovery. He has borne my delays with great patience; and we are therefore publishing it in October. The article is so long that something else must be omitted and as it is in the same field as yours I feel that for the sake of proportion, and out of justice to both yourself and him, it would be better not to print both in the same number. I am very sorry for the sake of the *Criterion*, because the October, which starts the New Year, will be inferior to the January one and if this arrangement inconveniences you or displeases you in any way I shall be very deeply grieved. It is simply the blunder of an inexperienced editor.[2]

I hasten to add, in the event of your not going to America this winter, that this need not and I hope will not affect the first of the future Studies in Genius.[3] We shall be ready to publish the latter in the April number if we can have it then, and I hope that we may. There are only a very few people whom the *Criterion* is anxious to publish as often as it can, and you are one of them.

If you are a reader of the *Nation*, I hope you will have paid your [*sc.* no] attention to an article about me by Mr Clive Bell,[4] which is incorrect in its facts and malignant in its insinuations, and which conveys an impression of intimacy which is far from being a faithful report of Mr Bell's relations with me.[5]

I hope that you will forgive my clumsiness, because the *Criterion* depends as much upon you as upon any of its contributors.

Yours very sincerely,
[T. S. E.]

1–According to Lawrence, 'no extant common theatre play of the period anterior to the second decade of the seventeenth-century presents any indication of the use of cornets by adult players' (82). On the basis of this 'new test', he offered some speculative dates for *The Merchant of Venice*, *All's Well*, and *Henry VIII* among other plays.
2–On 3 Oct., Robertson replied: 'Don't worry in the least . . . I have been an editor myself.'
3–Robertson said if his proposed American trip fell through, he would 'get on with the "Studies in Genius"'.
4–Clive Bell's review of *TWL*, 'T. S. Eliot', *N&A* 33 (22 Sept. 1923); reprinted the same month in *Vanity Fair* as 'The Elusive Art of T. S. Eliot', 53.
5–Bell claimed to have heard TSE read 'Prufrock' in 1916, and that he was 'one of the first in England to sing the praises of Eliot'.

TO *Mark Wardle* CC

1 October 1923 [London]

My dear Wardle,

I think it would be a good thing if we printed the alternative ending of *Le Serpent* together with your translation, as well as the usual ending. It should form a sort of appendix. Do you not agree? I hope to get my introduction written within a week or so and I should like then to arrange for a meeting and show it to you for your comments. Will you be in town when Valéry comes to lecture in the middle of the month?[1] I saw Whibley the other evening and he told me that he was going to take the Chair.

Yours in haste,
[T. S. E.]

TO *Stanley Rice* CC

1 October 1923 [9 Clarence Gate Gdns]

Dear Mr Rice,

(By the way my name is not Sanderson Eliot – you are confusing me with the *Criterion*'s publisher, Mr Cobden Sanderson.)[2]

Thank you for your letter of the 19th ulto. The subject you suggest is a very interesting one and is one of which I should very much like to read an article from you.[3] It is difficult for us absolutely to engage ourselves to accept an article which is not yet written or to accept an article for publication by any definite date. It is particularly difficult in the case of a subject the treatment of which affects so closely the policy of the paper. Such an article as you suggest would either fit in admirably with the design of the review or else, if treated in another way, would absolutely contradict it; and it is therefore only fair that I should explain to you the position of the paper. I am myself, having dabbled in Oriental languages,[4] very keen on the scholarly presentation of the Eastern world to occidental Europe which knows so little about it. But I am very much opposed to certain

1 – On 3 Oct., Wardle said he *was* going to Valéry's lecture, and he wondered whether TSE wished to discuss the '*affairs serpentine*' in French with Valéry, or in English with him. Valéry was due to talk on Victor Hugo at the French Institute, 16 Oct., under the chairmanship of CW.

2 – Rice's letter of 19 Sept. opened 'Dear Mr Sanderson Eliot'.

3 – Rice hoped to write on 'the artistic influences of Asia on Europe & of Europe on Asia'.

4 – At Harvard, TSE took courses in 'Elementary Sanskrit' in 1911–12, and Pali in 1912–13.

forms of Oriental influence which seem to me conducive to hysteria and barbarism.[1] You will have noticed probably that since the war, and indeed less forcibly for some years before the war, the Eastern ideas or rather paraphrases and corroborations of Eastern ideas, have been creeping into Western Europe through the gate of Germany. As the Germans are a very hysterical race they always select the most hysterical and unwholesome aspects of Oriental art and thought, and within the last few years they have been turning more and more toward the East, and more and more toward Russia apparently undeceived by the fiasco of the Treaty of Rapallo.[2] The effect of this, if the German Asiatic influence permeates Western Europe, will be to relax our hold on those European traditions without which I believe we should relapse into a state of barbarism equal to that of America or Russia.[3] My friend Hermann Hesse[4] for whose talent I have great respect is an example of the sort of orientalisation which I fear, and I have been tempted to write a denunciation of his book (which I commend to your interest) and of the author whom he so highly praises Dostoevsky.[5] Now the standpoint of the *Criterion* is distinctly Aristotelian and in a sense Orthodox.[6] As for Tagore,[7] I cannot read at all but his work in translation seems to me a miserable attenuation of the robust philosophy of early India.

Pardon my writing to you at such length, but the subject you suggest seems to me so important that I feel it is only right to give you some vague idea of its relations to the *Criterion*.

Sincerely yours,
[T. S. E.]

1–As examples of 'an Oriental tendency in European Art of late', Rice cited *Chu Chin Chow*, *Madame Butterfly*, the 'whole tone scale', and the 'vogue of Russia'.
2–At the Treaty of Rapallo (1922), Germany and Bolshevik Russia renounced all territorial and financial claims against each other in the wake of the Treaty of Brest-Litovsk (1918).
3–Cf. TSE's 'Notes', *C.* 2: 5 (Oct. 1923): '*all* European civilisations are equally dependent upon Greece and Rome – so far as they are civilisations at all'. It was 'as ridiculous for us to deny our ancestry as for India and China to reject their ancient literature, con Virgil, and compose Horatian odes'.
4–TSE had met Hesse in Switzerland in 1921.
5–Hermann Hesse, *Blick ins Chaos: Drei Aufsätze* (Berne, 1920), cited in the notes to *TWL*, ll. 366–76. TSE read Hesse's work in Lausanne in 1921, and persuaded SS to translate it into English. 'The Brothers Karamazov – the Downfall of Europe' was published in *Dial* 72: 6 (June 1922), and the remainder as *In Sight of Chaos* (Zurich, 1923). Hesse said: 'It seems to me that European and especially German youth are destined to find their greatest writer in Dostoevsky . . . The ideal of Karamazov, primeval, Asiatic, and occult, is already beginning to consume the European soul. That is what I mean by the downfall of Europe.'
6–In *ASG* (1934), TSE associates 'orthodoxy' with both Christianity and 'tradition'.
7–Rabindranath Tagore (1861–1941): Bengali poet, philosopher, playwright; Nobel laureate, 1913. Rice cited the 'cult of Tagore' as an instance of Oriental influence.

TO *John Burnet*[1] CC

1 October 1923 [*The Criterion*, London]

Dear Sir,

Thank you very much indeed for your kind letter of the 26th September. It will suit us very well if you can let us have an article in the Spring: we hope not later than in time for the July number.[2] I may say that if your health and leisure should permit, we should be of course delighted to publish anything that you might send earlier, but for the July number the date of receipt should be the 1st of June, and I sincerely hope that you will be sufficiently restored to health, and not too pressed by other obligations to let us have something by then.

The *Criterion* will consider any contribution from you a very great honour indeed.

I am,

Yours very sincerely
[T. S. E.]

TO *J. B. Trend* CC

1 October 1923 9 Clarence Gate Gdns

My dear Trend,

I am sorry to have been unable to answer your letter sooner. By all means do the article you suggest, only don't be afraid to make it too technical, because the *Criterion* makes no concessions to its readers in this way.[3] We either omit a subject altogether, such as mathematics or economics, or else we expect the reader to have some education and to take some trouble. I wish you could find the rest of the words that you quote and include the whole thing. But you will do the essay in your own way.

With many thanks,

Yours in haste,
[T. S. E.]

1–John Burnet (1863–1928) was Professor of Greek at St Andrews, 1881–1926. His works included a commentary on Aristotle's *Nicomachean Ethics* (1899); *Greek Philosophy: Part I: Thales to Plato* (1914); and a critical edition, in the Oxford Classical Texts series, of the complete works of Plato (1900–8).

2–Nothing by Burnet appeared in *C.*

3–Trend related (7 Sept.) that he would 'very much like to do an article, for I met some very queer people as well as queer music, and there would be no need to go into technicalities'.

TO *Ottoline Morrell* MS Texas

2 October [1923] [London]

My dear Ottoline

Many thanks for your kind letter and yr. wire. I was afraid you might already have gone, or be on the point of going.[1] Vivien wanted to see you before you went, but now I think she will be able to arrange it. I suppose you will be in London for a night on your way. No – as I said – I don't see how she can go until the new year – because I do not feel that it would be safe to let her go without me, even if Germany quietens down.[2] After a year of [Dr Hubert] Higgins, she has not the confidence or resistance – she would collapse before she got there. But meanwhile I want to keep in touch with Martin.

I will write you more fully later. There is so much to say. Thank you very much for Gordon's card – it is much more favourable than I shd have expected.[3] But so many things might stand in the way that I must not think about it.

I am *glad* you feel so about Clive's article. It made me feel as if I was covered with lice. But I don't want to say anything about it, because I take it the Woolfs consider it as a compliment[4] – and it is not the sort of thing one *resents* – it is too general and intangible – the vulgar and tasteless soul. *Please* don't mention it to Vivien – I have not shown it to her. I don't feel these things but she does, and she has quite enough to do to keep her body alive at present.

The dreadful thing about alien atmospheres is when one gets so used to them that one is not *conscious* of what is wrong – unconscious suffering is the worst for one – don't you think? – because one is denying oneself.

Always affectionately
Tom

1–OM went to Freiburg that autumn to attend the clinic of Dr K. B. Martin, whom VHE and TSE had consulted in the summer.

2–The situation in Germany was highly unstable as a result of the French occupation of the Ruhr earlier in the year, hyper-inflation, and the threat of a Communist rising in central Germany.

3–Presumably a ref. to TSE's request that she look out for a position for him at Oxford. G. S. Gordon (1881–1942) had been elected in 1922 Merton Professor of English Literature, Oxford University; later President of Magdalen College, and Vice-Chancellor, 1938–41.

4–On 14 Sept., VW had told Bell, who had written a favourable review of her work, that he was 'the best journalist, possibly critic, of the day' (*Letters of Virginia Woolf*, II, 70).

TO *Marianne Moore*[1] MS Rosenbach

4 October 1923 9 Clarence Gate Gdns

Dear Miss Moore

I have sent off to the *Dial* an article on you, long delayed by circumstances beyond my control.[2]

I hope you will like it. But it does you less than justice.[3]

When you are ready to publish another book here let me know – I think I could 'float' it better than the last which never got a fair show.[4]

Sincerely yours
T. S. Eliot

TO *Ezra Pound* CC

4 October 1923 9 Clarence Gate Gdns

Cher Ezra

Your article on Antheil is received.[5] It seems to be of excellent substance, so far as I can understand it; unfortunately music is what I know least about, but what is of general intelligibility is admirable.

But January, in any case, is impossible. I have promised Lewis all the possible space for as large a chunk as possible of his new book. He will never finish the damn thing, I must get what I can when I can get it. It is good stuff, Lewis is coming on. There shd. be a short essay of his in April, also the Proust *inédit* (not to my taste, merely a necessary sensation, we drop Proust after that, he is no part of the programme)[6] also Cocteau,[7]

1–Marianne Moore: see Glossary of Names.

2–TSE, 'Marianne Moore' (rev. of *Poems* and *Marriage*), *Dial* 75: 6 (Dec. 1923).

3–TSE could 'only think of five contemporary poets' whose work excited him 'as much as, or more than, Miss Moore's'. Moore told her brother that TSE's review was 'a very stately natively sweet natured affair . . . If bolstering by the profession can do one any good it certainly will advantage me' (*Selected Letters of Marianne Moore*, ed. Bonnie Costello and Cristanne Miller [1998], 205).

4–The next book of hers to be published in the UK was *Selected Poems*, with Intro. by TSE (Faber & Faber, 1935).

5–'George Antheil', *C.* 2: 7 (Apr. 1924).

6–Proust, 'The Death of Albertine', *C.* 2: 8 (July 1924). William Empson records TSE telling students at Cambridge 'I have not read Proust', but the following week giving a 'very weighty, and rather long, tribute' to Scott Moncrieff's translation, which he said was 'at no point inferior to the original' (*T. S. Eliot: A Symposium* [1948], 36–7).

7–Jean Cocteau proved elusive, but 'Scandales' was to appear (in French) in *NC* 4: 1 (Jan. 1926).

also two other things of which you will not approve, you shall therefore know nothing about it yet, lest you should talk against the *Criterion.* I know du Bos wont do us any good, I could have done better, and Huffer wont do us any bleeding good either.[1] I only could put him in because he insists upon one of our important principles, Anglo-French unity. He is rhetorical, verbose, and damn vulgar. He always has one or two good ideas and it is a pity he wont put them into decent English. Say what you will, there is a lot of the Hun about Huffer. I never knew a man who could make good ideas so unacceptable, exc. yrself. I wish you wdnt. sometimes write on his model. I want to publish yr. Antheil, but swear to me that Im not landing a catfish like Major Douglas,[2] the Messiah of Golders Green.[3] Anyway I gather that I shall have a chance of hearing him in London, and if I like him as much as I do Strawinskij,[4] I will print it in red ink. Antheil a Pole[5] he must have been born in Lodz or Kattowitz to have a name like that. Can you land any decent fiction. REMEMBER that I am prepared to publish a chunk of cantos as big as Sigismund every year until the ship sinks.[6] But if January dont sink it what with Lewis and Bain I don't know what will. Nobody can live off the *Criterion* even with the £2 you will get presently until there is a real tory government which there never will be.[7] Put no trust in Cecils.[8]

Yours ever
[T. S. E.]

1–'Huffer': Ford Madox Ford (formerly 'Hueffer'). TSE published nothing by Du Bos until Jan. 1935.
2–Major C. H. Douglas (1879–1952): engineer and economic theorist; author of *Economic Democracy* (1920). His theory of Social Credit was heavily promoted by EP, who decreed that Douglas should 'command the unqualified respect of all save those few cliques of the irresponsible and the economically guilty' (*Little Review* 6: 11, Apr. 1920).
3–Golders Green in London had a prominent Jewish community.
4–On 16 Sept., EP called Antheil 'a conscious Stravinsky, instead of an instinctive peasant-genius'; and in his article he said Stravinsky's 'merit lies very largely in taking hard bits of rhythm, and noting them with great care. Antheil continues this.' TSE was a strong admirer of Igor Stravinsky (1882–1971), and the composer later became a friend.
5–Pound's biographical notes began: 'George Antheil, born Trenton, N.J., July 8, 1901, of Polish parents; taken to Poland at age of four, returned to America at fourteen . . .'
6–Sigismundo da Montefeltro, protagonist of the 'Malatesta Cantos', in *C.* 1: 4 (July 1923).
7–On 6 Sept., Pound said that, if he had known of TSE's political allegiances earlier, he would have suggested the subtitle: 'The Criterium, or The Tory Review'.
8–There were two members of the Cecil family in Baldwin's Conservative government of 1923: Lord Robert Cecil, and James Edward Hubert Gascoyne Cecil, fourth Marquess of Salisbury.

TO *John Quinn* TS Berg

4 October 1923 9 Clarence Gate Gdns

My dear Mr Quinn,

There is absolutely no apology possible for my failure to write to you in August when I got your letter and draft. I only feel somehow that you meant what you said when you told me not to bother to write – though of course I did not intend to take you at your word.[1] But I don't know anyone but yourself who would say a thing like that, after such an action, and really mean it. Yet I ought not to impose on such rare generosity as I have done.

It is partly my inveterate habit of leaving important letters, which I want to be long and good letters, 'until I have time'. And doing all the paltry business ones. It is true that I have been harassed and constantly out of town. All summer I have been up and down to the country, skipping a day or two from work nearly every week, and having had about two months leave altogether besides. The bank have been extremely decent to me. For the last month I have been trying to get straight. I have written two things for the *Dial,* two for the *Criterion*, one for the *Nouvelle Revue Française*, and am sitting down to do a preface for Paul Valéry. These are all very old commissions. When I have got these done I must pay a lot of bills, make out my income tax, my American income tax (it comes to three dollars, but takes about three evenings work), review the situation and write to my mother. This will take me to the end of next week. Then I shall do no more writing except a quarterly article for the *Criterion*, for the next year.[2] I shall write nothing else. I have besides one preface to do within eighteen months. So I hope this winter to get time to start my play. No more articles for anybody, except the *Criterion.*

The *Criterion* does give a lot of trouble. I am very slowly learning the art of making other people work and only doing oneself what nobody else can do, but I am a slow learner. And you have to go slowly, or else they are either doing things you don't want done or referring things to you you don't want to know about, such as the size of a circular and how many to print. Then there is the trouble of trying to combine people who won't combine, Pound and Aldington, and defending one against the other, and everybody protesting against something and most jealous of each other,

1 – Quinn said there was 'no hurry about acknowledging this letter'.
2 – Apart from an English version of his 'Lettre d'Angleterre' in *Vanity Fair* 21: 6 (Feb. 1924), TSE published only his prose writing in *C.* in 1924.

and very few to be depended upon. Still, it is amusing, and will be for at least a year. Also there is satisfaction, for anyone who has been so much an object of charity as myself, in being able to put money in the hands of people like Lewis and Aldington and Pound (even though it is not very much) and not take any myself. It is harder to help Pound than anyone else. Apart from the fact that he is very sensitive and proud and that I have to keep an attitude of discipleship to him (as indeed I ought) every time I print anything of his it nearly sinks the paper. And he offers more than I want, thinking that he is helping. I am willing to sink the ship for things like cantos, which are great stuff whether anyone likes them or not, but it goes against the grain to do it for his articles. He always puts them in such a way that the errors stick out and the good points (there always are some) stick in, and he will imitate Hueffer, who writes vilely and who never omits to mention that he is an Officer (British) and a Gentleman. I have got one thing of Hueffer's that I took for Ezra's sake: it has good things in it too, but is twice as long as it need be.[1] I am simply getting execrated by all, but if one is going to edit a review at all I think the best one can do is to follow one's own faith and let things rip.

I am for the moment engaged in rather more tolerable work at the bank. I edit a daily sheet of Extracts (commercial and financial) from the foreign press, and have to be an authority on affairs in France, Italy, Spain, Roumania, Greece, Turkey and the U.S.A. And write a monthly article on foreign exchange. It is not bad. There is some possibility of a small job at Oxford, but I don't much bank on that.

I shall, of course, consider the money you sent as a trust, contingent upon my leaving the bank, and not dip into it unless in absolute need. I have been fairly near it, for my expenses in connexion with my wife's illness have been terrific, running a country cottage as well as this flat, doctors' bills, medicines, fares, motor car rides, and always feeding at least one extra person as she must always have some relative or friend with her to do house-keeping, see to preparation of her special food etc. I wanted her to be under a German physician [Dr K. B. Martin] who seems just the man – he was here for a week, but she is not fit to go to Freiburg, even if things settle down, unless I can go with her and stay with her, and this I cannot do. I am not looking forward to the winter.

1 – 'From the Grey Stone', *C.* 2: 5 (Oct. 1923). Quinn gave $1,000 that autumn to subsidise Ford's *The Transatlantic Review*, which was to be launched in Jan. 1924.

I have not attempted to express my thanks. It is really beyond words. But you have been a greater support and encouragement to me than I can possibly say. It is unique.[1]

I will write again.

Yours always gratefully
T. S. Eliot

TO *Charles Maurras* CC

4 October 1923 [9 Clarence Gate Gdns]

Cher Maître,

J'espère que vous pardonnerez mon hardiesse en vous écrivant à propos de cette revue anglaise trimestrielle *The Criterion*. Nous allons vous supplier de nous donner quelque chose d'inédit pour cette revue.

Jusqu'ici je crois que votre oeuvre étonnante a été ignorée et même supprimée en Angleterre. La cause suffisante, c'est que la plus grande partie de la presse littéraire est controlée par les Libéraux effectivement par des groupes qui sont de la gauche politique et presqu'ouvertement républicains. Je crois même que l'écrivain contemporain français qui est le mieux connu et le mieux gouté parmi les intellectuels de Londres c'est – André Gide.[2] Cela vous donnera quelqu'idée de la situation actuelle. C'est cette position que *The Criterion* veut renverser. Ici, même les journaux soi-disant conservateurs sont timides et maintiennent des vues plutôt flottantes. C'est seulement *The Criterion* qui avoue franchement une philosophie qui aux yeux de la démocrasserie[3] paraîtra réactionnaire, quoique c'est à notre avis la seule philosophie qui puisse, de nos jours, offrir le moindre espoir de progrès. Je suis certain que les opinions du groupe du *Criterion* sont celles qui se rapprochent le plus à l'Action Française. Il y a, naturellement, des réserves à faire dû aux circonstances variantes des deux peuples; mais *mutatis mutandis*, je crois que le font de notre philosophie, une philosophie Aristotélienne, est le même que le vôtre. Donc nous voulons établir des relations amicales.

1 – Quinn died on 28 July 1924, and this is TSE's last tribute to him.

2 – André Gide (1869–1951): novelist, diarist, man of letters; author of *L'immoraliste* (1911) and *La Porte étroite* [*Strait is the Gate*], 1909) among many other influential works.

3 – TSE took the term, as he took his tone, from RA. On 17 Sept., RA had advised TSE to 'discourse [to Maurras] of the iniquity of "La democrasserie"' – the term being probably derived from Flaubert, who used it in a letter to Taine in 1866: 'Je vous sais gré d'exalter l'individu si rebaissé de nos jours par la Démocrasserie' ['I am grateful to you for singing the praises of the individual, who is so denigrated nowadays by *La Démocrasserie*'].

Dans notre numéro d'Avril nous allons publier un grand article sur vous par Charles Whibley, écrivain éminent, duquel vous connaissez sans doute le nom. Or, cette article serait de beaucoup plus effectif si nous pourrions faire paraître quelqu'inédit de vous au même numéro. Pour un tel inédit nous pourrions vous indemnifier à raison de 700 francs les 5000 mots – honoraire bien au dessous de l'importance capitale d'une telle contribution. Un article ne devrait pas dépasser par beaucoup cette étendue.

Il faut qualifier en pratique l'idée que je vous ai donnée de notre revue. *The Criterion* n'est pas une revue de caractère directement politique. Nous ne nous occupons point des activités politiques. Nous nous abstenons complètement du jeu futile des partis; nous ne sommes partisans d'aucun gouvernement. Nous ne parlons pas politique. Nous ne nous présentons pas aux scrutins. Nous sommes simplement en train de labourer une philosophie générale d'où découlera une influence lente dans la politique, la théologie et la littérature. *The Criterion* est d'aveu simplement une revue littéraire.

Il convient par conséquent, qui si vous nous faites le grand honneur de collaborer à notre revue, votre article soit un article de critique générale ou plutôt littéraire.[1] En vous, nous saluons à la grande critique littéraire autant que le maître de politique.

En espérant un accueil favorable, je vous signale, Monsieur, ma grande admiration et mes hommages dévoués.

[T. S. E.][2]

1 – Maurras did not contribute to the following number, but his 'Prologue to an Essay on Criticism' appeared in *NC* 7: 1 (Jan. 1928), in a translation by TSE.

2 – *Translation*: Dear Sir, I hope you will forgive my boldness in writing to you in connection with the English quarterly review, *The Criterion*. We wish to urge you to let us have some unpublished text by you for this review.

Until now, I believe, your very remarkable work has remained unknown, or has even been suppressed, in England. Of this the sufficient cause is that the greater part of the literary press is controlled by Liberals, in effect by groups belonging to the political Left and almost openly republican. I would even say that the contemporary French writer who is best known to, and most appreciated by, London intellectuals is – André Gide. This will give you some idea of the present situation. It is this attitude that *The Criterion* wishes to reverse. Here, even the so-called Conservative papers lack boldness and profess rather indefinite opinions. Only *The Criterion* frankly proclaims a philosophy which 'democrassery' is bound to find reactionary, although, in our view, it is the only philosophy which offers the slightest hope of progress at the present time. I am certain that the *Criterion* group represents the body of opinion nearest to l'Action Française. There are, naturally, certain reservations to be made, because of the differing circumstances of the two nations; but *mutatis mutandis*, I think that the basis of our philosophy, an Aristotelian philosophy, is the same as yours. We wish therefore to establish friendly relations.

In our April number, we propose to publish a long article about you by Charles Whibley, an eminent writer whose name is no doubt known to you. This article would, of course, be

TO *Ford Madox Ford* TS Cornell

4 October 1923 *The Criterion*, 17 Thavies Inn

My dear Ford,

In reply to your letter of the 28th of September, I have after several attempts succeeded in sending off your manuscript of a history of literature to you, registered.[1] Please let me know when you get it. I have got many suggestions from it and if you don't publish it quickly you may see my plundering first.

Certainly, I should be delighted to write you an open letter for your paper, and welcome the prospect of its appearance;[2] but first I should like to have some idea of what it stands for in every important respect and what it aims at. The *Criterion* is developing a clearer general policy and I certainly hope that the two will be in harmony. As a matter of fact I intend to reduce my writing to the minimum this winter and beyond a quarterly contribution to the *Criterion* I don't think that I shall write at all.

Many thanks for your flattering remarks.[3] It is a great deal to find that there is one person, and that person is yourself, who regards the poem as

---

more effective if we could bring out some previously unpublished text by you in the same number. We could offer payment at the rate of 700 francs per 5,000 words – a fee not at all commensurate with the capital importance of such a contribution. The text should not greatly exceed the length indicated.

I must add a practical qualification to the description I have given you of our review. *The Criterion* is not a review of a directly political character. We do not deal with political activity. We stand completely aloof from the futile games of the parties; we do not lend support to any government. We do not discuss politics. We do not seek elected representation. We are solely engaged in working out a general philosophy which will exert a gradual influence on politics, theology and literature. *The Criterion* presents itself solely as a literary review.

It follows, therefore, that if you do us the great honour of contributing to our review, your article should concern itself with general criticism, or rather literary criticism. In you, we salute a great literary critic as well as an eminent political authority.

Hoping for a favourable reply, I assure you, Sir, of my great admiration and most respectful regards. [T. S. E.]

1–In his letter to TSE of 28 Sept., Ford asked for his 'short history of Brit. Lit. back': he wanted to print a 'slab of it'.

2–Ford was 're-starting on the weary road: founding a Review, monthly, in this city to be published in New York & London too'. *The Transatlantic Review* was launched in Paris in Jan. 1924. Ford wanted a word from TSE 'just to show we are a band of brothers: just a letter would do'.

3–Ford thought *TWL* 'all pretty level & a unit'. He liked 'personally *Death by Water* & from there to the end best' but would not have liked it so well 'if it hadn't come after the Shakespeherian rag & Mr Eugenides'. From 'April is the cruellest month' to '*mon frère*' was 'all very beautiful, but wouldn't be as beautiful if it was not a prelude to the rest'.

having any pretensions to coherence and unity at all. It has been unfavourably reviewed in this country; the critics here are too timid even to admit that they dislike it.[1] As for the lines I mention,[2] you need not scratch your head over them. They are the twenty-nine lines of the water-dripping song in the last part.[3]

With best wishes

Yours
T. S. Eliot

TO *J. M. Robertson* CC

4 October 1923 9 Clarence Gate Gdns

My dear Mr Robertson,

Very many thanks for your card. I am personally delighted by your news: and remember that anything you send will be acceptable but that we must have your big article on Tourgenev in any case.[4] It is an important part of the structure of the *Criterion*. But I should be very interested to see your opinions on Santayana.[5] I dislike his style and do not much like the man.

Yours very sincerely,
[T. S. E.]

1 – Clive Bell said 'How the man can write!' but noted TSE's 'disconcerting habit of omitting inverted commas' and thought the butter was 'spread unconscionably thin' (*N&A* 33, 22 Sept.); Edgell Rickword thought TSE's method had some 'theoretical justifications' but that *TWL* existed 'in the greater part in the shape of notes' ('A Fragmentary Poem', *TLS*, 20 Sept. 1923); J. C. Squire was unable 'to make head or tail of it', seeing only a 'vagrant string of drab pictures . . . interspersed with memories of literature, lines from old poets, and disconnected ejaculations' – a 'grunt would serve equally well' (*London Mercury* 7, Oct. 1923).

2 – TSE had told Ford (14 Aug.) there were 'about thirty *good* lines in *The Waste Land*', and asked if he could find them. Ford protested against 'the cruelty of the question': 'I DON'T KNOW!'

3 – 'What the Thunder Said', from 'Here is no water but only rock' to 'But there is no water' (*TWL*, ll. 331–58).

4 – Robertson published nothing on Ivan Turgenev (1818–83) in C. TSE had praised Turgenev for maintaining 'the role of foreigner with integrity', and called him a 'source of authority . . . but also isolation' ('Turgenev', *Egoist* 4: 11, Dec. 1917).

5 – George Santayana (1863–1952): Spanish-born American philosopher. TSE had taken his courses at Harvard on 'History of Modern Philosophy' (1907–8) and 'Ideals of Society, Religion, Art and Science in their Historical Development' (1909–10). In Aug. 1920, TSE told SS he had 'never liked Santayana', thinking him 'essentially feminine'. Later, when discussing Santayana's *Three Philosophical Poets* (1910), TSE said he was 'more interested in poetical philosophy than philosophical poetry' (*VMP*, 49).

TO *John Collier*[1] CC

4 October 1923 [*The Criterion*, London]

Dear Sir,

I must apologise humbly for not having written to you about the two drafts of a poem which you have submitted. I have read these with great care and several times over, and I was only waiting in the vain hope of finding time to submit to you a detailed criticism. I consider that the poem has merit; I merely don't think that it is sufficiently mature and significant to take its place in a periodical which hardly expects to publish more than two or three poems a year.[2] To tell the truth, it reminds me somewhat of the work of Mr Conrad Aiken,[3] which you probably have not read; it reminds me certainly of my own earlier verse. This is something which I have outgrown, and which I think you will outgrow also: I think that there is a great deal of sentimentality to be purged out of it. This particular type of fragmentary conversation (see page 4) was invented by Jules Laforgue[4] and done to death by Aldous Huxley.[5] Incidentally, Laforgue has made it impossible for anyone else to talk about geraniums.[6] I have been a sinner myself in the use of broken conversations punctuated by three dots.[7] But you have every reason for going on and you yourself will know, better than

1–John Collier (1901–80): British-born novelist and screenplay writer, famous for his stories in *The New Yorker*. He began as a poet influenced by the Sitwells and by JJ (as well as by TSE), but published only one collection, *Gemini* (1930), before making a successful career as a writer of fiction. He won attention with a satire, *His Monkey Wife* (1930); and a collection of his stories, *Fancies and Goodnights* (1951), won the first International Fantasy Award in 1952.

2–The only poems published in the first year of *C.* were *TWL* in 1: 1 (Oct. 1923), Valéry's 'The Serpent' 1: 3 (Apr. 1923), and Pound's 'Malatesta Cantos', 1: 4 (July 1923).

3–Conrad Aiken: see Glossary of Names.

4–Jules Laforgue (1860–1887), French poet, 'was the first to teach me how to speak, to teach me the poetic possibilities of my own idiom of speech' ('What Dante Means to Me', *TCC*, 126).

5–Reviewing Aldous Huxley's *The Defeat of Youth and Other Poems* (1918), TSE said AH had 'come down with a serious attack of Laforgue (which may be a good thing), and we must wait until he has worked it off' ('Verse Pleasant and Unpleasant', *Egoist* 5: 3, Mar. 1918).

6–Notable examples are in 'Pierrots', where Laforgue speaks of 'La bouche clownesque ensorcelé / Comme un singulier geranium', and *Derniers Vers* in which he addresses 'géraniums diaphanes'. Cf. TSE's 'Rhapsody on a Windy Night': 'Midnight shakes the memory / As a madman shakes a dead geranium'.

7–TSE employed this device in 'The Love Song of J. Alfred Prufrock' ('I grow old . . . I grow old . . .') and 'Portrait of a Lady' ('I shall sit here, serving tea to friends . . .'), as well as in 'Mr Apollinax' and 'Hysteria'.

anyone else, when you have actually done something. Meanwhile I should not recommend you to publish this poem.

I am,

Dear Sir,

Yours faithfully,
[T. S. E.]

TO *Otto Heller*[1]

MS Washington

5 October 1923 — 9 Clarence Gate Gdns

Sir,

Some time ago I read (I think in the *Post-Dispatch*) a review of my poem, *The Waste Land* by you.[2] It struck me as the most intelligent review of that poem that I have seen, and I have intended to write to thank you for it.

The poem is neither a success nor a failure – simply a struggle. Practically, one crucifies oneself and entertains drawing rooms and lounges. But the reception is irrelevant.

It is a pleasure to me that I remember you, although you are hardly likely to remember ever having seen *me*.[3]

I am,

Yr. obliged obt servt
T. S. Eliot

1–Otto Heller (1863–1941) was from 1892 Professor of German Language and Literature at Washington University, St Louis; literary editor of the *St Louis Post-Dispatch*, 1919–24; author of *Prophets of Dissent: Essays on Maeterlinck, Strindberg, Nietzsche and Tolstoy* (1918).

2–'Some critics deny emotion to Mr Eliot, others point out confusion in his thinking. The present writer disagrees, and finds the young poet altogether admirably equipped for his office. Only he's got into bad company for the time being, as young poets will . . . Mr Eliot betrays himself over and over again as the possessor of an orderly mind throwing itself not without difficulty into experimental disorder . . . enthusiasts are quick to read a marvelous temperamental response of its author to the passing tragedy of the period, the reflection of a civilization torn away from its moorings by deep and violent perturbations. They sense in *The Waste Land* a poet's intense suffering' ('News of New Books and Those Who Write Them', *St Louis Post-Dispatch*, 24 Feb. 1923, 10).

3–TSE went to school, 1898–1905, at Smith Academy, the prep school for Washington Univ.

TO *Stephen Gaselee*[1] CC

5 October 1923 [9 Clarence Gate Gdns]

Sir,

It has occurred to me that if you ever write at all, you would find the *Criterion* a suitable periodical in which to allow your articles to appear. The *Criterion* is a quarterly review founded by Lady Rothermere and edited by Mr Richard Aldington, the policy of which is directed by myself with the advice and assistance of Mr Charles Whibley. I enclose a recent circular, which will give you a partial, but only a partial, notion of its tendencies. You will gain a further perception when I inform you that we are publishing in the January number an essay on Disraeli by Mr F. W. Bain, and in the April number on Charles Maurras by Mr Charles Whibley.[2] We also hope for contributions from Mr Maurras himself and from Monsieur Pierre Lasserre,[3] and a paper on Aristotle's politics.[4]

It must be made clear, however, that the *Criterion* has no interest in actual politics but only in abstract ideas. On the other hand, in literature it supports such work as that of Mr James Joyce and Mr Wyndham Lewis. You will see that it is from the point of view of the usual Whig and semi socialist press of London an undesirable production.

I have suggested to Mr Saintsbury, who has already been a contributor, that he should write us a paper on Quintillian, or on Macrobius or on Charles II, or on some equally obscure subject. There are many subjects, such as Machiavelli,[5] which only await a well affected and properly qualified exponent. From what I have said, and from what you will find in the circular, there should suggest itself to you some subject in those fields of learning in which you have become eminent to the point of myth. If the prospect commends itself to you, and if you care to discuss the matter first,

1–Stephen Gaselee (1882–1943): Fellow and Pepys Librarian at Magdalene College, Cambridge, 1908–19; Keeper of the Papers at the Foreign Office, 1920–43; a classical scholar whose publications included *The Oxford Book of Medieval Latin Verse* (1928).

2–Bain's 'Disraeli' appeared in C. 2: 6 (Feb. 1924), but CW never wrote on Maurras.

3–Pierre Lasserre (1867–1930): French literary critic and essayist, influenced by George Sorel and Charles Péguy. A champion of French classicism, he was a leading literary critic in *L'Action Française*. He was the author of *Charles Maurras et la Renaissance classique* (1902), among other studies (though he broke with Maurras in 1914). He never wrote for C.

4–'By Mr F. S. Oliver' *del.*

5–Niccolò Machiavelli never featured as a topic in C. In 'Shakespeare and the Stoicism of Seneca' (1927), TSE praised WL for 'calling attention to the importance of Machiavelli in Elizabethan England' (*SE*, 128).

I should be happy if you would lunch with me or come to see me one evening.[1]

I am,

Sir,

Your obliged obedient servant,
[T. S. E.]

PS The rates of pay are insignificant, being £10 per 5000 words, and no contribution should exceed that length. If you do us the honour of accepting in principle, I will ask Mr Aldington [to] write to you.

TO *Richard Aldington* CC

5 October 1923 9 Clarence Gate Gdns

My dear Richard,

I merely meant that I thought the names ought to be uniform on the cover. I see your point, but it looks to me a little odd to see a list with Ker given simply as W. P. and Guignebert as Professor.[2] Inside, I think that we ought to make distinctions according to the notoriety of the contributor. Ker, to take the same example, needs no title, but I should give people like Guignebert their full designation, i.e. Charles Guignebert, and then below – Professor of such and such in the University of Paris. It is too late for this number but I think we might adopt it when we get to Lévy-Bruhl in the next.[3] What do you think?

Don't do anything about Vivante until I have had time to read it. Send me on the article by the Honourable George Sinclair.[4] I am still playing with the idea of approaching the Crown Prince of Sweden.[5]

I saw Lady Rothermere for a few moments. She is on her way to Vienna and thence is going to Rome and will see Mussolini. I suggest that when

1 – On 30 Nov., Gaselee proposed an essay pursuing 'an idea through classical antiquity to modern times' that he provisionally entitled 'The Soul in the Kiss': it was published under that title in C. 2: 7 (Apr. 1924), 349–59.

2 – In the contents for C. 2: 5 (Oct. 1923), W. P. Ker, 'Byron: An Oxford Lecture' was followed by 'Professor Charles Guignebert, "Concerning the Devil"'.

3 – In C. 2: 6 (Feb. 1924), the Contents gave L. Lévy-Bruhl, 'Primitive Mentality and Gambling'.

4 – On 3 Oct., RA described George Sinclair's article as 'a chatty travel-bore note on the portraits at Gripsholm' (Swedish Royal Palace, home to the National Portrait Gallery). There was 'no kudos to be got from publishing it, but it provides a first harmless liaison with Scandinavia'.

5 – TSE was to write to the Crown Prince on 30 Jan. 1924.

she has seen him I should get from her an introduction to him for you. I wish you would look about at Fashismo [*sic*], find out whether it has any general philosophy and if so whether its general ideas can in any way be attached to our own. I am still in a state of doubt. There is an immense faschista press which you might look at. Not only the *Popolo* but the *Critica, Faschista* and many others.[1] We are having a devil of a row now about the discipline of the local leaders or 'ras' and Mussolini seems to be getting the best of it. But so far as I can see, the whole movement is still fluid, and adapting itself to circumstances. In other words we do not know what it is until it has been in office for several years. But if there is anything to be said about it I don't see why you should not write an article as well as or better than any Italian.[2]

I have an embryonic notion of publishing in a year or so a book of essays by several hands: either essays reprinted from the *Criterion*, or essays by contributors to the *Criterion*. Half a dozen or so chosen as a collective statement of the *Criterion* position. For instance, if we reprinted, we might use my essay on Criticism, Bain's Disraeli, Whibley's Maurras, your article on Faschismo and Leonard Whibley's on Aristotle's politics if it is any good, perhaps an essay on art by Wyndham Lewis and so on.[3] On the other hand, if all the papers have appeared already in the *Criterion*, perhaps there would be no sale for the book. Tell me what you think of the idea in general.

I am sending to Heinemann to ask them for William Archer's book on the drama, because I think I can work it in nicely with my four essays.[4] Can you think of any other conspicuous contemporary whom I could work in in the same way and beat about the ears, or on the other hand use as a

1–*Il Popolo d'Italia* was Mussolini's paper. *La Critica* was edited by Benedetto Croce, who, after initial enthusiasm for the Fascist regime, became an opponent from 1925. *Critica Fascista* was a semi-monthly journal, 1923–43. The notes on 'Italian Publications' (C. 1924), by F. S. Flint, concentrated on literary items in *Il Convegno* rather than the Fascist press or journals.

2–RA did not meet Mussolini during his Italian trip, or write on Fascism for C. TSE later discussed 'British Fascism' in 'Commentary', *NC* 7: 1 (Jan. 1928), and 'The Literature of Fascism', *NC* 8: 31 (Dec. 1928).

3–Nothing came of this idea.

4–*The Old Drama and the New: An Essay in Re-valuation* (1923), by William Archer (1856–1924), theatre critic and journalist. In 'Four Elizabethan Dramatists', TSE said Archer's 'brilliant and stimulating book' had 'succeeded in making quite clear all of the dramatic faults of Elizabethan drama. What vitiates his analysis is his failure to see why these faults are faults, and not simply different conventions', C. 2: 6 (Feb. 1924), reprinted in *SE*, 109–17.

support? Is there anything in Lytton Strachey's essays[1] which you have read? Archer is a minion of the cocoa press you know.[2]

Yours ever
[T. S. E.]

PS I lunched with Cobden Sanderson today and passed for printing the new circular instead of sending it back to you. I did this to save time.

By the way, if you stop in Paris do not forget to make enquiries about Migne,[3] if you have time.

I have read Valéry's 'L'Ame et la Danse' and it is rubbish.[4] He knows nothing whatsoever about dancing, not much about the soul, and very little about Socrates. It is the usual sort of French bluff. (Monsieur Teste is also rubbish.)[5] Valéry's dialogue is followed by an article by Suarès which is pure imbecility.[6] There are also sketches by artists who are equally ignorant of dancing and which show up as humbug beside the few little drawings of Degas[7] who knew everything that a painter need know about dancing. I venture the idea that Valéry's poetry has merit, but the man cannot think.

TO *Herbert Trench*[8] CC

5 October 1923 [London]

My dear Mr Trench,

I hope you will pardon me for my delay in writing to you about your poem.[9] I have kept it a long time and am liking it very much indeed, while coming to a decision about the policy of the *Criterion* in publishing verse. The *Criterion* is a very small paper, and quarterly is a very infrequent publication, and our problem is that of a person stopping in a hotel who

1 – Lytton Strachey, *Books and Characters* (1922). TSE did not refer to Strachey in his article.
2 – The Liberally-inclined newspapers owned by the Cadburys and Rowntrees. Archer had been theatre critic of *The Star* and *Daily Chronicle*, both owned by George Cadbury.
3 – Jacques Paul Migne (1800–75), French publisher and patrologist.
4 – Valéry, 'L'Ame et la Danse' ('The Soul and the Dance') was published in a special supplement to *La Revue Musicale* 2: 1 (Dec. 1921), on nineteenth-century ballet, 1–32.
5 – *La soirée avec Monsieur Teste* (1896). TSE said 'M. Valéry's Teste is a monster' ('A Brief Introduction to the Method of Paul Valéry').
6 – André Suarès, 'Danse et Musique', 37–45.
7 – 'La Danseuse by Edgar Degas', 33–6.
8 – Frederick Herbert Trench (1865–1923): Irish poet and playwright who had died in Italy on 11 June. He had written to TSE on 24 Jan. 1923, with a poem and commentary. His *Selected Poems* appeared in 1924.
9 – 'Song of the Larks at Dawn': fragments of the poem had already appeared in anthologies.

has made many purchases and finds at the last moment that his luggage is inadequate. We shall therefore only publish two or three lots of verse during the year, and this will be either groups of poems or single poems of such a length as to preclude their publication in most other papers. Our idea is partly to publish work which is not likely to be suitable for, or [is] unacceptable to any other review: either because it is too radical, or because it is too re-actionnary [*sic*] or because it is by a foreigner, or because it is too scholarly. So I regretfully return to you this poem. I hope that we may meet again, but I imagine that you are very seldom in London.

Yours faithfully,
[T. S. E.]

TO *Hugo von Hofmannsthal*[1] CC

5 October 1923 [London]

Sir,

I welcome the opportunity of writing to you to inform you that your essay on Greece which Mr Scofield Thayer so kindly obtained for us is to appear in the *Criterion* next week.[2] A copy will be sent you and you should receive at the same time or a little later a fee for the equivalent of five guineas.

I admire this essay very much indeed and consider that the *Criterion* is very fortunate in being allowed to publish a translation in this country. But I have been an admirer of your work for the last thirteen years and your contributions to the *Dial* are to me the most interesting things in that paper.[3] I hope that we may have the opportunity of publishing further work of yours and I shall [ask] Mr Richard Aldington who is editing the *Criterion* under my direction to write to you next year. We only regret that the *Criterion*, being a quarterly and a very small one, can publish so little of any one contributor.[4]

1 – Hugo von Hofmannsthal: see Glossary of Names.
2 – 'Greece', C. 2: 5 (Oct. 1923), 95–102.
3 – TSE dates his admiration of Hofmannsthal's work back to his student year abroad in France, Germany and Italy in 1910–11. Later, TSE said he read him in Bavaria in 1911 ('Preface' to Michael Hamburger's trans. of Hofmannsthal, *Poems and Verse Plays*, 1962). In 'Marianne Moore', TSE ranked Moore with five other poets – American, English, Irish, French and German – who interested him (*Dial* 75: 6, Dec. 1923, 594). The unnamed German poet was Hofmannsthal (see Herbert Howarth, *Notes on Some Figures Behind T. S. Eliot*, 190).
4 – Hofmannsthal never contributed again.

Viscountess Rothermere, who is the founder and patroness of the *Criterion*, is now in Vienna, at the Hotel Bristol. She is also an admirer of your work and would be gratified if she might meet you. I am therefore giving you her address and expressing the hope that you will call upon her.[1]

With many thanks,

I remain,
Your obliged obedient servant,
[T. S. E.]

PS Is it the fact that none of your poetry has ever been translated into English?[2]

TO *George Saintsbury* CC

5 October 1923 [9 Clarence Gate Gdns]

Dear Mr Saintsbury,

Some time ago you held out to me the faint hope that you might again be persuaded to contribute to the *Criterion*. To this distant offer corresponds a firm determination on my part. Do you think that you could contribute a paper next year? There are many subjects on which no one is so qualified to speak as yourself: it has occurred to me that we should like to have from you an essay on Quintilian or on Macrobius[3] or on any of the excellent critics who in this age of darkness are neglected and unknown. But be assured that any essay on any subject at any time would be welcome from you. A defence of the character and rule of Charles II for example. I make this last suggestion in the knowledge that your political leanings are similar to my own.[4]

I am,

Dear Mr Saintsbury,
your obedient servant,
[T. S. E.]

1 – On 10 Oct., Hofmannsthal wrote that he was 'not near Vienna' but 'in the mountains, and writing very hard': he sent his regrets to Lady Rothermere.

2 – Hofmannsthal said that 'several of [his] lyric dramas and all [of his] poems (being very few)' had been 'translated and published in America'. He singled out Arthur Symons's 'masterly' translation of *Elektra* (1908).

3 – Quintilian (*c*.35–100): Roman rhetorician, author of *Institutio Oratoria*; Macrobius (395–423): Roman grammarian and Neoplatonist philosopher, author of a commentary on Cicero's *Dream of Cicero*. Saintsbury wrote *A History of Criticism and Literary Taste in Europe from the Earliest Texts to the Present Day* (3 vols, 1900–4).

4 – Saintsbury worked as a journalist on the *Saturday Review*, of which he was assistant editor 1883–94. According to *DNB*, 'The independent toryism of the *Saturday Review* was never

TO *Robert Graves* TS Morris

9 October 1923 9 Clarence Gate Gdns

My dear Graves,

I am very sorry that I have not let you know before. I kept the poems a long time and went through them pretty thoroughly, and then sent them to Aldington and discussed them with him.[1] But I could not make any selection that would do for the *Criterion* – what we want, as we only publish verse about twice a year, is always some one thing of some length or importance both positively, and relatively in [the] work of the author. So I sent them on to the Woolfs. Tonight I rang them up about the matter, and learned that they had just got back from the country, and had had a mass of stuff to deal with, and had not had time to read the poems.[2] They should write to you when they have done so.

What I suggest, if they do not want them – and I think they would only want to print a smaller book, selecting from these, or rather letting you select – is to try Harold Monro. I do not know whether he is publishing at all on his own account now, but I think he would like these. I don't know why, as I have had no personal dealings, but – without prejudice or responsibility – I have a slight prejudice against Blackwell.[3]

I was rather pleased with Squire's comments, to tell the truth. The man is honest.[4]

With all best wishes, and apologies,

Sincerely
T. S. Eliot

—

more vigorous than in the years when Saintsbury became a seasoned Fleet Street commentator.' Saintsbury never contributed to C. again.

1–See TSE's letters to Graves of 16 July and to RA of 23 Aug.

2–Later published as John Crowe Ransom, *Grace After Meat*, introd. by Robert Graves (1924).

3–Basil Blackwell (1889–1985): bookseller and publisher, who had joined the family bookshop of Blackwell & Sons in Oxford. In 1913, he launched the annual *Oxford Poetry*, which had published Graves.

4–In his review of *TWL* in *London Mercury* 7 (Oct. 1923, 655–6), the editor J. C. Squire thought it 'scarcely worthy of the Hogarth Press'.

TO *Richard Cobden-Sanderson* TS Beinecke

11 October 1923 *The Criterion*, 9 Clarence Gate Gdns

Dear Cobden-Sanderson,

Many thanks, the Criteria[1] are highly satisfactory, the only thing I can find wrong are some bad errors in the German quotations in Ker's article,[2] that's not *your* fault.

I have finished my preface, sent it to Wardle for comment, got it back, and sent it to Aldington for comment.[3] When I get it back it may have a few alterations made, and then it will be quite ready for you. Thank you for Valéry's address. I am supposed to be going to hear his lecture, but I haven't the slightest curiosity.[4]

Yes, please, pay Pound £2 more (in English cheque) for his cantos.[5]

I hope to have news of the results of July no. soon from you.

Yours ever
T. S. E.

TO *Arnold Bennett*[6] MS

11 October 1923 9 Clarence Gate Gdns

Dear Mr Bennett

Thank you very much. I shall be very happy to come on Tuesday at 9 o'clock.[7]

Sincerely yours
T. S. Eliot

1–The copies of *C.* 2: 1 (Oct. 1923).
2–There were mistakes in the German quotations from Eckerman's *Conversations with Goethe* in Ker's 'Byron: An Oxford Lecture', *C.* 2: 5, 4.
3–'A Brief Introduction to the Method of Paul Valéry'. Wardle wrote with detailed comments on 9 Oct. With reference to TSE's remark that he was not implying that Valéry was 'a derivative poet', Wardle asked whether 'the appearance of so many of Valéry's kinsmen from the vasty deeps does not leave a taste of derivation that needs a brief gargle to remove it?'
4–TSE was more enthusiastic when writing to Valéry on 6 Nov., after the lecture.
5–See TSE's letter to EP of 14 Sept.
6–Arnold Bennett: see Glossary of Names.
7–To discuss *SA*, among other matters.

TO *Ford Madox Ford*[1]

11 October 1923 9 Clarence Gate Gdns

Dear Ford,

I welcome with extreme curiosity the appearance of the *Transatlantic Review*.[2] If it is similar to the *Criterion* I shall take it as the best possible testimony of the blessings of the gods upon our enterprises; in so far as it be different, I hope that the differences will be complementary or at least antagonistic.[3]

But from the prospectus which you have sent me I take no prescience of antagonism. Personally, I have always maintained what appears to be one of your capital tenets: that the standards of literature should be international. And personally, I am, as you know, an old-fashioned Tory.[4] We are so far in accord.

The present age, a singularly stupid one, is the age of a mistaken nationalism and of an equally mistaken and artificial internationalism. I am all for empires, especially the Austro-Hungarian empire,[5] and I deplore the outburst of artificial nationalities, constituted like artificial genealogies for millionaires, all over the world. The number of languages worth writing in is very small, and it seems to me a waste of time to attempt to enlarge it. On the other hand, if anyone has a genuine nationality – and a genuine nationality depends upon the existence of a genuine literature, and you cannot have a nationality worth speaking of unless you have a national literature – if anyone has a genuine nationality, let him assert it, let the Frenchman be as French, the Englishman as English, the German as German, as he can be; but let him be French or English or German in such

1–Text from *Transatlantic Review* (Paris) 1: 1 (Jan. 1924), 95–6. Ford wrote: 'Mr T. S. Eliot, the editor of the only other purely literary periodical that reaches us shall answer with his definition of what is the task of the Perfect Editor.' On Valerie Eliot's copy, TSE wrote in 1958: 'I seem to have assumed an odd tone of authority in addressing a man older than myself!'

2–In the version of this letter written on 11 Oct. 1923 (Beinecke), the title was given as '*The Paris Review*' as in the draft circular Ford sent. This was changed in the published edition.

3–In the Oct. draft, TSE wrote: 'I hope that the differences will be complementary or else [and not *del.*] *antagonistic*'.

4–The circular made a point of stressing that the periodical would introduce 'into international politics a note more genial than that which, almost universally prevails to-day . . . The politics will be those of its editor who has no party politics save those of a Tory kind so old fashioned as to see no salvation but in the feudal system practised in the fourteenth century.'

5–Cf. TSE's letter to EP, 14 Sept., in which he said he wanted 'to see the Hapsburgs restored'. With the break-up of the Austro-Hungarian Empire in 1918, a large number of new states came into existence, including Austria, Hungary, Yugoslavia and Czechoslovakia.

a way that his national character will complement, not contradict, the other nationalities.[1] Let us not have an indiscriminate mongrel mixture of socialist internationals, or of capitalist cosmopolitans, but a harmony of different functions. But the more contact, the more free exchange, there can be between the small number of intelligent people of every race or nation, the more likelihood of general contribution to what we call literature.

I agree also that there can only be one English literature; that there cannot be British literature, or American literature.[2]

You say that you wish to provide another vehicle for the younger writers.[3] I object that this is an unnecessary discrimination in favour of youth. In America there seem to be a considerable number of periodicals, appearing more or less periodically, for this same purpose: and in England there do not seem to be any younger writers anyway. That is one advantage of living in England: one remains perpetually a very young writer. I have enquired after younger writers; but those who are young in years seem anxious to pretend that they are round about forty, and try as hard as possible to assimilate themselves to the generation which has just gone out of date. They have no politics, or liberal politics (which is much the same thing); and if they had any politics, they would mix them up with their literature instead of keeping their literature clean.[4] They have nothing. It is your business to help create the younger generation, as much as to encourage it. It does not need much encouragement.

But a review is not measured by the number of stars and scoops that it gets. Good literature is produced by a few queer people in odd corners; the use of a review is not to force talent, but to create a favourable atmosphere. And you will serve this purpose if you publish, as I hope you will find and publish, work of writers of whatever age who are too good and too independent to have found other publishers. I know that there are

1–In his letter, Ford said he wanted a situation where 'there are no English, no French – or for the matter of that, no Russian, Italian, Asiatic or Teutonic literatures, there will only be literature.'

2–Ford said: 'There is no British literature; there is no American literature: there is only English literature which embraces alike Mark Twain and Thomas Hardy with the figure of Henry James to bracket them.'

3–Ford said his first objective was 'widening the field in which young writers of the day can find publication'.

4–Cf. 'The Function of a Literary Review', C. 1: 4 (July 1923): 'It is the function of a literary review to maintain the autonomy and disinterestedness of literature, and at the same time to exhibit the relations of literature – not to "life" . . . but to all the other activities, which, together with literature, are the components of life' (421).

good writers, young and old, who belong in this category. In the *Criterion* we have endeavoured not to discriminate in favour of either youth or age, but to find good work which either could not appear elsewhere at all, or would not appear elsewhere to such advantage.

But I have only one request to make: give us either what we can support, or what is worth our trouble to attack. There is little of either in existence.

Sincerely yours,
T. S. Eliot

TO *W. R. Lethaby* CC

11 October 1923 9 Clarence Gate Gdns

Dear Mr Lethaby,

I think that I have not thanked you for your letter. Certainly it is right that you should not notice such an essay, and as you have that opinion of it I certainly should not let anyone else do so.[1] But we do indeed want something from you very badly; it is appalling that there should be no one else in England who can write sense about architecture, but it is the truth.

I have just seen your book on Roman London:[2] I congratulate you on an important and extremely interesting book: important I think as much by reason of the point of view toward architecture in general and the subject in particular, as by the erudition itself.

Sincerely yours,
[T. S. E.]

TO *His Mother*[3] TS Houghton

[? Mid-October 1923] [London]

Dearest Mother:

First let me thank you very much for the birthday cable and the birthday cheque.[4] It touched me very much that you should remember so exactly. I am using the cheque as a luxury: not for clothing but to buy a book that I have wanted for a long time.

1–On 5 Sept., TSE sent an unidentified essay on architecture to Lethaby to be vetted. He hoped it would stimulate him to write something, but Lethaby was never to write for C.
2–William Richard Lethaby, *Londinium: Architecture and the Crafts* (1923).
3–From a copy made by HWE.
4–TSE's 35th birthday fell on 26 Sept.

Every day that passes without my having written to you hurts me, and I know it must seem strange that I write so seldom. During the past month I have been alone here in London, only going down to Fishbourne at weekends, or occasionally for the night during the week. During that time I have been working very hard to make up some arrears of promises viz:

An article	for the October *Criterion.*[1]
An editorial	
An essay on Andrew Marvell	for the *Nation.*[2]
An essay on the drama	
An essay on James Joyce	for the *Dial.*[3]
An essay on Marianne Moore	
A 'chronicle'	for the *Nouvelle Revue Française.*[4]
A preface	for the poem of Paul Valéry to appear as a book published by the *Criterion.*
A review of the money market in France and Spain.	for the *Lloyds Bank Financial Monthly.*[5]
A digest of Roumanian debt legislation.	for my *Lloyds Bank Extracts from the Foreign Press.*

So now I am clear of old debts. I have also cleared up all my business correspondence (*Criterion*) to date, and am now ready to attack my income tax returns (English and American). My plans for the winter are to write nothing but one article for each *Criterion*, and to write nothing else. I have undertaken to write four articles for the *Criterion* on four Elizabethan dramatists: Webster, Tourneur, Middleton and Chapman; and as I want to make them pretty long and careful and scholarly, that will be quite enough to undertake, besides a few editorials, and to work in a

1 – The article was 'The Function of Criticism'; the editorial (signed 'T. S. E.'), 'The Classics in France – and in England', C. 2: 5 (Oct. 1923), 31–42, 104–5.

2 – 'Andrew Marvell', *N&A* 33: 26 (29 Sept.); 'The Beating of a Drum', 34: 1 (6 Oct.).

3 – '*Ulysses*, Order and Myth', *Dial* 75: 5 (Nov.); and 'Marianne Moore', 75: 6 (Dec.).

4 – 'Lettre d'Angleterre', *NRF* 21: 122 (Nov. 1923).

5 – [Unsigned], 'Foreign Exchanges', *Lloyds Bank Monthly*, Oct. 1923, 360. TSE noted, 'the main points of interest during the month have been directly connected with the political situation'. Fluctuations of the franc had 'long since come to be dominated by political, rather than economic movements, but the present ascent had long been less political than emotional'. Of the *coup d'état* in Spain: 'unlike that of the Italian fascismo', it had not been 'prepared by any gradual conversion and training of the middle classes, and must be judged by results'.

desultory way on preparations for my play, which involves studying Aristophanes and learning all I can about the Greek theatre.[1]

As for the work of the *Criterion*, I am very slowly learning how to make other people do the work, and only do myself what no one else can do as well. I have been very slow to learn this. But now I simply make decisions, about general policy and about important contributors. I have aimed to get together people whose bond should be myself, so that the power should remain in my hands. Richard Aldington is very useful and hard-working, and more suitable for my purpose than anyone else who I could have had. And I have managed to associate to myself certain allies, like J. M. Robertson and Charles Whibley, of an elder generation, whose support is very valuable. The paper is now pretty well established in opinion, though I shall not be satisfied until it pays its way apart from Lady Rothermere's subsidy. If it reaches that point, I shall be willing to entrust my livelihood to it; and until it reaches that point I prefer to do less work and draw no pay. Of course, if I could have at the same time some other editorial post, I would do that now. But if it comes – and such posts are few – I should prefer to be associated with a more Conservative paper than the *Nation* – though this did not influence me at the time, as it was quite clear that I was to be literary editor solely. But as you will see, the *Criterion* without descending to actual current politics, is developing a clearer programme and attitude than during the first year. I thought it wisest to be rather non-committal at first.

The work at the Bank is interesting, as interesting as bank work can be. Besides retaining what work there is left in connection with Enemy Debts under the Peace Treaties, I have to make myself a sort of authority on everything that goes on of financial and commercial interest in France, Belgium, Italy, Greece, Turkey, Roumania, and North and South America. I read a number of newspapers from the various countries every day, and make such extracts as I have shown you; and I have to make enquiries, and see people at the Board of Trade, and so on. It is a kind of writing.

Vivien has been in the country, having had a friend till now. She will have to come back shortly, and is dreading it; and I very much regret not having taken the *Nation*, because I could then have lived in the country. She gets more fresh air, and in the country she can be in and out, and in the garden and the fields, all day long, and it is wonderful what a difference it makes when one can spend most of the day out of doors. It would not be so bad in London if we had a house and a little garden of our own; but living in a flat one must dress up properly, and go out for a purpose, or else

1 – A further reference to what would become *SA*.

stay indoors; and at best the London air is not very good, especially in November and December, when there are so many fogs. I know too that her illness in the spring gave her a great nervous shock, as to any delicate person it must, to come so near to dying, and it will take her a long time to get over it. So the question is how she can survive a winter in London. It has been a strain for us both to have her in the country when I had to be in town, but still it was better than her being in London. She gains no weight at all – only three pounds in four months, and weighs only a little over 80 pounds. Yet she has been making the most heartrending efforts, eating all she can, and forcing herself to be up and go out and pay no attention to her feelings, when she only feels like staying in bed; because her great horror is invalidism, and being dependent upon other people. She needs quiet and fresh air, and a perfectly steady and peaceful routine of life, to get well. She still has very bad intestinal attacks, sometimes keeping her up most of the night.

I heard from Henry that you are likely to have the *Savonarola* printed. I hope so. I should like to have written a preface or introduction for it.[1] I should have been very proud.

Thank you a thousand times for all your sweetness and all the trouble you have taken about the will.[2]. It does indeed lift a load off my mind. I cannot tell you what a difference it makes, and if anything like the *Nation* should ever be offered again, I should feel able to accept. About the insurance I have been thinking about that.[3] While I am alive I do not like the idea of depriving you of any part of your income. I should like, for the present, to leave it like this: if I get a literary position offering less security than the Bank, and no pension (the Bank pension would be sixty pounds a year if I died now, and more in proportion to further years of service and salary) I should like to have the insurance on the terms you suggest. But until then I do not think that I ought to put you to that expense and privation.

The extra dividend was a godsend,[4] as my expenses have been enormous. The difference between running one establishment, and two –

1 – See Charlotte Eliot, *Savonarola*, with intro. by T. S. Eliot (1928).
2 – She had cabled: 'Can change will for Vivian's lifetime, will do so at once.' On 10 Sept., she said she would create a trust for VHE's benefit, in the event of TSE's prior death, with the income payable to her during her lifetime and with the principal payable at her death to Charlotte Eliot's other children and their descendants. 'With the change in my will you need not remain in the Bank for the small widow's pension.' He would be free to 'accept a two years' engagement with this guarantee'.
3 – CCE said it would enable him to accept such a position as that on *N.* if he 'took additional insurance' on his life and she 'paid the premiums'.
4 – CCE enclosed a cutting announcing that 'The Board of Directors of the Hydraulic-Press Brick Company yesterday declared two dividends of 1 per cent each, or $1 dollar a share.'

one in town and one in the country – is much more than one would think. And then the doctor's bills, and medicine, and special foods, and train fares up and down. And an extra person to feed at the cottage always, and a charwoman to pay, and Ellen to look after me. Of course, when Mrs Haigh-Wood has been there, which has been as much as she can, she has always paid all her own expenses, and some of ours too. But she has been very poorly herself, with bad arthritis, and I think the exertion of those first terrible weeks in April was a very great strain for her at her age.

I must stop now. Remember next spring.

Tom[1]

TO *Bertrand Russell*[2] — MS McMaster

15 October 1923 — 9 Clarence Gate Gdns

Dear Bertie,

I was delighted to get your letter.[3] It gives me very great pleasure to know that you like the *Waste Land*, and especially Part V which in my opinion is not only the best part, but the only part that justifies the whole, at all. It means a great deal to me that you like it.

I must tell you that eighteen months ago, before it was published anywhere, Vivien wanted me to send you the MS to read, because she was sure that you were one of the very few persons who might possibly see anything in it.[4] But we felt that *you* might prefer to have nothing to do with *us*. It is absurd to say that we wished to drop you.[5]

—

She thought TSE would be 'glad of an extra dividend', given that his 'expenses must be so excessive'.

1–CCE wrote at the foot of his copy: 'This letter of Tom's was a long one and it has taken me several hours to copy it. I think Tom has done wonders in the way of literary work under the circumstances.'

2–Bertrand Russell: see Glossary of Names. He quotes this letter in his *Autobiography: 1914–1944*, vol. 2 (1968), 173.

3–BR's letter does not appear to survive. After returning from China and getting re-established in Chelsea at the end of Aug., BR told OM on 14 Oct. that he was particularly excited to 'get hold of Eliot's *Wasteland*', recently published by the Hogarth Press.

4–BR claimed in his *Autobiography* that during the war, 'I used in imagination to see the bridges collapse and sink, and the whole great city vanish and I would wonder whether the world in which I thought I had lived was a mere product of my own febrile nightmares.' BR then took this credit: 'I spoke of this to T. S. Eliot, who put it into *The Waste Land*', 18.

5–VHE told OM in May 1919, 'I shall never try to see him again.' Having broken off all contact with him, VHE wrote on 1 Nov. 1921 to congratulate him on the birth of his son. In the same letter, she reported that TSE was 'having a nervous – or so called – breakdown' and was 'at present in Margate'. TSE was working on *TWL* at the time.

Vivien has had a frightful illness, and nearly died, in the spring – as Ottoline has probably told you. And that she has been in the country ever since. She has not yet come back.

Dinner is rather difficult for me at present. But might I come to tea with you on Saturday? I should like to see you very much – there have been *many times* when I have thought that.

Yours ever
T. S. E.

TO *Richard Cobden-Sanderson* MS Beinecke

15 October 1923 [London]

Dear C-S,

The second ending goes in (text and translation) as an appendix.[1] Wardle shd. tell you how it should be marked, or any note of explanation.

Yes, I shd send a copy to Paris.

A copy of October should go to

J. Middleton Murry Esq
The Adelphi
18 York Bldgs
Adelphi

And one to Wyndham Lewis Esq
61 Palace Gardens Terrace
Kensington, W.8

Many thanks.

Preface will be *reviewed* in a few days.

Yrs ever
T. S. E.

TO *Mary Hutchinson* MS Texas

[Postmark 19 October 1923] 9 Clarence Gate Gdns

Have been *trying* to get you on telephone for two days, as am going to Chich. tomorrow and shan't be here – dreadfully disappointed. Thank you

1 – Valéry's alternative ending to 'Le Serpent' was published as an appendix to *Le Serpent par Paul Valéry* (1924), 51. It was introduced by a note: 'The last strophe did not exist in the first edition. The poem ended with the preceding, or thirtieth, strophe, which then read . . .'

very much, I shd have *loved* to go. I want to see you soon and will telephone tomorrow morning before 10.

His Mother TO *Henry Eliot*

TS Houghton

17 October 1923 [24 Concord Ave]

Dear Henry:

I received your letter last evening and was very glad to have you write that you 'had as lief trust U.S. to pay their rent as an unknown party to pay a note.'[1] I wrote Terry last week that I preferred $25,000.00 cash to $26,500.00 with notes. I think I should accept a cash payment, but I am timid about taking notes up to $18,000.00 in value. Evidently Terry does not look up his 'parties' and if the party in question is not perfectly reliable, there will be difficulty in disposing of the notes. Before he sold note for 4446 Westminster the Banks had to look up Mrs Ledlie. Is Terry sure of being able to sell the thirteen thousand note? He says nothing about the second note. I should be anxious until both those notes were paid. To sell Bohn's $3500.00 note I had to pay 6%. If the 'party' has no security but the building itself, is that sufficient? I went in to consult Mr Martin at the Old Colony, and he agreed with me $8,000.00 was a small proportion of cash on a $26500.00 sale. If there was delay in disposing of the $13,000.00 note I should be very anxious.

I have been hesitating about telegraphing to Terry 'Get no more reports. Dun's all sufficient.' It seems to me outrageous for him to charge me $20.00 I think he is mad. I do not believe he would look up the 'party'. I think he should belong to Dun's and look up parties who give notes.

I am sorry as I have said before, to trouble you when you are so busy. It must be a problem to get a new bookkeeper. Women have been so flattered by their own sex, they expect more than men.

I should like you to return me Dun's report after you have shown it to business friends.

To turn from business, or shall I first write of codicil. I am waiting to sign until I receive your verdict. Is there any loophole by which Tom's share might go to Haigh-Woods?[2] Dana will charge me at least fifty dollars for

1–From HWE's letter of 5 Oct., it is clear that U.S. Army Stores had offered to lease her property at 812 Broadway again, but that she had also received an offer to buy it for $26,500.
2–Writing to TSE on 2 Oct., HWE said 'I have now in front of me a five-page codicil to her will (copied off by her on the typewriter!) creating a life estate for Vivien. I had supposed that was a matter of inserting seven or eight words.' Mrs Eliot was concerned that the money should not go to Vivien's family, the Haigh-Woods, in the event that Vivien predeceased them.

the long document. It seems to me to repeat much that is in the will. If he changes ten years to fifteen in the will it will have to be re-written and he will charge much more. I am sorry I went to him a second time.

Tom wrote me last the 15th August.[1] In that letter he said he did not know whether he wanted to take any more inheritance if Vivian was not included. I immediately prepared to have a codicil to my will including her if she outlived Tom. I cabled Tom I had done so. I have written him every Sunday since April because he reproached me for having discontinued doing so. He has never acknowledged as I told you my gift of one hundred dollars.[2] He has not replied to what I wrote him about the codicil. In giving him outright the dividends and having the codicil, I have disobeyed Father's instructions which I was loath to do [. . .][3] I wrote him just what property I had, and told him it was not as much as Lady Ottoline and Mrs Haigh-Wood supposed. Perhaps that offended him. I do not think you should send him money. His salary is probably four thousand, and he has dividends. I do not want you to give anything to Charlotte, but he has more than she. I want you to invest in gilt-edge bonds.

It is very nice in Tom to say he would write a preface to my book[4] if it is accepted, (if so probably with guarantee). If it should be I would pay him, but I would not like to tell him so. I am preparing a third copy which I will send you to forward to him. He can at least criticise or make suggestions. I infer that he thinks a preface by him would help in its acceptance. I shall discontinue writing except in reply to his letters. I am afraid I have written something he did not like, and if so I had better write less and less frequently. It is a dreadful thought if he avoids communication with me, it troubles me. You have been more than faithful – What should I do without you? Tom's last letter was written on 15th August.

I shall probably send the *Savonarola* in a week.

I am glad the firm is doing so well, but sorry you have so much to do. Get all the sleep you can. I am glad you enjoyed the concert. Hope you can go with Hambleton again. Marian is going to hear Pachmann.[5]

Do not forget your teeth. Are you having any more trouble? Do not think I am angry with Tom – only hurt because I am so fond of him. Vivian is fond of him too, how could she help being, but she eats his life out.[6]

1–TSE's letter of 15 Aug. does not seem to survive.
2–Sent as a present for his birthday on 26 Sept.
3–A heavily deleted and illegible phrase follows 'loath to do'.
4–*Savonarola: A Dramatic Poem.*
5–Vladimir de Pachmann (1848–1933): flamboyant virtuoso pianist.
6–Alongside this remark about VHE, Mrs Eliot wrote by hand 'Is that too strong?'

I am very glad Tom was kind to Nancy Porter[1] and her friend. I have given a young aspirant to literary fame a letter to him – the grandson of my neighbour, Mrs Spencer. I could not refuse.

Ever yours with love,
Mother.

<Do you endorse codicil? Shall I sign?>

When I do get a letter from Tom it will probably be a very affectionate one – but when? Christmas is on the way.

FROM *His Mother* TS Houghton

[20 October 1923] [24 Concord Ave, Cambridge, Massachusetts]

Dear Tom,

I have just finished copying your letter to send to Henry, and it has taken at least two hours, so I appreciate your sending me such a long letter.[2] If you only knew how much satisfaction and relief it has given me. I wish now you would write to Henry. I have to consult him about so much business, and he is so busy himself. He and I have been worried to know whether to sell the store on Broadway or to continue to lease it. The offer was only one-third cash and two notes. I am timid about notes. And I did not know about the would-be purchaser. The real estate has been a great care and anxiety to me. And I am so far away.

I noticed in copying your letter, that you speak of writing a preface or introduction for the *Savonarola*. Of course I should prefer the Introduction if you could find time for it. It suggests to me more weighty matter than a preface. How about the intellectual atmosphere of that period? However, do nothing if you are driven by more insistent and normal claims.

Give my love and sympathy to Vivien. She must have great resistive power of some kind to have gone through what she has. She wrote me she was more happy in London than in the country. I hope she will continue to improve. Tell her I often think of her.

I am glad you have your intellectual interests to stimulate and occupy your mind. It must be a great source of happiness to know that all you write will be read with interest. Miss Spencer, to whose nephew I gave the

1–HWE wrote to TSE on 19 Oct.: 'I appreciate highly your entertainment of Nancy Porter, as the Porters are my favorite cousins. The young ladies seem to have been delighted.'
2–TSE's letter of mid-Oct. 1923 above.

letter of introduction to you, tells me he admires your writings very much. I will end this with love. I hope you will keep me informed as to Vivien's health, and write me again of your interests and health.

Yours ever with much love,
Mother.

FROM *His Mother*

TS Valerie Eliot

21 October [1923]

24 Concord Ave

Dearest Tom:

I wrote you a short note yesterday on the receipt of your letter, and enclosed it in the envelope with the *Savonarola*. As I wrote you I had intended sending it to Henry with the request he forward it to you. I do not know, of course that it will ever be published, even with my guarantee. And I do not know that I shall ever be willing to use money for that purpose. I had been told (by Aunt Nellie), that I should receive a few thousand, two perhaps, from the Thomas Blood estate, two-thirds of which was to go to Aunts Mattie and Nellie. I found, however, when Thomas Jr. died, that Aunt Mattie had made Aunt Susie residuary legatee, and Aunt Nellie has like Uncle Will left everything to Aunt Susie, who will have quite a large estate. I may, however, get a few hundreds out of a separate small fund.

I would be much gratified if you would read through the manuscript and give me your opinion as did Drs. Grandgent and [Livingston] Lowes. Then if you can write me a preface which would enhance its value, I should like to pay you as would a magazine, for your time is valuable. However, if you are very busy do not try. I may have written this in yesterday's note.

It was a great relief to me to receive your letter yesterday, as I had been considerably troubled by your long silence. The photographs gave me a pleasanter impression than the picture I had formed in my own mind. The cottage especially at least in outward appearance was much more attractive, and the pictures of you and Vivian in the garden left a pleasant impression. She looks, of course, very thin, and I am sorry she does not gain more in weight. I do not wonder that her nerves are still shaken by her experience in the spring. And what a problem you have had to meet and are still having. Although Regent's Park is so near you one must, as you say, dress for an outing to go there.

Under the circumstances, going back and forth between Old Fishbourne and London, I think your literary output has been remarkable. You must have worked very hard. I was much interested in the two articles you sent. I should think your Bank Reports would be very interesting but very difficult. Have you a working knowledge of such languages as Roumanian? It appals me to think of these financial reports. They ought at the Bank to pay you well for such expert and difficult work.

I am glad you have transferred the more laborious and less important work on the *Criterion* to Mr Aldington and others. I am glad to have you write that you would like to be associated with a more conservative paper than the *Nation*. I feel as if radicalism would run us on to the rocks both in England and America. I fear what this next Congress will do with La Follette, Brookhart and Magnus Johnson working for the irrational Farmer-Labor party. And Senator Moses says Ford is the most popular man in the country – Ford with his hundred million when his advocates are against capitalism. He is most unfit for the Presidency.

I am not surprised to hear you say that your expenses have been enormous. One household is costly and two must be extreme. I fear you have had to spend the two thousand prize – it seems cruel. And doctors! How little they can do, and what prices they charge. Yet we must have them.

As to the insurance I suggested. If I gave you two hundred for a premium I must give each of the others the same. I still have three hundred shares of stock the dividends of which would give you two hundred dollars apiece. It is, of course, impossible to tell how long I or anyone else will live.

Charlotte has not been very well – housework is beginning to tell on her. She spends all her dividends on her children. Even if she could afford a maid it is difficult to obtain one in Millis, I wish they wd try to sell the place.

I have said nothing about your offer of writing an Introduction to the *Savonarola*. It would please me very much and I think would aid in its acceptance by the publisher and its sale. If I received anything from the Blood Estate I would use it as a guarantee, but I fear the amount will be very small. I should not want you to give too much time to it that you required for your legitimate promised work. Or if you did I should want to make it good. I am copying for the printer the text with the name of the character presented on the same line as the first line of his speech. It is so written in plays I have examined. I discovered that two of my concluding sonnets have twelve lines instead of fourteen. I find it difficult to introduce two more lines without all re-writing. All Michelangelo's sonnets have fourteen lines. They are not very interesting.

Remember if necessary to balance expenses I will pay for the next few months for Ellen. Vivian cannot be left alone and unattended.

Ever yours,
Mother.

TO *Dorothy Pound* — MS Lilly

27 October [1923] — 9 Clarence Gate Gdns

My dear Dorothy,

Do forgive me. I had not realised that I had let so much time elapse. As for your question, I don't think I will give you the name unless you ask me again, or unless you want to do somebody in.[1] He nearly put V. in her grave, she *just* escaped at the moment of expiring. Hence this year's disasters. She has an *excellent* man [Dr K. B. Martin] now – only unfortunately he is practising in Germany – being a German. I don't know who the best man is for *glands* – *that* man was not a specialist on the subject, but I can recommend this German to anyone who is willing to go to Freiburg. Vivien is fighting her way up, very slowly.

Of course I will have tea with you when you return. Let me know.

Yours aff.
T. S. E.

FROM *Paul Valéry* — MS Valerie Eliot

Mardi [30? October 1923] — 40 rue de Villejust, Paris

Cher Monsieur Eliot,

J'ai infiniment regretté que vous n'ayez pu dîner avec Whibley et moi, à l'University Club. Nous avons agité de vieux souvenirs qui vous auraient peut-être intéressé; et puis, j'aurais bien aimé faire avec vous plus profonde et plus parfaite connaissance. Mais je sais que la santé de Madame Eliot vous préoccupe beaucoup et que vous allez auprès d'elle aussi souvent que votre banque s'entr'ouvre. Je sais ce que c'est que l'esclavage et ce qu'est aussi qu'une femme malade . . .

1 – Dorothy Pound had asked for the name of VHE's doctor for treatment of her glands. Cf. *SA*: 'I once knew a man who did a girl in. / Any man might do a girl in' (*CPP* 124).

Vous voulez bien me demander mes notes sur Baudelaire.[1] Je vous les donnerais bien volontiers si elles existaient le moins du monde . . . Mais vous avez vu que je parlais comme je pouvais, et même un peu plus que je ne pouvais, car j'ai perdu tout à coup ma pensée, et je me suis égaré dans ma forêt. Il a fallu lire des vers pour orner le vide! Mes conférences sont des improvisations, qui ne sont pas toujours heureuses; et j'oublie ce que j'ai dit aussi vite que je l'ai dit. Ainsi, je ne me souviens plus d'avoir parlé d'*originalité*, et ce que j'en ai dit m'est inconnu. Si j'essayais de le reconstituer, je suis sûr que je formerais autre chose.[2]

Je penserai au *Criterion* aussitôt que ma terrible vie me donnera un peu de calme et de temps. Je sais que vous avez d'excellents traducteurs, et je suis encore émerveillé de la transposition du *Serpent* par Wardle.

Je vous dirai aussi à ce sujet que j'ai publié dans la *Revue Hebdomadaire* un article sur Pascal, qui a fait quelque scandale ici.[3] Peut-être, intéresserait-il le lecteur anglais? Si vous désirez le voir, je vous l'enverrai; et si le *Criterion* peut et veut le donner, je serai assez amusé de voir ce texte traduit.[4]

Je vous félicite de la forme et de la substance de votre excellente revue. Le dernier numéro que j'ai lu en passant la Manche, m'a extrêmement intéressé, et peut-être sauvé du mal de mer. La mer était fort sévère, mais le numéro du *Criterion* m'a rendu indépendant du mouvement. (Quelle belle *réclame*!)

1–On 16 Oct., Valéry gave a talk at the French Institute (chaired by CW) on Victor Hugo. TSE was present, and remembered Valéry speaking also about Baudelaire. As Valéry indicates, TSE missed out on the opportunity to dine with him because he had rush off to see to the sick VHE. Of his encounters with Valéry, TSE was much later to recall the utterly 'consistent' personality: 'The social qualities and the charm – such an unaffected modesty of manner, more impressive than any grandeur, and the kind of impish wit that indicates a man who needs no assumed dignity – these were apparent at once. But only gradually it struck me that these qualities of manner were integral to his type of mind. His modesty and his informality were the qualities of a man without illusions, who maintained no pretence about himself to himself, and found it idle to pretend to others' ('Leçon de Valéry', *Listener* 37 [9 Jan. 1947], 72).

2–Valéry lectured on Baudelaire again in Monaco in Feb. 1924: published as 'La situation de Baudelaire' in *Revue de France*, 15 Sept. 1924, with the note: 'Texte d'une conférence sur Baudelaire reconstitué d'après la sténographie' ['a text of a lecture on Baudelaire from a shorthand record']. The lecture was later reprinted in *Maîtres et amis* (1927).

3–'Variation sur Une Pensée de Pascal': a contribution to the 300th anniversary of Pascal, in *La Revue hebdomadaire* 7: 28 (14 July 1923), 161–70 (reprinted in *Variété*, 1927). In his distinctly sceptical essay, Valéry found 'something rather dubious, something rather facile' in Pascal's 'making a speciality of tragic themes and imposing subjects' (trans. Martin Turnell).

4–Valéry told a friend, 'The article on Pascal is everyday stuff, nothing worth communicating to any but the 40,000 readers of *Revue hebdomadaire*' (Pierre Féline, 'Souvenirs sur Paul Valéry', *Mercure de France* 1, 1954, 417). Although TSE did not take it up, a translation was published in Ford's *Transatlantic Review* 2: 7 (July 1924).

N'oubliez pas de me prévenir quand vous-même passerez cette mer. Rien de plus sot que de se manquer!

Croyez, mon cher Eliot, à toute ma sympathie et à mes sentiments véritablement les meilleurs.

Paul Valéry[1]

TO *Paul Valéry* — TS Valéry Estate

6 November 1923 — *The Criterion*, 17 Thavies Inn

Mon cher Valéry,

Merci infiniment pour votre charmante lettre, qui m'a donné tant de plaisir, que j'ose vous répondre en français. Quoique je n'ai jamais, hélas! bien parlé ou bien écrit en langue française je préfère l'employer en causant avec les personnes qui me sont sympathiques, parce que votre langue me donne une certaine liberté d'esprit et de sentiments que la langue anglaise me réfuse. En tout cas je me trouve moins gêné.

Je me suis bien aperçu que vous n'aviez pas de notes à votre Conférence mais je dois vous féliciter du succès prestigieux avec lequel vous avez comblé

1 – *Translation*: Dear Mr Eliot, I am extremely sorry you were unable to dine with Whibley and me at the University Club. We stirred up old memories that might have interested you; I would have very much liked to develop and deepen our acquaintance. But I know that you are greatly concerned about Mrs Eliot's health and that you go to her whenever you are released from the bank. I know what slavery is, and also what it is to have an ailing wife.

You do me the kindness of asking for my notes on Baudelaire. I would let you have them by all means, if in any sense they existed . . . But you saw that I spoke as best I could, and even a little more than I could manage, because my thoughts suddenly went astray and I became lost in my forest. I had to recite poetry to adorn the void! My lectures are improvisations, which do not always come off; and I forget what I have said as soon as I have said it. So, I no longer remember having talked about originality, and what I said about it is unknown to me. If I tried to reconstruct my remarks, I am sure I would say something different.

I shall think about the *Criterion* as soon as my terrible life allows me a degree of calm and time. I know that you have excellent translators, and I still marvel at Wardle's transposition of the *Serpent*.

I also mention in this connection that I have published, in *La Revue Hebdomadaire*, an article on Pascal, which has caused a slight scandal here. Perhaps it might interest the English reader? If you would like to see it, I will send it to you; and if the *Criterion* is able and willing to bring it out, I should be quite intrigued to see this text in translation.

I congratulate you on the form and substance of your excellent review. The latest issue, which I read during the Channel crossing, interested me greatly, and perhaps saved me from sea-sickness. The sea was fierce, but my copy of the *Criterion* made me independent of all motion. (What a splendid advertisement!)

Don't forget to let me know when you are about to make the crossing yourself. Nothing could be more stupid than to miss each other!

I send you, my dear Eliot, all warmest and sincerest regards. Paul Valéry

un vide qu'on ne soupçonnait pas, c'était bien l'improvisation, si c'etait une improvisation, d'un homme qui connaît son sujet à fond et qui peut le traiter d'un point de vue personnel. Mais j'espérais que vous avez un manuscrit, ou des notes, quelque part: si non, j'espérais que vous consentiriez rediger quelques unes de vos idées sur un sujet auquel, vous le savez, j'attribue une importance capitale pour la poésie. Je sais bien que dans votre vie vous avez peu de temps pour de tels *parerga*, mais si vous consentez à laisser paraître ici vos idées sur Baudelaire je peux vous assurer un succès retentissant.

Vous cherchez assez adroitement de me distraire avec votre Pascal;[1] *envoyez-le moi je vous en prie*; mais ne croyez pas que vous me ferez oublier l'autre.

J'espère bien vous chercher à Paris dans quelques mois.

Recevez, mon cher Valéry, l'expression de ma vive sympathie et également de mon admiration profonde.

T. S. Eliot[2]

TO *Gilbert Seldes* CC

6 November 1923 [London]

Dear Seldes

Thank you for your two letters and for the two cheques received.[3] I have also just received your November number with my note on *Ulysses*. I was

1 – 'Variation sur une Pensée de Pascal': Valéry enclosed a copy with his letter of 17 Nov.

2 – *Translation*: My dear Valéry, Very many thanks for your charming letter, which has given me so much pleasure that I dare to reply in French. Although I have never, alas, spoken or written the French language well, I prefer to use it in talking to people with whom I feel in sympathy, because your language gives me a certain freedom of mind and feeling that the English language denies me. At any rate, I find myself less embarrassed.

I noticed, of course, that you spoke without notes during your lecture, but I must congratulate you on the brilliant success with which you filled a void that no-one suspected. If the lecture was improvised, the improvisation was by a man who knows his subject thoroughly and can deal with it from a personal point of view. But I had hoped that there might be a manuscript or notes somewhere: if not, I hoped that you might consent to write down some of your ideas on a subject which, as you know, I consider to be of capital importance for poetry. I know that there is little time in your life for such *parerga*, but if you agree to your ideas on Baudelaire being published here, I can assure you of a resounding success.

You try, very cleverly, to put me off with your article on Pascal; *please send it to me*; but don't imagine that you will make me forget about the other.

I have great hopes of seeking you out in Paris in a few months' time.

I send you, my dear Valéry, my warmest regards together with the assurance of my profound admiration. T. S. Eliot

3 – Seldes had written on 4 and 17 Oct., with cheques in payment for TSE's '*Ulysses*, Order, and Myth' in *Dial* 75: 5 (Nov. 1923) and 'Marianne Moore' in 75: 6 (Dec. 1923).

certainly under the impression that you never wanted anything that had already appeared in any other periodical, and for this reason it never occurred to me to offer the *Dial* my papers in the *Nouvelle Revue Française*.[1] I therefore arranged with *Vanity Fair* to let them have all these papers for such publication in America; I could not very well ask the *Nouvelle Revue Française* to agree to simultaneous publication. I certainly hope after a few months to have another outburst of critical activity and to offer you either the article on prose and verse or something better.[2] I am pleased that you should want me to write about Saintsbury[3] and I should certainly be glad always of any opportunity of advertising him, but I feel that the notice on Saintsbury ought to appear immediately instead of in two or three months and that therefore you should get someone else to do it.

I have weighing on my mind a long article which I ought to write for the January *Criterion*.[4] If you hear no news of me for some time, you will not suppose that I am neglecting my promises in order to write for other papers – the *Criterion* excepted – but simply that as I warned you I am not writing at all.

I am still looking forward to your *Seven Arts*, I enjoyed very much your article on jazz music.[5] My play, if it is ever written, will certainly appear as a text, although I intend it for production with an orchestra consisting exclusively of drums.[6]

Sincerely yours,
[T. S. E.]

1–On 4 Oct., Seldes noted that *Vanity Fair* had published 'the essay on English prose' which was his 'first letter to the *NRF*' of 1 Dec. 1922. He hoped that in future TSE would give the *Dial* any such essays for 'simultaneous publication' in English. The reference is to 'A Preface to Modern Literature: Being a Conspectus Chiefly of English Poetry, Addressed to an Intelligent and Enquiring Foreigner', *Vanity Fair* 21: 3 (Nov. 1923).
2–Seldes hoped that 'after the moratorium of two months', TSE would feel like 'doing the essay on the development of prose and verse which is to be part of my series'.
3–On 17 Oct., Seldes said it would be 'a real service to George Saintsbury' if TSE would write 'a short thing about him'. Saintsbury had just published his *Collected Essays* (3 vols, 1923).
4–'Four Elizabethan Dramatists: A Preface', *C.* 2: 6 (Feb. 1924).
5–Gilbert Seldes, *The Seven Lively Arts* (1924). 'Toujours Jazz' appeared in *Dial* 75: 2 (Aug. 1923) as a response to Clive Bell's attack on jazz in *Since Cézanne* (1923).
6–Seldes had asked, 'Is the Jazz Oratorio [TSE's work-in-progress, *SA*] a work publishable in print or does it require something which the magazine page cannot offer?'

TO *Frank Crowninshield* CC

6 November 1923 [London]

Dear Mr Crowninshield,

Thank you for your letter of the 10th of October with the cheque.[1] I am sending you enclosed the English manuscript of another article which I have written for the current number of the *Nouvelle Revue Française* and which you may use any time if you like it.[2] May I say at the same time that I have not forgotten my promise to write something exclusively for you and that I intend to keep it at the first moment that the circumstances of my life permit.

Yours faithfully
[T. S. E.]

TO *Marianne Moore* TS Beinecke

7 November 1923 *The Monthly Criterion*,
24 Russell Sq, London W.C.1

Dear Miss Moore

I have just heard from Ezra Pound enclosing a letter of the 24th October which you wrote to him. I do not want you to delay any part of the Schloezer essay on our account.[3] I was as a matter of fact on the point of writing to you to ask you to let me know if you would immediately what point you would have reached in your issue of next March. I could not possibly use any of the book before that issue. But if there is part of it which you would ordinarily be publishing in that issue I wish you would let me know what part that is, as I should like to consider using it simultaneously. I will communicate with Pound on hearing from you.

Yours sincerely,
T. S. Eliot

1–Payment for TSE's 'A Preface to Modern Literature: Being a Conspectus Chiefly of English Poetry', *Vanity Fair* 21: 3 (Nov. 1923).

2–'Lettre d'Angleterre', *NRF* 21: 122 (1 Nov. 1923): in translation, 'A Prediction in Regard to Three English Authors, Writers Who, though Masters of Thought, Are Likewise Masters of Art'.

3–Boris de Schloezer (1881–1969): émigré Russian literary and music critic, translator and philosopher; author of studies of Scriabin, Stravinsky and Bach. Nothing of his appeared in the *Dial* in 1924 or in C. In 1923 he published a study of his friend Scriabin in Russian and a French translation of the critic Leo Shestov, *Les Révélations de la mort: Dostoevski–Tolstoi* (1923): this may be 'the book' to which TSE refers. EP's translation from the French of Schloezer's *Igor Stravinsky* was later serialised in the *Dial*, starting in 85: 4 (Oct. 1928).

TO *Virginia Woolf* MS Berg

Sunday [11 November 1923?] 9 Clarence Gate Gdns

Dear Virginia

I am disappointed that this week is no good, but may I come the first day next week – the 19th (Monday).[1] I am looking forward most keenly to seeing you again after such a long time. I am most anxious to know how you are and what you have been writing.[2]

I will come on the 19th unless I hear from you to the contrary. Tell Leonard that I *think* I can do a middle by Dec 15th,[3] but we will talk about that.

Yours always
T. S. E.

TO *His Mother*[4] TS Houghton

14 November 1923 [London]

Dearest Mother:

Your manuscript [of *Savonarola*] arrived safely last week, and I wired you to say that it had come. I should like very much to write an introduction for it and I think it is quite suitable that such a drama dealing with such an historical subject should have an introduction and I should like to do it thoroughly. It will take me several months to make a good job of it, but in any case you would not, I suppose, be bringing it out before the spring. What I suggest is that I should send back to you the play with the introduction and that prospective publishers should see the thing as a whole; as they would hardly be likely to accept a play without seeing the introduction if they knew that an introduction was to follow. We will then try several publishers; I think that Houghton Mifflin are very cautious people who seldom take any risks and like to be held guaranteed by the authors, so that we can probably do better in New York. It might be best in a limited edition.[5] As soon as the January *Criterion* is off my mind I shall tackle it seriously.

1 – On Monday 3 Dec. (*Diary*, II, 277), VW recorded a catastrophe then 'two weeks old', when her sister rang her up 'in the middle of dinner with Tom here' (i.e. 19 Nov.).
2 – VW was writing *Mrs Dalloway*.
3 – Unidentified.
4 – From a copy made by her for HWE: her own letter follows her transcription of TSE's letter.
5 – It was to be published in Mar. 1926 by RC-S, with TSE's intro., in an edition of 300 copies.

As I wired you I have been extremely busy at the bank. Until the last few weeks I had a colleague in conducting this small department; now he has been appointed to another post and I am running it by myself. It means that until they give me an assistant I am trying to do two men's work. The managers are quite aware of this and in a way I am glad of an opportunity, as it will be a conspicuous success if I manage to carry it on properly. But there is a great deal of work and responsibility of all sorts, as well as the work of the five other people who are under me. I sent you some specimens of a little publication which is part of the work.[1] This is not uninteresting as I have to keep in close touch with everything that happens in all European countries and at present have to read about twenty newspapers a day from all over the world.

London is not nearly so healthy in the winter as the country is, and the dampness and fogs are very bad for Vivien. She does not, however, need Ellen to go out with her, she goes out alone; but of course it is impossible to get the benefit from walking in London, especially London in the winter, that one gets in the country. I think I told you in my last letter more about Dr Martin, the great German Doctor who has been taking such an interest in her. He seems to me the wisest, as well as the most scientific Doctor that I have ever met. It is extraordinarily good of him and shows what an interest he takes in her case, that he agreed to send advice and prescriptions and medicines from Germany throughout the winter. Of course he said that he could not cure her of the chronic anaemia and defective circulation of so many years standing without seeing her every day, but he will be a great help even at a distance throughout the winter. I explained to him that I could not take her to him in Fribourgh [*sic*] this year for the reason that I had already had to have so much time away from my work that it had injured my standing and salary and that I could not ask for any more time now except by handing in my resignation.

So far I have dictated to my typist secretary. The rest I am writing myself because it is more private. I am very glad of this opportunity to have this work to do at the bank – two men's work, because I want to leave a good impression behind me. *I leave the bank in* January.[2] I need not go into all the reasons now; staying with the bank would mean and always did mean, giving up all writing. I think I can just manage expenses. My income will be reduced nearly half and what I do get will be precarious instead of sure. I must of course reduce expenses and the first thing to do will be to *let the*

1 – *Lloyds Bank Extracts from the Foreign Press.*

2 – TSE's intention to leave Lloyds in Jan. came to nothing: he did not leave until late 1925.

flat. But I shall let it only on a short lease so that it may be *free for you to come to in April.*[1] We shall have to dismiss Ellen of course and I do not think that she would care to stay on with the people who took the flat. But as I know how much you liked her I should be inclined to pay her a weekly wage pension until you came on condition that she comes back. She could take any work she liked meanwhile.

I want to have everything for you just as it was before: the flat and Ellen.

After I have left the bank we shall have to live *much* more cheaply and shall not be able to have a servant at all. Heretofore in the feverish life we have had to live, I have had to have certain comforts and luxuries simply to save time.

I am depending on the *Criterion* and a small salary from Lady Rothermere and what I can make by outside writing.

I am leaving the bank in January *not* because it is an opportune moment and *without* any such chance as I had in April – the *Nation* – which I bitterly regret having refused. I am leaving simply because I have got to the end of my strength and endurance. In fact, any time, up to this summer would have been a better time than this.

I do not want you to worry but to keep well so that you will be fit to come early in the spring *April.* And remember that I shall be able to be with you much more than last time.

Dear Henry:

It is a little hard for me to understand Tom's state of mind. His previous letter written while Vivien was in the country was quite cheerful. I have a theory that since her return she calls on him in the night. He is very dependent on his sleep. You know she is pretty exacting. The only excuse for his resigning would be that he was so run down physically and nervously he could not carry on.

I can not understand how they could give up having a servant unless they are going into lodgings. Vivien could not do the work. Now I have a plan. I do not want you to send any money to Tom. I have a plan which is to set aside a thousand dollars for Tom and give each of you a bond to that amount; yours will be subtracted from what you owe me on the store. I do not want Tom to know of the transaction. I will send in such sums as are needed. I have cabled him I will pay rent for six months so that they need not leave their apartments. I think I can give up the interest on six thousand as I shall [have] $1800.00 this year from Hydraulic. You notice

1 – CCE was to make a second visit to England the following spring.

Tom in enumerating his sources of income does not include Hydraulic which will have given him this year $1650.00. He does not seem to appreciate his stock. I hope he will not want to sell it unless he puts it immediately into bonds. He will spend otherwise his principal.

I want you to promise me if you buy the store you will leave it to me to look after Tom and will keep your money to pay your notes. I should like to have them paid during my lifetime. I think as you say Uncle Ed could draw up the deed of sale and the notes. That will save commission. If I pay Terry for commission that will leave you free to charge agency at any time you wish. They have been good about collecting. I certainly will not say anything to Terry about sale to you.

You will be here in less than four weeks. Wear one of your best suits. We have had our Thanksgiving dinner today with Charlotte and had the pleasure of telling her about the 6% dividend. Ada is putting her dividends into her house.

Of course I should not think of going to London before June. Margie thinks (so Marian tells me), that I ought to take her if I go again. She does not realize that I take Marian because of my age. Otherwise I would go alone. Margie would be a care lying in bed until one o'clock. She thinks of me as stronger than she. I absolutely *could* not take her.

I should hesitate to have Tom give so much time to *Savonarola*. I shall send for Christmas Tom $25.00 and Vivian $15.00. Do not you send. Save all you can for your notes.

Ever with love,
Mother.

I think before long Tom may get another offer similar to that of *The Nation*.

TO *Wyndham Lewis* — TS Cornell

14 November 1923 — *The Criterion*, 17 Thavies Inn

Dear Lewis,

Thanks for your letter.[1] I expect to be in my office up to one o'clock tomorrow, after that less certain. I am sorry you have had so much to do but it is really essential for this number of the *Criterion* to have your

1 – This may refer to an undated letter by WL in which he said he was 'working incessantly' on his *The Man of the World I* but that 'Zagreus will follow shortly' (dated 'October? 1923' in *Letters of Wyndham Lewis*, 136–7).

manuscript by Saturday. I would give you more time if I could but I don't think you will need to worry about its not being as finished as you would like.

Yours ever,
TSE

TO *Henry Eliot* — TS Houghton

14 November 1923 — 9 Clarence Gate Gdns

My dear Henry,

It is so long since I have written to you that I hardly know where to begin, and I shall only make this a short letter to break the silence and tell you that I have been thinking of you constantly and wanting to write every day.[1] At present I am so tired from having to do the work of two men in the bank for the last three weeks, and shall have to go on until they give me an assistant – that I hardly have energy now to take up the threads. First of all to thank you again and again for your generous thoughtfulness in the insurance.[2] This is a very big thing in itself because it will have, you shall see before very long, the effect which you intended and of course the only way in which I can compensate such a gift is by the work it will enable me to do. I have also your power of attorney which I will return to you as soon as I have found time to go to a commissioner for oaths and get it sworn.[3] I am writing to you again in a very few days. Several things have happened which require a very early decision, but remember that I am always,

Your appreciative and affectionate brother

Tom

I intend to write to you fully about my plans soon. Meanwhile I am very grateful for business data sent, but should like a long letter about yourself.

1–On 2 Oct., HWE wrote: 'We do not hear a great deal of news from you . . . and are rather in the dark as to your affairs.'

2–On 19 Oct. HWE asked: 'Did you ever get a policy (insurance) that I mailed you?' This refers to the certificate of the insurance on TSE's life, valued at $20,000. The first premium of $558 was paid by HWE on 28 July 1923.

3–On 2 Oct, HWE enclosed 'a new power of attorney prepared by Uncle Ed' which he wanted back as soon as possible. TSE was to sign as 'Thomas Stearns', as on the original certificate, rather than 'T. S. Eliot'. This covered the sale of 275 shares in the Hydraulic-Press Brick Company.

TO *Arthur Symons*[1] CC

14 November 1923 [9 Clarence Gate Gdns]

Dear Mr Symons,

As Mr Aldington has left for a holiday in Italy he has handed your story to me and asked me to read it and write to you. Anything that you write always interests me and I have very much enjoyed reading this story.[2] I wish indeed that we might have the honour of publishing it but the capacity of the *Criterion*, as you may have seen, is very small; and it attempts such a wide range – perhaps too wide a range – that it has had to make a rule of never printing more than one piece of fiction in each number.[3] This may be a mistake, but we are now committed to the acceptance of so many articles that we must pursue this policy for at least another year; and we have already accepted the stories to cover that period. That is why I am returning the story to you, with many regrets.

I hope you will not mind if I take this opportunity – as it is the first occasion on which I have written to you – of expressing my warm admiration both for your prose and for your verse. I have a peculiar debt of gratitude to your *Symbolist Movement*[4] for that was my introduction, for [which] I have never ceased to be grateful to you, to a poetry which has been one of the strongest influences on my life.

I am,
Yours very truly,
[T. S. E.]

1–Arthur Symons (1867–1945): poet, translator and critic; associated with the Decadent movement in England in the 1890s.

2–The unpublished sequel to two stories about 'Lucy Newcome' published in *The Savoy* in Apr. and Dec. 1896.

3–This was not strictly true. TSE published Pirandello's 'The Shrine' and Gómez de la Serna's 'From "The New Museum"' in *C.* 1: 2 (Jan. 1923); VW's 'In the Orchard' and Goold-Adams's 'The Obsequies' in 1: 3 (Apr. 1923); and Owen Barfield's 'Dope' and E. M. Forster's 'Pan' in 1: 4 (July 1923). The following year, WL's 'The Apes of God' and Stephen Hudson's 'Céleste' were both included in *C.* 2: 7 (Apr. 1924).

4–Symons's *The Symbolist Movement in Literature* (1899). TSE had come across the second edition of the book in the Harvard Union Library in Dec. 1908 (his own copy is now in Houghton). In 'The Perfect Critic', he described his encounter with it as 'an introduction to wholly new feelings, as a revelation' (*SW*). Elsewhere, he wrote: 'but for having read his book, I should not, in the year 1908, have heard of Laforgue or Rimbaud . . . So the Symons book is one of those which have affected the course of my life' (*NC* 9: 35 [Jan. 1930], 357).

FROM *Paul Valéry* TS Houghton

17 November 1923 40, rue de Villejust, Paris XVIe

Mon cher Eliot,

Vous écrivez délicieusement en français. C'est une révélation! Je vous avoue que je parle de vous ici, toutes les fois que l'occasion s'en présente – ou que je la crée . . .

Je lis en ce moment *The Waste Land* qui est un étrange monde lyrique.[1] La combinaison singulière de l'antique et du moderne donne des effets que je n'ai trouvé nulle part encore, et il me semble que la musique dont vous enveloppez votre sombre et érudite fantaisie soit, comme j'aime, toujours présente et vivante. Je vous remercie beaucoup de m'avoir envoyé ces poèmes, dont le physique, d'ailleurs, est charmant. Les Woolfs travaillent fort bien.

Je vous mets sous ce pli le Pascal mal famé.[2] Vous en ferez ce que vous voudrez.

J'ai appris que ma conférence sur Hugo avait fait des mécontents à Londres. Un de mes amis, qui est critique, a reçu une lettre anonyme et indignée, contenant un article indigné et anonyme de la *Chronique de Londres* . . . Il paraît que j'ai dit des horreurs sur Hugo.[3]

Mon Baudelaire est toujours quelque part dans l'univers. Je crois que vous avez eu une hallucination chez Mrs. Morley car je ne me souviens que d'un trou dans mes pensées, et c'est ce trou qui fut baptisé *conférence*.

1 – TSE inscribed a copy of *TWL* 'au grande poète français Paul Valéry, hommages de l'auteur T. S. Eliot. 1.xi.23.' ['to the great French poet Paul Valéry, with homage from the author T. S. Eliot. 1. xi. 23.'].

2 – See Valéry's letter of 30? Oct. for more details about the Pascal essay.

3 – See Michel Jarrety, *Paul Valéry* (2008): 'Le mardi 16 [Oct.] au soir, à l'Institut francais, sous la présidence de son vieil ami Charles Whibley, il prononce une conférence consacrée à l'oeuvre de Hugo qu'il a choisi d'envisager dans son progrès technique. Afin d'illustrer la vitalité du poète, il distrait son public de quelques anecdotes alors moins connues qu'aujourdhui – il mangeait les oranges avec leure écorce, et les langoustes avec leur carapace – et, pour souligner sa puissance de travail, raconte comment, le jour ou mourut François-Victor, il refusa de quitter son ouvrage tandis qu'on frappait à sa porte et attendit de l'avoir achevé pour descendre auprès de son fils – qui entre-temps était mort. En racontant cette anecdote tragique qu'il tient de Marcel Schwob qui lui-même la tenait peut-être de Georges Hugo, Valéry n'entend que marquer la nature surhumaine plutôt qu'inhumaine de Hugo. Mais, quelques jours plus tard, l'histoire donne lieu à un article de la *Chroniques de Londres* où on l'accuse d'avoir traité le poète de <<pere dénaturé>> et de <<goinfre>>. . .' (557). One member of the audience recalled him saying 'Hugo, hélas!' (Dwight MacDonald, *Esquire*, 1964). He must have spoken also about Baudelaire, a poet who fascinated TSE: 'The Lesson of Baudelaire' appeared in 'Notes on Current Letters', *Tyro* 1 (Spring 1921), and *TWL* is threaded with allusions to *Les fleurs du mal.*

J'ai bien des notes sur la littérature. Elles sont perdues dans les cahiers que je remplis de rêveries depuis trente ans. J'essaye, en ce moment d'avoir une dactylo pour copier et débrouiller ce chaos. Si je puis organiser cette opération coloniale, je trouverais, je pense, quelque chose pour le *Criterion*.

Au revoir, cher Eliot, n'oubliez pas de venir à Paris. Je vous serre les mains avec la plus grande sympathie.

Paul Valéry[1]

TO *Richard Cobden-Sanderson* MS Beinecke

20 November 1923 *The Criterion*, 17 Thavies Inn

Dear Cobden Sanderson,

Could you send yr. man for some MSS in the morning (before 3). Trend[2] is to be set up and I want to know no. of words in both Trend and Lewis as I don't think we have space for Pt. III of Lewis so I shd like to know number of words in each part of Lewis *separately*.[3]

1 – *Translation*: My dear Eliot, You write delightfully in French. This is a revelation! Let me tell you that I speak about you here, whenever the opportunity arises – or I create it . . .

I am busy reading *The Waste Land*, which is a strange and lyrical world. The curious combination of ancient and modern produces effects such as I have never seen anywhere before, and I have the feeling that the music in which you wrap your sombre and learned fantasy is, as I prefer, always present and vital. I thank you very much for sending me these poems, the physical presentation of which, incidentally, is charming. The Woolfs do very good work.

I enclose the notorious article on Pascal. You may do what you like with it.

I have been told that my lecture on Hugo caused some unhappiness in London. A friend of mine, a critic, has received an indignant and anonymous letter, containing an anonymous and indignant article from *The London Chronicle* . . . It seems that I said terrible things about Hugo.

My Baudelaire is still somewhere in the universe. I think you must have had a hallucination at Mrs Morley's since all I can remember is a gap in my thoughts, and this gap was dubbed a lecture.

I have a great many notes on literature. They are lost in the notebooks I have been filling with my musings during the last thirty years. I am trying, at the moment, to find a typist to copy and sort out this chaos. If I manage to organise this colonial operation, I think I might discover something for the *Criterion*.

Goodbye, dear Eliot, do not forget to come to Paris. With warmest regards, Paul Valéry

2 – J. B. Trend, 'The Moors in Spanish Music', *C.* 2: 6 (Feb. 1924).

3 – On 19 Nov., WL delivered what he called the third part (new to you) about 'Split-Man', saying it was about 9,000 words long. 'Use it all if you can.' 'Mr Zagreus and the Split-Man' appeared in shortened form in *C.* 2: 6 (Feb. 1924).

~~Will you please return this MSS with a slip (haven't any). Will ring you up in the morning.~~

Yrs
T. S. E.

TO *Mary Hutchinson* MS Texas

[early December 1923][1] [London]

My dear Mary,

I have read your list for Vivien and here is one of mine.[2] Of course both you and Vivien have read a good part of it and I have left out other things because they have been read – and I have left out French because there is enough English to keep one a lifetime to begin with – But please return it as I have not made a copy.

Always aff –
Tom

TO *Hugh Walpole*[3] TS Valerie Eliot

3 December 1923 *The Criterion*, 17 Thavies Inn

Dear Walpole

Thank you very much indeed for your kind letter of the 28th. You have no idea how much pleasure it gives me to receive an expression of approval of the *Criterion* such as *your* letter.[4] I have put a great deal of energy into it, a great deal of time which I could ill spare; and I often feel a great discouragement in thinking that such a paper will interest very few people indeed. And on the other hand, I realise fully how much better I could have made it had not more serious claims on my time, and the necessity of earning my livelihood by a very busy life in the City, hampered me, at times, to the point of hopelessness. The impartiality of which you speak[5] is certainly representative of my own taste, which I think is pretty catholic,

1 – MH dated this 'December 1923'. It probably predates the related card, postmarked 7 Dec.
2 – On 26 Aug. TSE thanked MH for saying she would give VHE a 'course of reading'. The lists themselves do not survive.
3 – Hugh Walpole: see Glossary of Names. Walpole went on to contribute 'The Old Ladies' to C. 2: 7 (Apr. 1924) and 2: 8 (July 1924)
4 – On 28 Nov. Walpole said C. 'went beyond any periodical we have had in English'.
5 – Walpole admired its 'avoidance of jealousies, back-bitings and clique opinions'.

and the paper would be more representative still were it possible to enlarge its size. But this impartiality subjects it to criticism from every quarter and deprives it of unanimous backing from any one set of people.

The *Criterion* is not directly in danger of stopping: it is only in danger of stopping insofar as it depends on my continuing. As I say, I have only been able to give to it my spare time, and for the work I have done I have not – as you may not know – accepted payment of any kind. Lady Rothermere has subsidised the cost of producing the paper, but my continuing depends on making it sufficiently successful to provide an income. In other words, I must sooner or later, and probably sooner, as my health has been going down for the last year, give it up unless it can be made a substantial thing and pay *me* a small but sure income. For this reason, every subscription counts, *and your suggestion would certainly be a very great help*.[1] If there are enough people in England who care enough for the *Criterion* to make it possible for me to continue, they will also help to make it possible for me to improve the paper. I should be glad of course to find some other work than that which keeps me in the City from 9 to 5 every day, so that I could have more time and freedom of movement, and which I could carry on at the same time as the *Criterion*; but I must look for something which would offer a reasonable hope of security, no matter how small the salary.

Please know in any case that your letter has given me great pleasure,

Yours sincerely,
T. S. Eliot

TO *Wyndham Lewis* TS Cornell

3 December 1923 *The Criterion*, 17 Thavies Inn

Dear Wyndham,

I am sorry about the cheque. You should have received it about four days ago but for distractions on my part.[2] I have seen Cobden-Sanderson today and have asked him to forward you today a cheque for the two sections we are issuing in this number: It comes to £23. I hope this is satisfactory. As I said, I should like to publish the third part in the April

1–Walpole wondered if it would help if supporters took out five or six subscriptions a year.
2–On 2 Dec. WL reminded TSE he had promised 'to pay me a cheque as soon as I handed you the MSS'. This was advance payment for 'Mr Zagreus and the Split-Man' in C. 2: 6 (Feb. 1924), for which WL was paid 'double rates'.

number.[1] I send you the manuscript herewith, as you say you want to work on it, but I hope you will see no objection to returning it to me by the end of February if you let me know *in time*. You will of course get the same rates and if you have it finished and send it sooner you shall have a cheque for it when we get it back, as I have had the number of words counted. Please let me know if you have received it.

Meanwhile there are two other points of importance. One is the short explanatory note which you promised me and which we ought to have at once.[2] Can you let me have it by tomorrow or the next day as otherwise we must go to press without it. You will get proof of the whole thing next week.

The other point is that you promised to ring me up one morning and arrange so that we could meet and so that I can see the manuscript, or part of the manuscript, of your book.[3]

And finally, you promised to let me know whether the copyright of *Tarr* and *the Caliph's design* was in *your name* or not.[4] Of course any arrangements made with Miss Weaver, in any case, will have to have your approval; and you understand that the whole matter is at present entirely confidential.

Let us discuss the second paragraph of your letter[5] when we meet.

I have only one objection to make to Adams' article[6] and that is that I hope he will not use the quotation which I have marked on page three. It is not a good passage.

Yours ever
T. S. E.

<Is there a Tyro soon?>[7]

1–The 'third part' was published as 'The Apes of God' in *C.* 2: 7 (Apr. 1924).
2–WL promised 'a few lines by way of explanation of this fragment'. They read: 'These few pages . . . belong to a book which will be finished I hope by next autumn. Mr Zagreus is an important ghost; he, however, remains attached to his disguises, a central myth. Krang is a subordinate character, but gives more development in the book than can be seen in the fragment.' *The Apes of God* was not published until 1930.
3–On 26 Sept. TSE had offered to have WL's essays published by *C.*
4–WL's *Tarr* (1918) and *The Caliph's Design* (1919) were published by Harriet Shaw Weaver's Egoist Press, which had recently wound up.
5–On 2 Nov., WL said TSE had promised him: 'To print a largish section of my book'. He did not want this 'printed in small bits'.
6–WL asked TSE to appraise a review by Adams of *TWL* commissioned for WL's *Tyro*. He asked TSE to let him know 'if it will pass muster' or 'return it'.
7–These words are scribbled in ink at the head of the letter. WL had published two issues of *The Tyro*. The first (1921) included TSE's 'Notes on Current Letters', and 'Song to the Opherian' by 'Guz Krutsch', while the second (1922) included TSE's 'The Three Provincialities'. There were no further issues.

TO *Richard Cobden-Sanderson* MS Beinecke

3 December 1923 [London]

As a special favour (not a precedent) please pay *immediately* Wyndham Lewis, 61 Palace Gardens Terrace, Kensington, W.8 for 'Mr Zagreus and the Split-Man' Parts I and II. This is (Hazell's estimate) 5724 words, which at *double* rates (giving exclusive periodical rights in England and America till Apr. 15) amounts to £23.

T. S. Eliot

TO *Mary Hutchinson* MS Texas

[Postmark 7 December 1923] 9 Clarence Gate Gdns

I forgot that I put in your list too. V. *wants it back* – at once!

You make notes on mine.[1]

T. S. E.

TO *Richard Cobden-Sanderson* MS Beinecke

9 December 1923 9 Clarence Gate Gdns

Dear C-S,

Here's mine.[2] It is short. There only remains my edit, as I enclose Aldington's. I will ring up or write tomorrow about what to omit.

Many thanks for yr Christmas gift! It is a beautiful book, and I am delighted to own it.

Yours ever
T. S. E.

1 – See TSE's letter of early Dec. relating to the reading lists he and MH had drawn up for VHE.

2 – Presumably TSE's 'Four Elizabethan Dramatists: A Preface', *C.* 2: 6 (Feb. 1924), 115–23.

TO *Lytton Strachey*[1] MS James Strachey via Michael Holroyd

10 December 1923 38 Burleigh Mansions[2]

. . . And once again – although I admire and enjoy your portraits in the *Nation*, it is to my interest to say that they are not *long* enough to do you justice. So – although you once refused – two years ago[3] – please remember that I should like to lead off a number of the *Criterion* with you, up to 5000 or 8000 words . . . I have thought that you ought to do Macaulay – but anything from you would ensure the success of a number, besides the pleasure it would give me. Could you?[4] . . .

[Incomplete]

TO *Richard Cobden-Sanderson* MS Beinecke

13 December 1923 *The Criterion*, 17 Thavies Inn

Dear C-S,

The order:[5]	Lewis (expurgations as per attached and with note)
	Lévy-Bruhl
How many pages?	Robertson
	Hauptmann
	Trend
	Eliot

Murry[6] must be postponed and announced in circular.

In haste

T. S. E.

1 – Lytton Strachey: see Glossary of Names. This fragment of a letter from TSE to Strachey is quoted in Michael Holroyd, *Lytton Strachey and the Bloomsbury Group: His Work, Their Influence* (revised edn, 1971), 777. Valerie Eliot records that by 1968 the original letter seen by Holroyd had 'disappeared and there is no copy of it'. She went to the late James Strachey's home in Marlow, but was unable to find it among Strachey's papers (letter to Dorothea Richards, 23 May 1968).

2 – According to Holroyd, TSE invited Strachey to a small party at his flat in 38 Burleigh Mansions in Dec. For VW's account of a dinner there with TSE at this time, see her diary entry for 19 Dec. 1923 (*Diary*, II, 278).

3 – VHE told MH in late 1922: 'T. wants *very much* to ask Lytton but does not think Lytton would be at all likely to consent to write for the *Criterion*.'

4 – Strachey did not write for *C*.

5 – The proposed running order for *C*. 2: 6 (Feb. 1924). The final order was different: TSE, WL, F. W. Bain, May Sinclair, J. M. Robertson, Lévy-Bruhl, Gerhart Hauptmann, J. B. Trend, and 'F. M.'.

6 – JMM, 'Romanticism and Tradition', was postponed to *C*. 2: 7 (Apr. 1924).

TO *Herbert Read* MS Victoria

16 December 1923 9 Clarence Gate Gdns

My dear Read

I got the *Speculations*[1] last night. Many thanks. I must have an article about it in the *Criterion* – if I can't think of anyone else I shall do it myself – certainly a congenial subject.[2] I shall also urge Leonard Woolf to give it a good notice.[3] It's a very fine thing – and it does you credit.

I have been wanting to see you, often, if you can, it can be realised after Christmas.

Cordially
T. S. Eliot

TO *Richard Cobden-Sanderson* MS Beinecke

[Postmark 19 December 1923 London W.I.]

Many thanks for various communications. Will you lunch with me – on business! – directly after Christmas? Thursday? There is one worrying point I want to ring you up about tomorrow and I think I have made a mistake.

TO *Hugh Walpole* TS Valerie Eliot

24 December 1923 *The Criterion*, 17 Thavies Inn,
London E.C.I
9 Clarence Gate Gdns, N.W.I

My dear Walpole,

I hope you will forgive my delay in answering your very kind letter of the 7th December.[4] I hope you will take it for what it is, an instance of the

1–T. E. Hulme, *Speculations: Essays on Humanism and the Philosophy of Art*, ed. HR (1924).
2–TSE was to write of the book: 'The posthumous volume of *Speculations* of T. E. Hulme . . . appears to have fallen like a stone to the bottom of the sea of print' but was 'a book of very great significance'. Calling Hulme 'the author of two or three of the most beautiful short poems in the language', TSE said that he 'appears as the forerunner of a new attitude of mind, which should be the twentieth-century mind, if the twentieth century is to have a mind of its own. Hulme is classical, reactionary, and revolutionary; he is the antipodes of the eclectic, tolerant, and democratic mind of the end of the last century', *C.* 2: 7 (Apr. 1924), 231.
3–There was no notice in *N&A*.
4–This does not appear to survive, but see TSE's letter to him of 3 Dec.

absurd and lamentable disorder of my life, that I cannot even answer such a letter immediately.

The *Criterion* is 14/- a year, so that five subscriptions would be three pounds, ten shillings. And I say again, that every subscription is a most valuable help. The present circulation is 800 to 1000, and I estimate that the *Criterion* could pay for itself, and pay me the sufficient basis of a living – with what I could write outside, on a circulation of 2500 to 3000 copies. That seems a moderate ambition; but it is only possible because we run the paper very economically, without an office or staff; but as we can afford very little advertising, and as 3000 is I suppose the limit of the number of persons who might be interested in such a paper, the progress is very slow indeed. Subscriptions should be sent to Cobden-Sanderson, whose address you see above.

I should welcome any criticism of the paper or suggestions from you. Of course I should be immensely grateful for anything you could do. I cannot afford to wait until the *Criterion* has a circulation of 3000. I need to find some secure position which would take only about half my time, and, preferably, which would allow me to live largely in the country and occasionally go abroad for considerable periods – on account of failing health. But I must in one way or another make 700 or 800 pounds a year. I can write for the *Times Literary Supplement* and the *Nation* and one or two American papers, but the total would produce only a part of what I need, and implies a precarious existence of continuous writing. I should like to get some editorial position or a readership or simply a commission for journalistic writing on a contractual basis. I sometimes think that it would be better if I had never gone into a bank at all. For I have been advanced very rapidly, and my prospects are, I suppose, from a banking point of view, almost 'brilliant', and the income is absolutely secure – it would go on till doomsday, with a pension at the end, and a widow's pension, and all of the inducements that enslave one. So that, when one has serious responsibilities, one simply feels that one has no right to surrender so much for an income which might be both much smaller and precarious. Yet there are only two things I really want to do – the *Criterion* and my own writing.

Forgive me for writing so openly to you – but you have really invited it.

With very cordial thanks,
Sincerely yours,
T. S. Eliot

Vivien Eliot TO *Sydney Schiff* MS BL

26 December [1923] 9 Clarence Gate Gdns

Dear Sydney,

We have just returned from a queer sort of Christmas spent in wandering about the country in Beasley's car, in search of a more convenient and accessible country cottage than our own. We are very tired, and have discovered nothing that is, in our opinion, worthy to be compared with Milestone Cottage.

In reading *Tony*[1] I noticed a development of a new style, of which I thought I saw the beginnings in *Prince Hempseed*.[2] I must say that at first I missed the extraordinary detachment and sort of cool indifference of the style in which you wrote *Elinor Colhouse*. Of course I think that you are writing of things too near to you in feeling as perhaps in time for *that* style to be a possible one. But, what has struck me *most* forcibly in the book is an extraordinary change of key in the writing, from (about) page 184 (or I think a little earlier) from which, to the end, it seems to me you have achieved a *most moving and serious* piece of work, an important document in the history of that period and a fine piece of character work. (I think 'the Rock'[3] is very cleverly done, and with such economy).

With very good wishes, yours always

Vivien Eliot

FROM *His Mother* [extract] TS Valerie Eliot

30 December 1923 24 Concord Ave, Cambridge, Mass.

Dear Tom:

Henry left last night having been here barely six days. They had an excess profits law suit in his firm and as he is Treasurer it was necessary for him to be in Chicago the last day of December. He was very tired when he came and I think the short vacation rested him somewhat. I was somewhat distressed when he told me he had sold one hundred shares of your stock. Had he consulted me I should have advised strongly against it, especially as the Company had made much money this year, a surplus. You

1 – SS's novel (published as by Stephen Hudson), *Tony* (1924) deploys the main characters of his previous novels, *Elinor Colhouse* (1921) and *Richard Kurt* (1922).

2 – Hudson, *Prince Hempseed* (1923).

3 – The nickname of the narrator's 'notorious pro-German' Uncle Fred who works in the City.

will realise what the difference means to you when I send the next dividend of $175.00 instead of $275.00. On the sale of one hundred shares you will lose this year $300. The stock at 6% would yield you $600 and the six bonds $300. If you sold all your Hydraulic you would receive $825.00 less income.

Now the 6% may not possibly continue more than a year or two, but this will probably be your hardest year, and I should advise you to hold on to the stock a while longer. If you decide to do so, you can write Henry to purchase back the hundred shares. He can certainly do so and make a hundred or so on the deal because the stock has gone down two points. He could watch the market.

[. . .]

I have faith that before the end of a year you will receive an offer of a position on some periodical that will yield you a far better income than the *Criterion*. Eleanor gave Henry a copy of a paper edited by J. Middleton Murrey [*sic*], called, I believe, *The Adelphi*.[1] I read or tried to read it and it is far inferior to the *Criterion* in contents, and what is of less importance, the cover was ugly and cheap. I looked through it and found the first article, a refutation of your theory of criticism, or rather of what the author termed classicism against romanticism, the only article worth reading.[2] The magazine was *cheap*.[3] The only articles I object to in the *Criterion* are those by Ezra Pound. They seem to me heterogeneous dry bones of literature. Are you obliged to publish his desiccated contributions? The next *Criterion* will be out in two weeks but it will be four before I receive it.

I am making another copy of *Savonarola* to submit to a publisher after your Introduction is ready. I should like to try Houghton & Mifflin,

1–JMM founded *The Adelphi*, a yellow-bound shilling monthly, in June 1923. He outlined its rationale in an editorial entitled 'The Cause of It All', *Adelphi* 1: 1 (June 1923). 'Eleanor' is TSE's much-loved first cousin on his mother's side: Eleanor Holmes Hinkley (1891–1971).

2–JMM took up the challenge laid down by TSE's attack in 'The Function of Criticism' in C. 2: 5 (Oct. 1923). He was pleased to have 'a real opponent, in Mr T. S. Eliot, the gifted editor of the *Criterion*', and said the debate between them was 'concerned with fundamentals' ('More About Romanticism', *Adelphi* 1: 7 [Dec. 1923], 557–69). For JMM, 'a man who has reached a condition of sufficient spiritual maturity to be a classicist or a Romantic, must be one or the other'. However, 'even Mr Eliot, the author of *The Waste Land*, the champion of *Ulysses*, is not a true-blue classicist in his bones; an English Tory is quite another thing'.

3–The *Adelphi* carried across its front page an advertisement for Remington typewriters, while other pages had advertisements, not only for publishers but department stores. C. carried no such advertisements.

although I think they would require a guarantee. If they refuse I should like you to help me try a New York publisher.

[. . .]

Ever your loving

Mother.

TO *Sydney Schiff* MS BL

Sunday [?30 December 1923] 9 Clarence Gate Gdns

My dear Sydney

I have not time to write a proper letter – this is just to *thank* you for two of yours to which I shall reply fully as soon as I can or when I can come to see you – but that must be *next* week, I am afraid. I think what you say about Hulme has a lot of truth in it, and hope to discuss that with you.[1]

I have just finished *Tony* and will get it back to you. There is a lot to talk about there. I am inclined to think you get your best effects *in spite of* your theory of the 'novel-document'! but you will deny that vigorously. I think 'the Rock' is extremely real and alive.[2]

With love to you both

Yours aff

Tom

Forgive this scrawl – am *very* run down and can do less and less now.

TO *C. K. Scott Moncrieff* CC

31 December 1923 [9 Clarence Gate Gdns]

Dear Mr Scott Moncrieff,

I have recently received from the Schiffs your translation of the Death of Bergotte.[3] I am very glad to have this, but very sorry to infer from what

1–On 29 Dec., SS said he had read T. E. Hulme's *Speculations* alongside *TWL* and saw 'a certain correspondence' between them. While he thought Hulme's volume 'a noteworthy contribution to certain aspects of modern thought', he found it occasionally 'superficial and frequently elliptical', and judged that 'a second grade logician would make short work of most of his theories'. He saw Hulme as '*un original* rather than original' and looked forward to discussing his 'provocative book' with TSE.

2–Cf. VHE's letter of 26 Dec. 1923.

3–Proust's account of the death of his fictional novelist Bergotte, in *La prisonnière*, the fifth book of *À la recherche du temps perdu*, published posthumously in French in 1923.

Mrs Schiff tells me that there has been a misunderstanding. Your letter to me did not go astray, but I gave it to Richard Aldington, who was assistant editor of the *Criterion*, and asked him to reply to you explaining the situation. He was just leaving for Italy and I thought that he would write to you from Rome. Evidently he did not do so, and as I received from him his resignation after he had left, it is possible that he overlooked the matter.[1]

The situation is this: Jacques Rivière arranged with Doctor Proust that we were to have a fragment from part of the book still unpublished in French, and I understand that we are to receive this fragment before the end of January. I thought that it would be so much more of a distinction for the *Criterion* to be able to publish some of Proust's work even before its appearance in French. This is what I asked Aldington to tell you and I asked him to say that we wished to send you the manuscript for translation as soon as received.

If the unpublished fragment arrives, will you consent to translate it especially for me?[2] I hope so, because, rather than have it translated by anyone else, I would even publish it in French. If, however, the promised fragment does not arrive, I should very much like to publish the Death of Bergotte. I am very sorry that this was not explained to you when it should have been, and I hope you will accept my apologies. Meanwhile, I of course wish to retain the manuscript you sent.

With all best wishes for the New Year.

Sincerely yours,
[T. S. E.]

TO *Gilbert Seldes* CC

31 December 1923 [London]

My dear Seldes,

Many thanks for you highly personal Christmas card and my wishes to you for the New Year.

I am very sorry to hear of your resignation from the *Dial*.[3] It gives me the hope, however, that you will now have more time to devote to writing,

1 – RA left for Italy in early Nov., and resigned soon afterwards.
2 – Proust, 'The Death of Albertine', trans. Scott Moncrieff, *C.* 2: 8 (July 1924).
3 – Seldes resigned his editorial position at *The Dial* in Dec., but continued to write 'Theatre' pieces until it ceased publication in 1929.

both in the *Dial* and out of it. I hope to hear that your book is published.[1] And finally, for the New Year, I hope that the *Dial* will continue to be as encouraging to me as you have always been.

I have been looking over the last two things of mine, and really I do not think that either the *Dial* or myself has any reason to be proud of them.[2] I am really ashamed to have sent you such badly written articles, and I feel again that I must stop writing and read and think for a long time before recommencing. Otherwise, I shall simply lose my reputation and disgrace the periodicals for which I write. For this reason you will see nothing of mine in the January *Criterion*: I have twice rewritten and finally scrapped an essay on a new direction for the drama which I hope some day to make fit for publication.[3] But it is no use squeezing a dry sponge and it is no use trying to work a tired and distracted mind. So I shall send the *Dial* nothing more until I feel certain that I have 'come back'.[4]

Again with all best wishes,

Yours always,
[T. S. E.]

TO *Wyndham Lewis* TS Cornell

31 December 1923 *The Criterion*, 17 Thavies Inn

Dear Lewis,

I have waited to answer your letter until I had the time to deal with it as thoroughly as I could.[5] The amendments to Zagreus are perfectly acceptable. The words in question were queried by the printer and not Cobden-Sanderson.[6] I should however have discussed the matter with you had you not so amiably sent in the alteration. The point is that your contribution is to be the first in the number, and therefore the questionable words would have been particularly conspicuous. Furthermore, I hold this

1 – *The Seven Lively Arts* appeared in spring 1924.
2 – '*Ulysses*, Order, and Myth', 75: 5 (Nov. 1923); 'Marianne Moore', 75: 6 (Dec. 1923).
3 – 'Four Elizabethan Dramatists: A Preface' did appear, presumably in rewritten form, in C. 2: 6 (Feb. 1924). With one exception, TSE published his prose only in C. in the following year.
4 – TSE's next prose contribution was 'Literature, Science, and Dogma', *Dial* 82: 3 (Mar. 1927).
5 – In the margin by the opening, TSE wrote: 'Dictating to a typist – therefore periphrastic'.
6 – On 13 Dec., WL told RC-S he found some of the queries about 'Mr Zagreus and the Split-Man' 'useful', and had 'rehandled' one passage to omit the word 'bugger' ('an ugly word that is however, I regret to say, often used, and perhaps sometimes justifiable').

principle: that in a book a writer can and ought to say anything he likes. But a periodical is a different matter. The majority of readers may be presumed to buy it because they believe that it will have good things in it and many of the readers buy it without knowing what any one contribution will be. Unless one aims at a very small and definite class of reader, an editor is not justified in risking offending harmless and otherwise desirable readers by anything except statements of principle. If we published your book, either here or in France, I should only do so on condition that everything was published in it which you wanted to put in it. I am perfectly in agreement with you about cunning people, but I must say that I think you are preposterously over-elaborating your suspicions of Lady Rothermere. This suspiciousness first took the form of a shyness of the *Criterion*, and now takes the form of a shyness toward her publishing your book.[1] I have always found her perfectly straight with me, and I am sure that she has nothing up her sleeve in connection with the publishing business. As a matter of fact, the idea of publishing books was suggested and developed entirely by myself, although she welcomed the idea with considerable enthusiasm. She does not pretend to want to make a martyr of herself or sacrifice everything to the cause of literature, but she has nothing whatever to get out of these enterprises except a certain distinction among a very small number of people. She has occasionally made suggestions but has never attempted to interfere or overrule my direction of the *Criterion* in any way. If you are now inclined to believe that you are dealing with me in the *Criterion*, you have just as much reason for believing that you are dealing with me in the publishing. The matter is perfectly simple. If you can get for your book of essays a publisher who will pay more and circulate it better there is no reason whatever why you should not do so. I never contemplated doing you out of a better engagement. I only meant that you should let us publish the book if Lady Rothermere could give you for it as much as you were likely to get elsewhere. If you have a good offer from a good publisher, and let me know what that offer is, I will see what Lady Rothermere will go to. That is all there is to it.

You do not seem to be aware that I have never taken any money for running the *Criterion*. The reason is that Lady Rothermere put down a definite subsidy, and I preferred to apply this to the paper and the contributors, rather than starve the paper to get a hundred or so a year

1 – In Nov., WL said 'I am rather shy with you' but 'I will give you everything I have for nothing, as you did did [*sc.* for] me' (for *The Tyro*).

while it lasted. It would not be worth my while to take so much trouble over a paper unless there was a chance of its perpetuation. If the paper establishes itself, I shall naturally see that there is enough in it for me to make it worth my while to go on with it. In any case it was not worth my while to cheapen the paper and reduce its chances of survival in order to take a hundred a year for three years. The paper is only worthwhile to me if it can establish itself sufficiently to give me the basis of a livelihood.

The publishing scheme does not relieve Lady Rothermere of expenses in any way, but on the contrary would considerably increase them. Sanderson would get his small percentage out of the publishing just as he does out of the *Criterion.* But I say again, this was not Lady Rothermere's idea, nor was it Sanderson's, but my own.

You surely know by this time that I have had a continuous and disinterested desire to push your work as far as in my power. I don't see why you shouldn't make a great deal more money by writing than you do; and I have urged you to write for the *Dial* and for *Vanity Fair* which are quite respectable papers in their way and are open to you as well as the *Criterion.* Of course I don't want to urge you into journalism, but at the same time I think that you would find more or less regular writing for the American public less antipathetic than incessant portrait-painting of people whom you despise and whom you cannot trust. And, of course every man has his own way of working, and I am a pretty slow writer myself. But I confess that I do not see where all your time goes. That is perhaps not my affair, but I am sure that everyone who admires your work as much as I do regrets that there is not more of it. Now, if you can get a better publisher for your books, I am the last person to stand in your way; It seems to me that after this book is published you ought to make a serious effort to beat up journalistic connections.

Yours ever,
Thomas Eliot

1924

TO *Mary Hutchinson* MS Texas

Tuesday [1 January 1924][1] 9 Clarence Gate Gdns

My dear Mary

Thank you so much for the lovely handkerchief which is very gay and buckish, and for the portrait of a lady resembling a lady of my acquaintance.[2] The latter has merits of its own, of an austere kind, but there are in existence informal views made on a picq-nicq with a small camera, which have more of the warmth of humankind. But I hope in a week or two to see the original?

T.

TO *Harold Monro* TS Beinecke

11 January 1924 *The Criterion*, 17 Thavies Inn

Dear Monro,

I have been waiting for the last fortnight for an opportunity to write or telephone to you and suggest your lunching with me, as I wanted to talk to you about the Wordsworth, and I am ashamed that I should have received your letter first. About the time: if your essay is under 3000 words I should like it by March 1st for the April number; if it is over that, I should like it by June 1st for the July number; but it should be exactly the length that you are inspired to make it.[3] It is to be about any part of Wordsworth's life or work or aspect of his work that you choose; his Youth would be perfectly suitable, but you need not confine yourself very closely to the matter of the books you get, if you wish to divagate. Only, I should like to know, as soon as you have got the scheme into shape, about what length you think it is *likely* to be.

I am sorry to have been so unbusinesslike, but I have been hopelessly tired out and run down for a long time, and not fit to be in charge of a

1–Postmarked 2 Jan. 1924.
2–The handkerchief and portrait were Christmas presents; the lady was MH.
3–'Wordsworth Revisited', C. 2: 8 (July 1924).

review at all. As I had to reduce correspondence and seeing people to the minimum, I had left it to Richard [Aldington] to arrange with you, but I don't think I said anything to him about time or length. That's my fault.

Will you not come and lunch with me one day in the City next week? Let me have a card to say what day would suit you, and what hour. My address is Lloyds Bank, 20 King William Street, near the Bank Station. We have not met for a long time.

Sincerely yours
T. S. Eliot

I'll try to get the other book for you.[1]

TO *Hugh Walpole* CC

23 January 1924 9 Clarence Gate Gdns

My dear Walpole,

Your kindness to me personally, and the great encouragement you have given me about the *Criterion*, make it possible for me to write to you to ask a favour which I should not have ventured to have asked before. In the early days of a new review, especially a review which cannot afford to pay very high rates to contributors an Editor like myself is forced to depend very largely on his personal friends for contributions. This is especially true when one wants stories;[2] it is always possible to get good scholarly or critical articles; but for fiction I have only dared approach writers whom I thought would be likely to let me have something as a personal favour. As the *Criterion* wants to keep its stories to the general standards of the paper I have thus the greatest difficulty of all; because I felt that it was undesirable to approach the best known writers prematurely. As the paper gets better known it will no doubt be easier but at present there are very few writers whom I want to publish and of these fewer still whom I am in a position to ask. But the *Criterion* needs more stories very badly and I therefore hope that you will forgive me if I now ask you if you will let us have something of yours either a short story, or (what would be equally interesting) a fragment of some unpublished novel.[3]

1–H. W. Garrod, *Wordsworth* (1923), one of three books Monro asked for.
2–On 29 Dec., Walpole wrote: 'for popularity's sake you might . . . have a little more good fiction' in *C.*
3–The first two chapters of Walpole's *The Old Ladies* appeared in C. 2: 7 & 8 (Apr. & July 1924).

If you would, I should be killing a number of birds with one stone, for I am sure that having had your name in the paper I should find it much easier to get contributions from others including the people you have mentioned.[1]

It would be a very great kindness on top of your previous generosity, but your interest in the *Criterion* encourages me to believe that you might be inclined to help it in this very substantial way. I shall be very happy if you assent in principle and still happier if you can let me have something at once. In any case please forgive my asking you.

Sincerely yours,
[T. S. E.]

TO *Lady Rothermere* CC

23 January 1924 9 Clarence Gate Gdns

Dear Lady Rothermere,

Thank you for your letter. Of course I only decided on the postponement very suddenly and wrote you at once.[2] I had not realised until I looked over the whole of the proof together that I was not at all satisfied with the number. It seemed to me so unsatisfactory that I preferred, and I felt sure that you would prefer, to postpone it for a few weeks rather than turn anything out under our usual standard. It was not that any of the contributions were bad, but rather that the number was badly put together and needed one or two things of a different kind, including an article by myself. It seems to me most important, until the *Criterion* has been running for a long time, that each number should be in some respect a little better than the last, and this number was no better than any of the others. I shall now have time to revise my article and get it into this number.[3]

The advertisements have been postponed so that there will be little if any extra expense, beyond the printing of two more contributions.

What has added to my delays and confusions has been losing my Assistant Editor and my Secretary at the same time and accordingly having had no assistance whatsoever. I am glad to report that I have just secured another Secretary[4] and as he has had wider experience and better opportunities than the last, I hope that he may be able to undertake in time

1–Walpole had mentioned May Sinclair, VW, Stella Benson, David Garnett and William Gerhardie.

2–The Jan. issue – C. 2: 6 – was postponed until Feb.

3–'Four Elizabethan Dramatists I: A Preface', C. 2: 6 (Feb. 1924), 115–23.

4–J. R. Culpin.

enlarged functions and relieve me of much of the routine work – so that I may be able to do without an Assistant Editor. This will be an ultimate economy – which is our great point – and keep the expense down, so that without increasing the cost of the paper we may be able to increase the pay to contributors.

Yes, everything is indeed muddle and confusion here but I really now begin to have hopes that things may turn out better than one expected.

Thank you for telling me that Miss Ireland is at 58; I am glad to know of it but I do not think that just at the moment there is anything I could discuss with her instead of with you.

Now, please let me know in advance of your movements and I will write to you again very shortly when I see better how things are going and just before the number comes out.

Yours always sincerely
[T. S. E.]

TO *Frederic Manning* CC

24 January 1924 [*The Criterion*, London]

Dear Manning,

Thank you very much for your letter of the 5th January. I was very glad to hear from you. I am afraid that I must confess ignorance of the Père Hyacinthe,[1] and I have put myself in a position where we have promised to print in the next three numbers more than we possibly can print; but I should like very much to be able to publish something by you. If you are going to write the article I should earnestly ask you to let us have the first sight of it. If you are not going to write until you have settled on publication might I ask that you will let me know to about what length you want to go and also inform my ignorance of the subject.

Thank you for mentioning my very rough and unsatisfactory article.[2] I should like to talk it over with you. I thank you for your invitation.[3] At

1 – Manning suggested he write on 'Le Père Hyacinthe' by way of a book by his friend Albert Houlin. Charles Loyson (1827–1912), known as 'Le Père Hyacinthe', was a French preacher who described himself as a priest without an altar; after being a member of three Roman Catholic religious orders, he was excommunicated in 1869 and became an Old Catholic pastor in Geneva. Ten years later, he founded the Gallican Catholic Church in Paris where he evolved his own version of liberal Christianity.

2 – Manning said that TSE's 'The Function of Criticism' (C. 2: 5 [Oct. 1923]) interested him 'in more ways than one', but that 'Most of Rémy de Gourmont's criticism' was 'essentially vicious'.

3 – Manning had invited TSE to stay at his sixteenth-century farmhouse near Woking.

present I have the whole work of the *Criterion* on my hands and cannot possibly get away from London but if I am freer in the spring I may write to propose myself.

Sincerely yours,
T. S. Eliot

TO *E. R. Curtius* CC

24 January 1924 [London]

My dear Curtius,

It was very pleasant to hear from you again after such a long silence and to know that you still think of the *Criterion* and want to write for us. I should very much like to publish something by you on Proust and it would be especially interesting if we could do so in the April or July number as I am expecting from Jacques Rivière an unpublished fragment which we shall publish in translation.[1] The April number is going to be a very crowded one and I shall have a great deal of difficulty with it; but your offer is so tempting that I am writing to ask whether you could, without unfairness to your own ideas, let us have a very short Essay on Proust – not more than 3000 words. If you will let me know at once about what you consider the minimum length for a satisfactory essay I will write to you definitely.

I am writing this in a great hurry, and I will write to you again soon about the rest of your letter and about the books that you will need for the series of English studies which I very much hope that you will make.[2]

With all best wishes,
Sincerely yours,
[T. S. E.]

1 – See Curtius, 'On the Style of Marcel Proust', *C.* 2: 7 (Apr. 1924), 311–20.
2 – Curtius had heard about D. H. Lawrence but had not read him. He also wanted to find out about 'the new literary movements in England' for the book TSE suggested on 14 Aug. 1923.

TO *Harold Joachim*[1] CC

24 January 1924 9 Clarence Gate Gdns

My dear Mr Joachim,

Forgive me for not having written to you immediately but I have for some time been deprived of both an Assistant Editor and a Secretary and it has been impossible for me to keep up with my correspondence. I should be very disappointed not to publish your Essay, and the only reason for our not doing so would be that you wished to publish elsewhere before we had had time to publish it in the *Criterion*. I had hoped to publish it sooner, but, handicapped as I have been, I have made numerous mistakes and have had to postpone a number of contributions. I count definitely upon publishing your Essay either in the April or the July number.[2] If that is alright, will you let me know and I will have a type-written copy made so that you may have the original back for your own reference. I should be very sorry to be deprived of such a distinguished contribution.

I take a late opportunity of wishing you and your family a happy year, and I hope that I may come down to Oxford at some time during the Summer term and that I may see you then.

Yours very sincerely,
[T. S. E.]

TO *Valery Larbaud* TS Vichy

24 January 1924 9 Clarence Gate Gdns

My dear Larbaud,

I do not suppose that you are in Paris – at least I hope for your own sake that you are much further south – but I hope that this letter will reach you. I have had no news of you for a long time and so have been wondering how you are and whether you have been able to work on Landor.[3] I was very happy to receive your book[4] and am cherishing it on the top of my pile, to read, and partly to re-read, at the first opportunity.

1 – Harold Joachim: see Glossary of Names.
2 – TSE listed 'Joachim: The Absolute etc' for possible publication in *C.* 2: 6 (Jan. 1925), but nothing came of this.
3 – Larbaud had promised an essay on Landor as long ago as Mar. 1922.
4 – *Amants, heureux amants* (1923), three novellas about love, was dedicated to JJ ('the only begetter of the form [the interior monologue] I have adopted'). Larbaud had written about *Ulysses* in *C.* 1: 1 (Oct. 1922).

Everything that you write is extremely important to me. Thank you very much indeed for thinking of me.

I do not want to worry you, but please do let me have a line to say how you are and where you are and when you think you will have the first part of Landor ready.[1] I do hope you are very much better than when I saw you last.

Yours always sincerely
T. S. Eliot

TO *The Reverend S. Udny* CC

24 January 1924 [*The Criterion*, London]

Dear Sir,

Please forgive me for not having replied at once to your second letter.[2] I should have written to you a long time ago but for a great pressure of work and I am sorry to have appeared very rude. It is very kind of you to offer us your translations of D'Annunzio's[3] verse but I am afraid that the *Criterion* is hardly the place for them. We publish very little verse and our space is so restricted in view of the number and variety of contributions which we wish to include that we are forced to rule out translations of foreign verse. If, however, you have access to any manuscripts of D'Annunzio which are *unpublished* in Italian we should be delighted if you let us consider them.[4]

Yours faithfully,
[T. S. E.]

1–On 4 Feb., Larbaud explained that before the war he had sent a volume, *Selections from the Works of W. S. Landor*, to Daniel O'Conor in England, but the war had prevented publication. If TSE could track it down, his notes for *C.* would be ready much sooner.

2–The Rev. S. Udny wrote twice (14 Nov. 1922; Jan. 1923) to offer to *C.* some of his 'renderings' of D'Annunzio's verse: they had originally been requested by the *Fortnightly Review*, but the editor had ultimately found himself 'cramped for space after all'.

3–Gabriele D'Annunzio (1863–1938), poet, playwright and nationalist politician, who, after establishing the short-lived Republic of Fiume, became a vocal supporter of Mussolini.

4–Nothing by D'Annunzio appeared in *C.*

TO *Charles Whibley* CC

25 January 1924 9 Clarence Gate Gdns

My dear Whibley,

I have asked Dr Cyriax[1] about Trigeminal Neuralgia and find he is quite familiar with it and has treated cases of it. I think that he might do you a great deal of good; in fact, I believe it is a sort of trouble with which he might be particularly successful. Of course he would not pretend that he could cure such a thing absolutely but there is always the possibility that he might and in any case I feel that it is more than probable that he could do you a great deal of benefit. And in that event it would be a comfort to know that you could always go back to him and get relief if you had later attacks. I feel almost sure that he could make it more possible for you to sleep and eat in comfort.

So I will leave it at that for the present, but if you are willing to give him a trial, I will at any time arrange an appointment for you. His address is 41 Welbeck Street.

I enjoyed immensely our evening and I am hoping that I may see you more frequently now, if you are coming to town from time to time. I should be glad for my own sake if you had a course of treatment with Dr Cyriax because you would be in London more often. I am looking forward with impatience to reading your Chesterfield,[2] and of course to your book.[3]

Yours affectionately,
[T. S. E.]

TO *Iris Barry* CC

25 January 1924 [*The Criterion*, London]

Dear Miss Barry,

I have by no means forgotten the story which you sent me last May and have been hoping that you would send us something else, but as you have not done so I am writing to remind you.[4] I hope that you remember that

1–Dr Edgar Ferdinand Cyriax (1874–1955): Swedish-born doctor, specialising in Swedish medical gymnastics and manipulative treatment. He was the son-in-law of Henrik Kellgren, a notable figure in the promotion of Swedish remedial gymnastics and massage. Cyriax lectured in physiology at the Central Institute for Swedish Gymnastics, London.
2–See Whibley, 'Lord Chesterfield', C. 2: 7 (Apr. 1924).
3–Presumably *Literary Studies* (1925).
4–See TSE's letter of 14 May 1923.

I liked your story very much although I did not find it quite suitable for the *Criterion* in the form in which I read it. One of the objections, which I mention again because it is a very important point with us, was that it was too long. I know by report that you have done better things since and I hope that among the products of the last year there is one suitable in brevity and in every respect for the *Criterion*. If you have something on hand of not more than 2500 words – and as I say to all contributors – as short as possible, will you not let me see it, and at once?[1]

Sincerely yours,
[T. S. E.]

TO *F. S. Flint* CC

28 January 1924 *The Criterion*, 9 Clarence Gate Gdns

My dear Flint,

The manuscript which I am sending you herewith[2] represents a favour which I am asking you. Would you mind reading it and giving me your opinion? If it is a very interesting essay we might publish it in the *Criterion*, if you would translate it. I have not had time to read it, and in any case I should hesitate to pronounce a verdict on the merit of such a composition from my faulty knowledge of the language.

I hope to have some stuff for you soon, including something by Cocteau if you will continue to give us the really invaluable benefit of your genius for translation. But let me say again that it is not fitting that a man of letters who has appeared so frequently in the *Criterion* as a translator and as an annotator of foreign periodicals should not from time to time be represented by an original article also. Will you not reconsider the subject which you suggested a long time ago, or if not, will you suggest a new one?

Sincerely yours,
[T. S. E.]

PS You need not return this typescript as I have another copy.

1 – She never contributed to C.
2 – A typescript article by Antonio Marichalar.

TO *Osbert Sitwell*[1] CC

28 January 1924 [London]

My dear Osbert,

Thank you very much indeed for the Essay on Baroque Architecture, which is extremely interesting, and which we shall be delighted to use.[2] I am never sure in which of two numbers anything can be published, but this will be either in the April or July number, and I will let you know later before sending proof.

Whenever you have a story ready which is not too long for us, do please let me see it at once. The most difficult thing in the world to find is a good short story.

I will write you again when I know where you are. Berners[3] reports that you are soon returning to London. I hope that is true.

Ever yours,

[T. S. E.]

PS If you have any story on hand of less than 6000 words, do let me see it now.

TO *Frederic Manning* CC

28 January 1924 9 Clarence Gate Gdns

Dear Manning,

Thank you very much for telling me something about le père Hyacinthe.[4] Now that you tell me, I remember quite well having had the usual vague hearsay knowledge of him. I have been thinking it over pretty carefully and it has taken a good deal to outweigh the benefit of having something from you. Were le Père Hyacinthe representative of something for which the *Criterion* definitely stood, I should jump at the opportunity. But my own position toward modernist movements in the Catholic Church is at best one of neutrality, as never having been a member of that Church

1–Osbert Sitwell: see Glossary of Names.

2–'A German Eighteenth Century Town', *C.* 2: 8 (July 1924), 433–47: a sketch of the architecture of Bayreuth, republished in *Discursions on Travel, Art and Life* (1925). It was Sitwell's last contribution to *C.*

3–Gerald Hugh Tyrwhitt Wilson, 14th Baron Berners (1883–1950), eccentric English composer.

4–On 26 Jan., Manning described Hyacinthe's work as 'a criticism of the ecclesiastical disclipline of the Roman Church, the preaching of a mystical non-sectarian Christianity, and later of a kind of theism (the unknown God)'.

I cannot adopt a more positive attitude. I was myself brought up in a strong atmosphere of the most liberal Liberal theology and I cannot but regard such tendencies as unsuitable to the needs of the time.[1] They have, rightly or wrongly, associations in the mind with liberalism in political thought, and my own position is too near that of Charles Maurras for me to have much sympathy with them. I read at one time a good deal of the modernist philosophy of Le Roy[2] and other Bergsonian clerics whose names I no longer retain, and I felt in them an ingenious *leger de main* of confusion of the better and worse which I disliked. This is of course a subject for an article by itself, and I should be extremely interested to know what your own position is.

The other things you tell me about interest me immensely.[3] I shall look forward to reading your article in the *Quarterly*[4] and I wish that we might have had the honour of printing it ourselves. I certainly welcome the suggestion that you make for sending a full article or study; please suggest some subject that you want to write about in order that we may waste no time. If you will read any number of the *Adelphi*, you will perhaps see why I am so shy of Father Hyacinthe.[5] I wish that we might talk these things over at length.

Sincerely yours,
[T. S. E.]

TO *Johan Mortensen*[6] CC

28 January 1924 9 Clarence Gate Gdns

Dear Sir,

I am glad to hear that you received the number of the *Criterion* which I had sent to you and thank you very much for your kind invitation to lunch. Unfortunately I am already engaged for lunch on Wednesday, and

1–TSE was 'brought up outside the Christian Fold, in Unitarianism; and in the form of Unitarianism in which I was instructed, things were either black or white' (*NC* 10: 41, July 1931, 771).
2–Edouard Le Roy (1870–1954), French philosopher and mathematician; Professor of Philosophy at the Collège de France and author of *A New Philosophy: Henri Bergson* (1913). A devout Catholic as well as 'modernist', he was later associated with Teilhard de Chardin, and his works were placed on the Index of prohibited books by the Vatican.
3–Manning was interested in the 'distinction between Fact and Value'.
4–'Critic and Aesthetic', *Quarterly Review*, 480 (24 July 1924), 123–44.
5–Despite TSE's reservations, 'Le Père Hyacinthe' appeared in C. 2: 6 (July 1924), 460–7.
6–Johan Mortensen: a translator from Danish and other Scandinavian languages.

as I am extremely busy at my vocation in the City at present, the National Liberal Club is rather far for me to go. Will you not therefore lunch with me on Monday next at the Cock in Fleet Street which should be an intermediate point for both of us? If Monday will not do, please suggest another day. Let us say one o'clock, unless some other time is more convenient for you. I hope that you will be able to come to meet me on Monday.

Yours very truly,
[T. S. E.]

TO *Miss J. C. Colcord*[1] CC

28 January 1924 [*The Criterion*, London]

Dear Miss Colcord,

Forgive me for not having answered your charming letter of the 6th December which my sister [Ada Sheffield] forwarded. The delay has been wholly due to pressure of other work. It is distressing to me to be obliged to decline such a flattering request. Had it been one of my other poems I should certainly have been inclined to accede although the power to give permission to reprint these rests with my American publishers.[2] But in the case of *The Waste Land* I feel very strongly against publication of any parts separately. The poem is intended to be a whole and if I allowed parts of it to be printed separately, it might not only spread the impression that it is merely a collection of unrelated parts, but might also appear to give sanction from myself of this impression. I do not want people to read the poem at all unless they read the whole thing, and it is quite impossible for any part of the poem to give a fair conception of the whole. It is with reluctance that I adhere to this decision and I sincerely hope that you will some day ask of me a favour which I shall be able to grant.

With all best wishes for the success of your anthology,

I am, yours sincerely,

[T. S. E.]

1 – Joanna Carver Colcord (1882–1960): social worker and author of *Broken Homes* (1919). She spent her first eighteen years at sea and was the editor of *Roll and Go: Songs of American Sailormen* (1924), the first comprehensive collection of American sea-songs. She wrote twice to TSE (12 Nov., 6 Dec. 1923), to request permission to include his 'beautiful poem "Death by Water"' in her proposed collection of 'poems by American authors about the sea and seafaring'.

2 – Boni & Liveright. TSE consistently opposed the publication of extracts from *TWL*.

TO *Douglas Ainslie* CC

28 January 1924 [London]

Dear Mr Ainslie,

Thank you for your card giving me your address. I should be glad if you would let me know, whether Mr Aldington, who has now resigned his position, suggested any particular date for the appearance of your translation of Croce's essay.[1] I am afraid that it will be impossible to use it in the April number, and expect to publish it in the following number which appears in July. Will you let me know if this [is] satisfactory as I should be very sorry if there were any misunderstanding. We look forward with great pleasure to publishing this essay.

I hope that you will be so kind as to keep me in touch with any change of address or else to give me some permanent address from which letters will be forwarded to you.

Yours very truly,
[T. S. E.]

PS We should of course be glad to use other writings of Croce but as the *Criterion* is so small and appears only quarterly, it is very rarely advisable or possible to publish work by the same author more than once a year.[2]

TO *May Sinclair* CC

29 January 1924 9 Clarence Gate Gdns

Dear Miss Sinclair,

I am writing to ask you whether you will continue your kindness to the *Criterion* by suggesting the names of any writers of fiction whom you think we ought to get into the *Criterion*. It is no flattery, but a simple statement of a situation which worries me a good deal, when I say that your stories have set such a high standard that it is difficult to find three other stories a year, and I dare not ask you for more than one story annually.[3] We get a good many sent voluntarily, but they are all very crude or hopelessly second rate. I never get time for any general reading myself and I simply

1–Croce's essay on Alfred Vigny, later published in Croce's *European Literature in the Nineteenth Century*, trans. Ainslie (1924).

2–The Vigny article did not appear, but Ainslie's translation of Croce's 'On the Nature of Allegory' was published in C. 3: 11 (Apr. 1925).

3–Sinclair's 'The Victim' appeared in C. 1: 1 (Oct. 1922); 'Jones's Karma' in C. 2: 5 (Oct. 1923).

do not know who are the writers worth asking, or who, amongst these writers, might be willing to let us have a contribution. I do not know of any promising new writers who ought to be helped, nor do I know, on the other hand, who are the established writers who are really good and whose names would help the paper. I have written to Walpole, but I do not know where he is at present and whether he can give us anything. He has been extremely kind to the *Criterion*, and has given me great encouragement and has even taken out five subscriptions, which is a very great help.

I calculate that the *Criterion* ought to appeal to about 3000 persons, and that if all of these unknown 3000 took it in, it could pay for itself amply, so that I could devote my time to it. At present I have been working practically singlehanded for some time and it is a real torment to feel that I could make the paper much better if I had the time to do so. But any suggestion from you for improving the paper would be extremely valuable.

I do not know whether you are in town now but I hope that some time you will let me come and see you again.

Sincerely yours,
[T. S. E.]

TO *His Royal Highness the Crown Prince of Sweden*[1] CC

30 January 1924 [*The Criterion*, London]

Your Royal Highness,

I am asking Messrs. Norstedt and Söner to forward this letter to Your Royal Highness, together with a copy of the *Criterion* which I am sending them. The *Criterion* is a literary quarterly review of an international character, aiming to bring together for the most discriminating public the best work of writers of all nationalities. While the *Criterion*, as I have said, is a literary review, its scope is wide enough to include almost everything of interest to people of culture with the exception of economics and contemporary politics. The paper has no political character and takes no part in political controversy. The list of contributors for the past year will, we think, maintain the claim of the *Criterion* to be the most choice and enlightened literary review in England. Although the review has been in

1 – The letter was sent to the Prince via Messrs. Norstedt and Soener, his publishers. Stockholm wrote back on 13 Feb.: 'I have the honour to tell You, that You seem to have made a mistake as far as the letter ought to have been addressed to HRH Prince Wilhelm of Sweden, to whom it today has been passed. HRH the Crown Prince has never written anything that has been published.' The reference is to Prince Wilhelm of Sweden (1884–1965).

existence only a year, it is not too much to say that it is appreciated not only in England but in France, in America, and gradually wherever English literature is read.

I do not know whether Your Royal Highness ever consents to publish articles in foreign reviews, but if so, I believe with confidence that the *Criterion* is more worthy than any other literary review outside Sweden to have the honour of publishing such contributions. I may add that a contribution from Your Royal Highness would be very much appreciated by a British audience which is already acquainted with some of Your Royal Highness's writings.

The *Criterion* has not yet been able to include any representative of contemporary Scandinavian literature, but is anxious to do so, and we should consider it a most fortunate beginning if we could publish a contribution from Your Royal Highness.

In any case the *Criterion* would consider it a greater error to have failed to ask for a contribution from Your Royal Highness than to ask even without the expectation of a favourable reply.

I have the Honour to be,

Your Royal Highness's

humble servant

[T. S. E.]

TO *May Sinclair* CC

31 January 1924 9 Clarence Gate Gdns

Dear Miss Sinclair,

Thank you so much for your kind letter. It is very good of you to take so much trouble and I should like to talk over with you the work of these writers of whom I confess I am completely ignorant.[1] Of course I know and admire the work of [D. H.] Lawrence[2] but there are reasons which I should like to explain to you why I feel that it is not quite suitable for the *Criterion*. Of course I should be only too happy to have your two poems,[3]

1–Sinclair suggested (29 Jan.) E. L. Grant Watson (1885–1970), Australian novelist and author of *Innocent Desires* (1924); Stacy Aumonier (1887–1928), author of *Miss Bracegirdle and Others* (1923); and John Gilbert Bohun Lynch (1884–1928), novelist, boxing writer and founder of P.E.N. Of these, only Grant Watson would publish in C. (as a reviewer).

2–Sinclair asked if TSE had written to DHL. TSE was to publish a number of pieces by DHL later, starting with 'Jimmy and the Desperate Woman', C. 3: 9 (Oct. 1924).

3–Sinclair had thought of sending 'two "poems" or chapters of a novel in free verse'. Her poem 'The Grandmother' was published in C. 2: 6 (Feb. 1924), 167–70.

the only possible question is the one of length as I have already nearly filled the April number and it will be a question of what can be postponed. Can you let me know how many lines there are to the poem and whether, if it is very long, it would be possible to publish one of the two chapters without the other?

I shall be very happy to dine with you on Thursday next and look forward to see[ing] you again with great pleasure.[1]

Sincerely yours,
[T. S. E.]

TO *Leonard Woolf* CC

6 February 1924 [*The Criterion*, London]

Dear Leonard,

Thank you for your card. I should like very much to write you a notice about *Hamlet* and promise to do so.[2] I am going on March 1st to the performance of the *Birds* in Cambridge.[3] Would you care to have me do a note about that too? Please let me know, as otherwise I shall write something and offer it elsewhere.

Yours ever,
[T. S. E.]

TO *Herbert E. Palmer*[4] CC

6 February 1924 [*The Criterion*, London]

Dear Sir,

Thank you very much indeed for letting me see your poem and for the interesting letter which we [you] wrote me. Unfortunately, it would be

1–The other guests were Stacy Aumonier, WL and the novelist Mary Webb (1881–1927).

2–LW had invited TSE to write 200–250 words on *Hamlet*, which he understood TSE was 'going to see at Oxford'. *Hamlet* was directed by J. B. Fagan at the Oxford University Dramatic Society (OUDS), 12–17 Feb., and was reviewed in *The Times* on 13 Feb. There was no notice of it in *N.*, but Jean de Menasce sent TSE his review of it.

3–Aristophanes' *The Birds* was to be performed in Greek at the New Theatre, Cambridge, from 26 Feb. to 1 Mar. 1924, and was reviewed in *The Times* on 28 Feb.

4–Herbert E. Palmer (1880–1961) submitted a long poem – 'about thirteen pages of the "*Criterion*", I think' – 'Cynewulf's poem of Constantine's Vision of the Cross'. The work had been accepted by the *London Mercury*, but the editor J. C. Squire had overfilled his next issue; and it was to be published early in 1924 by William Heinemann. Heinemann 'wanted

quite impossible for me even to consider it for the *Criterion* as we shall not be able to accept any more contributions until after the July number. Of course the space of the *Criterion* is very limited; being only a quarterly, it is much more restricted in capacity than a monthly. It is very seldom that we are able to publish contributions under six months after receipt.

With best wishes for the success of your book,

Yours faithfully,
[T. S. E.]

TO *Richard Cobden-Sanderson* CC

6 February 1924 9 Clarence Gate Gdns

Dear Cobden-Sanderson

I enclose one of the additional contributions, a poem by May Sinclair.[1] Will you please [have] it set up in galley and sent to me, because there are a few lines which I shall suggest to her that she take out. If it will save time, Hazell's need not submit any page proof.

I have made one draft of my article and will let you have it completed about the beginning of the week.[2] I may decide to omit the [John] Rodker article[3] and include one other short thing instead, but you will have everything by the beginning of the week.

Yours ever,
[T. S. E.]

—

to know if I was a Roman Catholic. No! I am not a Roman Catholic – I just followed my ancient or sub-conscious self, or whatever you like to call it, strengthened in that by an extraordinary manifestation I saw in a flaming sunset sky when I was walking with a friend away from the abbey. It was the bow of the Saxon harp . . . as clear and defined as a piece of blue and burnished steel.' In a later letter (10 Apr. 1925) – presumably referring to a different poem – Palmer asked for 'information about the poem I sent you some weeks ago. I propose now to change the title and call it "The copulation of Heaven & Hell"... The main theme is the *rape* of celestial inspiration by Demonic hate or evil passion. The Bible is full of its offsprings. I think nobody yet has written that sort of thing so clearly if my vanity be allowed.' A number of Palmer's poems were published by JMM in the *Adelphi*; and future publications were to include *The Judgement of François Villon* (1927) and *Cinder Thursday* (1931). His *Collected Poems* came out in 1933.

1–Sinclair, 'The Grandmother', *C.* 2: 6 (Feb. 1924), 167–70.

2–TSE, 'Four Elizabethan Dramatists: A Preface'.

3–TSE wrote to Rodker (7 Apr.) to apologise for not printing his 'Note on the Cinema'.

TO *Sydney Schiff* TS BL

[?7 February 1924] *The Criterion*, 9 Clarence Gate Gdns

Dear Sydney

This is just a line to say that I hope that you are much better and stronger and feeling able to work. I hope you can let me have the sketch soon;[1] I should like to have it by the end of this month in time for the April number. Is that possible? Do let me know how you are. <With love to Violet from both of us.>

Yours ever affectionately,
Tom

Vivien has been wondering every day how you are, and hoping to hear.

TO *Lady Rothermere* CC

7 February 1924 9 Clarence Gate Gdns

My dear Lady Rothermere,

Thank you for your letter and for letting me know your address. I rang up Miss Ireland and asked her to tell you about the present state of the *Criterion*. I think that it will be very much improved over what it would have been, had it appeared on the usual date. I have enough material on hand and definitely promised for the April number but I should be very glad if Cocteau could be induced to let us have his manuscript by the end of this month for translation. People are so undependable especially when they are at a distance. I asked Miss Ireland to explain about Valéry's book.[2] I had the preface all ready in November but Cobden-Sanderson warned me that there was an exceptionally large output of new books for Christmas and also that the booksellers were taking very little and reported a very bad trade. What with the election and the general unsettled conditions,[3] this Christmas was an especially bad time for bringing out books. I am also glad on my own account that we postponed the book as a preface to such a book is a very difficult and delicate matter, and on rereading what I had written, I was dissatisfied; so I have been rewriting it but I have had to lay it aside in order to get my article ready for this *Criterion*.

1–Schiff's sketch was published as Stephen Hudson: 'Céleste', *C.* 2: 7 (Apr., 1924).
2–*Le Serpent* was to have been published by *C.* in 1923 but came out only in Dec. 1924.
3–The General Election on 5 Dec. 1923 resulted in a hung parliament and the first ever Labour government, led by Ramsay MacDonald.

As soon as that is out of the way, I shall complete the revision of my preface and the book should be out toward the end of March, which will be a very good time, as it is slightly in advance of the bulk of the spring issues.

I have had one or two things in my mind for the next publication, but it seemed to me that it would be better not to decide on any step until after we see how the first book goes, as we may learn something from that. If, as I hope, you are back in Paris early in May, then I shall hope to see you there (or perhaps in London?) and discuss the next publication.

I have got the *American Mercury*.[1] I think it is dreadfully dull. The sight of publications like that is most encouraging!

I do hope that you will have good weather in the South[2] and that you will like the new *Criterion*.

Yours always sincerely,
[T. S. E.]

Vivien Eliot TO *Sydney Schiff*

MS BL

Sunday [February? 1924]

38 Burleigh Mansions,
St Martin's Lane, London W.C.2

Dear Sidney

Thank you for your letter. I do feel indeed grateful to you for allowing me to see one chapter of the new book. I must add, however, that I am by now so accustomed to reading typed MS and to having to form my opinions on it before I see it in print, that I do not think that it any longer makes the slightest difference to me, *although I know well what you mean*, and shd. probably feel exactly the same about any MS. of my own.

Anyhow, will you send any part or parts that you are willing to let me see, to Clarence Gate Gdns, and I shall look forward to reading it with tremendous excitement. *Of course* it is understood that all I tell you is absolutely and irrevocably in confidence, (and the same in your case with me) so that I feel I should like to, and perhaps ought to mention now, *before seeing yr. MS.* that from what you said of it in yr. letter it seems to

1–*The American Mercury* was founded in Jan. 1924 by H. L. Mencken and George Jean Nathan. The first issue sold more than 15,000 copies, and by the end of that first year circulation was over 42,000. Nathan left it the following year and Mencken in 1933, but it continued until 1981. Early contributors included Sinclair Lewis, Scott Fitzgerald, Langston Hughes, Conrad Aiken and William Faulkner.

2–Lady Rothermere had left Paris for Cap d'Ail, a seaside resort in the Alpes-Maritimes.

me possible that I have been trying out during the last two months or so, something in (possibly) the same *form* as your new book. But with this difference; I have not attempted to make each sketch from *the point of view* of a different person involved – but rather the attempt is to make them all from the point of view of a very interested, and a very *intimate*, outsider. (Or not necessarily even an *outsider*, but of someone who does not actually appear in the sketches).

Of course this is a very important difference indeed, and no doubt the only similarity is in that they are both a series of sketches which could appear separately, but which do, when all is finished (not yet, alas, with me!) make up a whole.

But the point is that I have not finished, not nearly. Only a little over half. And for this reason I have removed myself, sore throat and all, to this address. I cannot work, or find the atmosphere *I need*, at Clarence Gate. All the same, I shall be backwards and forwards and in and out, so it wd. be *safer* to send the MS. to *Clarence Gate*. I will send more news in a few days – meanwhile my love to both of you.

V.

TO *Pearl Fassett* CC

15 February 1924 9 Clarence Gate Gdns

My dear Pearl,

I have read your story called 'Mrs Pilkington visits Paris'. It is the best thing that you have done. If you are willing to make some alterations which I will suggest to you, I shall be able to print it in the *Criterion*.

I notice you say that you will get 'Mrs Pilkington or die'. But you have got Mrs Pilkington, so please do not touch her again or you will spoil her. Therefore there is no need for you to die. I consider that the letter with which you open the story is much too long. I have marked with red pencil the parts which I think would be better to omit; not only is it too long but it is not well handled. You are make statements on subject[s] of which you have not thought sufficiently about.[1]

In general your writing suffers very much from the fact that you have never thought enough, and that you have never formed any theories of your own. You write from observation and what you get is entirely from outside; nothing from inside. The only way for you to improve is to force

1 – The grammar in the copy is mangled.

yourself to think and to form theories on every subject even if at first they are wrong.

Will you try to rewrite the letter at the beginning of your story? – making it very short.[1] I am afraid I do not like the title of the story; can you think of another title or titles from which I could choose?[2] I should like the story not to be more than 1000 words. You could cut out a few words at the very end without hurting it.

[T. S. E.]

TO *Jean Cocteau*[3] CC

17 February 1924 9 Clarence Gate Gdns

Cher Monsieur,

Je suis ravi de recevoir votre petit volume sur Picasso;[4] surtout de posséder un exemplaire signé par l'auteur. Tout ce que vous écrivez renforce en moi l'impression que m'ont donné vos poésies et *Le Secret Professionel*.[5] J'ai cité ce dernier dans un article de théâtre, il y a quelques mois.[6] Je salue en vous une des intelligences les plus solides et créatrices de la France moderne. J'attends avec impatience d'aborder la lecture du *Thomas l'Imposteur*.[7]

Mais, voici mon inquiétude du moment; quand est-ce que nous allons recevoir le manuscrit inédit que vous m'avez si aimablement promis pour

1 – When published, the opening letter was only seven lines long.

2 – The story appeared as 'Mrs Pilkington', by 'Felix Morrison', in C. 3: 9 (Oct. 1924), 103–6. In choosing her pseudonym, TSE's secretary associated herself with VHE, who published as 'F. M.' in C. 2: 6 (Feb. 1924) and later used the pseudonyms 'Fanny Marlow' and 'Feiron Morris'.

3 – Jean Cocteau: see Glossary of Names.

4 – Cocteau, *Picasso* (1923). TSE's copy, inscribed 'à T. S. Eliot son admirateur Jean Cocteau 1924', is at Harvard. When he sent it to HWE in 1937, to be deposited at Eliot House, TSE described it as a 'somewhat rare pamphlet'.

5 – Cocteau's *Le Secret Professionnel* (1922) prescribed a return to the rules of classical versification.

6 – In 'Dramatis Personae', C. 1: 3 (Apr. 1923), TSE quoted Cocteau's remark: 'Le cirque, le music-hall, le cinématographe et ces entreprises qui, depuis Serge de Diaghilew, mettent de puissants vehicules aux mains des jeunes . . . conspirent, sans même connaître leur entente, contre ce que le théâtre est devenu, savoir: un vieil album de photographies' (303); [The circus, the music-hall, the cinema and these enterprises which, since Serge Diaghilev, put powerful instruments into the hands of the young . . . conspire, without even knowing their effect, against the theatre which has become: an old photograph album.]

7 – *Thomas l'Imposteur*: one of two novels Cocteau published in 1924.

le *Criterion* et que nous devions recevoir dans le mois courant?[1] C'est d'une importance capitale que ce que vous nous enverrez soit bien traduit. Je veux le remettre à Monsieur Flint, et je ne veux pas qu'il soit pressé dans un travail qui ne sera pas des plus faciles. Quandmême, j'espère que votre contribution donnera son éclat à notre numéro du quinze avril et je vous supplie de nous donner votre appui.

Dans l'attente de vos nouvelles,

Je me soussigne, cher Monsieur,
Votre admirateur dévoué,
[T. S. E.][2]

TO *F. S. Flint* CC

17 February 1924 9 Clarence Gate Gdns

Dear Flint,

As I have not heard from you, I am rather concerned to know whether you got my letter of the 28th January addressed to you at 65 Highbury New Park and containing a typescript article by Marichalar [on 'the art of criticism'], on which I wanted your opinion with a view to translation. Will you please let me know whether you got it? I am expecting a contribution from Cocteau very soon which I want to send you, as I had rather that you translated it than anybody else.

Yours ever,
[T. S. E.]

1 – Cocteau's promised contribution did not arrive. It was not until two years later that his 'Scandales' appeared in *NC* 4: 1 (Jan. 1926).

2 – *Translation*: Dear Sir, I am delighted to have your little book on Picasso; and especially a copy signed by the author. Everything you write strengthens in me the impression created by your poems and *The Professional Secret*. I quoted the latter work in a theatre article, a few months ago. I salute you as one of the most robust and creative intelligences of modern France. I am waiting impatiently to begin reading *Thomas the Imposter*.

But this is what is worrying me at the moment; when shall we receive the unpublished text that you so kindly promised for the *Criterion* and which was to reach us during the course of this month? It is of vital importance that what you send us should be well translated. I intend to entrust it to Mr Flint, and I would not like him to have to work hurriedly at a rather difficult task. At all events, I am hoping that your contribution will add its lustre to our issue on 15 April, and I plead for your support.

Waiting to hear from you, I sign myself, Sir, Your devoted admirer, [T. S. E.]

TO *E. R. Curtius* CC

17 February 1924 9 Clarence Gate Gdns

My dear Curtius,

Very many thanks for your letter of the 31st January and for the manuscript which has just arrived and which I look forward to reading within a few days. Even without having read it I can safely say that I would very much like to use it and I want to ask you whether it would still be possible to allow us to use it in the July number if, as I fear, it is impossible to make room for it in April. I think also that the unpublished fragment of Proust which Rivière has promised me is not likely to be ready and translated in time for the April number and it would be interesting if we could use your essay in the same number as the fragment of Proust.[1]

Will you let me know, in what way I can best help you in the preparation of your English Studies which I am very anxious to see written. If you would like any help, either in the selection of authors to be treated or in obtaining books, I shall be glad to do what I can. I will send you a copy of the *Adelphi* and you will see from [the] article in No. 5 of the *Criterion*, which I am also sending, something of my own attitude towards Mr Murry's philosophy.[2] I am sorry that you have not had the *Criterion* regularly.

Sincerely,
[T. S. E.]

TO *Humbert Wolfe*[3] CC

17 February 1924 [London]

Dear Wolfe,

I have just received your *Kensington Gardens*[4] from the publisher and have read it through with great pleasure. This is a double compliment

1 – Curtius's 'On the Style of Marcel Proust', was published in *C.* 2: 7 (Apr. 1924); Proust's 'The Death of Albertine' in 2: 8 (July 1924).

2 – Curtius requested copies of JMM's *Adelphi* and asked what TSE thought of JMM's *The Problem of Style*. TSE's article was 'The Function of Criticism', in *C.* 2: 5 (Oct. 1923), which offered a sustained critique of JMM's critical positions.

3 – Humbert Wolfe (1885–1940) – born Umberto Wolff – was a successful civil servant (working at the Board of Trade, the wartime Ministry of Munitions, and the Ministry of Labour), as well as a keen and versatile poet, translator, satirist, editor and critic.

4 – *Kensington Gardens* (1924) was a series of vignettes about flowers, trees, and people associated with the London park, mainly in quatrains.

because I very seldom read a book of poems through and almost never with the slightest pleasure. It seems to me that you have found an extremely good medium and that you have managed it with great skill, for the secret of such poetry is surely the delicacy with which it handles something which in clumsier hands would be fatuous – just as it seems to me that all artistic skill means going just to the frontier, and never a hair's breadth beyond the frontier, on the other side of which is some dreadful vice. Anyway I know that I like your poems and that I dislike heartily the sort of contemporary poetry which appears to be the nearest to it; which appears to bear out what I was saying.[1]

I have been and still am frightfully rushed with two numbers of the *Criterion* coming out on top of each other, but if, as a prelude to a more satisfactory evening, you would come and lunch again with me next week, I should be delighted. Would Wednesday or Thursday be possible for you?

Sincerely yours,
[T. S. E.]

TO *Frederic Manning* CC

17 February 1924 [*The Criterion*, London]

Dear Manning,

Thank you very much for letting me see your quarterly article.[2] I am returning it at once as you ask for it, although I have only been able to read it rather hurriedly. But I see that I want to read it very carefully when it appears and should like to have an opportunity of discussing it with you after that. I think that on the whole I am in agreement with you in opposition to Gourmont and I am certain that there is a lot to be done in restating and interpreting the Platonic doctrines.[3] I do hope that you will

1–Wolfe replied (23 Feb.): 'I had rather that you liked my verse than that the whole Squirearchy [J. C. Squire's faction] burst into unanimous song – which, as you may conjecture, is extremely unlikely.'

2–Manning, 'Critic and Aesthetic'.

3–Manning said (26 Jan.) he was 'concerned with the Platonic criticism of consciousness in *Theatetus* and *Sophist*, its development in Aristotle, and the distinction between Fact and Value'. Rémy de Gourmont (1858–1915), essayist, novelist, philosopher, playwright – whom TSE lauded in *SE* – was a major figure in the Symbolist movement; associate of Villiers de l'Isle Adam and Joris-Karl Huysmans; co-founder in 1889 of the influential *Mercure de France*; also co-founder of *L'Ymagier* and *La Revue des Idées*. Born in Normandy, he studied law at the University of Caen, and then worked for ten years from 1881 as an associate librarian at the Bibliothèque Nationale in Paris – though he was sacked for writing a supposedly 'unpatriotic' article 'Le joujou patriotisme' [Patriotism: A Toy], which argued,

not abandon your project of writing a whole book. I hope your note on Houtin is progressing.[1]

With many thanks,

Yours sincerely,
[T. S. E.]

TO *William Carlos Williams*[2] CC

17 February 1924 [London]

Dear [Wolfe del.] Williams,

Very many thanks for your letters and for sending me your manuscript on Marianne Moore which interested me extremely and made me feel that my own was very crude.[3] I am very proud of having had the honour of reading it in manuscript and if it were possible, I should like to print it in the *Criterion*. But we are absolutely full for the next six months. Furthermore, I think that your article ought to appear first in America because Marianne Moore is practically unknown here and your article really presupposes in the reader a mind already adapted to receive this kind of poetry. To me it is all the more interesting for that reason, but the public has to be educated very slowly.

I hope that you will remain in Europe all summer so that I may have a chance of seeing you. If you come to England, I shall of course expect that

---

against nationalists in both countries, for a rapprochment between France and Germany on grounds of their common culture and aesthetics. In *Physique de l'amour: Essai sur l'instinct sexual* (1903; translated as *The Natural Philosophy of Love*, 1904), he controversially argued that human love is fundamentally an animal instinct, scarcely a matter of heart and soul. However, his greatest influence upon modern European and American writers – including TSE, EP and the Imagists – derives from *Le problème du style* (1902), which argued for the primacy of the visual image in the work of poetry: poetry makes us literally *see*. See also Richard Aldington, *Rémy de Gourmont: Man of Letters* (1928) and Richard Sieburth, *Instigations: Ezra Pound and Rémy de Gourmont* (1978).

1 – See Manning on Albert Houtin's life of Charles Lyson: 'Le Père Hyacinthe', C. 2: 8 (July 1924).

2 – William Carlos Williams (1883–1963): poet and doctor; friend of EP and H. D. Author of *Spring and All* (1923) and *In the American Grain* (1925), he advocated an indigenous American modernism he opposed to TSE's *TWL*, which he described in his *Autobiography* (1915) as a 'disaster' for American letters.

3 – On 9 Dec. 1923, Williams had commented on the 'excellence as criticism' of TSE's review of Marianne Moore in *Dial* 75: 6 (Dec. 1923); he had been 'working upon the same theme' and 'somewhat similarly at the same time'. On 16 Dec., he sent TSE his 'essay on the work of Marianne Moore', which he had just finished 'writing over and over and over': see 'Marianne Moore', *Dial* 78: 5 (May 1925), 393–401; reprinted in *Imaginations* (1970).

pleasure but if you remain in Paris, there is always a chance of my coming over for a few days during the spring[1] and it would be a pleasure to be able to look forward to meeting one from whose poetry I have had so much pleasure.

Sincerely yours,
[T. S. E.]

TO *Owen Barfield* CC

17 February 1924 [London]

Dear Sir,

Thank you very much for responding to my request. I was of course interested in your story[2] as in everything you write but I do not feel that this one is quite suitable for the *Criterion*. It is very much slighter than the one which we published and I think that the proper place for it would be in a monthly or a weekly rather than a quarterly review. Nevertheless I am sure that amongst what you write, there will soon be something suitable for us and I shall be very glad if you will continue to let me see your manuscripts from time to time. I must say that in Dope, you got some extremely interesting rhythmical effects which I hope you will work upon and develop in subsequent writing.

With many thanks,
Yours very truly,
[T. S. E.]

TO *Henry Eliot* MS Houghton

18 February [1924] *The Criterion*, 17 Thavies Inn

My dear Henry

I am still hanging about after my illness. I don't seem to have anything like the strength I used to have. It is quite impossible for me to go away, because Vivien is too ill to go and too ill to be left. She broke down a week ago – after my illness on top of everything else – got out of bed and *fell down*, and has been sleeping most of the time ever since. Her condition of

1 – Williams hoped to see TSE when he was 'abroad this spring'. He gave his address as Shakespeare & Co., Paris.
2 – Unidentified.

anaemia and complete exhaustion is not merely a question of the moment but of the whole future, as it is a result not of the moment only but of the whole past.[1]

I am distracted by dilemmas of the most serious [kind], and I feel that you are the only person who can help me – because you are the only understanding person who knows me from the beginning and because you are in some ways like me and because you have good judgment. *When* can you come even for a short visit? Could you fly across this summer? I want to see you and talk to you – far more fully and intimately than three years ago. If *you* can't come then I shall have to come and see you (though it would be much more effective to see you *here*) but in order to do that I shall have to leave the Bank first, and I should prefer to see you first.

I am really in such a state that my mind and judgment and will are paralysed.[2] Please realise that I *mean* this: I *want to see you*, and as soon as possible. I wish to God you were here now.

Affectionately your brother
Tom

TO *His Mother*[3] — TS Houghton

[late February? 1924] [London]

My dearest Mother:

I am just recovering from influenza, and so am writing to you this way in pencil. I see no other way now than just to write on and on and set things down just as they come. There is too much to say for me to try to put things in the order of their importance.

Ever since November I have been overwhelmed with work. First Richard Aldington went to Italy, and I received his resignation from him the day he had left. There was pique and bad blood involved, and subsequent

1 – In an unpublished memoir of TSE, Osbert Sitwell recalled that in 1923/24 he spoke to TSE at a time when the Eliots' marriage had 'reached a state of despair and hopelessness'. Although TSE was always 'careful and kind in the way he referred to her', he spoke with 'some bitterness' about the fact that during his engagement to VHE 'she had never mentioned to him the appallingly bad health from which she had suffered as a small child'. Being 'afflicted with tuberculosis of the bones', she had undergone 'so many operations before she was seven, that she was able to recall nothing until she reached that age'. TSE thought she should have told him, 'and thus have prepared him in advance for her later illnesses, which were to impose so crushing an additional burden on him during many years' (Texas).

2 – Cf. 'Paralysed force, gesture without motion' ('The Hollow Men', l. 12)

3 – From a copy made by his mother.

correspondence and an endeavour on my part at least to set things right, but to no purpose.[1] So, although he nominally gave three months notice, I did not feel disposed to give him any work to do, and took it on myself. Then in January I lost my Secretary-typist, whom I had had for nearly a year. This again involved trouble. She had practically accepted my offer to her to take her as housekeeper to stay with Vivien in the country from March and to come and housekeep for you and go about with if you came to London. She was a quiet steady middle-aged woman and then when we came to the point of settling the date of leaving she said she must decline and had never intended to give the impression that she would definitely accept. So besides the disappointment of my plans, I could of course not keep her on as secretary. And Vivien and I have been doing all the work ourselves. Hence the January number had to be postponed to Feb 29th. It is ready now and I think pretty good, but at what cost![2] But we swore that we should at least complete Vol II *Criterion* and make it better than ever, so that the *Criterion*, while it lasted, should be the best literary review ever published in England. And I think we shall.

At the same time I have been made head of a Department at the Bank which has meant much more responsibility and *worry*. Four girls and three men under me, planning and tact and supervision and carrying on this newspaper for the bank and the printing press and also detailed work of my own – trying to read a dozen foreign papers a day and keep in touch with everything going on in a number of foreign countries, and be an authority on foreign bonds in certain complicated cases, and fight other departments that interfere with mine.

During all this time I have been tormented and torn with indecision, trying to settle in my mind my major problem as well as devote myself to

1 – RA left for Italy in the first half of Nov. 1923. In explanation of his subsequent resignation RA told Harold Monro (8 May 1924) he found TSE 'difficult to work with' and that he was 'paralysed mentally by the snobbish attitude of the *Criterion*'; his reward was 'a piffling little "attack" on something I said about Joyce, and the growing realisation that I was a "useful hack journalist"' (*Richard Aldington: An Autobiography in Letters*, 72–3). He is referring to TSE's remarks about RA's essay on Joyce, in '*Ulysses*, Order and Myth' (*The Dial* 75: 5 [Nov. 1923]). TSE said RA found the book 'an invitation to chaos, and an expression of feelings which are perverse, partial, and a distortion of reality' as well as a 'libel upon humanity'. While affirming their shared 'classicism', TSE questioned RA's idea that it was possible to 'libel humanity', his notion of 'Joyce's undisciplined talent', and 'pathetic solicitude for the half-witted'. Later TSE wrote: 'We were on the same side for a long time and I was the first to give offence, although unintentionally, which made a breach between us' (*Richard Aldington: An Intimate Portrait*, ed. Alister Kershaw and F.-J. Temple [1965], 25).

2 – On 19 Feb., RC-S said he despatched the final copy to the printers: copies should be with him by 27 Feb., for circulation on the 29th. This suggests a date for the letter of 20 Feb. or after.

the bank and to the *Criterion* and at the same time deal with the problems of our daily life. It has been so agonising that I have been completely paralyzed by it. I simply could not resign in January because just then the bank started this department which they would not have started at all except for me, because there is no one else available in the bank who has the education and width of experience to run such a thing. And during all this time I have been waiting and seeing Lord Rothermere now and then, to see if he would have anything to offer me; and he was in a panic over the prospect of a socialist government and kept telling me that this was no time to leave a good job, because there was no telling what might happen to the country, and to wait a few months and see them again. And I have made so many mistakes in the past, that I often feel no confidence whatever in my judgment, and act like a frightened rat.

I am trying to acquire a little capital by keeping dividends in [a bank] in America so far as I can do without them – that is why I cabled you to send the proceeds of my last dividend to Henry in order so that he might invest it for me. If I can build up a little income absolutely safe, then I shall feel more justified in giving up my bank salary. I hate to lose the good 6% on Hydraulic and if I was going to stay forever in the bank I should not dream of selling now, but I cannot leave the bank on the basis of an income which might cease altogether for a time just when I most wanted it. I do so want for the sake of my own work to be essentially independent and feel that I do not absolutely need to earn more than I certainly can earn.

Literary connections are always uncertain. I am no longer very popular with the *Nation* people, because my political and social views are so reactionary and ultra-conservative.[1] They have become gradually more so and I am losing the approval of the moderate and tepid whigs and Liberals who have most of the literary power. It is less offensive to be a Socialist nowadays than it is to be a Tory. I want to be able to say just what I think. But if I stay in the bank I shall never have *time* to say what I think. There is so much I want to do.

Vivien has made great progress this winter, considering that she has had nearly everything against her – the London winter and the flat where there is no fresh air and the worry of my decisions and the strain of the *Criterion*. She has only been able to keep up and make progress by going every day to Dr Cyriax, the Swedish doctor, who treats her for an *hour* with manipulation and hand vibration, getting her digestive organs into place

1 – TSE published no reviews for LW (*N&A*) for a period of over three years, between 'The Beating of a Drum' (34: 1, 6 Oct. 1923) and 'Whitman and Tennyson' (40: 11, 18 Dec. 1926).

and stimulating them to do their work. It is a wonderful system. Dr Cyriax treated Mrs Haigh-Wood for arthritis, but her special interest is the digestive system, colitis, etc. Vivien's colitis is very much better, but I think she is now at the end of the winter beginning to show signs of anaemia again. This is always the worst time of year for her – it is just a year ago that she broke down so badly as it often is with anaemic persons, and I want to get her to the country as soon as I possibly can.

I am sorry that Mrs Haigh-Wood thought fit to use the word 'drugs'. Vivien's drugs consist of a bismuth solution for the intestine, occasional doses of carbonate of magnesia and bicarbonate of soda and a mild sedative at night prescribed by Dr Martin. She has succeeded in doing without a stronger narcotic which was prescribed for her by the same physician who attended Mrs Haigh-Wood in her illness. Every bit of her doing without drugs is due to her own effort and persistence of will. I say this simply because I know that her mother will not have given her the credit for it.

I have been under Dr Edgar Cyriax the husband of Dr Cyriax who treats Vivien. He treats the nerves of my head and neck and spine, and stomach, three times a week, and I must say that I think he has been the cause of my keeping going through this terrible strain. He has come and treated me at home *for the same fee* during all this influenza, three weeks. I do not know how we should have got through without the two of them. No one knows what a struggle we have had, – what a fight. I have nothing to complain of, but it has been a struggle. Of course the treatment has been a great expense, although at reduced fees.

I am slowly getting over the influenza and am out and about. I had to wire instructions about a number of matters at the bank, all through it except the first week, and also about the *Criterion*. Vivien has handled a great deal of the latter business for me, and we have a young man in the[1]

[incomplete]

TO *Wyndham Lewis* — TS Cornell

24 February 1924 — 9 Clarence Gate Gdns

Dear Lewis,

I am sorry I did not answer the door this afternoon but I was in bed and did not want to get up or see anybody. Had I known it was you, I should

1 – CCE wrote (8 Mar.): 'I am glad you have a young man to do secretarial work in the evening' (see below). This is a reference to J. C. Culpin.

have let you in. It would really be better in future if you would telephone beforehand to say that you are coming.

As soon as I can possibly get the MS read,[1] including what you have just left, I will come to see you at your studio in the evening. I hope this will be by Friday of this week and I will send you a card or wire to let you know.

Yours,
T. S. E.

TO *Sydney Schiff* TS BL

24 February 1924 9 Clarence Gate Gdns

My dear Sydney

Thank you very much indeed for 'Celeste'.[2] The *Criterion* is very fortunate to have it, for it is a brilliant piece of work, and moved me extremely.

I have been laid up in bed with influenza, but hope to be out in a day or so. Largely fatigue – we have both been working at top pitch for the last [three *del.*] five weeks to get out the *Criterion* – it is all ready and will be sent out on the 29th. And now we must set to work at once on the April number.

We do indeed want to see you. There is so much to talk about after this long time. Vivienne has stood the winter in London far better than last year, and has kept up remarkably well, but this long spell of bitter cold weather is beginning to wear on her and she has been very feverish this afternoon, and is beginning to exhibit some of the old symptoms of this time last year. Nevertheless, when she is able to see friends, I think it is much better for her and more cheering to go to see them than for them to come here. I will ring you up on Tuesday evening, so you need not bother to answer this.

Affectionately,
Tom

1 – The second instalment of Lewis's new novel, for publication in C. 2: 7 (Apr. 1924).
2 – On 23 Feb., SS sent TSE his story 'Céleste', a study written 'from the point of view of a sentimental character'. It was based on Céleste Albaret, in Proust's *À la recherche du temps perdu*, who SS said was 'an excellent and tiresome woman, whose only value was her devotion to her master'. Despite some diffidence, Schiff thought 'its conscientious banality' might give it 'some historical interest'. It appeared, as by Stephen Hudson, in C. 2: 7 (Apr. 1924), 332–48.

PS Vivienne has had you both so much on her mind that she has been intending to ring up Lye Green[1] to ask how you were, but I forgot to mention that she has had an attack of influenza the last ten days and I think I caught it from her.

TO *Charles Whibley* CC

24 February 1924 9 Clarence Gate Gdns

My dear Whibley,

I have been in bed with influenza and am still feeling pretty miserable. I have been invited to Cambridge this weekend, to see *The Birds*, but I don't think I shall be up to it – and I don't suppose you will be there, which would be a strong inducement.

May we hope to receive 'Chesterfield'[2] in the next two or three weeks? Remember that we are depending upon it and shall be in a bad way without it. You will have the delayed January number on the 1st March.

Do you consider it desirable to invite Kerry to write on Shelburne?[3]

I did not tell you that what you said at our last meeting was a great encouragement to me. But I hope to say more about this at our next meeting. I also want to discuss my article in the *Criterion*[4] with you after you have seen it – I should have preferred doing so before I printed it, had that been possible.

Yours affectionately,
[T. S. E.]

TO *Italo Svevo*[5] CC

24 February 1924 [*The Criterion*, London]

Dear Sir,

I am sorry that I was not at home when you called, as I should always be very happy to meet any friend of Mr James Joyce. I am very much

1 – The Schiffs lived at Lye Green House, Chesham, Buckinghamshire.
2 – CW's 'Lord Chesterfield' appeared in C. 2: 7 (Apr. 1924), 236–57.
3 – See TSE's letter to RA of 20 Sept. 1923.
4 – 'Four Elizabethan Dramatists: A Preface'.
5 – Italo Svevo – 'Italus the Swabian' – pseudonym of Ettore Schmitz (1861–1928), Italian novelist from Trieste. JJ became his English teacher in 1907 and encouraged and promoted his novels. Like TSE, Svevo spent a period in a bank (Viennese Unionbank in Trieste in the

obliged to you for your book,[1] which I shall read with great interest, although I fear very slowly.

Could you lunch with me on Thursday next, at the Cock in Fleet Street, at 12.30? I should meet you just inside the entrance.

Yours very truly,
[T. S. E.]

TO *His Royal Highness, Prince Wilhelm of Sweden* CC

24 February 1924 [*The Criterion*, London]

I have to thank Your Royal Highness for Your letter of the 12th February and to express the hope that Your Royal Highness will reconsider judgment. The *Criterion* and its contributors would be in every way honoured by Your Royal Highness's collaboration. Your Royal Highness's letter indicates complete command of the English language, but if this should still be a difficulty, I have to inform Your Royal Highness that we are quite prepared to translate from Swedish any manuscript that Your Royal Highness might be good enough to allow us to use.

I remain Your Royal Highness's

obliged and obedient servant,
[T. S. E.]

TO *Richard Cobden-Sanderson* CC

25 February 1924 9 Clarence Gate Gdns

Dear Cobden-Sanderson,

Will you kindly debit the *Criterion* and send a cheque for £4.0.0 to J. R. Culpin at this address with a receipt form for four weeks secretarial work for the *Criterion*?

1890s), and combined a career as a businessman with writing. He lived in England early in the century and again after WW1. His impressions are recorded in *This England is So Different: Italo Svevo's London Writings*, ed. John Gatt-Rutter and Brian Moloney (2003).

1 – *La Coscienza di Zeno* (1923) – later translated into English by Beryl de Zoete as *The Confessions of Zeno* (1930) – which Svevo had delivered in person to TSE's flat in London. It was sceptically reviewed by G. B. Angioletti in his 'Italian Chronicle', *C.* 4: 3 (June 1926).

I hope that you will not have a great pressure of work in getting the *Criterion* distributed as I shall feel that it is my fault.

Yours ever,
[T. S. E.]

TO *Mrs Arnold Bennett*[1]

TS Keele

29 February 1924 *The Criterion*, 9 Clarence Gate Gdns

Dear Mrs Bennett

I am indeed deeply flattered at being asked by you to speak about Ronsard at the celebration of the Institut Français.[2] It is a great temptation to accept such an honour although I am only a humble admirer of Ronsard[3] and have no thorough knowledge or special competence to speak about him. I have learnt by experience that it is extremely dangerous to make such engagements, because, as I lead a life which never leaves me a free moment, I know that when the time comes, it is always very difficult for me to carry out my promises, and often they have had to be carried out in an inadequate way. Rather than take a risk which might involve either disappointing you altogether at the last moment, or else doing badly by the guests and by myself, I must regretfully decline the honour.

With many thanks and best wishes for the success of a celebration which I should be proud to support,

I am,

Yours sincerely
T. S. Eliot

1 – Marguerite Bennett, née Soulier, French wife of the novelist Arnold Bennett (who had left her the previous year). With Edith Sitwell and Helen Rootham, she launched the Anglo-French Poetry Society in 1920, though she soon fell out with them. Lytton Strachey described how at a meeting of the Society in June 1921, after TSE had read some poems, 'Mrs Arnold Bennett recited, with waving arms and chanting voice, Baudelaire and Verlaine till everyone was ready to vomit' (quoted in Michael Holroyd, *Lytton Strachey: The New Biography*, 497).
2 – She invited TSE 'as an English poetic admirer of French poetry' to give a talk at an occasion to commemorate the 'fourth anniversary [centenary] of the birth of Prince de Ronsard'. Pierre de Ronsard (1524–85), was a French Renaissance poet who, with du Bellay and others, founded the Pléiade. TSE had told RA on 17 Nov. 1921 that he thought du Bellay the 'better poet'.
3 – Writing as 'F. M.' in C. 2: 6 (Feb. 1924), VHE quoted Ronsard's 'Le temps s'en va'.

TO *F. S. Flint* CC

29 February 1924 9 Clarence Gate Gdns

Dear Flint,

Thank you for your letter. What you say about Marichalar's article seems to me entirely just and in accord with the impression a superficial examination gave me.[1] You need not bother to return the article as I have another copy.

The *Criterion* is out today and I trust that you will receive it tomorrow. The April number, by the way, should appear on the 15th April as usual so that we shall want your notes at the usual time.[2]

As for your remark about your inability to write;[3] that is entirely absurd and reprehensive and I shall have to see you soon and speak seriously to you about it. Otherwise, you will become as bad as Richard [Aldington] whose ideas of scholarship are so high, that he practically refuses to write at all. And remember that I am myself very poorly educated and have a smattering of a great variety of subjects. After the pressure of getting the April number to press is over, I shall ring you up and suggest a lunch.

Yours ever
[T. S. E.]

TO *Herbert Read* CC

29 February 1924 [*The Criterion*, London]

Dear Read,

Thank you for your letter. As the *Modern Quarterly* have been so polite and as you think well of it, you must certainly have it.[4] Would you mind writing to Cobden-Sanderson for me and asking [*sc.* saying] that I have asked you to ask him to put the *Modern Quarterly* on the exchange list? And if you would also write to the *Modern Quarterly* on my behalf and

1–On 25 Feb., Flint said Marichalar's article on 'the art of criticism' lacked 'the seriousness' at which TSE aimed in C. Given that it was 'largely derivative from current French writing', it would be better to 'go direct to Frenchmen for this, and not to a Spaniard'.
2–Flint's notes on 'Italian Periodicals' and 'Danish Periodicals' for C. 2: 7 (Apr. 1924).
3–Flint said: 'As for contributing something more serious than notes and translations, I'm afraid you've come to the wrong man. I'm not half educated, and I wonder at my cheek in ever having published anything at all.'
4–On 26 Feb., HR quoted V. F. Calverton, American Marxist critic and editor of *The Modern Quarterly* (Baltimore), saying 'I still believe the *Criterion* to be the best magazine that is now appearing in England', and said he wanted 'an exchange copy'. HR thought the *Quarterly* 'more of an ally than most of the American papers'.

tell them that the *Criterion* is coming, and ask them to send their review direct to you as I am extremely pressed for time. Sanderson will give you some subscriptions forms if you ask him.

I quite agree with you about the desirability of building up a circulation in America.[1] Would you let me know the names and addresses of what you consider the most important American periodicals with which we [do] not exchange?

I am sorry to have been so vague about the date when I wanted your article,[2] but as you also seem to be a busy man, and as I understood that you did not want to be pressed for time, I thought I would merely wait until you had it ready, and then fit it in the first number possible. Meanwhile I have more than filled up the April number, so that the only question is whether it can go into July or whether it should wait till October.[3] The difficulty with a Quarterly is that one cannot risk getting suitable material at short notice; consequently there has to be a sort of waiting list, as a result of which everybody has been appearing a quarter or so later than they should do. I must get the April number ready for press within the next fortnight. When the pressure is over I shall write to you and if meanwhile, you should be visiting East London, as you used to do, please ring me up at Central 8246 and arrange a lunch with me.

Yours ever,
[T. S. E.]

TO *Coningsby Disraeli*[4] CC

29 February 1924 [*The Criterion*, London]

Sir,

At the request of Mr F. W. Bain, I am having sent to you a copy of the *Criterion* containing Mr Bain's essay on the late Earl of Beaconsfield.[5] I hope that Mr Bain's essay and the paper in general will be of interest to you.

I am, Sir,

Your obedient servant,
[T. S. E.]

1–HR said 'it ought to be possible to build up an American circulation', and 'exchange copies' would help do this.
2–HR wanted to know when his article on 'Psychology and Criticism' was needed.
3–HR's 'Psycho-Analysis and the Critic' appeared in C. 3: 10 (Jan. 1925), 214–30.
4–Coningsby Disraeli (1867–1936): Conservative politician; nephew of Benjamin Disraeli.
5–F. W. Bain, 'Disraeli', *C.* 2: 6 (Feb. 1924), 143–66.

TO *Anabel M. Berry*[1] CC

29 February 1924 [*The Criterion*, London]

Dear Miss Berry,

Thank you very much for thinking of me and for sending me the tickets to Miss Sitwell's lecture.[2] I should very much like to come, both for the pleasure of hearing Miss Sitwell and for the purpose of supporting any undertaking of the Arts League of Service.[3] I have unfortunately made another engagement for Wednesday which will be difficult for me to break; but if I cannot come myself, I shall try to pass the tickets on to someone who would enjoy it. I hope on the next occasion to be able to come and see your new premises and I hope that your presence in London means renewed and beneficient activity on the part of the Arts League of Service.

[T. S. E.]

TO *Wyndham Lewis* MS Cornell

Sunday night [?2 March 1924] 9 Clarence Gate Gdns

Dear Lewis

Very many thanks. If you will send MSS.[4] as soon as ready there will always be someone here, or they will be quite safe in my letter box. I am not always here at night but you can always find me in the day, or *for lunch,* at 20 King William Street (Central 8246). *Come and lunch any day* in the City. In any case I shall want to see you three or four days after I receive MSS.

Yours
T. S. E.

Might there be another part of the *Zagreus* book for April or June?[5]

1 – Anabel M. Berry, organising secretary of the Arts League of Service; author of *Animals in Art* (1929) and *Art for Children* (1929).

2 – Edith Sitwell was to lecture on 'Forms of Expression in Contemporary Poetry', at the Arts League of Service, Adelphi Terrace House, London, on 5 Mar.

3 – TSE gave a lecture on poetry at the Arts League of Service on 28 Oct. 1919.

4 – In a letter dated by W. K. Rose to 'February 1924' WL speaks of 'leaving of the MSS': 'a section (roughly 50 pages) of a book Man of the World', delivered 'should the Apes of God by any mischance not turn up by March 10' (*Letters of Wyndham Lewis*, 139).

5 – 'The Apes of God' appeared in C. 2: 7 (Apr. 1924).

TO *Harold Monro* TS Beinecke

3 March 1924 *The Criterion*, 17 Thavies Inn

My dear Monro,

I do indeed wish that we could meet more often and what you call my politeness is certainly sincere. It is true my difficulties of seeing anyone any oftener than at long intervals are much greater than anyone understands, because few people realise what it means to have to put a whole day's work into an evening. Unfortunately, I cannot come to supper this Wednesday because I have made an engagement, but I should be very glad to come some other Wednesday to meet your friend. Of course I must explain in advance, that the *Criterion* cannot at present afford an Assistant Editor; it has had pretty heavy expenses lately and I am trying to run it with the utmost economy. That keeps me extremely busy of course but I must get along somehow with what help I can afford, as I do believe that the thing is worth while keeping up. But nevertheless I should be glad to make the acquaintance of the man you have told me about.

It will suit me capitally if you can let me have your article[1] by the 1st of June; but remember that I shall have to have it by that date in order to get it into the July number.

I am delighted to hear that you will be spending part of your time in my neighbourhood this summer. Do let me know how near to Chichester you are. I may be going down quite soon for a long stay and I shall be there through the summer for weekends and we shall look forward to having you as a neighbour. Do let me have your address. Meanwhile, I hope we may meet again in a week or two.

Yours ever,
T. S. Eliot

TO *Sydney Schiff* TS BL

3 March 1924 9 Clarence Gate Gdns

My dear Sydney,

I cannot tell you how touched we are by the inscription which you have put in the copy of *Tony*.[2] But I am writing for both of us and must make an attempt to express what we both feel. We should like you to believe

1 – Monro, 'Wordsworth Revisited', C. 2: 8 (July 1924).
2 – Stephen Hudson, *Tony* (1924).

that our encouragement is always ready for you if you need encouragement, because you must know that we can give much more than what is expressed by the word 'approval'. But we are really distressed at your giving us this book, because we had wanted to buy a copy for ourselves. We shall however nevertheless buy a copy and give it to someone whom we like very much and whom we think might understand it.

We are very much struck by your exposition of the fundamental idea of *Tony* as expressed in your letter to Sadleir.[1] It is the essential idea to keep in mind, I think, in reading the book and it is one with which I am very much in sympathy. I really wish that such a letter might have been published as a preface to the book itself. For I fear, that not many readers, however much they appreciate the skill of the story, will be able to draw this conclusion for themselves.

I am looking forward to a long talk with you later in the week. Meanwhile we both send our love and sincerest good wishes for *Tony*.

Affectionately,
Tom

TO *Wyndham Lewis* — MS Cornell

[Early March? 1924] — *The Criterion*, 17 Thavies Inn

Dear Lewis

Many thanks for the fresh MSS.[2] I will do as you say. I hope it will do if I return you the part you want when I come on Wednesday evening. I am afraid I have mislaid your new address. It is ? Holland Walk ?[3]

Yours
T. S. E.

Zagreus looks very well in the C. I think[4] –

1 – Michael Sadleir (1888–1957): book collector, writer, bibliographer, and SS's publisher at Constable; later author of *Fanny by Gaslight* (1940).
2 – Probably a reference to the second extract from 'The Apes of God', *C.* 2: 7 (Apr. 1924), 300–10.
3 – Lewis's letters were addressed from 61 Palace Gardens Terrace.
4 – 'Mr Zagreus and the Split-Man', *C.* 2: 6 (Feb. 1924).

TO *Charles Whibley* CC

5 March 1924 [London]

My dear Whibley,

I am sending the book registered and insured to Constable in Edinburgh as you requested.[1] I shall certainly do my best to get it finished by the autumn.

I for one can say that I enjoyed our lunch immensely.[2] I liked Baldwin[3] very much indeed. But there was much that I should have liked to have discussed with you which had to be left unsaid, and I hope therefore that you will come up to town soon as you promised and that we may have an evening together.

Affectionately,
[T. S. E.]

TO *Lady Rothermere* CC

5 March 1924 [London]

Dear Lady Rothermere,

This is just a note in great haste to enclose this letter from Cocteau.[4] It looks as if he meant to give us the slip. That would be a great pity, because I have already advertised him as a contributor and a contribution from him would have impressed many people here and in Paris. This letter arrived at the exact moment when he had promised a contribution. I wish you would let me know if you can think of any way of bringing pressure on him to send something. It is most unfortunate to lose this contribution.

Yours always sincerely,
[T. S. E.]

1–*Seneca: His Tenne Tragedies*, trans. into English by Thomas Newton, to which TSE had agreed to write an introduction for CW's Tudor Translations Series.
2–TSE and Whibley lunched on 2 Mar., together with an undergraduate named Wood.
3–Stanley Baldwin (1867–1947): Conservative politician. He became Prime Minister on 22 May 1923, but lost his majority in the General Election of Dec. 1923. Although he attempted to stay in office leading a minority government, his government was defeated on 21 Jan. 1924. Baldwin resigned but was confirmed as leader of the Conservative Party on 11 Feb. In a series of speeches over the following months he set out what came to be termed the 'new conservatism', and was returned to power in Oct. with a massive majority.
4–See TSE's letter to Cocteau of 17 Feb.

TO *Frank Crowninshield* CC

5 March 1924 [*The Criterion*, London]

Dear Mr Crowninshield,

Thank you very much for your note of the 20th and for continuing to think of me.[1] I have not by any means forgotten either *Vanity Fair* or yourself and I sincerely hope to become a more frequent contributor in the course of this summer.[2] I have been so busy with the *Criterion* this winter, that I have had no time for anything else; for several months I have been without an Assistant Editor and for most of the time without even a secretary. We have just brought out the number which should have appeared in January and I am now engaged in making up the number for April. Meanwhile I hope, that you can remember me for two or three months longer until I send you something which I have in mind to write. And if, as I hope, you are going to visit us again this year, you must let me know in advance and I shall hope to see more of you than I did a year ago.

[T. S. E.]

TO *Cecil Scott*[3] CC

5 March 1924 [*The Criterion*, London]

Dear Mr Scott,

I am returning herewith your manuscript on Rimbaud which I have retained for so long because it interested me.[4] But as it would be impossible for us, in any case, to publish an article of this length within the next nine months owing to our having accepted a great deal of material, I think that I had better now return it to you. It is an interesting subject, but I think that you need to develop it still further and make a very thorough study of it.[5]

1 – Crowninshield, editor of *Vanity Fair*, wrote (5 Mar.): 'You won't forget us, will you.' He was 'unable to forget' meeting TSE.
2 – TSE had published 'A Prediction in Regard to Three English Authors, Writers Who, though Masters of Thought, Are Likewise Masters of Art', in *Vanity Fair* 21: 6 (Feb. 1924). He published nothing further in *Vanity Fair*.
3 – Cecil Scott reviewed in the *Adelphi* and elsewhere.
4 – 'I wrote it in the first place with no intention of publishing it,' said Scott in an undated letter from Trinity College, Cambridge, 'but because of the indignation I felt at Mr Harold Nicolson's picture of the poet [Rimbaud] in his book on Verlaine . . . No French writer has traced the connection between de Nerval and Rimbaud; or made any direct reference to the Cabbala.'
5 – On 4 June Scott asked for TSE's views about a revised version that would include Baudelaire and de Nerval.

If you are in London during the vacation, I hope that you will let me know, so that we may renew our acquaintance and discuss these and other subjects. Do drop me a line in advance if you are expecting at any time to be in London for a few days.

Sincerely yours,
[T. S. E.]

TO *H. P. Collins*[1] CC

5 March 1924 [*The Criterion*, London]

Dear Sir,

Thank you for your letter of the 27th January enclosing MS of your essay on Housman.[2] I shall look forward to seeing the book and wish that we could use the MS. But unfortunately we have so much material accepted, that it is impossible even to consider any more contributions for the next six or nine months.[3]

With many thanks,

Yours faithfully
[T. S. E.]

TO *Gilbert Brooks*[4] CC

5 March 1924 [*The Criterion*, London]

Dear Mr Brooks,

I am very much pleased at receiving from you a copy of your poems inscribed with your name. I have not had time yet to read enough to venture on a criticism, but I think from what I have read, that if I did, it would be of a complimentary nature. I am extremely distrustful always of my own judgements in contemporary literature and therefore I never venture any until I have time for a thoroughly considered opinion. But

1–Harold Poulton Collins (1899–1985): English editor and critic; worked with JMM on the *Adelphi*.
2–Collins offered a chapter from his forthcoming *Modern Poetry* (1925); it appeared as 'A. E. Housman: A Retrospective Note', in *Adelphi* 3: 3 (Aug. 1925).
3–Collins contributed 'A Note on the Classical Principle in Poetry', C. 3: 11 (Apr. 1925), and numerous later reviews.
4–Benjamin Gilbert Brooks: poet and critic; author of *Camelot* (1919).

I shall look forward to reading your book and if possible to writing to you again about it.[1]

I remember very well having met you and look forward to some day having the opportunity of renewing our acquaintance.[2]

Yours sincerely,
[T. S. E.]

TO *Miss Kate Buss*[3] CC

5 March 1924 [*The Criterion*, London]

Dear Miss Buss,

Excuse me for not having answered your letter of the 12th January and for not having thanked you for your compliments. If you wish to send me the title page of Prufrock, I will gladly put my name on it and return it to you and I return herewith your postage stamp for that purpose.[4]

Yours faithfully,
[T. S. E.]

1–*Exile: Poems* (Dijon: Maurice Darantière, 1923). 'I am aware,' wrote Brooks (13 Feb.), 'that it may seem rather cavalierly [*sic*] to send such a book to you who, to judge from your critical writings, seem to have so rigid a system of selection to apply to poetry. Still, I have the courage of honest workmanship. I should be pleased to know how certain of the poems strike you.'

2–'I had the pleasure' wrote Brooks, 'of being introduced to you once at Oxford, at the home of Lady Ottoline, by Aldous Huxley, about the summer of 1920, shortly after the appearance of my first volume . . .'

3–Kate Buss: American writer; author of *Jevons Block* (1918) and *Studies in Chinese Drama* (1922). An early admirer of EP, she reviewed *Cathay* in the *Boston Evening Transcript* (6 Dec. 1916). In 1916, EP had told her: 'Do keep an eye out for Joyce and also for T. S. Eliot. They are worth attention.' She and EP corresponded about TSE and Bel Esprit in 1922.

4–'I have one of the rare and precious copies of your PRUFROCK,' wrote Buss. 'Do you think I might have your signature to add to its lustre? Or, should I enclose a title-page, would you write your name upon it? . . . Although you will never have heard of me I have listened to your praise frequently by your Paris friends. Also I read and, too rarely – you publish so seldom, review you . . . That I refrain from adding a stamp signifies inability to procure one in Boston!! Will this U.S. issue serve as the "fair exchange" in some American correspondence?'

FROM *His Mother* TS Valerie Eliot

8 March 1924 24 Concord Ave, Cambridge, Mass.

My dearest Tom:

I received yesterday your lovely letter and it made me very happy.[1] I feared you were offended with me because of what I had written regarding putting your Hydraulic stock in trust, and I felt I could not bear it in my old age. So night before last I lay awake many hours in much trouble. Your letter reassured me of your continued affection.

Some time today (I am awaiting a telegram from Henry,) I will send you a weekend letter. I have been thinking over what you wrote regarding my going to see you this summer, and your coming here in the fall. It seems to me that if there is any certainty regarding your coming here in the fall, that will be better for you than my going to London. Of course it will depend more or less on Vivien's condition, but fall ought to be her best time. I think the time spent on the ocean voyage would greatly benefit you. Charlotte was going with me, and she came in yesterday. She and Ada both thought you might be able to make profitable lecture engagements here especially in New York. Certainly you could deliver one here. What do you think? I think you could cover any loss of salary. If not I would pay that as well as your travelling expenses.

It wrings my heart to think what a hard time you have had this year. I am disgusted with Mr Aldington, but I have felt the situation was a delicate one. He would resent a superior over him being an author himself. I should expect a person in his position to desire to have his own contributions published, and perhaps to resent a controlling judgment in choice of articles. How you and Vivian must have worked! Must you do as much on July and October numbers, as you say you want to carry the magazine through its second year? It has seemed to me you could do more creative work if you did not have the editorship of the *Criterion*.

Do not suggest such a thing as that my affections or even Henry's could possibly be 'alienated' from you. Not while I possess conscious being. So long time elapsed that you did not write, I felt I had gone out of your life. And I knew that were you happy and untroubled you would write, which excited my apprehensions still more and caused many wakeful hours. For I had rather know the worst than be kept in ignorance. It seems to me I have written quite frequently, but when you were silent so long I did not know what to write. Your last letter I shall always treasure. I have all your

1 – TSE's letter of late Feb.

letters from the time you first went to Milton. I suppose I ought to destroy at least part of them.[1]

As to your income I intend soon as it can be done to advantage to sell 300 shares (all I have left of Hydraulic) and divide. Your portion I will put in trust with the Old Colony. I should like you to put in with it the bonds Henry has purchased for you. If you approve let us know later. I shall start also if I can a trust for Margaret. I wish Marian would put her money in trust, as she does not know much about business. Gradually I want to turn over to my children all I can spare from my income while still living. I have just had an offer for Locust Street and have telegraphed Henry. Congress (the House) wants a tax on gifts. I hope the Senate will not confirm.

Your work at the Bank must be tremendous. I am sorry the Socialists are so in the ascendant. There is a considerable amount of parlor Bolshevism here. I do not know how Shef[2] feels – I do not dare to talk freely with him.

I think you had better rent your apartments at once and will let you know by cable if I am not coming. Of course if you were prevented from coming I should be very greatly disappointed, but one can never be sure of the future. I want what is for your best good, and feel it would be a good thing in many ways for you. I am glad to know you are more conservative. I think many Social Reformers are destroying many of the finer qualities of the classes they desire to benefit.

I fear you will find it a slow process to regain your strength after Influenza. I feared you would go out too soon and contract Pneumonia which often happens. I hope that danger period is passed, as also I hope danger of Vivian's taking the disease from you. I am glad that the Swedish cure is benefiting you both. I believe in the treatment.

Please do not let so long time elapse again without writing. Write just a few lines. I cannot expect many such long delightful letters as the last with its warm expressions of affection. Since I came from the hospital I am on strict diet, but I think lying awake at night increases my trouble. I hope you will find another satisfactory person to stay with Vivian in the country. Charlotte would have gone about with me – she dearly loves sight-seeing. I could not have kept up with her. I should enjoy her company.

Is the April first or is it April 15th number of the *Criterion* still to be prepared by you and Vivian? I am glad you have a young man to do

1 – None of TSE's early letters from Milton Academy or Harvard survive: he destroyed them after her death. On 5 May 1930 he told HWE he was 'glad to have the letters to make ashes of'.

2 – Alfred Dwight Sheffield (see Glossary of Names), husband of TSE's sister Ada.

secretarial work in the evening. And I am very glad you think Vivian has improved this winter. Give her my love.

You have ere this received Henry's report of your finances. I should think it would be safe for you to keep your stock at 6% a while longer. It would not do to put it in trust in that form. It would be better, I should think to add it to the fund later.

If I went to London it would not be for sight-seeing but to see you. But as I previously have stated, if you *can* come in the fall it will be better for you. Of course I like Henry's protecting presence. I do not know whether he can come another year or for some time to come. He does not entirely trust the business judgment of the other two men. He says Buchen does not realize income must exceed outgo. He pledged his stock for them last year. I hope he will not do such a thing again.

I am glad that in the writing your essays on the Elizabethan Period in the *Criterion,* you are planning to expand them into a book.[1] I have always had that in mind for you in relation to that period. I wish too that poem. Perhaps you could write in crossing Atlantic – if you could get as Henry did a state room to yourself.

I wish to tell you in confidence that I have received a small inheritance from the Blood Estate, of which the bulk goes to Aunt Susie. It is five hundred dollars. I will tell you in confidence what I wish to do with it. Houghton & Mifflin may not be willing to publish my *Savonarola* on any terms, but if they will do so on my guarantee, I feel that I can use this money leaving not so much to take from my children's estate, from which I should not have liked to take the full amount. You say you will write a separate letter regarding the *Savonarola.* I know how horribly you are pressed, but wish to say you can make the Introduction as short as you please. I have a sentiment about having your name associated with mine, which will also be an advantage. I should like now as soon as possible to put my fortune to the test, 'to win or lose it all'. I do not think a long Introduction is necessary if you can just say the fitting word.

I think I will close this letter and write again very soon. I shall always keep your last letter. It was a delight to me to receive such a long communication. Remember you are always with me in spirit and thought. And I am anxious to do all I can to help you. And I am always

Your devoted Mother

1 – 'Four Elizabethan Dramatists: A Preface' in C. 2: 6 was to have been followed by a book. This never happened, though TSE did publish *Elizabethan Essays* (1934).

TO *Jean de Menasce*[1] CC

10 March 1924 [*The Criterion*, London]

Dear Menasce,

Thank you very much for your letter and for fulfilling your promise of a note on *Hamlet*.[2] Your note is extremely interesting and needs no apologies, and I hope to be able to use it. Meanwhile will you let me know as soon as possible when you will be passing through London and how long you will be here? I believe you told me that you are going to Paris for the Easter vacation, but I hope that you will be staying for a few days in London.

Sincerely yours,
[T. S. E.]

TO *E. M. Forster* CC

10 March 1924 [London]

Dear Forster,

Jean de Menasce has lent me the manuscript of some translations of poems of your friend Cavafy.[3] He has suggested that we might like to print some of them in the *Criterion* and tells me that you are the person to whom to apply. There are several which I like very much. Might we use them?

I understood from Menasce that you had given him the manuscript for the purpose of selecting a few poems for the [Oxford periodical] *Isis* but he has generously suggested, that if you agree to our using a few in the *Criterion*, I may have the first choice.[4]

1–Jean de Menasce (1902–73): born in Alexandria of a Jewish father; trained in law and philosophy at Alexandria, Cairo, and Balliol College, Oxford, 1921–4, where he came to know OM and her circle. He became secretary of the Zionist Bureau in Geneva, before converting to Catholicism in 1925 and being ordained a Dominican priest in 1935. He published a French translation of *TWL*, described as 'revuée et approuvée par l'auteur', in *Esprit* 1 (May 1926), as well as translations of parts of *Ash-Wednesday* in *Commerce* 15 (Spring 1928) and 21 (Autumn 1929). He became a professor of the history of religions and missiology in Fribourg. His missiological essays were collected in *Permanence et transformation de la mission* (1967).

2–On 1 Mar. de Menasce sent TSE his review of the OUDS production of *Hamlet*. He went on to discuss *Coriolanus* in musical terms, comparing it with *Boris Goudounov* and suggesting it was written 'on the same thematic principles as a Wagner opera'.

3–Constantine Cavafy (1863–1933), Greek poet from Alexandria. Forster met him there and on his return to England in 1919 helped to promote his work. Forster's essay on Cavafy's poetry in *Pharos and Pharillon* (1923) introduced Cavafy to the English-speaking world.

4–C. P. Cavafy, 'Ithaca', trans. G. Valassopoulo, appeared in *C.* 2: 8 (July 1924), 431–3.

If this is all right, please let me know the person or persons who ought to be paid for the translation apart from the payment to the author. It will not amount to very much for anybody, I am afraid, but we manage to pay [a] little higher rates for verse than for prose.

Now that I have the opportunity of asking, is there any chance of your being able to offer us anything of your own before very long? It is a long time since I have heard from you. We should very much like to print something more of yours.

Yours sincerely,
[T. S. E.]

TO *Richard Cobden-Sanderson* CC

10 March 1924 [*The Criterion*, 17 Thavies Inn]

Dear Cobden-Sanderson,

I am not quite certain about payment for Lévy-Bruhl,[1] as this was all arranged by Richard Aldington. The general terms decided upon for foreign contributions are that payment at the rate of 15/- per 1000 words to the translator should be deducted from the payment to the contributor; and that the contributor should then be sent a draft in his own currency. It is possible that Aldington in his correspondence with Lévy-Bruhl quoted some definite sum and I hope it is not troubling you too much to ask if you would not mind writing to Aldington to find out whether he made any such arrangement. But if he quoted a definite sum in Francs, I think that nevertheless Lévy-Bruhl ought to be given the advantage of the fall in the French exchange. Another point to find out from Aldington is the name and address of the person who made the translation.

I will write to Aldington later about the question of French periodicals.

There is also the question of payment on account of Hauptmann's notes.[2] I understood that Randall had the rights for this country. Could you write also to Randall and ask him, to whom the payment should be made and find out whether we should send a separate cheque to Hauptmann or an inclusive cheque to Randall?

I am very sorry to trouble you with these details but I have had no time at all lately as my wife is very seriously ill with influenza and I have been

1–L. Lévy-Bruhl, 'Primitive Mentality and Gambling', *C.* 2: 6 (Feb. 1924).
2–Gerhart Hauptmann, 'Notes on Art and Life', trans. by A. W. G. Randall, in the same number.

at home most of the time for the past three or four days. As soon as circumstances permit, I will telephone to you and arrange a meeting.

Yours ever,
[T. S. E.]

TO *Messrs. John Lane, The Bodley Head Ltd*[1] CC

10 March 1924 [*The Criterion*, London]

Dear Sirs,

I have to acknowledge receipt of several books which you have sent me for notice in the *Criterion*. I think that it is only fair to mention that the *Criterion* does not make a regular practice of reviewing current books but only notices such as are thought worthy of particular mention in articles or in editorial notes. I propose to give a notice of your excellent series of Bodley Head Quartos as soon as possible but I am afraid that it will be impossible to mention the other volumes which you have sent.[2] I should be glad if you would continue to send volumes of the series I have just mentioned, as they appear. But in general, I prefer to let publishers know when any volumes appear which we wish to mention. And you may be assured that when we ask for any book to be sent, it will receive due notice.

Yours faithfully,
[T. S. E.]

TO *G. Elliot Smith* CC

10 March 1924 [*The Criterion*, London]

Dear Mr Elliot Smith,

I am writing to remind you of a letter you wrote me on the 30th May last, in which you promised me, that at some time you would write a paper for the *Criterion* dealing with your views in Anthropology or with some particular problem in which you are interested. I should like to claim the fulfilment of this promise, as we have assured our readers that we should

1 – The Bodley Head Press, founded by John Lane and Elkin Mathews in 1887.
2 – In his 'Commentary' (*C.* 2: 7, Apr. 1924), TSE said: 'To the public spirit, or the sagacity of such publishers as John Lane and Routledge, has been left the publication of two recent excellent series.' He was referring to *The Bodley Head Quartos* (John Lane) and *The Broadway Translations* (Routledge & Co.). *The Bodley Head Quartos* were scholarly reprints of rare Tudor texts edited by G. B. Harrison.

publish something by you in Volume II. Do you think that it would be possible for you to let me have something by the 1st of June, that is to say for the July Number? I cannot tell you how highly we should appreciate the honour of publishing a contribution by you or how much good it would do the *Criterion*.[1] If you are able to do us this favour, I should like to have the title of your essay as soon as possible in order that we might advertise it in the April number.

I repeat that a contribution from you would be of the highest value to the *Criterion*.

Sincerely yours,
[T. S. E.]

TO *E. M. Forster* CC

12 March 1924

Dear Forster,

Thank you very much for your letter and the information about Cavafy.[2] I want to use at any rate the first poem which is called in the manuscript '*ITHACA*'. I only questioned one or two points of spelling and the translation:

'And beget the goodly merchandise.'[3]

But as I should not be able to use the poem until the July number, there is plenty of time. I might be able to use one or two other of the poems as well.

I am sorry that you do not feel in a fluent mood yourself but hope that after the influenza season is over, you will be able to let us have something. I am sure that you are able to make even Coleridge interesting.[4]

Sincerely yours
[T. S. E.]

1–See Elliot Smith, 'The Glamour of Gold', *C.* 3: 11 (Apr. 1925).

2–On 11 Mar., Forster provided Cavafy's address in Alexandria and the name of the translator, G. Valassopoulo. They had given some poems to Jean de Menasce for *Oxford Outlook* but otherwise 'left the English arrangements' in Forster's hands. He had placed 'The City' and 'Theodotus' with *N.*

3–When 'Ithaca' was published in *C.* 2: 8 (July 1924), line 18 read 'And procure the goodly merchandise'.

4–Forster wrote that he had 'nothing in mind at all' except for some possible reflections about when Coleridge 'fell off his charger three times in a week' and ended up helping a 'comrade in a workhouse near Henley'.

TO *Wyndham Lewis* PC Cornell

[Postmark 13 March 1924] [9 Clarence Gate Gdns]

¿ Apes[1] ?
Z.[2] is a masterpiece.
Want *Apes* at once –

TO *Virginia Woolf* MS Berg

17 March 1924 [9 Clarence Gate Gdns]

Dear Virginia

I am very happy to learn that I shall have the honour of your company at *King Lear* on the 30th (Sunday night) and have written for my tickets.[3] I had to find out whether you would come before deciding which performance to apply for.

Tell Leonard that I rang up again as he asked me to do, but got no reply, so your bell is evidently not in order yet.[4]

Always yours
T. S. E.

1–WL, 'The Apes of God, Extract from Encyclical Addressed to Daniel Boleyn by Mr Zagreus', *C*. 2: 7 (Apr. 1924).
2–'Mr Zagreus'.
3–The Phoenix Society production of *King Lear*, which TSE and VW attended on 30 Mar. Writing as 'Crites' (*C*. Apr. 1924), TSE applauded the production as 'almost flawless': 'It is commonly said that *King Lear* is not a play to be acted . . . It is more likely, to judge from the response of the audience, that *King Lear* is a work of such immense power that it offends and scandalizes ordinary citizens of both sexes.' On 5 May, VW recorded her sense of betrayal: 'He took me to Lear (unrecorded) & we both jeered & despised; & now he comes out in the Criterion with solemn & stately rebuke of those who jeer & despise. I taxed him, lightly with this: he sat tight & said that he meant what he wrote: then what does he mean by what he says? God knows. There's something hole & cornerish, biting in the back, suspicious, elaborate, uneasy, about him: much would be liberated by a douche of pure praise, which he can scarcely hope to get' (*Diary*, II, 302).
4–On 21 Mar., VW told Lytton Strachey she fled to Strachey's works when she heard the telephone 'ringing with Tom's sepulchral voice' (*Letters*, III, 94).

TO *Charles Whibley* CC

16 March 1924 [*The Criterion*, London]

My dear Whibley,

I regret very bitterly that I was not able to dine with you last week because I have a great deal to say to you and there are several important matters I should like to go into with you as soon as possible. It would give me great pleasure as well, if you would dine with me on the first possible evening from next Monday the 24th.

My wife has been dragged through a very bad attack of influenza by the Doctors Cyriax, in a most miraculous way, but as you know, the after-effects of influenza are so pernicious and dangerous, that she must be sent into the country as soon as possible, as they say that there is no chance for recuperation without sea-air and healthy surroundings.

I could arrange any night next week for dinner, but the earlier the better, if you would let me know as soon as you possibly can. I do hope that the warmer weather has brought you some relief.

Yours affectionately,
[T. S. E.]

TO *Charles Whibley* CC

17 March 1924 [London]

My dear Whibley,

Many thanks for letter which crossed mine. Wednesday the 26th will suit me capitally. You say Wednesday the 24th, but I take it that you mean the Wednesday and not the Monday, although either day would suit me. Do come as early as you can after 7 o'clock. I am delighted to be reassured about Chesterfield.[1]

Affectionately,
[T. S. E.]

1–Whibley, 'Chesterfield', *C.* 2: 7 (Apr. 1924).

TO *Ada Leverson*[1] CC

18 March 1924 9 Clarence Gate Gdns

Dear Mrs Leverson,

I have had it in mind for a long time to ask you for a contribution to the *Criterion*, but I am always naturally timid of asking anyone so well known and established as yourself to contribute to a new and comparatively unknown review. But now I feel that the *Criterion* is about to justify its existence, so may I hope that you will let me have something: in satiric vein? If you will do us this honour, I must explain, that having to run the *Criterion* alone and under so many difficulties, I can only manage it by having contributions in hand very well in advance. I should be very pleased if you could let me have something now, which I could use for April or July. I shall be having the July type set up within the next few weeks; in fact I often have three numbers in process at the same time, as it is such a great help in giving the year's volume the form which I should like it to have.

Sincerely yours,
[T. S. E.]

TO *Wyndham Lewis* MS Cornell

[Postmark 19 March 1924] [London]

Dear Lewis

You have surpassed yourself and everything. It is worthwhile running the *Criterion* just to publish these.[2] It is so immense that I have no words for it. I can only say that you have taken a weight off my mind, and off my chest, so that I breathe better after it.

Can I see you on Monday? I have a lot to do for the *Criterion* this week.

Yours
T. S. E.

1 – Ada Leverson, née Beddington (1862–1933), a sister of Violet Schiff; notable *salonière* (her friends included Beardsley and Beerbohm); novelist and contributor to the *Yellow Book* and *Punch*. She was a close friend of Oscar Wilde, who nicknamed her 'The Sphinx' and saluted her as 'the wittiest woman in the world', and she remained loyal to him after his imprisonment. See Julie Speedie, *Wonderful Sphinx: The Biography of Ada Leverson* (1993).
2 – 'Mr Zagreus and the Split-Man' and 'The Apes of God', from *The Apes of God* (1930), in *C.* 2: 6 (Feb. 1924) and 2: 7 (Apr. 1924). The main target of WL's satire is the 'very select closed club' of 'moneyed descendants of Victorian literary splendour', who differ from previous Bohemians by substituting 'money for talent as a qualification'. These 'Apes of God'

TO *Ada Leverson* MS NYPL

27 March [1924] [*The Criterion*, 17 Thavies Inn]

Dear Mrs Leverson,

I ought to have answered your letter at once, and should have done so had I had one moment. Of course I should like to have the Wilde as soon as possible,[1] but I can safely give you till three weeks from the end of this week – the 18th of April? Can you have it ready by then? *Please let me know.*

I am very pleased to hear about the 'Consultation' too.[2] I have been thinking about the Proust too. But in April and July, as it happens, we are having something *by* Proust and several things about Proust, and I don't think we can publish any more 'Proust' for a long time after that! And I think the sooner you can publish the thing you have in mind the better. You see I want you to write it, even if the *Criterion* can't publish it!

I do look forward to our next meeting. If we go away soon I shall write to you as soon as we return.

Sincerely yours
T. S. Eliot

I like the title very much – 'The Importance'.[3]
Have you seen what Middleton Murry has written about George Moore in the April *Adelphi*.[4] It is the filthiest low poisonous attack I have ever read. Do look at it.

—

are 'all "geniuses", before whose creations other members of the Club, in an invariable ritual, would swoon with appreciation' (307).

1 – On 24 Mar. Leverson suggested a sketch called 'The Last First Night', describing the first night of Wilde's *The Importance of being Earnest* on 14 Feb. 1895.

2 – As an alternative, she suggested 'a burlesque dialogue – medical consultation, between a retired Philistine soldier of 35 & his soul physician – an improvement on the Psycho-analyst doctor': the title would be 'Consultation Sentimentale'.

3 – She suggested 'First Night: or The Importance of Being Oscar' as another possible title for her 'Importance' article.

4 – JMM, 'Wrap me up in my Aubusson carpet', *Adelphi* 1: 11 (Apr. 1924), 951–8. This diatribe against the Irish novelist George Moore was prompted by his *Conversations in Ebury Street* (1924), which included an attack on Thomas Hardy's 'absurd' novels. 'In his treatment of Mr Hardy,' said JMM, 'he has surpassed his own previous triumphs in envy and vulgarity . . . He cannot help himself; he is possessed – but by such a mean, ugly, contemptible little demon that we can feel no pity for him' (958). On 28 Mar., Hardy congratulated JMM on his 'brilliant little article', but added: 'I doubt if he was worth such good powder and shot as you give him!'

TO *Richard Cobden-Sanderson* CC

28 March 1924 [London]

Dear Cobden-Sanderson,

Will you please send a cheque for four Pounds to Mr J. R. Culpin at this address in payment of secretarial work for the *Criterion* from 20th Febr. to 19th March.

Yours ever,
[T. S. E.]

TO *Messrs. Hazell, Watson & Viney* CC

28 March 1924 [London]

Dear Sirs,

I enclose herewith Mr Wyndham Lewis's 'The Apes of God'. I shall be obliged if you will immediately set it up for the April *Criterion* and send the proofs direct to me. Please print the selection entitled 'Encyclical' to come first.[1] I shall be glad if you will send me a card to acknowledge receipt.

Yours faithfully
[T. S. E.]

TO *C. K. Scott Moncrieff* CC

30 March 1924 [9 Clarence Gate Gdns]

Dear Mr Scott Moncrieff,

I am enclosing the Manuscript of Marcel Proust[2] which I have just received from Jacques Rivière and very much hope that you will be able to let us have the translation not later than the 15th of June, as we count upon this to be one of the most important contributions in the July number. We very much appreciate the honour that you are doing us in making this translation for the *Criterion* as it has been an essential part of

1 – On 29 Mar. the printers confirmed receipt of 'The Apes of God', 'Extracts from Encyclical' and 'Lord Osmond's Lenten Party'. 'The Apes of God' appeared in C. 2: 7 (Apr. 1924), ending with the sentence: '[Now, again, keep yourself free for the Lenten Party.]'. Despite this trailer, the third extract did not appear in a later issue.

2 – 'La Mort d'Albertine', which appeared in Scott Moncrieff's translation as 'The Death of Albertine', C. 2: 8 (July 1924).

my design of publishing the Manuscript of Proust, that the translation should be by yourself.

Sincerely yours,
[T. S. E.]

TO *Scofield Thayer* TS Beinecke

30 March 1924 [*The Criterion*, 17 Thavies Inn]

Dear Scofield,

I was very pleased to get your letter of the 11th February and the delay in answering represents only the extent to which I always undertake more than I can do. I have been under great difficulties in running the *Criterion* this winter as you may judge from the fact that the January number did not appear until the end of February. This delay has also embarrassed the April number since it has allowed me only six weeks instead of three months to get it ready. Now the April number is nearly finished and I have to complete an introduction which I have promised to the work of Paul Valéry and then I hope to get away for a month's rest.

This is to assure you that I have not forgotten the promised essay which I have not yet been able to write, but which nevertheless I shall attempt by mid-summer.[1] It is true that you have waited very patiently and I feel that I must have pretty nearly exhausted the patience of the *Dial* as well as of every other periodical and person with whom I come into contact.

I wish indeed that I had seen your folio.[2] I should like very much to do something about it, but the fact is that I could not put into the *Criterion* anything of any length until at least October. I should be delighted to write an Editorial paragraph meanwhile, but I quite realise that that would not do. You will by-the-way observe that in a new series of Editorial meditations which I have started,[3] I shall refer frequently to the *Dial* and

1–On 11 Feb., Thayer enquired after TSE's 'promised essay upon recent developments in English prose'. No essay of TSE's appeared in the *Dial* in 1924. His next, 'Literature, Science, and Dogma' came out only in 82: 3 (Mar. 1927).

2–Thayer said he was giving out 'a very few copies' of 'our folio *Living Art*', and wondered if C. might be interested. *Living Art* was a book of reproductions of paintings, sculpture and drawings by contemporary artists selected by Thayer, published by the Ganymed Press in Berlin for *The Dial* in 1923, at $60. It included work by Picasso, Matisse, Vlaminck, and other leading European and American artists. Nicholas Joost notes that 'securing a favorable reception for *Living Art*' was a 'difficult' task. See review by WL in 'Art Chronicle' in C. 3: 9 (Oct. 1924).

3–'A Commentary', the first of TSE's regular editorial statements, appeared as the opening item in C. 2: 7 (Apr. 1924).

to articles which appear in it. That will show you how much we depend upon the *Dial* for intellectual food.

When do you return to Europe?

Yours ever,
T. S. E.

TO *Richard Cobden-Sanderson* CC

30 March 1924 [London]

Dear Cobden-Sanderson,

I am enclosing a third receipt for the transcription of Hugh Walpole's Manuscript.[1] I think that when I sent you Chapters I and II, I enclosed receipts amounting to £1.3.7 so that the total which the *Criterion* owes me is now £1.14.7.

I have had a letter from Douglas Ainslie asking when the Croce article is to be published.[2] This is something which Aldington accepted with my consent and I feel therefore that I ought to read it before replying. Would you mind sending it on to me some time this week?

Yours ever,
[T. S. E.]

TO *Catherine M. Maclean*[3] CC

30 March 1924 [*The Criterion*, London]

Dear Madam,

I must apologise for the delay over your Manuscript ['The Art of Mr James Joyce'] and for the delay in answering your letter of the 12th inst. I have been very much interested in your essay on Mr James Joyce which strikes me as a valuable piece of criticism and it is wholly for that reason that I hesitated over it. But I feel that I had better return it to you, for in any case, it would be impossible for us to make use of it for nearly a year owing to the number of contributions already accepted. I feel therefore

1 – Hugh Walpole, 'The Old Ladies', I and II, in *C.* 2: 7 & 8 (Apr. & July 1924).

2 – Croce's essay on Alfred Vigny. Ainslie's translation of Croce, 'On the Nature of Allegory' appeared in *C.* 3: 11 (Apr. 1925).

3 – Catherine Maclean taught English at University College, Cardiff; later author of *Dorothy and William Wordsworth* (1927) and *Born Under Saturn: a Biography of William Hazlitt* (1943). She never contributed to *C.*

that I should be doing you an injustice by retaining it any longer and I hope that meantime you will succeed in finding another publisher.

Yours faithfully
[T. S. E.]

TO *G. Elliot Smith* CC

31 March 1924 [*The Criterion*, London]

Dear Elliot Smith,

Thank you very much for your letter. The title you have suggested suggests an extremely interesting paper and I shall be delighted to have an essay from you on that subject.[1] Our only qualification is that we do not deal with contemporary economics (or politics), so that I hope that what you have in mind is a treatment of a general or historical character rather than a discussion of contemporary problems. Of course, it is possible that your intention is to throw light on these problems and there would be no objection whatever if your essay does not go too deeply or technically into contentious contemporary questions.

May I hope that we shall receive your contribution about the 1st of May?

I hope that you will be visiting and lecturing at Harvard University as I spent some years there and have many friends and relatives among the faculty.

With many grateful thanks,

sincerely yours,
[T. S. E.]

TO *Jacques Rivière* TS Dr Gerd Schmidt

31 March 1924 *The Criterion*, 17 Thavies Inn

Cher Monsieur,

Je vous fais toutes mes excuses d'avoir négligé de vous remercier pour l'envoi du précieux inédit de Proust[2] et de vous remercier aussi de tout mon coeur de ma part et de celle de la Vicomtesse Rothermere pour tous

1–Smith, 'The Glamour of Gold', in *C.* 3: 11 (Apr. 1925), was an historical account of 'the most potent factor in the history of civilisation' (355).
2–Proust, 'The Death of Albertine', *C.* 2: 8 (July 1924).

les soins que vous avez pris pour nous. Je suis comme vous, toujours débordé de travail.[1] Dans les circonstances où vous vous trouvez, vous avez été infiniment gentil de vous occuper des intérêts du *Criterion*.

Je veux vous avertir que nous voudrions bien recevoir de vous une autre contribution inédite qui égalerait en importance la première.* Je vous signale encore une fois le bruit qu'a fait ici votre article sur Freud.[2]

Avec mes remerciements, je vous assure de mes sentiments les plus cordiaux,

T. S. Eliot

* vers l'automne – *est-ce possible*?[3]

Vivien Eliot TO *Sydney Schiff*

MS BL

30/31 March 1924[4]

9 Clarence Gate Gdns

My Dear Sydney,

I wanted to write to you sooner to thank you for your letter. But the weekend was a strain (our weekends always are) and today I have been to see *King Lear* (the Phoenix) and *that* has nearly done me in.

I am sure you will not give me away, you do not need to persuade me that anonymity is vital;[5] the more so as I have a very strong feeling that this

1 – On 17 Mar., Rivière said he was '*débordé de travail*' ['overwhelmed with work'].

2 – Rivière, 'Notes on a Possible Generalisation of the Theories of Freud', *C.* 1: 4 (July 1923).

3 – *Translation*: Dear Sir, I offer you my most sincere apologies for having neglected to thank you for having sent me the precious unpublished extract from Proust, and also to thank you, both in my name and in that of Viscountess Rothermere, for all you have done for us. Like you, I am always overwhelmed with work, and bearing in mind your situation, I appreciate all the more the great kindness you have shown me in looking after the interests of the *Criterion*.

I should like to let you know that we should be very glad to print another unpublished article by you, which, I have no doubt, would be as important as the first.* I am glad to let you know that your article on Freud has been widely acclaimed here.

With my thanks, please believe me, yours very cordially, T. S. Eliot

* towards autumn – *is that possible*?

4 – Schiff noted: 'answd 2d April'.

5 – A reference to VHE's authorship of an anonymously printed sketch in the latest *C.* This appeared as F. M., 'Letters of the Moment – I', *C.* 2: 6 (Feb. 1924), 220–2: the first of a series of fictionalised sketches she was to contribute at this time under a variety of pseudonyms, 'all beginning with F. M.'. (The others were 'Fanny Marlow' and 'Feiron Morris'.) 'Letters of the Moment – I', dated 'London, February 10th' was very of the moment, and referred to the Phoenix Society production of *The Country Wife* on the 17th. With its opening echoes of TSE ('My hyacinths are bursting clumsily out of their pots . . . And this is the essential spring – spring in winter, spring in London, grey and misty spring, grey twilights, piano organs . . .'), its quotation from Ronsard ('Le temps s'en va, le temps s'en va, madame'), its reference to

is a sort of flash in the pan – that it won't *go on* – that, in fact, it is being done *faute de mieux*. But what is *mieux*? Why life, of course, my dear Sydney. No one will ever persuade me that writing is a substitute for living.

And yet, it makes me very happy that this temporary aberration of mine has given such added proof of your, and Violet's friendship.

We *must*, please, meet before we both go away. The next *Criterion* however is blocking every moment until Saturday, when it MUST go to print. Until then – chaos!

With my love to you both

Ever affectionately

Vivienne

TO *Ada Leverson* CC

1 April 1924 [*The Criterion*, London]

Dear Mrs Leverson,

I am deeply distressed. I am expecting to go to the country on Friday at very short notice indeed and in order to do so I have had to fill up every moment of my time until then with duties and appointments which would otherwise have extended over a fortnight.[1] I am distressed however merely because you feel that it is necessary that you should discuss any details of your contribution with me, *not* because I recognise this is necessary. I must assure you that I am completely confident that anything you write will be a brilliant success and that your misgivings are entirely unnecessary. I cannot flatter myself that there might be anything about which you should need to consult me in advance. Had it been possible, I should certainly have come to see you but only for the pleasure of the visit and for the sake of assuaging your anxiety. But I do not believe that any impartial witness who knew your work would share these anxieties. Do write your contribution just as you would for any other periodical[2] and be assured of

'Volumnia' (a name drawn from *Coriolanus*), its discussion of artists and 'egoists', and its play on Whigs and Tories ('For Whigs rush in where Tories fear to tread'), VHE's piece suggests a strong convergence between husband and wife, even as it strikes a disturbing note of its own: 'Now one begins to beat against the bars of the cage: the typewriter and the telephone, and the sight of one's face in the glass' (220). The image of 'beating against the bars' is taken by VHE from Stravinsky's *The Firebird*.

1–On 31 Mar., Leverson asked for an opportunity to discuss her contribution on 'The Importance' before submitting it.

2–Leverson had been a frequent contributor to periodicals in the 1890s.

my confidence and of my desire to come to see you as soon as I am in London. Indeed I can tell you that any contribution that appears in the *Criterion* must be as the author would wish it to be.

Looking forward to seeing you on my [return].

[Sincerely yours,
T. S. E.]

TO *F. W. Bain* CC

1 April 1924 [London]

My dear Bain,

Thank you very much for your letter. I am very grateful to you for putting me in the way of such a contribution and should like very much to see it. It sounds like one of the sorts of thing that we want. Will you please ask your friend Mr Selby to send the essay to me?[1] I shall try to read it immediately and return it gratefully if we cannot use it.

I had been meaning to write to you to tell you what a brilliant success your Disraeli[2] has been and how grateful we are to you. But I wanted still more to say that we want another article from you this winter and as you have yourself put the temptation into my head, I should like to suggest that an essay by you vindicating either Charles the Second or George the Third would be truly appreciated.[3] Of course this is only a suggestion not a limitation.

Yours ever,
[T. S. E.]

His Mother TO *Henry Eliot* TS Houghton

4 April 1924 [24 Concord Ave]

My dear Henry:

I will write you and use a special delivery stamp in the hope that you will receive this Sunday evening, and can include in your night message your opinion and advice as to whether I shall go to England this summer or concentrate on the possibility of Tom's coming here. Under date of

1 – An essay on 'Bacon and Montaigne' by F. G. Selby. For Selby see TSE's letter of 8 Apr.
2 – 'Disraeli', C. 2: 6 (Feb. 1924).
3 – Bain did not take up TSE's suggestions; he contributed '1789' (C. 3: 9, Oct. 1924).

March 16th[1] he writes: 'Your cable on receipt of my letter leads me to believe that you have finally abandoned the idea of coming to England this spring. I told you in my letter that if you did not come to England, I would come to America and, of course, I will. That is obvious. You will of course realize that I cannot say when that will be, but it will be just as soon as I possibly can.

'Of course I must say that I am disappointed that you have given up all idea of coming to Europe again as I had looked forward to great happiness in having you here with me in the flat. You and I and Marion would have been here with Ellen and Vivian would simply have come up now and then from the country to see you. Of course it was out of the question her being in London the whole summer, as it is essential for her to have six months a year in the country. I realised naturally that you could not go about as you did before and I should not have encouraged you to do so, but at the same time I had hoped that you would be able to do a certain amount of sightseeing and little trips with me. I shall be here in the flat all alone during the summer and shall constantly think of how it would have been to have had you. Anyhow the flat will be here and ready if you should change your mind. *It will seem very lonely without you.* Will write soon about *Savonarola*.' This is the only important part of the letter.

Now I have written Tom in my letter before the last, that if his salary was not continued during his visit here, I would pay it. He had expressed doubt as to whether it would be paid. If I incur the expense of going this summer, I shall not feel as if I ought to pay both salary and expenses. Besides I understand that if I go this summer Tom will not come here, and I feel as if it would be an advantage to him to visit America and if possible, lecture. Can you advise me what you think would be for his best good. If so and you send a night message Sunday, please express an opinion therein.

I shall not mail the Deed until I hear from you, although I am going now to a Notary. I will wait to hear from you before I write to Zeibig, because I want to know about the notes, and I emphatically want you to *do what is best for yourself*.

With love,
Mother

1 – TSE's letter is missing.

TO *St John Hutchinson*[1] PC Texas

4 April 1924 9 Clarence Gate Gdns

Thanks very much. I am in great hopes of leaving London on Saturday for a month. However, if I am prevented, I will come with pleasure. Don't bother about lunch, because possibly I will have had it before I come.

Love to you both.

TO *Richard Cobden-Sanderson* CC

6 April 1924 [London]

Dear Cobden-Sanderson,

I enclose copy of my letter to Hazell, Watson & Viney Ltd, which will explain itself. I have been working up till the last moment arranging the make-up and correcting proof. I am afraid that this number will have to be pretty bulky and there is no help for it.[2] I shall try to ring you up tomorrow in case there are any points to discuss.

I was very sorry to miss your party, although not altogether sorry to have missed such a lamentable race.[3] I wonder how it happened!

Yours in haste,
[T. S. E.]

TO *Messrs. Hazell, Watson & Viney* CC

6 April 1924 [*The Criterion*, London]

Dear Sirs,

Herewith you will find the following enclosures:–

1.	Corrected proof of	'A Commentary'
2.	dto.	'The Old Ladies'
3.	dto.	'The Soul in the Kiss'
4.	Typescript of	'Letters of the Moment II'
5.	Corrected proof of	'George Antheil'
6.	Order of Contents	

1 – St John Hutchinson: see Glossary of Names.

2 – The April number was 140 pages, as against about 110 for the previous two.

3 – The Oxford and Cambridge boat race on 5 Apr.: Cambridge won by 4½ lengths.

You will observe that I wish 'A Commentary' to appear on the cover as inside and without the writer's pseudonym.[1] You need not send Galley proof of 'Letters of the Moment', but I should be glad to see Page proof if you can let me have it.

I may send you two or three more paragraphs to add to 'A Commentary' by express letter to-morrow morning. You need not send Galley proof of these either. I should not send it later than by express to-morrow morning.

If you have not yet sent out Galley proof of 'Lord Chesterfield', 'The Apes of God' and 'On the style of Marcel Proust', I should be glad if you would send one copy of the pull to me.

IMPORTANT. Of the 'Apes of God', please notice that only the Section entitled 'Encyclical Letter' is to be printed in this (April) issue. The other two sections are to be kept set up for July.[2] I should be obliged if you will kindly acknowledge receipt of the enclosures.

Yours faithfully,
[T. S. E.]

PS Please do not alter the punctuation of 'Letters of the Moment' in any way.[3]

TO *Sydney Schiff* — TS Valerie Eliot

6 April 1924 — 2 Milestone Cottages,
Old Fishbourne

My dear Sydney,

I must answer several letters at once. I did not mean to suggest that Hulme's point of view was tentatively held, or that his mind was in a state of suspense on main issues. Nor should I say that his philosophy was

1–TSE's pseudonym 'Crites' did appear at the foot of his 'Commentary'.

2–'Extract from Encyclical Addressed to Daniel Boleyn by Mr Zagreus' appeared in *C.* 2: 7 (Apr. 1924), but 'Lord Osmond's Lenten Party', the third extract, never followed.

3–This is an indication of TSE's close investment in VHE's anonymous contribution, dated '1 April', which included twenty lines of verse (described as 'obsequies' on 'the passing Movement') rescued from the rejected draft of 'The Fire Sermon', beginning 'When sniffing Chloe, with the toast and tea, / Drags back the curtains to disclose the day, / The amorous Fresca stretches, yawns, and gapes, / Aroused from dreams of love in curious shapes' (*C.* 2: 7, 360–1); see *TWL: Facs*, 39. VHE's 'letter of the moment' also refers to 'bawdy Caroline renovations' by Congreve, the 'gently undulating bog of Anglo-Saxon democracy', JMM, Proust, Stravinsky, Cocteau and the literary periodicals of the day, from the 'pink *Dial*' and 'austere *Nouvelle Revue Française*' to the 'lemon yellow *Adelphi*' and 'slim and elegant *Nation*'.

amorphous. It had not been elaborated; perhaps in logical structure it might always have been defective. But I should say that he did set down in essentials the only alternative directions that I can see to the directions of the nineteenth century.[1]

As you know, I have read very little of Proust, but I am so far as I am qualified to speak, of the opinion that he is not a 'classical' writer. Reconstruction of a past period and investigations of the unconscious do not appear to me relevant: they might be attributes of either classic or romantic. Proust appears to me, from what little I know of him, to be far too much a sensationalist. It is I am sure a wonderful commentary on the world that exists and has existed, not the discovery of a new one.

I should have included another section of my essay had I had the time or strength to write it. 'A Commentary' is no more than its name implies.[2]

I agree with what you say about democracy, though I see no necessary connexion between democracy and Christianity. Christianity as I see it is anti-democratic. But you are not to imagine that in this I am the spokesman for any religious sect.

One may be certain of directions although not knowing where they lead.

I have not seen the *Transatlantic Review*. I remember meeting Adams some weeks ago at your house, and had met him once years ago. Probably he thinks that he has written an original poem. He is poor and obscure, and no doubt industrious, and is welcome, like everyone else who is, to what he can borrow from me. I speak from fatigue and indifference.[3]

If I find that I am 'reproached' with having published such a perfectly justifiable article as Wyndham Lewis's 'Apes of God', I fancy that I shall know from what sources the trouble has sprung.[4] Had I been in London, I do not imagine that there would have been such a hue and cry set up about it. In fact, my absence from London at this moment has given the most excellent opportunity to all those people who bear me a grudge for one reason or another, to gather together and vent their spleen in a cause

1–TSE remarked, in 'A Commentary', C. 2: 7 (Apr. 1924), that T. E. Hulme's *Speculations* (1923), 'with all its defects . . . is an outline of work to be done, and not an accomplished philosophy'. Yet it was equally 'the forerunner of a new attitude of mind, which should be the twentieth-century mind, if the twentieth century is to have a mind of its own' (231).

2–This was the first 'Commentary' by TSE. It became an enduring editorial feature until 1939.

3–See John J. Adams, 'Dust' and 'Brainworm', in *Transatlantic Review* 1: 2 (Feb. 1924). 'Dust' combines visions of London and images of the desert: 'Hurrying along the path over Hell Rise, / Because of black clouds gathering and night descending. / Not knowing what loss or ruin might befall me'. Other lines include: 'What does it all mean? Who's there? Lord, it's you! /. . . The dry dust dancing beneath the moon corpse's candle!'

4–'The Apes of God' included much satire of Osbert Sitwell ('Lord Osmund') and others.

which, being impersonal, will seem to them to conceal their personal malice. In short, I have played into the hands of all my London 'friends' and given them an opportunity to display the hostility to the *Criterion* which without exception they have most obviously felt since it first made its appearance. Fortunately I am editing the paper for a woman of the world and a cosmopolitan, who is not interested in petty tribal vendettas, and whose idea of a quarterly is of one which will appeal not only to London but to England, to America and perhaps other countries.

Ever yours aff.
T. S. E.

TO *Ada Leverson* CC

7 April 1924 [*The Criterion*, London]

My dear Mrs Leverson,

I quite agree with you that there is likely to be a revival of the nineties and Vivienne and I are anxious to do all we can to help it forward.[1] So don't worry, but let us co-operate. I think you ought to send things to the *Dial* and to *Vanity Fair* in New York. Can you not write something else about the period soon and I will drop a line to Mr Crowninshield of *Vanity Fair*.

I am so sorry that you have been ill and I only pray that it will not interfere with your work. We both look forward very much to seeing you in May.

Sincerely yours,
[T. S. E.]

TO *John Rodker*[2] CC

7 April 1924 [*The Criterion*, London]

Dear Rodker,

I feel that I owe you an apology for the long delay in the matter of your Note on the Cinema. It has never quite seemed to fit in till now – you know

1 – On 5 Apr., Leverson wrote: 'this – nearly 30 years after the troubles – is the year there will be a great revival & so forth of interest in O. Wilde's work and life. So I long to have this thing done for your *Criterion*.' She reported meeting 'several co-idolators' of TSE's poetry at Edith Sitwell's flat, and hearing a 'mere child quote from *The Waste Land* & *Prufrock*'.
2 – John Rodker: poet and publisher, see Glossary of Names.

how these things are. I am going to be quite frank with you as to what has now happened. I had the type set up for this number. On seeing the proof however, I honestly felt that it was not the best you could do – that in fact it would not do you justice – and that I should ask you to write something else. I cannot feel that you cared for the subject or that you wanted to write this article, and such a feeling in any article always gives a lack of conviction. You must at any rate give me the benefit of frankness in this matter. I should be delighted to receive and to publish an article by you on some subject which you felt to be completely congenial, and an article you really wish to write and wish to appear in the *Criterion*.[1]

Yours ever,
[T. S. E.]

TO *Messrs. Curtis Brown Ltd* CC

7 April 1924 [*The Criterion*, London]

Dear Sirs,

I am returning to you enclosed story by Miss May Sinclair.[2] As you will see from the contents of past numbers of the *Criterion*, I have a very high opinion of Miss Sinclair's work and am anxious to publish it whenever possible. But we have already published two contributions by Miss Sinclair in the present volume of the *Criterion*[3] and as the *Criterion* aims to be a representative publication, it is impossible with only four issues a year, to include any contributor more than twice. It would therefore be impossible for us to publish anything more by Miss Sinclair in the present year and I can only express the hope that she could let us have something for the next volume.[4]

Yours faithfully,
[T. S. E.]

1 – On 8 Apr., Rodker thought he had asked TSE not to print his article, and was 'immensely relieved' it did not appear. He never contributed to C.
2 – On 18 Mar., Curtis Brown submitted May Sinclair's 'The Mahatma Story'.
3 – 'Jones's Karma' in 2: 5 (Oct. 1923) and her poem 'The Grandmother' in 2: 6 (Feb. 1924).
4 – Harold Monro wrote a warm review of her verse novel *The Dark Night*, in C. 3: 9 (Oct. 1924), but she never published in it again.

TO *F. G. Selby*[1] CC

8 April 1924 [*The Criterion*, London]

Dear Sir,

I thank you for sending me your manuscript on Bacon and Montaigne[2] which seems to me extremely interesting. I should like very much to publish it but owing to the fact that our April and July numbers are already filled, I cannot promise to use it before the number of October 15th. Will you let me know whether that suits you or not? I should very much regret the loss.

I am, dear Sir,

yours faithfully,
[T. S. E.]

Please let us publish it in October.

TO *Bertrand Russell* CC

8 April 1924 [London]

Dear Bertie,

I am sending you herewith proof of a little editorial about you which I am publishing in the next *Criterion* and is what, I suppose, most people would call an attack upon you.[3] I do not call it an 'attack' myself but simply a legitimate dispute and I hope you will take it as such; for you must know that I am not a likely person to make anything in the nature of a personal attack upon you. Anyway it is simply a point I am sure you would know that I should disagree with you, but I had rather you saw it before it appeared.[4] I enjoyed very much seeing you that Sunday

1–F. G. Selby, English historical scholar; editor of works by Bacon, including the *Essays* (1894), as well as Burke and other prose writers.

2–'Bacon and Montaigne' appeared in C. 3: 10 (Jan. 1925).

3–'The Honourable Bertrand Russell and Culture' – in 'A Commentary' (by 'Crites'), 2: 7 (Apr. 1924), 232–3 – attacked BR's assertion, in 'A Motley Pantheon' (*Dial* 76: 3, Mar. 1924), that science was the nineteenth century's 'only claim to distinction', and that its 'literary men were mostly second-rate, its philosophers sentimental, its artists inferior to those of earlier times'. On the contrary, said TSE, 'the man of "culture" of the present time is far too easily impressed and overawed by scientific knowledge and ability; the aristocracy of culture has abdicated before the demagogy of science' (233). TSE acknowledged BR as 'a great philosopher' but he deplored the 'vulgar conception of culture' in his article.

4–On 12 June, BR replied, 'There was absolutely nothing in it to vex me'; 'Your opinion is different from mine, but why shouldn't it be? Neither is founded on reason.'

afternoon.[1] I am going away in a day or two to the country but if you are in London when I get back, I hope that I may come to see you again.[2]

Yours always,
[T. S. E.]

TO *Allan Wade*[3] TS Valerie Eliot

8 April 1924 [*The Criterion*, 17 Thavies Inn]

Dear Sir,

As one of the original members of the Phoenix Society, I am writing to you to express my gratitude for the amazingly fine performance of *King Lear*. I am certain that it is the finest performance that the Phoenix Society has ever given; and since you are able to dispose of such fine actors as those who played *King Lear*, I hope that the Society will devote more attention to the less familiar plays of Shakespeare and his contemporaries rather than to Restoration Comedy.[4] I am aware of course that the latter is much more popular, but the performance of *King Lear* was enough in itself to justify the existence of the Society. I suppose that it is too much to hope that a supplementary performance with the same cast may be performed at the end of the season but I have voiced this hope in the April *Criterion*.

Yours faithfully,
T. S. Eliot

1–On 15 Oct. 1923, TSE had invited BR to 'come to tea' the following Saturday.
2–BR was lecturing in the USA from 1 Apr. to the end of May.
3–Allan Wade (1881–1954), English actor, manager and producer, founded the Phoenix Society and directed nearly all of its productions.
4–'F. M.', in 'Letters of the Moment – II', made great play with the vogue for Restoration Comedy represented by the Phoenix productions. Since their foundation, they had revived Dryden's *Marriage à la Mode* and *All For Love*, Wycherley's *The Country Wife* and Congreve's *Love for Love*. Wade replied to TSE (9 Apr.): 'I agree with you in thinking that there is much more useful work to be done in what for the sake of convenience one calls Elizabethan drama than in Restoration. At present, as you say, Restoration drama seems to be more popular . . . The supply of first rate Restoration comedy is – *pace* my friend & colleague Montague Summers – strictly a limited one, & unless our audience are prepared to support a good deal of experimental work we may find ourselves at the end of our tether far sooner than need be.'

TO *Duncan Yarrow*[1] CC

8 April 1924 [*The Criterion*, London]

Dear Sir,

Some time ago I wrote to express my appreciation of your magnificent performance of *Edward II*,[2] and I am now writing to tell you that your performance of Edgar in *King Lear* seemed to me equally fine.[3] I mean that I do not think that the part – and it seems to me a very difficult part – could have been better done. The play will remain in my memory as the finest performance in the history of the Society. I have written a short notice – very much limited by space for the next number of the *Criterion*.

Yours faithfully,
[T. S. E.]

TO *Hubert Carter*[4] CC

8 April 1924 [London]

Dear Sir,

I am taking the first opportunity which I have had to write to express my very great admiration for your performance as Lear, and I hope that the appreciation of a private individual who has attended the Phoenix Society performances since the formation of the Society will not be unwelcome. The performance was in my opinion much the finest that the Phoenix has ever given, and this is due chiefly to the prodigious vigour and subtlety with which you acted your part. I am mentioning the performance in the next number of the *Criterion* but space has made more than a very brief mention impossible. I hardly think that a finer representation of the title-role could be given.

Yours faithfully,
[T. S. E.]

1–Duncan Yarrow (b.1884): English actor.
2–Marlowe's *Edward II* was directed by Allan Wade for the Phoenix Society at the Regent's Theatre, 18–19 Nov. 1923. TSE's letter of congratulation to Yarrow for his performance as the king is missing, but it was acknowledged with thanks on 7 Dec. 1923.
3–In 'A Commentary' TSE commended the success of Yarrow as 'Edgar (a most difficult role)'.
4–Hubert Carter (1869–1934): English actor, who had played the title role in the Phoenix production of *King Lear*.

TO *Frank Cellier*[1] CC

8 April 1924 [London]

Dear Sir,

I am writing to express my appreciation of what seemed to me a really perfect interpretation of the role which you took in *King Lear*. It is difficult to believe that the play was not rehearsed for a very long time, and in any case it is obvious that your performance of the part of Gloucester was prepared with very great care. I hope it will not be unwelcome to you to receive a word of praise and admiration from one of the original subscribers to the Phoenix Society.

Yours faithfully,
[T. S. E.]

TO *F. S. Flint* TS Texas

8 April 1924 *The Criterion*, 17 Thavies Inn

Dear Flint,

I am looking forward to seeing you tomorrow but I shall be in a great hurry and in any case I should have preferred to write to you about this. As Richard has given up his criticism of French periodicals along with his position,[2] there is no one in London as competent to deal with this criticism as yourself. Of course, I consider the French reviews the most important part of the foreign reviews and it is really a question of finding someone competent to give a résumé of the activity of the French mind over three months. French reviews are of course more numerous than the others and the space devoted to France must be longer than that devoted to other nations. If you find the work too much for you, I really hope you will consider taking on the French and dropping the others, but I hasten to assure you that I much prefer that you continue to do what you have been doing as well.[3] Please think this over and let me know if you agree.

1–Frank Cellier (1884–1949): English actor, who played the part of Kent. TSE confused Cellier with Frank Cochrane, who played Gloucester. In his 'Commentary' TSE praised 'Frank Cochrane and Frank Cellier as Gloucester and Kent'.

2–Since RA's resignation, there had been no notes on French reviews in C. 2: 6 & 7 (Feb. & Apr. 1924).

3–Flint reported on German periodicals in C. 1: 4, on Spanish and Italian ones in C. 2: 5, on Danish and Italian in 2: 6 and 2: 7. In 2: 8 (July 1924), he would provide notes on 'an accumulation of six months' of French periodicals in addition to Italian and Danish ones.

In any case you cannot deny that you are the one person marked out for this, and that you will be carrying on the work in which you were a pioneer before the war; and remember that you will be able to say what you damned well please about Paul Morand without any objections from me.[1]

Yours ever,
T. S. Eliot

TO *Conrad Aiken*[2]

TS Huntington

8 April 1924 — *The Criterion*, 9 Clarence Gate Gdns

Dear Conrad,

The appearance in the *Dial* of your admirable essay on Emily Dickinson[3] has reminded me of our loss of this contribution and of the fact that I have not written to you. My wife only recovered from a severe attack of influenza in time for us to put all our energies into preparing the April *Criterion* which has now gone to press, but will be, I am sorry to say, a week or so late. Meantime I have been wondering how you are and whether you have been in London. I am very sorry indeed that we could not use your essay within the time limit which you set. I am now however advertising to *you* a vacancy in October. Will you promise me a critical essay for that number? I think we may leave the subject to you. In spite of your increasing laziness I think that you might be able to do me this kindness.[4]

1–Paul Morand (1888–1976): French diplomat, novelist, playwright and poet; author of *Ouvert la Nuit* (1922) and *Fermé la Nuit* (1923). During WW2 he was to be a prominent collaborator. TSE had already encouraged his wife to say what she 'damned well please' about Paul Morand in her pseudonymous 'Letters of the Moment – II'. In mischievous mood, VHE undertakes to parody one of the regular features of *C.*, the notes on the contents of other periodicals, domestic and foreign – 'the monthlies, weeklies, the quarterly reviews, set out in rows like a parterre'. While purporting to flip through the *Nouvelle Revue Française*, the *London Mercury*, the *Adelphi*, and so on, she chances upon an article, a 'Paris Letter' by Paul Morand, in the latest issue of the *Dial* (Mar. 1924, 265–73), and proceeds to burlesque the self-importance of Morand's address to the Americans: 'A postiche style, this, not too difficult to imitate . . . Mark my words well, we shall soon see plenty of little Paul Morands and little Pauline Morands too, scribbling for their suppers. And then, our Monsieur Paul, citizen of Paris in spite of all, with perfect facility will change his style, and leave them all *dans la purée*.'

2–Conrad Aiken: see Glossary of Names.

3–'Emily Dickinson', *Dial* 76: 4 (Apr. 1924); reprinted in Aiken's *Collected Criticism* (1968).

4–On 22 Apr., Aiken contested the charge of 'laziness', citing a book of short stories, a 2,000-line poem and a novel. He had 'nothing on hand or in mind' for Oct. He later wrote reviews of Osbert Sitwell and Gilbert Seldes, and a poem 'Psychomachia', for *C.* 3: 9 (Oct. 1924).

Do let me know also how you are and what your plans are for the summer. I shall be going away for a short time but anything addressed to me here is certain to reach me.

Yours ever,
Tom

TO *Wyndham Lewis* TS Cornell

8 April 1924 *The Criterion*, 17 Thavies Inn

Dear Lewis,

I presume that you received your proof direct this morning as I received one copy. If you have not already returned it, will you please do so at once direct to Messrs. Hazell, Watson & Viney Ltd., Printers, Aylesbury, Bucks. I have read over the Encyclical once more[1] and am more amazed at it than ever. There is one phrase which I think mars the effect because it is superfluous and weakens the effect. I think it is much better to leave the Bloomsbury accent at 'a queer exaggeration of speech' and omit the parenthesis 'bringing to one's mind the sounds associated with spasms of a rough Channel passage' which seems to me to cheapen it.[2]

I presume that you have deleted the word 'Bloomsbury' and altered the name 'Osmund'.[3]

Yours ever,
T. S. E.

<I am going to country will send my address.>

1 – 'Extract from Encyclical Addressed to Daniel Boleyn by Mr Zagreus'.

2 – The passage was thus amended to read: 'It was this rather scandalous shabbiness, and a queer exaggeration of speech, that cut them off from the outside world' (*C.* 2: 7, 308).

3 – In an undated letter to TSE, WL allowed: 'the name Stillwell (if too suggestive of certain people) could be altered to anything you like', and '"Bloomsbury" (only occurring once) could be deleted'. However, he also conceded in a postscript: 'I . . . think that in any case another name, for the purposes of this extract, had better be given to Lord Osmund.' Neither 'Osmund' (i.e., Osbert Sitwell) nor 'Bloomsbury' figure in the version published in *C.* Lewis re-introduced 'Osmund' and 'Bloomsbury' when publishing *The Apes of God* as a novel in 1930. When the Sitwells and the Schiffs did expostulate about WL's piece, he defended himself in another undated letter to TSE; 'There was no question about the "cap fitting" – they put it on and rushed out into the street exclaiming. Schiff this morning writes me that I shall be "molested" in consequence of my article by those I have "castigated" . . . The article is a very general statement, and (except for the bare truth of what it says) there is no excuse for the threatening noises that these outraged gentlemen have filled the air with. So tender with their own sweet selves, the least speck of dust blown they think purposely their way is, to our spoilt "children", a terrible offence. I hope they have not been disturbing you too much during your much-needed holiday?'

TO *Herbert Read* CC

9 April 1924 [*The Criterion*, London]

Dear Read,

I return herewith the letter from the *Modern Quarterly*.[1] I shall be very grateful if you will deal with it.

After the *Criterion* is out, I will ask Cobden-Sanderson to see about the exchanges. As the number of exchange copies must be kept down within reasonable limits, I think that we ought to select our exchanges with the whole world in view, not merely one country or language by itself, so I suggest that at our next fortnightly luncheon[2] I should produce a list of our present exchanges and then that we should all decide in committee what are the most important to add and how many new exchanges can be allocated to each country. I may write to you again before our next meeting. It is pleasant I think to have these luncheons even for people like you and myself whose time is so limited.

Yours ever,
[T. S. E.]

TO *Messrs. Hazell, Watson & Viney* CC

9 April 1924 [*The Criterion*, London]

For the attention of Mr Jowatt
Dear Sirs,

I hereby confirm our telephone conversation of this afternoon in which we arranged that you should get the bound copies of the April *Criterion* to the hands of Mr Cobden-Sanderson by Thursday morning the 17th inst. at the latest and if possible on Wednesday, the 16th inst.; and I confirm our arrangement that you should work overtime to the extent necessary to make this possible; and our arrangement that you should send me the page

1–On 10 Mar., HR listed the US periodicals with which they exchanged – *The Literary Review*, *The Dial*, *The Century*, *The Yale* and *The Modern Quarterly* – as well as other possible ones, including *North American Review*, *Scribner's* and *Harper's*.

2–HR later recorded: 'in order to preserve a regular contact, it was agreed that we should meet for lunch one day every week in South Kensington, and for the next seven years we forgathered at a pub called The Grove in Beauchamp Place. The Grove became the Mermaid Tavern to which, week by week (I think it was every Thursday), came not only some of the regular contributors to *The Criterion*, but also any sympathizing critics or poets from abroad' ('T.S.E. – A Memoir', in *T. S. Eliot: The Man and his Work*, ed. Allen Tate, 1966, 24).

proofs as printed and that I should make any alterations necessary by telephone to you on the day of receipt. It is understood that you will not delay paging on account of any corrected proof not yet received, and that you should take every possible means of accelerating production to the date named or even earlier if possible. I beg to express my obligation and appreciation of your courtesy and attention.

Yours faithfully,
[T. S. E.]

PS Referring to your letter of the 8th inst., please note that in my editorial the name is spelt *Athene Seyler*.[1]

TO *Richard Cobden-Sanderson* CC

9 April 1924 [*The Criterion*, 17 Thavies Inn]

Dear Cobden-Sanderson,

I enclose a carbon copy of a letter which I have posted to-night to Hazell Viney and Watson. I had a letter from them this morning saying that they could not get the copies to you much before the 25th. On account of the postponement of the January number I was particularly anxious that the April number should be out as near the time as possible, so I telephoned to Aylesbury and used every means to induce them to hurry it up. I told them that Lady Rothermere was very annoyed at the postponement of the January number and that if this number was delayed for Easter, she would be very likely to stop the *Criterion* altogether.

I hope that it will not be inconvenient to you to have the copies in on Wednesday or Thursday, but I do feel that it is very important to get this number out by Easter. I suppose that if you get the copies by the time agreed, the Inland subscribers will be able to receive them by Saturday morning. It is really a great pity that I could not have the number ready so as to be on sale before Good Friday, because of the Easter holidays. The delay is wholly due to the difficulties under which I work myself, and I take full responsibility for any expense incurred in hastening delivery.

I tried to ring you up today after telephoning to Aylesbury but could not get through.

1–TSE described Athene Seyler (1889–1990), who featured in the Phoenix Society production of Wycherley's *The Country Wife*, as 'probably the finest living actress of comedy in England'; 'She played the part of Lady Fidget with a cold ferocity, a pure and undefiled detachment which makes her worthy to rank in that supreme class which includes Marie Lloyd and Nellie Wallace' (C. 2: 7 [Apr. 1924], 234).

About the French reviews, I have arranged with Flint to do these, so will you post on to him all that come in. At your leisure, say after the *Criterion* is out, I should very much like to have a list of all periodicals with which we exchange.

I take it that there is no reason for altering the review list and the advertising list for this number? I am keen about the advertising scheme which you proposed. I am still hoping that we may be able to arrange for American distribution in some regular way; several people in the States have been complaining to me about the difficulty of getting copies.

Yours ever,
[T. S. E.]

TO *Dr K. B. Martin*[1] CC

9 April 1924 9 Clarence Gate Gdns

Dear Dr Martin

I am very much obliged to you for answering my wire and very much relieved to be assured that you are actually coming to London.

I shall be very grateful if you will let me know for how long a period you propose to be in London, and also what your London address will be. I understand that you will be staying at Lady Margaret Levett's.[2] It has been quite out of the question for me to get over to Germany this winter and I am afraid that it will be quite impossible next autumn and winter as well, and for this reason your visit to London is of the greatest importance to my wife and myself. May I ask you to be so kind as to consider how practically impossible it is to get abroad, and ask you to give as much time as you possibly can while you are in London to seeing my wife and myself? I am anxious to see you separately.

I quite agree with your suggestion about my seeing you first but that of course was in the circumstances even more impossible to carry out than for me simply to have brought my wife to Germany.

I am anxious to see you as often as possible while you are in London.[3]

With very grateful thanks for all your kindness.

Yours very truly
[T. S. E.]

1 – Dr Karl Bernhard Martin: see Glossary of Names.

2 – Martin, in reply (13 Apr.), thanked TSE for his 'X-mas present'; he would be staying at Mr Levett's house, 6 Eaton Square, for most of May.

3 – Martin said the length of his stay would give the Eliots 'a chance': he would try 'to see both as often as possible'.

TO *His Mother*[1] TS Houghton

[Received 17 April 1924] [London]

Dearest Mother:

The *Criterion* has this minute gone to press and I am so tired that I want to lie down and sleep for a year.

Today I received your two letters dated 25 and 23 March.[2] Thank you very much.

I enclose in this letter two copies of press cuttings which have been sent me from America. As one concerns Cousin Charles[3] and the other concerns your youngest son,[4] I am in hopes that they may have interest for you.

In a few days Vivien and I will go to the country for three weeks to the cottage at Fishbourne. Please continue, however, to write to this address.

Vivien is much better. She has been writing since Christmas and although her output is small she has met with extraordinary success. There is no doubt whatever that she has talent. She should have been encouraged to write years ago. She has already a very exceptional and individual style.

Please oblige me by keeping an *open mind* with regard to coming to London this summer. There is no need for you to make long and elaborate preparations. There is no need for you to give me long warning. I shall be here all the summer probably alone. So keep an *open mind*.[5]

1–This letter, transcribed within a letter from CCE to HWE of 17 Apr., was probably written over the weekend of 11–12 Apr., since TSE went to Fishbourne on Monday 13th.

2–On 23 Mar., CCE said she thought the last C. was 'one of the best', especially TSE's article on 'Elizabethan Dramatists'; and she was looking forward to 'the book'. She thought his style had 'improved', and noted he had 'given up parentheses'.

3–President Charles William Eliot of Harvard University, whose ninetieth birthday was celebrated at Harvard on 20 Mar. 1924. See *Charles William Eliot: The Man and his Beliefs, with a Biographical Study by President Neilson* (1926).

4–'T. S. Eliot in a Nutshell', *New York Herald* (Mar. 1924), reported that TSE was 'a man of abundant health and great vigor'.

5–Having transcribed TSE's letter, CCE told HWE: 'I have sent an immediate answer . . . that with increasing age I had become timid about going abroad with Marian, and that I had written you I had rather pay your passage and be away a month with you than a longer time with Marian . . . Tom's letter did not sound as though he expected me very much . . . I do not think he would have much time to give me. Vivien would have to be his first thought and I should be much alone. It does not look to me very attractive – I think I should be lonely.'

TO *C. K. Scott Moncrieff* CC

13 April 1924 [9 Clarence Gate Gdns]

Dear Scott Moncrieff,

Thank you for your letter. I am delighted to hear that you think so well of the selection which Rivière sent me; such a contribution will certainly be the making of our next issue, but I assure you that it would have failed to produce its full effect upon the public, had we not been so happy as to have you to translate it. I am sorry to feel that it will divert you from your other work[1] and hope very earnestly that you can let us have it by the 1st of June at the very latest. I am anxious to bring out the July issue on July 1st.

Yours ever,
[T. S. E.]

TO *Stephen Gaselee* CC

13 April 1924 [9 Clarence Gate Gdns]

Dear Mr Gaselee,

I owe you an apology, although in the circumstances I could not have done otherwise than I have done. There was considerable delay in getting to press the number of the *Criterion* which will be out next week and at the last moment it was necessary to decide what contributions should be postponed to the following issue. Before proofs of your article[2] were ready, I telephoned to your house and was informed that you were leaving Madeira in a few days, that the last post to catch you was that leaving the same night, and that thereafter you would be inaccessible until the 14th. I therefore took it upon myself to correct your proofs, and hope that you will not find many considerable errors. But my classical learning is of course much more restricted than yours and I am afraid also that I corrected your proof in great haste and I hope you will let me know of any errors which you remark.[3] A copy should reach you by the middle of next week.

1 – Scott Moncrieff was 'still ploughing through *Guermantes* II', though 'getting rather tired of the Guermantes dinner party'.
2 – 'The Soul in the Kiss', C. 2: 7 (Apr. 1924), 349–59.
3 – The essay traced the 'pretty conceit' that kisses join 'souls', all the way from the Greek anthology to John Galsworthy, and involved extensive quotation from Greek and Latin.

With very many thanks for so interesting an essay, I am,

Yours faithfully,

[T. S. E.]

TO *Lady Rothermere* CC

13 April 1924 9 Clarence Gate Gdns

Dear Lady Rothermere,

One copy of the April number will be sent to you at Cap d'Ail and the rest to Paris. The printers had assured me that the April number would be ready by the 16th, and I have been constantly in telephone conversation with them at Aylesbury to hurry the printing forward and give them every assistance; but you will see from the enclosed letter from Cobden-Sanderson that they now refuse to promise it before the 23rd. It appears that they do no work over the Easter holidays. This is extremely annoying to me, as I had done a great deal of work in order to make it possible to get this number out punctually; and I have given more time to it than to any previous number, even the last one.

I am sorry that you found the last number so dull,[1] as I had received numerous assurances that it was the best we have so far produced. I cannot say that the contributions from May Sinclair and J. M. Robertson were exciting, and I had no illusions about them at the time.[2] In my opinion what the *Criterion* now needs is chiefly a more distinct standpoint and a more topical quality; and you will see from the April number that I have made several innovations with this in view. Of course, it is much more difficult in a quarterly than in a monthly as the topics have to remain interesting for three months instead of one. But in so far as I can find the people to do it, I want to work in periodical comment on contemporary life, thought and manners, of a lighter and more satirical tone.[3]

It is particularly important to get exactly the right people from Paris, and that implies also getting them at the right moment, before they are stale here, and before they are stale in America – which is equally important. Cocteau[4] would have come just at the right moment; and had

1 – On 26 Mar., Lady Rothermere commented on 'the *severely* serious tone' of C.

2 – Sinclair, 'The Grandmother', and J. M. Robertson, 'The Evolution of English Blank Verse', in 2: 6 (Feb. 1924).

3 – This must refer to WL's contributions and the two 'Letters of the Moment' by 'F. M.' (VHE).

4 – Lady Rothermere had enclosed a note from Cocteau of 16 Mar., asking forgiveness for not doing anything: 'Pour vous, pour Eliot que ne ferai-je? Pardonnez moi. C'est une passe terrible

he behaved properly and done what he promised to do, I had in mind to offer him a regular chronique. It is as much his loss as ours, because there is not yet any other paper in England which is likely to want him, and our public would have given him a better hearing than any. But Morand I know is stale. He has already been taken up by the *Dial* and *Vogue*,[1] and that means that he would do us no good. I have watched him pretty carefully, and I think that he has nothing fresh to give. Stories of his are being sent about by press agencies, and I have refused several which arrived in that way. His things would annoy the larger and more dependable part of our English readers; and the small *coterie* who pretend to keep in touch with French literature would only despise us for printing him so late. In a short time he will be out of date, and we shall be better thought of for not having published him at all.

I am trying to find out whether Max Jacob[2] writes anything that might be translated into English. I have several other ideas for illuminating our sombre pages.

I am keeping Gleize's essay[3] to read in the country. I am sorry that I have been much too busy to interview the editor of *The Daily Express*,[4] and must go to the country for several weeks rest.

I hope that you will be coming to London in May or June, or at least to Paris: even one meeting is more useful than a great many letters.

Yours very sincerely,
[T. S. E.]

—

que je traverse' ['For you, for Eliot, what will I not do? Forgive me. It is a terrible time I'm going through']. Cocteau was '*impossible*, being *perfectly fit now* & enjoying himself down here [in the South of France]', she said.

1–See Morand's 'Paris Letter', *Dial* 75: 2, 5, 6 (Aug., Nov., Dec. 1923); 76: 3 (Mar. 1924).

2–Max Jacob (1876–1944): avant-garde poet and painter; author of *Le cornet à dés* (1917) and *Le laboratoire central* (1921). Jewish by birth, he converted to Catholicism in 1915, became a recluse in 1921, and perished in the concentration camp of Drancy. He never featured in C.

3–Unidentified essay. Albert Gleize (1881–1953) was a Cubist painter; author of *Le cubisme et les moyens de le comprendre* (1920).

4–Lady Rothermere enclosed a letter of 19 Mar. from Lord Beaverbrook, proprietor of the *Daily Express*: 'Will you ask Mr Eliot to go and see Blumenfeld at the *Daily Express* office? I have spoken to Blumenfeld about him.'

TO *Cecil Scott* CC

13 April 1924 [*The Criterion*, London]

Dear Mr Scott,

I was very glad to hear from you but have been so busy with the *Criterion* that I have had no time to reply. I was disappointed that you could not come to see me on your way through London, because I am going to the country tomorrow and probably shall not be back in London until some time in May. Nevertheless, when you do pass through London please drop me a line as there is a chance of my being here. And if we are unable to meet then, I shall still count upon seeing you when you come down in June.[1]

Meanwhile I hope that you will consider our acquaintance solid enough ground for letting me see the things that you are writing, and anything else that you may write.[2] In writing on the criticism of Baudelaire you have chosen a subject in which I am very much interested.[3] Do you know also 'Mon coeur mis à nu'?[4] There is a good book or at least a good essay to be written on the importance of Baudelaire for English poetry; and so far as I know there is nothing really good written about him in English.

I am also waiting for an opportunity to talk about your essay on Rimbaud with you.

Do not fail to let me know when you pass through London and write to me and do keep me in touch with your work in any case.

Sincerely yours,
[T. S. E.]

1–TSE's kind remarks speak to Scott's self-deprecation (25 Mar.): 'I want to renew our acquaintance very much, though there is nothing I can tell you which would be worth a discussion . . . I have a clumsy mind and a tremendous sincerity, and that combination is hopeless for the dialogic style.'

2–Scott said (25 Mar.) that he was working on a poem – 'and an article on the criticism of Baudelaire – L'Art Romantique and the Curiosités Esthetiques'.

3–TSE had published 'The Lesson of Baudelaire' in *Tyro* 1 (Spring 1921), and quoted from Baudelaire's writings on caricature in the 'London Letter', *Dial* 70: 6 (June 1921).

4–'My heart laid bare': from Baudelaire's *Intimate Journals*. Introducing Christopher Isherwood's translation of these in 1930, TSE called them 'indispensable for any student of his poetry', and noted that in 'Mon coeur mis à nu' Baudelaire had 'a great deal to say about the love of man and woman' and understood that seeing 'the sexual act as evil is more dignified, less boring than as the natural, "life-giving", cheery automatism of the modern world' (*SE*, 419–30).

TO *Douglas Ainslie* CC

13 April 1924 [London]

Dear Mr Ainslie,

I must apologize for the delay in answering your letter of the 21st March. I was overwhelmed with work and had to ask Mr Cobden-Sanderson to send me Croce's essay which Mr Aldington had chosen and which I had never read. I have finally managed to read it. As this matter had been left in Mr Aldington's hands, I am afraid that I had not appreciated the fact that the essay was to be part of a volume to appear in the near future; and I should be very glad if you would let me know how soon you wish the book to appear, because it will be impossible, owing to the number of contributions previously ordered and accepted, to print this essay before the October number.[1]

I hope you will not be offended if I say frankly that the essay does not interest me nearly as much as the essay on Heine which you previously sent and which I read. Of course this is a point of delicacy, as I am aware that Mr Aldington selected this essay from several others and I have no claim upon your patience or time. But as Mr Aldington has now for private reasons resigned from the *Criterion*, I feel that it is my duty to depend upon my own opinion; and if it is still possible I should very much like to see the Heine again and perhaps other essays. I put this quite frankly to you as a favour and hope that you will consider it as a request made in all courtesy and deference.

Sincerely yours,
[T. S. E.]

TO *Mrs S. A. Middleton* CC

14 April 1924 [*The Criterion*, London]

Dear Mrs Middleton,

I am extremely sorry for the repeated delay in answering your letter, but when you wrote I was just preparing the *Criterion* for press and have had to sacrifice everything to that up to the present moment. Since I last corresponded with you I have had your son very much in my mind. I know

1–On 21 Mar., Ainslie said he wanted his translation of Croce's article on Alfred de Vigny to appear prior to the publication of Croce's *European Literature in the Nineteenth Century*, trans. Ainslie (1924). RA had promised publication 'early in 1924'.

that it will be difficult for you to believe me if I told you the kind of life I lead. My history since this time last year is simply a record of one perpetual struggle with serious illness, expense far beyond my means and overwhelming work, done against every kind of obstacle and vicissitude. The *Criterion* itself has been torturingly uphill work, as one must expect with a purely literary quarterly which offers no political or other excitement and panders to no common taste and makes no bid for popularity. During the past winter I have run it myself for a considerable time without other help except a shorthand typist.

I have had no Spanish contributions whatever since that you translated for us;[1] otherwise I should assuredly have sent such contributions to you.

I am really interested to know to what point your son has arrived in the course of self training which I suggested, and which I think is very essential for him, and what he has been doing. I am just leaving for the country for about four weeks – my only holiday in the year. If your son cares to come down for a couple of days, any time after Easter week, to a very small cottage near Chichester, both I and my wife should be pleased to see him. He could choose his own date after that week. Not only I but my wife also have constantly thought of him and felt anxious about him, and I hope that you will convey to him our expression of interest.

If he does not come to see me in the country, I will allow nothing to prevent my seeing him within reasonable time after my return; I would certainly see him by the first of June.

With all best wishes,

Sincerely yours,
[T. S. E.]

Country address:- Milestone Cottages, Old Fishbourne, nr Chichester, Sussex

TO *Ada Leverson* CC

17 April 1924 [*The Criterion*, London]

Dear Mrs Leverson,

Thank you for your letter and for letting me know your address. I have been in the country for the last week and have had no letters forwarded and only came up last night, so that I did not get your letter until I came back. Vivienne has been here the whole time as she had a bad attack of

1–Marichalar, 'Contemporary Spanish Literature', C. 1: 3 (1923).

colitis and was too ill to come with me, but I am hoping that she will be well enough to come down with me on Saturday morning. I am so sorry to hear that you have been ill again and hope that this fine weather will set you right. It is most exciting to hear that you will include some unpublished letters in your Oscar Wilde.[1] I am looking forward keenly to the pleasure of reading it.

Yours always sincerely,
[T. S. E.]

TO *Jacques Rivière* CC

17 April 1924 [London]

Mon cher Rivière,

Dans quelques jours de repos à la campagne, je viens de lire votre article dans l'avant-dernier numéro de la *Nouvelle Revue Française* et je dois vous féliciter sur une belle exposition d'une idée d'une haute importance.[2] Vous avez posé un problème et vous avez énoncé un dogme très voisin à mon propre point de vue et j'ai l'intention de citer votre article dans quelque chose que je vais écrire pour attaquer les idées de Middleton Murry qui maintient une théorie opposée.[3]

J'espère que vous nous enverrez pendant l'été un article d'une égale importance. Je ressens même un peu de chagrin en sachant que l'article en question est inutilisable pour le *Criterion*, puisque à mon avis la philosophie que vous détruisez est même plus répandue en Angleterre qu'en France.

J'ai aussi admiré un bel article de Ramón Fernandez.[4]

1–'The Last First Night' (*NC* 4: 1, Jan. 1926) did not include any new Wilde letters.
2–Rivière, 'La crise du concept de littérature' [The Crisis of the Concept of Literature], *NRF* 11: 125 (1 Feb. 1924). Responding to Marcel Arland's article on a new 'Mal du siècle', Rivière attacked the legacy of the Romantic idea of the literary act as religious, or 'une sorte de tentative sur l'absolu' [a sort of attempt at the absolute]. He identifies this in the work of the Dadaists and Surrealists ('André Breton et ses amis'), the paintings of de Chirico, photos of Man Ray and post-Dadaist poetry ('toute la poésie post-dadaïste'). Rivière insisted instead on the 'strong limits' of literature, not confounding our unconscious with revelation, and not subordinating literature to transcendental ends ('des fins transcendantes').
3–In 'A Commentary' (*C.* 2: 8, July 1924), TSE attacked 'the alarming tendency in our time for literary criticism to be something else'. Citing JMM among other offenders, he observed: 'This particular heresy has lately been dealt with very ably by Monsieur Jacques Rivière in the *Nouvelle Revue Française* on the Crisis of the Concept of Literature' (373).
4–Ramón Fernandez, 'La garantie des sentiments et les intermittences du coeur', *NRF* 11: 132 (1 Apr.).

Est-ce loisible de demander si vous aurez une note sur *The Waste Land* ou non?[1]

Cordialement,
Votre
[T. S. E.][2]

TO *Charles Whibley* CC

17 April 1924 [London]

My dear Whibley,

I was very glad to get your kind letter although it reminded me that I have been waiting for about a fortnight for an opportunity to write to you. But what with the final work on the *Criterion* which was particularly heavy for this number, and what with preparations for removal to my country cottage, I have had not a moment to spare.

I am very happy to hear that you have been out of pain for so long and I hope that the weather will favour you. At any rate the cessation for so long is a very favourable omen and will give you greater strength to resist another attack if it comes. But these maladies often leave as suddenly and irrationally as they come and I hope that yours has left you for good.

I meant to write to you immediately after our dinner which I enjoyed so much.[3] For one thing I wanted to explain that I was really much keener about the London University than I gave you any hint of. If I did not express all the interest – and all the gratitude – which I felt, it was because I have habituated myself to regard these things as only remote possibilities

1 – There was no mention of *TWL* in *NRF* in 1924.

2 – *Translation*: My dear Sir, I have made use of my brief period of rest in the country to read the article which you published in the *Nouvelle Revue Française* of two months ago and I must congratulate you on your exposition of a most important idea. You have asked questions and you have expounded a point of view which is, in fact, extremely close to mine; so much so that I intend to quote your article in a paper in which I propose to attack the ideas of Middleton Murry, who upholds views opposed to mine.

I hope that during the summer you will send us an article of the same importance as this one. As, in my opinion, the philosophy which you seek to destroy is even more widespread in England than in France, I can't help feeling rather sad at the thought that the article in question cannot be used for the *Criterion*.

I also much admired an excellent article by Ramón Fernandez.

I wonder if I could ask you whether or not you hope to be able to say something about *The Waste Land*?

Cordially yours, [T. S. E.]

3 – On 15 Apr., CW recalled their 'very pleasant dinner at Kettner's'.

for myself. It is a movement of self-protection against disappointment, but please know that I am very grateful to you and that I should be overjoyed if anything came of it. Will you let me know if anything can be done or if I can do anything myself?

Also, I should like very much to join the Travellers Club.

The printers of the *Criterion* have disappointed me in not getting it out before Easter, but you will have your copy by the middle of next week. I have asked that a copy should be sent to Charles Strachey[1] as I hoped it might interest him. Of course, he will be glad to have your essay. I read it in the proof and admired it immensely.

I shall of course be very grateful for any criticisms you may care to make on any and as many of the contributions as interest you at all. I am trying now to give the thing a little more point, and I think you will see that several of the contributions are meant to fit in with each other. As for Middleton Murry, I shall have to write a short rejoinder to this apostle of suburban free thought.

Yours ever affectionately,
[T. S. E.]

TO *Ramón Fernandez*[2] CC

17 April 1924 [London]

Monsieur,

J'ai été extrêmement frappé par votre article dans le dernier numéro de la *Nouvelle Revue Française*[3] et je vous écris pour demander si vous ferez l'honneur de donner au *Criterion* une contribution inédite. Je vous ferai parvenir un numéro spécimen, et je vous fais remarquer que nous avons déjà publié des choses par plusieurs autres collaborateurs à la *Nouvelle Revue Française*, notamment Monsieur Jacques Rivière.

Malheureusement nous ne pouvons pas publier des choses qui ont déjà paru en France, sauf en cas exceptionnel; c'est que la plupart de nos lecteurs sont bien au courant de la littérature périodique de Paris.

1 – Sir Charles Strachey (1862–1942), brother of Lytton Strachey, was a diplomat; editor of *The Letters of the Earl of Chesterfield to his Son* (reprinted 1924).

2 – Mexican by birth but educated in France, Ramón Fernandez (1894–1944) was philosopher, essayist, and novelist; a regular contributor to *NRF*, 1923–43. His later publications include *Messages* (1926), *De la personnalité* (1928), and *L'homme est-il humain?* (1936). In the mid-1930s, he was a fierce anti-fascist, but during WW2 he became a collaborator.

3 – 'La garantie des sentiments et les intermittences du coeur', *NRF* 11: 132 (1 Apr.).

L'honoraire est £10 les 5000 mots, moins les frais de traduction pour les contributions reçues en langues étrangères; et une contribution quelconque ne doit pas par beaucoup dépasser cet étendue.

Puis-je vous proposer de me suggérer quelques sujets sur lesquels vous voulez écrire? C'est évident que vous connaissez très bien la littérature anglaise et vous seriez libre de choisir un sujet anglais si vous voulez: par exemple le Cardinal Newman.[1]

En espérant une réponse favorable, je me soussigne,

Monsieur, avec beaucoup d'admiration,

[T. S. E.]

PS Dans le numéro de juillet, nous allons publier la traduction d'un morceau fort intéressant de Proust, pour lequel nous sommes redevables à l'amabilité de Monsieur Rivière.[2]

TO *Henry Eliot* — MS Houghton

Friday 19 April [1924] — *The Criterion*, 17 Thavies Inn

My dear Henry

Thank you very much for your letter of the 5th instant, which arrived yesterday. I can only answer it briefly now – .

1 – On 19 July, Fernandez said he was working 'at the essay on Cardinal Newman', which he would send in French. Translated by RA, this appeared as 'The Experience of Newman' in *C.* 3: 9 (Oct. 1924): the first of a number of contributions by Fernandez.

2 – *Translation*: Dear Sir, I have been deeply impressed by your article which appeared in the latest issue of the *Nouvelle Revue Française* and I write to ask you if you could do us the honour of contributing something of yours, as yet unpublished, to the *Criterion*. I shall send you a specimen copy of this periodical, and I take the liberty of informing you that we have already published articles by various contributors to the *Nouvelle Revue Française*, among them Mr Jacques Rivière.

As most of our readers are well informed about French periodicals, we cannot, unfortunately, except in very exceptional cases, publish articles which have already been published in France.

The fee we could offer you is £10 per 5000 words, less translation costs for articles in a foreign language. The articles should not exceed 5000 words in length.

I wonder if you could propose to us some subjects about which you could write. It is evident that you have an extensive knowledge of English literature, and, if you like, you could write something on an English subject, Cardinal Newman for instance.

Hoping for a favourable answer, I send you the expression of my admiration. [T. S. E.]

PS In the July issue we shall publish the translation of a very interesting extract from Proust, which we owe to Mr Rivière's kindness.

I send you herewith the trust forms, signed, and will leave it to you to arrange with the State Street Trust Co.[1] when you get to Boston. You have not answered my other question – how I can keep my other money (investments) in America without *tying it up*. I want to keep *some* property liquid, in case of unforeseen emergencies.[2]

I do not want to despoil mother of any of her present income as long as she lives.

And as for you, I want you to keep every penny of your money for yourself, and to *retire* from this damned business at the first possible moment, when you have the barest minimum of subsistance.[3] As I shall show you eventually, you could be of far greater help to me by *being* free, and by being able once a year to come to England, to see me and *advise me*, than by gifts *however* generous and self-sacrificing.

My present anxieties are *not primarily* financial. I have a scheme which, *if it comes off*, will enable me in two months to leave the bank on about half my present salary, but give me much greater freedom. I should have to make up my income by outside work, but I can see my way – if other troubles do not interfere – for a year at least.

No, what I need you for is to come and view the whole situation – myself, my future, Vivien's health, and what sort of life is best for both of us. You understand *me* as no one here does, and you understand V. *in some ways*, perhaps better than I do, though no doubt in other ways – having seen so little of her in your short visit – you may be quite wrong! No matter – you *would* understand better than anyone *if you came* even for a very short time. Vivien has this instinct as strongly as I – that *you* could help us as no one else can, in the world.

And I feel that the next time I shall be able to get nearer to you than I did then. I think of that visit with regret as a wasted opportunity of mine. There is no one to whom I feel I should be nearer than to you.

This last illness of V.'s has been indescribable. She suffered more in spirit than ever before. I have not been able to leave her for three months. I have gone through some terrible agony myself which I do not understand yet, and which has left me utterly bewildered and dazed.

1–State Street Trust Co., one of Boston's long-established Trusts (it acquired the National Union Bank in the 1920s), is commemorated in *State Street Trust and Others, Sketches of Boston and New England*, vol. 3 (1930).
2–There is a marginal bracket to the left of the paragraph extending from 'how' to 'emergencies'.
3–TSE uses the archaic spelling of 'subsistence'.

Oh do come when you can. You know what you can do – I only know my own need, and merely cry out to you.[1]

This is all in *complete confidence*.

I will write again [?soon].

Ever affectionately
Tom

V. wants you *just* as much as I do –

TO *John Middleton Murry* — MS Valerie Eliot

19 [April] 1924[2] — *The Criterion*, 17 Thavies Inn

My dear John,

You know it is impossible for me to come to your wedding,[3] as I am in a bank and cannot get away at such an hour. I am sure that you have done the best thing for yourself in marrying again, but you know that it has always been impossible for me to understand any of your actions.[4]

Ever yours
T. S. E.

TO *Richard Cobden-Sanderson* — CC

24 April 1924 — 2 Milestone Cottages,
Old Fishbourne

Dear Cobden-Sanderson,

I approve the advertising scheme, and appreciate the detail and precision of it.[5] The only question I ask is: does the Post Office admit Imitation-Typewritten-Letters at half-pence rate? At Lloyds Bank we lately had some difficulty with a provincial Post Office about printed matter done on the

1 – Cf. 'And let my cry come unto Thee', *Ash-Wednesday* VI (*CPP* 99).

2 – Misdated 19 May.

3 – JMM married his second wife, Violet le Maistre (*c.*1901–31), on 24 Apr., fifteen months after the death of Katherine Mansfield. He had become engaged just before Easter.

4 – JMM had written on 10 Apr., without mentioning his forthcoming marriage, but saying he was going on a fortnight's holiday. He thought TSE's recent demeanour towards him was 'of mistrust once more', speculatively ascribing this to the 'Gertler affair' in which he was 'absolutely innocent . . . But . . . if you have anything against me, I shd. be told of it.'

5 – On 16 Apr., RC-S submitted an estimate (for £37 5s 10d or £35 15s 10d depending on whether the name of the paper was printed in red or black) for sending circulars to 5000 potential subscribers, inc. libraries in the UK and USA and Canada as well as clubs and universities in the UK.

Multigraph machine, which is not even an imitation of typing in intention, but simply has letters in standard typewriter sizes and shapes and of the same size for the whole alphabet (in order to compose mechanically).

Will you submit it to Lady Rothermere? She has returned to Paris.

I don't think I can make any estimate of your own charges, because I have no idea of the amount of time involved for your staff or of the rates of pay. So I am afraid that I shall have to leave that entirely to you. I shall be writing to Lady Rothermere in a day or two.

I am sorry to have left this so long, but country life in a cottage is arduous without servants and leaves little time for business.

It is distressing that the number could not have been got out before Easter. I cannot help harping on it, because I do feel that it will affect the sale and the interest very adversely, especially as this number was so much more topical than any before; and I feel that Lady Rothermere will have strong grounds for complaint. Do you think that Hazell's are as quick in their work as anyone who would do work of that quality at that price?

Yours in haste

[T. S. E.]

Sacheverell Sitwell: 2 Carlyle Square, S.W.3

FROM *His Mother* TS Valerie Eliot

24 April 1924 24 Concord Ave, Cambridge, Mass.

Dearest Tom:

After quite an interval I received your cablegram from Chichester. I am afraid you will suppose that I consider lecturing an important part of your visit to America, but I do not. I hope, O, I hope, you will come this late fall, just to see us and friends. Think how many years it is since you were here.[1] And I will meet all your expenses as I have written several times, and your salary. I can see it will be quite a while before you can write lectures. And with the *Criterion*, I do not see how you can write anything original. Especially since Mr Aldington is gone. It must be very difficult to find anyone to fill a position that requires so much learning and literary judgment and is far from lucrative.

I have just received a letter from Henry; Mr Bertrand Russell has been staying at his apartments for four days; the Dudleys introduced him to them. Whatever his morals and erraticisms are Henry found him a

1–TSE had not been back to the USA since July/Aug. 1915, soon after his marriage.

delightful and interesting companion. I mentioned him here to repeat one remark he made. It was as follows: He thinks editorial work is 'deadening to creativeness'. That has always been my idea. So I hope that you will not continue much longer on the *Criterion*. Russell says that when you return from the Bank you can put aside that work because it is unrelated to literary work, and you can forget it. But it is not so with editorial work. Now even Henry thinks Russell's judgment in politics is wrong, but I should think his opinion regarding editorial work was correct. At least it seems so to me. Mr Russell was much struck with Henry's resemblance to you.

I have never suffered more from uncertainty in plans than the last few weeks or is it months? I had quite made up my mind to go to England until Marian told me when she came out to see me at the Hospital that she did not feel well enough to go to England. I have been considering Charlotte who would enjoy going. Several times I have almost decided to take her, but she would not want to remain very long and if anyone of her family should be ill, I should feel I must send her home at once. Even at the last minute something might happen too late to get Marian a passport. I thought of going today and asking about passage, and then the thought occurred to me what if Charlotte should give out (through illness in her family), too late for Marian to get a passport. So I have been much agitated.

If you could come late fall, I paying your salary (for you have taken your vacation) I would do everything I could for you. I would want you to send me a list of all the people you wanted me to invite to meet you. I should love to be able to do something for you. I do not feel as if I ought to expect you to write an Introduction to my *Savonarola*, much as I should appreciate it. You must have other work waiting for you, like the Elizabethan authors. I would like to send it to Houghton-Mifflin early June, so as if they return it to have you send it to a New York publisher. Would Alfred Knopf[1] take it? I shall try Houghton-Mifflin first as Grandgent advised.

I hope you have been able to rest at Old Fishbourne. I hope you have someone to cook for you. Pegasus in harness[2] you are too much of the time. My poor boy. I hope you can sleep. I will finish this and let Margaret mail it.

Ever your loving
Mother

1–Knopf had published US editions of TSE's *P* (1920) and *SW* (1921).
2–'Pegasus in Harness' was the title of Bowring's translation of Schiller's 1796 poem.

TO *Lady Rothermere* CC

27 April 1924

At present: Milestone Cottages, Old Fishbourne, nr Chichester, Sussex

Dear Lady Rothermere,

In case this letter does not reach you before you leave Paris, I am wiring to you tomorrow to ask for your address in New York, and will immediately write to you there. This is the first moment, after moving to the country, that I have had for writing. I shall be back in London in about a *fortnight.*

I got the *Philosophies*, with the letter of M. Grenier in it, and I think his article is very good.[1] I shall write to him, but I think before accepting this thing for publication I must ask him if he can let me see the rest of it. He is dealing with a subject which seems to me very important and very interesting, and his essay ought to be just what we want. Certainly we ought to exchange with this review. It will take me some time to go through Gleizes,[2] because his essay would have to be cut very much to be possible for us. But you have got hold of two very good things. If you could find out (but probably you have not time) a variety of unprejudiced opinions of Jacob (without intimating that we have him in view as a Paris correspondent) it would be very useful; verbal opinions are so much better than those got by letters.

I am indeed aware that the *Criterion* has been on the dull side (my wife has reminded me of this fault every few days!) and I am not offended at your saying so.[3] I think that the new number is an improvement in this respect, but I want to do a great deal more. There will be at least two good things for July, a new play by W. B. Yeats[4] and the *inédit* of Proust[5] which is now in the hands of Scott Moncrieff. These two things alone ought to mean a column in *The Times*. But what I want to do is to reduce the number of 'star turns' and introduce more regular chroniques, etc., reviews of a very few books (say three books in each number) letters from Paris, Rome, Berlin or Vienna, and Madrid and perhaps New York (yes, certainly

1–Jean Grenier, 'European Nihilism', *Philosophies* 1 (Paris). On Grenier, see TSE's letter of 15 May.
2–See TSE's letter to her of 13 Apr. The French cubist never published in C.
3–Lady Rothermere said she appreciated all TSE did for her and C. – '& if I have found it a little high-brow & grave, perhaps it is my fault!'
4–WBY, 'The Cat and the Moon: A Play for Dancers', C. 2: 8 (July 1924), 395–408.
5–'The Death of Albertine', C. 2: 8 (July 1924).

New York).[1] A dramatic chronique and a review of English periodicals.[2] We should provide people with more opinions on current literary etc, events.

I was very much vexed and irritated and disappointed at the delay in publication. When you return I should like to discuss the whole question of the methods of publication and distribution with you. If you find any misprints or faults in the production of this number I wish you would let me know. Of course the manuscript was not all in the hands of the printers as early as usual, and I had myself to correct the proofs of two or three articles for writers who were abroad, but nevertheless the printers told me that they would get it out just before Easter, and then changed their minds. But all this involves points that can only be discussed when we meet.

In accord with your suggestion of some time ago, Cobden-Sanderson is submitting to you an estimate for sending out sample copies of back numbers and circulars. He asked me to suggest what I thought a proper commission for him to ask, but I told him that I had not the knowledge of his expenses (labour of his staff, rates of pay) necessary; I think that he might simply make a statement of what it costs *him* in this way, if he has to take his assistants off his own work to put them onto this, or else simply charge a small percentage toward covering these expenses. Of course, he does not get much out of the *Criterion* at present, in proportion to the work involved for him; but on the other hand the *Criterion* very much improves his prestige as a publisher, and it is to his own interest that it should prosper; if the advertising increases the sales it will increase his commission.

If you approve this scheme in general, I will draw up a letter and circular.

I think that it is most important and in every way good for the paper that you should be visiting New York; it ought to be possible to do a great deal there. I think that we ought to have 2000 subscribers in America. I should like very much to know how much the *Criterion* is now seen and read in New York, and how much trouble people have to get it. My mother (in Boston) has lately complained to me – and so have other people – of the difficulty of getting extra copies. It is certain that either an agent or a publisher in New York is a necessity. I know that Cobden-Sanderson has corresponded with several publishers over there without success; but with Americans much more can be done by conversation than by letter; and

1–From Oct., *C.* included a review section, 'Books of the Quarter'; and in Jan. 1925 TSE inaugurated a series, 'New York Chronicle', by Gilbert Seldes.

2–*C.* 3: 10 (Jan. 1925) included the first occasional report on Music, and the Stage. But no attention was paid to English periodicals.

also American men of business are used to such violent methods of pushing and being pushed, that they do not respond to the ordinary quiet approaches of English proposals! There are, as you know, two ways of spreading the *Criterion* in America. One is to have an agent who will either buy so many copies outright or take them on commission, and *advertise* himself and the magazine in the American papers, the other to arrange with an American publisher to take unbound copies, advertise the paper, print American advertisements in it if he likes.

The increase of the topical element, and an appeal to the snobbish desire of cultivated America to be *au courant* with what is being talked about, fresh, in Europe, ought to stimulate our circulation there. They should like local news from London and Paris etc. even about plays which they will never see and authors whom they will never read; but in order to compete with the *Dial* we must retain the character and appearance of a *London* quarterly, in order to remind Americans that our news is more first hand.

It might be possible to arrange with the *Dial* for a 'combined subscription' offer in America, sharing the cost of advertisement. We ought in this case to prepare our own advertising copy, and not leave it to the *Dial*. Any such arrangement with the *Dial* would have to be very carefully safeguarded, because the *Dial* is our most formidable competitor there. It pretends to be in very close touch with European affairs.

Please let me know your address in New York so that I can write immediately about anything else that occurs to me.

[On second] thoughts, that is a matter to go very carefully about. If arranged at all, it might be better with some other paper than the *Dial* (but of at least as good standing and at least as well known).

If no publishers cared to take up the *Criterion* direct, perhaps one or more New York people might like to guarantee the expenses of an American edition – which expenses would be chiefly advertising in American papers and extra payment to contributors for American rights. There must be people in New York who would be sufficiently flattered by having a hand in the paper to this extent, without having any control over the form or contents.

If you are going at once, bon voyage, and better weather than we are having here. I do hope you will get this in time to let me hear from you before you leave.[1]

How long do you expect to be in America?

Yours always sincerely,
[T. S. E.]

1 – She was leaving for the USA 'for a short stay on the 30th'.

TO *Hugh Walpole* MS Valerie Eliot

[28? April 1924] 38 Burleigh Mansions,
St Martins Lane, London W.C.2

My dear Walpole

I am glad to hear from you – delighted that you think so well of the last number.[1] I wish the *Old Ladies* book was not appearing so soon.[2] I look forward to discussing the future of the paper with you.

Any night I think wd do (not weekend) evening I cd come to you or where you like or come in here (this is two rooms and a washstand!) let me hear when you get back, at this address.

Always yours
T. S. Eliot

TO *Ezra Pound* TS Lilly

30 April 1924 *The Criterion*, 9 Clarence Gate Gdns

Dear Ezra

Your card just received with address. Antheil[3] has appeared in an inflated and shapeless number of the *Criterion* in a somewhat abbreviated form; as this was due to exigencies of amateur editorship I hasten to inform you that payment will be made for the complete manuscript.

I also inform you that for about four people there is money enough to pay for their best creative work at double rates. That is, for any stuff like the 'Malatesta [Cantos]' I should be able to pay you at the verse equivalent to £20 per five thousand words prose. I count each page of verse as four hundred words which is about what it would be if it was prose. This is on condition that the contribution is not printed in English in any other periodical in England, America or elsewhere for three months after its appearance in the *Criterion*. What have you got or what will you have?[4]

I have other things to write to you about but they must wait, meanwhile send me your various addresses, and if you have any notion yourself let me

1 – On 27 Apr., Walpole said he was 'delighted with the new number' (*C.* 2: 7, Apr. 1924), which included ch. I of his novel *The Old Ladies*.

2 – Walpole's book was due out in Oct., making it impossible to publish 'the four chapters' as planned; chap. II appeared as a last instalment in *C.* 2: 8 (July 1924).

3 – 'George Antheil', in *C.* 2: 7 (Apr. 1924).

4 – EP's next contribution was 'Antheil 1924–1926', in *NC.* 4: 4 (Oct. 1926), followed by 'Horace' in 9: 35 (Jan. 1930).

know *where you expect to be next winter*; I will keep the information to myself if so desired.

Yours,
T.

TO *Douglas Ainslie* CC

30 April 1924 9 Clarence Gate Gdns

Dear Mr Ainslie,

I am indeed deeply sorry for this unfortunate misunderstanding for which I must take the blame as I should have made full enquiries from Mr Aldington about his correspondence with you.[1] I am sending the manuscript of Croce's 'Alfred de Vigny' to Mr Arthur Waugh as you request. Let me express the sincerest hope that you will soon have something else of Croce's ready and that you will let me see it as we should like very much to have the honour of publishing something by Croce translated by you in the *Criterion*.[2] It is a loss to the review to have been unable to publish any of these things this year.

With many thanks and best wishes for the success of the volume to which I shall look forward,

Yours sincerely,
[T. S. E.]

TO *Leonard Woolf* TS Berg

1 May 1924 2 Milestone Cottages,
Old Fishbourne

Dear Leonard,

Please excuse me for not having thanked you for your cheque for £7. 5. 7 representing royalties on the sale of *The Waste Land*.[3] I am very glad that the book has already sold enough to cover expenses and I hope that you will be able to get rid of the whole edition.

1–See TSE's letter of 13 Apr.
2–See Ainslie's transl. of Croce's 'On the Nature of Allegory' in *C.* 3: 11 (Apr. 1925).
3–'We consider that the book has done extraordinarily well', wrote LW (12 Apr.), 'and I hope you feel the same.' 330 copies had been sold by 31 Mar. Total printing, binding, advertising and distribution costs were £25 6s. 3d, and TSE received 25% of the gross profit.

I should like very much to get something done for you soon.[1] Here in the country life has been intolerable and has consisted entirely in an unsuccessful struggle to keep warm and to keep fed. I look every day at a suitcase full of letters, papers, books, notes, unpaid bills, and unread manuscripts which I have not had time to disturb. I had hoped to get all my work for the next *Criterion* done, but I now see it is useless to attack it until I get back to London. I am afraid it is quite impossible for me to attempt anything else for the next month or more, but I hope to see you as soon as we return and then I shall report my progress.

Yours ever,
T. S. Eliot

TO *Virginia Woolf* — TS Texas

1 May 1924 — 2 Milestone Cottages

My dear Virginia,

Thank you for your card. Yes, I wished that we could have had that essay[2] in the *Criterion*, [even if *del.*] as you will not release your clutches on any sketch or part of a novel. I can only offer you two inducements, one noble and the other mercenary: the first that you might let me have something too long for the *Nation*, because you may be sure that there will be no limitations of length. (Indeed, what you gave me last year was far too short to represent such a distinguished name in the *Criterion*.) The other inducement is this: I am now at liberty to offer to the most desirable contributors, at my discretion, double rates for the first periodical rights in England and America; that is, I can pay £20 instead of £10 per five thousand words. There are at most four people to whom I should offer this, one of whom is of course yourself. When may I hope for something from you?

I am now struggling, in the few intervals one gets here in the terrible struggle for life in the country, with *Jacob's Room*,[3] with a view to chronique for the *Nouvelle Revue Française* on the evolution of the *roman contemporain anglais*.[4] But you do not make it easy for critics; one feels that a superhuman cleverness is called for or disaster is inevitable.

1–TSE published no further signed articles in *N.* until 29 Jan. 1927.
2–'The Patron and the Crocus', *N&A*, 35: 2 (12 Apr. 1924).
3–VW's *Jacob's Room* had been published by the Hogarth Press in Oct. 1922.
4–In 'Le roman anglais contemporain' (*NRF* 28: 164, 1 May 1927), TSE discussed the effect of psycho-analysis and the lack of 'Jamesian moral preoccupation' in contemporary fiction,

We are looking forward to seeing you in London and I subscribe myself, in starvation, cold and hopeless confusion,

Your obedient servant,
T. S. E.

TO *Henry Eliot* TS Houghton

1 May 1924 9 Clarence Gate Gdns

Dear Henry,

This is just a short note and will not deal with any of the important things about which I have to write to you and which every day I am struggling to find time to write about fully. This is simply to tell you that Lady Rothermere is going to New York and will be there by the time this letter reaches you.

I do not think I have ever explained to you fully the terms on which I run the *Criterion* or my relations with Lady Rothermere. The fact is that I was a damned fool ever to agree to run the review without a salary; or, in fact, to run it at all. Having in the first place shown my willingness, or perhaps eagerness to run the paper for her on the minimum amount of money and for no salary, I have never since been in the position to demand a salary. You will see this, I am sure. However, the general position becomes every day more impossible and I am certain that my health will give out completely if I go on with things as they are, for another year.

When the question of my leaving the Bank was first brought up and made public, Lady Rothermere expressed approval of my leaving and told me that she would guarantee me a salary of three hundred pounds a year (clear of anything I should make by *writing* for the *Criterion*) *on* my leaving the bank. In this way she has made my having a salary for the *Criterion* conditional, and I feel a certain resentment on this account, for in my view she has no right to impose any condition at all. If I am worth a salary, I am worth a salary whether I am in the bank or out of it. I am telling you this in order to get that side of the position quite clear. On the other hand, I want you to understand that I have never had the slightest difficulty with Lady Rothermere on the subject of the *Criterion* in any

—

drawing on VW, DHL, David Garnett and Aldous Huxley. VW deserved 'credit for having performed at Kew and at seaside watering places what Conrad performed in the tropics and the south seas'.

respect. She has given me an absolutely free hand, has made no criticisms, has agreed to every suggestion and has lately slightly increased the sum which she at first stipulated would be the utmost to which she could go for its expenses.

Lady Rothermere is always flying about the world and is scarcely ever in London at all. Although she keeps a large house in London she is never here for more than a month out of the year. She lives a great deal more in Paris where she keeps up a very luxurious flat. She is a very cosmopolitan woman without a trace of snobbism *and we have always without exception been on the friendliest terms*. She is curiously Americanised; so much so that at first I always thought she must be an American by birth. She is much more like an American than any English woman I have ever met and has got a great liking for Americans and America. I fancy, by the way, that most of the Rothermeres' money is invested in America and Canada by now.

One of my greatest pulls with her is being an American myself. When she decided to go to New York, she asked me to tell her of anything she could do or any people she could see that would be of use to the *Criterion*. I feel that it would be a very great advantage to me if she could meet some relation of mine while in America, and a great help to me to have my point of view shown to her by an American. In short, I should like you to meet her and you would be doing me a great favour if you could possibly arrange to see her, although I am afraid it would necessitate your going to New York. For this reason I hesitate to ask you. I am perfectly convinced that she would like to meet some relative of mine and also that you would like her. She is an extraordinarily intelligent woman, perhaps the most intelligent woman I have ever met, though *not* an intellectual. Although she is about fifty years of age, she is an extremely attractive and young looking woman, very smart and very gay.

If you could manage just two days in New York and would present yourself at the Plaza Hotel, I feel sure that everything would arrange itself and that you would be received with open arms.

There is no other member of my family whom I would ask to receive her for two reasons: there is no other who would be as likely to get on with her as you and there is no other who has anywhere near as much knowledge and understanding of my position as you have.

You know about the movement called Bel Esprit. Several years ago there were several wealthy people ready to provide annual payments to help me to live without working in a bank. I never had any of this money. In the form which the scheme took I could not have accepted it, I refused. It involved my leaving the bank for a very inadequate income without certainty of continuity, on the promises only without guarantees, and with indefinite obligations to various individuals each with his own conception of what was to be expected of me – instead of a definite contract for a definite job. The bank was preferable to that.

Now if, instead of this abortive scheme, this money which was once promised could be concentrated on providing me a decent salary for a definite task: *editing the Criterion*, it would be the true solution of my difficulties. The present position with the *Criterion* is a farce to make one laugh, if any Eliot could ever laugh. I am running a quarterly review which has to make the same appearances, get as good contributors, and give as good value as any other quarterly. The *Criterion* has to compete with reviews which have an editor and a sub-editor devoting all their time to it, a business manager, an office and a secretarial staff. The *Criterion* is run without an office, without any staff or business manager, by a sickly bank clerk and his wife. The latter has had to be on her back half of the time and the former has conducted all his work in the evening in his own sitting room, without even a *desk*, till Christmas! after a busy and tiring day, and subject to a thousand interruptions. Until the last few months I have paid my own secretary, a woman who came in three evenings a week. When I finally add that I have not only taken no salary but have actually been considerably out of pocket for payment of a secretary, and for the time that I might have spent on writing for other papers, it is enough to make any outsider believe that I ought to be certified a lunatic.

The *Criterion* work is increasing all the time, the correspondence increases, the thought and labour in attempting to make each number better than the last increases, and the editorship of the *Criterion* has now become really a full time job. I consider that it is worth a living wage of at least five hundred a year. And at that I should still be working without an editor's usual aids of an office, an assistant editor, a business manager and a full time secretary.

Lady Rothermere has been so little in England during the past year that I have never had an opportunity to make this position clear to her. Possibly she wonders why I do not leave the bank on her guarantee of three hundred a year for three years. I am sure that you will see without my saying more how impossible this would be.

If you see Lady Rothermere there is one point on which I wish to caution you. About two years ago when Vivien began to break up in health, Lady Rothermere sent her her own doctor, a very cranky and unstable individual who was the real cause of Vivien's final collapse this time last year.

Naturally this matter has caused a little embarrassment as Lady Rothermere still has an implicit faith in this charlatan. It would be better therefore to avoid all mention of Vivien, and that is the only warning I have to give you.

Lady Rothermere's address, as I mentioned above, is the Hotel Plaza.

Do you think you could possibly get to New York?

Always your affectionate brother,
Tom.

Lady R. has been very appreciative of the *Criterion* and regards it, quite rightly, as an asset to her own importance. Naturally she wants to keep this distinction for herself, and not share the ownership of the paper with others, but on the other hand it ought to make her anxious to do everything else possible to keep the paper alive.

If *I* give it up, I don't suppose she could find anyone else to run it on the terms on which I have run it!

PS If you can get to New York, *Cable* me (Eliot, Colforloyd, Cannon, London) and *I will cable to Lady Rothermere* to say you are coming to see her. T.

TO *Harold Monro* — TS Beinecke

2 May 1924

2 Milestone Cottages,
Old Fishbourne

Dear Monro

I have only just got your letter:[1] you see where I am. I would gladly turn up if I were in London, but I shall not be at home for another week. I rather thought you would be down in these parts yourself just now. I am very sorry to miss the party.

I have already had a torrent of abuse over Lewis's article ['The Apes of God'] in the *Criterion*, but probably only a shower compared to what is to come. Of course I knew this when I accepted the article. Anyhow, I trust you – as you say that the *Criterion* is 'on the upward grade' and that Lewis's article has 'great style' – to uphold it as an *impersonal* work of literature.[2] If people are going to take things like this with a petty personal

1 – On 30 Apr., Monro invited TSE to a party at the Poetry Bookshop on Tues., 6 May, in company with WL, the graphic designer E. McKnight Kauffer, Flint and the Sitwells.

2 – TSE's comment is canny: he knew that WL's piece was full of scarcely veiled attacks on real people, including the Sitwells.

bias, and make a grievance, it is not worthwhile trying to produce literature at all. It is thankless work running a literary review, at best: I say this to you because you have been through it yourself.[1] Of course I want the *Criterion* to be a good review, indeed to be the best review, and not simply a good review for a man in my circumstances; but it is interesting that nobody, even those who know the circumstances quite well enough, ever makes the slightest allowance. The *Criterion* is condemned if it is not better in every way than the *Mercury*, the *Quarterly*, the *English*, or any other.[2] It has to make the same appearances, get as good contributors, and give as good value as any other paper. It has to compete with reviews which have an editor and a sub-editor paid and devoting all their time, which have a business manager, an office and a secretarial staff. The *Criterion* is run without any office, without any staff or business manager, by a sickly bank clerk and his wife: the latter has had to be on her back half the time and the former has conducted all his work in the evenings in his own sitting room, after a busy and tiring day, and subject to a thousand interruptions: without even a desk until he bought a second hand one at Christmas! Until the last few months I have paid my own secretary, a woman who came in three evenings a week. I shouldn't mind if people thought me a lunatic for doing this (and without a salary) but they simply think me mercenary for staying in a bank instead of giving all my time to it. The whole thing is enough to make me laugh, if any Eliot ever could laugh. And after all to find that some people simply find in the *Criterion* an occasion for personal offense . . . . !

Anyway, I am glad that you like this number. When I get back I will ring you up, as I should like to see you soon (in that 'hollow' vale).[3] I do hope you have broken Wordsworth's back by this time.[4]

Yours ever,
T. S. E.

1–Monro launched *The Poetry Review* in 1912, and edited *The Chapbook*, 1919–25.
2–*The London Mercury* was founded by J. C. Squire in 1919; *The Quarterly Review* dated back to the nineteenth century; *The English Review* was founded by Ford Madox Ford in 1908.
3–Monro wrote, 'Please don't fail to meet me in this (what is it? – O choice of epithet!) *something* vale, next Tuesday.' The reference is to Bishop Henry King, 'The Exequy': 'Stay for me there; I will not fail / To meet thee in that hollow vale.'
4–Monro was thinking of calling his latest article 'Wordsworth: Our Grandfather'; it appeared as 'Wordsworth Revisited', in C. 2: 8 (July 1924).

TO *Frederic Manning* CC

3 May 1924 2 Milestone Cottages

My dear Manning,

I am very glad to hear from you and very sorry that I cannot accept your kind invitation.[1] I am down here in the country for a supposed rest but really dealing with past arrears of *Criterion* correspondence and my own writing. I still hope to be able to spend a weekend with you later in the year. I am staying here for some little time and on the other hand I may have to return to London at any moment, so it is safer to address me at 9 Clarence Gate Gardens, N.W.1.

May I have the note on Father Hyacinthe?[2] I wonder if the Murry muddle has any pathological interest for you. I am obliged to write some sort of brief reply to his article in the *Criterion*,[3] simply to make clear that everything that Murry believes in is anathema to me, but I shall not be able to go into everything at all thoroughly. It will hardly be more than a statement or creed. I have never found any writer whose views were so antipathetic to me as Murry's.[4] I agree with what you say about faith and religion.[5]

I want a long article from you: If you do not suggest a subject yourself, I shall probably before long suggest to you several which I think ought to be dealt with by the *Criterion*.

I am very sorry that we meet so seldom.

Yours sincerely,
[T. S. E.]

1–On 2 May, Manning had invited TSE to his farm in Surrey for a day or two.
2–'Le Père Hyacinthe', C. 2: 8 (July 1924), 460–7.
3–JMM's 'Romanticism and the Tradition', C. 2: 7 (Apr. 1924), a reply to TSE's 'The Function of Criticism', C. 2: 5 (Oct. 1923). JMM said that 'since the debate was originally opened in *The Adelphi*' of which he was editor, he had replied 'to Mr Eliot . . . in an article entitled "More About Romanticism" in *The Adelphi* for December.' However, he thought 'the more leisurely and expansive pages of *The Criterion*' offered 'a better chance of conducting this controversy to some issue'. See also David Goldie, *A Critical Difference: T. S. Eliot and John Middleton Murry in English Literary Criticism, 1919–1928* (1998).
4–JMM argued that 'the tradition of Romanticism is just as lofty and august as the tradition of Classicism' and 'in the present condition of the European consciousness is of more immediate importance'. He saw 'Religion and Literature' as 'branches of the same everlasting root', and construed Romanticism as 'something that happened to the European soul after the Renaissance', which was characterised by the assertion of man's 'independence' of the 'external spiritual authority' of the Church. Far from being 'impersonal', the work of art was, according to JMM, 'a manifestation of the rhythm of the soul of the man who created it'.
5–'Murry should distinguish between faith and religion,' wrote Manning.

TO *Richard Cobden-Sanderson* CC

3 May 1924 2 Milestone Cottages

Dear Cobden-Sanderson,

I am sorry that I have not had time hitherto to answer your letters or anybody else's for that matter. I hope that you managed to get the draft scheme into Lady Rothermere's hands before she left Paris, and got an answer from her about it.[1] I had a letter from her just before leaving but she does not mention this matter at all.

Do not think that I am not aware you had a very short time in which to get the number out and I must take my part of the responsibility for the delay. What I am more concerned about at present is the number of printers' errors or blemishes in the present number. There are a great many errors of a sort which have not occurred before and for which the printers themselves ought to be responsible and they are the sort of error which ought not to occur in a paper of our high quality. They show signs of haste in the composition which I should have quite excused had they been able to get the number out before Easter. But as Hazells had the usual amount of time for the final make up, I do not see that there is any excuse for errors of this sort. I have apologized for them to Lady Rothermere because I know that this is the sort of thing which annoys her particularly: You know yourself that she has always been very proud of the paper and sets great store by having it absolutely perfect. If this sort of carelessness were to continue she would just as likely as not throw the whole thing up, so I think that it ought to be brought to Hazells' attention in detail. The errors consist chiefly in irregularities in placing the letters and in unevenness of inking of certain letters. I am sending you herewith a copy in which I think most of these errors have been marked and I am sending another one to Hazell. We cannot be too particular on these points.

My secretary Mr J. L. Culpin will bring you this letter and a marked copy of the *Criterion* himself and I should be obliged if you would give him a cheque for £5 for payment of salary for the four weeks from March 19th to April 16th.

In case any press cuttings get lost in the post coming to me, I hope that you will have them all yourself. If the *Criterion* does not get good notices this time from all the Rothermere and Beaverbrook press, I shall draw

1 – A reference to the plan put forward by RC-S for 'circularising 5000 names'.

Lady Rothermere's attention again to this. I have not received any press cuttings yet,

Yours ever,
[T. S. E.]

PS Could you let me know the number of words in all the contributions to the April Number, so that we may get the contributors paid off?

TO *W. B. Yeats* CC

3 May 1924 [London]

My dear Mr [Yates *del.*] Yeats,

I am very much obliged at receiving from Messrs. A. P. Watt & Son your play 'The Cat and the Moon'.[1] You know how intense an admiration I have for all of your work and you know that I should be very happy to publish in the *Criterion* everything that you would give us. Also, I venture to hope that you will agree with me that the *Criterion* is far the most suitable review in this country in which your work could appear. Of course the *Criterion* is run on very scanty means and it is a hard struggle to make the appearance that we do with the capital at our disposal. In order to run it at all, I am working without a salary, without an Assistant Editor, without a business Manager, a staff or an office; doing all the editing at home in the evening. I remind you of this only to explain that my offer to Watts is not commensurate with my desire to get this play but only commensurate with the means at my disposal. I have offered £10.00.0 for the British Serial rights with the suggestion that I might be able to pay rather more if the play does not appear in America until after July 15th, the date of the issue in which I should publish it. If you will let me have the play, I shall consider it a favour and a kindness to my attempt to run a good literary review in London.

I look back with great pleasure to my lunch with you at the Savile Club[2] and I hope that I may have the pleasure of seeing you when you are next in London.

I suppose that *The Trembling of the Veil*[3] has been entirely distributed but I am just contemplating having in each number of the *Criterion*

1–WBY's 'The Cat and the Moon' appeared in C. 2: 8 (July 1924).

2–On 12 Dec. 1922 TSE had told OM he had lunched with WBY at the Savile Club. He found WBY 'very stimulating': 'one of a very small number of people with whom one can profitably talk about poetry'.

3–1000 copies of WBY's autobiography were privately printed in 1922. In reply, WBY offered to lend TSE a copy as there was none to be had. It was reviewed in C. 5: 3 (June

substantial reviews of a very small number of books.[1] Would it be possible for us to get a copy for that purpose? I admired and enjoyed immensely all that I read in the *Dial*.[2]

Sincerely yours,
[T. S. E.]

TO *Harriet Shaw Weaver*[3] CC

3 May 1924

2 Milestone Cottages,
Old Fishbourne

Dear Miss Weaver,

I am very glad and very sorry to hear from you: sorry to hear your news[4] and also sorry that I did not take this matter up with you before. I had been intending to do so for some weeks, but had to postpone it from day to day owing to pressure of other business; I have been waiting for an evening to come and see you.

I should like very much to discuss your proposal with you and I hope that the matter can wait for a week or so until I return to town. I shall come to see you as soon as I return. I should like to consider the possibility of our taking over the poets translation series and of arranging with Lewis about his two books as well.[5] When I see you, I hope that we can come to some arrangement which I could submit to Lady Rothermere for her approval. I am very sorry about the Joyce books.[6]

—

1927), after being reissued in *Autobiographies: Reveries over Childhood and Youth and The Trembling of the Veil* (1926).

1 – 'Books of this Quarter' first appeared in C. 2: 8 (July 1924).

2 – Instalments of WBY's autobiography appeared as 'More Memories' in *Dial* 73: 1–4 (July–Oct. 1922).

3 – Harriet Shaw Weaver: see Glossary of Names.

4 – On 1 May, Shaw Weaver said the Egoist Press had 'now reached that stage where to expand requires too much capital', and 'not to expand means . . . slow extinction'. She and Dora Marsden had decided 'to close down'.

5 – Weaver said that RA believed TSE might want to take over all or some of the Poets' Translations series, albeit of 'little commercial value'; 'the copyright and what remains of the stock of *Tarr* and *The Caliph's Design* are being made over to Mr Lewis who wants to concentrate on one publisher'.

6 – RA said TSE 'would be sorry that Mr Joyce's books have gone'. Sylvia Beach had taken *Ulysses*, while Cape took over the other four Joyce titles – *Dubliners*, *Portrait of the Artist as a Young Man*, *Exiles* and *Chamber Music*.

I want to put into the next *Criterion* a note commemorating the end of the Egoist Press.[1] For I am convinced that what you have done in publishing the *Egoist* through those years, in bringing out the books which you published, and in advancing the work of certain authors, is a work of very great importance and value. I doubt if you realise yourself how much you have done for English literature or with what unselfishness, modesty and public spirit you have done it.

Sincerely yours,
[T. S. E.]

TO *Hugh Walpole* — TS Valerie Eliot

3 May 1924 — at 2 Milestone Cottages,
Old Fishbourne

My dear Walpole,

I am very glad to hear from you and to know that the new number pleases you. I have been waiting to write to you for a very long time, but have had no address whatever. When I returned your manuscript to your Secretary, I asked for an address to which I could write to you but he did not reply. Had I been able to communicate with you I should have explained my intentions and asked your approval and should of course have sent you proof of 'the Old Ladies'. I hope you will understand that it is through no fault of mine that I was unable to do so.

I had hoped to publish two chapters in the April number and two more in the July issue in order to get in all that you gave me before your book appeared, but I found myself overwhelmed with material; Middleton Murry's article was twice as long as I expected it to be and several other things have turned up which I had imprudently promised to publish. In consequence the April number is really bigger than our means allow and I am afraid that the July number will also be bigger. So I am disappointed in only being able to publish one chapter in April and another in July; this is a pity as the four chapters are something rather complete in itself.

1 – In his 'Commentary', TSE said he had learnt with 'great regret that the Egoist Press has ceased to exist'. It had 'performed a service that is one function of a private press. It made possible the publication of the works of authors then unknown which would never have been accepted by the larger publishing houses.' Citing JJ's *Portrait of the Artist*, as well as volumes by WL, EP, Marianne Moore, and H. D., he added: 'With complete disintestedness and modesty the Egoist Press performed services to literature wholly out of proportion to its capital and position' (*C.* 2: 8 [July 1924], 372–3). TSE dedicated *SE* to Shaw Weaver, 'in gratitude and recognition of her services to English Letters'. See also his tribute, 'Miss Harriet Weaver', *Encounter*, Jan. 1962.

I think that you left England before I had an opportunity of telling you how much I liked and enjoyed 'the Old Ladies' and how grateful I am to you for letting me use it. I think that the portrait of Mrs Payne is extraordinarily good.

I am trying to improve the *Criterion* in various ways but it is difficult with the time and funds at my disposal. I find that it takes more and more time and thought, and I always see how much better it might be, had I more time to give to it. I have come down to the country for a supposed rest, but I find myself doing several hours' work on it every day, and yet I have a bag full of unanswered correspondence. I am dreading the point at which running the *Criterion* will obviously be too much for my time and strength.

I expect to be in town again in a week or so and I should be delighted to come and see you, or we could lunch somewhere together.

Lunch is an unsatisfactory meal for me at best, because it has to take place in the City and I am always too busy to spare more than an hour and a half at most but I do hope that we can arrange a meeting very soon.

Sincerely yours
T. S. Eliot

I hope the proof-reading was satisfactory?

TO *J. E. Spingarn*[1] — TS Berg

3 May 1924 — *The Criterion*, 17 Thavies Inn

Dear Sir,

Thank you very much for your book of poems[2] which I have just received and for your cordial greetings which I cordially reciprocate. I am indeed flattered that you should have paid me this attention and shall look forward with great pleasure to reading the poems as well as to having an inscribed copy. I should like very much to send you a copy of my prose book of criticism,[3] should you care to receive it but you may already have seen it and not care to encumber your shelves with a presentation copy.

1–J. E. Spingarn (1875–1939): Professor of Comparative Literature, Columbia University, 1899–1911.

2–Spingarn, *Poems* (1924): a limited edition of 40 copies.

3–*SW* (1920). Replying on 24 May, Spingarn said he would like a presentation copy: 'I know it well, but do not own a copy, and the American Edition seems to be out of print.' He had followed TSE's 'career as poet and critic from the beginning'.

I was pleased to see that your publishers had thought me worthy to be included in a volume of select essays in which you are represented, although a little annoyed that I should never have been notified of it and should have known of the fact only from a notice in *The Times*.[1] But that is the way publishers behave.

I have known and admired your book on the Renaissance for many years.[2]

Yours very truly,
T. S. Eliot

TO *Ramón Fernandez* CC

3 May 1924 [London]

My dear Sir,

I am very glad to have your letter of the 1st inst. and delighted by your having accepted my suggestion. I also appreciate very highly what you say about the *Criterion* and myself.[3]

I could ask for nothing better than the essay on Newman which you suggest and in fact I cannot think of anyone either here or abroad from whom I should prefer to have such an essay.[4] I may say that ever since the beginning of the *Criterion*, I have been looking for someone to write an essay on Newman: I have not had the time to do so myself and until I read your essay in the *Nouvelle Revue Française*,[5] I did not know whom to ask.

But I do not wish to hamper you; if there is some other subject on which you would prefer to write, please let me know.

Write in French or English as you please: if the former, we will have it translated; if the latter, we will have any corrections made that may prove

1–*Criticism in America, its Functions and Status* (1924) included essays by Irving Babbitt, Van Wyck Brooks, TSE and Spingarn, among others.

2–*A History of Literary Criticism in the Renaissance* (1899). TSE's annotated copy (2nd ed., 1908) is at Houghton,

3–Replying on 1 May to TSE's letter of 17 Apr., Fernandez said: 'I read the *Criterion*, value it highly, and follow and admire very much your personal work, both as a poet and as a critic.'

4–Fernandez would be 'delighted to contribute to the *Criterion* an essay on Newman as the master of concrete thought, which could stand as an indirect criticism of Russell's assertion concerning science and culture' (the subject of TSE's 'Commentary', *C.* 2: 7, Apr. 1924). On 16 Sept. 1921, TSE had told RA: 'I am not sure that the greatest Nineteenth Century *poets* (in your sense!) are not Ruskin and Newman.'

5–'La garantie des sentiments et les intermittences du coeur', *NRF* 11: 132 (1 Apr.).

necessary. I agree with you that it is difficult to write in a foreign language except while one is in the habit of thinking in that language.

I look forward to meeting you when I am next in Paris and look forward with impatience to your essay on Newman.[1]

Yours very sincerely,
[T. S. E.]

TO *Olivia Shakespear*[2] CC

3 May 1924 Milestone Cottages

Dear Mrs Shakespear,

On the contrary, it is possible that Ezra may curse me. To the best of my recollection the complete works of Thomas Jefferson were left at Holland Place Chambers.[3] Ezra had them for a long time and I think that when he went to Paris, we had some discussion as to whether he should return them to me. There are a great many volumes and my flat was already filled with books, so I think that he agreed to store them for me. At any rate I have not got the Jefferson now and I think that you will find them at Holland Place Chambers.

No, I have never met George Antheil.[4]

Yours sincerely,
[T. S. E.]

1 – Fernandez, 'The Experience of Newman', *C.* 3: 9 (Oct. 1924).

2 – Olivia Shakespear (1864–1938), mother of Dorothy Pound, made an unhappy marriage in 1885 with Henry Hope Shakespear (1849–1923), a solicitor. She published several novels including *Love on a Mortal Lease* (1894) and *The Devotees* (1904). Through her cousin, the poet Lionel Johnson (1867–1902), she effected a meeting with WBY, which resulted in a short love affair and a lifetime's friendship. WBY wrote at least two poems for her, and she was the 'Diana Vernon' of his *Memoirs* (ed. Denis Donoghue, 1972).

3 – TSE had acquired his father's *Complete Works of Thomas Jefferson* on his father's death in 1919. Jefferson was a crucial figure in EP's later intellectual Pantheon, featuring in *Cantos* XXXI–XLI entitled '*Jefferson Nuevo Mundo*', *Jefferson and/or Mussolini* (1935) and 'The Jefferson–Adams Letters as Shrine and Monument' (1937). The Pounds lived at 5 Holland Park Chambers from 1914 until their departure for Paris at the end of 1920.

4 – See EP, 'George Antheil', *C.* 2: 7 (Apr. 1924).

TO *E. R. Curtius* CC

3 May 1924 [London]

My dear Curtius,

Thank you for your letter of the 29th ult. I have taken note of your change of address.[1] You shall receive [a] cheque for the Proust article in due course.[2]

I am sorry that Mr Flint's note[3] has given offence to you. It did not occur to me that this would cause ground for complaint, but of course all such comments ought to be made either by the Editor himself or else to be submitted to the contributor for his approval. I quite agree with you about the principle involved.

I certainly look forward to meeting one day and meanwhile at more leisure I look forward to writing to you about your projected studies in English literature.[4] I feel that you take Mr Murry a little too seriously.[5] In his own paper the *Adelphi*, he has subsequently denied to Marcel Proust all importance.[6] Since the publication of the book which I sent you which, having been a course of lectures delivered at Oxford was comparatively restrained in tone, he has indulged in considerable loose and even vituperative criticism of writers who fall outside of his rather narrow sphere of sympathy.

I am writing a short rejoinder to his article in the *Criterion*.[7]

Yours always sincerely,
[T. S. E.]

1 – Curtius had recently been appointed Professor of German at Heidelberg University.
2 – 'On the Style of Marcel Proust', trans. F. S. Flint (C. 2: 7, Apr. 1924).
3 – Flint added a footnote to the phrase 'rocket-like effusion': '*Sie-raketenartige Aufsprühen*, or "rocket-like sparkling-up." It is questionable whether *effuser* is good French. Most French writers would say *fuser*, I think. In any case, it is hardly just to describe the lilac as rocket-like – F.S.F.' (314).
4 – TSE met Curtius only once or twice in their thirty-five years of correspondence, but counted him among his 'old friends' ('Brief über Ernst Robert Curtius', 1956). In his letters Curtius frequently alluded to a possible English sequel to his *French Literary Relations*.
5 – Curtius considered: 'Proust's style confirms Middleton Murry's affirmations in his suggestive and thoughtful book, *The Problem of Style*' (313) – a book that TSE had sent him.
6 – 'I saw Marcel Proust and James Joyce emerge . . . Essentially, from my point of view, they are nothing. Landmarks, perhaps, to tell me twice again that the intellectual consciousness is utterly *kaput* . . . There is more really profound thought-adventure in one of Tchehov's stories like *The Black Monk* than in all their work put together' ('Novels and Thought-Adventures', *Adelphi* 1: 6, Nov. 1923, 536).
7 – TSE did not publish a rejoinder to JMM's 'Romanticism and the Tradition', C. 2: 7 (Apr. 1924).

TO *Jean de Menasce* CC

3 May 1924 [London]

Dear Menasce,

I have only today received your letter.[1] By ill luck it must have been delivered by the next post after I had left for the country and before my instructions to the Post Office had taken effect; in consequence it remained at Clarence Gate Gardens until someone called there yesterday and brought it to me. I had been wondering when you would return but was afraid that I should be out of town at the moment of your passage. Thank you very much for the version of 'Ithaca'.[2] I hope to use two or three of these poems in the July number.

I hope to be back in London by the time you come up for a visit and look forward to seeing you and hearing about Paris.

I have never met Supervielle nor read any of his work, although I have heard much of him and once received a cheque for Fc 75- which was intended for him. I believe he belongs to a wealthy family of bankers in Montevideo.[3] *Antigone* must have been very interesting.[4]

Looking forward to seeing you,

Sincerely,
[T. S. E.]

TO *Messrs. A. P. Watt & Son* CC

3 May 1924 [*The Criterion*, London]

Dear Sirs,

Mr Cobden-Sanderson has forwarded to me your letter of the 22nd ult. together with a copy of Mr W. B. Yates' [*sic*] play entitled *The Cat and the Moon*. As you know, our uniform rates are £10.0.0 per 5000 words, but for such an important contribution from so distinguished a writer, I would make an exception. The play appears to me to be under 2000 words: I will

1 – De Menasce had written on 18 Apr.

2 – De Menasce sent a translation of Cavafy's 'Ithaca' by G. Valassopoulo, saying it will 'stand a good deal of sub-editing'. It appeared in *C.* 2: 8 (July 1924).

3 – Jules Supervielle (1884–1960), whom de Menasce had been 'glad to meet', was a French–Uruguayan poet, novelist and dramatist, whose collection *Débarcadères* appeared in 1922. His uncle, who adopted him in infancy, founded a bank in Montevideo.

4 – De Menasce had seen Cocteau's Sophoclean adaptation of *Antigone* performed in Paris in 1922, with scenery by Picasso and music by Paul Honegger.

take it upon myself to offer on behalf of *The Criterion* £10.0.0. This is the only occasion on which I have ever offered more than the standard rate; but I have very great admiration for Mr Yates' work and I am convinced that *The Criterion* is the most suitable periodical in England in which it could appear.

I should publish this play in the number to appear July 15th. If Mr Yates' arrangement with *The Dial* permits of the play appearing in America not before this date – that is to say, if *The Dial* could publish it not earlier than from the August number, I should be able to make a larger offer.

I should be glad to hear from you as soon as possible.

Yours faithfully
[T. S. E.]

TO *Dr Wilhelm Lehmann* CC

3 May 1924 [Fishbourne]

Dear Dr Lehmann,

I am in the country and separated from my letter files so that I am obliged to write to you care of your publishers to thank you for your book[1] which has just arrived. I have been looking forward for a long time to reading something of yours after our interesting correspondence and am delighted to have at last the opportunity. I hope to read it before returning to London. I have come away for a supposed rest but in reality am dealing with immense arrears of correspondence in connection with the *Criterion*.

I have been meaning to write to you for a long time and to send you one of the books that you asked for. I will at least do that when I return to London. Meanwhile, with many thanks and looking forward with great interest to reading your story.

Yours sincerely,
[T. S. E.]

1 – Presumably Lehmann's *Die Bedrängte Seraph. Novelle* (1924).

TO *Jacques Rivière* CC

4 May 1924 [Fishbourne]

Mon cher Rivière,

Merci de votre aimable lettre; il m'a beaucoup plu. Je suis enchanté de recevoir une promesse même un peu vague.[1] J'espère que nous pourrons publier quelque chose dans notre numéro d'octobre, parce que ça nous serait assez utile à cause de la conférence que vous proposez.[2] Je suis certain qu'on pourrait arranger une ou deux conferénces qui vous dédommageraient des frais de voyage. À présent je suis en villégiature – un repos illusoire parce que j'y ai apporté un paquet énorme de correspondance relative au *Criterion*. Dès mon retour, je ferai une enquête là-dessus. Si Lady Rothermere vient à Londres pendant l'automne, je suis sûr qu'elle donnerait son appui et nous pourrions peut-être avoir une conférence lancée par le *Criterion*. En tout cas nous pourrons probablement préparer la situation par un peu de réclame.

Je vous ferai parvenir un exemplaire du *Waste Land*.[3] C'est curieux que vous ne l'aviez pas encore reçu parce que j'ai insisté chez les editeurs qu'un exemplaire fut envoyé à votre revue.

J'ai reçu une très gentille lettre de Fernandez.

Cordialement, votre
[T. S. E.][4]

1 – On 22 Apr. Rivière promised a new article after he completed a novel.
2 – Rivière asked whether there would be an audience for a lecture on Proust in London the following year, and if it would cover his costs.
3 – On 17 Apr., TSE had enquired whether the *NRF* would do a note on *TWL*. Rivière said they had not received a copy (though on 21 May VW confirmed that one had been sent).
4 – *Translation*: My dear Rivière, Thank you for your kind letter, which gave me much pleasure. I was delighted to receive a promise from you, however vague it might be. I hope we might be able to publish something from you in the October issue, for, bearing in mind the lecture which you propose, this would be very useful to us. I am sure that we could organise one or two more lectures for you, so as to enable you to cover your travel expenses. For the moment I am supposed to be on holiday, but it is only an illusory rest, for I have brought with me an enormous amount of mail from the *Criterion*, which has to be dealt with. As soon as I am back in London, I shall look into the problem of your lectures, and if Lady Rothermere comes to London in the autumn, I am sure that she would give us her support and that we could perhaps organise a lecture under the auspices of the *Criterion*. In any case, we could probably prepare the ground by making some publicity out of it.

I shall let you have a copy of *The Waste Land*. I am surprised that you have not had a copy yet, for I had specifically asked the publishers to send a copy to your review.

I've had a very nice letter from Fernandez. Cordially yours [T. S. E.]

TO *Charles Whibley* CC

4 May 1924 2 Milestone Cottages,
Old Fishbourne

My dear Whibley,

I am delighted that you consider this *Criterion* so good.[1] I do think myself that it has much more character than any previous number, and for that reason am all the more glad to have had your Chesterfield in this number, as I think that nothing could fit any better with that character. You give me great encouragement.

As you say nothing about your health, I do hope that it continues as good as it was when we last met.

I return to London in a week or two.

Yours ever affectionately,
[T. S. E.]

TO *Lady Margaret Levett* CC

4 May 1924 2 Milestone Cottages

Dear Lady Margaret Levett,

You may remember that you kindly arranged last year two appointments for myself and my wife to see Dr Martin. I have been in communication with Dr Martin all the winter and he now informs me that he will be staying with you from the 10th till the end of the month. I asked him, in view of my difficulties in getting to Germany, whether he could not give me and my wife a number of appointments and I enclose a copy of his reply. Assuming that Dr Martin will arrive at the end of this week or the beginning of next, I should like particularly to arrange two appointments for myself for next week, and an appointment for my wife early in the following week.

As I am in the city during the day, the best time for me if possible is from 5.30 in the afternoon, but should there be any difficulty in fixing an appointment for this time or later, I could probably keep any other appointment that Dr Martin could give me.

I shall return to town at the end of this week and meanwhile I am at this address. I am very sorry to trouble you, but I know that Dr Martin's

1–On 1 May, CW said that TSE was 'giving the *Criterion* by degrees a distinctive character'. He hoped TSE's notes ('Crites') would become a permanent feature, praised the pieces by WL and Sitwell, and disparaged JMM as 'all soap bubbles & cotton-wool'.

time is likely to be very full, and as I have been looking forward to his coming all the winter, I am very anxious to miss no opportunity of seeing him.

I am yours faithfully,
[T. S. E.]

TO *Bonamy Dobrée*[1] TS Brotherton

4 May 1924 *The Criterion*, 17 Thavies Inn

My dear Dobrée

I have at last had the opportunity to read carefully your essay on Laforgue.[2] I am very sorry that it has been utterly impossible to deal with it before. I am very much interested by it and in my opinion it is well worth developing at greater length. It would be extremely interesting if you could go thoroughly into the philosophical basis of Laforgue's thought, which so far as I know has never been properly done. Of course no discussion of Laforgue would be complete without an analysis of his technical innovations in verse. But I think it might be a most valuable piece of work and it would be an interesting thing to make a short series including Rimbaud and Corbière. I do hope that you will go ahead with this essay.

As for the poems[3] you left with me, that will take more time, one cannot form an opinion on poetry in the time I have had at my disposal. So I should like to keep them a little longer and meanwhile if you want them back, please let me know. I should like very much to hear from you in any case. Do let me know when you are again in this country.

Yours always sincerely
T. S. Eliot

1 – Bonamy Dobrée: see Glossary of Names. At this time, prior to his academic career, BD was living in Larrau in the Pyrenees.
2 – BD responded (8 May) that he would try to develop the essay on Laforgue that TSE returned to him. 'I must, however, confine myself to a discussion of his material, as I am not competent to deal with his technical innovations in verse. Frankly I don't think his philosophic basis very profound: he fastened eagerly, I think, upon any scheme that seemed at the moment likely to assuage his tormenting sensibility. I should like to do Rimbaud also some time, but he is a more complicated problem. He made and destroyed sanctuaries as fast as Millamant said she could make and unmake lovers. I know too little about Corbière at present to want to write about him; I am curious now only to read him more thoroughly.'
3 – BD had sent TSE some poems by A. J. C. Brown that he admired.

TO *Ottoline Morrell* CC

4 May 1924

2 Milestone Cottages,
Old Fishbourne

My dear Ottoline,

I have forwarded your letter to Modern Medicines Ltd., Bush House, Aldwych, W.C.2. but these people are very undependable. They only get very small supplies of Mutaflor[1] and often one has to wait for a week or a fortnight. If you are in a hurry, I should advise you to write or telegraph to Robert Hanagarth, Apotheker, Freiburg, Breisgau, who will post the Mutaflor immediately, registered.

We have been living in such a muddle and have had so many disasters here, that Vivienne has simply not had the time or strength to write any letters whatever. The weather has been abominable, the domestic difficulties of keeping house in a small cottage with very undependable help, has simply meant slavery from morning to night. We are both longing to get back and are simply waiting for Dr Martin on whom we have been counting for so many months. I have written to Lady Margaret Levett and hope for an early appointment. It is very kind of you to ask us to Garsington while he is here; but I know that it would be impossible for either of us to leave London at all during that time. Vivienne will need to keep all the strength she can for the treatment, and as it is there will be a thousand and one things to be left undone during that time.

What a miserable spring we have had. You cannot be looking forward to Dr Martin's coming more eagerly than we. Vivienne wants to write to you as soon as she gets back to London and into the life which at least makes correspondence possible.

Always affectionately,
[T. S. E.]

PS Thank you very much for letting us know about Dr Martin's fees. At the rate at which I paid last year, we certainly could not afford to see him more than once or twice, and I am very anxious to get the maximum possible number of appointments.

1 – Mutaflor, a medication developed in Germany in 1917 by Prof. Alfred Nissle, is still used in the treatment of bowel disorders.

TO *Conrad Aiken* TS Huntington

4 May 1924 2 Milestone Cottages

Dear Conrad,

I am glad you are able to account for yourself so well but sorry that you remain so evasive in response to my demands. Please however, in your search for emoluments (with which I sympathise) remember that there is an emolument always waiting for you at the *Criterion*; also that you or I or the *Criterion* might disappear at any moment and that it would a pity that this should happen without your name ever having appeared in it. I hope that business if not pleasure will call you to London this summer. I have organised some fortnightly lunches at the Cock in Fleet Street at which several regular contributors usually turn up and we should be glad to have your company on one of these Wednesdays. I also should be glad to have your private company on another day. I hope things are going smoothly with you, barring the need for money which is perpetual. I have come down here for a short rest but as a matter of fact to deal with arrears of work and shall be in London again in a week or so.

Yours ever,
T. S. E.

TO *D. R. Gillie*[1] CC

4 May 1924 [*The Criterion*, London]

My dear Gillie,

I have only today received your letter. By a curious piece of ill luck, it seems to have been delivered on the evening of the day on which I left for the country together with a letter from Menasce and one or two others. In consequence it arrived too soon for my instructions to the Post Office to forward letters to have taken effect and was only discovered yesterday by someone who went into my flat. I am extremely sorry, although I was out of town in any case, on the days you mention. I suppose you will be too busy during this term to come up to London at all, and it is hardly likely that I shall get to Oxford. So I wish you the best of luck – for there is luck in your examinations – although I have not the slightest doubt of the result.

1 – D. R. Gillie: a student of Balliol College, Oxford; later translator of Joseph Pilsudski, *The Memories of a Polish Revolutionary and Soldier* (1931).

In any case I hope you will let me know when you have come down to London again with success behind you.[1]

Valery Larbaud lives at 70 rue du Cardinal le Moine, Paris V and you had better put '*faire suivre*' on the letter because I have not heard from him for some time and he may not yet have returned from Italy. When I spoke to him in November, he was very indefinite about coming to England but I think that if you wrote to him, it would serve as an additional inducement. He is more likely to come in June than at any other time of the year. Certainly use my name.

Sincerely yours,
[T. S. E.]

TO *J. Shand*[2] CC

4 May 1924 [*The Criterion*, London]

Dear Sir,

I am returning herewith your two essays on Hamlet and Satire, because although they are very interesting they do not very well fit in with the make-up of the several next numbers of the *Criterion*.[3] With your permission I will retain a little longer your very interesting paper on Conrad as it might be possible for us to use this.[4]

Yours faithfully
[T. S. E.]

1–On 18 Apr. Gillie recalled TSE mentioning at Christmas time that Larbaud was coming over in the summer and might be 'willing to come to the Ordinary'. 'I have more or less decided not to put off my schools and am watching the dreadful term approach with a sort of fatalistic indifference.' He hoped to be able to call on TSE in London on 22 or 23 Apr. if he was free.

2–John Shand (b. 1901) was an occasional contributor to C. He later wrote an essay 'Around *Little Gidding*', *Nineteenth Century* 136 (Sept. 1944).

3–On 25 May Shand submitted an essay on *Othello*, and on 16 June a dialogue on 'The Art of Acting'. He published 'Satire and Cynicism' in 'The Contributors' Club', *Adelphi* 2: 9 (Feb. 1925).

4–See Shand, 'Some Notes on Joseph Conrad', C. 3: 9 (Oct. 1924).

TO *Virginia Woolf* TS Berg

7 May 1924[1] Milestone Cottages

My dear Virginia,

Five thousand words are no drawback, when the words are yours; I wish for nothing better than to attract the sparkish wits[2] of undergraduates; I accept the article which you offer me.[3] May I have it at once, and set it up? You can fashion it to any cut you please when you get the proof. I shall print it in the July number. If you will send it to Clarence Gate Gardens I shall be there in time to receive it.

I hope indeed that the *Criterion* has improved. If so, it must be chiefly due to having an article by Murry.[4] Of course his contribution is probably not up [to] the level of his newest obstetric style under the name of Helen Thomas (vide the last *Adelphi*)[5] but it would be unreasonable of me to expect him to honour me with his very best – which is perhaps a little above the heads of the *Criterion* public. I should be interested to know

1–Misdated April 1924.

2–The phrase 'sparkish wits' had figured in VHE's 'Letters of the Moment – II', published in *C.*, Apr. 1924. In the course of her sketch, 'F. M.' quotes what she calls a 'few poor verses' – in fact, they were a modified extract from TSE's draft opening of 'The Fire Sermon' – including: 'But see, where Fresca in her boudoir sits, / Surrounded by a court of sparkish wits' (Vivien Eliot Papers, Bodleian: Eng misc. c 624, folios 107–8). The epithet 'sparkish' aptly picks up the name of a character in *The Country Wife* – the play that has supposedly sparked F. M.'s verses in the first place. It is probable that TSE gave VHE the term 'sparkish', since the word is written in his hand at the foot of folio 110^{v} in the Bodleian MSS. TSE evidently relished the private joke of devising a sketch that incorporated an adapted portion of his draft of *TWL*, since not only is VHE's piece dated '1st April', but TSE also pressed the printers to ensure that the issue in which it was to feature should be published on April Fool's Day: Hazell, Watson & Viney wrote on 3 Mar. 1925, 'We note that you are very anxious that this should be published on April 1st and we will do everything possible to work to this date.' See further J. Haffenden, 'Vivien Eliot and *The Waste Land*: The Forgotten Fragments', *PN Review* 175 (33: 5, May–June 2007), 18–23.

3–On 5 May, VW was 'flattered' that TSE wanted anything of hers in C. where she 'would rather appear than anywhere else'. The only thing she had was a lecture 'called Mr Bennett and Mrs Brown': 'the drawbacks are that it is elementary and loquacious, being meant for undergraduates . . . and that we are going to print it next autumn' (*Letters*, III, 106). See 'Character in Fiction', described as 'A paper read to the Heretics, Cambridge, on May 8, 1924', in *C.* 2: 8 (July 1924); it was reprinted as *Mr Bennett and Mrs Brown* (Hogarth Press, 1924).

4–VW said it 'was a very good number', but she experienced 'a complete failure as to what Murry means'. See JMM's 'Romanticism and the Tradition', *C.* 2: 7 (Apr. 1924).

5–Helen Thomas (widow of the poet Edward Thomas), 'Birth', *Adelphi* 1: 12 (May 1924). The piece began with a description of the birth of her son: 'I woke up in the night, and knew that at last my waiting was over. My baby was making ready for his mysterious entrance into life. I held my breath, and waited.' (1085–91).

your verdict on his essay when you have given it really adequate study, because I have not yet had time to read it. If your opinion accords with that of the *Times Literary Supplement*[1] (and I somehow divine your approval) I shall be glad to feel that I have been the humble instrument of reinstating Murry to his place in society, beside the hearths of civilised homes, from which he has wilfully strayed in recent years,

e cio gli fece
Romeo, persona umile e peregrina . . .

[2]

and I shall not have run the *Criterion* for two suicidal[3] years in vain.

I have already been 'warned' and 'put on my guard', in fact perhaps 'threatened' by our venerable and august friend Mr Sydney Schiff, that I may be met on my return at Victoria Station by a mass-meeting of protestants against my careless editing – in not having had time to read and expurgate Wyndham Lewis's article before publication, there being only twenty-four hours in a day. This armed and menacing mass-meeting of all those who feel that the 'cap fits' (I expect to recognise many friendly faces) will presumably be led by Mr Sydney Schiff himself in the costume and headpiece of a pseudo-Proust.[4] But when I am dismembered, like a hero of Grecian tragedy[5] (rather than a bungalow bride) it is you, my dear Virginia, whom I shall reproach and execrate with my last breath. For you are my oracle and counsel in matters journalistic, and did you not advise me (with the supporting opinions too of Leonard and Clive as junior counsel) that it was in pursuance of 'the best tradition of British

1 – 'Continuing his discussion of Classicism and Romanticism with Mr T. S. Eliot, the editor of *The Criterion*, Mr Murry sets out in some detail his theory of religion as a relation between the fundamental "I Am" in the soul and the greater "I Am" beyond, which imperatively demands the rejection of any external spiritual authority in its task of overcoming the antithesis between inner freedom and external necessity, and apprehending the mystical unity of the world . . . His theory is fertile enough of new ideas to demand careful attention even from those who reject his individualism' (*TLS*, 1 May 1924, 271).

2 – Dante, *Parad.*, VI, 135: 'and this was wrought / for him by Romeo, a lowly and an alien man' (Temple Classics). Dante's adjective '*peregrina*' re-appears in English guise as 'unappeased and peregrine' in 'Little Gidding'.

3 – On the carbon copy TSE wrote 'tedious'.

4 – In his satire on literary London, WL's narrator said: 'In a little artificial world of carefully-fostered self-esteem I will show you a pseudo-Proust'. Replying on the 11th, VW said she and LW had imagined this referred to JMM and had not 'connected the pseudo-Proust with Schiff'. She added: 'everyone – Lytton, Osbert Sitwell, Mary Hutchinson is claiming to be an Ape of God and identifying the rest of the pack'.

5 – A reference to the ritual dismembering of the hero in Greek tragedy, exemplified by Pentheus in Euripides' *The Bacchae*.

6 – VW replied that TSE's 'oracles and counsels, Virginia, Leonard and Clive [Bell] are fallible mortals', instancing their mistaken identification of the 'pseudo-Proust' with JMM.

journalism' to let one contributor say what he likes about another?[6]

But seriously, Virginia, how tired I am of being supposed to edit the *Criterion*, how tired of the very word *Criterion*! and yet you would be surprised how many substantial personages and men of weight, Oxford dons and grave statesmen, come and tell me what a lucky young man I am at my age to have a review to 'do as I like with'! Do as I like! as if there were any satisfaction in doing as one likes with editing a review in the fragmentary evening hours given at the cost of sleep, society, recreation and neglect of private affairs; having to make the same appearances, get as good or better contributors, as reviews provided with an editor and sub-editor (with *salaries* and devoting all their time to it) a business manager, an office and a staff; doing as one likes by editing a review in one's sitting room in the evenings, subject to a thousand interruptions: without staff, assistants or a business manager: only since Christmas with a Desk (the one Vivien shewed you: nine pounds ten second hand saved up for) and recently with a job secretary who performs domestic duties as well, so that I may have a little more time for my part of the work! I should not mind if people thought me a lunatic (and agreed that I was a harmless one) but they simply think me mercenary for staying in a bank instead of giving *all* my time to my lunacy.

I am glad to hear that Rodmell is purged, and clergy, as you may imagine, are always a temptation to me.[1] But what would happen, and how would you behave, if I were to extend my next visit to 20 hours? You would expire of boredom. I know my failings. Insensitive persons can endure me for 24 hours;[2] there is one old gentleman who, kept up by Port Wine, can even survive until the first Monday morning train: but 19½ hours is precisely the limit for less coarse and hardy natures. So you see there is method in my time-table. But if you sent me to Divine Service on Sunday Morning, and to walk with the Curate on Sunday afternoon, could you endure me a little longer? It would still be a risk.

Vivien, in one of her lightning changes of Policy, has decided not to return to London at all this summer. She sends you her love.

I have just faced and taxed the *Nouvelle Revue Française* with never having reviewed *The Waste Land*. With specious palaver, and filthy French knavery, they say they never received a copy. Would the Hogarth Press try the experiment of sending them another copy? If advised of its despatch, I will attempt my Arts and Browbeating ways on the Frenchmen again.

1 – VW had said that 'We remain in solitude with the clergy, which is as it should be.'
2 – Recalling his previous visits, VW had written: 'Please begin to set aside your 19½ hours for Rodmell in September.'

Meanwhile I retain my chronique, and have other cards in my sleeve.

I shall study my essays carefully on my return to London.[1]

Ever yours
T. S. E.

PS I will come to see you and fetch the manuscript on my return, instead of asking you to post it.

TO *Wyndham Lewis* — TS Cornell

13 May 1924 — 9 Clarence Gate Gdns

Dear Lewis,

I have got back and want to see you soon.[2] I cannot manage this week but will you let me know what evening next week you have free and I will come in about the usual time?

Yours ever,
T. S. E.

TO *Robert Graves* — TS Morris

13 May 1924 — *The Criterion*, 17 Thavies Inn

Dear Graves,

Please forgive me for not replying immediately to your letter.[3] I hope that the enclosed manuscripts will not reach you too late for your purpose. As a matter of fact I was in the country and could do nothing about returning the manuscripts until I came back to town yesterday.

I am very pleased that you should have thought of the *Criterion* and hope that you will send us something more. Of course we publish very little poetry and I am afraid that we should not be able to accept any more until next January; otherwise I should have clung to them.[4] I hope we may

1–On 5 May, VW wrote 'don't forget your essays': TSE's *Homage to John Dryden: Three Essays on the Poetry of the Seventeenth Century* was published by the Hogarth Press in Nov. 1924.

2–Probably to discuss the rumpus caused by 'The Apes of God'. The third instalment never appeared.

3–On 3 May, Graves asked if TSE would return the poems, if he did not intend to publish them in C. Edith Sitwell was staying with him in Oxford the following week and wanted to see them.

4–None of Graves's poems were published in C.

1 Pencil portrait of Eliot by Wyndham Lewis, 1922

2 Eliot in a garden at Bosham. Annotated on the reverse in Vivien Eliot's hand, 'Bosham/August 1922/Tom, looking like the Prince of Wales'

3 Eliot's workplace, Lloyds Bank, photographed by his brother Henry, with St Mary Woolnoth on the right

4 Vivien in the kitchen at 9 Clarence Gate Gardens

5 Richard Aldington. Photograph by Madame Yevonde

6 'Sunday afternoon': Eliot at Garsington with Anthony Asquith, Lord David Cecil, L. P. Hartley and Edward Sackville-West. Photograph by Lady Ottoline Morrell, 1923

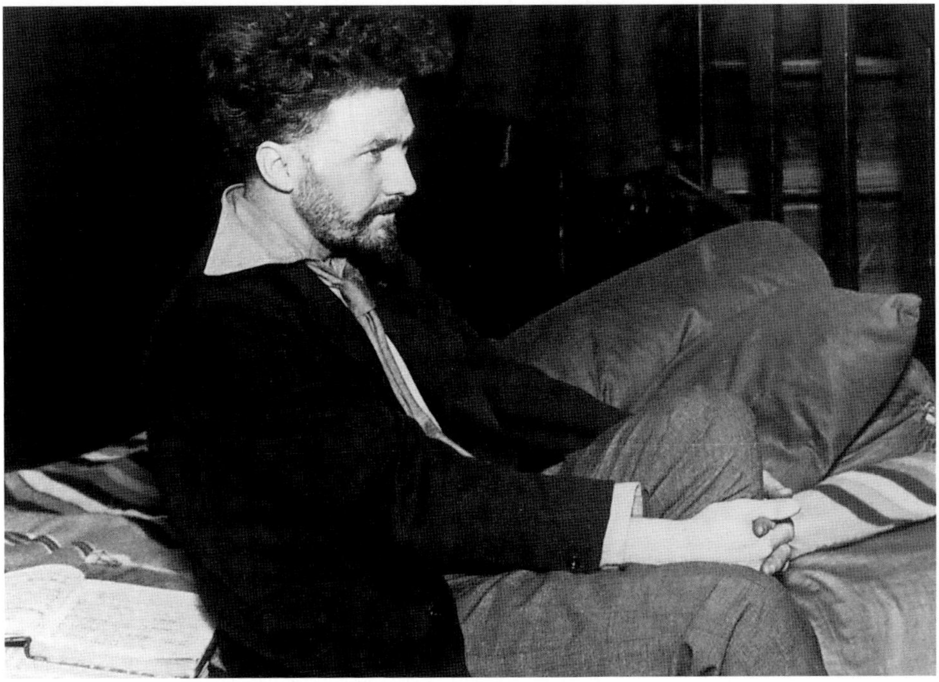

7 Ezra Pound in his Paris studio, 1923

8 Eliot in conversation with L. A. G. Strong

9 Mary Hutchinson with her lover Clive Bell (seated), Duncan Grant and E. M. Forster at Charleston, Sussex, 1923

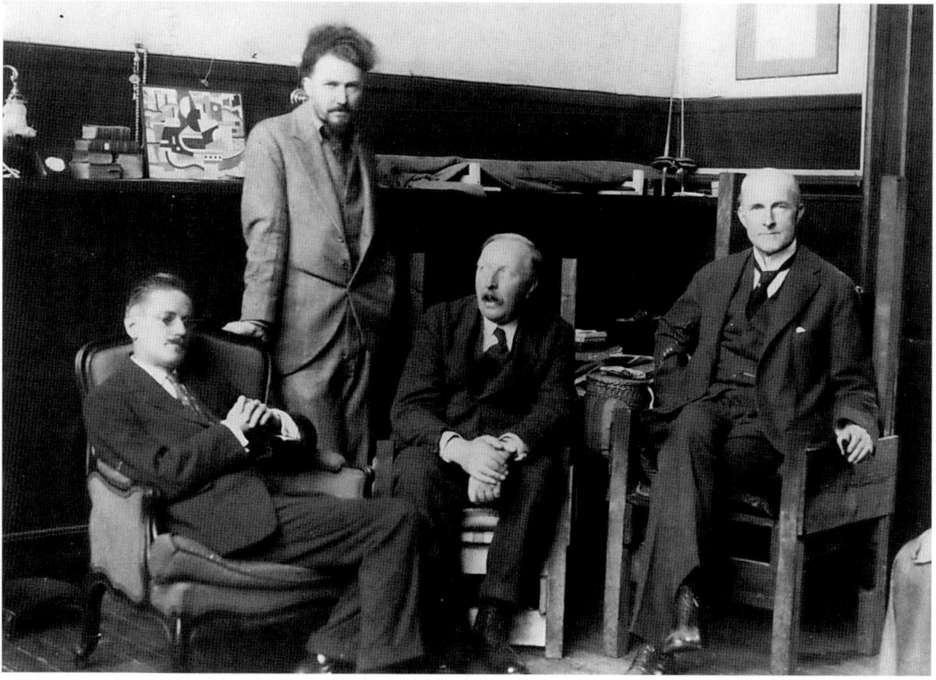

10 James Joyce, Ezra Pound, Ford Madox Ford and John Quinn in Pound's studio in Paris, 1923

11 Vivien with Lucy Thayer at Fishbourne, June 1924

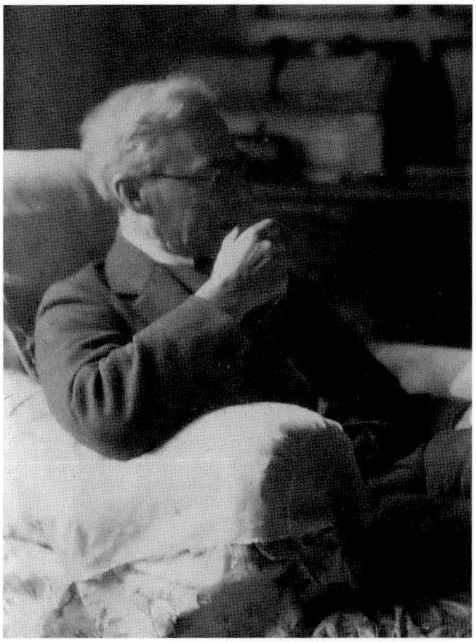

12 Bertrand Russell at Garsington. Photograph by Lady Ottoline Morrell, late 1924

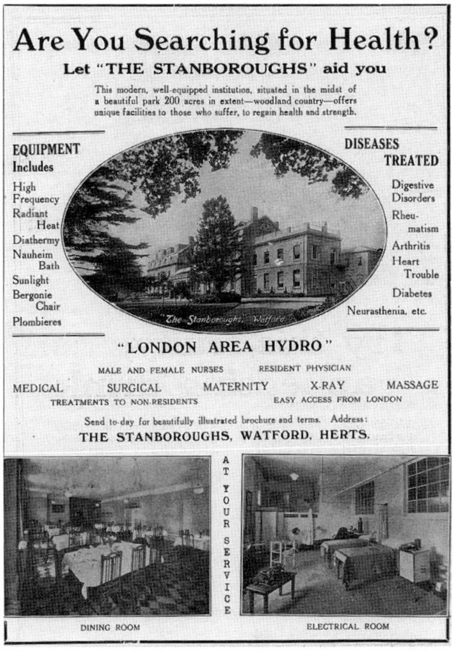

13 Advertisement for 'The Stanboroughs' Nursing Home, Watford, from *Good Health* magazine, July 1929

14 Aldous Huxley. Photograph by Edward Gooch, *c.*1925

15 Eliot with Virginia Woolf at Garsington.
Photograph by Lady Ottoline Morrell, June 1924

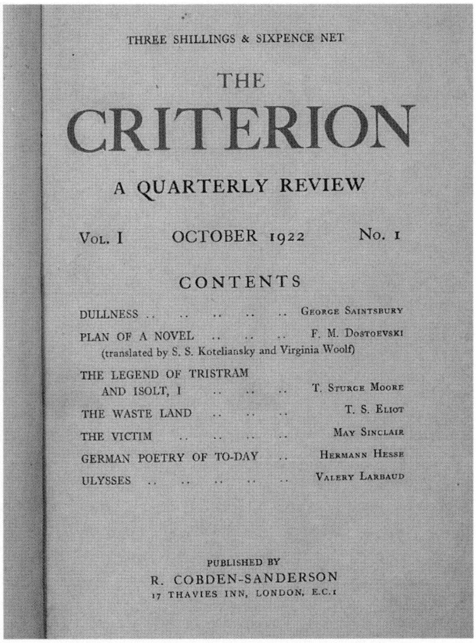
THREE SHILLINGS & SIXPENCE NET

THE
CRITERION
A QUARTERLY REVIEW

VOL. I OCTOBER 1922 No. 1

CONTENTS

DULLNESS	GEORGE SAINTSBURY
PLAN OF A NOVEL .. .. .. (translated by S. S. Koteliansky and Virginia Woolf)	F. M. DOSTOEVSKI
THE LEGEND OF TRISTRAM AND ISOLT, I	T. STURGE MOORE
THE WASTE LAND	T. S. ELIOT
THE VICTIM	MAY SINCLAIR
GERMAN POETRY OF TO-DAY ..	HERMANN HESSE
ULYSSES	VALERY LARBAUD

PUBLISHED BY
R. COBDEN-SANDERSON
17 THAVIES INN, LONDON, E.C.1

16 Cover of the first issue of *The Criterion*, October 1922

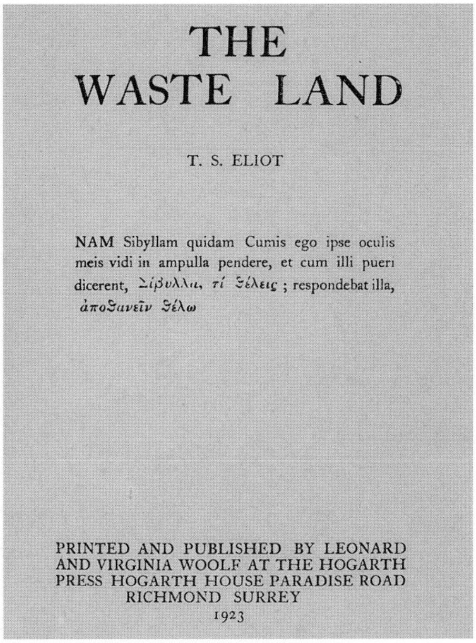
THE
WASTE LAND

T. S. ELIOT

NAM Sibyllam quidam Cumis ego ipse oculis meis vidi in ampulla pendere, et cum illi pueri dicerent, Σίβυλλα, τί θέλεις; respondebat illa, ἀποθανεῖν θέλω

PRINTED AND PUBLISHED BY LEONARD AND VIRGINIA WOOLF AT THE HOGARTH PRESS HOGARTH HOUSE PARADISE ROAD RICHMOND SURREY
1923

17 The first edition of *The Waste Land*, published by the Hogarth Press, 1923

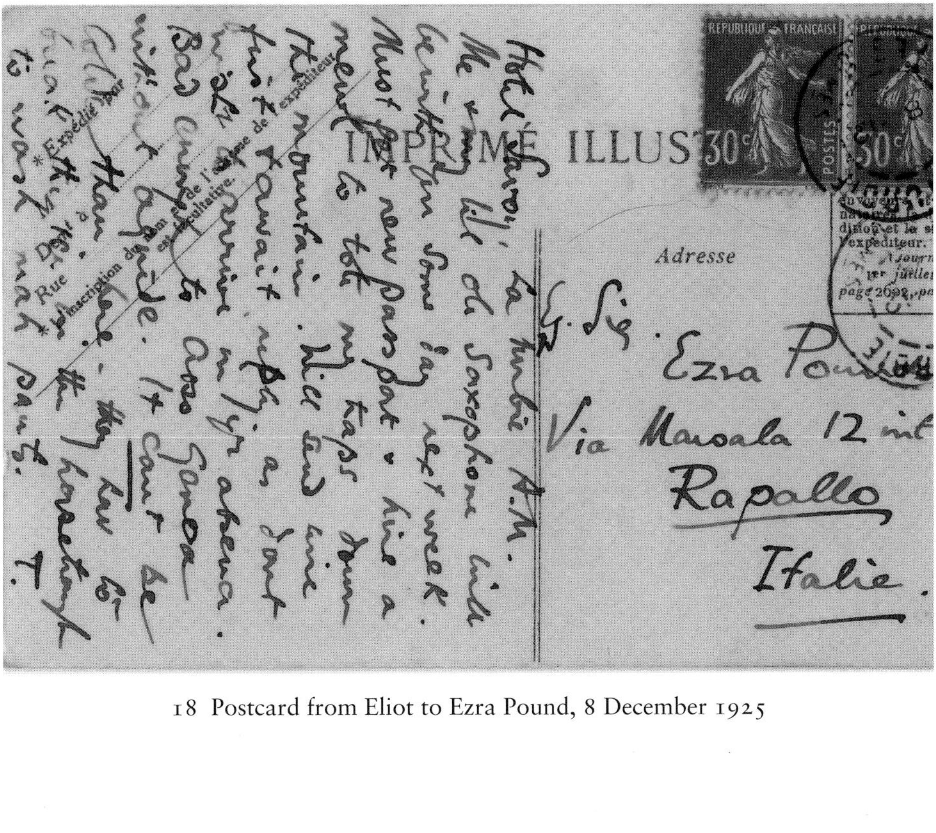

18 Postcard from Eliot to Ezra Pound, 8 December 1925

19 Eliot at his desk at Faber & Gwyer, 1925

20 Geoffrey Faber

21 Eliot outside the Faber & Gwyer offices. Photograph by Henry Ware Eliot

meet again within a reasonable time. I should like very much to see you but it does not look as if I were likely to visit Oxford again within the present generation.

Yours sincerely,
T. S. Eliot

Do send some prose *as well.*

TO *Frederick Etchells*[1] CC

14 May 1924 [*Criterion*] 9 Clarence Gate Gdns

Dear Etchells,

My sincere congratulations on the beautiful piece of work.[2] I think these things ought to sell very well at such moderate prices and I shall be glad to insert a note in the *Criterion* about them.[3]

I shall be delighted to make suggestions about reprints. I shall not be able to tell you what the first editions are like but I can recommend a few things which ought to be reprinted. It seems to me that wherever possible, it would be more useful to reprint things which are difficult to obtain in any form, and from this point of view I should suggest that less easily obtainable things could be found than any of Swift's pamphlets. One or two things of Bolingbroke's for example.

As soon as anything particularly suitable occurs to me I will let you know and I should like very much to see you later to talk it over.

With all success to your work,
Sincerely yours,
[T. S. E.]

1–Frederick Etchells (1886–1973), architect and writer, studied at the Royal College of Art and worked for a while at the Omega Workshops established by Roger Fry, and then as a Vorticist artist. Following WW1 he went into partnership with Hugh MacDonald and practised thereafter as an architect: by 1928 he was principal architect to the Grosvenor Estate. Haslewood Reprints was a short-lived publishing venture; but presently he undertook, at the behest of John Rodker, a translation of Le Corbusier's classic *Vers une architecture* (*Towards a New Architecture*, 1927).

2–Sir Thomas Browne, *A Letter to a Friend upon occasion of the death of his Intimate Friend* (Frederick Etchells and Hugh Macdonald, 1924).

3–'A new press which is welcome is that of Frederick Etchells and Hugh Macdonald, who announce the Haslewood Reprints. Sir Thomas Browne's *Letter to a Friend*, which is the first in the series, is an admirable reproduction of the first edition; and the volumes of the series are published at very moderate prices '('A Commentary', *C.* 2: 8, July 1924, 374).

TO *Owen Barfield* TS Barfield

14 May 1924 *The Criterion*, 17 Thavies Inn

Dear Mr Barfield,

Thank you for your letter of the 30th April and for the manuscript. I think I appreciate what you say about the rhythm of 'Dope' but all the same I believe in a fundamental rhythm of which one's original work gives variations and I think that this is very much stronger in 'Dope' than in anything else of yours I have seen. About the present story ['Mr Cayley's Bet']. There are things in it which I like very much[;] they are to me an exact statement of an aspect of the Cockney type. The first part seems to me very successful: the episode of the quarrel and the bet. But it seems to me that in the figure of the narrator you have invented a superfluous character and that in the episode of the death you have invented a conclusion dangerously near to the worst tricks of Dickens and Thomas Hardy. It seems to me that it was unnecessary to make the child into such a central figure. I am aware that the narrative manner is usually liked, but the restriction to exact statement seems to me a higher form of literature. It is rather like the difference between the battle of Waterloo described by Stendhal on the one hand and by Victor Hugo on the other.[1]

I have expressed myself very badly, but you will see perhaps that up to a point you have been working in a way which I very much like, and that after that point you have been working in a way which I very much dislike. But I do not think that the manner and tone of a public house quarrel has *ever* been better done and I wish that this might be re-cast in a form in which we might use it.[2]

With best wishes,

Yours truly
T. S. Eliot

1 – See Stendhal's account of Fabrice in the Battle of Waterloo (*La Chartreuse de Parme*), and the apocalyptic account of the same battle in the first book of Pt II of Victor Hugo's *Les Misérables*.

2 – On 10 May, Barfield had written that he did not want the 'rhythm of "Dope"' to be his 'permanent rhythm' and that the 'character of the narrator' was of 'paramount interest' in the new story. He was 'not ready to alter the thing yet awhile'. It was not published in *C*.

TO *Henri Bremond*[1] CC

14 May 1924 [London]

Cher Monsieur,

Je suis enchanté de recevoir votre charmante lettre et ensuite votre livre qui vient d'arriver.[2] Je connaissais déjà le nom de votre livre dont je viens d'aborder la lecture avec un grand intérêt. Tout ce que vous dites sur Boileau m'intéresse et me plaît.[3]

Je vous ferai parvenir avec beaucoup de plaisir les deux numéros de *Criterion* qui ont attiré votre attention.[4] J'ai l'idée que la discussion entre Monsieur Murry et moi a lieu sur tout autre terrain que votre admirable travail. Je ne suis pas de ceux qui croient à une distinction absolue entre le classicisme et le romantisme; je trouve qu'on peut même regarder plus souvent qu'on ne croit un seul auteur sous les deux aspects. Ce qui est en cause entre Monsieur Murry et moi, c'est plutôt qu'il confond à mon avis la littérature avec la religion et dans cette question çi, je me trouve fort heureusement appuyé par un bel article de Jacques Rivière sur la crise du

1 – Henri Brémond (1865–1933): French literary scholar and Catholic philosopher; author of *Newman* (1905) and *Histoire littéraire du sentiment religieux en France* (6 vols, 1916–22). His *The Mystery of Newman* (1907) was discussed in *NC* 4: 1 (Jan. 1926).

2 – On 6 May, Brémond wrote to say that Charles du Bos had alerted him to an article in the *TLS* about TSE's controversy with JMM about classicism and romanticism (*TLS*, 1 May 1924, 271). As a result he was sending TSE his book *Pour le Romantisme* (1923), which had aroused considerable public controversy in France: 'Le dernier document à ce sujet est dans le numéro du 1 mai de la *Revue des Deux Mondes* – l'article d'André Seaunier. Comme je compte revenir prochainement à la charge pour résumer le débat, je serais très curieux de connaître ce qui a été dit chez vous. Il serait en effet très intéressant de prendre sur le fait une même préoccupation littéraire des deux côtés de l'eau. Puis-je donc, sans être trop indiscret, vous demander de bien vouloir me faire envoyer ce qui a été écrit dans votre revue autour de la question' (MS Houghton). *Trans.*: 'The latest contribution is to be found in the 1 May issue of *La Revue des Deux Mondes* – the article by André Seaunier. As I intend to re-enter the fray in order to sum up the debate so far, I should be very curious to know what views have been expressed in England. It would, indeed, be very interesting to discover the same literary preoccupation at work on both sides of the water. Can I, without putting you to too much trouble, ask you to send me what has been written on the question in your review?'

3 – Brémond's opening chapter, 'La Légende de Boileau', disposes of the myth of Boileau as 'le classicisme fait homme' ['classicism made man'] in favour of a writer who is 'vivant, pittoresque, coloré, savoureux, sonore, le vrai Boileau enfin, tout différent de celui de la légende' ['living, picturesque, colourful, pungent, sonorous, the real Boileau, quite different from the figure of legend'] (p. 2). He says in the introduction that the aim of the book, with its studies of Scott, Lammenais, Sainte-Beuve and Barrès, is to dispel the 'absurd quarrel between Boileau and Victor Hugo' (x).

4 – TSE's 'The Function of Criticism' in *C.* 2: 5 (Oct. 1923), and JMM's 'Romanticism and the Tradition' in *C.* 2: 7 (Apr. 1924).

concept de littérature dans un des derniers numéros de la *Nouvelle Revue Française*.[1]

Quand-même je vous prie de me donner votre opinion quand vous aurez lu mon article et de ma part je ne manquerai pas de vous écrire à la longue dès que j'aurai terminé la lecture de votre étude.

En espérant vous voir à votre prochaine visite à Londres ou à ma prochaine visite à Paris, je vous prie, cher Monsieur Brémond, de recevoir l'expression de mes

hommages respectueux,
[T. S. E.][2]

TO *Alexander Porterfield*[3] CC

14 May 1924 [*The Criterion*, London]

Sir,

I was very much struck by a story which appeared under your name in the *Storyteller* magazine with the title 'The Old Guard Dies'.[4] I should very much like to see some of your other work with a view to publication in the *Criterion*.[5] On the one hand the *Criterion* probably does not offer competitive remuneration: our rates are £10.0.0 per 5000 words and

1–Rivière, 'La crise du concept de littérature' ['The Crisis of the Concept of Literature'], *NRF* 11: 125 (1 Feb. 1924): TSE alludes to it in his 'Commentary' in *C.* 2: 8 (July 1924).

2–*Translation*: Dear Sir, I am delighted to have your charming letter and, following it, your book which has just arrived. Its title was already known to me, and I have begun reading it with great interest. Everything you say about Boileau interests and delights me.

I shall have great pleasure in sending you the two issues of the *Criterion* which attracted your attention. I fancy that the discussion between Mr Murry and myself is concerned with quite a different area from that of your admirable study. I am not among those who believe in an absolute distinction between Classicism and Romanticism; I even find that, more often than is supposed, one and the same author can be looked at from both angles. What is at issue between Mr Murry and myself is rather that he, in my opinion, confuses literature with religion and, in this connection, I find very welcome support for my view in an excellent article by Jacques Rivière on the crisis in the concept of literature in one of the latest numbers of *La Nouvelle Revue Française*.

Nevertheless, please give me your opinion when you have read my article and I, for my part, will not fail to write to you in due course when I have finished reading your study.

Hoping that I shall see you during your next visit to London or my next visit to Paris, I assure you, dear Monsieur Brémond, of my most respectful regards. [T. S. E.]

3–Alexander Porterfield, an American short-story writer (resident in New York City) whose work appeared in *Harper's* and other magazines.

4–'The Old Guard Dies', *Saturday Evening Post* (22 July 1922); reprinted in *The Storyteller*.

5–See Porterfield, 'A Marriage Has Been Arranged', *C.* 3: 10 (Jan. 1925).

contributions should be under that length if possible. On the other hand the inducement is the appreciation of a different public.

The *Criterion* is a quarterly and publishes one or two pieces of fiction in each number.

I am, yours faithfully,

[T. S. E.]

TO *Jean Charles Grenier*[1] CC

15 May 1924 [*The Criterion*, London]

Monsieur,

Madame la Vicomtesse Rothermere m'a envoyé le premier numéro de votre review *Philosophies* qui contient la première partie de votre article sur le Nihilisme européen.[2] Voilà un sujet qui a déjà attiré mon attention et que je trouve d'une importance capitale. J'ai été énormément intéressé par votre article; je voudrais bien que cette question fut posée aux lecteurs anglais et je partage avec Lady Rothermere son admiration pour votre article. Pourriez vous m'indiquer l'étendue eventuelle de votre article et les conclusions générales? S'il est admissible, je voudrais bien voir la suite de cet article dont je prendrais tous les soins possibles.[3]

Nous serons heureux d'insérer une note sur *Philosophie* dans un numéro futur du *Criterion*[4] et je ferai parvenir le *Criterion* à votre bureau à Paris.

En vous félicitant encore sur la revue que vous avez initiée, je vous prie, Monsieur, d'agréer l'expression de mes sentiments tres distingués.

[T. S. E.][5]

1 – Jean Grenier (1898–1971): French philosopher, essayist and novelist.

2 – 'European Nihilism', *Philosophies* 1: 1 (1924).

3 – Grenier replied (23 May) that the two articles he had written were just a 'fragment' of a book he had been working on since Oct. 1923, and which would be published only after a few years.

4 – In his note on 'French Periodicals', F. S. Flint called it 'a new review for the discussion of ideas from all angles'. The opening numbers were full of 'interesting matter' and it promised to be 'valuable . . . for those not afraid of ideas, whatever their nature', C. 2: 8 (July 1924), 498.

5 – *Translation*: Dear Sir, Lady Rothermere sent me the first number of your review *Philosophies* which includes the first part of your article on European Nihilism. It's a subject which had already caught my attention, and is of capital importance. I was immensely interested in your article; I wish this question could be put before English readers and share Lady Rothermere's admiration for your article. Could you let me know the eventual scope of the article, and its general conclusions? If permitted, I would very much like to see the sequel of the article – which I would take great care of.

TO *Hugh Walpole* CC

15 May 1924 [*The Criterion*, London]

Dear Walpole,

I am back from the country and should like very much to see you. I could lunch on any day you like next week except Wednesday but a work-day lunch would necessitate your coming to lunch with me in the City, which as I said, would be rather hurried and crowded and I am afraid I could not give you a very good lunch either. On the other hand I could meet you for lunch on a Saturday, either next Saturday or the following, anywhere you liked. But if Saturday is not a good day for you, then I should suggest lunching with me on a weekday at the Cock in Fleet Street which is about as far west as I can get on a working day. I do hope in any case that you will choose one day within the next week.

Yours sincerely,
[T. S. E.]

FROM *Henry Eliot* TS Valerie Eliot

17 May 1924 David C. Thomas Company (Advertising), 28 East Jackson Bvd, Chicago

Dear Tom:

I received your long letter of May 1 on the 14th, and cabled you that day regarding making an appointment with Lady Rothermere. As I did not know how long she was to be in New York I later thought it might be best to write her a note, explaining the circumstances, your having suggested my meeting her, etc. From what you have written me I judged her to be extremely sensible and capable of understanding the business exigencies of correspondence. I did not in my note (which was purely formal) go into any reasons for wishing to see her, but based it on a common interest in your affairs. Today I received a telegram from her, 'Delighted if you will lunch with me 25th. Rothermere.'

At first I was not able to see in what way I could be of much help or exert much influence, but I was convinced from your letter that it would

—

We would be happy to insert a note about *Philosophies* in a future number of the *Criterion* and I will send the *Criterion* to your office in Paris.

With many congratulations again on launching your review, and my sincerest regards, [T. S. E.]

be agreeable to her and that in some indirect way it might have a good effect. At least I can give her an outline of your finances and your extreme difficulties. It is difficult to know just what course to steer. Her offer still stands, I take it, of 300 pounds a year if you leave the bank. I am not sure whether your present aim is to have her offer you the 300 pounds while you are still at the bank, or to increase the offer so that you can leave the bank. I do not see, myself, how the former would help you otherwise than financially. It would perhaps enable you to have more assistance (would enable you to hire helpers) but would not relieve you from the physical and nervous strain which you cannot support long.

It seems to me it would be better if she would increase the salary, or allow you money for assistants, or both, and you should then leave the bank, provided that the bank people are not still insisting that it is your sacred duty to stay. As I understand it, Lord Rothermere insists the same thing, and if this is so, he and Lady Rothermere are in conflict on that point. In this case, the difficulty is more than a money difficulty.

You have $1500 a year from your securities, which with 300 pounds would make about $2800 a year. To this I could add, as long as my affairs prosper, $1500 a year more. I get $1200 from my securities. I think that it would be better before very long for you to sell the rest of your Hydraulic. It has slipped off lately to about 67½. I believe it will fall off somewhat more during the summer, but it may come back in the fall or at the beginning of next year. This of course would reduce your income from securities to about $1200, which with my $1500 and the 300 pounds would mean about $4000 a year to you. Could you do with that?

Mother is contemplating dividing $18,000 in securities among the children. I should advise her dividing her remaining 300 shares of Hydraulic, as that will do away with a Missouri inheritance tax on them. That would give you $150 or $180 a year more. I think however that she wants first to have you put your securities in trust, and then she will put this $3000 with them. Her idea is to have you create a voluntary trust, making yourself the beneficiary, Vivien the beneficiary after your death, and the five children the beneficiaries in event of Vivien's death. Such a trust could be made revocable, but would become irrevocable on your death. I myself am in favour of such a trust, but whether you want to make the five children the ultimate beneficiaries or not I do not know. The principal reason for making it revocable, to my mind, would be on the chance that you would want to use the money to build a house, or to invest in a publishing venture. The latter course I hope you will never take, not that I do not believe in new ventures, but that neither your fortune (if such it can be called) nor mine is sufficient to allow of the least risk being taken with it. I would certainly put my own money in trust for myself if I did not have to be in a position to borrow on it in emergency. The fact of having ready money and borrowing power is one of my chief holds on this business and gives me an importance which I should not otherwise possess. In case of any split, it would theoretically be possible for Needham and myself to take most of the clients away and start a new agency. This keeps the other fellow in line. I should not like to have to make such an investment, but I am too old to go out and get a job and it might be the only course. It would not be a serious risk with a few good clients; this business can be run on amazingly little capital, and theoretically we are paid before we disburse, and practically we come pretty close to that. We can do a half million dollar business a year on three or four thousand dollars' capital.

My business is prospering at present. A month ago my salary was put up to $8000, and while the total of our salaries is staggering for so small a business we still continue to show a small profit each month. We have a back tax claim of $6000 against us, but expect to get that reduced by half, if not more. Relations are again amicable. The business still seems less precarious than it did, though we have new offices, at twice the rent, and a high payroll, which I believe we can reduce.

I mention all this because I feel that I am at present in a position where I can give you a good deal of help, provided the status quo continues. I can easily spare the income I get from securities, and more, provided everything goes well. It is the uncertainty bothers me. So I would like to know the minimum on which you can live, in order to have some basis to figure. I want to save a little each year.

When I have to quit business myself, will come the difficulty. Probably by that time you will be getting $2500 a year from securities, but I shall need all of my income from my securities. I am going to have an operation on my ear before very long, which will make me deafer. I do not want to work out my life. I can do on $3000, perhaps $2500, if I have few doctors' bills.

There are three dangers: business disaster, death and marriage. In the case of my death, you would receive two thirds of my estate, and I believe it would be advisable to leave the other third to you instead of to Charlotte. The others can help Charlotte, if they are minded to.

As to marriage, it is very difficult to prognosticate. It is a well known fact (to myself at least) that I would be putty in the hands of any decent looking woman who ever spoke two kind words to me, and that I have only escaped because no woman has ever happened to take a notion to speak kindly to me. I am equally certain that I shall never get married (and never want to get married) and that I am to be had for the whistling (and want nothing else in the world than to be married). However, forty-four years of immunity augurs well for the future.

IMPORTANT

1. Please give consideration to the trust matter as soon as possible, as that will release the $18,000 which Mother wishes to distribute.

2. Be sure to make out and mail the income tax return at once on receipt of this letter, if you have not done so, as by the time you receive this notice there will just barely be time to get it to Baltimore. Mail check with it and I will reimburse you.

Re Mother's visit:

My last letter from Mother, received today, says 'I have been enduring much mental suffering over the question whether to go or not to go to London. Now I have the refusal of a stateroom on the 21st of June, and one returning on the 23d of August.' She says she has cabled you to this effect.

In all of her recent letters she has spoken of the nervous strain of deciding the matter, and I have hoped for months that she would come to a final decision. I think it would be well for her to go, and my only doubt has been whether it would be better to wait till you are free of the bank and had leisure. I thought in that case you could even go to Italy for a week with her, which I am sure would delight her above all things. I hope that you can do this if she comes. I think that once she has made a final decision she will be relieved and will look forward to the trip. I shall write her today urging her going.

I do not believe that I have written you that Bertrand Russell spent two or three days at my flat on Rush Street. This was suggested to him by the Dudleys. I believe he was really pleased to get away from wherever he was at the time and preferred it much to a hotel. The place is shabby, but it is comfortable and we do have good food. He had the run of the place and no one disturbed him or tried to entertain him. My conversation with him was chiefly about you and Vivien. I confess to quite a feeling of affection or at least strong friendliness for him, wholly personal.

Naturally I shall be much interested in meeting Lady Rothermere, but I shall stick pretty close to the matter in hand and shall confine myself to sketching the situation rather than suggesting anything. I suppose I must not mention Russell? I shall play safe.

Affectionately,

Henry

TO *Allan Wade* MS Valerie Eliot

18 May 1924 *The Criterion*, 9 Clarence Gate Gdns

Dear Mr Wade,

I have not yet thanked you for your long and very important letter, but that is because I am waiting for the opportunity to reply fully.[1] I shall certainly do so.

I have asked your secretary if for the last performance of the season I could be given a box (Sunday night). Can you help me?[2]

I am looking forward with great interest to next year's performance.

With all best wishes,

Yours very truly,
T. S. Eliot

TO *F. W. Bain* CC

19 May 1924 [*The Criterion*, London]

My dear Bain,

I would have written before but have been away in the country. Of course we shall be delighted to have something from you on some subject connected with the French revolution early in the autumn.[3] May I depend upon you and would it be possible for you to let us have it by the 1st September?

Yours in haste,
[T. S. E.]

TO *Richard Cobden-Sanderson* CC

19 May 1924 [London]

Dear Cobden-Sanderson,

Thank you for your letter of the 19th enclosing Hazell's report which I will submit to Lady Rothermere.[4] I enclose [a] list of payments to

1 – See TSE's letter of 8 Apr. congratulating Wade on the Phoenix *King Lear*.

2 – Wade replied on 18 May, reserving a box for *The Old Bachelor* at the Regent's Theatre, and acknowledging TSE's appreciative notices of the last two plays in *C.*

3 – On 7 May, Bain said he 'could write you things worth reading on the French Revolution – a sealed book to most people in this country'. See '1789', *C.* 3: 9 (Oct. 1924), 43–71.

4 – The printers' report on the 'defects in printing' that TSE complained of in *C.* 2: 7 (Apr. 1924) blamed the problems in the printing of the issue on 'the pure carelessness of the

contributors with the exception of Ezra Pound's article[1] and the foreign reviews. As the foreign reviews are composed by different people, I am afraid I must ask for a statement of the number of words in the reviews of each country separately. As for the article by Ezra Pound, I forgot to say that as I cut out part of this without referring it to Ezra Pound first, I feel that it ought justly to be paid as for the whole article. Will you therefore ask Hazells to let me have the number of words in the complete galley proof of the Antheil article instead of the words actually printed in the number.

I enclose the manuscript of W. B. Yeats as he has agreed to our publishing it if the number can be printed by the end of June. I think that the stage directions at various points ought to be printed in small type.

I deposited with you the manuscript of an article by Osbert Sitwell. Will you please send this on to Hazells and call their attention to the fact that a large section at the beginning marked by the author has not to be printed.

I think you now have the following manuscripts:-[2]

Yeats,
Selby,
Cavafy,
Sitwell,
Proust,

I should of course like to have the number of words in each as soon as Hazells can count them.

I shall be obliged if you will have a copy of the October and of the April number sent to:

Monsieur Henri Brémond
7 rue Mechain
Paris XIV

I think that we ought also to send copies regularly to the publishers of any books noticed in the *Criterion*, especially as I am intending in future to have a few book reviews. So would you mind sending a copy of the February number of [*sc.* to] Messrs. Heinemann, re William Archer, *The Old Drama and the New*, discussed in my article and copies of the April number to Kegan Paul re Hulme's *Speculations* and to John Lane and Routledge re their series mentioned in my commentary.[3]

---

operator', and assured RC-S and TSE that everything would be done to prevent a recurrence.

1–EP, 'George Antheil', in C. 2: 7 (Apr. 1924).

2–WBY, 'The Cat and the Moon'; F. G. Selby, 'Bacon and Montaigne'; C. P. Cavafy, 'Ithaca'; Osbert Sitwell, 'A German Eighteenth-Century Town'; Marcel Proust, 'The Death of Albertine' – all in C. 2: 8 (July 1924), with the exception of the Selby (3: 10, Jan. 1925).

3–TSE wrote on Archer in 'Four Elizabethan Dramatists', C. 2: 6 (Feb. 1924), and praised the 'public spirit or sagacity of such publishers as John Lane and Routledge' for their Bodley

I am sorry to give you so much trouble.

Yours ever,
[T. S. E.]

TO *Conrad Aiken* TS Huntington

19 May 1924 *The Criterion*, 17 Thavies Inn

My dear Conrad,

Yes, it is true that I have no right to complain.[1] I return you herewith your Emily Dickinson with compliments and thanks. As for 'Psychomachia', I am still clinging to that with the desire of printing it in the autumn.[2] May I ask politely whether it has been or is likely to be published anywhere in America meanwhile? Also I press for your article. I shall be very disappointed if I do not eventually get Henry James from you,[3] but of course if you don't want to write about that subject, you must choose your own. As I don't think candidly that we could use anything very long about Williams or Miss Moore[4] I should like very much if you would do a review on either or both of them when any book of either appears. I am intending to introduce into each number reviews of three or four books of importance and have made a short and very select list of people to do this. Will you give your support? Would you by the way care to write a review on Rivers's last book?[5] Or is that somewhat outside your interest? I hope that you will be coming up soon if only for the day.

Yours in haste,
T. S. E.

Head Quartos and the Broadway Translations in 'A Commentary', *C.* 2: 7 (Apr. 1924); he also discussed T. E. Hulme. Book reviews began with the next issue, 2: 8 (July 1924).

1 – See TSE's letter of 4 May. On the 7th, Aiken responded to TSE's prompt, made 'so movingly (but surely a little pessimistically) that it would be a pity if you or I or the *Criterion* should cease, my name not having appeared there'. Aiken reminded TSE that he had had his poem 'Psychomachia' for a year and a half, in addition to the MS of his essay on Emily Dickinson.

2 – Aiken's 'Psychomachia' appeared in *C.* 3: 9 (Oct. 1924), 79–83.

3 – Aiken had written about James and American Criticism in 'A Letter from America' in *London Mercury* IV (June 1921). He later wrote a review of Theodora Bosanquet's *Henry James at Work, C.* 3: 11 (Apr. 1925).

4 – No review of William Carlos Williams appeared, but Marianne Moore's *Observations* was reviewed by RA in *C.* 3: 12 (July 1925).

5 – W. H. Rivers, *Medicine, Magic and Religion*, was reviewed by WL in C. 3: 10 (Jan. 1925).

TO *Cecil Scott* CC

19 May 1924 [*The Criterion*, London]

Dear Mr Scott,

I was very pleased by your sending me your poem which I liked very much.[1] I have only two criticisms to make. If you read it aloud I think you will see that certain lines are lacking in rhythm and that there is in general an absence of plan in the rhythm which very much weakens the effect. It is unsatisfactory to criticise the rhythm of a poem by correspondence; it is so much easier to explain what one means in a few minutes by reading aloud and one finds out very much more quickly what sort of rhythm was intended by hearing the author reading aloud. My second criticism is that you happen to have used a number of words which occur rather conspicuously in certain parts of my own work and although there is no question of borrowing, I think an association might suggest itself to some readers. I have marked some of these words so that you may see what I mean. These are both difficulties that one is apt to meet and can easily be corrected. Do go on and send me more.[2]

If I get down to Cambridge during the summer term I shall hope to see you; otherwise I hope you will let me know when you next come to London.

I am not surprised to hear that James Joyce is not read in Cambridge![3]

Yours always sincerely,
[T. S. E.]

TO *Messrs. Methuen & Co. Ltd* CC

19 May 1924 [*The Criterion*, London]

The Criterion would be pleased to receive for review copies of the recent books of Mr W. J. Perry. *The Criterion* proposes to give serious notices of

1 – 'I am writing a poem here, a Testament, which is very beautiful but which I cannot finish', wrote Scott (25 Mar.) from a hotel in Paris.
2 – Scott wrote back (undated letter) to apologise for bothering TSE with the poem: 'I shall destroy it and my borrowings and begin again.' Although there was one deliberate borrowing from Joyce – 'Paris nor Zurich nor Trieste' –TSE 'must have felt astonished and irritated' when he read it. Despite re-reading his work with TSE's 'scan' arrows, he still thought the rhythm was 'all right really'. He hoped TSE would visit him in Cambridge.
3 – Scott wrote from Trinity College, Cambridge, on 5 May: 'Nobody knows anything about it [the poem he had finished that morning] here, but then nobody here reads James Joyce.'

three or four important books in each number and it prefers to apply to the publishers for such books as it wishes to review rather than to receive books submitted by the publishers.

[T. S. E.]

TO *Hugh Walpole* CC

20 May 1924 [*The Criterion*, London]

My dear Walpole,

It is very disappointing that you are going away again so soon and cannot lunch with me and I wish that something more satisfactory could be devised than a visit to the city, but I want very much to see you and so I should be delighted if you would look in on me on Friday afternoon. The address is Lloyds Bank, 20 King William Street, on the corner of Cannon Street and the telephone number is Central 8246. If you can, ring me up in the morning to let me know about what time to expect you.

Sincerely yours,
[T. S. E.]

TO *Henry Eliot* Telegram Houghton

[Received 21 May 1924] London

DANGEROUS COMPLICATIONS ARISEN MAKING INADVISABLE FORCE DEFINITE FINANCIAL DISCUSSION[1] MAKE VISIT PURELY CORDIAL SOCIAL COURTESY OPPORTUNITY SEE HER AGAIN WHEN YOU COME FETCH MOTHER WILL GIVE MOTHER ALL TIME POSSIBLE YOU KNOW LIMITATIONS IMPOSSIBLE ACCEPT EXTREME GENEROSITY YOU[R] OFFER

[unsigned]

1 – In a telegram HWE asked whether TSE could leave the bank if he was assured of $1,500 a year from HWE himself in addition to his own income and *C.* salary.

TO *Osbert Sitwell* CC

22 May 1924 9 Clarence Gate Gdns

Dear Osbert,

As the Phoenix Society have seen fit to reward my services by giving me a box for the Congreve Play[1] on Sunday, June 1st, I should be honoured by the company of you and Sachie.[2] Richardson Wood[3] is coming and just possibly another man.

And if you – or any of your family – have any feeling of annoyance on any matter, it would be a good opportunity for discussing it frankly.[4]

Yours ever,
[T. S. E.]

I am sending this by messenger as I want to make up my party without delay.

TO *Virginia Woolf* TS Berg

22 May 1924 [*The Criterion*, 17 Thavies Inn]

My dear Virginia,

The article[5] has been received, read and forwarded, registered, to the printers. I have asked the printers your questions[6] and asked them to write direct to you in reply.

I must tell you how fully I appreciate your generosity in letting me have this article, especially at the present time. If the *Criterion* should be extinguished, I want it to go out at full flame and with your paper and unpublished manuscripts of Marcel Proust and W. B. Yeats, the July number will be the most brilliant in its history, and suitable to close the second volume.[7] It will help me to feel that the *Criterion* has not been altogether without value or distinction.

1 – William Congreve, *The Old Bachelour*, Regent's Theatre, 1 June: the first performance of the play since 1789.

2 – Sacheverell Sitwell.

3 – For Richardson Wood, see TSE's letter of 27 May.

4 – Presumably a reference to the Sitwells' reactions to WL's 'The Apes of God', in *C.* 2: 7 (Apr. 1924). Sacheverell Sitwell's 'Three Variations' appeared in the same number.

5 – VW, 'Character in Fiction', *C.* 2: 8 (July 1924).

6 – On 21 May VW asked for estimates from TSE's printers for printing her lecture as a pamphlet. On 30 Oct. it was issued as *Mr Bennett and Mrs Brown*, in Hogarth Essays, First Series, No 1.

7 – VW asked (23 May): 'But is there any danger that the *Criterion* is dying? I hope not.'

I do not suppose that as Editor I am required to expurgate your comments on myself but they do somewhat embarrass me as being excessive for what I know my own work to be.[1] Nevertheless they gave me great pleasure. Apart from these remarks, your paper seems to me a most important piece of historical criticism. It also expresses for me what I have always been very sensible of, the absence of any masters in the previous generation whose work one could carry on,[2] and the amount of waste that goes on in one's own work in the necessity, so to speak, of building one's own house before one can start the business of living. I feel myself that everything I have done consists simply of tentative sketches and rough experiments. Will the next generation profit by our labours?

Yours ever,
T. S. E.

<This is very badly written>

PS I cannot help writing this Postscript to make a suggestion, because I really feel that it is an opportunity which I should like you to know of. A very remarkable German Doctor, Dr Martin is at present in London for a fortnight. He was here last year for a short time and was able to do Vivienne a great deal of good, in fact made the turning point in that serious illness. I am going to him myself now. I have very great belief in him, he is not a specialist but I have never met a Doctor of such wide special knowledge. In addition he is a very charming man. I hope that you are perfectly well now, but even if you are, I really think that it would be worth your while to see him while he is in London because I feel that he might be useful to anybody and it would be an advantage to have seen him, should you ever want a first rate physician. Also he is extremely accommodating about his fees. He is staying at Lady Margaret Levett's, 61 Eaton Sq. I think so much of him that I should like any friend of mine to see him if they can. Do consider this, because I like him more than any physician I have ever had to do with.

1–VW named TSE, JJ, E. M. Forster, DHL, and Lytton Strachey as representative of the modern generation of writers who wrote after 'December 1910' when 'human character changed'. Of TSE: 'I think that Mr Eliot has written some of the loveliest lines in modern poetry. But how intolerant he is of the old usages and politenesses of society – respect for the weak, consideration for the dull!' (409–30).

2–VW said that 'the men and women who began writing novels in 1910 or thereabouts had this great difficulty to face – that there was no English novelist living from whom they could learn their business'. TSE wrote later that 'there was no poet, in either country [UK or USA], who could have been of use to a beginner in 1908. The only recourse was to poetry of another age and to poetry of another language' ('Ezra Pound', *Poetry* 78: 6, Sept. 1946).

TO *Conrad Aiken* TS Huntington

27 May 1924 [*The Criterion*, 17 Thavies Inn]

I shall expect you on Tuesday.[1] I don't think that Rivers's book which is entitled *Medicine, Magic and Religion* is at all unsuitable[2] but my idea is as much to have a small and select number of reviewers and have them review what they want to review, so that if you would prefer not to do this, please suggest something else. Meanwhile I should be still more grateful if you could do a short review say 1000 words on Sacheverell Sitwell's *Southern Baroque Art* for the July number, by the end of next week.[3] Would you do this for me as a kindness? Unless I hear from you by Thursday morning, I shall post the book to you.

Yours ever,
T. S. E.

TO *James Smith*[4] CC

27 May 1924 [London]

Dear Sir

Thank you for your kind letter of the 26th.[5] I shall look forward with pleasure in addressing your club and meeting the members on Saturday, November 8th.

Yours sincerely
[T. S. E.]

1–On 27 May Aiken said he was going to the 'Phoenix show' on 1 June and suggested lunch with TSE the following Monday.
2–Aiken said that Rivers's new book would 'require more technical knowledge' than he had.
3–See Aiken's review of Sitwell, *Southern Baroque Art*, in *C.* 2: 8 (July 1924).
4–James Smith (1904–72): English literary critic; author of *Shakespearean and Other Essays* (1974). A scholar of Trinity College, Cambridge, he took a double first in English and modern languages. According to a profile in *Granta* (which he edited, 1925–6), he revived the Cam Literary Club, 'and even presided over it for a year, in order to introduce Cambridge to T. S. Eliot' (quoted in John Haffenden, *William Empson: Among the Mandarins* [2005], 603). Smith was Vice-President of the club (the President being Professor Sir Arthur Quiller-Couch). Empson recalled having weekly supervisions with I. A. Richards, then treacherously 'listening to the James Smith group, who favoured T. S. Eliot and Original Sin' (195). Smith was to become an occasional contributor to *C.* (he wrote brilliantly on metaphysical poetry and on Empson's *Seven Types of Ambiguity*) and to *Scrutiny*.
5–An intervening letter by TSE seems to be lost: Smith initially invited TSE (letter of 21 May) to speak to the Cam Literary Club on 'any subject connected with the Elizabethan drama' on 8 Nov. According to a letter to OM of 30 Nov, TSE spoke on 'Chapman, Dostoevski and Dante'.

TO *Hugh Walpole* TS Valerie Eliot

27 May 1924 [17 Thavies Inn]

My dear Walpole,

I now understand that a letter I wrote you last week cannot have reached you,[1] a letter in which I said that in default of any other opportunity of seeing you, I should be delighted if you would come to see me on Friday afternoon last. I am so sorry that you have gone away again and I hope that you will let me know as soon as you get back. If you find an odd time you can get me on the telephone at Central 8246 during the day.

I enclose the proof of Chapter 2 of *The Old Ladies*. Will you please correct it and return it to R. Cobden-Sanderson Esq, 17 Thavies Inn, Holborn, London E.C.1. I am afraid that you will find a great deal of superfluous punctuation in it.

Yours sincerely
T. S. Eliot

TO *Osbert Sitwell* CC

27 May 1924 [London]

My dear Osbert,

I am delighted that you and Sachie are coming to the Phoenix on June 2nd [*sc.* 1st]. We are evidently in the same case in having so many annoyances that we have no time to be annoyed with anyone in particular.[2] That is exactly my dilemma. For the rest of your letter, I shall have to await elucidation until we meet for there is a key word which I am unable to decipher and I should love to know who it is who has behaved as you expected him to behave.[3] To me this habit seems a little tedious and I should be glad if my expectations were not always fulfilled.

Vivien wonders whether you went to Murry's wedding.[4]

1 – On 20 May, TSE said that he was disappointed that Walpole was 'going away again so soon' and couldn't have lunch. Walpole replied on 23 May that he had been expecting to hear from him, but was off to Cumberland the following day.

2 – With ref. to TSE's earlier enquiry as to whether he had 'any feeling of annoyance on any matter' (letter of 22 May), Sitwell had responded that he had 'too many annoyances ever to be annoyed with anyone in particular', and that "The Apes of God" was 'wonderful but dangerous'.

3 – The illegible word was 'Lewis' (whom Sitwell had not seen for eight months). He thought it better to stake his claim by writing to WL first: it 'always delighted when people behave as you would expect them to'.

4 – TSE was invited to JMM's wedding to Violet le Maistre on 24 Apr., but he did not go.

Richardson Wood is staying with me and I am hoping you and Sachie will come in and have a talk after the play. I shall ask Roger [Fry] and one or two others if they are there. We will meet you in the main entrance at 7.30.

Yours ever,
[T. S. E.]

TO *Humbert Wolfe* CC

27 May 1924 [London]

My dear Wolfe,

I am very glad to hear from you. I have indeed been immersed in what you may call a stupor but not at all for the reason you allege. It may rather be called a kind of paralysis. Will you help to release me from it by lunching with me on Thursday or Friday? I should be delighted if you would ring up Central 8246 one morning and tell me that you will come.

Yours ever,
[T. S. E.]

TO *Richardson Wood*[1] CC

27 May 1924 [London]

Dear Wood,

The 14th will suit me very well and I am willing to put up with the crowd of young ladies and young men.[2] I look forward to seeing you on Sunday.[3] Will you fetch me, not at this address but at 28 [38] Burleigh Mansions, St Martins Lane over Chatto & Windus' shop?[4] Trafalgar Square is your nearest station. I will be there at 6 o'clock and that is where we shall be staying the night.

I hope at all events that I have contributed to a small extent to helping you take honours in your examinations!

Yours sincerely,
[T. S. E.]

1–Richardson Wood (b. 1903): an American undergraduate at King's College, Cambridge, 1922–5; later editor and managing editor of *Fortune*, 1937–45, and a community economic consultant in New York City.
2–The date of TSE's proposed trip to Cambridge, Saturday 14 June.
3–At the Phoenix Society production of Congreve, *The Old Bachelor*, along with the Sitwells.
4–TSE's 'office' in central London.

TO *W. B. Yeats* CC

27 May 1924 [London]

My dear Mr Yeats,

I am very grateful to you for your permission to use 'The Cat and the Moon' in our July number.[1] Messrs. Watt & Son inform me that perhaps you did not understand that I had no objection to the fact that a private edition of 250 copies was to be published first; perhaps your hesitation was due to this. In any case I wish to say that I do not want the publication of the book to be delayed on account of the appearance of the play in the *Criterion* and it will not matter to me if the book appears first.

I hope that you will also make good your promise to let me have some prose from you later on.

With very many thanks,
Yours sincerely,
[T. S. E.]

TO *Leonard Woolf* CC

29 May 1924 17 Thavies Inn

Dear Leonard,

It is rather difficult to suggest proper terms without knowing the magnitude of the undertaking.[2] I should say that where the circulation of the paper is particularly stationary the percentage ought to be fixed, but if the circulation is highly variable, or if it is expected to increase, a higher scale should be devised. That is to say, the lower the circulation, the higher the percentage for the publisher in order that he should get anything out of it at all. For a periodical of large circulation like the *Adelphi*, I should say 10% on the sales or perhaps less, but for a periodical of small circulation and limited appeal, I should say from 10 to 15%. In any case

1–WBY wrote on 13 May that it was impossible to let TSE have his play, due to his sister's publishing schedule. However, on 19 May he telegrammed in reply to a telegram from TSE: 'I accept but my sister must publish a few copies not later than June 29th save copyright, Yeats.' This enabled TSE to publish 'The Cat and the Moon' in C. 2: 8 (July 1924), following its publication by the Cuala Press.

2–LW wrote on 29 May, 'A certain periodical has asked us to publish it', but he did not know 'what terms publishers ask in these cases'. He asked TSE 'in confidence what terms Cobden-Sanderson has in publishing the *Criterion*'.

I suggest you should work out your commission on the basis of the sales of the periodical in question.

Yours ever,
[T. S. E.]

TO *Charles Whibley* CC

29 May 1924 [London]

My dear Whibley,

I am delighted to hear from you after such a long time and to have such good news of your health. This is really a blessing and I am very glad that it has made it possible for you to do a good deal of work. When is the Manners book to appear?[1] I am looking forward to it eagerly. I am of course very disappointed not to have something from Oliver[2] in the July number; it breaks the continuity which I had hoped to establish of having in each number an important historical article on sound principles. May I hope that you will endeavour to get something out of him this summer that I can print in October? And if not, can you suggest anything else? I really depend upon you entirely in these matters.

I am trying to re-organise the *Criterion* somewhat and introduce some regular chronicles by regular contributors in the hope that it will give the paper more popularity and also that it will spare me part of the enormous correspondence involved in getting so many contributions. I believe that if I can reduce the star contributions to four or five and fill the paper up with reviews and chronicles, and notes by dependable people, it will save me trouble and increase the circulation. After all, what people want out of a review is criticism of books they are reading and the things they are talking about and to be provided with opinions to give material for dinner table conversation. From my point of view too, the work is increasing with every number and unless I can start some cooperative machinery, will soon be beyond my strength and time. Perhaps when some particularly important book appears you would consent to write a review for me? And I hope you will be able to let me have an essay at latest by January.

There are many things I am anxious to talk to you about. But I shall be at Cambridge not at Whitsuntide but on the 14th and I hope from your

1–CW, *Lord John Manners and His Friends* (2 vols, 1925).
2–F. S. Oliver had written (23 Aug. 1923) that he wanted to write an article for C.

letter that you will be there then. Could you let me have a line to say whether I may count on seeing you?

If not, I must write you a longer letter.

Ever yours affectionately,
[T. S. E.]

TO *M. Jean Grenier* CC

29 May 1924 [London]

My dear Sir,

Thank you for your letter of the 23rd inst.[1] I await with interest Number 2 of your review and will then write to you more fully about the two articles.

Yours very truly,
[T. S. E.]

TO *Herbert Bates*[2] CC

29 May 1924 [London]]

Dear Sir,

I have your letter of the 6th inst. You should have addressed yourself to Mr Knopf instead of myself as he has the powers of granting anthology rights for any of the poems of the volume in which the poem you mention is to be found. It is a poem which has been used by several anthologists and seems to be successful with children and the public for which anthologies are published and I do not believe that Mr Knopf will see any objection to its inclusion in another anthology.[3]

Yours faithfully,
[T. S. E.]

1–On 31 May, Grenier thanked TSE for his 'exaggerated praise', and said the second issue of *Philosophies* was appearing shortly. It was from a book to be called *Thèse de philosophie*, written from a purely speculative viewpoint, with no political or national bias. He was happy for TSE to translate it for *C.* if he wished, but nothing by Grenier was to appear there.

2–Herbert Bates (1868–1929): US critic and anthologist. He published *Poems of Exile* (1896), an annotated edition of *Palgrave's Golden Treasury* (1905), and *Books for Home Reading for High School and Junior High School* (1923); and he later compiled *Modern Lyric Poetry* (1929).

3–Bates said he was working on 'an anthology of modern verse', intended primarily for 'high school students', and requested permission to reprint TSE's 'La Figlia Che Piange'. As the publisher of *Poems* (1920), Alfred Knopf had the US rights to TSE's poems. 'La Figlia Che Piange' had also been included in *An Anthology of Modern Verse*, chosen by Algernon Methuen (1921).

TO *Wyndham Lewis* CC

29 May 1924 [*The Criterion*]

My dear Lewis,

Thank you for your letter. I really hope that this time you will let me have your thing in good season, that is to say by Saturday at the latest as I am very anxious to include it in the July number.[1] I hope that you will remember also that this is to be the first of a regular chronicle[2] and that I shall depend upon you for another on the 1st of September. If you can do this regularly it will really be the greatest help that you can give.

As for your proposal, I am very much pleased that you should have thought of this and appreciate the offer,[3] but apart from the iniquity of paying other contributors at the expense of my friends, I shall be able to give you several good reasons why it should not be done. I shall insist upon your being paid for these art notes at the same rates as other contributors and of course for special contributions at the double rates which I can give to a very few people.

Don't fail to let me have the article by Saturday morning and let me have a line from you as soon as you get back from France. I hope you will enjoy it and come back rested and ready to deal with publishers [incomplete]

TO *Mrs S. A. Middleton* CC

30 May 1924 [London]

Dear Mrs Middleton,

I am back in London and hasten to write to you as I promised. I have had your son's affairs very much on my mind and I should like first of all to come and see you before I see him. I could call upon you in the evening on Wednesday or Thursday next, preferably Thursday, if you will let me have a line to say whether I shall find you and which evening would be more convenient.

Sincerely yours,
[T. S. E.]

1–'Art Chronicle', C. 2: 8 (July 1924), 477–82.
2–WL wrote that newspapers refer politely to 'art' 'as though it still existed': 'I have been asked by *The Criterion* to write an art-chronicle, and am playing my part in the general pretence, as you see.' In the end, he wrote only one other art chronicle in 3: 9 (Oct. 1924).
3–WL's letter does not appear to survive. He seems to have offered to write for TSE gratis or at least at a lesser rate than other contributors.

FROM *Henry Eliot* Telegram Valerie Eliot

[Received 31 May 1924] Chicago

INTERVIEW WITHOUT RESULT[1] TWO OTHER GUESTS AT LUNCH BRIEF CONVERSATION ALONE AFTERWARD I OUTLINED FAMILY FINANCES CASUALLY AND SAID I WAS ANXIOUS TO HELP YOU LEAVE BANK LADY DISPLAYED COMPLETE RETICENCE SALARY NOT MENTION CORDIAL BUT UNCOMMUNICATIVE DOUBT IF FETCH MOTHER AS CHARLOTTE COMPETENT WRITING

[unsigned]

FROM *Henry Eliot* TS Valerie Eliot

2 June 1924 1037 Rush St, Chicago

Dear Tom:

I cabled you the other day the inconclusive results of my interview with Lady Rothermere, and had meant to write you earlier, but my life now is so ordered, or disordered, that I can get nothing done. I still drudge much in the evening at the office, write Mother about interminable things like your trust and her mortgage notes which I am to buy, and the rest of my time is devoured by people of no importance or advantage to me.

I arrived in New York Sunday morning, called at the Harveys first (H. B. Harvey, once my room-mate in Chicago, m. Dorothy Dudley) where to my surprise I found Bertrand Russell visiting. I went to the Plaza, and up to Lady Rothermere's apartments, where there were two visitors, a Mr Loewenthal (I think) and a Miss or Mrs Muriel Draper, who had been invited to luncheon. Mr Lowenthal seems to be a poet of sorts, a handsome young Jew, faultlessly dressed and rather pleasant. The Draper person was cleverish, smart-looking, gaily dressed, talkative and a bit noisy, hardly pretty, but entertaining. She seemed to know Lady Rothermere extremely well, called her Lillian, mauled her affectionately and smoked cigarettes end-to-end. After I got accustomed to the excessively histrionic New York manner of Mrs Draper I rather liked her.

Conversation started with people, Chicago, New York, the effects of arsenic, hotel service, and finally drifted around to the Gurdjieff dancers,

1–This telegram, relating to HWE's meeting with Lady Rothermere, is in answer to TSE's telegram (30 May): 'Please wire result interview also are you coming fetch mother or not important.'

around which topic it hovered pretty much throughout the visit. The Gurdjieff Dancers, and the Gurdjieff Institute for the Harmonious Development of Man, appeared in Chicago some months ago, and I attended, and found the dances very interesting (being ritualistic dances of antiquity), but found myself much bored with their memory tests. A pamphlet which I have somewhere elucidating their theory of harmonious development contains, as I remember it, some excellent common-sense ideas and a certain amount that has a flavor of quackery. As well as I could guess, Mrs Draper was trying to interest Lady Rothermere, [who,] while interested intellectually, was inclined to be very canny. I cannot imagine two philosophies of conduct more opposed than those of Mr Gurdjieff and those actually practised by people of Mrs Draper's type. However, you probably know more about this institution than I do.

After these two people left, I remained for about fifteen or twenty minutes, both because I wanted to see whether Lady Rothermere had [anything] to communicate to me and because I could not well do otherwise with courtesy. Naturally the conversation dwelt on the *Criterion*, on English literary magazines in general, and on you. I ventured the remark that you were intensely interested in the *Criterion*, and wished to give your whole time to it, and that I hoped you would soon be able to give up bank work, and that you had about $1200 a year from securities and that I was happily able to help you now to about the same extent but doubted whether that was enough for you to live on. I did not leave any embarrassing pauses for her to fill in nor did I ask her any point-blank questions about the management of the *Criterion* or intimate that you had ever told me anything about the financial details of the *Criterion*. I said incidentally that I was poorly posted on your affairs because you were so busy that you had little time except for cables, and that I wished she might give me some recent news of you. She expressed great delight at the management of the *Criterion* by you, and said she had a cable from you saying that the April number was a great success. We discussed the April number briefly and agreed that it was one of the best numbers. We discussed the *Adelphi* and the *American Mercury* and the advantages and disadvantages of advertising pages, and the possibilities of increasing circulation in America. I said that Mother was going over to England again and wished that she might meet Mother.

I made my visit appear, so far as was possible, casual, and said I had been planning for some time visiting some friends in New York and also seeing my mother in Boston. I was a little surprised that she did not ask me about ways and means of furthering the American circulation of the *Criterion* in America, though offhand I can think of no means but circularizing library and club lists and advertising in the *Dial* or the *Times* or *Transcript*.

Lady Rothermere was very cordial and very easy, but I have an impression of her treating my visit in a purely perfunctory and entirely social way, and displaying not very great curiosity about me, even a reflected curiosity. I have an impression of slightly strained reticence when I touched on your finances, and in general when we were alone, though always of amiability. I do not think she suspected me of coming there with ulterior motives, and certainly I gave her every chance of either discussing finances or avoiding the subject as she chose, without appearing to do so. I hardly think I could have been accused of hinting, though of course the mere fact of my being there could have been so construed, if she had a mind to do so. However, I did, I think, make it appear that I had other affairs in the East besides calling on her.

So I do not know whether anything was accomplished or not. I liked her and am glad to have met her, and it is possible that I may have dispelled some incorrect notions that she may have had about your family and your finances. I do not think that I am able to judge from this interview whether she is interesting or intelligent. Of course I cannot say that I like her as well as Russell, for whom I have a great admiration and a great feeling of friendliness. I told her that I had seen Russell that morning (having first ascertained from him that there was no political or other antagonism) and she said quite positively that she would like to see him. In fact I think she told me to tell him that she would like to see him.

I went down to Boston in the evening, and spent four hours next day with Mother, who seems very well and I think happy over the idea of going abroad again. Charlotte also is delighted. The Porters, by the way, invited me yesterday to go to Norway with them at their expense, which would land me in England July 23. A delightful trip, as there are some other rather pleasant people whom I know going on the boat. I could then stay in England and come back with Mother. The only trouble is that I can't do it, for business reasons already briefly outlined, and because anyway I should appear rather badly in Mother's eyes after having declared that I was unable to go with her.

This is all I can write, or think of to write, at the moment.

With much affection,

Henry

I agree with you that the present financial arrangement as to the *Criterion* is unreasonable and cruel. I should think you could throw yourself on her mercy. Has she no humanity?

TO *Barrett H. Clark* CC

2 June 1924 [London]

Dear Sir,

I regret that I am unable to understand your letter of the 21st ultimo.[1] I do not appear to have had any previous communication from you. The article by Hugo von Hofmannsthal on Greece was received by me direct from Vienna in the printed German text through the medium of Mr Schofield Thayer.[2] I sent it out to a gentleman in Switzerland who made the translation and both translator and author were paid direct by Mr Cobden-Sanderson. In the circumstances, you will understand that I am more [than] puzzled by your letter. If any further explanation is needed you will doubtless write again.[3]

Yours faithfully,
[T. S. E.]

TO *Conrad Aiken* TS Huntington

12 June 1924 *The Criterion*, 17 Thavies Inn

Dear Conrad,

I am glad that the book arrived,[4] but very sorry to hear that you have been under the weather. I hope this is nothing serious. But do let me know how you are getting on. I have been very seedy myself the last day or so, both in stomach and head.

I have no right to worry you about this book, but every day saved will now count, and the sooner you can let me have the review the more grateful I shall be to you. About a thousand words is enough. Next time I shall offer you a couple of months in which to do it.

It is very good of you to do this review at all, as I know how busy you are.

Yours ever,
T. S. E.

1–On 21 May, Barrett Clark asked about payment for his 'translation of Hugo von Hofmannsthal's article "Greece" in *The Criterion*'.
2–Hofmannsthal's 'Greece', in *C.* 2: 5 (Oct. 1923), in a translation by Charles Caffrey.
3–On 13 June, Clark apologised for his misapprehension: a friend had mistakenly thought the translation was one he had submitted to J. T. Grein, who 'offered to send it to English editors'.
4–Sacheverell Sitwell, *Southern Baroque Art*, was reviewed by Aiken in *C.* 2: 8 (July 1924). Aiken replied the same day that he had 'found it rather tiresome reading, for all the talent displayed': Sitwell's 'remarkable ability' entitled him 'to a kind word, – but not too kind'.

TO *Gilbert Seldes* TS Timothy and Marian Seldes

12 June 1924 *The Criterion*, 17 Thavies Inn

My dear Seldes,

This is to thank you for your book[1] to which I had been looking forward for so long and which I have now read through with great interest and pleasure.

Of course a great deal of it is obscure to me as I have never had the opportunity of seeing most of the comedians you mention; but when I come to New York I shall expect you to introduce me to Al Jolson and Fanny Brice and some of the others who in your pages have impressed my so deeply.[2] Anyway I like the book immensely and I wish you would come over again and do an English edition introducing some of the comedians of this country and of France.

I have now started having a few reviews in each number of the *Criterion*, and I intend to review your book myself in the October number.[3] I should have done so in the July number, but I was so pressed for time in getting it ready that I should not have been able to do the book justice.

I now want to make a suggestion. I design to have in the *Criterion* more regular features such as book reviews, art and music notes and dramatic articles. The number of ordinary contributions will accordingly be slightly diminished. Amongst other contributions I want to have a regular chronicle or letter from several of the principal capitals of Europe and also from New York. Of course we are very much cramped for space, and it will at present hardly be possible to have any one city represented more than twice a year – that is, in every other number. Eventually I hope that it may be possible to have a chronicle from each city in each number. These chronicles must be limited to two or three thousand words. Would you consent to undertake to report and comment upon the activities of New

1 – *The Seven Lively Arts* (1924).

2 – Seldes writes, in 'The Daemonic in the American Theatre': 'One man on the American stage, and one woman, are possessed – Al Jolson and Fanny Brice. Their daemons are not of the same order, but together they represent all we have of the Great God Pan, and we ought to be grateful for it' (191). He adds, 'the fury and exultation of Jolson is a hundred times higher in voltage than a Roosevelt', while 'courageous and adventurous women who shoot lions or manage construction gangs . . . remain pale beside the extraordinary "cutting loose" of Fanny Brice'. Al Jolson (1886–1950) was a Jewish-American singer, comic and actor, specialising in black-face roles, most famously in the film *The Jazz Singer* (1927); Fanny Brice (1891–1951), an American comedian, singer, entertainer and film actress, who starred in the Ziegfeld Follies, 1911–30.

3 – In fact it was reviewed by Conrad Aiken (C. 3: 9, Oct. 1924, 148–50).

York for the British public?[1] By a chronicle I mean, of course, an entertaining review of any events, exhibitions, theatres, shows, books, etc. which would give a reader the impression of being in touch with all the artistic activities of New York. There must often be new things in the theatres which we should like to have intelligently reported and commented upon. You would be of course quite as free in a choice of material as even Paul Morand when he writes for the *Dial*,[2] and I am sure that anything that you would write would be equally amusing and less superficial.

Our emoluments are of course insignificant compared to those of America, as they would work out at about five or six pounds per article. The only inducement would be that there is no one else doing quite the same thing here and you would therefore be able to impress upon the British public any opinion that you wished.

I do hope that you will undertake this. It ought not to be a difficult thing for you to do as you are so much in touch with everything that happens. Do let me hear from you as soon as possible.

Yours always sincerely,
T. S. Eliot

TO *Harold Monro* TS Beinecke

12 June 1924 *The Criterion*, 17 Thavies Inn

My dear Monro,

I am so sorry. Most unfortunately I was ill all of last night, and when I finally got to sleep I did not wake up until half past one. I have had to stop in bed the whole day, but if I had not slept so late I should have telephoned to you. Will next Wednesday be possible? I will drop you a line the day before.

I hope you are not taking too much trouble over your proof.[3] I hope that you will be able to let Cobden-Sanderson have it back with the additional paragraphs by Saturday, as we want the printers to start setting up the numbers in pages on Monday.

1–Seldes contributed a first 'New York Chronicle' to *C.* 3: 10 (Jan. 1925).
2–Paul Morand was contributing the regular 'Paris Letter' to the *Dial*.
3–Monro, 'Wordsworth Revisited', *C.* 2: 8 (July 1924). Monro wrote again on 16 June, saying it was still unfinished and needed more 'editorial attention'. He suggested it should conclude with 'To be continued'. The note was inserted, but the article was never continued.

I infer from your silence that you did not think Abercrombie's book worth reviewing.[1] I should very much like to have a review of *something* from you next time.

I am giving up my cottage at Fishbourne as soon as I can get rid of it. The house next door has been turned into a garage which also sells lemonade and sweets; what with being on the Portsmouth Road, the place has become quite uninhabitable. So I shall not be down any more except to move my furniture when I find somewhere to put it, but we must meet oftener in London.

Yours ever,
T. S. Eliot

TO *Virginia Woolf* TS Texas

12 June [1924] *The Criterion*, 17 Thavies Inn

My dear Virginia,

I have been annoyed about the delay of the printers in sending your proof, but today I have received a copy and so I trust that you have yours also.[2] I hope that you will be able to let Cobden-Sanderson have the proof back by Saturday, so that the number may come out by July 1st. But I don't want to worry *you*: on the contrary, you are a model, indeed *the* model contributor – no one else has ever taken the trouble to remind us about proof. And again I tell you how delighted I am to have this essay.

I have just got the final preparations for this number completed, and have taken to my Bed today and perhaps tomorrow. If I can struggle up by that time I must go to Cambridge on Saturday (*not* to lecture, but as a private individual) where I hope to make a good impression, or at least be tolerated, on the ground of being a friend and publisher of Mrs Woolf. Who seems to have made a permanent impression herself, to judge from the minds of the two undergraduates whom I have since seen.[3]

And we hope you are not going to Paris, or Spain, or Rodmell, in the immediate future? And that you *are* going to Rodmell in July. As our Cottage is now flanked by a Garage selling BP Motor Spirit at all hours, and faced by a Lemonade Stall, we have come to the conclusion that it is

1–Presumably Lascelles Abercrombie, *The Theory of Poetry* (1924).

2–'Character in Fiction', *C.* 2: 8 (July 1924). The proofs had not yet reached VW.

3–VW's 'Mr Bennnett and Mrs Brown' ('Character in Fiction') had been read to the Heretics, Cambridge, on 18 May. It is likely the undergraduates were Richardson Wood and Cecil Scott.

uninhabitable. It is possible that Vivien may be at Eastbourne, and also that we may be again in search of a cottage on the Downs.

Yours ever,
T. S. E.

Vivien tells me that she is writing to ask you and Leonard to dinner next week. I do hope you can come. Please do.[1]

Vivien Eliot TO *Virginia Woolf* TS Berg

13 June 1924 9 Clarence Gate Gardens

My dear Virginia

I telephoned, but you were out (as usual). I am very sorry that you cannot both come to dinner next week. We should love you to come alone on Thursday and yet we should so much like you both to come together, and I am afraid two occasions of us in rapid succession would be too boring for you and after the first occasion you might not feel equal to repeating it. Therefore will you keep Tues 24th for us? We shall look forward to seeing both of you then, if we may.

About the proofs, Tom thinks that the reason that Hazells said nothing to you about extra copies is because they are waiting to set it up in pages before they can tell you. *They promised him they would let you know.* Their telephone is Aylesbury 15. Will you let us know if we can do anything?

Yes I am going about about as much as I ever go about and I *want* to come and see your room. Please can I come, and when??? *Writing* – !? Editing, perhaps.

Yrs ever
Vivien

YES, please, a cottage near the downs, and quickly.

1–In her diary for 21 June, in a list of people recently seen, VW includes: 'Mrs Eliot – this last making me almost vomit, so scented, so powdered, so egotistic, so morbid, so weakly' (*Diary*, II, 304).

TO *May Sinclair* TS Pennsylvania

19 June 1924 *The Criterion*, 17 Thavies Inn

Dear Miss Sinclair,

I am delighted to have your book with your signature and incidentally to have such a beautiful edition.[1] I liked 'The Grandmother'[2] so much that I am certain I shall like the whole poem, to which I have been looking forward with great interest. It seems to me a very remarkable thing to have accomplished, and perhaps too an important step in the transition of the novel into some other form, which I feel is an inevitable development already foreshadowed in some of your own work as well as in that of Joyce and a few others. But I shall say no more about the poem until I have had time to study it carefully: I should not myself have cared for any criticism of *The Waste Land* which came from only a first reading.[3]

Thank you for troubling to return the books. Some day when you have time I should like to know your opinion of them.

I hope that you have had an interesting visit to America and that you are now settling down to fresh work. Thank you again for giving me *The Dark Night* which I shall always treasure.

Very sincerely yours,
T. S. Eliot

TO *Frederic Manning* CC

19 June 1924 [London]

My dear Manning,

Would you be willing to review any or all of these books for the October *Criterion*?[4] I am starting book reviews and intend to have three or four reviews, not more, in each number, of about 1000 words each. There will probably not be more than this number of books worth our reviewing and there certainly will not be more than a very limited number of people whom I should care to ask to review. If you will do this for me I shall be

1–May Sinclair, *The Dark Night: A Poem* (1924).

2–'The Grandmother', an extract from her verse novel, *C.* 2: 6 (Feb. 1924). Sinclair wrote (13 June): 'I'm afraid that it does not follow that because you liked *that* you will like the rest.'

3–*The Dark Night* was reviewed by Harold Monro in *C.* 3: 9 (Oct. 1924).

4–A. J. Toynbee, *Greek Historical Thought* and *Greek Civilisation and Character*; and T. D. Denniston, *Greek Literary Criticism*.

very grateful; if not, I shall not have them reviewed at all. I do not know anyone else to whom I should be willing to give them.[1]

I do not know what you mean about the left and the right in literature. From a literary point of view I do not recognise any left or right; only what I like. I do not much admire the work of Paul Morand but I give him the admiration which I should give to a brilliant designer of hats or gowns. But I should like to discuss this question of left and right in conversation with you rather than by correspondence.[2]

Yours always sincerely,
[T. S. E.]

I hope the *Criterion* will be out about the 1st of July.

TO *Leonard Woolf* CC

19 June 1924 [*The Criterion*, London]

Dear Leonard,

Forgive me for not answering your letter immediately.[3] I am glad to say that the whole question of American publication of Virginia's article is nonexistent. We do not purchase American rights for the purpose of separate publication in America. The idea is that the *Criterion* aims at increasing its American circulation which is already a considerable fraction of the total. It is therefore to our advantage that our best contributions do not appear also in American reviews, and I therefore secured from Lady Rothermere an additional small subsidy which makes it possible to offer a very small number of writers double rates for exclusive rights. Virginia's article will therefore be circulated in America only in those copies of the July *Criterion* which will reach America, and therefore there will be nothing to interfere with your publishing the book as soon after July as you choose.

Yours ever,
[T. S. E.]

1 – Manning's review appeared in *C.* 3: 9 (Oct. 1924), 134–7.

2 – On 18 May, Manning suggested an article on 'modern critical tendencies', but he suspected TSE would not want this because his 'sympathies with the left' were not his own. Manning said: 'I admire Paul Morand as a writer, I admire his diagnosis, but I do not think him an artist.'

3 – LW wrote (17 June) about 'some difficulties with regard to the American rights of Virginia's article' ('Character in Fiction', *C.* 2: 8). He understood TSE had taken both UK and US rights and was paying more than the usual rate. They intended to 'publish it as a pamphlet early in the autumn', but Knopf had asked for first refusal in the USA. If TSE could not

TO *F. W. Bain* CC

23 June 1924 [London]

My dear Bain,

In case I did not make it clear when I last wrote to you, may I hope to receive your essay called 'A Conspiracy of Silence' by the 1st of September?[1] I do hope that this may be possible and am looking forward to it with great eagerness.

Sincerely yours,
[T. S. E.]

TO *G. A. Porterfield* CC

23 June 1924 [*The Criterion*, London]

Dear Mr Porterfield

I am very glad indeed to hear from you. As you do not say exactly when you are coming back, would it be possible for you to send me one or two stories soon to look at? I should promise not to mutilate any of them without your permission.

I am very much pleased to learn that you like what you have seen of the *Criterion*. I am having a copy of the July number sent to you.

Yours faithfully
[T. S. E.]

TO *Frederic Manning* CC

23 June 1924 [London]

My dear Manning,

Thank you very much for your letter and for consenting to do the books. I will try to get Mackail's lecture also.[2]

—

arrange for serial publication in the US before 30 Sept., VW would be happy to 'accept ordinary rates' for its publication in *C.*

1 – On 29 May, Bain proposed to call his essay on the French Revolution 'A Conspiracy of Silence'. On 3 Aug., he changed it to '1789': this was adopted in *C.* 3: 9 (Oct. 1924).

2 – On 20 June, Manning said he would review the books on classical thought TSE had sent but wanted 'to include Mackail's lecture' mentioned in the previous *TLS*. See J. W. Mackail, *Bentley's Milton* (British Academy Warton Lecture, 1924): reviewed in *TLS*, 12 June 1924, 374.

I see that the reference to the left was my own blunder.[1]

I am very sorry indeed to hear that you have had appendicitis. An operation like that is an unpleasant shock to one's nerves at the very mildest but I judge from your letter that you have got through it as successfully as could be expected. Your present condition sounds very painful indeed.[2]

Yours very sincerely,
[T. S. E.]

TO *Johan Mortensen* CC

27 June 1924 [*The Criterion*, London]

Dear Mr Mortensen,

I did not answer your letter of the 22nd at once because I waited until I had had an opportunity of reading the story you so kindly sent me.[3] I am grateful to you for letting me see it because the story is extremely interesting and has moments of great power. I think that we can use it and it will certainly be a welcome change from the usual fiction. Will you let me know whether the author has left it entirely in your hands or whether I ought to communicate with the author direct? Address is not on the manuscript.

We usually divide the payment between the author and the translator; that is our payment is at the rate of £10.0.0 per 5000 thousand words and from this we deduct the translator's fee of 15/- per 1000 words, unless the author has made private arrangements with the translator. We also like to know the name of the translator as this is published. There are a few places where I think the English could be somewhat improved, and as it would not involve mutilation of the story, I presume there would be no objection.

I should like to hear from you on
[incomplete]

1–Manning said his 'reference to the left in literature' was apropos of a casual remark that TSE had made 'in town'.

2–Manning had spent three weeks in a nursing home; the coughing brought on by his bronchial troubles made it hard for his wound to heal.

3–On 22 June, Mortensen submitted 'a story of a young Swedish authoress' whose significance went 'beyond the limits of nationality'; it was by Anna Lenah Elgström (1884–1968): see 'Two of the Red Cross', *NC* 5: 2 (May 1927).

Vivien Eliot TO *Leonard Woolf* TS Berg

27 June 1924 9 Clarence Gate Gardens

Dear Leonard,

Thank you for your letter. It was good of you to write, but the whole thing is a complete fantasy. Neither Tom nor I have ever for one moment thought or imagined that you or Virginia have ever written or said anything insulting or unkind about *The Waste Land*. We cannot imagine what we did or said – but for a little crude and meaningless badinage – which has led you to suppose that we took offence on these grounds.

For myself, I have no idea whatever about the facts of private publishing; I should have no more idea of the success of the publication if I heard that forty copies had been sold by the Hogarth Press, or 4000. The subject of the sales of the Hogarth Press has never once been discussed between Tom and myself.[1] We have never conceived it possible that Tom or any good poet could be popular in this country or in any other country. We have never imagined that any money could be made out of good poetry. Therefore, we have never considered poetry as a financial asset, and that is why Tom earns his living in other ways.

We still cherish hopes of leisure and independence, bringing such a command of conversation as will make it impossible for misunderstandings of this kind to occur.

Yours sincerely,
Vivien Eliot

TO *Ramón Fernandez* CC

4 July 1924 [*The Criterion*, London]

My dear Sir,

I wrote to you last on the 3rd May expressing my pleasure at your willingness to let us have an essay on Cardinal Newman. I should very much like to publish this essay in our October number if possible and am therefore writing to ask if you could let me have it by the 1st of September in English or a fortnight earlier if you prefer to write it in French. As I say, I should particularly like to publish it in the October number.

Yours very sincerely,
[T. S. E.]

1 – See TSE's letter to Leonard Woolf, 1 May 1924.

TO *Louis Untermeyer*[1] CC

4 July 1924 [London]

Dear Mr Untermeyer,

Thank you very much for your letter of the 13th inst. Aiken was quite right about my willingness to be included in the American Miscellany.[2] I have not seen either of the numbers, but he has explained the scheme to me and it seems to be one which is very fair to the contributors.[3] The only obstacle to my contributing at present is the most insuperable obstacle possible; that is to say I have written nothing whatsoever for three years and I do not see any immediate likelihood of my writing. The writing of poetry takes time and I never have any time. With the prospects of the summer which I have before me, I can say definitely that it will be utterly impossible for me to write anything by next November.[4] I am however obliged to you for your proposal and hope that we may meet when you come to London.

Sincerely yours,
[T. S. E.]

TO *Harriet Shaw Weaver* CC

4 July 1924 [*The Criterion*, London]

Dear Miss Weaver,

Thank you very much for the books and for sending them so promptly.[5] I will send them on to Lady Rothermere and will let you know directly I hear from her. Meanwhile I will consult Mr Cobden-Sanderson about the possibilities of storage.

1–Louis Untermeyer (1885–1977): American poet and anthologist; author of *Collected Parodies* (1926), *Long Feud: Selected Poems* (1962), and a memoir *From Another World* (1939).

2–Untermeyer had already edited two anthologies: *American Poetry Miscellanies* (1920, 1922).

3–In his 'Foreword', Untermeyer explained that this volume of new poems by a dozen 'representative native authors' was based on a selection 'composed by the poets themselves' (*American Poetry 1925: A Miscellany*, 1925, iii.). The anthology was based on 'cooperative participation and divisions of royalties'.

4–In fact, TSE contributed 'Three Dream Songs' to *American Poetry 1925*: the version of Part I of *The Hollow Men* published in *Commerce* 3 (Winter 1924) and 'Doris's Dream Songs' published in *Chapbook* 39 (Nov. 1924).

5–WL's *Tarr* and *The Caliph's Design*, published by Weaver's defunct Egoist Press.

But I must say again that I think it is a public misfortune as well as a strong private regret to me that the Egoist Press should go out of existence. It will be some small compensation for me if the *Criterion* can to this extent carry on a little of your work.

I telephoned to Fladgates[1] this morning and found as I expected that your neighbour had an option on the office. They said they would know next week whether the option would be exercised. I very much hope not because I cannot imagine a more suitable place for the purpose. It would be a godsend. I do not suppose that the people would be inclined to give it up if they have an opportunity of getting it but it would be a sentimental pleasure as well as a practical advantage to have your office as well as your books.

We both enjoyed very much seeing you last night and hope that we may see something more of you this summer.

Sincerely yours,
[T. S. E.]

PS I enclose cheque for 6/9 for *Tarr* and the *Caliph's Design* with many thanks.

TO *Harriet Shaw Weaver* CC

7 July 1924 [*The Criterion*, London]

Dear Miss Weaver,

I am more grateful to you than I can express for all the trouble you have taken about the room.[2] I am sure that no one else would have taken so much trouble or managed it so neatly. The office is exactly what I want for the *Criterion* and will simplify the running of the paper very much indeed.

I hope that you will not bother yourself to have the room cleaned.[3] I should like to come in to see you soon and discuss the practical details of the sub-tenancy and if nothing prevents, I shall look in on you in your office hours this Wednesday. I say if nothing prevents, because I have just had a slight operation on my finger which has been giving me a good deal of trouble and for several days I am not able to move about as freely as I

1 – Messrs. Fladgates, the firm responsible for renting out the offices used by the Egoist Press at 2 Robert Street, which TSE wanted to take for C.

2 – On 7 July, Weaver said that, after consultations with the estate agents, TSE could 'definitely' have the former offices of the Egoist; she and Dora Marsden remained 'technically the tenants'.

3 – It was 'in a dirty state', Weaver reported.

should like. But as I understand you will be there on Wednesday and Friday mornings in any case, I will simply drop you a line the night before to say whether you may expect me.

My wife is anxious also to see the office. But I doubt whether she will be able to come in this week. She has her hands so full of this unfortunate business of preparing for my mother's arrival,[1] which all falls on her, and with her own preparations for going away in order that my mother may come here, that I doubt if she will have a moment to come in. She will take the first opportunity to come at a time when you are there, but it may be not for several weeks.

Thank you very much also for the lists,[2] of which we shall make full use. Again with very grateful appreciation and thanks,

Sincerely yours,
[T. S. E.]

PS My wife does not expect to be away from London the whole of the time this summer and we both look forward to seeing you oftener.

TO *A. B. Walkley*[3] CC

8 July 1924 [*The Criterion*, London]

Sir,

At the suggestion of Mr Scott Moncrieff, I have asked Mr Cobden-Sanderson to send you a copy of the July *Criterion* containing an unpublished fragment by Marcel Proust, which we think should interest you. We should of course be glad if you found it possible to mention this fragment, and this number of the *Criterion* in *The Times*.[4]

I am, Sir,

Your obedient servant,
[T. S. E.]

1 – TSE's mother was to arrive in London on 14 July.
2 – On 22 July she referred to sending a 'list of subscribers to the Poets' translations series'.
3 – Arthur Bingham Walkley (1855–1926): literary and drama critic; reviewer for the *Times* and *TLS*.
4 – On 11 July, *The Times* carried an advert for C. 2: 8 (July 1924), highlighting an 'unpublished fragment by Marcel Proust' as well as the pieces by WBY, VW and others. On 23 July, Walkley devoted his column to 'the latest manifestation' of Proust's novel in C., saying no novelist was more suited to 'the instalment plan' than Proust ('Albertine Dead. A Proust Fragment', *The Times*, 23 July, 12). On 30 July, Walkley returned to C. when he used his column to take issue with VW's 'Character in Fiction' under the headline 'Character in Fiction. Miss Virginia Woolf's Paper. Strange Occurrence in 1910' (*The Times*, 30 July 1924, 10).

TO *Frederic Manning* CC

8 July 1924 [London]

My dear Manning,

Thank you for your letter. I am sorry to hear that you are not recovering more rapidly but I hope that you are having no set-backs beyond the slowness of the wound in healing. I do not want to add another obstacle to your progress, but in spite of what you say, should very much like you to do these books.[1] I know that it is tiresome to have to think about books of this sort at all, but it seems to me very desirable that this sort of publication should be denounced. I am not surprised to hear what they are because I have always had the impression that Arnold Toynbee[2] was a noxious humanitarian. The point is that these books have been well spoken of in *The Times* and praised in the *Nation* and I think that some voice ought to be raised against this degraded culture.[3] If you do not think so, please let me know frankly; and perhaps you would prefer to devote to other tasks the little strength that you have at present.[4]

With all best wishes,

Sincerely yours,
[T. S. E.]

1–On 7 July, Manning said he did not think the books in the Library of Greek Thought 'useful' and that Toynbee wrote 'deplorable journalese'. He wondered if C. 'should notice them at all'.

2–Arnold Toynbee (1889–1975), English historian, had published *The Western Question in Greece and Turkey: A Study in the Contact of Civilizations* (1922, 2nd edn 1923). He was to become Professor of International History at University College, London, and author of *A Study of History* (12 vols, 1930–61). In a letter to *The Times* (3 Jan. 1924), he explained that he had resigned his Koraes Chair at the University of London in protest against 'the conduct of the Greek authorities' in Asia Minor.

3–Both *Greek Historical Thought* and *Greek Civilization and Character* were praised in 'The Good of Greek' (*TLS*, 19 June 1924, 382). The reviewer praised 'the abundance of material' not available elsewhere, and spoke of Toynbee as a 'thoroughgoing modernist, or man of his age, who must have his Greek authors to speak as if they were men now living'.

4–See Manning's review in C. 2: 9 (Oct. 1924): it was 'evident that such books are profitable . . . but their value is less obvious'. He criticised Toynbee's translations on the grounds that it was 'advisable that a translator from Greek into English should know at least one of the two languages with which he deals' (134–7).

TO *Jean de Menasce* CC

9 July 1924 [*The Criterion*, London]

Dear Menasce,

I am glad to hear from you at last.[1] I heard rumours in Oxford that you had not stopped in London and therefore imagined that you did not get my card.[2] Do let us meet when you return to London and we will see whether I can give you any introductions that will be of use to you. I am sure that the America tour will be a great success. And meanwhile write to me some time if you ever feel inclined.

Yours,
[T. S. E.]

TO *Conrad Aiken* TS Huntington

9 July 1924 *The Criterion*, 17 Thavies Inn, London E.C.1

Dear Conrad,

I am sorry that I missed you the other day. I have been having a great deal of trouble with my hand getting an abscess under the finger nail which became infected and I am not out of trouble yet. Nevertheless, I am in the city now nearly every day and hope that you will try again if you are in town. You had best ring me up at Central 8246.

Would you care to review Gilbert Seldes' book on the *Lively Arts* for the October number? I hope you will. Let me hear from you so that I may send it.[3]

Yours ever,
T. S. E.

1 – De Menasce's letter does not survive. TSE's letter is addressed to him in Paris.
2 – Writing on 18 Apr., de Menasce had hoped to see TSE when he got up to London, as he expected to 'fairly often during the term'.
3 – Aiken reviewed it in C. 2: 9 (Oct. 1924).

TO *May Sinclair* CC

9 July 1924 [London]

Dear Miss Sinclair,

Thank you for your letter.[1] I should very much have liked to see you before your departure and am extremely sorry that Monday night is impossible. Very unfortunately, my mother who is eighty-one is arriving on Monday from America to pay me a visit of a few weeks and I do not think that I ought to leave her on the evening of her arrival. We have been completely up-side-down with preparations for her coming as this flat has to be prepared for her and my wife and I must disperse for the time into other and much less comfortable quarters. In addition to these afflictions, I am at present hampered by an accident which has necessitated an operation to my hand.

I suppose that you will be away until the autumn. May I hope that you will let me hear when you return or that if you come to town meanwhile at any time for a few days, you might give me an opportunity of seeing you. There are several things which I should like to talk about.

Yours very sincerely,
[T. S. E.]

TO *Charles Whibley* CC

9 July 1924 9 Clarence Gate Gdns

My dear Whibley,

Although I enjoyed our boating expedition, it did not lend itself to conversation.[2] So I should like to hear from you and to hear when you are to be in London again.

I hope that your neuralgia has shown no sign of returning, so that you can steadily build up strength against next winter. I have been bothered lately by an abscess in my finger which has given me a great deal of pain and been an infernal nuisance. I have just had it operated upon and some of the nail and flesh removed and now hope that there will be no further consequences. It is extremely trying to have it happen at this time because we are domestically in chaos and mentally in nervous tension before the arrival next week from America of my mother who is eighty-one and

1 – On 8 July, Sinclair said she hoped to see TSE before leaving for Stow-on-the-Wold.

2 – On his trip to Cambridge of 14 June TSE had visited Whibley and gone punting on the Cam.

insists on coming over to visit me. I shall not be able to draw a peaceful breath or think an intelligent thought until the end of August.

Yours ever,
[T. S. E.]

PS I should like to know what you think of the July number. But there are many other things which I want to talk about which were in my mind at Cambridge but which of course I had no opportunity to mention.

[Richardson] Wood appears to be enjoying himself motoring about the continent. I imagine he is happier now than anyone can expect to be again.

TO *J. B. Trend* CC

9 July 1924 [London]

My dear Trend,

As you have honoured the *Criterion* with your collaboration, may I ask you three questions: (1) Do you think it would be possible for us to get an article on some musical matter from de Falla?[1] I should very much like to have something from him. If you encourage me to ask him, will you let me have his address and would you object to my mentioning your name? (2) I am proposing to have a set of regular chronicles of literary and other artistic events from various foreign capitals: Paris, Berlin, Rome, Madrid, New York. Each foreign representative would contribute a chronicle of 2 or 3000 words twice a year. I want in each case someone who is on the spot and active in the life of the capital. Do you think that Ortega y Gasset[2] would be a good man for Spain, and do you think that he would be inclined to do it? I only know that you and others have spoken highly of him to me and that he is the Editor of a review which I find sympathetic and with which I should like to be on closer terms.[3] (3) I am also intending to have regular chronicles on art, music and the drama when I can find the suitable people who will undertake them. These should be about 2000

1–Manuel de Falla (1876–1946): Spanish composer whose ballet *The Three-Cornered Hat* had been performed by Diaghilev's Russian Ballet in 1917. Trend, a friend of his, was author of *Manuel de Falla and Spanish Music* (1929). On 11 July Trend said he tried to persuade Falla not to write such articles because he took 'such immense trouble': 'a page of prose' took longer than 'a page of music'. But maybe Falla would dictate something when he visited him in Oct.

2–Trend replied that Gasset 'would be the very man for the chronicle from Madrid'. He would be 'gratified', since 'the *Criterion* was one of the few reviews he really liked'. For Gasset, see TSE's letter of ?13 July.

3–*La Revista de Occidente* was founded by Gasset in 1923.

words each and should appear in every number. I must explain that I do not want a summary of all the exhibitions, plays, concerts, etc which take place, for such are only suitable in periodicals appearing much more frequently. What I want, is really a short article by someone who can write with knowledge and interest, dealing with some event or aspect of that particular contemporary art. In this way the writer would have a good deal of latitude and would be able to make general reflections for which there might not be scope in for instance a weekly periodical. Would you care to honour us by undertaking music?[1] If you happen to be in Spain, you could write about Spanish music, if in Austria, on German music: there is no need to be comprehensive.

I hope you will not think all this an impertinence and a bore, I really should like to secure your regular appearance and closer collaboration in the *Criterion*. May I send you a copy of the July number which I think in some respects, the best that we have produced?

Yours sincerely,
[T. S. E.]

TO *Herbert Read* CC

9 July 1924 [*The Criterion*, London]

My dear Read,

I am so sorry that I was unable to meet you on Tuesday and also that I could not let you know so that you should not come in vain. Please accept my apologies. I have been having a great deal of trouble with my hand, getting an abscess under the finger nail which became infected and I am not out of trouble yet.

I have discovered a good and cheap restaurant called the Bell which is in Holborn near Chancery Lane. Is that a very inconvenient place for you? – or could you take the Piccadilly railway, getting out at Holborn? Monro's restaurant was not a success and Monro himself was not there to justify it.

I am sending you the Babbitt book.[2]

Yours ever,
[T. S. E.]

1 – Trend said TSE's 'view of musical criticism' interested him very much. He contributed a 'Musical Chronicle' to *C.* on a regular basis from 3: 9 (Oct. 1924) to 12: 49 (July 1933).

2 – Irving Babbitt, *Democracy and Leadership*, which Read reviewed in *C.* 3: 9 (Oct. 1924), 134. Professor of French at Harvard, Babbitt had been one of TSE's most influential teachers there: see 'The Humanism of Irving Babbitt' (1928), reprinted in *SE*.

TO *Alec Randall* CC

9 July 1924 [London]

My dear Randall

I do not know whether you are back yet, but I want to have this question ready for you on your return.[1] Can you tell me much about Fritz von Unruh,[2] and do you think he would be possible as a German correspondent? I have never read anything of his except some agreeable war reminiscences in the *Nouvelle Revue Française*.[3] I met him in London a short time ago and he struck me as chaotic but I hear that he has a considerable following in Germany. Is he what in journalism is called a representative writer of the present time?

Would you mind writing yourself to the Editors of the periodicals you want to exchange with?[4] If you have no *Criterion* paper, drop a line to Cobden-Sanderson and he will send you some.

Would a restaurant called the Bell in Holborn near Chancery Lane be a particularly inconvenient place for you? I lunched there the other day and found it extremely good and very cheap and have heard it highly recommended. I am writing to ask the others.[5] I hope you had a very successful holiday.

Yours ever
[T. S. E.]

PS You promised to send me the address of the *Revista* [*de Occidente*]. If you can find it, may I have it?

1 – Randall had been for a holiday in Brittany.

2 – Fritz von Unruh (1885–1970), son of a German Army officer, was an Expressionist dramatist, poet and novelist whose notable early works, inc. the play *Offiziere* ('Officers', 1911) and *Louis Ferdinand* (1913) – both produced by Max Reinhardt – and the narrative *Der Opfergang* ('Way of Sacrifice', written in 1916 during the siege of Verdun but published only in 1919), proclaimed his lifelong pacificist idealism. Winner of the Kleist Prize (1915), the Das Junge Deutschland Prize (1920), and the Grillparzer Prize (1923), he was to be an outspoken opponent of the Nazi Party. He left Germany in 1932, and lived, until 1962, in the USA. Randall replied (4 Aug.): 'Unruh is a good writer, but he has a political bee in his bonnet, which might awkwardly affect his writing of a chronicle.' Unruh never published in *C.*

3 – Fritz von Unruh, 'Fragments d'un Journal de guerre', *NRF* 19: 108 (1922).

4 – On 4 June, Randall complained that *Neue Rundschau* was no longer being sent to him; he suggested adding *Die Literatur* to the list of reviews for exchange.

5 – Randall was a regular attender at the weekly *C.* lunches, along with HR, Flint and TSE.

TO *Harold Monro* TS Beinecke

9 July 1924 *The Criterion*, 17 Thavies Inn

Dear Monro,

I am sorry to miss you at your restaurant last week. What happened? I have discovered another, which with all due respect seems to me remarkably good and cheap, called the Bell in Holborn near Chancery Lane Station. Would this be a possible rendez-vous for you in the future?

I hope you like the *Criterion*. Would you care to write a short notice of Campbell's poem[1] for the next issue? I should be very glad if you would, only I am afraid that it would be necessary for you also to review May Sinclair's poem as I cannot very well review verse and leave her out.[2] Would you be willing to tackle this and to deal gently with her? If not, I should have to see whether someone would be willing to review it as a novel.[3]

Yours ever,
T. S. E.

TO *Dr E. Classen* CC

9 July 1924 [London]

Dear Sir,

I learn from Dr Mortensen that you wish to revise your translation of Mrs Elgstroen's story[4] and I therefore return it to you herewith. I shall be glad if you will kindly acknowledge receipt and hope that you will be able to return it to me within the course of a few days.

Yours faithfully,
[T. S. E.]

1–*The Flaming Terrapin* (1924), by Roy Campbell (1901–57), South African poet and satirist.

2–May Sinclair, *The Dark Night* (1924).

3–Monro replied (29 July) that he would do 'a comparative review of Campbell's poem & May Sinclair's' and would not say anything derogatory. In his review (*C.* 3: 9, Oct. 1924), he noted Campbell's 'colonial flavour', calling him 'precocious and unweariedly exuberant' but with 'sufficient restraint not to become tiresome'. Sinclair's poem he put down as 'a novel in verse (free of a kind) of an accomplished novelist who has already expressed herself again and again in her natural medium and is now trying an experiment in a medium not naturally her own'.

4–See Anna Lenah Elgström, 'Two of the Red Cross' (*C.* 5: 2, May 1927, 202–13).

TO *Gilbert Seldes* CC

10 July 1924 [*The Criterion*, London]

My dear Seldes,

I was very glad to get your wire and today have your letter. I am very glad that you will do a chronicle for us. I hope that you can arrange them to fit in so as to arrive just in time for the two numbers in which they should appear. In future I hope to bring out the *Criterion* on the first day of Oct. January, April and July. That means we should have to receive the copy for the January number by December 1st at the very latest. Can you manage this? I was hoping that you would let me have something in time for the October number, but if this is impossible, can you not manage to get it into my hands by the latter part of November?[1]

I am glad to hear that you will be part of the time in Europe and felicitate you upon your marriage.[2] It appears possible that I may get over to Paris in the late autumn and certainly hope to see you there or in London before your return to America.

Yours sincerely,
[T. S. E.]

TO *Messrs. Curtis Brown*[3] CC

10 July 1924 [*The Criterion*, London]

Dear Sirs,

I have read with great interest Mr D. H. Lawrence's story entitled 'Jimmy and the Desperate Woman' submitted with your letter of the 8th inst. and if possible should like to publish it in the October number of the *Criterion*.[4] I should like first to know whether any arrangement has been made to publish this story in America and when it is likely to be published there. We should of course like to have prior or simultaneous publication. I should be glad to hear from you at the earliest possible moment.

Yours faithfully,
[T. S. E.]

1–Seldes's first 'New York Chronicle' appeared in *C.* 3: 10 (Jan. 1925).

2–Seldes married Alice Wadhams Hall in Paris on 21 June.

3–DHL's literary agency.

4–'Jimmy and the Desperate Woman', *C.* 3: 9 (Oct. 1924), 15–42: the first of five pieces by DHL.

TO *Richard Cobden-Sanderson* CC

10 July 1924 [London]

Dear Cobden-Sanderson

I enclose a list of the periodicals to be dropped or be taken up for exchange. I should be grateful if you could provide each of the colleagues concerned, i.e. Read, Flint and Randall, with a small quantity of *Criterion* paper to enable them to write to the reviews which they want to take up.

I have been having trouble with my hand. I bruised the finger a fortnight ago and rather neglected it; it developed an abscess under the finger nail which has had to be operated upon and I am not yet out of trouble with it.

The telegram from Seldes means that he accepts my proposal that he should write for us an occasional review of events in the world of arts in New York.

I am struggling to the city every day, so you ought to be able to get me on the telephone there when you want me.

Yours ever
[T. S. E.]

To be dropped:-

The New Republic	New York
The Nation	" "
Indice	Madrid
Les Ecrits du Nord	Brussels
Europe	Paris

To be taken up for exchange:-

American Mercury
North American Review
Atlantic Monthly
Philosophies, rue de Douai 50, Paris
Die Literatur, Munich
Le Disque Vert
Revista de Occidente
Le Crapouillot,[1] 3 Place de la Sorbonne, Paris

If you have not the addresses of any of these new periodicals, you can get them from Flint, Randall and Read respectively.

1 – *Le Crapouillot*: a satirical magazine launched in 1915 by Jean Galtier-Boissière; it lasted until 1996.

Vivien Eliot TO *Mary Hutchinson* MS Texas

10 July [1924] 9 Clarence Gate Gdns

Dear Mary

This is *too* disappointing. To miss the one party of the season – to be stuffily here – packing – while you are having, as I am sure it is, the most perfect party. Such a lovely night. I had three beautiful dresses laid out to choose from – and had *really* looked forward to it. Tom's hand is very painful, he had to have a piece of bone removed today from the top of his finger. He is feverish.

Very sadly yours
V

TO *Messrs. Curtis Brown* CC

13 July 1924 [*The Criterion*, London]

Dear Sirs,

I have your letter of the 10th inst. Whilst I should be very glad to use this story by so distinguished a writer as Mr Lawrence, I am afraid that for any contribution which is to be published separately in an American periodical, we can only offer our usual terms which are at the rate of £10.0.0 per 5000 words. If therefore you can place Mr Lawrence's story to much better advantage in some other British periodical, I shall be glad to hear from you without delay.

Yours faithfully,
[T. S. E.]

TO *Harold Monro* CC

13 July 1924 9 Clarence Gate Gdns

Dear Monro,

I think that it is time that I returned you these manuscripts of Prentis. You will remember what I said about them and I don't think he has done anything formed enough for us to publish but I trust that you are keeping an eye on his work because I do think that something may come of it. His vocabulary and syntax need a good deal of disciplining, don't you think. I should like to see his stuff from time to time and hope for another opportunity to meet him. At present I am in a state of chaos awaiting a visit from my mother who is crossing the Atlantic at the age of eighty-one and arrives tomorrow.

Did you get my last letter? I hope that you will be willing to review those two books as well as to let me have the continuation of your Wordsworth, the first part of which has contributed so largely to what I consider the best number of the *Criterion* so far.[1]

I shall not be able to lunch this week, but what about Wednesday week?

In haste, yours ever,
[T. S. E.]

TO *Lady Rothermere* CC

13 July 1924 9 Clarence Gate Gdns

Dear Lady Rothermere,

I have your second letter this morning. The matter of the publication[2] is of course *one* of the subjects which I wish to discuss with you and if you can manage to come to London, you shall hear all about it. This subject also includes the question of the Egoist Press. Of course it is difficult to go very far as a publisher under present conditions when one is also an Editor and it is simply a practical question of the amount of time at one's disposal. Our programme involves time and organisation which I suppose such a press as the Three Mountains[3] enjoys.

I never see Rodker and cannot carry messages to him and I am sure that he would feel more pleasure in hearing from you direct. His address is 4 Tooks Court, Cursitor Street, E.C.4.

Yours very sincerely,
[T. S. E.]

1 – Monro's 'Wordsworth Revisited' was set 'to be continued', but it never was. The 'two books' are those by Campbell and Sinclair.

2 – This apparently refers to the proposal that C. move into book publishing.

3 – The Three Mountains Press was a small press launched in Paris by the American journalist William Bird (1888–1963): its publications included EP, *A Draft of XVI Cantos*; Ernest Hemingway, *In Our Time* (1924); and William Carlos Williams, *The Great American Novel*.

TO *Sydney Schiff* CC

13 July 1924 [London]

My dear Sydney,

This is just a short note to enclose the manuscript verses of Mr Edward Moore.[1] I am very glad to have seen them but I remain of the same opinion and I think that on the whole you will agree with me that Moore's vehicle is much more philosophic prose than verse. I have been much interested by the two books you lent me[2] and I should very much like to meet him when he comes to this country.

I cannot write any more just now because we are in the convulsions of preparation for my mother's arrival. The whole business is unspeakably difficult to arrange and [we] shall be quite exhausted by the end of the summer.

Affectionately,
[T. S. E.]

TO *Arnold Bennett* TS Beinecke

13 July 1924 9 Clarence Gate Gdns

Dear Mr Bennett,

If you are in town and have the time, I should very much appreciate it if you would let me come and see you one day after 5 o'clock or in the evening. I shall be in town every day except Thursday and Friday of this week. I am sorry to trouble you but I have a scheme in view concerning which yours is the only advice which would be of any help.[3] So I hope that it will not be impossible for you to see me.

Yours very truly,
[T. S. E.]

1–Pseud. of Edwin Muir, Scottish poet and novelist: see TSE's letter of 12 June 1925.
2–Muir's first two books of essays were *We Moderns: Enigmas and Guesses* (1918) written under the pseud. 'Edward Moore', and *Latitudes* (1924).
3–On 10 Sept. Bennett recorded in his journal that TSE had visited him at the Reform Club the evening before: TSE was 'now centred on dramatic writing' and 'wanted to write a drama of modern life (furnished flat sort of people) in a rhythmic prose "perhaps with certain things in it accentuated by drum-beats". And he wanted my advice. We arranged that he should do the scenario and some sample pages of dialogue' (*Journals 1921–1928*, ed. Newman Flower [1933], 482). Bennett's remarks relate to *SA*.

TO *José Ortega y Gasset*[1] CC

[?13 July 1924] 9 Clarence Gate Gdns

Sir,

I am writing to you under the auspices of our friend Mr J. B. Trend, who is a regular contributor to the *Criterion*. I believe that we have another common friend in M. Valery Larbaud, who has often told me of your work.

I hope that you have seen the *Criterion*, which is sent to your review. I am writing to you in the hope that you may become one of our contributors, and that also in this way the two reviews may become more closely associated. It is one of the aims of the *Criterion* to establish international standards, and to publish work of British and foreign contributors equally. It is also our aim to establish close relations with one similar review in every country, such as the *Nouvelle Revue Française*, and the *Dial* in New York.

We now propose to publish a Literary Letter, twice a year, from each of the important foreign capitals.[2] This letter must be contributed by one of the most distinguished and authoritative men of letters in each capital; and I am assured that Madrid could have no better representative than yourself.

If you consent '*en principe*' I will immediately write to you more fully on the subject, and I trust that you will find the terms and conditions quite satisfactory. If I might appeal also to your public spirit, I would say that nothing could so assist the interest in and knowledge of Spanish letters of today, in England, as such a regular contribution to the *Criterion* from yourself.[3]

I have the honour to be,

Sir,
Your obedient servant,
[T. S. E.]

1–José Ortega y Gasset (1883–1955), Spanish essayist, philosopher, lecturer and journalist, was Professor of Metaphysics at Madrid University. He founded *La Revista de Occidente* in 1923, and was its director until 1936. He was the author of *España invertebrada* (1921); trans. as *Invertebrate Spain* (1937) and *La rebelión de las masas* (1930); trans. as *The Revolt of the Masses* (1932).

2–This plan never fully materialised, but chronicles from New York and some European capitals were published from time to time. The 'Spanish Chronicles' were undertaken by Marichalar.

3–In the event, Ortega y Gasset never published in *C*.

TO *May Sinclair* CC

13 July 1924 9 Clarence Gate Gdns

Dear Miss Sinclair,

You said in your letter that you were leaving town on the 17th. I should very much like to see you before you go, especially as I imagine that there will be no further opportunity of seeing you until the autumn. As Monday is impossible for me, could I come for a little while on Tuesday or Wednesday evening at 10 o'clock or 10.30? but if this time is inconvenient, especially when you are preparing to leave town, I do not want to disturb you.

Sincerely yours,
[T. S. E.]

TO *Osbert Sitwell* MS Mugar

15 July [1924] *The Criterion*, 17 Thavies Inn

Dear Osbert

I am writing for Vivien, to say that she is ill. We have had a very hard time and incredible complications caused by my family's arrival in England and occupation of Clarence Gate Gardens.[1] I have also been ill myself with a poisoned hand, and have to have two slight operations. Not having heard from you Vivien did not know whether you expected to see her tomorrow or not, but she is in bed with fever, and quite unfit to see anyone.

I should like to see you myself about several matters, but at the moment I am driven to death. *On what date* are you leaving London and what is the last possible date for seeing you? Could you have lunch with me (as the lunch hour is the only time I now have available) on Thursday or Friday of next week?

Yours ever
T. S. E.

1–CCE (with daughter Charlotte) arrived on her second visit on 14 July. According to Mrs Eliot's memoir, TSE 'engaged apartments for Vivien at Eastbourne' while 'Tom was with us this time sleeping on the lounge . . . His presence added *greatly* to my pleasure.' During her stay, Mrs Eliot met the Sitwells. In an unpub. memoir of TSE's marriage, Osbert Sitwell records that 'old Mrs Eliot' was a 'strait-laced, straightforward, conventional, but kindly lady' (TS Texas).

TO *Dorothy Pound* MS Lilly

[Postmark 21 July 1924] 9 Clarence Gate Gdns

Dear Dorothy

Excuse chaos. My *mother* is occupying this flat, we are in temporary slums and I am waiting to go to Eastbourne with Vivien who is completely exhausted.[1] I'll write early next week and come to tea if I may.

Yours ever
T.

TO *Wyndham Lewis* CC

5 August 1924 [*The Criterion*, London]

Dear Lewis,

I have just (yesterday) returned from Eastbourne, where I have been ill with influenza.[2] I have my mother here for several weeks to look after, but I am available at tea time, as you propose, if you telephone to Central 8246 during the day, or by arrangement the day before.[3] I am as much as possible in occlusion, but want to see you if you will meet me, and about the next *Criterion*.

Thanks for tip about Moore.[4] He has been writing to me, but I had no time even to reply. I will get hold of him if possible: I have no means of getting his present address except through Schiff, and I do not want to write to him, in case he should be in town, as I do not want to see people presently.

I am asking Sanderson to send you *Criterion*, it should come to you regularly.

Yours ever
[T. S. E.]

1–TSE's mother and sister joined them in Eastbourne, staying in a 'good hotel' on the front near the apartment they had rented. 'Altogether a delightful scene', noted Mrs Eliot.

2–In her memoir, CCE recorded that, during her visit to Eastbourne, TSE's physician told her that her son 'ought to remain in bed and rest for some time as he was very very tired from overwork'. The doctor 'urged as long as possible his giving up work'. CCE and Charlotte returned to London to do more sight-seeing, leaving TSE ill in Eastbourne. When he rejoined them in London, he 'seemed a little better, though not very strong'.

3–CCE said they were 'glad to have Tom with us at dinner time and in the evening when we sat with him in the study'. WL suggested tea 'if convenient' after TSE's day in the city.

4–Edwin Muir. WL wrote (undated letter): 'Edwin Moore is in London for a few days at Schiff's request. He doesn't seem overburdened with intelligence, but probably is a little more useful than Herbert Read.' He suggested TSE would 'find in MOORE a useful collaborator'.

TO *Harold Monro* TS Beinecke

5 August 1924 *The Criterion*, 17 Thavies Inn

My dear Monro,

The May Sinclair[1] has been sent to you today. I returned yesterday from Eastbourne, where I was in bed with an attack, or a recrudescence, of influenza.

About Wordsworth there seem to be three possibilities.[2] You can drop him altogether, and wait for a more inspiring subject to propose itself, or you can hang him over for the January number, which will give you plenty of time for new inspirations about him, or you can follow one of the lines you suggested. It seems to me that perhaps the exploration of his prose is the most interesting avenue. But shall we lunch next Wednesday, and perhaps you will have decided by then what you really want to do?

Many thanks for your letter; I am very glad to hear that you like the number in general. I shall be happy to have this review from you.

Yours ever
T. S. E.

TO *Frederic Manning* CC

5 August 1924 [London]

My dear Manning,

Circumstances have prevented me from correspondence altogether; I have not only had my family, but have been ill with influenza in Eastbourne, and other afflictions. I have never answered your question about the series of books: I should be very glad if *you* would do a short notice of it, for the January number, as the October number will have more than its share of reviews.[3]

How soon will it be convenient for you to let me have the review of Toynbee?[4]

1–May Sinclair, *The Dark Night* (1924), which Monro was reviewing.

2–Monro said (26 July) he did not know how to complete 'Wordsworth Revisited' which had been announced in *C.* 2: 8 (July 1924): torn between comparing him to Byron, discussing 'nature poetry', or confining himself to his 'prose writings', he was 'awfully inclined to drop him'.

3–See Manning's reviews of the Library of Greek Thought, *C.* 3: 9 (Oct. 1924).

4–On 14 July, Manning called Arnold Toynbee 'a vulgar scribbler', and hoped to 'have some fun with him' if 'well enough to feel vindictive'.

I understand from Sanderson that he has sent you the cheque for Le Père Hyacinthe.[1] Have you received it?

I am inclined to agree with you about Garrod and the others. Ker was the only one of any substance.[2]

I wish I could look forward to a definite date when I could see you. There would be a great deal to talk of. My present life is worst than an anchorite's, for I cannot meditate. I hope that you make progress physically?

Yours ever sincerely,
[T. S. E.]

TO *F. S. Flint* MS Texas

10 August 1924 *The Criterion*, 17 Thavies Inn

Dear Flint

I am forwarding book[3] to your abode in Atlantis. I am very tired of your damned modesty (cloak of laziness).[4] Not that I wish to disturb any man's holiday. I wd have kept it against your return.

I hope you are enjoying the menus plaisirs of life. N. Devon must be dreadful in summer. You know I dislike Americans, as a rule.[5]

Hope to see you in a 4tnight. Please do this book. Of course you can.[6]

Yours ever
T. S. E.

1–'Le Père Hyacinthe', C. 2: 8 (July 1924). Manning needed money for medical treatment.
2–H. W. Garrod (1878–1960): Fellow of Merton College, Oxford. Following the death of W. P. Ker, he became Professor of Poetry on the strength of his *Wordsworth: Lectures and Essays* (1923). Manning asked TSE whether he 'liked Garrod, who professes poetry'; he thought him 'a degree better than Gordon, who professes literature'. Manning mourned 'Ker, who, apart from *his* magnificent learning, could think like a man, and fight like a gentleman'.
3–RA, *Literary Studies and Relations* (1924), which TSE sent to Flint at Parracombe, Devon, where he was on holiday.
4–On 8 Aug. Flint said: 'I don't know that I am capable of writing a review for the *Criterion.*' Replying to TSE's charge in this letter, Flint said his 'damned modesty' was not 'a cloak for laziness' – he worked 'hard and exhaustingly' – but 'a tribute'.
5–On 8 Aug. Flint told TSE: 'You are so little of an American that it might amuse you to know that this is one of the parts of England that the Americans do in a few days.' After citing an American's derogatory remark about 'the natives', he added: 'Queer American tourists can't appreciate the sleepy shrewdness of these folk.'
6–Flint's review appeared in C. 3: 9 (Oct. 1924).

TO *Arnold Bennett* MS Beinecke

10 August 1924 *The Criterion*, 9 Clarence Gate Gdns

Dear Mr Bennett

I failed to thank you for your kind letter (I was ill at Eastbourne) but I hope I may have the pleasure of calling on you whenever you are in London and find it convenient see me.[1]

Yours sincerely
T. S. Eliot

TO *Hugh Walpole* CC

11 August 1924 9 Clarence Gate Gdns

My dear Walpole,

I hope that you have not forgotten that I am anxious to see you when you are in London and when you can arrange a meeting? And I want to hear your opinion and criticisms of the last *Criterion*.[2]

Yours sincerely,
[T. S. E.]

TO *Alfred Kreymborg* CC

11 August 1924 9 Clarence Gate Gdns

My dear Kreymborg,

I have often thought of you and have been on the point of writing to you. I am ashamed (as an amateur editor I have often cause to be ashamed) about the Puppets: I can only say that there are others – in fact nearly all of my contributors at one time or another – whom I do not dare to meet in the street. Conducting a Review after 8 p.m. in the back room of a flat, I live *qua* editor very much from hand to mouth, get myself into all sorts

1 – Bennett took TSE to lunch at the Reform Club on 9 Sept.
2 – C. 2: 8 (July 1924) included 'Character in Fiction', VW's critique of Arnold Bennett. Having returned from Bayreuth (26 Aug.), Walpole wrote the following day: 'I read the *Criterion* coming over and think that for variety and entertainment it is the best number yet – How far in advance (even though I am a contributor) it seems to me of every other publication. The *Adelphi's* egotism makes me ill, the *Mercury* sleepy and what else in English is there?' He took TSE to lunch on 11 Sept., recording in his diary: 'Enjoyed it very much. He is a very quiet man and of course I am a little afraid of him. But he was awfully kind and seemed genuinely to have enjoyed *The Old Ladies*.'

of hot water and predicaments, and offend everybody. At the end, the review is squeezed together somehow, and is never the number that I planned three months before. But I hope to get your Puppets in early next year.[1]

When are you coming back to London to let us see the puppets themselves, and hear the mandolute?[2] You know I have already expressed the hope that you would.

I have written nothing, but my 'commentary' in the *Criterion*. Otherwise, I have been speechless for nine months, until perhaps I have lost the power of speech.[3] The pressure of time is squeezing me out, like the walls of 'The Pit and the Pendulum'.[4]

I look forward to your book (it sounds almost as if you had become one of the 'elder men of letters' writing reminiscences!) and shall be flattered to find myself mentioned in it, even if in anything but the heroic role!

And why not more plays? Mine is in the same state.[5] But perhaps when you return there will be more of it to discuss with you.

Yours ever, with best wishes,
[T. S. E.]

TO *Virginia Woolf* — MS Berg

11 August 1924 — 9 Clarence Gate Gdns

My dear Virginia,

We had already retired to Eastbourne, before your letter arrived, and as no letters were forwarded, your party was already history long before we had knowledge of it – which was only a day or two ago, when on my return I seized it from the mass of letters, manuscripts and bills and

1 – On 6 Aug. 1923, Kreymborg had sent his article, 'Writing for Puppets'. On 12 July 1924, he asked whether it had appeared or was going to. But nothing by Kreymborg was to appear in C.

2 – Kreymborg had spent years after the war touring the USA, performing experimental puppet-shows and playing the 'mandolute'.

3 – Kreymborg wrote: 'Outside an occasional essay, one sees nothing of yours over here.' Apart from two 'Commentary' pieces in *C.* 2: 7 & 8 (Apr. & July 1924), TSE published almost no prose apart from 'Four Elizabethan Dramatists' (*C.* 2: 6 [Feb.]). As to poetry, the first poems to be published since *TWL* in 1922 were 'Doris's Dream Songs' (inc. 'The Hollow Men' III) in *Chapbook* 39 ([Nov.] 1924) and 'Poème ('The Hollow Men' I) in *Commerce* 3 (Winter 1924).

4 – Edgar Allan Poe's story, 'The Pit and the Pendulum'.

5 – A ref. to what became *SA*.

moneylenders' advertisements. I have only regrets, and apologies for my silence to be expressed. But for the disease which confined me at Eastbourne, there would have been a risk, of which you were ignorant, of a charabanc of American visitors arriving for tea at Rodmell; it was in question; but perhaps I shall perpetrate this expedition another year.[1] You have many admirers on the dark Continent; they have borrowed all of your works. So you will have to finish the new novel this summer, and let me have it in the autumn.[2]

Ever yours
T. S. E.

TO *Lady Rothermere* CC

11 August 1924 9 Clarence Gate Gdns

Dear Lady Rothermere,

This is merely to ask you whether you will be so good as to drop a line to Cobden-Sanderson to say that you approve of the scheme (which is of course your own invention!) which he outlined to you, for sending specimen copies and circular letters to a selected list of persons here and abroad and in America? I think myself that it is well worth trying, and I think that you thought so too.

Cobden-Sanderson tells me that the April number sold better than any previous number except Nos 1 and 2, and that the July number is selling still better, and *may* sell out, to judge from present appearances.

I am writing tonight to Massine, to ask him to come and see me when he returns. I should like to get some sort of notes from him, from Diaghilev, from Stravinsky and from Cocteau, if possible. There will not be any too much time, if the Ballet is definitely coming in the autumn.[3]

[T. S. E.]

1–TSE took his mother and sister on a series of expeditions from Eastbourne during their visit, including to Pevensey.

2–VW was finishing *Mrs Dalloway*.

3–Replying on 12 Aug., Lady Rothermere said she was in touch with the impresario Serge Diaghilev (1872–1929), and hoped 'to arrange Ballet for this Autumn'. In his 'Commentary' for *C.* 3: 9 (Oct. 1924), TSE noted: 'From November 27 the London public is to have the inestimable privilege of a season of the Diaghilev Ballet, and will be able to see again Leonid Massine and Lydia Lopokova, as well as several new acquisitions of the finest ballet in Europe.'

TO *Natalie Barney* TS Doucet

11 August 1924 [*The Criterion*, London]

Dear Miss Barney,

I am very very sorry that my mental peculiarities should have put you and the Princess Bassiano[1] to so much trouble in return for your kindness. I did indeed receive the cheque, from you, about Christmas time: here it is. At the time when Princess Bassiano sent it she was no doubt under the impression, as I was myself, that I was leaving my bank in January; or perhaps she thought that I had already left. Being in doubt, I postponed writing. I have been unable to change my mode of living until I could reduce certain expenses and pay off certain liabilities, and it has been impossible for me this year to forego my regular salary, as indeed all of my income, and somewhat more, has been covered by expenditures. My intentions are the same: but I do not know whether I can carry them out in three months or in six. Meanwhile I am not entitled to any support of this kind. I prefer to leave the money in your hands to retain or to return. It would certainly be of great value when the time comes, but Princess Bassiano may change her mind; and it is only fair that she should have the opportunity of acting upon her views. I only ask you to express to her my grateful appreciation, and to accept yourself the appreciation which I would wish to express to you.

It is possible that I may come to Paris for a weekend to see Lady Rothermere in the autumn: if so, I hope that I may find you there, and will certainly seek you. I should only be able to come for two days, as my holidays are exhausted.

Yours very sincerely,
T. S. Eliot

1 – Marguerite de Bassiano, Princess Caetani: see Marguerite Caetani in Glossary of Names. In 1924 she established the literary review *Commerce* (ed. Valery Larbaud, Léon-Paul Fargue and Paul Valéry) in which TSE placed 'Poème' ('The Hollow Men' I) later in the year (*Commerce* 3, Winter 1924 [/1925]). After WW2, she founded another international review, *Botteghe Oscure*, based in Rome. She and Natalie Barney had put up money for TSE in the event of his leaving Lloyds Bank.

TO *Gilbert Seldes* TS Timothy and Marian Seldes

11 August 1924 9 Clarence Gate Gdns

My dear Seldes,

Thank you for your letter of the 1st, which I have been considering. Your idea for a first chronicle sounds like just what I want.[1] The only question was whether it should appear in October or January. I should prefer October, but there are two reasons why January might be better. One is that I am more in the dark than usual as to how big the October number will be, and as the July number was unusually expensive (we had to pay something for an unpublished Proust!) although it has been selling extremely well, I want to keep October down as much as possible. A more important reason is that once the chronicles are started (and in any case they would start with yours), I don't want any hiatus: I have not yet definitely arranged any of the other chroniclers, and if you came on in October, there would be a risk of January appearing without any. Spaniards never write letters in the summer, because they go to the mountains and leave no addresses[2] (perhaps they are afraid of being sent to the Canaries), I am hesitating between two or three Germans, and I shall wait till I can get to Paris in October before I choose a Frenchman.[3] So I think January is better, but I hope that Ring Lardner's book will still be valid then.[4]

Yes, one can never strike the popular fancy, I'm afraid;[5] all one can do is avoid writing for intellectualsintelligenzzia [*sic*] by aiming at what OUGHT to be the popular fancy if there was a People (and in these days of democracy there isn't any people) and if it had a fancy.

Best wishes for your southern voyage.

Yours always
T. S. Eliot

1–On 1 Aug., Seldes suggested 'a general letter attached to a few specific phenomena', using *How to Write Short Stories* (1924), by the journalist and short-story writer Ring Lardner 'as a centre'.

2–J. B. Trend told TSE that Ortega y Gasset would be away for the summer. Cf. 'The Fire Sermon': 'The nymphs are departed. / And their friends, the loitering heirs of City directors; / Departed, have left no addresses' (*TWL* l. 179–81).

3–See Seldes, 'New York Chronicle', *C.* 3: 10 (Jan. 1925). The only other international chronicle to appear in the coming year was J. Kessel's 'A Note from Paris', *C.* 3: 11 (Apr. 1925).

4–Seldes called Lardner 'the last American who will be civilised (to wit, understood) by the English'; 'important, interesting and entertaining'; and 'as peculiar to America as a folk-song'.

5–According to Seldes, *The Seven Lively Arts* had 'failed to strike the most popular fancy'.

TO *Henry Eliot* CC

12 August 1924 9 Clarence Gate Gdns

My dear Henry,

I want to tell you something of mother and Charlotte, but first as briefly as possible to discuss my financial affairs in the light of your last letters and my conversation with mother. I am going to make some arrangement, because I have felt for a long time that I was placing far too great a burden and responsibility upon your already heavily burdened shoulders.[1] Beyond this, what I must consider are

Security of capital
Size of income
Convertibility of capital

With regard to the last, I wish to retain a certain amount of capital in a form in which it could quickly be realised, in the event of any emergency; furthermore, I do not like to tie up any more capital than can be helped in any one country, in view of the unsettled social conditions which will prevail everywhere during our lifetime.[2] There are three ways:

1. To put 8000 in the trust with mother's 6000, realise the Hydraulic and bring the balance over to London under my own supervision.
2. To put the whole of my money into a revocable trust of my own, and receive the income from mother's 6000 during her lifetime, the 6000 itself to be added to her trust for me after her death.
3. To realise and transport the whole of my capital, and receive the income from the 6000 in the way mentioned under (2).

There is also the way of putting all my capital into mother's trust, but this ties up all of my property in America whatever happens.

In any event, I think that it is best that the insurance you have taken out should be made payable to the trust, as you suggest, or to the trust to be established after mother's death, assuming that I survive her. In this way it would ultimately revert to the family, as it ought to do. The same disposition ought to be made of any property left me in your will.

1–HWE had offered to add $1500 a year out of his own pocket to the $1500 securities TSE should earn.

2–Since TSE was responsible for writing about 'Foreign Exchanges' for *Lloyds Bank Monthly*, he was well informed in this matter. In Aug. he said that 'in the present unsettled state of Europe, and the confused state of the exchanges', it was doubtful whether the world was 'reverting gradually to the conditions which obtained before the war', as observers claimed (*Lloyds Bank Monthly* No. 81, Aug. 1924, 325).

Before coming to any conclusion, I want to know to what extent my income would be reduced by putting it in the trust. I suppose that the range of securities allowed by law for trust funds would make it unlikely that I should get more than an average 5%, instead of the 6% bonds you have bought for me? This is an important point, and I should be grateful if you would let me know.

Taking the exchange at 4.60 which is slightly less favourable to me than the actual rate today, I work it out as follows:
(When I give proceeds of Hydraulic, I mean $15,000 shares @ 65).

Scheme 1:

14,000			10,000 (proceeds of Hydraulic)
.05			@ 4.60 . . . £2,173
700.00			.06
35			£ 130
665.00	@4.60 . . .	£144	
		£130	
		£274. . . total income	

Scheme 2:

18,000	(whole of my money)
.05	
900.00	
40.00	(trust co.'s commission?)
860.00	
300.00	(income from mother on 6000 @ 5%)
1160.00 @ 4.60 . . . £252 . . . total income	

Scheme 3:

18,000 (whole of my money)		
@ 4.60 . . .	£3913	300 from mother @ 4.60 . . . £65
	.06	
	£234	
	65	
	£299 . . . total income	

Or if I invested in government stock only here, total income wd. be £260.

It accordingly appears that under these schemes my income wd. be £274, £252 and £299 respectively, if my computations are correct. I therefore incline to either 1 or 3. Under 3, eventually, half my income would be from England, and on realisable capital, half from America, on unrealisable.

There is one more point. As the Old Colony[1] will be my trustee under mother's will, it might be safer to have any other trust with some other company: I might suggest the Bankers Trust Co. in New York, which has the advantage of a Paris office.

I may say that in the unlikely event of Vivien outliving me, my money would revert to the family in any case by her will. The property, if here, would be kept separate and in a different bank from any that she inherited on the death of her father and mother, which might amount to about £200 p.a. I think; it is hardly likely to be more.

I shall have the power of attorney sworn and returned to you in a few days, for dealing with the Hydraulic stock. In any case I want to realise my Hydraulic this autumn. Do you think that it is likely to rise any higher than 65?

Obviously, what I keep in America must be in some form of trust: English investments I can keep my eye on and have every facility for being informed about.

I did not state explicitly that if I do not form a trust with mother, she has offered to let me have the income on the 6000 during her lifetime, and add the principal to my trust in her will.

You will have learned that mother was ill on the voyage.[2] Since being here she has improved very much. The weather has been very warm for London, that is to say what to Americans is a fine temperate summer, and I think that it has been much better for mother than the hot summer in Cambridge. I do not think that she ought to be in Cambridge in the summer. Both she and Charlotte look very well now, and have good appetites, and I think that Charlotte also will have benefited by the change. Charlotte does not take the responsibility nearly as heavily as Marion, I believe; mother has told me that she was happier with Marion, which is natural. They make quite contradictory statements about themselves: Charlotte told me that she had dreaded coming and had wept on George's shoulder with relief when they heard at one moment that mother could not get passages. Mother, on the other hand, says that Charlotte wanted very much to come and that Charlotte told Marion that if she had not been taking this trip she would have had to use some of her capital in the autumn to stay in town for a time to rest from the fatigues of Millis. Charlotte says that she would have done so in any case, but that the

1 – Old Colony Trust Company, a Boston Bank.

2 – In her memoir, Mrs Eliot wrote that, after a day of rough sea, she woke up only able to 'utter one or two words at a time, which alarmed me'. The doctor reassured her that this was 'caused by sea-sickness', and the following day she recovered.

expense of the trip will make it impossible. So there it is. However, I am certain that the change is doing them both good.

It turned out rather unfortunate taking them to Eastbourne, as it led to a muddle, and it was impossible to get to the truth of the matter, whether they liked being there or not, and if so or if not so, which. They both said that the hotel was very comfortable. Before we went I suggested that they should stay ten days, as owing to a public holiday, and two holidays of my own, I should have been there all but three days in the middle; but after two days each one told me that the other one wanted to go back. This continued after I was sent to bed there by the doctor – I unfortunately assumed that they would want to stay until I was able to return. Charlotte (according to a note she wrote) persuaded mother to stay two days longer; mother said that she wanted to stay but did not want to keep Charlotte there; mother then declared that she would stay as long as I did, and Charlotte said that she must insist on going back because she herself was not sleeping and had indigestion.[1] I should not have minded that in the least if she had said so at once quite frankly, and if she had not waited until my return to inform me that that was not the reason at all, but a pretext for getting mother away because mother was not well there. I wish Charlotte would be more frank. She will probably tell you about this incident herself. I am used to people who deal openly and directly.

I will write again soon. I wish that mother and Charlotte would stay longer, as it seemed to me from the start a long journey and a great expense for only five weeks, and we should love to have them here – and it makes no difference whatever to us in the way of inconvenience – but mother says that Charlotte wants to get back – and I don't want to start that round again.[2]

I will write again soon.

Affectionately
[T. S. E.]

1 – In her memoir, Mrs Eliot recalled with pleasure their trips to Pevensey, Beachy Head, Old Eastbourne, and a 'tea house called Devonshire House' which reminded her of VHE's story 'Thé Dansant' (C. 3: 9, Oct. 1924). Recounting their departure, she said 'I left Tom with great regret but Charlotte thought life in a hotel did not agree with her.'

2 – TSE went with them by train to Liverpool to see them off when they sailed on 23 Aug.

TO *Conrad Aiken* MS Huntington

15 August 1924 9 Clarence Gate Gdns

Dear Conrad

Of what use are stuffed peacocks' tongues to him who has just feasted? The figure is not quite apposite, because *I* have the pleasure of reading; but *editorially* a surfeit. *Psychomachia*[1] in October, O Florentine[2] –

Wd you be willing also to do *Triple Fugue* (Osbert Sitwell) briefly 1000 words?[3] I hate to pile it on, but having already approached the only *other* person I should trust with it ('F. M.' [Vivien]) who is ill and can't or won't work, I wish you would. It is good – very good in parts, and not quite what you wd expect.

Yours ever
T. S. E.

TO *Ottoline Morrell* MS Texas

17 August 1924 9 Clarence Gate Gdns

My dear Ottoline

Vivien has been unable to write: she has had ten days in bed at Eastbourne and is only just up and went out yesterday; and she is anxious for news of you. I am all the more sorry to have missed you. It has been very trying for both of us – as I have had to be in London at weekends with my mother, and could only get down to see her by snatching a day now and again during the week. But there has been a great deal more to it than that. Do let us hear from you and news of you.

Affectionately
Tom

1 – Aiken, 'Psychomachia', *C.* 3: 9 (Oct. 1924), 79–83.
2 – See perhaps F. T. Palgrave, 'O Florentine, O Master, who alone / From thy loved Vergil till our Shakespeare came / Didst climb the long steps to the imperial throne' (*The Visions of England*, 1891).
3 – See Aiken's review of Sitwell's *Triple Fugue, C.* 3: 9 (Oct. 1924), 141–4.

TO *Harriet Shaw Weaver* CC

19 August 1924 9 Clarence Gate Gdns

Dear Miss Weaver,

Thank you for your letter.[1] The end of September will suit me quite well. Meanwhile shall I keep the key? I do not expect to have occasion to go to the office, so if you need the key please let me know.

I think that the enclosed agreement will do quite well, and it will not be necessary to submit it to Lady Rothermere before it is ready for stamping.

Thank you for the list of subscribers[2] etc. I suppose that there were no definite arrangements with Pound, Miss Moore etc.[3] You may of course say that we shall be responsible for the refund of the subscriptions if no more volumes are issued, but that continuation of the series is under consideration.

I should be very glad to have the use of the typewriter, and will see to having it put in order.[4] Thank you very much indeed.

Sincerely yours,
[T. S. E.]

TO *Leone Vivante* CC

19 August 1924 9 Clarence Gate Gdns

My dear Sir,

Thank you very much for your letter of the 15th. I must apologise to you very humbly. I am only an amateur editor: as a bank employee for my livelihood, I can only be an editor in the evenings and on Sundays, (I run this review solely because it interests me to do so) and owing to inexperience, illness and the very little time of which I [may] dispose, I have got into many difficulties. I had looked forward to publishing your essay (the first part) early next year. But at least let us give it a careful and considered review (either I or some quite competent person will write it) and let me hope that the book will have the success it deserves.[5] And

1 – On 4 Aug. Weaver said TSE could take over the *Egoist* office at the end of the week; she would give him a second key on 13 Aug. The official date of transfer would be the end of Sept.

2 – A list of the subscribers to the Poets' Translations series.

3 – Weaver replied (31 Aug.): 'There was no definite arrangement with Mr Pound or Miss Moore.'

4 – Weaver left behind a Remington no. 11 Typewriter that was 'not in the best order'.

5 – In Jan. 1923, EP sent TSE a copy of Vivante's *Della Intelligenza nell'Espressione* (1922), suggesting he might 'use' it in *C*. An English trans. of the book by Broderick-Bullock entitled

afterwards, may I hope to have something else from you that we may publish?[1]

With best wishes, I am,
Yours sincerely,
[T. S. E.]

TO *Douglas Ainslie* cc

19 August 1924 9 Clarence Gate Gdns

Dear Mr Ainslie,

Thank you very much for your kindness in sending me the 'Allegory',[2] and please accept my apologies for my delay in replying. I should like to publish this essay: I have filled the October number so full that part of the contents must be postponed until January, which also is overflowing. Would April be too late?[3]

When I started the *Criterion* I was afraid that I should not be able to fill it; now I find my greatest difficulty is keeping it within the limits of our purse. I find it necessary (it is what readers like mostly) to put in so much of immediate interest for the moment, that the more permanent work is limited. We hope that some day it may be turned into a monthly, but from present appearances, that requires to cover expenses a much larger public than such a review can ever hope for. The audience of the *Criterion* is not a large one.

Yours sincerely,
[T. S. E.]

—

Intelligence in Expression was imminent (1925): it was reviewed in C. 3: 11 (Apr. 1925), 463–4, by W. A. Thorpe, who described it as 'very welcome' as 'an application of Croce's theory of art to the wider problem of organic life'.

1–Vivante's 'The Misleading Comparison Between Art and Dreams' would appear in *NC* 4: 3 (June 1926).

2–On 24 May Ainslie sent his translation of Benedetto Croce, 'On the Nature of Allegory'–'one of his most interesting and original contributions to the higher criticism'. On 14 Aug., he enquired if TSE wanted it.

3–See 'On the Nature of Allegory', trans. by Ainslie, in C. 3: 11 (Apr. 1925), 405–12.

TO *Virginia Woolf* TS Texas

27 August 1924

38 Burleigh Mansions,
St Martins Lane, London W.C.2

My dear Virginia

Forgive the unconscionable delay in answering your charming letter and invitation.[1] I have been boiled in a hell-broth, and on Saturday journeyed to Liverpool to place my mother in her transatlantic, with the confusion and scurry usual on such occasions, and the usual narrow escape from being carried off to America (or at least to Cobh) myself.[2] In the tumult on the dock an impetuous lady of middle age, 'seeing off' a relative going to make his fortune in the New World, by way of the Steerage) stuck her umbrella in my eye, which is Black. I should love to visit you, seriously: the Prince of Bores to refresh his reputation: but the only pleasure that I can now permit myself is, that should I come to Eastbourne (which is doubtful) we might visit you by dromedary for tea:[3] if I leave London at all I am most unlikely to get done all the things that I ought to do (such as my 1923 Income Tax Return) and certainly not any of the things that you want me to do. I have done absolutely nothing for six weeks. One thing is certain: I MUST stay in London, where Vivien will be, after this week, is uncertain. But

When do you want to publish my defective compositions?[4]

When do you want the MSS?

I should like at least to provide a short preface, which might take two or three nights' work, and make a few alterations in the text to remove the more patent evidences of periodical publication.[5] These three essays are

1–VW wrote on 15 Aug.: 'You do not imagine, I hope, that you are going to escape your annual visit. The 6th September – will that suit you?'

2–In her memoir, Mrs Eliot described her leavetaking on 23 Aug.: 'The sad moment arrived when Tom was obliged to leave the boat as the whistle sounded. He left us with a last embrace and then we watched him standing on the dock until as we moved away we lost sight of him. An ocean seems such a long long distance away from those we love.'

3–In reply (3 Sept.), VW wrote: 'It is a dreadful pity the Prince of Bores can't come to keep his reputation on the boil . . . Come by dromedary (this leaves me quite mystified) rather than not at all' (VW, *Letters*, III, 128).

4–On 15 Aug. VW wrote: 'We want to know about your essay too for our pamphlet series. May we count on it and when?' It would 'lend to the prestige of the series'. The ref. is to *Homage to John Dryden*, published as the fourth in the Hogarth Essays series in Oct. 1924.

5–In his preface, TSE explained that the essays were written for the *TLS* and were to form part of 'a series of papers on the poetry of the seventeenth and eighteenth centuries: beginning with Chapman and Donne, and ending with Johnson'. This proved 'fruit of impossible leisure'. He had 'long felt that the poetry of the seventeenth and eighteenth centuries . . . possesses an elegance and a dignity absent from the popular and pretentious verse of the Romantic Poets and their successors' (9).

not very good (the one on Dryden is the best)[1] but I cannot offer you my 'Reactionary's Encheiridion' or my 'By Sleeping-Car to Rome: A Note on Church Reunion' because they will not be ready in time. But you shall see for yourself, as soon as you wish, whether you think these three papers good enough to reprint.

But what about a FRAGMENT of an Unpublished Novel from you to me?[2] One exists most of the time in morose discontent with the sort of work that one does oneself, and wastes vain envy on all others: the worst of it is that nobody will believe one. But no one regrets more that these moods should occur to Mrs Woolf (of all people) than

Yr. devoted servt.
Thos. Eliot

TO *Lady Rothermere* CC

27 August 1924 9 Clarence Gate Gdns

Dear Lady Rothermere,

I am just recovering from the exhaustion of seeing my mother off from Liverpool and have been recuperating at Eastbourne and as Cocteau would say, 'incapable of writing four lines'.[3] I am writing to him now. I infer however that his article is not about the Ballet. Now, is it certain yet that the Ballet is coming this autumn? And if so, the following would be useful: if Diaghilev would write us a letter even, that we could publish, about the ballets that he is to bring over – *some* inside information which would shew that the *Criterion* had privileged access to Ballet affairs. I do not suppose that Massine is back at his London address, as he has not answered my letter.

Would *you* write to Diaghilev? (According to Cocteau's letter he is [at] the Hotel de Paris, Monte-Carlo.)

1–The essays, dating from the year before *TWL*, were 'John Dryden' (*TLS*, 9 June 1921), 'The Metaphysical Poets' (*TLS*, 20 Oct. 1921), 'Andrew Marvell' (*TLS*, 31 Mar. 1921).

2–VW was writing *Mrs Dalloway*, but nothing from any of her novels appeared in *C*. On 15 Aug., she said: 'I have come to the stage where I can only tolerate plays & poetry: novels seem to me utterly loathsome.'

3–These appear to be Cocteau's exact words (see TSE's letter to him of 5 Sept.). Cocteau was grieving for the death by typhoid of his friend Raymond Radiguet (1903–23). On 7 Aug., he told Valentine and Jean Hugo: 'I am suffering – suffering in the sun, and this is atrocious' (Francis Steegmuller, *Cocteau: A Biography*, 1970, 332). He had also started smoking opium.

Do you know anything about Kessel?[1] Besides, Romeo has not been made into a ballet, has it: and apart from the ballet, I don't see why we should advertise Cocteau's work YET, do you?[2] If Cocteau's own essay is any good, however, I think we ought to have it.[3]

I can't think what more I can do about the Ballet, at present. Do let me know, if you think of anything else that *I* can do. If I only knew for certain when they were coming, and knew their programme as nearly as possible, I could write some editorial matter myself.[4] I propose, in the circumstances, to postpone publication for two weeks (to November 1st) unless you disapprove. The 1st of the month is always the best date, as the number thereby remains 'current' longer, and I could not possibly have got it ready by October 1st, this time.

Anyways, you have worked a miracle in getting something out of Cocteau! I hope that Walter Shaw will send his article.[5]

In haste,

always yours sincerely
[T. S. E.]

1–Joseph Kessel (1898–1979): French novelist and reporter born in Argentina; later author of *Les Captifs* (1926), *Les Secrets Parisiens* (1930), and *L'Armées des ombres* (1943) about the French Resistance. Kessel had proposed an interview with Diaghilev: although this did not take place, TSE later invited Kessel to write 'A Note from Paris' for C. 3: 11 (Apr. 1925).

2–Cocteau had written a balletic version of *Romeo and Juliet*, which was performed as part of Beaumont's season of 'Soirées de Paris' in June 1924. Designed by Jean Hugo, it had a score by Roger Désormière, and Cocteau played the part of Mercutio. Its homoeroticism earned it the soubriquet of *Roméo et Jules*.

3–An article by Cocteau, 'Scandales', appeared much later (in French) in *NC* 4: 1 (Jan. 1926).

4–TSE eventually wrote a paragraph on the 'inestimable privilege of a season of the Diaghilev Ballet', in 'A Commentary', C. 3: 9 (Oct. 1924).

5–On 5 Sept. Shaw offered TSE an article on the Soirée de Paris. Published as 'The Foreign Theatre, The Soirée de Paris', in C. 3: 9 (Oct. 1924), it included comments on Cocteau's *Romeo and Juliet* (described as 'a triumph', though it would have annoyed 'those whose interest in Shakespeare is purely literary') as well as work by Tristan Tzara and Massine.

TO *Jane Heap*[1] TS Beinecke

27 August 1924 *The Criterion*, 9 Clarence Gate Gdns

Dear Miss Heap,

Very many thanks for your letter and all the trouble you have taken.[2] I should very much like to discuss business with you, and shall welcome any suggestions for enlarging circulation in America or anywhere else. I hope that I can manage a weekend in Paris in October. I really know nothing whatever of Gertrude Stein's work, but should much like to see some of it.

Again thanking you,

Sincerely yours,
Thos Eliot

TO *Harold Monro* MS Beinecke

28 August 1924 *The Criterion*, 38 Burleigh Mansions

My dear Monro

I was afraid afterwards, from your recurring to the subject, that my mention of superabundant material might put you off the Wordsworth.[3] If so, I have done very badly by myself, for I want your continuation very much – please assure me that we shall have it. The superabundance, alas, is quantitative not qualitative. And in any case – I want your continuous collaboration.

Yours ever
T. S. E.

TO *Messrs. Curtis Brown* CC

4 September 1924 [*The Criterion*, London]

Dear Sirs,

I must apologise for my absence from town, and for not having answered your letters. Mr Lawrence's story is accepted at our usual rates,

1–Jane Heap (1883–1964): American publisher; co-editor (with her lover Margaret Anderson) of the *Little Review* (1916–29).

2–Heap wrote on 18 Aug. about Ford Madox Ford's attempts to induce Lady Rothermere to take over his magazine *Transatlantic Review*; she told TSE she had 'ideas that should work for our mutual good', and offered to discuss 'distribution and advertising' for *C*.

3–Monro never completed 'Wordsworth Revisited'.

as explained, which will bring the price to your figures (£18.00.0) subject to our printers' confirmation of the number of words; and we propose to print the story in the October number, which will probably appear November 1st.

I enclose a story which Mr Alexander Porterfield has asked me to forward to you, as we are unable to make use of it. Kindly acknowledge receipt.

Yours faithfully,
[T. S. E.]

TO *Miss Hope Clutterbuck*[1] CC

5 September 1924 [London]

Dear Madam,

It would always be a pleasure to me to be of service to any patient of Dr Cyriax,[2] although your enquiry is so general that it is difficult to answer. It is first necessary to decide what field of journalism one will enter. Usually one begins by writing about some subject which one knows, or which one is supposed to know: at one period a certain paper sent me for review all books on contemporary Asiatic politics, merely because I knew Sanskrit:[3] I did not then know or care about contemporary Asiatic politics, but by being supposed to have the knowledge I got the opportunity to acquire it. Then, when one is established in the minds of editors as an authority on one subject, one may gradually get the license (by another irrational process in editors' minds) to write about anything one likes. After a time one reprints a collection of one's essays or reviews as a book. But you must begin by being or by pretending to be an authority on some subject or other, by studying the style and tricks of the papers one is trying to write for, and adopting its tone and prejudices. I suggest that you are an authority on Music, and that you should send musical articles, preferably short ones, and shewing omniscience on the latest movements and

1–On 3 Sept., Hope Clutterbuck explained that 'owing to a breakdown' when 'studying music abroad', she had had to give up her studies. Being 'anxious to take up journalism which Dr Cyriax thinks would be an appropriate hobby', she wanted TSE's advice.

2–TSE and VHE were patients of the two Dr Cyriaxes. During her visit to England, TSE's mother met Madame Cyriax, whom she described as 'a lady of culture and charm'.

3–This account of TSE's early career as reviewer refers loosely to his occasional reviews for *International Journal of Ethics* from Jan. 1916 to July 1918. His output included reviews of anthropological, religious and occasionally Asian material (including *Brahmadarsanam, or Intuition of the Absolute Brahmadarsam, or Intuition of the Absolute* by Sri Ananda Achary).

composers, to such papers as you choose to write for. You should also get personal introductions to editors of daily papers, and here I fear I cannot help you. But if at some time you sent me a short article or criticism, and told me what sort of paper you intended it for, I would give you my brief opinion of it.

I have never known a journalist who had been to a school of journalism,[1] and I have known many journalists. In short-story writing the competition is of course tremendous. A few people make modest fortunes out of writing, many make some sort of living, and others, like myself, have to earn their living by working.

I am afraid that this letter is not very helpful, but it contains all that I know.

Yours faithfully,
[T. S. E.]

TO *Jean Cocteau* CC

5 September 1924 9 Clarence Gate Gdns

Cher Monsieur,

Madame la Vicomtesse Rothermere me transmet la triste nouvelle que vous refusez catégoriquement d'écrire 4 lignes sur le ballet etcetera – mais que, par un tour diplomatique dont nous serons complices, vous pourrez nous faire parvenir un article qui devait paraître aux *Annales*. Je ne sais pas si c'est un article *inédit* ou une conférence *inécrite*? Si vous avez le manuscrit sous la main, je serai heureux de le déchiffrer; si l'idée gît encore aux ténèbres corticales, donnez moi au moins le *titre* de l'article futur, afin que nous puissions rendre à nos lecteurs cette promesse de bonheur qui est la beauté.

Et recevez, cher monsieur, l'assurance de ma vive sympathie.

[T. S. E.][2]

1 – Clutterbuck wanted advice about the various 'Journalists' Schools' she had contacted.

2 – *Translation*: Dear Sir, Viscountess Rothermere has brought me the sad news that you categorically refuse to write four lines about the ballet et cetera, but that, thanks to a diplomatic trick in which we shall be your accomplices, you will give us an article which was intended to be published in *Les Annales*. I do not know whether this article is *unpublished*, or if it is an as yet *unwritten* lecture. If you have the text ready, I should be very pleased to read it; if on the other hand, the whole thing is still gestating in the dark cells of your cortex, then please do let me have at least the title of this forthcoming article, so that we might be able to offer our readers the promise of happiness which is beauty.

Accept, dear sir, the expression of my sincere friendship. [T. S. E.]

TO *Jacques Rivière* CC

12 September 1924 9 Clarence Gate Gdns

Cher Monsieur Rivière,

Voulez-vous me laisser avoir un mot pour dire en faveur de qui on devrait tirer le chèque au sujet du morceau de Proust?[1]

Cette 'Mort d'Albertine' a eu un succès énorme, et Scott Moncrieff a executé quelque chose de merveilleux en fait de traduction. Je vous remercie de tout mon coeur pour vos si aimables soins.

Et voulez-vous bien me rassurer à l'égard de votre article? Nous y comptons.[2]

Avec l'assurance de mes amitiés trés cordiales,

[T. S. E.]

J'espère descendre à Paris au mois de novembre. Il y a une possibilité minime qu'on m'envoie à Basle en qualité de représentant des créditeurs anglais de la ville de Budapest![3]

TO *Lady Rothermere* CC

12 September 1924 9 Clarence Gate Gdns

Dear Lady Rothermere,

I am delighted to hear of your progress so far. I have received the article from Shaw, and have sent it to be set up in type, although, should the ballet *not* come this autumn, I should hold it over till next time.[4] The interview with Diaghilev, and the programme, are just what we want. So the *Criterion* is nearly ready, for either contingency. I hope that the interview

1–'The Death of Albertine', C. 2: 8 (July 1924) had appeared through Rivière's mediation.
2–There was no further article by Rivière, who died the following year.
3–*Translation*: Dear Mr Rivière, Could you please let me have the name of the person to whom we should make out the cheque for the Proust extract?

This 'Death of Albertine' has had an enormous success, and Scott Moncrieff has done something wonderful with the translation. I thank you most sincerely for all the help you have given me.

Would you be kind enough to reassure me about your article? We rely on it.

Please believe in my very cordial friendship. [T. S. E.]

I hope to come to Paris in November. There is the faintest possibility that I might be sent to Basle as a representative of the English creditors to the town of Budapest!

4–Walter Hanks Shaw, 'The Soirée de Paris', *C.* 3: 9 (Oct. 1924): an account of the inaugural seven-week season at the Soirée de Paris of five ballets and two dramas, which included collaborative work by Milhaud, Satie, Massine, Picasso, Marie Laurencin, Cocteau and Tzara.

will take place soon, and that Kessel will send the notes of it quickly, and that then you will wire me if Rothermere and Diaghilev come to terms for this autumn.[1] Then perhaps it would be a good thing if I could have a short article about the ballet in the *Daily Mail*, just when it starts, and drag in the *Criterion* as well. Or in the *Standard*?

The last *Criterion* was rather more expensive, because of the high rates I had to pay for Proust and Virginia Woolf; both of them seemed to help a good deal to send up the circulation, but I shall keep the payment to contributors down a bit after this, and trim down the reviewers and chroniclers a little.

I should have sent you the office contract[2] with this letter, but that I have not a long envelope, and I will keep it till you come, if it is true that you will be here next week.

The Barnes story[3] does not seem to me first rate: I think that she can do better, and I know that there are one or two others who can. We shall see! Miss Heap has sent me two manuscripts of Gertrude Stein; they are not like the story, and they are quite meaningless to me.[4] It seems to me to be nonsense; I will shew them to you when you come. I am so glad that the Hindu is a success, and that you are feeling so well.

Yours very sincerely,
[T. S. E.]

TO *Conrad Aiken* — TS Huntington

12 September 1924 — *The Criterion*, 9 Clarence Gate Gdns

Dear Conrad,

Many thanks for the reviews, which are, as always, very much to the point.[5] I hope that you have returned corrected proof of 'Psychomachia'[6]

1–Rothermere and Diaghilev did come to terms for Diaghilev's company to offer a programme of ballet in London in Nov., but Kessel's projected interview with Diaghilev never came to pass.
2–The contract with Harriet Shaw Weaver for sub-letting the *Egoist* office.
3–Djuna Barnes (1892–1982): novelist, poet and short-story writer, who lived in Paris, 1920–32. Though her stories never appeared in *C.*, TSE wrote a preface to her novel *Nightwood* (1936).
4–TSE was to publish Stein's 'The Fifteenth of November' in *NC* 4: 1 (Jan. 1926). He reviewed her *Composition as Explanation* in 'Charleston, Hey! Hey!', *N&A* 40: 17 (29 Jan. 1927).
5–Aiken had sent his reviews of Osbert Sitwell, *Triple Fugue*, and Gilbert Seldes, *The Seven Lively Arts*, for *C.* 3: 9 (Oct. 1924).
6–Aiken's long poem in the same issue.

to Cobden-Sanderson, though you do not say so. Yes, I know the cheques are smallish, but I hope that some day they will be larger.[1]

I am very sorry to hear your news. Please give my sympathy and my felicitations to your wife – I may say that the former is much more profound than the latter.[2] I hope that things are clear enough now for you to work with as peaceful a mind as one can ever expect to have.

Yours ever,
Tom

TO *Richard Cobden-Sanderson* CC

12 September 1924 [9 Clarence Gate Gdns]

Dear Cobden-Sanderson,

There is a point I should have asked you before. Would the saving of space by putting the bulk of the book reviews in small type be any considerable saving of money as well? And even if not, from the point of view of typography do you as a publisher think that it would look better or worse?[3]

You can ring me up on Monday and give me your opinion. If you say small, I should leave the two most important (every time: this time Read and Manning) in large type and then run on in small. And in that case it would be necessary to reset the Flint review of Aldington in small, because it would be invidious to set Aldington in large and Sitwell and Seldes in small. The two enclosed by Conrad Aiken should go in small if small, and of course in large if all large.

There are two more to come, and my editorials.[4] And IF the ballet is coming (I have asked Lady R. to wire me) then the Walter Shaw goes in, and an interview with Diaghilev which would arrive.

1 – Aiken was grateful that RC-S had sent him his 'cheque (smallish)'.

2 – A 'daughter (Joan) has been added to the family' but Aiken's wife had had 'a bad time of it'.

3 – In C. 2: 8 (July 1924), the new 'Books of the Quarter' section was printed in the same type as the lead articles. In 3: 9 (Oct.), the issue being discussed here, the first two reviews were printed in larger type, while the rest were in the smaller type used in 'Foreign Reviews'. From 3: 10 (Jan. 1925), all reviews were printed in smaller type.

4 – IPF's review of E. M. Forster, *A Passage to India*, and Harold Monro's review of poems by Sinclair and Campbell. TSE's 'Commentary' dealt with the death of Joseph Conrad and the death of F. H. Bradley, as well as with the British Association for the Advancement of Science, folk-dancing, Bernard Shaw's *St Joan*, and the Russian Ballet.

I forgot to include the press-comment (enclosed) in my circular. Will you have a look and see if there would be room to insinuate them anywhere, or if you think the circular too verbose as it is . . . .

I have written to Rivière.

Yours ever
[T. S. E.]

TO *Richard Aldington* CC

12 September 1924 9 Clarence Gate Gdns

My dear Richard,

(1) Very many thanks. I should very much like to publish the Villon. It would probably be in January, though I have got into so many scrapes by this time, with promises and postponements, that I dare not swear it would not be April, but I think I can do it in January. Is that all right? I can swear it will be published, if you let me keep it. I suppose it is the first scholarly article on him in English.[1]

(2) Would you care to write a thing on English influence in France, based on some books (theses) from Champion[2] which have been sent and which you probably have (I believe you reviewed one). The last is on Swift.

(3) Would you be willing – and I know how busy you are, so don't mind refusing – to translate an essay by Ramón Fernandez on Newman for the next *Criterion*? I could give you a fortnight. Flint says he is incapable of understanding it, Manning sneers at it (without having seen it) and I am up a tree. But if you can't, for God's sake suggest someone who could and would.

Can you lunch one Wednesday. Next Wednesday I am alone; the following is the meeting at the Garrick.

Yours ever,
[T. S. E.]

1–RA's 'Villon', in *C.* 3: 11 (Apr. 1925), 376–88 – based on his reading of *François Villon, Oeuvres*, ed. Louis Thuasne (3 vols, 1923) – presents Villon as writing for 'a very small circle of *clercs*' and constantly using 'topical and local allusions . . . incomprehensible to us without a huge commentary'.

2–Éditions Honoré Champion, a scholarly publishing company founded by Honoré Champion (1846–1913). RA mentions Champion's *Histoire Poétique du Quinzième Siècle* in his essay.

TO *Richard Aldington* TS Texas

15 September 1924 9 Clarence Gate Gdns

My dear Richard,

Very good and very many thanks. I certainly don't think that the translation is beyond you! though the point of view may not be sympathetic to you the ideas are subtle and interesting.[1] I will post it tomorrow, accept my appreciation of your doing this.

If you are coming on Wednesday week, as I hope, and do bring Richmond if you can, I will give the French books then. I hope I get the Villon into January, '*dans l'hyver*'.

Scofield Thayer is now described as Editor of the *Dial*, and he is in New York, I am pretty sure.[2] Why not address it to him? I don't know whether you care to say I wanted the *Dial* to have it and urged you to send it, you probably know the *Dial* too well for that, but I used to know Thayer very well personally.

The Fernandez is in French.

Yours ever,
Tom

TO *Messrs. Alfred A. Knopf Inc.* CC

12 September 1924 [London]

Dear Sirs,

I am preparing an essay on the poetic drama, embodying a good many conclusions which I have come to since the publication of *The Sacred Wood*, which I intend to publish together with a series of verse dialogues (not a play) on the life of Savonarola, by my mother, and which I think is worth publishing.[3] It would be ready for publication in the spring and would make I think (together) about 125 to 150 pages at most. I do not intend to print my essay in any other form.

1–See RA's translation of Ramón Fernandez, 'The Experience of Newman', *C.* 3: 9 (Oct. 1924), 84–102.
2–RA wanted to send 'an article on Voltaire's poetry' to the *Dial*: it was not published there.
3–Knopf published *SW* (1921) and had first rights on his next prose book. TSE's introduction to his mother's *Savonarola* consisted of two sections. The first, 'Of History and Truth', argued that a historical work 'tells us more about the age in which it is written than about the past'; the second, 'Of Dramatic Form', discussed the medium within 'a line the termini of which are liturgy and realism'. Presenting Ibsen and Chekhov as 'drama at the extreme limit *beyond* which it ceases to have artistic form', TSE argued that 'the next form of drama will have to be a verse drama but in new verse forms' (*Savonarola: A Dramatic Poem*, 1926, xi).

I should be glad to know whether you would consider publishing this volume, and what terms you would offer.[1] It will be my first American publication since *The Waste Land*.[2]

Yours faithfully,
[T. S. E.]

TO *Jean Cocteau* CC

15 September 1924 9 Clarence Gate Gdns

Mon cher Cocteau,[3]

Très bien – quant au poème,[4] simple question de longueur – nous serons comblés de bonheur de publier un poème, mais certainement *dans le français*, puisqu'il n'y a personne capable de vous traduire et vous rendre un peu de justice – et pour cette raison le poème ne dois pas être une épopée! Voulez-vous bien m'avertir? Et l'article – vous n'avez pas répondu à ma question? Il est déjà écrit? Prière de m'envoyer tous les deux par retour de courrier.

En répétant l'assurance de mon admiration devouée

[T. S. E.][5]

1 – On 26 Sept., Blanche Knopf turned down the proposal. Knopf would 'like to continue to publish your prose over here', but 'combining the material would make a difficult book': it was not sufficiently 'saleable' or 'interesting'.

2 – Published in the USA by Boni & Liveright in Dec. 1922.

3 – TSE's previous letter (12 Sept.) was addressed to 'Cher Monsieur Cocteau'. Cocteau replied: 'Mon cher Eliot, (disons-nous Eliot, Cocteau), Ne sommes-nous pas poètes, donc rois, donc cousins?' ['My dear Eliot (let's say Eliot, Cocteau). Are we not poets, therefore kings, therefore cousins?']

4 – Cocteau had asked: 'voulez-vous un poème? J'ai une pièce inédite que je refuse partout' ['Do you want a poem? I have a piece which I have refused to everyone']. It was to appear in a book in Dec. (*Poésies 1916–1923*, 1924). Neither poem nor essay arrived in time. Cocteau's book was reviewed by RA along with Marianne Moore's *Observations*, in C. 3: 12 (July 1925).

5 – *Translation*: My dear Cocteau, Excellent idea – as for the poem, there is only the problem of its length, but we shall be delighted to publish it, and without any doubt in its original French, for there is no one capable of doing justice to you in translation; and that is why the poem must not be of epic length! Will you please give me some information about it? You have not answered my question about the article. Is it already written? Could you please send me both by return of post?

Renewing the expression of my faithful admiration for you [T. S. E.]

TO *S. S. Koteliansky* MS BL

21 September 1924 *The Criterion*, 17 Thavies Inn

Dear Koteliansky

I think the Tolstoy letters are extremely valuable and interesting, and should very much like to publish them, in *January*.[1] If you intend printing them in a book *before* then, will you let me know? I wish that the *October* number was not completely made up, as it wd have suited me to use them at once.

Have they been published in any other language than [German *del.*] Russian?

With many thanks.

Yours sincerely
T. S. Eliot

TO *Wyndham Lewis* MS Cornell

[Postmark 23 September 1924] 9 Clarence Gate Gdns

Very many thanks for punctual MS.[2] I shall expect the others during the week. Excellent. If you can send me this week all the things you promised to send, I want to see you again soon and discuss affairs.

T. S. E.

TO *Harold Joachim* CC

28 September 1924 9 Clarence Gate Gdns

Dear Mr Joachim,

Thank you very much for your kind letter. I did not expect that you would be able, at the moment, to write for us even a short obituary, I merely expressed the hope that you might do so later.[3] No doubt you

1–'A Few Extracts from Letters exchanged between Leo Nicolayevich Tolstoy and N. N. Strakhov relating to F. M. Dostoevsky', trans. S. S. Koteliansky, C. 3: 10 (Jan. 1925), 164–9.
2–See WL, 'Art Chronicle', *C.* 3: 9 (Oct. 1924).
3–F. H. Bradley had died in Oxford on 18 Sept., and TSE approached Harold Joachim as his Oxford colleague. Joachim thanked TSE on 24 Sept. for the 'kind offer to take an obituary or article on Bradley, *if I write one*'. His lecturing and other duties made it unlikely, he said, but Bradley 'was a *very great man* – greater perhaps than any of us have realised'.

will record the event in *Mind*;[1] but I should like to impress Bradley on a different public. I have succeeded in imposing a word about him upon such unlikely organs as *Vanity Fair* and *Vogue*![2] I shall send you a copy of the October *Criterion* containing my own notice: very inadequate, as it must be, when there is so much to say, and to so indifferent and so unprepared readers.[3] I enclose the notice from the *Nation*, which is just what I should expect from that implement of Cambridge free-thought, and which roused me to my own small effort.[4]

Always your pupil[5] –
[T. S. E.]

TO *Harold Monro* MS UCLA

30 September 1924 *The Criterion*, 17 Thavies Inn

My dear Monro

I am very very sorry.[6] I have been ploughing away at wiping off some much older debts, as C-Sanderson can testify, and also trying to get down a little verse, which is a hell of a sweat for anyone whose hand is so far out as mine (the latter wd be of no use to you or anyone in its present form). But I will still *try* to do that small piece, *if* there's time without holding you up. I do owe it to you indeed in return for all you have done (and I hope will do!) for me.

Yours
T. S. Eliot

1–The obituary article for *Mind* 34: 133 (Jan. 1925), 1–12, was by A. E. Taylor.
2–TSE had discussed F. H. Bradley in 'Contemporary British Prose', *Vanity Fair* 20: 5 (July 1923). On 13 Aug., the editor of *Vogue* asked to reprint TSE's piece.
3–TSE paid tribute to Bradley in his 'Commentary' (C. 3: 9, Oct. 1924, 1–2), calling him 'the last survivor of the academic race of metaphysicians': 'Few will ever take the pains to study the consummate art of Bradley's style, the finest philosophic style in our language, in which acute intellect and passionate feeling preserve a classic balance: only those who will surrender patient years to the understanding of his meaning. But upon those few, both living and unborn, his writings perform that mysterious and complete operation which transmutes not one department of thought only, but the whole intellectual and emotional tone of their being. To them, in the living generation, the news of his death has brought an intimate and private grief.'
4–See 'Omicron', in the column 'From Alpha to Omega', *N&A* 35: 26 (27 Sept. 1924), 777.
5–Joachim had been TSE's tutor at Oxford in 1914–15. On his death, TSE wrote 'Professor H. H. Joachim', *The Times*, 4 Aug. 1938.
6–On 18 and 26 Sept., Monro pressed for TSE's promised 'short contribution' (only two pages) to *Chapbook*, which was due on 30 Sept.: 'Please be in it for the sake of representation.'

Do you like Emily Dickinson and *if so* wd you care or be willing to review her book?[1]
Shall turn up *next* Wednesday.

TO *Wyndham Lewis* MS Cornell

3 October 1924 *The Criterion*, 17 Thavies Inn

Dear Lewis

I do not know in the least what you mean by 'some economic factor at work on my side'. I thought it was quite clear why I suggested next week.[2] You seem to have misunderstood me. As for the finances of the *Criterion*, they are entirely in Cobden-Sanderson's hands; he keeps the ledgers, which are audited by auditors, and reports to Lady Rothermere; and I only receive the ordinary rate of payment for my contributions, and have never received anything else from her or from the paper.

Also, I don't understand what you say about what you had hoped to do (for the Jan. no.).[3] You know quite well that I would publish *practically anything you gave me*, except anything which I thought would render us liable to prosecution, and that there is almost no one but yourself of whom I would accept so much.

I saw C.-S. today but his cheque books were in the bank, and he could not make out a cheque till tomorrow, that is why I enclose my own cheque for £10 which is all I can spare over the weekend and I will get C.-S. to pay me.[4] This is no inconvenience at all. If you can let me have up to 5000 to 6000 words for January, as well as chronicle, I will see that everything is paid for at once.[5]

Yours ever
T. S. E.

1–See Monro on *Selected Poems of Emily Dickinson*, ed. Conrad Aiken, in C. 3: 10 (Jan. 1925).
2–WL wrote (undated letter): 'As you suggested next week for this exceptional advance payment, I know that this must mean some "economic factor" is at work on your side.'
3–WL wrote: 'What I had hoped was to do you something of the length and importance of the *Apes* [*of God*], and I meant to ask you directly for a similar sum.'
4–WL, who had been penniless for a week, had asked TSE 'under the circumstances' to 'make the cheque as large as you can'.
5–In the event, neither an 'Art Chronicle' nor a substantial piece of fiction appeared in C. 3: 10 (Jan. 1925), only a couple of reviews.

TO *Harold Monro* TS UCLA

5 October 1924 9 Clarence Gate Gdns

My dear Monro,

I am afraid that I have not been able to do what I promised.[1] The subject you suggested is one that I want to write something about in a pamphlet which I have put down for future agenda,[2] but it is too much aside from what I have been working at lately for me to be able to get my mind onto it. I am sending you the only things that I have. Print them if you like or not, I dare say that they are bad enough to do the *Chapbook* no good and to bring me considerable discredit.[3] If you want them you are welcome, if not, I am very sorry that I have done nothing better that I could give you. They were all written for another purpose and perhaps would not look quite so foolish in their proper context as they probably do by themselves.[4]

I hope to see you on Wednesday. What about Emily Dickinson?[5]

Yours ever
T. S. E.

TO *E. R. Curtius* CC

[?6 October 1924] [9 Clarence Gate Gdns]

My dear Curtius,

You will think it very rude of me not to have written to you before, but during the summer I have been worried and ill, and since then have been very busy. I wish that I could have come to Pontigny, but I have not been out of England for a year, and am not likely to be: such is the life of a *Bankbeamte*.[6] I will see that you receive a copy of the last and the next (October) *Criterion*; the former will certainly interest you.

1 – See TSE's letter of 30 Sept.
2 – On 18 Sept., Monro said he was not 'sure about the Dawes exposition' that TSE had proposed, and suggested 'something about International Intellectualism, or Intellectual Internationalism'.
3 – 'Doris's Dream Songs' (*Chapbook* 39, 1924, 36–7). Along with 'Poème', in *Commerce* 3 (Winter 1924 [/1925]), these were the first poems to be published since *TWL* two years earlier.
4 – This may refer to the sequence that became 'The Hollow Men', first published as a whole in *P 1909–1925*.
5 – See TSE's letter of 30 Sept.
6 – 'Bank clerk'. Curtius had been to the annual literary conference at Pontigny, to which TSE had also been invited.

I am writing to Professor Jacobsthal,[1] and hope that he will let me see his essay. I wish that I might hear from you what work you are doing yourself, and whether you are any nearer to the English *Wegbereiter*?[2] I am bringing out a small book in January with the Hogarth Press, but that is only three essays written several years ago: but I shall send you a copy.[3]

With kindest regards,

Yours always
[T. S. E.]

TO *Paul Jacobsthal*[4] CC

6 October 1924 [London]

Sir,

Our friend Dr Curtius tells me that you have an essay on 'Bewertung und Wirkung antiker Kunst in Deutschland' which you might care to publish in England.[5] If it is not too long for the possibilities of the *Criterion* (our contributions ought not to exceed 5000 words) I should very highly appreciate the honour of examining this essay. May I hope to hear from you?

I am, Sir,

Your obedient servant,
[T. S. E.]

1–Curtius recommended an article by his friend Paul Jacobsthal, a scholar of Greek vases.
2–An allusion to their earlier discussions about an English version of Curtius's *Die literarischen Wegbereiter des neuen Frankreich* (1919), or *The Literary Precursors of the New France* (see TSE's letter of 14 Aug. 1923).
3–In fact, *Homage to John Dryden* came out on 30 Oct.
4–Paul Jacobsthal (1880–1957): German scholar of Greek vase painting and (in a later year) Celtic art; author of *Der Blitz in der Orientalischen und Griechischen Kunst: ein formgeschichtlicher Versuch* (1906), and *Ornamente Griechische Vase* (1927) and *Early Celtic Art* (1944). In 1912 he was appointed a professor at the University of Marburg. Of Jewish origins, he left Germany in 1935 and became a lecturer at Christ Church, Oxford; co-editor of Oxford Classical Monographs. He was Oxford Reader in Celtic Archaeology, 1947–50.
5–See Paul Jacobsthal, 'Views and Valuations of Ancient Art since Winckelmann, chiefly in Germany', trans. Charles Caffrey, *C.* 3: 12 (July 1925), 543–56; *NC* 4: 1 (Jan. 1926), 138–47.

TO *Ernst Bertram*[1] CC

6 October 1924 9 Clarence Gate Gdns

Sir,

Our friend Dr E. R. Curtius has made me acquainted with your *Nietzsche*, of which I admire both the matter and the style.[2] I should consider it an honour if you would consider contributing a critical essay to the *Criterion*, which would be happy to introduce your work in this country. Dr Curtius suggested that you might care to let us have an essay on Hölderlin,[3] but I should be delighted to consider any suggestions from you.

I must explain that as we give equal importance to foreign and to British contributors, we must ask that every contribution appear first in the *Criterion*, before appearing in the country of its origin. Our rates of payment are £10 per 5000 words, less translators' fees of 15 shillings per 1000 words. Perhaps Dr Curtius would tell you something of the character and standing of the review.

I am, Sir,

Your obedient servant,
[T. S. E.]

TO *G. A. Porterfield* CC

6 October 1924 9 Clarence Gate Gdns

Dear Mr Porterfield

I must apologise for not writing before. I have been very busy. What I should have told you is this: I should like to use the Colonel, if as you say you will allow me to cut it down considerably: I must go over it carefully again. There is much dialogue which I enjoy immensely. I choose this one, because the other would be much more difficult to cut. The third story struck me – I hope you will not mind my saying so – as much more superficial, and at the same time probably more acceptable to many other magazines, and I therefore sent it to Curtis Brown, and have his receipt. As I have no instructions from you, I shall hold the other story subject to your commands, and retain the Colonel for the *Criterion*.[4]

1–Ernst Bertram (1884–1957): poet and scholar: see note to letter to Scofield Thayer, 12 Jan. 1923.
2–*Nietzsche: Versuch einer Mythologie* (1918).
3–Bertram later edited Hölderlin's *Letters* (1935); he did not contribute to *C.*
4–TSE solicited stories from Porterfield on 14 May. Having chosen 'The Colonel', TSE later gave it another title. Its protagonist remains Colonel Bellamy, but it appeared as 'A Marriage Has Been Arranged, etc.', in *C.* 3: 10 (Jan. 1925), 193–213.

I am so glad that you like the *Criterion*, and grateful to you for making it better known in New York. That is what we need. One reason why I postponed writing was that I had hoped to see you in London this autumn.

Yours sincerely
[T. S. E.]

TO *G. Elliot Smith*[1] CC

6 October 1924 9 Clarence Gate Gdns

Dear Mr Elliot Smith,

I know that you will think me a great nuisance, but I cannot allow you to forget that you promised me an essay on 'The Glamour of Gold'[2] when you went to America. I did not want to bother you during the summer – I was much disappointed that the Association Meetings[3] did not include an address by you – but if you have now returned, I hope that you will be able to offer me the hope of something from you during the winter.

I think that Volume III of The *Criterion* promises to surpass the previous two volumes, but I shall not account it successful unless it contains something from you – and there are others whom I wish to ask – but who should be preceded by yourself.

Yours very truly,
[T. S. E.]

TO *Jean Cocteau* CC

6 October 1924 9 Clarence Gate Gdns

Mon cher Cocteau

Vous me présentez une coupe et vous me l'arrachez aux lèvres. Me voici en présence d'un beau poème que je ne peux pas publier.[4] Et

1–See letter of 28 May 1923.

2–Elliot Smith suggested this title in a letter of 30 May 1924. 'The Glamour of Gold' appeared in *C.* 3: 11 (Apr. 1925), 345–55.

3–Presumably the British Association for the Advancement of Science, as discussed in TSE's 'Commentary', *C.* 3: 9 (Oct. 1924): their published addresses were always 'a document of general importance'.

4–TSE seems to have misunderstood Cocteau's remark that his poem would appear with *NRF* to refer to the Nov. issue of *NRF*. Cocteau was in fact referring to its appearance as a book, viz. *Poésies 1915–1923*, published by *NRF* in late 1924.

pourquoi? Je veux exposer les raisons: Ce poème paraîtra dans *La Nouvelle Revue Française* au mois de novembre. Notre numéro d'octobre était déjà sous presse, donc votre poème ne pourrait paraître chez nous qu'au mois de janvier. Mais *La Nouvelle Revue Française* est la seule que nous ne pouvons absolument pas nous laisser dévancer. Notre public, plus étendu naturellement, comprend tous les lecteurs anglais de la *NRF*: il s'ensuit que trop de nos lecteurs auraient déjà vu le poème en question. Nous n'osons pas leur donner raison de dire que nous sommes arrièrés. J'espère que vous comprendrez ma position, parce que je suis comblé de désespoir.

Mais, à ce même titre, un INÉDIT de vous aura un succès retentissant, et nous enveloppera de gloire. Sinon un poème, permettez-moi de vous supplier de nous envoyer EXPRÈS votre prose lors de votre arrivée à Paris.[1]

Et recevez toujours l'assurance de ma profonde admiration.

Votre

[T. S. E.][2]

TO *Harold Monro* TS UCLA

6 October 1924 *The Criterion*, 17 Thavies Inn

My dear Monro,

Will you kindly give the bearer of this letter, my secretary, the three MSS. I sent you last night.[3] I promise that you shall have them back or their verse equivalent by hand in the evening. I know you are in a hurry, and

1–Cocteau's 'Scandales' appeared (in French) in *NC* 4: 1 (Jan. 1926).

2–*Translation*: My dear Cocteau, You offer me a full cup, and you snatch it away just when it reaches my lips. You offer me a fine poem and I cannot publish it. Why? Here are the reasons. The poem is to be published in the *Nouvelle Revue Française* in November. Our October issue is already at the printers, therefore your poem could not be published by us until the January issue. Now the *Nouvelle Revue Française* is the only review which we cannot allow to publish before us, things we ourselves intend to publish. Our reading public, which naturally is wider, nevertheless includes all the English readers of the *NRF*; therefore if this poem were published in the *NRF*, too many of our readers would already have seen it before it appears with us. We dare not offer them grounds to label us backward and slow. I am deeply distressed, and I hope you will understand my position.

For these very reasons, an unpublished text from you will have a resounding success which could only bring glory to us. If you cannot send us a poem, I beg you to send us by express post your prose article as soon as you reach Paris.

Please accept once more the expression of my deep admiration. Yours, [T. S. E.]

3–The three poems TSE sent to Monro for the *Chapbook* on 5 Oct.

I won't let you down, but I must have them back today. I will write to you fully tonight.[1]

In great haste,
T. S. Eliot

My secretary is authorised to give you a receipt for them.

TO *Douglas Ainslie* CC

6 October 1924 [London]

Dear Mr Ainslie,

This is only a hurried line to thank you for your letter of the 26th ultimo. I should not think that there was any doubt of the position which Croce has reached.[2] By the way, the *European Poetry* has *not* reached me, I should be very much interested to see it.[3] I am glad that the *Criterion* is of some interest to you, and that you do not think that it is too big.[4]

I have enjoyed reading your poems. Unfortunately, there is nothing for which there has been so little room in the *Criterion* as poetry; and I have imprudently accepted more than can, I think, be published within the next year! But I hope that that will not discourage you from sending more.[5]

Sincerely yours,
[T. S. E.]

TO *Ford Madox Ford* CC

6 October 1924 9 Clarence Gate Gdns

Dear Ford,

Thank you for your letter of the 18th ultimo. I quite understand your difficulties, which I share. I have not seen the current number of the

1–The later letter seems to be missing.

2–Ainslie wrote that 'Croce seems to be making his way to ever wider recognition'.

3–Ainslie named Croce's *European Poetry* (presumably *European Literature in the Nineteenth Century*, 1924) as the most recent of his translations.

4–Ainslie hoped C. would 'increase its bulk'.

5–Ainslie had sent TSE 'a few small poems', with sources in *The Vedanta* and *Upanishads*. His *Chosen Poems* appeared from the Hogarth Press in Mar. 1926, but no poem was used in C.

Transatlantic, but I assure you that I only consider it an honour to be gibed at therein.[1] Many thanks for your complimentary expressions.[2]

I cannot find in my records of Corrupted Contributors, or of Contributors-to-be and to-be-Corrupted, or of Contributors in Process of Corruption, any mention of one of your staff, nor can I think whom it would be that I should thus desire to entice. I have never made it a condition, to any of my contributors, that his or her name should never be seen in *The Transatlantic*: I am extremely liberal in such matters. And fourpence is really beyond our means.[3]

Sincerely yours,
[T. S. E.]

TO *Jane Heap* CC

6 October 1924 9 Clarence Gate Gdns

Dear Miss Heap,

I am returning to you Miss Stein's MSS. I have read them through several times and think I have grasped some at least of the intention: and they certainly produce a peculiar hypnotic effect upon me. But I do not think that they would do for us in the *Criterion*; and they seem to me much more for the professional, as a technical study, than for the ordinary reader. They are extremely interesting to *me*, as I have been working in a method of repetition and variation lately myself; and some day I should much like to meet the author.[4]

1 – On 18 Sept., Ford wrote: 'There is in the current number of this review a rather silly gibe at yourself . . . It is difficult to know how to deal with these matters. You ask a contributor to write for you on his general record and then he smacks in the eye your dearest and best . . . and you remain *planté là*. I hope you'll forgive.' Ernest Hemingway had written: 'It is agreed by most of the people I know that Conrad is a bad writer, just as it is agreed that T. S. Eliot is a good writer. If I knew that by grinding Mr Eliot into a fine dry powder and sprinkling that powder over Mr Conrad's grave Mr Conrad would shortly appear, looking very annoyed at the forced return and commence writing I would leave for London early tomorrow morning with a sausage grinder' ('Appreciations of Conrad', *Transatlantic Review* 2: 3 [Sept. 1924], 341–2). Ford made a public apology in a later issue, 2: 5 (Nov. 1924), 550.

2 – Ford said: 'You know in any case I have a great admiration for your poems and I will shortly make occasion to say so with great emphasis in the review.'

3 – Ford wrote: 'An eccentric rumour has reached me to the effect that you have offered one of my regular contributors an immense sum to go over to the *Criterion* . . . You might have me and the lot for about fourpence.'

4 – This may refer to the short poems such as 'Doris's Dream Songs' and the drafts of 'The Hollow Men', or to *SA*.

I am very sorry that you are returning to New York before November; as I am disappointed of my hope of meeting you, and also as a conversation would have been so much easier than a correspondence. We are getting out a new circular and letter toward the end of October, and propose to send it to 5000 selected names in England and America. I have composed a special letter addressed to prospective American subscribers. Could you make use of and distribute some of these circulars, or could you even slip one into each number of the next *Little Review*? I should not dream of asking such a thing, but that you have been so kind in offering help. I should like to see the *Criterion* firmly on its feet this year; anyway, I think that at the end of the third year it will have as brilliant a record of contributors as any magazine could have in the time; and I should like to see the subscription list at the same level.

And when you get back will you see that the *Little Review* is sent regularly to Herbert Read, 35 Beaumont Road, Purley, Surrey, who reviews all the American periodicals? I presume that you get the *Criterion* regularly.

With all best wishes, many thanks, and the hope of seeing you some day in London or Paris.

Sincerely yours,
[T. S. E.]

TO *Arnold Bennett* — TS Beinecke

8 October 1924 — *The Criterion*, 9 Clarence Gate Gdns

Dear Mr Bennett,

I hope that you have not forgotten your kind and inestimable offer to examine my work, and I hope that you realised that I would take full advantage of it.[1] I have five or six typed pages of dialogue, and a very brief scenario, which I should now like to submit to you. May I, as you proposed yourself, come to see you at your convenience? I could come to see you either Monday, Tuesday or Thursday evenings of next week, if any of those times is possible for you. I should be extremely grateful. Perhaps I shall have a little more dialogue by then.

Sincerely yours,
T. S. Eliot

Say nine o'clock?

1 – On 10 Sept. Bennett recorded in his journal that TSE had visited him at the Reform Club the evening before; see note to TSE's letter to Bennett of 13 July.

TO *Richard Aldington* TS Texas

8 October [1924] *The Criterion*, 17 Thavies Inn

My dear Richard,

Many thanks for lending me the Garnier book, and for giving me the tip about him.[1] Of course, I am genuinely extremely ignorant – my only strength is that I am not abashed to admit it.

If I can write English prose – and I imagine that there are more Americanisms in my prose than you wish to see[2] – it is due to two causes: an intensive study of two years of the prose of Bradley,[3] and an inherited disposition to rhetoric, from innumerable ancestors who occupied themselves with the church, the law, or politics! On the other hand, this gives my prose, I am aware, a rather rheumatic pomposity – I am conscious of this stiffness, but I do not trust myself elsewhere.

Would you be willing to review a book for January called *Contemporary Criticism of Literature* by Orlo Williams? It seems to me not a bad book, though I may be prejudiced by the fact that the author is not unfavourable to me, and in any case it gives scope for saying anything one wants to say about criticism.[4]

Yours ever
Tom

1–A. M. Witherspoon, *The Influence of Robert Garnier on Elizabethan Drama* (1924).
2–RA said that TSE's was the only prose by a native-born American where he could not 'scent the American "note"'. On 8 Oct. he replied to TSE that 'I have just re-read three of your essays, and still assert there is no Americanism in them!'
3–In the 1965 preface to his doctoral thesis, published as *KEPB*, TSE noted that his 'wife observed at once, how closely my own prose style was formed on that of Bradley and how little it has changed in all these years'.
4–Orlo Williams's chapter on 'Scientific Critics' includes an extended discussion of TSE's *SW* (*Contemporary Criticism of Literature*, 1924, 134–54), which he described as 'a small critical portmanteau admirably packed with controversial topics'. Williams (for whom see TSE's letter of 13 Oct.) noted that some readers found 'something repellent in the cold lucidity of [TSE's] critical prose as there is in the equally cold want of lucidity' in *TWL*, and described TSE as 'an elect mind consciously for the elect': 'Mr Eliot is not generous, especially to the art and enthusiasms of the present, but it is bad criticism to be annoyed with him instead of inquiring how near he comes to the truth' (145). In his review, RA called Williams 'a critic sitting in judgement upon other critics', who had 'accomplished the task with urbanity and impartiality' (*C* 3: 11, Apr. 1925, 453–6).

TO *Herbert Read* PC Victoria

[Postmark 9 October 1924] *The Criterion*, 9 Clarence Gate Gdns

The undersigned begs to express his humble penitence at continued default and absence from meetings of The Criterion Club,[1] but confesses to a state of utter mental unreliability owing to preoccupation with a piece of work which he hopes you will (later) consider extenuating: he forbears from alleging the strong practical reasons which exist. If the next meeting can be held on a Saturday he promises and undertakes to provide such quantity of Port as shall induce the plaintiffs to withdraw their process.

T. S. Eliot

TO *Lady Rothermere* CC

13 October 1924 9 Clarence Gate Gdns

Dear Lady Rothermere,

Diaghilev never responded to my wire *at all*,[2] and Kessel's story arrived three days too late, after everything had been finally set up. But it is very interesting, and I see no reason why it should not go into the January number.[3] January and April are now practically complete, except of course for the topical chronicles etc.

The October number should be out about the end of the week. It is I think the most alive of any that we have had: there is nothing of the costly showiness of Proust and Virginia Woolf (neither of which I cared much about myself), but there is a brilliant and ferocious essay by F. W. Bain, an extraordinary thing by Fernandez, and some first rate fiction and verse by very promising people; and the chronicles and reviews are exceedingly good.[4] The Shaw review comes in very well, and if you see him, do tell him that I like it.

1 – A reference to the weekly meetings of TSE, HR, Monro, and others associated with *C.*

2 – On 13 Sept., TSE told her: 'The interview with Diaghilev, and the programme, are just what we want.'

3 – Joseph Kessel sent from Paris an interview with one of Diaghilev's dancers about which Lady Rothermere had spoken to TSE; he was deeply interested in writing a regular Letter from Paris.

4 – The issue included: F. W. Bain, '1789'; Ramón Fernandez, 'The Experience of Newman'; DHL, 'Jimmy and the Desperate Woman'; John Shand, 'Some Notes on Joseph Conrad'; VHE's 'Thé Dansant'; IPF's 'Mrs Pilkington'; Conrad Aiken's poem 'Psychomachia'; WL's 'Art Chronicle'; J. B. Trend, 'Music'; Walter Hanks Shaw, 'The Soirée de Paris'; and Zoe Hawley, 'Celui qui reçoit les gifles', *C.* 3: 9 (Oct. 1924).

I am writing to Kessel about the chronique.[1]

Certainly, the Mardrus must be a small and special subscribed edition.[2] If you find it difficult, I could probably find someone to collaborate, but I am sure you can do it. The Valéry of course will be a test, but I am convinced that there is a market for limited editions of small books at high prices, and in America also.[3] Your friend Milbanke who has just been here has promised to make enquiries about the New York market. The Mardrus is just the sort of thing that Rodker would like to get.

Will you let me know whether the 15th would be an equally [convenient] date for me to come to Paris, as it would suit me much better, and I am not *sure* that the 21st is possible. The ballet, by the way, has been changed from the 27th to the 24th, so if you want to come – I hope you will, as it would be a good thing for us in every way – that is the night for a box.[4]

Yours always
[T. S. E.]

TO *Harold Monro* MS UCLA

13 October 1924 *The Criterion*, 17 Thavies Inn

Dear Monro,

The title is not good, but it has a connexion for me, and I can't think of a better.[5]

I shall appear on Wednesday week. Have you received Dickinson from Cobden-Sanderson?[6]

1–Kessel's 'A Note from Paris' appeared in *C.* 3: 11 (Apr. 1925).

2–Joseph Charles Mardrus (1868–1949): French doctor born in Cairo, famous for his translations into French of *1001 Nights* and the Koran: TSE is referring to his *The Arabian Nights* in 4 vols.

3–*Le Serpent by Paul Valéry* (1924) was intended to be the first of a series of *C.* publications.

4–On 24 Nov., the Russian Ballet performed at the Coliseum. They played *Cimarosiana*, based on music by Cimarosa, and *Le Train Bleu, une opérette dansée* about 'Flappers' and their 'Boys' by Darius Milhaud. It was choreographed by Mlle Nijinska, and starred Anton Dolin as the 'Beau Gosse' and Lydia Sokolova as his partner.

5–'Doris's Dream Songs', the title he gave to 'Eyes that last I saw in tears', 'The wind sprang up at four o'clock' and 'This is the dead land', in *Chapbook* 39. The 'connexion' is with the contemporary *SA*, in which Doris is the main female protagonist. 'Death's dream kingdom' and 'death's other kingdom' in the songs may be linked with Sweeney's declarations: 'He didn't know if they were both alive or both were dead' and 'Death is life and life is death' (*CPP*, 125).

6–Conrad Aiken's *Selected Poems of Emily Dickinson* (1924), which Monro was to review.

I am sorry to make trouble. But, as I *particularly* should *not* be willing to appear on the same page with anyone else, *I will immediately produce another ½ page of verse* if you have any difficulty with the *cul-de-lampe*.[1] Will you let me know? You can telephone Central 8246 if necessary.

Yours ever
T. S. E.

TO *Orlo Williams*[2] CC

13 October 1924 9 Clarence Gate Gdns

Dear Sir

I have to thank you for the book and for your kind letter of the 5th instant.[3] I have read your book, with an interest prompted by vanity but sustained by respect. Any opinion of mine is no doubt likely to be deflected by the honour which you do me, and is perhaps worthless. I am impressed by the justice with which you represent my point of view: I do not think that I have ever (as a critic) been treated more impartially and fairly. I have the same opinion of your treatment of the other writers discussed: the book seems to me to display very rare virtues of temperateness and understanding, and I do not think that one of your subjects has the slightest reason to complain of injustice. May Rhadamanthus[4] treat us as kindly.

Yes, I think, for what my opinion is worth, that the book is a valuable contribution, and that you display as valuable critical qualities as any of the persons in whom you interest yourself.[5]

1 – 'Doris's Dream Songs' occupies two pages in *Chapbook* 39. The first two poems (of fifteen and twelve lines) are on one page, while on the second page the third poem (of thirteen lines) is followed by a black-and-white vignette (or '*cul-de-lampe*') set in an otherwise empty lower half-page. The semi-abstract vignette suggests the 'cactus land' and 'stone images' of the poem, and their position on the page meant that TSE did not have to 'appear on the same page with anyone else'.

2 – Orlo (Orlando) Williams (1883–1967): Clerk to the House of Commons; scholar and critic; author of *The Clerical Organization of the House of Commons 1661–1850* (1954); *Vie de Bohème: A Patch of Romantic Paris* (1913); *Some Great English Novels: The Art of Fiction* (1926).

3 – Williams, *Contemporary Criticism of Literature* (1924).

4 – In Greek mythology, Rhadamanthus, son of Zeus and Europa, is a severe judge in the lower world.

5 – Williams also discussed Edmund Gosse, J. C. Squire, JMM, George Saintsbury and Percy Lubbock.

I do not mean that I agree with you in everything. Nobody likes being called a 'highbrow'.[1] But there are some things you say that positively delight me. Yours is the first expression that I have seen in print of the disgust with which I was inspired by the 'tributes' to Marcel Proust,[2] and what you say on pages 62–64 is a favourite cause of my own.[3]

I should like to see your name in the *Criterion* – please take this as a suggestion to send me, when you will, some critical essay, if you will.[4]

Yours very truly
[T. S. E.]

FROM *Herbert Read* — TS Valerie Eliot

18 October 1924 — 35 Beaumont Rd, Purley

Dear Eliot,

Perhaps I wrote hastily and it would be as well to withdraw.[5] I don't want to say anything that would offend you, and it is easy enough to criticise from an irresponsible position like mine. I realise that you have difficulties due to the necessity of making some sort of commercial show which wouldn't exist if free critical considerations only were in the field. Some degree of compromise is necessary and from that point of view

1 – Williams proclaimed: 'T. S. Eliot *is* a highbrow, and writes with admirable limpidity' (122). In a contemporary story by IPF, when Mrs Pilkington hears that Marion is reading a French novel '*in* French too', she says 'you were always a bit of a highbrow', which provokes Marion to say 'I hope not' (Felix Morrison, 'Mrs Pilkington', *C.* 3: 9, Oct. 1924, 104).
2 – *Marcel Proust: An English Tribute* (1923), collected by C. K. Scott Moncrieff. The twenty-one contributors included Conrad, Arnold Bennett and JMM. Several of the pieces were newspaper reprints, and two were extracts from letters to the editor. In his book, Williams asked: 'Could anything have been more unnecessary or ridiculous than this uncertain chorus of miscellaneous voices in honour of a remarkable and recently dead French novelist?' (173).
3 – Williams observed that in England, 'the critical biography, or monograph', involving 'the delineation of an author's worldly figure, gracefully and sympathetically carried out', prevailed over works which focus on 'the work of art alone' (63); 'we are bare of conclusions about the literature of the immediate past and the actual present.' Modern poetry is still 'a battlefield': 'The labour of tidying-up, were it seriously undertaken, would be colossal, and there is no inducement to undertake it. We seem to look in vain for an intellect large enough, a knowledge wide enough, and a disinterested energy powerful enough to force order upon this confusion' (63–4).
4 – Williams reviewed JMM's *Keats and Shakespeare* in *NC* 4: 1 (Jan. 1926), and became a regular reviewer and contributor.
5 – On 14 Oct., HR thanked TSE for suggesting a Donne book for review. He added: 'A phalanx – yes! That is the right image. I confess I have been a bit afraid, lately, that you were using forces too scattered in disposition. But there is no knowing how far strategy may be carried.'

I suppose even Hugh Walpole is permissible.[1] All that is fully granted and anything I can find to say is to that extent vitiated.

I don't know anything about the history of journals, but wouldn't it be true to say that reviews like the *Edinburgh*, the *Quarterly, Fraser's* at the period of their maximum force[2] were not the repositories of all possible brilliance, but rather well-disciplined teams even to some extent composed of rather dull units, but coherent, definite and decisive? At any rate, isn't that the ideal? The *Dial*, as I have heard you say, is a miscellany of accepted reputations. Isn't it a mistake to be a miscellany of any sort? I think you agree, and I have construed your present policy as one of experimental assortments – as though you had said: Let us be miscellaneous for a year or two and then gradually weed out, until only the coherent band remains, the phalanx of your own evocation.[3]

It is conceivable, of course, that there isn't a phalanx – that you simply can't see your way to a closing of the ranks. But there I shouldn't agree with you. I think there is just about enough talent of the right sort [to] make a show. (A little that you haven't tapped at all yet.) I think, too, that you are the only possible nucleus: that your critical standards are so adequately defined and so definitely orientated that it is possible for a good few of us to follow your track.

I'm really avoiding your direct question. Personally, I like Robertson and I like Whibley: they are at least objective.[4] Whether they like us is another question. I think you can rely (for standards) on Lewis.[5] I don't share the general disapproval of Ezra.[6] I think the foreign introductions have been excellent, and liaison with the right elements abroad will always be desirable. Virginia Woolf, E. M. Forster and Osbert Sitwell all fulfil their

1–Hugh Walpole's 'The Old Ladies', chs 1 and 2, appeared in *C.* 2: 7 & 8 (Apr. & July 1924).

2–*The Edinburgh Review*, *The Quarterly Review* and *Fraser's* were among the most influential nineteenth-century periodicals.

3–In 'T. S. E. – A Memoir', HR recalls the regular *C.* meetings as being meant 'to build up some kind of "phalanx" whose unity would be reflected in the pages of the magazine. I doubt if they achieved their purpose, but they were enjoyable and intellectually stimulating' (*T. S. Eliot: The Man and His Work*, ed. Allen Tate [1971], 24).

4–J. M. Robertson published 'The Evolution of English Blank Verse' in *C.* 2: 6 (Feb. 1924) and was to publish 'The Naturalistic Theory of *Hamlet*' in 3: 10 (Jan. 1925). CW contributed 'Bolingbroke', 1: 3 & 4 (Apr. & July 1923), and 'Lord Chesterfield', 2: 7 (Apr. 1924).

5–In addition to 'Mr Zagreus and the Split-Man' and 'The Apes of God' in 2: 6 & 7 (Feb. & Apr. 1924), WL contributed an 'Art Chronicle' to 2: 8 (July 1924).

6–EP had contributed 'On Criticism in General', 1: 2 (Feb. 1923), 'Malatesta Cantos', 1: 4 (July 1923), and 'George Antheil', 2: 7 (Apr. 1924).

function:[1] they amuse; and if they do not altogether illustrate, yet they do not contradict the larger function of the review. That doesn't leave, perhaps, so very many disconnected stragglers. Bain, Ford, (Murry was involved in the argument), May Sinclair, J. B. Trend, W. B. Yeats (?)[2] – and another whose contribution struck me as romantic irony in the worst Stracheyan manner: a little mind dancing round a big one.[3]

Don't take these opinions too seriously. I've only been driven to expressing them because you flatter me that I shall help you in doing so. And finally, there is no question of my faith being disturbed.

Yours ever,
Herbert Read

TO *Herbert Read* MS Victoria

18 October 1924 *The Criterion*, 17 Thavies Inn

Dear Read,

Thank you for your letter. I concur with nearly everything you say. It is quite true, that having to experiment with what the public would take, I have spent most of these two years in casting about. When I wrote to you I was indicating my belief that we were at last settling down to some kind of order.

It was a part of my original programme that if the *Criterion* was ever to become effective, it must make itself *independent* – and aim at just a large enough circulation to support itself (This of course is not yet the case). A certain amount of window dressing was necessary, and also the complicity of certain people was to be gained by publishing their contributions (I do not mean Walpole, whom I included on other grounds).

Also I have had Lady Rothermere nagging at me for '*dullness*' ever since the first issue[4] (not that I take any notice of that beyond what is politic). And there has been a small amount of unsuccessful experiment as well.

1 – VW, 'In the Orchard', 1: 3 (Apr. 1923), 'Character in Fiction', 2: 8 (July 1924); E. M. Forster, 'Pan', 1: 4 (July 1923); Osbert Sitwell, 'A German Eighteenth-Century Town', 2: 8 (July 1924).

2 – The second volume included F. W. Bain, 'Disraeli', 2: 6 (Feb. 1924); F. M. Ford, 'From the Grey Stone', 2: 5 (Oct. 1923): JMM, 'Romanticism and the Tradition', 2: 7 (Apr. 1924); May Sinclair, 'The Grandmother', 2: 6 (Feb. 1924); J. B. Trend, 'The Moors in Spanish Music', 2: 6 (Feb. 1924); and WBY, 'The Cat and the Moon', 2: 8 (July 1924).

3 – Unidentified.

4 – C. 1: 1 (Oct. 1922) opened with 'Dullness' by George Saintsbury.

I shd like your opinion of the new number next week, and especially of the work of several young writers, which I have included as being independent and promising.

I shall always be grateful to you for criticism, as I depend upon you for support and collaboration. We might continue this discussion perhaps after you have seen the next number.

Yours ever
T. S. Eliot

TO *Herbert Read*[1] TS Victoria

[18 October 1924] [London]

Dear Read,

I answered your letter immediately on receipt, this afternoon, because it was a letter which deserved immediate acknowledgement, and because I find that if a letter is not answered at once, it risks not being answered at all. But there was much more that might be said, and now, although I have sat down to another task, I am impelled to write again and impart some of what is in my mind.

I don't want to bore you with a lengthy Apologia; in any case the time has not yet come for that: I merely want to put a little more clearly what I have just said to you.

The ideal which you propose in your letter is very near to that which I proposed to myself when I undertook the review, and which I have kept in mind ever since. The ideal which was present to the mind of Lady Rothermere at the beginning was that of a more chic and brilliant *Art & Letters*, which might have a fashionable vogue among a wealthy few. I had and have no resentment against her for this, as I have no criticism to make of her conduct throughout: she has given me a pretty free hand, has been quite as appreciative as one could expect a person of her antecedents and connexions to be, and the game between us has been a fair one. I have I think given her as much as possible of what she wants, and she has given me the possibility of an organ. It is true that I have laid myself open to the censure both of persons who assumed that I was making money out of the work, and of those who knew that I was taking nothing for it – and who consequently believe that I am running the paper for other discreditable

1–HR quotes much of this letter in his 'T.S.E. – A Personal Memoir', where he calls it 'an apologia' and observes that 'it shows how early Eliot had formulated certain principles of personal conduct which he was to maintain for the next forty years' (*T. S. Eliot*, ed. Tate, 25).

reasons – which latter group of persons, by the way, includes my relatives in America. One does not like to explain oneself only to arouse the accusation of hypocrisy, to be associated with the other causes of impeachment, and one learns to keep silence.[1] I have another reason for keeping silence, and that is that I find that I sometimes give people an impression of arrogance and intolerant self-conceit. If I say generally that I wish to form a 'phalanx', a hundred voices will forthwith declare that I wish to be a leader, and that my vanity will not allow me to serve, or even to exist on terms of equality with others.[2] If one maintains a cause, one is either a fanatic or a hypocrite: and if one has any definite dogmas, then one is imposing those dogmas upon those who cooperate with one.

I wish, certainly, to get as homogenous a group as possible: but I find that homogeneity is in the end indefinable: for the purposes of the *Criterion*, it cannot be reduced to a creed of numbered capitals. I do *not* expect everyone to subscribe to all the articles of my own faith, or to read Arnold, Newman, Bradley, or Maurras with my eyes.[3] It seems to me that at the present time we need more dogma, and that one ought to have as precise and clear a creed as possible, when one thinks at all: but a creed is always in one sense smaller than the man, and in another sense larger; one's formulations never fully explain one, although it is necessary to formulate: I do not, for myself, bother about the apparent inconsistency – which has been made the most of – between my prose and my verse. Why then should I bother about particular differences of formulation between myself and those whom I should like to find working with me?

This is to make a little clearer my notion of a phalanx. When I *write*, I must write to the limit of my own convictions and aspirations: but I don't want to impose these on others, any more than I should be willing to reduce myself to the common denominator of my colleagues. What is essential is to find those persons who have an impersonal loyalty to some faith not antagonistic to my own.

1 – The Eliot family motto was '*Tacuit et facuit*' ('Be silent and act').
2 – For this 'phalanx', see HR's letter of 18 Oct.
3 – TSE's investment in Arnold was clear as early as the Introduction to *SW*, was implicit in 'The Function of Criticism' (*C.* 2: 5, Oct. 1923), and became explicit in 'Arnold and Pater' (1930) and 'Matthew Arnold' (*TUPUC*, 1933). In the last, TSE refers to Arnold as 'the poet and critic of a period of false stability', whose writing is 'a valiant attempt to dodge the issue, to mediate between Newman and Huxley' (106). He included Fernandez's 'The Experience of Newman' in *C.* 3: 9 (Oct. 1924), and paid tribute to F. H. Bradley in his 'Commentary' in the same issue, as well as in 'Three British Prose Writers' and *KEPB* (1964). In the first years of *C.* TSE had hoped for an article on Maurras by CW, but Maurras did not figure until his 'Prologue to an Essay on Criticism' (trans. by TSE) appeared in *NC* 7: 1 (Jan. 1928). In 1925 TSE thought of writing a book on him.

Now as to persons. I agree about those you mention, except Bain, whom I do not consider 'disconnected'. But I should like to discuss this when you have seen more of his work. In the absence of exactly the right person for the musical equivalent of what we want in literature, Trend represents, I think, a decent compromise. Three persons you rate higher than I do. Certain others represent the payment of an honest debt: Murry of course there is no need to discuss. The 'contribution' you allude to – if my guess is right[1] – represents an experiment in absorption – the question was whether that person would give the proper response to the new environment – the risk – I hope you will agree – was worth taking, even if the result be disappointing.

I think you must agree that in my commentary I have spoken more and more clearly in opposition to the factions which in the beginning – and still to some extent – I have attempted to placate.

For Whibley I have a warm personal friendship: we have much in common, though no doubt there are many countries in which we speak a different language. For Robertson I have a very great respect: he is I believe wholly honest; I do not mind if he be called dull. Manning[2] represents something valuable. So does, in a minor way, Stephen Gaselee.[3] Whibley and Robertson support us, and as they represent to the public such *antithetical* abstractions, to each other they are both valuable. They have both shewn more sympathy and kindness than anyone but myself is aware of. To both of them, and especially Whibley, I am constantly in debt. Harold Joachim too, though to the public he will mean only dullness, represents something to me.[4]

I shall welcome any suggestions of 'untapped talent' (to which you refer). I have thought of one Orlo Williams and an Edward Muir.[5] My anxiety about the latter is the fear that his mind has been fed too exclusively on contemporary and on German literature: that his culture, in other words, is too shallow. I should be glad of your opinion of these people, if you have one.

You flatter me by the word 'nucleus'. My conception of 'leader' or 'organiser' is simply of a necessary organ in a body, which has no

1 – The unidentified contribution which struck HR as 'romantic irony in the worst Stracheyan manner'.

2 – Frederic Manning's 'Le Père Hyacinthe' appeared in *C.* 2: 8 (July 1924), and he became a regular contributor.

3 – Stephen Gaselee, 'The Soul in the Kiss', *C.* 2: 7 (Apr. 1924): his only contribution.

4 – Writing to RC-S on 21 Oct., TSE mentions Harold Joachim's 'The Absolute etc.' as a possible item in the Jan. 1925 issue, but his Oxford tutor never published in *C.*

5 – TSE's attention had been drawn to Edwin Muir by SS (see his letter of 13 July).

superiority at all, but simply exercises a particular function, and makes it possible for the others to do their best work.

I hasten to write all this now, because I should like you to have it in mind when you see the October number next week, and let me have your criticisms in the light of it. And lastly, your assurances give me great encouragement in what may easily become a heart-breaking struggle. You help me to believe it possible that a 'trial of Faith' may 'overcome the world'.[1]

Yours ever,
T. S. Eliot

Vivien Eliot TO *Mary Hutchinson* MS Texas

19 October [1924]

38 Burleigh Mansions,
St Martin's Lane

Dear Mary

I would have telephoned you if I could, but I have a telephone complex which has been very active for the last few days. I have been struggling with it, for I have really wanted to speak to you.

Will you come and have tea with me at this address next Thursday? Do come. (about 4.)

With love

V. E.

TO *Sydney Schiff* TS Valerie Eliot

21 October 1924

9 Clarence Gate Gdns

My dear Sydney,

I hope that you will get your *Criterion* tomorrow – or rather, I am sorry to think, Thursday, as I suppose it will have gone to Cambridge Square. Had I remembered, in the rush, I should have told them to send it direct to Lye Green. I think it is a good number: it does not appear so brilliant, as a mere list of eminent names, as some of the others, but I should like you to regard it from the point of view of a unity of purpose, and see whether

1 – 'For whatsoever is born of God overcometh the world: and this is the victory that overcometh the world, even our faith' (1 John 5: 4).

you do not agree that there is a greater harmony – and even a common will – amongst the contributors – than ever before.

It is a weakness in the machinery, and I fear patent testimony of amateur production, that it is a week late. I hope to avoid this particular fault in future.

I wish that it had been out when I came to see you the other evening: I was feeling singularly vigorous and calm and energetic that night, and it would have been a good opportunity for discussion.

Vivienne has been belittling the contribution of Feiron Morris[1] and saying that it is trifling and insignificant; and I fear that she has said so to you.[2] This is quite the contrary of my own judgement, and she will have done you and it a great injustice if she has conveyed that impression in advance. You will observe in this and in subsequent numbers, that I want to give an important place to younger writers, to writers who can really speak for a generation which is maturing but as yet almost inarticulate, and who, however little their practise may be, will not merely ape the elder age. The majority of writers of any period seem to me – and often the most skilful, to be simply concealing themselves beneath a dead and past maturity of others, rather than expressing an immaturity which is at least interesting because genuine. This thing of Vivienne's may appear very slight, but it is an integral part of the whole book, and just as important in its place. It does I am convinced express a point of view which is original – and which is more than original – which is typical: typical of a very modern mentality which has not yet been expressed in literature, and of which Vivienne is the most conscious representative. I am fearful of saying much, for fear of misleading you in my turn: but I do want to say that this 'sketch' goes very much deeper than its deceptive surface indicates.

I am looking forward to another talk with you.

With love to both
yours ever
Tom

1–Feiron Morris, 'Thé Dansant', C. 3: 9 (Oct. 1924), 72–8.

2–VHE had written this (undated) note to SS: 'Fanny is the money maker – she spins on for ever like a spider. There is no *end* to Fanny! But Feiron will never make money. And he does not spin. He is a nasty fellow' (BL: Add MSS 52918). Deprecating her writing as 'this temporary aberration of mine', VHE confided to Schiff too that she feared her writing was merely 'a sort of flash in the pan – that won't *go on*'.

TO *Richard Cobden-Sanderson* CC

21 October 1924 9 Clarence Gate Gdns

Dear Cobden-Sanderson

Thank you for the copies.[1] I return herewith the proof of the circular, in which I have made, I am sorry to say, several improvements in the writing. I think it is very cleverly put together.

Conrad Aiken did not receive his copy of the last number, so will you see that he gets this one? I should like a copy of this one and of the last one to go to Ernst Curtius (whose address you have) but that can wait until the rest of the posting is off your hands.

Now about the next number! I think that you hold the following:[2]

PROOF:	Clive Bell
	F. G. Selby
MSS:	Robertson: Hamlet
	Elgström: Story
	Sturge Moore: Poem
	Aldington: Villon
	Read: Psychoanalysis etc.
	Joachim: The Absolute etc.
	Keith: Sanskrit Literature
	Croce: Allegory
	Tolstoi: Letters
	Johnson: Letters

Will you please confirm?

Selby and Bell are to go in to the January number. So are Robertson, Read and Tolstoi, which could go to Hazell's immediately, and I shall be sending you the other articles quickly. And Sturge Moore is to be set up. I want to get the next number under way at once, and will send my commentary early, so that they can start on the page proof as soon as the

1 – Copies of C. 3: 9 (Oct. 1924).

2 – TSE lists the following contributions, all of which appeared in C. 3: 10 (Jan. 1925), unless otherwise stated: Clive Bell, 'Prologomena to a Study of Nineteenth-Century Painting'; F. G. Selby, 'Bacon and Montaigne'; J. M. Robertson, 'The Naturalistic Theory of *Hamlet*'; Anna Lenah Elgström, 'Two on a Cross' (5: 2; May 1927); T. Sturge Moore, 'The Vigil of Julian's Friend by his Dead Body' (3: 11, Apr. 1925); RA, 'François Villon' (3: 11, Apr. 1925); HR, 'Psycho-Analysis and the Critic'; Harold Joachim, 'The Absolute', never appeared nor did anything by A. B. Keith (though TSE mentioned having a contribution from him, possibly on Sanskrit Drama, in a letter to RA of 20 Sept. 1923); Benedetto Croce, 'On the Nature of Allegory' (3: 11, Apr. 1925); L. N. Tolstoi and N. N. Strakhov, 'Extracts from Letters Relating to F. M. Dostoevsky'; 'Some Letters of Lionel Johnson' (3: 11, Apr. 1925).

galley proof of the articles is corrected. The chronicles and reviews I shall get in by the latter part of November, so that the number can be out by Christmas. The sooner the better, as the election will hit the October number, but the following ought to benefit by the revival immediately afterwards.[1]

Finally, will you please make out a cheque to J. R. Culpin (I have let this get frightfully in arrears) from the last day of payment to the end of this week @ 25/- per week, and send it to him here? By the way, he hopes that you do not include this in income tax returns. I shall be grateful if you can do this at once, as I am ashamed not to have attended to it.

Yours
[T. S. E.]

And last of all, will you ask Hazell's to give me an itemised statement of the number of words in each contribution, counting the reviews and the foreign review notes separately? Curtis Brown will expect to be paid quickly for the Lawrence story.[2]

FROM *Irene Fassett* — TS Valerie Eliot

22 October 1924 — [32 Pembroke Rd, Kensington, W.8]

Dear T. S. E.,

I have been thinking over your letter all the morning. I must say first that I think you are making me a very generous offer and I consider myself very lucky to have such a chance. I would rather do work connected with the *Criterion* than anything else.

I am sorry that I can't meet you at six tonight, but I have an appointment for that time which I must keep.

There are two or three points which I must put to you before agreeing definitely to your proposals – one of which worries me very much:

1. I arranged, some days ago, to give music lessons to the de la Voye children twice weekly from six to seven – I did this because I want to earn as much money as I possibly can without hurting my writing work in any way. Of course I am sorry now that I did this, but I *have* made the arrangement and am starting on the work tonight. I feel that I could persuade Mrs de la Voye to change one of the evenings to Saturday morning, though I know this would not really suit her, but until the end of

1–The General Election (29 Oct.) was won by the Conservative Party under Stanley Baldwin.
2–DHL, 'Jimmy and the Desperate Woman', C. 3: 9 (Oct. 1924).

this term I should really *have* to give her that hour on Monday or Tuesday evenings. If you could possibly let me leave at 5.30 on one night a week, I would of course make up the hour and a half at another time or forego part of my fifteen shillings. I am furious that I have to put this to you, but so far I can think of no other way out of the difficulty.

2. I have promised my mother to ask for next *Wednesday* afternoon off (this was when I was doing odd jobs for Saigie). For various reasons this was unavoidable.

3. I do hope that the above statements won't give you the idea that I should be constantly doing things like this. Once I had made a definite arrangement with you I should stick to it through thick and thin to the very best of my ability – and I should always be prepared to deal with any *particular* rush of work that might necessitate my staying late or working after dinner – I mean that I should not do the work with an eye on the clock, I would do my best to make your new arrangement as successful as possible.

If you would care to telephone to me tonight, I would answer the telephone at *9 o'clock*.

In haste,
I. P. F.

TO *Arnold Bennett* — TS Beinecke

23 October 1924 — 9 Clarence Gate Gdns

Dear Mr Bennett,

I am writing to tell you that I am reconstructing my play according to all of your suggestions.[1] I was tremendously encouraged by seeing you, and finding that you thought the thing worth going on with. There is no one else in London whose opinion on such an attempt would mean so much to me, and had you so advised me, I should have abandoned the project at once.

I cannot tell you how grateful I am, and how fully I realise the privilege of having the counsel and guidance of a man like yourself, and how highly I appreciate your generosity in giving your time and attention to teaching me. In any case, I shall feel that the play will be as much yours as mine; but if I cannot make a good thing of it with the advantage of help which anyone would envy me, it will be final evidence of my dramatic incapacity.

1 – See TSE's letter of 8 Oct., on the drafts of *SA* he had discussed with Bennett. 'Fragment of a Prologue' was first published in *NC* 4: 4 (Oct. 1926).

Now, I shall to my vexation have to postpone further work for several weeks. On the 8th I must go to Cambridge to read a paper which I have not yet prepared;[1] and on the 15th I have to go to Paris for the weekend to see Lady Rothermere. I shall begin work again immediately after that, and shall have something to show you by the 1st December. I shall write before that to ask when you can see me. If you are out of London I shall be utterly lost, as I depend wholly upon your advice.

Yours very sincerely,
T. S. Eliot

TO *J. M. Robertson* CC

28 October 1924

23 Alephi Terrace House,
Robert St, London W.C.

Dear Mr Robertson,

Thank you very much for your letter of the 5th. I asked Cobden-Sanderson to send you back the Arnold paper,[2] and I hope you received it safely. And I am counting on having the Turgenev essay when it is ready.

I have been trying to find out the names of the *Hamlet* books which I saw mentioned.[3] Unfortunately I did not make a note of them at the time and I have only been able to discover the George Macdonald book[4] which I do not suppose is worth reviewing by itself. If I can trace the other I shall get it for you, and if I see anything else that I think might interest you I shall write to you about it; because it would be an excellent thing for the *Criterion* to have a review from you.

Yours very sincerely,
[T. S. E.]

1–'Chapman, Dostoevski and Dante': TSE's paper to the Cam Literary Club, 8 Nov.
2–On 20 June, Robertson offered TSE a paper on Matthew Arnold in place of a piece on Turgenev. He hoped it would appear in C. in Oct., but then on 28 July suggested an alternative paper on 'The Naturalistic Theory of *Hamlet*'. Evidently, TSE replied on 8 Aug. (in a missing letter), accepting the new paper. Writing on 12 Aug., Robertson was glad TSE was 'inclined to "restore"' Arnold, and supposed he was 'right about *Culture and Anarchy*' though he himself had earlier attacked it. Replying to another missing letter on 5 Oct., Robertson said the 'whole of the Arnold paper' was now being sent to publishers and he would like it back.
3–On 5 Oct., Robertson said he would like to review the '*Hamlet* books' TSE mentioned.
4–George MacDonald, *The Tragedie of Hamlet . . . A Study, with the text of the Folio of 1623* (1924). Robertson's 'The Naturalistic Theory of *Hamlet*' came out in C. 3: 10 (Jan. 1925), but did not mention more recent studies.

TO La Revue de France — CC

28 October 1924 — 23 Adelphi Terrace House

Dear Sirs,

You have been sending *La Revue de France* regularly to *The Egoist* at this address. I have to inform you that *The Egoist* has been taken over by *The Criterion* and I shall be obliged if you will in future send *La Revue de France* to the publisher's office of *The Criterion*, 17 Thavies Inn, Holborn, London E.C.1. If you will do so, a copy of *The Criterion* will be sent to you regularly.

The principal contributions of your review will be noticed in *The Criterion*. I wish to point out that *The Criterion* is the only English literary review which pays serious attention to foreign periodicals and that a section in each number is devoted to notice and criticism of the principal reviews in foreign countries.

I am, dear Sirs,

Yours faithfully
[T. S. E.]

TO *Rollo Myers*[1] — CC

28 October 1924 — [*The Criterion*, London]

Dear Mr Myers,

Thank you for your letter of the 16th. I forwarded your cheque to Mr Cobden-Sanderson.[2]

The idea of a translation of *Le Secret Professionel* interests me as I like the book.[3] I wonder if you would mind trying to get hold of a copy for me as I have lent or lost the one which I had. When you see Cocteau next, you might suggest to him that he should mention the question to Lady Rothermere. I will mention it to her myself when I next write to her.

I am sorry to say that I did not see your book which I am sure would interest me.[4]

Yours very truly,
[T. S. E.]

1–Rollo Myers (1892–1985): music critic, with a special interest in French music.
2–Myers subscribed to C. on 16 Oct.
3–Myers had translated Cocteau's *Cock and Harlequin* for the Egoist Press, and proposed to translate *Le secret professionel* (1922). Myers's translation eventually appeared in Jean Cocteau, *Call to Order . . . written between the years 1918 and 1926 and including 'Cock and Harlequin', 'Professional Secrets' and other critical essays* (Faber & Gwyer, 1926).
4–Myers asked if TSE knew his *Modern Music: Its Aims and Tendencies* (1923).

TO *Wyndham Lewis* CC

28 October 1924 23 Adelphi Terrace House

My dear Lewis,

I hope you can let me have the complete manuscript by the end of next week at the latest.[1] The January number is to come out on the 1st of January and as the printers do no work for about a week at Christmas time, we have to be very early with it.

Is the enclosed cutting of any use to you for your chronicle?[2]

Would you be willing to do a review of a couple of Elliot Smith's new books for the same number? This ought not to give you very much trouble and I should be delighted if you would do it. I could send you a book of Rivers'[3] at the same time. Do let me know the moment you are ready to see me as I am very anxious to hear about your affairs.

Yours ever,
[T. S. E.]

TO *F. S. Flint* CC

28 October 1924 23 Adelphi Terrace House

Dear Flint,

I am sending you some more periodicals and hope to get the *Revue de France* regularly for you. I was disappointed that you did not turn up on Wednesday; only Monro and Read came. What was the matter with you?

Can you let me have your foreign periodicals notes for the January number by November 25th?[4] I want to have the number out punctually by the 1st of January.

Also would you be willing to translate a French manuscript relating to the adventures of a Russian dancer attempting to escape from Russia?[5] I should like to send you this at once. I hope you will.

1 – The substantial MS promised for *C.* 3: 10 (Jan. 1925).
2 – WL's 'Art Chronicle', in *C.* 3: 9 (Oct. 1924) proved to be his last.
3 – G. Elliot Smith, *Essays on the Evolution of Man*, G. Elliot Smith and Warren R. Dawson, *Egyptian Mummies* and W. H. R. Rivers, *Medicine, Magic and Religion* were reviewed by WL in *C.* 3: 10 (Jan. 1925).
4 – Flint contributed a short section on 'Danish Periodicals'; a longer one on 'French Periodicals'. In the latter, he welcomed *Philosophies* as 'the most interesting of the French reviews received', and *Commerce* as a new 'quarterly de luxe' run by Paul Valéry, Léon-Paul Fargue and Valery Larbaud.
5 – Unidentified.

Let me know how you are and whether you are going to fail us next time.

Yours ever,
[T. S. E.]

TO *Edith Sitwell*[1] CC

28 October 1924 23 Adelphi Terrace House

Dear Edith,

I have just seen Osbert who tells me that you have returned to London, so I am writing to you about your poems.

You sent me some time ago two poems.[2] One of them, 'Colonel Fantock', I saw lately in *The Spectator*:[3] that is very much our loss as I liked it extremely and wanted to publish it. If the other one, 'The Man with the Green Patch', has not yet been published anywhere I want to use it in the January number, but if it has already appeared, or if you now have anything else that you would rather publish first, please let me know.[4] In any case I am anxious to have something of yours in the January number and I should like to use this poem, but if not this, another. I should like to have it set up immediately so I hope you will answer as soon as you can.

I do hope that you are better now. This has been a miserable summer for all of us.

Always yours,
[T. S. E.]

TO *Conrad Aiken* MS Huntington

[? 28 October 1924] *The Criterion*, 17 Thavies Inn

Dear Conrad,

By all means: Thursday with great pleasure.

Criterion should reach you tomorrow but will bring one on Thursday in case. It is an Aiken number, which will add lustre to the name. Incidentally,

1 – Edith Sitwell: see Glossary of Names.
2 – Sitwell had sent the poems on 31 Mar.
3 – 'Colonel Fantock', *The Spectator*, 31 May 1924, 880.
4 – 'The Man with the Green Patch', *C.* 3: 10 (Jan. 1925). The ghost in the poem was based on 'our ghost at home in Derbyshire', said Sitwell.

your note on O. Sitwell is one of the most brilliant pieces of destructive criticism I have ever read.[1] It couldn't be better.

Yours ever
T. S. E.

TO *John Crowe Ransom*[2] CC

29 October 1924 23 Adelphi Terrace House

Dear Mr Ransom,

I was very pleased to receive your book with an inscription from yourself.[3] I have probably a higher opinion of your verse than you have of mine.[4] My attention was first called to something of yours by Robert Graves a year or so ago: he showed me a poem which I liked very much, and subsequently a quantity of manuscript which I had pleasure in giving to the Hogarth Press with a recommendation that they should publish it. You will understand, therefore, that I am very glad to have this book and hope that it will receive the praise that it deserves.[5]

Yours faithfully
[T. S. E.]

1–*C.* 3: 9 (Oct. 1924) included Aiken's poem, 'Psychomachia', and his reviews of Osbert Sitwell, *Triple Fugue*, and Gilbert Seldes, *The Seven Lively Arts*. In his review of Sitwell's stories, Aiken borrowed Henry James's criticism of Swinburne as 'a writer in quest of a theme'. He called the title story 'a disastrous failure' and considered the volume 'typical' of not only 'the Sitwells' but 'the momentary appetite for hard, bright colours and irony, for disillusionment that tries to laugh and satire which tries to injure'.

2–John Crowe Ransom, US poet and critic, see note to TSE's letter to Robert Graves, 16 July 1923.

3–*Grace After Meat*, with Intro. by Robert Graves (Hogarth Press, 1924).

4–Ransom published a critique of *TWL* as 'the apotheosis of modernity'. While praising the 'Sweeney' verses and 'Prufrock' as coming out of a 'fairly mature and at any rate an equal art', he dismissed *TWL* as 'one of the most insubordinate poems in the language and perhaps . . . the most unequal' ('Waste Lands', *New York Evening Post Literary Review* 3 [14 July 1923], 825–6).

5–It was not reviewed in *C.* However, Ransom's later *Two Gentleman in Bonds* (1927) was reviewed in *C.*; so too his critical studies, *God Without Thunder: An Unorthodox Defence of Orthodoxy* (1931) and *The World's Body* (1938).

TO *Zoe Hawley*[1] CC

30 October 1924 [*The Criterion*, London]

Dear Miss Hawley,

If you have in mind any subject similar to that of the short essay by you which appears in the October *Criterion*,[2] it would give me great pleasure to know of it; or else if you would send me 1000 words on some subject you think suitable, by *the 21st November*.[3]

I think that your little dramatic article reads very well, and I was sorry that it was absolutely necessary to cut it down as much.

Hoping to hear from you,

I am,

Yours very truly,
[T. S. E.]

TO *Conrad Aiken* PC Huntington

[Postmark 1 November 1924] 9 Clarence Gate Gdns

Let me know if you haven't got your *Criterion*. Exiguous payment follows next week. By the way, the F. M. who wrote the letters you liked is the author of 'Thé Dansant' – not the other.[4] I think it has a distinct quality, though apparently very slight. What do you think of Lawrence on Murry?[5]

[unsigned]

1 – Zoe Hawley was a writer and theatre critic.

2 – Hawley, 'Celui qui reçoit les gifles' came out under the heading of 'The Foreign Theatre' in C. 3: 9 (Oct. 1924): a review of a play by L. Andréieff at the Théâtre du Vieux Colombier, Paris.

3 – Her review of the play 'Fata Morgana' appeared as 'The Theatre', C. 3: 10 (Jan. 1925).

4 – In C. 3: 9 (Oct. 1924), 'Thé Dansant' by 'Feiron Morris' was by VHE, but 'Mrs Pilkington' by 'Felix Morrison' was by IPF. The two book reviews signed 'F. M.' in 2: 8 (July 1924) were by Frederic Manning.

5 – Jimmy, the hero of DHL's 'Jimmy and the Desperate Woman' (C. 3: 9 [Oct. 1924], 15–43), is 'editor of a high-class, rather high-brow, rather successful magazine' called *The Commentator* and 'in his own opinion' a 'Martyred Saint Sebastian with the mind of a Plato'. The story is based on an anecdote told by JMM about a London editor's visit to a miner's cottage to see his wife (David Ellis, *D. H. Lawrence: Dying Game 1922–30*, 165). It was evidently a satirical portrait of JMM.

TO *Viola Tree*[1] CC

4 November 1924 23 Adelphi Terrace House

Dear Madam,

In reply to your letter in which you ask for details of the kind of contribution I want from you, and also whether you should write under you own name Viola Tree or under a pseudonym.[2]

I should like you to give me a commentary on the affairs of the world you live in – a review of the events adducing between each issue of the *Criterion* which strike you as being in any way significant. I should like you to do this *from your own personal point of view*. This is the reason why I have asked you to write for me – for *your point of view* rather than for the information or material – because of the *personality* in what you write. The essential thing for me is that you should be Viola Tree. If you keep *that* in your mind then anything that you write will be interesting, and everything you mention will have its interest in your article.

I particularly liked a very short sketch in the *Evening Standard* about a week ago – I cannot remember the date – in which you described a 'dress show' or mannequin parade.[3] In this your own personality was very marked and that is what gave it its value. Chiefly I want notes about social functions, dress, or modern manners, and theatrical performances both public and private.

As to theatrical gossip, you have only yourself to consider. For myself you can be as extreme as you like, short of libel; but if you want to say anything about any play which you would not want to say under the name of Viola Tree, then I suggest that you should write a rather shorter contribution as Viola Tree, and a separate note under a pseudonym.[4]

1–Viola Tree (1884–1938): actress, singer and author; daughter of the actor-manager Sir Herbert Beerbohm Tree (1853–1917).

2–In an undated letter, Tree said that she was honoured to be part of TSE's wonderful 'Cast', but asked for a 'line' on what she should do: she could be much fairer, particularly in dramatic criticism, if not writing under her own name.

3–Viola Tree, 'The Frocks of To-day', *Evening Standard*, 20 Oct. 1924, 11.

4–As Viola Tree, she published 'Mayfair and Bohemia'; as Violet Ray, 'The Stage', in C. 3: 10 (Jan. 1925). In her reply, she said she chose the pseud. 'Violet Ray' because it was how her name sounded when said by Cockneys. In Jan., as 'Ray', she discussed the theatre at the time when her father and George Alexander died – 'the last of the older generation, and Granville Barker did as good as die' – and when 'people were left with Gerald du Maurier in charge of modern drama' (305). She wrote too a note, under her own name, on the Phoenix Society production of Jonson's *Epicoene*, a work that also featured in 'Mayfair and Bohemia'.

I hope I have made myself quite clear: if there is anything you want to know at any time do not hesitate to ask me; and please do not forget that we go to press on the 25th November.

Yours faithfully,
[T. S. E.]

I trust that you received my second letter (supplementary to that written by my secretary) addressed to 1 Percy Street.

TO *Mary Hutchinson* MS Texas

[Postmark 5 November 1924] 9 Clarence Gate Gdns

My dear Mary

Thank you very much for your letter, for the letter to Lucas, and for the cigarettes. I shall try to see Lucas, certainly.[1] His review interested me, it is on the right side, though I think he could have demolished Fausset more thoroughly with his own weapons – i.e. the 'philosophy' itself of Fausset is unsound and shallow.[2]

It *was* sweet of you to give me the cigarettes – the only kind I can smoke! And I hope you did enjoy the lunch, because I did.

Affectionately
Tom

TO *P. N. Rowe* CC

6 November 1924 23 Adelphi Terrace House

Dear Mr Rowe,

Thank you very much for your letter of the 26th ultimo, which gave me great pleasure. Such expressions of approval are a great support in what is indeed a heartbreaking labour.

1–F. L. Lucas (1894–1967): English literary critic, based in Cambridge.
2–Lucas's rev. of Hugh L'Anson Fausset, *John Donne: A Study in Discord* (1924), appeared as 'John Donne' in *NS* 24: 602 (1 Nov. 1924), 112–13. Lucas deplored Fausset's 'glib dogmatism' about 'creative purpose' and 'the life-force': 'Mr Fausset should decide whether he wants to write philosophy or biography, to follow M. Bergson or Mr Lytton Strachey. He cannot do both.' The book was adversely reviewed too by HR, who deplored its mixture of 'biographical' and 'mystical' interpretations of Donne (*C.* 3: 10, Jan. 1925).

I can reassure you about Wyndham Lewis. He is not only producing, but has just completed a large book which will be a work of the greatest importance, and is also engaged on several other creative works.[1]

I think I can say that there is a strong likelihood of the *Criterion* appearing more frequently. It is possible that next year it may be issued at intervals of two months instead of three.

Yours very truly,
[T. S. E.]

TO *Mona Wilson*[2] CC

6 November 1924 23 Adelphi Terrace House

Dear Miss Wilson,

Thank you for your letter of the 2nd instant. I should be very pleased to reconsider your manuscript,[3] but I must warn you that I am afraid it will be quite impossible for us to accept any more manuscripts for publication before July next. I only regret that the *Criterion* is not a monthly, and hope that some day it may be. But with our present small dimensions and small resources I find myself more and more embarrassed by having to refuse or to postpone contributions which seem to me really valuable. I should prefer it if you would wait a few months before sending your manuscript, which, however, I shall be very happy to have the opportunity of re-reading.

Sincerely yours,
[T. S. E.]

1 – According to Timothy Materer, 'Between 1921 and 1926 Lewis lived in semi-retirement and near poverty to write a gigantic anatomy of post-World War I called *The Man of the World*' (*Pound/Lewis*, 142–3). *The Man of the World* was never published, though parts of it contributed to *The Art of Being Ruled* (1926) and *The Lion and the Fox* (1927).

2 – Mona Wilson (1872–1954): English civil servant (she worked from 1911 for the National Insurance Commission, and from 1917 for the Ministry of Reconstruction; resigning from the civil service in 1919) and scholar; author of *These were Muses* (1924), followed by a series of biographies and biographical studies (inc. lives of William Blake, Jane Austen and Queen Elizabeth I). On 22 Mar. 1923 she had submitted '3 articles on Sara Coleridge, Mrs Trollope & Lady Morgan', all of which were rejected on 4 Apr. 1923 – 'in consideration of the very limited size of the *Criterion*'. Still, it was added in the rejection letter that TSE 'earnestly' hoped she would 'continue to submit manuscripts'. On 26 Jan. 1925 she was to submit a piece on 'Cressida the Inconstant Woman'. Along with TSE, she later contributed to *From Anne to Victoria: Essays by Various Hands*, ed. Bonamy Dobrée (1937). She did not appear in *C*.

3 – Unidentified.

TO *Ramón Fernandez* CC

6 November 1924 [*The Criterion*]
23 Adelphi Terrace House

Dear Mr Fernandez,

Thank you for your letter of the 27th. I can assure you that your 'Newman' has not only pleased me but has attracted a great deal of notice and has cast great credit upon the *Criterion*. I hope that you will be a constant contributor.[1]

I shall be in Paris on Saturday week, the 15th, and shall be staying with Lady Rothermere at 33 quai Voltaire. If you are in Paris on that Saturday afternoon, I shall certainly hope to see you, and I shall write to Rivière.[2]

Yours very sincerely,
[T. S. E.]

TO *Richard Aldington* TS Texas

6 November 1924 23 Adelphi Terrace House

Dear Richard,

Thanks for your letter of the 25th. I hope that you will not find the books uninteresting.[3] If I get any American cuttings I will pass them on to you, but my own cuttings bureau in New York is very irregular and unsatisfactory.[4] I have not seen Priestley's book or bothered about it, because it seemed to be second rate from the notices I have seen.[5]

What is the work which Ezra sent you?[6] He puzzled me very much some weeks ago by sending me a lot of manuscript of a new poet which consisted simply of competent but quite uninteresting exercises in the style of

1–'The Experience of Newman', C. 3: 9 (Oct. 1924). Fernandez made a few later contributions.

2–On 24 Nov., TSE told RA he had met Fernandez in Paris, and 'liked him very much': he thought him 'one of the most promising young men in Paris'.

3–Orlo Williams, *Contemporary Criticism of Literature*, and Cyril Falls, *The Critic's Armoury*, which RA reviewed in C. 3: 11 (Apr. 1925).

4–About RA's *Literary Studies and Reviews* (1924). RA was pleased with Flint's review in C. 3: 10 (Oct. 1924), and said there had been an excellent one in the *New York Times*, 'comparing Priestley's style unfavourably with mine'.

5–J. B. Priestley, *Figures in Modern Literature* (1924).

6–EP, *Antheil and the Treatise on Harmony* (1924). On 25 Oct., RA called it 'an extraordinary and incomprehensible work': he wished EP would 'stick to writing poetry'.

Swinburne and Dowson.[1] What is the meaning of this reactionary movement?

I don't understand about *The Times*.[2] Who is at the bottom of this and with what motive?

I have been working hard on something new until quite recently but I have had to put it aside in order to deliver a lecture at Cambridge next Saturday.[3] It is still in very rough shape and I did not want to write it and I don't want to read it and I don't suppose that the Cambridge undergraduates will want to hear it.[4]

I am looking forward keenly to your new poem, about which I have heard most interesting rumours.[5]

When are you coming up to town?

Yours ever
Tom

TO *F. W. Bain* CC

6 November 1924 23 Adelphi Terrace House

My dear Bain,

Thank you for your letter of the 22nd. Your '1789' has brought the *Criterion* a great deal of notice, and, I think, has made a sensation.[6] It seems to me even more brilliant than your 'Disraeli'.[7] If you write anything

1–On 28 Sept., EP said he was sending carbons of poems by Ralph Cheever Dunning: 'Very much in the tone of the 90s. the mans period; Rubaiyat, Swinburne, Dowson, but great verse.' EP pressed TSE to read Dunning's poems and 'if accepted, publish *soon*'.

2–Edmund Gosse asked RA to sign the English Ronsard centenary address, and the Royal Society of Literature asked him to contribute towards a gift for the Poet Laureate (Robert Bridges). RA observed that on both occasions *The Times* reports omitted any mention of his name. While not distressed by this 'slight', he was interested in tracing the 'hidden hand'.

3–TSE's lecture was 'Chapman, Dostoevski and Dante'.

4–According to the issue of *Granta* published the day before, 'the most discussed of contemporary highbrows' was due to appear at the Cam Literary Society at the Tea Shop the following day. 'Mr Eliot is notorious for his poem "The Waste Land", which has occasioned nearly as many disputes as Prohibition . . . ! The Secretary says that he had hoped to obtain larger premises, but he has not yet been able to. Members or guests are therefore advised to appear fairly punctually, unless they want to sit on the floor' ('The Waste-Landers', *Granta*, 7 Nov. 1924, 70).

5–RA, *The Fool i' the Forest: A Phantasmagoria* (1925).

6–Bain's essay '1789' (*C.* 3: 9, Oct. 1924) is a critique of the historiography of the French Revolution. 'The Terror was the Revolution': '*all* the Revolutionary protagonists might figure in the pages of the Newgate Calendar', 43–71.

7–'Disraeli', *C.* 2: 6 (Feb. 1924).

about the Russian revolution, I hope that you will give me the opportunity of publishing it.[1] I could not use anything of any length before next July. I should like a full contribution from you then, but meanwhile, if you thinking of writing any short notes, do let me know.

Sincerely yours,
[T. S. E.]

TO *Joseph Kessel* CC

8 November 1924 23 Adelphi Terrace House

Cher Monsieur,

Merci bien de votre aimable lettre.[2] J'ai consigné votre manuscrit aux mains de Monsieur F. S. Flint qui en fera une belle traduction, j'en suis sûr. C'est une histoire des plus intéressantes; je regrette, seulement, que nous ne l'ayons pas reçu à temps pour notre numéro d'octobre qui vient de paraître.

Je suis bien content que nous nous entendons au sujet d'une chronique. Quant aux conditions et aux sujets que vous y traiterez, je crois que nous pouvons nous mettre d'accord quand nous nous rencontrerons le samedi soir le 15 novembre chez la Vicomtesse Rothermere.

En vous remerciant de votre appui, je vous prie, cher Monsieur, d'agréer l'expression de mes sentiments tres distingués.

pp T. S. Eliot[3]

1 – Bain wrote of 'the sinister quality of 1789, which nineteenth-century Liberalism has studiously disguised, just as the sentimental democratic idealism of to-day turns a blind eye on the Bolshevik atrocities in Russia' (51). On 22 Oct., Bain suggested doing 'a short line or two on 1917 (Russia) or some literary thing'.

2 – See letter to Lady Rothermere of 13 Oct. above.

3 – *Translation*: Dear Sir, Thank you very much for your cordial letter. I have sent your manuscript to Mr F. S. Flint, who I'm sure will make a fine translation. It is a really interesting story; and my only regret is that we didn't receive it in time for the October number, which is about to appear.

I'm very happy to know that you would like to write a chronicle. As to the conditions and subjects you might address, I believe we can agree on that when we meet up on Saturday evening, 15 November, at Lady Rothermere's.

In thanking you for your note, dear Sir, I send you my warmest regards. pp. T. S. Eliot

TO *Edwin Muir* CC

10 November 1924 [London]

Dear Mr Muir,

I must apologise for not having written to you sooner, but I have had a great deal to do for the last few weeks. I return your manuscript with great regret because I should very much like to secure your collaboration.[1] I had already asked Ernst Bertram to write on the subject of *Hölderlin*.[2] I do not know whether he will do it or not, but meanwhile you no doubt prefer to place this essay somewhere else. But I should be glad if you would suggest some other subject on which you would like to write. I should be very glad to hear from you. It will probably be very difficult for me to accept any original contributions for publication earlier than July, but meantime would you care to help us with an occasional review if I find anything that is likely to appeal to you?[3]

Sincerely yours,
[T. S. E.]

TO *Marianne Moore* TS Rosenbach

10 November 1924 23 Adelphi Terrace House

Dear Miss Moore,

Thank you for your letter of the 1st ultimo.[4] I discussed the subject yesterday with Miss Weaver. I could not think of letting you *purchase* any copies of your book from the *Criterion* for the very good reason that Miss Weaver did not receive any money for them from us. At first I was under the impression that you wished to withdraw your book from circulation in favour of a revised edition, but I now understand that this is not the case. If you actually want any number of copies, I shall be pleased to send them to you, but it will suit me very well to keep as many as possible here

1–On 19 Sept., SS had sent Muir's essay on Hölderlin to TSE.

2–See TSE's letter to Bertram of 6 Oct.

3–See Muir's review of Conrad Aiken, *Bring! Bring!*, *C.* 3: 12 (July 1925).

4–On 1 Oct., Moore reported that Harriet Shaw Weaver had told her that *C.* had bought the remaining copies of her *Poems* (Egoist Press, 1921), and deplored 'the precariousness of the purchase'. She was preparing 'an American issue of the book with additions' and would like to buy them back from TSE. The new book was *Observations* (New York: Dial Press, 1924).

in the belief that there will eventually be a sale for them. You will of course share in the profits of any copies that we sell.

Sincerely yours,
T. S. Eliot

TO *E. R. Curtius* TS Bonn

10 November 1924 23 Adelphi Terrace House

My dear Curtius,

Many thanks for your letter of the 1st instant. I am delighted to hear that there is a possibility of your visiting England next year and am sure that it will result in a most interesting volume of English studies.[1] I shall look forward to welcoming you here. Meanwhile I hope that you will send me a copy of your forthcoming book for review in the *Criterion*.

I should be very glad to see some of your work translated into English.

Thank you very much for your offer about German books which I sincerely reciprocate. I have very little time for reading, but if anything appears in Germany which you think I ought not to miss, I hope that you will let me know, and I will send you anything that seems to me of real importance.

Yours always sincerely,
T. S. Eliot

TO *Ernst Bertram* CC

11 November 1924 23 Adelphi Terrace House

My dear Sir,

I thank you for your letter of the 21st ultimo and am much pleased to hear that we hope for your collaboration in the *Criterion*. For the subject you mention, I should be very glad to have an essay in the form of a short review, say a thousand words, but for a longer article I think that a more comprehensive subject would be desirable. Also it would give readers a better conception of your own standpoint. For a longer article I should suggest either a general essay on the work of one man or on a more general critical subject. But I should very much like to have a shorter article from you as well. The *Criterion* has only lately started a section of reviews of

1 – See TSE's letter to Curtius of 6? Oct.

books and it occurred to me that it would be an interesting innovation – for I do not think I have seen it done in any periodical – occasionally to have reviews of the work of foreign writers by critics of first rank among their own nation.[1]

With many thanks, and hoping to hear from you soon,

I am,

Yours faithfully,
[T. S. E.]

TO *Mark Wardle* CC

11 November 1924 23 Adelphi Terrace House

My dear Wardle,

I am returning you some poems which I have kept for a very long time, but I find that we are absolutely choked with material for at least nine months, so I think that these ought to have the opportunity of finding publication elsewhere. I part with them as always with great regret.

I can now somewhat furtively look you in the face again because the Valéry book is well on the way to publication. I have only released my introduction after holding it up for a year because I despaired of doing anything better, but do not suppose that I am pleased with it or that I feel anything but extreme dissatisfaction with what I have written.[2]

I hear from Cobden-Sanderson the good news that you are coming to London for several years at least. I do hope that we may see something more of each other.

Yours sincerely,
[T. S. E.]

TO *Wyndham Lewis* TS Cornell

12 November 1924 *The Criterion*, 17 Thavies Inn

Dear Lewis,

After two frantic letters from Schiff requesting and entreating me to grant him an interview on an exceedingly important matter connected with yourself (I can produce said letters if necessary) I had an hour's talk with

1 – Nothing by Bertram was published in *C.*

2 – 'A Brief Introduction to the Method of Paul Valéry', for *Le Serpent par Paul Valéry* (1924).

him tonight.[1] This was absolutely against my will and caused me infinite annoyance: I have to go to Paris on Friday on what is to me a most tedious and distasteful affair, and tear back to London on Sunday night; since I returned from Cambridge on Monday, I have had no time to sleep or eat.

I write now in haste merely to inform you that Schiff produced a paper on which he had typed out – or so he told me, for I did not read it – each sum of money you have had from him and the date.[2] The object of the interview was to coerce me into mediating between himself and you, and, as far as I gathered, to force or persuade you to behave in a proper manner towards him.

I refused to do so or to have any hand in the matter. Upon this he lost his temper and some disagreeable words passed between us.

I will tell you more of this when we meet next. *The purport of this letter is to warn you that if Schiff takes now what I expect will be his next step and vilifies me to you, or attempts to make mischief between you and me,* you will understand the reasons.

I write you this in the conviction that you will do nothing in the matter and *will treat this letter in confidence*.[3]

Thank you very much for both MSS. which are splendid stuff.[4] More about this when I get back.

COULD you use a stall at the Phoenix on Sunday night (Ben Jonson's *Epicoene*) and would you DEFINITELY go?[5] My secretary will wait for an answer, as I must know at once. Please say YES or NO and if YES don't fail to go. I should join you about the middle of the performance; would you wait for me?

Yours ever
T. S. E.

1 – These letters do not appear to survive.
2 – During his financial crisis of 1924, WL had been heavily dependent upon SS, who, after giving him £60 between Apr. and Aug., gave him a further £20 on 29 Aug., and then the same again on 17 Sept. and 13 Oct. When WL asked for more, SS said: 'I cannot go on giving you money at this rate.' (See Paul O'Keeffe, *Some Sort of Genius: A Life of Wyndham Lewis* (2000), 255–7.)
3 – TSE marked this and the preceding paragraph with double marginal lines.
4 – On 26 Nov., RC-S received 'The Perfect Action': it was over 20,000 words long.
5 – Ben Jonson's *Epicoene* was performed by the Phoenix Society at the Regent's Theatre on 16 Nov.

TO *Virginia Woolf* MS Texas

12 November 1924 9 Clarence Gate Gdns

My dear Virginia

I was delighted to find the author's copies on my return this evening; and must thank you and Leonard for giving my essays those advantages of print and form which I feel they need, but hardly justify.[1] May the appearance of the book, and the prestige of the Hogarth Press, give a value to the production which is lacking to the matter! But, avoiding indirections, I think the cover is charming – it only needs the signature of the designer.[2] The book gives me great pleasure – if I do not read it. And I *hope* that I have not made any abominable errors in proofreading.

I have been submerged – lately, in preparing a paper for Cambridge – but which, after all my labours, is unworthy of subsequent publication. Fortunately, it was not for the same audience as 'Mr Bennett and Mrs Brown', so I did not have *that* standard to contend with.

We are going to Paris on Friday, but I shall come back on Monday morning. May I be allowed to emerge from oblivion and see you before very long.

Yours always
T. S. (if you wish)
Eliot

TO *Wyndham Lewis* TS Cornell

13 November 1924 9 Clarence Gate Gdns

Dear Lewis,

Thanks for your letter. I am glad to hear that you will go and I shall see you there.[3] This is just to let you know that I have had a note from Schiff tonight, simply to enclose a copy of your letter to him (identical with the copy you sent me) and also a copy of his reply to you of today's date.[4]

1–*Homage to John Dryden: Three Essays on Poetry of the Seventeenth Century* was published by the Hogarth Press on 30 Oct.: it was the fourth of the Hogarth Essays.

2–The cover had a black-and-white design of a woman reading by Vanessa Bell.

3–The Phoenix Society production of Jonson's *Epicoene*.

4–Writing to Lewis on 13 Nov., SS attempted to make peace and offered further financial support ('£12 every four weeks for six months') – O'Keeffe, *Some Sort of Genius*, 256–7.

We must arrange a more satisfactory meeting as soon as soon as I have got back from this wretched visit to Paris[1] and have got the bulk of the *Criterion* off my hands.

Yours ever,
T. S. E.

ticket enclosed –
Remember that I shall be very late – so don't leave till I come –

TO *Harold Monro* — TS Beinecke

16 November 1924 — 9 Clarence Gate Gdns

My dear Monro,

Thanks very much for your letter.[2] I have only just got back from Paris and am writing in haste to catch the post. I agree that this thing ought to be done, but I am afraid it is too late for January 1st. But if you can let me know IMMEDIATELY the names of the publishers of these books I will send for copies and we shall see what can be done. It seems to me that I am in as difficult a position to review these anthologies as you are, because I am not in them: but can you suggest anyone else who could do it properly?[3] If so, let me hear at once.

What about the *Chapbook*?

I am very sorry about the Wordsworth: I meant it quite *literally* when I said we *could do* without it.[4] It won't embarrass me, but I hope you will do that or something you would like better to do – suggest something else when it occurs to you – soon.

Yours ever
T. S. E.

1 – TSE and VHE left for Paris on Friday 14 Nov. TSE was back in London by the Sunday evening.

2 – On 15 Nov., Monro reviewed a number of new anthologies of modern poetry: J. C. Squire, *Second Selections from Modern Poets* (1924); Laurence Binyon, *The Golden Treasury of Modern Lyrics* (1924); Joan Beauchamp, *Poems of Revolt* (1924); Jessie B. Rittenhouse, *The Little Book of Modern British Verse* (1924); L. A. G. Strong, *Eighty Poems: An Anthology* (1924). Monro called the first two 'infamous': 'Believe me, it really is your duty to write an article on these five works', though probably 'too late for the next number'. The anthologies were 'well worth being angry about', but 'in a reasoned manner'.

3 – Monro could not review them himself, being 'too much involved, and in the eyes of other persons, inherently or technically prejudiced'. They were not reviewed in *C*.

4 – Monro could not get on with the concluding part of 'Wordsworth Revisited'.

TO *G. Elliot Smith* CC

20 November 1924 23 Adelphi Terrace House

Dear Mr Elliot Smith,

I am delighted to hear from you at last, as I had been on the point of writing again to ask if you were back from your voyages.[1] What you say is extraordinarily gratifying as I am as anxious as ever to publish something by you.[2]

Now that I am writing to you, I should like to ask a favour. When recently in Paris I met a Doctor Mardrus, who seems to be a well known Orientalist and Egyptologist, and who, I am told, has made a remarkable translation of *The Arabian Nights* in French.[3] I hope you will not mind my asking you whether you know of him and whether you consider him to be a scholar of standing, as he has been recommended as a possible contributor, and as I am ignorant in these matters.

I hope you will forgive my asking you, even if you do not feel able or inclined to answer the question.

With many thanks,

Yours very truly,
[T. S. E.]

TO *S. S. Koteliansky* CC

22 November 1924 23 Adelphi Terrace House

Dear Koteliansky,

I hope you will forgive me for not answering your letter at once but I have been extra busy, and for the last week have been in bed with a cold. I should have let you know that there is no objection to the publication of the Tolstoy letters in America in January.[4] The enclosed Dostoevsky letter is also interesting, but as the Tolstoy letters form a whole without it, and as the January number is already so crowded that I am puzzled to distraction how to use everything I have promised to include, I must deny myself the pleasure of publishing this, at least in that number.[5] I hope that

1–See TSE's letter of 6 Oct.
2–A ref. to progress on 'The Glamour of Gold', for *C.* 3: 11 (Apr. 1925).
3–Joseph-Charles-Victor Mardrus's French translation, *Les Mille Nuits et une Nuit*, was published in 16 vols, 1898–1904. He never contributed to *C.*
4–On 4 Nov., Koteliansky asked if he could offer the *Dial* his translations of the 'Strakhov–Tolstoy letters'.
5–See 'A Few Extracts from Letters exchanged between Leo Nicolayevich Tolstoy and N. N. Strakhov relating to F. M. Dostoevsky', *C.* 3: 10 (Jan. 1925).

the *Dial* will be able to do so; it is so much easier to arrange the contents of a monthly than of a quarterly.

I hope that some time next year you will have something else as interesting and important as these Tolstoy letters.

Sincerely yours,
[T. S. E.]

TO *Edwin Seaver*[1] CC

24 November 1924 23 Adelphi Terrace House

Dear Sir,

Thank you for your letter (undated). I have not seen No. 1 of your magazine because it is forwarded directly to Mr Herbert Read who reviews American periodicals for us. So I shall be glad to have another copy, as well as 2 and 3, and I may be able to write you a note in reply to Mr Munson's essay.[2] As for exchange, it is entirely at the discretion of Mr Read, but I will put the question to him.

With all best wishes for success and looking forward to seeing your review.

I am,

Yours very truly,
[T. S. E.]

TO *Gilbert Seldes* CC

24 November 1924 23 Adelphi Terrace House

My dear Seldes,

Thank you very much for your admirable chronicle which arrived exactly at the right time to go to the printers.[3] It shall appear without alteration.

1 – Edwin Seaver (1900–87): Socialist critic; editor of a new magazine entitled *1 9 2 4*.
2 – In his account of US periodicals in C. 3: 9 (Oct. 1924), HR said of Gorham B. Munson's article 'The Esotericism of T. S. Eliot' (*1 9 2 4*, 1: 1, July 1924) that it was 'extremely able and comprehending criticism'; but he did not accept Munson's identification of *TWL* with the 'fatalism of Spengler', or the implication that there was a distinction between 'a sterile decayed Europe and an America of abounding energies and high spiritual potentiality' (152–3). For Munson, see TSE's letter of 3 Nov 1925.
3 – 'New York Chronicle', *C.* 3: 10 (Jan. 1925).

I will ask Cobden-Sanderson to have volume 2 of the *Criterion* bound up and sent to you, to be deducted from your insignificant payment. If you also wish volume 1, let me know, but I am afraid that numbers 1 and 2 are completely out of print.

Let me hear from you as soon as you reach Paris even if you do not feel moved to write to me before that. As your copy seems to have gone astray, I will have an October *Criterion* sent to you. Unfortunately I was too busy to be able to review your book adequately myself so I had to hand it over to Conrad Aiken.[1]

With all best wishes

Yours always,
[T. S. E.]

TO *Richard Aldington* CC

24 November 1924 23 Adelphi Terrace House

My dear Richard,

Thank you very much for your letter and for honoring me with a sight of the proof of your poem.[2] I have not had time yet to read it through, having been in bed with a cold, so may I keep it for a few days? What I have looked at I liked immensely.

Yes I dare say you are right about the preface and prefaces.[3] At any rate I am pleased to find that you still like the essays. I think that the one on Dryden is the only one which has any merit.

I think that Edith [Sitwell] has a sincere interest in and respect for good writing wherever she perceives it, and I agree with you that she is trustworthy. As for the others, I never supposed that any of them was deserving of the least confidence. The first two of them are purely parasitic. As for [John Gould] Fletcher, when I knew him years ago, he seemed to me always wavering between generous admiration and bitter envy of people who were in any way more successful than himself. I used to be very sorry for him.

I will look out for your Mark Twain with great interest. Something certainly needs to be said about him.

1–See Aiken's review of Seldes, *The Seven Lively Arts*, C. 3: 9 (Oct. 1924).

2–RA, *A Fool i' the Forest* (1925).

3–The one-page Preface to *HJD* (1924), in which TSE described the book as preserving 'in cryptogram certain notions which, if expressed directly, would be destined to immediate obloquy' (9). The essays were 'John Dryden', 'The Metaphysical Poets' and 'Andrew Marvell'.

I have sent a card to your friend[1] and asked him to come to lunch with me. You may depend on my doing anything I can.

I wish I might see you soon and have a talk about the *Criterion*. I should like to know your opinion of the Commentary, whether you think it is worth continuing or not.[2] I feel sometimes that it is nothing but a bid for unpopularity. When will you be in London again?

My lecture at Cambridge seemed to go off successfully, but as you say, lectures are a waste of time. I met Fernandez in Paris a week ago and liked him very much. He is one of the most promising young men in Paris I think.

About [Orlo] Williams, I hope you will not think it necessary to speak well of the book unless you like it. But I hope that you find it interesting enough to be worth writing about at all. Can I possibly have the review by Thursday?

[Alec] Randall has suggested that he would like occasionally to write a note about a German book. Would you ever care to review a French book when you come across one that seems to you to deserve a place?

Yours ever,
[T. S. E.]

1–George Dunning Gribble, whom RA described (25 Nov.) as 'a specimen of the Inglese Italianato di nostri giorni' and 'a really cultured man' who 'pretends he isn't'. RA admired Gribble's intro. to his translation of *The History of Manon Lescaut and the Chevalier de Grieux* (1925), which he had seen in proof.

2–RA thought the Commentaries 'excellent' (30 Nov.). His advice was to make C. the foremost literary review in England, and gradually to withdraw from politics. Most of the other reviews were attached to a party and 'most of them are Conservative'. With a strong Conservative government in power there was little point in advocating a 'Right view', and there was a danger that Commentaries would be 'tilting at windmills or knocking down open doors'. The Socialists were unlikely to be a threat for many years, but if they did emerge again, Crites [TSE] would be 'most valuable'. He suggested enlarging C. and bringing in a few more elements, especially 'les jeunes' if they could be found. In the post-war world most people sought peace, and 'intellectual harlots like ourselves must please rather by entertaining than by taking a hand in politics'.

TO *Geoffrey Faber*[1] TS Valerie Eliot

25 November 1924 9 Clarence Gate Gdns

Sir,

I understand from my friend Charles Whibley that he has conveyed to you his reasons for thinking that we should meet; and if you are so inclined, I should be happy to call upon you, if you would suggest an evening.[2]

I am, Sir,

Your obedient servant,
T. S. Eliot

TO *Messrs. Hazell, Watson & Viney* CC

25 November 1924 9 Clarence Gate Gdns

Dear Sirs,

I enclose herewith three further contributions to be set up for the January *Criterion*. Please note as to the pieces of theatrical criticism that the first is to be set up in large type and the two following notes in small type and that they are to run on continuously together without leaving any part of the page blank.[3]

The 'Diary of the Rive Gauche'[4] is to be set up in large type.

1–Geoffrey Faber: see Glossary of Names. At All Souls College, Oxford, GCF met Maurice Gwyer, whose wife had inherited the Scientific Press from her father, Sir Henry Burdett (1881–1943). It specialised in medical books and published a successful weekly paper, *The Nursing Mirror*. In 1922, with a view to expanding into general publishing, the Gwyers invited GCF to join the board as Chairman. They founded the firm of Faber & Gwyer in 1925.

2–They met on Mon., 1 Dec. at GCF's house, 21 Ladbroke Grove, London. At a memorial service for GCF, TSE was to recall nearly forty years later: 'For personal reasons, I found it necessary to change my means of livelihood, and to seek a new position which should also give some assurance of permanence. Faber, on the other hand, was looking only for a writer with some reputation among the young, who could attract promising authors of the younger generation as well as of our own, towards the newly founded firm of Faber & Gwyer. He wanted an informal adviser and, in fact, a "talent scout". My name had been suggested to him with warm commendation by my elder friend Charles Whibley, on an occasion when CW was a weekend guest at All Souls. I do not remember how it was, during the evening's conversation between Faber and myself, that our two designs became identical. I suspect that it was merely that we took to each other' (St Giles-in-the-Fields, Holborn, 10 May 1961; privately printed).

3–Viola Tree (as Violet Ray), 'The Stage: An Uninteresting Era', was printed in large type, followed by two short reviews: one by Ray on the Phoenix Society *Epicoene*, the other by Zoe Hawley on 'Fata Morgana', both in smaller type: *C.* 3: 10 (Jan. 1925), 305–10.

4–Fanny Marlow, 'Diary of the Rive Gauche I', in the same issue, 290–7.

All of these should be returned to myself for proof correction, except that a copy of the Fata Morgana note should be sent to Miss Zoe Hawley, 129 Church St, Chelsea, s.w.3.

You have now nearly everything except the Commentary and a few notes which shall follow in the course of this week. 'The Perfect Action'[1] should be set up immediately. I am anxiously awaiting from you a full statement of the number of words in *each* contribution which you have set up for the reason that something will have to be cut or postponed until the following issue and until I know the number of words, I cannot arrange the Number. Please note that I am anxious to get this Number out on January *1st*.

Yours faithfully,
[T. S. E.]

TO *D. H. Lawrence*[2] CC

25 November 1924 23 Adelphi Terrace House

Dear Mr Lawrence,

I like your stories very much and have just accepted from Messrs. Curtis Brown Limited a second story entitled 'The Woman Who Rode Away'.[3] I like your style and I like your perceptions. I should be glad if at any time you cared to contribute more regularly to the *Criterion*, as one of the half dozen or so writers who contribute to such an extent as to form the character of the paper. I mean that I should like to have something of yours in almost every number, shorter essays, notes or reviews.[4]

If you are ever in London and care to meet me, I should be glad if you would let me know. You could write to this address or to 9 Clarence Gate Gardens.

Yours very truly,
[T. S. E.]

1 – An extract from WL's long story, which ultimately never appeared.
2 – D. H. Lawrence (1884–1930): novelist, short-story writer, poet and essayist. He had published *Women in Love* (1920), *Kangaroo* (1923), *Studies in Classic American Literature* (1923), and *Birds, Beasts and Flowers* (1923).
3 – 'The Woman Who Rode Away' appeared in *C.* 3: 12 (July 1925) and *NC* 4: 1 (Jan. 1926).
4 – DHL made five contributions altogether before his death in 1930.

TO *Mary Hutchinson* MS Texas

[Postmark 25 November 1924] *The Criterion*, 9 Clarence Gate Gdns

It is true, dear Mary, that I have been more busy than is dreamt of in your philosophy (Hamlet)[1] and that I am more tired than I like to be, and have had more to think of than can be thought in the day and the night. But *all the same* I hope to see you next week. It is also true that Vivien is a very long way from recovery, and I don't expect she will be able to make any progress *during the winter*: but I think she would have rung you up, but that she has been making an exhaustive study of Clive's works,[2] in her thorough way, and when she has finished she wants to discuss them with you –

Affectionately
Tom

TO *Ottoline Morrell* MS Texas

30 November 1924 *The Criterion*, 9 Clarence Gate Gdns

My dear Ottoline

I am writing for Vivien. I wish she had *not* come back from Paris[3] – the journey, and the Ballet (which was *certainly not* worth coming over for!) resulted in a very alarming bronchitis which has settled at the back of the lungs. So she has been in bed with a high temperature ever since. The doctor was more reassuring today, but we are not yet certain whether the inflammation has been checked.

Par dessus le marché,[4] *I* have been in bed since Wednesday, with influenza. I am very weak still, and may not be up or out for several days yet. You can imagine what chaos and torment we have been living in! I think we must both have had a suppressed influenza for a long time – since July. I was in bed four days after my visit to Paris, a fortnight ago, then was up for three days, and then in bed again!

1 – 'There are more things in heaven and earth, Horatio, / Than are dreamt of in your philosophy' (*Hamlet* I. 5, 166–7).
2 – The works of Clive Bell (Hutchinson's lover) included *Art* (1913), *Since Cézanne* (1922), *On British Freedom* (1923) and *The Legend of Monte Della Sibilla* (1923). His 'Prologomena to a Study of Nineteenth-Century Painting' was to appear in *C.* 3: 10 (Jan. 1925), 231–44.
3 – TSE returned from their Paris weekend on 16 Nov. The Paris trip informed VHE's 'A Diary of the Rive Gauche' (*C.* 3: 10 & 11, Jan. & Apr. 1925), which she published as 'Fanny Marlow.' The first of these pieces, dated 'December', is set in an unnamed hotel, but ends up near quai Voltaire where the Eliots stayed in Lady Rothermere's apartment.
4 – 'Into the bargain' (French).

I think the Ballet was bad from *every* point of view, and we are very glad you think so too.[1] I am pleased that you like the poems[2] – they are part of a longer sequence which I am doing – I laid down the principles of it in a paper I read at Cambridge, on Chapman, Dostoevski and Dante – and which is a sort of avocation to a much more revolutionary [style *del.*] thing I am experimenting on.[3] But I dare not work on the latter except when *very well* and strong.

We are *both* bitterly disappointed not to see you this time. Vivien is too ill to be allowed to see anyone. She wants me to say that neither of us have heard anything about Philip's mother. We are very sorry indeed to hear of it. She must be a great loss to Oxford. Will you *please* give Philip our sympathy?[4]

We *must* see you the next time you come. With love from both.

Tom

I wanted to speak to you after the ballet – but I had Diaghilev[5] etc. on my hands.

1–On 24 Nov., TSE and VHE went to see Diaghilev's Ballets Russes in *Cimarosiana* and Cocteau's *Le Train Bleu* (starring Anton Dolin) at the Coliseum in London. TSE had heralded the London season of the Ballets Russes in his 'Commentary', *C.* 3: 9 (Oct. 1924).

2–'Doris's Dream Songs' [I–III], *Chapbook* 39 (Nov. 1924), 36–7.

3–The paper TSE gave to the Cam Literary Society on 8 Nov. was not published. 'A Neglected Aspect of Chapman' was due to be published in *C.* 3: 11 (Apr. 1925), but prevented by 'severe illness'. The 'longer sequence' is 'The Hollow Men'; the 'more revolutionary thing' *SA*. In his talk at Cambridge, TSE said of Chapman's plays that 'more or less consciously the personages are acting, and accepting, inevitable roles in *this* world, and the real centre of their action is in another Kingdom'. In Dostoevsky's novels likewise, 'there are everywhere two planes of reality . . . The characters themselves are partially aware of this division, aware of the grotesque futility of their visible lives, and seem always to be listening for other voices and to be conducting a conversation with spectres.' In conclusion, he said, 'Chapman and Dostoevski and ourselves are all part of a modern world' while 'Dante belonged to another and perhaps a wiser one' ('A Neglected Aspect of Chapman', unpub.).

4–Philip Morrell's mother died of pneumonia on 9 Nov.

5–TSE wrote that at 'the present time the ballet appears to depend almost wholly on Mr Diaghileff', and deplored the withdrawal of some of his best dancers. It was 'a public obligation . . . to continue to support Mr Diaghileff's ballet, and use our efforts so that on his next visit to London he may have the facilities for producing the *Sacré* and the newer work of Stravinski' (*C.* 3: 10 [Jan. 1925], 161–2).

FROM *Geoffrey Faber* CC

[2 December 1924] [London]

My [dear] Eliot

[I am] sending you a short memorandum of the [several words illegible] interesting conversation last night.[1] I hope [you] will make any alterations or additions to it that may suggest themselves to you. The whole idea is one that makes a great appeal to me personally, and I am not without hopes that something more definite may come of it, but you understand from what I said that I shall have rather to pick my foot-steps.[2]

I hope I did not keep you out of bed too long last night.

[Geoffrey C. Faber]

TO *J. M. Robertson* CC

2 December 1924 23 Adelphi Terrace House

My dear Mr Robertson,

I have a favour to ask you which I hope you will not have the slightest hesitation in refusing if you are too busy to grant it, inasmuch as it is one which I have no right to ask.

Two manuscripts have been offered to me for publication in the *Criterion*, the merits of which I have not the competence to decide. One is a theory of *A Lover's Complaint* by one R. L. Eagle, who, I believe, has recently made himself notorious by championing the Baconian heresy.[3] Nevertheless, to an uninstructed reader it appears interesting; but I do not wish to use [it] if it is patently absurd. The other is entitled 'Marvell's Hand in *Arden of Feversham*', by E. H. C. Oliphant, who writes from Melbourne and speaks of himself as a well known writer on Elizabethan drama.[4]

1–TSE and GCF met on the evening of Mon. 1 Dec. at GCF's house, 21 Ladbroke Grove. Unfortunately, the 'memorandum' GCF attached to this letter does not survive; and his diary entry for 1 Dec. reads merely: 'T. S. Eliot dined with me, & we had a long & interesting talk about the *Criterion*, recorded elsewhere' (Faber Archive).

2–GCF hints at the hope that TSE might be able to join his proposed firm of Faber & Gwyer.

3–William Shakespeare, 'A Lover's Complaint'. Roderick L. Eagle was author of *New Light on the Enigmas of Shakespeare Sonnets* (1916) and later studies in support of Bacon's authorship of Shakespeare, inc. *Shakespeare: New Views for Old* (1930). Replying on 3 Dec., Robertson called Eagle 'a quite exceptional Baconian'.

4–This should read 'Marlowe's hand in *Arden of Feversham*' (as Robertson pointed out to TSE). Robertson indicated his 'agreement with him on this point' in his recent *Introduction to the Study of the Shakespearian Canon*, and gave Oliphant the credit. Oliphant's 'Marlowe's hand in *Arden of Feversham*' appeared in *NC* 4: 1 (Jan. 1926), 76–93.

If you had time, immediately or later, to glance at these typescripts and give me your opinion of their value, I should be more than grateful to you. For even if I found it impossible to use both of these myself, I always feel a certain obligation to encourage anything that deserves publication and to recommend it to other reviews.

But I do not want to lay any burden on you, so if you cannot look at these yourself I should be grateful if you could suggest the name of someone else competent to decide.

The *Criterion* containing your '*Hamlet*' should appear on the 1st January.[1]

Sincerely yours,
[T. S. E.]

TO *Wyndham Lewis* TS Cornell

2 December 1924 9 Clarence Gate Gdns

Dear Lewis,

I have been ill in bed with influenza and bronchitis, hence the delay. Whibley says he does not *expect* to be in London again before Christmas, and suggests that if you will send him the complete manuscript he will send it to Macmillan personally.[2] If you do not like this will you write to him (Charles Whibley, Broomhill House, Great Brickhill, near Bletchley, Berks[3]) and try to arrange to see him when he next comes to town. I suggest writing to him first in any case, before sending MSS.

About your 'Perfect Action': I have just learned that it is 20,000 words.[4] I could only publish it all at once by arranging a number some time in advance, as it would otherwise involve putting off several contributors, and practically all in this number have been put off already for some months. *May I use it in parts? It is over twice* as long as anything we have ever published. I could print a *part* in this number (but let me know at once) and if the book came out before the next issue we could substitute the rest by something else of yours. You see I hope how I am fixed: I want

1 – 'The Naturalistic Theory of *Hamlet*', *C.* 3: 10 (Jan. 1925), 172–92.

2 – Presumably WL's huge new manuscript.

3 – Bletchley is in Buckinghamshire not Berkshire.

4 – The working title of WL's latest contribution.

you in more than everybody else, and if you could let me have 5,000 or 6,000 word lengths could use you in ~~practically~~ every number.[1]

Yours ever
T. S. E.

I know of a new publishing firm which is promising, but it won't even be formed for six months or so.

TO *Messrs. Hazell, Watson & Viney* CC

4 December 1924 9 Clarence Gate Gdns

Dear Sirs,

I enclose three reviews for small type, by[2]

Harold Monro
Feiron Morris
Frederic Manning

Also MS. of a poem by myself (large type).[3] In order to save time please send all the proof to me and a copy to Mr Cobden-Sanderson but send Mr Monro's proof to Mr Cobden-Sanderson.

The FOUR LETTERS of Tolstoi may be set up in a page to follow directly the COMMENTARY.[4] I shall let you have the remaining order [in] a few days time.

Yours faithfully,
[T. S. E.]

1 – 'The Perfect Action' was never to be published in *C.*

2 – Harold Monro on Aiken's *Selected Poems of Emily Dickinson* and Sacheverell Sitwell's *The Thirteenth Caesar*; Feiron Morris (VHE) on Virginia Woolf's *Mr Bennett and Mrs Brown*; and Frederick Manning on 'Collection Christianisme': all in *C.* 3: 10 (Jan. 1925).

3 – Thomas Eliot, 'Three Poems' in the same issue: I 'Eyes I dare not meet in dreams', II 'Eyes that last I saw in tears' and III 'The eyes are not here': the first poems TSE had published in *C.* since *TWL* in the first issue.

4 – 'L. N. Tolstoy and N. N. Strakhov: Extracts from Letters relating to F. M. Dostoevsky'.

TO *Marguerite Caetani* TS Galleria Nazionale d'Arte Moderna

5 December 1924 23 Adelphi Terrace House

Dear Princess Bassiano

It is very rude of me not to have written to you.[1] But first I hoped to meet you at Miss Barney's,[2] and second, I have been ill in bed, with intervals of a day at a time, (twice), ever since – with influenza following a chill on the journey.

I tried to explain to Miss Barney my scruples, but expressed myself very badly. If I saw you I could put the arguments better than in writing. The point is *not* that I don't need it. I need it very badly at the moment – but is chiefly that if I employed my spare time in other ways than I do, I could make more money out of *writing* than I do – that is almost nil.

I propose to send you, as soon as work and worry will allow me, MS copies of five new short poems. I.e. I compose on the typewriter, but there will be *no* other copies of these poems in *long hand*.[3] As I wish you to have something in return.

As I say, I could explain myself *much* better if I met you.

But, looking forward to that, some day.

I am

Very gratefully
T. S. Eliot

TO *Richard Cobden-Sanderson* CC

10 December 1924 9 Clarence Gate Gdns

Dear Cobden-Sanderson,

Enclosed is a statement of moneys owing to me from *The Criterion* on account of disbursements. Will you let me have a cheque for this £8.8.8d. at once, so as to settle all outstandings before Lady Rothermere arrives?

We will discuss other matters when we meet. I continue to enjoy the appearance of *The Serpent*. Let us hope that it is not a poisonous serpent.

1 – See TSE's letter to Natalie Barney of 11 Aug. Caetani and Barney had both put up money for TSE in the event of his leaving Lloyds Bank.
2 – During his visit to Paris in Nov.
3 – Presumably the 'Three Poems' in C. 3: 10, plus the other new poems in 'Doris's Dream Songs' in *Chapbook* 39 (Nov. 1924).

I am very sorry to hear that your wife is ill.

Yours ever

[T. S. E.]

TO *Lady Rothermere* cc

10 December 1924 [London]

Dear Lady Rothermere,

I have received your letter and will ring you up directly upon your arrival, when we can make all arrangements: including a meeting at Cobden-Sanderson's office to discuss all business and the accounts; also a visit to your own office in the Adelphi, which you have never yet seen![1]

Sincerely yours,

[T. S. E.]

TO *R. Cobden-Sanderson* cc

[11? December 1924] [London]

This is just suggestions for us to say – you may think too violent. But on the way we must arrange a system of *signs*, to communicate with each other, because if she is in a violent temper, I advise saying nothing at all.[2]

C-S

Now Lady Rothermere I have paid up everything and I have exactly £ . . . . . in hand as you can see by my books if you come to my office. The January *Criterion* is now ready and in my hands and complete. My publishing business lately has been widening out and I have been in discussion with other publishers and I have been very much criticised for running a review in this way. It is nothing to do with you personally but there are such things as accidents, illnesses etc. And supposing anything were to happen to you rendering you incapable of signing a cheque for three or four months I simply have not the means to LOAN THE MONEY temporarily. Of course, legally, I have no responsibility, but many of the contributors would press for payment instantly, specially the better known ones, and the printers. I am not legally bound to

1 – The new *Criterion* offices had been taken over from the *Egoist*.

2 – The first lines are written in pen. What follows is a typed memo in dialogue form to guide their discussion with Lady Rothermere about C. business.

anybody but at the same time possibly some people might think so and in that case proceedings might be started against me and in that case my position would be very awkward. I haven't money or time to engage in legal proceedings and to me time is money. It makes no difference to you whether you make a cheque in December or Jan. or in Feb. to pay off debts. Difference to me so much that I feel bound to ask whether you agree to pay for each issue in advance. There is nobody in the contract but yourself. What should I do if anything happened to you. You must have thought about that. I think that I may speak for Eliot that he has not either the cash or the time to attend to such a situation which might arrive. Let C.S. then turn to me and say I think I am right Eliot in saying that you are pledged quite nine months ahead to certain contributors. These contributors would have to be paid by law whether the *Criterion* was issued or not.

ELIOT says:

Quite so, I think every word C.S. has said is just and right, and I know myself that it is considered more than foolish and unbusinesslike for people to produce a review for which they will pay contributors and printers whatever happens. This has just been brought home to me and we know you will understand – same money only two months sooner. This as [*sic*] a matter of fact C.S. remarked on it and I have been thinking it over and the matter was brought to a head by a conversation I had with B[ruce] R[ichmond] of the *Times* and C[harles] W[hibley] and several other men of knowledge in these matters on that very unfortunate occasion of the first night of the Diaghilev season.

Which occasion of course needs explaining away. You had offered me your box and so I invited B. R. and C. W. and another man to join me and we found your box had been sold by your orders and this led to a discussion. That night was a ghastly catastrophe for the *Criterion*.

BOTH

If she cuts up we advise you to consult Lord Rothermere who is at least a man of business.

FROM *Geoffrey Faber* CC

12 December 1924 [London]

My dear Eliot

I am once more enclosing [a] copy of memorandum of the conversation between you and me. No doubt there are points in it which you will again wish to correct, but, on the whole, I fancy it gives a pretty accurate account of the general sense of what passed between us.[1]

I am afraid I was anything but at my best last night, but you will make allowances for the fact that I have been under considerable strain for the last ten days.

I have not said anything in the memorandum about what we agreed to call 'testimonials', but the more I think over the position, the more certain I feel that our hope lies in these. What I should like you to get for me, if you can, is *quantities* of opinions about yourself, from men whose names will carry weight with my Directors. Those you mentioned last night would do splendidly. Can you collect more of the same kind? Bruce Richmond, Hugh Walpole, Arnold Bennett and Robertson. What we do not want them to say is: 'Mr Eliot is a profound and scholarly critic.' What we want them to say is: 'Mr Eliot is a brilliant editor, as well as a brilliant writer and critic.' What will impress my directors favourably in the scheme, if anything will, is the sense that in you we have found a man who combines literary gifts with business instincts, who has a wide circle of literary friends, and who is quite as much at home on the lower levels as on the lonely peaks.

If you could deluge me with this sort of thing, and the sooner the better, I am not without hopes that we may not be able to make some arrangement but, of course, there is more than one lion in my path!

Yours sincerely
[Geoffrey C. Faber]

PS The memorandum is copied [the remainder is indecipherable].

TO *Richard Cobden-Sanderson* cc

13 December 1924 9 Clarence Gate Gdns

Dear Cobden-Sanderson,

I enclose title page. You will see that I have put much more on to the cover than usual; because it ought to attract purchasers and because it makes the paper look less arty and precious. I suppose the top will have to be shoved up and bottom down a bit?

Will you let Hazell's know at once, so that they can proceed with the page proof?

1–GCF and TSE met for a second conversation on Tues., 11 Dec. GCF's memorandum of the conversation does not survive, and he recorded in his diary merely, 'Eliot came to call about 9, & stayed till 11 discussing the *Criterion*.'

I also enclose circular copy to be slipped in. What do you think of having the prospectus on one side of a leaf and the *New Statesman* encomium on the other?[1]

Thursday at 5.15, in any case.

Yours ever
[T. S. E.]

TO *John Middleton Murry* MS Valerie Eliot

Monday 15 December 1924 9 Clarence Gate Gdns

Dear John,

If you are going to be in London, you will probably find a great many 'friends' to welcome you – and such a display of flags from ships not in stony places, that you may not find it necessary to recognise *my* ensign. So I shall not accept this letter as really a signal: but shall wait for another if, and when, you have use for me.[2]

But do you really consider it a good sign that the 'time of stony places is over'?[3] If so, you are luckier than the Saviour, who found things pretty stony to the last – and would, I believe, have continued to find them so, had he not been removed at an age less ripe than yours or mine.[4] I do not suppose that I share any other characteristic of the Founder of Christianity, but at least I have nothing but stony places to look forward to. This isolates me, of course, from those who can pass in and out of stony places with practised ease.

Yours ever,
Tom

1–For comments on *C.* by 'Affable Hawk', in *NS*, 22 Nov. 1924, 204, see TSE's letter to Desmond MacCarthy, 23 Dec. 1924.

2–Since his second marriage in the spring, JMM had been living at Abbotsbury, nr. Chesil Beach (a stony place). Evidently, in a missing letter JMM notified TSE he was visiting London.

3–TSE appears to be quoting from JMM quoting either the Bible ('And some fell on stony ground', Mark 4: 5) or *TWL* ('After the agony in stony places', l. 324).

4–JMM was born in 1889, TSE in 1888; both were older than Jesus at the time of the Crucifixion. JMM was working on his *The Life of Jesus* (1926).

FROM *Geoffrey Faber* CC

16 December 1924 [London]

My dear Eliot

Thank you for your letter of the 14th. I am glad you think I have a good memory, I have never thought so myself. I see your difficulty about testimonials. As far as we are concerned, provided you leave our name out, I do not mind what you say; but no doubt the difficulty is on your side. I do not want to raise your hopes unduly, but I do think, if we go about things in the right way, that there is a fair chance of something emerging at the end.

Yours sincerely
[Geoffrey C. Faber]

TO *John Middleton Murry* MS Valerie Eliot

17 December [1924] 9 Clarence Gate Gdns

Dear John

I hope you will not mind if I ask you to postpone our lunch till after this week? The fact is that I am at this moment so preoccupied and worried by certain affairs of my own, that I have not the energy or vitality to give to anything else – or to see you or *anybody*. If you will let me suggest a day next week, or better still after Christmas, I think it would be better from every point of view, and you will find me, I trust, less distracted. In fact, I had held this week clear over a month ahead, knowing that it wd need all my attention. As you are settled in London, there is no reason why we should not see more of each other, free from rush and hurry.

Yours ever
Tom.

TO *Wyndham Lewis* PC Cornell

[Postmark 18 December 1924] 9 Clarence Gate Gdns

I have been very harassed and occupied – Could we meet directly after Christmas – say Monday or Tuesday week? Am anxious to see you, but have had my hands full. Think can arrange my suggestion next week.

[Unsigned]

TO *Messrs. Hazell, Watson & Viney* CC

21 December 1924 9 Clarence Gate Gdns

Dear Sirs,

Criterion No. 10

I enclose herewith corrected page-proof of pp. 161–192; also corrected slip proof of Miss Sitwell's poem.[1]

There are three alterations to be made in three contributions viz. 'On the Eve', 'Diary of the Rive Gauche' and 'Mr Bennett and Mrs Brown', and I think that it will save time and trouble if you make them at once before setting up the pages:[2]

ON THE EVE Toward the end there is a song of four lines, followed by the words 'he sang savagely'. Delete the word *savagely*.[3]

DIARY OF THE RIVE GAUCHE Third line from the end 'attracting foreign visitors'. Alter to 'attracting American visitors'.[4]

MR. BENNETT AND MRS. BROWN (review). 1. Paragraph beginning 'But are we to accept James Joyce, T. S. Eliot and Wyndham Lewis . . .' Alter to 'But are we to accept these three nightmare figures, James Joyce, T. S. Eliot and Wyndham Lewis . . . etc.'[5] 2. Paragraph beginning 'Mrs Woolf's Mrs Brown is a romantic creature'. Third sentence from the end 'Modern young intellectuals . . . etc.' Alter to 'Modern young intellectuals – and here I distinguish between the minority of really modern young intellectuals and the semi-modern majority who still think that Katherine Mansfield's stories are "simply too wonderful for words" –

1–TSE, 'A Commentary'; Edith Sitwell, 'The Man with the Green Patch', *C.* 3: 10 (Jan. 1925).

2–These three contributions are credited: T. S. Eliot, 'On the Eve'; Fanny Marlow, 'Rive Gauche I'; Feiron Morris, 'Virginia Woolf, *Mr Bennett and Mrs Brown*'. Donald Gallup was to report – presumably on TSE's authority – that the story 'On the Eve: A Dialogue', was 'actually written, at least in part', by VHE, and 'extensively revised' by TSE (*T. S. Eliot: A Bibliography*, 1969, 211). However, on 24 May 1940, TSE had informed the Swiss critic Hans Häusermann (a friend of Herbert Read) that 'On the Eve', though published under his name, was 'written by my wife, who was then in a not very well balanced mental state; I did in fact help her in the writing of it, though, so far as I can recollect, not to the extent to which you would suppose'. It is very probable too that TSE helped VHE with both 'Diary of the Rive Gauche' and her review of VW.

3–See *C.* 3: 10, 281. The song is: 'It's the sime the whole world over – / It's the pore that gets the blime, / It's the rich what gets the pleashur: / Isn't it a ber-loody shime!'

4–Ibid., 296.

5–Ibid., 328. The inserted word turns TSE, Joyce and Lewis into 'nightmare' 'representatives of modern literature'. The knowledge that VHE (writing in concert with TSE) was responsible for this review of VW's essay gives a different status to sentences such as the following: 'Is it true that Mr James Joyce – for Mrs Woolf cites him – arrived at Bloom by observations in a Dublin tram?' and also: 'did Mr Eliot – for Mrs Woolf cites him – deduce Sweeney from observations in a New York bar-room?' (328).

refuse any longer to be filled with romantic interest in the doings and sayings of some patchwork Petrouschka . . . etc'.

Yours faithfully,
[T. S. E.]

TO *Ezra Pound*

TS Beinecke

22 December 1924

The Criterion,
23 Adelphi Terrace House

Dear Ezra,

Thanks for your two letters. I think you are probably quite right about Dunning but it means nothing to me.[1] Call it a blind spot if you like. Probably the fact that Swinburne and the poets of the nineties were entirely missed out of my personal history counts for a great deal. I never read any of these people until it was too late for me to get anything out of them, and until after I had assimilated other influences which must have made it impossible for me to accept the Swinburnians at all.[2] The only exception to the above is Rossetti.[3] I am as blind to the merits of these people as I am to Thomas Hardy.

The other thing you propose sounds very interesting but I think the necessity for diagrams rules it out.[4] I therefore should not dare to order a translation without seeing either translation or original beforehand.

1–Ralph Cheever Dunning (1878–1930): expatriate American poet settled in Paris since 1905. He published *Hyllus* (1910), and went on to publish parts of 'The Four Winds' in *Poetry* and *Transatlantic Review* (1924, 1925). On 28 Sept. EP wrote: 'I was called across the garden to look after a sick man, the day before yesterday. And have come back with the first poetry I have seen for a very long time . . . Very much in the tone of the 90s . . . single lines certainly as good as any we have done.' Two days later, he sent the carbon of *Four Winds*. TSE wrote: 'I dont understand – with all due respect – what *is* the disease? Should *prefer* your own unfinished inedita. Do you think I have brain softening? This gives me a jolt.' (In a draft, TSE asked whether EP had brain softening.) EP wrote on 'Mr Dunning's Poetry' in *Poetry* 26: 6 (Sept. 1925), and continued to champion him, to the amazement of friends. JJ talked later of 'Mr Dunning's drivel, which Pound defends as if it were Verlaine' (*Letters of James Joyce*, III, ed. Richard Ellmann, 155).

2–TSE discussed the influence on EP of 'the 'Nineties in general, and behind the 'Nineties, of course, Swinburne and William Morris' in his intro. to EP, *Selected Poems* (1926), ix. Of himself, TSE said later: 'I took the usual adolescent course with Byron, Shelley, Keats, Rossetti, Swinburne' (*TUPUC*, 33).

3–Dante Gabriel Rossetti (1828–82): poet and translator, whose 'The Blessed Damozel' TSE encountered in early adolescence, and echoed in 'La Figlia Che Piange'.

4–On 11 Dec. EP recommended an article by Samojloff of the University of Kazan on 'Die Anordnung der musikalischen Intervalle in Raume' ['The ordering of musical intervals in space'], published in *Psychologische Forschung*. EP said Vladimir Dixon was willing to translate it; it involved 'Technical mathematics with diagrams' but was 'very interesting'.

What I really want is a canto or two. Can you inform me as to present condition and prospects?[1] Also re appendicitis?

Yours,
T.

TO *Richard Aldington* CC

22 December 1924 23 Adelphi Terrace House

Dear Richard,

I did not have time to speak to you about your review the other day.[2] When I heard from you I withdrew it and substituted one or two other things which would otherwise have gone into the following number. I could, of course, have added yours as well, but this number is going to be twenty pages longer than any other and we must really try to cut down the size on account of the expense. I find that we tend to have more and more book reviews, and I think, at least to the extent to which this is done in the January number, that this is a good feature as well as a popular one. But this will make it necessary to have fewer contributed articles. In the January number I was unable to reduce the number of contributed articles for the reason that I had so many which had been accepted some time ago which could not be delayed any longer.

Now I am wondering whether you would be willing to revise your review of Williams so as to make it a review of his book and another book of criticism called *The Critic's Armoury* by Cyril Falls. I don't know that they have much in common, but probably neither is important enough to require an extended review separately. If you are willing, I will have it sent to you at once.[3]

Your 'Villon' is to appear in the next number after January.

Our meeting the other day was of course very unsatisfactory as luncheons usually are. I wish that it were possible to arrange a dinner, but you hold out no hope of being in London overnight.

Yours ever,
[T. S. E.]

1 – The next instalment, 'Cantos XVII–XIX', appeared in *This Quarter* 1: 2 (1925/6).
2 – On 4 Dec., RA thought he had done Orlo Williams an injustice: he wanted TSE to cancel the article and let him do another. Then on 12 Dec. he changed his mind.
3 – See RA on Cyril Falls, *The Critic's Armour*, and Orlo Williams, *Contemporary Criticism of Literature*, C. 3: 11 (Apr. 1925).

TO *Alec Waugh*[1] CC

22 December 1924 23 Adelphi Terrace House

Dear Waugh,

Thank you for your letter of the 8th instant. I have read Scott Moncrieff's story and like it very much indeed so am keeping it.[2] I think it would be necessary to publish it in two parts as it is rather long. I cannot let you know at the moment exactly when it will be possible to use it, but I think early in the Spring. Will you please let Scott Moncrieff know, or if you will let me have his present address I will write.

Yours very truly,
[T. S. E.]

TO *Walter Hanks Shaw* CC

22 December 1924 23 Adelphi Terrace House

Dear Mr Shaw,

Thank you for your letter of the 7th instant. I trust that your cheque reached you in good time as it was sent by Mr Cobden-Sanderson before your letter arrived.[3] If you care to submit any more articles or if you think of any subjects on which you would like to write, please let me know.[4]

Yours very truly,
[T. S. E.]

TO *Desmond MacCarthy*[5] CC

23 December 1924 23 Adelphi Terrace House

Dear MacCarthy,

Had I been able to do so I should have written to you immediately to thank you for your remarks in *The New Statesman* about the October

1–Alec Waugh (1898–1981): novelist and elder brother of Evelyn Waugh; author of *The Loom of Youth* (1917), and *Myself when Young* (1923).
2–C. K. Scott Moncrieff, 'Cousin Fanny and Cousin Annie', *NC* 4; 2 & 3 (Apr. & July 1926).
3–Payment for his 'Foreign Theatre', *C.* 3: 9 (Oct. 1924).
4–On 25 Jan 1925, Shaw was to offer an article, 'The Youngsters of the Moderns: Trois Enfants Prodigues'. His next piece was 'Cinema and Ballet in Paris', *NC* 4: 1 (Jan. 1926).
5–Desmond MacCarthy (1877–1952): literary editor and journalist; author of *Remnants* (1918). In 1920 he became literary editor of *NS*, for which he wrote a weekly column on 'Books in General' under the pseud. 'Affable Hawk'.

Criterion.[1] Such criticism is not only extremely flattering to the paper, but is the most useful attention which we could possibly receive. What you say about the difficulties is indeed true. The review is run most economically: the labour expended by Mr Cobden-Sanderson is much out of proportion to the commission he receives, and as for myself, I have never taken anything from the magazine except payment for my own contributions at the ordinary rates.

The proprietor, Lady Rothermere, was so impressed by your notice that she directed that it should be quoted on a leaflet for the next number.[2]

I was also pleased to see that Arthur Symons' book on *The Symbolist Movement in Literature* has at last received recognition through your criticism.[3] The book was my first introduction to modern French verse and in this way had the most immeasurable influence on my own poetical evolution.[4]

Yours sincerely,
[T. S. E.]

1–Desmond MacCarthy wrote: 'My respect for this magazine steadily increases; I find more good criticism in it than in any other . . . Altogether, this number, and the more recent numbers of *The Criterion* have made me wish to act as town-crier for it. It is not a popular kind of periodical; no doubt it exists with difficulty. It should therefore be supported by all who want to see current literature and art discussed by critics who care about distinguishing and expounding, and believe what they say. Though it appears only once a quarter, I know no magazine which enables its readers to keep in touch with so many aesthetic questions. If it dies, which I trust it will not, it will have set a standard to subsequent ventures of the same kind hard to reach.' 'Books in General', *NS* 24 (22 Nov. 1924), 204.

2–See letter to RC-S ,13 Dec. Lady Rothermere commanded the printer: 'Please have this excellent notice reprinted as a sheet of paper & sent to certain important & advisable people.'

3–In 'Books in General', *NS* 24 (13 Dec. 1924), 299), MacCarthy said: 'the young are apt to forget that it was Mr Symons who first praised writers like Laforgue and Rimbaud in English. We, who can no longer be called young, know that there was no one to touch him as a guide to the decadents . . .' After quoting a passage from Symons on Laforgue, MacCarthy asked: 'And, then, does it not also strike you that in this passage Mr Symons has been describing the latest kind of modern poetry itself? Nearly the whole of it is applicable to a poet and critic whose name I mentioned above, Mr T. S. Eliot. He, too, does not distinguish between irony and pity; he, too, makes his patter and his patterns largely out of the unconscious, is full of that self-pity which extends itself across the world . . . and he, too, belongs to the class of ironic sentimentalists, "metaphysical Pierrots", who invent a new way of being René and Werther.'

4–TSE described his encounter with Symons's work as 'an introduction to wholly new feelings . . . a revelation' (*SW*, 1920, 5).

TO *H. P. Collins*[1] TS Private Collection

23 December 1924 23 Adelphi Terrace House

Dear Sir,

In reply to your letter of the 12th instant, I wish to use your essay on Classicism from about page 9.[2] The first part seems to me a little too generalised, and the general principles laid down therein need a whole volume of elucidation rather than a few pages. Also, I am not quite sure of the soundness of your criticism of Milton. What I particularly like is the comparative analysis of poems by Marvell, Lionel Johnson and Doctor Bridges. This is all very much to the point and is the sort of thing that is very much needed.[3] In fact, I wish you might do a whole book by this method. It is only by sticking very close to the examination of specimens that any investigation of Classicism and Romanticism is likely to be fruitful. The terms are so elusive and alter their meaning so completely in different contexts that the majority of discussions, such as that between Mr Middleton Murry and myself, are quite futile.[4]

You shall receive proof in due course.[5]

Yours faithfully,
T. S. Eliot

With best Christmas wishes.

TO *Richard Cobden-Sanderson* CC

29 December 1924 23 Adelphi Terrace House

Dear Cobden-Sanderson

Will you please let Miss Fassett have a cheque for £2.9.0. The items consist of one pound salary to the 27th instant, nine shillings stamps and office expenses of which she will give you a list and one pound petty cash to go on with for stamps etc. You will observe that I have purchased a cash box (5.6d) and I propose that the secretary shall keep a petty cash account and render a full account to you when the cash is exhausted.

1–See note to letter of 5 Mar. 1924.
2–On 31 Aug. Collins had offered an extract on 'Classicism' from his forthcoming book, and on 9 Nov. he allowed TSE to choose an extract from it.
3–Collins compared Marvell's 'Horatian Ode' with Lionel Johnson's poem on Charles I, commenting on the 'groping feeling' of the latter 'when brought to the touchstone of Marvell's intellectual sanity'. Cf. TSE's comparison of Dryden and Shelley: 'John Dryden', *HJD* (1924).
4–See TSE, 'The Function of Criticism', *C.* 2: 5 (Oct. 1923); JMM, 'On Fear and Romanticism', *Adelphi* (Sept. 1923), and 'Romanticism and Tradition', *C.* 2: 7 (Apr. 1924).
5–H. P. Collins, 'A Note on the Classical Principle in Poetry', *C.* 3: 11 (Apr. 1925), 389–400.

I also propose that hereafter the secretary be paid two pounds fortnightly instead of one pound weekly, and that she come to you for the cheque and give you the receipt. This seems to me more businesslike than the previous method by which I paid her and recouped myself from you. There will accordingly be two pounds owing to her today fortnight.

I enclose a copy of a letter sent by Selfridge's to a lady who asked them to get her a copy of the October *Criterion*. This sort of thing is abominable and likely to do us harm. I propose to write very severely to Selfridge's but I should like to know first whether you have any knowledge of Selfridge's having made any attempt to get a copy from you.

[T. S. E.]

FROM *Geoffrey Faber* cc

30 December 1924 [London]

My dear Eliot

I write to say that I have to take my wife away for two or three weeks to the South Coast on Wednesday, January 7th. Will you have anything to say to me before that date? If not, I shall probably have to come up to town now and then from Eastbourne (which is where we are probably going) and could always do so for anything of real importance.

I saw Charles Whibley in the Club today, and I gathered from him that you are still taking the proposition seriously.

Yours ever
[Geoffrey C. Faber]

TO *Orlo Williams* cc

31 December 1924 23 Adelphi Terrace House

My dear Williams,

I have now finally read your story and should very much like to publish it.[1] I am only afraid that I cannot yet say definitely how soon we shall be able to use it – merely for the reason that we have so much material waiting to be published, and also there is always the question of fitting the right contributions together. But you shall of course receive proof in good time.

1 – Orlo Williams, 'Capitaine Ensorceleur', *NC* 4: 4 (Oct. 1926), 659–72.

I enjoyed very much lunching with you the other day and hope that you will again seek me out in the city.

Yours sincerely,
[T. S. E.]

TO *J. M. Robertson* CC

31 December 1924 23 Adelphi Terrace House

My dear Mr Robertson,

Thank you very much for your letter of the 26th.[1] I am really most grateful to you for the trouble you have taken and for your frank and satisfactory expression of opinion. I shall certainly accept the essay on *Arden of Feversham*.[2] I have neither the time nor the knowledge to read carefully and to judge essays of this kind, and your help is of the very greatest value to me.

Again with many grateful thanks,

Sincerely yours,
[T. S. E.]

TO *Humbert Wolfe* CC

31 December 1924 [London]

My dear Wolfe,

I have at last read your story and like it. I should like to keep it, though I cannot say yet at what date publication will be possible, for the reason that we have so much material waiting to be published, and there is always the question of fitting the right contributions together. But you shall of course receive proof in good time.[3]

1–On 26 Dec. Robertson reported that E. H. C. Oliphant's essay, 'Marlowe's hand in *Arden of Feversham*', was 'a solid and important piece of scholarship well worth publishing', but Roderick Eagle's piece on 'The Lover's Complaint' was the 'skinniest gammon of Bacon' he had ever seen.

2–See E. H. C. Oliphant, 'Marlowe's hand in *Arden of Feversham*', *NC* 4: 1 (Jan. 1926).

3–On 29 Dec. Wolfe enquired if TSE had had time to look at the article he had sent him for *C.* (having enquired on 27 May about the 'possibly odious contribution' he had sent). No story by Wolfe appeared in *C.*

I also like your dialogue, but I see less prospect of being able to use this within a reasonable time. So I am sending it back to you, as you may wish to use it elsewhere.[1]

If you are in London, will you not come and lunch with me again?

Sincerely yours,
[T. S. E.]

TO *Gilbert Brooks* CC

31 December 1924 23 Adelphi Terrace House

Dear Mr Brooks,

I was glad to get your letter of November 27th. I am very much interested by your poems and should like to keep them a little longer for consideration.[2] Meanwhile, I am merely writing to ask your permission to do so and to say I should be delighted if you would submit a note on the Norwich Theatre. I have, as a matter of fact, had in mind to try to get something written about it, so I hope you will let me have it soon.[3]

Yours faithfully,
[T. S. E.]

1–TSE published another dialogue by Wolfe, 'English Bards and French Reviewers', in *NC* 5: 1 (Jan. 1927).

2–No poems by Brooks came out in *C.*

3–See 'The Maddermarket Theatre, Norwich', *C.* 3: 11 (Apr. 1925): an account of recent productions – Shakespeare, Restoration drama, Noh plays, Stravinski's *L'histoire du soldat* – mounted on the Elizabethan stage at this theatre.

1925

TO *H. Dugdale Sykes* CC

[?early January 1925] 23 Adelphi Terrace House

Dear Mr Sykes

I was very much pleased to receive your volume of Elizabethan studies and am glad for my own purposes to have so much of you in a collected form.[1] I shall try to do you justice in a review in the *Criterion*, but, as you probably know, I am no scholar in these subjects and the weight of my opinion will probably not be so valuable as the book deserves.[2]

Sincerely yours
[T. S. E.]

FROM *Geoffrey Faber* CC

2 January 1925 [London]

My dear Eliot

Thank you for yours of New Year's Eve.[3] I go to Eastbourne next Thursday, not Torquay – which is rather too long a journey. We pray for better weather. Write to me as soon as you are ready to do so. I shall be very interested to see the January number of the *Criterion*.

Yours sincerely
[Geoffrey C. Faber]

1–*Sidelights on Elizabethan Drama: A Series of Studies dealing with the Authorship of Sixteenth and Seventeenth Century Plays* (1924).
2–It was reviewed by J. M. Robertson in C. 3: 11 (Apr. 1925).
3–TSE's letter of 31 Dec. 1924 does not appear to survive.

TO *Scofield Thayer* TS Beinecke

6 January 1925 *The Criterion*,
23 Adelphi Terrace House

Dear Scofield,

I am very glad to get your letter of the 17th ultimo and receive the news of the latest *Dial* award with satisfaction. I will say something about it in the *Criterion*.[1] I certainly cannot think of any more suitable recipient amongst our nationality – assuming, of course, that Ezra Pound was always disqualified as being over the age limit. But in any case, Miss Moore's award is fully deserved: to my mind she has made a very definite contribution to verse form and rhythm, and there are not more than half a dozen people living of whom one can say as much. I have thought that she was in danger of becoming monotonous and I hope that she will take advantage of the prize by travelling about a bit!

As for the embryos of the contributions which I have promised you at various times, they lie most uncomfortably on my brain at night. The fact is that I have done no writing whatever for the last two years except the scrappy contributions and editorials which you may have seen from time to time in the *Criterion*.[2] This is, from my point of view, a lamentable condition and greatly to my disadvantage. Had I had the time or strength during these years for my writing beyond the above mentioned scraps, you would have been the first to receive specimens; the scraps themselves have been drops of blood out of an exhausted stone. For every reason I should like to appear before long in the *Dial*. I may be able to send you some prose in a few months and meanwhile here are the poems you have heard of and possibly a few more. The ones marked 'A' have appeared in Harold Monro's *Chapbook*; the ones marked 'B' will have appeared in the January *Criterion* before you receive this letter; the one marked 'C' is to appear in *Commerce*, a French review.[3] There is at least another one in the series

1–The *Dial* award 1925 was given to Marianne Moore for *Observations*. Thayer thought TSE should hear in advance because of his 'championship' of her.

2–Thayer was disappointed not to receive any of the 'many manuscripts' from TSE he had been allowed to hope for. Apart from contributions to C., the previous year TSE had published only one essay, 'A Prediction in Regard to Three Authors', in *Vanity Fair* 21: 6 (Feb. 1924) and one poem, 'Poème', in *Commerce* 3 (Winter 1924[/1925]). His last contribution to *The Dial* was 'Marianne Moore' in 75: 6 (Dec. 1923).

3–'Doris's Dream Songs', I 'Eyes that last I saw in tears', II 'The wind sprang up at four o'clock', III 'This is the dead land', *Chapbook* 39 ([Nov.] 1924); Three Poems: I 'Eyes I dare not meet in dreams', II 'Eyes that last I saw in tears', III 'The eyes are not here', C. 3: 10 (Jan. 1925); and 'We are the hollow men' in *Commerce* 3 (Winter 1924[/1925]).

which is not yet written.[1] If the fact of publication here is no obstacle I should be glad to see them in the *Dial*.[2] But I hope you will let me know about this as soon as you can.

Vivien and I reciprocate cordially with best wishes for 1925 and the hope of seeing you in London.

Yours ever
T. S. E.

TO *D. H. Lawrence* CC

6 January 1925 23 Adelphi Terrace House

Dear Sir

Mr Cobden-Sanderson has handed me your letter of the 1st ultimo. I am very glad to hear that you like the *Criterion*[3] and can say in return that I very much admire your two stories – the one which I have already published and the one which I have accepted, 'The Woman Who Rode Away', for publication not before June. I hope that you will be a frequent contributor.[4]

Yours faithfully
[T. S. E.]

TSE/IPF[5]

1–At this stage TSE seems to have conceived all these poems as part of the same 'series' ('The Hollow Men'), but two were later transferred to 'Minor Poems'.
2–'The Hollow Men', I–III, in *Dial* 78: 3 (Mar. 1925), became 'The Hollow Men', I, II and IV in the full sequence, in *P 1909–1925* (1925).
3–On 1 Dec. 1924, DHL told RC-S he was relieved that C. had 'got some guts' and was not another *Adelphi* or *London Mercury*.
4–In reply, DHL said he thought the Jan. number 'a disappointment. It's all bits and bobs, like the rest of the literary magazines, and with no real raison d'être.' He liked F. W. Bain's '1789' and Fernandez's 'The Experience of Newman', in C. 3: 9 (Oct. 1924), but doubted whether anybody cared now about *Hamlet* or arranged marriages ('The Naturalistic Theory of *Hamlet*' by J. M. Robertson and 'A Marriage has been Arranged' by G. A. Porterfield in the current issue). It bored him 'to turn the very pages': 'If you're a quarterly, damn it, you ought to be a lonely bird and a fighter.' He berated the review for being 'the old barn-hen stuff' and too '*literairy*'.
5–Irene Pearl Fassett habitually marked the letters she typed for TSE in this way.

TO *Richard Aldington* CC

6 January 1925 23 Adelphi Terrace House

My dear Richard

I am very glad that my information was of service to you. It comes from the chief enquiry agency which is used by all the banks and I think, therefore, is as reliable as information can possibly be. I hope that the business will have at least indirect consequences for you. I am very glad to hear that your mother is beginning to mellow and treat you as she should. The new company ought certainly to be a good thing if well managed, and I hope that this gift is a prelude to further benefactions.[1] I should welcome anything that relieved you from the necessity of doing so much editing and translating which seems to me to have reached a point beyond which it will only be a hindrance to your more important activities.

Your letter is full of good news and arrived at a moment when it was very welcome. I am delighted to hear about the Mystery Play.[2] It struck me that Harold Monro was in a mood of asperity at the moment; at any rate he did not appear to take chaffing very amiably. I must tell you in confidence that I am not altogether satisfied with him as a critic of poetry and I should be glad to have your opinion after you see the next *Criterion*.[3]

About [Orlo] Williams and [Cyril] Fall[s], I should like about a thousand words, but I will leave it to your discretion if you think the two books deserve less or more. I should prefer to publish the English Influence article in June.[4] Will that suit you? Also would you care to do a shortish review of Rodker's reprint of Ned Ward's *London Spy*?[5] It is a very nicely printed book. I think you will find something about Ned Ward in one of Whibley's books; if I can find the place for you I will let you have it.[6]

1 – RA had enquired about a firm called Botterel & Roche on behalf of his mother who was entering into a business arrangement with it. On 3 Jan., RA said she had also begun 'to do the right thing' by transferring to him his father's books, some old pewter, and some shares: it was the 'first step towards economic independence'.

2 – Monro had 'sneered' at RA's transl. of *The Mystery of the Nativity* (1924), but there had been a few performances, and copies of the book had been selling well.

3 – Monro's review of *Selected Poems of Emily Dickinson* (ed. Aiken) was in the current issue, *C.* 3: 10 (Jan. 1925), 322–5.

4 – RA's article on 'the English influence in France'.

5 – See RA's rev. of Ward, *The London Spy Compleat*, *C.* 3: 11 (Apr. 1925).

6 – CW discusses Ward (1667–1731) in 'An Underworld of Letters', in *Literary Studies*, which TSE had reviewed: 'The Local Flavour', *A.* (12 Dec. 1919). For Ward, see H. W. Troyer, *Ned Ward of Grubstreet: A Study of sub-literary London in the Eighteenth Century* (1946).

I am very glad to hear that you are on with *Vogue* again, both for your own sake and my own.[1] I feel that my mind is too rheumatic to compete with most of the brisk wits who shine in that paper, or else my critical conscience is too acute, and the presence of a scholar like yourself may make it easier for me to edge in. I should certainly accept any offer from *Vogue* if I knew what they wanted of me and was sure that I could do it, and I shall certainly accept your intervention. At any rate it is a resource which, if genuine, may be very important to me before long. I am very grateful for your generous solicitude.

As touching the third paragraph of your letter – I hope that you will be in town soon and can talk things over with me.[2]

Yours ever,
[T. S. E.]

TO *Messrs. Selfridge & Co. Ltd* — CC

7 January 1925 — 23 Adelphi Terrace House

Dear Sirs,

I enclose a copy of a letter which you wrote on the 22nd ultimo to a lady [IPF] who had made enquiries for the current number (i.e. the number published in October) of *The Criterion*.[3] You will observe that you express your regret that the current number is out of stock at the publishers. I have to point out that this statement is quite untrue, and furthermore, that Mr Cobden-Sanderson the publisher and all of his office staff state that they have received no enquiry from you. In the circumstances, therefore, it appears astonishing that you should have provided one of your customers with this piece of information without having any knowledge whatever. Apart from the impression which this piece of misinformation gives of your business methods, I consider that an explanation is called for. Such misinformation is extremely damaging to the periodical, and if such a

1 – RA said the '*Vogue* affair' had blown over, and he was unwilling to lose his 'job' there, since it paid so well; TSE would have no difficulty in getting £100 a year from *Vogue* if he wished, and that Miss Todd was very impressed by his position in the world of letters. (Dorothy Todd was editor of British *Vogue*, 1922–6.) The 'brisk wits' writing for *Vogue* at this time included VW, AH, Clive Bell, and Raymond Mortimer.

2 – Bruce Richmond had hinted at possible developments and changes in *C.*

3 – The letter from Selfridges of 22 Dec. was addressed to Mrs Fassett: 'With reference to your order for *The Criterion*, we much regret that the current number is now out of stock at the publishers. We shall be glad to know, therefore, if you wish us to keep it on order for you.'

mistake is repeated we shall be obliged to issue a statement ourselves denying such rumours.

Yours faithfully,
[T. S. E.]

TO *Richard Aldington* CC

7 January 1925 23 Adelphi Terrace House

My dear Richard,

My wife tells me that you rang up today to give me a message and that she suggested your telephoning to the Bank in order to save time. She is very sorry, now, that she did not take the message herself because, if you were able to telephone, you evidently found it impossible to get on to me. I was there until half past five but was out of my room a great deal and it is possible that someone may have forgotten to tell me that you rang up. I am very sorry indeed and hope you have written. I am disappointed and regret that you should have been in town and I not seen you.

Yours ever,
[T. S. E.]

TO *Muriel Ciolkowska*[1] CC

7 January 1925 23 Adelphi Terrace House

Dear Madame Ciolkowska,

I was much pleased to hear from you again after such a long time and have read your essay on Rosny[2] with great interest. I should like to publish it, but I am afraid that it will be difficult to fit it in. A Quarterly does not give much scope as the contents must always exhibit as much variety and balance as possible, and contributions of any particular kind are very much limited. The paper is practically filled for several numbers ahead. But if

1–Muriel Ciolkowska was the author of *Rodin* (1912) and later *Blameless Man* (1926), and had contributed to *Poetry*, *The Nation* and *The Egoist*. Nothing by her appeared in C.

2–J.-H. Rosny was the pseud. of the brothers Joseph H. H. Boex (1856–1940) and Séraphin J. F. Boex (1859–1948), joint authors of a series of novels and stories published in French between 1886 and 1909. After 1909, they published separately as J.-H. Rosny *aîné* and *jeune*. They are considered among the founders of modern science fiction. 'I have not mentioned Rosny Jeune,' announced Mrs Ciolkowska (4 Dec. 1924), 'because there really is no such writer, though there is still a person. He has had no literary connection with Rosny *aîné* for years and years.'

you care to leave the manuscript with me I shall be glad to keep it for some time. If, on the other hand, you wish to publish it elsewhere as soon as possible, please let me know.

With all good wishes for the New Year, and hoping to see you again in Paris,

Yours very truly,
[T. S. E.]

TO *C. K. Scott Moncrieff* CC

7 January 1925 23 Adelphi Terrace House

Dear Scott Moncrieff,

Thank you for your letter of the 27th ultimo. If your story is divided, your indication shall be scrupulously observed.[1] I had not heard of Lawrence's story, but the similarity of title is of no importance.[2]

I should very much like to have the first chance of your article on *Pirandello*. The time would do nicely. I should also be glad to see anything by Norman Douglas.[3] I am ashamed to say that I have never read anything he has written, so I cannot accept in advance. But I should be extremely interested. I am very much obliged to you for having thought of *The Criterion*.

With best wishes for the New Year,
[T. S. E.]

TSE/IPF

1 – Scott Moncrieff's 'Cousin Fanny and Cousin Annie', in *NC* 4: 2 & 3 (Apr. & June 1926).
2 – DHL published a story, 'Fanny and Annie', in *England, My England* (1922).
3 – Norman Douglas (1868–1952), travel writer, worked for a while at the Foreign Office; then for *Cornhill Magazine* and *English Review*; author of *Old Calabria* (1915) and *South Wind* (1942).

TO *Mark Van Doren*[1] TS Butler

7 January 1925

The Criterion,
23 Adelphi Terrace House

Dear Mr Van Doren,

I was very pleased to get your letter of the 28th November and thank you for what you say about my essays. I take the opportunity of thanking you for the pleasure your book on Dryden gave me, and of expressing my admiration for it.[2]

I shall be very glad to review your book of poems, and only hope that the review will not arrive too late to be of any use to you.[3] I hope to get it done within a week or two. I am a very slow writer, and in the pressure of my affairs I have hardly been able to do any writing at all during the last two years.

With all best wishes,

Sincerely yours
T. S. Eliot

TSE/IPF

TO *Hugh Walpole* MS Valerie Eliot

8 January 1925

The Criterion, 9 Clarence Gate Gdns

My dear Walpole

I am writing this only to ask you if you will please let me know *where* I may write to you? As I have a favour to ask in the form of a testimonial![4] I wish you would come to London sometimes. I have several times wanted to consult you.

What about James-and-Conrad essay?[5]

Sincerely yours
T. S. Eliot

1 – Mark Van Doren (1894–1972): US poet and critic; Professor of English at Columbia University, New York, 1920–59; literary editor of *The Nation* (New York), 1924–8.
2 – *The Poetry of Dryden* (1920), which TSE reviewed in 'John Dryden', *TLS* (9 June 1921): 'an admirable book . . . which every practitioner of English verse should study.'
3 – Van Doren, *Spring Thunder and Other Poems* (1924). TSE sent off his review on 26 Feb.
4 – In relation to his appointment at Faber & Gwyer.
5 – Walpole never wrote on James or Conrad for C.

TO *Aldous Huxley* CC

8 January 1925 23 Adelphi Terrace House

Dear Aldous

I was delighted to get your letter of the 19th December and to have at last a contribution from you; though I still hope that you will write the one which we discussed.[1] This one, however, shall go in as quickly as possible, I hope in the March number which I am just on the point of making up.[2] No sooner is one finished than another begins: I used to think that running a Quarterly ought to mean two months' leisure and one month's work, but I have found it literally continuous.

I agree with you that one can dispense with almost anything in return for sunlight, although your picture of Italy in winter makes me wonder where that part of the year ought to be spent.[3] I cannot say that I have any mature plans, and I console myself at this season by thinking that I should prefer the summer for accustoming myself to your climate.

I am afraid I have no news for you of any importance. It is true that the *Adelphi* group is in some disorder and I gather that Murry is now producing that periodical without the group of friends who formerly supported him.[4] But you will probably find Sullivan a mine of information on this subject.[5] He promised to come and see me before leaving for Italy in January, and if he does not do so I will ask you to reproach him for me. John Franklin, by the way, is Sydney Waterlow, who lunched with me today and on that occasion broke his usual custom of subsisting entirely on fruit and omelettes.[6] So you were right in believing that there are no new luminaries in the sky of letters which you have not yet marked.

I am sending you a copy of the new *Criterion* because I think you will find it considerably altered since you last saw the review. I think myself that it is very much better, but you can judge that with a more detached mind than I or anyone living in London.

1 – See AH's story, 'The Monocle' in *NC* 4: 1 (Jan. 1926). But presumably TSE is here regretting the non-appearance of the 'essay on Wit' mentioned in his letter to AH of 14 May 1923.
2 – Unidentified.
3 – The Huxleys lived in Montici, Florence, from Aug. 1923 until June 1925.
4 – In late 1924 there had been dissension among the sponsors of JMM's *Adelphi*, which was seen as a vehicle for JMM's views and Katherine Mansfield's literary remains. This led to Koteliansky resigning as business manager.
5 – J. W. N. Sullivan (1886–1937): Irish scientist. A close friend of JMM, he had been an assistant editor of *A.* and later wrote *Beethoven* (1927). In a letter of 25 Jan., AH described him as 'a most interesting man' and 'stimulating companion'.
6 – Sydney Waterlow (1878–1944), diplomat, reviewed for *NS* under the pseud. 'John Franklin'; see Glossary of Names.

If you ever come across any new Italian books that interest you, do let me have a note on them, and let us have your Italian impressions from time to time. I am really delighted to have this sketch and also to have the prospect of having your name on the cover at last.

The festive season being thankfully over, Vivien and I send you both our best wishes for the New Year.

Yours ever,
[T. S. E.]

TSE/IPF

TO *Wyndham Lewis* — MS Cornell

[early January? 1925] [London]

Dear Lewis

I'm afraid you were right. I looked it up and found Lawrence was just under 9000 words.[1] I do understand your difficulty and hope you understand mine – 15,000 is impossible without special preparation.[2] But we might be able to hold this MS. as a hostage as before. Certain circumstances which have arisen which make it impossible to say definitely *at the moment:* but I should like to see you one afternoon early next week. I'm *very* disappointed over this. I *particularly* wanted an article or some long thing by you this time. I have sent an American publisher named Boni[3] (*no* longer connected with Liveright) to see you.

About Arch[4]– You will have something else in the Spring? We'll discuss that when we meet.

Yrs
T. S. E.

1–DHL, 'Jimmy and the Desperate Woman', for C. 3: 9 (Oct. 1924), 15–42.
2–Prob. a ref. to 'The Perfect Action', the 20,000 word MS Lewis left with C. in Dec.
3–*TWL* was published in the USA by Boni & Liveright (1922). Albert Boni had left the firm and founded another publishing house with his brother. WL was seeking potential publishers.
4–Prob. *Archie*, one of WL's many projected books. In a letter to EP (29 Apr. 1925), WL mentions it being 'complete' and 'thirty or forty thousand' words long. According to O'Keeffe, this lost novel 'followed the fortunes of a Jewish pupil at Joint's school and his relationship with his father in the East End of London' (*Some Sort of Genius*, 258).

TO *Messrs. Watson & Austin* CC

13 January 1925 23 Adelphi Terrace House

Dear Sirs,

I have just discovered with great regret that owing to the pressure of business and absence from town, your letter of the 1st instant has remained unanswered. I have known Mr Wyndham Lewis for many years. While I have no knowledge of his financial position, I can assure you that Mr Lewis is one of the most eminent painters and writers of the day and has a reputation amongst amateurs of these arts throughout the world.

These facts speak for themselves. As far as I know Mr Lewis should be a desirable tenant.[1] In all dealings that I have had with him I have found him highly honourable.

Yours faithfully,
[T. S. E.]

TO *Messrs. Selfridge & Co. Ltd* CC

13 January 1925 23 Adelphi Terrace House

Dear Sirs,

I have your letter of the 9th instant in reply to mine of the 7th instant.[2] I am interested in your explanation but hardly agree with the adjective which you employ. It was certainly 'excusable' for your messenger to be at the moment destitute of petty cash; and it would have been 'excusable' also if you had informed your customer that you had been unable to obtain *The Criterion* for her because your messenger was not provided with petty cash; but it does not appear to me 'excusable' to inform your customer that *The Criterion* was out of stock at the publishers when *The Criterion* was in stock at the publishers, and when the only reason for your not obtaining it was that your representative did not have the money to pay for it.

1–WL was evicted from his studio in 44 Holland Street in early 1925 for non-payment of rent. WL later vented anger about the lateness of TSE's reference on his behalf.

2–Selfridge & Co. Ltd had replied (9 Jan. 1925): 'We understand that a collector was sent for the copy, but Messrs. Simpkin Marshall were out of stock – at least they told our messenger so. He then went to your office at Thavies Inn and applied for a copy for Selfridge's but was not supplied as he was unable at that time to pay cash for it; unfortunately, he had used his petty cash prior to reaching the office. In all the circumstances, especially at a particularly busy season when the collector was more than ordinarily busy, we think you will agree that the letter to the customer was more or less excusable.'

I should suggest, without prejudice, that the substitution of a false explanation for a true one, whether deliberate or inadvertent, is a fact demanding explanation, and your letter of the 9th instant leaves your conduct in this matter more curious than before. Moreover, you have failed to give us any assurance that on future occasions your messenger will be provided with sufficient pocket money.

I have dictated the foregoing on the assumption that the statements contained in your letter of the 9th instant are correct. I would remind you, however, of my previous observation that neither Mr Cobden-Sanderson nor any of his staff has any recollection of your representative having called.

Yours faithfully,
[T. S. E.]

TO *E. M. Forster* CC

14 January 1925 23 Adelphi Terrace House

Dear Forster,

I have your letter and I am very glad to hear from you. I wish that people would write more frequently to express their opinions.[1] As for the *Rimbaud*, I only glanced through the book myself, but it did not impress me very favourably. Rimbaud happens to be an author whom I know pretty well and the translation struck me as bad.[2] I find that Flint's opinion of the book is supported by a reviewer in a recent number of the *Dial*, whose review is longer and consequently more thoroughly damaging.[3] But unless I hear from you to the contrary, I shall send your letter on to Flint as he might be interested to reply.[4]

I do hope you will have something to offer us before long.[5]

Yours sincerely,

1–On 12 Jan., Forster wrote to protest against F. S. Flint's 'scathing review' of Edgell Rickword's *Rimbaud: The Boy and the Poet*, in C. 3: 10 (Jan. 1925), 329–30. Forster said that 'the victim' was a 'young writer'; and while he knew 'little of Rimbaud', he found the book 'thrilling as a story, sound in psychology, and admirable in shape'.

2–Acc. to Edward J. H. Greene, TSE said that in his early work Rimbaud had 'une influence de plus et plus importante' ['a more and more important influence'] on him; he had read Rimbaud several times after the influence of Laforgue waned (*T. S. Eliot et la France* [1951], 63).

3–Lewis Galantière, 'The Problem of Rimbaud', *Dial* 78: 1 (Jan. 1925), 54–9.

4–Forster replied (18 Jan.) that he was 'an absolute outsider in the matter of French literature, and didn't want the letter to go directly to Flint'. If TSE thought it deserved notice, he would write to Flint directly.

5–Forster contributed 'The Novels of Virginia Woolf' to *NC* 4: 2 (Apr. 1926).

The above letter was dictated by Mr Eliot who was taken ill last night. In his absence I am talking the liberty of signing it on his behalf.

[I. P. Fassett][1]

Vivien Eliot TO *Mary Hutchinson* MS Texas

Monday [?19 January 1925] 9 Clarence Gate Gdns

My dear Mary

Thank you *very* much for bringing all those beautiful violets and snowdrops. It was charming of you. I wish I had seen you, but I could not have uttered a word yesterday as it happened. Tom has not been so well – it is not only influenza, of course! He has been working in a dark airless basement for the last six months and I think it has quite seriously affected his health. I am praying that *this* breakdown will bring our troubles to an end.

You must have had a fearful time moving into your new house. It sounded too awful. I am looking forward to seeing the house, but I feel it *can't* be as nice as River House, which I shall always regret!

Tom has seen no-one yet – he may not. I want to get him away to the country as quickly as possible, but the doctor does not think he is ready yet.

With love, and so many thanks from both of us for being so very kind.

Yrs,
V. H. E.

TO *Conrad Aiken* MS Huntington

Monday [26 January 1925] *The Criterion*, 17 Thavies Inn

Dear Conrad

Delighted to have your admirable review.[2] *Hope* you will do Huxley.[3]

Not yet up to reading stories.[4] Sit up a bit every day, but very weak.

1 – IPF reviewed Forster's *A Passage to India* in *C.* 3: 9 (Oct. 1924): 'Mr Forster is so very clever – what is it that his work lacks? What is it that we miss in *Passage to India*? Something that could lift it above the level of Sound Contemporary Fiction where it must inevitably lie' (138).

2 – Of Theodora Bosanquet, *Henry James at Work*, and Walt Whitman, *Criticism*, in *C.* 3: 11 (Apr. 1925), 465–8.

3 – Aiken's review of AH's *Those Barren Leaves* appeared in the same issue, 449–52.

4 – On 14 Jan., Aiken offered TSE a '*very* good short story'. His book of stories, *Bring! Bring!* (1925), was about to be set up, but he would hold it until he heard from TSE.

Drs. want to send me away for three weeks when I can get out. So I *might* be charmed to make a detour and burst in on you for two days at Rye (as p.g.) if that mention of a spare bedroom was sincere.[1]

But I am no use tomorrow.

Yours ever
T. S. E.

Would have asked you to do Richards for us, but Read asked for it long ago[2] –
Have read you in *Nation*.[3]
Shd like to discuss Read's article with you.[4]

TO *Aldous Huxley* CC

27 January 1925 23 Adelphi Terrace House

Dear Aldous,

Thank you for your letter of the 19th instant enclosing an essay on *Breughel*.[5] For several reasons, however, I prefer the previous essay which has gone to the printers.[6] Also, I am rather puzzled by your not mentioning the fact that there were several Breughels, all of whom are good, and who are difficult for the ordinary observer to distinguish from each other. No doubt you know a great deal more about the Breughels than I do, but I was tremendously interested in their painting ten years ago when I was in Belgium.[7]

1–Aiken moved from Winchelsea to Jeake's House, Rye, East Sussex, the previous year.
2–HR reviewed I. A. Richards, *Principles of Literary Criticism*, in C. 3: 1 (Apr. 1925), 444–9. While sceptical about Richards's 'frank acceptance of utilitarian or prudential ethics', he called it 'an important contribution to the rehabilitation of English criticism – perhaps, because of its sustained scientific nature, the most important contribution yet made'. TSE was to take up the debate with Richards in 'Literature, Science and Dogma', *Dial* 82: 3 (Mar. 1927).
3–Aiken reviewed I. A. Richards's book in *N&A* 36: 17 (24 Jan. 1925), 585–6.
4–Aiken wrote, 'Curse you for printing Read after rejecting my own treatment of that matter.' Referring to HR's 'Psycho-analysis and the Critic', C. 3: 10 (Jan. 1925). Aiken called HR's article 'more painstaking' than his own but 'less comprehensive and perceptive'.
5–See AH, 'Breughel' in *Along the Road: Notes and Essays of a Tourist* (1925).
6–This unidentified essay never appeared.
7–The most famous of the family was Pieter Breughel the Elder (*c*.1525–69), whose 'Census at Bethlehem', 'Fall of Icarus' and 'Massacre of the Innocents' TSE would have seen in Brussels in 1914. His sons Pieter Breughel the Younger (1564–1636) and Jan Breughel the Elder (1568–1625) were also painters. AH responded (30 Jan.) that there were 'of course three considerable Breughels', but that it was 'only the elder who counts'.

It might be suitable for Rickword's magazine[1] and for many others.

Considering the fact that both Vivien and I took the trouble to write very nice letters to you, in the midst of a life in which any sort of correspondence is almost impossible, your reply of the 19th seems to me inadequate.

Sincerely yours,
[T. S. E.]

TSE/IPF

TO *Conrad Aiken* PC Huntington

[30? January 1925] [9 Clarence Gate Gdns]

Very many thanks indeed.[2] I have had a sort of setback and don't know when I shall be out, and will write again. I have been shuddering over your stories, which have a terrible frisson.[3] How do you do it?

Unable to write, and very sick of myself.

T. S. E.

Look forward to seeing you.

TO *Wyndham Lewis* TS Cornell

31 January 1925 9 Clarence Gate Gdns

Dear Lewis

I have your letter dated the 30th January. You are certainly entitled to some explanation of the advertisement in question, and the tone of your letter seems to call for a clear statement of my attitude in this matter. The notice of 'The Perfect Action' was to have been followed by a letter to you which was unfortunately prevented by my illness; from which, as a matter

1–*Calendar of Modern Letters*: a literary journal (1925–7), founded by Edgell Rickword, Douglas Garman and Bertram Higgins. AH's 'Breughel' appeared in 1: 6 (Aug. 1925), 417–28.

2–Aiken said he would be glad to review AH, *Those Barren Leaves*: see *C.* 3: 11 (Apr. 1925).

3–Aiken had sent TSE three stories, 'Hey, Taxi', 'The Anniversary', and 'Bring! Bring!' They came out in *Bring! Bring!* (1925), reviewed by Edwin Muir in *C.* 3: 12 (July 1925). According to Muir, Aiken touched 'the fringe of a whole section of modern experience', working on 'the mass of data about the unconscious which psychoanalysis has discovered'.

of fact, I have not yet recovered.[1] The point is this. You will remember that I have repeatedly expressed my desire that there should be a contribution of some kind from you in every number of the *Criterion*; that is to say a chronicle and also a review (whenever any books appeared which you wished to review) in every number and a leading essay or piece of fiction as well in two numbers out of four. This is more than I care to take from any other contributor. Apart from the benefits of this regularity to the review and the benefits (upon which you will of course put your own valuation) to yourself, I had always in mind the benefit to us collectively. That is to say, there are as you are quite well aware a number of people who would be glad to see and to instrument any possible separation or disagreement between us for their own purposes. Such separation, or even the report of it, would I believe be harmful not only to ourselves but to the public good. The last number unfortunately contained nothing from you except a book review, which, although a valuable piece of writing and given the first place among the reviews, was not in my mind sufficient to keep the association before the public mind.[2] I therefore advertised the contribution from you for the next number and gave it the name which I had. I had proposed to write to you urging you, if you could not put the contribution into available form for the *Criterion*, to find or to write something of a possible length. I think that I made clear to you and that you understood that with the present resources of the *Criterion* it was impossible to publish contributions of this length from anyone whomsoever. I am quite well aware that you wish to devote the whole of your attention to the preparation of your books. I think that you ought to be convinced by this time that I have wished to do everything in my power to assist in the speedy completion and publication of your principal book. You will remember that on every occasion on which I have seen you, you have said that your book would be ready for the publishers within a week

1–On 22 Jan., WL asked IPF whether he could revise 'The Perfect Action' and if it would appear complete. She replied the following day on behalf of TSE, who was ill, to say WL could make revisions but they could use only 6,000 words. To TSE on 30 Jan., WL wrote: 'You advertised my article as appearing in the forthcoming number of the *Criterion* but Miss Fassett tells me you do not intend printing it after all . . . I hope the following statement will simplify matters. 1) "The Perfect Action" is no longer available for publication in the *Criterion*. I have just sold it to another paper. 2) You have still various fragments of mine, such as the Lenten Party. These fragments are no longer at your disposal for publication in the *Criterion*.' He would regard any attempt to publish these pieces as 'treachery rather than a harmless trick, or as the inadvertence of a harassed man' (*Letters of Wyndham Lewis*, 149). 'The Perfect Action' was an earlier title for 'The Dithyrambic Spectator', later published in book form as part of *The Diabolical Principle and the Dithyrambic Spectator* (1931).

2–WL's review of W. H. R. Rivers, *Medicine, Magic and Religion*, in C. 3: 10 (Jan. 1925).

or two, and that I have urged you to finish this book and get it published as quickly as was possible, and that this has gone on for some months. Everyone has his own methods of work and no one is entitled to say that another person's methods are mistaken. But I have felt very strongly that it would be in your own interest to concentrate on one book at a time and not plan eight or ten books at once, and I have endeavoured to intimate this.[1] On the other hand you are certainly entitled to respect, and you certainly have mine, for making every sacrifice to devote yourself to your main work and not disperse your activity.[2] But the dispersing in one direction seems to me possibly as unwise as a dispersal in another would be. And I cannot help feeling that it is possible, with organisation, for a man who is not engaged in any outside business merely for his livelihood to write a book and at the same time do a certain amount of current journalism without damage to his work and with advantage to his pocket. You will remember that I have occasionally mentioned to you American periodicals which pay well and would be glad to publish pieces of work from you on the subjects in which you have been interesting yourself. I have also assured you that, so far as the means of the paper permitted, you should receive better terms of payment than other contributors. Under present conditions even the ordinary rates are only made possible by my taking no salary or other remuneration for running the magazine. I only mention this fact because my friends seem sometimes to ignore it.

Please do not think that I am pressing upon you, in the manner of one of our friends whose name I need not mention, a reminder of supposed services.[3] I consider that anything I do is equalised by any support which you give to the *Criterion*. Furthermore I am not an individual but an instrument, and anything I do is in the interest of art and literature and civilisation, and is not a matter for personal compensation. But in the circumstances I cannot help feeling that your letter expressed an unjustified suspiciousness. I am unable to interpret your remark about your fragments finding their way into other hands than mine in any other way.[4]

1–WL was working on *Archie*, *Joint* and *The Man of the World*, none of which was finished. His next published books were *The Art of Being Ruled* (1926) and *The Lion and the Fox* (1927).
2–In an earlier Jan. letter WL wrote: 'I have quarrelled with almost everybody in order to get the money and time to write this and other books: and I have really worked very hard. My gesture, at the moment, may seem a foolish one (people are angry, and in consequence laugh): But there is an old saying, he laughs best who laughs last.'
3–Presumably SS (see TSE's letter of 12 Nov. 1924).
4–On 30 Jan., WL wrote: 'Should any of these fragments find their way into other hands than yours . . . I shall regard it as treachery.'

You say that your letter is not intended to be unfriendly and mine is certainly not so intended. If you are unable to do any work for the *Criterion* for an indefinite period, it will be very much to my disappointment and regret. I shall be very glad to know for the immediate future whether you prefer not to write at all or whether you care to continue the Art Chronicle and reviews for the next number.[1] If not, I can only wait until you have more leisure.

Charles Whibley is leaving England for some time on the 27th February, so if you want to get in touch with Macmillan's I should urge you to communicate with him as quickly as possible.[2]

I am still far from recovered from my influenza and my doctors wish me to go away for several weeks as soon as I have sufficient strength, but any correspondence from you would be forwarded. And if you feel any definite grievance in consequence of my behaviour I should be glad if you would make it clearer.

Yours,
T. S. Eliot

If you cannot review in any way the four books which you have I should be glad if you would write to my secretary and leave them ready at your house to be called for. I should of course much prefer to have a short notice of them from you.

TO *Hugh Walpole* — MS Valerie Eliot

2 February [1925] — 9 Clarence Gate Gdns

My dear Walpole,

This is merely to say that I am very glad that the first visit in my convalescence was yours, as it cheered me up particularly: and also to thank you – more distinctly than I did at the time – for your interest and encouragement. If a few more people took so practical an interest I should have no fears for the future of the *Criterion* – or at least of the same paper under a different name.[3]

1 – Lewis had written two 'Art Chronicles', for C. 2: 8 (July 1924) and 3: 9 (Oct. 1924). After his review in C. 3: 10 (Jan. 1925) and the present quarrel, WL published only one more piece, 'The Values of the Doctrine behind "Subjective" Art', in *NC* 6: 1 (July 1927).

2 – See WL's letter to CW, Mar. 1925 (*Letters of Wyndham Lewis*, 154–5).

3 – Faber proposed that his firm should publish a new quarterly under TSE's editorship.

Of course the new scheme must be kept quite in confidence – it's all very harassing. But my health, the doctor tells me, won't stand work in a dark basement indefinitely, or much longer.[1]

Will you do the James when you get back?[2] And meanwhile enjoy Egypt. And the testimonial [for TSE] will be as valuable as anyone's can be.

Sincerely yours
T. S. Eliot.

TO *Virginia Woolf*

MS Texas

4 February [1925] *The Criterion*, 17 Thavies Inn

My dear Virginia,

It is time that I wrote to thank you for your last letter. I am rather in the doldrums at present – I feel like a shell with no machinery in it, the moment I try to use my mind at all; it's no use, and then up goes the temperature. And Vivien is worse than I am by far, besides having to suffer now for the anxiety and strain of the first ten days of my illness. But as for *me*, I am to be congratulated rather than condoled with, as this has released me from the basement for a month.

Anyway, I wish that I could write as charming and perfect letters under influenza as you do. I don't know whether you are in London. I hope at Rodmell. Now what we want – again! – is a cottage, a barn, a stable, or a shed, or even a bit of land on which a sectional bungalow could be put up – it doesn't matter what, so long as it is in the *country*, and is *cheap*. Ever since we have been without even that miserable place at Fishbourne we have pined more and more. It's the only way to get out of London – however miserable, we want something of our own.[3] So if you *hear* of anything, or *can find* anything . . . . We only want to go and live in the country, and if Lady R. would only provide a possible salary – which is not to be hoped – we should go at once.

1 – TSE's offices at Lloyds Bank in Henrietta Street were below ground level. I. A. Richards visited him there: 'Within a foot of our heads when we stood were the thick, green glass squares of the pavement on which hammered all but incessantly the heels of the passers-by. There was just room for two perches beside the table' (*T. S. Eliot: The Man and His Work*, ed. Tate, 9–10).
2 – Walpole had been a friend of Henry James, but no such piece on James appeared.
3 – The Eliots had abandoned their cottage in Fishbourne the previous summer. VW wrote to RA on 16 Feb.: 'every letter I have had from Tom or Vivien lately has reiterated their desire to have a country cottage and his belief that most of their ill health is due to their not having one' (Woolf, *Letters*, III, 170).

Do let us know as soon as you return, and I hope we shall be fit to see and be seen – I want news of your work and of the Press. I was very pleased to hear Keynes's opinion of the Dryden[1] and flattered, but I will wager you 10/- that Mr Bennett[2] sells out first (what an advertisement for the actual Mr B. by the way).

V sends love.

Yours ever
T. S. E.

Don't lend us Rodmell – we want a *hovel of our own*, not the *House* of friends! I hope Leonard has escaped the flu.

FROM *Hugh Walpole* — TS Houghton

4 February 1925 — 90 Piccadilly, London W.1

My dear Eliot,

Forgive this typewritten note. I hope the enclosed letter[3] is what you require, it is at any rate absolutely sincere. Do look after your health; if I may say so without presumption your continued ability to do your work (critical and literary, not financial) is of great importance to a great many of us. You know that I will do anything in the world I can to help.

Yours ever,
Hugh Walpole

Vita Nicolson[4] was talking much of you yesterday. I think she'd help later if needed.

TO *Hugh Walpole* — MS Valerie Eliot

4 February [1925][5] — *The Criterion*, 17 Thavies Inn

My dear Walpole

Your letter is *absolutely perfect* for my purposes. It is so fine that I could hardly believe it was about myself. It is exactly what is wanted, and, a few

1 – *HJD* was published in the Hogarth Essays series the previous Oct.
2 – VW's 'Mr Bennett and Mrs Brown', the first of the Hogarth Essays.
3 – Hugh Walpole's letter of 4 Feb. is quoted in full in GCF's memorandum, 'Proposed publication of a Quarterly Review', 5 Apr. 1925, below.
4 – Vita Sackville West (1892–1962), English poet and novelist, married in 1913 the diplomat and writer Harold Nicolson (1886–1968).
5 – Misdated 3 Feb.

more, even half as enthusiastic, would make this a certainty. I cannot tell you how grateful I am for all your support including this letter. You've been a tremendous help to me. *Thank you again with all my heart.*

Of course I want as many as I can get – but I shall not get any to delight me so much as this, or to do me so much good.

I hope to see you as soon as you return? Please let me know. And *bon voyage.*

Yours ever
T. S. Eliot

I don't think I have ever met Vita Nicolson but have often heard of her.

TO *J. M. Robertson* CC

10 February 1925 9 Clarence Gate Gdns

My dear Mr Robertson,

My only justification for asking you the following favour is the paradoxical but practical reason that you have always been so kind to me in the past and have given me so much help and encouragement with the *Criterion*. In connection with a project about which the projectors wish me at present to give no details, but the nature of which will be sufficiently manifest, I should be extremely grateful if you could let me have some sort of letter stating anything favourable that you can honestly say of my abilities as an editor so far as they are visible to you. I do not so much need reference to anything I have done in verse or criticism, but rather to my capacity for running a magazine, business sense as an editor, and catholicity and discrimination in selection and composition of a review. For the purposes in question I do not wish to emphasise the appeal to a limited or exclusively intellectual audience, but if possible to a union of high standards with breadth of appeal.

This project, if it comes off, may improve my situation: I am reaching the point when it will no longer be possible for me to continue to be an editor and at the same time earn my living in the city. I am just recovering from a very severe attack of influenza and breakdown which will have kept me away from work for at least two months and my strength is no longer what it once was. I have been running the *Criterion* without remuneration and this position cannot very long be maintained.

I should feel distressed if this request embarrassed you, and I do not want to ask you for anything more than you can easily say. But I have ascertained that a word from you, together with others which I have received or shall receive, is one that would impress the group of people concerned. Of course for the present this project is wholly confidential and I have only mentioned it to the people whose testimonials I have asked for and particularly desire.

I hope, in any case, that you will forgive this importunity.

With very many thanks,

I am
Sincerely yours,
[T. S. E.]

TO *Wyndham Lewis*

TS Cornell

11 February 1925 — 9 Clarence Gate Gdns

Dear Lewis,

As I am unable to attend to much correspondence at present – indeed my last letter to you was much the longest that I have yet written – your letter of the 4th instant has remained unanswered for a week. I am sorry to find that your letter does not appear to me to deal satisfactorily with the points that I raised and I am sorry that your renewed assertion that you have no wish to be on anything but friendly terms is not embodied in a more friendly letter. You say that in the circumstances you do not care to continue your Art Chronicle, but you do not specify what the circumstances are, and it is not clear whether you imply any other reasons except lack of time, nor do I know what you mean by suggesting that I understand better than you do yourself why you have been compelled to the 'slight readjustment' which seems to mean declining to contribute regularly to the *Criterion*. I had certainly supposed that you were in contact with certain persons who would be pleased to find that you were no longer a contributor to the *Criterion*. Your denial of this fact leaves nothing more to be said.

You give no reason for wishing to have your name omitted from reviews. Your wish shall on this occasion be respected unless you prefer not to do the reviews at all, in which case I should be obliged for the return of the books. But I cannot understand your motive and the fact that you state none seems in itself an indication that you do not wish to be closely associated with myself or the other reviewers in the *Criterion*.

The tone of your two letters strongly suggests a definite grudge which you have not disclaimed. If you prefer to keep your reasons to yourself and merely adopt a mysterious and truculent manner, there is nothing more to be said.

Yours etcetera,
T. S. Eliot

TO *Herbert Read* TS Victoria

12 February 1925 *The Criterion*, 9 Clarence Gate Gdns

My dear Read,

The secretary has just shown me your letter of the 28th January.[1] I am very grateful to you indeed. As a matter of fact the material for the number was already in hand and arranged except for the reviews to come in which is a simple matter. So I do not think that there will be more than I can do or direct. But I am particularly grateful because I have often thought that in case of emergency I might want to call upon *you*, and now I feel that I *can* do so.

I should have gone to the country but my temperature is still very irregular and I am very weak. If I am in town and about before I return to work I shall hope to seek you out and have a leisurely meeting.

I am looking forward to reading your review of Richards.[2] If you don't want the copy of Ward's book I should be glad to see it, but there is no hurry because at present I can read very little.

With very grateful thanks,

Yours ever,
T. S. E.

TO *Conrad Aiken* TS Huntington

13 February 1925 9 Clarence Gate Gdns

My dear Conrad,

Thank you very much for the review of Huxley which is brilliant, eminently just, and covers the ground perfectly.[3] I have been meaning to

1–Worried that TSE's illness might delay publication of *C.*, HR offered to help.

2–HR reviewed I. A. Richards, *Principles of Literary Criticism*, and Stephen Ward, *Ethics: An Historical Introduction*, in *C.* 3: 11 (Apr. 1925).

3–Conrad Aiken, rev. of 'Aldous Huxley, *Those Barren Leaves*, *C.* 3: 11 (Apr. 1925). Though Aiken was wary of AH's 'incessantly frivolous' satire, blending the 'ingenious *morbidezza* of the "nineties" with the very latest fashions . . . from Paris and Vienna', he thought *Those Barren Leaves* AH's 'best work', and that it marked 'the sharpest single advance that he has made'.

write to you about your stories. I should like very much to use 'Hey, Taxi!', but I find that it will be impossible to get it in until October. The last number was so big and expensive that the next one must be smaller and I am having to postpone several contributions which should have gone in because of the length of time I have had them. In June I must publish two long stories, one by D. H. Lawrence, which I cannot afford to postpone because of the complication of American rights.[1] Will you let me know if there is any chance of October not being too late, as I should like to use it. I select this one not only because I like it but because the others, if published separately, would be more difficult for the English public to understand. I do hope you will let me use this and should like to know soon.[2]

It does not look as if I should be able to pay my long looked-forward-to visit to you for some time. I am still too variable in temperature to risk visits, my wife has broken down as the result of the long strain, and finally our servant seems to be on the verge of bronchitis. So as there is not much time remaining, I shall probably have to cancel all my visits, except possibly a short one to Cambridge which is principally a matter of business.[3] But I hope it may be possible for me to run down for a weekend with you either at the end of my leave or shortly after, if that is convenient. It seems to me that we have not had a proper conversation for ten years.[4]

Yours ever,
T. S. E.

TSE/IPF

<Your card just arrived. Have written to printers to return MS. to you. Send it back *soon*.>

TO *Herbert Read* — TS Victoria

16 February [1925] — *The Criterion*, 9 Clarence Gate Gdns

My dear Read,

Thank you again, for your last letter. It gave me much pleasure.

1 – DHL, 'The Woman Who Rode Away I', and JJ, 'Fragment of an Unpublished Work' (an extract from what would become *Finnegans Wake*) appeared in *C.* 3: 12 (July 1925).

2 – Aiken's story was published in *Bring! Bring!* (1925), too early for publication in *C.*

3 – See letter to JMM, 20 Feb.

4 – Aiken recalled that during the winter of 1921–2 he and TSE lunched together 'two or three times a week' (*T. S. Eliot: The Man and His Work*, 196).

I have read some of the chapters of Richards' book,[1] but cannot read very much yet. I found it hard going; it is badly organised, and I find the uncoordinated short chapters very bothering. I should like to talk or write to you about it again later. I have the same racial prejudice myself; and I am always inclined to suspect the racial envy and jealousy which makes that people inclined to bolshevism in some form (not always political) though I suspect something of this destructive instinct in Disraeli, in spite of the conventional Tory exaltation of him.[2]

Many thanks again.

Yours ever,
T. S. E.

TO *Mary Hutchinson* MS Texas

20 February [1925] 9 Clarence Gate Gdns

My dear Mary

I have had in mind to drop you a line for some time, but even cutting it down to the minimum I have had a certain amount of correspondence to deal with in one way or another each day, and quite enough of this business of family letter writing to exhaust one's energy. I am getting on, except for extreme feebleness of body and spirit. Vivien has been *very* ill – much iller than she realised or yet realises. Yesterday she seemed better, today I am not so sure, and it will be a long time before we see daylight. Meanwhile keep me in your mind as we do you.

Affectionately
Tom.

1–TSE later described *Principles of Literary Criticism*, by I. A. Richards (1924), as 'a milestone, though not an altogether satisfactory one'. Richards 'had difficult things to say' but 'had not wholly mastered the art of saying them' ('Literature, Science, and Dogma', *Dial* 82: 3 [Mar. 1927], 239).

2–HR's letter appears to be missing. In his 'Disraeli', F. W. Bain argued that Disraeli was 'the last great Tory leader': he had a 'passionate belief in his own race'; and 'in all his life, in all his works, he stood up for the Jews', C. 2: 6 (Feb. 1924).

FROM *Bruce Richmond* MS Valerie Eliot

20 February 1925 *The Times*, Printing House Square, London E.C.4

I have read *The Criterion* regularly, and have great pleasure in bearing testimony to the qualities shewn by its Editor. Mr Eliot has succeeded in impressing upon the paper as a whole the stamp of his own taste and intellectual keenness which, in a paper consisting mainly of signed contributions from writers who have their own firmly defined points of view, is difficult to do. He obviously has a full sense of the value of variety. For the uniformity of quality in *The Criterion* was never allowed to become monotony – either of subject-matter or of critical reaction. Mr Eliot found a place both for young new writers and for authors of established reputation. Technical literary and artistic criticism has been well balanced by historical & philosophical studies; and *The Criterion* has escaped the peril of making its readers feel that they have entered into a library. Mr Eliot has shown particularly in his choice of fiction that his sympathy is wide: he has published stories which would be read with pleasure by the 'general public' and has insisted only on a high level of workmanship as the necessary qualification for admission to *The Criterion*. It is reasonable to predict that the broadening of interest which has been a marked feature in the course of *The Criterion* would increase if he were called on to direct a paper of a less severely critical type. Though one would feel confident that, whatever variety and enlargement of interests he came to shew, he would retain as an editor the intellectual keenness as well as the integrity and solidarity of judgment which have been remarkable from his earliest days of writing.

TO *Ottoline Morrell* MS Texas

20 February [1925] 9 Clarence Gate Gdns

Dear Ottoline

I have a sure conviction that I offended you. I am not sure in what way, but I know it is so. I find (and Vivien finds) such silent estrangement unendurable. Will you not write and frankly? Because I have *never* had any desire or intention to hurt you in any way. This is much on my mind.

We have been very ill. I am still almost confined to the house, after six weeks of influenza, and it will be several weeks more before I can take up any work. I cannot read more than a few minutes and only write a few necessary notes. Some part of my strength, I know, has left me forever. Vivien collapsed just a fortnight ago – my illness coming on top of a very hard and worrying winter of great strain and anxiety. She simply got out of bed and fell down – both exhaustion of body and spirit like two years ago. Yesterday I thought she was better; today I am not sure. Even a few minutes' conversation sends her temperature up.

Affectionately
Tom.

I should like to know how you are.[1]

TO *John Middleton Murry* — MS Valerie Eliot

20 February [1925] — 9 Clarence Gate Gdns

Dear John

I do indeed appreciate your kindness in suggesting me for the Lectures at Cambridge.[2] I think it ~~likely~~ almost certain that I should accept. £200 would make ~~a vast~~ just all the difference to my inclination to jump out into the world this year – and the appointment is very attractive. Meanwhile could you let me know the terms and conditions – i.e. *subject* of lectures, expenses /whether one is put up at Trinity, whether fares paid etc – and anything else – whether it is definitely during the winter term? Yes, I *think* I should accept. *How soon would the offer be made, if at all?*

And in any case, I think it very kind of you – <a very feeble expression.> I should want to think a little, but I believe I should accept. It would get one through the first year.

I want to see you again before long.

Tom

1 – Acc. to her biographer, OM was depressed because she and her husband had temporarily moved out of Garsington into Black Hall in Oxford, which she hated. Her plan to take a house in St Leonard's Terrace in London also fell through in Feb. due to the influence of Logan Pearsall Smith and Alys Russell (Miranda Seymour, *Life on the Grand Scale*, 339).

2 – The Clark Lectures were inaugurated in 1884, with an endowment of £300 per year by a Fellow of Trinity College, William George Clark (1821–78). JMM gave lectures on 'Keats and Shakespeare' (1924–5): published as *Keats and Shakespeare* (1925), and reviewed by Orlo Williams in *NC* 4: 1 (Jan. 1926), 193–5. It was JMM, the vocal apologist for Romanticism, who nominated TSE, the proponent of Classicism, as his successor. The decision was the responsibility of Trinity College Council, who initially nominated one of their own Fellows, A. E. Housman, but ultimately opted for TSE.

<The incoherence of this letter shows the state of my mind.> V. is rather weaker again, after a bad night. She sends a message – will you keep her in your thoughts as much as possible, as she feels that does her good. She is feeling dreadfully ill and in extremity of body.
You must have *realised* that your proposal of my name, and the hope of this job, would come as a ray of hope just at the *blackest moment in my life*. I think there is no doubt I should accept.

TO *John Middleton Murry* — MS Valerie Eliot

[22? February 1925] 9 Clarence Gate Gdns

Dear John

Your *second* letter has just arrived. The answers are simple:

1. I should accept.

2. The subject you suggest was of course an intuition on your part. What I am aching to do <if acceptable> is to take the 17th C. metaphysicals (not only the poets, but the Cambridge platonists) and compare and contrast them with Dante and his school (Guido, Cino etc) and this wd be a big job – and primarily for the 'hypothetical'. What you say merely convinces me that I want to do this.[1]

And now I am inclined to retract my views about *friendship*. Other people have offered things, gifts, but no one, except you, has ever come with them exactly at *the* right moment. What is this except friendship? You came once with the *Athenaeum* – and I have since felt that this was a *gran rifiuto*[2] on my part, and that somehow, if we had been working together on it, we might have pulled it through and made things different, and that not at all out of vanity but, if you like, a superstition.[3] It was the idea of working *with* and *under* you. Anyway, I shan't make that mistake again.

1 – This is TSE's first account of the scope of the Clark lectures, published as *The Varieties of Metaphysical Poetry* (*VMP*), ed. R. Schuchard (1993).

2 – 'The great refusal'. Among the shades in the vestibule of Hell, Dante recognises 'colui / che fece per viltade il gran rifiuto' ['he who in his cowardice made the great refusal'], *Inf.*, 3: 59–60). This is generally taken to be a reference to Pope Celestino V.

3 – On 6 Apr. 1919, TSE told HWE that JMM had invited him 'to be his assistant editor at £500'. He turned it down because it was financially 'risky' and would have left him 'less energy for original work.' On 30 June 1922, TSE told RA he rejected JMM's offer on his 'own instinct' and against VHE's advice, and it had proved 'correct'. *A.* foundered two years after JMM took over.

Vivien said a couple of months ago (and has said *several* times) '*Murry was always your luck*'. I wish I might be *yours*. I have never known you to do or say anything against me. What I think now is: What can I ever do for Murry?

This *is* a symbolic event. It has just saved Vivien at this lowest moment and perhaps will have given her just what will save her life. I cannot explain how your two letters have affected her.

T.

I am always likely to be accessible by telephone here after 2 p.m. I am not *likely* to be out.

TO *John Middleton Murry* PC Northwestern

[Postmark 24 February 1925]

Thank you with all my heart. This would make *all the difference* to me. V.'s bronchitis very bad today. In haste.

T. S. E.

Will write later.

TO *John Middleton Murry* MS Valerie Eliot

[late February 1925] [London]

Dear John

I have done a damned and foolish thing. I was seeing Charles Whibley this week and I went and told him the whole thing about the Trinity Lectures – I suppose because I was so pleased about it, or I don't know why. I am beginning to feel very much like Vivien that from you I get good, and am becoming superstitious about it.

She (V.) hates Whibley and believes him to be the devil, although she has never so much as seen him.[1] I do hope I haven't done anything stupid

1–VHE's dislike of CW may possibly be explained, at least in part, by a recollection by Enid Faber: 'I don't know what she really felt for Tom. One day she said to me "What would you feel like if you were told you must not have any children" and described how Charles Whibley had warned her that financially, and so as to leave Tom freer[,] she must wait. She said that Tom's work had always been put first. But I do not know that that sentiment was any more real than her usual one which was "I think it must be dreadful to have children to think that you might pass on something of yourself"' ('Recollections of Vivienne Eliot', 10 Nov. 1950).

or to impede this thing which I believe to be the path leading out of the wilderness we are now stuck in.

V. is *very slowly* picking up again, but I don't think she would ever do that without your thoughts.

Tom.

TO *John Middleton Murry* — MS Valerie Eliot

[late February 1925] 9 Clarence Gate Gdns

Dear John

Thank you for your letter. I am very sorry (and rather superstitious) at having introduced the matter to another person, though it is only fair to say that I don't think Whibley would crab me. But it would have been only right and decent as well as prudent to have asked you before mentioning it to him.

I once met Q-Couch[1] at lunch at Whibleys in Cambridge. I don't know that that affects the matter one way or the other. Whibley once suggested to me – a year or so ago – that I might at *some* time be put up for the Clark, but it was very indefinite.

I shan't mention it to anyone else without speaking to you first, and I don't know of anyone I should be likely to. I understand how much trouble you are taking. The suspense and the issue are so great that I wonder, in my present state, whether I shall have the mind left to prepare the lectures, if I get it.

I am trying to see B. L. R.[2] next week, but about quite a different matter.

Gratefully
Yrs ever
T. S. E.

1 – Sir Arthur Quiller-Couch (1863–1944): King Edward VII Professor of English Literature at Cambridge 1912–44, and like CW a Fellow of Jesus College. He was editor of *The Oxford Book of English Verse, 1250–1900* (1900).

2 – Bruce Richmond, editor of *TLS*. This was in connection with TSE's negotiation with Faber.

TO *Lucia Joyce*[1] CC

26 February 1925 9 Clarence Gate Gdns

Dear Miss Joyce,

Thank you very much for your letter as we have been anxious for news of your father's health.[2] I am very sorry to hear that he has been having such acute trouble and that the physicians have not yet finished with him, but I sincerely hope that a few weeks will see him on the road to recovery. Please give our sympathy to him and to your mother and tell them that we have constantly thought and talked about your anxieties.

I am delighted to hear that I may soon have some of his work to publish. Will you tell him that I had refrained from bothering him but had been constantly hoping to hear. I should like to have the manuscript as soon as possible for the June number, as the April number has already gone to press.[3] Perhaps he will be so kind as to prepare it immediately he is able to work again so that I can send it to the printers at once and allow him plenty of time to deal with the proof.[4]

I should be very grateful for any further news of your father after he returns from the clinic.

With all best wishes,

Sincerely yours,
[T. S. E.]

TO *Bonamy Dobrée* TS Brotherton

26 February 1925 *The Criterion*,
23 Adelphi Terrace House

Dear Dobrée,

I am still kept to the house owing to this vile weather but I hope that you will be able to see me before you leave this country. I certainly expect to be about some time early next month and hope that you will drop me a line

1–Lucia Anna Joyce (1907–82): JJ's only daughter. She was to be diagnosed as suffering from hebephrenic schizophrenia in 1932, and spent her last thirty years in the care of St Andrew's Hospital, Northampton.

2–Lucia reported that her father had 'just returned from the *clinique des yeux*' after 'an attack of episcleritis'. He was due to return for a final operation on the left eye.

3–JJ said that TSE can 'have the piece for *The Criterion*' at three or four days' notice. 'Fragment of an Unpublished Work' was published in C. 3: 12 (July 1925).

4–Lucia said JJ hoped 'to revise the proof very carefully before he leaves Paris about the middle of next month'.

to let me know when you are in London as I understood from my secretary that you would be here about that time.

Let me express my appreciation of your book on *Restoration Drama* which is quite the best thing of its sort that I have seen. I have kept it in order to do an adequate review of it for the *Criterion*, but owing to my misfortunes I am afraid that I shall not be able to deal with it until the June number.[1]

Will you also let me know whether you still hold yourself responsible for the manuscripts of A. J. C. Brown. I have only recently looked them over, and while I think that there is some meat in them, I don't think that he has yet arrived at enough individuality for our uses. If you could let me know about this or drop a line to my secretary at 23 Adelphi Terrace House I should be grateful.

Yours sincerely,
T. S. Eliot

TO *Mark Van Doren* TS Butler

26 February 1925

The Criterion,
23 Adelphi Terrace House

Dear Mr Van Doren,

In fulfilment of my promise I am enclosing a review of your book of poems.[2] The delay is explained by the fact that the reading of the book and writing the notice have been one of my first occupations during convalescence after a long illness. I feel that my review fails to express the pleasure which your book gave me, but I was tempted by the fact that it proved such an excellent instance of a thesis. There is very little good verse in America of the kind that you write, and I sincerely hope that you will be able to let us have much more.

Sincerely yours,
T. S. Eliot

1–BD's *Restoration Comedy 1660–1720* (1925) was reviewed by RA in *NC* 4: 2 (Apr. 1926).
2–TSE's review of Mark Van Doren, *Spring Thunder and Other Poems* (New York, 1924) – 'Why Rural Verse?'– came out in the *Nation* (NY), 120 (15 Apr. 1925), 432. 'I enjoy Mr Van Doren's poems in the same way, I think, that English readers enjoy the poetry of Mr De la Mare and Mr Blunden. I believe that it is at least of the same excellence . . . [P]oetry like that of Mr Robert Frost and that of Mr Van Doren is a valuable antidote to the Manhattan brilliance and often sham originality by which American poetry has lately come to be known.'

PS If the allusions to Jews are undesirable you may omit them.[1]
TSE/IPF

TO *Wyndham Lewis* MS Cornell

[early March 1925] 9 Clarence Gate Gdns

Dear Lewis

My apology was for the one point which seemed to me to require an apology. For the rest, it is a pity that we have not a higher opinion of each other's characters, apart from the intelligences, as to which, I think, we have both formed an opinion which no dissensions can affect.

Whibley is in the Mediterranean with Lord Brabourne. He told me the day before he left that he could not be reached by letter, as he was on 'The Arcadian' the whole time, and that he was taking his holiday so that no correspondence *could* reach him. He expects to be back about April 1st – so I should write again to Broomhill House – I should ask Macmillans to send him the MSS. I think you might publish the book in five volumes if necessary.[2] I know another (new) publisher who might consider at least a part of it.[3]

Yours sincerely
T. S. E.

1 – TSE observed in his review: 'Racial migrations and the economic conditions of modern life have had one consequence which, among so many others, has been neglected. The universal and rapid growth of the reading public has produced a variety of cultures existing side by side in the same village, in the same street, exhibiting differences even between members of the same family . . . Moreover, literature has – partly for economic reasons, i.e., the necessity for grinding journalistic axes – tended to concentrate its activities in a few international capitals. There it becomes occupied chiefly with metropolitan emotions and sensations. And the metropolitan public, composed of various races and various social origins, has in common only these metropolitan feelings and emotions. Here too the metic plays a large part; for the metic, like the Jew, can only thoroughly naturalize himself in cities . . . I have no solution to offer for the problems of modern life. But . . . it is a good thing that rural verse should be written.'

2 – On 29 Apr., WL told EP he was dividing up his 500,000-word book *The Man of the World* into a series of shorter works: one on Shakespeare, *The Lion and the Fox* (published in 1927), one on 'contemporary sensibility' called *Sub Persona Infantis*, one on 'exoliti & sex transformation' called *The Shaman*, and others entitled *The Politics of Personality*, *The Politics of Philistia* and *The Strategy of Defeat*. WL would send them to Robert McAlmon of Contact Press (see *Pound/Lewis*, 142–5).

3 – The Scientific Press, shortly to become Faber & Gwyer.

TO *Virginia Woolf* TS Berg

Sunday [8? March 1925] *The Criterion*, 17 Thavies Inn

My dear Virginia,

If you *did* see the cottage at Ringmer,[1] I shall be glad to know, but in the present circumstances I shall rather be distressed to think that you should have taken that trouble. For at the moment I have no time even to think of houses. For the last three days Vivien has been in such agony as I have never seen, with the most terrific rheumatism all over her body. It came on quite suddenly, with no apparent cause, just as she was beginning to show signs of real progress. The doctor calls it rheumatism, but says that it is a most uncommon and peculiar variety, and she admits that she has never seen a case like it. She has hardly slept for three nights, and during the day also is in the greatest pain, almost delirious, so that it has seemed at times that she would simply expire from exhaustion.

So life is simply from minute to minute of horror. This is only to give you our news and explain any subsequent silence. The anxiety is terrible.

I recognised your imagination in the *Times* à propos of unicorns and jewellers.[2] If it was not you, who else could it possibly have been?

Yours ever,
T. S. E.

FROM *Geoffrey Faber* CC

[9 March 1925] [London]

My dear Eliot

I have been thinking over our conversation on Thursday, and am sending you the results; they may perhaps help you in formulating whatever proposal you ultimately make to us.[3]

It seems clear that the idea of a monthly must be abandoned. The market is glutted with them, and however good a new monthly was it would find

1–Ringmer is a village in East Sussex. VW was helping the Eliots to look for a country retreat.

2–'Notes on an Elizabethan Play', *TLS* (5 Mar. 1925), 145–6. All *TLS* articles were anonymous, but TSE was right to identify this as by VW: it was reprinted in *The Common Reader* (1925). Comparing Elizabethan drama and the modern novel, VW wrote: 'Thus, in spite of dullness, bombast, rhetoric, and confusion, we still read the lesser Elizabethans, still find ourselves adventuring in the land of the jeweller and the unicorn.'

3–GCF noted in his diary, 5 Mar.: 'Eliot lunched with me at the Club. He now proposes a Quarterly, & we talked till very late' (Faber Archive).

it very difficult indeed to make its way. The idea of publishing a quarterly was, when you broached it to me, new to my mind, but there is a good deal to be said for it. There is an obvious gap, at present filled, I think solely, by *The Criterion*.

What are the chances of a new quarterly, and what sort of character must it have? I should not think it worthwhile publishing such a review if its circulation is going to be limited to 1000. I have not the least idea what the circulations of the present *Quarterly Review* and *Edinburgh Review* are – not, I should imagine, very wide. But they are, it must be admitted, on the whole dull and heavy stuff; they seem, in their very nature, to cater for clubs rather than for the fire-side at home. They are almost entirely *reviews*, they do not give an opening, and I think never have given an opening, for creative or imaginative work, or indeed anything except full-length criticisms of history, literature, science, current politics and the like. This points to the gap which has got to be filled. There is a limit to the amount of criticism which one can read, even though it be very good, without a dulling of interest. But of the art itself which is the food of criticism one can never have enough, so long as it is genuine and fresh. It is to such art that a new quarterly must try to give a place. The attempt is, to some extent, being made in the better class monthly magazines, but one of the troubles is that it is made on too small a scale, the articles and the stories are too short to satisfy one's appetite. I do not mean, of course, that true criticism should be excluded from the ideal quarterly; let the proportions be about half and half. Of course, there is a sense in which art and criticism meet and are one, still, for journalistic purposes, it is right to make the distinction.

On the whole my readings of the *Criterion* have left me with a somewhat unsatisfied feeling. There has been a tendency to shortness in the items of the collection, and some of the long ones have been very obscure. That is, I think, to have things rather the wrong way round; the obscure articles, stories or poems should be brief. Another element in my judgment of the *Criterion* has been a faint feeling of being led through a somewhat exotic country. The ideal quarterly would have to stand a little more obviously on firm ground. When I get to this point in my reflections I begin at once to see the danger that in re-acting from what Robertson, I think quite rightly, called the exotic, one will plunge into what is merely dull and commonplace. I dare say if I were to edit such a Review myself that is what would happen. If you were to edit it I think you would avoid that danger and that is why I am tempted to insist rather that in scheming out your paper you will have to take more account of the average man than you have done in editing the *Criterion*. Would this mean losing the bulk of the *Criterion*'s circulation?

There is, however, no point in publishing a paper unless it is going to be unique, a leader of critical thought and of literary expression and, consequently, in some respects, irritating to the conservative mind. It is no good thinking of making it merely popular. If we did that there would be no point in approaching it from the publisher's point of view. I should want to use the Review first and foremost as a stimulus to young writers, so that having helped them to find their souls in print we should have a succession of the right sort to go on from the writing of articles and stories to the writing of books. One would like to repeat, in a healthier atmosphere and with stronger ideals, the kind of work that John Lane did with the *Yellow Book*.[1]

That is where the publisher comes in in this business.

So far, in talking together, we have both rather skirted round what is perhaps the really vital point, and that is the relation of the paper to the book publishing part of the show. Is it your idea that both are to fit in to each other with extreme nicety and that a rigid test is to be applied to every book, those which did not definitely tune in with the paper being refused publication? Something of this sort was, I think, in your mind to begin with when you spoke of the continental system. Personally I should not care to go so far as that. I do not think that it is at all necessary for an English publishing business to restrict itself in that kind of way. It is only necessary if the ideal set up is rigid, dogmatic, partial, of the school rather than of the people. That is not the natural English way, and when it is attempted in England something very limited and temporary results. Of course it may be true that there are times when the artistic instinct can only be roused by the weapon of a new dogma, but I cannot think that that is the case today. We have had nothing but a succession of attempts at new dogmas, and to add another would be to court obscurity. To my way of thinking what is wanted is, if anything so definite is wanted, the re-statement of the old eternal principles of Art which the new dogmatists have now, for many years, been trying to undermine. But more than a re-statement, perhaps, is wanted the active, continuous combination of the young men under the unifying principle not of a new dogma, but of a personality, and if our scheme comes to anything it is you who will supply that. The result would be nothing rigid, exclusive or artificial in the bad

1–John Lane (1854–1925) initially set up a London bookshop in partnership with Charles Elkin Mathews; their imprint, The Bodley Head (founded 1887), put out the *Yellow Book*, 1894–7.

sense of the word; but something organic, catholic, like Shakespeare's laugh in Meredith's Sonnet, 'Broad as ten thousand beeves at pasture'.[1]

As for the relationship between the paper so conditioned and the book publishing business, growing up side by side with it, that I think must be left to make itself. After all, a publisher is not either a preacher or a philosopher; he is a tradesman, and if he picks and chooses too much and gives the public nothing but what a rigid aesthetic theory thinks it ought to have, he ceases to be a tradesman and becomes a propagandist. I want to avoid deceiving myself with false logic; and I must admit that one has to draw the line somewhere. I do not want to publish anything that seems to me worthless or decadent or positively bad. So that one must apply some kind of criterion. The point which I am labouring to get at is this, that the criterion should be not a set of pre-conceived judgments, but the whole of one's intellectual life; but even now I fail to express myself very clearly, and must rely on your critical intuition of what is in my mind.

The Publisher must be much more of an opportunist than the Editor, at any rate to begin with. In order to get going at all one may have to publish books which one would send elsewhere later on. At any rate I do set this standard that whatever we publish shall have some virtue in it, even though it may not be of the very first order. My tentative suggestion that, if we entered into an alliance for the publication of a quarterly magazine or review, you might join us as a Director, would go a long way towards establishing the kind of organic connection between the paper and the books which I should hope to see grow up.

To go now to the question of finance. I should not like to commit the business to a probable loss of more than, say, £750 a year on the suggested paper, though we might perhaps be willing to spend some additional sums on preliminary advertisement, and I should certainly hope to see my way through the initial two or three years to such a circulation as would enable the paper to be run for a small profit. We shall have, therefore, to go very carefully into the costs of production, into the question of size, into the question of price and of advertising. On all these points I hope you will be able to give me fairly detailed information.

One thing more before I close. I want to say again, as I have said once or twice already, that once the thing is launched I should withhold criticism unless it was asked for, and put full confidence in you. The man who is actually steering the ship has to take into account all sorts of things which

1 – George Meredith, 'The Spirit of Shakespeare': 'Thence had he the laugh / We feel is thine: broad as ten thousand beeves / At pasture.'

the passengers know nothing about; but this being so I feel it to be essential that we should thoroughly understand what is at the back of each other's minds before we commit ourselves to the general undertaking; hence the length and, I am afraid, obscurity of this letter.

Yours sincerely,
[Geoffrey C. Faber]

TO *Mary Hutchinson* MS Texas

[Postmark 10 March 1925] 9 Clarence Gate Gdns

Thank you *very much* for the list of houses, which came at a most opportune moment, which I shall probably make use of. I cannot say more now but will write again when I have seen the doctor.

Love from us both.
T.

TO *Herbert Read* PC Victoria

[Postmark 10 March 1925] 9 Clarence Gate Gdns

Many thanks for sending Ward.[1] I will let you know as soon as I am about – have much to discuss with you. Do you think you could prepare those notes of Hulme, with your commentary, soon?[2] Fernandez (to whom I sent a copy of *Speculations*) has become very excited, and is writing an essay on him.[3] *We might have a Hulme number*?[4] Will reply more ceremoniously about G. W.[5]

Yours always
T. S. E.

1 – HR's review of Stephen Ward, *Ethics*, for *C.* 3: 11 (Apr. 1925), 444–9.
2 – See T. E. Hulme, 'Notes on Language and Style' (ed. by HR), *C.* 3: 12 (July 1925), 484–97. These notes had been excluded from *Speculations* (1923) for 'economic reasons', and because of the illegibility of the script.
3 – No essay by Fernandez on Hulme appeared in *C.*
4 – A special issue on Hulme never came to pass.
5 – On 8 Mar., HR enclosed a letter and poem by Grant Watson, saying it would make it easier for him to reply that he had shown them to TSE 'but that etc. . . .'

TO *E. R. Curtius* MS Bonn

13 March 1925 9 Clarence Gate Gdns

My dear Curtius,

Thank you very much for your kind letter. I will see that the January and April numbers are sent to you.

By the way, Fernandez (whom I like, and you would like, very much, he is one of the most intelligent of that group) has written an essay in the February *Nouvelle Revue Française* on my *prose*, which I like very much.[1] But *I* attach more value to my verse.

May I send you *either* Miss Weston's book or the *one volume Golden Bough* of Frazer?[2] The complete *Golden Bough* is quite beyond my means to possess – ten or twelve expensive volumes.

At present, my wife is very ill, so I have only leisure to send you my greetings and continued thoughts. How I wish we might *meet*! I hope to find a publisher here for one of your books. It is deplorable that your work is not better known in England.[3]

Yours ever sincerely
in friendship
T. S. Eliot.

1–Ramón Fernandez, 'Le Classicisme de T. S. Eliot', *NRF* 137 (1 Feb. 1925), 246–51. Fernandez began by saying: 'En un temps où le sentimentalisme, vainement combattu, triomphe encore sous des déguisements trompeurs, le poète américain T. S. Eliot nous propose un classicisme sévère, sain, authentique que les Français ne méditeront pas sans fruit' ['In a time when sentimentalism, combated in vain, still triumphs under deceptive disguises, the American poet T. S. Eliot proposes a severe, healthy, authentic classicism which the French might fruitfully reflect upon']. He described TSE as 'ni un poète critique, ni un critique poète: il est un poète qui analyse l'atmosphère pour la purifier' ['neither a poet critic nor a critic poet: he is a poet who analyses the atmosphere to purify it']. He praised the 'ardour and intellectual precision' of his accounts of Aristotle and Dante, affirmed his reading of *Hamlet* and, while comparing him to French writers like Lasserre and Benda, noted his 'précision presque angoissante' ['almost disturbing precision']. He alluded too to TSE's Bostonian family background of lawyers and clergymen, and the detestation of his family's belief in the 'transcendental atheism' of Emerson.

2–In his 'Notes' to *TWL* (1923), TSE acknowledged: 'Not only the title, but the plan and a good deal of the incidental symbolism of the poem were suggested by Jessie L. Weston's book on the Grail legend: *From Ritual to Romance*'. In addition, he acknowledged being 'indebted in general' to Sir James George Frazer's *The Golden Bough: A Study in Magic and Religion* (13 vols, 1890): the abridged, one-volume edition appeared in 1922. Curtius's German translation of the poem, *Das wüste Land*, was to come out in *Neue Schweizer Rundschau* (Apr. 1927).

3–It took some time for Curtius's works to be translated: among the first were *The Civilisation of France*, trans. Olive Wyon (1930), and *European Literature and the Latin Middle Ages*, trans. W. R. Trask (1953).

TO *Bonamy Dobrée* TS Brotherton

14 March 1925 9 Clarence Gate Gdns

Dear Dobrée,

Thank you for your letter. I still find myself unable to make any engagements because, although I am myself practically recovered, though very weak, my wife is so ill as to need exclusive attention. I not only cannot ask anyone here at present, but cannot even promise to be able to go out. I will keep your letter in front of me and will communicate with you at the Savile Club if I find there is any chance of our meeting. I should very much like to see you before you leave England.[1]

I hope that you never suffer from rheumatism and neuralgia, as I have been [*sc.* seen] in my wife's case[2] that the pain can be so great as almost to lead to delirium, and I have thought at moments that she would die of pure exhaustion. But the doctor says this is a very uncommon and peculiar case.

Sincerely yours
T. S. Eliot

I want you to send me something, or *suggest* a subject, for an essay for the *Criterion*.

TO *Mary Hutchinson* TS Texas

14 March 1925 9 Clarence Gate Gdns

My dear Mary,

I should have written to you sooner after sending you my card [of 10 March], but Vivien has been so very ill that there has been no time for anything else. She had been making progress, but for several days and nights has had such a fearful attack of what at first appeared to be rheumatism and neuralgia that I have never seen any human being in such agony. She has had practically no sleep for three nights and although she is having treatment continuously from her doctor, there seems to be nothing in the world that will stop the pain. The doctor says that she has never seen such a case and that it is a most uncommon thing; the nearest analogy appears to be rheumatism and neuralgia but this is very much more severe and continuous. She has been practically at death's door and

1–On 2 Mar., BD said he would be in London for four days from 20 Mar., before returning to the Pyrenees.
2–At this point, TSE changes from typewriter to pen.

at moments I have thought that she would die simply from exhaustion. There is no improvement yet. I will try to write again in a few days.

Affectionately
Tom.

I do appreciate your letters. V. has not been able to see them even.

TO *Herbert Read* MS Victoria

Sunday 15 March 1925[1] *The Criterion*, 17 Thavies Inn

My dear Read,

Good. Please consider it a definite commission.[2] I have always suspected a *tacit* conspiracy: and as the life of a review like *The C* is always fragile, I should like to perform this function as soon as possible.[3] (I have thought that there was a 'conspiracy of silence' in England, against Maurras also, to whom I have thought of devoting a future number. Who has ever heard of Georges Sorel but ourselves?)[4]

Should like to put the no. together by May 1st. Let me know how to get hold of Worringer and what subject to ask him for.[5]

Who do *you* think most suitable to write a short note on Hulme's poetry? R. A.?[6]

I am sending *Speculum Mentis* to Thorpe for the *next* no.[7] Given him something else for this no.[8] Should like to know what you think of a man

1–Misdated 13 March.

2–On 12 Mar., HR said he could send T. E. Hulme's 'unpublished notes & one or two unpublished poems' if he had 'a definite commission'. This resulted in T. E. Hulme, 'Notes on Language and Style', *C.* 3: 12 (July 1925).

3–HR said Hulme's *Speculations* (1924) had sold only 150 copies: he was almost driven 'to suspect conspiracies in Bloomsbury'.

4–Georges Sorel (1847–1922): French philosopher and theorist of revolutionary syndicalism. T. E. Hulme's intro. to his trans. of *Réflexions sur la violence* (1908) was included in *Speculations*. Sorel applauded Maurras and l'Action Française for their opposition to bourgeois democracy. In a list of six books that exemplified what he termed the tendency 'toward a higher and clearer conception of Reason', TSE was to include Sorel, *Réflexions sur la violence*; Maurras, *L'Avenir de l'intelligence*; and Hulme's *Speculations* ('The Idea of a Literary Review', *NC* 4: 1, Jan. 1926).

5–HR had been reading the German art historian Wilhelm Worringer (1881–1965), to whom Hulme owed 'a considerable debt'. He suggested inviting him to write for *C.* Worringer contributed 'Art Questions of the Day' to *NC* 6: 2 (Aug. 1927).

6–Richard Aldington.

7–R. G. Collingwood, *Speculum Mentis, or the Map of Knowledge*, was reviewed by W. A. Thorpe in *C.* 3: 12 (July 1925).

8–See Thorpe on Leone Vivante, *Intelligence in Expression*, *C.* 3: 11 (Apr. 1925).

named Collins when you see April no.[1] If I were living a more normal existence, I should try to confer with you much more often, and verbally, about the *Criterion* and things in general. I say this now because I want you to understand that I am *not*, in running a paper, naturally an autocrat, but that merely *lack of time*, and private preoccupations, make me play a much more solitary hand than I otherwise should. These causes have precipitated also a quarrel with Lewis, which distresses me: especially as a man like W. L., once set off, behaves so insolently that it is difficult to patch up.

At the moment I am distracted by my wife's illness: for three days and nights she has been in such agony – with something resembling, but far exceeding rheumatism that puzzles the doctor, that I can hardly think of anything else.

Yours ever –
T. S. E.

TO *Leonard Woolf* MS Berg

Friday [March? 1925] 9 Clarence Gate Gdns

My dear Leonard

Very many thanks for your sponsorship and your trouble.[2] I infer that Miss Fry refuses the gratification?[3]

I will do my best. I have not yet been able to get out, except with Vivien to the doctor. (The treatment, is, I think, good. At any rate, she is eating more and with some appetite.) In *any* case, would you be inclined to accept a pamphlet next winter? I could always do a few articles or reviews, base a pamphlet or book on them, and you could accept the articles only on the [private *del.*] informal understanding that you should have the book. But this is merely if you don't have the poems.[4]

Enclosed some reviews by a young man sent me by Yeats. MacGreevy.[5] Might he be of any use to you? I have accepted one thing from him and

1 – H. P. Collins, 'A Note on the Classical Principle in Poetry', C. 3: 11 (Apr. 1925), 389–400.
2 – LW had agreed to be one of TSE's referees for Faber's new firm.
3 – Joan Mary Fry (1862–1955): unmarried sister of the artist and art critic Roger Fry, who kept house for him until 1919.
4 – TSE was offering the Woolfs another prose pamphlet, in lieu of the new collection of poems they understood would be coming to them. On 1 June 1925, VW recorded that 'some old firm' would be publishing *The Criterion* in the autumn '& all his works must go to them – a blow to us' (*Diary of Virginia Woolf*, III, *1925–30*, 27).
5 – Thomas MacGreevy: see TSE's letter of 30 May. MacGreevy's poem 'Dysert' appeared in *NC* 4: 1 (Jan. 1926) under the pseud. 'L. St. Senan'.

suggested another. Of course I have not *seen* him, so cannot speak [for *del.*] about his personal appearance.

Love to Virginia. I have enjoyed very much my two visits.

Yours ever
T. S. E.

TO *Geoffrey Faber* PC Valerie Eliot

[Postmark 18 March 1925] 9 Clarence Gate Gdns

Please don't think I have neglected writing – but my wife has been so *very* ill with general neuritis that I have had no time to think of letters – and this must be a long one.[1]

T. S. E.

TO *Scofield Thayer* TS Beinecke

20 March 1925 9 Clarence Gate Gdns

Dear Scofield,

I was very glad to get your letter of the 10th. I had a bad time myself with influenza during January and February and Vivien has had a very much worse time with the same malady followed by bronchitis and a terrible attack of general neuritis.

I am glad that you like the poems.[2] I am not altogether satisfied with them myself. If, however, the other one is written, I will let you have it.

My note on Miss Marianne Moore in the April *Criterion*, which you will soon see, will be followed by a review of her book in the June number.[3]

1–A ref. to TSE's reply to GCF's proposals (9 Mar.) apropos *C.* and the new publishing house. GCF replied (19 Mar.): 'I am exceedingly sorry to get your postcard, and hear that your wife is so ill. Please do not worry yourself to think about writing to me until you are more at ease.'

2–'The Hollow Men', I–III, which appeared in *Dial* 78: 3 (Mar. 1925), became 'The Hollow Men', I, II and IV. In Jan., TSE sent them to Thayer, and on 10 Feb, Thayer congratulated TSE, saying he particularly liked the first two stanzas of the last (beginning 'The eyes are not here'). The 'other one' presumably refers to V, published in *P 1909–1925*.

3–'Our contemporary, *The Dial*, of New York, has justly bestowed its annual award for literature upon Miss Marianne Moore. In the dismal flood of affected and fantastical verse poured out in America within the last ten years, Miss Moore's poetry endures, "the wave may go over it if it likes." She is one of the few who have discovered an original *rhythm* – in an age when the defect of rhythm is the most eminent failure of verse both English and American. She has found a new verse-rhythm of the spoken phrase. Miss Moore's work is of international importance, and her book will be the subject of review in a later number'

Owing to the circumstances mentioned above, my essay on George Chapman has not been written. If it ever is written I will let you know and you can have it if you can arrange to publish it not earlier than it appears in the *Criterion*.[1]

I wish I could do an adequate review of Schnitzler.[2] Do forgive me for not having replied to this part of your letter at once, for I see that it may have inconvenienced you. Besides the fact that I am not able to do much work, I feel that this book ought to be reviewed by someone who is thoroughly well acquainted with Schnitzler's work which I know only in fragments. It is quite true that I was impressed by what I read in the *Dial*, and also, by the way, very much so by Thomas Mann's *Death in Venice*.[3] I wish indeed that I could do the Schnitzler for you but I actually have not at present the time or strength to do it properly even if I had the adequate knowledge. I have hopes, however, that I may be able to do more for you a few months hence, if you want me to.

Is there any chance of your coming to Europe this summer?

Yours ever,
T. S. E.

TO *Geoffrey Faber* — TS Valerie Eliot

22 March 1925 — 9 Clarence Gate Gdns

My dear Faber,

I am now replying to your letter of the 9th March.

It appears that we are agreed that for every reason a Quarterly is more desirable than a Monthly. With the means at your disposal a Monthly is impossible; a Quarterly may get hold of a part of the public which remains indifferent to the monthlies; people are more likely to take in a quarterly as well as a monthly, than they are to take in two monthlies; and in the end

—

('A Commentary', C. 3: 11, Apr. 1925, 343). Moore's *Observations* was reviewed by RA in 3: 12 (July 1925), 588–93.

1 – Thayer had enquired whether TSE's 'An Aspect of George Chapman' would be available for the *Dial*. In 'A Commentary', in C. 3: 11 (Apr. 1924), TSE announced that due to 'severe illness' he had been unable 'to prepare his essay on "A Neglected Aspect of George Chapman" for this number'.

2 – Thayer remembered TSE writing appreciatively about Arthur Schnitzler's novel *Dr Graesler*, and hoped he might review it in the *Dial* on its appearance in book form.

3 – See Schnitzler, 'Doctor Graesler', in *Dial* 73: 1–5 (July–Nov. 1922). Thomas Mann, *Death in Venice*, was serialised (trans. Kenneth Burke) in 76: 3–5 (Mar.–June 1924).

it is more feasible to turn a quarterly into a monthly than it is to transform a monthly into a quarterly.

A quarterly would not aim at quite such a large circulation as a monthly: the circulation which I have in view is 5000 within five years. With proper business management it might be more; and I think that there is a better chance of foreign (primarily American and colonial) circulation with a quarterly than with a monthly – it is less quickly out of date. The *Criterion* has of course been run in a amateur way; and it has been impossible to push its circulation in America (incidentally, if I were publicly and openly the editor, with my name on the paper, it would probably considerably assist the expansion in America).

As to the proportion of critical and creative work. I do not think that any review can carry the same amount of literary criticism that it could have carried a hundred years ago – in fact, that is self-evident. Two good critical articles (not meandering comment, but asserting principles) are enough. The critical attack must be developed by a fairly homogeneous but catholic corps of reviewers at the end of the review. Nowadays people like to read reviews, but they must not be very long, and they must be signed.[1] I should wish to continue the reviewing as it is at present done in the *Criterion*, and about the same proportion, not more.

But besides criticism and fiction, verse etc. there should be a place for good solid articles on subjects of general interest to the educated man: history, scholarship, review of current work in archaeology and anthropology etc., articles by foreign scholars such as Diehl[2] (Byzantine art), Picavet[3] etc. (these people can always be got, and fairly cheaply); English scholars such as John Burnet. One or two in each number.

As to the proportion of elder and known writers to younger and unknown ones, I should wish to select only such elder writers as might in one way or another serve as a stimulus or guide to the younger generation, and who would fit in with a new or nascent point of view. Here there is considerable latitude of opinion. But I should instance Frazer (as one of the oldest!) as a living force; whereas Saintsbury, with all his merits, has now

1–The *TLS* continued the tradition of anonymous reviewing, but it had been largely abandoned elsewhere. Since introducing reviews in 2: 8 (July 1924), *C.* had published signed reviews (though sometimes under a pseudonym).

2–Charles Diehl (1883–1944): expert on Byzantine Art at the Sorbonne; author of *Manuel d'art Byzantin* ('Manual of Byzantine Art', 1910) and *History of the Byzantine Empire* (1925).

3–Prob. François Picavet (1851–1921): French philosopher and expert on Kant; author of *Les Idéologues* (1891).

little point. Whibley has something to give, and Robertson who represents the opposition to sentimentality in criticism. Elliot Smith[1] will be one of the forces of our time. Most of the older writers of fiction and verse are meaningless from this point of view: Hardy, Kipling, Bennett, Yeats and many other names would be worthwhile only for advertising value (if desired) but would have no value in building up the character of a paper.

My belief is that much more catholicity should be maintained in the creative work than in the critical. Only in the smaller part of the paper which would be literary criticism would any uniformity of idea be aimed at. If you look over the reviews in the last and in the next *Criterion* I think you will see that there is no hint of a drilled uniformity even here. By selecting intelligent men who can write, and giving them each to review such books as will best bring out their points of sympathy with each other, enough homogeneity is obtained; but I do not suppose that any two of them would agree with each other, or with me, on more than a few cardinal points. Of course there are a few with whom I have more in common than others: Aldington, Manning, Read, Fernandez especially – but there is no dogma binding us.

In verse and fiction, as I suggested above, one would include almost anything that had life in it, without exacting conformity to any rules of taste or tendency.

I did not have in mind an exact correspondence between the publishing and the review. That would limit both too narrowly. I should think it only desirable to avoid any gross inconsistency i.e. publishing a book by some writer who had been consistently and steadily damned in the review. That is an unlikely contingency.

There are one or two points in your letter which I should like to hear more of. You refer to the 'old eternal principles of Art' which 'the new dogmatists' have been trying to undermine. That is allright – but the variations of opinion as to what *are* the eternal principles of Art are apt to constitute dogmata. What are yours and what are mine? And finally, who are the 'new dogmatists'? I hope we agree on the names of the reprehensible people. I do not want to form any critical 'school' so close that it will be able to contain and produce no creative writers: in fact, several critical attacks upon me (*vide* Murry) have been concentrated upon the point that I cannot really be a 'Classicist' at heart, because of my

1 – The first half of WL's essay 'The Dithyrambic Spectator' is an exposition of Elliot Smith's 'exhilarating and adventurous' book, *The Evolution of the Dragon*, which WL describes as a 'brilliant account of the origin of the fine arts' from the practice of mummification (*Calendar of Modern Letters*, I: 2, Apr. 1925, 89–107).

admiration for James Joyce and because of my own verse.[1] That is the weakness of the critique of the school of Maurras and Pierre Lasserre, that it is in a partial vacuum, and cannot support, correct, or develop any of the actual creative writing in France.

With what you say about the situation of the Publisher I am in agreement. And the Editor has to combine and reconcile principle, sensibility, and business sense. That is why an editor's life is such a bloody sweat.

If there are any points in your letter which I have not dealt with please let me know. There remains the capital question of cost. Certain expenses of the *Criterion* as at present run you would not have: there would be no publisher's commission; and perhaps you would have sufficient staff to provide a shorthand secretary. I assume that the publishing house would be able to attend to the business end and pushing the circulation without further staff. But £750 would just cover the expenses without any salary for the editor. The question to consider, therefore, is whether you or members of the firm have the opportunities for finding a few persons to subvention the rest of the money needed: I mean also that the position would be simpler if this were done through the firm, or through personalities associated with the firm, rather than through my personal friends – I think you will see this point?

Oh yes – there is one other question: I should like to be clearer as to what you term the 'exotic' element in the *Criterion*. A little more detailed criticism, quoting chapter and verse, would I think help us to – what I agree is of the first importance – to understand what is at the back of each others' minds. I believe, so far, from our conversations, that the financial problem is the most difficult; and that I imagine you can quickly decide.

Yours always sincerely,
T. S. Eliot

1 – In 'More about Romanticism', JMM wrote: 'And even Mr Eliot, the author of *The Waste Land*, the champion of *Ulysses*, is not a true-blue classicist, however much he might like to be', *Adelphi* 1: 7 (Dec. 1923), 557. The most developed expression of JMM's critique of TSE's classicism figures in his later essay, 'The "Classical" Revival', *Adelphi* 3 (Feb. 1926). Remarking on the 'profound and absolute contradiction' beneath TSE's 'professions of classicism', JMM identified him as 'essentially, an unregenerate and incomplete romantic'.

TO *Wyndham Lewis* MS Cornell

23 March 1925 9 Clarence Gate Gdns

Dear Lewis

Your essay reached me after – as I found by telephoning to Aylesbury – the April *Criterion* had already been set in pages.[1] The June number is the next available.

I cannot, however, consider this quite apart from your previous letter, and I cannot work with you so long as you consider me either the tool or the operator of machinations against you. The incident of the house agent I certainly much regret: owing to preoccupation with anxieties which concern only myself, I was not able to write the same night, and it entirely slipped my mind. When I found your letter I wrote immediately, and the agent can tell you that I did so; it was, however, two weeks late. If this lost you the flat, I am very sorry, and offer my apologies.[2]

As for the Bell episode, it did not strike me that an article which did not in any way appear to controvert your own opinions would be a cause for offence.[3] It might however have been better had you written at once to state your point of view: we might have come to an understanding for the future.

But until you are convinced by your own senses or by the testimony of others that I am neither conducting nor supporting (either deliberately or blindly) any intrigue against you, I do not see that we can get any farther.[4]

As for the *Calendar*, it would not have occurred to me that this required any justification on your part, without the elaborate defense which you present.[5] If you can discover any further evidence of my ill will, or of any plot to which you suppose me to be a party, please let me know.

Sincerely
T. S. Eliot

1–Unidentified. WL's 'Subjective Art' in *NC* 6: 1 (July 1927) was his last contribution.

2–See TSE's letter to Watson & Austin of 13 Jan.

3–See Clive Bell, 'Prolegomena to a Study of Nineteenth-Century Painting', *C.* 3: 10 (Jan. 1925). WL was offended it took the place that his 'Art Chronicle' had held in *C.* 3: 9 (Oct. 1924).

4–WL said their ten years of being 'vaguely associated' evidently counted little against TSE's 'passionate intrigue': if TSE did not reply soon, he would conclude that 'the devil' had him 'by the heel'.

5–On 30 Jan. WL withdrew 'The Perfect Action', originally intended for *C.* It appeared as 'The Dithyrambic Spectator: An Essay on the Origins and Survivals of Art' in *The Calendar of Modern Letters* I: 2 & 3 (Apr. & May, 1925). In Mar., WL said Harold Monro told him that in publishing there he was associating himself with a 'rival venture' to *C.*

FROM *Geoffrey Faber* CC

24 March 1925 [London]

My dear Eliot,

Many thanks for your letter of March 22nd.

Before I say anything in reply, I want to put the following questions:

(1) What size do you propose that the new Quarterly should be? Would you take as your standard the last number of the *Criterion*, or do you wish to make it rather larger?

(2) What amount have you been spending on contributors, or, say, what did the contributors to the last number cost you? I think you pay at present rather under a pound a page, do you not? This is perhaps rather under the rate that you would like to fix. If we do the thing at all, we ought to fix an adequate scale; but I suppose the rate would not be the same right the way through, from the first to the last page, or would it?

(3) Standard of Production: Do you wish to take the standard of the *Criterion* as your absolute standard? If we find it possible to produce a similar paper, of not quite such excellent quality, more cheaply, what would you say to that?

(4) Precisely what office accommodation would you need? One room for yourself I take it, and some sort of accommodation for a typist-stenographer. If we were unable to find you accommodation in our own premises, could you go on using your present offices, and if so, how much does that cost you?

(5) Do you need a whole-time typist, and if not, how much?

(6) What proportion of the present circulation of the *Criterion* is by private subscription, and what proportion is supplied through the trade, and what discount does the trade take? (Rates of discount vary considerably with the different class magazines; in the case of the ordinary shilling magazine the discount works out at something like 40%.)

These are all the questions which I have to put at the moment. Now for your letter. I find everything that you say in it to fit in with my own views. I agree with you on the proportion of critical and creative articles; on the desirability of articles on subjects of general interest; on utilising only those elder writers who have the spirit of the younger generation in them; on maintaining a more exact standard in the critical than in the creative part of the paper, and on avoiding the publication of books by writers consistently damned in the paper.

I think that we really are, so far as all points of importance are concerned, at one over the character which the paper is to have. I own I was rather afraid lest you might wish to cramp the book publishing side of the business into the Procrustean frame-work of the *Criterion*. This doubt your letter entirely removes, and I am glad I put the question to you point-blank; but I feel that I was extremely rash in making use of that old *cliché* about the eternal principles of Art. Your observation that the variations of opinion, as to what *are* the eternal principles of Art, are apt to constitute dogmata, is a nasty one. It reminds me of Bradley's observation, that the man who says he does not believe in Metaphysics is himself propounding a metaphysical theory.[1] You have, it is evident, the advantage of an amateur in these matters.

On the whole I suppose I meant something like this. Little effective art has ever sprung directly from theories about Art. Indirectly the theories, I suppose, do affect the minds of all intelligent people, and consequently (if we assume that artists are intelligent people) the work of the artist. But this is only (I am, of course, restricting my remarks to the best sort of work) when the influence of theory and criticism have soaked right down into the soul. The result is more in the nature of an unconscious physiological process, than of conscious rational effort. Unqualified this view is, of course, untenable, since a great deal of an artist's work is conscious, though it is perhaps rather a conscious process of selection amongst the suggestions provided from a source within himself but outside his conscious control than a process of conscious creation. There are also the technical methods which he has learnt, or elaborated for himself, most of which he applies unconsciously perhaps, but the acquisition of which was conscious and deliberate. But I think you would probably agree with me that both the selective process and technical methods are equally characteristic of all minor arts and handicrafts, as well as of Art with a capital A; and that what gives Art its capital A is the judgement of life or of the Universe which the selective process and the technical methods enable the artist to express; and that this judgement is, when it is a judgement of real value, formulated by the whole personality of the artist, and is far more an uncontrolled and involuntary reaction to the facts than a deliberate gesture. What I meant, therefore, when I used that unfortunate phrase about the eternal principles of Art was that the Artist ought always to seek to express his genuine re-action rather than make striking gestures;

1 – 'The man who is ready to prove that metaphysical knowledge is wholly impossible has no right here to any answer. He must be referred for conviction to the body of this treatise. And he can hardly refuse to go there, since he himself has, perhaps unknowingly, entered the arena. He is a brother metaphysician with a rival theory of first principles' (F. H. Bradley, 'Introduction', *Appearance and Reality* [1893], 1–2).

and what I meant by the 'New Dogmatists' was all those people who think out and practice new gestures, and try to convince themselves and the public that it is the gesture and the style of the gesture which matters for Art.

I hope this won't seem to you a farrago of nonsense. I have no intention of naming any names!

Of course the reactions must vary infinitely. For myself, I think I belong to that dwindling band which reads this world in the light of another. I am venturing to send you copies of two small books of poetry; and in the preface to the earlier volume you will find a rather obscure statement of my point of view.[1] But Art can certainly treat, and on the whole does nowadays tend to treat, the present world as self-complete. If that is the Artist's genuine reaction to his experience I have no sort of quarrel with it. I think there is, in fact, a dualism, difficult if not impossible to reconcile, and that the greatest Artists are those who are at home at both foci of the ellipse. There are very few, if any, such Artists living today.

But we are getting rather far away from the *Criterion*. One other question you asked me was what precisely I mean by the exotic element in the *Criterion*. I must reserve that for another time. But it was not I who first used the word 'exotic'; it was, I think, Robertson's word.

Yours ever,
[Geoffrey C. Faber]

PS I had a seventh question to put to you, about price. There seem to be three alternatives:

(a) To keep the price as it is now [3s 6d].
(b) To raise it to four or five shillings.
(c) To lower it to, say, half-a-crown.

I should like to know in what direction you think we ought to go. Three and sixpence seems to me rather an unsatisfactory sort of price, but at half-a-crown I do not think we could ever see our way to running the paper at much of a profit. If the price was put up to four or five shillings what do you think would be the effect on the present subscription?

Of course the paper would be publicly and openly edited by you, and would carry your name on the cover.

1 – GCF had published two books of poetry: *Interflow: Poems, Chiefly Lyrical* (1915) and *In the Valley of Vision: Poems Written in Time of War* (1918). In the 'Preface' to his first, he wrote: 'The sublimest Art, whether it be music or poetry or painting, is that which floods the soul with beauty . . . I will not conceal my belief that beauty, so understood, belongs not to this world of sense, but to another world of the spirit. It comes into being when the facts of this world are brought into sudden unsuspected union with the facts of that other world.' (xiii–xiv).

TO *Geoffrey Faber* MS Valerie Eliot

25 March 1925 9 Clarence Gate Gdns

My dear Faber,

I shall only attempt in this letter to answer your direct questions.

1. If the price were 2/6 I should say 125 pp. if 4/- or 5/- 180 to 200 – *not more*. The last (Jan.) *Criterion* was 180 – the April 140 – a better size for the *present* (3/6) production.

2. The Contributors have had £100 out of the Jan. no. I have pared the payt. for reviews to the minimum (£1.1.– to £2.2.–) really exploiting their loyalty or the advantage they get by association with the review. It could however be kept to this. My policy has been, as far as possible, only to have such reviewers as I could also publish articles by (what a sentence!) once or twice a year.

3. Personally, I should even prefer a less luxurious appearance, and I think that, aiming at a larger circulation, it would be *desirable*. I was assured that for a printing of only 1000 copies the saving by cheaper paper would be negligible. But I am all for a practical rather than a *luxe* appearance.

4. I should not need a *whole* time secretary. If you had an efficient and intelligent shorthand typist who could give half (at most) of his or her time to this, it would be an economy.

5. The present office is £20 a year, with some small extras, and could I think be retained. It might be dispensed with, if I had a desk in yours.

6. About 200 subscribers, the rest through newsagents. Discount: agents pay 2/- as a rule or 1/8 for larger orders. Smith's take about 300 copies.

7. I don't think that raising the price wd. lose many subscribers. It is very difficult to say. There are very few reviews as cheap as 14/- p. annum.

8. I don't like papers having the editor's name on them, but I think my name might do something in America – and it is the custom now. Personally, I prefer the old fashioned anonymity.[1]

I am in sympathy about the 'other world' in poetry. It was the theme of a lecture I gave at Cambridge in November (on Chapman) and wd. be of the Clark Lectures at Cambridge, which have been offered to me for next year. <I shd. lecture on the XVII Century metaphysicals.> But that is a

1 – In his Commentaries in *C.*, TSE had written in the guise of 'Crites'. When the review was relaunched as *NC* in Jan. 1926, it opened with 'The Idea of a Literary Review' by 'T. S. Eliot'. Though TSE's Commentaries were no longer signed 'Crites', neither they nor *NC* carried his name as editor.

practical question: I must decide before the end of April, and of course I could not give these lectures unless I abandoned my job in the city.

Therefore – how soon is the Scientific Press able to come to a decision and if affirmative agree upon the sum which could be assigned? After that, it seems to me that we should meet and discuss ways and means . . . It is this lectureship (which wd. give me perhaps £200 and some notoriety) which makes me pressed for time!

Yours ever
T. S. Eliot

<The [form *del.*] example of poetry which is particularly anathema to me is that of Sacheverell Sitwell. No other world there!>[1]

FROM *Geoffrey Faber* CC

27 March 1925 [London]

My dear Eliot

Many thanks for your letter of the 25th, and your reply to my questions. I think the price would have to go up. I am a little surprised at the large discount taken by the trade: which amounts, apparently, to over 50% in the case of large orders.

About time. If you want a decision before the end of April, of course we must give it you. I don't know that there is any real reason why we should not be able to make up our minds during the next three or four weeks; though I had hoped to be able to postpone the decision until the new control of the Company had found itself more completely than it will be able to do in so short a time. However I entirely understand that the question is, for you, an urgent one. I do hope very much that we may be able to give you an opportunity of delivering the Clark lectures. Will you give us the opportunity of publishing them if you do?[2]

I don't wonder that you were pleased with Fernandez' observations in *La Nouvelle Revue Française*, which I am very much interested to read.[3]

Yours ever
[Geoffrey C. Faber]

1–These sentences are added at the head of the page. TSE reviewed Sacheverell Sitwell's *The People's Palace* in *The Egoist* 5: 6 (June/July 1918), and published his 'Three Variations' in *C.* 2: 7 (Apr. 1924), 296–9: this was the only work by Sitwell to be published there.

2–The Clark lectures were published only posthumously (*VMP*, 1993).

3–Ramón Fernandez, 'Le Classicisme de T. S. Eliot', in 'Lettres Étrangères', *NRF* 12: 173 (1 Feb. 1925), 246–51.

TO *Mary Hutchinson* MS Texas

Thursday [2 April 1925][1] 9 Clarence Gate Gdns

My dear Mary

This is merely a line to signify that we are still alive – if this is life – but no more. How are you? I only go out myself for a few hours in the afternoon, and Vivien is in torture again with a return of neuritis in arms and legs. I was sorry to miss you yesterday at Viola Tree's, but we look forward to a time when there will again be haystacks and picnics. We *do* want to *rent* a cottage or hovel near Chichester.

With love from both of us

Affectionately
Tom.

We may be going to explore soon.

FROM *Geoffrey Faber* CC

3 April 1925 [London]

My dear Eliot

I am going away for ten days or so next Wednesday, and I think I shall have to broach the question of the quarterly to my Directors before I go away, that is to say probably next Monday afternoon. But before I do so, I should like to have a final conversation with you. Will you let me know if you can manage this? Perhaps you would come and see me at my house some time on Sunday?[2] I shall not be at the office again till Monday morning.

Yours ever
[Geoffrey C. Faber]

1 – Postmarked 3 Apr. 1925.
2 – GCF noted in his diary (4 Apr.): 'Eliot came to tea, & we talked "*Criterion*" till 7.' (Faber Archive).

TO *Sydney Schiff* MS Valerie Eliot

Sunday [5 April 1925] 9 Clarence Gate Gdns

My dear Sydney

Thank you for your letter. I am afraid that there is no chance of our meeting before Wednesday, but please let me know when you will be back, because it is hopeless to try to explain what things have been and what they are, until we meet: – I must depend upon your faith until then.

I should like *very much* to see Saurat's book.[1]

I wish we could have come today. For one or two weeks we are certain to be in a tormented condition, for certain reasons, *besides* the fact that my fate depends on events of the next few days. I don't know *when* I shall be able to read *Myrtle* – but Vivienne has told me something about it, and anything that she says in praise of a book is worthwhile, because it is always definite – the only kind of praise worth having, in my opinion.[2]

Yours aff'y
Tom

[Memorandum by Geoffrey C. Faber, 5 April 1925]

Proposed publication of a Quarterly Review
With some remarks on other methods of securing writers.

1. *Development of 'literary' side of business.*

In setting to work to build up a 'literary' connection *de novo* it has to be remembered that there are a great number of publishers competing for

1–Denis Saurat, *Milton: Man and Thinker* (1925), a translation of *La pensée de Milton* (1920): it was reviewed by H. P. Collins in *NC* 4: 1 (Jan. 1926), 196–202.

2–TSE was not letting on that he had already enabled VHE to poke fun at SS's novel *Myrtle* (1925), written under his nom-de-plume Stephen Hudson. Hidden behind the initials 'F. M.', in C. 3: 11 (Apr. 1925), VHE praises the novelist's gift of 'saturating one in an atmosphere', but then she moves on to joke that the trouble with *Myrtle* 'is that one cannot find Myrtle, and one is worried by looking for her all the time . . . The result is a collection of character studies of somewhat uninteresting and unsavoury persons. But, as one peers between these figures, hoping to catch sight of the supremely interesting figure of Myrtle, around which this odd assemblage is hung, one is perpetually baffled. Where is Myrtle?' Thus, laying waste to SS's fiction, VHE closes her review; but she had preceded that coup-de-grace with a lance in her first paragraph in which she suggests that Mr Hudson's 'work is a model of concentration . . . This looks to me like the dramatic gift. It seems to me that Mr Hudson might write very good plays.'

authors, and that there is a natural reluctance on the part of many authors to give their work to an unknown firm, and a disposition on the part of the copyright agents to deal with the established publishers to whom they have hitherto sent their clients' work. These difficulties will gradually disappear as the firm becomes known; but at the outset and for the first two or three years efforts of a special kind will have to be made in order, primarily, to make the name of the firm known in the right kind of way, and, secondarily, to attract individual authors into our orbit. In particular, great efforts must be made to get hold of young writers – the Kiplings and Bennetts of the next generation – and, having got them, to treat them sufficiently well to encourage their allegiance to the firm when their reputation has been made. It is perfectly clear that, while we may hope to recoup ourselves by some early successes, our right policy is to put that out of our minds, and deliberately spend money to begin with on building up the connection we desire.

Authors can be got hold of in various ways. There is (i) the method of direct personal approach. Nothing need be said of that here, except that, valuable as it is, and though we shall practise it to the fullest possible extent, it is limited in range and results and can only be one factor in the growth of the business; (ii) the establishment of friendly relations with the copyright agencies. This is being done already to some extent, and will become easier when we are well under way. No more need be said of it now. But there are two other methods, both of which I think it will be advantageous for us to use: namely (iii) the offer of substantial cash prizes for the best novels or other works submitted to us; and (iv) the publication of a literary periodical.

As to (iii) I think it would be better to wait until the name of the Company has been changed before we come to any decision or make any announcement. But I certainly think we should do something of the kind. Public competitions of this sort do stimulate public interest in a remarkable way and in exactly the right quarters for our purposes. Such a competition would do a great deal to bring us at one step into the limelight.

2. *History of the 'Quarterly' project.*
But the proposal which calls for immediate decision is (iv). I had not intended to bring it so suddenly to an issue, but events have forced my hand.

In November last I asked Charles Whibley if he could get me into touch with some of the younger writers. He replied by introducing me to Mr T. S. Eliot, of whom he wrote to me subsequently as follows:

Jesus College
Cambridge

Dec. 7th

My dear Faber,

I will gladly tell you what I know about Eliot. He is of American birth and is related to the Eliot Nortons and Norton Eliots of Boston and Harvard. (He is strongly anti-American, as you would suppose, and is now being naturalized.) He was educated at Harvard and Oxford, and is at present in Lloyds Bank, in the Foreign Department. The Bank thinks very highly of him, and I believe he is at the head of the Intelligence Department. So that you may take it that he has been trained in business. He has published several books – 'The Sacred Wood' (prose), and 'Poems' and 'The Waste Land'. As a critic, he is the best and most learned of his generation, and is respected (and a little feared) by the young. As a poet he is obscure and allusive, but I have faith that he will come out of his obscurity and write something really fine.

I know him intimately, and count him among my closest friends, and I have a perfect belief in his star. He knows all the young writers and is well able to discriminate among them. He gave a lecture here in Cambridge not long since, and met with a reception from the Undergraduates which surprised me.

Is that the sort of thing you wanted to know?

Yours always
Charles Whibley

In the meantime I had met Mr Eliot, and had a long conversation with him – the first of many which have steadily deepened my sense of his ability, sincerity and charm. E. is a man of about thirty-five. He has for something over two years been the editor of a Quarterly Review called *The Criterion*, which is in fact the property of Lady Rothermere, and has cost her about £750 a year. It is a rather 'rarefied' review, expensively and luxuriously produced, and is published by Cobden-Sanderson. It is priced at 3s. 6d. and has a circulation of about 1000. It has been very little advertised, and the business management has been very slight indeed. Nevertheless it has a growing readership, entirely the result of Eliot's editorship, hampered though that has been by the circumstances of the Review, and by the fact that he has had no remuneration and has had to find time to edit the paper in the intervals of a business life (which he would give up if he could).

The following letter from Hugh Walpole indicates the kind of impression which Eliot's editorship has made in literary circles.

90 Piccadilly,
London W.1

4th February 1925

Dear Sir,

I have been asked to say something of my opinion of Mr T. S. Eliot as an editor. I do this with great readiness because for myself and a number of others who are interested in the future of English letters Mr Eliot is by far the most important figure as an influence in contemporary literature now in England. It is, I suppose, not necessary for anyone to say much about Mr Eliot's gifts as a poet and critic. I can imagine that the austerity of his judgement and the beauty of such a poem as 'The Waste Land' must be sufficient evidence to anyone who really cares about English literature, but his great gifts as an editor have been a revelation to many of us during the publication of his Quarterly, *The Criterion.* That Quarterly started very austerely and in its earlier numbers appeared to make its appeal of necessity only to a small circle of readers. The question was how to broaden its appeal without losing its character, the real test of any editor. The later numbers of *The Criterion* have in my opinion shown Mr Eliot to be a really great editor because he has made his own paper acceptable to a much larger reading public and at the same time has impressed everything in the paper with the mark of his own personality. I venture to think that if Mr Eliot had editorial control of a literary monthly that had sufficient money behind it to allow of some enterprise and adventure we should have one of the most remarkable periodicals that English letters have yet seen. In spite of his very high personal critical standards he has a wide appreciation of the different tastes of our English reading public and he has that finest editorial gift of all, the power to extract the highest standard of work from his contributors because of the force of his own personality. I think that as editor of such a monthly he would gather round him a very fine band of contributors. I hope he will be given an opportunity for work of this kind.

Yours truly,
Hugh Walpole.

Similar letters have been written by Bruce Richmond, editor of *The Times Literary Supplement*, and other distinguished judges. Worth quoting is the following from a reference to *The Criterion* by 'Affable Hawk' in *The New Statesman* (November 22, 1924):

> My respect for this magazine steadily increases; I find more good criticism in it than in any other . . . Altogether this number, and the more

recent numbers of *The Criterion*, have made me wish to act as town-crier for it ... Though it appears only once a quarter, I know no magazine which enables its readers to keep in touch with so many aesthetic questions. If it dies, which I trust it will not, it will have set a standard to subsequent ventures of the same kind hard to reach.

Eliot's reputation is, in fact, growing very surely, and is not confined to this country. From a very remarkable appreciation of his critical work in *La Nouvelle Revue Française* by Ramón Fernandez occupying some six or seven pages I take the following:

> Je connais peu de juges mieux armés que lui: intelligence incisive, courageuse, toujours insatisfaite d'elle-même, soucieuse à la fois de se limiter et de toucher le tuf des réalités qu'elle considere; culture vaste et comprehensive ... fortes reactions traditionelles contre lesquelles il a du sans doute lutter afin de se conquérir moi-même, voilà des titres qui le désignent pour la tache, infiniment périlleuse de chasseur de nuces et de redresser des torts de l'esprit.

Such testimony speaks for itself. But it is as well to add that Mr Eliot, in spite of his unusual equipment, is anything but a paralyzing highbrow. On the contrary he has the faculty of stimulating work, and a personality which will certainly make itself more and more felt.

Eliot's desire, at the time of my first meeting with him, was to convert *The Criterion* into a monthly, and to get some firm or a private group to guarantee it. He could not go on editing it 'for love', and wanted a five-year contract at a fixed salary.

Subsequently we agreed that a new monthly was out of the question. There are too many already in the field. Some of these will die, and the way may be open later for the conversion of a Quarterly into a monthly. For a really good Quarterly, containing criticism, fiction, some poetry, articles of general interest to educated people, and reviews, there seems to be a definite opening. Both the *Edinburgh* and the *Quarterly* are massive and on the whole dull, as well as expensive (7s. 6d.). A quarterly can, doing the thing only four times a year, do it better and more fully than a monthly can; and it can get a bigger foreign and American circulation than a monthly, because it gets less quickly out of date.

We were still tentatively discussing this possibility, when Eliot was asked to deliver the 'Clark' lectures at Cambridge next year. He has till April 24 to accept or refuse. He cannot accept, unless he gives up his job at Lloyds; and he cannot afford to do that unless he knows whether we will back him or not. The lectures will add to his reputation, and to his value as an editor.

3. *Financial.*
I have been closely into cost. Clearly, while the immediate value of the Quarterly will be the publicity we shall get from it and the contact we shall hope to establish through it with new writers, it is undesirable to commit ourselves to an undertaking which could never pay its way. Allowing £400 a year for the editor's salary, £400 for contributors, £100 for typist-secretary (half-time), £200 for ordinary advertising, £40 for stationery and postage, and for free copies 'overs' and discounts, and taking the advertisement rates at £10 a page subject to 25% discounts, I have worked out the net annual loss or profit according to the attached table. The figures are, of course, only approximate estimates; but they are as exact as they can be made, and are based on the estimates I have obtained from different printers. They show clearly that the right policy is to price the paper higher than lower. I think it should be 5/-. It ought to be quite possible to work up to 3000. At that we should make a profit of over £500 a year. At 2000 it would just about pay for itself. At 1000 (of which we may be certain, I think) the loss at the very worst could not be more than some £700 – a good deal less than the loss on the *Hospital and Health Review*. It would be advisable to spend an additional £100 or so on preliminary advertising.

It is interesting to note that the advertisement revenue, while it might be of great assistance, would never justify low pricing. At 2/6 with a maximum circulation of 5000 and a maximum of 19 pages of advertisements the annual profit would only be £368. At 5/- with half that circulation and half that number of advertisements the profit would be about £480.

4. *Outlines of proposal.*
It is proposed to invite Mr Eliot to join the Board of Directors and to agree with him to publish a Quarterly Review, to be edited by him at a salary of £325 a year in addition to his remuneration as Director (£400 if he is not a Director). The agreement to be for five years, with the usual safeguards, and a proviso that we may cease publication within that period, provided we pay him his salary for the remainder of the period. The first number to be published in the autumn, and the agreement to take effect as from July 1 1925. Salary to be subject to revision, if and when the paper makes a sufficient profit.

Mr Eliot should prove a valuable member of the Board; his presence there would greatly assist us in making contact between the Company and the contributors to his paper.

Geoffrey C. Faber
April 5th 1925.

FROM *Geoffrey Faber* cc

6 April 1925 [London]

My dear Eliot

I am very glad to be able to tell you that at a meeting of our Board of Directors this afternoon, we decided to invite you to become the Editor of a new quarterly review, to be published by us, at a salary of £400 a year, to be reduced to £325 a year if it should be possible to offer you a seat on the Board of Directors at any time, carrying with it a remuneration of £150.[1] We are prepared to enter into an agreement with you for a period of five years with the proviso that we may cease publication of the review within that period on condition that we pay you the salary due for the remainder of the period. The first number to be published in the Autumn, and the agreement to take effects as from July 1st, 1925.[2] It is further understood that if and when the paper should

[. . .][3]

know you will be glad to hear of our decision, and to be able to make your plans accordingly.

To your own letter I can say nothing in reply, except that it is of the sort to warm the heart.

Yours ever,
[Geoffrey C. Faber]

TO *Richard Aldington* MS Texas

Tuesday, 8 April 1925[4] 9 Clarence Gate Gdns

My dear Richard

I have just seen the new *Vogue*, and re-read your article, and am more than ever overwhelmed by your 'generous pleasure in praise'.[5] This would

1–GCF wrote in his diary (5 Apr.): 'Special directors' meeting in the afternoon, to . . . decide about Eliot. We did decide finally to back him as editor of a Quarterly review. I am tremendously pleased. I wrote to E. tout de suite. He will now be able to give up his job at Lloyds.' (Faber Archive)

2–In the event, there was no Autumn number of C. There was a six-month interregnum between *C.* 3: 12 (July 1925), published under Lady Rothermere's patronage, and *NC* 4: 1 (Jan. 1926), published by F&G.

3–Five lines of this letter, taken from the faded carbon copy in GCF's letter-book, are worn out.

4–Misdated 7 April.

5–RA, 'T. S. Eliot, Poet and Critic: A Scholarly and Austere Modern Whose Classicism and Coherent Thought is of Serious Importance to His Generation', *Vogue* 65: 7 (Apr. 1925),

be the same even if I believed that every word of it was true! I think it is a most marvellous eulogy. What a man you are. My wife sends you a message:– that she is very glad that I have *you* for a friend, and that I ought to be very proud of your friendship. – But I *am*.

I don't suppose you will be in London till after your holiday, and I don't think you *ought* to come to this horrid town (*vide* Dr Johnson) yet, but I should like to see you when possible.

It is probable that I shall either have another quarterly or the *Criterion* on a salary, and leave the bank in June. I shall want you, and as much of you, as I can get. <Everything is very complex at the moment.> This is in confidence.

Would you have time this summer to do a Tudor Tr? I am seeing C. W.

Enclosed Bruce [Richmond]'s letter. I had to write as he was out of town. Will you write to Miss Todd, and get what scanty credit there is for the work? I wish I could have done something.

My wife is still very weak, and ought to get away, but I am tied hand and foot to London by the business I mentioned. She really broke down completely in health. She had been working very hard for some months, doing a lot of the *Criterion* work, and also writing. She is very diffident, and is very aware that her mind is quite untrained, and therefore writes only under assumed names: but she has an original mind, and I consider not at all a feminine one; and in my opinion a great deal of what she writes is quite good enough for the *Criterion*. She has not had the strength to do

–

70–1, 96. 'No English writer of his generation has exerted so intense an influence through so little published work. Mr Eliot's reputation and influence may not unjustly be likened to those of Mallarmé in the 'eighties and of M. Paul Valéry in our own time. He is not known to the crowd; he is not even very widely read by the educated classes; but his influence can be detected in many places. His work is incessantly discussed by those who are genuinely interested in modern literature. If he chose to play the game of Fashion he might easily aspire to the intellectual dictatorship of Mayfair. It is only ten years since he came here, quite unknown, from America with the manuscript of *Prufrock* in his baggage. Without any of the pleasing exaggerations of friendship one can say that within a decade his four small volumes have given him the reputation at least of showing more promise, both as a poet and as a critic, than any English writer of his generation' (71). His conversation, added RA, is 'as stimulating and brilliant as his writing'; so that altogether: 'here is a modern among moderns who is not scared of the past, who gladly acknowledges his immense debts to Aristotle and Dante; a man of culture who is intensely preoccupied with the problems of modern art. His thought is destructive because it attempts to annihilate Romanticism – aesthetic, moral and political; but it is constructive because it attempts to put something better in its place.' The piece was accompanied by a full-page photograph of TSE by Maurice Beck and Macgregor: he is dressed in an elegant suit, seated, reading a folio vol. and smoking a cigarette.

1 – Samuel Johnson, *London* (1738).

all this and lead a social life as well, and therefore has almost disappeared from the world. I intend to see that she gets training and systematic education, because there are so few women who have an un-feminine mind that I think they ought to be made the most of. You are the only person, except two of her friends, who now knows of her writing. But *I* see no reason now for concealment.

Ever yours
Tom

Let me have your news.
Tell me if you consider H. P. Collins, in the new *Criterion*, a likely recruit?[1]

TO *John Middleton Murry* MS Valerie Eliot

[mid-April? 1925] [London]

In the last ten years – gradually, but deliberately – I have made myself into a *machine*. I have done it deliberately – in order to endure, in order not to feel – *but it has killed* V.[2] In leaving the bank I hope to become less a machine – but yet I am frightened – because I don't know what it will do to me – and to V. – should I come alive again. I have deliberately killed my senses – I have deliberately died – in order to go on with the outward form of living – This I did in 1915. What will happen if I live again? 'I am I'[3] but with what feelings, with what results to *others* – Have I the right to be I – But the dilemma – to kill another person by being dead, or to kill them by being alive? Is it best to make oneself a machine, and kill them by not giving nourishment, or to be alive, and kill them by wanting something that one *cannot* get from that person? Does it happen that two persons' lives are absolutely hostile? Is it true that sometimes one can only live by another's dying?[4]

1–H. P. Collins, 'A Note on the Classical Principle in Poetry', C. 3: 11 (Apr. 1925), 389–400.
2–It was ten years earlier, on 24 Apr. 1915, that TSE told Eleanor Hinkley he had recently met an English girl named 'Vivien' in Oxford. TSE and VHE were married on 26 June 1915.
3–Cf. 'I am that I am' (Exodus 3: 14). 'Richard loves Richard; that is, I am I' (*Richard III*, 5. iii 183).
4–Cf. *SA*, in which Sweeney says 'Life is death':

He didn't know if he was alive
and the girl was dead
He didn't know if the girl was alive
and he was dead
He didn't know if they were both alive
or both were dead

'Fragment of a Prologue' appeared in *NC* 4: 4 (Oct. 1926).

<Answer *this*> During this illness she really *went away – for three days she felt that she had left her body. Is this wrong?* Should it be discouraged? Is there a way in which I can lay down my life and gain it? Must I kill her or kill myself? I have *tried* to kill myself – but only to make the machine which kills her. Can I exorcise this desire for what I cannot have, for someone I cannot see,[1] and give to her, life, and save my soul? I feel now that one cannot help another by *ruining* one's own soul – I have done that – can one help another and save it?

Does she want to die? Can I save myself and her by recognising that she is more important than I?

T. S. E.

TO *John Middleton Murry* MS Valerie Eliot

Easter [12 April 1925] *The Criterion,* 17 Thavies Inn

My dear John

I have wished daily that I might talk to you. But now I think I understand Vivien's illness a little better than when I saw you, and I want to put it to you now and get your opinion and advice.

I don't know yet what is the core, the egg, of the thing. I don't know what is the spring that is snapped, the formula of her mind, her temperament, personality, that has been isolated. What I *am* convinced of, however, is that *this* illness was directly precipitated and brought about by the interview she had with Dr Martin last June.[2] Dr Higgins, and indeed every previous doctor, had directed her mind *outward* and *forward*: Martin, seeing her *once*, deliberately turned it inward and backward. She has become a different person since that day. The process has continued, and the burden of this consciousness and introspection has become so great that she collapsed under it. It paralyses action, and as she sees more and more clearly and dwells more and more constantly on the past, she is overwhelmed by the *damage* that people have done her (and I am not the least important of them) and how her personal relations – with her family, with me, with friends – have been poisoned.

There are many things, my dear John, which I should like to ask you, because I know that in many ways – spiritually, you are much wiser than I. Intellectually, we are often, perhaps always, at opposite poles. To me

1 – Emily Hale.
2 – Both TSE and VHE saw Dr K. B. Martin in May and June 1924.

and you – not to the 'general public' – that is a small matter – it is *comparatively* easy to find *intellectual* sympathy.

We agree, I believe, about the danger and harm of psychoanalysis – tampering with minds.[1] This having been done by Martin, what is the way to put Vivien right again?

Yours
Tom

Do you know 'standing in another
person's light' (from either side)?[2]
How can I get out of hers?
At the moment she is *utterly* dependent.

TO *Ada Leverson* — MS Berg

Easter [12 April] 1925 — 9 Clarence Gate Gdns

Dear Mrs Leverson

Thank you very much for your note. I am so glad you like the new *Criterion* – I think it *is* a particularly good one. I believe you must have guessed that all the contributions signed by F— M— are by Vivienne and although the secret is *not out* yet, I have no objection to *your* knowing – in confidence. Vivienne has had a horrible time this winter with influenza and neuritis, and is *very* run down, and is going to the country at once to try to get over it. She sends you her love and best wishes. *Do* send me a contribution, I should be delighted to look at anything from you.[3]

Sincerely yours
T. S. Eliot

1 – In his 'London Letter' of Aug. 1922, TSE wrote of 'the soul of man under psychoanalysis'. He noted that 'there is no possibility of tapping the atmosphere of unknown terror and mystery in which our life is passed and which psychoanalysis has not yet analysed' (*Dial* 73: 3, Sept. 1922, 330).

2 – 'As if *officium* came of *officiendo*, of standing in another man's light, & doing other men hurt . . . There is no power given to any "to destruction", or to do harm' (Lancelot Andrewes, Sermon on Whit-Sunday 1622).

3 – Ada Leverson's memoir of Wilde, 'The Last First Night', appeared in *NC* 4: 1 (Jan. 1926).

TO *Richard Aldington* MS Texas

Wednesday [15 April 1925] *The Criterion*, 17 Thavies Inn

My dear Richard

I feel that I have failed to express my *appreciation* of your kindness in writing this article for *Vogue* – I do indeed realise the thought and generosity which have gone into it.[1] Incidentally, it says just what I should like to be said.

I want to show you the Rothermere correspondence when I come. I felt that it was safer for you as well as for me not to run any risk of pneumonia or bronchitis while on your hands, especially as my chest seems to be weakened by this illness.

If you hear of any cottage to let – or to sell *cheap* – let me know.

By the way, I can introduce you to a good broker if you wish. Without any personal interest at stake, I have an aversion for most foreign securities.

If you wish to come up on Wednesday I could arrange to wait till then and go back with you. – I want to see Bruce, but I had rather see you first.

Yours ever
Tom.

TO *Sylvia Beach*[2] MS Princeton

15 April 1925 *The Criterion*, 17 Thavies Inn

Dear Miss Beach

Thank you for your letter and for Mr Joyce's MSS. which I am delighted to have.[3] Will you, when you can, convey my and my wife's deep sympathy

1 – See TSE's letter of 8 Apr. (above).

2 – Sylvia Beach (1887–1962), American expatriate who in Nov. 1919 opened Shakespeare & Company, a bookshop and lending library, at 8 rue Dupuytren, Paris, moving two years later to 12 rue de l'Odéon. Her customers included Joyce (she published *Ulysses*), Gide, Maurois, Valéry, Pound, Hemingway and Gertrude Stein. TSE wrote in a tribute ('Miss Sylvia Beach', *The Times*, 13 Oct. 1962): 'I made the acquaintance of Sylvia Beach, and . . . of her friend Adrienne Monnier, on a visit to Paris early in the nineteen twenties, and thereafter saw them frequently during that decade. Only the scattered survivors of the Franco-Anglo-American literary world of Paris of that period, and a few others like myself who made frequent excursions across the Channel, know how important a part these two women played in the artistic and intellectual life of those years.'

3 – 'Fragment of an Unpublished Work' appeared in C. 3: 12 (July 1925), 498–510: this was an early version of *Finnegans Wake*, 104–25.

to him and to Mrs Joyce? I should be *very grateful* if you would let me know later the result of the operation.[1]

With all best wishes to yourself.

Sincerely yours
T. S. Eliot

The next *Criterion* should appear toward the end of June.

FROM *John Middleton Murry* MS Valerie Eliot

Thursday [? 16 April 1925] The Old Coastguard Station, Abbotsbury, Weymouth, Dorset

My dear Tom

Your letters have reached me only this morning. I am very sorry for the delay: but it was unavoidable.

Of one thing I am convinced. That it is your duty *absolutely* to come alive again. Absolutely, – this without regard to what may be the consequences for V. How you are to do it, and what may be those consequences for V., I cannot prophesy. You have done a great wrong to yourself, and a great wrong has been done to her. You are involved in a vicious circle, which thinking only tightens: you must break it by destroying the machine into which you have made yourself.

I know the consequences of this *may* be awful for V. I don't know that they will be. But I am sure that nothing but harm can come of your trying to kill yourself to keep her alive.

Don't misunderstand me. I am not saying you will not continue to make sacrifices for her, and great ones. But you must cease to sacrifice your inviolable self. What you choose to do *for* her, you must do with all yourself; what you refuse to do for her, you must refuse with all yourself. Let the giving and the refusing alike be your own wholly: the word being 'This *I* will do: this *I* cannot and will not do.'

Oh, Tom, I am almost afraid to say these things, because I do not feel certain that I could do what I tell you to do. But I think I know this. There

1 – On 23 Apr., Beach reported that JJ had had a capsulotomy operation on his left eye, which enabled him to see immediately but not at all afterwards, possibly owing to some haemorrhaging. As he was still suffering from conjunctivitis in the right eye, he could only read with the aid of three magnifying glasses. JJ had left hospital on 22 Apr. but would have to return twice a day for treatment; he told Beach that 'the only thing they had left to do with his eye now is to take it out and take it home with them'.

is a point at which the choice really is: she may die, I must die. Then you must say: I will not die.

That sounds terrible: it is terrible, but not in the way it sounds terrible. When you take your stand: 'I will not die', then indeed you do die – to all that you were. That choice is a self-sacrifice of the deepest.

Live, and let come what may. One of you two must go forward. It can't be V. She can only go forward by bodily death, in the state she is in now. And anyhow going forward is the man's job. If going forward for you means an end of some sort of your relation, still, go forward. Get out of her light that way. But try not to think about the future. You can't know what will be. And I am sure that there is no other way of helping her.

I see no good in discouraging her from 'going away'. It is only her particular form of a going away that is inevitable as between you. You will have to do yours but differently.

Give V. my love

John.

TO *John Middleton Murry* — MS Valerie Eliot

Friday [mid-April 1925] — *The Criterion*, 17 Thavies Inn

My dear John

Thank you for your letter. I think I understand it. What I do not know is whether I have put the case rightly without distorting it to my own point of view. I must ask: does it all correspond with what you have seen for yourself?

I know that the spring is Fear – a fear which I cannot account for.[1] And I know that I have killed *her*.[2] And this terrible sense of the most subtle form of *guilt* is itself paralysing and deadening.

At the moment, I want to ask one thing more. V. knew that I was writing to you – suggested it. She asked if I had heard from you. I don't think I can show her your letter – not now. Will you write to me *again* – what you think she should see – and more for her case than mine.

I give her nothing to live for, I have blocked every outlet.

We think of you constantly. We want to know when your child is born.[3]

Tom.

1 – Cf. TSE's draft title for *Murder in the Cathedral*: *Fear in the Way*. JMM had written 'On Fear; And on Romanticism', in *Adelphi* 1: 4 (Sept. 1923).
2 – Cf. *SA*: 'I knew a man once did a girl in'.
3 – A daughter, Katherine, was born to the Murrys on 20 Apr.

TO *Violet Schiff* MS Valerie Eliot

17 April 1925 9 Clarence Gate Gdns

My dear Violet

I am just writing a line to both as Vivienne is unable to sit up. On top of everything she has had the most excruciating neuralgia in her head and sinus – result of a chill – which is not only most weakening, but the pain puts her stomach all wrong too. I don't think anyone has ever had such a chain of misfortune. I have plans – but the immediate present and future are the anxieties.

She showed me your letter – I was delighted with what you say. She *must* come out and be known – she has another wonderful <and terrible> story, if she will *let* me print it![1]

We *must* meet (tell S.) when <*as soon as*> you come back. I think of you often.

Yrs affectionately,
Tom

She must be made to act – you can train her better than anyone.[2] Should we have more charades next winter?

TO *Allan Wade* MS Valerie Eliot

17 April 1925 9 Clarence Gate Gdns

Dear Mr Wade

Thank you for your time and flattering letter. I am writing to Mr Wilkinson to say that I shall be very glad to accept, and hope to be of more service in the autumn than I could be at present.[3]

Also, I shall look forward to meeting you.

Sincerely yours
T. S. Eliot

1 – VHE's story is 'The Paralysed Woman', which TSE was to send to the *Dial* for publication under the name of 'V. H. Eliot'. It tells the story of Sybilla, a writer who is in pain as she types, and realises she is envied by an immaculate and elegant young woman who lives across the way. The other woman is attended to by maids and chauffeurs, but is paralysed. Sybilla is staying with a friend in her seaside flat, while her husband comes at weekends, with his bowler hat and suitcases, one of which is full of books and periodicals and the other full of medicine bottles.

2 – Writing to SS on 31 Aug. 1920, TSE had asked about Vivien's 'success as an actress'.

3 – This may refer to TSE's offer to give advice about Renaissance plays to the Phoenix Society.

TO *Arnold Bennett* MS Beinecke

18 April 1925 9 Clarence Gate Gdns

Dear Mr Bennett,

I came to see you last in *November* with the outline and some dialogue of my play [*Sweeney Agonistes*]. I am writing now to explain that since December either I or my wife has been continually ill – I have had two months lately on end; – and my wife three months, of critical illness which is not ended; and I have had to let everything go.

I do not want you to think that I have troubled you for nothing. The help you gave me determined me to carry out this play: I have thought of it a great deal, and I shall finish it next winter.

And especially I wish that I may bring it to you again; I hope you will allow me to do so in the autumn – because, as I said before, and as I have proved, there is no one but yourself for whose opinion and advice I care, in such a venture.

<And may I remind you that you promised to let me publish, at some time, your observations on the art of fiction and *character*?[1] I still hope. I wish that I might see you, and have your criticism of recent fiction in the *Criterion*.>

Sincerely yours
T. S. Eliot

TO *Ottoline Morrell* MS Texas

Sunday, 19 April 1925 *The Criterion*, 17 Thavies Inn

My dear Ottoline,

Neither of us has heard from you for so long that we are rather concerned. Do let me know – if you can – how you are. I am afraid you have been very ill and harassed?

Vivien is still paying for the bad effects of the Cyriax treatment.[2] I am convinced that these people have done her damage that will take a *very*

1–This was conceived as a response to VW's critique, in 'Mr Bennett and Mrs Brown', published as 'Character in Fiction' in C. 2: 8 (July 1923). It never materialised.

2–The treatment given by the husband-and-wife team of Cyriax who attended VHE. HWE would write to CCE on 10 May 1925: 'What ill luck they do seem to have with doctors! They thought this Dr Cyriax was such a wonder at the time. Tom has indeed a dreadful time. I suppose it is cruel and unsympathetic to think of Tom's troubles more than Vivien's, but it is of course natural . . . I cannot believe that all the congratulation that Vivien receives on her writing is quite sincere' (Houghton).

long time to repair. Irritating and weakening the stomach, over-stimulating and exhausting the nerves. Her stomach is *persistently* relaxed and *out of place*, pressing on the heart and on nerves, and I think thereby causing the neuritis. She is now – for the last week – in *agony* with neuralgia of the sinus and antrim [*sc.* antrum]. And *you* know what that is, and the excruciation of any pain so near the brain.

The immediate future is giving me great anxiety. I cannot leave V. at present, and yet I ought to be in the City, for particular reasons. I have certain schemes which should mature before I see you – but when will that be? Vivien often speaks of you and longs to see you. When do you come? Please let me hear of you if not from you.

With love from both

Affectionately
Tom.

This neuralgia makes her almost *blind*, so that she cannot write a line. But she does want you to be one of her very first contacts in attempting to return to life.

TO *Virginia Woolf* — MS Texas

Sunday 19 April [1925] — *The Criterion*, 17 Thavies Inn

My dear Virginia,

You said you were going to France for a fortnight, but I am sure it is much longer than that.[1] If you are in London now, *why* do you not let me know? Do not deprive me of the hope of seeing one of the 'few people'. Especially as I don't know about the more distant future – we don't know where we shall be after June, but I hope not in London. May I come to see you?[2]

Vivien can't move, with violent neuralgia and neuritis. It will be months before she can get right again: only her brain is alive, at present.

How are you both?

Yrs ever
T. S. E.

Why are the Essays not out?[3]
<It has been a great distress to *me* to have seen so little of you.>

1 – The Woolfs were on holiday in France, 26 Mar. – 6 Apr.
2 – VW records in her diary that TSE visited them on the evening of Tues., 28 Apr.
3 – VW, *The Common Reader*, a collection of essays published by Hogarth Press on 23 Apr.

FROM *John Middleton Murry* MS Valerie Eliot

20 April [1925] The Old Coastguard Station,
Abbotsbury

My dear Tom,

A daughter was born this morning at 5.20, tell Vivien. A queer strange business. One is taken in hand, borne on the flood, by something far greater than we can know. One listens, and the cries of the woman upstairs are not *her* cries at all, not her voice: but the voice of something terribly strong and impersonal. Suddenly they are still – quite *suddenly* – and out of the tense stillness a queer, strange, *new* little cry. That moment of stillness is like a crack in the universe for the man listening – utterly unfathomable.

I am a bit tired. Therefore what I say may not be too coherent. But this is clear. Don't be afraid of coming alive: it is a fearful thing – it may, certainly will, involve consequences unknown, for you and V. You cannot foreknow them: when you think you do, you deceive yourself and increase the burden of your fear. You have to take a leap in the dark – nothing you can do, save the leap itself, will lighten the darkness. But, if you will really lead, take the decision and the responsibility, V. will follow. Every new shoot you can put out will, in some way or other be life-giving for her. She will only look forward, because you are going forward. A woman's direction is given only by her man: that is the law.

Even though your mind should tell you that the leap, or any move, forward towards your *self*, will be dangerous to V., still you must do it. Your mind doesn't know anything about it, because it can only speak of what has been, not of what will be. The truth is that if you can break through the circle, V. breaks through too. (You know I am not talking of happiness: I don't know whether you or she will be happy. But *happiness doesn't matter*. Life does.)

Nothing matters now, not even V., beside the question: will *you* go forward or not? (Show her this: she will understand.) *How* go forward? Do whatever thing your being says you must, and trample down what your mind says you ought. Put resolutely away from yourself all sense of guilt for the past: put that responsibility on to the universe. You may, and must. There is no past, once you begin to live: then there is only the present.

I wish, at this moment, you both were here, or I was there.

John

TO *Marianne Moore* MS Rosenbach

20 April 1925 9 Clarence Gate Gdns

Dear Miss Moore,

But for constant illness I should have written to you some time ago to express my pleasure at the *Dial* award – which confers a new and retroactive value upon the award itself. You must know that no choice could have pleased me more.

Sincerely yours,
T. S. Eliot

TO *Humbert Wolfe* CC

21 April 1925 9 Clarence Gate Gdns

My dear Wolfe,

Many thanks for your new poems and for the inscription.[1] I have been enjoying them. But you have given me a difficulty. I must try to find a reviewer with a muse as light-footed as your own and who will appreciate the kind of conversational grace which is pretty uncommon nowadays, and which makes me think of Calverley although I am not making any close comparisons.[2]

I am going to read your story at once.[3] Please forgive the delay, as both I and my wife have had a very long illness. When I return to the world again I hope I shall find you there.

Yours ever,
[T. S. E.]

TSE/IPF

1–Humbert Wolfe, *The Unknown Goddess* (1925).
2–It was reviewed by H. P. Collins, *C.* 3: 12 (July 1925), 584–6. Charles Stuart Calverley (1831–84): poet and parodist whose *Verses and Translations* (1862) and *Fly Leaves* (1872) combined academic scholarship and wit with parodies of the popular poets of the day.
3–TSE later turned down Wolfe's story 'Mr Fromage and George Gregory'.

TO *Gertrude Stein*[1]

MS Beinecke

21 April 1925 *The Criterion*, 17 Thavies Inn

Dear Miss Stein

I must apologise most humbly for the long delay, due to my and my wife's severe illness. I no longer, of course, have any claim on your poem, but I should like to use it. That would have to be in October,[2] as the unexpected receipt of two contributions from people whom I promised to print as soon as possible, has jammed the June.

I am immensely interested in everything you write.

Hoping that we may meet again before long.

Sincerely yours
pp. *The Criterion*
T. S. Eliot

TO *Arnold Bennett*

MS Beinecke

21 April 1925 *The Criterion*, 9 Clarence Gate Gdns

Dear Mr Bennett

Thank you very much for your kind letter. I should love to lunch with you on Saturday, but unfortunately under present conditions it is impossible for me to lunch or dine out. I should like to come to see you – if I may, one day at teatime (late) or after dinner. If that is possible in the immediate future could you leave word, and I will ring up? I am only not free on Tuesday next.

I am very sorry indeed that I cannot lunch with you.

With many thanks

Sincerely yours
T. S. Eliot

1–Gertrude Stein (1874–1946), American writer; author of *The Making of Americans* (1911) and other experimental essays in prose and drama; famous for her Paris salon and association with artists and writers inc. Picasso and F. Scott Fitzgerald.

2–The autumn C. did not appear. Stein's prose sketch 'Fifteenth of November' appeared in *NC* 4: 1 (Jan. 1926), 71–5.

TO *Bertrand Russell* MS McMaster

21 April [1925] 9 Clarence Gate Gdns

Dear Bertie,

If you are still in London I should very much like to see you.

My times and places are very restricted, but it is unnecessary to mention them unless I hear from you.

I want words from you which only you can give. But if you have now ceased to care at all about either of us, just write on a slip 'I do not care to see you' or 'I do not care to see either of you' – and I will understand.[1]

In case of that, I will tell you now that everything has turned out as you predicted ten years ago.[2] You are a great psychologist.

Yours
T. S. E.

FROM *Bertrand Russell* MS Valerie Eliot

23 April 1925 Carn Voel, Porthcurno, Penzance

My dear Tom

I am very sorry I am not in town now, as I should very much wish to see you, in view of your letter. If you can come down here, say at Whitsuntide, I should be more glad than I can say. My affection for you is what it always has been since I got to know you well.[3] So if there is any moment when your duties allow you to get away, do come and pay a visit here. Meanwhile, would you care to write more fully about what is wrong? Vivien has avoided me for the last seven or eight years, and I suppose still wants to do so, but if not I shouldn't like her to imagine that there is any

1–VHE had broken off relations with BR in early 1919, though she wrote again during TSE's breakdown on 1 Nov. 1921 to congratulate him on the imminent birth of his first child.

2–BR first met VHE on 9 July 1915, soon after the Eliots' marriage. It is possible that he was briefly her lover in the course of that summer. In Sept. 1915, he told OM that VHE had 'a great deal of mental passion & *no* physical passion, a universal vanity, that makes her desire every man's devotion, & a fastidiousness that makes any expression of their devotion disgusting to her' (Ray Monk, *Bertrand Russell: The Spirit of Solitude*, 440). The prediction to which TSE refers could be that which BR penned to OM on 10 Nov. 1915: 'she is really very fond of him, but has impulses of cruelty to him from time to time. It is a Dostojewsky type of cruelty . . . She is a person who lives on a knife edge, & will end as criminal or saint – I don't know which yet' (ibid., 440).

3–On 10 Nov. 1915, BR had told OM that he loved TSE 'as if he were my son'.

lack of friendliness on my side.[1] Whatever is the matter, you can count on me to help in any possible way.

You know, I suppose that I stayed with your brother in Chicago – he was very kind, and reminded me vividly of you.[2] With all affection,

Yours
Bertrand Russell

FROM *Geoffrey Faber* CC

23 April 1925 [London]

My dear Eliot

I am glad to be able to say that I have received the resignation of one of our Directors, and that at our Directors' Meeting this afternoon, you were appointed a Director of the Company. Our arrangements therefore with you will be on the lines which we agreed upon; namely, a salary of £325 as Editor and £150 as Director. The latter is paid half-yearly in arrear, so that you will, at the end of June, get two-sixths of £75, i.e. £25.

We must meet as soon as possible and celebrate the victory.

Yours ever
[Geoffrey C. Faber]

TO *L. H. C. Prentice* TS Reading

23 April 1925 *The Criterion*, 9 Clarence Gate Gdns

Dear Mr Prentice

The poems[3] which you sent me for my opinion have considerable merit. They suffer from a defect from which nearly all contemporary verse suffers, i.e. lack of an individual and mature rhythm. The versification is often rough, and the technique, though ingenious and showing a sense of experiment, is not accomplished. Bearing in mind what seems to me the

1 – According to Colette O'Niel, VHE wrote to BR in Jan. 1919 to say that she disliked fading intimacies and wanted to break with him completely (cited in Monk, *Bertrand Russell*, 544).

2 – BR had stayed with HWE for four days in Apr. 1924.

3 – On 16 Mar. L. H. C. (Charles) Prentice (an editor at the publisher Chatto & Windus) sent TSE some poems by Alec Brown ('a friend of Prince Mirsky's') which had 'flummoxed' him: he offered to pay TSE two guineas for his evaluation of the MS. Brown was a prolific translator from Russian and French; and author of *Beethoven Deaf, and Other Poems* (New York, 1927). See also Richard Aldington, *Pinorman: Personal Recollections of Norman Douglas, Pino Orioli, and Charles Prentice* (1954).

policy of your house, that is, I believe, to concentrate on rather a small number of writers and publish the whole of their work, I should not say that this writer had yet reached the point of being a safe and suitable investment for your house. When I say 'investment', I do not merely mean that the publication would not be remunerative; I mean that one cannot yet be certain of the author's future. The verse is too good to be popular and too crude to be distinguished. It seems to me, frankly, more suitable for one of the smaller publishing houses or private publishing firms which make more of a speciality of introducing new poetry.

I am returning the manuscript to you with this letter by hand.

Yours very truly,
[T. S. E.]
(pp IPF)

TSE/IPF

TO *S. S. Koteliansky* TS BL

24 April 1925

The Criterion,
23 Adelphi Terrace House

Dear Koteliansky,

Thank you for your letter of the 22nd sending me the new manuscripts of Dostoevsky.[1] They seem of great interest and I should like to use them. The July number is already filled to overflowing. Would October suit you?

Sincerely yours,
T. S. Eliot

TO *W. L. Johnston* CC

24 April 1925

23 Adelphi Terrace House

Dear Sir,

I have your letter of the 21st. I quite agree with you about the quality of Mr Bain's work and am taking the liberty of sending him your letter. We hope to have one or two contributions by Mr Bain regularly.

Mr Bain is not a prolific writer, and furthermore, you will understand that in a small quarterly review like the *Criterion* it is impossible to have

1–Koteliansky wrote on 22 Apr., enclosing an article, 'Dostoevsky on *The Brothers Karamazov*', a set of 'new, hitherto unpublished letters'.

many long contributions by the same writer. And it is necessary to appeal to a variety of tastes and interests. But I wish to assure you that on the subjects on which Mr Bain writes he is not only voicing his own opinions but is representing the policy of this paper, which is strongly reactionary and anti-romantic.

Yours faithfully,
[T. S. E.]

TSE/IPF

TO *F. W. Bain*

CC

24 April 1925 — 23 Adelphi Terrace House

My dear Bain,

I think that you ought to see the enclosed letter, and to know that I am as desirous as the writer that we should have more of your work.[1] I should have written to you and attempted a meeting this winter, but have been almost completely a recluse owing to a severe illness, followed by the much more severe illness of my wife.

By the way, a young Balliol man of my acquaintance, a clever Jew from Alexandria, named Jean de Menasce,[2] has written to ask me if you would allow your article on Disraeli[3] to be published in translation in *La Revue Juive*, which he is editing in Paris.[4] I told him to write to you and quote his terms.

With all best wishes, and looking forward to seeing you again and to having more essays from you,[5]

Yours very sincerely,
[T. S. E.]

TSE/IPF.

1–From W. L. Johnston.

2–See TSE's letter of 10 Mar. 1924.

3–'Disraeli', C. 2: 6 (Feb. 1924), 143–66.

4–In the first issue of *La Revue Juive* (15 Jan. 1925), the editor Albert Cohen proclaimed that it was 'fondée par des hommes qui ont conscience d'appartenir à une race vivante dont l'œuvre spirituelle n'est pas encore achevée' ['founded by men conscious of belonging to a living race whose spiritual work is not yet completed'].

5–Bain's only other contribution was a review of books on Napoleon, in 11: 42 (Oct. 1931).

TO *Douglas Ainslie* CC

27 April 1925 23 Adelphi Terrace House

Dear Mr Ainslie,

I must apologise to you for not having written to you about your poem but I have been ill for a long time and unable to attend to any correspondence. I am afraid that there has been some misunderstanding. While I expressed appreciation of your poem, I did not hold out to myself any hope of being able to use it.[1] We are unfortunately able to print only very little verse, and with the other contributions which have been accepted I am afraid that it will be impossible for us to accept any more verse for at least a year.

Pray forgive the delay in answering your letters.

With all best wishes,

Yours very truly,
[T. S. E.]

TO *John Middleton Murry* MS Northwestern

Tuesday [28? April 1925] 9 Clarence Gate Gdns

My dear John

Thank you very much for the essay.[2] As I said, it is too late for June. I can use it in October. I am eager to read it.

I very deeply appreciate your writing me such a letter as yours at a moment so vital to you.[3] I shall write to you, but meanwhile only say that we are *very glad* for your having a child, and successfully, I hope, in every way. We think of you very often.

Ever yours
Tom

The clouds have not lifted, and so forgive me for not writing sooner.

1 – Ainslie wrote on 19 Apr. to regret that his 'little poem' 'Idoch' had not yet appeared in C.; he thought TSE had 'agreed to print it eventually'.

2 – 'The Romantic Fallacy', a discussion of Tolstoy's *What is Art?* and Keats's *Letters*, *NC* 4: 3 (June 1926).

3 – See JMM's letter of 20 Apr. above.

TO *Adrienne Monnier*[1] MS Doucet

29 April 1925 *The Criterion,* 17 Thavies Inn

Mademoiselle,

Je vous remercie de votre aimable lettre du 21. Que les haruspices soient favorables à votre revue! Je veux bien que mon nom figure dans le premier numéro.[2] Je trouve votre traduction *excellente*, je n'ose pas essayer de l'améliorer! Je pense que 'Prufrock' se traduit en français mieux que 'The Waste Land', à cause du fait que l'influence de Laforgue y est pour beaucoup.[3]

(épuisé) *Prufrock* (écrit en 1911) est paru 1917 (The Egoist Press)
Poems Knopf, New York 1920
The Sacred Wood Methuen, London 1920
The Waste Land Hogarth Press, London 1923
Homage to John Dryden Hogarth Press 1925

Voilà la bibliographie complète!

Je vous félicite, vous et Mademoiselle Beach, et vous remercie de cette belle traduction.

'Coulons à pic' est très bien.[4]

Recevez, mademoiselle, l'assurance de mes sentiments les plus distingués.

T. S. Eliot

Vous êtes libre de parler du *Criterion.*[5]

1–Adrienne Monnier (1892–1955): French poet, bookseller and publisher. In 1915 she opened a bookshop called 'La Maison des Amis des Livres' in the rue de l'Odéon, which was across the road from Sylvia Beach's 'Shakespeare & Co'. In 1925 she launched a review, *Le Navire d'Argent*, the first issue of which appeared in June.

2–The translation of 'Prufrock' by Monnier and Sylvia Beach appeared as 'La Chanson d'amour de J. Alfred Prufrock' in *Le Navire d'Argent* 1 (June 1925), 23–9. It was the first translation into French of one of TSE's major poems.

3–On 18 Oct. 1938 TSE was to tell Edward H. Greene that 'Prufrock' was one of four poems written 'under the sign of Laforgue'.

4–'Coulons à pic' ('to sink like a stone'). The phrase occurs at the end of the French translation: 'Nous avons tardé dans les chambres de la mer / Devant les filles de la mer courronnées d'algues rouges et brunes / Jusqu'au jour où des voix humaines nous éveillent, et nous coulons à pic.' ['We have lingered in the chambers of the sea / By sea-girls wreathed with seaweed red and brown / Till human voices wake us and we drown.']

5–The translators described C. as 'la plus haute et la plus critique des revues littéraires anglaises' ['the highest and most critical of English literary reviews'].

Translation: Dear Mademoiselle, I thank you for your kind letter of the 21st. May the haruspices prove favourable to your review! I am quite willing for my name to appear in the first number. I find your translation *excellent* and would not presume to try to improve it! I think 'Prufrock' goes into French more easily than 'The Waste Land', because Laforgue's influence has a lot to do with it.

TO *Leonard Woolf* MS Berg

Wednesday, [29 April 1925] 9 Clarence Gate Gdns

My dear Leonard

I am writing to express my gratitude and appreciation of the interest you took last night in a matter which worried me very much.[1] If I find in the next week anything disturbing I shall consult [Henry] Head or [Maurice] Wright[2] without letting V. know. But I have been observing her since I saw you, and am convinced that it has been purely a nervous, *not* mental breakdown; that she acted with an instinct of self-preservation when she took to bed and gave everything up as she did; and that she is making a consistent effort to resume regular functioning. I think that the years of loneliness since marriage, the mental impressions of years coming to the surface in her weak condition, may be enough to account for the fear of being left.[3]

–

(out of print) *Prufrock* (written in 1911) appeared in 1917 (The Egoist Press)
Poems Knopf, New York 1920
The Sacred Wood Methuen, London 1920
The Waste Land Hogarth Press, London 1923
Homage to John Dryden Hogarth Press 1925

That is the complete bibliography!

I congratulate both you and Miss Beach, and thank you for the fine translation.

'Coulons à pic' is very good.

Yours sincerely, T. S. Eliot

You are free to mention the *Criterion*.

1–In her diary for 29 Apr., VW gave a long account of TSE's 'emotional rather tremulous & excited visit' the previous evening. She spoke of his 'release' from the Bank and 'heavensent appointment' at 4/5 of his present salary: 'He has seen his whole life afresh, seen his relations to the world, & to Vivien in particular, become humbler suppler more humane – good, sensitive, honourable man as he is, accusing himself of being the American husband, & wishing to tell me privately . . . what store V. sets by me, has done nothing but write since last June, because I told her to!' (*Diary*, III, 14).

2–Henry Head (1861–1940), FRCP, FRS, was consulted by VW in 1913. Consulting physician at the London Hospital, he was editor of the periodical *Brain*, 1910–25, and knighted in 1927. His works include *Studies in Neurology* (co-authored: 2 vols, 1920) and *Aphasia and Kindred Disorders of Speech* (2 vols, 1926). Dr Maurice Wright was also consulted by VW, and LW during the war. LW said in his next letter to TSE (30 Apr.) that on reflection he would recommend 'Wright rather than Head': Head could 'be rather brusque in manner'. See further: Stephen Trombley, *'All that Summer She was Mad': Virginia Woolf and Her Doctors* (1981).

3–VW records TSE asking LW whether he knew 'anything about psycho-analysis': 'Tom then told us the queer story – how Martin the dr. set V. off thinking of her childhood terror of loneliness, & now she cant let him, Tom, out of her sight. There he has sat mewed in her room these 3 months, poor pale creature, or if he has to go out, comes in to find her in a half fainting state' (*Diary*, III, 15).

There is one question I should like to ask you – (I know you will forgive me, as there is no one else I can trust). We shall go away within a month or so, and therefore it is out of the question to start a tutor or any other new regime until the autumn – the question is what she shall do until we do leave. She wants to begin writing again: do you think I should encourage this or not, and if so, should she try to write a little each day or in spells. Should you say that it is good or bad for her to write yet?[1]

It is a sign of my appreciation that I write to ask you this. I enjoyed seeing you and Virginia more than I can say.[2]

Yours ever
T. S. E.

TO *Leonard Woolf* MS Berg

Thursday [30 April 1925] 9 Clarence Gate Gdns

Dear Leonard

Thank you very much indeed.[3] There is one point however which complicates it. Vivien was (as I mentioned) never trained in regular habits of study. She is naturally immoderate. When she gets an idea she wants to work it out at once. If she postpones *writing*, the idea goes on fermenting in her brain, so that often it has *seemed* better to let her write. And with this neuralgia, she thinks and thinks the whole time, and because she must keep still there is no occupation one can substitute for that.

Would you begin by limiting and regularising her times of writing – or at the other end?[4]

Yours gratefully
T. S. E.

1–VW said TSE 'defended not writing which is her device he said, & went into her p[s]ychology' (*Diary*, III, 14).

2–VW found TSE's coming to them not merely touching to her vanity but to her 'sense of human worth'. She was conscious of his 'liking' for them, and 'trust in Leonard' (Ibid.).

3–For LW's letter of 30 Apr., see *Letters of Leonard Woolf*, ed. Frederic Spotts, 227–8. As to whether or not VHE should be encouraged to write, LW said it depended on the 'actual cause' of the disturbance. When VW was recovering from 'acute nervous exhaustion', she began by limiting her writing to half an hour a day, and gradually built up from there. LW's editor notes that at this time TSE and LW exchanged more than thirty letters and lunched together weekly.

4– LW responded (1 May): 'If the writing seems to decrease excitement or depression when she is no longer writing, then it is good; but if excitement and depression shows the slightest sign of increasing, it is bad.'

Of course V. would be delighted and flattered to have *The Common Reader*, and wd certainly read it! though *slowly*, at present.[1]

FROM *Geoffrey Faber* CC

1 May 1925

My dear Eliot

Thanks for yours of Thursday. Make what objections you think fit to make to the proposed Agreement. It is but a tentative draft. Of course Clause 5 was not intended in any way to prevent you from contributing to any papers you like; it was really meant to apply only to financial or editorial interest. I think, for example, that if you were to be offered a permanent post on the staff of some other periodical, it is reasonable that our consent should be asked. I should not however consider an arrangement under which you contributed regularly to any other paper as 'being on the staff' of such a paper; but editorial or quasi-editorial control or assistance or advice would, I think, come under that description.

How would the following substitute for Clause 5 do?

> 'Mr Eliot undertakes, during the continuance of this Agreement, not to acquire a financial interest in any other literary periodical or publishing house, nor to take any part in promoting or editing or managing any other literary periodical without the consent of the Company, and to give the option of publishing any work written by himself, at the terms upon which such work is offered to be published by any other publishing house in book form, to the Company. Provided that nothing in this Agreement shall restrict Mr Eliot from contributing to any periodicals or miscellanies published by any other firm.'

I hope you won't consider this clause unduly oppressive; knowing you I think it was hardly necessary to include it in the Agreement; but one has to think of other interested parties who have not that privilege.

About our name. We are waiting for a licence from the Board of Trade to change our name to 'Faber & Gwyer, Ltd,' and I hope that this change will be effected before June 30th.

Yours ever
[Geoffrey C. Faber]

1 – VW, *The Common Reader*, was published by the Hogarth Press on 23 Apr. VW asked LW to find out from TSE whether it would be 'all right' for VW to give a copy to VHE.

TO *Ottoline Morrell* MS Texas

1 May 1925 *The Criterion*, 17 Thavies Inn

My dear Ottoline,

I have been meaning to write to you for many days. I hope this will catch you before you leave Garsington.

Vivien has had a continuous torture with *neuralgia* – a peculiar neuralgia which comes from the back of the neck and affects all of one side of her face. It has never left her for three weeks. I think it is a little abated now, but it has been impossible for her to stir out of bed: any movement aggravates it. But the simple fact is that the Cyriax treatment has simply exhausted every nerve in her body to breaking point – had she gone on much longer I don't think she would ever have recovered. What doctors *can* do, in the way of criminal maltreatment, is incredible – and one can never prove it in a court of law. But I will explain to you more fully about the Cyriax treatment, and also about *Dr Martin* when we meet. I don't think anyone could have fought through and pulled herself out of such a terrible crash of nervous exhaustion more bravely and tenaciously than V. has. But it will take her a *long long* time to regain health. She has *years* to make up. I have seen, during the enforced leisure of this winter, many things which I never gave myself the *time* to see before.

It is true that I am leaving the bank almost immediately – but I shall only be telling a *very few* people at present. It had got to the point where I realised that neither of us could stand it any longer. I shall take a long rest – we shall disappear this summer; I have a new job to go to in the autumn – I am not in a position to divulge it yet, but shall be very soon. The fact is that I have been very much more ill than I knew – it was a real breakdown. I *had* to make a change. And I shan't be fit for any brain work for a long time.

Yes, it is true that V. wrote that poem.[1] In fact, she has been writing for a long time – and I have always suspected that you knew it! And *I* think that she is a *very* clever and original writer, with a mathematical and abstract mind which ought to be trained[2] – and I intend that it shall –

But this letter is merely an outline of some of the things I shall tell you when we meet. I *do* hope you are better and stronger, and will enjoy London. And to see you soon.

1–'Necesse est Perstare?' by 'F. M.', *C.* 3: 11 (Apr. 1925), 364. The poem's last lines are: 'Is it necessary – / Is this necessary – / Tell me, is it *necessary* that we go through this?'
2–On 28 May, TSE was to tell the Woolfs that VHE had 'the abstract, he the historic mind' (*Diary*, III, 15).

Ever affectionately with love from both

Tom.

Menasce's MS received[1]

TO *Herbert Read*

MS Victoria

1 May 1925

The Criterion, 17 Thavies Inn

My dear Read

Thank you very much for your two letters: I have wanted to answer them at length, but cannot do so even yet.[2]

I *expect* to be away from town for the whole summer: but must see you before I leave to discuss several important matters. I hope you will be in London throughout May.

Thorpe I like: I have sent him the Collingwood book.[3] I should like to try Willie King with something[4] – the Chesterfield goes to Aldington, who wanted it.[5]

Is there anything you would care to review? Collins I hope to keep and am sending one or two things to him.[6]

Richards does not *write* very well, I think; and lacks *ordonnance*.[7]

1–This may refer to Jean de Menasce's French translation of *TWL* – 'La Terre Mise à Nu' – which Menasce mentions in a letter of 22 Aug. It was published in *Esprit* I (May 1926).
2–HR wrote on 3 and 18 Apr. to discuss the T. E. Hulme notes he was preparing for C. 3: 12 (July 1925), and to give his reactions to 3: 11 (Apr. 1925).
3–On 18 Apr., HR asked: 'Do you approve of [W. A.] Thorpe?' See Thorpe on R. G. Collingwood, *Outline of a Philosophy of Art* and *Speculum Mentis* in 3: 12 (July 1925), 579–83.
4–See William King's review of RA's *Voltaire*, *NC* 4: 3 (June 1926): the first of many reviews.
5–Probably Roger Coxon, *Chesterfield and his Critics* (1925), but when approached for his review later in the year, RA had not done it.
6–HR thought H. P. Collins, 'A Note on the Classical Principle in Poetry' (C. 3: 11, Apr. 1925), 'excellent'. Collins reviewed Humbert Wolfe, *The Unknown Goddess*, and VW, *The Common Reader*, in 3: 12 (July 1925).
7–HR said that I. A. Richards had written him a 'very splenetic letter' following his review of *Principles of Practical Criticism* in 3: 11 (Apr. 1925). 'He does not, however, move me from my position and I feel that any misunderstanding of his work is excused by the manner in which it is expressed. I perhaps, in my desire for a contrast, gave [*Ethics* by Stephen Ward] rather too easy a show; Richards cries "Damn all this fine writing" and in a sense he is right. Ward is not exact enough, but his fundamental attitude is a better one than Richards'.'

I absolutely agree about 'Community' (re *NRF*).[1] Next winter I really hope we can organise some life. It is most important – but people must be trained to it! We must cooperate to that end. More later.

Yours ever
T. S. E.

TO *Bonamy Dobrée* MS Brotherton

3 May 1925 *The Criterion*, 17 Thavies Inn

Dear Dobrée

It was still more unfortunate for me. And circumstances have made it impossible for me to write, and now impossible for me to write more than a line. My wife is still very ill, but there is a possibility of our taking a long holiday in France. Where will you be this summer? And what do you consider the best make of cheapish small French car (new or second hand)?[2]

I should like to reply at length, but can only say this: *do* go on with the comparative 'Anthony and Cleopatra's' – the subject would interest me very much.[3] Or if not that, then something else soon!

Yes, I agree with you about Richards.[4]

Sincerely yours
T. S. Eliot

1–HR felt the lack of 'any valuable community' in their 'literary life', a fact borne in upon him when reading the issue of the *NRF* dedicated to Jacques Rivière, who had edited it from 1919 until his death in Feb. 1925. The issue was entitled *Hommage à Jacques Rivière 1886–1925*, *NRF* (1 Apr. 1925), and TSE had contributed a tribute, in French, entitled 'Témoignages Étrangers'.

2–BD recommended first a Michelin 'Mixte', then on 29 June, a Michelin 'Confort'.

3–On 10 Mar., BD said he intended to do a 'comparative critical study of the four Cleopatra plays of Daniel, Shakespeare, Sedley & Dryden', and wondered if TSE was interested.

4–BD said he had been reading I. A. Richards, *Principles of Literary Criticism*, with great interest but thought the chapter on Value needed 're-writing'. All that Richards had actually proved was that 'value = value', leaving us 'face to face' with the 'ultimates he tries to destroy'.

TO *Virginia Woolf* MS Texas

Sunday [3? May 1925] *The Criterion*, 17 Thavies Inn

My dear Virginia

Vivien has asked me to write to thank you for *The Common Reader*, which she is delighted to have, with the inscription, and which she *will* read. (But I shall probably read it first, for I see it as a most important document or text for a certain future work of my own. Are all writers such egoists as I?)

Vivien is not so well again, but in an illness like this, which is the fruit of so many years, she is bound to progress very slowly and have relapses for a long time to come. But I know that she would be delighted at any moment to have a letter from you – especially if *you* advised or instructed her about *writing*. But only if and when it occurs to you.

My love to you both
T. S. E.

TO *Leonard Woolf* MS Berg

Tuesday [5 May 1925] 9 Clarence Gate Gdns

Dear Leonard

I have not thanked you for your second letter and do so now. It puts the answer very clearly, and I am grateful.

Now could you give me the name of the best M.D. there is with psychoanalytic knowledge – if there is one? Would you say Wright[1] or someone else? This is obviously *not* for V. but for myself if anyone.

Yours ever
T. S. E.

TO *Bertrand Russell* MS McMaster

7 May [1925] *The Criterion*, 17 Thavies Inn

My dear Bertie,

Thank you very much indeed for your letter. As you say, it is very difficult for you to make suggestions until I can see you. For instance,

1 – Dr Maurice Wright (see TSE's letter of 29 Apr.). LW replied (8 May) that Wright, though not a practising psychoanalyst, was the best doctor he knew with psychoanalytic knowledge. He thought James Glover probably the best English analyst; for Glover, see note to TSE's letter to Charles Haigh-Wood, 12 July.

I don't know to what extent the changes which have taken place, since we were in touch with you, would seem to you material. What you suggest seems to me of course what should have been done years ago. Since then her health is a thousand times worse. Her only [choice *del.*] alternative would be to live quite alone – if she could. And the fact that living with me has done her so much damage does not help me to come to any decision. I need the help of someone who understands her – I find her still perpetually baffling and deceptive. She seems to me like a child of six with an immensely clever and precocious mind. She writes *extremely* well (stories etc.) and [with] great originality. And I can never escape from the spell of her persuasive (even coercive) gift of argument.

Well, thank you very much, Bertie – I feel quite desperate. I hope to see you in the autumn.

Yours ever
T. S. E.

TO *Frederic Manning* CC

11 May 1925 23 Adelphi Terrace House

My dear Manning,

Thank you for your letter of the 9th. I am returning the cheque herewith. Would you mind endorsing it to Miss Johnson[1] and, if you wish, return it to me and I will have it sent to her direct. Unless you have any special reason for wishing to have a new cheque made out to Miss Johnson, this is much the simplest way from the point of view of the *Criterion* accounts.

As for payment, I am very sorry indeed if my illness and the very little time which I have been able to give to the *Criterion* have made me overlook your previous correspondence or any tacit agreement between us. I will have the correspondence looked up. I do not consider that the figure you name is at all too high, but in the circumstances I should like to propose that the balance be paid on publication of a second selection of the letters.[2] For reasons, the explanation of which I cannot enter upon now as they are extremely involved, but which I should be glad to explain to you in conversation, this would not only simplify the accounts, but would be of great personal assistance to myself. I should propose to publish the

1 – This was in payment for 'Some Letters of Lionel Johnson', C. 3: 11 (Apr. 1925). Manning had forwarded the letters to TSE and acted on behalf of the executrix, Miss Johnson.
2 – No second selection appeared.

remaining letters in October, as it is absolutely essential to reduce the July number to the smallest possible compass.

Will you please let me know whether you concur?

Thank you for your expressions of sympathy. I am very sorry indeed to hear of your own illness:[1] please let me know how you get on, and I hope we may meet before the summer.

Yours very sincerely,
[T. S. E.]

TO *John Middleton Murry* CC

12 May 1925 23 Adelphi Terrace House

My dear John

I was very glad to hear from you and I think it is very kind of you to give me the option of using this article by Gorki.[2] I have read it, but I do not think that it is quite suitable for our readers either; it is a sort of general conspectus which, to tell the truth, I have always been anxious to avoid. What I should rather have, for instance, is specimens of original work by Russian writers which might have interest and value for European readers. However, I am very much obliged to you, and when I can reciprocate I will.

I shall be writing to you very soon: forgive this letter for being purely business.

SIGNED FOR T. S. ELIOT
(Secretary)

FROM *Geoffrey Faber* CC

13 May 1925 [London]

My dear Eliot

Many thanks for yours. The weekend after next, i.e. Saturday, 23rd, is perfectly all right for me. Unless I hear from you to the contrary I will take it that you will try to manage Saturday to Monday, which would on *all* accounts be best. If you can't do that, make it Saturday, stay to dinner and

1 – Manning was 'torpid with cold'.
2 – On 6 May, JMM offered TSE an article that Gorki had sent to *The Adelphi*: 'the most valuable & comprehensive synopsis of the present condition of Russian literature I have read'. However, JMM considered it 'too specialised and "literary"' for readers of *The Adelphi*.

go back by the last train, i.e. 9.22, which gets to Paddington at 10.46: this would *just* give you a chance to be seen, though a very brief one. [One-sentence insertion illegible.] If you had to go back on Sunday there are plenty of trains from 7.40 in the morning to 8.17 in the evening. The later ones are too bad to take. But if, best of all, you can stay till Monday morning, you could catch the 8.33 and be at Paddington by 9.

By the way, our next Directors' meeting is on May 26 at 2.30 or thereabouts. I hope you will be able to manage to attend this. You will have to take up a small number of qualifying shares. The present qualification is fixed at five £10 Preference Shares, bearing interest at the rate of 7%. I could let you have five of mine at par, if that suits you. The qualification may be altered in the new articles which we are about to adopt, and as you have two months grace from the date of your appointment as a Director you may prefer to let the matter stand over for a little.

About the *Criterion*: can you tell me when you are likely to see Lady R? I incline to think that the best name for the new paper would be *The New Criterion*. If it were possible I should like some announcement of the fact to appear in the June number of the *Criterion*. Will Lady R. be in England in time for that?

I hope your wife's health is benefiting by the change in the weather.

Yours ever
[Geoffrey C. Faber]

FROM *Geoffrey Faber* CC

15 May 1925 [London]

My dear Eliot

Yes, do try and make it Saturday and Sunday. It would be much better than going back by the 9.22 on Saturday night, since that would prevent you from seeing more than the two or three people you happened to sit next to at dinner.[1]

Try and come to our meeting if you can, even if it is only for a short time; but of course if you can't I will explain the circumstances to the other Directors.

Yours ever
[Geoffrey C. Faber]

1 – TSE was to be GCF's guest at All Souls College, Oxford, for the night of Sat., 23 May.

TO *Frederic Manning* CC

16 May 1925 23 Adelphi Terrace House

My dear Manning,

Thank you very much for your letter. I am glad to hear that you are progressing. I am also glad to settle the matter of the Johnson letters.[1]

My secretary is sending you the Newman book.[2] Take as much time as you need.

I should very much like to spend a weekend with you, but it is practically out of the question, I am afraid, until the autumn. I have a great deal of business to attend to here, and then I hope that my wife and I can get away for the whole summer. I am likely to be here for another month, and should you be coming to town during that time I hope that we might arrange a meeting. I suppose that you will be staying at Chobham all the summer and I hope that you will be there when I come back in the autumn.

Yes, but what you expect with a man like Churchill as Chancellor?[3]

Yours very sincerely
[T. S. E.]

TO *Ellen Thayer*[4] TS Beinecke

17 May 1925 9 Clarence Gate Gdns

Dear Ellen Thayer,

I am sending you herewith a story by Vivien, 'The Paralyzed Woman', which will appear in the July number of the *Criterion*, and which I think you would like for publication in the *Dial*.[5] It seems to me amazingly brilliant and humorous and horrible, and I have never read anything in the least like it. It is likely to attract a good deal of notice here, and it is the longest story she has yet published. You could publish it under her own name (V. H. Eliot), or 'Vivien Eliot', as you think best.

1 – See TSE's letter to Manning, 11 May.
2 – Bertram Newman, *Cardinal Newman* (1925). Manning's 'A French Criticism of Newman', in *NC* 4: 1 (Jan. 1926), 19–31, was primarily a response to Ramón Fernandez's 'The Experience of Newman', in C. 3: 9 (Oct. 1924).
3 – Winston Churchill (1874–1965) had become Chancellor the previous Nov., and recently delivered his first Budget. On 12 May, Manning said he was 'a little ashamed' of a Conservative Government 'indulging in more benevolence'.
4 – Ellen Thayer, Scofield Thayer's cousin, joined *The Dial* as Assistant Editor in May 1925.
5 – The story did not appear in C. or *The Dial*, though VHE's 'Fête Galante' was to appear under the name 'Fanny Marlow' in C. 3: 12 (July 1925), 557–63. In the event, VHE never published under her own name, and her story remained unpublished.

I am, as you know, printing Lawrence's 'The Woman Who Rode Away' (first part) in the *Criterion*, so the two cases are the same.[1]

Lucy[2] is still here, and we are sometimes a little worried on her account.

I hope for an opportunity of meeting you this summer.

If you cannot use this story there are others unpublished, but I think that this is the best up to date.

Sincerely yours,
T. S. Eliot

PS Vivien wrote 'Night Club' and also the poem by 'F. M.' in the last *Criterion*.[3] Did you read them?

TO *W. W. Worster* CC

22 May 1925 23 Adelphi Terrace House

Dear Sir,

I am very glad to hear from you again and very glad that you should consider contributing to the *Criterion*.

I should be very glad to have a review of a thousand words of the poetry of Gustav Fröding.[4]

I am afraid that it is impossible to consider at present your essay on *Buchholtz*[5] for the reason that I have already accepted several articles of this type from foreign authors – German and Italian – and it is impossible in a periodical of the size of the *Criterion* to print more than one such essay in each number.

I should certainly be interested to see an article such as you mention in your last paragraph.[6]

Yours very truly,
[T. S. E.]

1–DHL, 'The Woman Who Rode Away I', appeared in *C.* 3: 12 (July 1925) and in *Dial* 79: 1 (July 1925).

2–Lucy Thayer (Ellen's sister) had been a friend of VHE's since before she met TSE.

3–Feiron Morris, 'Night Club'; F. M., 'Necesse est Perstare?', in *C.* 3: 11 (Apr. 1925).

4–Gustav Fröding (1860–1911): Swedish lyric poet, whose *Guitarr och dragharmonika* appeared in 1891. On 12 May, Worster offered to review *Guitar & Concertina* (1925), a selection trans. C. D. Lockwood, but no review ever appeared in *C.*

5–Worster enclosed an article on Johannes Buchholtz (1882–1940): Danish novelist. Worster had translated his *Egholm and his God* (1921) and *The Miracles of Clara van Haag* (1922).

6–Worster proposed an article based on certain books published in recent months 'which seem to fit together as showing the general trend of thought in Denmark, namely a reaction from radical atheism to a more aristocratic and more spiritual view. Several deal with Brandes and his school from different angles (two novels by different writers and three critical works);

TO *J. M. Cohen*[1] CC

22 May 1925 23 Adelphi Terrace House

Dear Sir

I am sorry that illness prevented my answering immediately your letter of the 18th February.

I find your poem interesting and hopeful but, if you will allow me to say so, I think that you still need to digest the influences to which you have subjected yourself.[2] The influences themselves I cannot help considering very good ones, and we must all develop our originality in the same way; that is by steeping ourselves in the work of those previous poets whom we find most sympathetic. I think that the best antidote to the almost contemporary sources whom you mention is Dante – and perhaps Virgil.[3]

The forgoing implies that I should like to see more of the your work from time to time.

Yours faithfully
[T. S. E.]

TO *Allen Tate*[4] CC

22 May 1925 [London]

Dear Mr Tate

I am sorry that illness prevented my answering immediately your letter of the 28th February. I am sorry that we cannot find room for the enclosed poems, but I should be interested in following your work and I should be

—

one with feminism, one with the study of Child Psychology, and one which I consider specially important as an indicator of modern Danish thought is called "Fællesaanden" (the Collective Spirit) and offers a kind of practical working gospel that supplements the negative element of the rest.'

1–John Michael Cohen (1903–89): critic and translator, later editor of Penguin Classics.

2–The influences mentioned by Cohen included the Belgian symbolist Emile Verhaeren (1855–1916), Jules Laforgue, Heinrich Heine, and 'perhaps *Prufrock* and *The Waste Land*'.

3–TSE had already written an essay on Dante in *SW* (1920). In his influential 'Dante' (published as a Faber pamphlet in 1929), he was to propose that 'more can be learned about how to write poetry from Dante than from any English poet'. In an unpublished memoir, Mary Hutchinson mentions that he usually carried an edition of Dante or Virgil in his pocket. TSE's views of Virgil were articulated in 'Virgil and the Christian World' (1951), in *OPP* (1957).

4–Allen Tate (1899–1979): US poet and critic. He was to be editor of *T. S. Eliot: The Man and his Work* (1966). His *Reactionary Essays on Poetry and Ideas* (1936) was reviewed in *NC* 15: 61 (Apr. 1936).

very much pleased if you would continue to let me see portions of it from time to time with a view to publication in the *Criterion*.[1]

Yours faithfully
[T. S. E.]

TO *R. P. Blackmur*[2] CC

22 May 1925 23 Adelphi Terrace House

Dear Sir,

I am sorry that illness prevented my answering immediately your letter of the 16th December.

I think your poem[3] is very promising and I have taken the trouble to read it several times. The scheme which you mention is all right and it is highly desirable, in my experience, to have a kind of scheme or scaffold; but usually this scheme is useful chiefly to oneself. I think that your verse tends to diffuseness and to use of words of too general a meaning. Your poppy is not a definite poppy seen in a particular place or associated with particular circumstances and emotions. I think that you need to work the precise image. '*Laughter like hot ashes in the throat*' is not a very good comparison because one does not know what hot ashes in the throat are like and they do not suggest any kind of laughter. I think that a study of the similes of Dante might help you.[4] Later, I should very much like to see more of your work.

Yours faithfully,
[T. S. E.]

TSE/IPF

1–No poetry by Tate came out in *C.*, but his essay 'The Fallacy of Humanism' appeared in *NC* 8: 33 (July 1929).
2–R. P. Blackmur (1904–65): US poet and critic. His *The Double Agent: Essays in Craft and Elucidation* (1935) was to be reviewed by Michael Roberts in *NC* 15: 61 (July 1936), alongside Tate's *Reactionary Essays*.
3–'In a Falling House', written Oct. 1924.
4–In his Clark lectures (1926), TSE was to note the 'rational necessity' of Dante's similes and metaphors. None of Blackmur's poems or essays appeared in *C.*

TO *Herbert Read* CC

25 May 1925 9 Clarence Gate Gdns

My dear Read,

Thank you for your card and for letting me know about your absence from town. I think we shall have to wait until you come back, when I shall make a determined effort to get hold of you.

Thank you for returning your proof punctually.[1]

The next number of the *Criterion* will have to be rather a small one and therefore I have had to forego the idea of including several essays about Hulme. But I will explain the whole position to you when we meet.

Yours ever,
[T. S. E.]

TSE/IPF

TO *Ada Leverson* CC

25 May 1925 9 Clarence Gate Gdns

Dear Mrs Leverson,

Thank you very much for sending me the interesting material for your essay on Oscar Wilde. I have looked it over but have not read the whole because I have found it necessary to make a rule never to read any contributions that are not typed. If you will put your material together for me and have the whole essay typed, I think that I am safe in assuring you that we should be very happy to make use of it, because I am certain that any original and first hand reminiscences of Oscar are always of very great interest to the public. I should like to know about how long an essay you wish to make of it.[2]

Always yours sincerely,
[T. S. E.]

1–T. E. Hulme, 'Notes on Language and Style', *C.* 3: 12 (July 1925).

2–'The Last First Night', an account of the opening of *The Importance of Being Earnest*, appeared in *NC* 4: 1 (Jan. 1926), 148–53. Leverson was disappointed that TSE published only the second part of her article, because she felt Wilde's less well known jokes worth recording.

Vivien Eliot TO *Lucy Thayer* CC

25 May 1925 9 Clarence Gate Gdns

Dear Lucy,

I am sending back your letter because I cannot read the greater part of it and the part which I can read I cannot understand. I may add that I have never understood anything you have said or done since you last made your appearance in England. I do not think yours is a mind I should ever understand, nor a mind which I particularly wish to understand.[1] Now that the cause, or causes, for your preferring to keep away from Paris have been removed or are no longer active, and you are returning there so soon, I think, in view of everything, and after thinking it over for a long time, that it would be better to take this moment permanently to break off our relationship. I am sure you will agree. In so far as there is any relation to break off it is an impossible one on every count. I shall probably be in Paris myself before long. I have a great many friends in Paris, friends who know me well and in whom I have confidence, and in whom I should not hesitate to confide.

I hope your future will continue to prosper.

Yours
[V. H. Eliot][2]

FROM *Geoffrey Faber* CC

27 May 1925 [London]

My dear Eliot

Many thanks for your two letters, and the promised copy of *The Waste Land*, which I shall be most interested to read. I am so glad you enjoyed your brief stay at All Souls; it was a great pleasure to entertain you there. I hope we may see you tomorrow afternoon. There is a General Meeting at 2.30; the Board Meeting will follow, and will probably not begin much before 3 o'clock.

Yours ever
[Geoffrey C. Faber]

1 – See TSE's letter to Lady Rothermere, 18 June 1925.
2 – This letter may have been typed by TSE: VHE rarely typed letters.

FROM *Geoffrey Faber* CC

27 May 1925 [London]

My dear Eliot

A postscript to my other letter of today's date, though not connected with it.

You asked to see a list of contemplated books. I enclose a rough list, without much detail, but just enough to show you how the thing is shaping.[1] I am not satisfied with it by any means. There is almost nothing there of real literary merit, I want, very badly, to get hold of two or three (or more) striking things, or things that are really good without being striking, to publish in the autumn. Novels or other kinds. If you can help me to get onto anything, I should be very grateful; and I should, of course, be ready to pay a fee (£2.2.0) for anything that came to us through you, that we took.

Yours ever
[Geoffrey C. Faber]

Mr Eliot's poems of course excepted!![2]
Of course there are other possibilities I haven't put down and not all on the list will necessarily materialise.

TO *William Plomer*[3] CC

27 May 1925 23 Adelphi Terrace House

Dear Sir

The Editor of *The Criterion* has directed me to return to you the enclosed manuscript.

Mr Eliot thanks you for the compliment and has made pencilled observations on the manuscript of the poem.[4] He recognises a certain

1 – The list does not survive.

2 – *Poems 1909–1925* was to be published by F&G on 23 Nov.

3 – William Plomer (1903–1973): poet, novelist, and librettist; later author of the novel *Turbott Wolfe* (Hogarth Press, 1926); co-founder and editor of *Voorslag* (1925–6), the first bilingual South African literary journal; publisher's reader for Jonathan Cape; and collaborator with Benjamin Britten (*Gloriana*; *Curlew River*; *The Burning Fiery Furnace*; *The Prodigal Son*).

4 – Plomer wrote from Zululand on 3 May that he would regard it as 'a very great honour' if TSE would tell him what he thought of his poem 'The Ballad of John Cotton', since he believed TSE was 'as good a judge of poetry as any man alive'.

feeling and some sense of rhythm, but he thinks you should pay more attention to the exact sense of words and phrases. He thinks that you should read a great deal of good poetry and cultivate your ear.[1]

Faithfully yours
For the Editor of *The Criterion*
[I. P. Fassett]
Secretary

FROM *Geoffrey Faber* — MS Valerie Eliot

28 May 1925 — 21 Ladbroke Grove, London W.11

[Extract]
My dear Eliot,

I am v. glad to have *The Waste Land*. You won't think it unkind of me to say that I am excitedly groping in it. You *are* obscure, you know! with an obscurity compared to which Meredith at his most bewildering (and *he* can baffle, too) is the purest ray serene. I wonder if you realize how difficult you are? and alternatively I wonder if I am specially stupid. Is it that you are using a language of which I have learnt only the vocabulary but not the syntax? – I haven't yet got the key to your poetry, I say frankly. You try the stranger a bit high: only those who have trod the same labyrinth as yourself can follow the clue. The others must put too much detective-work into their reading, to lose the sense of the chase in the understanding of the thing captured – and, moreover, one asks oneself if it isn't really something quite other than one has at first thought.

Please understand me – this is *not* criticism. I am profoundly sensible, in reading *The Waste Land*, as I was in reading your three-fold 'Eyes' poem in the *Criterion*, of a meaning not the less truly there because I can only grasp it fragmentarily – of astounding vivid glimpses now of the pit beneath the human mind, and now of beauties seen and painted in the sharp startling precision of which, at your best, you are master.

> There the eyes are
> Sunlight on a broken column . . .

How thin my own stuff must seem to you!

Well, I write like this, tho' it may be an odd way of thanking you for a gift, because I will not pretend to understand where I don't understand;

1 – TSE pencilled this paragraph on Plomer's letter, beginning 'Say – I thank him for the compliment' etc.

and I suspect that a good many people have praised *The Waste Land* who hadn't the faintest atom of an idea what it was all about!! You have the pull on them – but more on me. I daresay posterity will wonder that anybody cld. have found you obscure – we puzzle at people's obtuseness over Browning now.

Having said that, you won't suspect me of flattering you, when I reiterate that you *do* impress, and impress with a sense of a new way of seeing and relating things, which will be understood all in good time; and meanwhile gives bright unforgettable landing-places.

I wonder if I dare send you all this!

[. . .]

Geoffrey C. Faber

FROM *Geoffrey Faber* CC

29 May 1925 [London]

My dear Eliot

Under the new Articles which were adopted yesterday and will be finally adopted at a confirmatory meeting on June 18th, the qualification of a Director is to be the possession of a single £10 share. I suggest that I should transfer a £10 Preference Share to you at the next Board Meeting, i.e. June 25th. This will be exactly two months after your original appointment as Director. The Articles require you to take up your qualification within two months; but I think we may take it that the formal requirement will be adequately satisfied in this way, and nobody is in the least likely to raise any objection. If you would prefer to take up five £10 shares, by all means do so; but I expect you will prefer the smaller amount. The purchase money will be £10 per share, and you will, I suppose, have to pay a trifling stamp fee in addition.

Yours sincerely,
[Geoffrey C. Faber]

Geoffrey Faber TO *Charles Whibley* CC

29 May 1925 [Scientific Press, 28 Southampton St, Strand, London W.C.2]

My dear Whibley,

I have been on the look out for you lately in the club, but when I saw you the other day I was tied by a guest.

I expect Eliot has told you about his arrangement with us; we are going to take him on as Editor of *The Criterion* or its successor, and he is also joining our Board of Directors.[1] I want to say to you how very glad I am that you have made us acquainted. He is a most attractive fellow, and if only his health holds out I am convinced that he will make a considerable name for himself. I am running him for a research fellowship at All Souls next November, and with great difficulty got him to spend last Saturday with me at Oxford. His health really does rather alarm me; the strain of looking after his wife seems to be telling on him severely. I do hope now that he will soon be in the way of earning a reasonable income, by congenial means, that both he and she will climb rapidly out of the melancholy state they had got into.

All is going pretty well here. We are changing our name to 'Faber & Gwyer Ltd', and are moving in September to new premises at 24 Russell Square. Rather a fine house; we have got to build up as fine a publishing business as we can to inhabit it! Amongst the many schemes which chase each other through my mind is one for a series of monographs on the great foreign writers, rather after the style of the Macmillan's English Men of Letters. I should like to find a good man to edit such a series. Do you think Eliot might do it? I haven't asked him; or would it be better to get the nearest approach we can find to a John Morley?[2] But I suppose a modern John Morley, if he exists, would have a very full sense of his own value.

Yours ever,
[Geoffrey Faber]

1 – TSE was elected to the Board on 23 Apr.

2 – John Morley (1838–1923): politician and biographer; editor of *The Fortnightly Review* and *Pall Mall Gazette*, as well as of 'English Men of Letters', a series of biographical studies.

TO *Thomas MacGreevy*[1] MS TCD

30 May 1925 9 Clarence Gate Gdns

Dear Mr MacGreevy

Please excuse my not having acknowledged at once your letter of introduction from Mr Yeats.[2] Illness at home has made it difficult for me to make appointments. I hope that you will be in London permanently, or long enough for us to meet, though I am not likely to be here throughout the summer. Meanwhile I like your poems, and should like to use your 'Dysert' – probably in October.[3] I will not mention it to Mr Yeats until it is published. I should like to know about your critical work too, what you have written, and what you propose to do, and what you are interested in.[4]

Yours very truly
T. S. Eliot

Is the name ST SENAN?

TO *Alfred Kreymborg* MS Virginia

30 May 1925 *The Criterion*, 17 Thavies Inn

My dear Kreymborg

Many thanks – I am delighted to have your book and inscription, and overcome by the portrait of myself.[5] The only adequate recognition would be to write my own biography and give my view of the meeting! But that I shall never do – my own aim is to suppress my own biography – even otherwise I could not make mine as interesting as yours. But may there be

1–Thomas MacGreevy (1893–1967): Irish poet, literary and art critic, curator; served in the Royal Field Artillery in WW1; graduated in history from Trinity College, Dublin; met JJ and began a lifelong friendship with him; forged a very close friendship with Samuel Beckett; taught in Paris, then at the National Gallery, London; contributed to periodicals inc. *C.*, *Formes*, *The Studio* and *TLS*. From the 1940s he lived in Dublin, where he was appointed Director of the National Gallery of Ireland, 1950–64. In 1948 he was made a chevalier of the Légion d'honneur. His works included *Thomas Stearns Eliot: A Study* (1931) and *Richard Aldington: An Englishman* (1931), as well as monographs on Jack Yeats and Poussin.

2–On 11 May 1924, WBY introduced MacGreevy as a 'cultivated man and subtle critic, especially of painting, of which he has great knowledge'. On 16 Aug. 1926 MacGreevy would tell George Yeats that TSE was 'a Unitarian Athenian, very Unitarian but more Athenian'.

3–There was no issue of *C.* in Oct. 1925, but 'Dysert' appeared under the pseudonym 'L. St. Senan' in *NC* 4: 1 (Jan. 1926), 94; it was reprinted as 'Homage to Jack Yeats', in *Poems* (1934).

4–MacGreevy contributed a number of reviews and essays, starting with a review of George Moore in *NC* 4: 2 (Apr. 1926).

5–Kreymborg, *Troubadour, An Autobiography* (1925), 396–7.

another meeting, and a long post-autobiographical life for the mandolutanist.[1]

Ever yours
T. S. Eliot

TO *Marianne Moore* MS Rosenbach

30 May 1925 9 Clarence Gate Gdns

Dear Miss Moore,

In spite of your prohibitive clause, I wish to thank you for your letter, which gave me much pleasure. It is also very gratifying to have your approval of my 'Dryden',[2] although those essays were written so long ago as to cease to belong to me. But I hope to be in a position to resume work in the autumn, and in that event I shall not fail to give you an opportunity to sit in editorial judgement.

I shall only regret your association with the *Dial* if it leads you in mistaken modesty to print less of your own poetry in it. Please don't let it do that.

I gather that you are actually Literary Editor[3] and Miss Thayer Managing Editor? I sent Miss Thayer some MSS. by my wife which I think rather remarkable and am using in fact in the *Criterion* (*not*, as I told her, in July, but in October); but presumably if she likes it she will pass it on to you.[4]

I hope you will like Aldington's review of you in the July *Criterion*.[5]

Sincerely yours
T. S. Eliot

1 – The mandolute is a combination of mandolin and lute, with the solo register of the violin and mandolin and the tone of the lute. Kreymborg describes being introduced to the instrument by Franklin Hopkins, as well as his tours of the USA giving recitals and poetry readings with it.

2 – On 3 May, Marianne Moore wrote: 'I cannot say how rich in entertainment and in analysis I find your *Homage to John Dryden* . . . and at the risk of seeming to retract the understanding which I have of your statement that "one learns to conduct one's life with greater economy", I venture to hope that you will yet write criticisms of other poets of the seventeenth and eighteenth centuries.' She pressed him for a contribution of this kind for the *Dial*.

3 – Moore joined the *Dial* as acting editor on 27 Apr.

4 – See TSE's letter to Ellen Thayer of 17 May, and to Moore of 18 June.

5 – RA reviewed Moore's *Observations* alongside Jean Cocteau's *Poésie 1916–1923*, in C. 3: 12 (July 1925), 588–94. Describing them as 'two rare birds, modern poets of originality', he yet considered Moore 'the subtler and more important': she was 'the most high-brow poet in the world' and 'best poet now living in America'.

TO *Richard Aldington* MS Texas

30 May 1925 *The Criterion*, 17 Thavies Inn

My dear Richard

Many thanks. I am grateful to you for doing this admirable review[1] at a time when, returning from your holiday, you must be under considerable pressure of work. I quite agree with your opinions – but I wonder if you would mind slightly modifying, or allowing me to modify, the [asperity, no, *del.*] the strength of your judgment on Cocteau – I mean, by all means preserve the judgment, but delete a phrase or two so as not to rub it in so much? It is merely that I have accepted some notes by Cocteau on the Theatre[2] – he is much better at this sort of thing than at verse.

But if you prefer to leave it as it is, I shall print it as it is. It is only a question of removing a phrase here or there, anyway.

This is all I have time to write. More news later. I should be very glad to know how you are after your walk, and any other news.[3] I agree about the Welsh![4]

Ever aff.
T. S. E.

TO *Mary Hutchinson* MS Texas

Wednesday [1 June 1925?] 9 Clarence Gate Gdns

I see there has been some misunderstanding. Ellen is very stupid *indeed* about taking messages on the telephone. I find we shall be kept in London for some considerable time, for reasons which I will explain later; but at any rate we ought to see each other a good deal. Vivien is 'unwell' just at the moment, and is feeling particularly knocked out by it, as she is having a most frightful and terrifying treatment by a new doctor who is really clever, very modern, and who has at last seen her case as it really is. There is much more the matter with her than we suspected. She will write a long letter to Mary directly she has finished being unwell, and

1 – RA's review of Cocteau and Moore, C. 3: 12 (July 1925), 588–94.

2 – Cocteau, 'Scandales', published in French, *NC* 4: 1 (Jan. 1926), 125–37.

3 – RA said he was going for a three-week walking tour in Wales.

4 – On 23 May RA had written: 'The Welsh are the most poisonous Puritans I have yet struck', and 'still subject to the grossest superstitions and vices'.

then we must really arrange to have more meetings and some long talks all four of us.

Love to Jack
Tom

TO *Herbert Read* MS Victoria

[June? 1925]

It is odd that we should both have been following the same rather unknown trail. Have you seen Bourquin's *Julien Benda*?[1] Do you know anything about Gonzague Truc, or Jules de Gaultier, or Henri Massis?[2] There are other things I am pining to talk to you about also.

T. S. E.

Please don't offer your book anywhere until I can see you or write to your about it (soon). I have a publisher in mind.[3]

TO *F. S. Flint* CC

4 June 1925 9 Clarence Gate Gdns

My dear Flint,

I find that Cobden-Sanderson failed to mention in sending you your cheque that it was in payment for both the Danish notes and the translation.[4] The translation amounted to 1415 words and the Danish notes to 547 words, so that I made it a guinea for each. I wish that the

1–Constant Bourquin, *Julien Benda, ou le point de vue de Sirius*, with an Intro. by Jules de Gaultier (Editions du Siècle, 1925).

2–Gonzague Truc (1877–1972): essayist, critic, biographer; author of *Charles Maurras et son temps* (1917). On 19 June RA described him as a scholar 'of immense erudition in French literature'. TSE cites his *Les mystiques espagnols* in the Clark lectures (*VMP*, 65). Jules de Gaultier (1858–1942): philosopher, and author of a number of books on Flaubert including *Le Bovarysme, la psychologie dans l'œuvre de Flaubert* (1892) and *La Sensibilité métaphysique* (1924). Henri Massis (1886–1970): literary critic and historian, closely associated with Charles Maurras, who had recently published *Jugements II: André Gide, Romain Rolland, Georges Duhamel, Julien Benda, les chapelles littéraires* (1924) and *Jacques Rivière* (1925). A defender of Mussolini and Salazar, Massis's later books included *Chefs: les dictateurs et nous* (1939) and *Maurras et notre temps* (2 vols, 1951). His 'Defence of the West' appeared in *NC* 4: 2 & 3 (Apr. & June 1926).

3–HR's book of essays, later entitled *Reason and Romanticism* (F&G, 1926).

4–'Danish Periodicals', *C.* 3: 11 (Apr. 1925). The translation may have been of J. Kessel's 'A Note from Paris' in the same issue, for which no translator was named.

Criterion could pay better, but please remember that I have always wanted to get a great deal more work out of you than you have ever been willing to do! Will you *never* suggest something that you would really like to write about, or are you becoming more and more absorbed in official activities? That is what all your friends wish to prevent.

Also I wish we could meet oftener, but, as you know, I have been able to see almost no one for several months, but when I emerge you shall hear from me.

Ever yours,
[T. S. E.]

TSE/IPF

FROM *Geoffrey Faber* — MS Valerie Eliot

4 June 1925 — 28 Southampton St, Strand, London

My dear Eliot,

I am most awfully sorry to hear that you have such a serious report of your wife's health: though it is something to know that her doctor sees a definite line of treatment to be followed. I hope to goodness you will follow it strictly, even if it means some financial stringency. If I had any resources of my own I would offer you a loan; but almost every penny I have is now locked up in the business, and I have very shallow waters to negotiate myself before Xmas! We can let you have an advance at the beginning of July. You ought to be able to spare the necessary two hours for our Board meeting on the 25th June; and that will assure you of a few pounds. You will also, I hope, be able to come to the following meeting, on the 4th Thursday in July. In August there is no meeting; and we shall not meet you again till the 4th Thursday in September.

About Lady R. I am of opinion that, under the circumstances, you must *write*.[1] Several people now know that you are coming to us to edit a successor to the *Criterion*. These things can't be kept hidden; and it would be most unfortunate if news leaked round to her, before she heard of it from you. Even if she doesn't answer your letter you will at any rate safeguard yourself against *that* contingency. I should most strongly advise you to write at once, and tell her of the offer you have had, which you

1–GCF's diary (7 May): '[TSE] thinks Lady R. wld give up *Criterion* if we could publish a sort of "overflow" irregular paper, together with certain expensive editions, she standing expense.'

were not in a position to refuse; going on to say that you (and the publishers) would like to continue as much as possible of the best traditions of the *Criterion*, and to embody its name in *The New Criterion*; but this, of course, depends on her; and then developing your suggestions for continuing her interest in publishing. Saying, too, that some amount ought to go into the next no. of the *Criterion*, and therefore you would be glad if she could write or wire her agreement (or otherwise) with your letter. I enumerate the points of importance to *us*; don't imagine I wld. be dictating the form of your letter. But I am absolutely clear that you have no alternative but to write, and that your letter should cover the points I have mentioned, and that it should go immediately.

It is not, as a rule, a wise thing to anticipate the future; but I have great hope that All Souls will take you at the end of October.[1] That will mean £300 a year, if it comes off, less Income Tax, of course, and some necessary expenditure in College. You would get the Nov–Dec portion in February; but I can always make advances to Fellows, so long as the advance is covered by the period which has run. Otherwise emoluments are paid annually in February in respect of the twelve months ending the previous Dec. 31.[2]

Yours ever
GCF

TO *Mary Hutchinson* — MS Texas

[Postmark 9 June 1925] — 9 Clarence Gate Gdns

I got a confused message about dinner tonight, but could get no reply from your telephone. We are having a very intensive treatment now, in order to get to the South as quickly as possible and soak in the heat in a car, and on to Rome.[3] V. much hopes to see you before we go: at the moment nothing is possible. I hear J[ack] is having a glorious time in Italy.

Love from both,
T.

1–Despite GCF's support, TSE was not elected to a research fellowship at All Souls.
2–GCF was Estates Bursar at All Souls.
3–This trip did not materialise but the Eliots visited Rome the following summer.

FROM *Geoffrey Faber* cc

9 June 1925 [London]

My dear Eliot

Many thanks for your letter and the letter from Leonard Woolf, which I return herewith.[1]

I should certainly like to publish your [poems in][2] the Autumn, about the time when the *New Criterion* starts, [and] I am quite prepared to give you the terms offered by the Woolfs.[3] I hope, however, that by complying with the conditions of our agreement you won't upset your relations with your friends. I should be very sorry to think that we had put you in such a position.

As regards the lectures; these too we should certainly want to publish.[4] I should suggest £50 on advance of a 10% Royalty; a higher on subsequent editions, if any. I doubt if the C. U. P. would give you a 15% Royalty throughout, and I am quite confident that the Oxford Press would not give it. We can defer the decision as to terms until the lectures are in the process of being delivered. Will this be all right?

Yours ever
[Geoffrey C. Faber]

TO *Arnold Bennett* TS Beinecke

9 June 1925 *The Criterion*, 9 Clarence Gate Gdns

Dear Mr Bennett

It is my misfortune that after making myself such a nuisance to you I have been unable to worry you still further by coming to see you. We are going abroad in July, and I should very much like to see you before we go. Could you give me the pleasure of dining with me, at the Savoy Grill, one evening soon? I suggest Friday or Saturday of this week, or Tuesday of next week.

1–VW records that TSE visited them on 31 May: he was to be the editor of a new quarterly, which 'some old firm' was publishing in the autumn, and 'all his works must go to them – a blow to us' (*Diary*, III, 27).
2–The paper of the carbon copy in GCF's Letter Book (E/2) is torn here.
3–*Poems 1909–1925*, published by F&G on 23 Nov. 1925. The first issue of *NC* was postponed until Jan. 1926.
4–The Clark lectures.

I will confess that I also want to take that opportunity – if I may have it – of asking you some more questions in connection with my play [*Sweeney Agonistes*].

Sincerely yours,
T. S. Eliot

TO *W. E. Süskind* CC

11 June 1925

[*The New Criterion*,
24 Russell Square, London]

Dear Sir,

I owe you many apologies for the delay in replying to your letter of the 15th April. I have myself been away for reasons of health, and my office was not for a long time in touch with me. I read with great interest your essay on the 'Tänzerische Generation' which I took abroad with me.[1] I confess that I was very much tempted, but our policy has always been to print only inedited matter or at any rate to print simultaneously with some foreign periodicals, and I feel that it would be a dangerous precedent for us to republish an essay from so well known a periodical as the *Neue Merkur*. We recently, however, modified this principle so far as to publish an essay by Monsieur Henri Massis, a part of which had already appeared in *La Revue Universelle*; but Monsieur Massis modified and extended this essay for us so as to give it new value.[2] If it interested you to write for us another essay similar to the one you sent me, I should be very happy indeed; and I should also be very glad to see more of your work.

With many thanks,

Yours sincerely,
[T. S. E.]

TSE/IPF

1 – W. E. Süskind, 'Die tänzerische Generation' ['The Dancing Generation'], *Der neue Merkur*, 8: 2 (1925), 586–97: an article about the democratic pleasure of dancing to jazz bands. See further Guy Stern, *War, Weimar, and Literature: the story of the Neue Merkur, 1914–1925* (1971), 129.

2 – Henri Massis, 'Defence of the West', *NC* 4: 2 & 3 (Apr. & June 1926).

TO *Thomas MacGreevy* MS TCD

11 June 1925 *The Criterion*, 17 Thavies Inn

Dear Mr MacGreevy

I have written to my friend Leonard Woolf, literary editor of *The Nation*, and he says he thinks he could use reviews by you.[1] Will you ring up *The Nation*, and go and see him when he is there.

Many thanks for Ballet – excellent – will write later.

Sincerely
T. S. Eliot

TO *Harold Monro* TS Beinecke

12 June 1925 *The Criterion*,
23 Adelphi Terrace House

My dear Monro,

Very many thanks for your post-card. Is it true that I failed to answer your last letter? If so, I am very, very sorry. On the contrary, it is a great pleasure to me to be importuned, as you call it, and to think that I have a few friends who still remember my existence after such a long disappearance. My wife is still ill and has just started on a new and very drastic treatment for a serious liver trouble which all the doctors until the present one failed to discover. Hence I have been very much preoccupied, but you have been in my mind lately and I had already made a note to suggest a meeting at dinner one evening as soon as practicable. Let me know should you be intending to leave town so that I may not miss you.

Ever yours,
T. S. E.

1 – 'Mr Woolf has been as kind as could be to me. I am very grateful to you for that introduction,' MacGreevy replied on 24 Sept. MacGreevy was to write regular (usually unsigned) pieces in the 'Alpha and Omega' column in *N&A*, as well as reviews, from 27 June 1925 to 13 Aug. 1927.

TO *Edwin Muir*[1] CC

12 June 1925 23 Adelphi Terrace House

Dear Mr Muir,

I am extremely grateful for your very thorough and convincing criticism of the adaptations from *Hölderlin*.[2] You really have taken much more trouble than was necessary, as merely a word from you would have satisfied me whether the translations were good or bad.

Your letter has so impressed me that I am inclined to ask you whether you are interested yourself in translating some of Hölderlin into English.[3] If you would, I should like to publish some of them in the *Criterion*, and I think it probable that I could find a good publisher for a volume of such translations by you, together with an introductory essay by you. Does this appeal to you?

Has your essay on Hölderlin ever been published? Because, if not, I should like to have the opportunity of working it into the *Criterion* next winter.

I am glad to see that you are living nearer to London. I do not know whether you ever come to town, but when I have an opportunity – but I am afraid not very soon – I shall make an attempt to arrange a meeting with you.

Sincerely yours,
[T. S. E.]

TSE/IPF

1–Edwin Muir (1887–1959): Scottish poet, novelist, critic and prolific reviewer, and translator (with his wife Willa) of Kafka. He had been an editorial assistant to A. R. Orage on *The New Age*, and spent the early 1920s in Prague, Germany, Italy and Austria. His *First Poems* was published by the Hogarth Press in Apr. 1925. TSE came to think his criticism 'the best of our time' (*The Times*, 7 Jan. 1959), and was impressed by 'the power of his early work', even though he considered the later work 'the most remarkable'. See TSE, 'Edwin Muir: 1887–1959 An Appreciation' (*Listener* 71, 28 May 1964, 872), reprinted with modifications as the 'Preface' to Muir's *Selected Poems* (1965).

2–On 3 June, IPF sent Muir a set of translations of Hölderlin by Pierre Loving, with a request for his 'opinion'. On 8 June, Muir replied that 'it would be a gross injustice if these little scraps torn from the work of the greatest after Goethe of German poets . . . should purport to give to English readers, and for the first time, too, a notion of Hölderlin's quality'.

3–Muir was one of the first to introduce the Romantic poet to the English-speaking public, in his 'A Note on Friedrich Hölderlin', *Scottish Nation* (Sept. 1923). In his reply to TSE, Muir said he had not yet tried to translate him, but would try a version of 'Patmos'. Neither Muir's essay nor any translations appeared in C. His *Essays on Literature and Society* (1949) included 'Hölderlin' and 'Hölderlin's Patmos', and Muir's poem 'Hölderlin's Journey' appeared in *NC* 16: 63 (Jan. 1937).

TO *F. S. Flint* TS Texas

12 June 1925 *The Criterion*,
23 Adelphi Terrace House

My dear Flint,

Many thanks for your letter, compliments and manuscript. I like your poem very much except that I am not certain whether I like the fourth part, the part which is rather in the manner of James B. V. Thomson which seems to me at first two readings to jar a little with the rest.[1] However, I should like to keep the poem for publication. The only difficulty is that the title and subject make reason for delay. If you were an editor, which you should thank God you are not, you would know that the public will tolerate almost anything except the publication of a spring ode in the autumn. I think, however, that it might make the public feel pleasant to read about spring in January. Do you agree?

I hope that the pleasant days of beef steak and beer and discussion may return to us.

Ever yours,
[T. S. E.]

TO *Ronald Davis*[2] CC

12 June 1925 23 Adelphi Terrace House

Dear Sir,

Thank you for your letter and the copy of your book which has just arrived.[3] I am asking Mr Cobden-Sanderson to send you the copies of *The Serpent* which you require, together with the invoice.

Allow me to compliment you on the delightful appearance of your translation and to express my great pleasure at the inscriptions by Monsieur Valéry and yourself. I should like to take up the question of the publication in this country with Lady Rothermere when I next see her. Have you translated any other of Monsieur Valéry's essays? I am asking

1–Flint sent his poem 'Spring Ode' in response to TSE's letter of 4 June. It appeared in *NC* 4: 3 (June 1926), minus its fourth (and last) section.

2–Ronald Davis was a translator, and co-editor (with Raoul Simonson) of *Bibliographie des oeuvres du Paul Valéry 1895–1925* (1926).

3–Paul Valéry, *An Evening with M. Teste*, trans. Ronald Davis, '*avec une préface inédite de l'auteur*' (Paris, 1925): the first English translation of Valéry's 1919 essay, in a limited edition of 208 copies.

because it has occurred to me that there might be some demand for a larger publication of Valéry's prose work.

Yours very truly,
[T. S. E.]

TO *L. A. G. Strong* CC

12 June 1925 23 Adelphi Terrace House

Dear Strong,

Many thanks for your letter which is so amiable that I am disposed to accede to your request.[1] I should be inclined to ask three guineas as a fee for republication. Will you let me know if you agree?

I have, however, another short poem in the same series which has been published in Paris and New York but not here.[2] It seems to me better than the ones you have seen. I should prefer to substitute for this series a series containing the other poem, as it appeared in the *Dial* last March.[3] If we are in agreement on both points, I will send you the copy.

Thank you for the rest of your letter. Be sure that I look forward to a meeting when possible. Unfortunately my illness, and subsequently my wife's illness, still make it a little difficult, but in any case I hope you will let me know when you are in London and we will see what we can do.

Sincerely yours,
[T. S. E.]

TO *Mansfield Forbes*[4] TS Clare

12 June 1925 *The Criterion*,
23 Adelphi Terrace House

My dear Mr Forbes,

Thank you very much for your kind letter. I am looking forward very keenly to visiting Cambridge and to making your acquaintance while there.

1 – Evidently a request to reprint TSE's 'Three Poems', from *C.* 3: 10 (Jan. 1925).
2 – 'Poème', *Commerce* 3 (Winter 1924 [/1925]), reprinted in *The Dial*, became Part I of 'The Hollow Men'.
3 – 'The Hollow Men, I–III', *Dial* 78: 3 (Mar. 1925), was reprinted as 'The Hollow Men', Parts I–II, and IV, in *P 1909–1925* (1925).
4 – Mansfield Forbes (1890–1936): Fellow in English of Clare College, Cambridge. See Hugh Carey, *Mansfield Forbes and his Cambridge* (1984).

It is unfortunately true that both my wife and myself have been in very bad health and have been almost shut off from the world for some months, but I hope that next winter we may have the pleasure of seeing you in London as well as Cambridge.

With many thanks,

Yours sincerely,
T. S. Eliot

TO *H. P. Collins* CC

12 June 1925 23 Adelphi Terrace House

Dear Mr Collins,

I hope that my testimonial will be of some use.

Had I had the opportunity I should have written to you before to explain that I was obliged to cut down your review of Mrs Woolf's book.[1] For certain reasons it is necessary to make the forthcoming issue of the *Criterion* of as small a compass as possible, and it is solely on this account that your review, as well as other contributions, has been reduced. I hope that in future numbers such restrictions will not be necessary. I should be very interested to hear whether you get the job you are after.

With all best wishes,

Sincerely yours,
[T. S. E.]

TSE/IPF

FROM *Henry Eliot* TS Valerie Eliot

12 June 1925 1037 Rush St, Chicago

Dear Tom:

You ask me to write about myself. That is what I am going to do. I think you are the only person to whom I can express my innermost thoughts and feelings with complete candor, and without fear of being misunderstood. It may be that soon I shall not be able to express myself with complete candor. I sometimes doubt if any married man can. Sometimes in their cups or in their grief married men have talked freely about marriage to me, but have always recanted.

1 – See Collins, rev, of VW, *The Common Reader*, C. 3: 12 (July 1925).

I am engaged to be married.[1] See attached memo. Also attached photo. I am very proud of this, and very happy, and very frightened lest I fail to measure up to expectations. I am quite in love with her, but of course not as much in love as if she had flouted, scorned, deceived, cheated and ridiculed me. However, the kind of affection which I have for her is rare, solider, more lasting and more certain of bringing happiness than the kind with which I have usually nourished my masochistic tendencies. This is the kind of girl of whom I could, and probably did (though my memory is indistinct) say, before romance had begun to cloud my judgment, that she would be an ideal person for me to marry. I said to her lately (and it seemed to please her greatly) that if she had been a man, or I a girl, she would have been my best friend.

She is a most happy combination of the kind of qualities that I like with qualities that make her wholly acceptable to such a fanatically conservative family as ours is. I have to accept the facts that she is a mildly devout church-goer, that she does not bob her hair, nor smoke cigarettes. She is, however, no proselyte; as to point two, the way she does her hair is so excellent and has so much distinction of its own that I should view with alarm any suggestion of change; and as to point three (due largely to filial affection) I do not care either way. I cannot think of anyone I know who would not like her unreservedly. You and Vivien would both find her tonic and sympathetic – I do not mean sentimentally, merely, but mentally sympathetic.

I shall not be my own master, but at least I shall be under a benevolent, affectionate, and intelligent rule. The most astonishing thing – and one which it is a constant effort to realize – is that she is quite fond – indeed, I might almost say, quite in love with me. This is too seemingly preposterous a statement for me to commit myself to unqualifiedly. To me it is an almost frightening and disconcerting phenomenon. It never happened before, although at times I have been under the illusion of it.

I am not quite clear why either of us wants to get married. We should both probably be better off for the material comforts if we remained single. I have as frequently convinced myself that under no circumstances could I possibly get married, as of the contrary thesis that I was predestined to get married. Of course I should be better off unmarried; and yet something has always driven me counter to reason. Hence Winifred, Ethel, Eunice, Mary, Bess, Rosamond, Geraldine, Katharine, and Joan. Il catalogo. Thank God none of them ever loved me – enough, at least. Two people would have been miserable.

1 – HWE and Theresa Garrett were to be married on 15 Feb. 1926.

In time, if I remained single, I might achieve freedom – I might save enough to live on, to go abroad, to read and think. I have always desiderated the luxury of thinking; as a pastime it is without equal. And yet that may have been a mirage. If I had leisure, I should be frightfully lonely, because no one else has leisure; I should become soft, introspective and misanthropic. Here is a companion who openly countenances such fruitless occupations as reading, thinking, working at what you like, and enjoying life intelligently. Few people (I did not say merely few women) have ever seemed to me so completely simpatico. The thought of her – her sincerity, honesty, vitality, joyousness, and courage – is very comforting.

Perhaps she will make a Man out of me. I never had any very strong ambition toward that end. The field is already overcrowded. I had rather be the freak nature meant me to be. It is bad news for the disagreeable hobgoblin inside of me who claims to be me, and who has been laughing cynically over the whole business. He will have to retire into my Cimmerian sub-consciousness.

Good God, how does anyone get married? I would not accept a job as a traffic manager or shipping clerk because I know nothing about it, and yet here is a job which every man accepts apparently on the blithe assumption that knowledge of the business is innate in him. Should I take a course in obstetrics, infant feeding and household management? On top of my present duties, and the necessity of making a change in my whole mode of life, I cannot casually pick up these things. I have often puzzled over the marriage relationship, which seemed to me the most incongruous, impossible, and inconsistent thing ever conceived. One must translate an iridescent fantasy into the hardest and ugliest of facts. One goes to a bourne of which no traveller ever tells. It is the most secret of all secret cults.

Once I learned to ride a horse. Nothing seemed to me at the time so preposterous as the idea that I could learn to ride a horse. Yet some automaton inside of me did learn, after a fashion, to ride. It was not I; I do not know that person. Whoever he was, would probably have made some sort of a soldier out of me, had I ever by unkind fate been elected to that lot. Whoever he is, he will probably see me through married life.

If you have any advice to give me, now is the time. You can probably help me. Please do. I am very fond of you, and very fond of Vivien. You and Theresa are the only persons by whom I have any hope of being understood.

Affectionately your brother,

Henry

TO *Herbert Read* MS Victoria

[17? June 1925] [London]

My dear Read

We shall probably be here most if not all of the summer. My new doctor has found my wife's liver and intestine so nearly paralized [*sic*] that he does not dare to let us move for the present.

I am anxious to see you when we both can. Meanwhile:-

1. What do you think of Fernandez on Maritain?[1] It seemed to me a little specious and Bergsonian.[2] I have sent for Maritain's book.[3]

2. You spoke once of making a book including your two essays in the *Criterion*, one on the Brontes, and perhaps more. Will you let me know about it? I have a reason.[4]

Ever yours
T. S. Eliot

TO *Violet Schiff* MS Valerie Eliot

17 June [1925] 9 Clarence Gate Gdns

My dear Violet

Why do V. and I never hear from either of you? How are you? V.'s new treatment continues, but will be very hard and very long. She was just on the verge of paralysis of the intestine and some terrible functional liver trouble. The doctor said he had never seen so bad a liver on a woman, or an intestine so nearly dead.

I am sure she would like to hear from you.

Ever aff
Tom

1 – Ramón Fernandez, 'L'intelligence et M. Maritain', *NRF* 12: 141 (1 June 1925), 986–94.
2 – Fernandez found an equivalent to scientific enquiry rather than Thomist reason in modern works such as Einstein's writings, Bergson's *La Matière et Mémoire*, Cézanne's paintings and Proust's novels. On 19 June, HR said that while the article initially gave him 'firm ground', he agreed it was 'very specious'.
3 – Maritain's *Réflexions sur l'intelligence et sur sa vie propre* (1924): HR had been reading it and *L'art scholastique*, and found them 'extremely interesting'.
4 – HR's proposed book was to include 'The Nature of Metaphysical Poetry' (from *C.* 1: 3, Apr. 1923) and 'Psycho-analysis and the Critic' (from 3: 10, Jan. 1925) as well as 'Charlotte and Emily Bronte' and eight other essays. In reply, HR reaffirmed that he wanted to write a book.

TO *Sydney Waterlow* MS Private Collection

17 June 1925 9 Clarence Gate Gdns

My dear Sydney

Will you listen to a voice from the tomb? I don't know whether news from any source has reached you, as I have been inaudible and almost invisible for nearly six months. Vivien has had a frightful illness, which is now proved to be some liver disorder and intestinal infection – and the new doctor has just told me that she will probably recover – he was very doubtful, as she must have had it for many years. I have literally hardly left the house for months, except to see doctors, and a few imperative visits which had to be arranged carefully. In July we must go abroad, ~~not Germany~~. Will you be accessible in the autumn – I should like to continue our conversation. I saw Murry once in March.

Meanwhile will you do me a favour? You once signed a naturalisation form for me. I am *now* only completing it, but have *lost* the form you signed.[1] Would you be willing to sign another? I particularly wanted you on it.

Please remember me to your wife, and I'd like to know what you are thinking about and how you are.

Ever yours
T. S. E.

TO *The Collector of Inland Revenue, Baltimore, MD* CC

17 June 1925 9 Clarence Gate Gdns

Sir,

I enclose my income return for the year 1924 together with cheque [for] $12.44. I regret the delay, which is due to very exceptional difficult personal conditions.

This is as accurate a return as I have been able to prepare in the circumstances. The inaccuracies and omissions are only such as would, if corrected, *reduce* the tax payable by me. For instance, you will observe that I have made no deduction on account of income tax paid here. Had I made all inclusions and allowances the tax, to the best of my knowledge and belief, would have been something between four and five dollars.

I have the honour to be, Sir,

Your obedient servant,
[T. S. E.]

1 – TSE was eventually naturalised in Nov. 1927.

TO *Marianne Moore* CC

18 June 1925 [London]

Dear Miss Moore,

I have your letter of the 4th June. I am surprised at hearing from you when I wrote to Miss Thayer, and I observe the insulting tone of your letter.[1]

I wrote personally to Miss Thayer, who had privately expressed strong admiration for some of my wife's earlier work. I now know that Miss Thayer has made use of you in order to insult me and my wife for personal reasons. You may or may not know the facts of the influences which have converted Miss Thayer from admiration to hostility, and for her reasons for replying in this fashion through you instead of writing herself. It is indifferent to me whether you know these reasons or not; it is enough that you have lent yourself to this plot, and have written to me in a manner which I can only call insulting. It is an insult that you wrote to me, when my letter was *pointedly to Miss T.*

I have hitherto praised your work both in America and here, without reserve, especially here: where the literary public sees in it no merit whatever. I have championed you in the face of derision and indifference, and I had the right to expect better treatment from you.[2] In future, I shall take a different course, and I intend to see that justice is done and the balance righted.

I am surprised that Scofield Thayer should leave a woman in charge who is merely the tool of such a woman as Ellen Thayer.

I have already observed, in connection with your own work, that opinion as to what is good writing is utterly different here and in America, and this story will be published here in the autumn.

1–On 17 May TSE had sent VHE's story 'The Paralyzed Woman' to Ellen Thayer at the *Dial*. Moore replied on 4 June: 'We are sorry not to publish in America, Mrs Eliot's story . . . which you were so good as to let us see at the hand of Miss Ellen Thayer. Your opinion, as you know, is held in the most profound esteem by the editors of *The Dial*, and we could not be insensible to the resilience and grace, of this story; yet, it has not for us, that finality which you feel it to have.' Although TSE was furious that it was rejected by the *Dial*, neither did it appear in *C.* – even though he had already despatched it to be set up by the printers: it is possible that he came to agree with Moore's judgement. The story is preserved under the nom-de-plume 'Feiron Morris' among VHE's papers in the Bodleian (MSS Eng. Misc. c.624).

2–TSE had recently championed Moore in *C.* 3: 11 (Apr. 1925), when she won the *Dial* award. Despite this letter, normal relations were soon resumed, and TSE went on to publish Moore's *Selected Poems* (1935).

I do not intend to endure this manoeuvre, and I propose to put all the readers of the *Dial* whom I know – and I know a good many – in possession of the facts.

Yours faithfully,
[T. S. E.]

TO *Lady Rothermere* CC

18 June 1925 [London]

Dear L. R.

This is to warn you against a person named Lucy Thayer, an American, aged thirty-eight but looks younger, who is now loose in Paris and who is anxious to injure me. She is (I am convinced) *mad*.

She was some years ago a friend of my wife.[1] She has been alone in London for the past two years, and has been persecuting my wife during that time with her very obscene attentions. Two years ago in the country she came down to see my wife, and told her that she was going to kill her father, against whom she had a perfectly unwarranted grudge. My wife is devoted to her own father, and this woman saw the horror in her face and changed the subject abruptly. Since then, having lived under the influence of several psycho-analysts whom she saw every day she became madder. She is psycho-analysis mad, and cannot even speak now except in the language of psycho-analysis.

Several months ago this woman lay in wait for my wife at her doctor's, when she was very ill, and told her in so many words that she had killed her father at last. I have another witness for this. She then made violent love to my wife, kneeling at her feet. She is perverted. My wife was *prostrated* by this shock, especially as she was then in a state of great anxiety about her own father. She has been very ill ever since, and nearly lost her reason for a time. Her doctor knows all about this. Consequently I forbade the woman the house and forcibly removed her and have prevented her from communicating with my wife in any way.

This is her grievance against me. She is in Paris and burning to injure me in every way possible. She is a cousin of the editor of *The Dial* and has

1 – VHE met Lucy Thayer in Vevey in 1908, some years before meeting TSE. Lucy Thayer was a witness to the Eliots' wedding in June 1915.

already done me in in this quarter, so that I have lost a very important part of my income.[1]

She is now busy in defaming and libelling me and my wife everywhere where harm can be done us. She knows about you and about the *Criterion*. You may hear of her activities, and she is quite likely to seek you out for the purpose of telling you lies about us. Hence this letter.

Always very sincerely,
[T. S. E.]

Vivien Eliot TO *Ezra Pound*

TS Beinecke

[June 1925] [London]

Ezra Pound. Excuse length of letter.

Dear Ezra,

This is odd. I was just going to rite to you on another matta. Very import. to me.

Meanwhile damn Sco.'s cousin. But she has done me in. I think she hates Tom more than death. She came to my doctor's (Where I used to go every day to have my stomach punched which is now sed to have done me in) and told me her Pa was dead at larst & as she had already told me she ment to kill him it upset me. Then she nelt down beside me and asked me if I loved her, & made love. I could not get at anyone to help me & so nearly went mad. Helpless. Not dressed. Alone. So Tom afterwards removed her. He sent her a chit to say she should never seee me againe. She then left England, to poison France.[2]

Meanwhile I *MUST* explain that I have been riting (writing!) for a long time under various names and nomenclatures. Have written a lot of stories. Very peculiar. I wrote nearly the whole of the last '*Criterion*' – except anything that was good in it, if there was such – under different names, all beginning with F. M. I thought out this skeme of getting money out of the

1 – VHE told EP that TSE 'cursed Ellen and Marrrriannnne and Lucy, and so ends the *Dial* for us'. TSE's next contribution to the *Dial* was 'Literature, Science, and Dogma' in 82: 3 (Mar. 1927).

2 – Surprisingly, Ellen Thayer would write to TSE again two years later, on 31 Jan. 1927: 'Lucy writes me good news of Vivien, and seems herself very happy' (MS Valerie Eliot). However, Carole Seymour-Jones sums up the fate of Scofield's cousin: 'Lucy . . . was unbalanced and, like Scofield, now under analysis with Sigmund Freud in Vienna, and . . . like Vivien, would end her days as a psychiatric patient' (*Painted Shadow: The Life of Vivienne Eliot* [2001], 403).

Criterion a year ago. Because was always annoyed by spouse getting no salary. So thought what a good idea will receive money for contributions. Have received money. No one knows. But *unfort.* I was mis-led into telling Sco's cousin Lucy (it *is* the one we went on the river with in a punt).

Nearly finished now cheer up[1]

Sco's cousin professed great admiration & fuss about writings, made great scene. She wrote to her sister *Ellen* ELLEN (age about 41) who Sco has left the Dial to, & her sister Ellen expressed much joy & sed my stories made her laugh & laugh & split her sides etc. etc. So I got ambitious & sent a long story to the Dial (O hell-blood why did I) thinking that Ellen Thayer was a just woman & knew her sister to be mad & bad & insane & shocking and murderous.

Ellen Thayer *immediately* returned my story which is damn good *by means of a gastly female* called Marrriannnnne Mooooore or (sum such name) a POETESS (Christ!) & who is left in co-partnership of Dial. Spouse had written letter concerning story to Ellen Thayer & at same time enclosed my doctor's diagnosis of present disease, to explain why her sister was dangerous to me, but as the reply (curt & rude) *came via Marrrriannnnne Moore*, he rote & cursed her out. He cursed out Ellen and Marrrriannnne & Lucy & so ends the Dial for us.

Other matter (most important).

Am ill (*still* ill) not ill again (always ill)

Became *exceeeedingly* ill nearly ded just after Xmas. Took to swoons & trances etc. Much horror. Other doctor considered necessary. Spouse having remembered that *your* spouse was much sett up by man called W E S T (& being convinced) (as am I) that all ordinary medical men are *fools*) fetched W E S T. After long exam. & screams by *West* he sed –

This female is starved to death. This female has very very strong h a r t
No spine fuss, <u>*but*</u> [underlined 7 times] this female has got the most terrible huge vast hideous gastly rock-like shocking incredible
LIVER
I have ever
seen or hard of or her
tell of in life or on any
living or ded female. MUST
go V I C H Y in the end.
I think, well – praps.

1 – Last two words added by hand.

Drag self to W. who treats me 3 times per week always yelling about one thing or another. Become slightly sickened.

Convinced had nervous breakdown owing to various causes will *not bore* you with. Certainly starved. Being anxious to due took to trances. (Am very *hypnotic, always was*. Could be 1st class *MEDIUM*).

Enjoyed trances. Went off for 2 or 3 weeks at a time. (Had *very queer* experiences in sum other Place).

Spouse explained trances to W. who sed starvation induces trances in mediumistics.

Dislike West terribly. Is improving *health* – but terrible dislike grows. *Hate* his manner, hate his ways, *hate* his mind, hate his house & the row & his lowness (is really *very LOW Irish* from W. America). Hate going to him. Now he says I shall be fit to got to *Vichy* (where he goes twice a year) in Aug. I still feel very unwell. Tired. Hav not been in a *train* for 3 years. Only hired car. Am too nervous to shop *alone*. He ses Vichy, I say *no*. Spouse all of a dither. Fearful clinch. Have got *suspiciouns* about Vichy business. Also *suspiciouns* about liver. *Kant* believed in L I V E R. *Cant* think it true. Crying with rage.
Loathe indecision. Give me advice on a post card quick.
Is West alrite?
Do you know?
Do you believe in Vichy?
Do you believe in Liver?
Please E. P. relieve a tormented Celt (Am ½ Welsh ½ Irish).

Believe West gets commission on patients taken to Vichy. (Know this is case at Evian). Was *warned* once years ago, by best doctor ever had, against Vichy.

Just relieve me on a p. card on 3 points.[1]

o – o – o – o - o – o – o – o – o – o

[Unsigned]

1–EP wrote to TSE on 28 June 1925: 'Am sending V. a long screed part serious, and part intended to be diverting.

'As to West's diagnosis of liver; the phantasms might very well indicate liver, i.e. liver does make one see things.

'AND starvation produces visions (less vigorous than liver visions) & it produces tears, dither, agoraphobia etc. . . .

'She says West is doing her good . . . If it is hard liver, I don't KNOW anything, merely; West's diagnosis sounds plausible; see nothing against it; but it ought to be controllable by fecal analysis (though there may be special liver troubles that aint.)'

EP's response to VHE herself has not been found.

TO *Wyndham Lewis* MS Cornell

19 June 1925 [9 Clarence Gate Gdns]

Dear Lewis

I return your MS as you request,[1] but bear in mind that it would have suited me perfectly for October, and will still do so. For certain reasons I have had to make the July no. very small.

As soon as circumstances permit me to make engagements more freely, I shall suggest a meeting. Meanwhile, I should be glad to know what is the position about your books, and especially the Arch-Zagreus etc. cycle.[2] I have something in view (new).[3]

Yours
T. S. E.

TO *Herbert Read* MS Victoria

21 June 1925 [London]

My dear Read

Pending a meeting, will you tell me what you think of this idea (in confidence) – This is *not* in any way a substitute for the present *Criterion* or its equivalent, but as well.

A *small* periodical (say 60 pp.) quarterly or six times a year, and possibly irregularly i.e. four numbers during the year but not necessarily at regular intervals; each no. to contain essays by four or six writers of various nationalities on the same (set) subject;[4] the subject to be one within literature or the sphere of general ideas and of European (not merely local) interest. The writers might also append their views of each others views.

It could hardly have more than a very small circulation. The question is its interest, utility and influence. Writers to be paid of course.

1 – Unidentified.

2 – TSE had published 'Mr Zagreus and the Split-Man' in C. 2: 6 (Feb. 1924); and 'The Apes of God' in 2: 7 (Apr. 1924), both of which became part of *The Apes of God* (1930). On 29 Apr., WL told EP he had completed two volumes of *The Apes of God* and *Archie*. The latter was never published, but the MS is in the Olin Library, Cornell University.

3 – Presumably a ref. to possible publication by F&G.

4 – TSE has written 'Symposium' vertically in the left margin. This letter indicates that he was considering the possibility of running two parallel reviews; one, a continuation of C. financed by F&G; the other a 'Symposium' (which he refers to on 31 July as 'the *Cahiers*') financed by Lady Rothermere.

There seems to me to exist (1) great ignorance and indifference here to continental ideas (2) a certain waste in that writers in modern Europe tend to apply themselves too narrowly to local aspects of general problems. Mediaeval Europe was more economical.

More French names, of course, occur to one than of other nationalities. But we might scrape together half a dozen here; there are few enough who think at all.

The tendency in England is of course (vide *Vogue*, Lytton Strachey et other phenomena)[1] to avoid thought altogether.

If this were done it *might* be published in Paris (in French) also.

If you see *anything* in this rough outline we will discuss it further. It would never of course pay for itself, but it is entertained by me as a possible line for certain funds which would otherwise be spent at Deauville and Cannes.[2]

Ever yours
T. S. E.

TO *Richard Aldington* — MS Texas

Sunday [21 June 1925] — [9 Clarence Gate Gdns]

My dear Richard

I was very disappointed to have so unsatisfactory an afternoon.[3] I should have been very glad to see S[ydney] W[aterlow] at another time, but the coincidence – when you come to town so seldom – was deplorable. I wanted not only to hear more of your affairs but to tell you privately about my own designs. For the energy to write six close pages is lacking – if there is any hope of your coming again within the month.

I was discussing our plans for Ezra with my wife last night – she thought that a book of essays was no good unless we could get a good number of big names – and I don't see where they are to come from. Even Yeats is not likely to be of much use. She thought that a smaller book – a critical study – by one man – would be better – i.e. either

by me with a preface by you }
" you " " " me } but

1 – RA, writing to HR in June, wondered 'why TSE is so very bitter against Lytton Strachey' ('Richard Aldington's Letters to Herbert Read'). Strachey, like RA, published in *Vogue*.
2 – An allusion to Lady Rothermere.
3 – On 19 June, RA said he would call on TSE the following day (Saturday).

when will either of us have the time? I should like to get something done. But it seems as if Ezra would have to wait for his luck until after he is dead.[1]

– Nevertheless, I much enjoyed seeing you, even under unsatisfactory conditions.

Ever yours
Tom

TO *Theodore Spencer*[2] MS Harvard

25 June 1925 9 Clarence Gate Gdns

Dear Mr Spencer

I should be happy to have a talk with you. Unfortunately, my circumstances are such at present that it is difficult for me to make engagements ahead, and I am also very busy. If you will write to me when you come to London, and tell me what times are possible for you (not the morning or evening) I will try to arrange it.

Sincerely yours
T. S. Eliot

Criterion Contract TS Valerie Eliot

25 June 1925

AN AGREEMENT made the 25th day of June One thousand nine hundred and twenty-five BETWEEN THE SCIENTIFIC PRESS LIMITED of 28 and 29 Southampton Street London W.C.2 (hereinafter called 'the Company') of the one part and THOMAS STEARNS Eliot of 9 Clarence Gate Gardens in the County of London (hereinafter referred to as 'Mr Eliot') of the other part

WHEREBY IT IS AGREED as follows

1. THE Company will employ Mr Eliot and Mr Eliot will serve the company as sole Editor of a quarterly literary periodical the property of the

1–TSE had published *Ezra Pound: His Metric and Poetry* (1917), and was to publish EP's *Selected Poems*, ed. T. S. Eliot (1928). The mooted book of essays never materialised.

2–Theodore Spencer (1902–49), poet, critic, Shakespearean scholar, taught English at Harvard, 1927–49, and was close to TSE there during his Charles Eliot Norton professorship 1932–3.

Company intended to be shortly published for a period of five years from the First of July One thousand nine hundred and twenty-five.

2. THE Company will pay Mr Eliot by way of remuneration so long as he shall remain a Director of the Company a salary in addition to his remuneration as such Director at the rate of Three hundred and twenty-five pounds per annum by quarterly payments on the usual quarter days of One hundred and eighteen pounds fifteen shillings to be paid on the Twenty-fifth day of March and the Twenty-ninth day of September respectively and the sum of Forty-three pounds fifteen shillings to be paid on the Twenty-fourth day of June and Twenty-fifth day of December respectively the first payment of One hundred and eighteen pounds fifteen shillings to be made on the Twenty-ninth day of September One thousand nine hundred and twenty-five Provided that if Mr Eliot shall **not** cease to be a Director of the Company during the continuance of this Agreement then the said salary of Three hundred and twenty-five pounds per annum shall be increased to Four hundred pounds per annum payable by equal quarterly payments Each quarter's salary may be paid wholly or partly in advance provided no such payment in advance shall be made in respect of any half-yearly period except within that period A half-yearly period is a period from the First day of January to the Thirtieth day of June and from the First day of July to the Thirty-first day of December in any year.

3. Mr Eliot shall during his employment hereunder secure contributions for and decide the contents of the said periodical at such remuneration as may be agreed between the contributor and Mr Eliot not exceeding Two pounds per thousand words except with the specific consent in writing of the Chairman of the Company and shall endeavour as far as possible to obtain from the various contributors and to correct and prepare for press and deliver to the Company the manuscript of the several contributions to be included in each issue of the said periodical at such times as the Company may require.

4. ALL expenses of and attending the preparation compilation and publication of each issue of the said periodical including the remuneration of the contributors shall be borne by the Company who will provide Mr Eliot with such secretarial assistance as may be necessary. The Company will be responsible for the mechanical production of the said periodical.

5. Mr Eliot shall not during the continuance of this Agreement without the previous sanction in writing of the Company acquire a financial interest in any other literary periodical or publishing house or without the like consent edit or assist in editing or take any part in the

preparation or production of any publication of a similar nature to and calculated to compete with the said periodical but Mr Eliot shall be at liberty at all times to contribute to any other publication or periodical.

6. Mr Eliot agrees to offer in the first place to the Company for publication in book form by them upon terms not less favourable than those offered by any other publisher all or any original works written by him.

7. If Mr Eliot shall be incapacitated by illness from editing two consecutive issues of the said periodical then this Agreement may be determined by the Company upon their giving six calendar months' notice in writing to that effect.

IN WITNESS WHEREOF the Company has caused these presents to be signed on its behalf and the said Thomas Stearns Eliot has hereunto set his hand the day and year first above written.

[Signed by
Geoffrey C. Faber
Witness A. S. Ward
Secretary]

FROM *Geoffrey Faber* CC

30 June 1925 [London]

My dear Eliot,

(1) *The New Criterion*

I want as soon as possible to have a meeting here between you and me and our Publications Manager, to settle definitely the form of the paper. Our Advertisement Manager wants to have as exact answers as he can to the following questions:-

1. Title, size, style, type area and number of pages.
2. Date of the first number.
3. Scope of contents.
4. Number to be printed each quarter and probable readers.

He also wants to know as far ahead as possible what books will be under review in the first and all succeeding numbers, so that he can make arrangements to secure advertisements from the publishers concerned. All these points we can discuss when we meet.

We have also got to consider what steps ought to be taken with regard to sales overseas; especially, I suppose, in Paris and the United States. Any information you can give us on these points will be welcome.

We shall, as soon as possible, for the sake of the Advertisement Manager, have to get out dummy copies showing the cover design and a page or two of text matter. This we ought to do if possible during the next fortnight.

(2) Books

About the various suggestions you made to me the other day. They were all sound; and I should be grateful if you would take whatever steps you can to bring any of them nearer realisation. I should like to have as much as possible fixed up before the end of July so that we shall have sufficient in hand for the Autumn and Christmas season.

Yours ever,
[Geoffrey C. Faber]

TO *L. A. G. Strong* CC

30 June 1925 23 Adelphi Terrace House

Dear Strong,

I apologise for not having replied immediately to your letter of the 14th instant. But I am still in doubt as to how I wish this suite to be arranged; as a matter of fact, it is not quite complete.[1] Therefore I should be very glad if you would use only the poem which provides the title, i.e. Part I of the three poems printed in the *Dial*.[2] This is the only one with which I am at present satisfied. I should therefore ask only two guineas, as the original subject of negotiation was a set of three.

Write to me when you come to London, and if I have not left town we will meet.

Yours sincerely,
[T. S. E.]

TSE/IPF

TO *Wyndham Lewis* TS Cornell

6 July 1925 9 Clarence Gate Gdns

Dear Lewis,

This is the first opportunity I have had to reply to your letter. I shall be very glad to discuss the matter of the books with you as soon as you are

1 – 'The Hollow Men'.

2 – Parts I–II and IV of the final 'suite' were published in *Dial* 78: 3 (Mar. 1925). The opening of I reads: 'We are the hollow men / We are the stuffed men'.

ready to negotiate.[1] Meanwhile I want to say that I know nothing whatever about Whibley's actions. I have not seen him for a very long time and although I have had letters from him, he has not alluded to this business in any way.[2] I should therefore be very glad if you would let me know what has happened. If the negotiations for this book have fallen through, I should be very glad to take it to the people I have in mind.

Sincerely yours,
T. S. Eliot

TO *Richard Aldington* CC

6 July 1925 9 Clarence Gate Gdns

My dear Richard,

I waited in the hope that you might get up to town and I shall now continue to wait. Our last interview was so unsatisfactory that I hope we can meet again as soon as possible. I am very sorry that you disliked S. W.[3] He is a peculiar person, but when one understands him I don't think that there is very much to dislike seriously. But he was very kind to me at one time years ago, and was in fact the first person to give me any writing to do.[4]

This note is merely to tell you that I am waiting for you.

Ever yours,
[T. S. E.]

PS I am sending you a little book on verse translation from Latin. If you think it is worth a note in the *Criterion* I shall be delighted to have it. At any rate this is your book if it is anybody's.

1–See TSE's letter of 19 June, asking for 'the position' about *The Apes of God* and *Archie*.
2–WL wrote to CW in Mar. about his offer to introduce WL to Macmillan in connection with his 100,000-word MS *The Politics of the Personality* (*Letters of Wyndham Lewis*, 154–5).
3–Sydney Waterlow (see letter of 21 June).
4–Waterlow was on the editorial committee of *International Journal of Ethics*, 1914–16, and had invited TSE to write his review of A. J. Balfour's *Theism and Humanism*, in *IJE* 26: 2 (Jan. 1916). This had been TSE's first review (with the exception of those in *Harvard Advocate*).

FROM *Geoffrey Faber* CC

7 July 1925 [London]

My dear Eliot,

Thank you for your secretary's letter and the enclosure from Scott Moncrieff from which I gather that there is nothing in immediate prospect that we can hope for. I note that you have asked for an option on the books mentioned if they are declined by Chatto & Windus.[1] Many thanks for the trouble you have taken. I hope your interview yesterday with Lady R. eventuated and was successful.

We enjoyed the rehearsal on Sunday very much, and were able to use all four tickets.

Yours ever,
[Geoffrey C. Faber]

TO *George Rylands*[2] CC

7 July 1925 23 Adelphi Terrace House

Dear Mr Rylands,

I have had your poem in my hands for some little time and must apologise for not having written to you about it.[3] I like it very much on the whole but should like to make certain comments in the margin if you will allow me, and return it to you for consideration. I have considered the possibility of using it in October if the Woolf's are not going to publish it before I could do so, but in the case of verse I cannot be certain very long in advance.[4] What would be best would be if we could meet some time

1 – In a postcard (Nov.? 1925) Scott Moncrieff was to ask whether TSE proposed to use his story ('Cousin Fanny and Cousin Annie', which would appear in *NC* 4: 2 & 3, Apr. & June 1926) or Pirandello's *Black Shawl*. He also offered one of Pirandello's recently published one-act plays. Since Chatto & Windus continued to publish Scott Moncrieff's translation of Proust, the letter may refer to the Pirandello translations.

2 – George 'Dadie' Rylands (1902–99), literary scholar and theatre director, was elected in 1927 a Fellow of King's College, Cambridge, where he became renowned for his expressive and inspirational teaching and theatrical productions; in later years he became a governor of the Old Vic Theatre, London, and chairman (from 1946) of the Cambridge Arts Theatre.

3 – 'Russet and Taffeta'.

4 – The Oct. *C.* never appeared. *Russet and Taffeta* came out as an eight-page pamphlet with the Hogarth Press in Dec. 1925. (Rylands had worked with the Woolfs at the Hogarth Press for six months in 1924.) Humbert Wolfe, in a review of it, regretted that, despite its 'easy happy grace', it did not offer the 'puzzled critic more to bite on' (*NC* 4: 2 [Apr. 1926]).

late in the summer and discuss it. But meanwhile I will offer my criticisms and shall be glad to hear what you think of them.

Yours sincerely
[T. S. E.]

TO *Herbert Read* — TS Victoria

7 July 1925 — *The Criterion*, 9 Clarence Gate Gdns

My dear Read,

I have not had time even to thank you for your valuable notes and suggestions.[1] I shall do everything I can to realise such a project and if anything comes of it your words will have had a formative influence.[2]

I should particularly like to start something along these lines, because it seems an appropriate vehicle for the kind of thought in which we have both become interested. You are not to suppose that I know any more about Thomism than you do, but in fact rather less. Hulme's book[3] awakened in me certain desires of exploration which had slumbered during many years of Lombard Street. The only qualification I have, but for which I am very thankful, is that I was pretty well grounded at one time in Aristotle.[4] Beyond this I have nothing more at present than an instinct. Of course the religious difficulty is the great one and it is impossible to tell what one's solution will be. All that one can do at present is conscientiously to avoid anticipating the conclusions to which one may come five or ten years hence. I mean that one must be on guard against the prejudices of one's training on the one hand and any emotional collapse on the other. I certainly do not want to fall into the pit of obscurantism. But one way or the other it will need an heroic effect to keep from allowing oneself illicit conclusions.

I think that you have found the weak spot in Fernandez.[5]

You may hear from me in a short time about the practical side of this matter.

Ever yours,
T. S. E.

1–These notes do not appear to survive.
2–A ref. to TSE's plan to run another review in tandem with C.
3–T. E. Hulme, *Speculations: Essays on Humanism and the Philosophy of Art* ed. by HR (1924).
4–TSE took courses on Aristotle with J. A. Smith, R. G. Collingwood and Harold Joachim in 1914–15.
5–Ramón Fernandez, 'L'intelligence et M. Maritain', *NRF* 12: 141 (1 June 1925), 986–94.

Yes, I do feel that important things are possible, but that the possibilities may somehow evaporate.

TO *Conrad Aiken* TS Huntington

7 July 1925 *The Criterion*, 9 Clarence Gate Gdns

Dear Conrad,

I was very pleased to get your letter of the 23rd June and apologise for my inability to answer it at once. I am afraid that it will be impossible for me to get away from town for a considerable time, but nevertheless, it is most cheering to have such an invitation at my disposal. I should like nothing better than to share your seaside pleasures.

How are you? What are you thinking and writing about? And when David Garnett's new book appears may I send it to you?[1] You are the man to deal with him. I should like to get from you a complete and destructive study of this author, as good as your one of Huxley.[2] I can send you his two earlier books if you have not got them.[3]

And another suggestion for you to consider. There is a remarkable unity about things you have done for me about Huxley, the Sitwells, etcetera.[4] Would you consider the gradual preparation of a book of papers on contemporary British authors, or perhaps more particularly authors of fiction? I think that I can almost guarantee the publisher, and, if I may say so, I believe a better publisher than Secker.[5] With this in view I should like to send you Virginia Woolf's new novel also.[6]

Do let me hear from you again, and remember that sooner or later I shall descend upon Rye.

Ever yours,
Tom

1–David Garnett, *The Sailor's Return* (1925).
2–Aiken reviewed AH's *Those Barren Leaves* in *C.* 3: 11 (Apr. 1925). While considering it AH's 'best work', and 'admirably, if ornately written', he yet complained that it offered not so much 'a story' or 'series of character studies' as 'another tremendous example of Mr Huxley's highly cultured conversation'.
3–Garnett, *Lady into Fox* (1922) and *Man in the Zoo* (1924).
4–Aiken's other reviews had been of Gilbert Seldes, *The Seven Lively Arts*, and Osbert Sitwell, *Triple Fugue*, in *C.* 3: 9 (Oct. 1924).
5–Aiken had published with Secker *Nocturne of Remembered Spring* (1922), *Punch: The Immortal Liar* (1921), *The Pilgrimage of Festus* (1924) and *Bring! Bring!* (1925). On 9 July, he said he was negotiating a book of verse with Hogarth Press and had agreed to give them first refusal of his prose. Aiken's *Senlin: A Biography* came out with Hogarth Press in July 1925.
6–VW, *Mrs Dalloway* (May 1925).

TO *Edmund Wilson* CC

7 July 1925 [*The Criterion*, London]

Dear Sir,

Mr Eliot is very sorry that the length of your story precludes the possibility of considering it for the *Criterion*. Also, in view of the fact that the *Criterion* publishes very little fiction, and has already published one war story and accepted another, the subject happens to be rather a disqualification.

Mr Eliot hopes very much that you will send him more contributions, both fiction and critical essays.[1]

Yours faithfully
For the Editor of *The Criterion*
Secretary

TO *Harold Monro* TS Beinecke

7 July 1925 9 Clarence Gate Gdns

My dear Monro,

Thank you very much for your last letter and for your good wishes. I think that 'Lost Sheep' might be a better phrase than 'Lost Leader'.[2] At any rate you may be certain that this lamb of Lombard Street has not left you for a handful of silver and that he intends to keep his wool and eventually return to the fold.

I wish I could definitely arrange a luncheon with you, but it is cheering to know that you will be in London more or less the whole summer, and please be sure that I shall ring you up as soon as a meeting is possible.

Meanwhile, I am ashamed to have been unable to do anything for the *Chapbook* in the Bloomsbury quarter, but I don't suppose that it would have altered the result. I must also say that I have not a shred of verse or prose which would be of any use to you. If I had time, I should make a

1 – Wilson never appeared in C.

2 – On 1 July, Monro wrote: 'With "gangs" so strong one does want to see something of you again – however detestable the expression "lost leader" may ring to you.' 'The Lost Leader' is a poem by Robert Browning, from *Dramatic Romances and Lyrics* (1845), which begins: 'Just for a handful of silver he left us, / Just for a riband to stick in his coat'. It refers to Wordsworth in later life. 'The Lost Sheep' refers to the parable in Matthew 18: 10–14.

great effort to fabricate something. But last year you gave me until November. What is your absolutely final date this year?

Believe me,
Ever yours,
T. S. E.

FROM *Geoffrey Faber* CC

8 July 1925 [London]

My dear Eliot,

Many thanks for your letter. I conceive that your interview [with Lady Rothermere] must have required an amazing amount of tact on your part. I shall hope to hear fairly soon that she has agreed with you, or at any rate that you have got the title, and the right to insert a notice in the July number. As soon as that is settled we must have a meeting here and decide various points which I mentioned the other day.

Yours ever,
[G. C. F.]

TO *Leonard Woolf* TS Berg

Wednesday 8 July[1] [1925] 9 Clarence Gate Gdns

My dear Leonard,

As I may not be able to come in tomorrow after all, and as you were so helpful to me, I am writing to tell you this. I took your advice and went to [Dr Henry] Head, before Vivien saw a doctor at all, but he did not seem to me modern enough. Although we have got her apparently over her fear of doctors, it has not yet been successful. On each occasion on which she has seen doctors since then the first effects have been apparently good, but have been followed by collapses, and she has been very ill indeed. I have now working together a big specialist and a consultant who agree that the effect of Dr Martin (the German doctor I told you of) upon her was much more serious than at first supposed. I may write to you again about this.

1 – Misdated '10 July'.

I should consider suing Dr Martin but understand it would mean my going to Germany, which I cannot do.

Yours ever
T. S. E.

PRIVATE.

TO *Rollo Myers* CC

10 July 1925 23 Adelphi Terrace House

Dear Mr Myers,

Thank you for your letter of the 2nd July. I shall be very glad to undertake the arrangement for publication of *Le Secret Professionel* translation if possible.[1] At the moment, everything is rather fluid and I cannot speak definitely, but I should be glad if you would bring your manuscript over and I will take charge of it. I should certainly be able to give you something much more definite within about ten days' time.[2]

With all best wishes,
Yours sincerely,
[T. S. E.]

TSE/IPF

TO *Wyndham Lewis* TS Cornell

10 July 1925 *The Criterion*, 9 Clarence Gate Gdns

Dear Lewis,

I have your letter of the 8th instant. As I know nothing whatever about the matter of Whibley and your book, and as neither of you has given me any hint as to what happened, I shall not myself raise the question with either of you. As you make no suggestion of the book being available for publication, I presume that you have made your arrangements.

I may say that the publishing firm which I have in mind is one consisting of persons whom I believe to be not only unknown to you but quite out of

1–Jean Cocteau, *Le secret professionel* (1924). Myers said his translation was still at TSE's disposal; but he now had an American offer and wanted to know whether TSE was interested in publishing it.

2–It appeared as *A Call to Order, written between the years 1918 and 1926 and including 'Cock and Harlequin', 'Professional Secrets', and other critical essays*, trans. Rollo Myers (F&G, 1926).

touch with anyone of whom you have suspicions. It is probable that any manuscript placed in my hands would fall under the eyes of a man named Faber and possibly under the eyes of a man named Burdett,[1] but no one else. There is no possibility that anyone could assert that he was rendering you a service, and the assertion is not one that I should have any advantage whatever in making myself.[2]

In my opinion, and so far as I know anything of either side, the firm is a suitable one, but as it is just starting its existence as a general publishing firm, I have no means of proving this assertion nor you of testing it. Your book has certainly not been offered to this firm. It is of course impossible for me to guarantee their acceptance, nor until they had seen the manuscript could I possibly suggest any definite sum as an advance. I should be glad to hear from you further.

Thanking you for your good wishes, I am,

Yours,
T. S. Eliot

TO *Herbert Read* — TS Victoria

10 July 1925 — *The Criterion*, 9 Clarence Gate Gdns

Dear Read,

Thank you for your letter. I had already observed J. F. Holms and noted that the review in question is a better one than any I have seen;[3] is indeed

1–Osbert Burdett (1885–1936): author of *The Idea of Coventry Patmore* (1921), *The Beardsley Period* (1925), and *Critical Essays* (1925). Maurice Gwyer, GCF's partner, was married to Alise Burdett, who had inherited the Scientific Press from her father Sir Henry. GCF reflected in his diary (18 Nov. 1924) upon Burdett, whom he 'liked very well', that he seemed 'the rather unpractical writer, full of ideas, some valuable others not' (Faber Archive).

2–WL desired 'the strictest secrecy' regarding *The Apes of God*. He confessed (8 July): 'there are two or three people that I have offended who would not pass the "suspiciousness" test, if "suspiciousness" were given a really free hand as inquisitor . . . [O]f late I have had what in my wild brain has seemed a proof of flagrant hanky-panky. – Under these circumstances would you mind my asking you for an assurance that your offer (re books) is entirely your own affair; and that – with however blameless intentions – you are not seeking to render me a service at the instigation of anyone in England who could subsequently claim that *your* assistance was *his*?' WL's letters to EP (11 June) and McAlmon (24 July) are equally suspicious of the motives of would-be publishers and promoters (see *Pound/Lewis*, 150–1; *Letters of Wyndham Lewis*, 161).

3–J. F. Holms's review of *Mrs Dalloway* appeared in *Calendar of Modern Letters* (July 1925). Though Holms thought it 'the best book she has written', he asked how could 'such talent co-exist with a sentimentality that would be remarkable in a stockbroker, and inconceivable among educated people?' Though the novel had 'the design, apparent intensity, and

better than the one I have by Collins for the next *Criterion*.[1] It is perhaps hardly fair to judge Collins by this, especially as I have never yet seen him nor given him a direct line on what we want, but at the same time a review is often a pretty good test of independence and fearlessness.

Muir's essay is also good.[2]

The other elements you suggest, and more still, might be useful later if one could bring out such a publication more frequently, but it seems to me that at the beginning one would have to limit oneself to such people as could be made to fit in pretty clearly with a general policy. What do you think? Of course nothing may come of it, but if it does I shall try to arrange a meeting with you at the earliest opportunity.

I am trying to get the Keyserling book[3] for you if it is not too late to secure a review copy. At the moment I do not know of anything else worth your trouble. I should like also to discuss your suggestion which appeals to me: the only objection which occurs to me at the moment is something which I always have to keep in mind, i.e. the awakening of jealousy amongst other contributors. You will understand this I am sure. Otherwise it appeals to me very much.

Yours ever,
T. S. E.

TO *Messrs. Peter Jones* CC

10 July 1924 [?1925] [London]

Dear Sirs,

57 Chester Terrace[4]

In reply to your letter of the 9th inst., I have been advised by my solicitors that I should pay a deposit upon completion of the contract and

---

immediate aspect of a work of art', he thought it 'an interesting problem of aesthetic psychology to explain so self-subsistent a mirage entirely unconnected with reality'.

1–H. P. Collins reviewed Humbert Wolfe, *The Unknown Goddess*, and VW, *The Common Reader*, in C. 3: 12 (July 1925).

2–Edwin Muir reviewed Conrad Aiken's *Bring! Bring!* in C. 3: 12 (July 1925).

3–Count Hermann Keyserling, *The Travel Diary of a Philosopher*, trans. J. Holroyd, (1925). HR's review of it (*NC* 4: 1, Jan. 1926, 189–93) deplored its '*orientalism*' – which he described as not so much a 'direct advocacy of the philosophies of the East' as an implicit 'reflection on the adequacy of Western thought' from their standpoint – and its Rousseau-like 'subjectivism'.

4–On 12 July 1925, TSE spoke of moving VHE into Chester Terrace that week which suggests that the present letter may be misdated. In the event the Eliots did not move from Clarence Gate Gardens to 57 Chester Terrace until spring 1926.

the balance upon transference of the lease. My solicitors are taking up the matter with Mrs Tollemache's solicitors.

With regard to the articles which Mrs Tollemache wishes to dispose, Mrs Eliot would be disposed to take them over and would be glad to know the value to be set upon them.

Yours faithfully,
[T. S. E.]

TO *Charles Haigh-Wood*[1]

TS Valerie Eliot

12 July 1925 [London]

Dear P.,[2]

Just a line as I never have time for more. To say V. thanks you for your kind and sympathetic letter and begs you not to return earlier on her account. She will be very much upset if you do, and I should think it better you should not. I should like her to be a little better when you see her. We have Dr Glover[3] (17 Fitzjohns Avenue) with Dr Barris (of 50 Welbeck Street) directing him and have settled into some sort of routine. They are both fine men, and gentlemen, and we have full confidence. We *want* to get her to Chester Terrace this week as both of them agree she will be better moved away from such unhappy surroundings.

I will just tell you that the whole murder is out. To begin with it is agreed that the Cyriax treatment caused her to starve for nearly two years. Mrs Cyriax although knowing she was getting thinner and lighter the whole time never once suggested her taking food. On the contrary, whatever article of food V. mentioned such as milk, toast, meat, veg. etc., her invariable reply was that it was not good for the stomach. So V. quietly gave up one food after the other until in the end she gave up eating altogether.

1–Charles Haigh-Wood, TSE's father-in-law: see Glossary of Names.
2–It is uncertain whether VHE's father saw this letter because he had left his French hotel before it arrived, and though re-addressed to his London home, it was probably returned to TSE who had registered it. Furthermore, TSE recalled by wire the copy he had sent to his brother-in-law, Maurice, in Rome marked '*Please keep*'; it came back with the words, 'Dear Tom – Here is the letter. Much love M', pencilled on the original envelope.
3–Dr James Glover (1882–1926): pioneering British psychoanalyst whom LW recommended to TSE in May. Glover qualified as a surgeon in Glasgow at twenty-one, but transferred his interest to psychotherapy. After being in analysis with Karl Abraham, he became a member of the newly formed Psychoanalytic Society in 1922, and would arrange for the transfer of the International Library of Psychoanalysis to the Hogarth Press.

1. So you have long starvation, with long *periods* (there were many intervals) of the most exhausting stomach treatment which all four doctors I have in all consulted agree tended to wear out the nerves.
2. The German brute of a doctor [K. B. Martin] whom I took her to (against her will) in the spring of last year. He never saw her starvation symptoms, and *always* urged her to continue the Cyriax treatment. She never went alone (I always [went] with her) until one day last July. Then she went alone, and he was in some hysterical state, and in a diabolical rage for reasons of his own. He began to psychoanalyse her and poke into her childhood and youth, and told her finally that she was living on Will, that she had a terrific will which kept her alive, and that if this will ever collapsed she would be nothing but a feeble minded little snivelling invalid, asking only for a little pity and led about by an attendant. He even pointed to the corner of the room and said she would be sitting there and painted in words a filthy picture of a semi-idiot. She sat still and looked at him and said nothing at all, and this must have infuriated him more, for when they came out of the room I noticed at once that his forehead was heavily beaded with sweat. V. seemed quite calm and appeared to take no notice whatever of his words. In fact, she did not tell me what he had said until a long time afterwards.

Shortly afterwards they went to Eastbourne as you know, and there she continued to starve, and most unfortunately there lived opposite her window a paralysed woman, who somehow joined up in her mind the horrible ideas which the German doctor had planted there. She very seldom went out and spent a lot of time watching the paralysed woman and feverishly writing stories, always starving. I was completely taken up with my mother and sister and neither Jack nor Pearl is fully developed or responsible, and certainly unfit to be with anyone in such a state. When she returned she soon got into a depressed and gloomy state. She went fitfully to the Cyriax woman who never saw anything wrong with her to the very end. She was bitterly disappointed that some of her stories were rejected, and she continued to starve, and I am ashamed to say that I was on the verge of a nervous breakdown myself and didnt notice it at all. As you know I had influenza just after Christmas and I was scarcely out of bed before V. suddenly rushed into bed and refused to get up any more. From that time for eleven weeks she refused to get up and insisted on sleeping at any cost, nearly all the time. Whenever she was awake she made me promise never to let a doctor see her again, and it got to the point where she wouldnt even let her family see her; and I know her mother blames me for this, but this is the true reason which I couldnt state. She was in such a shocking state in between the long sleeps she had, of terror that she was becoming an idiot, that her only idea was that if anyone saw her they would realise that she was becoming an idiot. For this reason she had a particular horror of a doctor seeing her, for she constantly said that she knew a doctor would say she was becoming an idiot.

I must say that I had very grave fears that her reason would go altogether, and I was in a state of horror and tension indescribable to you, who have never gone through anything like it, I am sure. I dared not fetch a doctor, I dared not fetch one of you into her room, I was paralysed. She became more and more frantic as time went on and took to making the most shocking faces and hypnotising herself. I can say no more of this; it is too horrible. I leave it to your imagination.

As you know, we got her up and out, but she had small collapses at the slightest thing, and still flatly refused to see a doctor. The mania was still strong in her mind. At last I thought of a scheme by which I could get outside help. I pretended that there was something wrong with her spine, and that she ought to see an osteopath. She did not raise objections, she was not afraid of an osteopath – for some reason, heaven only knows. I got in an osteopath at once and told him the whole story. At last we got her out to him regularly three times a week, and I must say he stood by her very well, and was a very decent fellow, extremely clever. However, he underestimated her condition, both mental and physical. In endeavouring to force her to attend to her body, instead of constantly thinking whether she was an idiot or not, and to force her to eat enough food, he shouted at her and frightened her so that she had another most frightful and serious collapse so that I thought she would die. However, this brought good in its train, although she was more ill than I can possibly tell you, for a fortnight. The reaction from the osteopath at last broke down her horror. She consented to see a doctor. Having been recommended most tremendously by our friends the Schiffs, a consultant by the name of Dr Barris of Welbeck Street, I instantly sent for him, and we sat up till 12 o'clock waiting for him to come. Vivien was in bed in a state of most complete collapse, shewing terrible symptoms. (In any mental strain her nervous breakdown and idiot-mania symptoms return, even to the hour). At last Dr Barris came at 12 o'clock and we found him a most charming and delightful creature. After a little conversation he went in to Vivien, and quieted her down within an incredibly short time, making her perfectly adore him at the same time. He took away all her fears, sympathised with her, and has the most courtly and charming manners. All the same, afterwards, he said to me, that of course a great deal of this was caused by starvation, and that he thoroughly disapproved of the Cyriax method and treatment on any account whatever. He seems fully to understand the case, and feels that Vivien ought to have some attendant or maid or nurse, some responsible elderly female who will never leave her, until she is perfectly strong again, which will be several years. He considers her extraordinarily undeveloped, in fact all doctors do, every one has commented on her extreme youth and almost childishness. And have said that this largely accounts for what the German doctor said to her having taken such terrific hold on her mind. Dr Barris being a surgeon-consultant cannot of course attend to her regularly, and we have had some difficulty in finding a perfectly suitable practitioner, clever, modern, experienced, and kind. But Dr Barris has been very kind in helping in this matter, and we have taken his advice and have now Dr Glover in consultation with him all the time. I have told them about her brother being in Rome and both are agreed that it is most advisable, in fact almost necessary, to send her abroad to a good climate in three or four months time, as that will strengthen her. They think the companionship of Maurice would be good for her, and I myself am of that opinion. The dreadful part is that for a whole year I have paid the rent of a flat and a house.

You now see the reason why I left the bank. Of course I have never dared leave Vivien for one second up to now. I really am nearly ruined. I bled my mother white for money, and you know yourself what a generous woman she is. The future fills me with horror. I do not know what I shall do. The unfortunate part is that the expenses are not by any means at an end; I have doctors to pay, bills not in yet, Vivien to be sent to Rome, in luxury, a maid or nurse to pay for, God knows how I can let this flat, I don't, I shall never be able to sit all day here, which is the only way to let a flat; I have thrown up the *Criterion*, as I did not get a farthing out of it, and I have thrown over Lady Rothermere for good. You have often offered me help, and I have always promised to come on you in an hour of need, and I may have to come on you before long, but [you] may be sure I will keep my expenses to the absolute minimum.

Vivien sends love, and is very happy to have her mother's letters and little presents, but of course has to stay in bed, keep absolutely quiet, sees no one and knows nothing. As for Jack and Pearl they are practically useless, and I have practically cast them out; Pearl is the more useful of the two.

With love from
Tom

FROM *Henry Eliot* TS Valerie Eliot

[mid-July 1925] Chicago

Dear Tom:-

I have just seen Theresa off on the train. This is no cool-headed affair de convenance. Yet sometimes I feel that I am doing a fine bit of acting. How one can act under the stimulus of emotion! Who is it that is doing it? And my letters – I wish I did not perceive how absurd they are.

For most of us – for those who must lead a life of action, of contacts and conflicts – success in life is largely a matter of histrionic ability. All self-improvement, all self-development, is histrionic. You create the mental image of the kind of hero you wish to be, and then proceed to play the part. After you have played it for years, you almost become it. Few – including yourself – can distinguish the real self, the puppet-master, behind you. That is what I must do. I must act. Acting and action are alike foreign to my nature. I prefer to be a still mirror of contemplation.

Already I know the loss of liberty, the little encroachments on one's time, the seemingly senseless expenses, of life with another person. And there is the sordid business of picking out a ring; not imposed by her so much as by custom. For she is intensely unselfish. She wants to earn money to set aside for a trip abroad; she wants to pay her mother's living expenses; she wants to work if I am ever sick and unable to earn.

But I have never known liberty anyway. Cutting myself off as much as possible from social life for its own sake, I am still unable to find an evening when I can sit down and read. In this country one has no choice between constant senseless activity and the life-in-death of a hermit.

On July 23 the premium on your policy will be due. I want to do just what you wish about this: to pay it, or send you the money itself. It is not that I begrudge the money, I only want it to be of the most good. Do you think, now, that the insurance is worth the price? The policy was written, you know, before Mother changed the terms of her will. It seems to me that the cash in hand is worth more than the protection against the contingency of your death before Vivien. Please write me when you get this letter.

I told Theresa I wish to send you $1000. She assented gladly. Mother has a bond which I sent her to make up for selling 100 shares of Hydraulic before it went up ten points. She will not take it, and is going to return it to me. I shall compromise by sending the money to you. You can, if you wish, add this to the trust she is having drawn up, that is to say, the one you sent me signed. Or you can use it to tide you through the difficult period of which you wrote.

The rest of my money I shall certainly put in trust. I shall bend my efforts toward getting out of the business what I have in it. I shall look for a job in New York or Boston. What I hope for is a place in a small but successful business where I can be treasurer as well as write advertising copy. I suppose it will entail some sacrifice, but eventually I am certain to be eliminated from the present business by Buchen. He has already picked out a man whom he wished to bring into the business in about a year. He has already suggested a cut in both our salaries; he can carry this down to a point where I will have to go elsewhere, and then pay himself back salary after I am out. But the crux of the matter is that I hate him with a bitter hatred, and he hates me; we cover it up, but we know it.

Ever affectionately,
Henry

FROM *Geoffrey C. Faber* CC

17 July 1925 [London]

My dear Eliot,

(1) I send you a copy of the memorandum which has gone to the other Directors and chief shareholders. This is the only copy I have, so that I shall be glad if, after digesting it, you would kindly return it to me.

(2) There will be a formal Directors Meeting at 3.15 next Thursday afternoon; but there is no need for you to attend that if it is not convenient for you, though of course we should like to see you; the important Directors Meeting will be held on Tuesday July 28th, at 2.30; and that I hope you will be able to attend.

I have been anxiously awaiting for news about *The Criterion*; time is getting infernally short, and I devoutly hope that I may hear, before Monday, what Lady R's attitude is to be.[1]

Yours ever,
[G. C. F.]

1–GCF noted (diary, Sat. 19 July): 'Telephoned to Eliot: the *Criterion*, alas, comes out on Monday, without our notice in it; Lady R. having behaved in an exasperating manner.'

TO *St John Hutchinson* TS Texas

18 July 1925

Very many thanks. I had not wished to hurry you, but wanted to be sure you have received it.

V. never hears from Mary?

T. S. E.

TO *George Rylands* MS King's

18 July 1925 9 Clarence Gate Gdns

Dear Mr Rylands

Here are my comments, for what they are worth; you may ignore them all! In any case, let me see the poem again when you are ready.[1]

I am sorry to have missed you, but look forward to meeting you later, and, meanwhile, success to the Fellowship.

Sincerely yours
T. S. Eliot

I think the second two pages are almost allright as they stand.

TO *Conrad Aiken* MS Huntington

Sunday [19? July 1925] 9 Clarence Gate Gdns

Dear Conrad

Please accept my sincere apologies and deep regrets at not having answered your card – it was absolutely impossible for me just then, and very difficult even to write. And I think I have also failed to answer a previous letter. I am sorry about the book, dispirited about the reviewing, but glad that if you are fixed up it is with the Woolfs.[2] They did *Senlin* quite well, I thought.[3]

1 – Rylands, *Russet and Taffeta*, appeared from the Hogarth Press in Dec. 1925.
2 – Aiken responded on 9 July to TSE's letter of 7 July that he could not offer TSE a book of essays on fiction because the Hogarth Press had first refusal. He was suffering from 'paralysis of the critical faculty' and 'an intense hatred of reviewing', and could not face reviewing the novels by David Garnett and VW that TSE had suggested.
3 – Aiken's poem *Senlin: A Biography* was published by the Hogarth Press earlier in July.

But as I can't get away from London, when will there be another chance of seeing you here?

Ever yrs.
T. S. E.

FROM *Geoffrey Faber* CC

27 July 1925 [London]

Dear Eliot,

Many thanks for your letter of yesterday's date. You blame yourself unnecessarily; there are certain kinds of inertia against which the best of men spend themselves in vain.

But I am afraid that we have now got to a point when it would be foolish to attempt to bring the paper out in October. Nothing can be usefully settled now before the end of July, and we have then the dead period of August and September before us. If the paper is to be brought out under the best conditions, with the whole of the business side of the undertaking explored and properly mapped out, we must, as you suggest, wait till the New Year. I cannot however, think of leaving you stranded during these five or six months. For one thing if we publish in January your salary would certainly begin to run from the end of September, and could, under the terms of our agreement, be drawn upon in advance. The best way out of the difficulty that I can see, if you agree to it, is that you should take your salary for the current quarter as payment for the task of planning and starting a series of studies on foreign writers, of the sort we were discussing the other day; what do you think of this suggestion?

I am looking forward to seeing you tomorrow.

Yours ever,
[Geoffrey C. Faber]

TO *Leonard Woolf* MS Berg

[late July? 1925][1] [London]

Dear Leonard

I am sorry I could not answer at once, but circumstances have been very difficult indeed. I don't see how I can do any work for some weeks, and then I must attend to

{ my new job
the bank
my Camb. lectures

In addition I have the Tudor Translation introduction and another commission and a preface to write for my mother's poems![2] So I don't see how, *at best* (and things don't look very bright) I can get you a pamphlet before the latter part of Nov. What I have in mind is a reply to Graves' analogy (misleading I think) between poetry and politics.[3] But if you prefer to avoid controversy between one of your pamphleteers and another, let me know – I have other ideas. All these difficulties affect the poems – because I have no time to write anything else, i.e. I shall have nothing to give them *but* the poems, which increases the difficulty.[4] The fact that they are advancing my salary aggravates it further. But more later. You shall have a pamphlet in any case, the only question is when.[5]

Love to Virginia. When do you go to Rodmell? I want to see you once before you go.

Yours ever
T. S. E.

1–The Woolfs, who went to Rodmell for eleven weeks on 28 July, suggested a date in late July.

2–In addition to the Clark lectures to be delivered at Cambridge in spring 1926, TSE is referring to *Seneca: His Tenne Tragedies*, trans. into English by Thomas Newton, with intro. by TSE (1927) and Charlotte Eliot, *Savonarola, A Dramatic Poem*, with intro. by TSE (1926).

3–Robert Graves, *Contemporary Techniques of Poetry, A Political Analogy* (1925).

4–On 1 June VW regarded it as a 'blow' that all of TSE's works would have to go from the Hogarth Press to F&G (*Diary*, III, 27).

5–In the event, having published *Poems* (1919), *TWL* (1923) and *HJD* (1924), the Hogarth Press published nothing else by TSE.

TO *Richard Aldington* MS Texas

[?29 July 1925] [9 Clarence Gate Gdns]

Dear Richard

I miss your letters. How are you? We have been having an anxious time for a fortnight. I think it is a little better now.

When you write, can you suggest any bibliography of

Marini[1]
Marinism
Góngora[2]
Góngorism

for my lectures on XVII C. poets (English). I must be well fortified.

Ever yours aff.
Tom.

TO *John Middleton Murry* MS Valerie Eliot

31 July 1925 9 Clarence Gate Gdns

My dear John

You are so often in our thoughts and in our conversation that I was very surprised to realise how long a time it is since I have written. I find myself making the assumption, often, that you (though no one else) will somehow know what one is going through without being told. And, somehow, there is nothing that can be told – only facts that give no indication. And there is nothing essential to tell which you don't know already.

Vivien has been terribly ill – and we have had terrible practical difficulties. And it all seems to mark the end of an epoch – a period of awful changes. A great deal of structure seems to have collapsed. Here I feel that you have given me immense help for which I shall always be grateful – the Cambridge Lectures are something definite and firm to hold on to in the midst of dissolution: they will keep my mind together if anything will.[3]

1 – Giambattista Marino, or Marini (1569–1625): Italian religious poet. In his Clark lectures, TSE argued that the influence of Marino, St Theresa and John Donne combined to inform the poetry of Richard Crashaw. His views developed after reading Mario Praz's *Secentismo e Marinismo in Inghilterra* (1925), which he reviewed in the *TLS* (17 Dec. 1925).
2 – Luis de Góngora y Argote (1561–1627): Spanish poet and priest. TSE noted that 'for English poetry the influence of Gongorism' was 'much less than that of Marinism' (*VMP*, 181–2).
3 – JMM had put TSE's name forward to be Clark lecturer. In the lectures, TSE spoke of 'the tendency toward dissolution' in Donne's poetry, and noted that 'dissolution so frequently begins within', and talked of 'the spectacle of thought in dissolution' (*VMP*, 76, 80, 155).

Vivien had a terrible breakdown – the climax came long after the time when you saw her. She is fighting most courageously.

Ever yours aff.
Tom

I should like a *line* to know how you are, and your family?[1]

TO *Richard Aldington* MS Texas

31 July 1925 9 Clarence Gate Gdns

My dear Richard

Thank you very much for your letters. The information about Marini is most useful.[2]

We have been going through the same sort of vicissitudes – I won't bother my friends with monotony – which have made correspondence impossible. But I often think hungrily when shall I see you? and alone. There will be a new quarterly in the new year – which will depend very much on you, if it may – instead of the *Criterion*. It is not secrecy, only fatigue, which prevents me from giving details in this letter.

Also – *Confidential*

Would you be disposed, next year, and for a reasonable sum, to write a short critical and expository book (40,000 words) on Rémy de Gourmont? I may be editing a series of Foreign Men of Letters. You are the only man who could de Rémy in English.[3] Epicurus on Epicurus. You would not need to do much reading – you have it all in your head.

Let me have a line to say how you are, and whether you will ever be in London in these dog days.

Ever your aff.
T. S. E.

1 – On 7 Aug., JMM replied that TSE and VHE were constantly in his thoughts, and that his daughter Katherine was 'flourishing now and a great delight'.

2 – See TSE's letter of 29 July.

3 – RA had corresponded with de Gourmont as well as helping him financially; see his *Rémy de Gourmont: A Modern Man of Letters* (1928), and his later translations from de Gourmont: *Selections from All His Works* (1929) and *Letters to the Amazon* (1931).

TO *Herbert Read* MS Victoria

31 July 1925 9 Clarence Gate Gdns

My dear Read

Many thanks for your letter. I wish indeed that I had been present when you were at Aldington's.[1] I hope that we may have some triangular conversations this autumn. We might hatch a few eggs. I have several to bring for joint incubation.

Meanwhile I am still hoping for a meeting with you. The *Criterion* is to be succeeded, in the new year, by a new quarterly which I have undertaken, in which I hope to keep all that is worth preserving. It is an opportunity for revision, so far as revision is needed, and I shall wish to take your counsel.

As for the *Cahiers*, that is still in the air.[2]

What are you reading and thinking?

Ever yours
T. S. E.

TO *George Rylands* MS King's

Sunday [2? August 1925] 9 Clarence Gate Gdns

Dear Mr Rylands

I must apologise for not having answered your letter. I agree with your alterations and am persuaded by your defenses.[3] I like the poem very much. I cannot see that the quotation is sentimental, and it seems to me to make the poem more intelligible.

I should like to print it, but if Leonard is to bring it out before Christmas, I am afraid it is impossible. For there will be no *Criterion* in the autumn, so far as I am concerned, or ever again. In January I am to edit a new quarterly – very similar, as I made the one and shall have the making of the other – and I am glad to receive contributions for that. So if the Woolfs should happen not to publish first, I should like to be able to use this: otherwise, I hope you will send me your next.[4]

1–On 30 July, HR said he had spent a weekend with RA, and had much 'profitable discussion', but they needed 'a third point of view'.

2–The proposal for a 'Symposium'-style review to run alongside *NC*.

3–A reply to the suggestions sent with TSE's letter of 18 July for revisions to Rylands's poem 'Russet and Taffeta', provisionally accepted for the autumn *C*.

4–Rylands's *Russet and Taffeta* appeared from the Hogarth Press in Dec. 1925. Rylands did publish one further book of poetry, *Poems* (1931), but none of his verse appeared in *C*.

I dare say you have left Cambridge now, but I hope this will be forwarded.

Sincerely yours
T. S. Eliot

Do you want the MS back?

Vivien Eliot TO *John Middleton Murry* MS Valerie Eliot

[8? August 1925] 9 Clarence Gate Gdns

Dear Murry

The message you sent me in your letter to Tom has made me feel that I may write to you, as I have been wishing to do for so long.

Up till now, it has seemed to me impossible that you would care to hear that I have thought about you constantly for the last month. And that I have had what has happened incessantly in my mind.

Perhaps we may meet some day, and be able to talk.

I am afraid Tom's terrific life takes all my energy, and I can only lie still and wait for it to end.

With all my thoughts and wishes for you

Vivien Eliot

TO *Dorothy Pound* MS Lilly

Tuesday, 11 August [1925] Ty Glyn Aeron, Ciliau Aeron, Cardiganshire[1]

Dear Dorothy

Your kind note has just reached me here. I am sorry, I shall not be back in London till the 17th, and have dinner engagements on the 17th and 18th – am free for tea on 18th and at any time on any day after that. So you can either ask me to tea or dinner, *or* will you please name a day *to lunch with me*? I have a lovely p.c. for you but left it in London not knowing where you were: six cows killed by lightning under a tree in Gloucestershire.

Yrs. devotedly
Possum.

1 – TSE was visiting the Fabers in Wales.

TO *H. P. Collins*

MS Private Collection

11 August 1925

9 Clarence Gate Gdns

Dear Mr Collins

I apologise for not replying at once. I am afraid it is impossible to use your 'Romanticism' in October, for the reason that there will not be any *Criterion* in October.[1] There will be a new quarterly in *January* (not under the auspices of Lady Rothermere) which I shall edit and which will welcome and solicit your contributions, so I hope you will have something for me – the 'Milton' at least.[2]

I am sorry that you have been ill. I look forward to your book,[3] and shall write to propose a meeting as soon as I have a little more leisure.

Sincerely yours
T. S. Eliot

TO *Geoffrey Faber*

TS Faber

14 August 1925

9 Clarence Gate Gdns

My dear Faber,

Here is a programme of Foreign Men of Letters for you to mull over at your leisure. The prospectus is not supposed to be in printable form, but merely to contain suggestions to which you may add or from which you may detract. After we have arrived at some formula on which we agree, I propose to shew it to one or two of the men whom I want to write, and get their opinions.

I may have forgotten somebody very important. You will notice that I have omitted Tchehov and Dostoevski for the present.

I see that a good deal of correspondence will be necessary, first and last, with the writers enlisted.

Incidentally, the series might help us to secure the rights of translation of some of the authors, if and when we want them.

My own inclination is to keep the number of words on the short side. I have the E. M. of L. 'Ben Jonson' in front of me,[4] and it runs to 302

1 – Collins's 'fragment on Romanticism and Language' (as he termed it on 2 Aug.) was not published, but he reviewed Lascelles Abercrombie, *Romanticism*, in *NC* 5: 1 (Jan. 1927).
2 – Collins reviewed Denis Saurat, *Milton: Man and Thinker*, in *NC* 4: 1 (Jan. 1926), 196–202.
3 – Collins, *Modern Poetry* (1925).
4 – On 29 May GCF told CW they were contemplating 'a series of monographs' on foreign writers in 'the style of the Macmillan's English Men of Letters'. TSE reviewed G. Gregory Smith's *Ben Jonson* in the series, *TLS* (13 Nov. 1919).

pages in small type. I think that is much too long for this purpose. Also, it seems possible nowadays to sell very small books for absurdly high prices (vide the Hogarth Pamphlets @ 2/6 and the preposterous Kegan Paul 'Future of . . .' series at the same price). I suggest about 200 pages of somewhat larger type than the E.M.L. at 2/6 or 3/6 preferably. But here my opinion is of no more value than anyone else's.

Lady R. seems to have gone into the Bush, or gone native; I have written again.

I am seeing Stewart about my poems as soon as he is back.[1]

Meanwhile I hope that you are free from all cares and that your family is flourishing.

Ever yours
T. S. E.

FOREIGN MEN OF LETTERS

The design of this series is to introduce the British reader to the most important movements of thought and literary art on the continent of Europe. It will include studies of both living and dead authors: the principle of inclusion being that each volume shall consider an author – or a group of authors – representative of some living force or tendency; an author who has made an important contribution to the thought of contemporary Europe. While the series is not limited to a definite number of volumes, it aims nevertheless at a certain unity.

For the moment, authors on whom any considerable work in the English language has recently appeared will be excluded. The aim of the series, however, differs both from that of any single biography or critical study, or from that of any existing series. The studies do not attempt to replace any works on the authors considered, which already exist in any foreign language. They are written for English readers, as an introduction to the work and influence of foreign writers. For this reason the volumes will for the most part be written by English critics of the younger generation, who are themselves representative, and who have experienced the influence of the authors of whom they treat.

A few works will be included by foreign critics of international reputation and international point of view.

Each volume will contain the necessary minimum of biographical material, and a critical and expository account of the author's work, emphasising its international, rather than its local importance.

1 – Charles W. Stewart was Publications Manager at Faber & Gwyer Ltd, and Company Secretary; later a director.

PRELIMINARY LIST OF SUBJECTS AND WRITERS SUGGESTED

Henri Bergson	Herbert Read
Rémy de Gourmont	Richard Aldington
Henrik Ibsen	Edwin Muir
*Maurice Barrès	Ernst Curtius[1]
G. D'Annunzio	Aldous Huxley
Loisy and French Modernism	Frederic Manning
Marcel Proust	Ramón Fernandez
*Friedrich Nietzsche	Ernst Bertram
Ernest Renan	Frederic Manning
Charles Maurras	T. S. Eliot[2]
Pirandello	Orlo Williams (?)
Perez Galdos	
(or some other Spaniard)	J. B. Trend
French Symbolist Poetry	Bonamy Dobrée
Hugo von Hofmannsthal	Edwin Muir
Paul Valéry	Mark Wardle
*Julien Benda	Constant Bourquin[3]
André Gide	B. Cremieux (?)
G. Verga	D. H. Lawrence[4]

*In existence. To be translated and abridged.

Possible: Fustel de Coulanges,[5] Knut Hamsun, Gerhardt Hauptmann, Benedetto Croce.

1–Ernst Robert Curtius, *Maurice Barrès und die geistigen Grundlagen des französischen Nationalismus* ['Maurice Barrès and the intellectual foundations of French Nationalism'] (1921).

2–TSE's proposed study of Maurras, like many of the projected studies, never appeared. He published 'The *Action Française*, M. Maurras and Mr Ward' in *NC* 7: 3 (Mar. 1928).

3–Constant Bourquin, *Julien Benda, ou le point de vue de Sirius* ['Julien Benda, or the viewpoint of Sirius'] with an Introduction by Jules de Gaultier (1925).

4–DHL's transl. of the Sicilian novelist Giovanni Verga's *Mastro-Don Gesualdo* was published in New York in 1923. He later translated Verga's *Cavalleria Rusticana, and Other Stories* (1928), for which he wrote a Preface.

5–Numa Denis Fustel de Coulanges (1830–89): French historian; author of *La cité antique* (1864) and *Histoire des institutions politiques de l'ancienne France* (6 vols, 1874–92).

Vivien Eliot TO *John Middleton Murry* MS Valerie Eliot

[mid August? 1925] [London]

Dear John

Thank you for writing.[1] I always like to have a letter from you and the yellow envelope of the *Adelphi* is an *extraordinarily comfortable* sight, yet altho' I don't want you to feel you've *got* to write to me, or anything, it will always be a particular joy and help to get a letter from you. I am beginning to believe now that I have really got a little niche in your thoughts, and that's what I want. When things are *extra* bad I shall always write and ask you to give me as much of your attention as you have time for. Anyhow you wrote me a perfect letter, and I thank you for it.

Really John I think of you for ever, constantly, and I know, by thinking, lots of little things about you that it seems to me nobody else knows now. I think, in certain cases one can know a person much better by seldom meeting and constantly thinking than by being with them all the time.

I am so furious and worried about this Whibley, and *why* did – O well. W. is an evil genius if ever there was one.

Vivien

TO *Geoffrey Faber* TS Valerie Eliot

16 August 1925 9 Clarence Gate Gdns

My dear Faber,

I enclose a copy of a letter today received from Lady R. I am no more certain than you will be whether this is lunacy or cunning. At any rate, if it is the latter, it seems to indicate that she realises that it is not worth her while to try to continue on her own.[2]

I shall be writing to her to say that we agree, if she will sign the enclosed form of agreement, which I have today (letter by hand) asked my solicitor to draw up. If she does not change her mind, but returns me the signed agreement, we shall be in the following position:

1–JMM wrote to TSE on 7 Aug.: 'I have you both constantly in my thoughts: & sometimes the strong desire to see you & talk to you. That moment will doubtless come when it ought to come . . . Give my love to Vivien. Often I think of writing to her: and then I don't because I feel that what little I have to give is given otherwise & better just now than by letters.'

2–Lady Rothermere declared on 14 Aug. that TSE had best '*take on "The Criterion" for another year* at any rate & see what happens'. However, if F&G could offer her a '*better price*' than RC-S, she might consider giving it up, but meanwhile it would be better to remain with RC-S.

It will be undesirable to get her to assign the name of *The Criterion*, for she appears to be a nominalist and more attached to names than to realities. If I have the agreement, she cannot compete; I should take the style and format of *The Criterion* for the new review, and produce something quarterly for her under the title of *The Criterion*, but in a different shape and of content approximating what I proposed. When my ideas are clearer on this subject you shall have them. My point at the moment is that it is better to humour her, and arrange a scheme for transferring the subscribers etc. later.

The agreement would be simply to appoint myself as editor for another year with advance quarterly payments covering the cost (I have said £700) to be made to Faber & Gwyer Ltd. For *The Criterion*, a [review *del.*] periodical of literary and artistic character. Published for the *Criterion* Press by Faber & Gwyer Ltd. Out of the £700 some remuneration to myself and a commission to Faber & Gwyer Ltd.

We can settle details when you return – the important thing at the moment is to get her pinned down.

Did you get a letter from me with outline of Foreign Men of Letters? You don't need to answer it.

Ever yours,
T. S. E.

PS If *The Criterion* name continues, is not *The Critic* too similar a name? Will you try to think of another? My wife suggests *The Metropolitan*.[1]

TO *Messrs. Broad & Son*[2] CC

16 August 1925 9 Clarence Gate Gdns

Dear Sirs,

I enclose copy of the original agreement between Lady Rothermere and myself for the *Criterion*.

1 – It had been VHE who came up with the name *The Criterion* in 1922. These names are for the other periodical TSE was to edit, which he referred to earlier as a 'Symposium' or 'Cahier'. GCF responded (18 Aug.): 'I think you are right about "The Critic". I'm not sure that I like "The Metropolitan" very much: it has an uncomfortable flavour to my foolish mind – a X between the Underground & the Roman Catholic Church! If anything better comes to me I will send the result to you. But Mrs Eliot is prolific in ideas: I expect she will think of another.' See further TSE's postcard to GCF, 21 Aug., below.

2 – TSE's solicitor, J. Moxon Broad, Broad & Son, 1 Great Winchester Street, London, E.C.2.

Referring to my recent interview with Mr Moxon Broad on this subject, I have just heard from Lady Rothermere asking me to 'continue *The Criterion* for a year'.

I should be obliged if you would kindly provide me with a short letter or form of agreement, to be signed by Lady Rothermere, appointing me editor of *The Criterion* for one more year, and guaranteeing £700 for the year payable in quarterly instalments in advance of each number, the first payment to be made one month in advance of the first number. The first (or next) number to be produced as soon as I can arrange for publication, but not before October 1925.

The sums to be paid to Messrs. Faber & Gwyer Ltd., to be held in a special account called '*Criterion* Press Account', and to be operated by Faber & Gwyer Ltd. for the purpose of the magazine solely.

I am to be entitled to arrange with Faber & Gwyer Ltd. for their commission and for my salary out of the £700 and any receipts from sales and advertisements.

Clauses 2 and 3 can stand I think as in the original, except that it seems worthwhile to add to 2 'The accounts are to be audited, if I desire and on my written request to Messrs. Faber & Gwyer Ltd etc' . . . .

I should like it also to be clear that the form and contents of the magazine are wholly within my control (except that the paper is to be primarily literary and artistic and not the organ of any political party), and that disposal of the funds for printing, advertising, payment of contributors etc. is to be made by Faber & Gwyer with my approval.

I want it to be such that any process for non-payment of funds would be between Faber & Gwyer Ltd. and Lady Rothermere, not between myself and Lady Rothermere.

For your own information I will state that I am a Director of Faber & Gwyer Ltd.

I should be very grateful – if you can do so on the basis of this letter – if you could draw up this agreement as quickly as possible, before Lady Rothermere changes her mind. Brevity is desirable! but at the same time I wish to be clear on the points mentioned, and wish – without its being so expressly stated, to be free to alter the form and content and size of *The Criterion* as I choose, while keeping it to a literary and artistic character.

Yours faithfully,
[T. S. E.]

[Attachment]

TO *Geoffrey Faber* MS Valerie Eliot

18 August 1925 9 Clarence Gate Gdns

My dear Faber

I should like a line from you, to know whether you have had my letters, and because I do not wish to move in the Rothermere matter without your concurrence.

I might not make a penny out of this scheme myself – for I might have to, and indeed wd. prefer to – pass the work (and remuneration) over to someone like Herbert Read and concentrate on the more important things – but I think it would be a better advertisement – both for F. & G. Ltd. and for myself – if we produced something for *her*, as well as our own, *for a year* – than if the *Criterion* simply ended in a mess. I hope you will be in town before the date when she promises to arrive, and we should have a triangular meeting. *If* we cannot agree *then* – by that time she will probably be so sick of it all that she will let it all go!

And if we do something for a year, it may not only be conspicuous, but will lead to absorption instead of breach.

My F. M. L. plan is a fluid one. I have just discussed it with Whibley (who said you had told him of it) and with Aldington, who will do Rémy de Gourmont.

But do let me hear, as I want to reply to Lady R. How are you?

Ever yours

T. S. E.

Yr. letter just arrived after sealing this – That is all right.[1] I will proceed. I agree about Sr. D. J. Carramba's biography.[2] St Augustine bathed after the death of his mother; may you bathe again on receipt of this letter.[3] *Salve.*

1 – GCF approved (18 Aug.) TSE's prospectus for the series. He thought 50,000–60,000 words the right length and suggested each should begin with a 'succinct biographical statement'. He found TSE's list 'admirable', but would like to see Hauptmann and Croce in from the start and suggested it might eventually include 'the big omissions' including 'Checkov, Dostoevsky, Tolstoy, France'.

2 – With his letter GCF sent a brief outline life of the fictitious 'José Carramba (1878–), Spanish novelist and theologian' as a model for the sort of thing he had in mind.

3 – GCF said that while in Norfolk he wrote letters all morning, and then bathed. TSE recalls St Augustine's account, in *The Confessions*, of going to the baths after his mother's funeral.

TO *John Middleton Murry* MS Northwestern

Tuesday [August 1925] *The Criterion*, 17 Thavies Inn

Dear John

Certainly I shall read it, and I *should* like another copy for review, for it is impossible for me to take the time to do that adequately myself.[1] I should not dream of giving it to Aldington.[2] Orlo Williams asked for it long ago. I don't know whether he is competent or not. Is there anyone, suitable for the *Criterion*, whom you would prefer? If so, name him.[3]

This will probably be published in *January*. I am taking on a new quarterly for Faber & Gwyer Ltd. which will be virtually the *Criterion*. I am also continuing the *Criterion* for Lady R. but the form must be substantially altered. All this tedious business would be much more easily explained (if you care to hear) if I could see you.

I often wish I *could* see you. I have several times re-read your letters.[4]

Ever yours
Tom

I hope you can find time to answer my previous letter.

Vivien Eliot TO *John Middleton Murry* MS Valerie Eliot

[August? 1925] [London]

Dear John

How sweet of you to send your book to Tom and me. It *was* kind of you. I shall read it, some day soon, but at present I cant read and dont want to read. I hope you understand that feeling. I had the most terrific nervous breakdown after I saw you in Jan. and lay as one dead for eleven weeks. I really dont know what happened because one minute I was standing up talking and the next I had gone on a *very* long and peculiar journey. Poor Tom. He says you have helped him. I came out of this all the wrong way up. That was the worst part. It has taken me months and months to get

1 – In an undated letter (Aug.), JMM said he had asked Oxford University Press to send TSE his *Keats and Shakespeare*, based on his 1924 Clark lectures and published in Aug. He told TSE he would like it reviewed in *C.*, and could send another copy ('I know you can't review it yourself').

2 – JMM requested that it not be given to RA, 'who won't have an idea what it is about'.

3 – Orlo Williams reviewed JMM's book in *NC* 4: 1 (Jan. 1926), 193–6. While noting that JMM's prose made 'some little minds cross', Williams said that no book of his had so 'completely proved' his qualities of 'absolute sincerity, deep sensibility, passionate conviction' and 'profound loyalty to apprehended truth'.

4 – See their correspondence of 12–20 Apr.

myself at all straightened out. I tell you this not because I suppose it will interest you much, but to explain why at present I hardly dare to read. I have so much to *do* to get strong and fit again that I daren't take my eye off the ball. That seems a terrible complication in life to me, i.e. how to keep one's eye on the ball. It gets off without one's knowing it. I often feel I shall have to turn into a farm labourer or a mechanic or something like that.

Tom and I speak of you *very often*. He is not well. He seems to me again to have involved himself in too much work. It is so hopeless – one can't *live*, like this.

I hope your baby is flourishing. I hope you will let her be fond of animals and accustomed to deal with them. There are times when animals are the only companions one can have. *Thanking you again.*

I read your article: 'Man's faith in Man' – yes.[1] But what about the times when we are not on this earth. Who, or what are we to look to then? Cant there be a God, yet not a God the Father? The latter idea may have been created by Christ but there may still all the same be a God whom *He* could not conceive?

Yrs.
V. H. E.

TO *Geoffrey Faber* — PC Valerie Eliot

[Postmark 21 August 1925]

The Albany is a possible title, but I still think *The Metropolitan* better – wd. appeal to provincials. One must think of a future amalgamation '*The X. and the Criterion*' how it would sound. On the other hand, I am not sure that *The Critic* is not still as good as any.

Yours ever
T. S. E.[2]

1–JMM, in 'Christ or Christianity?' (*Adelphi* 2: 4, Sept. 1925, 233–41), scorned to believe in 'God the Father', a figure who exacts blood-sacrifice but is hailed as a God of Love. Yet one can believe in Jesus, the figure of 'infinite love' who accepted 'a shameful and atrocious death' so as to create 'a loving God who was a man'. 'There will, there must, come the time when all men will create within themselves the infinite love that he had. Man may, in the long run must, believe in man.'

2–GCF responded (23 Aug.): 'I don't much care about *The Albany* which seems to lack meaning. *The Metropolitan* is certainly better, & is rather popular here; tho' I cannot rid my own mind of a certain discomfort about it. *The Critic* is good; but is open to the objection that it suggests too rigidly critical a paper, excluding original imaginative work, which we are both anxious to include. Of the three I wld. vote for *The Metropolitan*, & will agree to this if a better cannot be found.'

TO *George Rylands* MS King's

21 August 1925 9 Clarence Gate Gdns

Dear Mr Rylands,

Here is your MS.[1] Perhaps I shall be able to ask for it back later. I am glad that you are not a fluent poet: fluency is fatal.

Will you let me know when you are next in London and come to see me and we will discuss the future. In the odd muddle of literary ventures in which I find myself, it is possible that something will turn up.

If you will tell me what you would like to review, and mention any books as they come out. I will give you some reviews to do. I think it would be a good thing if you had later a 'heavy', i.e. a serious critical essay. The chief advantage of publication in the *Criterion*, or any of the humble ventures with which I am or will be associated, is that the right people see it, and a good thing attracts offers from elsewhere. And I would help personally also.

Good verse is only recognised after five years, at least. Good criticism is noticed at once. The cultivated public prefers critical to creative work.

Come and see me.

Yours sincerely
T. S. Eliot

TO *Signora G. Celenza*[2] CC

22 August 1925 [London]

Dear Madam,

Thank you for your letter of August 10th and for sending me the article by Signor Liuzzi.[3] Before accepting articles on any musical subject I always submit them to the gentleman who has charge of such matters, Mr J. B. Trend, and it may, therefore, be some little time before I am able to report to you about this.[4] It is, however, very welcome.

1–Rylands's poem *Russet and Taffeta* was issued by the Hogarth Press in Dec. 1925.

2–Giulia Celenza taught at the University of Florence; her publications included an Italian translation of Swinburne's *Atalanta in Calydon*.

3–An article on Italian opera by Fernando Liuzzi (1884–1940), Italian composer and musicologist; author of *Estetica della Musica* (1924). He did not contribute to C.

4–J. B. Trend adjudged (9 Sept.) that while Liuzzi offered some 'good things', he assumed 'everyone to be familiar with contemporary Italian works, & also Italian operas of the last twenty years or so, most of which have never been given out of Italy'. His view seemed just 'too parochial to be of real interest, while it would need very careful – & artful – translation'.

I am sorry to hear that you have had a severe illness and hope that you will soon be well enough to prepare an article for me to read on one of the subjects which you suggest.[1]

Please accept my thanks, also, for your kind remark about my own verse.

Yours sincerely,
[T. S. E.]

TO *Henry Eliot* — MS Houghton

22 August 1925 — [9 Clarence Gate Gdns]

My dear brother

Thank you a thousand times for the money.[2] Some day I will explain to you how it has saved me – for it is wrong for me to take it when you need it most yourself. Thank you for your letters and affection. I am glad you are to be married[3] – but I know this – that if you are happy (as I expect) you will not need me, and if you are unhappy your pride will cut you off from me. But nothing can destroy the deep and essential affection.[4] I want to know Theresa.

If you *could* come, I could tell you much more than in letters. It would be a great happiness too. But I shall try to give you more in my letters.

Ever your devoted brother

Tom

1 – On 10 Aug. she proposed articles on (a) recent Italian poetry; (b) 'the structure of Modern Prose (English, French & Italian): the psychology of its technique'.

2 – A gift of $1,500, cabled on 17 July. HWE explained that it was separate from the insurance and investments discussed in his other letters.

3 – On 12 June, HWE said he was 'very proud', 'very happy', 'very frightened', 'quite in love' with Theresa Garrett. On 9 Aug., he thanked TSE for his 'kindly letter' about the engagement: but TSE's letter has not been located.

4 – HWE wrote on 9 Aug.: 'I have written to you frequently with a degree of self-revelation which I have never even approximated with any other person . . . Any other person than yourself would undoubtedly misunderstand me completely and censure me severely. My faith persists that you do, in a measure at least, understand me. I have a similar faith that I can understand anything that you might wish to write me about yourself.'

TO *L. Tilden Smith* CC

24 August 1925 [London]

Dear Sir,

Thank you for your letter of the 11th inst and for sending me Mr Wortham's story.[1] While I find it very clever and amusing, it does not strike me as emphatically suitable for the *Criterion*, and therefore, as I have much other material on hand, I am returning it herewith. I should, however, be very glad to see any other work by Mr Wortham, or indeed anything whatever that strikes you as likely to interest the *Criterion* audience.

Yours faithfully,
[T. S. E.]

TO *Gilbert Seldes* CC

24 August 1925 23 Adelphi Terrace House

My dear Seldes,

I find that I failed to acknowledge your letter which was dated the 1st July. As your letter contained a most interesting chronicle, this is all the less excusable on my part. I can only say that I have been more than usually occupied by a bewildering variety of affairs. I do not expect to be able to use this letter until January, for reasons of publication which I can explain to you more fully later.[2] If there is anything in it which you would wish to bring up to date let me know, but so far as we can see here it needs no alteration.

I hope that you will be able to finish your long and remunerative work this winter and come abroad in April as you suggest.

Faithfully yours,
[T. S. E.]

1–Hugh Evelyn Wortham (1884–1959), music critic of the *Morning Post*; author of *A Musical Odyssey* (1924). The story in question was 'Mr Jaspar Fell's Strange Complex', of which Tilden Smith, Wortham's agent, related (11 Aug.): 'Messrs. Faber & Gwyer are publishing Mr Wortham's first novel in the autumn. Mr Faber has suggested that I should send this story to you; but he has not seen it, and he tells me that he makes no attempt to influence you in any way over individual contributions.' Wortham was not to be a contributor to *C*.

2–Seldes's 'New York Chronicle' was published in *NC* 4: 1 (Jan. 1926), 170–7.

TO *Geoffrey Faber* MS Valerie Eliot

Monday, 24 August 1925 9 Clarence Gate Gdns

My dear Faber

Without having seen the book, I should support [Osbert] Burdett's opinion; only, I should stress even more strongly the importance of the play.[1] That will carry it; otherwise, I should be adverse.

Is there any danger of another translation, or are the rights sound and exclusive? But the only person to eclipse Koteliansky would be Constance Garnett.

In general, in the case of translations done for *succès d'estime*, I should incline to authors, even if less famous here, whose names were not already associated with another publishing house.

Let's leave the title till the time comes, waiting for possible inspirations. Six to one Lady R. will change her mind and drop the *Criterion* anyway.

I quite understand and agree about not disbursing money on the F. Writers in 1925. It would hardly be possible to get the first lot ready before spring in any case. I agree about the price 5/-.

Ever yours
T. S. E.

TO *Richard Cobden-Sanderson* CC

24 August 1925 [London]

Dear Cobden-Sanderson,

I have at last heard from Lady Rothermere from an address in Arcachon. As of course she gives no explanation of her movements and does not say how long she has been there, how long she is going to stay or where she is going next, it is impossible to say whether she got your letter or not. But if she got it she probably forgot all about it in the excitement of travel. I am writing to her but as I have quite enough to say for her mind to take in, and because of what I am saying, I think it would be better, if you don't mind, for you also to write again separately and address it to 33 quai

1–Koteliansky offered a translation of *The Wood-Demon: A Comedy in Four Acts*, which was eventually published by Chatto & Windus (1926). GCF pursued (26 Aug.): 'The Tchehov play is a one act thing, never intended for publication, & I gather from Burdett not up to much.' Constance Garnett's *The Plays of Tchehov* had been published by Chatto & Windus in 2 vols (1922–3).

Voltaire. I should like to see you and tell you all about it when you have come back to town – I don't want to bother you more than is absolutely necessary on your holiday. Do make the most of it.

Ever yours,
[T. S. E.]

TO *James Joyce* CC

24 August 1925 9 Clarence Gate Gdns

Dear Joyce,

I was glad to have a letter from you after being without news of you for a long time.[1] I hope that I may be able to get to Paris before the end of the year, but I am not certain and therefore it is good news to hear that you are likely to be in London in January. I am very sorry to hear about your past and future operations and I hope that the next one will be the last.[2]

I have taken note to tell Cobden-Sanderson to send your cheque to Miss Sylvia Beach for your account.[3]

I congratulate you on having found a flat. My wife and I send our best wishes and sympathy to Mrs Joyce and yourself.

Yours sincerely,
[T. S. E.]

TO *Ada Leverson* MS Berg

25 August 1925 9 Clarence Gate Gdns

Dear Mrs Leverson,

I am very glad to hear from you. I do indeed hope you will be able to get ahead with Oscar now and let me have it soon.[4] And Vivienne says to tell you not to go abroad so much but stay in London and write more. I am looking forward to reading your Oscar soon.

1 – The letter does not appear to survive. JJ was on holiday in Arcachon, from where he wrote to Harriet Shaw Weaver (15 Aug.) with a parody of *TWL*: 'But we shall have great times, / When we return to Clinic, that waste land / O Esculapios! / (Shan't we? Shan't we? Shan't we?)'

2 – Joyce was due to have a further operation on his eyes in Paris in Sept.

3 – Payment for 'Fragment of an Unpublished Work', *C*. 3: 12 (July 1925), 498–510.

4 – 'The Last First Night' appeared in *NC* 4: 1 (Jan. 1926), 148–53.

We really have moved to S.W. but are back here temporarily on account of servant troubles.[1] Vivienne was quite recovered and was getting rapidly stronger when she came down with shingles, which of course will weaken her and keep her back.

I am so pleased that you liked the *Criterion* and her sketch.[2] You know how we both value your opinion.

Vivienne sends her love, and I my kindest regards.[3]

Sincerely yours
T. S. Eliot

Vivien Eliot TO *Ottoline Morrell* MS Texas

[late August? 1925] (Temporarily) 9 Clarence Gate Gdns

My dearest Ottoline

Thank you *so* much for your charming and affectionate letter. It was the greatest pleasure to hear from you. Especially as when one is ill for a very long time one begins to feel that one has no friends left – a fearful feeling of isolation. It is indeed *awful* that you have been in London for months and that I have never seen you. It is a dreadful catastrophe, because you so seldom settle in London for any length of time. *Of course* I have seen *no one* but a lot of miserable doctors. I *was* much better and we had moved to the house in Chester Terrace, where I was looking forward to being your neighbour for a time, when suddenly my parents arrived in England, (when all the worst was over!) and bore down on me and settled down in a hotel with nothing on earth to do but to interfere with me and shout advice in my ears and sit over me and make my life a hell. I very soon got

1 – The Eliots did not in fact move into their house in 57 Chester Terrace until 1926.

2 – 'Fête Galante', which VHE published as by 'Fanny Marlow' in *C.* 3: 12 (July 1925). It was an account of a late-night literary party in London, featuring the 'Sibylla' who had figured in 'Night Club' (*C.* 3: 11, Apr. 1925), as well a society hostess known as 'The Macaw' (OM), a 'great art critic, white locks gleaming in the moonlight' (Roger Fry), and an 'American financier', with a 'thickly powdered' face, who speaks in 'a muffled, pedantic, and slightly drunken voice'. The latter (who resembles TSE) is said to be 'the most marvellous poet in the *whole world*', which provokes Sibylla's retort: 'He might be if he ever wrote anything.'

3 – Leverson wrote in an undated letter to Osbert Sitwell: 'I have an affection for her [VHE] & she is amusing tho' I wouldn't exactly like to live with her, she's very nice really. It must be very chilly living on the Bostonian heights with Mr Eliot. I shouldn't like it at all, though I also like *him*. Their innocent snobbishness is quite touching, & like something in an American book' (Julie Speedie, *Wonderful Sphinx*, 253–4).

shingles then, owing I believe, to the extra dose of misery and as we had *great* difficulty with servants there, the only thing was to rush back to cover in this flat. We had, and do intend to let this flat furnished as it would be a dead loss to *give it up*. (We have a fairly long lease, and they let furnished very well). To continue this boring tale of afflictions I have been laid up with shingles ever since and am all stuck up with bandages and ointments and loathsomeness. My father and mother are still sitting over me and driving me to desperation but they are leaving on Monday. But *you* are leaving on Sunday. I might have seen you at the last minute but I am too involved in parental toils to call a moment my own. Isn't it *horrible*? Being helpless I can do nothing. They come *every* day, or *twice* a day. If I live till Monday I shall be surprised.

All the same I feel too degraded and bandaged and in a mess (with my hair about three inches down my back) even to see *you* with satisfaction. One of the worst features of this complaint is that you may not have a bath. You can scarcely *wash*, and to move is intolerable.

Yes, Tom is learning at a motor school, although we shall never be able to afford a car. My one, my *only* remaining ambition is to have a car and drive to Garsington to see you!

With ever so much love dearest Ottoline, and the most bitter regrets – (I can hardly say how I have felt it)

Your affectionate old friend

Vivien

I have *not* lived in a wonderful world for years. I was soon dragged out of that. I have lived in a world of unpleasant realities. I have . . . . . . nothing interesting and only law statistics, constitutional history I may yet turn into a barrister.

Tom felt he needed some very *hard* food for my mind and I have always hankered after the [law] he turned me into it – it really *is*, to me, fascinating.[1]

TO *Curtis Brown Ltd* CC

25 August 1925 [London]

Dear Sirs,

I regret that it has been impossible for me to give you an earlier decision about Mr D. H. Lawrence's sketch, which is the subject of your letters of

1 – The last two paragraphs are difficult to make out.

the 13th January and the 13th August.[1] I now find that for certain reasons it will be impossible for me [to] decide this question until the latter part of September at the earliest. It is therefore only fair to yourselves and to Mr Lawrence to suggest that if you wish to attempt to dispose of it elsewhere in the meantime, I should return it to you. Please bear in mind, however, for the future, that I shall always be glad to use as much of Mr Lawrence's work as I possibly can.

I should be glad to know when and where this sketch is to appear in America, if any arrangements have been made. I should be able to use it at a later date if not in January. But if it is to appear in America in December or January, and if I cannot use it myself until April, or later, I should of course prefer to have then some other contribution by Mr Lawrence if one was available.[2]

Yours faithfully,
[T. S. E.]

TSE/IPF

TO *Geoffrey Faber* — MS Valerie Eliot

Thursday, [27 August 1925?] — 9 Clarence Gate Gdns

My dear Faber,

I know nothing of Ludovici's published work[3] or of its sale. This is the sort of book which one feels one could write oneself better than anyone else! but I must say that the outline seems to me *excellent*, and predisposes me very favourably. I should like to see this published. But it ought to be of a size to be published at a moderate price – more useful and more saleable than a large tome of 15/- or a guinea. Even 12/6 is rather high.[4]

1–DHL, 'Saturday'.

2–Curtis Brown replied that there was no American publisher for 'Saturday', but TSE did not use it. 'The Woman Who Rode Away', which had been postponed because of the cancellation of the autumn number, appeared in *NC* 4: 1 (Jan. 1926), 95–124.

3–Anthony M. Ludovici (1882–1971): English political philosopher; author of *A Defence of Aristocracy: A Text-Book for Tories* (1915) and *The False Assumptions of 'Democracy'* (1921).

4–Ludovici's book was published at the price of 12/6d as *A Defence of Conservatism: A Further Text Book for Tories* (F&G, 1927). TSE, who reviewed it (*NC* 6: 1, July 1927), said Ludovici had much to say which 'everyone interested in political theory should study'; he sympathised with 'so many of his views'. Nonetheless, he objected to the isolation of politics from economics and religion, and particularly disliked his account of 'the relation of Toryism to the Church', arguing that 'Toryism is essentially Anglican' rather than Catholic (69–71).

The idea of a 'Fabrian Society'[1] is very good – if such a thing were ever realised we ought to try to secure the publication of its treatises pamphlets or periodicals.

Tell me what you think of the enclosed essay.[2] Do you know the author? It is dully written but praiseworthy, and I think we might use it in the X. review at some time.

Ever yours
T. S. E.[3]

FROM *Lady Rothermere* TS Valerie Eliot

28 August 1925

Dear Sir,

I confirm the arrangement we have come to for the continuance of your editorship of *The Criterion* for a further period of one year to include the next four successive quarterly issues of the magazine.

The terms of such arrangement are as follows:-

(1) I will provide the sum of £700 for the year to meet with any receipts from sales and advertisements the expenses involved in getting up, printing, issuing and advertising the magazine. You are entitled to any surplus which the £700 and any such receipts may give in excess of the expenses as remuneration for your services up to the sum of £100 (one hundred pounds).

(2) The said sum of £700 will be paid by me by equal quarterly instalments of £175 to Messrs. Faber & Gwyer Ltd., the first of such instalments to be paid one calendar month in advance of the next quarterly number which number is to be produced as soon as you can arrange for publication but not before October 1925.

1 – The 'Fabrian Society' would presumably have offered a conservative alternative to the Fabian Society, the Socialist society founded in 1884 in which Sidney and Beatrice Webb played a leading part.

2 – 'Dalway Turnbull's 'Aristotle on Democracy and Socialism' (see TSE's letter of 2 Sept.).

3 – GCF replied (29 Aug.): 'I am glad you like Ludovici's synopsis – I thought it good. L. has a name &, I think, a public; tho' I should have thought him a rather unstable mind. (A gt. Nietzschean – at least he used to be.) I am told his *Lysistrata: or the Future of Woman* has been very successful.' Of Turnbull's essay: 'It is excellently clear & easy reading, & – tho' I am not an Aristotelian student – I should say very sound. I think it wd. do well for the X; tho' as you say it is not exciting!'

(3) Messrs. Faber & Gwyer Ltd., are to place the quarterly payments to be made by me to a special account with their bankers to be called 'Criterion Press Account' to be operated by them for the purposes of the magazine solely and subject to your direction. All receipts are to be paid in the same account.

(4) Messrs. Faber & Gwyer Ltd., are to keep separate and detailed accounts of all matters connected with the publication and sale of the magazine including all receipts and disbursements, and if I desire I am to be at liberty to nominate an accountant to audit either annually or semi annually as I think fit the said accounts all facilities for the audit to be afforded by Messrs. Faber & Gwyer Ltd.

(5) Except with my express consent all expenses including commissions and payments to contributors are to be made out of the said sum of £700 provided by me and any such receipts as above mentioned.

(6) During the said period of one year the contents of the magazine are to be within your entire control (except that the magazine is to be primarily a literary and artistic magazine and not the organ of any political party) and you are to have the sole authority to solicit, accept and reject contributions.

Yours faithfully
Lilian Rothermere

I will instruct Lloyds Bank to make the quarterly payments.

TO *John Middleton Murry* MS Northwestern

29 August 1925 9 Clarence Gate Gdns

My dear John,

I was very much struck by your leader in the last *Adelphi*, which Vivien read first and pointed out to me.[1] It seemed to me clearer and sharper and bolder, and somehow more *assured*, than anything of yours for some time. There are some things I agree with – some I don't – what I want to ask is: did you also write the note on 'Life and Death' by one 'Wilmshurst'?[2] The

1–'Christ or Christianity?', *Adelphi* 3: 4 (Sept. 1925), 233–41. JMM asked his readers to bear in mind two things: 'The first is: that I am fully conscious of the debt that I owe the Church . . . The second is: that I now hold that the finer conscience of mankind has now passed definitely outside the Church' (233).

2–W. L. Wilmshurst, 'On Life and Death and Science', 290–4. Although not written by JMM it built on his 'Science and the Control of Life' (*Adelphi* 3: 3, Aug. 1925, 155–66). Comparing Buddhism and Christianity, Wilmshurst sought to clarify the meaning of the terms 'life' and 'death' by way of ten propositions. In the final one, he asserted that the idea of

latter I admired very much, and I detected some of your ideas in it; but some of the conclusions strike me [as] *incompatible* with those of the article signed by you. The Wilmshurst is to me more Christian as well as more Buddhist, in its view of progress and temporal vs. non-temporal values. It seems to me that one must either ignore the Church, or reform it from within, or transcend it – but never attack it. The Wilmshurst seems to me to go beyond the creed of any church.

You see I happened to be brought up in the most 'liberal' of 'Christian' creeds – Unitarianism: I may therefore be excused for seeing the dangers of what you propose, more clearly than I see the vices of what you attack. If one discards dogma, it should be for a more celestial garment, not for nakedness.[1]

I wish I could discuss this with you for hours. I also liked 'The Journeyman' very much;[2] I disliked intensely the Diary of H. T.[3]

I will write again – I like to keep a letter to one subject

Ever yours aff.
Tom

TO *Virginia Woolf* MS Berg

[2? September 1925] at 9 Clarence Gate Gdns

My dear Virginia

How are you? We both envy you in the country. It makes us quite ill to see the evening skies. I can't write much now as I am exceedingly busy. From January I shall be running two periodicals at once, and there is no need to tell you how much work that involves.

May I beg pray and entreat that you will help me? What can I have of yours? Could you possibly let me have a story sketch essay or criticism

---

'creative evolution' is a 'complete fallacy': 'Real Being is outside evolution, outside time-space-causation, although *in*volved in them. The true gospel therefore is, and can only be, *liberation* of our involved permanent Self from the sphere where alone flux, evolution and the time-order obtain. "My kingdom (real Being) is *not* of this world" and can never *evolve* from it' (293).

1 – Cf. TSE's remark about Blake: 'if there was nothing to distract him from sincerity, there were, on the other hand, the dangers to which the naked man is exposed' (*SW*, 155).

2 – JMM (writing as 'The Journeyman'), 'Round and About Sincerity', criticised Horace Thorogood's 'Concerning God' in the current *Hibbert Journal*.

3 – Helen Thomas, 'As It Was', the second of three extracts from the narrative of her courtship and marriage to the poet Edward Thomas, who had been killed at the Battle of Arras in 1917. *As It Was* was published as a book in 1926.

and send it to me in good time. I feel my new venture will never succeed unless you are represented in the first number.[1] Will you give this matter your *earnest* consideration for the rest of the time you are in the country. Please do not fail me.

Vivien is very much better indeed, although she has just had a bad attack of shingles which tied us here for most of this month. She is over it now and I am thankful to say she looks like being much stronger, in the end than she has been for many years. She sends her love to you and wishes me to say, what a blessing your ear stoppers have been.[2] I can testify that she has slept better since she had them than for about four years.

With love from
Tom

<Will write soon about certain other matters.>

TO *H. G. Dalway Turnbull*[3] CC

2 September 1925 23 Adelphi Terrace House

Dear Sir,

I have just read your essay on Aristotle[4] and apologise for the delay. It seems to me extremely suitable for my review and in fact I cannot think of any other periodical for which it would be so suitable. At the moment the *Criterion* is about to undergo considerable changes; its character will probably be altered but I am to bring out in January the first number of another Quarterly Review for Messrs. Faber & Gwyer, Limited, which will pursue a similar policy and in which I should like to use your essay. It is difficult, however, at the moment of starting a new periodical and reorganising an old one, to state definitely when any one contribution can be published; and I shall therefore be very grateful if you are willing to leave the essay in my hands, and I will let you know at the first possible moment in what number I can publish it.

1–VW replied (3 Sept.) that it would be an 'honour' to be in the 'first number' of '*Criterion Junior* – waiting for the demise of *Criterion Senior*'.
2–VW replied that the ear plugs had changed her life too.
3–H. G. Dalway Turnbull, author of *Shakespeare and Ibsen* (1926).
4–'Aristotle on Democracy and Socialism' appeared in *NC* 4: 1 (Jan. 1926), 7–18.

I had been obliged to leave a huge number of manuscripts unread, but Mr Bain, in a recent letter, referred to your essay and I immediately looked for it and read it.

Yours faithfully,
[T. S. E.]

TSE/IPF

TO *Herbert S. Gorman*[1] TS Morris

2 September 1925 *The Criterion*, 9 Clarence Gate Gdns

Dear Mr Gorman

I am very glad to hear from you. In fact I have reproached myself several times in the last few years because I had intended to write to you and express my appreciation of your review of *The Waste Land* which gave me a great deal of pleasure and satisfaction.[2] I should very much like to see you. I am not very well myself and my wife is ill with Shingles, but if it is possible to get hold of you on short notice I will try to suggest in a few days a meeting at my office, 23 Adelphi Terrace House, Robert Street, W.C.2, for a talk and a cup of tea.

I have not seen your book on Joyce[3] but I am sure that it would interest me very much indeed and I wish you would let me know who published it, and when, so that I may get a copy. As for influence, that is a very important matter in any case.

With all best wishes

Sincerely yours
T. S. Eliot

1–Herbert Gorman (1893–1954): US novelist, critic, journalist; later author of *James Joyce: The Definitive Biography* (1941).
2–'The Waste Land of the Younger Generation', *Literary Digest International Book Review* 3 (Apr. 1923), 46, 48, 64.
3–*James Joyce, His First Forty Years* (1925).

TO *Major Desmond Chapman-Huston*[1] CC

4 September 1925 [London]

Dear Sir,

I like your essay on Lord Curzon very much and should like to publish it. It strikes me as eminently suitable for my review, perhaps more so than for any other.

I should like to publish it in January and hope to be able to do so but cannot bind myself to publish it before April. Will you kindly let me know if you have any reason for wishing to have it published sooner?[2]

Yours faithfully,
[T. S. E.]

TO *Wyndham Lewis* MS Cornell

5 September 1925 [9 Clarence Gate Gdns]

Dear Lewis –

I simply don't understand you at all. If you are dissatisfied please explain with figures. No malevolence on my part – I simply *don't understand.*[3]

T. S. E.

TO *Virginia Woolf* MS Berg

5 September 1925 at 9 Clarence Gate Gdns

My dear Virginia

This is sad news, to be in bed at Rodmell in such weather as we have been having. But now the weather has turned to the worse, I hope you are turning to the better. I fear that this means that you were overdoing during the Season, before you left town.

But I shall not relax my petitions.

1 – Desmond Chapman-Huston (1884–1952): Irish biographical writer; author (with Owen Rutter) of *Sir John Cowans: The Quartermaster-General of the Great War* (1923).
2 – 'Lord Curzon the Man and the Orator' appeared in *NC* 4: 2 (Apr. 1926), 313–28.
3 – WL's letter does not survive. As early as 15 Mar., TSE spoke to HR of 'a quarrel with Lewis'. The present crisis seems to be about not being paid for contributions to C. (see TSE's letter of 24 Sept.).

But first – I think I detect an overtone of disapproval in your critical voice. Certainly it sounds irrational, to run two reviews.[1] The truth is simply this: Lady R. (Visc.) hasn't 'cut up' anything but smooth.[2] When she had recovered from the blow of my appointment to run another Quarterly, she wrote and asked me to take on the *Criterion* as well for another year. As I had offered to do anything I could for her, I agreed. It is understood that it must assume some form in which it will not conflict with the other (which we will call for the moment the Heavy Review) and should be in fact a kind of supplement. In fact, it is far less of a task to run two things in this way as twins, with one proper office and full secretarial assistance, and a firm to deal with the whole of the business part, than to run Lloyds Banks Extracts from the Foreign Press in the City in the day and the *Criterion* here at night.

I don't know yet quite what form the Light will take. I want the contribution from Mrs Woolf for the Heavy, and it will be anything she pleases to give, and she can sell it in America too, if it does not appear in America before January or preferably February, as my infolio will appear abt. Jan. 15th. Can she not provide an essay, a story, a sketch, or a chapter of a novel, at any length she thinks fit, and let me have it by November 1st?[3]

Truly there is much to discuss, but September wanes already, the nights are drawing in, and it is impossible for me to get away from London during this month, even for a night – and probably October also. Alas, there is too much and too many for me to get away at all. So *when do you return*? I want to come to see you as soon as you are here, and then we will discuss (among other things) publishing in all its aspects. I don't want my House to be a competitor of the H. Press, and I don't think it is at all likely to, judging from our list – unless you go in for Nursing and Indian Education.[4]

Ever yours
T. S. E.

V. sends love, and is picking up rapidly after her Shingles.

1 – On 3 Sept., VW asked TSE why he had 'two magazines on [his] shoulders?'

2 – VW asked if he had 'ever cornered the Countess – Is she only a Baroness? & whether she cut up rough'. As TSE indicated, Lady Rothermere was in fact a Viscountess.

3 – VW had in mind 'a story, an article on some thing like Painting & Writing, & another undecided' promised to America.

4 – Specialities of F&G, inherited from the Scientific Press. With the Hogarth Press in mind, VW wrote in her diary on 14 Sept. that TSE had treated them 'scurvily': 'On Monday I get a letter that fawns & flatters, implores me to write for his new 4ly; & proposes to discuss press matters as soon as we get back; on Thursday we read in the *Lit. Supt.* that his new firm is publishing *The Waste Land* & his other poems – a fact which he dared not confess, but sought to palliate by flattering me' (*Diary*, III, 41). The *TLS* reported that F&G had

TO *Geoffrey Faber* — MS Valerie Eliot

7 September 1925 — *The Criterion*, 17 Thavies Inn

My dear Faber

I hope you have returned after killing innumerable birds. I am looking forward to seeing you; if you will let me know that you are back. I will arrange to come in one morning toward the end of the week.[1] (I have to be gassed and have my teeth out one day this week, and I don't yet know which). I want to discuss with you the various alternatives to lay before Lady R. when we interview her, etc. I will have a talk with Stewart about the poems at the same time.[2]

I have not much to report to you meanwhile.

There is one small matter. An old friend of Oscar Wilde, Mrs Leverson, has given me some reminiscences of Oscar (The First Night of *The Importance of Being Earnest*) which I think quite good and amusing. If I take these for the Quarterly I can also probably get the option on her book on O. W. if you want it (I suppose [Osbert] Burdett could give an authoritative opinion about this). I have promised her £10 for the reminiscences which I have. But she is a mad and improvident person, and wants the money *at once*, before her daughter Mrs Guy Wyndham comes back on Wednesday and finds that she is overdrawn at the bank (her daughter is her financial guardian). I would not promise, but I said I would put it to my principal, and if he was agreeable ask him to send a cheque for £10 at once to Lloyds Bank, 81 Edgware Road, W.C.2 for a/c Mrs Ernest Leverson. She is in a panic, and has been sending me express letters twice a day. So there it is, and I leave it to you.

By the way, you might ask Burdett what he thinks of the Letters of Lionel Johnson for a book. Would it sell at all? I could probably get them. The two in the April *Criterion* are samples out of a lot.[3]

Ever yours
T. S. E.

When do you move?

—

announced 'a new volume of *Critical Essays* by Osbert Burdett' and '*Collected Poems* by T. S. Eliot, containing *The Waste Land*, now out of print, together with many pieces no longer obtainable, and some not previously collected' (*TLS*, 10 Sept. 1925, 581).

1–TSE and GCF talked in person in the morning of 9 Sept.

2–TSE, *Poems 1909–1925* published by F&G on 23 Nov.

3–'Some Letters of Lionel Johnson', C. 3: 11 (Apr. 1925), 356–74: TSE had acquired these through Frederic Manning. Johnson's *Some Winchester Letters* came out in 1919, but it was not until 1988 that his *Selected Letters* appeared.

TO *Violet Schiff* CC

Wednesday, 8 September [?1925] 9 Clarence Gate Gardens

Dear Violet

Your letter does not bore me. What you tell me is not altogether news to me, although it gives me a fresh and stronger impression. And I think that it is tragic (I do not use such words frivolously).

I know perhaps more than you realise about the general case. And I think (whether you know it or not) that it is precisely this experience which is the bond between you and Vivien. I say that you may not know it, because she *never* speaks, even to someone who could best understand, about her own case. She is quite aware, as I am aware, that she is not primarily and primitively a *writer* – this has only come to her (lately) as a *partial* compensation for what she wanted. There were several things which came to her more naturally – *painting* – then bad eyesight – *music* – then an operation which crippled, for musical purposes, her right hand: but deepest and strongest, *dancing*. She had a genius for dancing – it was not until after she was married – too late for success, and with a constitution already ruined by neglect and misunderstanding – that she was even free enough to take up ballet training. Even then, and knowing that it was *too late* to *succeed* in that profession – her dancing gave her *far more* satisfaction and fulfillment than her writing has done or ever can do: until the unwise discouragement of a doctor, and *lack of encouragement* from anyone else, put an end to it. When she had that – even what she *did* have – she needed nothing else, and no other realisation of personality was necessary to her. You have only really known her *since* this failed. Lately, and only lately, she has created, by pure force of character, another occupation: it represents an immense victory of will.

You are, like her, essentially a *professional*: you are essentially a singer. I can understand what it means to you to be able to *train* someone else – to *create* someone else, for the material was *nil* – to do something of what you can no longer do. But you will I hope forgive me, if I say that I do not believe that *this* is your real compensation. It is not enough. You will, I hope and believe, find some other more direct means of expressing yourself – like Vivienne – in some other art or profession, rather than in training someone else in your own (for the people one trains are always disappointing – they are passive, inert, they never bring that intensity and conviction one has oneself, they live only with the life one infuses into them, they live on your blood – Vivienne knows *this* too).

You may say that even if you and Vivienne know these things, that I have no right to discuss them – because I have had a straight road, with no obstacles and no substitutions. It may be so, certainly it looks so, and I have *no grounds for regret*. I am not sure however that I have not been *forced* into poetry by my weakness in other directions – that there is not something else that I want – but at all events, I took this direction very young, and learned very early to find my life and my realisation in this curious way, and to be obtuse and indifferent to my reality in other ways. So it has been much easier for me. The admission of this fact may help you to admit that I understand in part the tragedy of others. But your letter seemed to require my explaining to you for Vivienne – as she never explains herself – the degree of resignation and the force of will and character which her present activities represent.

Yours ever aff.
[T. S. E.]

TO *Herbert Read* — MS Victoria

[9? September 1925] [London]

My dear Read

Thanks for your notes. I appreciate the force of your criticisms – some of the objections had already occurred to me. I had also thought of 'Cahiers de la Quinzaine' such as you suggest.[1]

Could you now suggest
approx. length of each Cahier –
four or six Cahiers p. annum?

A few names of people who *might* contribute? *Who* is there in this country?

I want to get all the suggestions out of you I can now, because I may be bringing this matter to a head *next week*.

Yours ever
T. S. E.

I will send you Bourquin's book.[2] It is not important, if you have read *Belphégor*.[3]

1 – The poet Charles Péguy published his *Cahiers de la Quinzaine* ['Fortnightly Notebooks'] from 1900 to 1914. On 31 July, TSE suggested *Cahiers* to HR as a title for his alternative review.

2 – Constant Bourquin, *Julien Benda, ou le point de vue de Sirius* (1925).

3 – Julien Benda, *Belphégor: essai sur l'esthétique de la présente société française* (1919).

TO *Wyndham Lewis* MS Cornell

[mid? September 1925] [London]

Thanks for yours. I am ill, harassed, impoverished, and am going to have five teeth out. I have managed to avoid seeing anyone for a very long time. I have several enemies. But the little matter you mention shall be attended to.[1] Best wishes.

T. S. E.

TO *Herbert Read* MS Victoria

14 September 1925 [London]

My dear Read

I am very glad to have your notes in. It is probable that the *Criterion* will be very late or else skip a number, but your notes will be used in any case.[2] It is also probable that the reorganisation of the *Cr.* will be instead of the additional periodical for which you sent me notes. Your notes shall be preserved, being most valuable, against the time when we can get someone to finance the scheme.

The details are not very interesting so I shall save them till we meet, when we must discuss the future programme of the *Criterion.*

Also, I have a proposal to make to you for writing a short book on *Bergson and his Critics* for a series on Foreign Writers.[3] I intend to do one on Maurras and get Aldington to do Gourmont. Etc. Can I persuade you to tackle this during the winter? Payment on receipt of ms.[4]

Yours in haste
T. S. E.

1–On 14 Sept., IPF sent WL a cheque for two guineas in payment for reviews for *C.* received from him the previous Apr. (but not published).

2–HR, 'American Periodicals', *NC* 4: 1 (Jan. 1926), 210–13.

3–GCF wrote to Mrs Gwyer, 9 Oct. 1925: 'we are now in a good way to coming to a definite arrangement with Lady Rothermere, under which she will continue her subsidy of £700 a year to "The New *Criterion*". I have not time to go into all the details of the arrangement; but I shall be very glad to have the use of this money, since we shall of course have to find a good deal of cash both for our book developments and for the weekly paper. Eliot himself has been through a bad time, and has not yet been able to help me very much outside "The *Criterion*"; but he is getting together what will, I believe, prove to be an important and valuable series of monographs on Foreign Writers, which we shall probably begin to publish next autumn. One or two other things are also coming to us through him – not money-makers but reputation-makers' (Faber Archive).

4–RA, whom HR consulted about this approach by TSE, wrote on 16 Oct.: 'Yes he approached me in the publisher's line and I believe I am vaguely committed to a Gourmont

TO *John Gould Fletcher* MS Arkansas

15 September 1925 9 Clarence Gate Gdns

Dear Fletcher

I have not written to you heretofore about your poem, because the *Criterion* is passing through a certain reorganisation. It was a question whether, with all the prose already accepted or ordered, I could find room for so long a poem. Probably the *Criterion* will not appear again till January – then in a larger form. But this means a still greater congestion of accepted stuff. Anyway – may I hold it? If not room for whole, could the Mississippi section appear alone?[1] I like it very much indeed.

Also, would you be interested in doing a book in a series in view, of which I am to be the general editor – a series on foreign writers. They will be short *critical* books (not much biographical matter) for English readers. Aldington will do Rémy de Gourmont, I shall do Charles Maurras – we thought you might do a Rimbaud. There is nothing in English that I know of but an atrocious book by Rickword.[2] Let me know if this interests you. Payment on receipt of ms.

Yours sincerely
T. S. Eliot

—

and a translation. But I never start a commission book until the contract is signed, so he won't get anything from me till he sends it . . . I suspect him, Herbert, most vehemently. There isn't an honest man in the whole goddam American race. *Il se fiche de nous*. We are his claque, his suite, his ladder, his footprints in the sands of Time, his stepping-stones to higher things . . . Eh lad, goo yer own weay, an' fook 'im . . .' ('Richard Aldington's Letters to Herbert Read', 20–1). RA had earlier grumbled to HR (17 Aug.): 'Make up your mind to this – T. S. E. sees nothing in any of us, we are a mere chorus of Theban old men useful as celebrators and disciples'; and he would return to this resentful theme on 2 Oct.: 'You know I've backed him very warmly, in public and in private; and shall continue to do so. But I have lost faith in him and I feel suspicious – I mean that I do most vehemently suspect him of condescension to us all and of making us his cat's paws' (ibid., 8–9). But see TSE's fuller proposal to RA, 26 Nov., below.

1 – 'The River Flows', *NC* 4: 1 (Jan. 1926), 46–7. As a native of St Louis, TSE may have relished Fletcher's account of the Mississippi: 'At St Louis we waited all morning with the roar of the trucks cutting across the cobbles, / The river swirling through the great arches of the bridge above us, / The mules flicking their ears aganst the flies'. Fletcher acknowledged to TSE (7 May) that it was influenced by *TWL* ('a poem no contemporary can afford to neglect'). TSE returned to his own memories of the river in *The Dry Salvages*, which he once said 'begins where I began, with the Mississippi' ('The Influence of Landscape upon the Poet', *Daedalus* 89: 2, Spring 1960, 422).

2 – Edgell Rickword, *Rimbaud: The Boy and the Poet* (1924).

TO *Richard Aldington* MS Texas

15 September 1925 *The Criterion*, 17 Thavies Inn

My dear Richard

Good.[1] It shall all be 'commission' work, with the Gourmont to begin with. Should like to have the anthology also – wd. urge it strongly on my people – *Can it be done so that the Introduction and the Book don't overlap*?[2]

About your series for *Vogue* – answer this at once – they have asked me to do an essay on contemporary American poetry, but I won't *if it will conflict in any way*.[3] Can you give me a better idea of what you are doing, with any suggestions for what I can do? Or I will offer some other topic.

Glad to hear all is well with you both.

Ever aff.
T. S. E.

TO *Antonio Marichalar*

MS Real Academia de la Historia

16 September 1925 *The Criterion*, 9 Clarence Gate Gdns

Mon cher ami

Vous êtes bien aimable de me prévenir – je serai ravi de vous voir. Malheureusement, je suis casé demain dans un 'nursing home', sous les soins de mon médecin et mon dentiste, pour une opération assez grave. *Si je suis assez rétabli* je vous enverrai une dépêche le vendredi matin, en espérant vous voir dans l'après-midi. Mais je vous prie de rester à Londres *jusqu'au dimanche*, afin que nous puissions nous faire la connaissance.

Bien cordialement votre
T. S. Eliot

<J'aurai beaucoup à vous dire.>[4]

1–On 1 Sept., RA said he would be grateful for 'any remunerative work'.

2–In addition to taking on the study of Rémy de Gourmont commissioned by TSE on 31 July, RA wanted to do an anthology; he later published *Selections from all his Works* (1929).

3–RA published 'Modern Free Verse' – 'The First of a Series of Articles Dealing with the Free Verse Movement in England and America, its History and its Results' – in *Vogue* 66: 6 (Late Sept. 1925), 57, 90: 'The only English poet . . . with much interest in Paris is the American T. S. Eliot.' The second appeared in *Vogue* 66: 11 (Early Dec. 1925) and included photographs of TSE, EP, Flint, JJ, H. D. and T. E. Hulme. TSE did not publish anything in *Vogue* in 1925–6.

4–*Translation*: 'My dear friend, It is very kind of you to let me know in advance – I shall be delighted to see you. Unfortunately, tomorrow I shall be shut up in a nursing-home, and in

TO *Richard Cobden-Sanderson* MS Texas

Received 21 September 1925[1] [London]

My dear Cobden

I am convinced that by this time I am either

1. Insane, and in concealment
2. Perpetually drunk and in concealment
3. Avoiding the Police and in concealment

It is however a fact which can be proved by application to the matron of the nursing home at 3 Mandeville Place, that I have had a damnable operation on my jaw. No-one warned me how serious it would be. I thought I should be well as ever the next day – went blithely and found two dentists, a doctor, an anaesthetist and a swarm of Scotch nurses and male coolies waiting for me – they chiselled and chipped and scraped at my jaw for an hour and I came out of the ether in the middle of the afternoon, cursing God. Now I am ordered to keep quiet for *several* days with an occasional hypodermic in my arse, as a treat.

However, I will come to see you by Thurs or Friday and meanwhile send my apologies and this list, which I cannot alter much. I have ticked those who ought to be paid first. Meanwhile I can write to you, at least. You will certainly be glad to see the last of me. What a blessing for you (and for many others) if I had never come out of the ether at all! I don't think anyone's patience has ever been tried more than yours.

Yours ever
T. S. E.

—

the care of my doctor and my dentist for a fairly serious operation. *If I have recovered sufficiently*, I shall send you a telegram on Friday morning, with the hope of seeing you in the afternoon. But please stay in London *until Sunday*, so that we can get to know each other.

Most cordially yours, T. S. Eliot

I shall have lots to tell you.

1 – Noted by RC-S.

TO *Geoffrey Faber* MS Valerie Eliot

21 September 1925 9 Clarence Gate Gdns

My dear Faber

Many thanks.[1] The operation was in fact more than expected – they were sawing away at my jawbone (under ether) for over an hour, and the doctor has kept me in bed ever since. I did not stay in the nursing home, I am back here.

I expect to be out tomorrow but it is unfortunate for me that the board meeting is fixed for Wednesday. My wife's doctor has just returned from his holiday and has fixed Wed., 3.15 for the first appointment, and I'm afraid I really must go with her. What I propose to do is to come to see you in the morning (Wed.) but if you prefer will come the following morning (Thurs.). I'll discuss the Cocteau business with you then.[2] I will write to Manning about the [Lionel] Johnson letters.

I return the draft agreement. I have been through it three times and fail to pick any holes in it – it seems to me *excellent*.

Are you settled yet?

I will see you on Wednesday unless I hear to the contrary.

Ever yours
T. S. E.

I am awfully sorry about Wednesday. Let me know if there is anything very important?

I have arranged three volumes of F. writers so far, besides my own.[3]

I will see Stewart when I come.

Vivien Eliot TO *Ottoline Morrell* MS Texas

Undated [late September 1925] [9 Clarence Gate Gdns]

Dearest Ottoline

Thank you *so* much for your letter, and for the previous letter which I liked very much indeed. I should have answered, but was upset and ill over

1 – GCF wrote (17 Sept.): 'When I wrote to you yesterday about Lady Rothermere, sending you my draft proposals for the contract, I had quite forgotten, under the stress of my own affairs, that you must be feeling very sorry for yourself after your encounter with the dentist; it is, as I know well, a miserable condition for the first few days. I hope you will soon get over that and I don't doubt that you will benefit immensely in the long run.'

2 – Rollo Myers's translations of Cocteau's prose appeared as *A Call to Order* (1926).

3 – The Foreign Men of Letters series outlined on 14 Aug.

Tom's operation. Thank you for your sympathy. He had some *terrible* trouble, of very long standing, under some dead stumps. Abcesis or osseoposis (or whatever it is called!) anyhow it was quite a *big* dental operation and they had to take a bit of the bone away too.

I have felt frightfully ill ever since – so shaken. Incredibly violent neuralgia. Tom is full of poisoning from his teeth and is now feeling *very* ill indeed and is having deep injections every day from our doctor. Let me write again in a few days. I am not very well today. I want to thank you and tell you how much I value your friendship.

Very affectly.
Vivien

Vivien Eliot TO *Ada Leverson* MS Berg

Undated [late September 1925] [9 Clarence Gate Gdns]

My dear Ada

Thank you so much for your kind letter, and your other very kind letters which I am afraid I did not answer at the time. You are very sympathetic. My husband's operation on the jaw *was* very bad, and it has made him feel very ill ever since. He has to have deep injections from his doctor every day, and you know what a horrid thing that is, it is so painful. I am not very happy at the moment, there are many worries, but soon we shall be going to Cambridge where my husband has a lecturing post and I am looking forward to it.

How exciting about your play! Of course it will be an immense success. Lucky for you to be going to Rapallo – everyone we know is at Rapallo at the moment.

Yes we hope Sachie will be happy with his bride.[1] I thought the Huxleys would be still in Paris as they were there so recently. I think Osbert will feel lonely, if they are going to have such a long honeymoon.

With love, and best wishes – and yes certainly its allright about the German rights –

Love from
Vivien

1 – Sacheverell Sitwell married Georgia Doble in Paris on 12 Oct. 1925.

TO *Thomas MacGreevy* MS TCD

22 September 1925 *The Criterion*, 17 Thavies Inn

Dear Mr MacGreevy

I must apologise for not answering your postcard. I have been in a nursing home for an operation.

The *Criterion* is being reorganised and will appear from another firm. Therefore it will probably not be published in October. How soon the first of the new series will appear I cannot yet tell. You may be sure I shall try to get your poem into the first issue.[1]

Meanwhile I shall be interested to see more of your work whenever you care to let me see it.

Sincerely yours
T. S. Eliot

TO *Herbert Read* MS Victoria

22 September 1925 *The Criterion*, 17 Thavies Inn

Dear Read

Many thanks for your letter. I will expose the situation to Faber at once, and I have no doubt he will be ready to sign a contract at once.[2] I will write to you in Yorkshire. You could then truthfully and without risk say that this volume has already been promised. I don't like to cut across the Woolfs in any way, but it means a tremendous lot to me to have your name in any way associated with mine.[3]

The Bergson book wd. be very short, and it wd. be £50 down. I do intend the series to have a purpose, though it will be necessary to include a few names without the purpose. I will explain fully when I write again.

Ever yr
T. S. E.

1 – MacGreevy's 'Dysert' was published, as by 'L. St. Senan', in *NC* 4: 1 (Jan. 1926), 94.
2 – TSE offered to publish a book of HR's essays in June.
3 – HR published *Mutations of the Phoenix* with Hogarth Press in 1923; and *In Retreat* was due from Hogarth Press in Oct. 1925. HR had also promised the Woolfs his next book. In her diary for 30 Sept., VW said they were 'on Tom's track, riddling him and reviling him': 'He won't let Read off that book, has been after him for three or four months' (*Diary*, III, 45).

TO *Geoffrey Faber* MS Valerie Eliot

[22? September 1925] *The Criterion*, 17 Thavies Inn

Dear F

Enclosed for your consideration before I see you. I think it is well worthwhile to make him an offer.[1] He is to do 'Bergson' for FML and I have already spoken of him to you.

Yrs in haste
T. S. E.

TO *Bonamy Dobrée* MS Brotherton

22 September 1925 *The Criterion*, 9 Clarence Gate Gdns

My dear Dobrée

I send this at random, hoping that it will reach you somewhere – perhaps you are in London! I am delighted to hear that you will be lecturing and working with Nicoll.[2] That is very good news.

I am in six minds about your brilliant dialogue.[3] I will explain when I know whether I am in communication with you. And I wonder whether it would interest you to do a small book – a critical essay – for cash – for a series of Foreign Writers which I am to edit? say on Pirandello? or whom? It is restricted only to writers of *living* influence on the Continent, whether alive or dead. e.g. I am doing Maurras and we shall probably include Ibsen, Renan – but the dead ones must be people who have not yet been adequately treated in English.

In any case, let me know that you get this letter.

Haven't bought a car yet. No money. Many thanks for tips, though. Come to the 'Show' on Oct. 9th!

Sincerely yours
T. S. Eliot

1 – The 'enclosed' must be a synopsis or MS of HR's book, published by F&G as *Reason and Romanticism* (1926).
2 – In 1925–6, BD was a lecturer at East London College (London University), where Allardyce Nicoll (1894–1976), author of *Restoration Drama* (1923), was Professor, 1924–33.
3 – 'Sir John Denham', a conversation between Bishop Henry King and Edmund Waller, *NC* 4: 3 (June 1926), 454–64.

TO *Herbert Read* MS Victoria

[late? September 1925] *The Criterion*, 17 Thavies Inn

My dear Read

My people are very anxious to arrange with you and ready to give a contract.[1] Will you let me know what sort of terms you want, and how much you ask as cash advance on delivery of MS. and I can probably get it settled at once.

Yours in haste
T. S. E.

TO *Wyndham Lewis* MS Cornell

24 September 1925 9 Clarence Gate Gdns

Dear Lewis

I enclose a statement from Cobden Sanderson of moneys paid you.[2] The extra £3.14.– can very well go in as additional payment for the reviews of January '25, which were long and very good. I will ask C.-S. to return you the cheque for two guineas which I sent on to him with your letter. This makes us square. Hereafter I have nothing to do with the financial end.

Yours
T. S. Eliot

TO *H. P. Collins* MS Private Collection

27 September 1925 *The Criterion*, 17 Thavies Inn

Dear Mr Collins,

I am very sorry about the delay which the contributors are enduring. It is due to the reorganisation of the *Criterion* and the absence abroad of one of the principals. I hope you can be paid soon. The *Criterion* is not to be discontinued, but there will probably be an interval before the appearance of the next no. with your *admirable* review of Saurat.[3]

1–See letter to HR, 22 Sept.

2–The statement of 'Contributions by Wyndham Lewis to *The Criterion*' itemised all of WL's contributions, from 'Mr Zagreus and the Split-Man' (Feb. 1924) to 'Art Chronicle' (Oct. 1924), and including three reviews for Jan. 1925 – the last two being marked as unpaid.

3–Collins, rev. of Denis Saurat, *Man and Thinker*, *NC* 4: 1 (Jan. 1926), 196–202.

I am very sorry indeed to hear of your illness. I hope it is not merely a *rest*, and not a source of any kind of worry to you?[1] We must meet in a month or two. I have just had an operation in a nursing home myself.

All best wishes

Sincerely yours
T. S. Eliot

TO *Viola Tree* CC

30 September 1925 9 Clarence Gate Gdns

Dear Miss Tree

Thank you for your letter. I had been meaning to write to you to warn you to hold up your Dramatic criticism for the next *Criterion* until you hear from me again. The reason is that the paper is being reorganised on a somewhat larger scale, and owing to the machinery of reorganisation we shall have either to postpone the October number or miss it out altogether. In any case I will let you know in good time.

As the new *Criterion* will be somewhat heavier and less frivolous than the old, I think that we shall have to omit the Mayfair and Bohemia gossip from its programme,[2] but on the other hand I should be very glad if you could continue to do the same, or rather longer, Dramatic notes on the same terms as before.[3] I assure you I consider that we are very fortunate to have you in charge of the Dramatic reviewing.[4]

If you are going abroad before Christmas, I hope that you will let me know, and that you will be able to let me have something before you leave. I look forward to seeing you again; as a matter of fact I have just come out of a nursing home where I had an operation on my jaw, so that I do not expect to be fit for much for some little time.

Yours sincerely
[T. S. E.]

1–Collins explained (29 Sept.) that he had been suffering from 'perpetual dyspepsia arising from a kind of nervous breakdown'.

2–Tree had contributed 'Mayfair and Bohemia' to C. 3: 10 (Jan. 1925), 282–3.

3–As 'Violet Ray', she was to write 'The Theatre', *NC* 4: 1 (Jan. 1926), 161–9: a discussion of contemporary plays by John Galsworthy and Fred Lonsdale as well as *The White Devil* ('a play of iridescent beauty like the multi-coloured water on the blackness of a morass'), *Dr Faustus*, and *The Wild Duck*.

4–Tree responded ('25th'): 'I shall have time to send you a slight notice on *Hamlet* as Violet Ray early tomorrow morning if you care to add it to the Theatrical News from New York (under Violet Ray of course).'

TO *Orlo Williams* CC

1 October 1925 9 Clarence Gate Gdns

Dear Williams,

I must apologise for the series of vicissitudes which prevented me first from reading your essay and second from writing to you – culminating in a minor operation since which I have only just left a nursing home. But I have read your essay and I want to keep it. On the other hand, I do not know just when I can use it. Owing to reorganisation under a new publisher, it is probable that we shall omit the October number, which is inconvenient in that it means a plethora of stuff of all sorts accepted for early publication. And I have your story which I want to work in as soon as I can, and it is rather a long one too.[1] So if you want to publish 'Tom Jones' quickly, and have an opportunity of doing so elsewhere, I do not want to stand in your way, though I should surrender it with great regret.[2] I shall keep it, therefore, for ultimate publication unless you now, or at any time, command me to return it. Incidentally, it makes me ashamed of being unacquainted with any other of Fielding's novels besides *Tom Jones*.

The whole volume ought to be a very interesting one. Is it already arranged for, or is there any possibility of my obtaining it for the new publishing firm with which I shall be associated – Messrs. Faber & Gwyer Limited? I should be very proud if I might lay it before them.

Yes, I hope we can meet before long and I will drop you a line when conditions are possible for me. Meanwhile, I should be delighted to hear from Carlo Linati.[3]

Yours sincerely,
[T. S. E.]

1 – See Orlo Williams's story 'Capitaine Ensorceleur', *NC* 4: 4 (Oct. 1926), 659–72.

2 – Williams had indicated on 4 May 1925: 'My attitude to T. J. is one of calculated admiration tempered by a personal inability to find it really entertaining.' He included a study of Henry Fielding's *Tom Jones* in *Some Great English Novels: Studies in the Art of Fiction* (1926), but his essay did not appear in *C*.

3 – Carlo Linati (1878–1949): Italian author and literary critic; translator of JJ, DHL, WBY and others. JJ sent him a famous plan of *Ulysses* which became known as 'The Linati Schema'.

TO *Thomas MacGreevy* TS TCD

2 October 1925 9 Clarence Gate Gdns

Dear Mr MacGreevy,

Thank you very much for your kind letter and for sending me the new poems which I shall write to you about later on.[1] I hope you may soon have a book ready.

I will do what I can to turn anything your way that may appear, but I cannot hold out very much hope at present in connection with the *Criterion*.[2] It will continue to be run for the present in a pretty modest way although on more businesslike lines than heretofore, and the chief difference for the present will be that I shall myself get just enough salary to be able to give a good deal of time to it. I ran it for three years without any salary and did practically all the work at home in the evenings. That is too much for anybody. I also have been a clerk and a schoolmaster in my time and I should not like to see you forced into either of those professions.[3] Of the two I think it is better to be a clerk.

As soon as I begin to get about and keep office hours, I shall ask you to come and see me. Meanwhile, write whenever you care to. I hope you have had your cheque by now.

Yours sincerely
T. S. Eliot

1–On 24 Sept., MacGreevy sent what he deprecated as 'rather frivolous' poems, which he hoped might 'divert a convalescent'. They included 'Evening Recalled', which he described as 'all that came of trying to write an essay' on TSE.

2–As 'L. St. Senan' MacGreevy reviewed George Moore's *Héloise and Abelard*, in *NC* 4: 2 (Apr. 1926), 368–71; and in subsequent issues he contributed articles on 'The Ballet'.

3–MacGreevy asked, 'is it beastly of me to ask whether there is any possibility of my being fitted in anywhere in the reorganisation [of the *Criterion*]? I must try to get regular work . . . And I don't want to clerk or schoolmaster if I can help it.' He had had 'a ridiculous job' at Lucerne in the summer, 'taking lower middle class English Nonconformists up the Alps'. When the Yeatses had dined with him there one day, Mrs Yeats asked 'Dare I eat a peach?' and declared him a 'poor Eliotite' when he had to guess at the source of her quotation.

TO *John Hayward*[1] TS King's

2 October 1925 9 Clarence Gate Gdns

My dear Sir,

I am much pleased and flattered by your kind invitation on behalf of your committee to read a paper to the 'Heretics'.[2] I should very much like to allow myself this privilege. But at present I cannot see my way to accepting definitely for either this term, next term or the summer term. As to the first, I am just recovering from an illness and have an enormous amount of writing and organising work ahead of me; as for the second, it will be all that I can do to deliver my Clark lectures and attend to my other business as well; as for the third, I should be delighted to speak then if I were in England, but it is possible that I may take at that time a much needed holiday abroad.

Knowing the reputation of your Society for merciless criticism of your speakers' weaknesses, I should want to be pretty carefully prepared; so that, esteeming it a great compliment to be invited, I am in effect paying you a compliment by declining – that is to say I dare not accept any engagement so important for another year.

With many thanks,

I am
Yours faithfully,
T. S. Eliot

1–John Hayward (1905–65), editor, critic and anthologist, studied modern languages at King's College, Cambridge. Despite the early onset of muscular dystrophy, he became a prolific and eminent writer and editor, bringing out editions of the works of Rochester, Saint-Évremond, Jonathan Swift, Robert Herrick and Samuel Johnson. Other publications included *Complete Poems and Selected Prose of John Donne* (1929), *Donne* (1950), *T. S. Eliot: Selected Prose* (1953), *The Penguin Book of English Verse* (1958), and *The Oxford Book of Nineteenth Century English Verse* (1964). Celebrated in addition as the learned and acerbic editor of *The Book Collector*, he was made a chevalier of the Légion d'honneur in 1952, and a CBE in 1953. He became one of TSE's closest friends, and shared a flat with him, 1946–57. Writers including Graham Greene and Stevie Smith valued his keen editorial counsel; and Paul Valéry invited him to translate his comedy *Mon Faust*. Hayward advised TSE on various essays, poems, and plays including *The Cocktail Party* and *The Confidential Clerk*, and (especially) *Four Quartets*. See Helen Gardner, *The Composition of 'Four Quartets'* (1978).

2–The Cambridge Heretics Society, founded by C. K. Ogden and others in 1908, boasted a distinguished list of visiting speakers, including VW – whose talk 'Character in Fiction' was published in C. 2: 8 (July 1924).

TO *Bonamy Dobrée* CC

2 October 1925 9 Clarence Gate Gdns

My dear Dobrée,

I am very glad that my letter reached you;[1] I felt almost certain that you must be in England, but it was quicker to write to your old address than to make enquiries.

I don't remember whether I congratulated you in my last letter on your new appointment – if not, it would be because I had not yet heard of it.[2] In any case let me say that I am delighted to think that we may have you fixed in London for a part of every year.

Ibsen is certainly a possibility and I want to talk to you about that as soon as I can, though I should have liked you to do Pirandello in any case. I can't make any engagements at present – I am just recovering from an operation – but I will write to you as soon as I can.

Yours sincerely,
[T. S. E.]

TSE/IPF

TO *Walter H. Shaw* CC

2 October 1925 [London]

Dear Mr Shaw,

Thank you very much for the interesting article.[3] I shall be delighted to use it if I can. I say 'If I can' because it is probable that owing to reorganisation under different publishers the *Criterion* will not reappear until January. It is a little difficult to know so far in advance what, and how much, I can accept, particularly in the way of more or less topical notes. But I should like to keep your article and use it if I can. As you are going to America it is impossible to consider bringing it up to date in any way for January, but I think the matter may retain its interest.

1–On 29 Sept., BD said he '*might* do Pirandello' for the Foreign Men of Letters series, but would prefer Ibsen if he was not already 'preoccupied'.
2–BD had been appointed lecturer in English at East London College (London University).
3–Shaw's 'Cinema and Ballet in Paris', *NC* 4: 1 (Jan. 1926), 178–84, covered Marcel l'Herbier's *L'Inhumain*, Picabia's *Entracte*, Satie's *Relâche*, and Cocteau's *Le Train Bleu*, among other films and ballets.

Please let me know at what address or addresses I can reach you for the rest of the year.

Yours sincerely
[T. S. E.]

TO *W. A. Thorpe* CC

2 October 1925 9 Clarence Gate Gdns

Dear Mr Thorpe,

It would give me great pleasure to have your criticism of the *Tess*,[1] but there are two reasons why it is difficult for me to accept. One is that owing to reorganisation the *Criterion* will probably not appear again until January, and it is difficult to plan for Dramatic criticism so far ahead. The other is that we have a standing agreement with a lady who prefers to write under a pseudonym[2] to provide Dramatic notes in every number, and I feel that it would be hardly fair to her to use Dramatic criticisms by anyone else, however interesting and valuable they were and however different the point of view.

I am very sorry about this because I want to interest you in the *Criterion* as much as possible. I hope that you will not only continue to review, but that you will also submit independent contributions. Will you let me know the moment you have any other ideas in mind for writing?

Sincerely yours,
[T. S. E.]

TO *Kate Buss* TS The Rev. Karl Schroeder, SJ

2 October 1925 *The Criterion*, 9 Clarence Gate Gdns

Dear Miss Buss,

I shall be very glad to inscribe your copy of my book on Ezra Pound.[3] If you will send it I will do this at once.

1 – A stage adaptation by Thomas Hardy of *Tess of the D'Urbervilles* which had been playing at the Barnes Theatre since early Sept.

2 – Viola Tree, alias Violet Ray.

3 – *Ezra Pound, His Metric and Poetry* (Alfred Knopf, 1917): it had been published anonymously in Jan. 1918, and its authorship made public in Knopf's *The Borzoi 1920* (New York, 1920).

Should I ever reprint this book I should of course put my name to it.[1] It did not seem advisable at the time for the reason that when I wrote it my name would have carried no weight whatever and would have probably have done the book more harm than good. That is to say it might have been suspected to be a bit of log rolling or back scratching or whatever one chooses to call it, instead of an independent piece of criticism. What I want to do is eventually to re-write it and bring it up to date and make it more of a critical study: because I have never yet adequately expressed my admiration of Pound as a poet and my *debt* to him as a tutor and critic.[2]

Sincerely yours,
T. S. Eliot

TSE/IPF

TO *Leonard Woolf* MS Berg

Thursday, 8 October [1925] [London]

Dear Leonard

I am very sorry indeed to hear that Virginia is in bed.[3] Please give her all my sympathy.

I am also sorry if my postcard was misconstrued. I did not for a moment suppose that Virginia had been able to do any work this summer. Therefore there was no suggestion: I was merely paying a clumsy compliment on a brilliant piece of writing.[4] No one living can write like that.

I should like to see you soon, but won't bother you in your present circumstances.

V. is much better.

Ever yours
T. S. E.

1–TSE never reprinted the book, but the text was included in *To Criticize the Critic and Other Writings* (1965). TSE later wrote: 'Ezra was then known only to a few and I was so completely unknown that it seemed more decent that the pamphlet should appear anonymously' (*The Cantos of Ezra Pound: Some Testimonies*, 1933).

2–Though TSE never revised *Ezra Pound, His Metric and Poetry*, he wrote an Intro. to EP, *Selected Poems* (F&G, 1928), and publicly declared his 'debt' to EP in the dedication of *TWL* first inserted in *P 1909–1925* (1925): 'For Ezra Pound, *il miglior fabbro*'.

3–VW's doctor was sent for on 5 Oct., and she was confined to bed for Oct. and much of Nov.

4–Unidentified: the postcard appears to be missing. TSE may have complimented VW on her lead essay on 'Swift's Journal to Stella', published anonymously in the *TLS* (24 Sept. 1925).

TO *John Gould Fletcher* MS Arkansas

9 October 1925 9 Clarence Gate Gdns

Dear Fletcher

I did not answer your letter because I thought you had left. I am very pleased indeed. The letter arrived punctually.

The book should be 30,000 to 40,000 words.[1] My people (Faber & Gwyer Ltd) want to *purchase* outright, in order to keep the series intact – the books ought to go on selling for many years. The terms (to all) are:

£50 – in two instalments –
£25 on recpt. of MS.
£25 on publication -

and 10% royalty on all sales after the first 3,000.

In haste

T. S. E.

The others so far are Aldington, Read, Dobrée, Muir and myself.[2]

TO *Ezra Pound* MS Beinecke

13 October 1925 9 Clarence Gate Gdns

Cher E.

Re enclosed,[3] esp. II III and IV can you tell me by return

(1) Is it too bad to print?

(2) If not, can anything be done to it? Can it be cleaned up in any way? I feel I want something of about this length (I–V) to end the volume as post-Waste,[4] but if you think it is

[incomplete]

1 – TSE had asked whether Fletcher was interested in writing on Rimbaud for the proposed Foreign Men of Letters series.

2 – RA was booked to write on Rémy de Gourmont; HR on Bergson; BD on French Symbolist Poets, Edwin Muir on Hugo von Hofmannsthal, and TSE on Maurras.

3 – Evidently 'The Hollow Men' I–V, due to appear in full in *P 1909–1925*.

4 – 'The Hollow Men' was the only work in *P 1909–1925* to postdate *TWL*.

TO *Marguerite Caetani* MS Caetani

13 October 1925 9 Clarence Gate Gdns

Dear Cousin

Very many thanks. I must tell you that I showed the Bioplastina circular to my doctor – he is an *Italian* and a very fine doctor – and he told me that he has a very high opinion of it and was actually the first doctor to introduce it in England – and he is giving *my wife* injections of it![1] He is giving me injections a little different, with iron.

I am afraid Virginia Woolf is very ill – I have not seen her, but her husband tells me she is in bed and must not work. When she is better I will try again. Meanwhile I will think of others.[2]

Yes, I will look in on Quaritch[3] and nose about. *Exactly what is he supposed to do?* Perhaps I could get my own firm to take it on – they are very active *new* people – if I knew what was wanted – and they could also arrange advertisements here etc. I think I could help in Oxford and Cambridge. You know I am going to lecture next term at Cambridge – and my principal, Geoffrey Faber, is a Fellow of All Souls College.

Always sincerely yours
T. S. Eliot

TO *Herbert Read* PC Victoria

[Postmark 17 October 1925] 9 Clarence Gate Gdns

I applaud with cheers your criticism of Keyserling. The true gospel. It shall lead off in January.[4] I will give you more news next week.

Yrs
T. S. E.

1–Bioplastina Serono. Serono was an Italian pharmaceutical company founded in Rome in 1906 by Cesare Serono, a doctor in chemistry and medicine, who extracted lecithin from egg yolks to create a tonic called bioplastina. It was used to treat anaemia and other conditions.
2–A ref. to possible contributors to *Commerce*, the Paris-based review financed by Caetani, 1924–32.
3–Bernard Quaritch, London booksellers.
4–HR's review of Count Hermann Keyserling, *The Travel Diary of a Philosopher* was the lead review in *NC* 4: 1 (Jan. 1926), 189–93. HR argued: 'To deny the objective reality of the content of knowledge can only lead to this now too familiar cult of the self – to this gospel of inwardness, to this denial of science, to "the ideal of personal perfection as opposed to that of professional efficiency."' Although Keyserling does not mention Rousseau, HR identified this as 'the same solitary voice that once broke the silence of the groves of Ermenonville!' (192).

<There are one or two good men on *The Calendar*[1] – only – we ought to absorb them. But I think W. Lewis is *indulging* himself – in style. Difficult and *lazy*.>[2]

TO *George Rylands* MS King's

20 October 1925 9 Clarence Gate Gdns

Dear Mr Rylands

I had been speculating for a long time about you, as you never answered the letter (enclosing MSS) which I sent in your envelope to an address near Bristol.[3] Will you set my mind at rest about this?

I shall be a little more at leisure next week, although I am still very much handicapped by my and my wife's ill health. I should like to drop you a line early next week, suggesting that you should call here or that you should have tea with me somewhere – meals are still rather difficult. I shall be very glad to meet you at last.

Sincerely yours
T. S. Eliot

TO *Geoffrey Faber* MS Valerie Eliot

Tuesday morning [20? Oct. 1925] 9 Clarence Gate Gdns

My dear Faber

This is to say that my solicitor has found a good deal of trouble. He considers that the triple agreement assumes me to be a proprietor – not a servant, etc: and in short he proposes to draft two agreements: F&G and Lady R., and F&G and myself (based on the one which I hold from you). He then wants to discuss these with me, and afterwards take it up with your people. This is all very tiresome.[4]

1 – *The Calendar of Modern Letters*, a literary review ed. Edgell Rickword and Douglas Garman, ran from Mar. 1925 to July 1927.
2 – WL's essay 'The Foxes' Case' appeared in *Calendar of Modern Letters* 2: 8 (Oct. 1925): divided into seven sections, it was later reprinted (with revisions) in *The Art of Being Ruled* (1926) and *The Lion and the Fox* (1927).
3 – TSE was returning the MS of *Russet and Taffeta*, published by the Hogarth Press in Dec.
4 – GCF responded (21 Oct.): 'I do think that it would be a great pity to insist on replacing the triple agreement by two other agreements, and I gather from his letter to you that he has now abandoned this idea.'

I was very glad to see you yesterday.

Yrs ever
T. S. E.

TO *Geoffrey Faber*

MS Valerie Eliot

Tuesday evening [20 October 1925] [London]

Dear Faber

Yes, I should like [you] to see Lady R. (Tinkerbell)[1] on Thursday and have so appointed with her. She is a fool and needs the impact of your impressive presence.[2] I think you can manage her allright, but she actually suggested that F&G ought to pay her something for the 'goodwill'. I pointed out that if there was any question of 'goodwill' for a review which I had built, I myself should come down on somebody for £300 representing the minimum loss to myself of running it for three years for nothing: also that F&G would have me anyway, and therefore would not consider the market value of the title, without me, very great. This left her rather pensive, but I think you should give her a final blow very quickly. She also wanted to turn it into a monthly at once – I replied that I should want more salary *and* an assistant editor, and that F&G would need more money to launch it.

On the other hand she is willing to sign an agreement for a much longer time, and to increase her subsidy later. However . . . .

I will have a word with you on Thurs. first. Have made appt. with her for 5.

Ever yours
T. S. E.

1 – Tinkerbell is a cantankerous fairy in J. M. Barrie's *Peter Pan*.

2 – GCF replied (21 Oct.): 'I will do my best to live up to the character which your letter ascribes to me; but I *am* sorry to say that I have a bad cold which may detract from the intended effect!'

TO *Geoffrey Faber* MS Valerie Eliot

[late October 1925] [London]

Dear Faber

I was very distressed about this morning, especially as you did not ring up again. I shall be in tomorrow and Sat. a.m. if he cares to come. Next week I shall be freer.

Bookshelf about 5 ft. high I should think, along one wall. Later we will cover the top with objets d'art.[1]

Graves – a good thing, I think:[2] will you ask him to write to me about it? Or as you please – if you prefer I will write to him.

I have asked my secretary to post you two copies of *Commerce* – which will remind you to remind me etc. I think there might be a little money and some good connexions in it. But we need not mention it for the present (in any case) to Lady R., as she and the Princess B.[3] are best kept apart.

Yrs. in haste
T. S. E.

TO *Herbert Read* PC Victoria

[Postmark 21 October 1925] [London]

Thanks for your card. I have not wanted to keep you (or anyone) in the dark, but have simply not had time to write. I shall now wait till after Thursday when there is a meeting of myself, Lady R. and Faber & Gwyer and can I hope give further news. Then I really want to see you as soon as the negotiations are over, next week and have a long talk.

My mistake – You were to hear from me. I was to find out from you how big a book[4] (how many words approx.) as the size of the cash in adv. royalty depends on that. Can you give me some details?

<T. S. E.>

Do you know what terms L. W.[5] would give? <I think we ought to better them.>

1–This was in connection with furnishing TSE's office at the new premises of F&G at 24 Russell Square, London.

2–See TSE's letter to Robert Graves, 27 Oct. (below).

3–Princess Marguerite Caetani di Bassiano, who financed *Commerce*, 1924–32.

4–HR's book of essays, to be published by F&G the following year.

5–LW wanted to publish HR's book with Hogarth Press. GCF proposed (23 Oct.) 'a £40 advance on a 10% royalty . . . pretty good terms for a book of essays which is not likely to

TO *E. M. W. Tillyard*[1] MS King's

26 October 1925 9 Clarence Gate Gdns

Dear Sir,

I am very sorry not to have answered your letter at once.

I cannot give you an outline of my lectures, which have not yet taken definite shape. But I shall deal especially with Donne, Crashaw and Cowley (three different types); only touching Marvell lightly, and shall mention Benlowes and Cleveland.[2] I shall make no attempt to be *comprehensive* – I only take representatives. An acquaintance with Waller and Denham ('Cooper's Hill') would be useful.[3]

Cowley's 'Mistress'; Crashaw's 'Weeper' and 'St Teresa' – it is impossible to select any one poem of Donne's.[4]

With thanks for your good wishes.

Yours very truly
T. S. Eliot

—

have more than a somewhat limited sale . . . Of course Woolf's terms "a quarter of the profits" are very much less advantageous to the author of a book like this, than a royalty with an advance.'

1–E. M. W. Tillyard (1889–1954): Renaissance scholar, Fellow of Jesus College, Cambridge and Secretary of the English Faculty; later author of *The Elizabethan World Picture: A Study of the Idea of Order in the Age of Shakespeare, Donne and Milton* (1942) and *Shakespeare's History Plays* (1944). Basil Willey dated the beginning of 'climatic change' in Cambridge English from the day Tillyard said 'there was a new chap called T. S. Eliot for whom one should be on the look-out' (*Cambridge and Other Memories* [1968], 267).

2–TSE devoted four of the eight Clark lectures to Donne (lectures 2–5), with the sixth devoted to Richard Crashaw (1612–49) and the seventh to Abraham Cowley (1618–67). He had written about Marvell in *HJD* (1924), and Marvell scarcely figured in the lectures: TSE argued that Marvell was 'not at his best really metaphysical at all'; he was 'verbally conceited, but not metaphysical in spirit' (135). In the same lecture he declared the poetry of John Cleveland (1613–58) 'not very remunerative', and said of Edward Benlowes (?1602–76) that 'his verses, like those of Miss Gertrude Stein, can, for anyone whose taste has already been disciplined elsewhere, provide an extremely valuable exercise for unused parts of the mind' (137).

3–Edmund Waller is scarcely mentioned. In the lecture on 'Cowley and the Transition',TSE quoted 'Cooper's Hill' by John Denham (1615–69) as an instance of the 'new poetry' arising alongside Cowley's (195).

4–In the lecture on Cowley TSE emphasised 'the vast difference between the lyrics of Donne and the *Mistress* of Cowley' (187). This is a reference to *The Mistress: or, Several Copies of Love-Verses* (1647). In the lecture on Crashaw TSE discussed his 'Sainte Mary Magdalene or The Weeper' from *Steps to the Temple* (1646), and argued that his two 'most remarkable poems' are those to St Theresa: 'To the Name and Honour' and 'To the Book and Picture' (178).

TO *Herbert Read* MS Victoria

27 October 1925 [London]

My dear Read

I put the cards on the table: see enclosed. So why not just decide what are the best terms for you, and let Woolf and myself know on that basis?[1] I don't want to embroil you, or myself for that matter, with the Woolfs who are old friends of mine, and this seems to me perfectly fair – So make up your mind!

More later about other matters.

Ever yours
T. S. E.

But remember that I am very keen to have the essays![2]
Please return enclosure.

TO *Robert Graves* MS Morris

27 October 1925 9 Clarence Gate Gdns

Dear Graves

Thanks for your very interesting letter. I should be honoured to collaborate in such a work: my only doubt is whether, with the little time at my disposal, and the multitude of tasks undone, I can ever find the time for it.[3]

I have promised to write a short article for *Vogue*, in which, dealing with American poets alone, I should classify in three groups according to sophistication of sensibility.[4] This might be somewhat on the line –

It would not matter, I think, if we did not altogether agree, so long as we made our differences conspicuous and *interesting*.

I am not quite clear as to whether this is to be an *anthology* or merely essays with specimens? I should incline to the latter: there have been many anthologies, and I believe that a friend of mine is now preparing a new one of *American vers libres*.

1 – See note to postcard of 21 Oct.
2 – The essays by HR that would comprise *Reason and Romanticism*.
3 – Graves invited TSE to collaborate on a study of modern poetry – GCF had referred to it earlier, in a letter to Graves (14 Oct.), as a 'critical survey'. Although this came to nothing, Graves went on to collaborate with Laura Riding on *A Survey of Modernist Poetry* (1928).
4 – TSE's projected article was not written.

I approve of most of your names, but should add Gertrude Stein, without doubt, and perhaps Mina Loy.[1] I question Aldous Huxley and Bynner,[2] and I don't know Davidson;[3] there are two or three more Americans: Wallace Stevens, W. C. Williams, and I think Lindsay ought not to be out of it.[4] Frost (though very good at times) seems to me for this purpose obsolete.[5] I should not like to omit T. E. Hulme. What about Wilfred Owen?[6]

Might there be a chapter on the relation of such verse to certain modern prose – Joyce etc.?

These are merely suggestions. I hardly know whether to wish you to Liverpool or Cairo[7] – in either case you are lost to Oxford and London. But I wish you whichever you want.

What do you think of an *international* survey – English, French, German – or is it too ambitious and troublesome? One would have to include Cocteau, Cendrars, Sternheim, and the like.[8]

Ever yours sincerely
T. S. Eliot

1–Mina Loy (1882–1966): British/American poet and polemicist; author of *Lunar Baedeker* (1923) and 'Feminist Manifesto'. She was a friend of Gertrude Stein and Djuna Barnes, and much admired by William Carlos Williams.

2–Witter Bynner (1881–1968): US poet and scholar. In 1916 he was responsible for the *Spectra* hoax – a parody of *Imagism* – and later for influential translations from the Chinese, including *The Jade Mountain* (1929).

3–Donald Davidson (1893–1968): US poet and critic. With John Crowe Ransom, he was a founding contributor to *The Fugitive* magazine and a leading Southern Agrarian.

4–Wallace Stevens (1879–1955): US poet; author of *Harmonium* (1923). TSE later published his *Collected Poems* (1955). Although TSE did not publish William Carlos Williams, he seems to have shared some of Pound's enthusiasm. Vachel Lindsay (1879–1931) was the author of the hugely popular *General Booth Enters Heaven and Other Poems* (1913).

5–On 9 Aug. 1920 TSE had told his mother he had 'never had much interest in Frost's poetry' – though he was 'better than most others'. Graves later introduced *Selected Poems of Robert Frost* – 'the first American who could be honestly reckoned a master-poet by world standards'.

6–Wilfred Owen (1893–1918): poet of WW1. This is a rare mention of Owen by TSE.

7–Graves took up a Chair at the University of Cairo in 1926.

8–TSE published Cocteau's 'Scandales' in *NC* 4: 1 (Jan. 1926), and *A Call to Order* (F&G, 1926). Blaise Cendrars (1887–1961) was a French-Swiss novelist who had recently published *L'or* (1925), trans. H. L. Stuart as *Sutter's Gold* (1926). Carl Sternheim (1878–1942) was a German dramatist and short-story writer.

TO *Ezra Pound* MS Beinecke

28 October 1925 9 Clarence Gate Gdns

Cher E –

Havnt all of your works here i.e. have (or V. has) *Provença* but not *Personae* or *Exultations*.[1]

Canzoni:[2]	*include*	'Of Incense'
		'Of Angels'
		'Na Audiart'✓
Provença:[3]	*include*	'Famam Librosque'✓
		'In Temp. Senect.'
		'Camaraderie'
		'Idyll for Glaucus'
		'Piccadilly'
		'Night Litany'✓
		'Altaforte'✓
		'Planh for the Y.K.'✓
		'Alba'
		'Laudantes'
Ripostes:[4]	*include*	'Akr Çaar'✓
		'Portrait d'une Fme.'✓
		'N.Y.'✓

1 – At EP's request TSE compiled this list for possible inclusion in a UK edn of *Personae* (New York, 1926). EP's ticks on the letter are shown. None of the suggested omissions was accepted and some of the proposed inclusions were rejected. See TSE's intro. to EP's *Selected Poems* (F&G, 1928): 'Mr Ezra Pound recently made for publication in New York a volume of "collected poems" under the title of *Personae*. I made a few suggestions for omissions and inclusions in a similar collection to be published in London; and out of discussions of such matters with Pound arose the spectre of an introduction by myself' (vii).

2 – *Canzoni* (London: Elkin Mathews, 1911). 'Na Audiart' was first published in *A Lume Spento* (1908); 'Canzone: Of Incense' and 'Canzone: Of Angels' in *Canzoni* (1911). 'Of Incense' was included in *Selected Poems* (1928) under the heading of 'Early Poems Rejected by the Author and Omitted from his Collected Edition'.

3 – *Provença* (Boston: Small, Maynard, 1910) was the first US edition of EP's work and included poems from *Personae* (Elkin Mathews, 1909) and *Exultations* (Elkin Mathews, 1909). The poems listed are: 'Famam Librosque Cano', 'In Tempore Senectutis', 'Camaraderie', 'Idyll for Glaucus', 'Piccadilly', 'Night Litany', 'Planh for the Young English King', 'Alba Innominata' and 'Laudantes Decem Pulchritudinis Johannae Templi'. Of these, 'In Tempore Senectutis', 'Camaraderie' and 'An Idyll for Glaucus' were included as 'Early Poems Rejected by the Author' in *Selected Poems*.

4 – *Ripostes* (London: Stephen Swift & Co., 1912). The poems named are: 'The Tomb at Akr Çaar', 'Portrait d'une Femme', 'N.Y.', 'A Girl', 'Quies', 'The Seafarer', 'Echoes', 'An Immorality', 'Δωρια', 'A Virginal', 'Pan is Dead', 'The Picture', 'Jacopo del Sellaio' and 'The Return'. All except 'An Immorality' were included in *Selected Poems*.

'A Girl'✓
'Quies'✓
'Seafarer'✓
'Echoes'
'An Immorality'
'Δωρια'✓
'A Virginal'✓
'Pan is Dead'✓
'The Picture'✓
'Jacopo del S.'✓
'The Return'✓

Include *Cathay*[1] entire.

From *Lustra*[2] omit 'Millwins'
'Bellaires'
'Cake of Soap'
'Simulacra'
'Social Order'
'Ancient Music'
'Contemporaries'
'Housman's Message'

Include everything else.

Omit 'Contemporanea'[3]
Except 'I Vecchi[i]' and
'The Old Lady'.

Include Mauberley[4] entire.

I think these are all my suggestions. Send me a review copy. Many thanks for suggestions. The good Eliots do not understand the conduct of this world's affairs. In fact, they understand them *so* badly[5] –

Yrs
T.

1 – *Cathay* (1915): seventeen poems from *Cathay* were included in *Selected Poems*.

2 – *Lustra* (London: Elkin Mathews, 1916; New York: Knopf, 1917). The omitted poems are: 'Les Millwin', 'The Bellaires', 'The New Cake of Soap', 'Simulacra', 'The Social Order', 'Ancient Music', 'Our Contemporaries' and 'Song in the Manner of Housman' ('Mr Housman's Message'), originally published in *Canzoni* (1911).

3 – 'Moeurs Contemporaines', published in *Quia Pauper Amavi* (London: The Egoist, 1919). 'I Vechii' is number VII, 'Ritratto' ('The Old Lady'), number VIII in the eight-part sequence, all of which was included in *Selected Poems*.

4 – *Hugh Selwyn Mauberley* (1920) was included in full in *Selected Poems*.

5 – With the substitution of his surname TSE is quoting the opening lines of 'The Bellaires', one of the poems (from *Lustra*) that he proposed to omit. It begins: 'The good Bellaires / Do not understand the conduct of this world's affairs. / In fact they understand them so badly / That they have had to cross the Channel' (*Poems and Translations*, 276).

TO *Virginia Woolf* MS Texas

28 October 1925 9 Clarence Gate Gdns

My dear Virginia

It was a delight to see your handwriting again. We are so glad that you are so much better. I have intended for days and days to look in and ask how you were – because I know what a nuisance the telephone can be; but I have been *very* busy, not very well, and Vivien has had a bad chill.

I will write again shortly – meanwhile, if you can let me have the essay within a fortnight that would be capital, and it wd appear *in the middle of January.*[1] And after that, I want another one for *Commerce*![2]

Ever yours
T. S. E.

TO *Robert Graves* TS Morris

2 November 1925 9 Clarence Gate Gdns

Dear Graves,

Many thanks for your second letter which makes the subject still more interesting.[3] I return your list with a few names added which I think inadvisable to omit. Some of these people, as you yourself suggested, could be dealt with together. I have also marked with an X the people whom I should like to tackle myself. I notice that neither of us is tempted by D. H. Lawrence. I still query Frost because although he has done good work it does not seem to me modern enough to fall within the scope of this book, but I may be wrong.

I think now that an international study is too ambitious, and perhaps confusing, but I think that I should like to touch on certain foreign writers in my essay.

There is one thing which is certain and that is that I cannot tackle such a work for a full year. After I have finished my Cambridge lectures I must try to write a book on Charles Maurras. So that if you can do the book before then by yourself, by all means do it: it will be none the worse for the lack of my collaboration.

1 – See VW ,'On Being Ill', *NC* 4: 1 (Jan. 1926), 32–45.
2 – See TSE's letter to Caetani, 13 Oct.
3 – See TSE's letter to Graves, 27 Oct. Graves's letter appears to be missing.

I have crossed out my own name. It seems to me that we shall have to forego the pleasure of doing each other!

Yours ever sincerely,
T. S. Eliot

I enclose a circular of the *Criterion* simply to let you know what is happening.

TO *W. G. Johns*[1] CC

2 November 1925 [London]

Dear Mr Johns,

This letter is private. I have no objection to your shewing it to Mr Crofton,[2] and making any use of it that may be necessary; but afterwards I should be glad if you would destroy it.

This letter is to convey, first, the resignation which you must have been expecting for several months. It is of course not so much the resignation as the delay in resigning which demands explanation.

I wrote to you long ago to say that I must seek some employment which would give me the time to attend to my domestic anxieties. This I have found. I should have written this letter weeks and weeks ago but that I quite literally have had no moment of time in which to write it. The inevitable term has come to this situation, my wife has been sent to a nursing home in the country by Sir William Willcox,[3] and I am being sent on a voyage by the insistence of my doctor and the kindness of friends.

For a long time, even after recognising that I must resign, I was the dupe of my own conscience, and hoped that I should be able to return to give the Bank a month or two of work. This I regarded and regard as the only honourable course. From week to week I was deceived by appearances of improvement, alternating with regression. I ought to have recognised the facts much sooner than I did.

As for myself, I shall earn a sufficient income if I have the strength and brain to do so. If not, at any rate I shall not be encumbering the Bank, and I shall be in a position where my defaults can no longer provide a bad example to others. It will be the publishing firm of Faber & Gwyer Limited, and Trinity College, Cambridge, that will suffer, not the Bank, which has already suffered too much.

1 – W. G. Johns: Assistant General Manager (Administration), Lloyds Bank Head Office.
2 – H. C. Crofton: senior manager in the Colonial & Foreign Department at Lloyds.
3 – Sir William Willcox, KCIE (1869–1941), consultant physician.

I had two other reasons, besides honour, for wishing to return for a time. First, I should have liked to see the Intelligence Section a reality – it has never been more than the aspiration of a few persons, including myself. If I may now speak frankly, as an outsider, it seemed to me unfair that this Section should be charged upon the Colonial and Foreign Department – unfair to the Section, which was starved, and unfair to the Department, which was taxed. I should have liked to see the Section established on a proper basis before I left. And I should have liked to see it detached from the Credit Information Service with which it has no sort of relation.

My other reason is still more compulsive. Fearing – without conceit, for I reflected that a bad excuse serves in the world better than none – that my resignation would be made the excuse for further indefinite postponement, very likely even for the destruction of the rudimentary section which exists, I have felt very gravely my obligations toward my colleague Mr J. D. Aylward.[1] I am quite aware that his 'case' has already been fully considered. But – with all respect and without prejudice – injustice not only remains injustice, but has been enormously aggravated. For Mr Aylward has performed his work and that which was mine, alone since January; he has had one week of holiday and no more, and this only in October; he has had the responsibility without the authority of the Head of a Section, with scant respect and little aid, I sincerely believe (for this is my belief based on previous observation, not on complaints from him; he has not complained to me) from those who dislike to take orders or advice from a 'supplementary' man. It is bad enough that he should remain in his present situation; it would be worse if he were now degraded to some inferior or less agreeable post. It would be the source of endless regret and self-reproach to myself. In his letters to me, Mr Aylward has aimed even to conceal his own fatigue and anxieties, and has aimed always to raise my spirits and divert my mind from my troubles. The very least I can do – and it is no more than the most detached critic would do – is to make a final plea for the reform and improvement of his status.

But this concern does not blind me to the fact that in *my* relations with the Bank, the position is quite the reverse. It is only an instance of the invariable irony of life that I, who have done so shabbily by the Bank and deserved so little of it, should have met with such uncommon and consistent kindness there. From Mr Harrison,[2] of whom many spoke with animosity, I received the most unusual consideration from the moment

1–James de Vine Aylward (1871–1966).

2–E. J. Harrison was secretary to the Bank when TSE joined it; in 1919 he became Joint General Manager.

when he took me into the Bank with no enquiry for the credentials which I might have provided; I, from my own experience of him, must hold his memory in respect. For Mr Stevenson[1] and Mr Crofton, I have an intimate and affectionate regard; their abundant generosity and sympathy I shall never forget. It was a great pleasure to me to work under the supervision of Mr Paine[2] and Mr Barchard.[3] There are many who have been kind to me, few whom I have disliked. It is only because it is you to whom I write, that I put your name at the close: I have not forgotten your generous patience when I came to you at one or two moments of great distress of mind.

At this time, all my feelings are numb; but I know that it is, and I fear always will be, very painful to me to have severed my connection with Lloyds Bank in this way – a way which could justly be qualified as desertion rather than resignation.

Sincerely yours,
[T. S. E.]

I am not at my own address; at my doctor's solicitation I removed at once; and am this week at 58 Circus Road, St Johns Wood, N.W.8.[4]

TO *Signora Celenza* CC

2 November 1925 [London]

Dear Madam,

I must apologise for not having let you know more quickly about the enclosed manuscript.[5] As I think I told you, I submit all contributions on musical subjects to the editor of our Musical Chronicle. He speaks very highly of this article but considers that it requires more familiarity with contemporary Italian operatic work than can be assumed on the part of an English audience. That, of course, is the difficulty about any critical essay on foreign work – that it is apt either to tell the British Public what it knows already or to tell it what it does not understand. It is not meant that this essay is not of very high critical value; the author is obviously a first rate musical critic; only that it is not perfectly fitted to our audience.

1 – W. M. Stevenson was a General Manager's Assistant.
2 – W. W. Paine was a Joint General Manager 1919–25; Director, 1925–45.
3 – E. H. Barchard was a Principal in the Legal Department.
4 – Lady Rothermere's London residence. On 8 Dec., Dr Hubert Higgins recommended TSE to return there again after his trip to France.
5 – A MS on Italian opera by Fernando Liuzzi.

I am still hoping to receive some contribution from yourself,[1] but anything you can send us by other Italian writers, whether critical or creative, will always receive a welcome.

Sincerely yours,
[T. S. E.]

TO *Ellen Taylor*[2] CC

2 November 1925 [London]

Dear Madam,

Mr Eliot is very sorry indeed that he has not been able to see you but he has had to leave London for some weeks under doctors' orders. He asked me to say that he very much enjoyed your story[3] but that he felt that the atmosphere was too emphatically American to be intelligible to the majority of readers of the *Criterion*. He hopes that you will have other material to submit later.

Yours faithfully,
For the Editor of the *Criterion*,
[I. P. Fassett]
Secretary

FROM *Vivien Eliot* MS Valerie Eliot

[Postmark 2 November 1925] Elmsleigh, Bassett, Southampton[4]

Dear Tom

Please give access to Mother to see to my clothes. Do not let the flat. I must also *have Ellen* and I can pay her wages if you do not wish to keep her.

I apologise for having upset you. But I take it you are being helped over it. Try not to allow yourself to be led around by the nose by Higgins and Rothermere. It is undignified. Remember you go all out for things and we must both do our *own* thinking. Alone. I have such good clever nurses that I am glad now to be here.

1 – She never contributed to *C.*
2 – Ellen du Pois Taylor contributed to *The American Mercury* and the *Transatlantic Review*; she wrote to TSE from London, where she was visiting, with a request for an interview.
3 – 'One Crystal and a Mother', which Ford Madox Ford suggested she send to TSE.
4 – Dr Hubert Higgins had arranged for VHE to be treated at a nursing home near Southampton.

Will you please arrange at once to send me my *cheque book*. Put *Jack* [Culpin] in our flat while you go away if you are going.

Leopard skin coat. *Money cheques books* and Lulu must not be sacrificed. She also has her rights. The only safe thing I can think of if you are going away is to put her in the hands of the best Vet you know.

I am sorry I tortured you and drove you mad. I had no notion until yesterday afternoon that I had done it. I have been simply raving mad. You need not worry about me. I am really being saved but its hard work [illegible word]. Get the money from Father.

[Incomplete; unsigned]

<Please write to this doctor instantly and tell him the truth, that we have had sexual relations>[1]

<if you can>

<Do these things for me. Especially about our married life and make him see it *had* been good. All here believe not. Also explain about the scars on my back. I don't *blame* West now. I wish I could see him.>

FROM *Geoffrey Faber* — MS Valerie Eliot

3 November 1925 — 7 Oak Hill Park, Hampstead N.W.3

My dear Eliot,

I am only just back from Oxford to find your letter waiting for me, and being rather weary I am writing and not – the obvious thing to do – ringing you up.

I am glad, for your sake and I include in that phrase your wife's sake, that your doctor has had his way. But I can understand your own state of mind. You have fought a losing battle, and you feel the reaction now that the issue is decided. It must have been a very bitter experience, and – oh well, what can I say except that I am sorry for you both from the very bottom of my heart? Anyhow, you have done your best and the responsibility is now on other people's shoulders, and I can't but think that your wife will find herself more quickly again in a nursing home than she ever could in the familiar round of associations. As for you, I am thankful to hear of your Riviera voyage. Do not make it too short. We will see to the mechanical production of the paper – if you will make sure of the copy.

I don't know if Lady R. has responded to my letter, to the office. But the affair *must* be settled now; and I want to see you about this and one or two

1 – This and the following passages are written in the margins of the two-page MS.

other matters. I wonder if you wld. come to dine here with my wife and myself early tomorrow. A new maid, and the nurse is out – but you won't mind that, I expect? Ring me up (if you can get my number!) at the office tomorrow morning. Gerrard 2734.

About All Souls. I do think it will ultimately go through: but we will talk of this when we meet.[1]

Yours ever
GCF

PS Certainly we will take the cat; and eke the maid – or at any rate can find her the right sort of place. So don't despatch her till I see you!
Your letter is combusted.
<PPS My wife says – please, if you can, ring me up *here* (Hampstead 4839) *before* 9.30 a.m.>

TO *Gorham B. Munson*[2] CC

3 November 1925 [London]

Dear Mr Munson,

I have had my eye on you for some time, clearly enough to ensure a welcome to any contribution you send. I accept your article on Irving Babbitt,[3] whose work I have always wished to make better known here. I cannot tell how soon we can use it, and I hope you will not be impatient with me if there is some months' delay.[4] When one issue of a quarterly

1 – GCF recorded in his diary (Sat., 31 Oct.): 'Coll. Meeting. Eliot's election [as Research Fellow] postponed at Simm's instance. Fairly no doubt; but a disappointment.' On 3 Nov.: 'College meeting. Elected Rowse & Makins, both historians & both of the House [Christ Church, Oxford].' (Faber Archive)

2 – Gorham B. Munson (1896–1969): American critic; founder-editor of the magazine *Secession*. He taught at the New School for Social Research, New York; and his publications included *Destinations: A Canvas of American Literature since 1900* (1928) and *The Awakening Twenties: A Memoir-History of a Literary Period* (1985). He published 'The Esotericism of T. S. Eliot' in *1924* 1 (July 1924), 3–10.

3 – At Harvard, TSE took Irving Babbitt's course on Literary Criticism in France. He wrote later that Babbitt's 'ideas are permanently with one, as a measurement and test of one's own' (*Irving Babbitt: Man and Teacher*, 1941, 103–4). His essay 'The Humanism of Irving Babbitt' appeared in *Forum* 80: 1 (July 1928); reprinted in *SE*.

4 – In 'The Socratic Virtues of Irving Babbitt' (*NC* 4: 3, June 1926, 494–503), Munson argued that Babbitt was a 'figure to be reckoned with in any discussion of "culture and anarchy"'; to be read in conjunction with Matthew Arnold, Paul Elmer More, Pierre Lasserre and Julien Benda.

review is omitted, as the enclosed circular will show, a frightful congestion of material ensues.

Yours very truly,
[T. S. E.]

TSE/IPF

TO *B. G. Brooks* CC

3 November 1925 [London]

Dear Mr Brooks,

I owe you many apologies for not answering your first letter and for not acknowledging your manuscript.[1] I am all the more to blame as I feel that I have given you unnecessary trouble. I can only say that I have been so engaged in personal business for the last two months that I have hardly been able to attend to editorial duties at all. The reorganisation of the *Criterion*, also, has taken a great deal of time. You will see from the enclosed circular that no number has appeared this autumn, and for that reason the January number will be a very bulky one. Had there been an October number I should have sent your manuscript to J. B. Trend. It interested me very much, but as I have given all musical matters into his control I could not accept any contribution without his approval. I hope that you will forgive me and that you will make other suggestions and will send other contributions of both verse and prose.

Yours sincerely
[T. S. E.]

TSE/IPF

TO *F. S. Flint* CC

3 November 1925 *The New Criterion*, 24 Russell Sq, London

My dear Flint,

I am sorry to spring this on you so abruptly, but I really have not had the opportunity to write to you or to anybody before now. Could you let us have some French, Italian, Scandinavian and Brazilian notes by the 15th

1–On 1 Oct., Brooks sent an article on the Venice Festival of Chamber Music held in Sept. This piece was never published, and Brooks did not publish in C. again.

November? At any rate as much as you can manage.[1] And if so would you please send it direct to Faber & Gwyer, see enclosed circular. I have been struggling to realise this design for some months. The *Criterion* will go on just as before and I hope that it will eventually become more lucrative for the regular contributors who have made it what it is.

I am writing in great haste as I expect to leave in a few days for a short holiday. I should like very much to see you when I get back.

With all best wishes,

Yours,
[T. S. E.]

TSE/IPF

TO *T. Sturge Moore*[2] CC

3 November 1925 23 Adelphi Terrace House

Dear Mr Sturge Moore

I am very much honoured at receiving an unsolicited contribution from you, and one of so much interest. The January number is already made up but I should like very much to publish this essay later if possible.[3] On the other hand I should not like to stand in the way of your publishing it elsewhere in the meantime if you wish to do so, but I think we could certainly bring it out in April, or in April and July.

I am leaving for a short holiday, but am giving your manuscript into the hands of my secretary for safe keeping. If you should wish to publish it elsewhere, will you write to her at 23 Adelphi Terrace House, Robert Street, W.C.2. But I hope to find the manuscript still here on my return.[4]

1 – For *NC* 4: 1 (Jan. 1926), Flint contributed notes on Italian and Danish Periodicals, but said that 'owing to an accident' he was unable to contribute as usual on French Periodicals.
2 – Thomas Sturge Moore (1870–1944), English poet, playwright, author and wood engraver, published his first book of poems, *The Vinedresser and Other Poems*, in 1899. His brother was the philosopher G. E. Moore. A friend of many writers, including A. E. Housman and Aldous Huxley, he also designed bookplates and bookbindings for W. B. Yeats. See *W. B. Yeats and T. Sturge Moore: Their Correspondence, 1901–1937*, ed. Ursula Bridge (1953); and Frederick L. Gwynn, *Sturge Moore and the Life of Art* (1951).
3 – Sturge Moore, 'A Poet and his Technique' (on Paul Valéry), *NC* 4: 3 (June 1926), 421–35.
4 – Moore replied (10 Nov.) that he was 'quite content to wait'.

I presume that the enclosed circular has already been sent to you. The review will go on just as before, except that I shall now have a salary and shall be able to devote more time to it.

With very many thanks,
[T. S. E.]

TSE/IPF

TO *Herbert Read*

TS Victoria

3 November 1925 — *The Criterion*, 9 Clarence Gate Gdns

My dear Read,

This is a hasty note to thank you for your post card and to say that I had done nothing yet about any of the Russian writers for the reason that many books about them have appeared in the last few years. There is, for instance, Gerhardie's *Chekov*,[1] but I think that they ought certainly to be dealt with, though not in the first batch, and I should like to know about your man.

I have sent your letter on to Faber and asked him to communicate with you direct as to when he wants your manuscript, etc. I have also recommended him to accept the poems.[2] I should have liked to see you. I may be going away within the next few days, but if I see any opportunity I shall ring you up at the Museum.

Ever yours,
T. S. E.

TSE/IPF

TO *Orlo Williams*

CC

3 November 1925 — 9 Clarence Gate Gdns

Dear Williams,

I must apologise for the delay in sending you the Murry book[3] which is due to the preoccupations of private business. In the circumstances I have no right to press you, but if you could possibly deal with this in about a thousand words and send it direct to Messrs. Faber & Gwyer Limited

1–William Gerhardie, *Anton Chekhov: A Critical Study* (1923).
2–HR, *Collected Poems, 1913–25* (F&G, 1926).
3–JMM, *Keats and Shakespeare* (1925).

(28 Southampton Street, Strand, W.C.2) by November 15th at the latest, I should be very grateful indeed. I particularly want this book to be done and I particularly want you to do it – and of course to do it with perfect frankness – and we must have it by that date in order to get it into the January issue.[1] The reason for sending it to Faber & Gwyer is shown in the enclosed circular. The reason for not sending it to me is that I shall probably be away on a short holiday. After that we must arrange a meeting.

In haste,

Yours cordially,
[T. S. E.]

TSE/IPF

TO *C. K. Scott Moncrieff* CC

3 November 1925 23 Adelphi Terrace House

Dear Scott Moncrieff,

Many thanks for your letter and good wishes. Of course I should like to see the Pirandello or anything else you care to send.[2] I am slightly embarrassed by the cheque you sent me. The latest news is contained in the enclosed circular. So I leave it to you to decide about the other six shillings and meanwhile will have your cheque kept here.

I am attempting to clean up an enormous correspondence before going away for a holiday and will write to you again at more leisure.

Ever yours,
T. S. Eliot

TSE/IPF

1 – See Williams's review, in *NC* 4: 1 (Jan. 1926), 193–6.

2 – Scott Moncrieff had asked whether TSE proposed to use Pirandello's *Black Shawl*. He offered in addition one of Pirandello's recently published one-act plays. Neither was published in C.

TO *H. Baugh*[1] TS H. Baugh

5 November 1925 *The Criterion*,
23 Adelphi Terrace House

Dear Sir,

I have read the enclosed study of Rimbaud with very great interest but after due reflection have decided that I cannot use it. A good deal has been written about Rimbaud in the past few years and therefore, to speak quite frankly, I cannot feel justified in accepting anything on the subject unless it is also first rate.

The matter of your article is extremely interesting but I think that you ought to put in a good deal of work on the style. As you get to the heart of your subject your style on the whole becomes more simple and clear, but the writing, especially at the beginning, seems to me heavy and involved. Pardon me for speaking so frankly; ordinarily I do not take the trouble to do so; but the material which you have presented speaks so well for your brain power that I feel that it would be a great pity if you did not take the trouble to learn more about the writing of English prose. Study Swift and Newman.

I hope very much that I may hear from you again.

Yours faithfully,
T. S. Eliot

TSE/IPF

TO *Rollo Myers* CC

5 November 1925 9 Clarence Gate Gdns

Dear Myers,

Thank you for your letter. I am just off for a sea voyage tomorrow and have not time to write to Cocteau now but will try to do so on the boat. I was completely mistaken about 'Scandales'. It was only because I assumed that it was going into the book that I had not had it translated for the January number which has been made up.[2] I shall be very grateful if you

1–Hansell Baugh, critic; editor of *The Figure in the Carpet*, a magazine published by the New School of Social Research (1928–9), and of *Frances Newman's Letters* (1929).

2–Jean Cocteau's 'Scandales' appeared, in French, in *NC* 4: 1 (Jan. 1926), 125–37. A polemical autobiographical essay, it chronicled the scandals precipitated by the first performances of Stravinsky's *Rite of Spring*, Satie's *Parade*, Darius Milhaud's *Le Boeuf sur le Toit*, and Cocteau's *Mariés de la Tour Eiffel* and other works. The essay was not included in Cocteau's *Call to Order* (F&G, 1926).

will explain this to him meanwhile and say that we are going to try to shove it in in French if there is room.

I have discussed the question of payment again with Messrs. Faber & Gwyer. I have come to the conclusion that the most satisfactory method of contract is to pay a certain cash sum in advance of royalties to the translators, all royalties beyond this amount to go to the author.

If you have the manuscript ready within a month, will you send it direct to Geoffrey Faber Esqre., Messrs. Faber & Gwyer Limited, 28 Southampton Street, Strand, London W.C.2 instead of to me. I have handed him your translated 'Professional Secrets'. He will then write to you and to Cocteau, making a definite proposal for the cash advance and royalties.

Yours always sincerely,
[T. S. E.]

TSE/IPF

TO *Paul Jacobsthal* CC

5 November 1925 23 Adelphi Terrace House

My dear Sir,

I must apologise for not having written to you for a very long time but private affairs have made it almost impossible for me to attend to business.

You will see from the enclosed circular the reasons for the postponement of our next issue until January. This January issue will contain the conclusion of your essay. I very much regret this unavoidable break in the continuity of your essay.[1]

As the business is now changing hands, I cannot at present answer your enquiries. It is probable, however, that the next issue will be in the hands of different printers, which of course will make it more difficult to obey your original request for separate copies of your essay. So that I suggest that we should send you the required number of copies of the two issues of the *Criterion* and deduct them from the next payment to you at the lowest wholesale price.

Yours very truly,
[T. S. E.]

1–Part I of Paul Jacobsthal's 'Views and Valuations of Ancient Art since Winckelman' appeared in *C.* 3: 12 (July 1925), 543–56; Part II in *NC* 4: 1 (Jan. 1926), 138–47.

TO *Ottoline Morrell* MS Texas

5 November 1925 9 Clarence Gate Gdns

My dear Ottoline

I opened your letter to V. in case it required an immediate answer. V. has just gone to the country – we called in other opinions, according to which the country was absolutely necessary; and a very good local man is to keep his eye on her. And I am going tomorrow morning for a short sea voyage. I have never quite got over that operation. I shall write to you when I am back; I don't think V. will be in London again till Christmas. This Cambridge business[1] will make it difficult for me to get out of London again till the spring.

I should have loved to see you – and so I know wd V. Perhaps we can both come to Garsington, later. I think so.

Very much love
Tom.

FROM *Vivien Eliot* PC Valerie Eliot

5 November 1925 Elsmleigh, Bassett, Southampton

Thank you very much for cheque book and letter. I will write fully tomorrow. I hope you are getting ready to go. If sending things, the books in my bedroom – only Synge and all of E.P.[2] – [are *del.*] what I should like to have very much. I hope you are better. I am getting on well.

I. P. Fassett TO *Richard Aldington* CC

14 November 1925 23 Adelphi Terrace House

Dear Sir,

Thank you for your letter of the 9th November and for the two books.[3]

1 – The Clark lectures.
2 – VHE had been enthusiastic about EP's poetry since before her marriage to TSE.
3 – IPF wrote on 7 Nov. asking RA to send the review he was holding for *C.* RA replied (9 Nov.) that he had not known until a day or two previously that *C.* was resuming and was unable to review the two books 'at a moment's notice'. He therefore returned the books with apologies to TSE. On 16 Oct., RA had told Read he had not looked at the books TSE had sent him, and did not see why he should 'whore unprofessionally at half the regular Piccadilly rate in exchange for Mr E's patronage' ('Richard Aldington's Letters to Herbert Read', 20–1).

I must apologise for my two letters of the 7th and 12th November, which were written, it seems, upon a misunderstanding. Mr Eliot left England a week ago to take a short sea voyage under strict medical orders.[1] I understood from him that he had written to you himself before he left, and I understood also that the reviews in question were ready for us when we wanted them. Mr Eliot left in a great hurry after a great rush of work and I have no doubt I misunderstood him. I expect to be in touch with him in about three weeks' time, when I will explain to him what has taken place.

Yours faithfully,
For the Editor of the *Criterion*,
[IPF]
Secretary.

Vivien Eliot TO *Henry Eliot* MS Houghton

14 November [1925]

c/o Dr Hawkesworth,
Elmsleigh, Bassett, Southampton

Dear Henry,

I do hope Tom has let you know, before this, that I am here in a nursing home, and that he has gone abroad. The last I heard from him was that he was leaving for an eight days trip on the water, going, I think to the S. of France via Gibraltar. After that I do not know. I wish I [were] able to write more fully to you, but I cannot. I wish you and Theresa were here. Can't you come? Of course I know you do intend coming but if only you could come now, just now, it is so necessary. My own people are all in Rome. I cannot get out to buy you anything – but please will you give the enclosed handkerchief to Theresa – with my love. Please write Henry – and soon.

Yrs. ever,
Vivien Eliot

1 – TSE left England on 6 Dec, and stayed away until 24 Dec. He sailed to Marseilles, then went on to spend a month at Lady Rothermere's apartment at the Savoy Hotel in La Turbie in the Alpes Maritimes, before crossing the border to pass a few days with EP in Rapallo.

Vivien Eliot TO *Mary Hutchinson* MS Texas

15 November 1925 c/o Dr Hawkesworth,
Elmsleigh, Bassett

Dear Mary

I don't know if you have heard that I am here. I wish you would write to me. And please send me Virginia's address, I have stupidly forgotten the number. Tom is abroad. I don't know how long I shall be here.

Do write, Mary, and give my love to Jack.

V. H. E.

FROM *Dr T. A. Hawkesworth* MS Valerie Eliot

18 November 1925 Elmsleigh, Bassett

Dear Sir

At Dr Higgins' request I am writing you a short report of Mrs Eliot's progress. I may truly say she has improved since she came – as on her arrival she was in an acutely restless and hysterical condition. Sleep is as yet uncertain, but she gets a reasonable amount every night even when broken, and on some nights gets six hours or more undisturbed. She is taking a full diet perfectly well. As to the nervous condition – that is variable at present but there are indications now of some wish to get back to a reasonable state of mind and she is willing to admit her mistakes and to wish for a better state of balance. The hysterical state, when it recurs, is now very much less acute and less prolonged.

So that altogether the outlook is brighter and I hope we shall see continued progress.

Yrs faithfully
T. A. Hawkesworth

FROM *Dr Hubert Higgins*[1] MS Valerie Eliot

18 November 1925 [London]

Dear Eliot

Your wife is doing very well. She is most anxious to get your address, doubtless to belabour you. They are always full of [?furies] against their

1 – Hubert Higgins, the Eliots' doctor.

'slaves'. Considering that her will to take drugs is being systematically opposed, she is a good case and most favourable.

I am going to Paris on Friday till the following Tuesday

Hotel Terminus
Gare St Lazare

I do hope you are not feeling too exhausted by your reaction. The only way is to lie down and rest as much as possible and grin and bear it. It'll go off. The worse you feel now the better you will be when you come back. You don't mean to tell me that you haven't got a reaction – after all these awful experiences. If you haven't it'll be astonishing. I wish I was there to have a chat with you. Write to me about Lady Rothermere's studio at Paris. She arrives there on Sunday and may want to know. The best of good luck.

Yours very sincerely
Hubert Higgins

PS Let me know, very fully, how you are and, if possible, your symptoms in the [illegible word] H. H.

TO *Herbert Read* — TS Victoria

[20? November 1925] — Savoy Hotel, La Turbie, Alpes Maritimes

My dear Read,

It was kind to write to me at Marseilles, and relieved my mind considerably. I reread the article on the boat, at more leisure, and was pained by more than one passage.[1] The author does not really take seriously what he is writing about; his tone is as much as to say, 'I know it seems odd that I should be writing about this sort of thing; but it is really quite inoffensive, and rather quaint and charming'. That sort of person is not of much use. I have ventured to hint this to [Bruce] Richmond.

1 – 'The Margins of Philosophy', *TLS*, 5 Nov. 1925, 725–6: a review of Robert Sencourt, *Outlying Philosophy*; Etienne Gilson, *St Thomas D'Aquin*; F. Olgate, *L'anima del umanismo e del rinascimento*; Etienne Gilson, *The Philosophy of Thomas Aquinas* (a transl. of *Le Thomisme*); Aelred Whitacre and others, *St Thomas Aquinas*; Jacques Maritain, *Réflexions sur l'intelligence*; Etienne Gilson, *La philosophie de Saint Bonaventure*; Henri Ghéon, *Le triomphe de Saint Thomas D'Aquin*. On 9 Nov., HR wrote to 'disown' the piece: 'not mine the *lux beatissima*!' He acknowledged it was a curious coincidence, because he had thought of writing about these books; in his view, the writer failed to bring out the 'contrast between the mediaeval standpoint & the modern'.

I am glad you have settled with Faber about the essays. A good title.[1] He took a great fancy to you, and he ought to be delighted to get the Poems. (I have asked them to send you a copy of mine as soon as they are ready, so you will be able to criticise their production).[2]

I have written to him to say that I think the F.M.L. series[3] ought to be between 30,000 and 40,000 words according to the wish of the writer. My first estimate of 25,000 was I think rather short.

I want to interfere as little as possible. But the general idea is critical in a humane sense, rather than biographical or expository. To put the English reader in contact with some world-current. So I thought it would be interesting (and I think has never been done) if you could trace some of the influences and oppositions: such as the *NRF* on the one hand and Benda and Maritain etc. on the other.

Of course we shall have to include some pretty dull folk in the series: Hauptmann for instance (though I think Muir can make him interesting if anyone can). But I hope that the series as a whole and on the whole will have some significance, and certain volumes – a sort of inner circle – ought taken together to have more than that. I think that some of the bigger people of the last generation should eventually be included – such as Taine and Renan[4] (by the way I have Lasserre's book, and can lend it to you later; it is interesting); later, if the series proved a success, we could dare to present quite unknowns, such as Fustel de Coulanges, or even men of our own generation abroad. The difficulty is, that when it comes to a foreign writer whom I really care about having done just right, there are so few men in this country with the knowledge or the ideas. Barrès would be good if well done, awful if badly done.

I will write again when I have time, but I am just facing two weeks' correspondence forwarded from London, and a good deal of the time I merely lie in the sun (when there is any). I shall be back within a month.

Ever yours
T. S. E.

1–*Reason and Romanticism*: *Essays in Literary Criticism* (F&G, 1926).
2–TSE, *Poems 1909–1925*, published by F&G on 23 Nov.
3–The projected Foreign Men of Letters series.
4–Hippolyte Taine (1828–93): French positivist critic, author of *Origines de la France Contemporaine* (1875–93) and *History of English Literature* (1871). Ernest Renan (1823–92): cultural theorist and orientalist; author of *La Vie de Jésus* (1863).

TO *Mario Praz*[1] TS Galleria Nazionale d'Arte Moderna

23 November 1925 Savoy Hotel, La Turbie

Dear Sir,

I have just read your *Marinismo e Secentismo in Inghilterra*[2] which I am about to review for the *Times Literary Supplement*.[3] I shall also make copious reference to it in some lectures which I am to give during the winter at Trinity College, Cambridge, on 'the metaphysical poetry of the XVII Century in England'.[4] I am writing to tell you that I have found nothing by any of our scholars – even by Saintsbury or Grierson or Gosse, which can challenge comparison with your book for critical taste and judgement and for width (*envergure*) of learning.[5] I am a little jealous indeed that you have forestalled me on several points: in your criticism of Miss Ramsay, in your comparison and contrast of Donne and Guido Cavalcanti, and in your insistence on the importance of the Society of Jesus in England at the time.[6] All of these points had occurred to me, but you have spoken first.

I wish to extend to you an invitation to contribute a critical essay to *The New Criterion*. I do not know whether you know the *Criterion* (yes, you referred to it in a footnote) which I have directed from the beginning. I will send you the next issue in January.

1–Mario Praz (1896–1982): Italian scholar of English literature; later author of *The Romantic Agony* (1930). At this time, he was Senior Lecturer in Italian, Liverpool University.
2–*Secentismo e marinismo in Inghilterra: John Donne – Richard Crashaw* (Florence, 1925).
3–TSE, 'An Italian Critic on Donne and Crashaw', *TLS*, 17 Dec. 1925, 878. 'The best study of Crashaw that I know, and a very fine and suggestive essay, is that by Mario Praz', wrote TSE.
4–In the Clark lectures, TSE frequently cites Praz's study, putting it at the head of his reading list after the first lecture (*VMP*, 64).
5–TSE wrote later: 'I immediately recognised these essays – and especially his masterly study of Crashaw – as among the best I had ever read in that field. His knowledge of the poetry of that period in four languages . . . was encyclopaedic, and, fortified by his own judgement and good taste, makes that book essential reading for any student of the English "metaphysical poets"' (*Friendship's Garland: Essays Presented to Mario Praz On his Seventieth Birthday*, ed. Vittorio Gabrieli, 1966).
6–In his lectures – esp. 'Donne and the Middle Ages' (67–72) – TSE criticised Mary Paton Ramsay's *Les Doctrines médiévales chez Donne, le poète metaphysicien de l'Angleterre* (1917). Following Praz, he drew 'parallels and comparisons between Donne and his group on the one hand and Guido Guinizelli, Guido Cavalcanti, Cino da Pistoia on the other' (58). On the Society of Jesus, TSE observed: 'Jesuitism came to Donne through the intellect, and in his mind and memory it had to compete with Calvinism, Lutheranism, and everything else. It entered Crashaw's mind through poetry . . . and it found practically nothing in his mind to struggle against' (163–4).

I presume that you write English as well as you read and no doubt speak it; if you prefer to write in Italian or French we of course undertake the translation. Only, in that case, we are obliged to deduct the translator's fee from the payment (which is at the rate of ten pounds per 5000 words: articles should not much exceed 5000 words). I should be very much pleased if you cared to suggest a subject. We only publish *inédits*, but have no objection to any contribution appearing elsewhere, in a language other than English, six weeks after appearing in *The New Criterion*.[1]

I beg you to accept my compliments and admiration for your book.

Yours very truly,
T. S. Eliot
Editor of *The New Criterion*

I shall be at this address for two or three weeks. When I return to London the address is

care of Faber & Gwyer Limited,
28 Southampton Street,
Strand, W.C.2
London.

TO *Ezra Pound* PC Beinecke

[Postmark 24 November 1925] Savoy Hotel, La Turbie

Here for two or three weeks. If in Rapallo, write – perhaps we could meet somewhere? But don't give my address to *anyone*.

T. S. Eliot

FROM *Dr Hubert Higgins* MS Valerie Eliot

Wednesday morning [25 Nov. 1925] Hotel Terminus, rue St Lazare, Paris

Dear Eliot,

I liked your letter. Your symptoms are good. They are a normal, healthy reaction from your imprisonment.

1–Praz contributed a number of essays and reviews to *C.*, starting with 'Chaucer and the Great Italian writers of the Trecento' in *NC* 6: 1–3 (July–Sept. 1927).

I say imprisonment advisedly because you were forced, by your higher instincts of protection and chivalry,[1] into a region of restricted contacts with reality.

This is imprisonment of the mind. You are like a man who, for a considerable part of your life, was shoved, by authority, into an oubliette.

There is no difference.

Provided your mind can survey the two worlds: the world of restricted contacts, on the one side, and that of wide unrestricted contacts, on the other, and can see these worlds from the aspect rather of comedy than tragedy your experience is a precious experience and one you can use to help humanity to step out of the little into the great world – only don't argue – don't think – just submit to the exigencies of your strained and tired brain which is readjusting and admirably healing itself.

This is written in great haste.

I shall, all being well, see your wife tomorrow. I will wire a message.

Yours ever
H. H.

TO *Richard Aldington* MS Texas

26 November 1925 Savoy Hotel, La Turbie

My dear Richard,

I am writing sooner and therefore (my typewriter is *abîmée*[2] and the mechanic in Nice has not improved it much at a cost of 200 francs) ther efore the r therefore more briefly than I intended and shall do when I get to Nice again and hie h ir e hire a typewriter *merde*.

I thought I wrote to you just before I sailed.[3] But I dic-dictated forty letters and meant to write to you myself as I did not want to dictate it; and was writing till 3 a.m. before departure so cannot remember whether I wrote to you or not. Anyhow, I THOUGHT you wrote to me that you had written a review of Chesterfield, so I told my secretary to get it from you.[4]

1 – In early Dec., Higgins wrote again: 'I must confess that the "new England conscience", especially your brand thereof, claims, through its fruits, my most respectful admiration. At the same time irrelevant and impertinent enquiries into "motives" and hair-splitting weighings and measurings of "unworthy ingredients", can't help the business end of your mind.'

2 – 'Ruined' (French). The typescript is erratic, with the lower part of individual letters missing.

3 – See IPF's letter of 14 Nov.

4 – On 1 May, TSE told HR that RA had asked to review 'the Chesterfield' – probably Roger Coxon, *Chesterfield and his Critics* (1925).

It is just one of the things that have gone wrong. Of course you could not write a review in two days; but I am very disappointed because I particularly wished your name to appear in the first new number. It cannot be helped. Is there anything you have or want to write that I could publish (not a review, I mean an essay etc.) in the following Number?[1] I hesitate always to ask you because there is no less lucrative occupation than writing for the *Critero Cr Criterion*. This type looks just like Hebrew. But I hope soon to pay a little more. So in any interim between more remunerative occupations remember the *Criter Criterion*. You see what has happened. It is the *abutaboutissement* of my efforts for some months. As I had to leave the bank anyhow it is the best thing for me in the circumstances. The pay is less than Richmond once said an editor ought to get but there will be some perquisites from Faber & Gwyer. They combine with Lady R. to own and manage the review and I get a five years contract. So I am a director of Faber & Gwyer and a humble publisher at your service. NOW what about GOURMONT? Did I tell you that the terms offered are 25 pounds on recpt of MS and 25 more on publication, and a royalty of 10% after 3000 copies? Length 30,000 to 40,000 words and model model the English Men of Letters, but more criticism and less biography, and of course more explanation of the milieu influence etc. My scheme is to deal with writers of living influence whether alive or dead within a generation. I should like to have Renan, Taine and perhaps Sainte-Beuve later. I cant think of anyone to do Barrès. I shall do Maurras next autumn, and hope to have a book by Dobrée and one by [John Gould] Fletcher (at your instigation) in the autumn, but should LIKE to start in the spring with you, and with the Bergson of Read and the Hauptmann of Muir which are promised for then. How busy are you going to be this winter? I shall write a more pussnel[2] (as Ezra would say) letter later, but must lie down and rest. I can't stand this typewriter very long at a time. The Côte d'Azur is DAMNED COLD.

Ever yours aff
T.

1–RA contributed a review of five books by BD to *NC* 4: 2 (Apr. 1926).
2–'personal'.

TO *Richard de la Mare*[1] CC

7 December 1925 — 23 Adelphi Terrace House

Dear Mr de la Mare,

I have made a few tentative corrections on the 'Scandales' proof, but I do not feel at all competent to correct it as a whole.[2]

Mrs Leverson wants a space of a few lines after a paragraph ending 'some chill presentiment' and a space of one line after 'frame of mind at the last', omitting the phrase 'something of the sort'.[3] I think it is quite likely that Mrs Leverson will have made these corrections herself already and merely writes to me to confirm them.

Yours sincerely,
[T. S. E.]

FROM *Dr Hubert Higgins* MS Valerie Eliot

Tuesday 8 December [1925] — 46 Brook St, London W.1

Dear Eliot

I met your wife at Waterloo and saw her through to Euston.

Lady Rothermere has now contributed £50. She is willing to let you live at 58 Circus Road when you return *but* you must pay for your food.

I should strongly advise you to stay there and let me arrange some slight disciplines for you. Mainly learning to relax and thought control no more. Nothing in any way difficult, but brains like yours want little sensible disciplines and tips. I am *most* alarmed about the cold – that is very bad for you. All the other symptoms are exactly what are to be expected. I will go down to see your wife in a day or two and will let you know all about everything. I should like to see the lectures.

My 'Master Craft' is shaping itself even better than I thought.

With congratulations for your
Excellent reactions.

1–Richard de la Mare (1902–86) – son of the poet Walter de la Mare – joined Faber & Gwyer as production manager in 1925 and was to be made a director in 1928; ultimately he would be Chairman and later President of Faber & Faber.

2–Jean Cocteau, 'Scandales', *NC* 4: 1 (Jan. 1926), 125–37.

3–'The Last First Night', in the same issue (148–53).

There will also be some hydrotherapy for you – I have a most skilful assistant who has made a thorough study of this and also some electricity – I think I can borrow a friend's machines for you.

Yours very sincerely
Hubert Higgins

TO *Ezra Pound* PC Beinecke

[Postmark 8 December 1925] Savoy Hotel, La Turbie

Me and my lil ole saxophone will be with you some day next week.[1] I must get new passport and hire a mewl to tote my traps down the mountain. Will send wire first and await reply as dont wish to arrive in yr absence. Bad enough to cross Genoa without a guide. It *cant* be colder than here – they hav to break the ice in the horsetrough to wash mah pants. T.

TO *Ezra Pound* TS Beinecke

11 Dec[ember 1925] Savoy Hotel, La Turbie

Questo mio primo amico[2]

It doan matter a toad's fart whether your village is Syracuse Aggrigentum or Buffalo, the point is it aint in France, my passport expired with a sigh on the 7th instant, I had to go to Nice which is a hell of a journey down the mountain in a brokendown motor bus orijinly a U.S.A. army lorry it aint got no springs & you shd see the priests bouncing up and down when we take the hairpin curves on the Cornishe with ole Fernand singin and shoutin & flirtin with the girls in the seat behind him. Then when you get to Nice you gotta find the American consulat which is a long walk and they keep the door locked. After waitin ½ hour there I was told they would have to apply to Paris & it wd take 10 days. & I had to get a photo so I went to a photographe and jes as he wasstartin to take me his damn electric light died, and while he was tinkrin with it I nearly lost my bus back, and had to run my balls off across the Place Messena because you have to be there ½ hour ahead to get a seat, and it takes 1½ hrs to get back here because it is up hill and the bus breaks down and the lamps go out when he takes a corner and me with a baby with a bad cold and a bottle of wine with no

1 – The Pounds were in Rapallo, just over the border from TSE at La Turbie.

2 – 'This first friend of mine': ref. to Cavalcanti in Dante, *La Vita Nuova* XXIV: 3. 6.

cork in it in my [?] lap, and a parcel of medicaments wch I had bought for chilblains awful on my feet & so has the rest of the local population of this commune, and for constipation because of the cold and for neuralgia and insomnia and Enos Fruit Salt on principle, but I am much better here is my photo to prove it. Well, then when I do get my passport which may be sooner because I forgot to tell you I hear from London my new one from Wash has arrived so I have wired to them to send it to Nice consul. and Nice consul. are to wire me when it arrives. Well then I got to hire my mule 48 hrs ahead to take my luggage down the mountain from Monsieur Grinde NEGOCIANT EN TRANSPORTS wch means mules. So I will wire you when I can get away & I hope I dont have to cross Genoa bt can leave same station. Dont worry about calorifero,[1] people who been living on top of a mountain can keep warm in a refrigerator.

Yours truly
T.

TO *Richard Aldington* TS Texas

11 December 1925 Savoy Hotel, La Turbie

My dear Richard,

I wired you today and hope I made it clear that I was returning in two weeks in any case, and hoped that that would do. I am held up here waiting for a new passport, and cannot stir till it arrives. Then I want to spend a night with Ezra in Rapallo – not having seen him for four years – I had intended to take a few days in Paris more on business than pleasure, but being delayed here and having your news it will be better for me to come straight back and return to Paris for a week later.

What you say sounds incredibly perfect, and if it comes off will require a bottle of fizz to precede the Cockburn. Your influence over Routledge must be immense. As you say, it would advantage me in every way. Whatever happens, you have my sincere and respectful gratitude.[2]

1–'Radiator' (Italian).

2–See David S. Thatcher, 'Richard Aldington's Letters to Herbert Read', 7–8: 'In 1923 Aldington was asked by the publishing firm of Routledge to collaborate on a series of critical biographies, to be called "The Republic of Letters" and edited by William Rose. Aldington asked Eliot and Read to contribute, but both declined. Eighteen months later Eliot initiated a similar scheme as director of Faber & Gwyer. Routledge, after consulting Aldington, proposed to combine the two series under the joint editorship of Eliot and Rose, and the joint imprint of the two rival publishers. Aldington felt bitter because Eliot's venture was backed by the very people who had shown no interest in the project when Aldington himself

No good writing to me here any more. Will communicate immediately I reach London. By the way, should a Migne[1] not be beyond our joint purses, I would be glad to split one with you, if we can agree as to who should possess which volumes, lending the others reciprocally. What I want chiefly is XII and XIII century philosophy,[2] and Erigena; Prudentius and Tertullian[3] and the fathers I should be content to borrow!

By the way, to get away from here I have to hire a mule to take my luggage down the mountain. The mule belongs to Monsieur Grinde, who accordingly calls himself NEGOCIANT EN TRANSPORTS.

Ever affectionately
Tom

—

had canvassed support. Once it began to look as if Eliot would accept the new arrangement, Aldington wrote to Read: "This affair is the biggest setback I have had since the war and loses me the fruit of years of work. Not only is this editorship a big thing in itself, but it would have led me to a permanent connection with Routledge and would have lifted me out of the mire of journalism and poverty. However, it is no use crying over split milk; and the right thing to do is to smile and congratulate Tom" (13 Dec. 1925).' RA had told Harold Monro, in confidence, on 26 Nov. that Routledge had appointed him editor of a new complete section of the Broadway series of translations as well as joint editor of 'The Republic of Letters'. He thought it would be a 'big thing' and provide a 'certain counterpoise to the Gang [associates of TSE and Faber & Gwyer]'. The series would be devoted to 'historical figures' and therefore not cut across TSE's projected series, which was to be devoted to contemporaries. (*Richard Aldington: An Autobiography in Letters*, ed. Norman T. Gates [1992], 75–6.)

1–Jacques Paul Migne (1800–75): French priest and publisher responsible for inexpensive and widely distributed editions of early theological works. The most important of these were the Latin *Patrologiae cursus completus* (*Patrologia Latina*) in 221 vols (1844–5) and the *Patrologia Graeca*, with Greek text and Latin translation (165 vols, 1857–8). In his lecture on 'Donne and the Trecento' TSE refers to Richard of St Victor's works occupying 'the greater part of one volume in Migne's *Patrologia*' (*VMP*, 101).

2–Noting that the generation of Dante was 'nourished on *mediaeval* Latin culture', TSE declared that 'no one who has read even a little of the Latin of the twelfth and thirteenth centuries can doubt that the delight in ideas, the dialectical subtlety, the intensity with which ideas were felt, and the clarity and precision of the expression, came partly from this source' (99).

3–Johannes Scottus Erigena (*c.*800–*c.*877), Irish theologian, author of *Periphyseon* and translator of the Pseudo-Dionysus; Marcus Aurelius Clemens Prudentius (348–*c.*410), the best-known of the early poets of the Christian Church, author of *Cathemerinon Liber*; Tertullian (*c.*160–230), the first Christian theologian to produce major works in Latin. In the Clark lectures TSE said he thought he had an 'inability to feel devotional verse' before he 'had read the *Paradiso*, or any of the Latin hymns from Prudentius to Aquinas' (167).

TO *George Rylands* TS King's

11 December 1925 Savoy Hotel, La Turbie

Dear Mr Rylands,

Your letter has just reached me here. I shall look forward to seeing your book.[1] I leave in about a week and expect to be in London about Christmas time. I will let you know as soon as I am back, and you will I hope come and lunch with me. We will then see what we can arrange – I have some hopes, but very indefinite. I shall have an office at 24 Russell Square, quite near to you.[2]

Sincerely yours,
T. S. Eliot

TO *Herbert Read* TS Victoria

11 December 1925 Savoy Hotel, La Turbie

My dear Read,

The reply to your letter has suffered a common fate. I had to postpone it for a few days, during which it grew and grew to a size beyond either the time or energy at my disposal for writing it out. If I could dictate as I lie in bed at night my letters might be written and be complete; what issues is merely a series of fragments.

First, thank you very much for the tip about Routledge. I had never realised the possible conflict. I wrote at once to Aldington, without indicating in any way that I could have been warned by you. The result is first that he was pleased and relieved, second that he has made a *démarche* [an approach] with Routledge, and they are favourably disposed toward an understanding. So I am to interview Routledge's immediately on my return. For this I am obliged to you.

I am inclined to concede another season, especially as I shall not know for two or three weeks how we shall break with Routledge, and as I do not wish to rush you but am anxious that your book should be in the first lot.[3] So do not consider your work hurried, but take as much time as you need. It is not as if the work were lucrative enough for you to devote yourself to it exclusively. If you think the terms need revision we will discuss that as soon as I return and I will see what can be done.

1 – Rylands, *Russet and Taffeta*.
2 – Rylands wrote from 37 Gordon Square.
3 – HR's projected book on Bergson for F&G's Foreign Men of Letters series.

I will give you the Constant Bourquin book on Benda when I get back.[1] You will not find very much use for it, except that there is a certain amount of controversial gossip showing the relations between the different camps. It would appear from that book that Benda was at one time well thought of by the Maurresiens, but that he has kept himself very much *à l'écart*. At the end of *Belphégor* an appendix has some acid words about the romanticism of the anti-romantics, which is probably aimed at Maurras.[2] As for religion, I should say he was very much the Jew, no doubt a very emancipated Jew, but perhaps still responsive to *le mysticisme juif*.[3] He was a detached and critical Dreyfusard.[4] His circle of friends is rather a Jewish circle – Spire etc. and at one time there was a Jewish review – not this tedious *Revue Juive* – but I think called the *Revue Blanche* – with which he was associated.[5] I can lend you some of his books.

I have never read any Renouvier,[6] I know that William James thought a good deal of him, and borrowed from him. That is hardly a recommendation.[7] I think Maine de Biran[8] is a more likely name; he is always turning up. I have not read any of him either. When I do the Maurras book I shall have to look into Comte, Joseph de Maistre[9] etc.

1 – Constant Bourquin, *Julien Benda, ou le point de vue de Sirius* (1925).

2 – In Note J ('The Romanticism of Reason') Benda said of Maurras: 'The eulogies bestowed daily on the high-priest of the *Action Française* for "returning to the manners of the classic style" make us smile when we consider his enthusiasm for his own doctrines, the violence of his arguments, and especially the virulent, contemptuous tone he uses towards his adversary' (*Belphégor*, trans. S. J. I. Lawson, with an intro. by Irving Babbitt [1929], 156).

3 – 'Jewish mysticism' (French). Benda's parents were both Jewish. Acc. to Anthony Levi, he disliked Jewish assumptions of supremacy and Zionism, preferring the Judaism of his mother, 'the little Jewess of the Paris Marais, scribbling and petulant', to that of his father, 'a Jew of the Orient in antiquity, in love with eternity' (*Guide to French Literature* [1992], 98).

4 – See Benda's defence of Dreyfus and reflections on the affair, in *Dialogues à Byzance* (1900).

5 – Benda was one of a group of talented writers (including Debussy, Léon Blum and Mallarmé) associated with *La Revue Blanche*, 1891–1903. André Spire (1868–1966) was a Jewish poet, friend of Charles Péguy and author of *Poèmes Juifs* (1919). Valery Larbaud thought Spire France's only successful satirical writer. *La Revue Juive* was founded in Jan. 1925 under the direction of Albert Cohen; TSE's friend Jean de Menasce worked on it.

6 – Charles Renouvier (1815–1903): French neo-Kantian philosopher and student of Comte. His books included *Essais de critique générale* (1854–64) and *La Science de la morale* (1869), and he figures in Maritain's *Réflexions sur l'intelligence* (1924).

7 – TSE's judgement of William James was largely sceptical. He once praised the fact that 'what seems scepticism or inconsistency or vagueness in others, James has the knack of communicating as a sense of sincere adventurousness' ('William James on Immortality', *NS* 9: 231, 8 Sept. 1917).

8 – Maine de Biran (1766–1824): French philosopher. Starting out as a follower of Locke and Condillac, he subsequently became an intellectualist and then a mystical theosophist.

9 – Joseph de Maistre (1753–1821): political philosopher; author of *Considérations sur la France* (1796), a critique of the French Revolution; *Du Pape* (1819), a defence of papal infallibility; and *Soirées de St Pétersbourg* (1821).

Do you know anything about a contemporary named Ernest Seillière?[1]

I am delighted about the poems as well as the essays.[2] About the dedication: for myself, modesty is not proof against such a compliment, and I am candidly immensely flattered and pleased. I know no greater compliment. Dedications are too often used for paying off worldly debts; as there is no debt at all in this case, I am all the more honoured. There is only one point that occurs to me as an objection, which I will put to you: namely: whether the statement of a certain community of interest and point of view implied by such a dedication is, from the point of view of efficacy, good or injurious? For the purpose of implanting the right ideas in the public mind, is an obvious intimacy a good thing or does it raise the spectre of a Gunpowder Plot? I have doubts. As you say, my knowledge of your wish is the main thing: and I hope you will base your decision on your judgment of what is most to the public interest! After all, no harm is done by your *not* dedicating the book![3]

I have read Maritain's book,[4] and other books, since I have been here. I think it a valuable and significant book, but nevertheless am a little disappointed with it. I feel that the man has been somehow in too great a hurry to arrive, that he has with good intentions fallen into the trap of zealotry; and in his satisfaction at having found a point of view, is inclined to indulge himself in a political activity, and slanging his opponents. The attack on James[5] is well conducted, and brings some amazing follies to light, but is used more to gain a temporary platform victory than to consolidate his own position. If he had made it part of a thorough historical defense of thomism or of the Church – to show that *any* philosophy except that of the church leads to heresies which ordinary common sense condemns – it would be more permanent (this is what I should attempt if I put myself in his place). But Maurrasism, an excellent thing within its limits, is too exciting for a rather emotional philosopher

1 – Baron Ernest Seillière (1866–1955); French critic and philosopher who was an opponent of romanticism and an exponent of imperialism; author of *La Philosophie de l'impérialisme* (4 vols, 1903–8) and *Essais critiques sur la psychologie du romantisme français* (1933).

2 – In 1926, F&G published two books by HR: *Collected Poems 1913–1925* and *Reason and Romanticism: Essays in Literary Criticism.*

3 – In the event, HR dedicated his *Collected Poems* to William Prior Read.

4 – Jacques Maritain, *Réflexions sur l'intelligence et sur sa vie propre* (1924). In his 'Commentary', in *NC* 5: 1 (Jan. 1927), TSE called Maritain 'the most conspicuous figure, and probably the most powerful force, in contemporary French philosophy' (3).

5 – In ch. 8, 'La Nouvelle Théodicée Americaine', Maritain mounted a critique of William James's pluralism and pragmatism, in opposition to what he called in the next chapter 'Le Réalisme Thomiste': the Thomist realism of Aquinas.

who was converted from Protestantism by Léon Bloy[1] (as the Tharauds say in their reminiscences of Péguy which are appearing in the *Revue Universelle* – very interesting too – Maritain was a friend of Péguy, so was Sorel).[2]

I feel more and more, with the example of these impetuous Frenchmen before us, the necessity of proceeding very slowly, never anticipating or faking the cards. What has been done, is to make the work of S. Thomas and others more accessible and more intelligible: but this is only the *material* of neo-thomism. The great – perhaps the only – analogy being the transformation performed by Thomas himself upon Aristotle; and keeping in mind that in respect of the matter to be ordered, the données of life, science and society, our time differs far more from that of Aquinas than the time of Aquinas differed from that of Aristotle; the work to be done on Thomas therefore exceeds that which he did himself. Modern psychology is tiresome, misleading and full of humbug; but you cannot push it aside; you have to get straight through it somehow: for it has called into existence a thousand new questions which are potential in the humblest mind today, and which indefinitely complicate – to take one group of phenomena alone – any problem of religious belief. Meanwhile – to make more possible the required patience, attentiveness and anonymity – one needs of course some tentative scheme which shall simply go far enough to make action possible, and give to action a kind of moral and liturgical dignity.

I feel certain of one thing however, and that is that taking things 'as they stand' the XII and XIII centuries offer the finest – and perhaps the only training one can give oneself at the moment. If it only serves as an analogical stimulant to the mind and imagination, that is a great deal in itself. If we can add it, in our self education, to our knowledge of Greece, then it gives a second point of orientation, a standard of perfection to direct and enlarge, without prejudicing, our purposes.

This is really the theme of my lectures on Donne etc. which I should very much like to show you on my return. The idea is briefly this: to take the XIII century – in its literary form, Dante – as my *point de repère*, to

1–Léon Bloy (1846–1917): prolific essayist, novelist and religious polemicist. TSE later confirmed his characterisation of Maritain as 'rather emotional' when he wrote: 'I have never seen a more romantic classicist, or a Thomist whose methods of thought were less like those of Aquinas' ('Three Reformers', *TLS*, 8 Nov. 1928, 818).

2–Jean and Jerome Tharaud, 'Notre cher Péguy' was serialised in *La Revue Universelle* XXIII, in late 1925. It was at the suggestion of Péguy that Maritain attended Bergson's lectures at the Sorbonne.

treat subsequent history as the history of the disintegration of that unity – disintegration inevitable because of the increase of knowledge and consequent dispersion of attention, but bringing with it many undesirable features.[1] Disintegration, which, WHEN the world has crystallised for another moment into a new order, can be treated as a form of generation; but which the historian at the present time, who does not anticipate, must regard partly as the history of corruption. That is to say, to consider and criticise the poetry of the XVII century from the point of view of the XIII.[2] It seems to me that such an examination should bring out some curious things. I am far from sure that I have succeeded.

I am leaving here in a week – if I have written four lectures[3] and if my new passport arrives, shall go Rapallo for a few days, and probably come straight back from there.

I have asked my secretary to ask you whether there is any new book you care to review for April; but if there is, don't wait for her, but write to her (Miss Fassett, at 23 Adelphi Terrace House) and ask her to send for it.

Ever yours
T. S. E.

Truc has a new book *Notre Temps* (Renaissance du Livre)[4] I have not seen it, but I think rather well of him.

Vivien Eliot TO *Ezra Pound* MS Beinecke

14 December [1925] The Stanboroughs,[5] Watford

Ezra. I wrote *today* to T. care of you. *I have a* feeling it wont arrive. I *want you to let me know at once if it doesn't.* Tell T. not to be a fool. He pretends to think I hate him, but its just a lie. All this is the handiwork of Lilli Anne.

1 – In his Preface to *VMP*, TSE presented the book as part of a trilogy with the general title 'The Disintegration of the Intellect'.
2 – This argument is particularly prominent in the third lecture, 'Donne and the Trecento'.
3 – The first of TSE's eight Clark lectures was to be given on 26 Jan. 1926. On 12 Jan., TSE said he had written three of the lectures by the time he returned to England from Italy.
4 – Gonzague Truc (1877–1972): critic and biographer, associated with l'Action Française and author of *Charles Maurras et son temps* (1917). *Notre Temps* was published by Éditions du Siècle in 1925. TSE cites his *Les mystiques espagñoles: Sainte Terese – Saint Jean de la Croix* (1921) in his reading list at the end of the first Clark lecture.
5 – 'The Stanboroughs: A Modern Hydrotherapeutic Health Institution' described itself as a 'medical and surgical institution employing all the curative agencies recognized in rational medical science. Nervous complaints and all forms of rheumatism treated successfully.'

Bless L. A. O bless her. Speak to Tom. Ask him, dear Ezra, *make* him rescue me before Xmas. I am well now. At least I *shd* be well with/given one half grain of happiness, peace of mind, assurance, & time & opportunity to read & think. But O the starvation with all these things missing. I dont know where I am. I want a few books, my liberty, & peace. Is that too much? T. *is* unbalanced, & is *in the toils* of Lily & one Higgins. Pull him up O Ezra. *S. O. S. Mrs.* [? *Yrs*] V. H. Eliot

TO *Ezra Pound*[1] PC Beinecke

[Postmark 15 Dec. 1925] Savoy Hotel, La Turbie

I feah ma passpo't prob'ly arrive at Nice. Have been laid up with bad cold, but a hot grog & a hot brick wrapped in the *Morning Post* v. comfortable. Hope to join you by end of week.

Yrs
Tar Baby[2]

FROM *Dr Hubert Higgins* MS Valerie Eliot

Sunday [December 1925] 46 Brook St, London W.1

Dear Eliot,

Your wife is really better and, I am sure, very keen and eager to do her best to get thoroughly well. She has been at Stanborough Park now for nearly a week. Lady R's contribution of £50 has paid for the Dr. Your wife paid £21 herself and I paid £52 in addition to this there was travelling expenses and Willard's fee making about £15 extra, leaving a balance. The matron at Stanborough Park is an old friend of mine, a kindly, competent woman who has lived a long time in the U.S. and acquired, *more Britannica*, some of your more desirable characteristics. I am most annoyed about the cold, it's a beastly waste of time for you. I wish you were at Rapallo.

On the whole, bar the tiresome and annoying cold, you are all the better for your rest. I will complete your [?cemetarium] against wastage of 'vital force' (so called for want of a better phrase) as well as [illegible] for its

1–Addressed to 'Ole Marse Ezra Pound'.
2–Like the Possum, the Tar-Baby is a character in Joel Chandler Harris's *Uncle Remus*. It is a doll made of tar and turpentine, used to trap Br'er Rabbit in the second story.

creation &c &c & storage. Please let me know whether it was or was not, in your judgment, a mistake to have loaded my stuff on to your brain. Has it clarified things? If it has, I hope it has operated unconsciously.

With my best wishes and heartiest congratulations for your restoration

Yours sincerely
Hubert Higgins

PS I should be obliged if you could send a P.C. for me to Miss Fanny Gilbertson, Hotel Washington, Lugano, Swizzera, giving details about prices and hotels. She is a favourite patient of mine about eighty-three.

Vivien Eliot TO *Sydney and Violet Schiff* MS Valerie Eliot

16 December 1925 The Stanboroughs, Watford

Dear Violet and Sydney,

I have always looked upon you as friends. Am I right? I am in a very great difficulty, and in a most lonely and precarious situation. I do not know what to do, and I can think of no people who could advise me better than yourselves.

Would it be possible for you to motor here and see me any afternoon during the next week, from today? You can ring me up here – *1.30* is the best time, or 6 oclock to 9. If you come, come about 2.30 or 3, not morning when I have treatments. When you come, ask to see the matron, and ask her if you may take me out for a short drive and return me.

You must not be upset at my looks – I look worse than I am. This is chiefly worry and fear and torment. Send me *a line* directly in return for this, and tell me *what you will do*. I am going quite gray. Do help me. Do write and then do *come*.

Yrs ever
Vivienne[1]

TO *Gorham B. Munson* CC

16 December 1925 Savoy Hotel, La Turbie

Dear Mr Munson

I am just on my way back to England, but I have today received your letter, forwarded from London, and I cannot forbear writing a line to say

1 – This letter was forwarded by the Schiffs to TSE: see SS's letter to TSE, 27 Dec.

I do hope you will go on along this line with your investigations.[1] That is exactly the conclusion I had come to from Babbitt's last book,[2] and I thought no one had seen it except myself. It has been growing on him, but one only sees it clearly in the *Democracy and Leadership* book.[3] There, it is almost enough to *faire craquer le système*[4] – this constant leading up to the point of Christian ethics – just avoiding the bankruptcy of the '*inner* check'. The Holy Ghost always descends in the nick of time, and always in disguise.[5]

It is no use, I feel, calling *his* attention to this. And the Frenchmen have not got any farther from *their* direction (though please examine Maritain's books). I should like to recommend to you one who seems honest as well as learned – Gonzague Truc (*La retour à la scholastique, L'avenir de la raison, Notre temps* just out, I have not seen this last).[6] But you are on the right line anyway. I hope you will let me see anything you write.

Sincerely yours
[T. S. E.]

TO *Leonard Woolf* TS Berg

17 December [1925] Savoy Hotel, La Turbie

Dear Leonard

I have just seen your review of my poems, which my secretary has sent me; it is the only review I have seen.[7] This is merely to say that it gave me great pleasure, and I much appreciate the whole of it, but especially your

1–See Munson. 'The Socratic Virtues of Irving Babbitt', *NC* 4: 3 (June 1926), 494–503. Munson wanted to uncover the 'crucial problem Babbitt presents, namely whether religious virtues, which in spite of several denials and qualifications he appears to claim for humanism, can really be achieved by the habitual practise of a humanistic technique'.
2–Probably *Rousseau and Romanticism* (1919).
3–Munson's essay is largely a response to *Democracy and Leadership* (1924).
4–'Make the system crack' (French).
5–TSE returns to the argument in 'The Humanism of Irving Babbitt', *Forum* 80: 1 (July 1928), taking issue with the doctrine of the 'inner check' which runs through Babbitt's work. He argues too that Babbitt's humanism is 'alarmingly like very liberal Protestant theology of the nineteenth century' and a 'by-product' of 'Protestant theology in its last agonies' (*SE*, 475).
6–Gonzague Truc, *Le Retour à la scolastique* [The Return to Scholasticism] (1919); *L'Avenir de la raison, prolégomènes à une histoire de la raison* [The Future of Reason, Prolegomena to a History of Reason] (1922); *Notre Temps* ['Our Time'] (1925).
7–LW – in '"Jug Jug" to Dirty Ears', a review of *P 1909–1925* (*N&A* 28, 5 Dec. 1925, 354) – called TSE 'a long way the best of the modern poets . . . a real poet'; 'the spirit of the age is breathed' into *TWL*, 'much as the spirit of 1850 was breathed into "In Memoriam"'.

generously extra-critical remarks at the beginning! Your stricture does certainly apply to the whole book, but I purposely omitted some incomplete things to which I think it would not apply, because I thought it better to wind up and liquidate this phase and start afresh.[1] The book gives me no pleasure – and I think *The Waste Land* appears at a disadvantage in the midst of all this other stuff, some of which was not even good enough to reprint. But I regard the book merely as an ejection, a means of getting all that out of the way.

I hope to be back about Christmas time, and hope that I shall find you and Virginia both very well.

Yours ever
T. S. Eliot

TO *Richard Aldington* — TS Texas

17 December [1925] — Savoy Hotel, La Turbie

My dear Richard

I expect to arrive in London on Christmas Eve. I should like to see you (for one reason) before I see Routledge.[2] IF convenient for you and your wife, I think the best way would be for me to spend a night with you the following week. IF that suits you, will you drop me a line to 9 Clarence Gate Gardens to say what nights are NOT convenient – I think any would do for me, but of course cannot tell what I shall have to do till I arrive. IF not convenient for me to come at all, please say when and where we can meet.

I don't know about Whibley. I had a letter from him the other day, quite agreeable, but making no mention of the book I had sent him. I got a vague impression of depression from the letter – whether the Tudors[3] (as I suspect) have not gone well, or ill health, or old age, or the feeling of failure which I think he gets from time to time, I don't know. I shall go down to see him before long, and find out what's wrong.

1–LW's only criticism of TSE's poems was 'that the theme which he plays on these subtle strings is always the same and is very old. The splendour and romance of our desires and imaginations, the sordidness of reality – that is the theme of Prufrock, of Sweeney, of Burbank, of The Waste Land, of the Hollow Men.' TSE's reference to omitting 'incomplete things' may refer to *SA*: 'Fragment of a Prologue' was to come out in *NC* 4: 4 (Oct. 1926).
2–To discuss the relation between F&G's 'Foreign Men of Letters' and The Republic of Letters for Routledge.
3–The Tudor Translations series, ed. by CW.

Best cordial Christmas wishes to you both,

Ever affectionately
Tom

Please let me inscribe my book for you when we meet. I have only seen one review – Leonard Woolf's.[1] It is very kindly, but it does not encourage me.

TO *Vivien Eliot*[2]

MS Valerie Eliot

18 December [1925] Savoy Hotel, La Turbie

My dear Wee,[3]

Very pleased to get yr. letter of the 18th from Stanborough. I am leaving tomorrow and arrive Rapallo tomorrow night. It only costs 10/- first class. I must find out about trains Rapallo–Calais when I get there, but if nothing goes wrong I shall arrange to arrive in London on 24th (Thursday). I shall send you a wire from Dover just to let you know I have crossed safely; you will not hear from me again till then unless some alteration has to be made. Could not leave sooner as passport has only just arrived, and had to get Italian visa.

My love till then

T.

Vivien Eliot TO *Ellen Kellond*[4]

MS Valerie Eliot

Sunday night [20? Dec. 1925] The Stanboroughs, Watford

Dear Ellen,

Don't say anything about Lady R. to anyone, *or to Mr Eliot*. You understand. But Ellen dear tell him his wife does love him and still loves him and always always has loved him, (*he does not believe I do*). Ask him to be kind to me, and to forgive me for any wrongs I've done him. *Ask*

1–LW, '"Jug Jug" to Dirty Ears'.
2–From a handwritten copy by VHE, enclosed with her letter to Ellen Kellond, [21? Dec.].
3–The origin of this pet name is not known.
4–Ellen Kellond had been the Eliots' maid since 1918, and the letter was addressed to her at 6 Elgin Avenue, Maida Vale, London W.9. TSE said that part of 'The Game of Chess' was 'pure Ellen Kellond' (*TWL: Facs*, 127). When Ellen left their service the following Mar. to get married, VHE told OM (27 Mar.): 'She has been my greatest – best – almost only friend for nine years.'

and *beg* him to come *quickly* and fetch me away and have me with him for Xmas. And to put me right with these people here, for Ellen I am in such an *awful* position. The humiliation of it. Dr Higgins is very angry, and I fear Mr Eliot will be angry. *O dont let him. Promise* me I can come home for Xmas. Order *Beasley's* car for Thursday or perhaps it will be engaged.

If Mr Eliot does not arrive till night, what shall I do? I shall go mad Ellen.

Vivien Eliot TO *Ellen Kellond*

MS Valerie Eliot

Monday morning [?21 Dec. 1925] The Stanboroughs, Watford

Dear Ellen

Here is a copy of Mr Eliot's letter to me, which has just this moment arrived.[1] This is an answer to *two of mine* which were *long* letters and *most affectionate* and in which I *begged* him to have me home for Xmas. *So now you can see for yourself*. Is this like the Mr Eliot you used to know? You see, he no longer wants me and no longer cares for me. O Ellen what shall I do what shall I do. And I am kept here *in the pretence* that it is *to get me well*, while they torture me with neglect, and cruelty, and despair. I have not slept at all for the last two nights, and for the last four nights I think I have only slept about six hours in all.

Yet I am kept here *for my health*. I am banished from my home, from my husband, from my parents, from all and everything that makes life worth living, by the will of one man and one woman, who [*sc.* you] know who – so that they may secure my husband and turn him from me for ever. Well Ellen, this is the end of it. I mean to take my life. At the first opportunity I shall do so. It is difficult here, but I shall find a way. This is the end.

V. H. Eliot.

Keep all my letters. *You will need them soon.*

1 – TSE's letter of 18 Dec.

Vivien Eliot TO *Dr Hubert Higgins* MS Valerie Eliot

Tuesday 22 December [1925] The Stanboroughs, Watford

Dear Dr Higgins

I have very good news of my husband from Mr Pound with whom he is staying – telling me that he is in *excellent health* and *spirits*. Mr Pound has known him for twelve years, so he can judge, (he has also been very ill himself for years and *knows* about health).

I know how pleased you will be. You need no longer make him out an invalid (or an imbecile). Thank you for your letter. I have an idea which I think will meet *everybody*'s wishes, *and I shd. like to discuss it with you when* I have seen my husband. (Brighton – yes).

You see, the first time you came to see me here you said I was to stay two or three months, and the next time you said you had never intended that I shd. stay here. So in points of consistency there is nothing to choose between us.

If I find you have induced my husband to disbelieve my statements I shall kill myself. I feel so ill and so worried that I have gone and *kept* the nurse another week, Dr Rubli also thinking it advisable.

I need to go to the dentist at once, *and* the oculist at once. I am all *falling to pieces* and to keep me anywhere in this state is certainly not for my *health*.

Will you help me to get all these things seen to. And Xmas! If am left here alone over Xmas I shall [sentence unfinished]

If my husband *won't* help me you can rely on J. R. Culpin Esq. C/o Anglo-Argentine Bank, 24 Lombard St, E.C.3 (Royal 4020) to do any business and arrangements for me.[1] He will always help in any way.

Some friends of ours [Sydney and Violet Schiff] who have known us since we were married and who have known Lady Rothermere for many many years are motoring down to see me today as they are anxious. They will find me a dreadful sight.

1–J. C. Culpin told TSE (25 Nov.) that he had seen IPF, who had given him 'an account of what had happened & of her news of Vivien . . . [A]s far as can be judged by Vivien's letters, she appears to have passed through the crisis.' He had been to see Ellen Kellond at Clarence Gate and looked in at the other flat in Burleigh Mansions (which TSE had offered for his use) and found everything 'satisfactory'. He would be happy to attend to any of TSE's affairs if needed.

I am in constant communication with the Eliot family, who, oddly, are fond of me! They are very worried over all this.

With sincere good-feeling
Yours
V. H. Eliot

PS I was unhappy here and I did write to my husband asking to be sent to Margate with a *good elderly* nurse. I take it he communicated with you.

Later. When I think of all that my husband has done for me, and of all the life I smashed up (as I do think of it, all night and much of the day) I do not know why I dont go out and hang myself.

There is so much opportunity for sorrow and brooding here and the atmosphere fosters it. I feel *absolutely* <u>done</u>.

Vivien Eliot TO *Ellen Kellond* — MS Valerie Eliot

Undated [late December 1925] — The Stanboroughs, Watford

Don't trust Miss Fassett – she is *not altogether my friend*. You could better trust Mr and Mrs Schiff
Mrs Hutchinson
the Sitwells
Mrs Woolf
Lady Ottoline *Morrell*
Dr <u>Miller.</u>[1]

Vivien Eliot TO *Ottoline Morrell* — MS Texas

23 December 1925 — The Stanboroughs, Watford

Dearest Ottoline

I am only writing to wish you a very very happy Christmas and to tell you that I am now nearly well. I am leaving here in a few weeks, and going to Brighton, to finish the cure.

I have thought of you very often. I hope you have not forgotten me. I should love to see you. If you go to London, do let me know in time. Do write, anyhow, and tell me how you are.

1 – Dr Raymond Miller, one of VHE's doctors, had a practice at 110 Harley Street. On 10 Feb. 1926, he reported on VHE's progress to TSE. He was not worried about her fears, and recommended that they move into their new house together. VHE 'liked to be a sort of dressed up doll', and she felt 'in her mind' that she must 'dominate' TSE or he would dominate her. He told TSE he regretted the tendency to 'make the circles of your lives too coincident'.

I feel so much better.
With ever so much love.

Affectly
Vivienne Eliot

Vivien Eliot TO *Mary Hutchinson* MS Texas

23 December 1925 The Stanboroughs, Watford

Dear Mary

Your letter was forwarded to me here, and I have been intending to write to you, but I have been so busy arranging my next plans.

How sad that you have given up Eleanor.[1] Only I think in the long run every change is good – don't you!

I am *nearly* well now, and going to London soon, and then to Brighton, or abroad. Perhaps I shall see you then, before long. I do hope so.

Of course I have no news, but you must have a great deal. I should love to meet you again, after such ages. It will seem like starting a new life, to me.

Do write again. *Write anything*, about yourself.

My love
Vivien

FROM *Sydney Schiff* MS Valerie Eliot

27 December 1925 18 Cambridge Square, Hyde Park, London

My dear Tom

There is no letter so far from Vivienne though (exceptionally) there was a post this morning. The enclosed is the one that caused our visit.[2] The agitation apparent therein was less in evidence than the letter would have led one to anticipate and passed away gradually during the afternoon until – towards the end – she became perfectly reasonable.

Recalling her long account of her experiences, the point she seemed most concerned to emphasize was that her habit of taking chloral during many

1–Eleanor House, which the Hutchinsons had rented in West Wittering.
2–The Schiffs had visited VHE at the Stanboroughs, as she had implored them to do: SS enclosed her letter of 16 Dec.

years was the cause of all her troubles and she repeated several times that though she still slept very badly and could not dispense with a night nurse, nothing would induce her ever to take a narcotic again.

Yours ever affectly
Sydney

TO *Ezra Pound*

TS Beinecke

27 December 1925 9 Clarence Gate Gdns

caro lapino,[1]

jes to reassure you – its as I thought – all moonshine. But delighted at the idea of coming with me later in hot weather and bathing. Physically fitter than I have ever seen her, I think. Otherwise, much to be desired, Im not so optimistic as I might be. She is to go to Brighton in a furnished flat with a nurse. But there are *some* very good signs.

Yew dropped a brick for a minute in telling her I look in exclnt health. Itll come out in the wash, but dr. was trying to impress her I had been on the verge and was just pulling round with care and treatment, people in this state always inclining to vampire.[2]

Anny way, I shll thank God when the next six months is over, if still alive.

Coming to Rapallo was well wuth it, for me. Shall communicate shortly about finances. Comfortable journey.

Finding myself having to explain how I heard a bit of Antheil, said you played me bits on the barroom piano.[3]

ever
T.

Find she may have written letters and spread undesirable (and untrue) rumours about me.* If you shd at any time hear such, youll be ready for them, & will have to say she has had a nervous breakdown. And you might let me know. Im ready to wipe up after these rumours when necessary.
<It appears that at the first place they had to remove your works as she would read em the whole time?>[4]
*<But on the whole I found her extremely affectionate.>

1 – 'Dear Rabbit' (Italian) – an equivalent to 'Br'er Rabbit'.
2 – See VHE's letter to Dr Higgins of 22 Dec.
3 – EP was continuing to promote the US composer George Antheil, on whom he wrote his next piece for TSE, 'Antheil, 1924–1926', *NC* 4: 4 (Oct. 1926), 695–9.
4 – The 'first place' was Elmsleigh, nr. Southampton, where VHE was treated for a while.

TO *Arnold Bennett* MS Beinecke

Tuesday, 28 December [1925] *The Criterion*, 17 Thavies Inn

Dear Mr Bennett

I was extremely sorry to fail, especially after your kindness in making a second appointment. I shall be out again soon, and if it is not too importunate should like to come next week (or I could come to tea on *Saturday*). But unless the latter, please don't bother to answer. I will write again and ring up afterwards.

With apologies and regrets

Yours very sincerely
T. S. Eliot

TO *Ottoline Morrell* TS Texas

29 December 1925 9 Clarence Gate Gdns

My dear Ottoline,

This is just to say that I got back late on Christmas Eve, and found your little diary, which gave me very great pleasure – more than I can tell you; for indeed I expected that you would forget me this year. Also a parcel and a letter which I took out to Vivien; I do not know what you gave her, but I know that both present and letter made her very happy, and she has expressed great affection for you. I cannot tell you how much I appreciate and value your friendship and loyalty.

So I hope you got the volume of my poems which I sent you from France?

I am frightfully rushed at the moment, and will write more fully in a week or so. I should like very much to see you, and I should like to see you before Vivien does.

Ever affectionately
Tom

Vivien Eliot TO *Ottoline Morrell* TS Texas

30 December 1925 The Stanboroughs, Watford

Dearest Ottoline,

I only sent you a card, in haste, to thank you for your very *very* beautiful present. I was so *touched* that you remembered me, after so long!

Being away from everyone for a long time makes one realise who really are the friends of one's *choice*, and who one needs to keep. I do need yr. friendship, and hope you will give it to me – will you? I have thought of you very often. I feel there is so much in you I have never really appreciated.

I have been busy arranging to move from here – that's lucky I did not write sooner. I am much *better*, only not yet *strong*, or up to much effort. I leave here on *Monday*, and go to *9 Clarence Gate for a week* or so. *Then to Brighton* for a long stay, to get really strong. Can I see you? You *do* go to Brighton you know. Get yr. husband, or a nice rich friend or relation to take you there for a long visit! *Please do*. Tom will be down each week.

[Enclosed]:

O Ottoline how could you?
How could you Ottoline
How could you take me in like that
And make feel so 'green'.

O what a truly Otto-trick
Upon a friend to play
To make her feel as green as grass
Upon a Christmas Day!

For when I got your letter
In which you said 'Alas!
I've done no Christmas shopping
So let's let the Season pass'.

I turned again to 'regimen'
And thought 'how wise is she'
I won't send ANY present
And let d—d Christmas be'.

But as I sniff your glorious scent
My one pet Luxureee
I say 'thank Heaven Ottoline
Has played this trick on me'!

December 26th,
With apologies and great love.

FROM *Vivien Eliot* Telegram Valerie Eliot

11.30 30 December 1925 Watford

AFRAID HIGGINS[1] CHOOSING OUT-SKIRTS BRIGHTON TERRIFIED ISOLATION MELANCHOLIA CAN YOU WIRE HIM DO HELP DIVISION
[incomplete]

Vivien Eliot TO *Charlotte Eliot*[2] TS Victoria

Received about 30 December 1925 [The Stanboroughs, Watford]

My dear Mrs Eliot:

Today I have received your nice kind letter, dated November 29. I hope you have heard frequently from Tom. He is at La Turbie, which is a small place over Monte Carlo. I believe he is leaving there within the next few days and going to see Ezra Pound in Italy, and then to Paris on his way back. It should have done his health good. I do not know exactly *when* he is returning to England.

I have left the home in Southampton, where you sent your letter. I did not like it very much, although in many ways my health was greatly improved there. I am now at a Sanatorium which is under an American doctor, and which is run by people who belong to a religious sect call the Seventh Day Adventists. The food is entirely vegetarian. There are very elaborate treatment rooms where one may have every possible kind of electrical treatment, heat and light and galvanism, and baths of every description, and massage. There is a staff of well trained nurses who give the treatments. As I am still far from well, and unable to sleep, I have a nurse of my own, who sleeps in my room. She is very nice to me. I should be most unhappy but for that. Of course it costs me more, and soon I fear I must do without her.

How I wish I could see you. Do not let Tom come to America without me. I *must* come. My family are all in Italy – in Rome, and with Tom also abroad I feel very very lonely.

Yes, Tom is still to edit the *New Criterion*, and under different circumstances, but as it is all so complicated – all his new business arrangements, I shall leave it to him to tell you of them.

1–Dr Hubert Higgins. TSE told CCE (12 Jan. 1926) that VHE was back at Clarence Gate with a nurse.
2–The text is from a typed copy, made and dated by CCE for HWE.

So Henry is to be married in February. I wish we might be present at the wedding. I think of you with great devotion. Do not forget me. Keep well for my sake. *Never die.*

FROM *Geoffrey Faber* TO *Lady Rothermere* CC

30 December 1925 [London]

Dear Lady Rothermere,

I have now got from our solicitors the various documents which require your approval, or the approval of your representatives before we can go ahead with the formation of 'The New *Criterion* Ltd'.[1] Will you kindly let me know whether you wish these to be sent direct to you or if not, whom do you wish to act for you? The agreement you and we signed recently provides that the Memorandum and Articles of Association shall be approved by your legal advisers. Will you, if you wish them to consider the Articles on your behalf, kindly send me their name and address. Alternatively, of course, I can send them to Mr Horne.[2] But that is just as you desire.

Eliot has just returned from La Turbie and is a different man after the change. But I fear he has a difficult time ahead of him.

Yours sincerely,
[Geoffrey C. Faber]

1 – At a Directors' Meeting to be held on 21 June 1928, Geoffrey Faber opened proceedings by rehearsing the circumstances under which the Company was founded:

'The Criterion had hitherto been operated solely upon the private generosity of Lady Rothermere, and at a cost to her in the neighbourhood of £750 per annum. This figure was borne in mind when the preliminary agreement between herself and Messrs. Faber & Gwyer Limited, which led to the founding of The New Criterion, was drawn up. The arrangement was of the following character: The number of Ordinary Shares in the new company was fixed at 20,000 Ordinary one shilling shares, of which 10,500 were allotted to Messrs. Faber & Gwyer Limited and 9,500 to Lady Rothermere. The money received from these shares was paid to Lady Rothermere and to Messrs. Faber & Gwyer Limited as consideration for the copyright and the undertaking to publish. The working capital was provided by 5,000 £1 Preference Shares of which 3,500 were allotted to Lady Rothermere and the balance in effect to Messrs. Faber & Gwyer Limited. It was hoped that this would be sufficient to finance the publication of the review for five years, the deficit on publication being estimated to amount to £1,000 a year. In effect this would mean that Lady Rothermere would find £700 and Messrs. Faber & Gwyer £300 a year. Under the new arrangement provision was made for the payment of a salary to the Editor, no salary having previously been paid. At the formation of the Company the amount of 8s. per share was called up, and the Company therefore started operations on a working capital of £2,000. The first number was published in January 1926.' – 'Memorandum of a Directors' Meeting' (Present: GCF, TSE, the Company Secretary)

2 – H. S. Horne, Solicitor, 74 Park Street, London W.1.

TO *F. Scott Fitzgerald*[1]

TS Princeton

31 December 1925

Faber & Gwyer Ltd,
24 Russell Sq, London W.C.1

Dear Mr Scott Fitzgerald,

The Great Gatsby with your charming and overpowering inscription arrived the very morning I was leaving in some haste for a sea voyage advised by my doctor.[2] I therefore left it behind and only read it on my return a few days ago. I have, however, now read it three times. I am not in the least influenced by your remark about myself when I say that it has interested and excited me more than any new novel I have seen, either English or American, for a number of years.

When I have time I should like to write to you more fully and tell you exactly why it seems to me such a remarkable book. In fact it seems to me to be the first step that American fiction has taken since Henry James.[3]

I have recently become associated in the capacity of a director with the publishing firm whose name you see above. May I ask you, if you have not already committed yourself to publish *The Great Gatsby* with some other publishing house in London, to let us take the matter up with you?[4] I think that if we published the book we could do as well by you as anyone.

1–F. Scott Fitzgerald (1896–1940): novelist and short-story writer; author of *This Side of Paradise* (1920), *The Beautiful and the Damned* (1922), and *The Great Gatsby* (1925). This letter from TSE was reproduced, with the third paragraph omitted, in F. Scott Fitzgerald, *The Crack-Up*, ed. Edmund Wilson (1945).

2–TSE's copy was inscribed: 'For T. S. Elliot [*sic*] / Greatest of Living Poets / from his enthusiastic / worshipper / F. Scott Fitzgerald. / Paris. / Oct / 1925.' Replying in early Feb. 1926 Fitzgerald said that 'A Portrait of a Lady' was his 'favourite modern poem'. He also described the 'elation' he had felt when Edmund Wilson had given him the proofs of *TWL* to read.

3–Fitzgerald wrote to Maxwell Perkins (20 Feb. 1926): 'Now, confidential. T. S. Eliot for whom you know my profound admiration – I think he's the greatest living poet in any language –wrote me. He'd read Gatsby 3 times *and* thought it was the *1st step forward* American fiction had taken since Henry James' (Matthew J. Bruccoli, *F. Scott Fitzgerald: A Life in Letters*, 1994, 137). TSE's praise, he believed, 'was easily the nicest thing that's happened . . . in connection with *Gatsby*'; and he later told Ernest Hemingway it made him feel like 'the biggest man in my profession . . . everybody admired me and I was proud I'd done such a good thing' (quoted in Scott Donaldson, *Hemingway vs. Fitzgerald: The Rise and Fall of a Literary Friendship* [2000]).

4–*The Great Gatsby* was committed to Chatto & Windus: it was published in Feb. 1926.

By the way, if you ever have any short stories which you think would be suitable for the *Criterion* I wish you would let me see them.[1]

With many thanks,

I am,
Yours very truly,
T. S. Eliot

PS By a coincidence Gilbert Seldes in his New York Chronicle in the *Criterion* for January 14th has chosen your book for particular mention.[2]

TO *F. L. Lucas*[3] cc

31 December 1925 [London]

Dear Mr Lucas,

I hope that you will remember that I had the pleasure of coming to see you one Sunday last year at King's. In any case you probably do not know that I have become associated with the publishing firm of Faber & Gwyer who also publish the *Criterion*. I am writing to you in my role of publisher because I have heard indirectly that you have recently written a novel, the publication of which, I hope, is not yet arranged. If the rumour is correct and if my hope is justified, may I ask you to consider letting us see your manuscript?[4]

1–None of Fitzgerald's stories appeared in *C*.

2–Gilbert Seldes, in 'New York Chronicle' (*NC* 4: 1, Jan. 1926, 170–7), observed that the American press had been not 'too enthusiastic' about Fitzgerald's novel, but said it was 'a brilliant work' which 'has structure, and . . . has life'. *The Great Gatsby* was reviewed later by Conrad Aiken in *NC* 4: 4 (Oct. 1926). Though Aiken called it 'a highly coloured and brilliant little novel', he was less impressed: 'It is not great, it is not large, it is not strikingly subtle . . .'

3–F. L. Lucas (1894–1967): English classical scholar, literary critic, and poet; Fellow and Librarian of King's College, Cambridge; author of *Seneca and Elizabethan Tragedy* (1922) and *Euripides and his Influence* (1924).

4–Lucas's novel *The River Flows* was published by the Hogarth Press in Oct. 1926.

I hope that you will be in Cambridge during the winter term as I have been looking forward to meeting you again when I come up to lecture at Trinity.[1]

Sincerely yours,
[T. S. E.]

TSE/IPF

1–Lucas had published a hostile rev. of *TWL*: 'a poem that has to be explained in notes is not unlike a picture with "This is a dog" inscribed beneath'; he added, 'the borrowed jewels he has set in its head do not make Mr Eliot's toad the more prepossessing' (*NS* 22, 3 Nov. 1923, 118). According to E. M. W. Tillyard, Lucas was 'openly hostile' to TSE at Cambridge (*The Muse Unchained* [1958], 98); and according to T. E. B. Howarth, Lucas 'would not even allow Eliot's work to be bought for the library' (*Cambridge Between Two Wars* [1978], 166). See TSE on *The Complete Works of John Webster* (4 vols), ed. Lucas, in *NC* 7: 4 (June 1928), 443–6.

GLOSSARY OF NAMES

Conrad Aiken (1889–1973): American poet and critic. Though he and Eliot were a year apart at Harvard, they became close friends, and fellow editors of *The Harvard Advocate*. TSE said he had 'gone in for psycho-analysis with a Swinburnian equipment' and did not 'escape the fatal American introspectiveness' ('Reflections on Contemporary Poetry', *Egoist* 6: 3, July 1919). Aiken wrote a witty memoir of their times together, 'King Bolo and Others', in *T. S. Eliot: A Symposium*, ed. Richard Marsh and Tambimuttu (1948), describing how they revelled in the comic strips of 'Krazy Kat, and Mutt and Jeff' and in 'American slang'. His writings include volumes of poetry among them *Earth Triumphant* (1914); the Eliot-influenced *House of Dust* (1921); and *Selected Poems* (1929), which won the Pulitzer Prize 1930; editions of *Modern American Poets* (1922), and *Selected Poems of Emily Dickinson* (1924); and essays gathered up in *Scepticisms* (1923) and *Collected Criticism* (1968). His eccentric auto-biographical novel *Ushant: An Essay* (1952) provides a satirical portrait of TSE as 'Tsetse'.

Richard Aldington (1892–1962): poet, critic, translator, biographer, novelist. A friend of Ezra Pound, he was one of the founders of the Imagist movement; a contributor to *Des Imagistes* (1914); and assistant editor of *The Egoist*. In 1913 he married the American poet H. D., though they were soon estranged. In 1914 he volunteered for WW1, but his enlistment was deferred for medical reasons; he went on active service in June 1916 and was sent to France in December (TSE replaced him as literary editor of *The Egoist*). During the war, he rose from the ranks to be an acting captain in the Royal Sussex Regiment. He drew on his experiences in the poems of *Images of War* (1919) and the novel *Death of a Hero* (1929). After WW1, he became friends with TSE, working as his assistant on the *Criterion* and introducing him to Bruce Richmond, editor of the *TLS* (for which TSE wrote some of his finest essays). From 1919 Aldington himself was a regular reviewer of French literature for the *TLS*. In 1928 he went to live in France, where, except for a period in the USA (1935–47), he spent the rest of his life. He is best known for his early Imagist poetry and translations. In 1931, he published *Stepping Heavenward*, a lampoon of

TSE – who is portrayed as 'Blessed Jeremy Cibber': 'Father Cibber, O.S.B.' – and Vivien (as 'Adele Palaeologue'). This ended their friendship. His growing estrangement from Eliot was further publicised in an essay written in the 1930s but published only in 1954, *Ezra Pound and T. S Eliot: A Lecture*, which takes both poets to task for their putatively plagiaristic poetry. He also wrote an autobiography, *Life for Life's Sake* (1941), controversial biographies of D. H. Lawrence and T. E. Lawrence; and *Complete Poems* (1948). See also *Richard Aldington: An Intimate Portrait*, ed. Alister Kershaw and Frédéric-Jacques Temple (1965), which includes a brief tribute by Eliot; 'Richard Aldington's Letters to Herbert Read', ed. David S. Thatcher, *The Malahat Review* 15 (July 1970), 5–44; Charles Doyle, *Richard Aldington: A Biography* (1989); *Richard Aldington: A Life in Letters*, ed. Norman T. Gates (1992); *Richard Aldington & H. D.: Their lives in letters 1918–61*, ed. Caroline Zilboorg (2003).

Francis William Bain (1863–1940): author and scholar; educated at Christ Church, Oxford; Fellow of All Souls College, Oxford, 1889–97; Professor of History and Political Economy at the Deccan College at Poona, India – where he came to be considered 'not only as a professor but also as a prophet and a philosopher' – 1892–1919. An old-style High Tory, enthused by the writings of Bolingbroke and Disraeli, his publications included *The English Monarchy and its Revolutions* (1894) and *On the Realisation of the Possible and the Spirit of Aristotle* (1897), and a series of 'Hindu love stories' purportedly translated from Sanskrit originals. See K. Mutalik, *Francis William Bain* (Bombay, 1963).

Julien Benda (1867–1956): journalist, political and social philosopher, and critic. Born into a Jewish family in Paris, he studied history at the Sorbonne, and was quickly recognised as a noted essayist and '*intellectuel*', writing for a variety of periodicals including *Revue Blanche*, *Nouvelle Revue Française*, *Mercure de France*, *Divan* and *Le Figaro*. A passionate upholder of the Graeco-Roman ideal of rational order and disinterestedness – Eliot said that Benda's 'brand of classicism is just as romantic as anyone else's' – his works include *Dialogues à Byzance* (1900), complete with pro-Dreyfus pieces; *Le Bergsonisme: ou, Une Philosophie de la mobilité* (1912); *Belphégor: Essai sur l'esthétique de la présente société française* (1918); and *Le Trahison des clercs* (1927; trans. by Richard Aldington as *The Treason of the Intellectuals*, 1928). See Ray Nichols, *Treason, Tradition, and the Intellectual: Julien Benda and Political Discourse* (1978).

Arnold Bennett (1867–1931), author and journalist (and son of a weaver and tailor who eventually qualified and practised as a solicitor), grew up among 'the five towns' of the Potteries and began work at the age of sixteen in a solicitor's office; but he swiftly made a name for himself as a journalist and prolific author. His best-selling novels include *A Man from the North* (1898), *Anna of the Five Towns* (1902), and *The Old Wives' Tale* (1908) – the first book in the Clayhanger trilogy. His plays, including *The Great Adventure* (1913), were just as successful, with much naturalistic and effective dialogue; and it was in his capacity as a capable dramatist that TSE consulted him in the early 1920s – ironically when Eliot was attempting to write a determinedly (and ultimately unrealised) experimental play, *Sweeney Agonistes*. It says much for Bennett that he took TSE seriously and gave him advice that was valued. See *The Journals of Arnold Bennett*, ed. N. Flowers (3 vols, 1932–5); and Margaret Drabble, *Arnold Bennett: A Biography* (1974).

Marguerite Caetani, née Chapin (1880–1963) – born in Connecticut, she was a half-sister to Katherine Biddle, and a cousin of TSE – was married in 1911 to the wealthy Roffredo Caetani, 17th Duke of Sermoneta and the Prince of Bassiano. A generous patron of the arts, she founded in Paris a review called *Commerce*, 1918–39; and then, in Rome, *Botteghe oscure*, 1948–60, a biannual review featuring poetry and fiction from many nations – Britain, Germany, Italy, France, Spain and the USA – with all contributions being published in their original languages. Among the many celebrated authors gathered up in the journal were André Malraux, Albert Camus, Paul Valéry, Ignazio Silone, Robert Graves, Archibald MacLeish, e. e. cummings and Marianne Moore.

Richard Cobden-Sanderson (1884–1964), printer and publisher, was the son of the bookbinder and printer, T. J. Cobden-Sanderson (1840–1922), who was Bertrand Russell's godfather; and grandson of the politician and economist Richard Cobden (1804–65). He became the publisher of the *Criterion* from its first number in October 1922 until it was taken over by Faber & Gwyer in 1925. He also published three books with introductions by TSE: *Le Serpent* by Paul Valéry (1924), Charlotte Eliot's *Savonarola* (1926), and Harold Monro's *Collected Poems* (1933). In addition, his firm produced books by Edmund Blunden and David Gascoyne, editions of Shelley, and volumes illustrated by Rex Whistler. He became a dependable friend as well as a colleague of TSE.

Jean Cocteau (1889–1963), playwright, poet, librettist, novelist, film-maker, artist and designer, was born near Paris and established an early reputation with two volumes of verse, *La Lampe d'Aladin* [*Aladdin's Lamp*] and *Prince Frivole* [*The Frivolous Prince*]. Becoming associated with many of the foremost exponents of experimental modernism such as Proust, Gide, Picasso, Stravinsky, Erik Satie, Amedeo Modigliani and Sergei Diaghilev, he turned his remarkable energies to many modes of artistic creativity ranging from ballet-scenarios to opera-scenarios, as well as fiction and drama. 'Astonish me!' urged Diaghilev. A quick collaborator in all fields, his works embrace stage productions such as *Parade* (1917, produced by Diaghilev, with music by Satie and designs by Picasso); *Oedipus Rex* (1927, music by Stravinsky); and *La Machine Infernale* (produced at the Comédie des Champs-Elysées, 1934); novels including *Les Enfants Terribles* (1929; translated as *Enfants Terribles*, 1930); and the screenplay *Le Sang d'un poete* (1930; *The Blood of a Poet*, 1949).

Ernst Robert Curtius (1886–1956), German scholar of philology and Romance literature. Descendant of a line of famous scholars, he studied philology and philosophy at Strassburg, Berlin and Heidelberg, and taught in turn at Marburg, Heidelberg and Bonn. His most substantial work was *Europäische Literatur und Lateinisches Mittelalter* (1948), a study of Medieval Latin literature and its deeply fructifying influence upon the literatures of modern Europe.

Bonamy Dobrée (1891–1974), scholar, editor and critic, was to be Professor of English Literature at Leeds University, 1936–55. After early service in the army (he was twice mentioned in despatches and attained the rank of major), he read English at Christ's College, Cambridge, and taught briefly in London and as a professor of English at the Egyptian University, Cairo. His works include *Restoration Comedy* (1924), *Essays in Biography* (1925), *Restoration Tragedy, 1660–1720* (1929), *Alexander Pope* (1951), and critical editions and anthologies. From 1921 to 1925, Dobrée and his wife Valentine resided at Larrau, a village in the Pyrenees, where he worked as an independent scholar. He was one of TSE's most constant correspondents. See Jason Harding, *The* 'Criterion': *Cultural Politics and Periodical Networks in Inter-War Britain* (2002).

Charlotte Eliot (1874–1926), TSE's third eldest sister, married George Lawrence Smith, an architect, in September 1903. She studied art at college in St Louis and then in Boston, with sculpture being her especial interest.

Charlotte Champe Stearns Eliot (1843–1929), the poet's mother, was born on 22 October in Baltimore, Maryland, the second child and second daughter of Thomas Stearns (1811–96) and Charlotte Blood Stearns (1818–93). She went first to private schools in Boston and Sandwich, followed by three years at the State Normal School, Framingham, Massachusetts, from which she graduated in 1862. After teaching for a while at private schools in West Chester, Pennsylvania, and Milwaukee, Wisconsin, she spent two years with a Quaker family in Coatesville, Pennsylvania. She then taught at Antioch College, Ohio, 1865–7; at her Framingham School; and at St Louis Normal School. It was while she was at the last post that she met Henry Ware Eliot, entrepreneur, whom she married on 27 October 1868. She was secretary of the Mission Free School of the Church of the Messiah for many years. As her youngest child (TSE) was growing up, she became more thoroughly involved in social work through the Humanity Club of St Louis, whose members were disturbed by knowing that young offenders awaiting trial were being held for long periods with adults. In 1899, a committee of two was appointed, with Mrs Eliot as chairman, to bring about reform. It was in large part due to her campaigning and persistence over several years that the Probation Law of 1901 was approved; and in 1903, by mandate of the Juvenile Court Law, a juvenile court was established with its own probation officer and a separate place of detention. As a girl, Charlotte had nursed literary ambitions, and throughout her life wrote poems, some of which (such as 'Easter Songs' and 'Poems on the Apostles') were printed in the *Christian Register*. In 1904 she published *William Greenleaf Eliot: Minister, Educator, Philanthropist*, a memoir of her beloved father-in-law; and it came as a great joy to her when TSE arranged for the publication of her *Savonarola: A Dramatic Poem*, with an introduction by himself (London, 1926). When she was shown the issue of *Smith Academy Record* containing TSE's 'A Lyric' (1905), she said (as TSE would remember) 'that she thought it better than anything in verse she had ever written'. TSE reflected on that fine declaration: 'I knew what her verse meant to her. We did not discuss the matter further.' Inspired by a keen ethic of public service, she was a member of both the Wednesday Club of St Louis and the Missouri Society of the Colonial Dames of America, serving successively as secretary, vice-president, and president. She chaired a committee to award a Washington University scholarship that required the beneficiary to do a certain amount of patriotic work; and in 1917–18 she did further service as chair of the War Work Committee of the Colonial Dames. After the death of her husband in January 1919, she moved home to Cambridge, Massachusetts.

Henry Ware Eliot, Jr (1879–1947), TSE's elder brother, went to school at Smith Academy, and then passed two years at Washington University, St Louis, before progressing to Harvard. At Harvard, he displayed a gift for light verse in *Harvard Celebrities* (Cambridge, Mass., 1901), illustrated with 'Caricatures and Decorative Drawings' by two fellow undergraduates. After graduating, he spent a year at law school, but subsequently followed a career in printing, publishing and advertising. He attained a partnership in Husband & Thomas (later the Buchen Company), a Chicago advertising agency, from 1917 to 1929, during which time he gave financial assistance to TSE and advised him on investments. He accompanied their mother on her visit to London in the summer of 1921, his first trip away from the USA. In February 1926, he married Theresa Anne Garrett (1884–1981), and later the same year the couple went on holiday to Italy along with TSE and Vivien. He was one of TSE's most regular and trusted correspondents. It was not until late in life that he found his true calling, as a research fellow in anthropology at the Peabody Museum, Harvard. He was instrumental in building up the T. S. Eliot collection at Eliot House. Of slighter build than his brother – who remarked upon his 'Fred Astaire figure' – Henry suffered from deafness owing to scarlet fever as a child, and this may have contributed to his diffidence. Unselfishly devoted to TSE, whose growing up he movingly recorded with his camera, Henry took him to his first Broadway musical, *The Merry Widow*, which remained a favourite. It was with his brother in mind that TSE wrote: 'The notion of some infinitely gentle / Infinitely suffering thing' ('Preludes' IV).

Vivien Eliot, née Haigh-Wood (1888–1947). Born in Lancashire, she was brought up in Hampstead from the age of three. Having met TSE in company with Scofield Thayer in Oxford in the spring of 1915, she and TSE hastened to be married just a few weeks later, on 26 June 1915. She developed close friendships with Mary Hutchinson, Ottoline Morrell and others in TSE's circle. Despite chronic personal and medical difficulties, they remained together until 1933, when TSE finally resolved to separate from her during his visit to America. She was never reconciled to their separation, became increasingly ill and unhappy, and in 1938 was confined to a psychiatric hospital, where she died in 1947. She is the dedicatee of *Ash Wednesday* (1930). She published a number of sketches and stories in the *Criterion* (under various pseudonyms with the initials 'F. M.'), and collaborated with TSE on the *Criterion* and other works. See Carole Seymour-Smith, *Painted Shadow: The Life of Vivienne Eliot* (2001).

Geoffrey Faber (1889–1961), publisher and poet, was educated at Malvern College and Christ Church, Oxford, where he took a double first in classical moderations (1910) and *literae humaniores* (1912). He was called to the Bar by the Inner Temple (1921), though he was never to practise the law. In 1919 he was elected a prize fellow of All Souls College, Oxford, which he went on to serve in the capacity of estates bursar, 1923–51. Before WW1 – in which he served with the London Regiment (Post Office Rifles), seeing action in France and Belgium – he spent eighteen months as assistant to Humphrey Milford, publisher of Oxford University Press. After the war, he passed three years working for Strong & Co. Ltd, brewers (there was a family connection), before going in for publishing on a full-time basis by joining forces with his All Souls colleague Maurice Gwyer and his wife, Lady Alsina Gwyer, who were trying to run a specialised imprint called the Scientific Press that Lady Gwyer had inherited from her father, Sir Henry Burdett: its weekly journal, the *Nursing Mirror*, was their most successful output. Following protracted and difficult negotiations, in 1925 Faber became chair of their restructured general publishing house which was provisionally styled Faber & Gwyer. After being introduced by Charles Whibley to T. S. Eliot, Faber was so impressed by the personality and aptitude of the 37-year-old American that he chose both to take on the running of the *Criterion* and to appoint Eliot to the board of his company (Eliot's *Poems 1909–1925* was one of the first books to be put out by the new imprint), which was relocated from Southampton Row to 24 Russell Square. By 1929 both the Gwyers and the *Nursing Mirror* were disposed of to advantage, and the firm took final shape as Faber & Faber, with Richard de la Mare and two additional Americans, Frank Morley and Morley Kennerley, joining the board. Faber chaired the Publishers' Association, 1939–41 – campaigning successfully for the repeal of a wartime tax on books levied by the government – and helping to set up the National Book League. He was knighted in 1954, and gave up the chairmanship of Faber & Faber in 1960. His publications as poet included *The Buried Stream* (1941), and his major works of non-fiction were *Oxford Apostles* (1933) and *Jowett* (1957), and an edition of the works of John Gay (1926). In 1920 he married Enid Richards, with whom he had two sons and a daughter. He died at his home in 1961.

Frank Stuart ('F. S.') Flint (1885–1960), English poet and translator, and civil servant, left school at thirteen but persevered with educating himself in European languages and literature as well as in history and philosophy; in 1908 he started writing articles and reviews for the *New Age*, then for the *Egoist* and for *Poetry* (ed. Harriet Monroe). Quickly gaining in regard and authority (especially on French literature: his influential piece on 'Contemporary French Poetry' appeared in Harold Monro's *Poetry Review* in 1912), he soon became associated with T. E. Hulme, Ezra Pound, Richard Aldington and Hilda Doolittle; and he contributed poems to the *English Review* (ed. by Ford Madox Hueffer, later Ford) and to Pound's anthology *Des Imagistes* (1914). With TSE and Aldous Huxley, he was one of the contributors to *Three Critical Essays on Modern English Poetry*, in *Chapbook* 2: 9 (March 1920). Between 1909 and 1920 he published three volumes of poetry, though his work as essayist, reviewer and translator was the more appreciated: he became a regular translator and reviewer for the *Criterion* from the 1920s till the 1930s – and a member of the inner circle gathered round TSE – even while continuing to work in the statistics division of the Ministry of Labour until his retirement in 1951.

Ford Madox Ford (1873–1939) – originally Ford Hermann Hueffer (his father was German, his mother English) – novelist and editor, grew up in London and quickly became associated with a wide circle of talented friends including Edward Garnett, Henry James, Stephen Crane, H. G. Wells, Ezra Pound and Joseph Conrad; he was the discriminating founder-editor of the *English Review*, and later of the *Transatlantic Review* – for which he selected pieces by writers ranging from Conrad (see *Joseph Conrad: A Personal Remembrance*, 1924), D. H. Lawrence and Wyndham Lewis to James Joyce and Gertrude Stein. His novels include the celebrated 'impressionist' novel *The Good Soldier* (1915), which drew on his experiences at a German sanatorium following a nervous breakdown in 1904; and the four-volume sequence *Parade's End* (1924–8), which took fire from his experiences as an officer in the Welsh Regiment during WW1 (he had been involved in the bloody conflicts of the Somme in 1916 as well as at Ypres). See Max Saunders, *Ford Madox Ford* (2 vols, 1996).

E. M. Forster (1879–1970), novelist and essayist, was educated at King's College, Cambridge, where he gained a second in the classics tripos (and where he was elected to the exclusive Conversazione Society, the inner circle of the Apostles). Though intimately associated with the Bloomsbury Group in London, where his circle of friends and acquaintances came to include Edward Marsh, Edward Garnett, Duncan Grant, Roger Fry, Lytton Strachey and Leonard and Virginia Woolf, he derived much from visits to Italy, Greece, Egypt and India – where he worked for a while as private secretary to the Maharaja of Dewas: that experience brought about one of his most acclaimed novels, *A Passage to India* (1924), which sold around one million copies during his lifetime. His other celebrated novels include *Where Angels Fear to Tread* (1905), *A Room with a View* (1908), *Howards End* (1910), and the posthumous *Maurice* (1971, written 1910–13), a work that addressed his homosexuality. He gave the Clark Lectures at Cambridge in 1927 – in immediate succession to TSE – which were published as *Aspects of the Novel* (1927). Though he turned down a knighthood, in 1953 he was appointed a Companion of Honour; and he received the OM in 1969. See also P. N. Furbank, *E. M. Forster* (2 vols, 1977, 1978); *Selected Letters of E. M. Forster*, ed. Mary Lago and P. N. Furbank (2 vols, 1983–5); Nicola Beauman, *Morgan: A Biography of E. M. Forster* (1993).

Charles Haigh-Wood (1854–1927): TSE's father-in-law. Born Charles Haigh Wood, in Bury, Lancashire, the son of a carver and gilder who prospered, he was educated privately, at the local grammar school, and (from 1873) the Royal Academy School in London. He started exhibiting in the Academy three years later. He became a member of the RA, and pursued a successful career as a minor portrait and genre painter. On his mother's death, he inherited her properties in Kingstown (Dún Laoghaire) in Ireland, as well as Eglinton House, and thereafter he was supported by the rents of his tenants. In 1885 he married Rose Esther Robinson (1861–1941). They moved to Hampstead in 1891, settling at 3 Compayne Gardens, where they lived for the rest of his life. According to TSE (Oct. 1920), Vivien was 'particularly fond of her father; she takes more after him and his side of the family, and understands him better than the others do'.

Maurice Haigh-Wood (1896–1980): TSE's brother-in-law. He was six years younger than his sister Vivien, and after attending Ovingdean prep school and Malvern School, trained at Sandhurst Military Academy, before receiving his commission on 11 May 1915 as a second lieutenant in the 2nd Battalion, the Manchester Regiment. He served in the infantry for the war, and on regular visits home gave TSE his closest contact with the nightmare of life in the trenches. After the war, he found it difficult to get himself established, but became a stockbroker, and he remained friendly with, and respectful towards, TSE even after his separation from Vivien in

1933. In 1930 he married a 25-year-old American dancer, Ahmé Hoagland, and they had two children.

John Hayward (1905–65), editor, critic and anthologist, studied modern languages at King's College, Cambridge. Despite the early onset of muscular dystrophy, he became a prolific and eminent writer and editor, bringing out in quick succession respectable editions of the works of Rochester, Saint-Évremond, Jonathan Swift, Robert Herrick and Samuel Johnson. Other publications included *Complete Poems and Selected Prose of John Donne* (1929), *Donne* (1950), *T. S. Eliot: Selected Prose* (1953), *The Penguin Book of English Verse* (1958), and *The Oxford Book of Nineteenth Century English Verse* (1964). Celebrated in addition as the learned and acerbic editor of the *Book Collector*, he was made a chevalier of the Légion d'honneur in 1952 and a CBE in 1953. Writers including Graham Greene and Stevie Smith valued his keen editorial counsel; and Paul Valéry invited him to translate his comedy *Mon Faust*. Hayward advised TSE on various essays, poems and plays including *The Cocktail Party* and *The Confidential Clerk*, and most helpfully of all on *Four Quartets*. See also Helen Gardner, *The Composition of 'Four Quartets'* (1978).

Hofmannsthal, Hugo von (1874–1929), Austrian dramatist and poet, was educated at the University of Vienna, where he studied law before transferring his attention to Romance philology (writing a dissertation on the Pléiade poets, followed by a thesis on Victor Hugo). Inspired by French symbolism and Viennese neo-romanticism, he launched his career as a poetic dramatist and became a full-time writer in 1901. He enjoyed huge success through his operatic collaborations with Richard Strauss: the works they produced together included *Elektra* (a remodelling of Sophocles which was acclaimed upon its first production in Berlin, 1903), *Der Rosenkavalier* (1911), and *Ariadne auf Naxos* (1912). He became too a virtuoso of dramatic adaptation, starting out in 1912 with *Jedermann* (a version of the English morality play *Everyman*) and culminating with the tragedy *Der Turm* ('The Tower', adapted from a play by Calderón, 1927), which sought to portray a society in a crisis of materialistic violence. In 1919 he was co-founder, with Max Reinhardt, of the Salzburg Festival (Reinhardt was to produce no fewer than nineteen of his plays). E. R. Curtius said of Hofmannsthal that after 1914 he 'ceased to be a romantic aesthete and became a "conservative-revolutionary", seeking to set up intellectual authority based on spiritual motives'.

Mary Hutchinson, née Barnes (1889–1977): a half-cousin of Lytton Strachey, married St John ('Jack') Hutchinson in 1910. A prominent Bloomsbury hostess, she was for several years the acknowledged mistress of the art critic, Clive Bell, and became a close, supportive friend of both TSE and Vivien. TSE published one of her stories ('War') in the *Egoist*, and she later brought out a book of sketches, *Fugitive Pieces* (1927) under the imprint of the Hogarth Press. She wrote a short unpublished memoir of TSE (Harry Ransom Humanities Research Center, Austin) and was for a time in the late 1910s a very intimate friend of his. See David Bradshaw '"Those Extraordinary Parakeets": Clive Bell and Mary Hutchinson', *The Charleston Magazine* 1997/1998, 16 & 17.

St John ('Jack') Hutchinson (1884–1942): barrister-at-law; husband of Mary Hutchinson. Educated at Winchester and Magdalen College, Oxford, he was an unsuccessful Liberal parliamentary candidate, but acted as a legal adviser to the Ministry of Reconstruction, 1917; and was Recorder of Hastings from 1930.

Aldous Huxley (1894–1963): novelist, poet, essayist, whose early novels *Crome Yellow* (1921) and *Antic Hay* (1923) were immensely successful satires of post-war British culture. While teaching at Eton, Aldous told his brother Julian in December 1916 that he 'ought to read' Eliot's 'things', which are 'all the more remarkable when one knows the man, ordinarily just an Europeanized American, overwhelmingly cultured, talking about French literature in the most uninspired fashion imaginable'. For his part, Eliot thought Huxley's early poems fell too much under the spell of Laforgue (and of his own work), but Huxley went on to become not only a popular comic novelist, but, as the author of *Brave New World* and *The Doors of Perception*, a highly influential intellectual figure. See Nicholas Murray, *Aldous Huxley: An English Intellectual* (2002); and Aldous Huxley, *Selected Letters*, ed. James Sexton (2007).

Harold Joachim (1868–1938): fellow and tutor in philosophy in Merton College, Oxford, 1897–1919; British Idealist philosopher and follower of F. H. Bradley; author of *The Nature of Truth* (1906), an influential account of the 'coherence theory' of truth. TSE recalled buying Joachim's *The Nature of Truth* at Harvard, and taking it with him in 1914 to Oxford, where Joachim was his tutor. According to Brand Blanshard, it was claimed that 'if you started any sentence in the *Nichomachean Ethics* of Aristotle, Joachim could complete it for you, of course in Greek' ('Eliot at

Oxford', in *T. S. Eliot: Essays from the Southern Review*, ed. James Olney, 1988). TSE wrote an obituary letter in *The Times* (4 Aug. 1938; 'to his criticism of my papers I owe an appreciation of the fact that good writing is impossible without clear and distinct ideas'), and also paid tribute to him in the introduction to *Knowledge and Experience in the Philosophy of F. H. Bradley* (1964). In a late letter, he said 'he taught me more about how to write good prose than any other teacher I have ever had' as well as revealing 'the importance of punctuation in the interpretation of a text such as that of the *Posterior Analytics*' (24 June 1963: TS Merton College). TSE's systematic notes on Joachim's lectures on Aristotle's *Nichomachean Ethics* at Oxford 1914–15 are at Houghton.

James Joyce (1882–1941), expatriate Irish novelist, playwright and poet. Having lived in Zurich and Trieste, Joyce moved to Paris in 1920, where he became a centre of expatriate writers, including Pound and Stein. In *Blasting and Bombadiering* (1937), Wyndham Lewis recounts his and TSE's first encounter with Joyce there in August 1920 when bringing him a parcel of shoes. Joyce's *A Portrait of the Artist* was serialised in the *Egoist*, and *Ulysses* in the *Little Review* up to 1920. When *Ulysses* appeared in book form in 1922, the same year as *The Waste Land*, TSE called it 'the most important expression which the present age has found' – 'a book to which we are all indebted, and from which none of us can escape' ('*Ulysses*, Order and Myth', *Dial* 75: 5, November 1923). TSE published in the *Criterion* a number of pieces by and about Joyce, and at Faber he was responsible for the publication of *Finnegans Wake* (1940). See *The Letters of James Joyce*, ed. Stuart Gilbert and Richard Ellmann (3 vols, 1957, 1966); Richard Ellmann, *James Joyce* (2nd edn, 1982).

Valery Larbaud (1881–1957): French poet, novelist, translator and essayist, of independent means and with erudition and good taste. He translated, among other works, James Joyce's *Ulysses*. Pseudonymous author of *Poèmes par un riche amateur* (1908), *Le Journal Intime de A. O. Barnabooth* (1913), and *Ce Vice Impuni, la Lecture* (1925). In a letter of 20 March 1922, TSE called him 'a great poet and prose author'. Larbaud's essay 'The "Ulysses" of James Joyce' appeared in *Criterion* 1: 1 (October 1922).

Wyndham Lewis (1882–1957) was a painter, portraitist, novelist, philosopher and critic; and one of the major modernist writers. A friend of Ezra Pound, Lewis was the leading artist associated with Vorticism, and editor of *BLAST*, the movement's journal, 1914–15, in which TSE's

'Preludes' and 'Rhapsody on a windy night' appeared (in issue 2, July 1915). Lewis served as a bombardier and war-artist on the Western Front, 1916–18, and later wrote memorable accounts of the period in his memoir *Blasting and Bombardiering* (1937), including brilliant portraits of TSE, Pound and Joyce, and wartime and modernist London. TSE reviewed Lewis's first novel *Tarr* (1918) in the *Egoist* 5: 8 (Sept. 1918), describing him as 'the most fascinating personality of our time', in whose work 'we recognize the thought of the modern and the energy of the cave-man'. Lewis considered Eliot 'the most interesting man in London society' (7 Nov. 1918). TSE went on to publish Lewis in the *Criterion* and, even though Lewis was notoriously querulous, carried on a lifetime's friendship and correspondence with him. Lewis did a number of drawings of TSE, one of which hung in Eliot's flat, and his portrait of TSE is in the National Portrait Gallery. On Lewis's death, TSE wrote 'The Importance of Wyndham Lewis' in the *Sunday Times* (10 March 1957), and a memoir in *Hudson Review* X: 2 (Summer 1957): 'He was . . . a highly strung, nervous man, who was conscious of his own abilities, and sensitive to slight or neglect . . . He was independent, outspoken, and difficult. Temperament and circumstances combined to make him a great satirist . . . I remember Lewis, at the time when I first knew him, and for some years thereafter, as incomparably witty and amusing in company . . .' See *The Letters of Wyndham Lewis*, ed. W. K. Rose (1963), and Paul O'Keeffe, *Some Sort of Genius: A Life of Wyndham Lewis* (2000).

Horace Liveright (1884–1933): American book publisher and (later) stage producer. With Albert Boni, he founded Boni & Liveright in 1917, which published not only *The Waste Land* (1922) but Ezra Pound's *Instigations* (1920) and *Poems 1918–21* (1921), as well as works by Ernest Hemingway, Theodore Dreiser, Djuna Barnes, Bertrand Russell and Hart Crane. He was a strong campaigner against literary censorship. Pound considered him 'a jewel of a publisher'. See Tom Dardis, *Firebrand: The Life of Horace Liveright* (1995).

Desmond MacCarthy (1877–1952): literary and dramatic critic, intimately associated with the Bloomsbury Group. Literary editor of the *New Statesman* 1920–7, he moved in 1928 to the *Sunday Times*, where he stayed until his death.

Frederic Manning (1882–1935): Australian writer who settled in 1903 in England, where he came to know artists and writers including Max

Beerbohm, William Rothenstein, Ezra Pound and Richard Aldington; author of *Scenes and Portraits* (1909). Despite being an asthmatic, he served in the ranks (Shropshire Light Infantry) in WW1, being involved for four months in heavy fighting on the Somme: this experience eventually brought about his greatest achievement, a novel about the Western Front, *The Middle Parts of Fortune* (privately printed, 1929; standard text, 1977; expurgated as *Her Privates We*, credited pseudonymously to 'Private 19022', 1930; republished in full, with intro. by William Boyd, 1999). In a letter to Aldington (6 July 1921), TSE described Manning as 'undoubtedly one of the very best prose writers we have'. See V. Coleman, *The Last Exquisite: A Portrait of Frederic Manning* (1990).

Dr Karl Bernhard Martin lived at Dorfstrasse 15, Freiburg-Günthersthal, Germany, and ran a clinic called Sanatorium Hoven, Lengenhardstrasse. The treatments he meted out combined starvation dieting with psycho-analysis. One of his most socially prominent British patients was Lady Ottoline Morrell, who chose to submit herself to his ministrations for several years. Lytton Strachey, who met Martin at Morrell's country house, Garsington, thought him 'a miserable German doctor—a "psycho-analyst" of Freiburg' (letter to Dora Carrington, 3 June 1923). According to Miranda Seymour, Morrell's biographer, 'It was as a doctor, not as an analyst, that Marten [*sic*] was an unfortunate choice. "He thinks he has found out my trouble – some old germ left from typhoid years ago," Ottoline reported to Bertie [Russell] in November 1923, "and now he is injecting me with all sorts of injections of milk and other things in advance of England." The milk injections did her no good; Marten's belief in starvation diets, dutifully followed by Ottoline over the next ten years whenever she felt ill, did her considerable harm. No woman of her age and complicated medical history should have expected an improvement in health from fortnightly régimes of fruit and water which left her so weak that she could scarcely sit up, but that was Dr. Marten's panacea for all ailments' (*Ottoline Morrell: Life on the Grand Scale* [1992, 1998], 448–9). In due time, Virginia Woolf too would encourage Roger Fry to consult Dr Martin. Another such sorry patient was Edward Sackville-West (novelist, music critic, patron of the arts; heir to the grand Knole House in Kent) – at a dinner party in June 1923, he gaily declared to Virginia Woolf that 'Mr. Eliot was his favourite poet, and the favourite of all his friends' – who spent some weeks in Freiburg under Martin's odd orders in the hope of getting a 'cure' for his homosexuality. Strachey subsequently mocked Fry's efforts, in a letter to Carrington: 'After 4 months and an expenditure of £200 he found he could just bear the thought of going to bed with a woman' (quoted in Michael De-la-Noy, *Eddie: The Life of Edward Sackville-West* [1988, 1999], 87).

Harold Monro (1879–1932): poet, editor and publisher. In 1913 he founded the Poetry Bookshop at 35 Devonshire Street, London, where poets would meet and give readings and lectures. In 1912 he briefly edited the *Poetry Review* for the Poetry Society; then his own periodicals, *Poetry and Drama*, 1913–14, and the *Chapbook* (originally the *Monthly Chapbook*), 1919–25. From the Poetry Bookshop, Monro published the five volumes of *Georgian Poetry*, ed. Edward Marsh (1872–1953) between 1912 and 1922, and the first volumes of poetry by writers including Richard Aldington and Robert Graves, and some of his own collections including *Children of Love* (1915) and *Strange Meetings* (1917). He married in 1920 Alida Klemantaski (daughter of a Polish-Jewish trader), with whom he never cohabited but who remained loving, loyal and supportive to him; both endeared themselves to Eliot, who would often use the premises of the Poetry Bookshop for meetings with contributors to the *Criterion*. After his death, TSE wrote a 'Critical Note' to *The Collected Poems of Harold Monro* (1933). See Joy Grant, *Harold Monro and the Poetry Bookshop* (1967); Dominic Hibberd, *Harold Monro: Poet of the New Age* (2001).

Harriet Monroe (1860–1936): American poet and editor, based in Chicago. Monroe was the editor of *Poetry: A Magazine of Verse*, which she founded in 1912 – when she was already over fifty – and continued to edit until 1936. It provided a crucial launching place for many modern poets, including Eliot (whose 'Prufrock' was published there in 1915), Ezra Pound, Wallace Stevens, William Carlos Williams, Marianne Moore, W. B. Yeats and Robert Frost. She was co-editor, with Alice Corbin Henderson (first associate editor of *Poetry*), of *The New Poetry: An Anthology* (New York, 1917), which TSE reviewed in *Egoist* 4: 9 (Oct. 1917). Her autobiography, *A Poet's Life: Seventy Years in a Changing World*, appeared posthumously in 1937. See also *A History of Poetry in Letters*, ed. Joseph Parisi and Stephen Young (2002).

Marianne Moore (1887–1972), American poet and critic, contributed to the *Egoist* from 1915. Her first book, *Poems*, was published in London in 1921. She went on to become in 1925 acting editor of the *Dial*, then editor, 1927–9, and one of the most important and influential modern poets in America. Writing to her on 3 April 1921, Eliot said her verse interested him 'more than that of anyone now writing in America'. In his introduction to her *Selected Poems*, which he brought out at Faber & Faber in 1935, Eliot declared that her 'poems form part of the small body of durable poetry written in our time'.

Lady Ottoline Morrell (1873–1938): daughter of Lieutenant-General Arthur Bentinck and half-sister to the Duke of Portland. In 1902 she married Philip Morrell (1870–1941), Liberal MP for South Oxfordshire 1902–18. A patron of the arts, she entertained a notable literary and artistic circle, first at 44 Bedford Square, then at Garsington Manor, nr. Oxford, where she moved in 1915. She was a lover of Bertrand Russell, who introduced her to TSE, and her many friends included Lytton Strachey, D. H. Lawrence, Aldous Huxley, Siegfried Sassoon, the Woolfs, and the Eliots. Her memoirs (ed. Robert Gathorne-Hardy) appeared as *Ottoline* (1963) and *Ottoline at Garsington* (1974). See Miranda Seymour, *Life on the Grand Scale: Lady Ottoline Morrell* (1992, 1998).

John Middleton Murry (1889–1957): influential English writer, critic and editor, founded the magazine *Rhythm*, 1911–13, and worked as a reviewer for the *Westminster Gazette*, 1912–14, and the *Times Literary Supplement*, 1914–18, before becoming editor from 1919 to 1921 of the *Athenaeum*, which he turned for a time into a lively cultural forum – in a letter of 2 July 1919, TSE called it 'the best literary weekly in the Anglo-Saxon world'. In a 'London Letter' in *Dial* 72: 5 (May 1921), Eliot said he considered Murry as editor 'genuinely studious to maintain a serious criticism', but he disagreed with his 'particular tastes, as well as his general statements'. After the demise of the *Athenaeum*, Murry went on to edit the *Adelphi*. 1923–48. In 1918, he married Katherine Mansfield, who died in 1923. He was friend and biographer of D. H. Lawrence; and as an editor he provided a platform for writers as various as George Santayana, Paul Valéry, D. H. Lawrence, Aldous Huxley, Virginia Woolf, and TSE. His first notable critical work was *Dostoevsky* (1916); his most influential critical study, *The Problem of Style* (1922). Though as a Romanticist he was an intellectual opponent of the avowedly 'Classicist' Eliot, Murry offered Eliot in 1919 the post of assistant editor on the *Athenaeum* (which Eliot had to decline); in addition, he recommended him to be the Clark lecturer at Cambridge in 1926, and was a steadfast friend to both TSE and his wife Vivien. See F. A. Lea, *The Life of John Middleton Murry* (1959); and David Goldie, *A Critical Difference: T. S. Eliot and John Middleton Murry in English Literary Criticism, 1919–1928* (1998).

Dorothy Pound née Shakespear (1886–1973), the daughter of Yeats's mistress Olivia Shakespear, married Ezra Pound in 1914 and remained with him for the rest of his long life. Having started as a landscape watercolourist, like her father, she began to visit Wyndham Lewis's Rebel Art Centre, and adopted a Vorticist style. Her 'Snow Scene' appeared in *BLAST* 2, and she designed the cover of *The Catholic Anthology* (1915). She was a friend of TSE and Vivien during the Pounds' London years. See *Ezra Pound and Dorothy Shakespear: Their Letters 1909–1914*, ed. Omar Pound and A. Walton Litz (1984)

Ezra Pound (1885–1972), American poet and critic, was one of the prime impresarios of the modernist movement in London and Paris, and played a major part in launching Eliot – as well as Joyce, Lewis, and many other modernists. Eliot called on him at 5 Holland Place Chambers, Kensington, on 22 Sept. 1914, with an introduction from Conrad Aiken. On 30 Sept. 1914, Pound hailed 'Prufrock' as 'the best poem I have yet had or seen from an American'; and on 3 October called Eliot 'the last intelligent man I've found – a young American T. S. Eliot . . . worth watching – mind "not primitive"' (*Selected Letters of Ezra Pound*, 40–1). Pound was instrumental in arranging for 'Prufrock' to be published in *Poetry* in 1915, and helped to shape *The Waste Land* (1922), which Eliot dedicated to him as '*il miglior fabbro*'. After their first meeting, the poets became friends, and remained in loyal correspondence for the rest of their lives. Having initially dismissed Pound's poetry (to Aiken, 30 Sept. 1914) as 'well-meaning but touchingly incompetent', Eliot went on to champion his work, writing to Gilbert Seldes (27 Dec. 1922): 'I sincerely consider Ezra Pound the most important living poet in the English language.' He wrote an early study of Pound, *Ezra Pound: His Metric and Poetry* (1917), and went on, as editor of the *Criterion* and publisher at Faber & Faber, to publish most of Pound's work in the UK, including *Selected Shorter Poems*, *The Cantos* and *Selected Literary Essays*. After his move to Italy in the 1920s, Pound became increasingly sceptical about the direction of TSE's convictions and poetry, but they continued to correspond. After Eliot's death, Pound said of him: 'His was the true Dantescan voice – not honoured enough, and deserving more than I ever gave him.' See A. David Moody, *Ezra Pound: Poet: A Portrait of the Man and his Work* I: *The Young Genius 1885–1920* (2007), Humphrey Carpenter, *A Serious Character* (1988), and *The Selected Letters of Ezra Pound 1907–1941*, ed. D. D. Paige (1950).

John Quinn (1870–1924): Irish-American corporate lawyer in New York; major patron of modernist writers and artists; and collector of manuscripts. He afforded generous support, both financial and legal, to writers including Conrad, Yeats, Joyce and Ezra Pound. TSE began corresponding with him at the urgent prompting of Pound, who had read about him as a patron, in the *New Age* in January 1915: the correspondence ran until Quinn's death. Pound urged TSE's importance upon Quinn ('I have more or less discovered him,' he proclaimed). Quinn bought from TSE (for a fair price) the drafts of *The Waste Land*, which he later bequeathed to the New York Public Library. Though a supporter of the Irish nationalist cause, he worked for the British intelligence services, helping to report upon *agents provocateurs* who were working in the USA to mobilise anti-British groups of Irish and Germans. See B. L. Reid, *The Man from New York: John Quinn and His Friends* (1969).

Herbert Read (1893–1968): English poet and literary critic, and one of the most influential art critics of the century. Son of a tenant farmer, Read spent his first years in rural Yorkshire; at sixteen, he went to work as a bank clerk, then studied law and economics at Leeds University; later still, he joined the Civil Service, working first in the Ministry of Labour and then at the Treasury. During his years of service in WW1, he rose to be a captain in a Yorkshire regiment, the Green Howards (his war poems were published in *Naked Warriors*, 1919); and when on leave to receive the Military Cross in 1917, he arranged to dine with TSE at the Monico Restaurant in Piccadilly Circus. This launched a life-long friendship which he was to recall in 'T. S. E. – A Memoir', in *T. S. Eliot: The Man and his Work*, ed. Allen Tate (1966). Within the year, he had also become acquainted with the Sitwells, Ezra Pound, Wyndham Lewis, Richard Aldington and Ford Madox Ford. He co-founded the journal *Art & Letters*, 1917–20, and wrote essays too for A. R. Orage, editor of the *New Age*. In 1922 he was appointed a curator in the department of ceramics and glass at the Victoria and Albert Museum; and in later years he was to work for the publishers Routledge & Kegan Paul, and as editor of the *Burlington Magazine*, 1933–9. By 1923 he was writing for the *Criterion*: he was to be one of Eliot's regular leading contributors and a reliable ally and advisor. In 1924 he edited T. E. Hulme's posthumous *Speculations*. His later works include *Art Now* (1933); the introduction to the catalogue of the International Surrealist Exhibition held at the New Burlington Galleries, London, 1936; *Art and Society* (1937); *Education through Art* (1943); and *A Concise History of Modern Painting* (1959). In 1947 he founded (with Roland Penrose) the Institute of Contemporary Art; and in 1953 he was knighted for services to literature. Eliot, he was to recall (perhaps only half in jest), was 'rather like a gloomy priest presiding over my affections and spontaneity'. See Herbert Read, *Annals of Innocence and Experience* (1940); James King, *The Last Modern: A Life of Herbert Read* (1990); *Herbert Read Reassessed*, ed. D. Goodway (1998); and Jason Harding (*The* 'Criterion': see citation under Dobrée above), who states that Read contributed sixty-eight book reviews, four articles, and five poems to the *Criterion*.

Bruce Richmond (1871–1964), editor, was educated at Winchester and New College, Oxford, and called to the Bar in 1897. However, he never practised as a barrister. Instead, George Buckle, editor of *The Times*, appointed him an assistant editor in 1899, and in 1902 he assumed the editorship of the fledgling *Times Literary Supplement*, which he commanded for thirty-five years. During this period, the *TLS* established itself as the premier academic and critical periodical in Britain. He was knighted in 1935. TSE, who was introduced to Richmond by Richard Aldington in 1919, enthused to his mother that year that writing the leading article for the *TLS* was the highest honour 'in the critical world of literature'. In a tribute, he recalled Richmond as possessing 'a bird-like alertness of eye, body and mind . . . It was from Bruce Richmond that I learnt editorial standards . . . I learnt from him that it is the business of an editor to know his contributors personally, to keep in touch with them and to make suggestions to them. I tried [at the *Criterion*] to form a nucleus of writers (some of them, indeed, recruited from the *Times Literary Supplement*, and introduced to me by Richmond) on whom I could depend, differing from each other in many things, but not in love of literature and seriousness of purpose. And I learnt from Richmond that I must read every word of what was to appear in print . . . It is a final tribute to Richmond's genius as an editor that some of his troupe of regular contributors (I am thinking of myself as well as of others) produced some of their most distinguished critical essays as leaders for the *Literary Supplement* . . . Good literary criticism requires good editors as well as good critics. And Bruce Richmond was a great editor' ('Bruce Lyttelton Richmond', *TLS*, 13 Jan. 1961, 17).

Jacques Rivière (1886–1925), writer and periodical editor, was born and brought up in Bordeaux (where he befriended the writer Henri Alain-Fournier, who was to become his brother-in-law). In Paris, he taught for a while at L'École Saint-Joseph des Tuileries, then at the College Stanislas, before taking a higher degree at the Sorbonne. By 1907 he was writing for the *Occident*; and from 1909, for *Nouvelle Revue Française* (founded in 1908 by André Gide), which he made into the premier French intellectual review. His elegant essays were collected in *Études* (1912). During WW1, in which he served in the infantry, he was captured and held for four years in German prisoner-of-war camps until being repatriated in 1918. From 1919 until his death, he was the esteemed editor of *NRF*. He helped bring the work of Proust to prominence. TSE extolled him after his death ('Rencontre', *NRF* 24: 139 [1925], 657–8) as '*une personnalité charmante et gracieuse, un esprit si alerte and si enthousiaste que déjà alors il semblait presque une menace pour le corps délicat qui l'abritait*'. As opposed to someone with a temperament like his own – '*trop disposé à mesurer toutes choses selon les règles d'une conception dogmatique qui tendrait de plus en plus à devenir rigide et formelle*' – Riviere's large-mindedness, his precise but supple thinking, seemed an 'excellent discipline'. See Jean Lacouture, *Une adolescence du siècle: Jacques Rivière et la NRF* (1994).

J. M. Robertson (1856–1933), Scottish author, journalist, politician, began his career as a clerk; then worked as a journalist on newspapers including the *Edinburgh Evening News* and *National Reformer*. He was Liberal MP for Tyneside, 1908–18. Though self-taught, he published more than a hundred books and pamphlets. See M. Page, *Britain's Unknown Genius: The Life-Work of J. M. Robertson* (1984).

John Rodker (1894–1955): poet, novelist and publisher. Born in Manchester, of an immigrant Jewish family, he published his *Poems* in 1914. During WW1, Rodker was a conscientious objector, and after going on the run, sheltering with the poet R. C. Trevelyan, he was imprisoned in Dartmoor Prison. In 1919 he started up the Ovid Press (a small press which lasted about a year), and published TSE's *Poems* (1920), Ezra Pound's *Hugh Selwyn Mauberley*, and his own *Hymns* (1920), as well as portfolios of drawings by Wyndham Lewis, Henri Gaudier-Brzeska, and Edward Wadsworth. In 1919, he took over briefly from Pound as foreign editor of the *Little Review*. In the 1920s he spent time in Paris on the second edition of Joyce's *Ulysses* and set up the Casanova Press. He published his *Collected Poems, 1912–1925* (1930), and later worked with Anna Freud on the Imago Press in order to publish translations of Freud.

Viscountess Rothermere (Mary Lilian Harmsworth, *née* Share) (d. 1937). The daughter of George Wade Share, in 1893 she married Harold Sydney Harmsworth, first Viscount Rothermere (1868–1940). It was owing to Scofield Thayer, whom she met in New York, that she became the patron and financial backer of TSE's quarterly review the *Criterion* 1922–5. Discussion of her backing for TSE's review, a successor to Schiff's *Art and Letters*, was first floated in July 1921, and became a reality when the first issue of the *Criterion* appeared in Oct. 1922, featuring the first UK publication of *The Waste Land*.

Bertrand Russell (1872–1970): one of the most influential twentieth-century British philosophers; co-author (with Alfred North Whitehead) of *Principia Mathematica* (1910–13), and author of innumerable other books including the popular *Problems of Philosophy* (1912), *Mysticism and Logic* (1918) – which was reviewed by TSE in 'Style and Thought' (*Nation* 22, 23 March 1918) – and *History of Western Philosophy* (1945). In 1914, Russell gave the Lowell Lectures on 'Our Knowledge of the External World' at Harvard, where he encountered Eliot. On 27 March 1914, Russell described Eliot as 'very well dressed and polished, with manners of the finest Etonian type'. He later characterised him as 'proficient in Plato, intimate with French literature from Villon to Vildrach, and capable of exquisiteness of appreciation, but lacking in the crude insistent passion that one must have in order to achieve anything'. After their accidental meeting in 1914, Russell played an important role in introducing TSE to British intellectual life, as well as getting him launched as a reviewer for *International Journal of Ethics* and the *Monist*. However, it has been alleged that, not long after TSE's marriage, Russell may have had a brief affair with his wife Vivien. The three friends shared lodgings for a while at Russell's flat in London. Russell was a conscientious objector and vocal opponent of WW1, which led to a brief prison sentence in Wandsworth. In later years, TSE saw little of his one-time professor and friend, and he later attacked Russell's philosophical and ethical views, in his 'Commentary' in the *Criterion* (April 1924), and elsewhere. Russell provides a partial account of his relationship with the Eliots in *The Autobiography of Bertrand Russell* II: *1914–1944* (1968). See also Ray Monk, *Bertrand Russell: The Spirit of Solitude* (1996).

Sydney Schiff (1868–1944): novelist and translator, and patron of the arts. In 1911 Schiff married his second wife Violet Zillah Beddington (1874–1962), sister of Oscar Wilde's friend Ada Leverson, and a gifted musician who had studied singing under Paolo Tosti. Schiff soon began writing fiction and engaging in patronage of the arts. His first novel, *Concessions* (1913), was published under his own name, but *War-Time Silhouettes* (1916) and later novels appeared under the *nom-de-plume* 'Stephen Hudson'. The pseudonym was adopted in anticipation of the appearance of *Richard Kurt* (1919), the first of a sequence of autobiographical novels – the series would be gathered up in a volume advisedly called *A True Story* (1930). Schiff came from a wealthy Jewish family (his father having been a successful stockbroker), and he chose to support Isaac Rosenberg among other writers and artists; he would subsidise the short-lived but notable periodical *Art & Letters* (1918–20), as well as contributing to it and editing one issue. He was a major champion of Marcel Proust (and he would ultimately translate *Le temps retrouvé*), a friend of several other writers (Vivien Eliot dubbed him 'the Sitwells' Holy Ghost'), and a supporter of Wyndham Lewis (who painted a commissioned portrait of him and then went on to satirise him in *The Apes of God*). He and his wife were to become close friends of the Eliots: his first surviving letter to TSE dates from 3 May 1919. Though always ready to salute greater talents than his own, Schiff was still his own man, with decidedly independent views: he was for example prompt to dispute with TSE the value of the posthumously collected writings of the philosopher T. E. Hulme. On the death of Violet Schiff, TSE wrote in tribute to the couple: 'In the 1920s the Schiffs' hospitality, generosity, and encouragement meant much to a number of young artists and writers of whom I was one. The Schiffs' acquaintance was cosmopolitan, and their interests embraced all the arts. At their house I met, for example, Delius and Arthur Symons, and the first Viscountess Rothermere, who founded the *Criterion* under my editorship. Middleton Murry and Katherine Mansfield knew their house, and Wyndham Lewis and Charles Scott-Moncrieff, and many others . . . I write primarily to pay homage to a beloved friend, but also in the hope that some future chronicler of the history of art and letters in our time may give to Sydney and Violet Schiff the place which is their due.' (See 'Mrs Violet Schiff: All-Embracing Interest in the Arts', *The Times*, 9 July 1962.) See also Richard Davenport-Hines, *A Night at the Majestic: Proust and the Great Modernist Dinner Party of 1922* (2006).

Gilbert Seldes (1893–1970), journalist, editor and critic, graduated from Harvard in 1914 and was a war correspondent before becoming for a while editor of the *Dial*, 1920–3. His works include the influential study *The 7 Lively Arts* (1924) – on popular arts, embracing the comic strip and popular songs as well as cinema and vaudeville – and *The Stammering Century* (1928). In later years he was prolific as an essayist; he also wrote for the Broadway theatre, and became the first director of TV programmes for CBS News, and the founding Dean of the Annenberg School for Communication at the University of Pennsylvania. See Michael G. Kammen, *The Lively Arts: Gilbert Seldes and the Transformation of Cultural Criticism in the United States* (1996).

Alfred Dwight ('Shef') Sheffield (1871–1961), husband of TSE's eldest sister Ada (1869–1943), taught English at University School, Cleveland, Ohio, and was an English instructor, and later a Professor, of Group Work at Wellesley College. His publications include *Lectures on the Harvard Classics: Confucianism* (1909), and *Grammar and Thinking: a study of the working conceptions in syntax* (1912). He later joined the editorial staff of *Webster's International Dictionary*.

May Sinclair, pseud. of Mary St Clair (1863–1946): English novelist; active in the movement for women's suffrage, and an early apologist for psycho-analysis; author of *The Three Sisters* (1914), *Mary Olivier: A Life* (1919), and *The Life and Death of Harriet Frean* (1922) – which TSE thought 'a most interesting specimen' of modern English fiction, and which 'made all the use that is possible' of psycho-analysis. TSE reviewed her *A Defence of Idealism: Some Questions & Conclusions* (1917) in *New Statesman* 9 (22 Sept. 1917), while she reviewed *Prufrock and Other Observations* in *Little Review* 4 (Dec. 1917). She was a good friend to TSE, who printed her work in the *Egoist* and her story 'The Victim' in the *Criterion* 1 (Oct. 1922). According to Valerie Eliot, in TSE's play *The Elder Statesman* (1959) the phrase that Mrs Carghill remembers 'reading somewhere' – 'Where their fires are not quenched' (*CPP*, 553) – is a 'deliberate allusion' to 'Where their fire is not quenched' in Sinclair's *Uncanny Stories* (1923). See Suzanne Raitt, *May Sinclair: A Modern Victorian* (2000).

Edith Sitwell (1887–1964): poet, biographer, anthologist and novelist; editor of *Wheels* 1916–21. Her collection, *The Mother and Other Poems* (1915), was followed by *Clown's Houses* (1918) and *The Wooden Pegasus* (1920). In 1923, her performance at the Aeolian Hall in London of her cycle of poems, *Façade* (1922), with music by William Walton, placed her briefly at the centre of modernistic experimentation. Other writings include *Gold Coast Customs* (1929), *Collected Poems* (1930), *Fanfare for Elizabeth* (1946), *The Queens and the Hive* (1962), and a tart autobiography, *Taken Care Of* (1965). She was appointed a DBE in 1954. See John Lehmann, *A Nest of Tigers: Edith, Osbert and Sacheverell Sitwell in their Times* (1968); John Pearson, *Façades: Edith, Osbert and Sacheverell Sitwell* (1978). TSE published one of her poems in the *Criterion.*

Osbert Sitwell (1892–1969): English poet and man of letters. Early in his career, he published collections of poems, including *Argonaut and Juggernaut* (1919), and a volume of stories *Triple Fugue* (1924), but he is now celebrated for his remarkable memoirs, *Left Hand, Right Hand* (5 vols, 1945–50), which include a fine portrayal of TSE. TSE published one sketch by him in the *Criterion.*

Sacheverell Sitwell (1897–1988): English writer, poet and art critic; the youngest of the Sitwell trio. T. S. Eliot thought him the 'most important and difficult poet' in the anthology *Wheels* (1918). Reviewing *The People's Palace*, he praised its 'distinguished aridity', and said he 'attributed more' to Sacheverell Sitwell than to any poet of his generation (*Egoist* 5: 6, June/July 1918). However, it was not as a poet but as an idiosyncratic writer of books about travel, art and literature, including *Southern Baroque Art* (1924), that he came to be best known. TSE published one poem by him in the *Criterion.*

Lytton Strachey (1880–1932): English critic, biographer, and essayist, associated with the Bloomsbury Group. After early journalistic work, including *Landmarks of French Literature* (1912), he came to prominence with *Eminent Victorians* (1918), an exercise in cultural iconoclasm which launched the 'New Biography'. This was followed by *Queen Victoria* (1921) and *Elizabeth and Essex* (1928). TSE wrote that he 'invented new sensations from history, as Bergson has invented new sensations from metaphysics' (*Dial* 71: 2 [August 1921]). See Michael Holroyd, *Lytton Strachey: The New Biography* (1994), and *The Letters of Lytton Strachey*, ed. Paul Levy (2005).

Scofield Thayer (1890–1982): American poet and publisher; pioneering editor of the *Dial.* Thayer came from a wealthy Massachusetts family, which enabled him to travel and act as a patron of the arts. He was a friend of TSE from Milton Academy, where he was his junior by a year. Like TSE, he went on to Harvard and Oxford, where from 1914 he spent two years studying philosophy at Magdalen College: it was at his rooms there that TSE met Vivien Haigh-Wood in 1915. From 1919 to 1925 he was editor of the *Dial*, having joined forces with Dr James Sibley Watson (who became president of the magazine) to save it from closure. Re-launched as a monthly in January 1920, the *Dial* became the most enterprising and innovative cultural and arts magazine in the USA. It published TSE's 'London Letters' and *The Waste Land* as well as important essays by him such as '*Ulysses*, Order and Myth'; Yeats, Pound, cummings, Joyce and others of the most important Anglophone modernists; and influential European writers including Mann, Hofmannsthal and Valéry. A meeting with Lady Rothermere prompted her to finance the *Criterion*, with Eliot as editor. In 1921, Thayer settled in Vienna, where, while continuing remotely to edit the *Dial*, he underwent analysis with Sigmund Freud. He suffered a series of mental breakdowns, resigning from the magazine in June 1926. Certified in 1930, he spent the remainder of his life in care. Watson kept going with the *Dial*, and Marianne Moore took over as editor until its final issue in 1929. Moore judged Thayer to be 'very quiet friendly polished and amusing', and 'in his discernment and interplay of metaphor . . . very brilliant' (*Selected Letters of Marianne Moore*, ed. Bonnie Costello [1998]). See also Nicholas Joost, *Scofield Thayer and 'The Dial'* (1964).

Paul Valéry (1871–1945), poet, essayist and literary theoretician, was born near Marseilles (his father was French, his mother Italian) and educated at the University of Montpellier, where he read law. After settling in Paris in 1894, he developed close friendships with André Gide and Stephane Mallarmé (from whom he took inspiration). For many years, 1900–22, he worked for Edouard Lebey, director of the Press Association and Havas news agency; and he co-edited the review *Commerce*, 1924–32. His early reputation was built on his symbolist poems and some reviews, supplemented by two prose studies, *Introduction à la méthode de Léonard de Vinci* (1895), and *La Soirée avec Monsieur Teste* (1896) – an abstract, rational figure in search of quintessences. After a delay of nearly twenty years, Valéry then published a poem entitled *La Jeune Parque* (1917) and a volume titled simply *Charmes* ('Incantations', 1922) which gathered up his poems of the period 1913–22, and which included his most celebrated work, 'Le Cimetière Marin' ('The Graveyard by the Sea'), a symbolical, classically strict, modulated and musical meditation upon the essence of death and life. In 1925 he was elected an *académicien*, and from 1937 he held the post of Professor of Poetry at the Collège de France. Later writings include numerous elegantly composed essays distilled from the pages of the vast number of *cahiers* that he filled out—over a period of almost forty years – with reflections upon literary theory and philosophy. Works translated into English include *Le Serpent* (for which TSE wrote a preface in 1924). Eliot came to know Valéry fairly well over a 21-year span from 1923, and later said of him that his '"philosophy" lays itself open to the accusation of being only an elaborate game. Precisely, but to be able to play this game, to be able to take aesthetic delight in it, is one of the manifestations of civilised man . . . His was, I think, a profoundly destructive mind, even nihilistic. This cannot, one way or the other, alter our opinion of the poetry; it can neither abate nor magnify the pleasure or the admiration. But it should, I think, increase our admiration of the man who wrote the poetry. For the *agony* of creation, for a mind like Valéry's, must be very great . . . It is strange, but my intimacy with his poetry has been largely due to my study of what he has written about poetry. Of all poets, Valéry has been the most completely conscious (perhaps I should say the most nearly conscious) of what he was doing . . . It is he who will remain for posterity the representative poet, the symbol of the poet, of the first half of the twentieth century – not Yeats, not Rilke, not anyone else' ('Paul Valéry', *Quarterly Review of Literature* 3, 1946).

Hugh Walpole (1884–1941): prolific, popular novelist. Born in New Zealand but educated from the age of ten in England, he graduated from Emmanuel College, Cambridge, in 1906. He put out his first novel, *The Wooden Horse*, in 1909, and thereafter produced a best-seller – almost without exception, they were old-fashioned, honest, unpretentious tales – at the rate of almost one a year. Later successes include the five novels in the Herries series, beginning with *Rogue Herries* (1930) and concluding with *The Bright Pavilions* (1940). 'I know that I am sentimental, romantic and slipshod,' he good-humouredly conceded; and certainly exponents of more modernist experimental fictions did not much value his work – though the wealthy Walpole was the well-regarded acquaintance of numerous writers from Henry James and Joseph Conrad to Dorothy Richardson. Though wary of the modern, Walpole had a good deal of keen respect for certain modernist writers and their endeavours, including Eliot's *Criterion*. In 1918 (while working in the Department of Information at the Foreign Office), he wrote a letter of support for Eliot in his negotiations with the US Navy; and in 1925 he wrote a further testimonial to support Eliot's bid to get the *Criterion* taken over by Geoffrey Faber and the Gwyer family at the Scientific Press. When Eliot invited him to contribute a work for serialisation in the *Criterion*, Walpole was pleased to submit *The Old Ladies*, which was published in two parts (2: 7, April 1924, and 2: 8, July 1924), and in book form later the same year. Knighted in 1937, he died in 1941.

Sydney Waterlow (1878–1944): British diplomat and writer. Educated at Eton and Trinity College, Cambridge (where he gained a double first in classics), he joined the diplomatic service in 1900 and served as attaché and third secretary in Washington. TSE met him in 1915, when Waterlow, as a member of the editorial committee of *International Journal of Ethics*, invited him to review for it. In 1919 Waterlow served at the Paris Peace Conference (helping to negotiate the Treaty of Versailles), and in 1920 was re-appointed to the Foreign Office, later serving as British Minister to Bangkok, 1926–8; and Athens, 1933–9. In January 1920, Eliot told his mother he was 'fond of Sydney', who had been 'kind' to him. See Sarah M. Head, *Before Leonard: The Early Suitors of Virginia Woolf* (2006).

Harriet Shaw Weaver (1876–1961): English editor and publisher, and political activist, whom Virginia Woolf described as 'modest judicious & decorous' (*Diary*, 13 April 1918). In 1912, Weaver began by giving financial support to the *Freewoman*, a radical periodical founded and edited by Dora Marsden, which was renamed in 1913 (at the suggestion of Ezra Pound) *The Egoist*. Weaver became editor in 1914, turning it into a 'little magazine' with a big influence in the history of literary modernism. Following in the footsteps of Richard Aldington and H. D., TSE became assistant editor in 1917 (having been nominated by Pound) and remained so until it closed in 1919. When Joyce could not secure a publisher for *A Portrait of the Artist as a Young Man*, Weaver in 1917 converted the *Egoist* into a press to publish it. She went on to publish TSE's first book, *Prufrock and Other Observations* (1917), Pound's *Dialogues of Fontenelle* and *Quia Pauper Amavi*, Wyndham Lewis's novel *Tarr*, and Marianne Moore's *Poems*, and other notable books. (She played a major role as Joyce's patron and confidante, and went on to be his literary executor and to help to put together *The Letters of James Joyce*.) TSE wrote in tribute in 1962: 'Miss Harriet Shaw Weaver . . . was so modest and self-effacing a woman that her generous patronage of men of letters was hardly known beyond the circle of those who benefited by it . . . Miss Weaver's support, once given, remained steadfast. Her great disappointment was her failure to persuade any printer in this country to take the risk of printing *Ulysses*; her subsequent generosity to James Joyce, and her solicitude for his welfare and that of his family, knew no bounds . . . [Working for her at the *Egoist*] was all great fun, my first experience of editorship. In 1932 I dedicated my *Selected Essays* to this good, kind, unassuming, courageous and lovable woman, to whom I owe so much. What other publisher in 1917 (the Hogarth Press was not yet in existence) would, I wonder, have taken

Prufrock?' See also Jane Lidderdale and Mary Nicholson, *Dear Miss Weaver: Harriet Shaw Weaver, 1876–1961* (1970).

Charles Whibley (1859–1930) took a first in classics from Jesus College, Cambridge, in 1883 and embarked on a lifelong career as journalist, author and editor, and as a well-connected social figure (his chums were to include Lord Northcliffe and Lady Cynthia Asquith). After working briefly for the publishers Cassell & Co., he wrote for the *Scots Observer* and the *Pall Mall Gazette* (he was posted as Paris correspondent for some while in the 1890s, which enabled him to become acquainted with Stéphane Mallarmé, Paul Valéry and other considerable figures), and for the *Daily Mail*, and above all for *Blackwood's Magazine* – where he produced for over twenty-five years a regular commentary, 'Musings without Methods', of sharp High-Tory substance and style. TSE hailed his column as 'the best sustained piece of literary journalism that I know of in recent times'. His several books included *William Pitt* (1906), *Political Portraits* (1917 and 1923), and *Lord John Manners and his Friends* (1925).

Leonard Woolf (1880–1969): writer and publisher, and husband of Virginia Woolf, whom he married in 1912. A friend of Lytton Strachey and J. M. Keynes at Cambridge, he played a central part in the Bloomsbury Group. He wrote a number of novels, including *The Village and the Jungle* (1913), as well as political studies, including *Socialism and Co-operation* (1919) and *Imperialism and Civilization* (1928). As editor, with Virginia Woolf, of the Hogarth Press, he was responsible for publishing TSE's *Poems* (1919) and *The Waste Land* (1922). In 1923 he became literary editor of the *Nation & Athenaeum* (after TSE had turned it down), commissioning numerous reviews from him, and remained a friend. See *An Autobiography* (2 vols, 1980); *Letters of Leonard Woolf*, ed. Frederic Spotts (1990); and Victoria Glendinning, *Leonard Woolf: A Life* (2006).

Virginia Woolf (1882–1941), English novelist, essayist and critic, was the author of *Jacob's Room* (1922), *Mrs Dalloway* (1925), and *To the Lighthouse* (1927), among many experimental and influential novels, as well as of *A Room of One's Own* (1928), a classic of modern feminist criticism, and *The Common Reader* and other collections of essays. Daughter of the biographer and editor Leslie Stephen (1832–1904), she married Leonard Woolf in 1912, published her first novel *The Voyage Out* in 1915, and founded the Hogarth Press with her husband in 1917. The Hogarth Press published TSE's *Poems* (1919), *The Waste Land* (1923), and *Homage to John Dryden* (1923). For his part, TSE published in the *Criterion* Woolf's essays and talks including 'Kew Gardens', 'Character in Fiction', and 'On Being Ill'. In addition to being his publisher, Woolf became a friend and correspondent; and her diaries and letters give a detailed first-hand portrait of him. See Hermione Lee, *Virginia Woolf* (1996).

William Butler Yeats (1865–1939): poet and playwright. According to TSE, he was 'one of those few whose history is the history of their own time, who are part of the consciousness of an age' (*On Poetry and Poets*). TSE met Yeats soon after arriving in London, but despite their mutual admiration of Pound, they had little contact until late 1922, when TSE told Ottoline Morrell that Yeats was 'one of a very small number of people with whom one can talk profitably of poetry'. In his review of *Per Amica Silentia Lunae*, TSE said 'One is never weary of the voice, though the accents are strange' ('A Foreign Mind', *Athenaeum*, 4 July 1919). He was keen to publish Yeats in the *Criterion*: see a 'Biographical Fragment' in *Criterion* 1: 4 (July 1923), 'The Cat and the Moon' in 2: 8 (July 1924), and 'The Tower' in 5: 3 (June 1927). Yeats was instinctively opposed to TSE's work, but discussed it at length in the Introduction to *Oxford Book of Modern Verse* (1936), and declared after the publication of *The Waste Land* that he had found it 'very beautiful' (January 1923). See also Roy Foster, *Yeats: A Life:* I *The Apprentice Mage* (1997), and *Yeats: A Life:* II *The Arch-Poet* (2003).

INDEX OF CORRESPONDENTS AND RECIPIENTS

CORRESPONDENTS

RECIPIENTS

GENERAL INDEX

Page references in **bold** indicate a biographical note